ISBN 978-1-5285-3575-5
PIBN 10918778

AGREEMENT RELATING TO THE RESOLUTION OF CONFLICTING CLAIMS TO GERMAN ENEMY ASSETS

*by Ely Maurer
and
James Simsarian*

The United States, Canada, and the Netherlands signed at Brussels on December 5, 1947, the "Agreement Relating to the Resolution of Conflicting Claims to German Enemy Assets," the first comprehensive, multilateral agreement on the problem of conflicting claims by governments to German external assets. The agreement was designed to avoid the vexatious and lengthy litigation and negotiations which took place after the first World War. The article below summarizes the main provisions of the agreement.

The United States, Canada, and the Netherlands signed on December 5, 1947, at Brussels the "Agreement Relating to the Resolution of Conflicting Claims to German Enemy Assets", the first comprehensive, multilateral agreement on the complex and important problem of conflicting claims by governments to German external assets. The agreement is designed to avoid the vexatious and lengthy litigation and negotiations which took place after the first World War. The agreement does not become binding on the United States before it has been approved by Congress.

The types of claims covered by the agreement are those where the alien property custodians of two countries both claim the same German external asset or where an alien property custodian claims that certain property is a German external asset and a national of a friendly country claims the property is owned by him beneficially through an intermediate corporation.

The types of property covered by the agreement over which conflicts may arise are securities, negotiable instruments, currency, warehouse receipts, foreign currency bank deposits, decedents' estates, trusts, and the property in one signatory country of corporations organized under the laws of another signatory country or under the laws of Germany.

Of most importance are the provisions on securities, bank deposits, and the property of corporations. The agreement provides that if a security, owned by a German, was issued by an entity organized in one signatory country, and the certificate is physically located in another signatory country, the security shall go to the alien property custodian of the signatory country where the entity is organized. Bank deposits maintained in one signatory country by a bank located in another signatory country for the benefit of a German customer will, with certain exceptions, be divided equally between the custodians of the countries concerned. In the case of property in one signatory country belonging to a corporation organized under the laws of another signatory country or of Germany, the general rule is laid down (subject to exceptions for administrative practicality) that the signatory country where the property is located is entitled to that portion of the property corresponding to the German interest in the corporation, while that portion corresponding to the nonenemy interest will be free from seizure.

The agreement will enable the United States Office of Alien Property, Department of Justice, to secure without undue delay clear title to assets which might otherwise be the subject of extended and complicated litigation and negotiations with other governments or their nationals. The agreement, furthermore, will carry out the established policy of the Department of State of protecting the interests of United States nationals in assets outside Germany owned either by a corporation in which there is a German interest or by a corporation organized under the laws of Germany.

In the event a dispute arises between signatory countries regarding the interpretation, implementation, or application of the agreement, provision is made for compulsory and binding conciliation.

The agreement is the outcome of approximately 18 months of discussion and negotiation with other countries, members of the Inter-Allied Reparation Agency.[1] In these deliberations the United States Representatives took a responsible part. It was appreciated early in 1946 that it would be desirable to have a multilateral agreement for the purpose of resolving the problems of conflicts between custodians or between custodians and nationals of another country relating to German external assets. Accordingly discussions were first held of a preliminary character, in the Committee of Experts of IARA from June to July 1946, and then the matter was taken up for the purpose of arriving at a multilateral agreement in the Ger-

---

[1] Mr. Maurer and Mr. Simsarian served as advisers to Russell H. Dorr, U.S. Minister and Delegate to the Inter-Allied Reparation Agency, who represented the United States Government in the course of the negotiations leading to the agreement. Other advisers were from the Office of Alien Property, Department of Justice, Henry Hilken, Malcolm Mason, Donald Sham, and Leon Brooks; and from the Treasury Department, Elting Arnold and I. G. Alk. In the last part of the negotiations, Alex B. Daspit, Alternate U.S. Delegate to the Inter-Allied Reparation Agency, took Mr. Dorr's place in the latter's absence.

[2] The organization of IARA provides a convenient forum for these discussions. The Committee of Experts was provided for under part I, article 6F, of the Paris agreement on reparation of Jan. 14, 1946 (Treaties and Other International Acts Series 1655), "in order to over-

Part III concerns property situated within the jurisdiction of one party (secondary country) and owned by an enterprise (primary company) organized under the laws of another party (primary country), in which enterprise there exists a German interest. Where the German interest in the property in the secondary country or the primary company amounts to control (as defined in detail in article 11B), it is provided that, with certain exceptions, the property shall be released in kind but the secondary country shall be entitled to receive reimbursement from the primary country in an amount representing that portion of the value of the property in the secondary country corresponding to the percentage of German interest in the primary company (articles 11, 12, 13).

These exceptions concern German controlled production enterprises in a secondary country, considered by it to be necessary to its national security; cases involving property in a secondary country belonging to dummy or closely held holding companies; and cases where the parties agree that release in kind is not practicable or that administrative difficulty or other special circumstances require the liquidation of the property in the secondary country. In these cases provision is made for the retention and liquidation of the property or the German interest in the property and for protection of the nonenemy interests in the primary company, rather than for release of the entire property and reimbursement (articles 13, 15, 16).

The nonenemy interests in a primary company are entitled to that portion of the property in the secondary country corresponding to these interests (articles 15, 16, 17).

If the property in the secondary country and the primary company are not German controlled, the property must be released without reimbursement (articles 11, 12), unless the primary company is a dummy or a closely held company (article 16).

Part IV concerns property within the jurisdiction of a party and owned by an enterprise organized under the laws of Germany, in which enterprise nonenemy nationals of parties have an interest (article 21). The agreement provides that this property shall be released to the extent of the interests in the enterprise of the nonenemy nationals and pursuant to arrangements to be made between the parties concerned, if the nonenemy nationals directly or indirectly own 25 percent or more of the shares in the enterprise, or control the enterprise (article 22).

Release shall be made in kind except in the cases of German controlled enterprises in a signatory country considered by that country to be necessary to its national security, and in the cases where the parties agree that release in kind would not be practicable. In these cases provision is made for the release of the proceeds of sale or liquidation in substitution of the property which would otherwise have been released in kind (article 24).

Part V contains a number of miscellaneous provisions which supplement the substantive provisions of the first four parts. Thus a party is not obliged to release an enemy interest in property if this interest will not be treated by the recipient party as German enemy (article 26A). The release of property may be affected by the existence of judicial or administrative proceedings as to the property (article 26H). In determining whether property is owned or controlled by a German enemy, certain transfers need not be recognized if they occurred after the institution of wartime emergency measures or after the occupation of a country; or if they were "forced transfers" in Ger-

many; or if they were forced transfers outside Germany within the meaning of the inter-Allied declaration of January 5, 1943, against acts of dispossession (article 27). Property which is cloaked for a German enemy shall be regarded as directly owned by that German enemy (article 28). Nothing in the agreement may be construed to confer any right on a person to prosecute a claim in any court or administrative tribunal against his government or any other party (article 33).

Part VI concerns the machinery and procedure of conciliation to be followed if a dispute with respect to the interpretation, implementation, or application of the agreement is not resolved by negotiation between the parties. Provision is made for a panel of seven conciliators to be elected by the parties (article 35). A party may request the appointment of a conciliator from this panel to decide a dispute. This conciliator will hear the parties and formulate a solution which is, in his opinion, the best possible solution in the spirit of the agreement, and the solution so formulated will be binding and final (article 37A). The question whether the national security of a country requires retention of property is not subject to the procedure of conciliation (article 38).

TEXT OF AGREEMENT[1]

The Governments Parties to the present Agreement,
Desiring to resolve conflicting claims to German enemy assets within their respective jurisdictions and to facilitate the disposal of such assets to the common advantage,
Have agreed as follows:

Article 1

In dealing with German enemy assets the Parties to the present Agreement (hereinafter and in the Annex hereto referred to as Parties) shall be guided as far as possible, in their relations with each other, by the provisions set forth in the present Agreement and in its Annex (hereinafter and in the Annex hereto together referred to as the Agreement), and shall take such action to give effect to the Agreement as may be necessary and appropriate.

Article 2

The Agreement shall not supersede any prior agreements concluded between any two or more Parties, or between a Party and another Government not a Party; provided that no such prior agreement between any of

the Parties shall adversely affect the rights under the Agreement of another Party not party to the prior agreement, or those of its nationals.

When a prior agreement between a Party and another Government is deemed by a Party, not party to the prior agreement, to affect adversely its rights under the Agreement or those of its nationals, the Party who is also party to the prior agreement shall approach the other Government in order to secure, if possible, such modification of the relevant provisions of the prior agreement as will render them consistent with the Agreement.

Article 3

Nothing in the Agreement shall preclude any Party or Parties from concluding in the future any separate agreement; provided that such subsequent agreement shall not affect adversely the rights under the Agreement of another Party not party to the subsequent agreement, or those of its nationals.

Article 4

If a dispute arises between two or more Parties with respect to the interpretation, implementation or application of the Agreement, such Parties shall endeavour by every means possible to settle such dispute by negotia-

[1] Text printed from Department of State press release 944 of Dec. 4, 1947.

tion between themselves, which may include the use of a mutually acceptable conciliator with such powers as the Parties in dispute may agree. If the dispute is not resolved within a reasonable time by such negotiation, the dispute shall be settled in the manner provided in Part VI of the Annex.

Article 5

The Agreement shall come into force, as respects Governments which have signed it before it comes into force, as soon as it has been signed at any time before September 1, 1948, on behalf of Governments which, under Part 1, Article 1 B of the Paris Agreement on Reparation of January 24, 1946, are collectively entitled to not less than 35 percent of the aggregate of shares in Category A of German reparations.

The Agreement shall remain open for signature by other Governments Members of the Inter-Allied Reparation Agency for a period of six months from the date upon which it comes into force, and shall become effective with respect to those Governments immediately upon signature.

Article 6

If any Government which is not a member of the Inter-Allied Reparation Agency signifies in writing to the Government of Belgium within nine months of the date upon which the Agreement comes into force that it desires to become a Party to the Agreement, or to a similar agreement, the Parties will consider in consultation with one another and with that Government its participation in such an agreement; provided that nothing in this Article shall be deemed to qualify any right of any Party under Article 3 above.

Article 7

Any Government to which the Agreement is open for signature may, in lieu of signing, give notification of accession, in writing, to the Government of Belgium, and a Government making such notification of accession shall be deemed to have signed the Agreement on the date of receipt of the notification by the Government of Belgium.

Article 8

Any signatory Government may, at the time of signature or later, declare by notification in writing to the Government of Belgium that it desires the Agreement to apply to all or any of its overseas territories or colonies or territories under its suzerainty or protection or territories in respect of which it exercises a mandate or trusteeship, and the Agreement shall apply to the colonies and territories, named in the notification, from the date of receipt thereof by the Government of Belgium or from the date on which the Agreement comes into force in respect of the notifying Government, whichever is the later.

In witness whereof the undersigned, being duly authorized by their respective Governments, have signed this Agreement.

Done in Brussels on December 5, 1947, in the English and French languages, the two texts being equally authentic, in a single original which shall be deposited in the Archives of the Government of Belgium. The Government of Belgium will furnish certified copies of the Agreement to each Government Signatory of the Paris Agreement on Reparation of January 24, 1946, and to each other Government on whose behalf the Agreement is signed, and will also inform those Governments of all signatures of the Agreement and of any notifications received thereunder.

    For the Government of Canada

    For the Government of the Netherlands

    For the Government of the United States

ANNEX

Part I: Property Owned by German Enemies

Article 1

A. For the purpose of this Article, "security" means any stock, bond, debenture, share or, in general, any similar property known as a "security", in the country of issue.

B. Where a security owned by a German enemy has been issued by a Party or by a governmental or private organisation or person within its territory but the certificate is in the territory of another Party, the certificate, whether in registered or in bearer form, shall be released to the former Party.

C. A German enemy owner of a certificate issued by an administration office, voting trustee or similar organisation or person, and indicating a participation in one or more specifically named securities, shall be regarded as the owner of the amount of securities specifically indicated, and Paragraph B of this Article shall apply to these securities.

D. A Party obliged under this Article to release a certificate shall not be required to release the income (in cash or otherwise) which has before July 1, 1947, been received

in its territory by the releasing Party or by any person acting under its authority. Income received by such Party or person on or after July 1, 1947, shall be released to the Party entitled to the release of the certificate.

E. A Party obliged under this Article to release a certificate shall not be required to release the proceeds of any liquidation by sale, redemption or otherwise, which were, on December 31, 1946, in the form of cash or of securities issued by that Party or by a Governmental or private organisation or person within its territory, even if such cash was reinvested or such securities were sold or traded after that date. If the proceeds were, on December 31, 1946, in the form of securities issued by another Party or by a Governmental or private organisation or person within its territory, such securities (or the proceeds of their liquidation after that date) shall be released to the latter Party.

Article 2

A. For the purpose of this Article, "currency" means any notes, coins or other similar monetary media except those of numismatic or historical value.

B. Where currency has been issued by a Party or by a Governmental or private organisation acting under its authority but the currency is owned by a German enemy and is in the territory of another Party, the currency shall be released to the former Party.

C. Where currency has been sold before January 1, 1947, no release shall be required; but release of the proceeds shall be required if sale has taken place on or after January 1, 1947.

D. Nothing in this Article shall prejudice any rights or obligations which Parties may have under Part III of the Paris Agreement on Reparation.

Article 3

Where a negotiable instrument (such as a bill of exchange, promissory note, cheque or draft), not covered by Article 4 of this Annex, owned by a German enemy, is in the territory of a Party and the principal obligor is resident in the territory of another Party, the instrument shall be released to the latter Party.

Article 4

Where a bill of lading, warehouse receipt or other similar instrument, whether or not negotiable, owned by a German enemy, is in the territory of a Party but the property to which it relates is located in the territory of another Party, the instrument shall be released to the latter Party.

Article 5 ·

A. A foreign currency account ("primary account") maintained in favour of a German enemy by a financial institution in the territory of a Party ("primary country") covered in whole or in part by an account ("cover account") with a financial institution in the territory of another Party ("secondary country") shall be treated as follows:

(i) The cover account shall be released and the primary country shall reimburse the secondary country in an amount equal to 50% of the cover account applicable to the primary account. Such reimbursement shall be made in accordance with the terms of Article 14 of this Annex.

(ii) Where the secondary country has vested or otherwise taken under custodian control the income from German enemy property situated in the secondary country or the proceeds of the liquidation of German enemy owned securities issued by the secondary country or by a Governmental or private organisation or person within its territory and which securities were held in a custody or depot account, such income or such proceeds may be retained by the secondary country and sub-paragraph (i) of this Paragraph shall not apply thereto.

B. For the purpose of this Article, accounts shall include named, numbered or otherwise specially designated accounts and sub-accounts as well as undesignated accounts and sub-accounts.

Article 6

Where property covered by this Part is owned partly by a German enemy and partly by a non-enemy, the method of segregating the respective interests and releasing the enemy interests shall be determined by agreement between the interested Parties. The German enemy interests shall then be released to the Party which would have been entitled to the property if it had been wholly German enemy owned.

Part II: Deceaseds' Estates, Trusts and Other Fiduciary Arrangements Under Which a German Enemy Has an Interest

Article 7

A. Except as provided in Paragraph B of this Article, property within the jurisdiction of a Party, forming part of the estate of a non-enemy person who has died domiciled in the territory of another Party, in which estate a German enemy has an interest whether as a beneficiary or creditor, shall be released from control of the custodian authorities of the former Party with a view to facilitating normal administration of the estate in the territory of the latter Party. Property so released shall be subject to the application of the laws of the releasing Party governing administration and distribution of the deceaseds' estates. When under such laws distribution of the deceased's estate is made directly to the persons who have an interest in the estate, the releasing Party shall take appropriate action to assist in making available to the other Party the distributive share of each German enemy.

B. Notwithstanding the provisions of Paragraph A of this Article, where a non-enemy domiciled in the territory of one Party has died owning immovable property in the territory of another Party and an interest in the property devolves upon or is to be distributed to a German enemy under the will of the deceased or under the applicable laws of descent, the interest may be retained by the latter Party, subject to the rights of non-enemy creditors of the deceased or of non-enemy heirs to whom, under applicable law, a portion of the immovable property is reserved.

C. This Article shall not apply to any property in the estate of a deceased if the property was administered and distributed before the Party in whose territory the property was located instituted war-time emergency measures applicable to the administration and distribution of the property of the deceased.

D. For the purposes of this Article, the domicile of a deceased shall be determined according to the law of the Party within whose jurisdiction the property is located.

Article 8

Property within the jurisdiction of a Party which is held under a bona fide trust or other bona fide fiduciary arrangement in which a German enemy has an interest as a beneficiary or otherwise, and which trust or fiduciary arrangement is being administered under the laws of another Party, shall be released from the control of the custodian authorities of the former Party, except that such Party may retain any interest of a German enemy in immovable property located in its territory. Such release shall not be obligatory under this Part of this Annex in cases where the trust or other fiduciary arrangement was established by a person resident in Germany, or a German enemy, or a person who subsequently became a German enemy.

Article 9

The Party in favour of which property is released under this Part of this Annex shall recognise the rights of non-enemies in the estate, trust or other fiduciary arrangement.

Article 10

The principles of Part I of this Annex shall not be applicable to property released under this Part or distributed to the custodian authorities of a Party from an estate, bona fide trust or other bona fide fiduciary arrangement governed by this Part.

Part III: Property Owned by Enterprises Organised Under the Laws of a Party

Article 11

A. This Part shall apply to property situated within the jurisdiction of a Party and owned by an enterprise organised under the laws of another Party in which enterprise there was a direct or indirect German enemy interest on the material date. The Party within whose jurisdiction the property is situated shall be referred to as the "secondary country" with respect to that property. The enterprise owning the property shall be referred to as the "primary company" with respect to that property. The Party under whose laws the enterprise is organised shall be referred to as the "primary country" with respect to that property. The terms "enterprise" and "company" shall include any firm or body of persons, whether corporate or unincorporate. Property of an enterprise organised in the form of a trust, and property of a banking or financial institution other than the foreign currency cover accounts governed by Article 5 of this Annex, shall be dealt with under this Part. However, this exception with respect to cover accounts shall not be construed to imply that any cover accounts are or are not the property of the institution.

B. An enterprise shall be deemed to be German controlled if at the material date German enemies held directly or indirectly:

(i) 50 percent or more of the voting rights, outstanding capital stock or other proprietorship interests, or

(ii) participating rights in a voting trust arrangement which rights represented 50 percent or more of such voting rights, outstanding capital stock or other proprietorship interests;

or if at the material date German enemies directly or indirectly controlled the policy, management, voting power or operations of the enterprise. The property in the secondary country shall be deemed to be German controlled if at the material date German enemies directly or indirectly controlled the policy, management, use, or operation of the property.

Article 12

Except as otherwise provided in this Agreement, all property in a secondary country owned by a primary company shall be released by the secondary country and the secondary country shall be entitled to receive reimbursement from the primary country in an amount representing that portion of the value of the property in the secondary country which corresponds to the percentage of direct and indirect German enemy interest in the primary company on the material date. Release in each case shall take place as soon as an agreement has been reached between the countries concerned on whether either the property in the secondary country or the primary company shall be treated as German controlled and on the general limits of, and method of calculating, the percentage of direct and indirect German enemy interest in the primary company on the material date. If the property in the secondary country and the primary company are not German controlled, the property shall be released forthwith without reimbursement.

Article 13

A. Release of property in a secondary country shall be made in kind unless:

(i) the property has been liquidated by the secondary country prior to the date on which the Agreement comes into force in respect of that country; or

(ii) the primary and secondary countries concerned agree that release in kind would not be practicable or the primary company consents to the sale or liquidation of the property by the secondary country; or

(iii) the property in the secondary country is a production enterprise or a substantial interest therein, and such property or the primary company concerned is German controlled and, after full consideration of the economic interest of the primary country, the secondary country determines in exceptional cases that its national security nevertheless requires retention of the property and gives notice to the primary country to that effect.

B. Where release is not made in kind, the secondary country shall release in substitution the proceeds of the sale or liquidation of the property which would otherwise have been released in kind. If such property has not been sold or liquidated within one year after agreement or consent under sub-paragraph (ii) of Paragraph A of this Article or the giving of notice under sub-paragraph (iii) thereof, or within an agreed extension beyond that period, the value of the property retained as determined by accepted principles of valuation shall be released.

Article 14

Reimbursement shall be paid to the secondary country by the primary country in the currency of the secondary country within two years after the date of release of the property. Payment may be delayed, however, in accordance with foreign exchange restrictions applicable generally to payment of capital obligations from time to time in effect in the primary country, provided that such restrictions are maintained in accordance with the Articles of Agreement of the International Monetary Fund and provided further that in any event full payment shall be made within seven years after the date of the release. Interest at the rate of 2 percent per annum shall be paid

January 4, 1948

771892—48——2

to the secondary country by the primary country on such balance of reimbursement as remains unpaid at and after the end of the two year period.

Article 15

Where administrative difficulty to the secondary country requires it or in other special circumstances the secondary and primary countries concerned may agree that the secondary country shall retain that proportion of the value of the property in the secondary country to which it is entitled under the provisions of Article 12 of this Annex. In such event, the secondary country shall release the excess of the property above the amount to which it is entitled and such excess shall inure to the benefit solely of the non-enemy interests in the primary company.

Article 16

Where the primary company is a dummy company or is a holding company whose outstanding stock is closely held or is not regularly traded in a recognised financial market, the secondary country, notwithstanding the provisions of Article 12 of this Annex, may retain that proportion of the property in the secondary country which corresponds to the percentage of direct and indirect German enemy interest in the dummy or holding company on the material date. In such event, the secondary country shall release the excess of the property above the amount to which it is entitled and such excess shall inure to the benefit solely of the non-enemy interests in the primary company.

Article 17

It is contemplated that the proportion of the value of the property in the secondary country which corresponds to the percentage of the direct and indirect' non-enemy interests in the primary company shall inure to the benefit of such non-enemy interests. In arrangements for release and reimbursement made under this Part between two or more Parties, the Parties shall make reasonable provisions to avoid injury to interests in the primary company of non-enemies who are nationals of a third Party.

Article 18

In applying the rules of this Part to a case involving a chain of companies, releases of property and reimbursement payments shall be made between secondary countries and their respective primary companies and countries. On the other hand, in calculating the percentage of direct and indirect German enemy interest in each of the successive primary companies, such interests shall be traced through the entire chain of companies.

Article 19

With respect to the types of property covered by Articles 1 to 4 inclusive of this Annex, owned by enterprises governed by Part III of this Annex, that country which would be entitled to obtain release of property under the principles of such Articles shall be regarded as the secondary country for the purposes of Part III; in the case of foreign currency accounts under Article 5 of this Annex, maintained in favour of an enterprise governed by Part III, the country where the primary account is maintained and

the country where the cover account is maintained shall each be regarded as the secondary country for the purposes of Part III to the extent of 50 percent of the foreign currency cover account.

Article 20

An enterprise organised under the laws of Germany shall be considered as wholly German enemy for the purpose of administering this Part, but property which is received in reimbursement or retained by any country under this Part shall be available for the protection of non-enemy interests in such enterprise, in accordance with the provisions of Part IV of this Annex.

Part IV: Property Owned by Enterprises Organised Under the Laws of Germany

Article 21

This Part shall apply to property within the jurisdiction of a Party owned by an enterprise organised under the laws of Germany in which enterprise non-enemy nationals of Parties directly or indirectly have, and on September 1, 1939, had an interest. Non-enemy nationals of Parties referred to in this Part must have been nationals of Parties as of September 1, 1939.

Article 22

For the protection of the interests in the enterprise of non-enemy nationals, referred to in Article 21 of this Annex, the property to which this Part applies shall, subject to the provisions of Articles 23 and 24 of this Annex, be released to the extent of those interests and pursuant to arrangements to be made between the Parties concerned, if non-enemy nationals of Parties directly or indirectly:

(i) own and, on September 1, 1939, owned 25% or more of the shares in the enterprise; or

(ii) control and, on September 1, 1939, controlled the enterprise.

Article 23

No Party shall be obliged to release property under this Part, in respect of which no claim, sponsored by another Party, has been received by the former Party within one year after the coming into force of the Agreement between the respective Parties. Before sponsoring a claim under this Part, a Party shall be satisfied by a claimant, being one of its nationals, that Article 22 of this Annex applies. Where a claim is filed with the Party in whose jurisdiction the property is located and Article 22 of this Annex applies, such Party shall notify all other Parties and shall consider the claims of all non-enemy nationals of Parties who qualify under Article 21 of this Annex.

Article 24

A. Release of property under this Part shall be made in kind unless:

(i) the property has been liquidated prior to the date on which an eligible sponsored claim is filed with respect to the property pursuant to Article 23 of this Annex; or

(ii) the Parties concerned agree that release in kind would not be practicable; or

(iii) the property to be released is a production enterprise or a substantial interest therein, and such property or the enterprise organised under the laws of Germany is German controlled and, after full consideration of the economic interests of the other Party or Parties concerned, the Party in whose jurisdiction the property is located determines in exceptional cases that its national security nevertheless requires retention of the property and gives notice to the other Party or Parties to that effect.

B. Where release is not made in kind, there shall be released in substitution the proceeds of the sale or liquidation of the property which would otherwise have been released in kind. If such property has not been sold or liquidated within one year after agreement under sub-paragraph (ii) of Paragraph A of this Article or the giving of notice under sub-paragraph (iii) thereof, or within an agreed extension beyond that period, the value of the property retained as determined by accepted principles of valuation shall be released.

Article 25

With respect to the types of property covered by Articles 1 to 4 inclusive of this Annex, owned by enterprises governed by Part IV of this Annex, property shall be regarded as being within the jurisdiction of the Party which would be entitled to obtain the release of such property under the principles of such Articles; in the case of foreign currency accounts under Article 5 of this Annex, maintained in favour of an enterprise governed by Part IV, the country where the primary account is maintained and the country where the cover account is maintained shall each be regarded as having jurisdiction over the property to the extent of 50% of the foreign currency cover account.

Part V: Interpretation and Application

Article 26

A. A Party shall not be obliged to release an enemy interest in property to another Party or to an enterprise organised under the laws of that other Party except to the extent that such interest will be treated directly or indirectly by the recipient Party as German enemy.

B. A Party obliged under the Agreement to release property shall not be required to reverse any act of liquidation which has been carried out by sale, redemption or otherwise. The vesting, sequestration or confiscation of property shall not be regarded as constituting liquidation for the purposes of the Agreement.

C. Except as otherwise expressly provided in the Agreement, a Party obliged to release property shall, if the property has been liquidated, release the proceeds of such liquidation.

D. Except as otherwise expressly provided in the Agreement, a Party obliged to release property shall release all income or other benefits (in cash or otherwise) which have been received by it or by any person in its territory acting under its authority in respect of that property.

E. The Party to which property is released under the Agreement shall fully recognise bona fide liens or pledges thereon legally obtained within the territory of the releasing Party which became effective prior to the date when the recipient Party took war-time emergency

measures to prevent the acquisition of liens or pledges with respect to such property or the date when the territory of the recipient Party was invaded by Germany and were valid under the laws of the recipient Party in effect prior to such date. A releasing Party shall not be obliged hereby to take any measures to set aside any bona fide lien or pledge valid under its laws which arose or was created either (a) prior to the date on which the releasing Party took war-time emergency measures to prevent the acquisition of such liens or pledges with respect to the property involved, or (b) after such date under license or other authorisation by such Party.

F. Administrative charges and expenses of conservation and liquidation shall be borne by the recipient Party unless that Party requests the releasing Party to bear a portion thereof. In such event the obligation of the releasing Party shall be limited to the amount of the income or other benefits (if any) which the recipient Party establishes were received and were retained under the Agreement by the releasing Party or by any person in its territory acting under its authority with respect to the specific property released.

G. Where property is subject to release under the Agreement the method of delivery and the payment of any delivery costs shall be arranged between the Parties concerned.

H. (i) A Party shall not be required under the Agreement to make a release of property so long as there is pending any judicial or administrative proceeding in the territory of:

(a) The releasing Party, if the proceeding requires retention of the property by that Party or may result in a determination that the property is not directly or indirectly German enemy owned or controlled;

(b) the recipient Party, if the proceeding may result in a determination that the property is not directly or indirectly German enemy owned or controlled and may thus prevent that Party from treating the released property as German enemy.

(ii) If, after property is released under the Agreement:

(a) the recipient Party is obliged as a result of litigation in its territory to surrender custodian control of the property, the releasing Party may reassert its custodian control over the property in order to make an independent test of the litigated issue;

(b) the releasing Party is obliged as a result of litigation in its territory to make a disposition of the property which release has prevented it from making, that Party may reassert custodian control over the property in order to comply with the obligation imposed by the litigation.

If reassertion of custodian control by the releasing Party is required under this sub-paragraph, the recipient Party shall take appropriate action to facilitate such reassertion.

(iii) At the request of the releasing Party, appropriate arrangements shall be made by the recipient Party prior to the release of any property:

(a) assuring the releasing Party that it will be able to regain custodian control over the property or of the proceeds of sale or liquidation or of the value thereof, if required under the terms of sub-paragraph (ii) above;

(b) for indemnification of charges or expenses which may be incurred by the releasing Party with respect to the released property after the date of release.

I. The release of property under the provisions of the Agreement shall not terminate or otherwise affect the dedication of patents to the public, the placing of patents in the public domain or the grant of licenses to patents with or without royalty, pursuant to the provisions of Articles 1 or 2 of the German Patent Accord signed in London on July 27, 1946, or other agreement, when such action is taken prior to the release of the property.

J. A Party shall be entitled at its discretion to refuse to accept a release under the provisions of the Agreement and in such event shall not be liable for payment of the charges and expenses referred to in Paragraphs F and G and sub-paragraph (iii) of Paragraph H of this Article.

Article 27

A. Nothing in the Agreement shall oblige any Party to recognise:

(i) any transfer of, or other transaction relating to, a German enemy interest, occurring after the institution of war-time emergency measures by that Party or after the invasion of the territory of that Party by Germany;

(ii) any transfer of non-enemy property in Germany to German enemies, or any assumption by German enemies from non-enemies, of control over property in Germany, which was forced without adequate consideration by action of the Government of Germany whether before or after September 1, 1939. This sub-paragraph shall apply only to property of, or controlled by, non-enemies who were nationals of Parties at the time of the transfer of the property or the assumption of control over the property.

B. In determining whether any property is owned or controlled by a German enemy no transfer to a German enemy or dealings with a German enemy shall be taken into account which represent looting or forced transfers within the meaning of the Inter-Allied Declaration of January 5, 1943, against Acts of Dispossession.

Article 28

Property which is held for the benefit of a German enemy by any individual or body of persons, corporate or unincorporate, as a cloak, nominee, agent, trustee or in any other capacity, shall be regarded as directly owned by that German enemy. The question of recognising any interest which the holder of such property may claim therein shall not be prejudiced by the foregoing but shall be resolved in each case by negotiation between the Parties concerned.

Article 29

The assertion of custodian control over a German enemy interest in property within the territory of one Party shall not be deemed to have destroyed the German enemy interest in property within the territory of another Party.

Article 30

A branch or other similar office within the territory of a Party of an enterprise organised under the laws of another country shall be regarded as a separate entity located within the territory of the Party. A partnership having its principal office in the territory of any Party shall be regarded as an enterprise located in that territory regardless of the residence or domicile of the partners.

Article 31

Where under the Agreement special problems arise respecting a complex organisation having subsidiary or affiliated organisations with properties within the territories of several of the Parties, a committee composed of representatives of each of the interested Parties may be constituted to consider the problems and make recommendations for their solution.

Article 32

Parties shall exchange information and otherwise co-operate for the purpose of giving effect to the Agreement; provided that information given pursuant hereto shall be regarded as confidential by the Party receiving it which undertakes to use it exclusively for the purpose of implementing the Agreement and the Paris Agreement on Reparation of January 24, 1946.

Article 33

Nothing in the Agreement shall be construed to confer any right on an individual or body of persons, corporate or unincorporate, to prosecute a claim in any court or administrative tribunal against his or their Government or against any other Party.

Article 34

In this Annex:

(i) the term "property" shall include all rights, titles and interests in property;

(ii) the expression "war-time emergency measures" means the measures for the control of German enemy owned property, or of transactions by or on behalf of German enemies taken by a Party on or after September 1, 1939 whether or not taken prior to that Government's actual participation in the War;

(iii) the expression "the material date" means the day on which the secondary country as defined in Part III of this Annex came into the war or took war-time emergency measures, whichever is earlier.

Part VI: Conciliation

Article 35

In order to give effect to the provisions of Article 4 of the Agreement to which this is the Annex, a Panel of Conciliators consisting of seven members shall be established in the following manner:

(i) Each Party which has signed the Agreement before the expiry of six months after its coming into force may, by written notice to the Secretary General of the Inter-Allied Reparation Agency, nominate not more than three candidates for election to the Panel, and the Secretary General shall not accept any nomination after the expiry of that period.

(ii) The Secretary General shall, by secret ballot, conduct an election of the Panel of Conciliators and only those Parties which have signed the Agreement before the expiry of six months after its coming into force shall be entitled to vote.

(iii) Each Party shall be entitled to cast one vote in respect to each vacancy on the Panel. A Party shall not cast more than one vote for any one candidate.

(iv) The seven candidates receiving the highest number of votes shall be elected to the Panel; provided that no candidate shall be elected who has not received the vote of at least two-thirds of the Parties voting, and provided that not more than two nationals of the same country shall be elected.

(v) From the seven members of the Panel so elected, the Parties entitled to vote, exercising one vote each, shall elect by secret ballot a President of the Panel by a majority of at least two-thirds of the votes cast.

(vi) In case of the death or retirement of the President or any other member of the Panel, the vacancy shall be filled by vote of the then Parties. Each Party may nominate one candidate, and election shall be by a majority of at least two-thirds of the votes cast.

Article 36

Immediately upon its election the Panel shall formulate, for its internal organization and its work, such basic rules as it deems necessary. A fee therefor shall be paid to the members of the Panel by the Parties specified in sub-paragraph (ii) of Article 35 at a rate fixed by the Secretary General of the Inter-Allied Reparation Agency.

Article 37

A. If a dispute is not resolved within a reasonable time by negotiation as provided in Article 4 of the Agreement to which this is the Annex, a Party may request the President of the Panel of Conciliators referred to in Article 35 of this Annex to appoint from the Panel an impartial Conciliator who shall hear the Parties and may call for additional evidence. The Conciliator shall formulate a solution which is in his opinion the best possible solution in the spirit of the Agreement, and the solution so formulated shall be binding upon the Parties concerned and final.

B. The President shall, upon application of any of the parties in dispute, determine whether a reasonable time has elapsed before submission of the case to conciliation under Paragraph A of this Article; provided that a period of less than one year from the commencement of negotiations between the Parties in dispute shall not be considered a reasonable time for the purposes of this Paragraph.

Article 38

The question whether in the opinion of the secondary country, its national security requires the retention of property under sub-paragraph (iii) of Paragraph A of Article 13 of this Annex and sub-paragraph (iii) of Paragraph A of Article 24 of this Annex shall not be subject to the procedure of conciliation.

Article 39

The Conciliator shall not be entitled to grant any modification of the obligation to make full payment in the currency of the secondary country within seven years after the date of the release as required by Article 14 of this Annex.

Article 40

Each Party in dispute shall pay to the Conciliator such fees and expenses as he may determine. Any such Party may request the President of the Panel to review the fees and expenses fixed by the Conciliator, or their allocation between the Parties. The decision of the President on the matter shall be final.

THE UNITED NATIONS AND SPECIALIZED AGENCIES

Tensions in the United Nations

BY WARREN R. AUSTIN [1]

U.S. Representative at the Seat of the United Nations

Before launching upon the subject of our discussions, I wish to express the deep appreciation of the American Delegation for the service rendered our cause by one of your distinguished citizens, Mr. Adlai Stevenson. He played a significant role in the drafting of the United Nations Charter at San Francisco, in the initial period of organization at London, and as a member of the American Delegation to the first and second sessions of the General Assembly in New York. I personally, and my colleagues in the United States Mission to the United Nations, are indebted to Mr. Stevenson for his counsel on the broad range of our problems as well as his competent handling of the specific responsibilities entrusted to him. He has won the admiration and friendship of foreign delegations as a spokesman for his country who in his person displays the qualities of leadership.

The most important problem of our generation is that of preventing and abolishing war and of building and maintaining peace. I want to say at the outset that in attempting a realistic analysis of this problem, giving frank recognition to the difficulties we must surmount, I do not waiver in my conviction that we can and shall succeed in using the United Nations to achieve collective security. My conviction is based on a very simple proposition—namely, the people of the world want peace more than they ever have before in human history. Where there is a will there is a way. I am persuaded that there is not only a desire but also a powerful will to peace in all countries and that we can find the way to make peace prevail.

Yet it will not serve our cause to underestimate the difficulties in the way nor to overestimate the gains we are able to make in the short run. Our support of the United Nations must rest upon a realistic appraisal of the problem and the forces operating within the international organization. In spite of the road-blocks in the way of our central goal of collective security, we continue our support and persist in exercising our influence within the counsels of nations. Why? We are determined to reach the goal, and therefore we hold steadfastly to the best means of reaching it.

The very fact that we have a vast international organization meeting in conferences in various places all over the world enables us to see in bold relief the differences and tensions between nations as they appear and as they reflect realistically the situation in the international world today. We have a unique opportunity to study at close range, in open forums, both the tensions and the conditions they reflect.

I should like to discuss with you frankly the tensions in the United Nations, suggest how we might act to relieve these tensions and how we might hasten the realization of collective security envisaged in the United Nations Charter.

We have just concluded a significant session of the General Assembly in New York. During this Assembly, we have had an opportunity to observe the expression of opinions—so violent at times that many people wondered whether any common ground could be found for agreement. Let us look for a moment at a few of the achievements and then face up to the frustrations.

[1] Address delivered before the Chicago Council on Foreign Relations at Chicago, Dec. 17, 1947, and released to the press by the U.S. Mission to the United Nations on the same date.

is threatened with paralysis by the veto, it is natural for nations to lean more heavily on the unfettered arm of the Assembly.

By a vote of 43 to 0, another significant step was taken by the Assembly in the case of Korea. It created a commission to help prepare for and observe an election and to recommend steps leading toward unity and independence. The mere presentation of the stalemated Korean situation to the Assembly produced an immediate reaction on the part of the Soviet Union. In committee, the Soviet Union offered proposals with the obvious hope of avoiding or at least delaying Assembly action. When these proposals were turned down, it refused to participate in the vote. Once again the process of exposure of the issues and claims was made, and it is clear who wanted to submit the problem to the world community and who did not.

In the case of Palestine, the Assembly took a far-reaching step by its vote for partition with a United Nations trusteeship over Jerusalem. The full gamut of Assembly methods was used: a special Assembly last spring which set up a commission of disinterested parties to investigate and recommend; review of the long history and on-the-spot study of the case by that commission; the formulation of minority and majority recommendations; full debate of both reports in committee and plenary session of the regular Assembly; and finally, the taking of the decision by two-thirds vote. The United States and the Soviet Union stood together in this case.

The Palestine case was the *only* crucial issue on which the United States and the Soviet Union found common ground. Although dramatic divisions have been widely publicized, they have not been as numerous as is generally supposed.

The very existence and present development of the United Nations rests on a rather broad area of agreement and a willingness of nations, particularly the great powers, to compromise their views and accommodate themselves to majority positions. We have thus been able to set in motion the most ambitious organization for peace ever conceived. We have built up an efficient Secretariat, introduced novel methods of breaking down barriers of language, developed fact-finding facilities and arsenals of information for combating such ancient evils as disease, hunger, and ignorance. We have created commissions and specialized agen-

15

cies to deal with a whole range of vital problems through international consultation:

> the problem of control of atomic and other weapons of mass destruction;
> of reduction and regulation of armaments;
> of human rights;
> of finance and trade;
> of health and narcotics;
> of food and agriculture;
> ˋof economics and employment;
> of education, science, and culture;
> of labor standards;
> of displaced and stateless persons.

The crowded calendar of United Nations conferences this year bears eloquent testimony to the progress we have made in a very short time in submitting problems to international treatment. I do not share the cynical view that all these conferences, although they do involve interminable talk and endless drafting of documents, are of little consequence. They are of *great* consequence, even when they fail to reach agreements or to take actions which some regard as the only test of their success. They assemble together responsible political leaders and experts to grapple with practical problems. Only through this gradual process of consultation and discussion can we hope to develop the understandings essential to common programs of action. By this means we associate people of different experiences and views. Together they seek a world view and build up a body of knowledge which is used by specialists in all nations and eventually through education becomes a foundation for public opinion. There is no short-cut to world order. The concepts and understandings must be built patiently in the minds of men.

Not only do we need to understand what will help build world order but also what will disrupt it. In this Assembly the delegates after historic debates repulsed at least three adventures by the police states to extend the reach of their system of regimentation through the United Nations.

The first and most important was a demand for world-wide suppression and censorship—a direct blow at freedom of speech wherever it exists in the world. The resolution embodying this invasion of human rights was put forward as the major drive of the Soviet Union under the pretext of preventing war-mongering and propaganda disturbing to peaceful and friendly relations among nations.

formulating specific proposals on the functions and powers of an international control agency. Here we have a second major obstruction to collective security.

We have carried on extensive discussions in the Military Staff Committee on peace forces to implement the Charter provisions for enforcement of Security Council decisions, but there is as yet no basis for agreement.

Peace settlements, control of atomic energy, and an acceptable formula for peace forces are essential prerequisites to negotiations for the reduction and control of national armaments in general. The opposition by the Soviet Union to majority proposals in these four fields presents a formidable blockade on the road to collective security.

In the recent Assembly a small minority, led by the Soviet Union, vigorously opposed proposals supported by large majorities, such as those dealing with the Greek border, the Interim Committee, and Korea. When these proposals were adopted by more than the required two-thirds vote of the Assembly, the minority of 6 out of 57 made declarations of noncooperation on the ground that these measures violated provisions of the Charter. According to the majority interpretation of the meaning of the Charter, the actions taken were consistent with the letter and spirit of the basic law. However, a suggestion was made that the Court of International Justice be asked to rule on differences of interpretation. It was rejected by the minority. The members of the minority claimed they were right and the majority was wrong. In the view of the Soviet Union, there the matter rests.

The division within the United Nations is serious because it strikes at the central issue of collective security. That concept was based on the unanimity of the large powers. That unity is lacking on crucial issues. The Soviet Union has demonstrated an unwillingness on most vital matters to join with the majority. Rather, it has insisted that the majority accept the uncompromised position of the minority, which it claims is the only right one. In the face of this division, the Soviet Union accuses the majority of blocking the will of the minority and thus endangering peace and security.

It goes still further. It makes use of the United Nations as a sounding board to conduct a propaganda attack on member states, particularly the United States. In vitriolic and intemperate terms, it charges that the United States is seeking to dominate other nations, that certain circles, including government officials, are conducting a propaganda campaign for a new war and attempting to build up military power for aggression.

The record of discussion and voting in the United Nations makes it clear that the division is not correctly put as one between the Soviet Union and the United States. It is rather a division between a tiny minority of border states dominated and led by the Soviet Union on the one hand and most of the rest of the world on the other.

Most of the significant points over which seemingly irreconcilable differences develop concern the question of security. Collective security means that the member nations must be willing to trust their individual security primarily to the collective defense facilities of the Organization. Obviously the Soviet Union is not yet ready to do this. It hesitates to take any of the risks involved in the establishment of collective security. It gives evidence of a purpose to rely on its own national defense.

I can understand the fear and apprehension which undoubtedly exists in the Soviet Union, a fear which, as long as we lack real collective security, will exist to some degree everywhere. People and nations can only have real security together, mutually. One does not have to ascribe motives of aggression to explain expansionist tendencies. They can be explained as defensive moves. Yet, putting the best construction on the motives does not make the moves less dangerous to all concerned.

The fear of the Russian people feeds on vivid experience. They have suffered two destructive invasions in 30 years. They are naturally security-conscious. They are likely to be apprehensive of any proposal which they think might weaken their existing defenses.

This understandable fear is constantly stimulated by the ruling group through a rigidly controlled press and radio. The Russian people live in the presence of publicity playing up foreign hostility. They are told that the large majority votes in the United Nations show that they are surrounded by hostile forces. On the other hand, they are also told that these votes do not really represent the will of these countries but are cast under duress.

The Soviet leaders visualize a rather unique defense mechanism. As a first line in the outer defenses they rely upon the Communist Parties in various countries to oppose any moves they consider contrary to Soviet interests. If the Communist Party in a given country could actually become the government, the "hostile majority" would lose one vote in the United Nations and the Soviet Union would gain a dependable ally. Thus step by step they would move toward unanimity—Communist unanimity—in the United Nations, and achieve *their* brand of collective security.

A great part of the tension in the United Nations grows out of the fact that the economic and social instability in the wake of war has favored the growth of Communist Parties in many countries. Communist leaders in those countries try to exploit chaotic conditions to seize power. They are properly regarded as fifth columns.

Whether these parties are part of a Soviet plan for world domination through world revolution or merely outposts convenient to Russian defense makes no difference in ultimate consequences. It is obvious that their existence and prospects for their ultimate success must encourage intransigence on the part of the Soviet Union on all matters involving collective security.

The United States does not seek any particular brand of unanimity in the United Nations, nor any particular political or economic system in the individual member states. But we do seek to assist in the restoration of conditions that will safeguard the freedom of member nations.

The second line of Soviet defense consists of buffer states subject to her domination. She would no doubt rather have them "friendly" of their own free will, but "friendly" they must be. And the ruling group in Russia decides precisely how a border state must demonstrate its friendliness. This bear hug of "friendliness" seeks to embrace all distressed, frightened, and despairing neighbor states.

The third and inner line is, of course, the military organization and economic support of it inside Russia. Whether you assume that the motive of the Soviet action is one or another of the three I have mentioned—namely, the Politburo's purpose to maintain its grip on the Russian people, or world domination, or national defense—the conclusion is irresistible that the consequent need is

the United States, economic isolationism will become highly unattractive to eastern Europe. The people of that area will reach out for their customary trade. They will build business bridges over which manufactured goods and farm products can be exchanged. The second line of buffer states will be hard to hold under those conditions.

New power relationships in the world will develop because in the last analysis power is based on productivity. There will be a strong America and Western Hemisphere which have demonstrated by their acts that they are not engaged in dominating others nor preparing for assaults. The term "preventive war" will be forgotten. Those who startle people by talking about it will be recognized as irresponsible elements tolerated but not followed. There should be a strong British Commonwealth once again active in the growing trade of the world. There should be a reconstructed Europe rising to new levels of living by adapting the methods of modern technology and science to a large and free market.

Tensions reflect unstable and unbalanced conditions. We are planning definite acts to change those conditions. But these tensions also reflect a state of mind—a sickness of spirit. Merely changing the physical conditions will not suffice to release the full powers of the human spirit for peaceful progress.

We must overcome fear with faith. We must break the vicious circles of recriminations and accusations by our own emphasis on the positive, the constructive, the creative. It is by our faith that our world will be made whole.

Money and materials can contribute to reconstruction only if the hands which make use of them are moved by a human spirit expressing faith in great purposes and plans. The purpose is not merely to build a material foundation for life but to cultivate a good life.

For this reason we put stress on freedom and responsibility. Europe wants more than economic recovery. It wants a new birth of freedom. Our faith in the power of free men to act rationally in the common interest is the true basis of the coming collective security.

Alien Correspondents at United Nations

STATEMENT BY ACTIN

[Released to the press December 24]

The Department of State has received the communication from the United Nations regarding the case of Nicolas Kyriazides and intends to pass this communication on to the Justice Department today. In so far as the case of the Indian student, Syed Sibtay Hasan, is concerned, it is our understanding that the United Nations has requested the Immigration and Naturalization Service to allow Hasan to depart voluntarily from the United States.

I should like to refute any imputation or allegation that this Government has violated in any way the United Nations Headquarters Agreement which was enacted into law by joint resolution of Congress dated August 4, 1947. We have adhered not only to the letter but to the spirit of this agreement even before the recent action of the United Nations in ratifying it.

In order to keep the record straight, it should be stressed that Kyriazides, in so far as this Government was concerned, ceased being a *bona fide* journalist at the United Nations on October 18, the date the Greek Government closed the two Athens Communist newspapers which he represented at United Nations. We were advised informally this week, after the Immigration and Naturalization Service took action against him, that Kyriazides on October 24 requested United Nations accreditation in representing himself as correspondent for a weekly newspaper published in Cyprus. We were informed this week that a clerk in the United Nations accreditation office accredited Kyriazides without referring the matter to the higher officials or notifying anyone.

The United Nations Headquarters Agreement provides, of course, that accreditation of alien correspondents at United Nations shall be only *after* consultation with the Department of State. This Government, of course, has in no way yielded up its sovereign rights to challenge the *bona fides* of any alien journalist seeking to enter this country or already in this country. It has in no way yielded its sovereign rights to investigate, to hold

Fourth Meeting of Preparatory Commission for IRO

ARTICLE BY GEORGE L. WARREN

The Preparatory Commission for the International Refugee Organization (PCIRO) met for the fourth time at Geneva, Switzerland, on October 21, 1947. It had, on July 1, 1947, assumed operating responsibilities on behalf of the International Refugee Organization for the care, repatriation, and resettlement of displaced persons.[1] The purpose of this session was, therefore, to consider the report of the Executive Secretary on the activities of the Preparatory Commission since July 1 and the status of adherences to the IRO Constitution.

Budget Discussions

The chief problem confronting the Commission was the apparent inadequacy of funds for resettlement—the only available solution for the majority of refugees remaining in the assembly centers. Analysis of the budget showed that $80,000,000 of the total 1947-48 budget of $115,645,000 was set aside for the care and maintenance of displaced persons as compared with approximately $14,840,000 for resettlement. The Executive Secretary reported that 660,000 refugees had been taken under care and maintenance, and that 50,000 to 60,000 in-camp displaced persons remained to be taken over from the occupying authorities. The Executive Secretary presented a new budget for 1947-48 to the Commission, approximately $14,000,000 in excess of the budget adopted in May, and requested that government members consider additional contributions to meet the expanded budget. Practically all members of the Commission reported, however, that they were not in a position to make additional contributions to the IRO, and the Preparatory Commission decided that in order to avoid a deficit in operations the budget for the fiscal year July 1, 1947, through June 30, 1948, should remain at $115,645,000, the anticipated income for the year.

Eligibility Provisions for Care and Maintenance and Resettlement

The Executive Secretary also proposed that the Commission give serious consideration to the settling of a date, such as January 1 or July 1, 1948, after which displaced persons eligible for care under the constitution of IRO would not be accepted for care. This proposal was in line with two "freeze orders" which had already been issued by the administration, one restricting intake of new cases to those suffering extreme hardship and the other restricting resettlement activities solely to in-camp displaced persons. The restriction of resettlement services to in-camp displaced persons was rejected by the Commission, which took the view that this policy would penalize refugees who have become self-supporting but who require PCIRO assistance in finding new homes, and the Executive Secretary was instructed to cancel the administrative order. With respect to the "freeze order" restricting the number of displaced persons to be accepted for care, the Executive Secretary declared that it had been adopted with extreme reluctance for overwhelming reasons of a purely budgetary nature. The Preparatory Commission requested the Executive Secretary to interpret the hardship exception as liberally as possible and to report further to the Commission at its next meeting.

International Conference on Resettlement

The Executive Secretary proposed that the members of the United Nations be called upon to implement the United Nations Assembly Resolution of December 15, 1946, which urged each member to take its fair share of displaced persons. A detailed discussion on the calling of an international conference to determine specific numbers of refugees which receiving governments might agree to accept demonstrated the desirability of coordinating such plans with the International Labor Office and the Economic Committee for Europe and the wisdom of consulting governments as to the time,

[1] For the report on the Third Meeting of the Preparatory Commission for IRO, see BULLETIN of Sept. 28, 1947, p. 638.

place, sponsorship, and specific objectives of such a conference. The Executive Secretary was consequently instructed to consult governments and international organizations concerning these matters and to report to the next meeting of the Commission.

Assistance to Refugees in France

The French Delegation introduced a draft resolution to organize a program of assistance for the several thousand refugees now living in France who were refugees before the outbreak of the second World War, for reasons of race, religion, or political opinion. Included in this group are political refugees from Spain and refugees from Nazi persecution as well as the "Nansen" refugees of Russian and Armenian origin. The Preparatory Commission directed the Executive Secretary to undertake a more adequate program of assistance for needy persons in these categories as soon as possible.

International Tracing Service

The Commission recognized the importance of establishing a single unified international tracing service for displaced persons; this would coordinate all the separate tracing services now in existence. The Executive Secretary was therefore directed to invite all interested governments, whether or not members of the Preparatory Commission, as well as voluntary societies engaged in tracing persons, to relate their tracing activities to the work of the International Tracing Service whose functions will include mass tracing activities and the tracing of children.

International Travel Document

Large numbers of refugees and displaced persons are without travel documents of any kind. The Preparatory Commission discussed the advantages offered by an internationally valid travel document similar to the Nansen passport and instructed the Executive Secretary to insure that persons within the mandate of the organization be provided with identity papers and travel documents without which the formalities of travel prerequisite to resettlement cannot be completed.

Recognition of the Work of Voluntary Organizations

The Preparatory Commission took special note of the valuable work which was being carried for-

The Provisional Frequency Board is an international body formed under agreements made at the Atlantic City International Radio Conference of 1947. The Board was established to prepare a proposed international frequency list for presentation to a special administrative conference of the International Telecommunication Union, tentatively scheduled to be held in 1949. In accomplishing this work the Board will examine world requirements for radio frequencies with a view to reassigning them on the basis of good engineering practices and in conformity with the radiofrequency allocation table drawn up at the Atlantic City conference. Any country which is a member of the International Telecommunication Union may participate in the work of the Provisional Frequency Board.

of Interim Commission of WHO

Dr. Morton Kramer, Chief, Research Branch, Office of International Health Relations, U.S. Public Health Service

John Tomlinson, Assistant Chief, Division of International Organization Affairs, Department of State

The Interim Commission of the World Health Organization, set up at the International Health Conference at New York in July 1946, has met four times: at New York in July 1946, and at Geneva in November 1946, March and April 1947, and August and September 1947. The purpose of the Commission meetings is to consider urgent health problems arising during the period prior to the establishment of the World Health Organization and to formulate plans for setting up the permanent organization.

The American representative on the Interim Commission of the World Health Organization is Dr. Thomas Parran, Surgeon General, U.S. Public Health Service.

FOREIGN AID AND RECONSTRUCTI

Providing for the Admi

By virtue of the authority vested in me by the Constitution and statutes of the United States, particularly the Foreign Aid Act of 1947, and as President of the United States, it is hereby ordered, in the interest of the internal management of the Government, as follows:

1. The Secretary of State is hereby authorized and directed:

(a) To perform the functions and exercise the powers and authority vested in the President by the Foreign Aid Act of 1947 (hereinafter referred to as the Act), exclusive of sections 11 (b) and 11 (d) thereof:

Provided that—

(1) In designating, under section 3 of the Act, the existing departments, agencies, or independent establishments of the Government through which certain functions, powers, and authority under the Act shall be performed or exercised, the Secretary shall act with the concurrence of the department, agency, or establishment concerned in each case.

(2) In promulgating, under section 4 of the Act, any regulations controlling the purchase or procurement of commodities, and in promulgating, under section 10 of the Act, any rules and regulations necessary and proper to carry out any of the provisions of the Act, the Secretary shall, to the extent that any such rule or regulation affects the operations of any agency, establishment, or department other than the Department of State, act with the concurrence of the agency, establishment, or department concerned in each case.

(3) In making the determinations, required under paragraphs 2 and 3 of section 4 of the Act, whether commodities to be purchased or procured under the Act are in short supply in the United States, the Secretary of State shall act on the advice of the heads of the appropriate departments, agencies or establishments.

(4) In making the determinations required

---

[1] Ex. Or. 9914 (12 *Federal Register* 8867).

alendar of Meetings[1]

djourned During Month of December

:AO (International Civil Aviation Organization): Second Session of Council.	Montreal . . . .
ARBA (North American Regional Broadcasting Agreement): Meeting of Technicians.	Habana . . . .
NESCO (United Nations Educational, Scientific and Cultural Organization): Second Session of General Conference.	Mexico City . . . .
FM (Council of Foreign Ministers):	
Meeting of Deputies for Germany	London . . . .
Fifth Session	London . . . .
Inited Nations:	
Ecosoc (Economic and Social Council):	
Subcommission on Employment and Economic Stability	Lake Success . . . .
Subcommission on Economic Development	Lake Success . . . .
Subcommission on Protection of Minorities and Prevention of Discrimination.	Geneva . . . .
Human Rights Commission: Second Session	Geneva . . . .
Trusteeship Council: Second Session	Lake Success . . . .
ECAFE (Economic Commission for Asia and the Far East)	Baguio, Philippines . . . . .
ifth Meeting of Inter-American Bar Association	Lima . . . .
CEF (International Children's Emergency Fund): Executive Board .	Lake Success . . . .
'reliminary Discussions on Treatment of German Trade-Mark Rights .	London . . . .
LO (International Labor Organization):	
Joint Maritime Commission	Geneva . . . .
103d Session of Governing Body	Geneva . . . .
ifth Meeting of Caribbean Commission	Trinidad . . . .
nternational Wheat Council: 17th Session	Washington . . . .

n Session as of December 31, 1947

'ar Eastern Commission	Washington . . . .
Inited Nations:	
Security Council	Lake Success . . . .
Military Staff Committee	Lake Success . . . .
Committee on Atomic Energy	Lake Success . . . .
Commission on Conventional Armaments	Lake Success . . . .
Security Council's Good Offices Committee on Indonesia	Indonesian territory . . . .
Trade and Employment Conference	Habana . . . .
General Assembly's Special Balkan Committee	Salonika . . . .
ierman External Property Negotiations (Safehaven):	
With Portugal	Lisbon . . . .
With Spain	Madrid . . . .
nter-Allied Trade Board for Japan	Washington . . . .
FM (Council of Foreign Ministers):	
Meeting of Deputies for Italian Colonial Problems	London . . . .
Commission of Investigation to Former Italian Colonies	Former Italian Colonies . . .

[1] Prepared in the Division of International Conferences, Department of State.

Scheduled for January–March 1948		1948
Third Pan American Congress of Ophthalmology	Habana	Jan. 4–10
United Nations:		
Interim Committee of the General Assembly	Lake Success	Jan. 5–
Ecosoc (Economic and Social Council):		
Commission on the Status of Women	Lake Success	Jan. 5–16
Sixth Session	Lake Success	Feb. 2–
Subcommission on Economic Development	Lake Success	Mar. 8–
Subcommission on Employment and Economic Stability	Lake Success	Mar. 8–
World Conference on Freedom of Information	Geneva	Mar. 22–
Social Commission: Third Session	Lake Success	Mar. 30–
Ece (Economic Commission for Europe): Third Session	Geneva	Mar. 31–[1]
Meeting of the Inter-American Coffee Board	Washington	Jan. 5–
Ninth Pan American Child Congress	Caracas	Jan. 5–10
Icao (International Civil Aviation Organization):		
Statistics Division: First Session	Montreal	Jan. 13–
Aeronautical Maps and Charts Division	Brussels	Mar. 8–
Airline Operating Practices Division	Montreal	March
Provisional Frequency Board	Geneva	Jan. 15–
Who (World Health Organization):		
Committee on Administration and Finance	Geneva	Jan. 19–
Fifth Session of Interim Commission	Geneva	Jan. 22–
Expert Committee on Tuberculosis	Geneva	Feb. 17–
Iro (International Refugee Organization): Fifth Part of First Session of Preparatory Commission.	Geneva	Jan. 20–
International Telecommunication Union: Meeting of Administrative Council.	Geneva	Jan. 20–
Meeting of Special Committee to Make Recommendations for the Coordination of Safety Activities in Fields of Aviation, Meteorology, Shipping and Telecommunications.	London	Jan. 27–
American International Institute for the Protection of Childhood: Meeting of International Council.	Caracas	January
IUBS (International Union of Biological Sciences): Executive Committee.	Geneva	Feb. 2–3
FAO (Food and Agriculture Organization):		
Regional Meeting of Technical Nutritionists	Baguio	Feb. 9–15
Regional Meeting to Consider Creation of Councils for Study of the Sea.	Baguio	Feb. 9–15
Rice Meeting	Southeast Asia	Feb. 16–28
Second Meeting of Council	Washington	Mar. 18–31
Sixth Pan American Railway Congress	Habana	Feb. 28–
Praha International Spring Fair	Praha	Mar. 12–21
First Meeting of Planning Committee on High Frequency Broadcasting.	Geneva	Mar. 22–
Ninth International Conference of American States	Bogotá	Mar. 30–

[1] Tentative.

Facilitation of International Inland Transport in Europe

STATEMENT BY ACTING SECRETARY LOVETT

[Released to the press December 24]

One of the most progressive steps in the advancement and facilitation of international inland transport in Europe since the end of the war was developed at the December meeting of the Inland Transport Committee of the Economic Commission for Europe in Geneva.

Eight European governments together with the three western zones of Germany have agreed to grant or maintain freedom of operation for six months for highway trucks engaged in transit movements through any of the following participating countries: the three western zones of Germany; France; the Netherlands; Sweden; Switzerland; Italy; Denmark; and Czechoslovakia. This means, for example, that it will now be possible for trucks from Italy, en route to the Netherlands, to pass through Switzerland, France, and western Germany without transferring their loads to locally operated carriers.

The three German zones, Denmark, the Netherlands, Sweden, and Switzerland also agreed to grant or maintain freedom of movement for all other international transport of goods by highways for a six-month period. Belgium, Czechoslovakia, France, and Italy agreed to the most liberal application of their present systems of authorization. Adherence to this accord permits delivery of goods by highway transport from the factory or farm in one country direct to the consumer in another.

The only restrictions connected with these two agreements are:

(a) The road services of countries and zones granting such facilities shall enjoy reciprocal facilities in the beneficiary country;

(b) The carriers shall conform to existing laws and regulations of a technical or administrative character now in force.

Significance is attached to these agreements as evidence of the desire of European countries to promote economic cooperation among themselves. Increased use of highway transport will help relieve the presently overburdened continental railroads.

Action was also taken by the Inland Transport Committee to have custom offices reduce customs formalities and delays at frontiers.

The Committee recognized the urgent importance of obtaining the fullest utilization of available road transport, particularly during the next six months, of conserving fuel, tires, vehicles, and materials for road maintenance, and of reducing the burden of transport costs on commodity prices. It recommended that participating governments take all practical steps to reduce the ratio of empty loads to revenue loads, and that governments and international organizations should notify the Secretariat periodically of the capacity of vehicles utilized and the load actually carried in both directions over the principal international routes.

Consideration will be given to adopting a long-range program for the facilitation of the international movement of highway transport at a meeting in Geneva in January. Continuation of certain aspects of the present short-term program will also be covered in the January meeting.

Agreement With Burma on Educational Exchange

[Released to the press December 22]

An agreement putting into operation the program of international educational exchanges authorized by the Fulbright act (Public Law 584, 79th Congress) was signed in Rangoon on December 19 between the Minister of Foreign Affairs, U Tin Tut, on behalf of the Government of Burma, and R. Austin Acly, Chargé d'Affaires ad interim of the American Embassy, on behalf of the Government of the United States. This is the Republic of Burma's first agreement with any foreign country to be signed in Burma.

This agreement establishes the United States Educational Foundation in Burma to administer certain funds resulting from the sale of surplus property to Burma. The Fulbright act, which amends the Surplus Property Act of 1944, is predicated on a desire to cement international understanding and good-will by developing interchanges of students, specialists, and scholars on an unprecedented scale, and on the knowledge that many countries are not able to make complete payment for purchases of these supplies in United States dollars. It provides that partial payment may be made in local currencies which will then be used by the United States for educational purposes.

The present agreement places at the disposal of the Government of the United States the equivalent in Burmese national currency of $200,000 a year until the equivalent of 3 million dollars in United States dollars has been deposited for such activities. These include the financing of "studies, research, instruction, and other educational activities of or for citizens of the United States of America in schools and institutions of higher learning located in Burma, or of the citizens of Burma in United States schools and institutions of higher learning located outside the continental

Cuba–U.S. Tariff Concessions To Be Effec

[Released to the press December 22]

The Department of State announced on December 22 that Cuba and the United States will each make provisionally effective on January 1, 1948, the tariff concessions of principal interest to the other and will on that date generally apply the provisions of the exclusive agreement signed by the two countries supplementary to the general agreement on tariffs and trade, which was signed at Geneva on October 30, 1947, by 23 countries, including Cuba and the United States.

Cuba signed on December 17, 1947, at Lake Success the protocol of provisional application of the general agreement. Cuba is thus the first country

---

[1] For agreement with China see BULLETIN of Nov. 23, 1947, p. 1005.

EXCLUSIVE AGREEMENT BETWEEN THE UNITED STATES OF AMERICA AND THE REPUBLIC OF CUBA SUPPLEMENTARY TO THE GENERAL AGREEMENT ON TARIFFS AND TRADE

The Governments of the United States of America and the Republic of Cuba,

Having participated in the framing of a General Agreement on Tariffs and Trade, hereinafter referred to as the General Agreement, and a Protocol of Provisional Application, the texts of which have been authenticated by the Final Act adopted at the conclusion of the Second Session of the Preparatory Committee of the United Nations Conference on Trade and Employment, signed this day,

Hereby agree as follows:

1. The Convention of Commercial Reciprocity between the United States of America and the Republic of Cuba signed December 11, 1902, and the Reciprocal Trade Agreement between the United States of America and the Republic of Cuba signed August 24, 1934, with its accompanying exchange of notes, as amended by the supplementary trade agreement signed December 18, 1939, with its accompanying protocol and exchange of notes, and by the supplementary trade agreement signed December 23, 1941, with its accompanying exchange of notes, shall be inoperative for such time as the United States of America and the Republic of Cuba are both contracting parties to the General Agreement as defined in Article XXXII thereof.

2. For such time as the United States of America and the Republic of Cuba are both contracting parties to the General Agreement, the products of either country imported into the other shall be accorded customs treatment as follows:

(a) The provisions of Part II of Schedule IX of the General Agreement shall apply exclusively to products of the United States of America, and the provisions of Part II of Schedule XX of the General Agreement shall apply exclusively to products of the Republic of Cuba.

(b) Products of the United States of America described in Part I, but not in Part II, of Schedule IX of the General Agreement, imported into the Republic of Cuba, and products of the Republic of Cuba described in Part I, but not in Part II, of Schedule XX of the General Agreement, imported into the United States of America, shall be subject to the customs treatment provided for in Part I of the applicable Schedule.

(c) Subject to the principles set forth in Article 17 of the Draft Charter for an International Trade Organization recommended by the Preparatory Committee of the United Nations Conference on Trade and Employment—

(i) any product of the United States of America not described in either Part of Schedule IX of the General Agreement which would have been subject to ordinary customs duty if imported into the Republic of Cuba on April 10, 1947, any temporary or conditional exemption from duty to be disregarded, and which is of a kind which the Government of Cuba shall determine to have been imported into its territory as a product of the United States of America in any quantity during any of the calendar years 1937, 1939, 1944, and 1945, shall be entitled upon importation into the Republic of Cuba to a margin of preference in the applicable rate of duty equal to the absolute difference between the most-favored-nation rate for the like product existing on April 10, 1947, including any such rate temporarily suspended, and the preferential rate likewise existing on that date in respect of such product of the United States of America; and

(ii) any product of the Republic of Cuba not described in either Part of Schedule XX of the General Agreement, which would have been subject to ordinary customs duty if imported into the United States of America on April 10, 1947, any temporary or conditional exemption from duty to be disregarded, and which is of a kind which the Government of the United States of America shall determine to have been imported into its territory as a product of Cuba in any quantity during any of the calendar years 1937, 1939, 1944, and 1945, shall be entitled upon importation into the United States of America to a margin of preference in the applicable rate of duty equal to the absolute difference between the most-favored-nation rate for the like product existing on April 10, 1947, including any such rate temporarily suspended, and the preferential rate likewise existing on that date in respect of such product of the Republic of Cuba.

(d) Any product of the United States of America or of the Republic of Cuba for which customs treatment is not prescribed above shall be dutiable, when imported into the other country, at the most-favored-nation rate of duty of the importing country for the like product.

(e) Nothing in this Agreement shall require the application to any product of the Republic of Cuba imported into the United States of America of a rate of ordinary customs duty higher than one and one-half times the rate existing in respect of such product on January 1, 1945, any temporary or conditional exemption from duty to be disregarded.

3. The term "most-favored-nation rate" in this Exclusive Supplementary Agreement means the maximum rate which may be, or could have been, applied consistently with the principles set forth in Article I of the General Agreement to a product of a country which is a contracting party to that Agreement.

IN WITNESS WHEREOF the representatives of the Governments of the United States of America and the Republic of Cuba, after having exchanged their full powers, found to be in good and due form, have signed this Exclusive Supplementary Agreement.

DONE in duplicate, in the English and Spanish languages, both texts authentic, at Geneva, this thirtieth day of October, one thousand nine hundred and forty-seven.

For the Government of the United States of America:

WINTHROP G. BROWN

For the Government of the Republic of Cuba:

S. I. CLARK

Termination of Trade Agreement Procla

By the President of the United States of America

A PROCLAMATION[1]

WHEREAS (1), pursuant to the authority conferred by section 350 (*a*) of the Tariff Act of 1930, as amended by the act of June 12, 1934 entitled "An Act To amend the Tariff Act of 1930" (48 Stat. 943 and 944, ch. 474) the President of the United States of America entered into the following trade agreements:

(a) With the Belgo-Luxemburg Economic Union on February 27, 1935 (49 Stat. (pt. 2) 3681 to 3716), which trade agreement was proclaimed by the President on April 1, 1935 (49 Stat. (pt. 2) 3680 to 3717),

(b) With the Government of the French Republic on May 6, 1936 (53 Stat. (pt. 3) 2237 to 2290), which trade agreement was proclaimed by the President on May 16, 1936 (53 Stat. (pt. 3) 2236 to 2291), and

(c) With Her Majesty the Queen of the Netherlands on December 20, 1935 (50 Stat. (pt. 2) 1505 to 1557), which trade agreement was proclaimed by the President on December 28, 1935 (50 Stat. (pt. 2) 1504 to 1558) and was the subject of a supplementary proclamation by the President of April 10, 1937 (50 Stat. (pt. 2) 1559);

WHEREAS (2), pursuant to the authority conferred by said section 350 (*a*), the period within which such authority might be exercised having been extended by the Joint Resolution approved March 1, 1937 (50 Stat. 24, ch. 22), the President entered into the following trade agreements:

(a) With His Majesty the King of Great Britain, Ireland and the British dominions beyond the Seas, Emperor of India, in respect of Canada, on November 17, 1938 (53 Stat. (pt. 3) 2350 to 2392), which trade agreement was proclaimed by the President on November 25, 1938 (53 Stat. (pt. 3) 2348 to 2394) and was the subject of a supplementary proclamation by the President of June 17, 1939 (53 Stat. (pt. 3) 2394 and 2395), and

---

[1] Proc. 2763, 12 *Federal Register* 8866.

America, acting under the authority conferred by the said section 350(a) of the Tariff Act of 1930, as amended, do hereby proclaim that each of the proclamations listed in the 1st or the 2nd recitals of this proclamation shall not be in effect after December 31, 1947 except insofar as it relates to the termination on six months' notice of the trade agreement with respect to which it was issued.

IN WITNESS WHEREOF, I have hereunto set my hand and caused the Seal of the United States of America to be affixed.

DONE at the City of Washington this twenty-fourth day of December in the year of [SEAL] our Lord nineteen hundred and forty-seven and of the Independence of the United States of America the one hundred and seventy-second.

By the President:
ROBERT A. LOVETT
Acting Secretary of State

Panama Rejects Ratification of Defense-Sites Agreement

[Released to the press December 23]

According to official reports the National Assembly of Panama has rejected the ratification of the defense-sites agreement signed on December 10, 1947, by the Governments of the Republic of Panama and the United States of America. This agreement was reached in accordance with the 1936 treaty of friendship and cooperation providing for joint responsibility of the two countries for the effective protection of the Canal.

Throughout the period of more than 15 months during which negotiations for a defense-sites agreement have taken place, the United States Government has endeavored at all times to share with the Government of Panama its estimates of the minimum defense needs of the Canal. It has been the constant aim of the United States negotiators to consult with the appropriate Panamanian authorities in all frankness with respect to the considerations underlying these estimates which

have provided the basis for the recent defense proposals of this Government.

Substantial and repeated concessions were made during the lengthy negotiations on the agreement in an attempt to reconcile Panamanian desires with the defense requirements of the Canal. The negotiations were concluded on December 10 by the signature of the agreement in terms which were intended to take into account the legitimate interests of both countries.

In accordance with oral statements made to the Panamanian Government in the course of the negotiations, the necessary steps will be taken immediately with a view to evacuation of all sites in the Republic of Panama outside the Canal Zone where United States armed forces are now stationed. This withdrawal will be completed as quickly as possible, consistent with the number of personnel and the amount of matériel involved.

Failure to conclude an agreement will not, of course, affect the normal friendly relations between the two countries.

Visit of Guatemalan Educator

Dr. Carlos Martínez Durán, rector of the University of San Carlos, Guatemala, has arrived in the United States to confer with officials of American universities concerning university organization and administration, in order to aid in planning a university city at the University of San Carlos.

Dr. Martínez Durán is one of a distinguished group of specialists from the other American republics who have been awarded grants by the Department of State under its program for the interchange of professors, specialists, and distinguished leaders between the United States and the other American republics.

THE DEPARTMENT

Departmental Regulations

290.5 **Procedure for the Handling and Settlement of Certain Tort Claims:** (Effective 11-1-47) This regulation delegates authority to settle claims for personal injury or property damage under the Federal Tort Claims Act (60 Stat. 842; 28 U.S.C. 921) and the Small Claims Act (42 Stat. 1060; 31 U.S.C. 215–217), and claims for property damage under the Act of June 19, 1939 (53 Stat. 841; 22 U.S.C. 277e), and to establish and provide the exclusive authorization and procedure whereby claims arising from the negligent or wrongful acts or omissions of employees of the Department of State or of the United States Section, International Boundary and Water Commission, United States and Mexico, and claims for property damage not based on negligence and cognizable under the Act of June 19, 1939, may be considered, adjusted, determined, or settled within the Department or the Commisson.

I DELEGATION OF AUTHORITY FOR ADJUDICATION AND SETTLEMENT OF CLAIMS. The Legal Adviser is hereby authorized to settle all claims cognizable, as the case may be, under the Federal Tort Claims Act (60 Stat. 842; 28 U.S.C. 921) or the Small Claims Act (42 Stat. 1060; 31 U.S.C. 215–217), arising out of the negligent or wrongful acts or omissions of employees of the Department in accordance with the authority vested in the Secretary pursuant to those Acts, except those claims arising out of the negligent or wrongful acts or omissions of employees of the Commission. The Commissioner is authorized to settle those claims which arise out of the negligent or wrongful acts or omissions of employees of the Commission, and claims for property damage not based on negligence cognizable under the Act of June 19, 1939. The approval or disapproval, in whole or in part, of any claim by the approving authority constitutes final action in the case so far as the Department or the Commission is concerned, and no further review in the Department or in the Commission may be obtained.

II GENERAL PROVISIONS.

A *Definitions.* As used in this part—

1 The word *Secretary* refers to the Secretary of State.

2 The word *Department* refers to the Department of State, its offices, bureaus, and divisions and its Foreign Service establishments abroad.

3 The word *Commission* refers to the United States Section, International Boundary and Water Commission, United States and Mexico.

4 The word *Legal Adviser* refers to the Legal Adviser of the Department of State, or his designee.

5 The word *Commissioner* refers to the United States Commissioner, International Boundary and Water Commission, United States and Mexico.

6 The word *employee* includes officers or employees of the Department or of the Commission, and persons acting on behalf of the Department or of the Commission in an official capacity, temporarily or permanently in the service of the Department or of the Commission, whether with or without compensation.

7 The words *approving authority* refer to the Legal Adviser or to the Commissioner, as the case may be.

B *Action by Claimant.*

1 CLAIMS FOR DAMAGE TO, OR LOSS OF, PROPERTY, OR FOR PERSONAL INJURY OR DEATH. Claims for damage to, or loss of, property or for personal injury or death may be presented by the individual or firm sustaining injury or damages in his or its own right, by a duly-authorized agent or legal representative, or by an attorney. The claim, if filed by an agent or legal representative, must

c   Personal Injury. In support of claims for personal injury or death, the claimant should submit a written report by the attending physician, showing the nature and extent of injury, the nature and extent of treatment, the degree of permanent disability, if any, the prognosis, and the period of hospitalization or incapacitation, attaching itemized bills for medical, hospital, or burial expenses actually incurred.

d   Damage to Real Property. In support of claims for damage to land, trees, buildings, fences, and other improvements, and similar property, the claimant should submit an itemized receipt, if payment has been made, or an itemized signed statement or estimate of the cost of repairs. If the property is not economically reparable, a statement as to its value both before and after the accident should be included. If the damages to improvements can be readily and fairly valued apart from the damage to the land, the damage to such improvements should be stated separately from the damage to land. The value of such improvements at the time of loss or destruction should be stated, as well as the date the improvements were made and the original cost of such improvements.

e   Damage to Crops. In support of claims for damage to crops, the claimant should submit an itemized signed statement showing the number of acres, or other unit measure, of the crops damaged, the normal yield per unit, the gross amount which would have been realized from such normal yield and an estimate of the costs of cultivating, harvesting, and marketing such crops. If the crop is one which need not be planted each year, the diminution in value of the land beyond the damage to the current year's crop should also be stated.

f   Claims of Subrogees and Lien-holders. The rights of subrogees or lien-holders will be righted according to the law of the jurisdiction in which the accident or incident occurred.

g   Signatures. The claim and all other papers requiring the signature of the claimant should be in affidavit form signed by the claimant personally or by a duly-authorized agent or legal representative. The claim should also be signed by the insurance company as one of the claimants, where the claim is covered by insurance in whole or in part and the contract of insurance contains a provision for the subrogation of the insurance company to the rights of the insured, in accordance with paragraph II B 2 hereof. Section 35 (A) of the Criminal Code (18 U.S.C. 80) imposes a fine of not more than $10,000 and imprisonment of not more than 10 years, or both, for presenting false claims or making false or fraudulent statements or representations in connection with making claims against the Government. A civil penalty or forfeiture of $2,000 plus double the amount of damages sustained by the United States is provided for presenting false or fraudulent claims (see 31 U.S.C. 231).

C   Approval of Claim. Claims under paragraph II are approved, or disapproved, in whole or in part, by the Legal Adviser, after transmittal to him, with recommenda-

tions, by the head of the office, bureau, division, or Foreign Service establishment of the Department out of whose activities the accident or incident arose. Claims under paragraph II arising out of the activities of the Commission are approved or disapproved, in whole or in part, by the Commissioner.

D   Acceptance of Settlement by Claimant. The acceptance of the settlement by the claimant shall be final and conclusive on the claimant, and shall constitute a complete release by the claimant of any claim against the Government and against the employee of the Government whose act or omission gave rise to the claim, by reason of the same subject-matter.

III   FEDERAL TORT CLAIMS ACT.

A   General. The Federal Tort Claims Act (60 Stat. 842; 28 U.S.C. 921) conferred upon the head of each Federal agency, or his designee, acting on behalf of the United States, authority to ascertain, adjust, determine, and settle certain claims against the United States for money only, accruing on and after January 1, 1945.

B   Allowable Claims. Claims are payable by the Department or by the Commission under the Federal Tort Claims Act and paragraph III, on account of damage to or loss of property or on account of personal injury or death, where the total amount of the claim does not exceed $1,000, caused by the negligent or wrongful act or omission of any employee of the Department or of the Commission, while acting within the scope of his office or employment, under circumstances where the United States, if a private person, would be liable to the claimant for such damage, loss, injury, or death, in accordance with the law of the place where the act or omission occurred. The Department or the Commission does not have legal authorization to consider administratively claims in excess of $1,000 which are otherwise cognizable under the Federal Tort Claims Act. The claimant's remedy, if any, in such cases is by suit in the United States District Court for the district wherein the act or omission complained of occurred, including the United States District Courts for the Territories and possessions of the United States.

C   Exclusions. As provided in section 421 of the Federal Tort Claims Act, claims, among others, not payable under that act and paragraph III include:

1   Any claim based upon an act or omission of an employee of the Government, exercising due care, in the execution of a statute or regulation, whether or not such statute or regulation be valid, or based upon the exercise or performance or the failure to exercise or perform a discretionary function or duty on the part of a Federal agency or an employee of the Government, whether or not the discretion involved be abused.

2   Any claim arising out of the loss, miscarriage, or negligent transmission of letters or postal matter.

3   Any claim arising out of an act or omission of any employee of the Government in administering the provisions of the Trading-with-the-Enemy Act, as amended.

4   Any claim for damages caused by the imposition or establishment of a quarantine by the United States.

5   Any claim arising from injury to vessels, or to the cargo, crew, or passengers of vessels, while passing through the locks of the Panama Canal or while in Canal Zone waters.

6   Any claim arising out of assault, battery, false imprisonment, false arrest, malicious prosecution, abuse of process, libel, slander, misrepresentation, deceit, or interference with contract rights.

7   Any claim arising in a foreign country.

D   *Application to Claims Not Previously Adjusted.* The provisions of paragraph III shall apply to all claims otherwise within its scope, not heretofore adjusted, including claims formerly payable under provisions of laws and regulations now superseded, arising out of accidents or incidents occurring on or after January 1, 1945. Claims arising out of accidents or incidents occurring prior to January 1, 1945, or claims not cognizable under paragraph III, including, among others, claims arising in foreign countries, will be settled under the provisions of the Small Claims Act, the Act of December 28, 1922 (42 Stat. 1066; 31 U.S.C. 215–217). See paragraph IV. Claims for damage to lands or other private property of any kind by reason of the operations of the United States, its officers or employees, in the survey, construction, operation, or maintenance of any project constructed or administered through the Commissioner, not based upon the negligence or wrongful act or omission of any employee of the United States while acting within the scope of his office or employment, will be settled under the provisions of the Act of June 19, 1939 (53 Stat. 841; 22 U.S.C. 277e). See paragraph V.

E   *Statute of Limitations.* Claims under the Federal Tort Claims Act and under paragraph III must be presented in writing to the Department or to the Commission, as the case may be, within one year after the claim accrued, or by August 2, 1947, whichever is later.

F   *Payment of Claims.* When an award is made, the Legal Adviser or the Commissioner, as the case may be, will transmit the file on the case to the appropriate fiscal office for payment out of funds appropriated, or to be appropriated, for the purpose. Claims under the Federal Tort Claims Act shall be paid in accordance with the provisions of General Regulations No. 110, General Accounting Office, February 12, 1947.

G   *Withdrawal of Claim.* A claimant may, in accordance with the provisions of section 410 (b) of the Federal Tort Claims Act, withdraw his claim from consideration upon fifteen days' notice in writing to the Legal Adviser or to the Commissioner, as the case may be.

H   *Attorneys' Fees.* In accordance with section 422 of the Federal Tort Claims Act, reasonable attorneys' fees may be paid under paragraph III out of, but not in addition to, the amount of the award or settlement. If the award or settlement is $500 or less, reasonable attorneys' fees, but not in excess of $50, may be allowed. If the award is $500 or more, reasonable attorneys' fees, but not in excess of 10 percent of the amount of the award or settlement, may be allowed. Attorneys' fees under this paragraph may be fixed only on written request of either the claimant or his attorney.

thereupon be transmitted by the Commissioner through the Department to the General Accounting Office for settlement.

PUBLICATIONS

Department of State

For sale by the Superintendent of Documents, Government Printing Office, Washington 25, D. C. Address requests direct to the Superintendent of Documents, except in the case of free publications, which may be obtained from the Department of State.

The London Meeting of the Council of Foreign Ministers, Nov. 25–Dec. 16, 1947. 10 pp.

> Report on the result of the recent meeting of the Council of Foreign Ministers in London by George C. Marshall, Secretary of State. Broadcast from Washington, D. C., on December 19, 1947.

Air Transport Services. Treaties and Other International Acts Series 1587. Pub. 2764. 29 pp. 10¢.

> Agreement Between the U.S. and Peru, and Accompanying Notes—Signed at Lima December 27, 1946; entered into force December 27, 1946; and agreement effected by exchange of notes signed at Washington May 6 and 8, and July 21, 1947; entered into force July 21, 1947.

Haitian Finances. Treaties and Other International Acts Series 1643. Pub. 2945. 5 pp. 5¢.

> Agreement Between the U.S. and Haiti—Effected by exchange of notes signed at Port-au-Prince July 4, 1947; entered into force July 4, 1947.

Passport Visa Fees. Treaties and Other International Acts Series 1644. Pub. 2946. 2 pp. 5¢.

> Agreement Between the U.S. and Norway—Effected by exchange of notes signed at Washington July 7 and 29, 1947; entered into force July 29, 1947; effective August 1, 1947.

National Commission News, January 1, 1948. Pub. 3003. 10 pp. 10¢ a copy; $1 a year.

> Published monthly for the United States National Commission for the United Nations Educational, Scientific and Cultural Organization.

Contributors

Ely Maurer and *James Simsarian*, authors of the article on the
agreement relating to conflicting claims to German enemy assets, are
respectively an Assistant to the Legal Adviser, Department of State,
and Special Assistant to the U. S. Delegate to the Inter-Allied Reparation Agency.

George L. Warren, author of the article on the fourth meeting of the
Preparatory Commission for Iro, is Adviser on Refugees and Displaced Persons for the Assistant Secretary of State for Occupied Areas.
Mr. Warren was the American Delegate at the meeting of the Preparatory Commission.

The Department of State bulletin

Vol. XVIII, No. 445 • Publication 3015

January 11, 1948

The Department of State BULLETIN, a weekly publication compiled and edited in the Division of Publications, Office of Public Affairs, provides the public and interested agencies of the Government with information on developments in the field of foreign relations and on the work of the Department of State and the Foreign Service. The BULLETIN includes press releases on foreign policy issued by the White House and the Department, and statements and addresses made by the President and by the Secretary of State and other officers of the Department, as well as special articles on various phases of international affairs and the functions of the Department. Information is included concerning treaties and international agreements to which the United States is or may become a party and treaties of general international interest.

Publications of the Department, as well as legislative material in the field of international relations, are listed currently.

For sale by the Superintendent of Documents
U.S. Government Printing Office
Washington 25, D.C.

Subscription:
52 issues, $5; single copy, 15 cents

Published with the approval of the
Director of the Bureau of the Budget

Habana Meeting of U.N. Conference on Trade and Employment

STATEMENT ON QUANTITATIVE RESTRICTIONS BY VICE CHAIRMAN OF U. S. DELEGATION [1]

The issue now before us, Mr. Chairman, must will be forthcoming if trade is rigorously re- be narrowly defined.

It is *not* whether quantitative restrictions are to be abolished, immediately and completely. That there must be exceptions to the rule against QR everybody is agreed.

It is *not* whether undeveloped countries should be developed. On this question there has never been any dispute.

It is *not even* whether QR may be used for development. Under the present draft of Article 13 it may.

The issue, simply and solely, is whether QR for protection may be freely used by everybody all the time or may only be used where and when there is no superior alternative.

The United States has reluctantly come to the position that QR may be used for purely protective purposes in exceptional cases with appropriate safeguards. It cannot agree, however, to the proposal that is contained in certain amendments that are now before this Committee. Under these amendments, any country would be completely free, at any time, to impose on the imports of any product from any other country any quantitative limits that it might desire. There is only one way in which this proposal can be described: it is a prescription for economic anarchy.

If QR is to be fastened on the commerce of the world without let or hindrance, the restrictionism of the fifties and the sixties will make the restrictionism of the thirties look like absolute free trade. If this is to be the outcome of our negotiations here, I say that all our hopes for expanding trade, for raising standards of living, for promoting economic development, for achieving economic peace are doomed to failure.

I must confess to a total inability to follow the logic of those who have argued here that we can expand trade by forbidding exporters to sell and importers to buy. I find it equally difficult to understand how we can raise standards of living by making goods so scarce that people can't get them and so expensive that they can't afford to buy them.

So, too, with economic development. A reading of the verbatim record of these proceedings might lead one to the conclusion that an undeveloped country could achieve a rapid and far-reaching industrialization simply and solely by imposing quantitative restrictions on its trade. Nothing could be further from the truth. Industrialization requires capital. It requires equipment. It requires technology. It requires know-how. And one wonders to what extent any of these requisites will be forthcoming if trade is rigorously restrained. For investors will not be attracted to new industries unless they promise to succeed. New industries will not promise to succeed unless they have access to adequate markets. And they will not have access to adequate markets if every-

[1] Made on Dec. 23, 1947, and released to the press in Habana on the same date. Clair Wilcox, Director of the Office of International Trade Policy, Department of State, is Vice Chairman of the U. S. Delegation.

body, everywhere, resorts to QR. QR does not open markets; it closes them. That is what it is for. And when it spreads, through example and retaliation, to the point where every little country and every undeveloped country on earth is isolated from every other by a tight wall of prohibitions, the chances of vigorous industrial development will finally have been destroyed.

One way for a man to grow strong is to observe the proper diet, take plenty of sleep, and get plenty of exercise. Another way to present a superficial appearance of animation is to take an injection of a powerful drug. The former is slower and harder, but it lasts longer. The latter is quicker, but it is transitory, habit-forming, and may end in stupefaction. QR is a shot in the arm. A moderate dose may put an industry on its feet. An overdose can lay a whole economy flat on its back.

Several delegates, in the course of this debate, have referred to QR as a "weapon" and have said that the "weapon" is one of which they must not be deprived. The metaphor is all too appropriate. For a weapon is something that one uses in a war, and economic war will be the normal state of trade relations when everybody resorts to QR. What we are dealing with here—and we might as well recognize it—is the psychology of conflict, not the psychology of peace. A weapon is something that someone uses to hurt someone else. And I think it might be well for us to consider, if we place this weapon in the hands of every nation, big and little, strong and weak, and turn them all loose on the field of battle, who is going to be hurt and how much.

It should be clear that countries differ markedly in their ability to adapt themselves to a situation which closes the markets of the world to their products. A small, highly industrialized country depends upon its exports of manufactured goods to purchase the very food that is required to maintain the life of its people. A small, relatively undeveloped country, specializing in the production of one or two commodities—minerals or foodstuffs—depends upon foreign markets for the sales that enable it to acquire capital equipment and manufactured consumers' goods. Even a large country, if it specializes in a few export crops, may find its whole economic life seriously affected by its ability—or inability—to sell abroad. For any of these countries the general imposition of QR

around the world might spell disaster—unemployment, bankruptcy, and wide-spread distress, with all of the social and political consequences that they entail. If however, a country were large, if it had a great diversity of resources, if it had an extensive domestic market, and if it depended only to a minor extent on foreign trade, this would not be the case. For such a country, the general imposition of QR around the world would be annoying and inconvenient. But it would not be disastrous. The moral of this is plain. If we are to arm the nations of the world with this "weapon" of QR and send them into economic battle, the advantage will *not* be with the smaller and the weaker adversaries. It will be with the big and the strong. And this, I submit, is why every small country and every weak country should insist that this "weapon" be outlawed or, at least, if it cannot be outlawed, that its edge be blunted and its use controlled.

The debate in this Committee seems to have proceeded on the assumption that the smaller countries and the weaker countries will be accorded complete freedom to employ QR while the larger and the stronger ones will voluntarily forego its use. This, I fear, is the sheerest phantasy. One amendment would confine QR to "countries that have not reached an advanced stage of industrialization *as a whole*". Another would confine it to "countries in an early stage of industrial development". Just what do these terms mean? How would they be defined? How, for instance, would they apply to the United States? Certainly there are 12 of our 48 States that have reached an advanced stage of industrialization. But the "whole" of our Union includes 36 other States, not to mention the Territory of Alaska, which is an undeveloped country in itself. I invite the authors of these amendments to drive through the States that lie south of the Potomac and east of the Mississippi, to roam the whole area that lies between the Mississippi and the Rockies from Canada to Mexico, to fly over the vast reaches of Alaska, and then to report on the extent to which the industrialization of these areas is really "advanced". It would be instructive, too, to interview the Governors of these 36 States and the Chambers of Commerce in their cities to ask them whether they consider their stage of industrial development to be "early" or late. If QR for protection is open to one it will be open to all, including the United States. And nobody is likely to introduce a form of words that would prevent it.

My Government offered, in the Proposals which it published in December of 1945, to enter into an international agreement under which it would surrender its freedom to use QR for protective purposes. It maintained this offer at London. It maintained it at Geneva. It will maintain it at Havana. If this offer is accepted, no nation need fear that the United States will ever employ QR in ways that would be harmful to them. But if the offer is rejected, what then?

If the offer were rejected, I assure you that my Government would do everything within its power to prevent the general employment of QR by the United States. But I cannot assure you that it would succeed. For as QR spreads around the world, and as one group after another in the United States came to feel its effects, there would be angry reactions and insistent demands for retaliation. If QR were everywhere accepted in principle and widely employed in practice, it is less than likely that these demands could be resisted. If the United States, however reluctantly and however tardily, were to join in the procession that marched behind the banner of QR, how would this affect the welfare of the other countries of the world?

Let us take the case of Country A. Country A is a *small* country. It is highly industrialized. It specializes in the manufacture of semi-durable consumers' goods. It relies upon its export of this goods to pay for a large part of the goods which it imports. It finds a major part of its market for this goods in the United States. But this article is also manufactured in the United States. And our own factories could be so expanded as to meet *all* of the requirements of our market. Suppose that we finally were to yield to persistent pressures to impose upon imports of this article a quota which would cut our imports to a half or a third of their present size. Who would suffer most from this action—the big country or the little country? Would the unfettered use of QR *really* serve the interests of this little country? I think not.

Take the case of Country B. Country B is also a *small* country. It produces a basic raw material. It ships this material into our market in large quantities. Its whole economy is heavily dependent on these sales. It finds in them a source

of dollars that it can use in developing its industries and raising its standard of living. But we have developed, in the United States, a synthetic substitute for this raw material. By expanding our productive capacity we could satisfy the entire demand of our domestic market. Suppose that we yield to pressure to increase our output of the synthetic product by imposing stringent quotas on our imports of the natural product. Who would suffer most from this action—the big country or the little country? Would the interests of the little country *really* be served by untrammeled freedom to use QR? I think not.

Take the case of Country C. Country C is a small country. It sells us, in large quantity, a type of foodstuff that is closely competitive with foodstuffs produced in many of our agricultural states. Our own farmers, with little effort, could completely satisfy our appetites for this element in our diets. Suppose that we were to yield to pressure to give them a monopoly or a near-monopoly of our market by cutting down our imports of the foreign food. Who would suffer—the big country or the little country? Would the welfare of Country C *really* be advanced by the general application of QR? I think not.

Take the cases of Countries D and E. These are large countries, but they are, as yet, relatively undeveloped. Both of them sell us, in quantity, raw materials which constitute a large part of their export trade. In the case of Country D, we produce the same material in smaller quantity. In the case of Country E, we produce a substitute that will serve the same purpose at a slightly higher cost. Suppose that we impose quotas on these imports and expand production at home. Who would suffer most—the developed country or the undeveloped countries? Would the exercise of freedom to use QR *really* be helpful to Countries D and E? I think not.

Mr. Chairman, these are not imaginary cases. In every one of these cases there has been agitation for the use of QR in the United States. In every one of them, its employment would have been harmful, if not disastrous, to the country concerned. And in every one of them, the delegate who represents that country in this Committee has spoken in glowing terms of the blessings of QR.

Let me carry the argument a step further. Country F produces a raw material that it does not sell to the United States. But the *price* of that material is nonetheless influenced by the fact that we are making heavy demands upon the world market. Suppose that we impose a quota that cuts our imports from Countries D and E. Obviously, Countries D and E are hurt. But what about Country F? Is it immune? Certainly not. When our demand is withdrawn from the market, the price falls. And the goods that Country F sells elsewhere in the world bring it a smaller return. Is our use of QR *a good thing* for Country F? I think not.

One final case:—The United States imports a product from Countries G and H. Suppose that we inaugurate a quota system without cutting our total imports at all. But we give a bigger quota to G and a smaller quota to H. G may gain in the process or it may lose. That will depend entirely on whether we exact a price for the favor we confer. But certainly nobody will contend that Country H is better off because every country on earth is free to use QR.

It is probable that somebody will remind me, in the course of this debate, that certain products imported into the United States have been and are subject to QR. In a few cases,—a very few cases—, I am aware that this is true. If the rules of the Charter are adopted, these cases will be *only* those in which domestic production is similarly controlled. And QR will *not* be used to expand our own producer's share in our own market. But even in these cases, and even under such rules, I have gathered from these proceedings that our employment of QR has met with something less than universal acclaim. There are even those who have said that they don't like it. If we were to extend this principle to the whole range of our import trade, would the general enthusiasm for its employment be increased?

I have always supposed, Mr. Chairman, that the future economic policy of the United States is a matter of great importance to the other nations of the world. I have been led to believe that an increase in our tariffs or the general imposition of import quotas would be regarded as a serious blow to their essential interests. If this is indeed the case, I must ask other countries to consider for a moment the direction in which some of them are asking us to go, and what the consequences would be.

If the trading pattern now written into the

Meeting of International Meteorological Organization: Conference of Directors

ARTICLE BY JOHN M. CATES, JR.

The Conference of Directors of the International Meteorological Organization closed its twelfth session on October 11, 1947, with an impressive record of nearly 75 years of uninterrupted international service.[1] In the short space of three weeks the Conference had adopted 220 technical resolutions dealing with the science of meteorology, concluded an international convention by which the Imo is to be reorganized into an intergovernmental organization, and approved a procedure for the establishment of relationship as a specialized agency of the United Nations. In accomplishing this last step toward specialized-agency status and consequent relationship with the United Nations, the Imo prepared the way for the conclusion of an early agreement with the Economic and Social Council and close cooperation with the United Nations. The World Meteorological Organization will thereby take its place with the closely related transport and communications organizations in the aviation, telecommunications, and postal fields as a member of the family of the United Nations. The relationship thus to be established between the United Nations and the international technical organizations is expected to provide the basis for the coordination of the closely related activities of these organizations with consequent benefits to the specialized agencies themselves, to the United Nations, and to the world at large.

The Imo has for three quarters of a century been composed of the directors of meteorological services of the various states and territories of the world, with almost universal membership. Of its 88 members, 55 attended the Conference:

Anglo-Egyptian Sudan	French Equatorial Africa	Norway
Argentina	French West Africa	Pakistan
Australia	French West Africa	Palestine
Belgian Congo	Greece	Paraguay
Belgium	Guatemala	Philippines
Bermuda	Hong Kong	Portugal
Brazil	Hungary	Rhodesia
British East Africa	Iceland	Siam
Burma	India	Sweden
Canada	Indo-China	Switzerland
China	Ireland	Tunisia
Colombia	Italy	Turkey
Cuba	Malaya	Union of Soviet Socialist Republics
Czechoslovakia	Mauritius	
Denmark	Mexico	United Kingdom
Ecuador	Morocco	United States
Egypt	Netherlands	Uruguay
Finland	Netherlands East Indies	Venezuela
France	New Zealand	Yugoslavia

Four additional members were represented by observers:

Chile	Poland	Union of South Africa
Dominican Republic[a]	Rumania	

The representation at the Conference of both sovereign states and territories indicates the dual nature of the Conference. It was both a conference of meteorological directors, members of a nongovernmental technical organization convened to consider meteorological regulations essential to the accomplishment of the Organization's primary

[1] "Final Report (mimeographed edition), Twelfth Conference of Directors", International Meteorological Organization, Washington, Sept. 22–Oct. 11, 1947.

[a] Attended by invitation although not a member.

functions, and a conference of plenipotentiaries convened to conclude an international convention under which there might be established an intergovernmental organization eligible for status as a specialized agency with formal relationship with the United Nations.

The United States Delegation,[2] headed by Dr. Francis W. Reichelderfer, Chief of the United States Weather Bureau, urged that consideration be given to the following points:

(1) That an intergovernmental status was essential to assure to a world meteorological organization the prestige it deserved in its relationships to other intergovernmental organizations and to assure its accomplishment of the various responsibilities placed upon it; (2) that a formal relationship with the United Nations was in the best interests of both the Wmo and the United Nations; (3) that the membership of the new organization should conform to any decisions of the United Nations relating to membership in specialized agencies; and (4) that the Imo should continue in existence until such time as the convention establishing the intergovernmental Wmo should come into force.

With regard to technical matters, the United States Delegation directed its efforts toward obtaining the highest possible degree of uniformity in procedures and symbols used in reporting meteorological data and toward a clarification of the relationship between the Imo and the International Civil Aviation Organization.

The problems before the Conference of Directors thus fell into two general categories: (a) technical meteorological questions and (b) organizational and policy questions.

Technical Questions

Immediately preceding the Conference of Directors in Washington, there had been held in Toronto joint meetings of the so-called technical commissions of the Imo through which the basic work of the Organization is accomplished. There are presently 11 Commissions: Agricultural Me-

[2] The United States Delegation, in addition, consisted of: H. R. Byers, University of Chicago; John M. Cates, Jr., State Department; Commander G. Van A. Graves, U.S.C.G.; Delbert M. Little, Weather Bureau; Capt. Howard T. Orville, U. S. N.; Ivan R. Tannehill, Weather Bureau; and Brig. Gen. D. N. Yates, U.S.A.A.F.

The Conference, recognizing that the new governmental organization would not come into existence for several years, agreed that the Imo should carry on its usual functions until the entry into force of the convention of the Wmo in order to insure the necessary continuity in the world-wide cooperation of meteorological services. Further, to bridge the gap between the Imo and the proposed Wmo the Conference directed its Executive Council to prepare and submit to the first meeting of the congress of the Wmo recommendations governing the administration of the new organization and the transfer to it of the functions and activities of the Imo.

Organizational and Policy Matters

The Conference, sitting in its capacity as a conference of plenipotentiaries to consider a convention for the establishment of a world meteorological organization, had before it a draft convention prepared by a committee of the previous meteorological conference and individual drafts prepared by Canada, France, the United Kingdom, and the United States. Before consideration of the convention itself, the Conference argued at length upon the relative merits of an intergovernmental organization as against a more informal nongovernmental organization of the type of the Imo. The proposed relationship with the United Nations and the possibility that the organization would thereby lose some of its autonomy and suffer from the injection into its technical affairs of the disturbing influence of international politics were the main points upon which the opponents of the convention and of the Wmo based their arguments. The final decision of the Conference to adopt a convention and change the status of the Imo to that of an intergovernmental organization was due in great part to the strong beliefs, as expressed by Argentina, France, the United Kingdom, the United States, and the Union of Soviet Socialist Republics, in the advantages which would follow not only from placing the organization upon a convention basis but also from a relationship to the United Nations, which relationship was in turn dependent upon the adoption of a convention.

The convention, as adopted, follows in general the form of the conventions of Icao, the International Telecommunication Union, and other specialized agencies, although its specialized purposes and functions and its unique membership and voting articles give it particular interest. The basic purposes of the organization are set forth in the preamble, whereby the contracting states "with a view to coordinating, standardizing, and improving world meteorological activities, and to encouraging an efficient exchange of meteorological information between countries in the aid of human activities" agree to the present convention. These purposes are to be accomplished through facilitating the establishment of a world-wide network of weather-observation stations, the establishment of systems for the rapid exchange of weather information, the promotion of the standardization of meteorological observation, and the furtherance of the application of meteorology to aviation, shipping, agriculture, and other human activities.

Membership in the organization is not limited to sovereign states, as is the case with most intergovernmental organizations, nor is provision made for associate members. Membership in the organization is open to states represented at the Conference as listed in annex I of the convention; members of the United Nations having meteorological services; states not members of the United Nations but having meteorological services, upon approval of two-thirds of the members; any territory or group of territories as listed in annex II whose mother countries were represented at the Conference; and any territories not listed in the annex but maintaining meteorological service on behalf of which the convention is applied by the state having responsibility for their international relations and upon approval of two thirds of the members. In the discussions of this membership clause, a great point was made that only sovereign states could become parties to an international convention and members of the organization set up under the convention. However, with the recent experiences of the Universal Postal Union and the International Telecommunication Union in mind, the meteorologists, whether representing sovereign states or territories, were determined to maintain as fully as possible the world-wide-membership concept of the International Meteorological Organization. This concept had made no distinction between the directors of meteorological services of states, territories, or other forms of political and even geographic divisions. The requirements of international law and the demands of certain states were met by providing that only

those members of the organization which were
sovereign states could vote upon reserved subjects;
namely, the amendment or interpretation of the
present convention or proposals for a new convention; membership in the organization, relations
with the United Nations and other intergovernmental organizations; and the election of certain
officers of the organization. It is believed that
this membership formula, unique in the annals of
international organizations, is practicable and will
serve to meet not only the needs of the WMO but
also the requirements of the formalities of international law and practice. This provision of virtually full membership for territories is particularly appropriate in view of the fact that the territories, almost without exception, support their
own activities in the organization without aid
from the mother country.

The vexatious question of membership in the
new World Meteorological Organization of states
not fully recognized as being sovereign was met
by providing that only states represented at the
Conference, as listed in annex I of the convention
could become members merely by signing and ratifying; all others, except members of the United
Nations, must secure approval of two thirds of the
members. Among this latter group are the states
and would-be states, the status of which has so
complicated the conferences of other specialized
agencies during the year.[4] The postponement of a
final decision of these questions until the WMO
itself becomes established expedited the business
of the Conference considerably.

The question of Spanish participation in the
WMO was handled by a protocol similar to those
adopted by the International Telecommunication
Conference and the Universal Postal Congress.[5]

The question of Spanish participation in the
Conference of Directors of the IMO, a nongovern-

[4] International Civil Aviation Organization (ICAO),
BULLETIN of June 15, 1947, p. 1145; International Telecommunication Union (ITU), BULLETIN of Nov. 30, 1947,
p. 1033; also, Universal Postal Union (UPU) Congress
held in Paris, May–June 1947.

[5] "It is hereby agreed that Spain may, as soon as the
Resolution of the General Assembly of the United Nations
dated December 12, 1946 shall be abrogated or shall cease
to be applicable, accede to the Convention of the World
Meteorological Organization by complying with the provisions of Article 33 of the said Convention, without having
to comply with the provisions of Article 3(c) of the said
Convention". (Article 3(c) requires approval of two
thirds of the members for admission to membership.)

Expression of Faith in United Nations as Means of World Peace

EXTEMPORANEOUS REMARKS BY PRESIDENT TRUMAN[1]

I want to wish all of you a happy and prosperous 1948 and to say to you that I think 1947 has been a good year—not as good as we would like to have had it, none of them ever are—and that I am still confidently looking forward to a world peace on which all the nations can agree, and the proper implementation of the United Nations.

I always think of the Constitution of the United States and the difficulties that took place in the Colonies between 1781 and 1789, and then the difficulties that took place between 1789 and 1809. If you carefully look over that situation, you will find that they had tremendous difficulties in those days, almost exactly the same difficulties with which we are faced now both in Europe and here.

It took just about eighty years, really, to get the Constitution properly implemented. In fact it was not the Constitution of the United States until 1865.

So I don't think we ought to be discouraged at things that sometimes get in our way in making this tremendous peace organization work. I did not intend to make you a speech, but I am very much interested in peace, and I have every faith in the final working of the United Nations as a means of general world peace, for the simple reason that we can't afford anything else. It is to our selfish interests and to the selfish interests of every country in the world that we do have a workable world peace.

Presidential Appointments to U.N. Interim Committee

[Released to the press by the White House January 3]

The President on January 3 appointed Warren R. Austin, United States Representative at the seat of the United Nations, as United States Representative in the Interim Committee of the General Assembly of the United Nations; and Philip C. Jessup, Hamilton Fish professor of international law and diplomacy at Columbia University, as Deputy United States Representative. The Interim Committee of the United Nations General Assembly was established in accordance with a resolution adopted on November 13, 1947, at the Second Session of the United Nations General Assembly and will meet on January 5, 1948, at United Nations headquarters, Lake Success, New York.

The proposal for the establishment of an Interim Committee was placed on the agenda of the General Assembly by the United States after the Secretary of State, speaking in the Assembly on September 17, 1947, had suggested that such

a committee be created. The resolution on the Interim Committee, adopted 41-6, with six abstentions, provides that the Interim Committee shall assist the General Assembly by considering matters specifically referred to it by the Assembly; by considering disputes or situations placed on the Assembly's agenda by a member state or by the Security Council; by making studies on how the general principles of international cooperation in the political field and in the maintenance of international peace and security shall be implemented; and, within the scope of its jurisdiction, by conducting investigations and appointing commissions of inquiry. The Interim Committee has also been instructed to undertake a study of the veto, in consultation with any committee which the Security Council may designate.

Mr. Austin, formerly Senator from Vermont,

[1] Made before the President's press and radio conference at the White House on Dec. 31, 1947.

holds the rank of Ambassador. In addition to his duties as Permanent Representative at the Seat of the United Nations, he was a member of the United States Delegation to the Second Part of the First Session of the General Assembly and to the Second Regular Session of the Assembly.

Professor Jessup recently served as the United States Representative on the United Nations Com-

mittee for the Progressive Development of Inte national Law and Its Codification. He has ha long experience in international affairs. Follo ing service in 1943 as a division chief in the D partment of State's Office of Foreign Relief, D Jessup acted as Assistant Secretary General to tl Unrra and Bretton Woods conferences in 19 and 1944.

Review of Facts Regarding Accreditation of Bona Fide U.N. Correspondents

NOTE FROM THE UNITED STATES MISSION TO THE UNITED NATIONS

[Released to the press December 31]

Text of the communication delivered December 31 by this Government, through the United States Mission to the United Nations, to the Secretary-General of the United Nations concerning the subject of accreditation of correspondents

Excellency:

I have the honor to refer to your telegrams of December 22 and 23, regarding the detention and proceedings in connection with possible deportation in the cases of Nicholas Kyriazidis and Syed S. Hasan, which state that both these persons have been accredited as press correspondents by the United Nations. On instructions from my Government I beg to reply as follows:

"The Government of the United States intends to abide fully, both in letter and spirit, with the Agreement of June 26, 1947, regarding the headquarters of the United Nations which became effective November 21, 1947, as authorized by Public Law 357 of the 80th Congress and by the resolution of October 31, 1947 of the General Assembly.

"Although the Agreement became generally effective on November 21, its specific applicability to the interim headquarters of the United Nations at Lake Success and Flushing was not effective until the execution of the Supplemental Agreement of December 18. It is not entirely clear, therefore, whether the agreement was technically in force at the time of Mr. Kyriazidis' detention on December 17. My Government appreciates, however, the desirability of giving the fullest pos-

sible effect to the Agreement regardless of any su technicality.

"Under Section 13 (b) of the Agreement, tl United States retains the right to deport any pe sons who, in activities outside their official capa ity, have abused the privileges granted und Section 11 and 13. It is provided that deportatic proceeding shall not be instituted except with tl prior approval of the Secretary of State, whic shall be given only after consultation with tl Secretary General (or the appropriate Memb Nation if a representative of a Member is i volved).

"In considering the application of the Hea quarters Agreement in the instant cases, it is perl nent to note that the individuals were accredit by the United Nations without the 'consultatic with the United States' referred to in Section 1 Since accreditation took place before the Agre ment became effective, there was no legal oblig tion on the United Nations to hold such consult tions. Absence of consultation does, howev leave unconsidered any view of the United Stat on the question of whether the individuals co cerned are legally entitled to the privileg granted by Section 11 and as to whether the Unit States was consequently under obligation to co sult the Secretary General pursuant to Secti 13 (b) before instituting the proceedings.

"The application of Section 13 (b) to the pr ent cases may be uncertain for another reason. T issue may be not whether the individuals m have abused their privileges in activities outsi of their official capacity, but whether their pri leges may be void on account of misrepresentation of, or failure to disclose, material facts bearing on their accreditation or the issuance of their visas.

"While my Government does not believe that it has failed to comply with the Headquarters Agreement, it recognizes that it was unfortunate that the status of these persons was not clarified by an exchange of views before the exercise of discretion by the United Ñations to accredit them and before the cases reached the stage of legal proceedings.

"It is the view of my Government that the following steps should be taken to avoid any further misunderstandings: (1) The entire list of representatives of the press, radio, film or other information agencies accredited by the United Nations in its discretion should be reviewed by the United Nations in consultation with the United States, so as to bring all *bona fide* representatives clearly under the protection of the Agreement; (2) Procedures, data and criteria for handling future accreditations should be worked out jointly between officials of the United Nations and of the United States; (3) In all future cases where there appears to be any question as to compliance with or interpretation of the Headquarters Agreement, every effort should be made by both parties to settle the matter by informal discussion without taking steps that might be construed as engaging in public controversy. Representatives of the Government of the United States are available for early discussion of all these matters at the convenience of United Nations officials at Lake Success.

"Meanwhile both Mr. Kyriazidis and Mr. Hasan have been released from custody. It is our understanding that Mr. Hasan plans to leave the country voluntarily in the immediate future. No further steps will be taken in either case without consultation with the Secretary General.

"In conclusion let me assure your Excellency that my Government is deeply conscious of its obligations as host to the United Nations and is fully confident that the problems which may arise in implementing the Headquarters Agreement can be readily solved by mutual understanding and good will without prejudicing either the security of the United States or the stated purposes of the Agreement 'to enable the United Nations at its headquarters in the United States, fully and efficiently to discharge its responsibilities and fulfill its purposes.' "

Accept [etc.]   WARREN R. AUSTIN

January 11, 1948

772309—48——3

The General Assembly and the Problem of Greece

[Released to the press January 4]

The Department of State on January 4 released a special supplement to the BULLETIN entitled *The General Assembly and the Problem of Greece*. This publication supplements the materials issued by the Department in September 1947 under the title *The United Nations and the Problem of Greece*. It summarizes the lengthy General Assembly discussion of the question of relations between Greece and its northern neighbors, analyzes the voting on the various resolutions offered on this subject, and describes the positions adopted by Greece's northern neighbors, the U.S.S.R., and Poland. The current publication also contains an analysis of the evidence developed by the Subsidiary Group of the Balkan investigating commission from April to September 1947. This material shows that foreign assistance to the Greek guerrillas was continued on a considerable scale even during the period of active consideration of the Greek problem by the Security Council, and that Albania, Bulgaria, and Yugoslavia consistently refused to cooperate in any way with the work of the United Nations Subsidiary Group.

The supplement is being issued as Department of State Publication 2986, Near Eastern Series 12. Copies may be purchased from the Superintendent of Documents, Government Printing Office, Washington 25, D.C., for 25 cents each.

U.S. Delegation to IRO Preparatory Commission

[Released to the press December 31]

The Department of State announced December 31 the composition of the United States Delegation to the fifth part of the first session of the Preparatory Commission for the International Refugee Organization (IRO), which is scheduled to be held at Geneva, Switzerland, from January 20 to approximately January 30, 1948. The Delegation is as follows:

Chairman

George L. Warren, Adviser on Refugees and Displaced Persons, Department of State, and United States Representative on the Preparatory Commission of Iro

(Continued on page 63)

49

FOREIGN AID AND RECONSTRUCTION

Interim Aid Agreement

REMARKS BY AMERICAN *

[Released to the press January 2]

Since liberation France has made encouraging progress towards economic recovery. It has become increasingly apparent, however, that, due to the unprecedented wartime destruction and exhaustion of stocks, combined with two disastrously short crops, complete recovery would take longer than previously anticipated. The reconstruction task has been a heavy one and progress has been at the cost of the near-exhaustion of France's external financial resources and of the credits received from the United States and other sources.

When the special session of Congress convened last month at the call of the President of the United States, France was facing a situation in which her dollar resources were not adequate to procure the quantities of food, fuel, and materials needed from abroad to keep her people and her economy going during the winter and early spring. It was evident that unless something could be done and done quickly, wheat imports would have to be reduced and shipments of coal and petroleum decreased or eliminated entirely. A crisis was impending which, unless resolved, would have resulted in a further reduction in the already inadequate diet of the French people; in the closing of factories with resulting unemployment; and in impairment of transportation through lack of fuel,

The agreement which we have signed today is in pursuance of the response of the American

[1] Made upon the occasion of his signing the interim aid agreement with France in Paris on Jan. 2, 1948. Jefferson Caffery is the American Ambassador to France. For text of agreement see Department of State press release 3 of Jan. 2, 1948.

[2] Public Law 389, approved Dec. 17, 1947. The Secretary of the Senate reported that on Dec. 16 he presented to the President the enrolled bill (S. 1774).

indeed, if we were indifferent to the plight of less fortunate peoples overseas.

"We have supplied part of their needs and we shall do more. In this we are maintaining the American tradition.

"Because of our efforts people of other lands see the advent of a new day in which they can lead lives free from the harrowing fear of starvation and want.

"With the return of hope to these people will come renewed faith—faith in the dignity of the individual and the brotherhood of man."

AMBASSADOR TO ITALY[1]

program based on self-help and cooperation. The assistance to the Italian people is being given freely by the people of the United States, with the firm belief that this help will assure the development of Italy as a free and independent nation. My Government has only this as its objective.

The action of the American Congress in authorizing these shipments of wheat, coal, and other supplies demonstrates the confidence of the American people that the will to work of the Italian people will overcome the economic difficulties and problems which have resulted from the war.

IAN GOVERNMENT ON JANUARY 3, 1948

the will of the American people to help alleviate suffering in the war-devastated countries.

A program of assistance made possible by the Foreign Aid Act of 1947, passed by Congress on December 17, 1947, has but one major purpose— to provide immediate assistance in the form of food, fuel, and other commodities urgently needed by the people of Italy, France, Austria, and China

---

[1] Made upon the occasion of his signing the interim aid agreement with Italy in Rome on Jan. 3, 1948. James C. Dunn is the American Ambassador to Italy. For text of agreement see Department of State press release 9 of Jan. 3, 1948.

[4] For text of agreement of July 4, 1947, see BULLETIN of July 13, 1947, p. 97.

to alleviate conditions of intolerable hunger and cold, and prevent serious economic retrogression which would jeopardize any general European economic program based on self-help and cooperation. This element of the intention of the United States is again brought out in the preamble of the agreement just signed by representatives of the two Governments: "The Government of the United States of America and the Government of Italy considering the desire of the people of America to provide immediate assistance to the people of Italy and considering that the enactment by the United States of America of the Foreign Aid Act of 1947 provides basis of such assistance to the people of Italy, have agreed as follows".

Assistance to Italy under this act follows a program initiated by the United States in July 1947 whereby approximately $120,000,000 worth of food, fuel, and medical supplies were provided

REMARKS BY UNITED STATES HI

[Released to the press January 3]

For the second time within the space of approximately six months, it is my privilege and honor to sign, on behalf of the United States Government, an agreement with the Austrian Government to provide urgently needed basic commodities designed to contribute to Austria's reconstruction and rehabilitation.[5] The effects of the initial aid agreement signed in June of last year are in evidence in the noticeable progress which Austria has made to restore stable economic conditions.

The purpose of these aid agreements is to help you help yourselves. The Americans, acting through their elected representatives in Congress, have appreciated the problem faced by Austria and

---

[5] Made upon the occasion of his signing the interim aid agreement with Austria in Vienna on Jan. 3, 1948. General Geoffrey Keyes is the United States High Commissioner in Austria. For text of agreement see Department of State press release 6 of Jan. 2, 1948.

[6] For text of agreement of June 25, 1947, see BULLETIN of July 6, 1947, p. 39.

THE RECORD OF THE WEEK

D L. THORP [1]

for Economic Affairs

itous and incomplete sample data? What is the fair proportion between the United States and India for the shipment of raw cotton to Japan under present controlled trade conditions—a problem in which the accepted guiding principle requires the finding of a "representative base period" out of a most abnormal series of years? What is the relationship between the availability of tobacco products in the Ruhr and the production of coal and steel—a problem of psychological measurement since the proposal as made by several Senators rests in the allegation that tobacco products are particularly effective as incentive goods? What amount of goods sent to Russia under the lend-lease program was presumably unused and undestroyed at the end of the war and thus subject to a negotiated settlement—a problem in wartime and peacetime property life tables, and attrition, and depreciation rates? This random list of a few problems may serve to establish the inference of the presence of statistics in the State Department, but the record will be clearer if we consider' two illustrations in somewhat fuller detail.

In a world where there are desperate shortages of commodities, the problem of allocation has become a matter of prime importance. Countries have become competing purchasers, and even, in a few tragic cases, competitors for relief assistance. The shortages are wide-spread and severe, and for many commodities there are few countries with an exportable surplus. Foodstuffs are in this category, and no government with any claim to responsibility can look away while its people are hungry. The State Department has probably received more *aide-mémoire*, notes, memoranda, and formal and informal visitations from Prime Ministers, Ambassadors, foreign technicians, and even self-appointed representatives concerning the subject of

---

[1] An address delivered before the American Statistical Association, New York, N.Y., Dec. 29, 1947. Mr. Thorp is president of the Association.

food allocations than any other single topic during the last two years. The White House too has had distinguished callers on the same subject.

The development and application of the concept of equitable food allocation, based on a careful examination of requirements and availabilities, was done first by a small international committee, then by the International Emergency Food Council, and is now in process of being taken over by the Food and Agriculture Organization, one of the specialized agencies of the United Nations. This international body makes recommendations to the supplying countries as to the proper distribution of their surpluses, and these recommendations are followed with little variation.

The problem is a most complex one. The basic unit for comparing food levels is the calorie, but unfortunately the simple definition in Webster that a calorie is the amount of heat required to raise the temperature of one kilogram of water one degree centigrade has not been so exact and indisputable when applied in the field of nutrition. Two caloric tables for valuing foods are in general use now, one by the United States Army and one by the International Emergency Food Council. There are at least half a dozen other tables used in various parts of the world. The two principal ones vary in caloric content from 10 to 15 percent. Similarly, the effort to measure various types of grain in "wheat equivalent" opens the door to a thorough state of confusion. It is self-evident that when statisticians of many countries meet together to discuss a given problem, a primary requirement is that there be some common measure for setting down the facts, and this has been a major task in the food field. Although this does eliminate one standard area for professional controversy, there will always remain enough other factors of disagreement to permit full self-expression.

Obviously, the first information required for making international allocations is that pertaining to the requirement and the indigenous supply in each country. If these can be satisfactorily determined, the import requirement follows merely by subtraction. At once it is necessary to remark that in many countries where industrial production is lagging, the production of statistics is also below prewar, both in quality and quantity. Unfortunately, statistical organizations have been disorganized at the same time that the items to be measured have been subjected to wide varia-

night. New foods are not easily introduced, even to a starving people, and established prejudices are surprisingly tenacious. For example, corn is not regarded as a proper food for human beings in a number of European countries, nor are potatoes in the normal diet of Italy, while rice is consumed much more than wheat in Cuba. Differences are not merely the result of taste. Countries with long winters have different requirements from those in the Tropics. And even in our own experience as an occupying power, we have recognized that a much higher caloric requirement is needed for Germans than for Japanese to maintain the same health level. So the statistician, in figuring the amount of wheat to allocate to any deficit nation, must have a clear picture of that country's historical eating habits and be familiar with its preferences and prejudices.

Finally, in considering the amount which is to be permitted to come from abroad, the allocations must not work in such a way as to punish the country which brings its maximum to the market place, or all enterprise and initiative in the direction of improved collections from the farms will be destroyed. Conversely, there must be some penalty for failure to use the indigenous supplies most efficiently.

Since the beginning of the allocation procedure, it has always been true that the screened requirements for foodstuffs for all the deficit countries have totaled to substantially more than the availabilities, and here the really painful job begins—the effort to determine where the requirements can be cut with the minimum of hardship. The figures of each country are reviewed again and again, and here are many conferences to explore various aspects of the situation more thoroughly. Finally, the allocations are announced. At least, the process has made everyone aware of the limitations on supply and the urgency of the demands from other countries.

These random comments about the allocation machinery may make the task appear exceedingly complex. But the fact remains that the job must be done. These formidable calculations, aimed to take into consideration both the over-all requirements and supply situation and the peculiar circumstances in each case, are the only hope of providing some basis of fairness and equity in the distribution of scarce things to people who are in desperate need of them.

There is no question but that living for millions of individuals, for the next few years at least, will have to continue under rationing and allocations of critical, scarce commodities. The peoples in these countries know that death from starvation is just as permanent as death from bombing. They know that allocations and rationing are protections to their lives—that the rationing of milk, for instance, may cut down the number of fancy dishes served in fine hotels, but it does get the needed food to more mothers and infants for whom it is an essential. The international allocations in the same way are an effort more nearly to equalize the burden of the shortage on the people of the various countries, not leaving the distribution solely to ability to offer the highest bid or to the appeal of political sympathy, obligation, or reward.

The decision having been made to disregard economic bargaining or political discrimination and to place allocations on an objective basis, the key to this whole process becomes the little-heralded statisticians—both those who must present the case for their countries, and those who must screen the competing claims and bring them into a reasonable relationship with each other. The day and night work and worry is theirs, but they have built in large part upon the work of other statisticians whose work has gone before. I hesitate to think how impossible it would be to handle this problem had it not been for the continued collection and analysis of agricultural statistics and nutritional data in many countries for many years.

As a second illustration may I speak briefly about the European Recovery Plan? The last six months have seen a most difficult and complex statistical undertaking in Washington—the examination of the requirements for European recovery and the study of the capacity of the American economy and other economies to carry the European deficit in the meantime. This task has absorbed the full energies and capacities of many experts in many government agencies. The only relief for the central group directing the project was temporary when in a lighter moment they decided to call themselves the Technical Wizards on the European Recovery Program, or the TWERPS, for short.

Anyone familiar with Washington during wartime can easily visualize the time and energy required to develop the details of a plan involving

16 countries and a four-and-a-quarter year period. I remember in the late twenties being told by a Russian economist about the tremendous efforts required and the manpower devoted to drawing up the Five-Year Plan. Last summer, I saw French economists and statisticians in a state of near exhaustion from working on the so-called Monnet Plan. No one should regard an undertaking of this kind lightly. There have been no days, and even at times no nights, of rest.

This project stems back, of course, to the suggestion by Secretary Marshall that the countries of Europe get together, examine what their requirements will be over a period of time sufficient to permit them to put their economies on a self-supporting basis, determine how much of these requirements they can meet separately and collectively, and thus indicate what additional help is needed to accomplish the program.

Sixteen of the western European nations met in Paris last summer and in an incredibly short period of weeks drew up a program on which they could all agree. Undoubtedly, this agreement was possible because the essential elements of European recovery are beyond dispute—that production must be substantially increased, sound currencies must be established, and the restrictions on trade must be reduced. Their national requirements were presented and assembled. After some slight screening and reduction where the requirements were clearly beyond the possibility of supply, the so-called deficit was calculated. This was all incorporated in the report of the Committee of European Economic Co-operation which, together with a number of technical annexes, was sent to Washington in September.

Work was already well under way in Washington by that time, particularly with reference to the capacity of our own economy to meet such foreign demands and the effect of such an operation upon our own economic operations. But the review of the European plan has proved to be a most complicated undertaking. Covering a period of four-and-one-quarter years, the program for each of 16 countries and western Germany had to be consistent as between its internal program and its export and import programs. For the total of all countries, the requirements from abroad and the availability of supply had to balance. Similarly, for the various individual commodities,

the commodity committees into a coherent system from which balance-of-payments estimates could be derived fell, as it happened, to the Department of State. An early courageous attempt was made to grapple with it by assembling the adding and calculation machines of which the Department can boast only a sparse and scattered population and by amassing at the same time the clerical assistance necessary to man or woman these machines. The attempt was futile. The traditions of the Department of State and its personnel training are oriented more toward the accurate and careful phrasing of a memorandum than the well-multiplied, checked, and proven statistical table. Resort was necessarily had to punch cards and automatic sorting and addition. It may be that the Foreign Office of 10 years hence will boast a full line of international business machines with operators in 24-hour attendance. As of today, it was necessary to work the calculations in on the graveyard shift at Census, Bureau of Labor Statistics, and finally in the Department of National Defense.

One further difficulty was to establish the price assumptions to be used for the future period. Here the crystal ball was particularly cloudy. The Paris conference had used the prices then current, July 1, 1947, as the basis for both exports and imports for the first year (1948) and had then assumed that European export prices would remain firm, while import prices would decline by 7½ percent in 1949, 10 percent in 1950, and 12½ percent in 1951. The American reviewers have felt that the only way out of this dilemma was to present a range. Actually, the basic calculations were made in July 1, 1947, prices, but the totals have been adjusted globally to meet different sets of price assumptions.

For the first 15 months, all exports from Europe and imports to Europe from the Western Hemisphere, except the United States, are calculated at 5 percent above July 1, 1947, prices, while United States and non-Western Hemisphere shipments to Europe are 7.5 percent above July 1, 1947. In the later years, the calculations on the high-price assumption hold the price level constant with the level for the initial period, while the calculations for the low-price assumption are based on a marked decline, particularly for the items imported to Europe. These different assumptions explain the presence of a range in the total requirement for the program of 15.1–17.8 billion dollars.

The projections are, of course, not blueprints which can be followed during operation. Actually, this is a sketch rather than a blueprint. Its purpose is to provide Congress and the public with as accurate an estimate as possible of what the program may in fact turn out to be and the general magnitude of the requirements from abroad, if the European Recovery Program is to be accomplished. If some of the items are not available in the quantities indicated, there may be substitution. If availabilities increase, prices will fall, or if they decrease, prices will rise. In either event, the dollars involved will tend to be more nearly constant than the constituent elements. And with so many commodities and countries, we can fall back on the protection of all statisticians, the hope that the deviations will be somewhat compensatory.

In the original undertaking, five sets of questionnaires were drawn up by the European group to obtain information on food, fuels, machinery, iron and steel, transport, and balance of payments. This information has been available to us in Washington, and to it has been added further information which we requested, plus the vast reservoir of knowledge accumulated in our own Government. However, it is unfortunately clear that there are some serious gaps in the basic information required.

Even with the most complete information possible, there could be no assured results. The most that we can do is to achieve consistent and logical results from as reasonable assumptions as can be made. As I have already pointed out, assumptions had to be made as to price levels. Another uncertainty is created by the necessity to estimate crops. Should we assume that the weather will continue to be as un-cooperative with the farmer in Europe as it has been since the end of the war? And there are many other unknowns, such as, at what point the processes of commodity hoarding will cease and money will be used again as a store of value.

It is clear that the Recovery Program will have to be a dynamic and flexible operation. As was true during the war, programs will have to be changed from time to time as conditions change both as to countries and as to commodities. To achieve the most effective use of the available resources, there will need to be continued and detailed statistical recording of progress made and forecasts of the short- and long-run prospects. The injection of statistical methods into foreign policy is therefore no temporary expedient but promises to be a continuing necessity.

Certain conclusions are now apparent concerning our capacity to reduce the problems which I have been discussing to exact measurement. The first is the common complaint of the statistician—that we do not have adequate data. This is, of course, particularly true of the countries where the effects of the war are still felt so severely. On the American side, we know much too little about the statistical quality and relevance of much of the foreign data. It is clear that these international projects require cooperation and understanding between the statisticians of all participating nations. And time can be used up most rapidly if one is skipping about among long tons, short tons, and metric tons, not to mention bushels, quintals, hundredweights, barrels, and imperial gallons.

On this point, that of the development of statistical data and the effort to achieve greater uniformity, there is much that the United Nations can do, supplemented by the private international statistical organizations. The establishment of a Statistical Commission by the United Nations and the international statistical meetings held in Washington last September may give us some encouragement. This is a long-time job—it calls for continuous support and stimulation. If much is to be accomplished, the statisticians in the United States must take the lead. We must continually be prepared to demonstrate that, in this modern world, many problems can be faced properly and solved economically only when measurement is respected as a fundamental characteristic of the analysis.

But beyond these points, there is a continuing frustration because too few relationships have been reduced to calculable form. It is obvious that planning really requires both cost and market data, that the requirements in the form of materials must be readily related to capacity, that labor supply and working capital requirements must all be part of such consideration. Here the statistician can make endless contributions, substituting detailed analysis for the rule of thumb or

Communist Attempt To Overthrow Recognized Greek Government

[Released to the press December 30]

The claim of certain Communist guerrilla leaders that they have established at some unknown point a "First Provisional Democratic Government of Free Greece" is a transparent device, the true purpose of which will be clear to everyone. It is only a phase in the familiar effort of certain elements to overthrow the legitimate and recognized Greek Government and to threaten the territorial integrity and political independence of Greece. It came as no surprise. In itself, it would not materially change the existing situation.

But if other countries were to recognize the group, this step would have serious implications. It would be clearly contrary to the principles of the United Nations Charter. And if the country concerned were one of Greece's neighbors to the north, the act would constitute an open disregard of the recent recommendations of the United Nations Assembly, as set forth in the resolution of last October.

Negotiations for Revision of Schedule I of Trade Agreement With Mexico

ANNOUNCEMENT OF PUBLIC NOTICES

[Released to the press December 31]

The Acting Secretary of State on December 31 issued formal notice of intention to conduct negotiations for the revision of Schedule I of the trade agreement between the United States of America and the United Mexican States which was signed on December 23, 1942, and entered into force on January 30, 1943. Schedule I relates to the customs treatment accorded United States products upon importation into Mexico.

The Committee for Reciprocity Information simultaneously issued a notice fixing the dates for submission to it of written information and views about the projected negotiations and of applications to appear at public hearings before the Committee. The notice sets forth the time and place for the opening of the hearings. Representations which interested persons may wish to make to the Committee may cover any articles of actual or potential interest in the export trade of the United States with Mexico.

On December 13, 1947, the Government of Mexico announced the immediate provisional conversion of the specific rates of duty on products enumerated in Schedule I to ad valorem or compound rates at levels equivalent to those prevailing in 1942, as a means of correcting the disequilibrium in its balance of international payments and of giving a more reasonable measure of protection to Mexican industries. The Government of the United States consented to this action, pending a more definitive revision of Schedule I immediately following the termination of the United Nations Conference on Trade and Employment now in session at Habana. The negotiations announced on December 31 are for the purpose of considering that definitive revision. They will include discussion of an expansion of the list of items now included in Schedule I and adjusted concessions in the converted Mexican tariff rates on United States products presently included in Schedule I. Export interests are urged to let the trade-agreements organization know at the public hearings what concessions they feel should be requested in these negotiations.

PUBLIC NOTICE OF THE DEPARTMENT OF STATE

[Released to the press December 31]

Pursuant to section 4 of an act of Congress approved June 12, 1934, entitled "An Act to amend the Tariff Act of 1930", as extended and amended by Public Law 130, 79th Congress, approved July 5, 1945 (48 Stat. 945, 59 Stat. 411; 19 U.S.C. Supp. V, 1354), and to Executive Order 6750, of June 27, 1934, as amended by Executive Order 9647, of October 25, 1945 (3 CFR, 1945 Supp., ch. II), I hereby give notice of intention to conduct negotiations for the revision of Schedule I of the trade agreement between the United States of America and the United Mexican States which was signed on December 23, 1942 and entered into force on January 30, 1943.

All presentations of information and views in writing and applications for supplemental oral presentation of views with respect to such negotiations should be submitted to the Committee for Reciprocity Information in accordance with the announcement of this date issued by that Committee concerning the manner and dates for the submission of briefs and applications, and the time and place set for public hearings.

ROBERT A. LOVETT
Acting Secretary of State

WASHINGTON, D.C.
December 30, 1947.

PUBLIC NOTICE OF COMMITTEE FOR RECIPROCITY INFORMATION

[Released to the press December 31]

Closing date for submission of briefs, January 30, 1948
Closing date for application to be heard, January 30, 1948
Public hearings open, February 11, 1948

Submission of Information to Committee for Reciprocity Information

The Committee for Reciprocity Information hereby gives notice that all information and views in writing, and all applications for supplemental oral presentation of views, in regard to the negotiations for the revision of Schedule I of the trade agreement with Mexico, which relates to the customs treatment accorded United States products upon importation into Mexico, in respect of which notice of intention to negotiate has been issued by the Acting Secretary of State on this date, shall be submitted to the Committee for Reciprocity Information not later than 12 o'clock noon, Friday, January 30, 1948. Such communications should be addressed to "The Chairman, Committee for Reciprocity Information, Tariff Commission Building, Eighth and E Streets, Northwest, Washington 25, D.C."

A public hearing will be held, beginning at 10 a.m. on February 11, 1948, before the Committee for Reciprocity Information, in the hearing room of the Tariff Commission in the Tariff Commission Building, where supplemental oral statements will be heard.

Ten copies of written statements, either typewritten or printed, shall be submitted, of which one copy shall be sworn to. Appearance at hearings before the Committee may be made only by those persons who have filed written statements and who have within the time prescribed made written application for a hearing, and statements made at such hearings shall be under oath.

Persons interested in items of export may present their views regarding any tariff concessions that might be requested of the Government of Mexico in the negotiations.

By direction of the Committee for Reciprocity Information this 30th day of December 1947.

EDWARD YARDLEY
Secretary

WASHINGTON, D.C.,
December 30, 1947

---

[1] The text of Proclamation 2764, 13 *Federal Register* 21, was issued as Department of State press release 5 of Jan. 2, 1948. For documents relating to pineapple slips, avocados, and palm beach cloth also see press release 5. The text of the exclusive agreement was printed in the BULLETIN of Jan. 4, 1948, p. 29.

Establishment of the Union of Burma

[Released to the press December 30]

Message from President Truman to Sao Shwe Thaike, Saopha of Yawnghwe, President of the Union of Burma, on the occasion of the establishment of the Union on January 4, 1948

It is fitting that on this day, the day of the birth of a new nation, a sovereign independent republic, the Union of Burma, I should extend to you, to the Prime Minister and to the people of the Union, on behalf of the people of the United States of America, my sincere best wishes. We welcome you into the brotherhood of free and democratic nations and assure you of our firm friendship and goodwill, anticipating that the Union of Burma will take its rightful place among the nations of the world and by constructive participation will assist in the advancement of the welfare of all mankind. We in this country have confidence in the people of Burma and in their leaders. I am sure that our friendship will continue in the future and will be expressed in the same close and cordial relations as have existed in the past.

[Released to the press January 4]

Robert A. Lovett, Acting Secretary of State, addressed the following message to the Ambassador of Burma on the occasion of the flag-hoisting ceremony at the Embassy of Burma in Washington on January 4, 1948

This is a memorable occasion for the world as well as for Burma itself, for on this day the Union of Burma, a sovereign independent republic, has joined the family of nations. I extend to Your Excellency and to the people of Burma the welcome of the people of the United States. May the flag first flown today be dedicated to democratic principles of freedom, to the cause of peace, and to the advancement of all peoples. It is of singular pleasure to us here in the United States that you have seen fit to use the colors red, white, and blue, and to represent your various peoples by white stars on a blue field. Needless to say red, white, and blue and white stars on a blue field are especially dear to all Americans. We are confident that this new flag will symbolize the cordial meeting of the East and the West for the betterment of the entire world.

[1] For text of treaty see BULLETIN of Sept. 21, 1947, p. 565, and for an article by Ward Allen on the subject see BULLETIN of Nov. 23, 1947, p. 983. The report of the Acting Secretary of State is printed in the BULLETIN of Dec. 14, 1947, p. 1188.

U.S. Delegation to 9th Pan American Child Congress

[Released to the press December 31]

The Department of State announced on December 31 that the President has approved the composition of the United States Delegation to the Ninth Pan American Child Congress, which is scheduled to be held at Caracas, Venezuela, January 5–10, 1948. The Delegation is as follows:

Chairman

Katharine F. Lenroot, Chief, U. S. Children's Bureau, Social Security Administration, Federal Security Agency

Delegates

Dr. William J. French, County Health Officer, Anne Arundel County, Annapolis, Md.
Hazel Gabbard, Specialist in Extended School Service, U.S. Office of Education, Federal Security Agency
Kathryn D. Goodwin, Assistant Director, Bureau of Public Assistance, Social Security Administration, Federal Security Agency

Secretary

Mrs. Elisabeth Shirley Enochs, Director, International Cooperation Service, U.S. Children's Bureau, Social Security Administration, Federal Security Agency

The Child Congress will consider the following topics:

(1) pediatrics; (2) maternal and child health; (3) social welfare legislation; (4) education (in rural localities, preschool child, progressive education, vocational training and welfare, and recreation for the child outside of school); and (5) inter-American cooperation in the protection and welfare of children.

The First Pan American Child Congress was held at Buenos Aires in 1916, and the Eighth Congress was held at Washington in May 1942.

Letters of Credence

Ecuador

The newly appointed Ambassador of Ecuador, Señor Augusto Dillón, presented his credentials to the President on December 31, 1947. For translation of the Ambassador's remarks and for the President's reply, see Department of State press release 998 of December 31, 1947.

Bulgaria

The newly appointed Minister of Bulgaria, Dr. Nissim Judasy Mevorah, presented his credentials to the President on December 29, 1947. For translation of the Minister's remarks and for the President's reply, see Department of State press release 991 of December 29, 1947.

The action of the American Government (which is limited to this particular instance) will enable the Finns to claim compensation for Finnish ships requisitioned during the war through the same channels as are available to American and foreign shipowners. Compensation is pending on 17 Finnish ships, which were requisitioned during the war. Such of these ships as were afloat at the end of the war were returned early in 1947 to Finland pursuant to Presidential order.

IRO Delegation—*Continued from page 49*

Advisers

Roswell D. McClellan, Economic Analyst, American Legation, Bern, Switzerland

John Tomlinson, Assistant Chief, Division of International Organization Affairs, Department of State

Administrative Assistant

Eleanor Burnett, Secretary to the Adviser on Refugees and Displaced Persons, Department of State

Among the important items to be considered at this meeting of the Preparatory Commission are the reports of the Executive Secretary on (1) the status of organization and finance; (2) the budget for the fiscal year 1948–49; and (3) the establishment of semi-judicial machinery on the eligibility of displaced persons.[1]

The Preparatory Commission for the International Refugee Organization was established in order to insure continuity of service to displaced persons after July 1, 1947, when UNRRA and the Intergovernmental Committee on Refugees went out of existence, and to take the necessary measures to bring the permanent organization into operation as soon as possible.

The constitution of the International Refugee Organization was adopted by the General Assembly of the United Nations in December 1946 and deposited for signatures with the Secretary-General of the United Nations. It will come into force when 15 states whose contributions amount to 75 percent of the operational budget have signed it. The United States Congress has approved this Government's participation in the International Refugee Organization. The President signed the legislation authorizing participation on July 1, 1947, and the instrument of acceptance of membership was forwarded to the Secretary-General of the United Nations on July 3, 1947.

THE DEPARTMENT

Appointment of Officers

Leland Barrows as Deputy Director of the Office of Information and Educational Exchange, effective January 9, 1948.

THE FOREIGN SERVICE

Consular Offices

The American Consulate at St. Stephen, N.B., Canada, was closed to the public on December 15, 1947.

PUBLICATIONS

Department of State

For sale by the Superintendent of Documents, Government Printing Office, Washington 25, D.C. Adress requests direct to the Superintendent of Documents, except in the case of free publications, which may be obtained from the Department of State.

The London Meeting of the Council of Foreign Ministers, November 25–December 16, 1947, Report by Secretary of State Marshall. 10 pp. Free.

A description of what went on in the meeting and why it failed to formulate peace treaties for Germany and Austria.

Relief Assistance: Foreign Relief Program in Italy. Treaties and Other International Acts Series 1653. Pub. 2958. 24 pp. 10¢.

Agreement and Exchange of Notes Between the United States of America and Italy—Agreement Signed at Rome July 4, 1947; entered into force July 4, 1947.

Air Transport Services. Treaties and Other International Acts Series 1656. Pub. 2967. 7 pp. 5¢.

Agreements Between the United States of America and Portugal Amending Agreement of December 6, 1945—Effected by exchanges of notes signed at Lisbon June 28, 1947; entered into force June 28, 1947.

The Program of the Interdepartmental Committee on Scientific and Cultural Cooperation. Inter-American Series 37. Pub. 2994. 42 pp. 20¢.

A series of articles by State Department officials and others on various aspects of the activities of the Interdepartmental Committee.

National Commission News, January 1, 1948. Pub. 3003. 12 pp. 10¢ a copy; $1 a year.

Published monthly for the United States National Commission for the United Nations Educational, Scientific and Cultural Organization.

[1] For an article by Mr. Warren on the 4th meeting of the Preparatory Commission, see BULLETIN of Jan. 4, 1947, p. 21.

John M. Cates, author of the article on the International Meteorological Organization, is an officer in the Division of International Organization Affairs, Office of Special Political Affairs, Department of State.

The Department of State bu

VOL. XVIII,

Ja

The Departm
a weekly pu
edited in the
Office of Pu
public and
the Governm
development
relations and
partment of
Service. Th
press releases
by the White
ment, and s
made by th
Secretary of
of the Depar
articles on ι
national affa
the Departm
cluded conce
ternational a
United State
party and tr
national inte
Publication
well as legisla
of internatio
currently.

For sale by the Superintendent of Documents
U.S. Government Printing Office
Washington 25, D. C.

SUBSCRIPTION:
52 issues, $5; single copy, 15 cents

Published with the approval of the
Director of the Bureau of the Budget

;URY WILLOUGHBY

commercial policy have changed little through the years. As early as 1778 in the treaty with France, each nation accorded to the other any privileges granted any third nation. Then, there was the Jay treaty of 1794 where Great Britain and the United States agreed to establish commercial relations on a nondiscriminatory basis. Washington, when he admonished us in his Farewell Address to treat all nations alike in our commercial relations, expressed our historical policy. Like principles are embodied in the various treaties of friendship, commerce, and navigation drawn up during the course of the last century.

The trade agreements act of June 12, 1934, which is the statutory basis for all tariff negotiations since that date, specifically requires that any tariff reduction made under authority of the act be extended unconditionally and immediately to all countries not discriminating against the United States. Agreements have been concluded with more than 30 countries under the provisions of this act.

In the light of this history it is clear why the United States has taken such an active part in sponsoring the formation of the International Trade Organization. The basic requirement of the principal commercial-policy provisions of the charter for an International Trade Organization is that all members agree to extend to all other members unconditionally "any advantage, favour, privilege or immunity" accorded to any other member country on any product. Certain preferences, such as those between territories related by a common sovereignty or between specified neighboring states, are exempt. However, all members agree to carry on negotiations to reduce tariffs and eliminate preferences on a mutually advantageous basis. In general, no preferences can be increased nor can new ones be added. The benefits resulting from these reductions in tariffs and preferences must not be offset by the imposition of internal taxes, regulations, or other hidden forms of protection.

Probably the most important provisions of the charter are those which prohibit the imposition of quantitative restrictions [1] limiting the volume of exports and imports and having the effect of nullifying the tariff and preference reductions. Since such restrictions throttle competition and foster economic isolationism, the charter renounces the concept and strictly limits the use of such controls.

There are a number of exceptions to the ban on quantitative restrictions, including one authorizing their use on agricultural or fisheries products when needed to implement governmental measures for limiting domestic production and marketing or for facilitating surplus disposal programs. The most important exception to the basic rule against quota restrictions is when a member is faced with balance-of-payments difficulties, as evidenced by a serious decline in its monetary reserves, or the need to increase its already low reserves. Under such conditions it may levy import restrictions.

Members are enjoined from frustrating by trade restrictions the exchange provisions of the articles of agreement of the International Monetary Fund, or by exchange actions the provisions of the charter relating to quantitative restrictions. Members of the Ito must either become members of the International Monetary Fund or enter into a special exchange agreement with that organization. Ito members must also furnish necessary information to the Fund if they do not belong to the Fund organization.

The charter as drafted at Geneva last summer by the Preparatory Committee provides that if any member pays a subsidy to increase exports or reduce imports, it must notify the Ito and agree to negotiate with any member which believes it-

[1] For statement on quantitative restrictions by the vice chairman of the U.S. Delegation to the Habana conference, see BULLETIN of Jan. 11, 1948, p. 39.

member must request the Iro to consult with the other members whose trade would be affected by the action and obtain a limited release. The same must be done in order to use quotas. The charter is replete with statements making it incumbent upon all members to deviate as little as possible from the basic policy of the program it enunciates. In most cases, the charter explicitly requires that where a member is forced to place restrictions on trade it must do so in as nondiscriminatory a manner as possible.

In some respects, notably the elimination of discrimination, the basic objectives of our foreign commercial policy have changed little throughout the history of our country. In the matter of tariff duties, on the other hand, there has been a major reorientation. The changed position of the United States from a debtor to an active creditor country created a strong motive to reverse the trend toward higher and higher tariffs in favor of a selective reduction through negotiation with other countries. Under the reciprocal trade-agreements program the rates on a large part of our dutiable imports have been reduced.

This process of reducing our tariff rates in exchange for similar or comparable concessions by other countries has been carried a long step forward by recent negotiations at Geneva. While the drafting of the charter for an international trade organization was in process at Geneva in the spring and summer of 1947 more than a score of the participating countries undertook to give concrete evidence of the sincerity of their belief in the principles of the charter by undertaking simultaneous negotiations on tariffs and other trade barriers.

At this history-making conference the representatives of 23 countries, including, of course, those of the United States, were able to negotiate reductions in barriers to world trade on the most comprehensive scale ever undertaken. There was almost six months of continuous negotiating which required over 1000 formal meetings and an even greater number of less formal discussions. The delegates agreed to tariff concessions covering products which account for almost half the world imports, and at the same time they worked out general rules of trade to safeguard and make these concessions effective. They dealt with trade controls of all kinds—not only tariffs, but also prefer-

ences, quotas, internal controls, customs regulations, state trading, and subsidies.

It was not only the volume of world trade affected by this conference which made these activities of such striking importance, but also the fact that such comprehensive trade negotiations were conducted on a multilateral basis. The general articles on matters affecting international commerce were worked out as a joint effort. The initial discussions of tariff negotiations were undertaken product by product between the principal supplier and the principal importer, but, once a concession was agreed upon, that concession was automatically extended to all other negotiating countries. By the time the negotiations were completed, and as far as the end product was concerned, the country-by-country and product-by-product negotiations had little significance.

The so-called general provisions of the general agreement on tariffs and trade, that is, provisions which do not relate to specific duties, constitute a sort of code of fair competition for the conduct of international trade. They are similar to provisions in the proposed charter and to the general provisions of our own reciprocal trade agreements. The general agreement has provisionally replaced some of the individual reciprocal trade agreements which the United States already had with a number of the negotiating countries.

In addition to developing the charter, the United States is also broadening the scope of its treaties of friendship, commerce, and navigation, the basic bilateral instruments defining our treaty rights in foreign countries. The China treaty, already referred to, is representative of the newer spirit of these treaties of friendship, commerce, and navigation. Among the major improvements is clearly defined coverage for corporations, both the rights of American corporations in China and the rights of Americans participating in Chinese corporations. For the most part the rights provided in the treaty are mutual. There is a new provision specifying the treatment that must be accorded in the administration of exchange controls. The treaty also limits the use of quantitative controls and lays down rules to govern state trading. There are provisions designed to facilitate the settlement of commercial disputes by arbitration.

In the financial field, the United States has actively liberalized its approach. Through the International Monetary Fund, the United States is helping to provide an instrument for the stabilization of currency and thus reduce monetary hazards in the flow of goods across national boundaries. Through the International Bank, it is participating in, among other things, the promotion of "the long-range balanced growth of international trade" and the encouragement of foreign investment. The United States has consistently sought a multilateral approach to both the technical and the commercial aspects of civil aviation.

It is particularly encouraging that many countries have been willing to go on record against freezing into perpetual conditions certain existing constrictive and retarding practices in commercial relations, and with us to set their sights toward a broader and brighter horizon. This is of special importance as we move forward with the Marshall Plan. The principles enunciated in the charter of the Iro are complementary to the objectives of the program for European economic recovery. Though the emphasis in the Recovery Program is on the immediate crisis, the goal is to achieve a measure of equilibrium by 1951 that will assure for the future a satisfactory degree of economic stability and an adequate basis for continuing economic development. The Marshall Plan recognizes that European industries must be rehabilitated and that Europe must become self-supporting. This does not mean that Europe must become self-sufficient. She has not been so in the past and will not be so in the future. Climate and lack of adequate supplies of raw materials make it impossible for her to produce everything she needs. Even as Europe moves forward toward normalcy she must continue to have large imports and sustain herself by multilateral trade.

Trade must be a two-way street. In the long run, the only way Europe can import is by exporting sufficient goods and services to pay for these imports. In other words, it becomes axiomatic under the Marshall Plan that international trade must be facilitated, and it is instruments like the charter of the Iro which do just that. The reduction of tariff barriers and the expansion of nondiscriminatory trade relations will assist Europe

Assistance to European Economic Recovery

STATEMENT BY GEORGE C. MARSHALL [1]
Secretary of State

On December 19 the President placed before you the recommendations of the Executive branch of the Government for a program of United States assistance to European economic recovery.

This program will cost our country billions of dollars. It will impose a burden on the American taxpayer. It will require sacrifices today in order that we may enjoy security and peace tomorrow. Should the Congress approve the program for European recovery, as I urgently recommend, we Americans will have made an historic decision of our peacetime history.

A nation in which the voice of its people directs the conduct of its affairs cannot embark on an undertaking of such magnitude and significance for light or purely sentimental reasons. Decisions of this importance are dictated by the highest considerations of national interest. There are none higher, I am sure, than the establishment of enduring peace and the maintenance of true freedom for the individual. In the deliberations of the coming weeks I ask that the European Recovery Program be judged in these terms and on this basis.

As the Secretary of State and as the initial representative of the Executive branch of the Government in the presentation of the program to your committee, I will first outline my convic-

tions as to the extent and manner in which American interests are involved in European recovery.

Without the reestablishment of economic health and vigor in the free countries of Europe, without the restoration of their social and political strength necessarily associated with economic recuperation, the prospect for the American people, and for free people everywhere, to find peace with justice and well-being and security for themselves and their children will be gravely prejudiced.

So long as hunger, poverty, desperation, and resulting chaos threaten the great concentrations of people in western Europe—some 270 millions—there will steadily develop social unease and political confusion on every side. Left to their own resources there will be, I believe, no escape from economic distress so intense, social discontents so violent, political confusion so wide-spread, and hopes of the future so shattered that the historic base of western civilization, of which we are by belief and inheritance an integral part, will take on a new form in the image of the tyranny that we fought to destroy in Germany. The vacuum

---

[1] Made before the Senate Committee on Foreign Relations on Jan. 8, 1948, and released to the press on the same date. This statement will be printed in Department of State publication 3022.

which the war created in western Europe will be
filled by the forces of which wars are made. Our
national security will be seriously threatened. We
shall in effect live in an armed camp, regulated
and controlled. But if we furnish effective aid
to support the now visibly reviving hope of
Europe, the prospect should speedily change. The
foundation of political vitality is economic recovery. Durable peace requires the restoration
of western European vitality.

We have engaged in a great war. We poured
out our resources to win that war. We fought it
to make real peace possible. Though the war has
ended the peace has not commenced. We must
not fail to complete that which we commenced.

The peoples of western Europe have demonstrated their will to achieve a genuine recovery
by entering into a great cooperative effort. Within
the limits of their resources they formally undertake to establish the basis for the peace which we
all seek, but they cannot succeed without American
assistance. Dollars will not save the world—but
the world today cannot be saved without dollars.

The Paris report of the Committee of European
Economic Co-operation was a notable achievement. For the first time in modern history representatives of 16 nations collectively disclosed their
internal economic conditions and frailties and
undertook, subject to stated conditions, to do certain things for the mutual benefit of all. The
commitments each made to the other, if faithfully
observed, will produce in western Europe a far
more integrated economic system than any in previous history.

The report revealed the measure of outside
assistance which in their judgment would be
necessary to effect a lasting recovery of the participating nations. The Executive branch, with
help and advice from a great many sources, has
developed from this report a program of American aid to Europe which gives substantial promise
of achieving the goal of genuine recovery. The
program is *not* one of a series of piecemeal relief
measures. I ask that you note this difference, and
keep it in mind throughout our explanations. The
difference is absolutely vital.

I believe that this measure has received as concentrated study as has ever gone into the preparation of any proposal made to the Congress. The
best minds in numerous related fields have worked

transportation lines and equipment and thus made the ability to move goods and people inadequate. It was the war which destroyed livestock herds, made fertilizers unobtainable, and thus reduced soil fertility. It was the war which destroyed merchant fleets and thus cut off accustomed income from carrying the world's goods. It was the war which destroyed or caused the loss of so much of foreign investments and the income which it has produced. It was the war which bled inventories and working capital out of existence. It was the war which shattered business relationships and markets and the sources of raw materials. The war disrupted the flow of vital raw materials from southeast Asia, thereby breaking the pattern of multilateral trade which formerly provided, directly or indirectly, large dollar earnings for western Europe. In the postwar period artificial and forcible reorientation to the Soviet Union of eastern European trade has deprived western Europe of sources of foodstuff and raw material from that area. Here and there the present European situation has been aggravated by unsound or destructive policies pursued in one or another country, but the basic dislocations find their source directly in the war.

The inability of the European workshop to get food and raw materials required to produce the exports necessary to get the purchasing power for food and raw materials is the worst of the many vicious circles that beset the European peoples. Notwithstanding the fact that industrial output, except in western Germany, has almost regained its prewar volume, under the changed conditions this is not nearly enough. The loss of European investments abroad, the destruction of merchant fleets, and the disappearance of other sources of income, together with increases in populations to be sustained, make necessary an increase in production far above prewar levels, even sufficient for a living standard considerably below prewar standards.

This is the essence of the economic problem of Europe. This problem would exist even though it were not complicated by the ideological struggles in Europe between those who want to live as free men and those small groups who aspire to dominate by the method of police states. The solution would be much easier, of course, if all the nations of Europe were cooperating.

But they are not. Far from cooperating, the Soviet Union and the Communist Parties have proclaimed their determined opposition to a plan for European economic recovery. Economic distress is to be employed to further political ends.

There are many who accept the picture that I have just drawn but who raise a further question: "Why must the United States carry so great a load in helping Europe?" The answer is simple. The United States is the only country in the world today which has the economic power and productivity to furnish the needed assistance.

I wish now to turn to the other questions which we must answer. These are "how much" aid is required and "how" should that aid be given.

II. HOW MUCH?

Three principles should determine the amount and timing of our aid. It must be adequate. It must be prompt. It must be effectively applied.

Objective: Recovery

The objective of the European Recovery Program submitted for your consideration is to achieve lasting economic recovery for western Europe: recovery in the sense that, after our aid has terminated, the European countries will be able to maintain themselves by their own efforts on a sound economic basis.

Our assistance, if we determine to embark on this program to aid western Europe, must be adequate to do the job. The initial increment of our aid should be fully sufficient to get the program under way on a broad, sound basis and not in a piecemeal manner. An inadequate program would involve a wastage of our resources with an ineffective result. Either undertake to meet the requirements of the problem or don't undertake it at all.

Time Is Vital

I think it must be plain to all that the circumstances which have given birth to this program call for promptness in decision and vigor in putting the project into operation. The sooner this program can get under way the greater its chances of success. Careful consideration and early action are not incompatible.

The interim-aid law which the Congress enacted last December was designed as a stopgap measure to cover the period until April first of this year. In the meantime it would be possible to consider the long-term recovery measure which we are now discussing. Unless the program can be placed in operation on or soon after April first, there will undoubtedly be a serious deterioration in some of the basic conditions upon which the whole project is predicated.

It is proposed that the Congress now authorize the program for its full four-and-one-quarter-year duration, although appropriations are being requested only for the first 15 months. Annual decisions on appropriations will afford full opportunity for review and control. But a general authorization now for the longer term will provide a necessary foundation for the continuing effort and cooperation of the European countries in a progressive program of recovery.

Amounts of Required Assistance

The amounts, form, and conditions of the recommended program of Américan aid to European recovery have been presented in President Truman's message to the Congress on December 19, 1947. They were further explained in the proposed draft legislation and background material furnished to this committee at that time by the Department of State. Taking as the basis genuine European cooperation—the maximum of self-help and mutual help on the part of the participating European countries—the program aims to provide these countries, until the end of June 1952, with those portions of their essential imports from the Western Hemisphere which they themselves cannot pay for. These essential imports include not only the food, fuel, and other supplies but also equipment and materials to enable them to increase their productive capacity. They must produce and export considerably more goods than they did in prewar times if they are to become self-supporting, even at a lower standard of living.

During the first 15 months, exports from the European countries will provide current revenue sufficient to cover almost their entire import needs from sources outside the Western Hemisphere and also about one third of their requirements from the Western Hemisphere.

than the ability of the United States to provide assistance in the magnitudes proposed. Both in terms of physical resources and in terms of financial capacity, our ability to support such a program seems clear. Representatives of the Executive branch more closely familiar than I with the domestic economy will provide further testimony on this issue, but I should like to remind you of the conclusions of the three special committees which explored this matter in detail during the summer and fall.

The proposed program does involve some sacrifice on the part of the American people, but it should be kept in mind that the burden of the program diminishes rapidly after the first 15 months. Considerations of the cost must be related to the momentous objective on the one hand and to the probable price of the alternatives. The 6.8 billion dollars proposed for the first 15 months is less than a single month's charge of the war. A world of continuing uneasy half-peace will create demands for constantly mounting expenditures for defense. This program should be viewed as an investment in peace. In those terms, the cost is low.

III. HOW?

The third main consideration which I feel should be borne in mind in connection with this measure is that relating to conditions or terms upon which American assistance will be extended. It is the obvious duty of this Government to insure in so far as possible that the aid extended should be effectively used to promote recovery and not diverted to other purposes, whatever their nature. This aspect of the program is perhaps the most delicate and difficult and one which will require the exercise of a mature judgment and intelligent understanding of the nature of the problem faced by the European governments and of our particular position of leadership in this matter. We must always have in mind that we are dealing with democratic governments of sovereign nations.

We will be working with a group of nations each with a long and proud history. The peoples of these countries are highly skilled, able and energetic, and justly proud of their cultures. They have ancient traditions of self-reliance and are eager to take the lead in working out their own salvation.

We have stated in many ways that American

aid will not be used to interfere with the sovereign rights of these nations and their own responsibility to work out their own salvation. I cannot emphasize too much my profound conviction that the aid we furnish must not be tied to conditions which would, in effect, destroy the whole moral justification for our cooperative assistance toward European partnership.

We are dealing with democratic governments. One of the major justifications of asking the American people to make the sacrifice necessary under this program is the vital stake that the United States has in helping to preserve democracy in Europe. As democratic governments they are responsive, like our own, to the peoples of their countries—and we would not have it otherwise. We cannot expect any democratic government to take upon itself obligations or accept conditions which run counter to the basic national sentiment of its people. This program calls for free cooperation among nations mutually respecting one another's sincerity of purpose in the common endeavor—a cooperation which we hope will long outlive the period of American assistance.

The initial suggestion of June fifth last, the concept of American assistance to Europe, has been based on the premise that European initiative and cooperation are prerequisite to European recovery. Only the Europeans themselves can finally solve their problem.

The participating nations have signified their intention to retain the initiative in promoting their own joint recovery. They have pledged themselves to take effective cooperative measures. They have established ambitious production targets for themselves. They have recognized the need for financial and monetary stability and have agreed to take necessary steps in this direction. They have agreed to establish a continuing organization to make most effective their cooperative work and the application of American assistance. When our program is initiated we may expect that the participating European countries will reaffirm as an organic part of that program their multilateral agreements.

The fulfilment of the mutual pledges of these nations would have profound effects in altering for the better the future economic condition of the European continent. The Paris conference itself was one major step, and the participating nations have not waited on American action before taking further steps, many of which required a high order of political courage. They have moved forward toward a practical working arrangement for the multilateral clearing of trade. France and Italy, whose financial affairs suffered greatly by war and occupation, are taking energetic measures to establish monetary stability—an essential prerequisite to economic recovery. British coal production is being increased, more quickly than even the more hopeful forecasts, and there is a prospect of the early resumption of exports to the Continent. The customs union among Belgium, the Netherlands, and Luxembourg is now in operation. Negotiations for a Franco-Italian customs union are proceeding.

Application of American Aid

Our aid will not be given merely by turning money over to the European governments. The European countries will prepare periodic statements of their needs, taking into account the developing programs of mutual aid worked out through the CEEC continuing organization. After review by the specialist economic-cooperation officers in each country and by the special U.S. Ambassador to the continuing CEEC organization, they will be transmitted to the Administrator of the American agency carrying out our program of assistance.

The Administrator, in collaboration with other appropriate agencies of the Government, will determine to what extent the European requirements are justified and to what extent they can safely be met. The Administrator will also decide which specific requirements from among the over-all requirements will be financed by the United States, taking into account the ability of the country concerned to pay for some portion or all of its total needs. For those needs which cannot be paid for in cash, the Administrator will further decide, in consultation with the National Advisory Council, whether aid will be provided in loans—where a sound capacity to repay in the future exists—or in outright grants. When the program has been determined in detail, the Administrator will either advance requisite funds to the participating country concerned to enable the purchase of the

to meet adverse emergencies, or to cushion the impact of the program on the domestic economy.

It has been suggested in some quarters that the administering agency should be established in the form of a Government corporation. It is claimed that a corporation can be vested with broader powers and flexibility than an independent Executive agency. I do not believe that this is necessarily so. The legislation establishing an agency can clothe it with any or all of the beneficial attributes of a Government corporation. On the other hand an Executive agency under the responsible direction of one man, and fitted into the existing machinery of government, will be better able to meet the requirements of the situation than a corporation directed by a board. This task of administration clearly calls for administration by a single responsible individual.

Finally, the operation of the program must be related to the foreign policy of the Nation. The importance of the recovery program in our foreign affairs needs no argument. To carry out this relationship effectively will require cooperation and teamwork, but I know of no other way by which the complexities of modern world affairs can be met. It should, I think, be constantly kept in mind that this great project, which would be difficult enough in a normal international political climate, must be carried to success against the avowed determination of the Soviet Union and the Communist Party to oppose and sabotage it at every turn. There has been comment that the proposed organization, the Economic Cooperation Administration, would be completely under the thumb of the Department of State. This is not so, should not be so, and need not be so. I have personally interested myself to see that it will not be so. The activities of the ECA will touch on many aspects of our internal American affairs and on our economy. In the multitude of activities of this nature the Department of State should have no direction.

But the activities of the ECA will be directly related to the affairs of the European nations, political as well as economic, and will also affect the affairs of other nations throughout the world. In this field, the constitutional responsibility of the President is paramount. Whether or not he chooses to ignore or eliminate the Secretary of State in the conduct of foreign relations is a presidential decision. I think that in our effort to restore the stability of the governments of western Europe it would be unfortunate to create an entirely new agency of foreign policy for this Government. There cannot be two Secretaries of State. I do not wish to interfere in the proper operations of the ECA. The organizational structure we have proposed provides a means for giving appropriate direction and control in matters of foreign policy to the Administrator of the ECA with least interference in the businesslike conduct of his task. In this connection he must coordinate his affairs with the legal responsibilities charged to the Secretaries of Commerce and Agriculture.

The man who accepts the challenge of the great task of administering the European Recovery Program must be a man of great breadth, ability, and stature. I have no qualms but that with such a man, and the able aides he will choose, I and my staff can form a smoothly working team for handling the complicated problems in foreign relationships which will arise in the course of the program. In my judgment, the organizational proposals which have been put forward represent a sound and practical arrangement of functions and a framework for successful administration.

Conclusion

What are the prospects of success of such a program for the economic recovery of a continent? It would be absurd to deny the existence of obstacles and risks. Weather and the extent of world crops are unpredictable. The possible extent of political sabotage and the effectiveness with which its true intentions are unmasked and thus made susceptible to control cannot be fully foreseen. All we can say is this program does provide the means for success and if we maintain the will for success I believe that success will be achieved.

To be quite clear, this unprecedented endeavor of the new world to help the old is neither sure nor easy. It is a calculated risk. But there can be no doubts as to the alternatives. The way of life that we have known is literally in balance.

Our country is now faced with a momentous decision. If we decide that the United States is unable or unwilling effectively to assist in the reconstruction of western Europe, we must accept the consequences of its collapse into the dictatorship of police states.

American Aid in Restoring the European Community

BY CHARLES E. BOHLEN [1]

Counselor

During the war and since the end of hostilities, the United States has taken the lead in almost every movement designed to further world cooperation and to bring about the substitution of the rule of law for anarchy and force in international affairs. The Charter of the United Nations, as well as the basic idea on which it rests, was in large measure the result of United States initiative. The International Bank, the International Monetary Fund, UNRRA, and virtually every other international organization for a constructive purpose bears a strong imprint of American leadership and idealism. It would be false to pretend that the hopes which found expression in these endeavors have as yet been fulfilled. But it can be asserted with confidence that if the world today is still far from the realization of these hopes it has not been due to a lack of genuine effort on the part of your Government.

It should be a matter of pride to our people that the United States took the lead in these constructive efforts. It is because of its record in this respect—notwithstanding the disappointments that have been encountered—that the United States now enjoys the support and confidence of the free peoples of the earth. As a result of that record, we can with clear conscience proceed to do what is necessary in the present world situation. And in doing so, we must face the world as it is—not as we would like it to be.

In the past year and particularly in the last few months, the harsh outlines of the present world situation have emerged with greater clarity. It is a matter of tragic fact that the United States and the western democracies, in their efforts to bring about a free and prosperous world community, have encountered at every step opposition and obstruction on the part of the Soviet Government.

The record of the western Allies in earnest attempting to find a secure foundation for such common action is convincing testimony to the good faith and their sincerity of purpose. It is cause of profound regret that the sentiments that motivated their efforts were not reciprocated.

It is in relation to Europe that the deep cleavage between the aims and purposes of the western democracies on the one hand and those of the Soviet Union on the other find clearest expression. The fundamental facts of the European situation and the cause of our disagreements with the Soviet Union in that area have been clearly outlined on number of occasions by the President and the Secretary of State as well as other officials of the United States Government. A thorough understanding on this point, however, is so vital to understanding of our foreign policy as a whole that, at the risk of appearing repetitious to many of you, I shall restate these facts.

The basic cause of the present state of affairs Europe is of course the war itself. This most destructive of all wars quite literally shattered the European community.

It left behind it, as Secretary Marshall stated in his report to the nation on December 19th, continent whose economic and political life completely disrupted. The essential question confronting the major Allies at the close of hostilities was what policies were to be adopted in relation to this shattered continent. Was a helping hand to be extended to the European nations assist them in rebuilding an independent community of free nations? Or was their weakness and misery to be exploited for purposes of domination

[1] Excerpts from address made before the centennial celebration of the State of Wisconsin at Madison, Wis., on Jan. 5, 1948, and released to the press on the same date.

FOREIGN AID AND RECONSTRUCTION

and control?˙ The answer was not slow in coming and is now, I think, plain to all.

If the cooperation of all the major Allies could have been enlisted in this task of reconstruction, it would obviously have been far simpler and less costly. To this end, during the war and postwar conferences, the western democracies with patience and persistence sought the cooperation of the Soviet Union in this task. Despite freely negotiated agreements at Yalta and Potsdam to further the revival of a free and democratic European community, the Soviet Union, at first by devious means and later openly, has consistently sought to block the realization of that aim. The United States, the United Kingdom, and the western democracies have sought a revival of Europe, free from outside pressure or threat. The Soviet Union on the other hand has sought not the revival of the European community but the perpetuation of conditions there most favorable for the extension of its control.

The issue in regard to Europe is as simple as that. It is the cause of the present division which tragically stares at us from the map of Europe today. It has been the underlying reason for the failure to agree on a peace settlement for Germany and Austria.

Against this background the European Recovery Program represents no new departure in United States policy towards Europe. It is merely the application of that same policy to conditions as they exist today.

Through no fault of the United States, or any of the participating countries, only 16 European nations plus the area of Germany under western occupation have felt free to join in the cooperative effort for the restoration or, more accurately, the continuance of their civilization. The original suggestion of Secretary Marshall on June 5th of last year for a joint European program for recovery contained no geographic or political limitations, nor did the original invitation by the British and French Governments to the Paris conference last summer. The fact that only 16 and not all of the European nations are involved in this great constructive endeavor is the responsibility of the Soviet Government. Soviet refusal and outright opposition, however, must not and will not prevent this great effort from going forward.

We know now that we cannot count today upon any assistance from the Soviet Union or groups politically subservient to it in the task of European reconstruction. On the contrary, we know that the disruption of this program is high on the list of immediate Soviet objectives. This is not a mere supposition, but a matter of public record in the form of a declaration by one of the leading officials of the Soviet Union. This opposition has been reflected in word and deed by the Communist parties of Europe and of the world.

I think it worthwhile to digress briefly, to point out that when we use the term communism, we need to know just what we mean. Alertness to the threat represented by a highly organized group whose loyalties are to a foreign government rather than to their own country does not in any sense warrant a witch-hunt. Any loose definition of communism which would embrace progressive or even radical thought of native origin is not only misleading but actually dangerous to the foundations of any democratic society. Confusion on this issue and the suspicion which can be sown between Americans of different political views but of equally sincere patriotism would be of great advantage to the Communist purpose. In fact, such confusion and suspicion are a by-product of the Communist movement which is welcomed by its leaders, who cultivate "muddying the waters" as a fine art.

The economic recovery program now before the Congress is the latest concrete manifestation of our policy directed towards the restoration of the European community. No other step in our foreign relations has received closer analysis or more careful study than the measure that the President has recommended. During the hearings before Congress, every aspect of this proposal and its effect upon the United States and its foreign policy will unquestionably and quite rightly be explored by the Congress.

It is obviously impossible in one short speech to attempt to discuss the multiplicity of detail involved in this undertaking. Nothing approaching it in scope and magnitude—affecting the daily lives of millions of people and involving the resources of continents—has ever been attempted for peaceful purposes in the world's history.

To begin with, the representatives of 16 European countries with different languages, institutions, economies, and currencies met together in Paris and analyzed the needs and potentials of these countries, in terms of commodities, production, manpower, trade, and finances, and then projected these estimates four years into the future. These estimates were then carefully appraised in relation to each other and to world supplies, and were correlated into a comprehensive program which was presented to the United States Government for its consideration. As a statistical feat alone, the Paris report ranks as a major accomplishment, but it was much more than that. It outlined a course of action calculated to enable these 16 countries and western Germany, over a four-year period, to achieve a reasonable standard of living which could be sustained without further abnormal assistance from abroad.

Even the full achievement of the ambitious goals set by the Paris report—most of them calling for production surpassing that prevailing before the war—would hardly restore the European standard of living to prewar levels. The reason for this is that the European countries have been forced to liquidate most of the foreign investments and have lost the shipping fleets that formerly helped pay for imports, while their combined population has increased almost 10 percent. Britain, for example, must surpass its prewar exports by an estimated 75 percent in order to sustain its present population. Evidence like this makes it clear that the recovery program envisaged by the Paris report represents neither merely an appeal for continued relief nor an attempt to enable Europe to enjoy a life of ease.

The Paris report emphasized that the maximum collective effort of the European countries could not succeed without this additional support and that prompt action was essential in order to prevent a rapid deterioration of Europe's already precarious situation.

When the Paris report reached this Government, the Krug, Nourse, and Harriman committees were concluding their studies, at the direction of the President, of the probable effect of foreign aid on the economy and resources of the United States. More than 200 members of Congress had visited Europe to obtain first-hand information on conditions there. The Executive branch had organized a corps of specialists from the various departments and agencies to carry out the mass of

to make sacrifices with no immediate prospect of return and certainly no possibility for profit. In fact, one of the chief obstacles to public understanding of the program in this country is the difficulty some experience in understanding why we should expend large amounts of our substance, in the form of dollars and goods, when all that we can expect in return is expressed in intangibles. What we must realize is that these intangibles—the dividends we will receive in terms of peace, security, well-being, and the right to live in the kind of world we desire—represent values perhaps even more real because they cannot be expressed directly in terms of money.

The President has proposed a program estimated to require a total of about 17 billion dollars over four and a quarter years, ending in the middle of 1952. Of this amount, 6.8 billions would be provided in the first 15 months, beginning next April 1, with a progressively smaller expenditure during the next three years. The money would be used by the 16 participating countries and western Germany to pay for necessary imports, which would be bought in Latin America, Canada, and other parts of the world as well as in the United States, in order to lessen the drain on this country as much as possible. The funds will be made available both as free grants and loans, with ability to repay as the determining factor in each case.

The countries receiving our aid will sign an agreement among themselves formalizing their undertakings set forth in the Paris report, and will sign separate bilateral agreements with this country reaffirming these commitments and adding others which will vary in individual cases. Among other things, the European countries will be asked to agree to set aside amounts of their own money equal to grants from the United States, and use these special funds to stabilize their currencies and combat inflation. Those countries having exportable supplies of raw materials suitable for our stockpiling program will agree to make such materials available to us.

These are some of the prominent features of the proposed program. More fundamental, however, are two questions with which, I believe, the American people are primarily concerned. One is: What will be the effect of this far-reaching measure on

the internal economy of the United States? This aspect of the matter has been uppermost in the minds of the authors of this proposal from the beginning, as evidenced by the President's appointment of the three committees to explore that subject thoroughly.

The general conclusion of the Krug, Nourse, and Harriman groups, after the most intensive study, was that a program of this magnitude could be safely undertaken by this country without undue strain upon our internal economy or damaging depletion of our natural resources. These conclusions will undoubtedly be subjected to the closest scrutiny by the Congress. There is one factor in this connection, however, that can be stated now: That is, that under the first year of the proposed program, for which proportionately the largest annual appropriation is being asked, the total export of United States products will not exceed the level of similar exports in 1947. This in effect means that no greater quantity of American commodities will be diverted through export from the American domestic supply than during the preceding two years, when our people enjoyed the highest standard of living in history. Viewed in this light, the program will not by itself add to the existing pressures on American sources of supply.

Another basic question is: Will this program succeed in establishing a genuine recovery of western Europe? On this point, Secretary Marshall has referred to the program as a calculated risk. Even under the best of circumstances, the imponderables of any long-range program of this character—such as future agricultural conditions and other natural phenomena, to say nothing of the political and human factors involved—make it impossible to guarantee automatic success.

In so far as it is humanly possible to do so, however, the program contemplates, with a good chance of success, the laying of a solid foundation for European recovery which would definitely end the dependence of western Europe on the United States for extraordinary aid. In this sense, it is not only a recovery program but a blueprint for European economic independence.

The opponents of recovery in Europe seem to have little doubt of the feasibility of the European recovery program. They are indeed fearful of its success. Otherwise it would be inconceivable that so much time and energy would be devoted to a concerted assault by word and deed on the cooperative proposal to unite the strength of the United States with that of the participating countries in order to assure the recovery of Europe.

We are all in agreement, I think, that the continuance of piecemeal relief rather than a program of genuine recovery would be possibly the worst way of dealing with the situation. Secretary Marshall said at Harvard last June 5th that any such measure "should provide a cure rather than a mere palliative". The decision now rests with the United States—its people and its Congress.

The war and its aftermath imposed upon this country a vast responsibility for the future of the world. History has placed us in a position of world leadership which, since we have a large measure of choice, we can either accept or refuse to recognize.

I do not believe that there is any danger that the United States will shrink from this responsibility and turn its back on the outside world by refusing to do anything in the present circumstances. The issue is rather whether or not we will take prompt and effective action in meeting this responsibility or whether the tragic specter of too little and too late will be the judgment of history.

I do not believe it is necessary here in the State of Wisconsin, which has benefited so much by the energetic and progressive settlers from the continent of Europe, to elaborate on the vital stake the United States has in the preservation of a free and prosperous Europe or what that means to the United States. There is no need to justify to you the main objectives of this program or to dwell on what its success will mean to the security, prosperity, and every day well-being of the citizens of this country.

Certainly there are risks, but this country has not grown to greatness by the avoidance of risks. We must calculate most carefully what we can afford to do, but we must calculate even more carefully what we cannot afford *not* to do.

The risks and burdens which this country will assume in adopting the European Recovery Program have been calculated. The consequences of failure to meet this challenge and to act boldly and decisively in our enlightened self-interest might well be incalculable.

If western Europe, as we know it, falters and goes under, such a cataclysm would automatically

THE UNITED NATIONS AND SPECIALIZED AGENCIES

Economic Accomplishments of the General Assembly

BY WILLARD L. THORP [1]

Assistant Secretary for Economic Affairs

. . . The daily newspapers deal in large measure with the spectacular events of today and yesterday. The eruption of a volcano will be described on page one, but you will find no progress report on the formation of a coral island.

. . . There were few headlines about the economic discussions at the Second Session of the General Assembly. There was the work of Committee II, but, so far as the Assembly itself was concerned, economic debates occupied a relatively minor portion of its time. This is in no way surprising. The economists were rather proud not to make the headlines. To achieve international cooperation in solving problems of an economic and social nature is not a matter of periodic and dazzling leaps. Progress is made chiefly as the result of steady, day-to-day application to specific problems. The individual problems are often technical and may seem fairly limited in their significance, but their cumulative importance is fundamental.

This necessity for intensive work in the economic field has in fact been recognized in the evolving structure of the United Nations and its agencies. The recent Assembly established in the political field four commissions . . . but there are already in existence more than a dozen U.N. commissions and subcommissions to consider various problems in the economic and social fields under the supervision of the Economic and Social Council. To these bodies, and particularly to the specialized agencies, which are related to the U.N. through the Ecosoc, the job of bringing about international cooperation in their respective areas has been entrusted.

The very fact that the volume of debate on economic topics was less at the second General Assembly than at the first is an indication that these subsidiary and specialized bodies are moving through their organizational phases and themselves coming to grips with the substantive international problems with which they are charged. . . .

This whole system of diversified operation was severely challenged at the last Assembly. In the first round of speeches, there were a number of expressions of dissatisfaction with the work of the Economic and Social Council, which some speakers felt had very few concrete accomplishments to which it might point. . . . The Council has a membership of 18 so that most of the countries represented at the General Assembly had no first-hand knowledge of its operations. For this reason the discussion of whether Ecosoc was doing its job properly was valuable as a method of reemphasizing what that job should be.

The discussions served to make it clear that Ecosoc is not itself to be in any sense an operating organ of the United Nations; it is rather to supervise the multifarious international activities in the economic and social fields In this connection it has two main functions: first, to coordinate the

[1] Excerpts from an address made before the American Association for the United Nations, Inc., at New York, N. Y., on Jan. 10, 1948, and released to the press on the same date. William Fowler of the U.S. Mission to U.N. read the address for Mr. Thorp.

work of its own commissions and of the specialized agencies so that possible conflicts may be resolved and duplication of effort, particularly in research and staff work, may be avoided; and secondly, to stimulate work by these bodies in fields which may seem from time to time to be neglected.

'In reemphasizing these functions, the Assembly discussions pointed the way to the conclusion that criticism of Ecosoc for its failure to move mountains was at least premature. The specialized agencies and the commissions of the Council have not gone so far in their own substantive work to make overlapping or duplication an urgent problem. Moreover, it was pointed out that analysis of a problem by two different bodies from two different points of view was likely to be more helpful than damaging and that liaison between secretariats was the primary instrument for guarding against inefficient repetition of basic information gathering and research. It also became apparent that until the commissions and specialized agencies had time to launch their own substantive projects it was not appropriate for the Economic and Social Council to urge specific projects upon them, as this would come close to usurping the functions for which they were created.

The effect of the discussion of this subject will, I am sure, be a healthy one. As I have mentioned, there is now a more wide-spread awareness of what the Ecosoc is supposed to do and, equally important, of what it is supposed to leave in the first instance to other groups. But the debate and the resolution also put Ecosoc and the specialized agencies on notice that, as the formative period comes to an end and the various bodies begin to operate on their own power, the General Assembly will be looking at them closely and critically and will be expecting results. This machinery is really an extraordinary experiment. It must be watched closely and will certainly be susceptible of improvement. We must find just the right coefficient of impatience—one which will maintain the feeling of urgency, yet will not lead to discouragement.

The Assembly also recommended that Ecosoc should consider at least once a year, and at other times if deemed necessary, a survey of world economic conditions and trends, together with a study of major dislocations of supply and requirements.

it was pointed out that all European countries except Spain had been asked to participate, that only the eastern European countries had refused, and that their refusal had not been based on a failure to use U. N. machinery but on the alleged infringement of national sovereignty by the proposed international cooperation.

United States participation in this particular debate was limited, because the target of criticism was the Committee of European Economic Co-operation and because defense of this body was more appropriately the task of representatives from among its members. There can be no question but that the European Recovery Program is thoroughly consistent with the purposes of the United Nations. It therefore in no way tears down any of the principles of the Charter. Whether or not such an operation should be carried on directly through the United Nations is a matter of choice by the nations concerned. In this instance the European nations felt under a great urgency. The United Nations had no agency established for this type of task, and, it should be remarked, the first session of the Economic Commission for Europe, which was almost contemporaneous, failed even to complete its agenda. Furthermore, five of the participating countries have not been admitted to the United Nations, and certain United Nations countries in Europe have refused to cooperate.

However, the United Nations agencies should also carry a most important share in accomplishing the goal of European recovery. The Economic Commission for Europe already has important tasks in various fields, notably coal, inland transport, and certain chemicals. The FAO has a real concern with the food and fertilizer problems. The International Bank for Reconstruction and Development and the International Monetary Fund must both be closely related to the processes of recovery. This is no project outside the United Nations. Much of its success will depend upon the contributions made by these agencies. And the achievement of European recovery will in turn greatly increase the opportunities and effectiveness of the U. N. agencies.

At the last session the debates indicated once again the major concern of many member states with the matter of economic development. It becomes increasingly apparent in the meetings of the various U. N. economic bodies that this topic will command over the next few years a large portion of the attention of specialized agencies, of the Ecosoc and its commissions, and of the Assembly itself.

The problem of economic development has various aspects, and the emphasis given by different countries to different methods of approach and to different schedules of relative priorities appeared time and again in the opening debate in Committee II. This eagerness for industrialization and diversification has formed the foundation of the proceedings in the Economic Commission for Asia and the Far East, has arisen constantly in discussion of the formation of a similar commission for Latin America, and was of course paramount in the recent session of Ecosoc's Subcommission on Economic Development. The desire of these countries to be permitted free use of infant industry protection is currently one of the most important issues before the Conference on Trade and Employment, which is working at Habana to create an International Trade Organization.

Today economic blocs tend to form along lines of degree of economic development, with the largest group those who regard themselves as underdeveloped countries. Earlier sessions paid particular attention to the countries devastated by the war. This was, of course, to be expected. From a humanitarian point of view, relief programs for these countries was a matter of first concern, and this state of mind was reflected in the consideration of economic reconstruction as well. However, the enormous scope of any reconstruction program has become apparent, and it is now realized that the needs of reconstruction alone can absorb huge quantities of materials, supplies, and resources for a long time to come. It is at this point that some other countries begin to raise questions.

For example, even before the war many of the Latin American countries felt that their well-being was hampered by a relatively low level of economic development. Many had become increasingly aware of the desirability of expanding their activities in this field and had taken steps to promote both industrial and agricultural development. During the war great efforts were made to expand Latin American production of a variety of materials, and in that period of emergency shortages it was often impossible or undesirable to carry out a balanced development program. In this area, therefore, though there was no direct war devastation, the war years did not permit steady progress in a planned and orderly process of economic development, and the countries involved feel that much remains to be done. They wish to move ahead without delay on this unfinished task, which it is recognized will be substantially speeded up by assistance from abroad.

A similar problem exists in Asia. The war resulted in severe material damage in many areas, though by and large the destruction to industrial plant did not compare with that in Europe. But, more important, the war accelerated the transition from colonial to independent status, and the new governments in that area are rightly eager to launch programs for their own economic development and, in support of those programs, to draw upon other parts of the world for assistance in money and in goods. The same desire exists in the Middle East and in other areas that have been in the past relatively undeveloped from an economic point of view.

The cumulative effect of this desire for economic development is an enormous demand for money and for goods. The demand is vigorously pressed because the desire is urgent, and no area or country is predisposed to subordinate to another what it feels to be its own legitimate needs. Much of this is not very realistic. Imaginations reach much further than documented projects. And there is little realization of the many elements which must be developed more or less simultaneously to achieve industrialization and diversification. But no one can argue with the objectives. It is the course of economic progress.

But let us return to the problem of nations like those of western Europe, which before the war had high levels of production and economic activity but which suffered enormous material losses by way of military destruction, exhaustion, obsolescence, and want of upkeep. It is persuasively argued that the world-wide demand for goods is so large, so out of proportion to present availabilities, that the first step in a general raising of the economic level should be the rehabilitation of existing plant in areas

(Continued on page 95)

INTERNATIONAL ORGANIZATIONS AND CONFERENCES

Activities and Developments

Report on the First Consultation of the Commission on History

ARTICLE BY ARTHUR P. WHITAKER

Delegations representing 19 American governments took part in the First Consultation of the Commission on History of the Pan American Institute of Geography and History at Mexico City from October 18 to 26, 1947. The only American republics not represented were Chile and Paraguay. There were also observers from other governments and from the United Nations, the United Nations Educational, Scientific and Cultural Organization, the Pan American Union, and the Pan American Institute of Geography and History; and about 50 delegates representing universities and learned societies. Only government delegates (one for each member state) had the right to vote, but all delegates were entitled to participate in the discussions.

Purposes and Program

The main purposes of the meeting were to organize the Commission on History on a permanent basis and to plan its future activities. This is one of the three commissions (one each on cartography, geography, and history) through which most of the activities of the Pan American Institute of Geography and History are now carried on. The Commission on History was created by resolution XXVII of the Fourth General Assembly of the Institute at Caracas, August 25–September 1, 1946. This resolution outlined the purposes and structure of the Commission and entrusted its preliminary organization to the Government of Mexico through the Instituto Nacional de Antropología e Historia of that country.

Permanent Organization

The first of the two main purposes of the Mexico City meeting was accomplished by the adoption of a permanent organization and by-laws. Silvio Zavala, Mexican historian and Acting Chairman of the Commission, was confirmed as Chairman. Provision was made for an executive committee, special committees, a secretariat, and periodic consultative meetings of the full Commission, to be held at intervals of one or two years. The next meeting was scheduled to be held at Santiago, Chile, in 1950 in connection with the Fifth General Assembly of the Pan American Institute of Geography and History. It was felt that on this first occasion the interval should be somewhat longer than the statutory "one or two years" in order to provide adequate time for initial work on the numerous projects adopted by the Mexico City meeting.

Permanent Committees

The second purpose of the Mexico City meeting—the planning of the program of activities of the Commission on History—was carried out mainly within the framework of the four permanent committees of the Commission, which were created at the Institute's Caracas assembly of 1946. Each of these committees was set up under the auspices of a particular country, but all of them retain an international character and remain dependencies of the Commission. The Mexico City meeting defined their composition more precisely by stipulating that each committee shall have active members in five or six of the American states and corresponding members in the rest, so that all the American states will be represented on the committees.

The four committees created at Caracas, and

the countries to which they were assigned, are as follows: Committee on the Origins and Development of the Independence Movement and the Congress of Panama, Venezuela; Committee on the History of the Americas and the Revision of Text Books, Argentina; Committee on Archives, Cuba; Committee on Folklore, Peru. The meeting of the History Commission generally followed the committee pattern in the conduct of its discussions, dividing itself into four sections, each of which corresponded to one of the four committees.

Resolutions Adopted

The new Commission conducted its discussions on a professional level, and its decisions were marked by moderation, realism, and breadth of vision. The results of the meeting are set forth in the final act, which consists of three parts, namely, resolutions, by-laws, and budget. Of the 34 resolutions contained in the final act, only the last four (nos. XXXI–XXXIV) relate directly to the four committees and constitute the core of the document.

Independence Movement

The resolution (no. XXXI) on the Caracas Committee on the Independence Movement recommended that the Committee's attention be concentrated on the preparation and publication of . two bibliographies: one of the origins and development of the independence movement, and the other of the Congress of Panama, 1826. In accordance with recent trends in historical writing, the Committee was also advised to promote the study of economic and social factors in the independence movement. The purpose of this recommendation was to break the quasi-monopoly of historical writing on this subject which has been exercised by military campaigns and the careers of Bolívar and a few other *próceres*.

History of the Americas

The results are set forth in resolution XXXII. This resolution contains two declarations on the History of the Americas, the first of which states the purposes of the "History" and provides, among other things, that the "History" shall in no sense be official, that the Commission

created the Commission on History and its dependent committees.

In addition, the third section recommended that the Committee on Folklore study the possibility of publishing guides and manuals in that field and promote the collection of folk music.

Archives

The resolution (no. XXXIV) emanating from the fourth section, on archives, falls into two main parts: one proposing the establishment of National Councils on Archives, in connection with the Commission's Committee on Archives (Cuba), and enumerating the activities in which they should engage; the other outlining a program of activities for the Cuban committee itself. The national councils are to concern themselves with internal, domestic matters and the Cuban committee is to serve as a central coordinating agency for the national councils. Both are to study such matters as the preservation, organization, and publication of archives and the reproduction of documents for the use of scholars.

Other Commission Actions

There were a number of resolutions which encouraged the broadening of the concept of history in accordance with current trends, as well as resolutions relating to social and economic history. Others related to various aspects of cultural history, particularly historiography (resolution I), the history of American universities (resolution XII), and the history of "ideas, thought, and philosophy" (resolutions XVI, XVII, and XVIII).

Various provisions were made looking toward the more systematic use of the *Revista de Historia de América* for the dissemination of news notes and articles relating to the activities of the Commission on History and its committees. Formerly published under the general authority of the Institute, this journal has been placed under the Commission on History since its establishment, and the Institute makes a contribution to the Commission's budget for support of the publication.

This meeting of the Commission was strongly marked by a recognition of the interdependence of the American states with the rest of the world and by a desire to cooperate with individuals and agencies outside the immediate region, particularly through the United Nations. For example, the Commission resolved to cooperate with UNESCO, offered its cooperation to that body (resolution XIX), and took steps to establish immediate contact with UNESCO in the preparation of the Buenos Aires committee's report on the revision of textbooks. Other illustrations are the article in resolution XXXI authorizing the Caracas Committee on the Independence Movement to solicit the cooperation of historians in non-American countries and resolution XXIII, which directs the Executive Committee of the Commission to study, in the light of the decisions taken by the forthcoming Ninth International Conference of American States at Bogotá, the relations that ought to exist between the Commission on History and the non-American nations which are interested in the history of the Americas. In short, while it was the consensus that inter-American cooperation can be of great value in promoting the study of the history of the Americas, there was not the slightest tendency toward an exclusive regionalism in this matter.

The budget for 1948 tentatively adopted by this meeting was fixed at 123,180 Mexican pesos, of which 50,000 pesos were to be contributed by the Mexican Government and 45,000 pesos by the Institute (for the support of the *Revista de Historia de América* and other publications), leaving a deficit of 28,180 pesos. It seems reasonable to expect that this small deficit would be made up either from an increase of quotas as a result of the Bogotá conference or, failing that, from some other source.

Conclusion

The new Commission on History made a very successful start at its first consultative meeting. It adopted a sound program which augurs well for the future development of its activities. These activities can be of considerable value to the member states and to the international group of scholars interested in the history of the Americas. Government support enables scholars to carry on cooperative studies which would otherwise be difficult, if not impossible; and cooperative enterprises of this kind among scholars from various countries are one of the best means of attaining international good-will and understanding.

THE RECORD OF THE WEEK

Mr. President, Mr. Speaker, Members of the 80th Congress:

We are here today to consider the state of the Union.

On this occasion, above all others, the Congress and the President should concentrate their attention not upon party but upon country; not upon the things which divide us but upon those which bind us together—the enduring principles of our American system, and our common aspirations for the future welfare and security of the people of the United States.

The United States has become great because we, as a people, have been able to work together for great objectives even while differing about details.

The elements of our strength are many. They include our democratic government, our economic system, our great natural resources. But these are only partial explanations.

The basic source of our strength is spiritual. For we are a people with a faith. We believe in the dignity of man. We believe that he was created in the image of the Father of us all.

We do not believe that men exist merely to strengthen the state or to be cogs in an economic machine. We do believe that governments are created to serve the people and that economic systems exist to minister to their wants. We have a profound devotion to the welfare and rights of the individual as a human being.

The faith of our people has particular meaning at this time in history because of the unsettled and changing state of the world.

The victims of war in many lands are striving to rebuild their lives, and are seeking assurance that the tragedy of war will not occur again. Throughout the world new ideas are challenging the old. Men of all nations are re-examining the beliefs by which they live. Great scientific and industrial changes have released new forces which will affect the future course of civilization.

The state of our Union reflects the changing nature of the modern world. On all sides there is heartening evidence of great energy—of capac-

---

[1] Excerpts from the message delivered by the President before a joint session of the Congress on Jan. 7, 1948, and released to the press on the same date by the White House.

clear objectives and with firm determination, we can, in the next ten years, build upon the accomplishments of the past decade to achieve a glorious future. Year by year, beginning now, we must make a substantial part of this progress.

Our first goal is to secure fully the essential human rights of our citizens.

The United States has always had a deep concern for human rights. Religious freedom, free speech, and freedom of thought are cherished realities in our land. Any denial of human rights is a denial of the basic beliefs of democracy and of our regard for the worth of each individual.

.   .   .   .   .

Our second goal is to protect and develop our human resources.

The safeguarding of the rights of our citizens must be accompanied by an equal regard for their opportunities for development and their protection from economic insecurity. In this Nation the ideals of freedom and equality can be given specific meaning in terms of health, education, social security, and housing.

.   .   .   .   .

Another fundamental aim of our democracy is to provide an adequate education for every person.

Our educational systems face a financial crisis. It is deplorable that in a Nation as rich as ours there are millions of children who do not have adequate schoolhouses or enough teachers for a good elementary or secondary education. If there are educational inadequacies in any State, the whole Nation suffers. The Federal Government has a responsibility for providing financial aid to meet this crisis.

.   .   .   .   .

The Government's program for health, education, and security are of such great importance to our democracy that we should now establish an Executive department for their administration.

Our fourth goal is to lift the standard of living for all our people by strengthening our economic system and sharing more broadly among our people the goods we produce.

.   .   .   .   .

Our fifth goal is to achieve world peace based on principles of freedom and justice and the equality of all nations.

Twice within our generation, world wars have taught us that we cannot isolate ourselves from the rest of the world.

We have learned that the loss of freedom in any area of the world means a loss of freedom to ourselves—that the loss of independence by any na-

tion adds directly to the insecurity of the United States and all free nations.

We have learned that a healthy world economy is essential to world peace—that economic distress is a disease whose evil effects spread far beyond the boundaries of the afflicted nation.

For these reasons the United States is vigorously following policies designed to achieve a peaceful and prosperous world.

We are giving, and will continue to give, our full support to the United Nations. While that organization has encountered unforeseen and unwelcome difficulties, I am confident of its ultimate success. We are also devoting our efforts toward world economic recovery and the revival of world trade. These actions are closely related and mutually supporting.

We believe that the United States can be an effective force for world peace only if it is strong. We look forward to the day when nations will decrease their armaments. Yet so long as there remains serious opposition to the ideals of a peaceful world, we must maintain strong armed forces.

The passage of the National Security Act by the Congress at its last session was a notable step in providing for the security of this country. A further step which I consider of even greater importance is the early provision for universal training. There are many elements in a balanced national security program, all inter-related and necessary, but universal training should be the foundation for them all. A favorable decision by the Congress at an early date is of world importance. I am convinced that such action is vital to the security of this Nation and to the maintenance of its leadership.

The United States is engaged today in many international activities directed toward the creation of lasting peaceful relationships among nations.

We have been giving substantial aid to Greece and Turkey to assist these nations in preserving their integrity against foreign pressures. Had it not been for our aid, their situation today might well be radically different. The continued integrity of those countries will have a powerful effect upon other nations in the Middle East and Europe struggling to maintain their independence while they repair the damages of war.

The United States has special responsibilities with respect to the countries in which we have occupation forces: Germany, Austria, Japan, and Korea. Our efforts to reach agreements on peace settlements for these countries have so far been blocked. But we shall continue to exert our utmost efforts to obtain satisfactory settlements for each of these nations.

Many thousands of displaced persons, still living in camps overseas, should be allowed entry into the United States. I again urge the Congress to pass suitable legislation at once so that this

Nation may do its share in caring for homeless and suffering refugees of all faiths. I believe that the admission of these persons will add to the strength and energy of this Nation.

We are moving toward our goal of world peace in many ways. But the most important efforts which we are now making are those which support world economic reconstruction. We are seeking to restore the world trading system which was shattered by the war and to remedy the economic paralysis which grips many countries.

To restore world trade we have recently taken the lead in bringing about the greatest reduction of world tariffs that has ever occurred. The extension of the provisions of the Reciprocal Trade Agreements Act, which made this achievement possible, is of extreme importance. We must also go on to support the International Trade Organization, through which we hope to obtain worldwide agreement on a code of fair conduct in international trade.

Our present major effort toward economic reconstruction is to support the program for recovery developed by the countries of Europe. In my recent message to the Congress, I outlined the reasons why it is wise and necessary for the United States to extend this support.

I want to reaffirm my belief in the soundness and promise of this proposal. When the European economy is strengthened, the product of its industry will be of benefit to many other areas of economic distress. The ability of free men to overcome hunger and despair will be a moral stimulus to the entire world.

We intend to work also with other nations in achieving world economic recovery. We shall continue our cooperation with the nations of the Western Hemisphere. A special program of assistance to China, to provide urgent relief needs and to speed reconstruction, will be submitted to the Congress.

Unfortunately, not all governments share the hope of the people of the United States that economic reconstruction in many areas of the world can be achieved through cooperative effort among nations. In spite of these differences we will go forward with our efforts to overcome economic paralysis.

No nation by itself can carry these programs to success; they depend upon the cooperative and honest efforts of all participating countries. Yet the leadership is inevitably ours.

I consider it of the highest importance that the Congress should authorize support for the European Recovery Program for the period from April 1, 1948, to June 30, 1952, with an initial amount for the first 15 months of $6.8 billion. I urge the Congress to act promptly on this vital measure of our foreign policy—on this decisive contribution to world peace.

We are following a sound, constructive, and

the distribution of available industrial assets from within Japan. These schedules have reflected the general political judgments of the Department of State as to the over-all contribution to victory over Japan, and losses suffered due to Japan's aggression, by each member country. All of these proposals have been rejected and therefore do not constitute commitments of the United States.

During 1946 the Far Eastern Commission declared certain industrial capacity in Japanese munitions and war-supporting industries to be clearly surplus to the peaceful needs of that country and to be available for removal as reparations. In view of the prolonged delays in reaching any decision at all on the distribution of Japanese reparations and in recognition of the urgent need for assistance in relief and rehabilitation in devastated Far Eastern countries, the United States Government in April 1947[1] directed the Supreme Commander for the Allied Powers to distribute 30 percent of the initially available reparations pool to the four principal war-devastated countries as follows:

China	15 percent
Philippines	5 "
United Kingdom (for Malaya Burma)	5 "
Netherlands (for Netherlands East Indies)	5 "

This unilateral directive constitutes the only United States policy now in force as to the distribution of Japanese reparations shares at this time.

Supply of Food for Civilian Consumption in Japan [2]

1. The Far Eastern Commission, having considered the question of the supply of food for civilian consumption in Japan in the light of—

a. the measures already taken by the Supreme Commander since the beginning of the occupation to improve Japan's production and distribution of indigenous food; and

b. the acute shortage of food which is not confined to Japan, but is causing serious hardship in countries which suffered as a result of Japanese aggression;

hereby adopts the following policies with respect to this matter.

2. The Supreme Commander should ensure, by all practicable means, that the Japanese Government take the necessary measures—

a. to attain the maximum production of indigenous food; and

b. to ensure equitable distribution of indigenous food supplies by maintaining and improving the system of collection, rationing, and price control.

3. In view of the acute world shortage, imports of food for Japan during the present crop year (November 1, 1947–October 31, 1948) should be the minimum required to prevent such starvation and widespread disease and civil unrest as would endanger the safety of the occupation forces, and no imports exceeding this minimum should be permitted which would have the effect of giving preferential treatment to the Japanese over the peoples of any Allied Power or liberated area.

4. The Far Eastern Commission recommends to its member governments that they take all steps within their power to assist the implementation of this policy.

Belgium Signs German Enemy Assets Agreement

[Released to the press January 8]

The Department of State announced on January 8 that the Government of Belgium signed on January 5, 1948, the agreement relating to the resolution of conflicting claims to German enemy assets.

Belgium is the fourth country to sign, the other three countries, Canada, the Netherlands, and the United States, having signed the agreement on December 5, 1947. The agreement remains open for signature by the governments of the 14 other countries which are members of the Inter-Allied Reparation Agency. The agreement does not become binding on the United States until it has been approved by the Congress.

The Department made an announcement on December 4, 1947, giving details and text of the agreement and the earlier signatures.[3]

Norway Extended Time for Renewing Trade-Mark Registrations

The extension until June 30, 1948, of time for renewing trade-mark registrations with respect to Norway was granted by the President in Proclamation 2765 (13 *Federal Register* 111) on January 6, 1948.

---

[1] BULLETIN of Apr. 13, 1947, p. 674.
[2] Policy decision approved by the Far Eastern Commission on Dec. 11, 1947, and released to the press by FEC on Jan. 2, 1948. A directive based upon this policy decision has been forwarded to the Supreme Commander for the Allied Powers for implementation.
[3] BULLETIN of Dec. 14, 1947, p. 1192. For text of the agreement and for an article on the subject by Ely Maurer and James Simsarian, see BULLETIN of Jan. 4, 1948, p. 3.

U.S.–Canadian Provisional Seal Agreeme

[Released to the press January 6]

The United States and Canada, by an exchange of notes dated December 26, 1947, have provided for the continuance of the present provisional fur-seal agreement between the two countries until a permanent convention can be arranged for the protection of the fur-seal herd of the North Pacific.

The original sealing convention for the protection and preservation of the fur-seal herd of the North Pacific Ocean was signed in 1911 by the United States, Great Britain, Japan, and Russia. In October 1941 this convention was abrogated by Japan. During the war the Governments of Canada and the United States felt it advisable that the two countries should continue the protection of the herd. They therefore entered into a provisional agreement for the duration of the emergency and twelve months thereafter in order to carry on the fur-seal conservation program during the war.

The fur-seal conservation program was designed to rehabilitate the stock of fur seals in the North Pacific, which had become seriously depleted by the practice of ruthless pelagic sealing. The original convention was intended to rebuild the herd, primarily by the prohibition of pelagic sealing. In 1912, the first year that the convention was in effect, the size of the Pribilof Islands herd was about 216,000; by sound conservation and management practices the herd has now increased to over 3,600,000, according to the annual census taken in August 1947. The sealing operations in these islands are administered by the Fish and Wildlife Service of the Department of the Interior. The herd is estimated to be worth in excess of $100,000,000, and the fall 1947 semi-annual auction of fur-seal skins yielded gross proceeds to the Federal Government of over $1,470,000.

The texts of the notes follow:

December 26, 1947

EXCELLENCY:

I have the honor to refer to conversations which have taken place between representatives of the Government of the United States of America and representatives of the Government of Canada with regard to the possibility of amending the Provisional Fur Seal Agreement between the United States and Canada effected by exchange of notes signed at Washington, December 8 and 19, 1942, with a view to assuring continuing protection of the fur seal herd.

I am glad to inform you that legislation has recently been enacted by the Congress of the United States of America which provides for the extension for an indefinite

Deadline Extended for Registration of Foreign Capital in Brazil

[Released to the press January 8]

An instruction of the Brazilian Banking Superintendency published on December 19, 1947, extended to March 31, 1948, the deadline for the registration of private foreign capital that entered Brazil before October 8, 1947. The requirement that private capital entering the country after October 7, 1947, be registered within 30 days of the date of its entrance was not altered by the instruction.

As indicated in the Department's announcement of December 2, 1947, foreign capital already invested in Brazil, or which may be invested in the future, will lose the right of exit as well as transfer of profits abroad if it is not registered with the Banking Fiscalization Department within the specified periods.[1]

Albert M. Day Appointed to International Pacific Salmon Fisheries Commission

[Released to the press January 5]

Secretary of State Marshall announced on January 5 that the President has designated Albert M. Day, Director of the Fish and Wildlife Service of the Department of the Interior, as a United States member of the International Pacific Salmon Fisheries Commission, United States and Canada, to fill the position left vacant by the death of Fred J. Foster. The other United States members of the Commission are Edward W. Allen and Milo Moore, both of Seattle, Washington. Mr. Day will receive no compensation for his work as a member of the Commission, and he will maintain his position as Director of the Fish and Wildlife Service.

The International Pacific Salmon Fisheries Commission functions under the convention between the United States and Canada signed at Washington on May 26, 1930, for the protection, preservation, and extension of the sockeye salmon fishery of the Fraser River system.

Economic Accomplishments of the General Assembly—*Continued from page 86*

where the tradition of production and high economic activity existed in the past and can be revived more readily. And these countries can provide the markets for the goods which the material-supplying countries are presently able to produce.

Both lines of argument, those of the underdeveloped countries and those of the devastated countries, are cogent and convincing. They are deeply felt and sincerely and vigorously urged by their respective proponents. They are addressed primarily to countries like the United States, which are highly productive and which have had the fortune to escape the direct material destruction of the war.

The sad truth is that there are not enough resources, financial, material, or human, to do all the urgent jobs at once and right away. Under these circumstances the only salvation is to examine the various needs critically and continuously, so that the maximum can be accomplished in an orderly and resolute manner. Those whose aims must be deferred must be convinced that all the reasons advanced for various possible courses have been considered on their merits. Those whose needs are first taken care of must

realize that their opportunity carries a commensurate obligation to advance the general economic development to which all nations aspire.

For these reasons it is important that the various views of the different countries should be given the widest currency and should be tested against one another as fully as possible in the same place and at the same time. At the last Assembly, representatives of 38 countries spoke in the general debate in Committee II on the economic questions raised by the Ecosoc report. To the best of my recollection all of them touched in one way or another on the problems of reconstruction and development. This represents one of the great values of the General Assembly. It is not the place to solve the detailed problems of technical complexity which must be worked out before economic programs can be carried through. But it is a forum in which every country can make known its own basic economic concerns and come to a fuller realization of those of others. Such knowledge is the essential foundation for the achievement of international cooperation in economic matters.

[1] BULLETIN of Dec. 14, 1947, p. 1191.

Woodbury Willoughby, author of the article on U.S. postwar commercial policy, is Acting Chief of the Division of Commercial Policy,
Office of International Trade Policy, Department of State.

Arthur P. Whitaker, author of the article on the First Consultation
of the Commission on History, served as Chairman of the United States
Delegation to that meeting. Dr. Whitaker is Professor of History at
the University of Pennsylvania.

The Department of State

For sale by the Superintendent of Documents
U.S. Government Printing Office
Washington 25, D.C.

SUBSCRIPTION:
52 issues, $5; single copy, 15 cents

Published with the approval of the
Director of the Bureau of the Budget

TOWARD A WORLD MARITIME ORGANIZATION

Part I. Developments From 1897–1946

ARTICLE BY EULA MCDONALD

Government officials and private individuals concerned with ocean shipping and ocean travel are keenly interested in the preparations for the international conference scheduled to meet in February 1948 to establish an Intergovernmental Maritime Consultative Organization. An even half-century of developments in this field has led to the creation of this new organization that will provide machinery for multinational cooperation in merchant shipping.

Among the problems that have demanded international discussions have been: (1) the rendering of assistance to vessels in distress; (2) salvage of shipwrecked cargoes; (3) determination of legal responsibility and civil jurisdiction in collisions; (4) settlement of disputes between states on maritime matters; (5) standardization of tonnage measurements, rules of the road, and code signals; (6) deciding upon the right of inland states to possess merchant fleets; (7) treatment of foreign vessels in ports and harbors; and (8) wartime international coordination and allocation of tonnage for troop transport and for shipment of war supplies.

This article deals primarily with the program and structure of the significant bilateral and multilateral organizations created to deal with international shipping problems; in addition, however, to these organization aspects, it presents a consolidated treatment of one problem of outstanding importance which has been dealt with by international conferences and has resulted in the adoption of international conventions, namely, the promotion of human safety at sea. This topic, which has a universal, humanitarian appeal and which has been the object of international attention for

over 50 years, is closely integrated with the program to be considered at the February conference, and will also be the subject of a special diplomatic conference to be held in London in April 1948.

The agreements adopted and discussions held at the various marine conferences, and the several maritime organizations themselves—some of which operated for a time and then vanished or were absorbed, others being but transitory outgrowths of the exigencies of war—all served a highly useful purpose. It has now become clear, however, that a partial attack on the complexities of maritime activity cannot solve the difficult and pressing problems emerging in present-day global shipping. To those who have studied the subject the necessity for a greater degree of continuity than was possible under previous arrangements has become increasingly apparent, and the solution appears to be the permanent international maritime organization for the creation of which the conference in February has been summoned.

International Maritime Committee

Among the earliest of the international organizations established to deal with maritime matters was the International Maritime Committee, unofficial in character, which was formally created in 1897. Nineteen conferences of this international committee, all concerned with legal phases of merchant shipping, were held from 1897 to 1937, inclusive. Among the subjects dealt with were collisions at sea, salvage and assistance at sea, limitations of shipowners' liability, maritime mortgages and liens on ships, immunity of state-owned ships, and exemption clauses in bills of lading.

This committee assisted in the work of several diplomatic conferences, including the Third International Conference on Maritime Law, held at Brussels, at which were signed the conventions of September 23, 1910, for the unification of certain rules of law with respect to assistance and salvage at sea, and for the unification of certain rules relating to collisions at sea.[1] The first of these is still in force with respect to the United States and other countries. The second, which the United States did not ratify, is also in force with respect to many governments.

The committee also assisted in the drafting of the convention for the safety of life at sea, signed at London on January 20, 1914. At its 1937 meeting, which was held at Paris, the committee adopted draft conventions for consideration by the interested governments relating to penal and civil jurisdiction in matters of collision and the attachment of vessels.[2] It was contemplated that these 1937 draft conventions would be submitted to a diplomatic conference, but they have been held in abeyance awaiting a suitable opportunity for their presentation.[3]

Allied Maritime Transport Council, 1917–1919

The Allies in the years 1914 to 1917 fully recognized the importance of shipping as a vital factor in waging war, but agreements for emergency allocations of tonnage prior to 1917, according to

---

[1] Treaty Series 576, 37 Stat. 1658; *Treaty Information Bulletin*, No. 21 of June 1931 (Department of State publication 213), p. 22. See also *Bulletin* No. 24 of the Comité Maritime International, April 1911, p. ix.

[2] League of Nations Secretariat, *Handbook of International Organizations* (Geneva, 1938), p. 246.

[3] It is not believed that the valuable work which has been done by the International Maritime Committee on an unofficial basis will be carried on by the proposed Intergovernmental Maritime Consultative Organization. It seems probable, rather, that satisfactory arrangements for cooperation will be made by which the proposed organization will recommend to its member governments the adoption of various proposals of the International Maritime Committee.

[4] *Foreign Relations of the United States*, 1917, supplement 2, vol. I, pp. 334 ff. and 413–415. In August 1918 Japan was invited to participate in the deliberations of the group (*ibid., 1918*, supplement 1, vol. I, p. 526).

[5] *Ibid.*, 1917, supplement 2, vol. I, p. 422.

[6] *Ibid.*, 1918, supplement 1, vol. I, p. 512.

ing the most practical and most productive allocation of available vessels. The transocean and coastal shipment of troops, food, and equipment was materially aided and expedited by the council's activities.

With the signing of the Armistice the Allied Maritime Transport Council and the Allied Maritime Transport Executive ceased to play important roles in the control of shipping. Other organizations and other methods began gradually to be utilized in meeting the postwar seagoing transport problems. The council ceased to function on April 7, 1919, when it became a part of the Supreme Economic Council. The executive, with changed duties and changed personnel, continued in existence until February 7, 1920.

League of Nations Organization for Communications and Transit, 1921–1946

In article 23 (e) of the Covenant of the League of Nations (part I of the Treaty of Versailles) the signatories agreed that they would "make provision to secure and maintain ·freedom of communications and of transit", bearing in mind "the special necessities of the regions devastated during the war of 1914–1918". Part XII of the Treaty of Versailles, entitled "Ports, Waterways and Railways", provides (1) in article 338 that the régime for European inland waterways established by article 332–337 "shall be superseded by one to be laid down in a General Convention . . . approved by the League of Nations", and (2) in article 379 that Germany shall "adhere to any General Conventions regarding the international régime of transit, waterways, ports or railways which may be concluded . . . with the approval of the League of Nations".·

The Assembly of the League on December 9, 1920, resolved to call a conference to carry out the provisions of the treaty.[7] The conference met in Barcelona in March and April 1921 and drew up a number of conventions including those contemplated in part XII of the Treaty of Versailles.[8] The conference also formulated a set of rules for the organization of general conferences on communications and transit and of an advisory and technical committee. These rules were revised by the Third General Conference on Communications and Transit, in the summer of 1927, in the form of

a Statute for the Organization for Communications and Transit and Rules of Procedure for the General Conferences.[9] Finally a new statute, giving the Organization greater autonomy within the League, was approved by the Council of the League of Nations on January 29, 1938.[10] Under this statute the work of the Organization was to be carried out by (1) a committee for communications and transit, of an advisory and technical character; (2) permanent or temporary special committees; (3) a permanent secretariat provided by the Secretary General of the League; and (4) general conferences and other meetings.

The Committee for Communications and Transit provided for by the 1938 statute was the successor of the Advisory and Technical Committee for Communications and Transit created under the earlier organic provisions. This committee was in one respect a subsidiary of the Communications and Transit Organization, in that it carried out the Organization's work; in another respect it was independent of the Organization in that its composition was determined by the Assembly of the League.[11] It was empowered to study and propose measures for insuring freedom of communications and transit; collect from the states which had taken part in the conferences information regarding the signing and ratification of conventions adopted by the conferences, as well as the accessions to such conventions; consider questions of conciliation and inquiry, falling. within its competence, in disputes between states; and exchange information concerning communications and transit with appropriate tech-

[7] League of Nations, *Official Journal*, Special Supplement, January 1921, p. 14.

[8] *The Treaty of Versailles and After; Annotations of the Text of the Treaty* (Conference Series 92, Department of State publication 2724), p. 689.

[9] League of Nations, *Third General Conference on Communications and Transit, Geneva, August 23rd to September 2nd, 1927* (4 volumes, Geneva, 1927), IV, 60. Although not mentioned in the title of these rules, an advisory and technical committee is provided for in them.

[10] League of Nations, *Official Journal*, January 1938, pp. 218–226.

[11] Articles 3 and 4 of the 1938 statute. Under article 4, the Assembly was to elect the states whose nationals were to form the Committee for Communications and Transit.

nical ministries of the states members of the organization and with certain other international bodies. It was also to prepare an annual report on the activities of the Organization for Communications and Transit and to forward the report to the members of the organization and to the council and the Assembly of the League, together with an indication of the program of the organization for the following year.[12]

This committee and its predecessor, the Advisory and Technical Committee, carried out their purposes during the 1920's and the fateful 1930's until the outbreak of war. It met for the last time in June 1939, after which its work was carried on as far as possible by the League Secretariat.[13]

The statute made provision, as stated above, for special committees in addition to the foregoing general committee. Of these special committees, one group consisted of seven subcommittees of the general committee, which were specifically named in the statute. They were to deal with air navigation, electric power, transport by rail, inland navigation, maritime ports and navigation, road traffic, and law. The members of these permanent subcommittees and also their chairmen were to be selected by the parent committee. In addition to the seven subcommittees mentioned, the committee was empowered to ask individual experts or temporary committees to undertake studies or submit information coming within the scope of the Organization.[14] These permanent and temporary subcommittees or special committees conducted studies and prepared drafts for consideration on the subjects which were assigned them. A draft set of international regulations for the ton-

[12] Article 7 of the statute.

[13] League of Nations, *Report on the Work of the League During the War* (Geneva, 1945), pp. 44–45.

[14] Articles 10 and 11 of the statute.

[15] *Report on the Work of the League*, p. 47.

[16] League of Nations, Secretariat, Information Section, *Essential Facts About the League of Nations* (Geneva, 1938), p. 235.

[17] *Report on the Work of the League*, pp. 54 ff.

[18] United Nations, *Resolutions Adopted by the General Assembly . . . 10 January to 14 February 1946* (London, 1946), pp. 35–36.

[19] League of Nations, Board of Liquidation, *First Interim Report* (Geneva, 1946), pp. 3, 4, 14, 17, and 18.

[20] Articles 17, 19, and 20 of the 1938 Statute.

fourth, at Geneva, in 1931.[21] Regarding these meetings, one observer noted in 1931 that the communications conference, after the labor conference, was the most important of those which sat regularly in direct connection with the League.

Among the accomplishments of the Organization for Communications and Transit may be mentioned its adoption at Barcelona of a declaration recognizing the right of states having no seacoast to possess a merchant fleet; the preparation at Geneva in 1923 of a convention on the international regime of maritime ports, which established the principle of the equality of treatment of vessels in maritime ports, irrespective of flag; and the preparation of draft international regulations and uniform methods covering the tonnage measurements of ships.[22] The Organization also assisted in the settlement of disputes concerning communications and transit matters, a function not paralleled in the case of any other technical organ of the League.

The residual responsibilities of the Organization for Communications and Transit have been channeled into the United Nations. The activities of the appropriate organs of the United Nations in this field are outlined on subsequent pages.

Combined Shipping Adjustment Board, 1942

On January 26, 1942, the White House announced the creation of the Combined Shipping Adjustment Board by President Roosevelt and Prime Minister Churchill, "to adjust and concert in one harmonious policy the work of the British Ministry of War Transport and the shipping authorities of the United States Government".[23] By an Executive Order of February 7, 1942 (no. 9054), President Roosevelt established a War Shipping Administration in the Executive Office of the President, which comprised the American section of the board. Although this bilateral board was created primarily to coordinate the work of the shipping authorities of the two countries, it was agreed that its members would confer with representatives of the Union of Soviet Socialist Republics, China, and such others of the United Nations as it might be necessary to consult in order to provide for the most effective utilization of the joint shipping resources of the United Nations.[24]

During its period of most active operation, in 1942–45, the board sought not only to obtain the fullest possible utilization of the available shipping but also to increase the available supply, in order to achieve the speedy and successful transportation of goods from raw-material sources to industrial centers and from the latter to the fighting fronts in the form of war essentials.

The board was able to exploit a vast pool of vessels. All American and British ships except certain coastal vessels were under requisition to their respective Governments. Moreover, the majority of ships under the flags of other United Nations, also under requisition by their governments, had been chartered for the duration of the European war to the British Ministry of War Transport or the War Shipping Administration or had been made available in some other way for utilization by one or the other of these bodies.[25]

The board continued in existence after the termination of active hostilities, and still maintains at least a *pro forma* existence, although in 1944 agreement was reached for the subsequent coordination of Allied shipping arrangements by a multilateral body, known as the United Maritime Authority.

United Maritime Authority, 1945–1946

Representatives of eight Allied countries which had agreed to coordinate their available shipping in the interests of the war effort met at London from July 19 to August 5, 1944. Their purpose was to discuss the best methods for insuring the continued availability of the tonnage resources of the various nations in the light of the changed conditions anticipated during the latter phases of the war. The countries represented were Belgium, Canada, Greece, the Netherlands, Norway, Poland, the United Kingdom, and the United States. Rep-

[21] *American Delegations to International Conferences . . . Fiscal Year Ended June 30, 1932* (Department of State publication 425, Conference Series 13), p. 18. The United States was represented at the third and fourth of the general conferences.

[22] *Essential Facts About the League of Nations* (1939 edition), p. 247. For text of convention, see League of Nations Treaty Series, vol. 58, p. 285.

[23] BULLETIN of Jan. 31, 1942, p. 88.

[24] BULLETIN of Jan. 31, 1942, pp. 87–88, and Jan. 16, 1943, p. 69.

[25] BULLETIN of Oct. 1, 1944, p. 357.

resentatives of Denmark and of the French Committee of National Liberation also participated in the session, the Danish delegate being present in the capacity of an observer.[26]

In order to bring about the necessary adjustments in the already existing arrangements, the conference drew up, and signed on August 5, an agreement on principles having reference to the continuance of co-ordinated control of merchant shipping.[27] In paragraph 1 of the agreement the contracting governments declared that they accepted as a common responsibility the provision of shipping for not only the military tasks but also for all other tasks necessary for the completion of the war in Europe and the Far East, and for the transport of supplies to "the liberated areas as well as . . . the United Nations generally and territories under their authority." Under the terms of paragraph 7(a) of the agreement, a central authority to exercise control was to come into operation upon the general suspension of hostilities with Germany. A planning committee was to begin work in London as soon as possible after the signing of the agreement, for the purpose of working out, on a basis satisfactory to the contracting governments, the details of the machinery required to enable the new agency to begin to discharge its functions. Paragraph 14 of the annex to the agreement made the Governments of the United States and the United Kingdom responsible, in consultation with the other contracting governments, for determining the date of the coming into operation of the central authority in accordance with paragraph 7(a) of the agreement.

Provision was made for the implementation of the principles laid down in the agreement by the establishment of a United Maritime Council and a United Maritime Executive Board, together constituting the central authority (which became known as the United Maritime Authority).[28] The annex to the agreement provided that each contracting government should be represented on the

[26] BULLETIN of Aug. 13, 1944, p. 157.
[27] BULLETIN of Oct. 1, 1944, pp. 358–361.
[28] BULLETIN of Oct. 1, 1944, p. 359, and Dec. 3, 1944, p. 655.
[29] BULLETIN of Feb. 3, 1946, p. 171, and Mar. 24, 1946, pp. 487–488. This meeting was also considered to be a session of the full Council of the United Maritime Authority, as all the member governments were represented.

destinations. The board decided unanimously that further coordination was necessary until normal international shipping could be resumed. The result was a recommendation that governments represented on the United Maritime Authority should enter into a new but temporary agreement under which there would be established (1) a voluntary pool of shipping for the transportation of relief and rehabilitation cargoes, and (2) a consultative council to serve as a forum for the discussion of the shipping problems which might arise prior to the return to normal peacetime shipping activities.

The United Maritime Authority was terminated on March 2, 1946, in accordance with its decision to set September 2, 1945, as the date on which "the general suspension of hostilities" took place, such date beginning the last six months of its control over world merchant shipping.[30]

United Maritime Consultative Council and the United Nations

Prior to the termination of the United Maritime Authority and its recommendation for the establishment of an interim consultative council to succeed it, the United Nations had already come into being and had begun to consider plans for promoting international maritime cooperation. Since the actions of the United Nations in this field in the year 1946 not only occurred simultaneously with the setting up and operation of the recommended consultative council, but also bore in part directly upon it, the two sets of parallel developments are treated together, in chronological sequence, in this section.

The Charter of the United Nations, signed at San Francisco June 26, 1945, provided, among other things, for the promotion of conditions of economic progress and development (article 55), and to that end it made provision for an Economic and Social Council and "such subsidiary organs as may be found necessary" (article 7). The Preparatory Commission which met at London in December 1945 to bring the United Nations into full operation suggested the establishment of a temporary or nuclear Transport and Communications Commission to review "the general field of international transport and communications in order to advise the Council on any machinery which it will be necessary to establish either as part of the United Nations or as a new specialized agency."[31]

February 1946

As stated above, the Council of the United Maritime Authority met in London from February 4 to 11, 1946, and decided to recommend the establishment of a temporary successor agency. Five days later, on February 16, 1946, the Economic and Social Council of the United Nations, also meeting at London, adopted a resolution creating a Temporary Transport and Communications Commission, as recommended by the Preparatory Commission in December 1945. The Economic and Social Council, in its resolution, expressed the opinion that establishment of formal relationships with existing intergovernmental agencies in the field of transport and communications would be premature, but it took into account the need for some form of preliminary contact with such organizations. It also recognized the need for advice on the practical problems involved and on the adequacy of the international structure in those fields. The functions of the Temporary Transport and Communications Commission were delimited to implementing these understandings.[32] By further action of the council on February 18, 1946, the initial membership of the Temporary Commission was determined.

March 1946

On March 2 the United Maritime Authority expired, and on March 3 the United Maritime Consultative Council came provisionally into being. Part "A" of the relevant agreement provided that all the nations which had made a regular contribution of tonnage to the common tasks under the United Maritime Authority should continue to provide shipping on a voluntary basis for the imperative needs of UNRRA and the liberated areas. Part "B" of the agreement provided for the establishment of the United Maritime Consultative Council as a forum for the exchange of information and the discussion of mutual problems with the hope that the knowledge thus gained of the methods by which other governments met current shipping problems would be valuable to the individual governments in forming their own policies. The agreement also provided for a Ship-

[30] BULLETIN of Dec. 16, 1945, pp. 965–966.

[31] U.N. press release B–7, Apr. 26, 1946.

[32] U.N. doc. E/42, May 20, 1946, p. 38.

ping Coordinating and Review Committee to consider and review UNRRA's shipping requirements, and a Contributory Nations Committee, which was assigned the task of actually meeting the ocean-transportation requirements of UNRRA and of the liberated areas in an orderly and effective manner by adjusting ship space and cargoes.[33]

May 1946

The newly created Temporary Transport and Communications Commission met in New York in May and made its first report to the Economic and Social Council of the United Nations on May 25, 1946. In connection with a general survey of intergovernmental organization in the field of transport and communications, the report pointed out that aside from the United Maritime Consultative Council, which was temporary in character, the only standing intergovernmental bodies in the shipping field were the International Hydrographic Bureau and the International Commission for the Maintenance of the Lighthouse at Cape Spartel. The commission believed that in view of the lack of an over-all international organization in the field of shipping, an intergovernmental body should be set up to deal with technical matters in that field. The report outlined the general responsibilities which such a body should have.[34]

The commission also engaged in considerable discussion concerning the desirability of establishing a permanent Transport and Communications Commission of the Economic and Social Council of the United Nations. It was argued that such a commission could serve as a conciliatory body when disputes arose and would be in a position to indicate to the council when new agencies or agreements were needed. The temporary commission finally agreed unanimously to recommend the establishment of a permanent Transport and Communications Commission which should not act as an intermediary between the council and specialized agencies, but should serve in an advisory capacity, particularly with respect to coordina-

[33] BULLETIN of Mar. 24, 1946, pp. 488–489.
[34] U.N. doc. E/42, May 20, 1946 (report submitted May 25), pp. 5–13.
[35] Ibid., pp. 7, 8, and 9.
[36] BULLETIN of July 14, 1946, pp. 64–65.

le responsibility of advising the Economic and
ocial Council in general matters concerning
:ansport and communications; of receiving spe-
ial delegations of authority from the Council on
:rtain questions, particularly those for which no
pecialized agency exists; and of dealing with
pecific problems with respect to specialized
gencies, on the request of the Council.[37]

On June 23, 1946, the Chairman of the first ses-
on of the United Maritime Consultative Coun-
l informed the Secretary-General of the United
ations by telegram, in response to his cable of
une 21, that the question of a world-wide ship-
ing organization was already included in the
genda of the meeting and that the United Mari-
me Consultative Council had discussed the ques-
on with the result that a resolution had been
dopted to the effect that (1) the council took
ote of the view generally expressed that an in-
rgovernmental body was likely to be required,
nd (2) the council would appoint a committee
consider in greater detail the possible con-
titution, scope, and procedure of such a body.
he chairman added that the committee was to
port its findings to the second session of the
nited Maritime Consultative Council, which
ould be convened prior to October 31, 1946, to
nsider the report and to make recommendations
the member governments.[38]

September 1946

The Department of State announced on Sep-
mber 26, 1946, that pursuant to the wishes ex-
ressed by the member nations of the United
aritime Consultative Council at their June
eeting it had invited those nations to the second
d final session of the United Maritime Con-
ltative Council at Washington from October 24
30, 1946. In addition to the consideration of
e working committee's report and the resultant
commendations, the United Maritime Consul-
tive Council had on its agenda the preparation
a reply to the United Nations concerning its
quest for the views of the United Maritime Con-
ltative Council on the establishment of an inter-

[37] U.N. doc. E/58/Rev. 2, July 1, 1946, pp. 2–4.
[38] U.N. doc. E/CN. 2/4, Jan. 10, 1947, pp. 4–7.
[39] BULLETIN of Oct. 6, 1946, p. 631.
[40] BULLETIN of Dec. 15, 1946, pp. 1092–1098.

governmental maritime organization; a review of
the working of the machinery set up by the
former United Maritime Executive Board for the
orderly transportation of certain cargoes after the
termination of the United Maritime Authority;
and a review of the progress made in the restoration of normal processes of international merchant
shipping.[39]

October 1946

The United Maritime Consultative Council met
at Washington according to schedule for its final
session and agreed to recommend to its 18 member
governments the establishment through the machinery of the United Nations of a permanent
shipping organization. It also agreed, as a temporary measure pending the creation of the permanent body, on the desirability of forming a
further interim body designed particularly to
handle such problems as might arise during the
period of transition to the permanent organization. The interim body was denominated a Provisional Maritime Consultative Council.[40] The
four recommendations adopted on October 30,
1946, provided that—

"(1) an Inter-Governmental Maritime Consultative Organization should be established as a
specialized agency of the United Nations, as set
forth in the draft convention for an Inter-Governmental Maritime Consultative Organization annexed hereto;

"(2) each Member Government take appropriate action in requesting the Economic and Social
Council to convene a conference of all interested
governments for the purpose of adopting a constitution for an Inter-Governmental Maritime
Consultative Organization as set forth in the annexed draft convention;

"(3) in view of the fact that the United Maritime Consultative Council will cease to exist on October 31, 1946, a Provisional Maritime Consultative Council should be set up forthwith in accordance with the annexed Agreement for the establishment of a Provisional Maritime Consultative
Council;

"(4) government members of the United Maritime Consultative Council should accept as soon
as possible the Agreement for a Provisional Mari-

(Continued on page 115)

FOREIGN AID AND RECONSTRUCTION

The Stake of the Businessman in the European Recovery Progra

ADDRESS BY GEORGE C. MARSHALL [1]
Secretary of State

During the past week I have appeared before Congressional committees of the Senate and the House to discuss the European Recovery Program recently recommended by the President. Other officials of the Executive branch are now testifying before the same committees as to the details of the program. It has been widely publicized and discussed. Its purpose and principal features are now well known. Therefore, I am reluctant to add another statement to the mass of material on the subject. But this issue is of such great national importance that I feel justified in referring tonight to some aspects that may be of especial interest to the leaders in business.

Businessmen quite naturally are concerned about the possible effects on their own position—about how this program will affect the supply of raw materials, prices, sales, profits, and the conditions of doing business. Measures affecting the national economic interest in the long run will influence the private affairs of all of us. In considering the effect of this particular measure upon our individual or collective lives and fortunes, it seems logical first to appraise the present position of the United States in world affairs.

In order to put current events in proper perspective, it is necessary to go back at least to the Council of Foreign Ministers at Moscow last spring. We met there, as you know, to consider peace treaties for Germany and Austria. That effort to reach agreement failed utterly because the Soviet Union insisted upon conditions which the three western powers could not in good conscience accept. The reasons for the Soviet attitude have now become clearer and were well defined at the recent London conference, where resort to similar obstructive tactics and propaganda appeals led again to failure.

Our experience at Moscow was productive in

one sense at least. It necessitated a complete appraisement of the situation in Europe which steadily deteriorating, and brought us to the portant conclusion that we faced the choice of qu ting Europe altogether or of completing the t of European recovery. We had no intention quitting.

Once the basic decision was taken, the Uni States put into effect certain measures suscepti of immediate application. These concerned C many, where we have major responsibilities as occupying power. It was apparent that there no immediate prospect of a German peace tre nor any likelihood that the Soviet Union wo cooperate in establishing a balanced economy all of Germany as provided in the Potsdam ag ment. Therefore, we had to take what steps could to enable the Germans to pull their o weight in Europe and at an early date to termin reliance upon Britain and the United States the essentials of existence now lacking in west Germany.

The British and American zones were then be integrated economically in the interest of efficie and economy. This process was accelerated. addition, the two Governments decided upon appreciable increase in the level of industry. T is a rather technical matter which is not read understood. It should be remembered that Potsdam agreement called for the economic ir gration of all four zones of Germany. To ena Germany to be self-supporting, a stipulated p tion of the German industrial capacity, factor machinery, etc., was to be retained in Germa Industrial capacity in excess of this requirem was to be destroyed or distributed among the lied nations as reparations.

But the refusal of the Soviets to cooperate establishing a unified economy for Germany validated the level of industry and reparation culations made at Potsdam. It soon became parent that the plants and equipment origina

[1] Delivered before the Chamber of Commerce at Pittsburgh, Pa., on Jan. 15, 1948, and released to the press on the same date.

problem confined to the narrow purview of each nation.

The response of the Soviet Union and the states under its domination was revealing. Their reaction was immediate, sharp, and defensive. Our proposal to Europe contained no geographical or ideological qualifications of any kind. Any government sincerely desirous of entering into a combined effort to promote the rehabilitation of Europe was free to participate. It was made clear, however, that we would not aid—in fact, we would vigorously oppose—any nation or group which sought to delay or impede recovery.

This was the suggestion: the nations of Europe were left to their own choice—so far as they were free to do so. Sixteen countries, led by Britain and France, rallied together at Paris to work out a joint program to which each pledged itself to contribute what it could. The Soviet Union, though invited to serve as a co-sponsor of the conference, spurned this invitation and refused to participate. Moreover, the Soviet Government evidently directed the eastern European countries subject to its influence or control to refrain from attending, even after some of these had indicated a desire to participate and one had actually accepted. Subsequently, a high Soviet official, a member of the ruling Politburo, made a public statement that it would be the policy of his Government to oppose and attempt to defeat the European Recovery Program by every possible means. That statement has been confirmed by the actions of the Communist parties in several European countries, notably France and Italy.

The 16 western nations set up the Committee of European Economic Co-operation and proceeded to draft a program for achieving recovery to a self-sustaining basis in a four-year period. Far from interfering with the sovereign rights of the countries involved, as hostile propagandists have alleged, the United States refrained throughout the summer from any suggestion or advice to the European representatives at Paris, despite the fact that repeated and urgent appeals for such counsel were made. We were determined that the initiative in this phase of the procedure should be confined entirely to the European countries involved. Only at the conclusion, and then at the insistence of the participants, did we express our views on some aspects of the preliminary draft of the Paris program as they might relate to the prospect of American support or aid.

After the Paris program was submitted to our Government, it was given an intensive and critical examination. No peacetime project in Government history has received more careful attention and study from a large number of highly qualified individuals both in and out of Government. Numerous modifications were made in the Paris program, as the result of studies made by various groups from the Executive branch and by the Krug, Nourse, and Harriman committees. As a result, the measure recommended to the Congress represents the combined judgment of a large number of the nation's best talent. It is the plan, we believe, best adapted to serve the interests both of the United States and the European countries we wish to help.

There may be flaws of omission or phrasing and no doubt the proposal will be improved in some particulars in the light of Congressional hearings and debate, but the principal features have been shaped with utmost care to meet many vital considerations affecting the national interest. Radical alteration of the basic structure would, I fear, jeopardize the prospect that the measure will successfully accomplish the purpose for which it is designed. There is a general determination to secure the most efficient administration of this program that is humanly possible, taking into full account the unavoidable factors of governmental legal requirements and diplomatic relationships.

The proposal is now under close scrutiny in Congress and the resulting publicity should keep the nation well informed as to the issues. This is especially desirable because we are dealing with a matter which may largely determine the course of history—certainly the character of western civilization—in our time and for many years to come.

The American people frequently hear assertions that events have thrust our nation into a position of world leadership which imposes on us unprecedented responsibilities. There is truth in these assertions. The practical question is: Shall we acknowledge and accept the obligations and exactions of leadership and, if so, in what manner shall we exert that leadership?

I dare say no group is more determined to assert its leadership in vigorous and decisive fashion

American dollars actually will constitute but a small proportion of Europe's total requirements—perhaps on the order of 5 percent. Our aids will be marginal, but that margin is absolutely necessary to enable the European economy to gain sufficient momentum to make real progress towards a pay-as-you-go basis. It is, in effect, the proverbial nail for lack of which the battle of European recovery may be lost.

The fatal deterioration and collapse of Europe economically and therefore politically would result in consequences of a most serious nature for this country. The situation we then would face would necessarily impose on us such burdens in the way of taxes, discomforts, sacrifices, and impairments of the rights and privileges we now enjoy as to make those that now confront us seem trivial by comparison.

In the field of foreign trade, for example, this Government is pressing for international agreements to remove or minimize arbitrary restraints in business between nations and to eliminate harmful discriminations. Many of the restrictive practices we oppose appear in the system known as state trading, where the foreign commerce of a country is conducted by the government as the sole or dominant buyer and seller. We recognize that many of the present state-imposed restraints are defense mechanisms, resorted to as a result of abnormal conditions caused by the war, and susceptible of correction when stability is assured.

The long-term significance of state control of foreign trade, however, is a matter for serious concern. Thus, business has a special stake in European recovery by virtue of what this recovery may mean for the practices and atmosphere of world trade. There is no doubt that if the countries of Europe should be forced to meet their present problems without further assistance from this country, the result could only be a radical increase in the restrictions and controls in force throughout that area affecting international trade and investment. And more important, perhaps, than the actual restrictions themselves would be the deterioration in the atmosphere in which international business would have to be conducted. If the businessmen of this country are again to enjoy the former facilities for residing, traveling, and doing business among the European peoples, then it is essential that the Europeans retain their confi-

dence in this country and in the soundness of liberal institutions in general. It is idle to think that a Europe left to its own efforts in these serious problems of recovery would remain open to American business in the same way that we have known it in the past.

I have been talking about Europe, but the situation is even more serious than that. Europe was at the heart of a great world trading and financial organization. Her failure to recover would have disastrous effects in many other areas. The economies of Latin America and Canada, for example, are organized on the basis of having markets in Europe. If Europe fails to recover, and she certainly cannot do so without our aid, the repercussions will be felt throughout the entire world.

The cumulative loss of foreign markets and sources of supply would unquestionably have a depressing influence on our domestic economy and would drive us to increased measures of government control.

By contrast with these possibilities, the cost and temporary adjustments required by the European Recovery Program appear reasonable, as I think they are. I have attempted only to present an estimate of the stakes the businessmen of America have at issue in this matter.

We are all stockholders in the same company—the United States of America. The paramount question before us, I think, can be stated in business terms. We are required to make a decision as to which is the wiser course: Whether to make a capital investment in European recovery involving a sum that though large is well within our means, with a good prospect of realizing long-term gains; or whether to spend our abundant capital for the satisfaction of our immediate wants, in the hope that the day of reckoning can be indefinitely deferred.

I am not a businessman, but I have some knowledge out of my experience of what has been required in the past to preserve certain of our national assets in security, peace, and freedom. I consider the prudent course in this situation is prompt and effective action to assure solvency and stability in Europe. I think that is our role as a leader in a distressed world. I think we must judge ourselves in our present security and abundance in comparison with distressed people, sick and suffering, but already inspired by a great hope that the New World will help redeem the Old.

Relation of European Recovery Program to American Foreign Policy

‣ STATEMENT BY GEORGE C. MARSHALL[1]

Secretary of State

The President on December 19 presented to the Congress a proposal for a European Recovery Program. Subsequent documents submitted to the Committee from the Executive branch provide amplification and detail. Further explanation will follow.

For my part, this morning I wish to place this proposal for economic assistance to the free countries of Europe in what I believe is its broad perspective.

The European Recovery Program necessarily must be considered in relation to the foreign policy of the United States, which in its simplest form is concerned with those conditions abroad which affect or could later affect the future security and the well-being of our nation. What we desire, I think, is a stable, cooperative, and confident world. But such a world does not exist today. We must deal with the existing situation in our effort to promote peace and security. The situation in Europe has not yet developed to the point where the grim progression from economic uncertainty to tyranny is probable. But without United States support of European self-help this progression may well become inevitable. Therefore, it is proposed that our Nation take vigorous action now to assist in setting in motion the processes of recovery in the second most productive area in the world.

The aid suggested is designed to prevent the economic strangulation which now threatens western Europe and through that vital area endangers the free people of the world. This aid must cure the illness without impairing the integrity of the nations we wish to support. The challenge of our task is great.

We are faced with the necessity of making [ ] historic decision. The proposed program will i[ ] pose burdens upon the American people, but t[ ] quantity of exports contemplated is less than th[ ] of the past 15 months. The decision should [ ] made on the basis of our most fundamental int[ ] ests, and I submit that none of these are more co[ ] pelling than enduring peace and individu[ ] freedom.

Europe must be restored if a durable peace [ ] to be attained. The United States has expend[ ] vast resources in the quest for peace. If by t[ ] expenditure of an additional amount, small [ ] proportion to the investment already made, we c[ ] finish the job, certainly we should do so in o[ ] own interest as well as that of the world at lar[ ]

To a far greater extent than, I believe, is n[ ] recognized, the western European countries, [ ] their own efforts, have made a well-organized st[ ] towards recovery. We have witnessed the u[ ] precedented sight of 16 sovereign nations s[ ] ordinating their diverse individual interests t[ ] broader objective. The work of the Commit[ ] of European Economic Co-operation is a dem[ ] stration of the will of those European nati[ ] to work out with our help their own salvati[ ] The recent actions taken by several of the part[ ] ipating nations without awaiting hoped-for [ ] sistance from us is heartening. The pledges [ ] this European group promise a far more [ ] operative system than has ever before existed [ ] that continent.

The European Recovery Program is designe[ ] reinforce the joint efforts of the free peoples [ ] Europe. It is not a series of piecemeal re[ ] measures. I ask you and the whole Congres[ ] keep in mind the great difference between rec[ ] ery and mere relief.

To be effective, our action should meet f[ ] tests. It must be prompt. It must be adequ[ ]

[1] Made before the House Committee on Foreign Affairs on Jan. 12, 1948, and released to the press on the same date.

results from complex calculations. It takes into account the anticipated production, exports, and imports of the participating countries in their relation to all parts of the world and the availability of supplies both in the United States and elsewhere.

I have so far stressed that the size of the program must be adequate to its purpose of supporting genuine recovery. It is equally important that the program be administered in a businesslike way that commands the confidence of the American people and the peoples and governments of Europe.

In its operations it must be primarily a business, technical, and engineering job. The requirements of the European participants must be continuously screened as to need and availability. The efficient use of available funds must be assured. The utilization of the aid provided must be reviewed. These functions of business management we propose be assigned to an Economic Cooperation Administration. In exercising these functions we should expect the Eca to consult with other agencies of Government where appropriate.

The European Recovery Program is intimately related to the foreign policy of the United States and to our relationship with the participating countries. It will become the most important single expression of American foreign relationships in this part of the world. Its efficient administration will have far-reaching influence on our foreign policy. For this reason, as Secretary of State I am vitally interested in finding the best possible organization and management for the program.

It has never been my intention that the administration of the program be hampered by unnecessary controls or interference from the Department of State. I have said before that I have an open mind, both on the specific machinery of administration and on the wording of legislation. I believe, however, that the authority for the administration of the program should be vested in a single individual and not in a commission or board and that matters of foreign policy must be subject to control and direction of the Secretary of State.

Finally I turn to the inevitable questions: "What does the United States get out of this? Why should the people of the United States accept European burdens in this manner?"

European economic recovery, we feel sure, is

essential to the preservation of basic freedom in the most critical area in the world today.

European economic recovery is essential to a return of normal trade and commerce throughout the world.

The United States is the only nation today with the strength to lend vital support to such a movement.

We want peace. We want security. We want to see the world return to normal as quickly as possible. We are in a position of leadership by force of circumstance. A great crisis has to be met. Do we meet the situation with action or do we step aside and allow other forces to settle the pattern of future European civilization?

Country Studies on ERP Released

[Released to the press January 14]

A report comprising country studies has been prepared by the Executive branch for use in connection with the consideration of the European Recovery Program.[1] These studies deal in the first instance with the economic and political backgrounds of the 16 countries represented at the Paris conference as well as western Germany. Attention has been focused particularly on those background elements which seem most pertinent to the recovery program.

The background statements are accompanied by separate analyses of the prospective part of each country in the recovery program. Since increased production is the keystone to European economic recovery, particular attention is given in the studies to the production programs contained in the report of the Committee of European Economic Co-operation. These programs have been analyzed and evaluated by United States technical working groups, after further explanations of the Paris report by CEEC representatives who came to Washington early in October for this purpose.

---

[1] These studies include chapter I, Introduction; chapter II, Austria; chapter III, Belgium and Luxembourg; chapter IV, Denmark; chapter V, France; chapter VI, Greece; chapter VII, Iceland; chapter VIII, Ireland; chapter IX, Italy; chapter X, The Netherlands; chapter XI, Norway; chapter XII, Portugal; chapter XIII, Sweden; chapter XIV, Switzerland; chapter XV, Turkey; chapter XVI, The United Kingdom; chapter XVII, Western Germany.

No Provision for Military Bases in European Recovery Program

[Released to the press January 17]

In view of the misquotations of Secretary Forrestal's testimony before the Senate Foreign Relations Committee on January 15 in relation to a possible connection between the European Recovery Program and overseas bases, the Secretary of State issued the following statement on January 17:

"The program of United States assistance to European recovery which is now being considered by the Congress does not provide for nor contemplate the acquisition of military bases for the United States in return for economic assistance to the European countries. The intent of the American aid is only to enable the European nations participating in the recovery program to re-establish their economic health and vigor."

There is no contradiction between the purpose outlined above and the statements of Secretary Forrestal. In reply to a question concerning the importance of overseas bases, Mr. Forrestal, as Secretary of National Defense, stated he would not quarrel with this thesis and added:

"I am sure that the Secretary of State will have it in mind. I simply want to underline my own belief that in order of priority I would place the fundamental recovery of national confidence and the belief in survival on the part of these nations that we are trying to help."

Charles E. Moore Consultant to AMAG

The Department of State announced on January 8 the appointment of Charles E. Moore, an authority on machine-tool techniques, as a consultant to the American Mission for Aid to Greece.

Mr. Moore, who recently joined the Mission in Athens, will make a study of the utilization of machine tools in the Greek-aid program, including the approximately one million dollars of machine tools brought by UNRRA into Greece. He will supervise distribution of machine tools and determine Greece's additional machine-tool requirements for aiding reconstruction and rehabilitation.

Burton Y. Berry Assigned to AMAG

The Department of State announced on January 13 the assignment of Burton Y. Berry, a veteran Foreign Service Officer, as special assistant to Dwight P. Griswold, Chief of the American Mission for Aid to Greece. Mr. Berry sailed on January 9 and is scheduled to arrive in Athens on January 26.

China To Send Mission to U.S. on Aid Program

[Released to the press January 15]

The Chinese Government recently informed the Department of State that it was prepared to send a small technical mission to the United States in connection with the aid program for China. The Department of State replied that it would welcome such a mission. It is expected that the mission will be of assistance to the Department of State and other concerned Government agencies and that it will be prepared to discuss the present economic situation in China and measures that the Chinese Government is undertaking.

It is understood that Mr. Pei Tsu-i, former Governor of the Central Bank of China, who will head the technical mission, is scheduled to arrive in Washington on January 16.

World Maritime Organization—*Continued from page 107*

World Maritime Organization—*Continued from page 107*

time Consultative Council by notification to the government of the United Kingdom in accordance with Article V (1) thereof." [41]

Annexed to the recommendations were a draft convention for an intergovernmental maritime consultative organization and a document headed "Agreement for Provisional Maritime Consultative Council".

In a telegram of October 30, 1946, the chairman of the second session of the United Maritime Consultative Council informed the Secretary-General of the United Nations of the action taken.[42]

[41] BULLETIN of Dec. 15, 1946, p. 1094.
[42] U.N. doc. E/CN.2/4, Jan. 10, 1947, p. 7.

THE UNITED NATIONS AND SPECIALIZED AGENCIES

Necessity for International Cooperation in Aviation Matter

STATEMENT BY LAURENCE S. KUTER [1]
U. S. Representative to ICAO

[Released to the press January 13]

The report of the President's Air Policy Commission is a remarkable American document. The five members of the Commission should be congratulated for a demonstration of vision, realism, and foresight which matches that of the Morrow board a quarter of a century ago.

Most of the report is addressed to the domestic aviation problems of the United States, military and civil. In order properly to approach those problems, the Commission naturally found it essential to consider fundamental questions of the national security.

I heartily agree with the Commission that the United States must work to achieve world peace through support and development of the United Nations and the specialized agencies such as ICAO. Meanwhile, as the Commission says, unilateral disarmament by the United States is out of the question.

This viewpoint is related to the committee's recognition and endorsement of a "double-barreled" policy and is also singularly appropriate to the position of the United States in ICAO. In this organization we take a leading position in whole-hearted support to the basic premise in the convention "whereas the future development of international civil aviation can greatly help to create and preserve friendship and understanding among the nations and peoples of the world", meanwhile honestly acknowledging that civil commercial air strength is an important element in the air power of the nation.

In its recommendations dealing with civil commercial air transport, the Commission lays prim emphasis upon the need for greater safety and reg ularity of airline operations. I agree with th Commission that even though airline travel much safer than is generally realized, the recor must be improved. Such improvement is a matt of the greatest urgency.

The figures as to the typical experience of reg lar air travelers with respect to late departures an late arrivals as published by the Commission ca only be described as shocking. It is obvious th: this problem must continue to receive an increa ing amount of attention by the airlines.

As the Commission says, however, the basic r quirement for substantial improvement in safe and regularity of the airlines is an adequate sy tem of air-traffic control navigation and landir aids. I agree with the Commission that the d velopment and financing of such a system of ai should be given top priority.

This problem must be met and solved not on within the United States. It is equally acute on : of our international air routes. While few inte national routes carry as much traffic as certain our domestic routes, the technical facilities to a sist air navigation on most of the world routes a far from adequate even for present traffic leve

It was my privilege to bring this problem to t attention of the Commission when I appeared t fore it. I am naturally delighted that the Co mission has given so strong an endorsement to t ICAO program for the joint international financir where it is truly necessary, of air-navigation : cilities along world air routes. This is a progr: which, in my opinion, is a good investment i the United States.

[1] Made in Montreal, Canada, on Jan. 13, 1948, upon release of *Survival in the Air Age, A Report by the President's Air Policy Commission.*

U.S. Rejects Yugoslav Demand for Immediate Release of Frozen Assets

EXCHANGE OF NOTES BETWEEN THE SECRETARY OF STATE AND THE YUGOSLAV AMBASSADOR

[Released to the press January 14]

Text of note from Secretary Marshall to the Ambassador of the Federal People's Republic of Yugoslavia delivered on January 14

The Secretary of State presents his compliments to His Excellency the Ambassador of the Federal People's Republic of Yugoslavia and has the honor to acknowledge the receipt of the Ambassador's note Pov. Br. No. 1 of January 2, 1948 concerning Yugoslav assets frozen in the United States and claims of the United States and its nationals against Yugoslavia.

Claims of United States nationals against Yugoslavia for compensation for properties expropriated by the Yugoslav authorities through nationalization or on other bases exceed 42 million dollars. In addition the United States claims compensation for two United States airplanes shot down by Yugoslav forces in August 1946. United States accounts with Yugoslavia in regard to lend-lease, pre-UNRRA civilian relief etc. are also still outstanding. Several further minor matters are likewise unsettled.

The Ambassador will recall that, following various previous informal approaches, the Yugoslav Government in March 1947 indicated its desire to negotiate with a view to the settlement of outstanding problems relating to the expropriation of American interests in Yugoslavia and to Yugoslav blocked assets in the United States. In its reply the United States Government stated that it would welcome the early initiation of such negotiations and added that in its view such negotiations should simultaneously also cover the settlement of lend-lease accounts between Yugoslavia and the United States and any other financial claims of one Government against the other which had arisen subsequent to the outbreak of war. On that basis negotiations were undertaken on May 19. During these negotiations the United States has consistently sought a general settlement of this nature.

In an effort to achieve a satisfactory compromise solution the United States offered to accept a lump sum of 20 million dollars as settlement for expropriated American property in Yugoslavia and in compensation for other outstanding United States claims except for the lend-lease and civilian relief accounts with respect to which it also offered to accept a reasonable amount in Yugoslav currency. This offer constituted an earnest effort to expedite a settlement of the matters at issue with Yugoslavia in this regard. The Yugoslav Government summarily dismissed this effort. The Ambassador will recognize that in so doing the Yugoslav Government manifestly relieved the United States of any further obligation with regard to such offer.

The Yugoslav Government for its part made an obviously unrealistic counter offer of 5,187,000 dollars in reimbursement for losses suffered through expropriation by a strictly limited category of claimants. It excluded from this offer the claims, among others, of United States citizens naturalized during and since the war even though such claimants were United States citizens at the time their properties were expropriated. With respect to these excluded claims the Yugoslav Government proposed to postpone consideration until some later time, leaving the sum of 2,500,000 dollars of its assets in this country pending a final agreement.

The Yugoslav Government also expressed willingness to settle the lend-lease and pre-UNRRA civilian relief accounts in local Yugoslav currency but has offered only 300,000 Yugoslav dinars for that purpose. The United States lend-lease expenditures on account of Yugoslavia amounted to 32 million dollars and its share in pre-UNRRA civilian relief over 6 million dollars.

The Yugoslav Government bases its figure of 5,187,000 dollars on a publication regarding American interests in Yugoslavia issued by the United States Department of Commerce in 1942. As the Ambassador has been previously informed, the Department of Commerce considers that figure as constituting only an unsupported estimate concerning a limited category of such investments. In the view of the Department of

Commerce any reliance which might have been placed upon that figure becomes unrealistic by comparison with the subsequent survey published by the United States Treasury in 1947 which lists American-owned assets in Yugoslavia as of May 31, 1943 at 50,300,000 dollars. The latter figure includes certain assets registered in the United States which were not at the time the property of American citizens and is subject to revision in the light of developments since May 31, 1943. That it is more accurate than the earlier Department of Commerce figure is confirmed, however, by the total of 42,300,000 dollars which the Department of State's records indicate as the total claims of United States nationals for expropriated property in Yugoslavia as set forth above.

The Ambassador's note under acknowledgment contains a number of allegations concerning United States motives in these negotiations. All of these allegations have previously been dealt with in oral discussions with the Ambassador and it should not be necessary to refute them once again. It may be noted, however, that the Ambassador charges that the United States by continuing to freeze Yugoslav monetary reserves intends to obstruct the economic reconstruction of Yugoslavia and to hinder Yugoslavia's participation in the general reconstruction of Europe. In this connection, it will be recalled that the United States has already freely contributed to the economic reconstruction of Yugoslavia some 288 million dollars as its share (72 percent) of UNRRA's expenditures in that country, advanced approximately 6 million dollars to Yugoslavia in pre-UNRRA civilian relief and is now further sharing substantially in the program of the International Children's Emergency Fund which has established a major allocation for Yugoslavia. In addition, material charitable donations have been made to Yugoslavia by various relief organizations in the United States. As for Yugoslavia's part in the economic reconstruction of Europe, the Yugoslav Government has not only declined to participate in, but has even actively attacked, the common European recovery program.

The Ambassador also charges that the United States is violating the Bretton Woods Agreement. The Secretary of State is unable to comprehend the applicability of the Bretton Woods Agreement to this situation.

The Secretary of State notes that the Yugoslav Government is prepared to continue the negotiations with regard to compensation for American enterprises in Yugoslavia. In assuring the Ambassador that the United States, on its part, is equally anxious to attain an expeditious solution of all the various matters at issue between the two Governments in this connection, the Secretary of State expresses his confidence that, if the Yugoslav

represented an unquestionable violation of the Bretton Woods Agreement, signed in Washington by forty-three (43) Allied nations, including the United States and Yugoslavia.

Nevertheless, at the beginning of November, 1947, the Government of Yugoslavia made another effort, prepared for a great sacrifice in order to reach an agreement. The representatives of the Yugoslav Government offered the immediate payment of $5,000,000 for the prewar American investments, with a substantial guaranty for the remaining claims. When this offer too was rejected, it was asked how it was that the American Government did not unfreeze and put at the disposal of the National Bank at least that part of the monetary reserve which exceeded the amount of the American claims. This question remained unanswered.

From the end of the war up to this date the Government of the United States has unfrozen the monetary reserves of all the Allied and neutral countries. Yugoslavia is the only country which so far has been unable to recover the property which it entrusted to the United States to save from the fascist plunderers. Recently a decision was reached, with the Government of the United States participating, that the gold which Hitler had seized throughout Europe be returned to its former owners. Under this decision, not only Italy is receiving back its gold, but also the former enemy nation, Austria, with which a peace treaty still has not been signed.

For all these reasons, the Government of the Federal Peoples Republic of Yugoslavia considers it necessary once again to draw the attention of the Government of the United States to this question, and, before undertaking other means for the settlement of this problem, wishes to stress the following:

(1) The Government of the Federal Peoples Republic of Yugoslavia again asserts its readiness to continue negotiations on compensation for American enterprises nationalized in Yugoslavia, such compensation being guaranteed by the Law of Nationalization. But the Government of the Federal Peoples Republic of Yugoslavia firmly refuses to concede that the question of the unfreezing of the monetary reserves and the other assets of the National Bank be contingent upon previous agreement on the other questions.

(2) Further delay in the unfreezing of these reserves, under whatever pretext, can be interpreted only as an intention to obstruct the economic reconstruction of Yugoslavia and to hinder her participation in the reconstruction of European economy, thus hampering the reconstruction of Europe in general.

WASHINGTON, D.C.,
January 2, 1948.

Status of General Agreement on Tariffs

[Released to the press January 15]

The general agreement on tariffs and trade negotiated at Geneva has been brought into force provisionally by the United States and eight other countries. These countries are: Australia, the Belgium-Netherlands-Luxembourg Customs Union, Canada, Cuba, France, and the United Kingdom.

On the part of the United States, the agreement became provisionally effective to the extent specified in the President's proclamations dated December 16, 1947 [1] and January 2, 1948 [2] (Department's press releases 973 and 5, respectively).

According to the latest available information, the present status of the general agreement in each of the other countries named above is as follows:

Australia

The Australian Government gave provisional effect to the general agreement on November 18, 1947, including all of the tariff concessions provided for in schedule I of the agreement. These agreement rates apply to all countries to which Australia extends most-favored-nation treatment, irrespective of whether or not they are parties to the agreement.

Belgium-Netherlands-Luxembourg Customs Union

The Customs Union of Belgium, Luxembourg, and the Netherlands (Benelux) gave provisional effect to the general agreement on January 1, 1948, including the rates of duty appearing in schedule II, section A, of the general agreement, covering Luxembourg and the metropolitan territories of Belgium and the Netherlands. At the same time, for a temporary period, certain of these rates applicable to a number of highly essential products are being suspended in whole or in part. The new rates of duty are applicable to imports from the countries which participated in the Geneva negotiations and to imports from such other countries as enjoy most-favored-nation treatment. At present most-favored-nation treatment is granted to all other countries.

With respect to the rates of duty in sections B to E inclusive of schedule II, covering the Belgian Congo and Ruanda-Urundi, the Netherlands East Indies, Curaçao, and Surinam, respectively, the Governments of Belgium and the Netherlands have indicated that they expect it will be administratively possible to put these rates into effect by June 30, 1948, and possibly sooner.

---

[1] Proclamation 2761A (12 *Federal Register* 8863).
[2] Proclamation 2764 (13 *Federal Register* 21).

More detailed information may be obtained from the Office of International Trade, Department of Commerce, including the following: (1) products on which the Benelux and French rates of duty are for the time being suspended; (2) Canadian tariff concessions included in schedule V not yet made effective.

The remaining countries represented at Geneva have until June 30, 1948, to give provisional effect to the general agreement. These countries are: Brazil, Burma, Ceylon, Chile, China, Czechoslovakia, India, New Zealand, Norway, Pakistan, Southern Rhodesia, Syro-Lebanese C u s t o m s Union, and the Union of South Africa. As each of them signifies its intention to put its tariff concessions into effect a further proclamation will be issued by the President giving effect to United States rates of duty in schedule XX now withheld on items of primary interest to such countries.

Nonenemy Status of Italy, Bulgaria, Hungary, and Rumania

STATEMENT BY THE SECRETARY OF THE TREASURY

[Released to the press by the Treasury Department January 16]

The Secretary of the Treasury announced on January 16 that the Governments of Italy, Bulgaria, Hungary, and Rumania, and nationals thereof, are no longer deemed to be "enemy nationals" within the meaning of general ruling no. 11.[1]

Treasury officials pointed out that this action, which is in the form of an amendment to public circular no. 25, was taken in view of the ratification of the treaties of peace with Italy, Bulgaria, Hungary, and Rumania. The amendment does not authorize transactions under certain Treasury licenses, nor does it in any way affect the definitions appearing in Executive Order 9193, which established the Office of Alien Property.

It was also announced that the Treasury Department is prepared, in appropriate cases, to grant licenses for payments to creditors resident in the United States of business organizations and individuals in Bulgaria, Hungary, and Rumania from blocked accounts in this country in which the debtors have an interest. It was recalled that on May 20, 1947, a similar announcement was made concerning payments to creditors of persons in Italy.

Treasury officials explained that the step with respect to Bulgaria, Hungary, and Rumania is

[1] General ruling no. 11 was issued under Ex. Or. 8389 (7 *Federal Register* 2168).

being taken even though the final disposition of the blocked assets of these countries has not been determined. They pointed out, however, that in taking this step the Treasury Department is in substance applying to its unblocking procedures the principles of Public Law 671, 79th Congress, which authorizes the Office of Alien Property to pay debt claims of American citizens out of vested assets of their Bulgarian, Hungarian,'and Rumanian debtors.

It was stated that, in general, licenses will be issued only in those instances where the debt was incurred either prior to the date of the blocking of the country involved or as a result of a transaction entered into subsequent to that date pursuant to a license specifically authorizing the use of blocked funds.

U. S. Representative and Advisers to ITU Council

[Released to the press January 8]

The Department of State announced on January 8 that the President had appointed the United States Representative and Advisers to the Administrative Council of the International Telecommunication Union (ITU). The Council is scheduled to meet at Geneva on January 20, 1948.

Francis Colt de Wolf, Chief of the Telecommunications Division, Department of State, will se as the United States Representative. Helen Kelly, Telecommunications Division, and J. D. Tomlinson, Assistant Chief of the Division International Organization Affairs, both of Department of State, will serve as Advisers.

The Administrative Council was provided by the new international telecommunication c vention drawn up at Atlantic City this past si mer, which revised the structure of the ITU. Council is charged with implementing the p visions of the Atlantic City convention and re lations, coordinating the work of the Union, considering and solving problems arising in interim between plenipotentiary conferen which meet every five years. There are 18 g ernments, elected by the conference, represen on the Council.

Although the convention setting forth the r ganization of the Union does not go into effect til January 1, 1949, a protocol to the convent was signed at Atlantic City providing for the mediate establishment of the Administrat Council on a provisional basis. It is expected t the Council will normally meet at least once a y at Geneva, the seat of the International T communication Union.

Transfer of Nondemilitarized Combat Matériel

[Released to the press January 5]

The following is a list of authorizations and transfers of surplus nondemilitarized combat matériel, effected by the Department of State in its capacity as foreign surplus and lend-lease disp agent, during the months of February, May, Ji August, September, October, and November 1 and not previously reported to the Munitions visions.

AUTHORIZATIONS AND TRANSFERS OF SURPLUS NONDEMILITARIZED COMBAT MATÉRIEL

Country	Description of matériel	Procurement cost	Sales price	Date of tr
				1947
Brazil	Spare parts for armored light car M8, and half-track car M2.	$16, 227. 81	$8, 113. 91	Nov. .
	Spare parts for light tank M3A1	387, 205. 07	19, 860. 25	"
Canada.	VT fuzes (time fuze)	4, 149, 936. 00	5, 000. 00	"
	Spare parts for tanks	935, 491. 65	99, 274. 58	"
Chile	Eight AT-11 aircraft (trainers)	667, 208. 00	160, 000. 00	Sept.
	Drill cartridges, miscellaneous equipment .	37, 629. 88	3, 640. 45	Nov.
Cuba	One patrol craft, escort	1, 786, 700. 00	33, 500. 00	"
Denmark	10 German "E" (motor torpedo boats) (awarded to the United States by the Tripartite Naval Commission).	Captured enemy equipment	42, 500. 00	June 2
Ecuador.	12 P-47D, one AT-7 or AT-11 aircraft . .	1, 275, 654. 00	98, 000. 00	May 7
Egypt	9 minesweepers.	5, 240, 250. 00	540, 000. 00	Sept.

Country	Description of matériel	Procurement cost	Sales price	Date of transfer
				1947
Salvador	One AT–11 aircraft (advanced trainer). . .	$83, 401. 00	$20, 000. 00	Oct. 7
	Spare parts for tanks	11, 609. 76	580. 56	Nov. 13
	Metallic belt link and miscellaneous cartridges.	3, 576. 98	358. 18	" 24
	Miscellaneous cartridges, metallic belt link, shells, shot, rifle grenades, signals.	58, 892. 16	5, 075. 11	Oct. 28
reece	11 minesweepers	6, 404, 750. 00	660, 000. 00	Sept.
Iexico	4 patrol frigates.	9, 408, 000. 00	50, 000. 00	Nov. 5
	5 patrol crafts, escort	8, 933, 500. 00	150, 000. 00	" 5
orway.	10 German "E" motor torpedo boats (awarded to the United States by the Tripartite Naval Commission).	Captured enemy equipment	42, 500. 00	June 17, Aug. 4
urkey	7 minesweepers.	1, 590, 000. 00	1, 078, 000. 00	Feb.
ruguay	One AT–6D aircraft (advanced trainer) . .	25, 029. 00	5, 000. 00	Oct. 2

AUTHORIZATIONS FOR RETRANSFER OF LEND-LEASE ARTICLES IN BRITISH MILITARY INVENTORY, APRIL 1 THROUGH SEPTEMBER 30, 1947

Retransferee government	Item	Quantity
elgium	Engines, aircraft, Packard Merlin 266 (installed in British fighters on loan to Belgium, equipment for two squadrons).	
hina	Gunsights, gyro, Mark XIV	18
zechoslovakia	Propellors, Hamilton	4 [1]
	Spare blades for Hamilton propellors	4 [1]
)enmark	Ammunition, .5-inch	68,000 rds.[1]
	Guns, .5-inch Browning	18 [1]
	Spare barrels for .5-inch Browning guns	36 [1]
	Spare parts for the above guns, three years' requirements	
rance	Ammunition, 3-inch .50 cal. low-angle practice cartridges	451 [1]
ireece	Ammunition:	
	.5-inch AP incendiary	500,000 rds.
	.5-inch ball	500,000 rds.
	.5-inch incendiary and tracer	150,500 rds.
	9 mm. ball	210,400 rds.
	.45-inch ball	91,882 rds.
	.30-inch ball	20,000 rds.
	Equipment surplus to British needs located in Greece, blanket authority, details of items and quantities not yet determined.	
lew Zealand . . \	Machine guns, Colt .5-inch (exact number undetermined, small quantity).	([1])
weden	Explosive composition, RDX A and A2	1,000 tons [1]
urkey	Ammunition, .5-inch.	2,100,000 rds.

[1] Retransfer approved as outright sale; other retransfers approved subject to continuing U. S. right of recapture.

THE CONGRESS

Third Supplemental Appropriation Bill for 1948: Hearngs Before the Subcommittee of the Committee on Appropriations, House of Representatives, 80th Cong., 1st ess., on the Third Supplemental Appropriation Bill for 1948. ii, 415 pp. [Department of State, pp. 223–336.]

Third Supplemental Appropriation Bill for 1948: Hearngs Before the Committee on Appropriations, United States Senate, 80th Cong., 1st sess., on H. R. 4748, a bill

making supplemental appropriations for the fiscal year ending June 30, 1948, and for other purposes. ii, 289 pp. [Department of State, pp. 119–153, 170–187, 272–3.]

Investigation of the National Defense Program: Hearings Before a Special Committee Investigating the National Defense Program, United States Senate, 79th Cong., 2nd sess. . . . Part 36, Surplus Property Abroad, and Part 39, Return of Overseas Surpluses, Maintenance of

Naval Establishments, Canol Project, Emergency Housing Program, Renegotiation of War Contracts . . . [Both parts indexed.]

Hearings Regarding the Communist Infiltration of the Motion Picture Industry: Hearings before the Committee on Un-American Activities, House of Representatives, 80th Cong., 1st sess., Public Law 601. October 20, 21, 22, 23, 24, 27, 28, 29, and 30, 1947. iv, 549 pp.

Consolidation of International Air Carriers (Chosen Instrument): Hearings Before a Subcommittee of the Committee on Interstate and Foreign Commerce, United States Senate, 80th Cong., 1st sess., on S. 987, a bill to amend the Civil Aeronautics Act of 1938, as amended, to provide for the creation of a consolidated international air carrier for the United States, and for other purposes. May 19, 20, 21, 22, 23, 24, 26, 28, June 2, 3, 4, and 5, 1947. iv, 821 pp. [Department of State, pp. 708–729, 804.]

Transfer of Property to the Philippines

By Executive Order 9921 (13 *Federal Register* 171), the President on January 12 authorized the Philippine Alien Property Administrator to transfer certain property to the Republic of the Philippines. The provisions of Executive Order 9921 are as follows:

1. The Philippine Alien Property Administrator is authorized to transfer to the Republic of the Philippines in accordance with the provisions of section 3 of the Philippine Property Act of 1946, as soon as practicable after final payment of claims, costs, and expenses of administration, any property, or proceeds thereof, vested in or transferred to him pursuant to the Trading with the Enemy Act, as amended, and the Philippine Property Act of 1946.

2. The Philippine Alien Property Administrator is authorized to transfer to the Republic of the Philippines in accordance with the provisions of section 3 of the Philippine Property Act of 1946, prior to final adjudication of claims, costs, and expenses of administration when he deems it to be administratively feasible, and without further consideration for such transfer, property, or proceeds thereof, vested in or transferred to him pursuant to the Trading with the Enemy Act, as amended, and the Philippine Property Act of 1946, against which, in the judgment of the Administrator, no substantial claims, expenses, or costs of administration are likely to be chargeable.

THE FOREIGN SERVICE

Consular Offices

The American Vice Consulate at Aruba, West Indies, was raised to the rank of Consulate on January 1, 1948.

Effected by exchange of notes signed at Tegucigalpa May 13, 1947; entered into force May 13, 1947; effective from May 1, 1947.

Treaty of Peace With Italy. Treaties and Other International Acts Series 1648. Pub. 2960. 511 pp. $1.25.

Dated at Paris February 10, 1947; ratified by the President of the United States June 14, 1947; proclaimed by the President September 15, 1947; entered into force September 15, 1947.

Paris Peace Conference 1946: Selected Documents

[Released to the press January 17]

The Department of State released on January 17 a volume which contains a selection of documents setting forth the deliberations and recommendations of the Paris peace conference of 1946 attended by 21 nations. The conference was held for the purpose of considering the draft treaties of peace with Italy, Rumania, Bulgaria, Hungary, and Finland which had been prepared by the Council of Foreign Ministers. Although the proceedings of the Paris conference have not been restricted they were prepared only in a few copies for official use and have therefore not previously been available to the general public.

Photographic reproduction has been employed in producing this volume, thus making available to the public facsimile copies of the documents in their mimeographed form as distributed at the conference. The compilation is divided into two main categories, dealing with (1) the participants, organization, and procedures of the conference, and (2) consideration of each of the five draft treaties in the primary commissions and in plenary sessions. There is also included an appendix of three supplementary documents concerning the statute of the Free Territory of Trieste.

This volume is for sale by the Superintendent of Documents, United States Government Printing Office, Washington 25, D.C., for $6 a copy.

Foreign Agriculture

The Office of Foreign Agricultural Relations, Department of Agriculture, has consolidated its two monthly periodicals, *Agriculture in the Americas* and *Foreign Agriculture*, effective in January 1948. The combined publication is entitled *Foreign Agriculture*. Paid subscriptions are obtainable from the Superintendent of Documents, Government Printing Office, Washington 25, D.C. For a sample copy write to the Office of Foreign Agricultural Relations, Department of Agriculture, Washington 25, D.C.

Erratum: Habana Meeting of U. N. Conference on Trade and Employment

Bulletin of January 11, 1948, page 39, first column, first paragraph, second line: Delete "will be forthcoming if trade is rigorously re-".

THE DEPARTMENT

President's Budg[

Our new international programs for European aid have been fully presented to the Congress in recent messages. The appropriation already enacted will provide "stopgap" assistance through next March to the European countries in most urgent need—France, Italy, and Austria—as well as aid to China. It is essential that we move as soon as possible to a positive program for promotion of European recovery.

In addition to the European Recovery Program, other international-aid programs for several countries, including China, are provided for under proposed legislation. Definite recommendations on these programs will be transmitted shortly. Also, I urge again enactment of the inter-American military cooperation bill proposed last May. Estimates of appropriations and expenditures for this group of programs have been included in the budget.

Expenditures. By far the largest international expenditures in the fiscal year 1949 will be under the European Recovery Program—4 billion dollars, in addition to 500 million dollars in the fiscal year 1948. Expenditures under other proposed legislation for aid are estimated at 60 million dollars in the fiscal year 1948 and 440 million dollars in the fiscal year 1949.

The Export-Import Bank will continue in the fiscal year 1949 to make loans to expand international trade and promote economic development, particularly in the Western Hemisphere. The need for such loans will decline, however, when the dollar problem of Western Hemisphere countries is eased as a result of purchases in these countries under the European Recovery Program. Disbursements of the Bank's funds will also decline because its large loan authorizations to several European countries are rapidly being exhausted during the current fiscal year. Plans for the European Recovery Program call for use of the Bank's facilities to administer loans made under the new program.

The largest expenditures for foreign relief now fall under the occupied-areas program. These expenditures are handled by the Army and are

¹Excerpts from *The President's Budget Message for 1949 and Selected Budget Statements* which was released to the press by the White House on Jan. 10, 1948. See also S. Doc. 106, 80th Cong., 1st Sess.

ent problems indicates that the margin between ie recommended appropriation and the 4.5-bilon-dollar expenditure estimate during the same eriod is reasonable. To permit systematic and :onomical placement of orders for later delivery, ppropriations must be substantially greater than rpenditures in the initial phase of the program. 1 addition, bills for a portion of the goods iipped in one fiscal year are not paid until the)llowing year, and this lag of expenditures is articularly significant in a large new program. Other recommended 1948 supplemental approriations, to be spent mainly in 1949 and later ears, include 300 million dollars for other foreignid programs, 65 million dollars for the loan to

the United Nations for headquarters construction, and smaller amounts for Department of State programs.

Because of the large supplemental appropriations for international activities recommended for the fiscal year 1948, appropriations for 1949 total only 2.1 billion dollars. The two main items are 1,250 million dollars for the Army programs in occupied areas and an estimate of 450 million dollars for aid programs under proposed legislation. Recommended appropriations totaling 133 million dollars for Philippine programs are below estimated expenditures because a portion of the appropriations for the current year will remain available for expenditure next year.

INTERNATIONAL AFFAIRS AND FINANCE

[Fiscal years. In millions]

Program or agency	Actual, 1947	Estimate, 1948	Estimate, 1949	Appropriations, 1949
	Expenditures			
econstruction and stabilization:				
European Recovery Program (proposed legislation)	. . . .	$500	$4,000	(¹)
Other proposed aid legislation	. . . .	60	440	² $450
Export-Import Bank loans	$937	736	500	. . . . .
Treasury loan to United Kingdom	2,050	1,700	. . . . .	. . . . .
Subscriptions to International Bank and Fund	1,426	. . . . .	. . . . .	. . . . .
Reconstruction Finance Corporation loans to United Kingdom . .	−38	−40	−40	. . . . .
U.S. Commercial Company	−47	63	. . . . .	. . . . .
Greek-Turkish aid (act of 1947)	. . . .	275	119	. . . . .
oreign relief:				
Foreign (interim) aid (Foreign Aid Act of 1947)	. . . .	375	165	. . . . .
Army (occupied countries)	514	998	1,250	1,250
Relief assistance to war-devastated areas (post-UNRRA)	. . . .	272	60	. . . . .
UNRRA	1,489	201	1	. . . . .
International Refugee Organization	. . . .	71	71	71
Other	3	(³)	. . . . .	. . . . .
hilippine war damage and rehabilitation:				
Present programs	73	95	180	116
Proposed legislation for veterans' benefits	. . . . .	. . . . .	16	16
Iembership in international organizations:				
Present programs	17	25	24	24
Proposed legislation	. . . . .	15	34	4
oreign relations:				
Department of State:				
Present programs	111	160	164	151
Proposed legislation	. . . .	20	16	20
Other	6	7	7	1
Total	6,540	5,533	7,009	2,104

¹ A 1948 supplemental appropriation of 6.8 billion dollars is anticipated for the period from Apr. 1, 1948, to June 30,)49.

² A 1948 supplemental appropriation of 300 million dollars is also included in this budget.
³ Less than one-half million dollars.

Contributors | *Eula McDonald*, author of the article on a world maritime organization, is a foreign-affairs analyst in the Division of Historical Policy Research, Office of Public Affairs, Department of State.

The Department of State bulletin

VOL. XVIII, No. 448 • PUBLICATION 3036

February 1, 1948

The Department of State BULLETIN,
a weekly publication compiled and
edited in the Division of Publications,
Office of Public Affairs, provides the
public and interested agencies of
the Government with information on
developments in the field of foreign
relations and on the work of the Department of State and the Foreign
Service. The BULLETIN includes
press releases on foreign policy issued
by the White House and the Department, and statements and addresses
made by the President and by the
Secretary of State and other officers
of the Department, as well as special
articles on various phases of international affairs and the functions of
the Department. Information is included concerning treaties and international agreements to which the
United States is or may become a
party and treaties of general international interest.

Publications of the Department, as
well as legislative material in the field
of international relations, are listed
currently.

uperintendent of Documents
Government Printing Office
Washington 25, D.C.

SUBSCRIPTION:
sues, $5; single copy, 15 cents

shed with the approval of the
of the Bureau of the Budget

TOWARD A WORLD MARITIME ORGANIZATION

Part II

ARTICLE BY EULA McDONALD

Part I of this article, which appeared in the BULLETIN of January 25, gave a résumé of the antecedents and accomplishments of some of the significant organizations concerned with ocean shipping from 1897 to 1946, inclusive. Part II of the narrative continues with an account of major activities in this field since the end of 1946, the plans for the proposed Intergovernmental Maritime Consultative Organization, and a special section on the problem of safety of life at sea.

Provisional Maritime Consultative Council and the United Nations

As in the case of the concurrent activities in 1946 of the United Maritime Consultative Council and the Temporary Transport and Communications Commission of the Economic and Social Council, likewise in 1947 both the Provisional Maritime Consultative Council and the permanent Transport and Communications Commission of the Economic and Social Council met independently but aware of each other's functioning.

The Government of the United States had notified the Government of the United Kingdom of its acceptance of membership in the Provisional Maritime Consultative Council in November 1946.[43] The Economic and Social Council, at its session of December 10, 1946, in New York, had appointed the representatives of 12 countries who had been duly nominated by their respective governments to the permanent Transport and Communications Commission.[44]

The permanent Commission began its first session on February 6, 1947, in New York. The provisional agenda, which had been prepared by

the Secretariat of the United Nations, contained a proposal for the establishment of a world-wide intergovernmental shipping organization. This proposal was included in the agenda pursuant to the resolution adopted by the Economic and Social Council on June 21, 1946.[45] In connection with this item of the agenda, the permanent Commission took note of (1) the comprehensive report of May 25, 1946, submitted by the Temporary Transport and Communications Commission in favor of an intergovernmental shipping organization, and (2) the similar recommendations of the United Maritime Consultative Council. The permanent Commission did not consider a more detailed study necessary. Accordingly it decided, in compliance with its terms of reference, to recommend to the Economic and Social Council the establishment of a world-wide intergovernmental organization to deal with technical matters in the realm of shipping. Since, however, the draft recommendations of the United Maritime Consultative Council were not limited to the technical field, the Commission proceeded to adopt a draft resolution which contemplated a range of activities broader in scope than those confined to technical aspects alone.

---

[43] BULLETIN of Dec. 1, 1946, p. 1002; United States membership was effective Nov. 20, 1946. Of the other countries which had participated in the Washington meeting of October 1946, a sufficient number to bring the new Council into existence informed the Government of the United Kingdom of their acceptance of the "Agreement for Provisional Maritime Consultative Council".

[44] U.N. doc. E/CN.2/SR.1, Feb. 6, 1947, p. 2.

[45] BULLETIN of Jan. 25, 1948, p. 106.

This resolution requested the Economic and Social Council to take action to the effect that the Secretary-General of the United Nations be instructed to call a conference for the purpose of establishing an intergovernmental shipping organization and to circulate with the invitations to the conference the draft convention prepared by the United Maritime Consultative Council, which should form the basis for discussion at the conference.[46] The resolution specified, that the conference should be held in Europe, preferably in the fall of 1947.[47]

The Economic and Social Council, meeting on March 28, 1947, took note of the report of the first session of the Transport and Communications Commission and adopted a resolution requesting the Secretary-General of the United Nations among other things to convene a conference for the purpose mentioned; to circulate the draft convention prepared by the United Maritime Consultative Council to all of the invited governments with the notation that any comments or amendments which they might wish to offer in advance of the meeting should be sent to the Secretary-General for submission to the other governments and for later consideration at the conference; and to draw up a provisional agenda for the conference. The resolution also expressed the hope that the invited governments would give their delegations full powers to sign the convention.[48]

At this juncture the newly created Provisional Maritime Consultative Council, replacing the defunct United Martime Consultative Council, began its activities. Its first meeting was held at Paris from May 16 to 20, 1947, at the invitation of the French Government.

Under the terms of the agreement annexed to the recommendations adopted by the United Maritime Consultative Council at its Washington meeting in October 1946, the Provisional Maritime Consultative Council was designed to function temporarily, pending the establishment of the proposed world-wide organization, and in particular "to provide machinery for cooperation among Governments in the field of Governmental

[46] U.N. doc. E/270, Feb. 24, 1947, pp. 13–15, 30.
[47] U.N. doc. E/270/Add. 1, Mar. 7, 1947, p. 2.
[48] U.N. doc. E/408, Apr. 9, 1947, pp. 2–3.
[49] BULLETIN of Dec. 15, 1946, p. 1098.

Lanes for steamers on frequented routes, with
special regard to the avoidance of steamer
collisions and the safety of fishermen;

Night signals for communicating information
at sea;

Reporting, marking, and removing dangerous
wrecks or other obstructions to navigation;

Notices of changes in lights, buoys, and other
day-and-night danger marks;

Uniform system of coloring and numbering
buoys; and

Establishment of a permanent international
maritime commission.

The last-named topic represents perhaps the
earliest suggestion considered at a formal international meeting for a permanent multilateral
maritime body. However, the conference resolved
"That for the present the establishment of a permanent international maritime commission is not
considered expedient".[52]

The maritime nations were made acutely aware
of the urgent need for closer international cooperation in the field of safety at sea by the *Titanic*
disaster of 1912. This tragedy was the immediate
cause for the convening of a diplomatic conference
in London in the latter part of 1914 to consider
measures to prevent the future occurrence of such
calamities.[53] The conference drew up the convention of January 20, 1914, for the safety of life
at sea. The intervention of World War I as well
as other less influential factors prevented the convention from coming into force completely, although several of the signatory countries adopted
portions of it.[54]

[52] *Protocol of Proceedings of the International Marine
Conference Held in Washington, D.C., . . . October 16
to December 31, 1889* (3 vols., Washington, Government
Printing Office, 1890), vol. I, p. 1.

[51] These regulations, which are a modification of the
International Rules of the Road as adopted in 1884 by
England and of those adopted by the United States in
1885 (23 Stat. 438), were enacted into law by the Congress
of the United States in 1890 (26 Stat. 320) and, with
some changes throughout the years, are still in force
(33 U.S.C. 61 ff.).

[53] *Protocol of Proceedings of the International Marine
Conference*, vol. II, pp. 1365 ff.

[53] S. Doc. 463, 63d Cong., 2d sess. (Washington, Government Printing Office, 1914). See also BULLETIN of Nov.
3, 1946, p. 816.

[54] *Foreign Relations of the United States*, 1929, vol. I,
p. 368.

The Government of the United States did not ratify the convention of 1914, but it did undertake the direction of the services of derelict destruction, study and observation of ice conditions, and the conduct of the international ice patrol in the North Atlantic, which it was invited to do by article 7 of the convention. Pursuant to an Executive order these services were performed by the vessels of the United States Coast Guard. Foreign nations contributed *pro rata* shares for the maintenance of the services.[55]

The years brought added knowledge in the technical matters covered by the convention of 1914 as well as marked advancements in ship construction. These changed conditions prompted the British Government to make proposals for the convening of a conference to revise and amend the convention of 1914.[56] The proposals were made in the autumn of 1927 to the Government of the United States, which replied in January 1928 agreeing that consideration should be given to the revision of the convention and suggesting that the conference be held in the spring of 1929.[57]

Before the conference met, another tragedy at sea focused the attention of the world on the importance of immediate safety measures. On November 12, 1928, the steamship *Vestris* sank off the Virginia Capes with the consequent loss of 110 lives.

The conference was held in London from April 16 to May 31, 1929. Out of its deliberations grew the existing convention for promoting safety of life at sea, which was signed on the last day of the meeting by the delegations of 18 governments. The United States became a party to this convention on August 7, 1936 (effective November 7), subject to three understandings bearing on American standards of safety.[58]

Another international conference concerned

[55] *International Conference on Safety of Life at Sea, London, April 16–May 31, 1929; Report of the Delegation of the United States of America and Appended Documents* (Department of State publication 14), p. 16. See also Executive Order 2458, Sept. 20, 1916.

[56] *Foreign Relations*, 1929, vol. I, p. 379.

[57] *International Conference on Safety of Life at Sea*, pp. 16–17.

[58] Treaty Series 910, 50 Stat. 1121.

[59] Department of State, *Press Releases*, May 10, 1930, pp. 224–225; *ibid.*, Sept. 6, 1930, pp. 155–158. Treaty Series 858, 47 Stat. 2228.

[60] U.N. doc. E/270, Feb. 24, 1947, p. 16.

manent organization, that a Provisional Maritime Consultative Council be established.

The "scope and purposes" of the permanent organization, as set forth in article I of the draft convention, are identical with the purposes of the Provisional Maritime Consultative Council as set forth in the interim agreement and digested hereinabove. In full, they are as follows: [65]

"i. to provide machinery for cooperation among Governments in the field of Governmental regulation and practices relating to technical matters of all kinds affecting shipping engaged in international trade, and to encourage the general adoption of the highest practicable standards in matters concerning maritime safety and efficiency of navigation;

"ii. to encourage the removal of all forms of discriminatory action and unnecessary restrictions by Governments affecting shipping engaged in international trade so as to promote the availability of shipping services to the commerce of the world without discrimination;

"iii. to provide for the consideration by the Organization of any shipping problems of an international character involving matters of general principle that may be referred to the Organization by the United Nations. Matters which are suitable for settlement through the normal processes of international shipping business are not within the scope of the Organization;

"iv. to provide for the exchange of information among Governments on matters under consideration by the Organization."

In article II the draft convention prescribes the functions of the organization as follows:

"Section 1. The functions of the Organization shall be consultative and advisory.

"Section 2. In order to achieve the objectives set out in Article I, the functions of the Organization in relation to matters within its scope shall be—

"(a) to consider and make recommendations upon matters arising under Subsections i and ii of Article I that may be remitted to it by Mem-

[61] *Ibid.*, pp. 16–17.
[62] U.N. doc. E/408, Apr. 9, 1947, p. 3.
[63] BULLETIN of Oct. 5, 1947, p. 676.
[64] BULLETIN of Dec. 15, 1946, pp. 1092 ff.
[65] BULLETIN of Dec. 15, 1946, p. 1094.

ber Governments, by organs of the United Nations, or by other intergovernmental organizations, or upon matters referred to it under Subsection iii of Article I;

"(b) to draft conventions, agreements, or other suitable instruments, and to recommend these to Governments and to intergovernmental organizations, and to convene such conferences as may be necessary;

"(c) to provide machinery for consultation and exchange of information among Member Governments.

"Section 3. In those matters which appear to the Organization suitable for settlement through the normal processes of international shipping business, the Organization shall so recommend."[46]

The draft convention provides that the organization shall consist of an Assembly; a Council; a Maritime Safety Committee and such other subsidiary organs as may be established by the organization from time to time; and a secretariat.

The Assembly is to consist of delegates of all the member governments, each member government being entitled to one vote. Regular meetings of the Assembly are to be held at least every two years. Extraordinary meetings may be convoked when one third of the member governments notify the Secretary-General that such a meeting is desired, or at any other time if considered necessary by the Council.

The functions of the Assembly will include the establishment of any temporary or, upon recommendation of the Council, permanent subsidiary bodies it may deem necessary; election of the member governments to be represented on the Council; deciding upon questions referred to it by the Council; consideration of the Council's reports; determination of the financial arrangements of the organization after studying the budget estimates and financial statements; referral to the Council of appropriate matters within the organization's scope; providing opportunity for exchange of information and of views among the member governments; and exercise of certain powers in connection with the establishment of the Maritime Safety Committee.

The Council of the organization will consist of

---

[46] *Ibid.*, p. 1096.

The new organization, it may be pointed out, is expected to cooperate with the International Civil Aviation Organization in some phases (especially safety phases) of air transport across the world's seas. In discussing the transocean carriage of goods and passengers both by surface vessel and by air William L. Clayton, then Under Secretary of State for economic affairs, spoke as follows at the October 1946 session of the United Maritime Consultative Council:

"The power-driven vessel plying the free seas is the cheapest form of transportation in the world. For many years we shipped cotton from Houston to Shanghai at less cost than it took to bring it from Oklahoma to Houston. Man himself can now fly over the seas quicker than he can travel on the surface, but it seems safe to say that his goods will for the most part always travel on and not above the water." [70]

In a domain of such paramount importance to the welfare of mankind, the economic, humanitarian, and political benefits derived from international cooperation may well comprise a significant part of the mosaic of friendly interrelationship which the United Nations is steadily forming.

Addresses on European Recovery Program

On January 22 the Secretary of State made an address before the National Cotton Council in Atlanta, Ga.; for the text of this address on European aid, see Department of State press release 52 of January 22, 1948.

On January 22 Assistant Secretary Thorp made an address before the National Industrial Conference Board in New York City; for the text of this address on European aid, see Department of State press release 51 of January 22, 1948.

---

[67] BULLETIN of Jan. 25, 1948, p. 107.
[68] See U.N. doc. E/Conf. 4/2, Oct. 2, 1947, p. 1.
[69] U.N. doc. E/C. 4/3, Sept. 16, 1947, p. 8.
[70] BULLETIN of Nov. 3, 1946, p. 817.

FOREIGN AID AND RECONSTRUCTION

British Foreign Secretary Asks for Union of Western Europe

STATEMENT BY THE DEPARTMENT OF STATE

[Released to the press January 23]

Mr. Bevin has proposed measures which will enable the free countries of western Europe further to concert with one another for their common safety and good.[1] As in the case of the recovery program the United States heartily welcomes European initiative in this respect and any proposal looking to a closer material and spiritual link between the western European nations will serve to reinforce the efforts which our two countries have been making to lay the foundation for a firm peace.

New Interim Aid Allocation to France, Italy, and Austria

[Released to the press January 23]

The Department of State announced on January 23 an additional allocation of $97,121,000 to France, Italy, and Austria under the $522,000,000 Interim Aid Program. The new allocation will be used, in large part, to cover February procurement of vitally needed cereals and coal. France will receive $49,539,000; Italy, $35,477,000; and Austria, $12,105,000.

A breakdown of the new allocation, on which procurement has already started, is as follows:

	Quantity (long tons)	Estimated cost and freight value ($000)
Austrian program:		
Cereals	39, 000	5, 478
Coal (offshore)	240, 000	3, 800
Peanuts	7, 000	2, 827
		12, 105
French program:		
Cereals	165, 000	[2] 22, 789
Coal (U.S.)[4]	1, 300, 000	26, 750
		49, 539

[1] In address before the House of Commons in London on Jan. 22, 1948.

[2] Includes $1,000,000 additional for transportation against the January allocation of cereals from the United States.

[3] January allocation.

[4] See Department of State press releases 3, 6, and 9 of Jan. 2 and 3, 1948.

The International Labor Organization Regional Meeting for the Near and Middle East

ARTICLE BY IRWIN M. TOBIN

Introduction

The International Labor Organization Regional Meeting for the Near and Middle East, held at Istanbul, November 24–29, 1947, represented a significant extension of the work of the International Labor Organization. Taken together with the regional meetings held at Mexico City (April 1–16, 1946) and New Delhi (October 27–November 8, 1947), Istanbul demonstrated the intention of the ILo to extend the frontiers of its activity along regional lines and take fuller account than hitherto of the special problems involved in raising living standards in areas still in the early stages of industrial development.

The Istanbul meeting, modest as it was in composition and objectives, also marked a new departure in the approach of the governments of the Near and Middle East toward the solution of their economic and social problems. It provided for the first time an opportunity for officials of the states of the area to exchange experiences and information about social problems and progress in their countries and to examine from a regional viewpoint the standards to which the peoples of the area should aspire.

Originally invited by the Egyptian Government to meet in Cairo, the ILo was obliged either to transfer the site elsewhere owing to the cholera epidemic or to postpone the meeting indefinitely because of other ILo commitments. The ILo, with the full cooperation of the Egyptian Government, decided upon the former course. By its readiness to make arrangements for holding the meeting at Istanbul on very short notice, the Turkish Government made it possible to proceed on the original schedule.

Attendance

The independent states of the Near and Middle East represented at the conference were: Egypt, Iran, Iraq, Lebanon, Syria, and Turkey. Unlike the full-scale conferences of the International Labor Organization, in which representatives of industry and labor take part together with representatives of governments, the Istanbul meeting, because of its preliminary character, consisted only of government delegates. The wish was widely expressed among those present that future regional meetings of the Near and Middle East area should also include representatives of industry and labor in line with the classic ILo pattern.

In addition to the participating governments, a number of other governments and international organizations were represented by observers. The United States was represented in this capacity by William S. Tyson, Solicitor of the Department of Labor, and William J. Handley, Labor Attaché at the American Legation, Cairo. Other Governments similarly represented were Afghanistan, France, Greece, India, Pakistan, and the Union of South Africa. Observers were also present from the United Nations and the United Nations Food and Agriculture Organization.

In addition, an influential role was played at the meeting by the tripartite delegation—representing government, employers, and workers—appointed by the Governing Body of the International Labor Office. Sir Guildhaume Myrddin-Evans, Chairman of the Governing Body, headed the ILo group and delivered one of the principal opening addresses. F. L. Yllanes Ramos of Mexico, of the employers' group, and O. Lizzadri of Italy, of the workers' group, took part in committee discussions and were able, as a result of their industrial experience, to make a number of practical suggestions in the course of the formulation of resolutions. The meeting elected Tahsin B. Balta, Minister of Labor of Turkey, as its President and Ibrahim Istuany, Syrian Delegate, as its Vice President. N. Sadak, Minister of Foreign Affairs of Turkey, addressed the opening session of the meeting on behalf of the Turkish Government. Jef Rens, Assistant Director General of the Ilo, served as Secretary General.

Objectives

The Istanbul meeting was by its very nature a preliminary gathering intended to pave the way for full-scale regional conferences in the future and lay the groundwork for more intensive activity by the Ilo in the region of the Near and Middle East. Although the essence of the meeting was an exchange of views and information, there was in fact adopted an elaborate set of resolutions which, while having no binding effect, were to be transmitted to the member governments as proposals for action in the social and economic field within the shortest possible time. Furthermore, the meeting proposed to the Governing Body of the Ilo a considerable number of practical steps designed to expand the interests and activities of the Ilo in the Near and Middle East.

Resolutions

The Istanbul meeting unanimously adopted five principal resolutions on the following subjects:

(1) the development of the work of the Ilo in the Near and Middle East; (2) labor policy; (3) social security; (4) conditions of life and work of agricultural workers; (5) economic policies designed to further in the Near and Middle East the social objectives of the Ilo.

1. *Development of the Work of the Ilo in the Near and Middle East*

Recognizing the need for concerted effort to improve living and working conditions of the peoples of the Near and Middle East and to institute vigorous Ilo action in that region, the Istanbul meeting proposed to the Ilo that it convene at an appropriate time a regional conference to review the progress made in the fields covered by the policy resolutions summarized below; send an Ilo mission to the Middle East in preparation

each of the Near and Middle Eastern countries should prepare a national program of action for the progressive application of the standards outlined over a given number of years and submit periodically reports on the action taken by them to the International Labor Office for consideration at a future regional meeting.

3. *Social Security*

Acknowledging, as did all the policy resolutions, the "special conditions" existing in the countries of the Near and Middle East, the proposals on social security called for the progressive expansion and systematic application of legislation for the promotion of health and nutrition, income security, and benefits covering employment injuries, sickness, invalidity, old age, and death. Special attention was given to the position of rural workers, with the suggestion that crop insurance might be developed together with organized schemes of relief to prevent famine in times of scarcity. With regard to medical care it was proposed that the aim of national health policies should be to make adequate medical care available to the whole population as a public service without contribution or means test and that steps should be taken to provide for preventive medicine and environmental hygiene.

4. *Conditions of Life and Work of Agricultural Workers*

In view of the fact that some 70 percent of the population of the countries of the Near and Middle East are engaged in agriculture and that marked differences exist between conditions of life and work in industry and those prevailing in agriculture, special attention was given to means of improving the conditions of life and work of agricultural workers. It was urged that studies should be made on particular aspects of raising the standards of living of the agricultural population and that further consideration be given to that subject by the ILo Permanent Agricultural Committee and future regional meetings. The Food and Agriculture Organization of the United Nations and other specialized agencies concerned with such problems were also encouraged to engage in further studies. Recognizing that the present condition of the agricultural population of the area does not correspond to the great potentialities of the region and to the general desire for higher standards of living, it was suggested that "carefully planned intervention by the State" would alone be able "to devise, coordinate, and enforce the necessary measures for the best utilization of the human and material resources of the countries concerned in the interests of the welfare of the people". It was further proposed that in order to meet the needs of the agricultural population "it is necessary that the national economy as a whole should find possibilities of expansion through development works, increase in production, initiation of new lines of output, and a parallel planning of industrial and agricultural developments".

Specific suggestions were also put forward for the use of modern methods to increase the productivity of the soil, the improvement of systems of land tenure and relationship, the organization of agricultural credit, the stimulation of cooperative organizations, the protection of wage-paid labor, the expansion of health and education, and the development of small-scale rural industries to supplement income from agriculture.

5. *Economic Policies Designed To Further in the Near and Middle East the Social Objectives of the* ILO

Perhaps the most significant of the resolutions adopted at Istanbul was that concerned with economic policies, since only economic development will enable the nations of the Near and Middle East to make any appreciable social progress. Recognizing that "improvements in the standards of living, means of production and the health of the population of the countries of the Near and Middle East are urgently required and are a matter of concern to the whole world", the meeting made a number of proposals designed to encourage governments to increase their productivity and develop their natural resources. The delegates at Istanbul hope to enlist the cooperation of the Economic and Social Council of the United Nations, the Food and Agriculture Organization, and the World Health Organization in achieving these goals.

Concrete proposals were made with regard to improvement in nutrition and agricultural output and distribution; price policy for agricultural products and the maintenance of reserves; improvement in the methods of agricultural production; and the encouragement of additional imports of agricultural equipment. The govern-

strife. It recognized that the development of responsible organizations of employers and workers is more important in the attainment of social progress than formal adherence to even the most elaborately phrased conventions. And it recognized that however much international organizations and friendly neighbors might contribute, the primary responsibility for concrete progress must rest upon the states of the region.

Istanbul therefore represents a first stage in a venture which may, if it prospers, contribute significantly to the welfare of peoples and stability of governments in an area important to the maintenance of world peace and stability. The Governing Body of the ILO, at its 103d session held in Geneva in December 1947, has already adopted the Istanbul recommendations for the extension of ILO activity in the region. There is every likelihood that in the long run the activities of the ILO, thus inaugurated at Istanbul, will have a measurable impact on the economic and social evolution which is, given all the circumstances, inevitable in the Near and Middle East. Yet as the immediate future of social and economic progress in the area is contemplated, it would be well to keep in mind the warning of one of the delegates who, at the final Istanbul session, emphasized that political stability is a necessary prerequisite for any substantial achievement in the direction of social progress.

Resolution Relating to Kashmir Situation [1]

The Security Council

HAVING HEARD statements on the situation in Kashmir from representatives of the Governments of India and Pakistan;

RECOGNIZING the urgency of the situation;

TAKING NOTE of the telegram addressed on January 6 by its President to each of the parties and of their replies thereto and in which they affirm their intention to conform with the Charter:

Calls upon both the Government of India and the Government of Pakistan to take immediately all measures within their power (including public appeals to their people) calculated to improve the situation and to refrain from making any statements and from doing or causing to be done or permitting any acts which might aggravate the situation

And further requests each of those Governments to inform the Council immediately of any material change in the situation which occurs or appears to either of them to be about to occur while the matter is under consideration by the Council and consult with the Council thereon.

American Interest in Settlement of Netherland-Indonesian Dispute Through Security Council's Proposals

[Released to the press January 20]

The United States Government has received with much gratification the news that Netherland and Indonesian delegations have accepted the proposals of the Security Council's Committee of Good Offices as a basis for the settlement of the Dutch-Indonesian dispute.

The United States Government regards these proposals as eminently just and practical, and believes that they will provide a sound basis for political and economic development of the Indies, beneficial not only to the Indonesians and Dutch, but also to the rest of the world.

The United States Government wishes to congratulate the Committee of Good Offices on its excellent work and to congratulate both Netherlanders and Indonesians on the spirit of high statesmanship with which they have concluded the negotiations before the Committee.

The United States Government will continue to follow with deepest interest the progress of reconstruction in the Netherlands East Indies and is exploring ways and means of extending economic and financial assistance to this reconstruction.

[1] U.N. doc. S/651, Jan. 17, 1948. Adopted on Jan. 17, 1948.

INTERNATIONAL ORGANIZATIONS AND CONFERENCES

Calendar of Meetings [1]

Adjourned During Month of January		1948
Third Pan American Congress of Ophthalmology	Habana	Jan. 4–10
United Nations: Ecosoc (Economic and Social Council): Commission on the Status of Women.	Lake Success	Jan. 5–16
Ninth Pan American Child Congress	Caracas	Jan. 5–10
American International Institute for the Protection of Childhood: Meeting of International Council.	Caracas	Jan. 5–10
Icao (International Civil Aviation Organization): Statistics Division: First Session.	Montreal	Jan. 13–
Who (World Health Organization): Committee on Administration and Finance.	Geneva	Jan. 19–21
In Session as of January 31, 1948		**1946**
Far Eastern Commission	Washington	Feb. 26–
United Nations: Security Council	Lake Success	Mar. 25–
Military Staff Committee	Lake Success	Mar. 25–
Committee on Atomic Energy	Lake Success	June 14–
		1947
Commission on Conventional Armaments	Lake Success	Mar. 24–
Security Council's Good Offices Committee on Indonesia	Indonesian Territory . .	Oct. 20–
Trade and Employment Conference	Habana	Nov. 21–
General Assembly's Special Balkan Committee.	Salonika	Nov. 21–
		1948
Interim Committee of the General Assembly	Lake Success	Jan. 5–
Commission for Palestine.	Lake Success	Jan. 9–
German External Property Negotiations (Safehaven):		**1946**
With Portugal	Lisbon	Sept. 3–
With Spain	Madrid	Nov. 12–
Inter-Allied Trade Board for Japan	Washington	Oct. 24–
		1947
cfm (Council of Foreign Ministers): Commission to Investigate Former Italian Colonies.	Former Italian Colonies .	Nov. 8–
		1948
pfb .(Provisional Frequency Board)	Geneva	Jan. 15–
iro (International Refugee Organization): Fifth Part of First Session of Preparatory Commission.	Geneva	Jan. 20–
itu (International Telecommunication Union): Meeting of Administrative Council.	Geneva	Jan. 20–
who (World Health Organization): Fifth Session of Interim Commission .	Geneva	Jan. 22–

[1] Prepared in the Division of International Conferences, Department of State.

EEC (Committee on European Economic Co-operation): European Manpower Conference.	Rome . . . .
Meeting of Special Committee to Make Recommendations for the Coordination of Safety Activities in Fields of Aviation, Meteorology, Shipping and Telecommunications.	London . . . .
Tripartite Discussions on Western Germany	London . . . .

Scheduled for February–April 1948

United Nations:

ECOSOC (Economic and Social Council):	
Sixth Session	Lake Success . . . . .
Subcommission on Economic Development	Lake Success . . . . .
Subcommission on Employment and Economic Stability	Lake Success . . . . . .
World Conference on Freedom of Information	Geneva . . . .
Social Commission: Third Session	Lake Success . . . . . .
ECE (Economic Commission for Europe): Third Session	Geneva . . . .
Transport and Communications Commission: Second Session . . .	Geneva . . . .
Subcommission on Statistical Sampling	Lake Success . . . . . .
Economic and Employment Commission: Third Session	Lake Success . . . . . .
Statistical Commission: Third Session	Lake Success . . . . . .
Permanent Central Opium Board	Geneva . . . .
UBS (International Union of Biological Sciences): Executive Committee .	Geneva . . . .
UNESCO (United Nations Educational, Scientific and Cultural Organization): Sixth Session of Executive Board.	Paris . . . .
WHO (World Health Organization): Expert Committee on Tuberculosis .	Geneva . . . .
Inter-governmental Maritime Consultative Organization	Geneva . . . .
ILO (International Labor Organization):	
Permanent Committee on Migration	Geneva . . . .
104th Session of Governing Body	Geneva . . . .
FAO (Food and Agriculture Organization):	
Regional Meeting to Consider Creation of Councils for Study of the Sea .	Baguio, Philippines . . .
Regional Meeting of Technical Nutritionists	Baguio, Philippines . . .
Rice Meeting	Baguio, Philippines . . .
Second Meeting of Council	Washington . . . . . .
ICAO (International Civil Aviation Organization):	
Aeronautical Maps and Charts Division	Brussels . . . .
Personnel Licensing Division	Montreal . . . .
Rules of the Air and Air Traffic Control Practices Division	Montreal . . . .
Facilitation Division	Europe . . . .
Prague International Spring Fair	Prague . . . .
First Meeting of Planning Committee on High-Frequency Broadcasting .	Geneva . . . .
Sixth Pan American Railway Congress	Habana . . . .
Ninth International Conference of American States	Bogotá . . . .
Conference to Plan for an International Institute of Hylean Amazon . .	Tingo María, Peru . . .
ICAC (International Cotton Advisory Committee): Seventh Meeting . . .	Cairo . . . . A
Fifth International Leprosy Conference	Habana . . . . A
Lyon International Fair	Lyon . . . . A

¹ Tentative.

Royal Netherlands Industries Fair	Utrecht	Apr. 6–15
26th Milan Fair	Milan	Apr. 12–27
International Conference on Safety of Life at Sea	London	Apr. 16–
22d International Brussels Fair	Brussels	Apr. 17–28
Third Inter-American Travel Congress	Buenos Aires.	Apr. 18–28
Rubber Study Group: Fifth Session	Washington	Apr. 26–
International Conference on Social Work . . `.	Atlantic City.	April
Arts and Handicrafts Exhibition of American Elementary School Children.	Montevideo	April
Ccir (International Telephone Consulting Committee): Technical Meeting.	The Hague.	April
Fifth Pan American Highway Congress	Lima	April [2]
Tripartite Discussions on Western Germany	Paris	April
Fourth Pan American Consultation on Cartography	Buenos Aires.	April–May
Pan American Institute of Geography and History: General Assembly . .	Buenos Aires.	April–May

[2] Tentative.

First Inter-American Conference on the Conservation of Renewable Natural Resources

[Released to the press January 20]

The Department of State announced on January 20 that the First Inter-American Conference on the Conservation of Renewable Natural Resources is scheduled to be held at Denver, Colorado, from September 7 to 20, 1948. After many other sites had been considered, the Governing Board of the Pan American Union and the Department of State decided to hold the conference at Denver. The presence of many conservation projects in the surrounding territory was one of the factors contributing to the selection of Denver as the site. The conference is being held pursuant to a resolution adopted at the Third Inter-American Conference on Agriculture held at Caracas, Venezuela, from July 24–August 7, 1945.

The conservation conference, the first international meeting of its kind, will bring together delegates from the American republics to consider the development and use, on a sound scientific basis, of the renewable natural resources of the Hemisphere. It is anticipated that leading government officials, scientists, and other interested groups from the entire Hemisphere will attend.

Among the problems to be discussed will be those arising out of deforestation, soil erosion, overgrazing, wildlife destruction, floods, and fail-

ing water supplies. These problems are year growing more serious throughout the Hemisphe because of inadequate conservation practic mounting populations, and attempts to raise livi standards. They are of world-wide significan because of the increasing needs of Europe an Asia.

The conference will consist of a series meetings to discuss conservation problems t gether with field trips to study land-manageme practices. The delegates will have an opportuni to view at first hand soil-conservation distric forest and range experiment stations, the Roc Mountain National Park, and other places of i terest. Irrigation projects will be studied, alo with their relationship to agriculture, grazing, a forestry practices on the land from which irrig tion waters are derived.

Warren Kelchner, Chief of the Division of I ternational Conferences, Department of State, h been appointed executive vice president of t conference, and William Vogt, Chief of the Co servation Section of the Pan American Unio secretary general. An organizing committee co posed of representatives of interested Governme agencies has been established to formulate pla and coordinate arrangements for the conferen

ourth International Cancer Research Congress

ARTICLE BY LEONARD A. SCHEELE

The Fourth International Cancer Research ongress, sponsored by the Union Internationale ontre le Cancer and the American Association for 'ancer Research, was held at St. Louis, Mo., from eptember 2 to 7, 1947.[1] It was attended by offi- ial country delegates, members of both sponsor- 1g organizations, and individual scientists who ame to present reports of significant research. 'hirty-nine countries were represented.[2]

The general purpose of the Congress was to resent, as inclusively as possible, the most recent chievements in cancer research, including both linical and laboratory phases. To all those who lanned and attended this convention, a further urpose was clearly recognized: the renewal of iternational participation and cooperation in ancer research, which had been seriously retarded y the war, and the stimulation of efforts more itensive than had ever before been applied in the ght against this disease.

During the Congress President Truman sent a elegram to the assembled scientists which con- eyed an announcement of special interest to hem. The President's telegram stated:

"It is now possible for the United States to take n important forward step toward greater inter- ational cooperation in the field of medical and iological research. On behalf of the people of he United States, I am pleased to announce to he Fourth International Cancer Research Con- ;ress that progress in the production of radioiso- opes by the United States Atomic Energy Com- nission now permits limited distribution to quali-

fied research workers in other countries. . ..
I know that the representatives of the United States attending the Cancer Research Congress share my hope that the open, impartial and truly international character of medical research will carry over into the realm of other problems of world concern. The sharing by and among all nations of both the means and the results of can- cer research will reduce the loss of life and human suffering from disease throughout the world."

History and Organization of the Cancer Research Congress

Three international cancer research congresses have been held in past years under the auspices of the Union Internationale contre le Cancer. The first congress was held at Madrid in 1933, the second at Brussels in 1936, and the third at At- lantic City in 1939. World War II was costly in equipment and trained research workers and im- posed such barriers to travel and communication that it disrupted the work of the Union Inter- nationale and of other agencies and persons en- gaged in cancer research. As a result activity in

[1] For members of the U. S. Delegation, see BULLETIN of Sept. 7, 1947, p. 472.

[2] The countries represented were: Argentina, Australia, Belgium, Bolivia, Brazil, Canada, Chile, China, Colom- bia, Czechoslovakia, Denmark, Egypt, El Salvador, France, Greece, India, Iran, Iraq, Italy, Korea, Luxembourg, Mexico, the Netherlands, Nicaragua, Norway, Palestine, Peru, the Republic of the Philippines, Portugal, Spain, Sweden, Switzerland, Tunisia, Turkey, the Union of South Africa, the United Kingdom, the United States (and Ha- waii), Uruguay, and Venezuela.

this field was slowed in some countries and halted in others. Scientists the world over, however, were fully aware that the lack of international correspondence was a serious deterrent to their investigations and the exchange of information. As soon as it was possible, the American Association for Cancer Research, a scientific society which numbers in its membership most of the cancer research workers in the United States and Canada, assumed the leadership in providing* for an assembly of scientists to review progress made in the study of cancer during the war and to arrange for future cooperative investigation.

The Association met in April 1946 and appointed a committee to formulate preliminary plans for a Fourth International Cancer Research Congress to be held in the United States in 1947. This committee advised the Department of State of its intention to hold such a meeting and of the world-wide interest in the project. The Department agreed that in behalf of the Congress it would extend invitations to the various countries through diplomatic channels.

On October 13, 1946, at New Haven, Conn., the Board of Directors of the American Association for Cancer Research, acting upon the recommendations of the committee, voted to invite the Union Internationale contre le Cancer to cooperate in sponsoring the Congress. At this time it was decided to hold the meeting at St. Louis in September 1947. Dr. E. V. Cowdry, professor of anatomy at Washington University and director of research at Barnard Free Skin and Cancer Hospital, St. Louis, was elected president of the Congress.

The International Cancer Research Commission

One of the most significant results of the Fourth International Cancer Research Congress was the creation of a permanent international agency for cancer research, the International Cancer Research Commission.

At an organization meeting of the Congress on September 2, 1947, attended by representatives from the various countries, it was unanimously decided, after full discussion, that the duty of making recommendations be assigned to a smaller

*The Union Internationale contre le Cancer will publish the reports and proceedings of the Congress in a special edition of *Acta*, the Union's cancer journal.

Until such a program is established, the work of the newly created Commission is well defined by the recommendations of the Fourth Congress. The Commission wishes, of course, to cooperate closely with the World Health Organization (WHO). As of December 1947 no definite cooperative program had been established with WHO, although officials of the Union Internationale contre le Cancer have been in touch with the medical staff of the Interim Commission at Geneva.

Today the sum of information is so large and cancer research involves studies in so many fields of science that no one investigator can comprehend it all. We need, therefore, not only brilliant researchers with analytical minds, but also investigators who can sympathize and interpret the products of that research. The process of synthesis, however, requires that information be first assembled and presented to the investigator in comprehensive form. It was apparent to all who attended the Fourth International Cancer Research Congress that this had been accomplished. The findings from years of research in many lands were so collected and presented that the process of synthesis was certainly advanced. For the future, extensive collaborative research, firmly directed, adequately financed, and carried forward by the teamwork of many men, must be initiated in even larger measure than before, if better ways to prevent, detect, and cure cancer are to be found.

Ambassador Pawley To Assist in Preparatory Work for Inter-American Conference at Bogotá

[Released to the press January 20]

The Secretary of State announced on January 20 that William D. Pawley, American Ambassador to Brazil, who has recently been in the United States, will remain in Washington for the time being to assist the Secretary in the work now going on in preparation for the forthcoming Ninth International Conference of American States at Bogotá. Ambassador Pawley's wide experience in inter-American relations as well as his practical knowledge of economic problems will, the Secretary said, contribute in an important way to the progress of this preparatory work.

THE RECORD OF THE WEEK

German War Documer

[Released to the press January 21]

The Department of State announced on January 21 the publication of a volume of German war documents bearing on Soviet-German relations during the period 1939–1941. These documents are part of the great mass of materials from the German Foreign Office which were captured by British and American arms toward the end of hostilities.

As has previously been announced, the Department of State, along with the British and French Foreign Office, is sponsoring the publication of a series of volumes of documents from the archives of the German Foreign Office with a view to giving a complete and accurate account of German diplomacy relating to World War II for the enlightenment of American and world opinion. Staffs of eminent American, British, and French scholars have been working on these archives for a number of months, and it is expected that the first two volumes of the series, beginning with 1937, will be published within the next year.

The series of volumes is planned as a tripartite

Agreement Signed With Canada Relating

[Released to the press January 12]

Various problems have arisen with respect to the division of waters which are of common interest along, across or in the vicinity of the international boundary between Canada and the United States in Montana and North Dakota in the United States and in the Provinces of Manitoba, Saskatchewan and Alberta in Canada.

A conference of representatives of the two Governments was held at Ottawa on August 25–26, 1947. Draft terms of reference to the International Joint Commission—United States and Canada—under article IX of the boundary waters treaty signed at Washington on January 11, 1909, were prepared for consideration by both Governments.

Agreement has now been reached on the text of the terms of two references, one of which covers "waters which are of common interest along, across or in the vicinity of the international boundary from the Continental Divide on the west

In the conduct of its investigations, and otherwise in the performance of its duties under this Reference, the International Joint Commission may utilize the services of engineers and other specially qualified personnel of technical agencies of Canada and the United States, and will, so far as possible, make use of information and technical data which has been acquired by such technical agencies or which may become available during the course of the investigation, thus avoiding duplication of effort and unnecessary expense.

Very truly yours,

PUBLICATIONS

Department of State

For sale by the Superintendent of Documents, Government Printing Office, Washington 25, D. C. Address requests direct to the Superintendent of Documents, except in the case of free publications, which may be obtained from the Department of State.

Paris Peace Conference, 1946—Selected Documents. Conference Series 103. Pub. 2868. 1442 pp. $6.

A selection from the documents of the Paris Peace Conference of 1946, reproduced by offset lithography.

Armistice with Italy, 1943. Treaties and Other International Acts Series 1604. Pub. 2963. 34 pp. 15¢.

Italian military armistice, together with other pertinent documents.

Treaty of Peace With Roumania. Treaties and Other International Acts Series 1649. Pub. 2969. 157 pp. 35¢.

Dated at Paris February 10, 1947; ratified by the President of the United States June 14, 1947; proclaimed by the President September 15, 1947; entered into force September 15, 1947.

Treaty of Peace With Bulgaria. Treaties and Other International Acts Series 1650. Pub. 2973. 150 pp. 35¢.

Dated at Paris February 10, 1947; ratified by the President of the United States June 14, 1947; proclaimed by the President September 15, 1947; entered into force September 15, 1947.

Treaty of Peace With Hungary. Treaties and Other International Acts Series 1651. Pub. 2974. 165 pp. 35¢.

Dated at Paris February 10, 1947; ratified by the President of the United States June 14, 1947; proclaimed by the President September 15, 1947; entered into force September 15, 1947.

Diplomatic List, January 1948. Pub. 3018. 192 pp. 20¢.

Monthly list of foreign diplomatic representatives in Washington, with their addresses.

Eula McDonald, author of the article on a world maritime organization, is a foreign-affairs analyst in the Division of Historical Policy
Research, Office of Public Affairs, Department of State.

Leonard A. Scheele, author of the article on the Fourth Interna-
tional Cancer Research Congress, served as Chairman of the United
States Delegation to the Congress. Dr. Scheele is Director of the
National Cancer Institute, United States Public Health Service, at
Bethesda, Maryland.

Irwin M. Tobin, author of the article on the International Labor
Organization Regional Meeting for the Near and Middle East, is a
member of the staff on foreign labor problems in the Division of
International Labor, Social and Health Affairs, Department of State.

The Department of State bulletin

VOL. XVIII, No. 449 • PUBLICATION 3047

February 8, 1948

For sale by the Superintendent of Documents
U.S. Government Printing Office
Washington 25, D.C.

SUBSCRIPTION:
52 issues, $5; single copy, 15 cents

Published with the approval of the
Director of the Bureau of the Budget

The Department of State BULLETIN, a weekly publication compiled and edited in the Division of Publications, Office of Public Affairs, provides the public and interested agencies of the Government with information on developments in the field of foreign relations and on the work of the Department of State and the Foreign Service. The BULLETIN includes press releases on foreign policy issued by the White House and the Department, and statements and addresses made by the President and by the Secretary of State and other officers of the Department, as well as special articles on various phases of international affairs and the functions of the Department. Information is included concerning treaties and international agreements to which the United States is or may become a party and treaties of general international interest.

Publications of the Department, as well as legislative material in the field of international relations, are listed currently.

SOVEREIGNTY AND INTERDEPENDENCE IN THE NEW WORLD

Comments on the Inter-American System

ARTICLE BY WILLIAM SANDERS

Like so many institutions shaped by the pragmatic interplay of stability and change, the Inter-American System defies adequate definition. It has the substance but in many respects lacks the form of the closest union of sovereign and independent states known to history.

Within its present stage of development, it retains forms and methods it has outgrown but not completely discarded, as well as incipient mutations of a more vigorous and promising life. It is not always possible to distinguish clearly in the evolving and complex structure of the System between the deadwood of evolutionary or experimental phases of development and new growth, which may deceptively lie dormant for long periods awaiting the right moment for full activity.

The ever present problem of semantics also creates its own peculiar hazards to understanding. The title itself, for example, is still in debate. Some say it should not be called a system because it is not an astronomical phenomenon, and should therefore not be associated with solar or galactic systems. Others claim that the System is in fact a union of states, and should therefore be called that. Again, the prophets of glory and of doom, the Pollyannas and the Cassandras, work at cross purposes and distort perspective by claiming for the System more or less than it deserves.

The present is an especially promising moment for an over-all appraisal of the System. After almost sixty years of Topsylike growth, plans are now underway for its complete overhauling at the ninth general conference of the System, to be held at Bogotá this coming March, and for the determination of its relations with the United Nations. The latter circumstance, in particular, should help in reaching a broad perspective, since it will compel an examination of the role of this regional system within the world system.

This is not to say that only with the establishment of the United Nations has the System acquired extra-regional significance. In fact, the historical and political background of the System is world-wide, and its context is nothing less than mankind's persevering search for permanent peace and security. In a world of independent national states in which, until recently, balance of power was the only challenge to the more ancient but still endemic idea of peace through universal domination, the Inter-American System bespoke with growing conviction and confidence through the years the concept of collective security crystallized in the United Nations. The Western Hemisphere began to test in an organized and purposeful manner the theory and practice of this approach to international relations during a period still dominated by the old *Realpolitik* of alliances, ententes, and spheres of influence.

Many factors contributed to the creation in the new world of virtually ideal laboratory conditions for the initial experiments and for the testing and gradual development of the institutional and ideological foundations of collective security.

Somewhat similar experiences in occupying the new world; relative freedom from involvement in local conflicts of the old; similar theories, if not always practices, of republican and democratic government; analogous national beginnings in the violent dissolution of colonial status through revolution, as well as a persistent sense of geographical propinquity—all these factors tended to give the peoples of the Western Hemisphere a sense of community of interest and of a new beginning, which was translated into a more optimistic belief in man's ability to break the pattern of the past.

In international affairs this fresh approach took the form of an attempt to apply new political and legal theories regarding the problem of peace and security.

In the south these were worked out at a series of five political conferences held by the Latin American states from 1826 to 1865. Although none of the treaties signed at these conferences entered into effect, most of the principles and many of the organizational characteristics of the Inter-American System of today are found in them. These include the establishment of an international organization, in the form of an assembly, for consultation and agreement on matters of common interest, and the undertaking of mutual obligations for defense against aggression; for the renunciation of war; for the peaceful settlement of disputes through mediation, investigation, conciliation, arbitration, and consultation; for the adoption of sanctions against a law-breaking member of the community; for reciprocal respect of territorial integrity and political independence, and for observance of the principle of nonintervention.

In the north the United States sought security through a self-denying injunction to stay out of conflicts in other parts of the world and through a demand that non-American powers seek no political or territorial gains or advantages in the Western Hemisphere. These were the two sides of our national security shield, each complementary to the other, both nonaggressive in spirit and intent. Time soon demonstrated that, as interpreted and applied, these policies were not adequate of themselves to achieve the purposes they were designed to serve.

Thus the United States soon found it difficult, and indeed was not permitted, to abide by the first self-restraining injunction and to live according to St. Paul's admonition to be in the world but not of it. It discovered that isolationism ignored the fundamental historical and political reality that the world was not yet free of the danger of a mad-dog drive for universal domination by one or more states. For compelling reasons of national security the United States repeatedly discarded isolationism when the world was threatened by domination. It now seeks security through collective action by the United Nations in conjunction with

structure of the system built during the last 15 years and developed three principal organizational features: the conferences, the Pan American Union, and other permanent or special-purpose or temporary organizations. Developments in the last 15 years have simply brought those organizations to rapid maturity under the forcing processes of the age in which we live.

The end of World War II and the proposed establishment of a new world organization led the American republics to agree on a broad program for the "reorganization, consolidation and strengthening of the inter-American system", in order that it might become more effective in solving inter-American problems and in assuming its appropriate responsibilities in harmony with the principles and purposes of the United Nations. Under this plan, approved at the Inter-American Conference on Problems of War and Peace held in Mexico City a few months prior to the meeting of the United Nations conference in San Francisco, the System is to have three basic "charter" documents: a treaty on reciprocal assistance in the event of an attack or threat of aggression from within or without the Continent against an American republic; an over-all charter or organic pact of the Inter-American System, which will establish the organizational elements of the system and state its basic principles and purposes (including as annexed documents two declarations on the rights and duties of states and of man); a treaty which will coordinate, integrate, and bring up to date the inter-American procedures of pacific settlement.

The first basic instrument, the treaty on reciprocal assistance, was concluded at the recent conference at Petropolis, Brazil. The other two treaties and their supplementary and complementary declarations and resolutions are to be negotiated at the Ninth International Conference of American States to be held at Bogotá this coming year. Drafts of these documents have been prepared by committees of the Governing Board of the Pan American Union and by the Inter-American Juridical Committee at Rio de Janeiro.

These three fundamental organizational features of the Inter-American System are examined here in the light of the decisions reached at Mexico City, of the proposals made by the governments for consideration at the Bogotá conference, and of the probable impact on them of the new functions and responsibilities of the System. The section on the institutions of the System is followed by a discussion of inter-American cooperation in the political and nonpolitical fields and of the relations of the System with the United Nations. The article concludes with a summary of the principal issues at the conference.

This analysis of the System will be made against the background of the historical development of its institutions, principles, and purposes. This method has been chosen over a less pedestrian approach on the theory that it will bring out more adequately how deep the roots of the System reach back into the past and how the plans for Bogotá reflect and are the product of the process of growth in mutual understanding and confidence which has made this regional association possible.

The Organs of the System

The draft organic pact prepared by committees of the Governing Board of the Pan American Union for the conference provides that "The inter-American system carries out its objectives through the following organs: *a.* The Inter-American Assemblies (Conferences); *b.* The Pan American Union; *c.* The specialized inter-American organizations".

The Conferences

The conference method is a fundamental and essential characteristic of the Inter-American System. Through this technique the member states have agreed upon basic policies and worked out ways and means of carrying them into effect. Until recently there were two main types of conferences: the International Conference of American States and the special and technical conference. A third type, the Meetings of Consultation of the Ministers of Foreign Affairs, was added in the late 1930's.

The International Conferences of American States are the over-all policy-making or constituent body of the System, and they in fact legislate on the organs of the System and their functions. Eight of these conferences were held in the first half century of the Pan American movement. The last one was held in Lima, Peru, in 1938, and the next will be held at Bogotá early in 1948. The conclusions of these conferences have taken the form of 40 treaties and several hundred recommendations, resolutions, and declarations. These documents have defined the basic principles and policies of the System, as well as objectives to be achieved through individual or collective action under the inter-American treaties on collective defense and pacific settlement. The specialized conferences will continue their present role. They will be held, as provided in the draft organic pact, "to consider special technical questions or to further specific aspects of inter-American cooperation". Probably the recent trend toward greater coordination of technical activities will be crystallized, in the form, perhaps, of a provision calling for a decision either of a general conference, a meeting of Foreign Ministers, or the Governing Board of the Pan American Union, before a specialized conference can be held.

The Pan American Union

Between 1890 and 1910 the name of the international association established at the first conference was contracted to Union of the American Republics, and the Commercial Bureau first became the International Bureau of the American Republics and finally the Pan American Union, and as such became the permanent organ of the Association, that is, of the System.

The Bureau created at the conference of 1890 was under the supervision of the Secretary of State of the United States. This arrangement, under which the host government supplied the secretariat and managed the affairs of the organization, was typical of the unions of this initial period of international organization. The second general conference in 1902, however, decided that the "management" should be in the hands of a governing board composed of the diplomatic representatives in Washington of the member states, under the chairmanship of the United States Secretary of State. At Habana in 1928 the formula was changed to provide that each government would appoint a special representative, but could at its option designate its diplomatic representatives in Washington. This arrangement continued until 1945, when the Mexico City conference resolved that the Governing Board should thereafter be composed of delegates especially designated by the member states rather than composed of their diplomatic representatives in Washington.[1] The same Conference agreed on the prin-

---

[1] Only approximately six governments have given effect to this resolution and on the insistence of certain member states, final decision has been deferred until the Bogotá conference.

ciple that the Chairman of the Board should not
be eligible for reelection. It likewise agreed that
the Director General and Assistant Director of
the Pan American Union should be chosen for a
term of 10 years and be ineligible for reelection,
and also that neither could be succeeded by a person of the same nationality. These provisions
foreshadowed for the first time a Chairman of the
Board and a Director General of the Union not a
citizen of the United States.

These changes in structure and internal organization parallelled simultaneous and expanding
changes in functions. From being a center for
the collection and distribution of information on
commercial matters the Bureau was transformed
gradually into a center for similar activities in
other fields, including economic, social, cultural,
legal, and technical. It also evolved from being
simply the custodian of the records of the general
conferences into the permanent commission of the
conferences, with greatly enlarged secretariat
functions. As a result of this evolution it acquired
broad informational, promotional, research, and
secretariat responsibilities and passed from being
simply a technical agency representing the
Association or Union into its permanent organ.

During this process the Pan American Union
became more representative and more international. It became more representative because the
control of the institution soon passed from being
the sole responsibility of the host country to a
governing body on which all the member states
were represented. It became more international
in that as this transformation in control occurred
and as its functions expanded, it became more and
more the instrument of the collective will of the
association as expressed in the international agreements reached at the general conferences. Although there has been a tendency to disassociate
the Governing Board and the Pan American
Union, identifying the latter only with the administrative offices headed by the executive officer or
Director General, the Union has been in fact the
composite of these two organs.

In theory the Pan American Union has been the
executive body of the System, but in reality it has
had few operational responsibilities and has served
principally in two capacities: as an international
secretariat and as a center for the exchange of information and the promotion of inter-American
cooperation in nonpolitical matters.

Under a pre-Bogotá agreement reached recently by the governments through the Pan American Union, it is contemplated that the Conference will create these organs and outline their functions, and that the Governing Board will organize them after the Conference on the basis of the decisions at Bogotá.

Should the plans for these councils be approved, the Pan American Union, after Bogotá, will be the composite of the Governing Board, the four organs or councils, and the secretariat. As such the Union would be in fact as well as theory the central and permanent organ of the entire System and its general secretariat, with broad advisory and promotional responsibilities for inter-American cooperation in the economic, social, cultural, and technical fields.

(b) POLITICAL FUNCTIONS

In one important respect the Pan American Union became a case of arrested development: it was not permitted to discharge political functions. This apolitical, or more strictly speaking non-political, character was inherent in its technical beginnings, but with its expansion into the permanent organ of the system it might have been expected that it would acquire such functions. The reason often taken for granted that this did not occur was because of its location in Washington and consequently, the suspicion of being under the shadow if not actually a branch of the Department of State. Its location had its inhibiting effect and was unquestionably responsible for the express stipulation prohibiting the organization from undertaking political functions. This was introduced into the statutes of the Pan American Union at the sixth conference in 1928, during the high tide of Latin American reaction to United States interventions in the Caribbean area. Another explanation offered has been that the bar to the exercise of political functions was a deliberate method used to protect the Pan American Union from the stresses and strains of political and therefore controversial issues which might destroy it. The logic of this was that these stresses and strains should be borne by *ad hoc* or especially created organizations which could disappear without doing permanent damage to the System.

An additional and perhaps more fundamental explanation may be found in the fact that the

System as a whole, and this means specifically the general conferences, assumed executive political responsibilities only very recently. The two major aspects of international political activity with which the Inter-American System has been concerned relate to peace and security and to the formulation of principles of international conduct. In the first category are the treaties and conventions on pacific settlement such as those concluded at the fifth and seventh general conferences and at the special conciliation and arbitration conference of 1929; in the second are found the resolutions and declarations which deal with such problems as nonintervention and inter-American solidarity. With respect to both of these matters the general conferences, so far as they discussed these issues, limited themselves to the formulation of principles and policies, and of procedures by which the states could give them effect. The application of these principles and policies and the use of the procedures was left in the hands of the member governments acting individually or through special implementing agreements. There was no international compliance machinery. Thus the procedures of pacific settlement contained in the treaties referred to are essentially bilateral in character, and the general conferences themselves had no continuing or general responsibility for initiating them, for assuring their application, or for taking over when they failed.[2] The functions of the System on these matters were therefore considered to have been discharged when it achieved multilateral agreement on a principle or a procedure. From then on the success or failure of the principle or procedure depended on the good will and the good faith of the parties. If this was absent in a given case, through failure of a state to abide by an agreed standard of international conduct or through failure to utilize pacific settlement procedures, the problem had to be handled on an *ad hoc* basis.

The Pan American Union, as the executive-

---

[2] The permanent diplomatic commissions provided for in the Gondra treaty of 1923 and the conciliation convention of 1929, composed of the three longest accredited diplomatic representatives of the parties to these instruments in Washington and Montevideo, have certain rudimentary conciliation functions pending the setting up of the *ad hoc* bilateral commissions. This is, however, an essential part of the bilateral mechanism, there being no tie-back to the conferences.

probably entail a reduction in the number of these organizations and the establishment of coordinated relations among those that remain and between these and the Pan American Union.

The specialized organizations differ from the councils of the Pan American Union in three aspects. As a general rule they are separate and autonomous bodies forming a distinct organizational group in the system; they will have their own secretariats, and they will have narrower subject and functional assignments than the councils. There will probably be such variation and departure from the norm, however, that in some cases the distinction may be somewhat meaningless. It is quite likely, for example, that the military defense agency, a dependent organ, will have its own secretariat; whereas the Inter-American Commission of Women, a specialized agency, may rely on the Pan American Union secretariat.

It is evident that an important issue is involved in these apparent contradictions in which a basic principle of structure and function is qualified in many ways. In the United Nations this issue is dealt with in articles 57 and 63 of the Charter, which recognize the principle of autonomy in the specialized field but contain a flexible formula which permits agreements for a lesser or greater relationship between the specialized organizations and the United Nations. The factors responsible for certain contradictions in the inter-American problem of devising a coherent and workable organizational pattern are already operating to produce a similar situation in the United Nations. These factors are the need for economy and the need to avoid duplication and overlapping of effort. These problems arise from multiplicity of secretariats and the impossibility of rigidly compartmentalizing the different specialized fields.

An added factor in the inter-American situation is the feeling that some of these roving satellites of the System either have occasionally dissipated their energies because of the lack of an over-all perspective or objective or have simply occupied a "paper" position in the System, creating a false appearance of planning and activity which tended to inhibit by preemption constructive thought on the problems which they were supposedly handling. If these regional organizations are to perform effectively the responsibilities which may devolve upon them as regional agencies or offices of, or under

CHART I

PRESENT INTER-AMERICAN SYSTEM

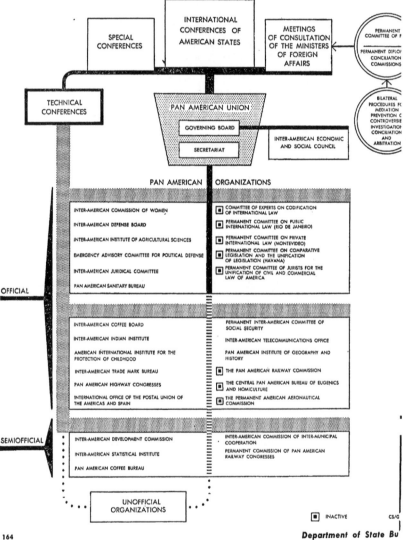

cooperative agreements with, world organizations, a greater over-all integration must be planned within the region as a whole.

Should certain ideas now current prevail at Bogotá, there will be a considerable degree of supervision and control by the Governing Board over the specialized organizations. The draft organic pact contains provisions that these organizations shall be registered in the Pan American Union, that they shall make reports to the Governing Board and that the Board shall have general supervision over their activities, with due regard for the principle of technical autonomy. A uniform or common fiscal system administered by the Union for all inter-American organizations is also being considered. A strong tendency toward centralization with respect to the specialized conferences, the conference counterpart, and indeed in many cases the conference aspect of specialized organization activity is apparent.

It is not anticipated that Bogotá will take decisions regarding the details of the reorganization of individual specialized organizations, with the exception of the Inter-American Commission of Women.[3] The Bogotá conference will probably nevertheless reach general conclusions regarding the elimination or integration of certain organizations, including specifically the large number of relatively inactive agencies in the legal field, which will be combined in the Juridical Council.

Principles and Purposes of the System

In the preceding discussion of the three basic organizational characteristics of the Inter-American System the emerging outline of the reorganized system can be seen. This outline is a rough composite of proposals made by the governments for consideration at Bogotá. (See Chart II.)

Political Cooperation

The political activities of the Inter-American System culminated in the treaties on pacific settlement, the agreements on consultation and obligations for the maintenance of peace and security, the protocol of nonintervention of 1936, and the declarations on principles of inter-American solidarity and cooperation and of rights and duties of states.

The process by which these results were achieved usually began in an initial statement by a conference of a desirable rule of international conduct

in the form of a declaration of a self-evident truth or categorical imperative, or of a recommended course of practical action. This initiative was followed by a series of formulations and reformulations, of affirmations and reaffirmations of the initial statement in the form of conference recommendations and resolutions. Through this seemingly highly redundant process, new forms of law and policy were evolved, and refinement of language and basic accommodation of divergent views were achieved for eventual incorporation in a treaty or convention. This process still continues.

(a) SECURITY AND PACIFIC SETTLEMENT

In the field of security and pacific settlement the initiative was taken originally by the first general conference in Washington in 1890, in its recommendations that the participating governments denounce the principle of conquest and agree upon a uniform treaty for compulsory arbitration subject only to the restriction then current on matters affecting independence. The trends which these recommendations set in motion finally resulted in a series of treaties, concluded between 1923 and 1936, on good offices and mediation, prevention of controversies, inquiry, conciliation, and arbitration. As indicated previously, these treaties provided for *ad hoc* machinery for the bilateral settlement of disputes but gave the System itself no continuing responsibility. A hesitant step toward collective action was taken in 1933 when the seventh general conference recommended that the participating governments adhere to the anti-war treaty of non-aggression and conciliation, which had been signed the same year at Rio de Janeiro by six American republics. This treaty condemns wars of aggression, stipulates the principles of pacific settlement of disputes and of non-recognition of territory acquired by force, and binds the parties, in the event of a violation of these principles, to "adopt in their character as neutrals a common and solidary attitude", to "exercise the political, juridical, or economic means authorized by international law," and to "bring the influence of public opinion to bear" without resorting to intervention,

---

[3] Approval of the statutes of this organization is specifically on the agenda by reference from the Mexico City conference of 1945.

CHART II

SUGGESTED REVISION OF INTER-AMERICAN SYSTEM

(TO BE CONSIDERED AT BOGOTA CONFERENCE, 1948)

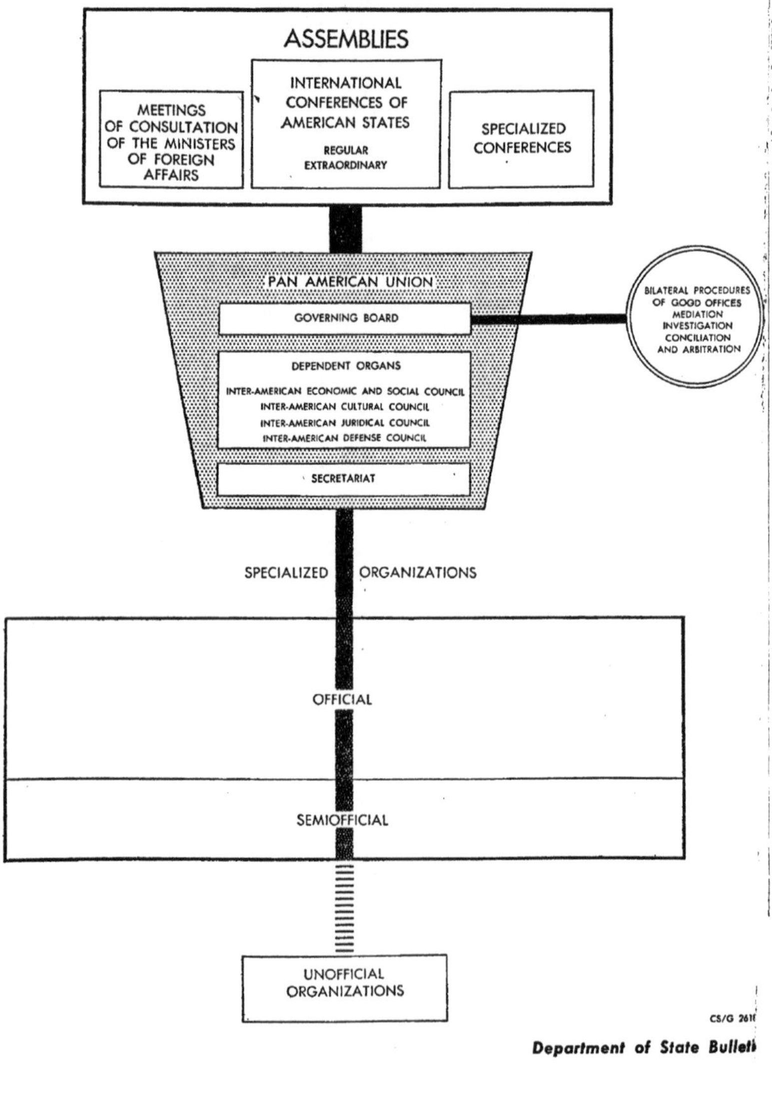

ASSEMBLIES

MEETINGS OF CONSULTATION OF THE MINISTERS OF FOREIGN AFFAIRS

INTERNATIONAL CONFERENCES OF AMERICAN STATES

REGULAR
EXTRAORDINARY

SPECIALIZED CONFERENCES

PAN AMERICAN UNION

GOVERNING BOARD

DEPENDENT ORGANS

INTER-AMERICAN ECONOMIC AND SOCIAL COUNCIL
INTER-AMERICAN CULTURAL COUNCIL
INTER-AMERICAN JURIDICAL COUNCIL
INTER-AMERICAN DEFENSE COUNCIL

SECRETARIAT

BILATERAL PROCEDURES OF GOOD OFFICES
MEDIATION
INVESTIGATION
CONCILIATION
AND ARBITRATION

SPECIALIZED ORGANIZATIONS

OFFICIAL

SEMIOFFICIAL

UNOFFICIAL ORGANIZATIONS

CS/G 2611

by the Second Consultative Meeting in 1940. In this document it was agreed:

> "that any attempt on the part of a non-American state against the integrity or inviolability of the territory, the sovereignty or the political independence of an American state shall be considered as an act of aggression against the states which sign this declaration."

It was further agreed that the signatory states would consult among themselves in order to agree upon advisable measures to take in the event an act of aggression was committed, or if there was reason to believe that an act of aggression was being prepared by a non-American nation against an American nation. Immediately upon the attack on Pearl Harbor this undertaking was invoked and the Third Meeting of Consultation was thereupon held at Rio de Janeiro in January of 1942, at which agreement was reached on the bases for cooperation in the war against the Axis.

In this development of the principle and procedures of consultation for peace and security, a distinction emerged between an intra- and an extra-continental situation. In an intra-American situation, consultation was a vehicle for collective mediation for pacific settlement purposes and for reaching a collective understanding to take individual action to deprive the parties engaged in hostilities of the means by which they could continue the war. Inter-American action in such a situation stopped short of an identification of the aggressor and application of sanctions, that is, of collective enforcement action. In the case of an extra-continental situation, the principle of one for all and all for one had developed during the war and had become the basis of collective and individual political, economic, and military action against aggression.

This distinction may be explained as the product of two factors: first, a lag in the transition from the principle of maintaining the internal peace of the Continent by mediation and moral suasion to the concept that aggression, from whatever source, can and should in fact and in principle be met by coercive action; secondly, the fact that external aggression would directly engage the vital security interests of the entire Continent and that attempting to meet it by an appeal to pacific settlement or by an impartial embargo on the aggressor and victim was patently unrealistic.

The special conference of Mexico City of 1945 eliminated the distinction between the two situations, by the Act of Chapultepec in which it was agreed that for the duration of the war any attack, regardless of the place in which it originated, would be considered an attack against all the American republics. The principle of the Declaration of Habana therefore would apply regardless of the source of the attack, whether by an American state or by a non-American state.

This basic principle was given permanent form in the treaty of reciprocal assistance signed at the special conference at Rio de Janeiro this year.[4] The Rio treaty constitutes a regional arrangement for the maintenance of peace and security under articles 52 through 54 of the United Nations Charter. It also invokes the right of individual and collective self-defense under article 51 in the case of an armed attack, pending the taking of the necessary measures by the Security Council to maintain international peace and security. Besides incorporating the principle of the Act of Chapultepec that an attack against one is an attack against all, the treaty provides for consultation in the event of an act or threat of aggression against an American state or of any fact or situation which might endanger the peace of the Americas. Under the terms of the treaty, decisions may be taken to recall chiefs of diplomatic missions, break diplomatic relations, break consular relations, interrupt in partial or complete form economic and communications relations, and to use armed force. These decisions are binding on all parties, including those not concurring, when taken by a two-thirds vote, except that no state is required to use armed force without its consent. The decisions are to be taken by the organ of consultation, which is either the meeting of Foreign Ministers of the signatory states that ratified the treaty or, provisionally, pending such a meeting, the Governing Board of the Pan American Union.

In the case of an armed attack from any source made within a Western Hemisphere area delimited in the treaty or within the territory of an American state outside the area, an obligation is placed upon the parties to assist in meeting the

[4] For an analysis of this treaty see report by the Senate Committee on Foreign Relations, Dec. 5, 1947, 80th Cong., 1st sess. See also article by Ward P. Allen, BULLETIN of Nov. 23, 1947, p. 983.

This provision does not violate the principle that there shall be no difference in the treatment to be accorded aggression, regardless of its origin, nor does it mean that individual' assistance prior to consultation may not be given. Its essential feature is that the first objective of consultative action will be to separate the contending parties and to bring them together in peace. In this latter respect, the Rio treaty carries the issue to the threshhold of pacific settlement, where the procedures for the peaceful solution of controversies will take over. These will be of two interrelated categories: the bilateral and the collective.

The first raises for Bogotá the problem of coordinating and improving the existing bilateral procedures of good offices and mediation, investigation, conciliation and arbitration, and of relating these to judicial settlement by reference to the International Court of Justice. There appears to be substantial agreement on the problem of coordination, which arises primarily from the fact that the existing procedures are unrelated to each other and are included in a variety of treaties. The problem of "improving" the procedures, on the other hand, will probably give rise to differences of view, particularly on the role of arbitration and its relation to judicial settlement. Perhaps the principal issue to come up at the conference in this connection is raised by proposals that in the event other means of pacific settlement fail, the parties to the dispute shall be bound to arbitrate, regardless of whether the controversy is political or legal in character. Matters of domestic jurisdiction are excluded in these proposals, but some of them provide for adjudication of the domestic or international character of a case. In advancing the thesis of unlimited compulsory arbitration of all disputes, these proposals go considerably beyond the principle of compulsory arbitration of legal' disputes agreed upon in the inter-American treaty of 1929. The Bogotá conference must also decide, in view of the existence of the International Court of Justice, of which all the American states are parties, and of provisions in its statutes for chambers of the Court to meet elsewhere than at The Hague, whether elaborate bilateral arbitration machinery is necessary.

The collective aspect raises the problem of determining the procedure, scope, and objective of consultation, in other words, the organ of consultation, and its functions and powers in the field of pacific settlement. It is not unlikely that the organizational pattern of the Rio treaty will be followed and that the organ will be the meetings of Foreign Ministers, with the Governing Board of the Pan American Union empowered to act provisionally in that capacity. The powers of the organ of consultation will include, in all probability, the type of good offices and mediation agreed upon in the Buenos Aires conventions of 1936. This method will involve not only the attempt to bring the parties together but also recommendations of procedures of pacific settlement which they may use, and perhaps encompass *post office* and interim conciliation functions similar to those granted the permanent diplomatic commissions created by the conciliation convention of 1929.

The emphasis throughout will unquestionably be on encouraging the parties to settle by means of their own choice. The question immediately will be raised regarding the circumstances under which consultation will be invoked. Perhaps the formula will be that consultation shall apply, either on request of one of the parties or on the initiative of the organ of consultation, to disputes susceptible of endangering the maintenance of peace and security. Another point will be whether collective action should be limited to moral suasion or should include such functions as investigation and recommendation of terms of settlement, on the analogy of those given the Security Council of the United Nations. This action would in effect empower the organ of consultation to act as a conciliation body. The transition from consultation for pacific-settlement purposes to consultation for coercive action will also be considered. No difficulty should be met here since the criterion has already been established in the Rio treaty that consultation shall apply in all cases of armed attack or threats or other acts of aggression or any fact or situation that might endanger the peace of America.

This entire structure must be designed to satisfy a long-felt need in the System for the improvement and coordination of the treaties on pacific settlement,[5] and to give full effect to the provisions

---

[5] See Resolution XV on "Perfection, Coordination of the Inter-American Peace Instruments", approved by the Eighth International Conference of American States at Lima in 1938.

fused or otherwise frustrated recourse to arbitration. The so-called Porter amendment to the Drago Doctrine was included in the Hague convention of 1907 on the subject. This exception was countered by the condition formulated by several Latin American states that arbitration would apply only if the remedies offered by local law and tribunals had been exhausted, and a denial of justice had been established. This series of moves showed that a firm meeting of minds even on this narrow issue had not been reached.

A broader approach designed to establish a new frame of reference for the major issue of unilateral use of force or coercion was meanwhile being developed through the inter-American codification techniques, taking the form of a draft resolution on the rights and duties of states submitted initially at the sixth general conference in 1928. This draft contained the proposition that "no state has the right to intervene in the internal affairs of another." The immediate question was whether this language correctly stated the applicable rule of international law. The United States maintained that it contravened a generally accepted rule which permitted intervention under certain circumstances. No agreement was possible at that conference.

However, the progressive acceptance in theory and in practice of the principles of sovereign juridical equality, of repudiation of force, of pacific settlement, of good faith and of cooperation for the promotion of common interests, which are all standards of a highly developed and responsible community of nations, made possible the eventual adoption of the nonintervention rule. The crystallization of these principles in the good-neighbor policy and the assumption of common responsibility for the maintenance of peace and the territorial integrity and political independence of the American states further established conditions favorable to the adoption of that principle.

Only five years after the sixth conference, agreement was reached at the seventh conference at Montevideo in 1933 on the principle, incorporated in the Convention on Rights and Duties of States, that "No state has a right to intervene in the internal or external affairs of another." Three years later, at the special conference at Buenos Aires for the maintenance of peace, the principle of nonintervention was accepted as a treaty obligation in the following unequivocal and sweeping terms: "The High Contracting Parties declare inadmissible the intervention of any one of them, directly or indirectly, and for whatever reason, in the internal or external affairs of any other of the Parties."

There was nevertheless a general realization that the dynamics of a developing peaceful order require not only rejection of the old but also construction of the new. The question remained: With the rejection of the use of force or coercion as final arbiters in these matters, what collective responsibility and what rules of law should take their place? Awareness of this problem was shown by the rapid assumption, as described previously, of collective responsibility for the security and peace of the Western Hemisphere in the event of any fact or situation which might affect them. Under the Rio treaty on mutual assistance and the proposed organic pact, members of the Inter-American System will be able to act on the basis of predetermined principles, obligations, and procedures agreed upon and to be executed in the exercise of the sovereignty and independence of each state as a member of an interdependent community of nations. Action under these arrangements will consequently not constitute intervention since arbitrary action of any kind is precluded. This principle is stated in the draft organic pact as follows: "Collective action provided for in this Pact and in the Charter of the UN does not constitute intervention."

There still remains, moreover, the need to reach full agreement on whether certain existing international principles or practices fall or should fall within the general prohibition of the principle of nonintervention. Two specific issues relate to the diplomatic protection of citizens and the recognition of governments.

With respect to the first, treaty agreements of limited duration for the reference to arbitration of pecuniary claims of citizens of one state against

---

⁴ These questions include: What recourse has the creditor state in the case of public debts when there is inability to pay, and how is the *bona fides* of this to be determined? What constitutes denial of justice, and under what circumstances is diplomatic interposition justified? Does the Calvo clause—under which the citizens of one country doing business in another are required to agree not to invoke diplomatic assistance for the recovery of contractual debts or of claims for loss or damage to property or life—validly foreclose diplomatic interposition of any kind?

sultation for the purpose of exchanging views and reaching a common understanding prior to individual decision on recognition of *de facto* governments. This appears to be a generalization of the established custom under which the governments of neighboring countries and those most directly interested ordinarily consult informally among themselves before granting recognition.

Under a specific topic on the agenda of the Bogotá conference, the problem of *de facto* governments is to be examined in the light of two concrete proposals which were referred for consideration to the ninth conference by the Mexico City conference. One of these projects, formulated by the Ecuadoran Delegation at the latter conference, provided for the "abolition of the practice of recognizing *de facto* governments," on the ground that this practice violates "the autonomy or domestic sovereignty of the states and constitutes arbitrary interference or intervention in their affairs." The other project, submitted by the Guatemalan Delegation, recommended that the American republics "refrain from granting recognition to and maintaining relations with antidemocratic regimes," particularly those resulting from a *coup d'état* against legitimately established governments of a democratic character. This proposal was justified on the ground that antidemocratic régimes constitute "a serious danger to the unity, solidarity, peace and defense of the continent."

In these two proposals the conference will have before it the specific issues of whether the practice of recognition is *per se* arbitrary interference in the domestic affairs of the state as maintained by Estrada; whether uniform rules can be elaborated which will mitigate the possibility that recognition may be used in individual cases unduly and improperly to influence changes of government in other states; and whether nonrecognition should be used as a collective means by which the establishment of antidemocratic governments in the Americas may be discouraged. The latter point will not of course raise the specific question of whether nonrecognition or withdrawal of diplomatic representatives is an appropriate collective measure against a state which threatens or breaks the peace or commits an act of aggression. This question has already been settled in the affirmative in the Charter of the United Nations and in the Rio treaty of mutual assistance.

Inter-American cooperation in non-political matters has been characterized by a gradual but certain expansion and intensification in all fields. It has been like a mountain stream which broadens and deepens into a great river as it is fed by tributaries in its course toward the sea.

As indicated in the introduction to this article, the conclusions of the first conference in 1890 related chiefly to interchange of information and technical cooperation, particularly in commercial and economic matters. Its principal recommendations dealt with such matters as the adoption of a uniform system of weights and measures, nomenclature of merchandise, improvement of transportation and communication, patents and trademarks, consular fees, and custom and sanitary regulations. However, the outlines of more ambitious ideas were sketched. These were so far-reaching that they still remain, after more than half a century, in the realm of ideals. They included an intercontinental railway, an inter-American bank, an inter-American customs union, and an inter-American monetary union.[7]

Cultural cooperation was mentioned only in a resolution creating a Latin American library to commemorate the conference in which should be deposited all documents relating to the history and civilization of the Americas. Legal cooperation was limited to recommendations for the conclusion of treaties on the extradition of criminals and for adherence to the South American treaties of 1888 on private international law and civil, commercial, and procedural law.

To this frame of reference succeeding conferences kept adding specific subjects in the economic, social, cultural, and legal fields until comprehensive programs and suitable techniques were evolved. The underlying purpose has been to obtain not only the material advantages of this cooperation but also the international understanding and cooperation which is basic to increased friendly relations among nations.

(a) ECONOMIC AND SOCIAL

While continuing to study and make recommendations on the technical subjects considered by the

---

[7] The last two topics were on the agenda of the conference by specific direction of the act of Congress of the United States which authorized the calling of the conference.

ished in 1915 to study the economic problems created by World War I, but disappeared in the early 1930's. With the advent of World War II certain emergency and permanent agencies were created. Chief of these was the Inter-American Financial and Economic Advisory Committee. This has become the Economic and Social Council, which, as an organ of the Governing Board of the Pan American Union, will function as a permanent over-all body for economic and social cooperation. Another wartime agency, the Inter-American Development Committee, will probably be absorbed by the Council. The Inter-American Institute of Agricultural Sciences was also established during the war as a permanent agency, with a comprehensive technical program of research and education in its important field.

Under the draft organic pact to be considered at Bogotá, the Council will "promote the economic and social well-being of the American nations through effective cooperation among them for the better utilization of their natural resources, their agricultural and industrial development and the elevation of the standards of living of the peoples".

The Council has in fact begun to exercise these responsibilities. By request of the special conference for the maintenance of peace and security held in Rio de Janeiro, it is drafting the basic economic agreement to be considered at Bogotá. This draft will establish the principles which will guide inter-American economic cooperation. Under the terms of the resolution of Rio de Janeiro, an economic conference will be held the latter part of 1948 to consider specific methods by which these principles may be given effect through individual and collective action by the governments.

An important question at Bogotá will concern the respective roles of private investment and intergovernmental financial assistance in the development of the natural resources and the progressive industrialization of the countries of Latin America. Another related problem will concern the broad objective of facilitating international commerce. This will entail agreement on principles by which trade discrimination can be eliminated and trade barriers reduced.[8]

The most important question in the social field for the Bogotá conference will be the Declaration on the Rights and Duties of Man. It will also consider a number of other questions, such as improvement of public health, social security and insurance, and a charter of social guaranties.

(b) CULTURAL

The only direct concern expressed by the First Conference with cultural cooperation was the recommendation for the establishment of the Latin American library, previously mentioned. From this almost total neglect, interest in this subject progressed steadily. The Buenos Aires conference of 1936, which was a special conference for the maintenance of peace, agreed on a large number of resolutions on the subject and five of the eleven treaties which it concluded dealt with cultural cooperation. At the last general conference at Lima in 1938, on the eve of the war, almost a third of the 112 resolutions dealt with cultural matters. The same conference also included cultural exchange among the fundamental principles of the System, considering it basic to the creation of mutual understanding and of conditions necessary to peaceful relations among nations.

As in the case of economic cooperation, the main stress at first was on the removal of restrictions and obstacles to interchange. This explains the concern with copyright protection, which has been on the agenda of all the general conferences since 1902. Although preoccupation with the removal of restrictions to interchange has continued, a growing interest has developed in the promotion of exchange of skills or "know-how," students, teachers, and professional and scientific personnel in all fields.[9]

The chief means by which the general policies agreed upon at the general conferences have been carried into effect have been the Pan American Scientific Congresses, of which the first was held in 1915 and the eighth in 1940; the Division of Intellectual Cooperation of the Pan American Union, which has effectively functioned as the central, permanent body in this field; and the Pan American Institute of Geography and History, created in 1929 as an organ of cooperation between geographic and historical societies. Moreover, in

[8] For an address by Assistant Secretary Armour on the economic aspects of the Bogotá conference, see BULLETIN of Dec. 21, 1947, p. 1214.

[9] See Cooperation in the Americas, Report of the Interdepartmental Committee on Scientific and Cultural Cooperation, July 1946–June 1947, Department of State publication 2971.

1939 and 1940, the first and second Inter-American Conferences of National Committees of Intellectual Cooperation of the League of Nations were held in Chile and Cuba under the auspices of the host country in each instance and the Paris Institute of Intellectual Cooperation. By this means a link was established in these endeavors with the work of the League of Nations in the same field.

Chief interest at Bogotá in cultural matters will relate to the creation of the Inter-American Cultural Council, as an organ of the Governing Board of the Pan American Union. The draft organic pact provides that the Council is "to promote the development of teaching, education, and culture of the American peoples and to stimulate cooperation among them in these fields". The Council will meet every two years and will be, in effect, a type of specialized conference. The appropriate divisions of the Pan American Union will act as its permanent secretariat. There is also some support for the establishment of a permanent commission of the Council in the Pan American Union composed of persons designated by countries selected by the Governing Board of the Union.

Coordination of activities in this field will relate specifically to the relations of the Council with the Scientific Congresses and the Institute of Geography and History, on the one hand, and to UNESCO on the other. A contemplated agreement between the Institute and the Union should avoid the possibility of duplicating activities, so far as the former organization is concerned. A different type of problem will arise in connection with the relations of the Scientific Congresses to the Council. Two conferences in the same field would appear to be redundant. However, any plan to integrate or coordinate the two should take into account the fact that the former are conferences which include not only governments, but private organizations and individuals as well. The active and direct participation of private organizations and individuals should be maintained to avoid giving a purely official character to these activities.

Coordinated relations will be established between the activities of the Cultural Council and UNESCO. A directive to this effect is included in the draft organic pact, which requires the organs of the Governing Board to "establish close relations of cooperation with appropriate organs of the United Nations and with national and in-

tional law and of private international law; and, insofar as possible, to promote uniformity of legislation among the different American countries." It is to meet whenever convoked by the Governing Board of the Pan American Union.

Among the tenets of the codification movement in the Americas is the idea that the work should be the result of a gradual and progressive process involving the conclusion of special agreements or declarations in the various fields of international law; that the work should be coordinated with the labor in the same field undertaken in other parts of the world; that private agencies interested in this subject should be asked to cooperate; that the agencies of codification should not modify the principles of inter-American conventional law; and that, whenever the nature of the subject makes it possible and expedient, inter-American conventions should be generalized by inviting the adherence of non-American states.

There are profound implications for both national and international law in the present period of unrest and upheaval in the world. New forces, new political, social, and economic ideas, are pressing against established legal principles and concepts. Any activity of codification and unification in the international sphere, as in the national, must necessarily take this situation into consideration. In the Americas it is recognized that law cannot remain static, but the point of departure is that the change in the law must come about by agreement and not through unilateral action.

Relations With the United Nations

Support of the United Nations is a cornerstone of the foreign policy of the United States. Support of the Inter-American System is likewise a fundamental principle of American foreign policy. There would be contradiction in these two objectives if the regional system pursued purposes or rested on principles incompatible with the world system, or if it in fact tended to qualify support of the latter.

The objective of peace and international cooperation through the application of principles and purposes such as those incorporated in the United Nations Charter is not novel to the members of the Inter-American System. In their own experi-

---

[10] For a more detailed treatment of this subject, see William Sanders, "The Pan American Program for Juridical Unity", the *Inter-American Quarterly*, April 1940.

ence of cooperative endeavor through the last half century they have reason to attach validity to and to recognize the practical effectiveness of such principles and purposes. It' is therefore understandable that the American states see in the Inter-American System not only a means by which their traditional close ties of friendly cooperation can be strengthened but also a constructive factor in the world effort through the United Nations to maintain peace and promote human welfare.

The recently signed Rio treaty is a concrete example of the position of the American republics on the vital problem of the relations between the System and the United Nations in security matters. In this area, where there are concrete signposts and directives in the articles on regional arrangements of the Charter of the United Nations, every effort was made to insure the closest possible legal and functional relation between the regional security treaty and the world system. As indicated previously, this was done by specific and general linking of the principles, purposes, and obligations of the treaty to those of the Charter. This regional arrangement did not in any manner localize or regionalize the responsibility for world peace assumed by the parties to the treaty under the Charter of the United Nations.

In the nonsecurity field, the San Francisco conference refrained from providing for regional arrangements, on the ground that such a reference was unnecessary. This decision did not of course imply that regional cooperation in economic and social matters was considered undesirable. In fact, among the chief proponents of the strongest possible role for the Economic and Social Council were members of the Inter-American System, who would have opposed any such interpretation. The decision at San Francisco, however, did not imply indifference. Though the Charter gives no specific guidance on this important question, it is clear from the discussions at San Francisco and from the Charter itself that no dualism exists between security and nonsecurity matters in the basic world approach to peace through the United Nations. The interdependence of the two factors is clearly recognized, as is the consequent corollary that only through the interaction of the two can the objectives of the United Nations, of promoting human welfare and maintaining peace, be achieved.

Implicit in the Charter premise that peace is in-

the System shall maintain cooperation with the United Nations and appropriate international organizations. It imposes on the Governing Board the duty to "promote and facilitate collaboration between the Pan American Union and the United Nations, as well as between the specialized inter-American organizations and similar international organizations". It specifically provides in connection with the inter-American specialized organizations that this cooperation shall be for the purpose of effectively coordinating and harmonizing their activities with those of their world counterparts.

The manner in which these provisions are given effect will determine the extent to which inter-American economic, social, and cultural activities will in fact "supplement and complement rather than contradict" those of the United Nations and its specialized agencies. The intent to avoid overlapping and duplication and to do nothing which will detract from the prestige and effectiveness of the world approach to the interrelated problem of human welfare and maintenance of peace will not be enough. This intention must and surely will be given practical expression in the development of formal and informal relations between the component elements of the Inter-American System and their global counterparts. The responsibility for avoiding duplication rests both on world agencies and regional organizations—it must be a two-way concern. Unquestionably increasingly effective relations must be established on the basis of experience and in the light of needs. This will no doubt entail variations in degree and kind of relationship, depending on the organizations and problems involved. (See chart III.)

In the development of these relations in the nonsecurity field, the following general considerations will apply:

1. The indivisibility of peace and its indispensable economic and social foundation mean that regional arrangements cannot take the place of the United Nations in promoting human welfare and enduring peace.

2. Regional arrangements for dealing with economic and social matters are appropriate for regional action provided they are compatible with and recognize the foregoing principle.

3. The maintenance of consistency between these two principles requires continuing good faith, constant vigilance, and the application of working

CHART III

INTER-AMERICAN SYSTEM AND THE UNITED NATION

(TO BE CONSIDERED AT BOGOTA CONFERENCE, 1948)

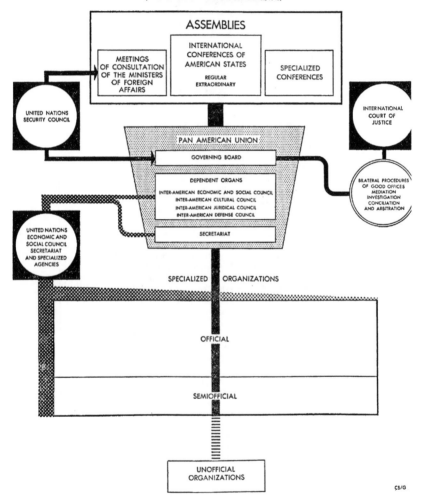

CS/G

extensive powers, as a provisional organ of consultation, for the maintenance of peace and security, which gives the System for the first time a permanent or continuing political agency. Moreover, it is quite likely that at Bogotá the Union will be given a similar role in the field of pacific settlement. In addition, it is presently contemplated that the Union will be given a broad grant of power along the lines of the formula in resolution IX of the Mexico City conference, under which it would deal, within the limitations set forth in the organic pact and other inter-American treaties, with any matter affecting the functioning or the purposes of the Inter-American System.

However, it is not unlikely that the question of the exercise of political functions by the Pan American Union, apparently settled by the decision of the Mexico City conference and the provisions incorporated in the treaty at Rio, will be brought up at Bogotá in terms of a proposal by one of the governments that all political and security responsibilities be lodged in a "council of solidarity" of the System located elsewhere than in Washington.

In the nonpolitical field the Pan American Union will also have greatly increased authority and responsibility. Through the addition of the new organs of the Governing Board, the Union will have broad responsibilities for implementing conference decisions and for taking action on its own initiative within the terms of the organic pact in the economic, social, cultural, and legal fields. Also its Defense Council will act in an advisory capacity to the governments and to the organ of consultation on military cooperation for the defense of the Western Hemisphere. Still unresolved, however, is an issue raised, by one of the governments who holds the view that the Defense Council should not be an organ of the Governing Board of the Pan American Union but an autonomous specialized organization. Should this view prevail, it would constitute a significant departure from the trend toward centralization.

The relations of the Union with the other two principal organs of the System, the assemblies or conferences and the specialized organizations, will be drawn tighter. To an even greater extent than in the past it will serve as the permanent secretariat of the general conferences and meetings of Foreign Ministers and, as indicated, will have an expanded role in proposing means by which their conclusions may be applied. This should avoid the need for the creation of new permanent or *ad hoc* agencies. Within the same tenor of ideas the Pan American Union will probably be given a greater degree of over-all supervision over the specialized conferences, formerly the technical conferences. Should this tendency be crystallized at Bogotá, it will be important that the Union not become a bottleneck inhibiting desirable activities in the specialized fields. The objective is a degree of over-all supervision which will prevent duplication of effort and unnecessary activity without curtailment of technical autonomy.

The same objective will hold with respect to the specialized organizations. The Pan American Union apparently will have closer relations with them than in the past and a degree of over-all supervision, the details of which will be worked out in agreements between the Union and such agencies. The objective of this supervision will be avoidance of overlapping activities either in the form of duplicating or competing organizations or functions.

The basic motivation for the trend toward centralization has been the desire to create a more effective and efficient System. As always in an endeavor of this kind, a good idea can be run into the ground. With this in mind the architects of the plans for reorganization have stressed as one way in which rigidity may be avoided the principle already alluded to of technical autonomy for the new organs of the Board and for the specialized conferences and organizations. In this same connection, but with wider implications applicable to the entire problem of reorganization at Bogotá, there has been an ever-present concern lest the flexibility which has been so constructive a factor in the development of the System to date be completely lost.

Bogotá should allow for elbow room in which the System can operate freely and grow in the light of experience and needs. This will be particularly important since it is planned to formalize in a treaty at Bogotá the organs, principles, and purposes of the System, which will mean that modifications cannot subsequently be introduced except through an international instrument of the same category. The wisest formula, therefore, will be one which achieves a desirable degree of centralization and integration but leaves an open door for

ica. The item on European colonies is on the agenda in terms of a proposal by the Guatemalan Government that the American Governments declare that the continued existence of European colonies in America constitutes a danger to hemispheric security. The topic relative to defense of democracy in the Americas concerns the proposal by Guatemala that the American republics agree not to enter into diplomatic relations with anti-democratic regimes.

Although listed under the first chapter, the proposed treaty on pacific settlement properly belongs in the chapter on political and juridical problems and will probably be considered by the conference committee on this chapter or by a special committee. As indicated previously, the chief questions here will concern the problem of compulsory arbitration, the relation of this procedure to juridical settlement under the International Court of Justice, and the role of inter-American consultation for pacific settlement purposes.

On the vital question of the relations of the System and its component organs to the United Nations and world specialized agencies, the conference will in all probability not attempt to supply in detail the answer to what these relations should be. If the articles already alluded to of the draft organic pact are accepted, the problem of working out satisfactory relationships will be a post-Bogotá problem that will be processed in the light of those articles and of experience and needs in each case.

Conclusion

The empiricism which characterized the beginnings of the System in 1890 continues, but the ideals and larger purposes which were then seen as "through a glass darkly" have given dynamic meaning and direction to the Pan American movement. They have increasingly become the warp and the woof of inter-American relations.

It is perhaps difficult for those brought up in the tradition which regards war as inevitable to believe in the sincerity with which the peoples of the New World hold to the cardinal principles and purposes of the Inter-American System. Measured against the stark background of rules of the game based upon conflict and domination and balance of power, these principles and purposes appear naive and unrealistic. They would indeed be so in the absence of a common determination that they shall in fact control the relations of the members of the System. They have produced results because, beneath the rhetoric and exaltation which seems always to accompany these endeavors, there has been a hard-headed conviction that these principles and purposes would best advance the enlightened self-interest of each American nation.

This approach to international affairs is the very substance of the search for peace and human welfare through the United Nations. Impatience with the slow progress being made through these methods in the wider arena of the world, where the obstacles loom almost insurmountable from today's perspective, could lead to a pessimistic denial of the universal validity of such methods.

The major conclusions to be drawn from the experience in inter-American relations described in this article may be useful in assessing the advantages and limitations of such methods in overcoming these apparently greater obstacles. These conclusions are that machinery and procedures are secondary to the willingness and decision to use them; that the "know-how" of working out difficult and sometimes apparently insuperable problems can be acquired, but not overnight; that constructive international cooperation is the product of many years of patient effort, of a spirit of give and take, and of unwavering determination to break with the defeatism of the past which holds that man is doomed by his nature and environment to perpetual strife.

A belief in the final triumph of the moral order is a helpful handmaiden of the policies which seek the objectives of the United Nations and the Inter-American System. This belief must be based, however, on something more than wishful thinking. It must take into account that peace, like liberty, can be achieved and maintained only through the labor and struggles and eternal vigilance of many generations. Man has the ingenuity and the resourcefulness to create peace, provided he so wills it and is not dismayed.

ERP To Aid in Industrial Development in Latin America

[Released to the press January 30]

The American Delegate before the Economic and Social Council of the Pan American Union made the following statement on January 30

European recovery requires fundamentally an increase in production levels to a point where basic economic needs can be met and still leave a surplus for export to cover essential imports. Without European recovery there can be no general world prosperity. The restoration of Europe will be of particular assistance to Latin America where foreign trade comprises a relatively large proportion of the national income and where strong European markets for exports are essential to continuing prosperity. The resumption of European exports particularly in the field of capital equipment will also facilitate industrial development in Latin America by easing present shortages of these items which will continue as long as the United States is the only important source.

In the first year or two of ERP, before increases in European production make possible a considerable expansion of exports, available supplies of the tools of production will continue to be inadequate to meet in full the requirements of all countries. The difficult problem of determining the most effective distribution of these short supplies must be faced. The objectives of European recovery and of Latin American development often will coincide. Goods and equipment which will make possible a prompt and efficient increase in Latin American production and export of items essential to European recovery should be supplied to the greatest extent possible. It is essential, moreover, that such export controls as are required should be administered in an equitable manner with a view to maintaining, in so far as possible, the continuity of industrial development in the other American Republics.

emoval of Industrial Plants From Germany by Reparation

LETTER TO THE SPEAKER OF THE HOUSE OF REPRESENTATIVES
FROM UNDER SECRETARY LOVETT

January 24, 1948

Y DEAR MR. SPEAKER:

By his letter of December 19, 1947, the Honorle John Andrews, Clerk of the House of Repreitatives, forwarded an attested copy of House solution 365 of the Eightieth Congress, adopted the House of Representatives on December 18,)47. The Resolution requests the Secretaries of tate and of Defense to transmit to the House of :epresentatives at the earliest practical moment artain information, specified in eleven questions at out in the text of the Resolution, regarding the amoval of industrial plants from Germany by ay of reparation.

The Department of State, for itself and the Deartment of Defense, herewith respectfully subits a basic reply to the questions asked by the Iouse of Representatives. Every effort has been iade to obtain to the fullest extent and as rapidly s possible the information requested by House tesolution 365. Because of the urgency of putting the requested information before the House, he submission has not been cleared with the Bueau of the Budget, to which, however, copies are eing sent.

It will be observed that much of the detailed nformation requested is lacking regarding the 3ritish, French and Soviet Zones of Occupation n Germany. Through both diplomatic channels nd through the Office of Military Government US), the British and French Governments have been asked to supply the additional information needed. These Governments have not been able to comply quickly with this request, because their occupation authorities have not maintained such data in the form in which it is desired by the House of Representatives. The representatives of these Governments have given assurances, however, that they will make every effort to obtain the information which is presently lacking. This additional information and the checking of the information herewith submitted will probably require further communications to the House of Representatives from the Department of State and the Department of Defense.

No official information on reparation removals is available for the Soviet Zone of Occupation in Germany, nor has there been in response to the Resolution a request to the Government of the Soviet Union for such information. Since the Soviet Government has repeatedly, the most recently at the meeting of the Council of Foreign Ministers at London in December, 1947, refused to comply with requests of this nature, it was not considered that a reiteration would be effective.

Sincerely yours,

ROBERT A. LOVETT
Under Secretary

The Honorable
JOSEPH W. MARTIN, JR.,
Speaker of the House of Representatives.

INFORMATION REQUESTED BY HOUSE RESOLUTION 365, DECEMBER 18, 1947

QUESTION 1. How many of the six hundred and ighty-two plants in Germany recently announced s surplus and available for reparations have actually been dismantled and removed from Gernany? How many from the British Zone? How nany from the Russian Zone? How many from he French Zone?

ANSWER

The list of 682 plants and parts of plants, announced on October 16, 1947, as representing caacity surplus to the needs of the German econmy, applied only to the Bizonal Area of Gernany. Of these, 186 are in the U.S. Zone and 496 n the British Zone. The French on October 10,

1947, announced a provisional list of 176 surplus plants in their Zone. No equivalent list is available for the Soviet Zone. Copies of the Bizonal and French lists are attached. (Attachments 1 and 2.[1])

Forty plants have been completely dismantled and removed from the American Zone, and the same number from the British Zone. In addition other plants have been dismantled and partially removed. This information is given in answer to question 3 below. No information is presently available for either the French or Soviet Zones.

QUESTION 2. What was the character and capacity

[1] Attachments not printed.

of the removed plants in each zone? Which ones could have contributed to the economic reconstruction of Germany and Europe within the scope of the so-called Marshall Plan?

ANSWER

Character and Capacity of the Removed Plants

Of the 40 plants removed from the American Zone, 32 were war plants, i.e., plants designed exclusively for the manufacture of war materials. Only general purpose equipment from them, readily convertible to civilian production, was shipped out as reparation. Equipment usable only for the manufacture of war materials was destroyed.

No information on the capacity output of war materials of these war plants is available, nor is it believed that such information would be relevant to the purpose of House Resolution 365. Since the plants were not designed for civilian use, and since important elements of them were destroyed prior to shipment of the general purpose equipment as reparation, no information is available concerning their capacity for production of civilian goods.

Of the 8 non-war plants already removed from the American Zone, 3 produced machinery; 2 were power plants; and there were 1 each in the fields of optical goods, diesel engine production, and shipbuilding. All of these 8 non-war plants were on the so-called "advance list" of plants to be removed as reparation. This list was drawn up in 1945, prior to the preparation of the original Level of Industry Plan of March, 1946, in order to permit an immediate start on the reparation program established by the Potsdam Agreement of August 2, 1945. Capacities of the non-war plants removed from the U.S. Zone are shown in Table "A" attached.

No detailed information on the types and capacities of plants already removed from Zones other than the American has as yet been received. It is believed, however, that removals from the British Zone, as from the American, have consisted chiefly of war plants. Since it is known that only a very small tonnage of material has been shipped from the French Zone, it is believed that but few plants have been completely removed.

Possible Contribution of Removed Plants to German and European Reconstruction

While full information is not available, it is known that a large proportion of the plants and equipment already removed from Germany are now in operation in the recipient countries, and are contributing to their reconstruction. Of particular importance has been the receipt from Germany of critical types of machines, not procurable elsewhere within less than two or three years, which have served to break industrial bottlenecks,

The capacity of the plants listed for reparation from the Bizonal Area, other than war plants, is summarized by types of industry in a table included in the attached list of "Plants and Part Plants Listed for Reparations from the U.S. and U.K. Zones." No capacity data have been received from the French Zone.

Detailed capacity data for individual plants are presently available only for the U.S. Zone. Figures for the capacity of each plant, except war plants, yet to be removed from the U.S. Zone are shown in Table "B" attached.

QUESTION 4. How many of those remaining to be dismantled or removed could be converted to peacetime production? For example, from making nitrogen explosives to making nitrogen fertilizers?

ANSWER

All of the plants and equipment remaining to be removed are either capable of peacetime production in their present condition, or can be converted thereto. Such use or conversion is, of course, a basic objective of the reparation program, which envisages the transfer of German plants and equipment useful for civilian production from Germany to the countries whose industries Germany looted, damaged and destroyed. Equipment useful only for military production is destroyed in Germany.

As has been pointed out above, a number of transfers have already taken place, and former German plants and equipment are now producing civilian products in the recipient countries.

On the particular question of nitrogen explosive plants, all plants in the Bizonal Area capable of making synthetic nitrogen for fertilizers are being utilized for that purpose, and no such plant is on the Bizonal reparation list.

QUESTION 5. How many of these plants remaining to be dismantled and removed are capable of making a substantial contribution to the export trade envisioned as necessary if Germany, or the bizonal area of Germany, is to balance her imports of food by export of goods in the year 1952?

ANSWER

As was noted in the Revised Plan for Level of Industry in the US/UK Zones of Germany, published on August 29, 1947, a copy of which is attached (Attachment 5), "the over-riding requirements" in developing the Plan were "to provide the level of industry necessary to make the area self-supporting". Full allowance was made for the necessity of retaining in Germany sufficient industrial capacity to permit development of an export trade sufficient to balance essential imports, not only of food but of raw materials and other commodities. General Clay has said, in a statement the full text of which is attached, that:

". . . it is doubtful if the industrial capacity left in Germany (under the Revised Plan) can be put fully to use in less than 5 years, and it would be indeed many years before the full capacity, including that made available for reparations, could be put to use. . . . It is my sincere conviction that . . . we have left to Western Germany all the industrial capacity it can use". (Attachment 6.[2])

The Revised Plan, therefore, leaves in the Bizonal Area sufficient industrial capacity to pay for needed imports. In view, however, of shortages of fuel, raw materials, manpower and other factors of production, it will require the utmost efforts of the Germans to achieve by 1952 full utilization of even this capacity.

The list of plants remaining to be dismantled or removed was drawn up in accordance with the Revised Plan, and their capacity as a whole is, therefore, surplus to that required by Germany to pay for needed imports. Many individual plants on the reparation list, other than war plants, are, of course, similar or identical in character to plants to be retained in Germany under the Revised Plan for the purpose of meeting German needs, whether through production for domestic use or through production for export. Thus a number of individual plants listed for reparation could, if retained in Germany *and if given necessary supplies of coal, raw materials, etc.*, contribute to German domestic or export needs.

While this holds true for individual plants, however, it cannot be applied to all plants listed for reparation *as a group*. To retain *and* put into production any substantial number of the plants now listed for reparation would simply mean that other plants scheduled to be retained in Germany would fall idle, or be run far below capacity, because of shortages of the essential factors of production.

QUESTION 6. On what basis was the determination made that a particular plant was surplus? That is, was the surplus character of the plant determined in relation to German domestic products or in relation to available raw materials, or in relation to manpower? Or in relation to exports readily salable abroad?

ANSWER

As stated in answer to question 5, the Revised Plan for Level of Industry in the US/UK Zones of Germany was drawn up to provide for the retention in Germany of sufficient industrial capacity, including that required for exports, to permit self-support and the development of a reasonable standard of living. The *difference* between the retained capacity provided for under the Revised Level and the *total* capacity actually

_____
[2] Not printed.

ments of foodstuffs that may have occurred are believed to have been negligible in quantity.

It is known that considerable quantities of foodstuffs have been, and are now being, removed from the Soviet Zone. No comprehensive data concerning such shipments are, however, available.

QUESTION 10. To what extent have harbor facilities and transportation equipment been removed from Germany and is any replacement of these facilities or equipment contemplated in the proposals for supplying by the United States as a part of economic recovery for Europe?

ANSWER

Railway Transport Equipment

Locomotives and freight cars must of necessity continually cross international boundaries in the ordinary course of operations, and, at any given time, substantial quantities of German rolling stock would be outside Germany and corresponding quantities of rolling stock of foreign ownership would be inside Germany. This situation prevailed at the end of the war.

Several countries which, as the Germany army was driven from their territories, found themselves in possession of large numbers of German locomotives and railway wagons have retained them; and have insisted that under the terms of existing international agreements they were entitled to do so. American and British military authorities in Germany have been attempting to negotiate the return of these cars to Germany, in exchange for the foreign rolling stock now held in the Bizonal Area. These negotiations have so far been only partially successful. No German railway rolling stock has been removed from the Bizonal Area since the end of the war, except such as has crossed the German borders in the course of normal operations.

The situation is further complicated by the severe shortage of railway repair facilities in the Bizonal Area, a shortage largely due to concentrated Allied bombing. Despite utmost efforts, it has been impossible to prevent deterioration in the German transport situation because of the inability to maintain and repair available rolling stock properly.

It is possible that imports of new rolling stock into the Bizonal Area will be necessary. The necessity for such imports, however, derives to a considerable degree from the shortage of repair facilities.

Ocean-Going Shipping

In accordance with the Potsdam decision made on grounds of military security, Germany has been prohibited from building or maintaining an ocean-going fleet. The entire German merchant fleet has, therefore, been distributed among Allied nations as reparation by the Tripartite Merchant Marine Commission and the Inter-Allied Reparation Agency. The great majority of ships distributed are now in operation under Allied flags. The remainder are being repaired.

No replacement of these ships is contemplated in the proposals for European recovery.

Coastal Shipping

A proportion of the German coastal fleet, determined at the time to be in excess of German minimum needs, has been distributed among Allied nations as reparation. A re-examination of requirements has led to the conclusion that it may be necessary to replace some of this tonnage. No firm figures, however, are yet available.

Inland Water Transport

Inland water transport equipment is similar in character to rolling stock, in that it frequently crosses international boundaries in the course of normal operations. A number of foreign owned barges which have been removed from the Danubian Basin have been delivered from Germany not as reparations but under restitution procedures. Negotiations have been in progress for some time for the purpose of arranging exchange of certain other German inland waterway craft now held by liberated countries for foreign craft now held in Germany. No replacements of German craft are contemplated under the proposals for aid to European recovery.

Harbor Facilities

No major fixed harbor facilities have been removed from the Western Zones of Germany, nor are any removals planned. Approximately 60 percent of such facilities have, however, been destroyed, in accordance with decisions of military security. No replacement is contemplated as part of aid to European recovery. No information is available concerning the Soviet Zone.

QUESTION 11. Has the Government of the United States taken appropriate steps to delay temporarily the further dismantling of plants in western Germany so as to permit further study by the appropriate committees of Congress in order to determine whether such transfers are prejudicial to any general recovery program for western Europe?

ANSWER

The U.S. Government has taken no steps to halt the general dismantling program pending Congressional study of its economic effects, but is now engaged in discussions with the British regarding the question of further reparation deliveries to the east. It will be recalled that General Clay stopped deliveries of additional reparations plants

U.S.-U.K. Begin Consular Treaty Negotiations

[Released to the press January 30]

The Department of State announced on January 30 that representatives of the United Kingdom have begun direct negotiations with representatives of the United States for the preparation of a consular treaty between the two countries. The treaty will define and clarify for the first time the rights and privileges mutually extended to consular representatives of the United States and the United Kingdom and will enable them in a more satisfactory manner to perform their official functions while serving abroad.

The proposed treaty, when ratified, will be the first consular convention concluded by the United Kingdom. It is expected to follow the same general lines as the recently announced consular treaty with Costa Rica.[2] The importance of the convention now under negotiation is also evidenced in the fact that it will apply to the United States and all its territories and possessions, and to the United Kingdom and all British colonies and other dependent territories, and it will therefore cover a wider area and include more consular posts than any other similar consular convention. The current negotiations are the outgrowth of written exchanges which have been carried on between the two Governments for some time.

The United Kingdom representatives and the key United States representatives are as follows:

UNITED KINGDOM REPRESENTATIVES

(*Chairman*) W. E. Beckett, C.M.G., K.C., Legal Adviser to the Foreign Office
R. W. Urquhart, C.M.G., O.B.E., Minister at the British Embassy
R. S. B. Best, Legal Counselor at the British Embassy
D. J. Mill Irving, Consular Department, Foreign Office

UNITED STATES REPRESENTATIVES

Department of State

(*Chairman*) Herbert P. Fales, Assistant Chief, Division of British Commonwealth Affairs

Department of Justice

D. E. Feller, Attorney, Office of Alien Property

Maritime Commission

Charles E. Moody, Chief Agency and Port Service Section

Treasury Department

Raphael Sherfy, Attorney, Tax Legislative Council

---

[1] Not printed.
[2] For text of convention with Costa Rica, see Department of State press release 33 of Jan. 13, 1948.

William Sanders, author of the article on the Inter-American
System, is directing and coordinating the preparatory work on the
Bogotá conference for the Assistant Secretary of State for political
affairs.

The Department of State bu

Vol. XVIII, N

Feb

For sale by the Superintendent of Documents
U.S. Government Printing Office
Washington 25, D.O.

SUBSCRIPTION:
52 issues, $5; single copy, 15 cents

Published with the approval of the
Director of the Bureau of the Budget

The Departm
a weekly pu
edited in the
Office of Pu
public and
the Governm
development
relations and
partment of
Service. Th
press releases
by the White
ment, and st
made by th
Secretary of
of the Depart
articles on t
national affa
the Departm
cluded conce
ternational a
United State
party and tr
national inte

Publication
well as legisla
of internatio
currently.

es P. Hendrick

sion was made for promoting respect for human
rights and fundamental freedoms, and later at
the Inter-American Conference on Problems of
War and Peace, held at Mexico City in 1945, resolutions were passed recognizing the essential importance of human rights in the Inter-American
System.[2] Plans were made for an inter-American
declaration, which is to be considered at the forthcoming Ninth International Conference of American States, scheduled to convene in Bogotá, Colombia. Finally, in the United Nations Charter as
drafted at San Francisco, reference was made no
less than seven times to human rights, and provision was specifically made for the setting up of a
Commission on Human Rights.[3]

First Session of the Economic and Social Council

When the Economic and Social Council assembled for its first meeting, in London in January
1946, for the purpose, among others, of constituting a Commission on Human Rights, two draft
declarations of rights were presented to it, one
by Panama[4] and the other by Cuba.[5] Later Chile
presented a draft declaration to the Commission
on Human Rights[6] and since then a substantial

zations and individuals in the United States for the creation of the Commission on Human Rights and work on an
international bill, is given in an article on "The Charter
and the Promotion of Human Rights" by Alice M. Mc-
Diarmid, BULLETIN of Feb. 10, 1946, p. 210. See also *Year-
book of the United Nations*, 1946–47, p. 523.

[4] U.N. docs. E/HR/3, Apr. 26, 1946, or A/148, Oct. 24,
1946. The declaration was written under the auspices of
the American Law Institute.

[5] U.N. doc. E/HR/1, Apr. 22, 1946.

[6] U.N. doc. E/CN.4/2, Jan. 8, 1947, prepared by the Inter-
American Juridical Committee, working under the mandate of the Mexico City resolution.

number of other bills have been presented formally or informally.[7]

The Economic and Social Council set up the Human Rights Commission on February 16, 1946. Nine members were elected to serve as a nuclear group.[8] The Commission's terms of reference, as approved by the Economic and Social Council, included "work . . . directed towards submitting proposals, recommendations and reports to the Council regarding . . . an international bill of rights".[9]

Nuclear Commission Session

The nuclear commission met at Hunter College, New York, from April 29 to May 20, 1946. Beset by many difficulties,[10] the nuclear commission

---

[7] Included among the bills which have been prepared are the following: International Bill of Rights, proposal submitted by the American Federation of Labor (E/Ct. 2/2, Aug. 20, 1946) ; draft General Assembly resolution submitted by India (U.N. doc. E/CN 4/11, Jan. 31, 1947) ; Draft Charter of International Human Rights and Duties submitted by Ecuador (U.N. doc. A/341, Aug. 21, 1947) ; Report of the UNESCO Committee on the Philosophic Principles of the Rights of Man (UNESCO/Phil/10, Paris, July 31, 1947) ; Draft International Bill of Human Rights, prepared by the Committee on Human Rights, Commission to Study the Organization of Peace; National Catholic Welfare Conference—A Declaration of Rights; Declaration of Human Rights, submitted by the American Jewish Committee, January 1945; Draft of the International Bill of Rights, by the American Association for the United Nations and the American Jewish Conference; Declaration of the Rights of Man, London *Daily Herald*, Apr. 20, 1940; Enumeration of Subjects for Consideration as to an International Bill of Rights, by the American Bar Association; A charter for the United Nations—The Rights of Every Man, recommended by *Free World;* Declaration of the International Rights and Duties of the Individual, by Gustavo Gutierrez: An International Bill of the Rights of Man, by H. Lauterpacht, Columbia University Press, New York; International Bill of Rights; Principles of the Rights and Duties of Individuals, by Irving A. Isaacs; International Bill of Rights, suggested by Rollin McNitt; An International Bill of Rights, by Rev. Wilfred Parsons, S.J.; Declaration of the Rights of Man by H. G. Wells; National Resources Planning Board: A New Bill of Rights. See also U.N. doc. E/600, Dec. 17, 1947, p. 8, par. 28, referring to communications concerning human rights from writers whose identity may not (under Economic and Social Council ruling) be divulged.

[8] The members of the nuclear commission were chosen to serve as individuals rather than as government representatives. Except for the U.S.S.R. and Yugoslav members, they were elected by name by the Economic and Social Council at its first session. The membership of

upon pressed strongly for the adoption of her suggestion [16] that a working group should prepare an initial draft, to be submitted to the second session of the Commission. This suggestion was accepted and the Commission adjourned, having, in addition to the work on the bill, established a Subcommission on Freedom of Information and of the Press and a Subcommission on Prevention of Discrimination and Protection of Minorities.

Definitive Plan for Drafting of the Bill

The Economic and Social Council considered the Commission's report and an eight-point program was adopted for the drafting of a bill envisaging (1) secretariat preparations; (2) consideration by the Human Rights Drafting Committee; (3) consideration by the Human Rights Commission; (4) submission for comment to all member nations; (5) reconsideration by the Drafting Committee; (6) reconsideration by the Commission; (7) consideration by the Economic and Social Council; and (8) consideration by the General Assembly.[17] The first four steps of this program have now been taken.

First Session of the Drafting Committee

The Human Rights Drafting Committee convened on June 9, 1947.[18] Before it was a secre-

---

[14] U.N. doc. E/CN.4/SR8, Jan. 13, 1947, p. 4.

[15] Dr. Malik of Lebanon (U.N. doc. E/CN.4/SR9, Feb. 1, 1947, p. 3). Miss Sender, Representative of the American Federation of Labor, whose draft declaration had been specifically criticized by Dr. Ribnikar, stated that Dr. Ribnikar had placed greater importance upon common interest than that of the individual, and had considered the idea of individual liberty obsolete. The American Federation of Labor considered that individual liberty was perfectly compatible with the interests of the community. (U.N. doc. E/CN.4/SR8, Jan. 31, 1947, p. 5).

[16] U.N. doc. E/CN.4/4, Jan. 28, 1947.

[17] Resolution 46 (IV), fourth session of the Economic and Social Council. The first session of the eight-member Human Rights Drafting Committee was held in June 1947; the second session of the Human Rights Commission, in December 1947. The Commission's report was submitted to member nations for comment in January 1948. The second session of the Human Rights Drafting Committee is scheduled for May 1948; the third session of the Commission for May 1948; the seventh session of the Economic and Social Council, for July 1948; and the third session of the General Assembly for September 1948.

tariat outline of a bill with annotation to constitutions of member states—a document of over 400 pages.[19] The secretariat outline contained 48 articles. It was designed to cover most of the rights commonly contained in constitutions of member states or in drafts of international bills of rights. The United States, accepting the secretariat outline as a basis for discussion, filed a memorandum suggesting amendments.[20] Other members made suggestions from the floor. The difficulty of handling a detailed task of drafting with eight members in formal session became evident. A subcommittee was appointed; thereafter the subcommittee designated one individual—Professor Cassin of France—to prepare the initial redraft. Professor Cassin's redraft contained 46 articles.[21] Subsequent redrafting reduced the Declaration to 36 articles.[22] The Declaration did not purport to be legally binding.

The United Kingdom, however, had filed with the Drafting Committee a proposed covenant (convention)[23] on human rights which set forth in the form of a treaty obligation certain of those civil rights which are presently recognized in the local laws of "civilized nations".[24]

This document, when formally ratified by states, would impose a definite legal obligation. It would,

---

[18] Membership of the Human Rights Drafting Committee was as follows: chairman, Mrs. Franklin D. Roosevelt; vice chairman, P. C. Chang; rapporteur, Charles Malik; other members were W. R. Hodgson (Australia); H. Santa Cruz (Chile); René Cassin (France); V. Koretsky (U.S.S.R.); Geoffrey Wilson (U.K.).

[19] U.N. doc. E/CN.4/AC.1/3/Add.1, June 2, 1947.

[20] U.N. doc. E/CN.4/AC.1/8, June 11, 1947.

[21] U.N. doc. E/CN.4/21, annex D, July 1, 1947.

[22] *Ibid.*, annex F. The substance of these articles is summarized in *Concerning Freedom of Information*, Department of State publication 2977, p. 12.

[23] The term "covenant" is used in this article in lieu of the more ordinary terms "convention" or "treaty", in view of a decision to this effect reached by the Human Rights Commission at its second session (U.N. doc. E/600, Dec. 17, 1947, p. 6, par. 18). No distinction has been made by the Commission between the three terms, which have been used by its members to designate a legally binding document, to be ratified by states in accordance with their constitutional processes. The United Kingdom wished to use the term "bill". Other members objected to its use in lieu of "covenant" on the ground that the word could not be adequately translated into any other working language. (The French translation is *charte*, which also means "charter".) They were, however, willing to use the word "bill" to cover both the Declaration and Covenant. Since the decision on terminology was not reached until

I. Civil Rights

Eighteen articles deal with civil rights, which may be summarized as follows:

Personal Liberty: Right to life, liberty, and security of the person (article 4); freedom from slavery (article 8); freedom from torture, cruel or inhuman punishment, or indignity (article 7); freedom from interference with reputation, privacy, family, home, correspondence (article 9); liberty of movement and free choice of residence within states; right to leave country (article 10).

Legal Status: Right to recognition as a person before the law (article 12); equality before the law (article 3).

Provisions Applying to Civil and Criminal Cases: Access to independent and impartial tribunals; fair hearing; aid of qualified representative;[31] use of foreign language when necessary (article 6);[32] freedom from wrongful arrest;

[30] In general the Declaration follows the form of the Human Rights Drafting Committee's declaration—it is a rather lengthy document with a certain amount of technical detail included. The advantages of a short declaration (which could be easily memorized by any school child) were apparently considered to be outweighed by the advantages of a statement which, in the event that governments refused to become parties to the convenant in any substantial numbers, would furnish a guidepost for United Nations action. In addition, special interest in individual articles and the shortness of time at the declaration working groups' disposal made for length rather than brevity in drafting (a common enough experience in the United Nations and other fields). The U.S. submitted to the Commission a "short form" declaration consisting of 10 brief articles, describing in 350 words the rights sought to be covered (U.N. doc. E/600, Dec. 17, 1947, p. 25; BULLETIN of Dec. 7, 1947, p. 1076). While the decision of the working group was to produce a substantially longer draft, the Commission toward the close of its session recognized that the definitive declaration must be as short as possible (*ibid.*, p. 16, par. 50).

[31] Originally provision was made for "aid of counsel". This provision was changed however in view of the fact that in certain administrative cases lawyers are not available as of right to the parties concerned.

[32] Provision is made for having procedure explained in a manner which the party can understand, and the party is given the privilege of using a language which he can speak. This provision was warmly advocated by the Philippine member. The U.S.S.R. member would have preferred an even stronger provision. Certain of the civil law countries opposed the provision adopted regarding explanation of procedure, since it was not provided for under their laws and regarded as undesirable.

right to immediate judicial determination of legality of detention (habeas corpus) and to trial within reasonable time (article 5).[33]

Additional Provisions Applying to Criminal Cases: Presumption of innocence; fair public trial; freedom from *ex post facto* laws (article 7).[34]

Freedom from Discrimination: Freedom from discrimination in relation to the rights set forth in the Declaration "without distinction of any kind, such as race, (which includes colour), sex, language, religion, political or other opinion, property status, or national or social origin";[35] equal protection against "any arbitrary discrimination, or against incitement to such discrimination" (article 3).[36] Provision is also made that men and women "have the same freedom to contract marriage" (article 13); that women shall work "with the same advantages as men" and "receive equal pay for equal work" (article 24).[37]

---

[33] It will be noted that a distinction is made between a "fair hearing" for civil and criminal cases, and a "fair public trial" for criminal cases.

[34] Special explanation is made covering cases of war criminals.

[35] The quoted provision departs from the language employed in arts. 1 (3), 13 (1, b), 55 (c), 76 (c) of the Charter—"without distinction as to race, sex, language, or religion". The view expressed by the United States was that the four categories described in the Charter were not meant to be exclusive, since the Charter refers to "human rights . . . for all".

[36] Cf. art. 17, Draft Declaration proposed by Panama, U. N. docs. E/HR/3, Apr. 26, 1946, or A/148, Oct. 24, 1946.

[37] In the Declaration working groups' article, provision was made that "women shall have the right to work under the same conditions as men", but an official comment was inserted that legislation providing protection for Women, particularly in regard to heavy or harmful work, may be necessary. (U.N. doc. E/CN.4/57, Dec. 10, 1947, art. 30.) The change in the article as approved by the full commission was made on the suggestion of the Uruguayan member, Dr. Juan J. Carbajal Victorica.

[38] Art. 21—Everyone "without discrimination" has the right to participate in government; art. 25—Everyone "without distinction as to economic and social conditions" has the right to preservation of health; art. 27—There shall be access for higher education "without distinction as to race, sex, language, religion, social standing, financial means, or political affiliation."

[39] The article on religion makes it clear that this right is not limited to the act of worship, but extends to teaching and observance. The freedom of information articles were adopted from the Human Rights Drafting Committee's declaration without change and without discussion with the understanding that they would be referred to

made to state responsibility in connection with the enumeration of civil rights, except in the article dealing with participation in government.[44] Thus everyone is entitled to personal liberty, to a fair trial, and to other rights of this character, but nothing is said about the duty of the state to insure these rights.[45]

As presently drafted, therefore, the Declaration shows a curious lack of balance, superficially indicating that the state must be more concerned with social and economic rights than with civil rights.

III. Miscellaneous Rights

Included under the category of miscellaneous rights are the two rights in the declaration which are of a purely international character and rights of minorities. The international rights deal with

---

actively interested in social and economic rights. These members laid stress upon the importance of state action with respect to social and economic rights; and they were unwilling to conceive of the present need for a covenant or covenants. It was the pressure of their arguments which gave impetus to specific wording relating to state responsibility in the social and economic field.

For example, the proposal that marriage be protected by the state was made by the Byelorussian member (addition of the responsibility of society—which would include the church—was not suggested by him) ; the proposal that the state take all necessary steps to prevent unemployment was also made by the Byelorussian member; on the other hand the change from a requirement that the state insure higher education to a statement referring to higher education "as can be provided by the state or community" was made by the United Kingdom member. The U.S.S.R. member evinced great interest in one civil right—freedom from discrimination. He proposed the following article (which was not accepted):

"All people are equal before the law and shall enjoy equal rights in the economic, cultural, social and political life, irrespective of their race, sex, language, religion, property status, national or social origin.

"Any advocacy of national, racial and religious hostility or of national exclusiveness or hatred and contempt, as well as any action establishing a privilege or a discrimination based on distinctions of race, nationality or religion shall constitute a crime and shall be punishable under the law of the State."

This article had originally been proposed by Mr. Borisov (U.S.S.R.) in the first session of the Sub-commission on the Prevention of Discrimination and the Protection of Minorities (U.N. doc. E/CN.4/Sub. 2/21, Nov. 26, 1947).

asylum and nationality (articles 11 and 15).[46] The
provision on minority rights (article 31) presented
an extremely difficult problem; the Commission refrained from approving or disapproving a provision for them.[47]

A further right, the right to resist tyranny and
oppression, is to be considered for inclusion in the
preamble.[48]

Articles of Limitation

Although there was detailed discussion of what
rights could to some extent be abridged in connection with the covenant and mention was made
of freedom from torture as being one which could
not be abridged in any way [49] the Commission
made no effort to affirm in the Declaration any
"absolute" rights other than individual freedom
of thought and conscience.[50] It was recognized
in article 2 that rights are limited, first, by the
"rights of others" and, second, by the "just requirements of the democratic state".[51]

The provision for rights of others is designed
to take care of what might be described as con-

[46] In each case a change was made from the Human
Rights Drafting Committee's wording. The right of
asylum, formerly limited to seeking asylum from persecution, is now extended to the right to "seek and be granted"
asylum. One of the strongest proponents of this change
was the French member, who cited the case of Spanish
loyalists finding refuge on French soil. In the case of
nationality a provision is added to the assertion of everyone's right to a nationality, to the effect that the United
Nations shall protect those who do not enjoy the protection of any government. These rights may be noted as
particularly vivid examples of the distinction between a
declaration and a covenant. While the principle of granting asylum and granting nationality is recognized, it is
obvious that a very clear definition of how these rights
are to be construed must be worked out before any state
will be willing legally to enforce them within its own
jurisdiction.

[47] In the Human Rights Drafting Committee, a redraft
of the original secretariat provision (U.N. doc. E/CN.4/21,
July 1, 1947, p. 23, art. 46) was made by Professor Cassin
(ibid., p. 65, art. 44) and approved with minor changes
without any prolonged attempt on the Committee's part
to agree on a definitive version (ibid., p. 81, art. 36). The
Committee referred this draft to the Sub-commission on
the Prevention of Discrimination and the Protection of
Minorities. In the Declaration as submitted by the Commission, both the Drafting Committee's version and the

dividual articles [59] for purposes of emphasis: the over-all limitation clause (article 2) could easily construed to authorize their imposition without tailed enumeration.

COVENANT

The Covenant differs from the Declaration in that it is clearly intended to constitute a legally binding obligation and in that it covers a relatively small number of rights. In addition, in its present form it spells out, where appropriate, specific limitations to each right.[60]

[59] Freedom of movement and choice of residence may limited by laws adopted for security or in general interest (art. 10) ; the right of asylum is not to be granted iminals or those acting against the aims of the United itions (art. 11) ; a similar limitation is placed on United itions protection of stateless persons (art. 15).

[60] The United States stated its preference for having e substantive articles of the covenant expressed without ly limitations but to have a single limiting clause expressed as follows:

"The full exercise of these rights requires recognition of the rights of others and protection by law of the freedom, general welfare and security of all".

This view was agreed to by certain other members (U.N. doc. E/600, Dec. 17, 1947, p. 37, par. 4). The United Kingdom, although strenuously opposing a general over-all limitation clause on the ground that it would render the covenant "innocuous" and bring the United Nations as well as the covenant into discredit (ibid., p. 37, par. 5), sponsored successfully the insertion of an article allowing a state in time of "war or other public emergency' to take measures derogating from its obligations under the covenant "to the extent strictly limited by the exigencies of the situation" (ibid., p. 30, covenant art. 4).

Substantive Rights

The specific rights contained in the Covenant and their limitations may be summarized as follows with cross references to the Declaration articles in parentheses:

SUMMARY OF COVENANT ARTICLES

Article	Right	Right not applicable in case of—
5	Right to life (declaration article 4)...	Proper criminal conviction.
6	Freedom from mutilation or scientific experimentation (no corresponding declaration article).	No exception.
7	Freedom from torture, cruel or inhuman punishment, or indignity (declaration article 7).	No exception.
8	Freedom from slavery or forced labor (declaration article 8, referring to slavery only).	Proper criminal conviction, military service,[61] emergency service, communal service.
9	Right to personal liberty (declaration articles 4 and 5; right to "liberty and security of the person"; freedom from wrongful arrest).	Arrest in proper court proceedings, retention of insane, custody of minors.
	Prompt information of charges in case of arrest (no corresponding declaration provision).	No exception.
	Trial within reasonable time (declaration article 5).	No exception.
	Habeas corpus (declaration article 5).	No exception.
	Compensation for false arrest (no corresponding declaration provision).	No exception.
10	Freedom from imprisonment for debt (no corresponding declaration article).	No exception.

[61] Provision is made for conscientious objectors performing service of a nonmilitary character. A provision that conscientious objectors should be "compensated with adequate maintenance and pay" was defeated (ibid., p. 39).

Article	Right	Right not applicable in case of—
11	Liberty of movement and free choice of residence within state (declaration article 10).	Laws adopted for security or general interest.
	Right to leave country (declaration article 10).	Lawful deprivation of liberty; obligation of military service.
12	Freedom of alien from arbitrary expulsion (no corresponding declaration article).	Illegal entry.
13	Fair hearing in all cases (declaration article 6).	No exception.
	Public trial in criminal cases (declaration article 7).	No exception.
14	Freedom from *ex post facto* laws (with special explanation in regard to war criminals) (declaration article 7).	No exception.
15	Right to juridical personality (declaration article 12, "recognition as a person before the law").	No exception.
16	Freedom of religion (declaration article 16).	Laws protecting public order, welfare, morals, rights of others.
17	Freedom of information and expression [62] (declaration articles 17, 18.)	Publications inciting to alter government by violence, to promote disorder or crime; obscenity; suppression of human rights; publications injurious to fair conduct of legal proceedings; libel; slander; advocacy of national, racial, or religious hostilities inciting to violence. [63]
18	Right of assembly (declaration article 19).	Assembly which is not peaceable. Restrictions may also be imposed to protect life or property; to prevent disorders or obstruction of traffic and free movement of others.
19	Right of association (declaration article 19).	Promotion of interests which are not legitimate or lawful objects.
20	Freedom from discrimination in relation to rights set forth in the Covenant, equal protection against arbitrary discrimination or incitement thereto (declaration article 3).	No exception.

[62] As in the case of Declaration arts. 17 and 18, the Covenant article on freedom of information and expression was taken from the Human Rights Drafting Committee's draft and was not specifically passed on by the Commission. An alternate version suggested by the United States is also printed. The United States version does not contain specific limitations but relies on an over-all limitation clause.

[63] This last limitation is not contained in art. 17; it is set forth separately in art. 21.

(article 31); right to nationality (article 15); right of petition (article 20).[65]

In other words, the Covenant deals exclusively with civil rights whereas the Declaration deals with civil, social and economic, and miscellaneous rights.[66]

It is worthy of note also that the Covenant does not include all civil rights. Even such elementary rights as ownership of property and participation in government have not been included. The reason given for this was that the beginning must be relatively modest; that nations will not be willing to enter into a covenant which contains rights whose definitions vary considerably in different countries. Under the circumstances it is surprising that a majority of the Commission was able to agree on as many rights as are contained in the Covenant; and the possibility must be envisaged that in subsequent re-examination the Covenant may be narrowed rather than broadened in scope.[67]

Responsibilities of States

The undertaking of each state which becomes a party to the Covenant is expressed in article 2: that its laws should secure the enjoyment of the rights set forth in the Covenant; that it should insure that any person whose rights are violated has an effective remedy, enforceable by independent judiciary and supported by police and executive officers. As an instrument ratified by na-

tion. Analysis of the constitutions of member states compiled by the U.N. secretariat at the time of the first meeting of the Human Rights Drafting Committee (U.N. doc. E/CN.4/AC. 1/3/Add. 1, June 11, 1947) makes this point clear. In the case of certain Commission members who expressed more interest in the social and economic rights than in the civil rights, this was one reason for their voting against the proposed Covenant; but these members made no counter-proposal for a covenant dealing with social and economic rights.

[67] The Covenant is to be open to accession by all states (article 23). Provision is made for General Assembly approval in the case of states not members of the U.N. or parties to the International Court of Justice. A U.S. alternative article in the body of the text contains no such limiting provision. It will come into force as soon as two thirds of the U.N. members have acceded to it. The disability of federal-state governments to bind states, provinces, or cantons is recognized in article 24, the wording of which is derived from that successfully worked out in international labor conventions. A special provision is also inserted with respect to colonies and territories (article 25).

tions in accordance with their constitutional processes and containing detailed provisions rather than statements of general principles, it would constitute a legally binding obligation. This obligation extends not only to the passage of laws but to the insurance of their enforcement.

IMPLEMENTATION

Within the lapse of less than two years, the United Nations has made considerable strides in working out the details of a declaration and the substantive articles of a covenant. When it comes to the all-important question of what the United Nations can or should do when a right is violated, a majority of the Human Rights Commission members have been quite unwilling to commit themselves. At the first session of the nuclear commission, the significance of this problem was recognized.[68] At the first session of the full Commission, only three members made formal, specific suggestions for implementation.[69] At the first session of the Human Rights Drafting Committee, these suggestions and two additional suggestions [70] were set forth in an information memorandum produced by the secretariat on request,[71] but no committee action was taken with respect to them.

At the second session of the Human Rights Com-

---

[68] See discussion of nuclear commission session, *supra*.

[69] The U.S. originated the proposal that implementation be accomplished by one or more treaties or conventions (U.N. doc. E/CN.4/4, Jan. 28, 1947). But it did not offer specific suggestions as to what means of implementation should be contained in the conventions. Australia proposed an International Court of Human Rights (U.N. doc. E/CN.4/15, Feb. 5, 1947). India proposed investigation and enforced redress by the Security Council in the case of all violations of human rights (U.N. doc. E/CN.4/11, Jan. 31, 1947, par. V).

[70] Proposals made in the Covenant for consideration of violations by the General Assembly, and obtaining of advisory opinions by the International Court of Justice, suggested by the U.K. (U.N. doc. E/CN.4/21, July 1, 1947, art. 6, p. 32) ; general proposals for protection of rights "by the commonwealth of nations" and the constitution of "an appropriate International organ with a view to ensuring effective observance of those rights" made by France (*ibid.*, annex H, p. 95).

[71] *Ibid.*, annex H.

[72] Of the six members assigned to work on this group, one (the member from Uruguay) was unavoidably detained and did not arrive in time to participate. Another (the Ukrainian member) refused to participate in any

As at present drafted, even without the inclusion of specific articles on implementation along the lines suggested by the Implementation Working Group, it is possible that the Covenant would be considered to have removed the barrier imposed by the Charter's domestic jurisdiction clause.[83] At the very least, one country which has ratified the Covenant might complain, outside of the United Nations, of violations by another country which has ratified the Covenant; and in view of the essentially domestic nature of the Covenant's obligations, this could concern matters within the offending country's domestic jurisdiction. According to the opinion of the Working Group, such complaint could be made in the forum of the United Nations.[84]

It would not seem, however, that any such removal of the barrier would apply to the Declaration.[85] Indeed, the project of having recommendations made as to specific violations of an instrument which is an expression of aspirations and is not binding could present considerable difficulties.[86]

---

of the General Assembly, the Economic and Social Council, and the Commission on Human Rights to make inquiry and recommendation could in such event apply.

[82] U.N. doc. E/600, Dec. 17, 1947, p. 44.

[83] Art. 2, par. 7 of the U.N. Charter provides: "Nothing contained in the present Charter shall authorize the United Nations to intervene in matters which are essentially within the domestic jurisdiction of any state or shall require the Members to submit such matters to settlement under the present Charter; but this principle shall not prejudice the application of enforcement measures under Chapter VII." (Chapter VII deals with Security Council action with respect to threats to the peace, breaches of the peace, and acts of aggression.)

[84] *Ibid.*, pp. 47–53.

[85] See letter of Ernest A. Gross, Legal Adviser to the Secretary of State, to the Attorney General, dated Nov. 4, 1947, regarding *Shelley* v. *Kraemer* (no. 72, U.S. Supreme Court), submitted as an exhibit in the brief of the United States as *amicus curiae;* see also Secretary of State's *Report to the President on the Results of the San Francisco Conference*, Department of State publication 2349, p. 115.

[86] In this connection the question must be considered whether the complaint against South Africa because of its treatment of Indians would have been the proper subject of U.N recommendation had it not been for treaties and clearly international subject matter involved. See proceedings of the General Assembly, first session, second part.

The Commission on Human Rights has produced a Declaration, designed to be a statement of aspirations, that summarizes the civil, social and economic, and other rights which the Commission members felt to be most important. It could be regarded as complete except for a preamble. Whether it will be further expanded, or contracted, whether its emphasis should be on the right of the individual or the right of the state, are among the principal questions facing the Commission and other bodies which will recast it in shape for presentation to the General Assembly.[87]

The Commission has also produced a partial draft of covenant, which is designed to set forth individual rights which member states would be legally bound to observe. The Covenant contains a limited number of civil rights. A principal question to be decided in connection with the Covenant is (as in the case of the Declaration) whether it is to be expanded or contracted.[88] Another question is to what extent failures to comply with the Covenant's provisions shall warrant international action.

In addition the Commission has authorized the circulation of a working paper on implementation, approved by four of its members.

The work on the international bill of human rights [89] has reached the half-way mark. Mem-

---

[87] See discussion of definitive plan for drafting of bill, *supra*.

[88] In this connection attention may be given to the proposal originally made by the United States (U.N. doc. E/CN.4/4) for a series of covenants, which was favorably discussed at the Commission's second session.

Current United Nations Documents: A S

Economic and Social Council

Report of the Activities of the Interim Commission of the World Health Organization in 1947. E/593, January 14, 1948. 26 pp. mimeo.

[1] Printed materials may be secured in the United States from the International Documents Service, Columbia University Press, 2960 Broadway, New York City. Other materials (mimeographed or processed documents) may be consulted at certain designated libraries in the United States.

Sixth Session of the Economic and Social Council

STATEMENT BY WILLARD L. THORP [1]
U.S. Representative to ECOSOC

MR. CHAIRMAN: As you all unhappily know, we have an agenda before us of 45 items, and it is rather difficult to anticipate adequate consideration of all these items in the length of time we will have in the next several weeks.

I think before I discuss particular items I would merely want to make one general observation. On the document each one of these items looks to be of equal importance. I think we should remember that there are some items here which do indicate a rather new opportunity for our work. For the first time we will have an opportunity to discuss together a careful analysis of general economic conditions and trends. Unfortunately, for reasons which we all understand, we have not had a chance to study these documents in advance, but I know as soon as we have them we will all be very much concerned and interested in them. At the same time we have a series of subjects relating to coordination, and we also have the reports of a number of specialized agencies and of commissions and subcommissions. Now these things together mean that we at last have the opportunity which all of us have been anticipating ever since the Council started to undertake the task of reviewing the economic problems, the social problems of the world, reviewing the work of the United Nations and its related agencies, and seeking as best we can to increase the effectiveness and efficiency of the United Nations with respect to these problems. I think the exciting thing about the agenda is hidden away in these small items—small in the number of words on the agenda—and the opportunity to do this task. At the last meeting we were looking forward to the time when we could move toward a consideration of the basic economic conditions in the world and the effectiveness of our own agencies. Apparently that time has come.

With respect to the individual items on the agenda, I should like to divide my remarks into two general groups: first, with respect to the matter of whether certain items should or should not be on the agenda and, secondly, with respect to the sequence of items on the agenda.

With respect to the items that are on the agenda, we see very little that can be done to change the grouping. I would like to comment on item 8. Item 8 is the one entitled "Damage Caused to the Federal People's Republic of Yugoslavia by the Withholding of its Gold Reserves by the United States of America". This is an item which implies that the Economic and Social Council is an agency for resolving disputes between two nations. I shall not discuss in any way the content of this matter, but I should like to say that it is a matter on which negotiation has been taking place between ourselves and Yugoslavia. No resolution has yet been reached of the group of problems of which the item on the agenda is one. The Economic and Social Council has certain functions and powers which are defined in the Charter. There is nothing in the Charter which authorizes the Council to act in an arbitration or a conciliation or a judicial determination. In the Charter you will find all references to the settlement of disputes and situations relating to the work of the Security Council, not relating to the work of the Economic and Social Council. The notion that

[1] Made at the opening session on Feb. 2, 1948, and released to the press by the U.S. Mission to the U.N. on the same date. Mr. Thorp is Assistant Secretary of State for economic affairs.

this agency should become an agency for resolving bilateral economic disputes was certainly not contemplated at San Francisco, and one can find no such indication of a function for us in the Charter. So, for technical grounds, I carefully question the propriety of items of this type appearing on our agenda.

I just should like to speak in a sense for more practical reasons as to why it is somewhat unfortunate to have such items on the agenda. Those of you who have engaged in negotiations are well aware of the fact that your negotiations are made increasingly difficult by the degree to which positions are taken by either Government publicly. In a full discussion of a problem of this sort in public, both Governments involved, I think, will find themselves in a greater difficulty when it comes to ultimately resolving the issue. So, for technical grounds and practical grounds, I regret that this item is on the agenda. However, the United States is a party with respect to this matter. The United States does not wish to take any position which would indicate that it is unwilling to have its acts discussed. We are prepared to discuss the merits of positions taken by our Government, and, therefore, with respect to this item, I shall not oppose its inclusion on the agenda although I do believe that it is most unfortunate to find it there. I cannot take the position of approving it being on the agenda, and, therefore, when we ultimately approve the agenda, Mr. Chairman, I shall ask to be recorded as abstaining with respect to this particular item.

The question has been raised with respect to two items having to do with the specialized agency of Icao. Nothing that I say on this matter should be regarded as indicating the position of the United States Government with respect to these items. But I should like to support the position taken by the representative of the Secretary-General before the Agenda Committee. That position is reported in full on page 7 of the Agenda Committee's report, and it indicates that the Secretary-General holds that the agreement came into force in May 1947 on action taken by the First Assembly of Icao to amend its constitution so as to debar Franco Spain from membership and on the withdrawal of the Spanish Delegation from that Assembly; that the coming into force of the agreement had been reported to the General Assembly at its second regular session, to which no objection

later documentation proves that that is the more appropriate place where it should be included.

Finally, I should like to talk about coordinating items in general. As the agenda comes before us, the fourth group of items from 32 on are grouped together as coordination problems. This agenda is set up this way on the assumption, I believe, that we are virtually going through the entire agenda rather quickly group by group, getting the items into committees for more detailed work. In that case I have no difficulty with this structure. If, on the other hand, we follow the practice which we have had in the past of going on down through the agenda more carefully, I would be inclined to feel that we ought not to leave coordination and its problems to the very end. I agree with the Representative from Australia that emphasis should be put on this point. It should not be incidental; it should be one of our major responsibilities. I am not sure that we ought not to give consideration to coordination problems before we move into the problems of the individual agencies. At any rate, we should have it in mind at that time. While I am not suggesting a change in the agenda with respect to these items, I do suggest that we all keep in mind the fact that we are most concerned ourselves with the problem of coordination and not have it the tail end of our consideration here at our meetings, but have it something that is going along with the substantive consideration of the particular matters before us.

H SESSION OF ECOSOC [1]

Nations Headquarters, Lake Success. Item proposed by the representative of the United Kingdom

8. (31) Damage caused to the Federal People's Republic of Yugoslavia by the withholding of its gold reserves by the United States of America. Item proposed by Yugoslavia

---

[1] Recommendations of the Agenda Committee to the Council subject to reservations and comments contained in section I of the report of the Agenda Committee, U.N. doc. E/631, Jan. 31, 1948.

* Numbers in parentheses represent numbers of items as in U.N. doc. E/607.

Agenda for the Sixth Session of ECOSOC—Continued

9. (new Addition to Article concerning the use of the
item) United Nations "laissez-passer" to the agreement between the United Nations and the
ICAO

10. (15) Report of the second session of the Social Commission

11. (16) Report of the second session of the Population Commission

12. (17) Report of the second session of the Commission on Narcotic Drugs

13. (18) Report of the Permanent Central Opium Board

14. (19) Report of the Executive Board of the International Children's Emergency Fund

15. (20) United Nations Appeal for Children

16. (28) Report by the Secretary-General on the question of the establishment of Research Laboratories of the United Nations

17. (6) Report of the *ad hoc* Committee on the proposal for an Economic Commission for Latin America

18. (7) Question of the establishment of an Economic Commission for the Middle East

19. (5) Report of the Economic Commission for Asia and the Far East

20. (4) Interim report of the Economic Commission for Europe

21. (8) United Nations Scientific Conference on Conservation and Utilization of Resources

22. (3) Surveys of World Economic Conditions and Trends

23. (33) Co-ordinated action to meet the continuing world food crisis. Item proposed by the FAO

24. (10) Report of the second session of the Statistical Commission

25. (new Resolution of the United Nations Trade and
item) Employment Conference at Havana on employment (if accepted and passed by the plenary conference at Havana in time)

26. (12) Report of the second session of the Commission on Human Rights

27. (14) Report of the second session of the Sub-Commission on Freedom of Information and of the Press

28. (34) Survey of forced labour and measures for its abolition. Item proposed by the American Federation of Labor

29. (new Report of the second session of the Commission
item) on the Status of Women

30. (35) Principle of equal pay for equal work for men and women workers. Item proposed by the WFTU

31. (13) Genocide

32. (22) Relations with and co-ordination of specialized agencies

33. (23) Work programmes of Commissions of the Council for 1948 and draft calendar of meetings and conferences in 1948

34. (24) Reports of the specialized agencies

[1] BULLETIN of Jan. 11, 1948, p. 59.

larification of Status of Certain Discussions Within Far Eastern Commission

[Released to the press by the FEC on January 30]

The attention of the Chairman of the Far Eastern Commission has been called to reports recently appearing in the press, purporting to disclose the status of certain discussions within the Commission. In response to numerous queries regarding these reports, which carry inaccurate and totally misleading implications, the Chairman has authorized the following statement.

The Chairman desires to make clear that no member of the Far Eastern Commission has "blocked consideration" of any increase in Commission membership, or of any other proposal.

In regard to the disarmament of Japan, as was explained in the report of the Secretary General released to the press on July 17, 1947,[1] this subject has been under active discussion within the Commission for some months, looking towards the formulation of principles based upon pertinent sections of the Commission's basic policy agreement. In the course of these discussions representatives have from time to time introduced proposals that naturally reflect differing points of view. Here, as with other matters, negotiations have been carried on within the Commission in an effort to arrive at Allied agreement.

The manner in which these negotiations have been conducted over many months has not changed. Personal relations between representatives continue to be courteous and reasonable. Such differences of opinion as have appeared have been, and continue to be, aired in full and friendly fashion. This procedure has not been modified as a result of changes in personnel that have taken place over the course of two years. Its success is attested by the Allied agreements that have thus far been reached on some 46 policy questions.

In his capacity as United States Representative, the Chairman last week presented to the Commission a statement on the economy of Japan which was subsequently made public. In that statement the Chairman had occasion to observe that the United States Government recognizes "that the cooperation of the Far Eastern Commission and its member states is essential to the successful accomplishment of a program for bringing about a self-supporting economy in Japan." American policy toward Japan, political and economic, is directed toward the creation of conditions that make for lasting peace. Cooperation with our Allies through the machinery of the Far Eastern Commission is an essential part of that policy.

U.S. Asks For Resumption of Austrian Treaty Negotiations

[Released to the press February 2]

The Secretary of State has requested the Secretariat of the Council of Foreign Ministers to transmit to the Government of the United Kingdom, the Union of Soviet Socialist Republics, and France the following proposal concerning the resumption of the discussions by the Deputies of the Council of Foreign Ministers on the Austrian treaty:

"The Secretary of State refers to the agreement of the Deputies for the Austrian Treaty in their sixty-third meeting on December 17, 1947, that the United States Deputy, as next Chairman, would indicate within five days of the receipt of the Soviet proposals on German assets in Austria the date of the next meeting of the Deputies which if possible would be held no later than February 1, 1948. The United States Deputy considered that this agreement would permit the various governments sufficient t me prior to the convening of the Deputies to study the Soviet proposals which, as he understood, would be transmitted through the Secretariat of the Council of Foreign Ministers

early in January. The Soviet proposals were received by the United States Government on January 26. The Secretary of State believes that it would be difficult to give proper consideration to the Soviet proposals by the date set by the Deputies in their meeting of December 17. The Secretary of State therefore proposes, with the concurrence of the other governments, that the Deputies meet in London on or about February 20.

"If the other governments see no objection, the United States is prepared to discuss at this meeting the French and Soviet proposals on German assets in Austria, as well as any other proposal designed to solve this problem and the other unagreed Articles in the draft Austrian Treaty."

The Secretary of State has designated Samuel Reber, Deputy Director for European Affairs, Department of State, as Deputy for the Austrian Treaty at the forthcoming meeting.

[1] *Activities of the Far Eastern Commission, Report by the Secretary General*, Feb. 26, 1946–July 10, 1947 (Department of State ppublication 2888).

[Released to the press January 28]

The Secretary of State announced that the President signed on January 28 the Joint Resolution (H. J. Res. 232)[1] authorizing United States membership and participation in the South Pacific Commission. The President also signed the instrument accepting, on behalf of the United States Government, the agreement establishing the South Pacific Commission.[2] Accordingly, the Secretary is taking steps to deposit the instrument of acceptance with the Australian Government, which will in turn notify the other signatory governments of this action.

Purpose. The purpose of the Commission is to provide the means by which governments which administer non-self-governing territories in the South Pacific may cooperate with one another to promote the economic and social advancement of the peoples of these territories. This purpose is in accord with the obligations assumed by the members of the United Nations under chapter XI of the Charter with respect to the non-self-governing territories which they administer, namely, to promote the economic, social, and educational advancement of the inhabitants of these territories, to promote constructive measures of development, to encourage research, and to cooperate with one another with a view to the practical achievement of these objectives. The peoples of the non-self-governing territories in the South Pacific, including those administered by the United States, have common economic and social problems, many of which can be solved more expeditiously and economically through joint research and action by the governments administering them.

The South Pacific Commission, assisted by its auxiliary bodies, will provide machinery for such joint research and action. It will serve primarily as an advisory and consultative body to the participating governments, but it also may, if all the governments agree, take executive action.

Membership. The six member governments of the South Pacific Commission, as envisaged by the agreement signed *ad referendum* at the South Seas conference in Canberra on February 6, 1947, are Australia, France, the Netherlands, New Zealand, the United Kingdom, and the United States. The agreement will enter into force when accepted

---

[1] Public Law 403, 80th Cong., 2d sess., approved Jan. 28, 1948.

[2] For article analyzing the agreement, see BULLETIN of Mar. 16, 1947, p. 459.

the Department of Agriculture to accept a position in private industry. Mr. Dodd is serving as chairman of the Delegation. Other Delegates are Edward G. Cale, Associate Chief, Division of International Resources, Department of State; Leroy K. Smith, Director, Grain Branch, Production and Marketing Administration, Department of Agriculture; and Leslie A. Wheeler, Director, Office of Foreign Agricultural Relations, Department of Agriculture.

The International Wheat Council, composed of major wheat importing and exporting countries, was established in 1942 to administer certain provisions of an interim international wheat agreement and to facilitate the negotiation of a broader agreement following the termination of the war.

THE FOREIGN SERVICE

U.S. and Nepal To Exchange Ministers

[Released to the press February 3]

The United States and the Kingdom of Nepal will shortly enter into formal diplomatic relations by an exchange of Ministers. This important development in United States–Nepalese relations follows the agreement of friendship and commerce entered into by the United States and Nepal on April 25, 1947. The agreement was negotiated in Kathmandu, the capital of Nepal, by a special United States diplomatic mission headed by Joseph C. Satterthwaite. During the visit of this special mission, preliminary arrangements were made for the exchange of diplomatic and consular representatives.

The Government of the Kingdom of Nepal has now designated Commanding General Sir Kaiser Shum Shere Jung Bahadur Rana to be the first Nepalese Minister to the United States. General Kaiser, at present the Nepalese Ambassador to the Court of St. James, will represent his country concurrently in Washington and London with residence in the latter capital. The Nepalese Minister-Designate plans to come to the United States in February to present his credentials to President Truman.

THE DEPARTMENT

Appointment of Officers

Durward V. Sandifer as Deputy Director of the Office of United Nations Affairs, effective February 3, 1948.

THE RECORD OF THE WEEK

Violations of Treaty of Peace by Rumania

LETTER FROM THE UNITED STATES MINISTER TO RUMANIA TO THE RUMANIAN MINISTRY OF FOREIGN AFFAIRS

[Released to the press February 4]

Rudolf E. Schoenfeld, United States Minister to Rumania, transmitted the following note to the Rumanian Ministry of Foreign Affairs on Monday, February 2, 1948. Copies of this note, which sets forth violations of the treaty of peace by Rumania, have been communicated to the British and Soviet Chiefs of Mission in Bucharest with a request for their respective comments

The United States, pursuant to the principles for which it stands, in consequence of its undertakings at Yalta with the Union of Soviet Socialist Republics and the United Kingdom, and by virtue of its joint responsibilities with these Powers as a member of the Rumanian Armistice Commission, has striven constantly since the withdrawal of Rumania from the war against the Allies to assist the Rumanian people in obtaining a broadly representative and responsive Government which would secure for them their basic rights and fundamental freedoms.

The United States together with the Union of Soviet Socialist Republics and United Kingdom agreed at the Moscow Conference of Foreign Ministers in December 1945 to assist in a broadening of the Rumanian Government and in obtaining guarantees of such civil liberties. In January 1946, in compliance with the Moscow Agreement, representatives of the National Peasant and National Liberal Parties were included in the Rumanian Government. The Rumanian Council of Ministers thereupon made a solemn written declaration that free general elections would be held in the shortest possible time, on the basis of universal suffrage and secret ballot, in which all democratic and anti-Fascist parties would have a right to participate and to present candidates. Likewise, the declaration of the Rumanian Government pledged that freedom of the press, speech, religion and assembly would be assured. In an oral amplification of this declaration, the President of the Rumanian Council of Ministers, Petru Groza, made explicit the application of these assurances to all the parties represented in the reorganized Government, thereby acknowledging the National Peasant Party headed by Mr. Iuliu Maniu, the National Liberal Party led by Mr. Constantin Bratianu, and the

Social Democratic Party under the direction of Mr. Constantin Petrescu as democratic and anti-Fascist.

The Rumanian Premier also gave explicit assurances that these parties would be entitled (1) to participate in the elections and to put forward candidates, (2) to have representatives present for the examination of the balloting procedure and the counting of the ballots, (3) to be accorded equitable broadcasting facilities for the presentation of their political views, (4) to have equal opportunity to print and distribute their own newspapers and political publications and to obtain newsprint on a fair and equitable basis, (5) to organize associations, to hold meetings and to be allowed premises for this purpose, and (6) to be consulted by the Council of Ministers in order to reach agreement concerning the assured freedoms of press and speech as well as on the drafting of an electoral law and on the conduct of the elections.

However, notwithstanding the categorical nature of these international commitments the Rumanian Government undertook at once to subvert them, and throughout 1946 steadily violated their spirit and letter. All manner of chicanery, and extreme physical violence was employed by or with the consent of the Rumanian Government to reduce the legitimate political activity of any elements not subservient to the controlling minority. Every one of the assurances given was either ignored or sabotaged. The representatives of the Peasant and Liberal Parties were effectively excluded from decisions of the Government and from any real voice in the preparation of the elections. Broadcasting facilities were wholly denied to all but the minority Government bloc. Through the inequitable distribution of newsprint, the denial of freedom to print, publish and distribute and by various other artifices and official censorship, the legitimate opposition press was relegated to a point of virtual extinction. Party meetings of the opposition were prevented by violence. Government officials, employing compulsion and forgery, wrested the control of the Social Democratic Party from the majority of its members.

During nine months which preceded the general elections, numerous eligible candidates were disbarred from participation and large sections of the

devotion to democratic ideals over a period of many years and whose struggle for civil liberties in Rumania are well known.

Reports reaching the United States Government over a period of several months demonstrated convincingly that the political prisoners apprehended as a result of the mass arrests in Rumania were being subjected by the Rumanian authorities not only to physical conditions of starvation and disease but in some instances to methods designed to extract "confessions" in anticipation of forthcoming trials. The United States Government in a public statement on August 15, 1947 [2] took note of this inhuman treatment of Rumanian political prisoners and the methods employed to predetermine their conviction—methods which had already been clearly revealed by the Rumanian mass trials of allegedly subversive organizations which had taken place in November 1946.

On September 15, 1947 the Treaty of Peace with Rumania came into force with its consequent obligation upon the Rumanian Government to secure the specified rights and freedoms to all people under its jurisdiction. Nevertheless, in October and November 1947, the Rumanian authorities tried, convicted and sentenced for treason Mr. Iuliu Maniu and other members of the National Peasant Party of Rumania. The transparent political motivation of this "judicial process" was manifest. The recent threats by the Rumanian authorities against the National Liberal and Independent Socialist Parties, which have been reduced to impotence, give further evidence of the Rumanian Government's intent to wipe out the last vestiges of democratic opposition in Rumania.

By its actions over a period of almost three years since March 1945, the Rumanian Government placed the legitimate and patriotic opposition elements in Rumania in a position of seeming to constitute a clandestine, subversive movement. Activities on their part to bring about, through constitutional means, a democratic alteration in the Government of Rumania so that it might be broadly representative of the Rumanian people were construed as subversive and treasonable. Associations or communications about Rumanian conditions with two of the Powers which had rights and responsibilities in Rumania by virtue of the Yalta, Potsdam, and Moscow Agreements, the Rumanian Armistice and the Rumanian Peace treaty, were made to appear as conspiracy.

The trial of Mr. Maniu and his co-defendants, which was concluded on November 11, 1947, itself was specifically prejudiced in the following respects which, by generally recognized standards of civilized procedure, precluded the free exercise of justice:

---

[1] TIAS 1649 (Department of State publication 2969).
[2] BULLETIN of Aug. 17, 1947, p. 329.

1) The possibility of an impartial trial was excluded by the appointment of a presiding judge known to be thoroughly compromised by improper acts as a military judge during the recent war and lacking in judicial integrity.

2) The defendants were effectively deprived of their right to be represented by counsel of their own choice which, except for intimidation, might have been available.

3) defense of the accused by the appointed counsel was inadequate, despite an apparently spirited summation in the single instance of Maniu.

4) Excessive restrictions were placed upon the preparation of the defense, on the testimony of the defendants and on the interrogation of state witnesses by or for the defendants.

5) A violent campaign of excitation against the defendants was conducted before and during the trial through the officially controlled press, labor, professional and Government organizations, which not only had the effect of intimidating w nesses and influencing the judges but which al by its scope and nature revealed that it was i spired, directed and assisted by the Rumani. Government for the evident purpose of supportir a pre-arranged verdict.

Aside from the lack of validity of a trial carri out under such conditions, the prosecution failed substantiate the charges of treasonable activiti upon which the defendants were found guilty, evidence other than that of highly questional "confessions" which had been drawn from certa defendants following their arrest.

The United States Government considers it n essary to state that in its view the actions of t Rumanian Government recited in this note ma it clear that there have not existed, and do n now exist in Rumania those human rights a fundamental freedoms which the Rumanian G ernment is obligated by the Treaty of Peace secure to all persons under its jurisdiction.

Visits of U. S. Naval Vessels to Italian Ports

EXCHANGE OF NOTES BETWEEN THE UNITED STATES AND THE U.S.S.R.

[Released to the press February 2]

January 28, 1948.

Sɪʀ:

In recent months the Italian press has repeatedly reported the presence of naval vessels of the United States of America in the ports of Taranto, Leghorn, Genoa, Spezia, Venice, and Naples. In January 1948 reports also appeared in the American and Italian press that the military authorities of the U.S.A. dispatched on these vessels sizable units of American Marines. These reports were later confirmed by statements of official representatives of the Government and Military Command of the U.S.A., according to which units of American Marines were dispatched on naval vessels of the U.S.A. in the Mediterranean Sea allegedly for the purpose of conducting training exercises.

According to information at the disposal of the Soviet Government, the reports mentioned by the foreign press concerning the presence of naval vessels of the U.S.A. in Italian ports and in the territorial waters of Italy correspond to the facts.

Whereas, under Paragraph 1, Article 73, of the Treaty of Peace with Italy, all armed forces of the Allied and Associated Powers should have be withdrawn from Italy by December 15, 1947, te continued presence of the naval forces of te U.S.A. in Italian ports and in the territorial wat's of Italy after this date constitutes a violation f the reference provision of the Treaty of Peace ad should not take place. The Soviet Governmt expects that the Government of the U.S.A. wl adopt measures without delay toward the elimi: tion of the reference violation of the Treaty f Peace.

The Soviet Government is forwarding sim taneously to the French Government a copy the present note with the request that it bringt to the attention of the Allied and Associad Powers which signed the Treaty of Peace wh Italy.

A. Panyushkin
Ambassador of the USSR to the USₐ

The Secretary of State,
  George C. Marshall,
    Department of State,
    Washington.

This is the first comprehensive commercial treaty concluded by the United States with a European country since 1934, and the first treaty of its type signed by Italy since the conclusion of peace. It replaces the treaty of commerce and navigation concluded with Italy in 1871, following the unification of that country. The former treaty was terminated December 15, 1937, by mutual agreement, but efforts to work out a more modern and comprehensive treaty at that time proved unsuccessful.

The treaty, which is based in general upon the principle of mutuality, establishes standards to govern relations between the two countries in many fields of activity. It includes articles relating to the status and activities of persons and corporations, protection of persons and property, landholding, freedom of information, treatment of vessels, commercial principles comparable to those in the proposed charter for an International Trade Organization, and provisions concerning such matters as exchange control, transit, industrial property, et cetera.

Preliminary conversations on the treaty were held in the Department with the Italian Financial and Economic Delegation, which was headed by Mr. Lombardo, in May and June of 1947, while formal negotiations were opened in Rome on September 16.

For the text of the treaty, see Department of State press release 77 of February 2, 1948.

Indictment of Dimiter Gitchev in Bulgaria

[Released to the press February 6]

In response to press inquiry concerning reports from Sofia in respect to forthcoming trial of Dimiter Gitchev, the Department of State made the following comment

The Department has received reports from the American Legation at Sofia concerning the indictment, calling for the death penalty or life imprisonment which has been brought against Dimiter Gitchev, prominent Agrarian opposition leader. Mr. Gitchev has a long and impressive record as a defender of democratic principles in Bulgaria.

Viewed against the background of the present Bulgarian regime's past and current record and recent statements by Bulgarian officials, the charges against Mr. Gitchev and the preparation for his trial, resemble so closely the case of Nikola Petkov as to suggest strongly the Bulgarian Government's intention again to disregard its treaty obligations with respect to securing to its citizens the most basic human rights.

Use of Mellaha Airfield by the U.S. Air Force

EXCHANGE OF NOTES BETWEEN THE UNITED STATES AND THE U.S.S.R.

[Released to the press February 3]

January 21, 1948.

SIR:

Upon instructions of the Soviet Government I have the honor to communicate to you as follows.

In recent days reports were published in the press of Great Britain and the U.S.A. to the effect that the Government of Great Britain agreed to place at the disposal of the Government of the United States an air base at Mellaha, Tripolitania. These reports were confirmed on January 14 of this year by official representatives of the Ministry of Foreign Affairs of Great Britain and of the Department of State of the U.S.A.

The Soviet Government calls your attention to the fact that the conclusion of a separate Anglo-American agreement on the creation of a military air base of the United States in a former Italian colony under provisional British administration contradicts the peace treaty with Italy and in particular Annex XI to the treaty entitled "Joint Declaration of the Governments of the Soviet Union, the United Kingdom, the United States of America and France Concerning Italian Territorial Possessions in Africa", on the strength of which the Soviet Government can not recognize the agreement mentioned as having legal force.

Accept [etc.]

A. PANYUSHKIN
Ambassador of the USSR to the USA

The Acting Secretary of State,
Mr. ROBERT A. LOVETT
Department of State, Washington, D.C.

February 3, 1948.

EXCELLENCY:

I have the honor to refer to your Excellency's Note No. 13 of January 21, 1948 regarding the airfield at Mellaha, Tripolitania.

The Government of the United States wishes to point out that the continuation of the arrangement with regard to the use of Mellaha Airfield by the United States Air Force for communications purposes extends only for the period during which the present administration remains responsible for the territory. In the circumstances, the Government

---

[1] BULLETIN of Apr. 7, 1946, p. 587.

of the United States does not consider that such an arrangement is in any way inconsistent with the provisions of Annex XI or any provision of the Treaty of Peace with Italy.

Accept [etc.] ROBERT A. LOVETT

His Excellency
ALEXANDER SEMENOVICH PANYUSHKIN,
*Ambassador of the Union of
Soviet Socialist Republics.*

Air Agreements Signed

Air Transport Agreement With Italy

[Released to the press February 6]

The Department of State announced on February 6 the conclusion of a bilateral air-transport agreement between the United States of America and Italy which was signed in Rome on February 6, 1948, at 12 noon by duly appointed representatives of the respective Governments.

The agreement closely adheres to the so-called Bermuda principles incorporated in the agreement consummated by the United States and the United Kingdom at Bermuda on February 11, 1946,[1] and provides for the exchange of full fifth-freedom rights by designated air carriers of the two countries. It is the twenty-third formal bilateral air transport agreement signed by the United States in accordance with the Bermuda pattern which since its inception, has been widely accepted as the most satisfactory formula for the orderly development of international civil aviation based upon reciprocal rights and the broadest possible freedom consistent with national security and sound economic principles.

The agreement further signifies the desire of Italy to take its place in the ranks of countries which recognize the importance of the fullest development of international civil aviation and to contribute, through its international airlines, to the creation and preservation of friendship and understanding among the nations and peoples of the world.

The text of the agreement will be released in full at a later date.

DEAR SENATOR GURNEY:

I refer to your letter of January 14, 1948 requesting that the Committee on Armed Services be informed of further steps which the Department of State contemplates taking with respect to the horses claimed by the Hungarian Government.

The Department of State and the Department of the Army have agreed that the horses in question will not be returned to Hungary but will be retained by the Army as property of the United States. The two Departments concur in the conclusion of the Committee that this Government has a legal right to retain the horses. The desirability of so doing for reasons of national interest has been brought out by new evidence adduced at the hearings of your Subcommittee. This result has adequate basis in Article 32 of the Treaty of Peace with Hungary, by which Hungary waived all claims against the United States arising out of the purported exercise of belligerent rights.

I am glad that the Department of State is able to reach a conclusion on this subject compatible with the views of the Committee on Armed Services, and I wish to state that the Department appreciates the courtesy with which the hearings were conducted by the Chairman of the Subcommittee, Senator Morse.

Sincerely yours,

ROBERT A. LOVETT
Under Secretary of State

The Department of the Army has written a similar letter to Senator Gurney indicating its agreement with this decision.

rom French,

ferred to other Governments, namely, France, Belgium, and Luxembourg, this Government, as the Committee is aware, has assumed an active and continuing interest in their repatriation. As a result of an approach made by this Government early in December 1946 to the three Governments concerned, all such prisoners of war transferred to Luxembourg and Belgium have been released, and in France substantial numbers have been released and repatriated under the agreed program which has been in operation since last March. As the Committee was accorded special status in supervising the repatriation program in the latter country, I know that you are fully aware of the progress which has been made, as well as the practical difficulties which have been encountered in implementing the program.

"It is my sincere hope that all Governments still

---

[1] Not printed.

holding prisoners of war will find it possible to act favorably on the Committee's humanitarian appeal." [1]

The agreement with the French Government referred to above provided for the release of these men by two means: (1) repatriation at the rate of 20,000 a month and (2) release in France as free workers of those voluntarily choosing to remain. The program initiated by this agreement was made applicable to all German prisoners of war in French custody, including those captured by French forces as well as those transferred by this Government. Information just received in the Department from official French sources indicates that the number of German prisoners of war in French custody, as of January 1, has been reduced to 301,440. Between March 14 and December 31, 1947, a total of 278,006 were released from prisoner-of-war status. Of the total number released during this period 181,645 were repatriated while 96,361 were transferred to free-worker status. In this latter category there are an additional 43,700 now being processed for release. Some reduction in the total number held has also occurred as a result of escapes. The minimum rate of repatriation has been increased to 25,000 per month.

The Department of State, through the American Embassy at Paris, is maintaining an active interest in this matter and will continue to do so

American Ambassador to Venezuela to A

of Venezuelan President-Elect

[Released to the press February 2]

The Government of the United States of Venezuela has invited this Government to be specially represented at the inauguration ceremonies of the President-elect of Venezuela, Señor Don Rómulo Gallegos, which will be held at Caracas February 13 to 18. The inauguration will be on February 15.

The President has designated Walter J. Donnelly, the American Ambassador to Venezuela, as his personal representative with the rank of special Ambassador to the inauguration of President-elect Gallegos. Ambassador Donnelly will be accompanied, as members of the United States Delegation, by Archibald MacLeish with the rank of Minister; Lt. Gen. Willis D. Crittenberger, Commanding General of the Caribbean Defense Command; Vice Adm. Daniel E. Barbey, Commandant, Tenth U.S. Naval District; John Willard Carrigan, First Secretary of the American Embassy at

[1] Signed by Robert A. Lovett on behalf of the United States Government.

EORGE V. ALLEN [1]

bassador to Iran

We are interested in two things. In the first place, we hope that Iran will spend what funds it has to the best possible advantage for Iran itself, because we are anxious for Iran to become strong and to remain independent. Our second and more important interest is that Iran should remain entirely free to make its own choice in this matter, unhampered by threats and menaces.

I recognize fully that an entirely honest division of opinion may exist among Iranians both as regards what military supplies you need and whether you desire American advisers. Whatever your decision may be, it will not affect in any way the friendly relations between Iran and the United States.

The communication which your Government has just received disturbs the calm atmosphere in which you will need to consider these important questions. I am confident that no self-respecting and patriotic Iranian will be deterred by this communication from doing his duty as he considers best. The allegations in the note are so clearly false that they do not require consideration in detail. I would merely ask: where are the plans for an American airport at Qum, where are the American storage tanks in southern Iran, the barracks being prepared for American troops, or any other of the things alleged in the note?

I am reminded in this connection that history repeats itself. There is considerable essential similarity between the present communication which your Government has received and one which was delivered to you in 1912 when Morgan Shuster was exerting every effort to assist Iran to become strong and independent of foreign domination. Fortunately, however, the world situation is vastly different today from what it was in 1912. Iran and all other independent countries of the world today are bound together in a world organization based on equality and respect for their sovereign independence. The entire structure of the United Nations is built on the principle that no nation shall any longer have to stand alone as Iran did when it received the 1912 note.

I regret sincerely the injection of foreign interference in the question now before the Majlis, and I hope the deputies will consider the matter with appropriate calmness and dignity. The only important consideration is that the decision, whatever it may be, should be a free Iranian decision.

---

[1] Delivered before the Tehran Press Club in Tehran on Feb. 4 and released to the press in Washington on Feb. 5, 1948.

*Contributors*

James P. Hendrick, author of the article on an international bill of
human rights, is Acting Associate Chief of the Division of International Organization Affairs, Office of United Nations Affairs, Department of State. He has served as adviser to Mrs. Franklin D. Roosevelt, United States Member of the Commission on Human Rights, at
all sessions of the Commission, and of its Drafting Committee.

The Department of State bulletin

VOL. XVIII, No. 451 • PUBLICATION 3061

February 22, 1948

For sale by the Superintendent of Documents
U.S. Government Printing Office
Washington 25, D.C.

SUBSCRIPTION:
52 issues, $5; single copy, 15 cents

Published with the approval of the
Director of the Bureau of the Budget

The Department of State BULLETIN, a weekly publication compiled and edited in the Division of Publications, Office of Public Affairs, provides the public and interested agencies of the Government with information on developments in the field of foreign relations and on the work of the Department of State and the Foreign Service. The BULLETIN includes press releases on foreign policy issued by the White House and the Department, and statements and addresses made by the President and by the Secretary of State and other officers of the Department, as well as special articles on various phases of international affairs and the functions of the Department. Information is included concerning treaties and international agreements to which the United States is or may become a party and treaties of general international interest.

Publications of the Department, as well as legislative material in the field of international relations, are listed currently.

ULES FOR ACCOUNTING FOR GERMAN ASSETS IN COUNTRIES IEMBERS OF THE INTER-ALLIED REPARATION AGENCY

By James Simsarian

Agreement was reached at the Inter-Allied eparation Agency in Brussels on November 21,)47, with respect to the German assets in the)untries members of this Agency [1] which should } accounted for by them as German reparations nder article 6A of the Paris reparation agree- ent.[2] Article 6A of the Paris agreement pro- des that each IARA country shall "hold or spose of German enemy assets within its juris- iction in manners designed to preclude their turn to German ownership or control and shall arge against its reparation share such assets" et of certain deductions permitted. This pro- ision stems from the decision made at Potsdam lat "appropriate German external assets" should a one of the sources for reparations from ermany.

Rules relating to the German assets which should a accounted for by IARA countries were drafted nd recommended by the Committee of Experts on nemy Property Custodianship of the Inter- llied Reparation Agency as the result of meetings f the Committee in October 1946 and from July , 1947, to September 13, 1947. The rules recom-

mended by the Committee of Experts were changed in only minor respects by the IARA Com- mittee on German External Assets and adopted by the Assembly of IARA on November 21, 1947.[3]

The accounting rules are divided into eight parts. Part I of the rules defines Germany as the territory within the boundaries of that country as of December 31, 1937.

Under part II of the rules, each IARA country must, as a minimum, account for all assets within its jurisdiction which on January 24, 1946 (the date of the coming into force of the Paris repara- tion agreement), were owned by any of the follow- ing, subject to certain exceptions provided in other parts of the rules:

1. The German state, Government, municipal and other public authorities and organizations, and the German Nazi Party;

2. An individual who had German nationality on January 24, 1946, and who on that date was physically inside Germany or had his residence in Germany;

3. An individual who, as a German national,

---

[1] The 18 countries members of the Inter-Allied Repara- on Agency are Albania, Australia, Belgium, Canada, zechoslovakia, Denmark, Egypt, France, Greece, India, uxembourg, Netherlands, New Zealand, Norway, Union ! South Africa, United Kingdom, United States, and ugoslavia. Russell H. Dorr is U.S. Minister and Dele- ate to the Inter-Allied Reparation Agency.

[2] For the text of the Paris reparation agreement of an. 24, 1946, see Treaties and Other International Acts eries 1655.

[3] The proposal of the Committee of Experts that the ales adopted relate solely to the question of what German ssets should be accounted for and not to the question f what are or are not "German enemy assets" under the aris reparation agreement was accepted by the Assembly

of IARA. It was agreed that the latter question would be considered separately at another time if necessary. Ac- cordingly, the adoption of these rules does not necessitate any change in the provisions of the U.S. Trading with the Enemy Act. Approval was given by the IARA Assembly to the explanation that the rules are designed to present an expeditious arrangement for accounting for German assets in IARA countries under the Paris reparation agree- ment and are without prejudice to any other issues which may arise between countries.

It was also decided by the IARA Assembly that separate consideration will be given at IARA to accounting problems relating to German railway rolling stock and other means of transport and that in the meanwhile the accounting rules adopted Nov. 21, 1947, would not be applicable to these assets.

has been compulsorily repatriated to Germany since January 24, 1946, or is intended to be compulsorily repatriated to Germany;

4. A corporation organized in Germany. If, however, there are non-German`interests in the corporation, an IARA country need not account for assets of the corporation to the extent that the assets proportionate to the non-German interests in the corporation are released to the non-German interests. This provision is consistent with part IV of the agreement relating to the resolution of conflicting claims to German enemy assets, which was recently signed in Brussels by Belgium, Canada, the Netherlands, and the United States.[4]

In addition to the above minimum to be accounted for, each IARA country must also account for all assets within its jurisdiction which have been seized because of a German interest in the assets and are not intended to be released, provided that:

1. These assets were owned directly or indirectly on January 24, 1946, by an individual other than those described above who had German nationality, or by a corporation in which there has been a German interest, at any time between the date on which the IARA country was occupied or annexed by or entered World War II against Germany and January 24, 1946; or

2. The assets were owned directly or indirectly by an individual of German nationality who died before January 24, 1946.

Accordingly, in general, although an IARA country must account for assets in its country owned by all Germans residing in Germany, the IARA country need not account for the assets of a German residing outside Germany unless the IARA country seizes and does not intend to release the assets of such a German. The term "seized" is

---

[4] For text of this agreement see BULLETIN of Jan. 4, 1948, p. 6. The agreement was signed on Dec. 5, 1947, by Canada, the Netherlands, and the United States, and on Jan. 5, 1948, by Belgium. The agreement was signed on behalf of the United States subject to the approval of Congress. It has not as yet come into force.

Under part IV of the agreement, if nonenemy nationals of parties to the agreement own at least 25 percent of the shares in or control the corporation organized in Germany, the assets in the IARA country of the corporation will be released to the extent of the interests in the corporation of all nonenemy nationals of parties.

[5] For text of the London patent accord on German-owned patents, see BULLETIN of Aug. 18, 1946, p. 300.

governments with which they are at war or which belong or have belonged, to persons, including juridical persons, resident in such territories." It was pointed out in the Declaration that "This warning applies whether such transfers or dealings have taken the form of open looting or plunder, or of transactions apparently legal in form, even when they purport to be voluntarily effected."

Although there were many instances of direct looting by the Germans, when force or duress was applied directly to the owner of an asset, there was a great deal of plundering of the economy of the occupied countries by indirect looting as well. By obliging the occupied countries to accept chronically unfavorable clearing balances between themselves and Germany and by levying exorbitant occupation costs, the Germans obtained almost limitless amounts of purchasing power, which were used to purchase assets without the necessity of intimidating the seller. The seller received payment in local currency and frequently did not know that the assets were sold to a German. Through this process, the exchequer and the national economy of the occupied countries were indirectly looted. The billions of Reichsmarks poured by Germany into the occupied countries in exchange for local currency were, in general, useless to the occupied countries, since imports from Germany for these Reichsmarks were generally unavailable to replace the vast amounts of property purchased in the occupied countries by the Germans.

Accordingly, part VI of the accounting rules adopted by IARA provides in general that an IARA country need not account for any assets acquired by a German after the invasion or annexation of territory of that country by Germany. This rule was adopted because of the widespread character of direct and indirect looting by Germans in the occupied countries. It was agreed, however, that assets brought into an IARA country by a German during the occupation should be accounted for by the IARA country. For example, if assets, such as machinery, were exchanged by a German with a national of the Netherlands dur-

[6] Union of South Africa, United States, Australia, Belgium, Canada, China, Czechoslovakia, United Kingdom, U.S.S.R., Greece, India, Luxembourg, Netherlands, New Zealand, Norway, Poland, Yugoslavia. For complete text of declaration see BULLETIN of Jan. 9, 1943, p. 21.

.ing the occupation of the Netherlands for a house owned by the latter, the Netherlands would account for the value of the machinery as the consideration for the house and not account for the house itself.

Part VII provides that an IARA country may deduct from the value of assets to be accounted for any sum which it has paid or intends to pay in the following categories:

1. Accrued taxes.
2. Liens.
3. Expenses of administration already incurred.
4. *In rem* charges against specific assets.
5. Unsecured legitimate contract claims against the German former owner of assets,[7] provided that these have been paid or are to be paid in accordance with laws or administrative rules of the IARA country already in force and provided also that the claims are:

(a) Those of nationals or residents of the IARA country within whose jurisdiction the assets are situated;

(b) Filed with the IARA country before January 24, 1949, or within two years after the vesting, sequestration, or confiscation of the assets involved; and

(c) In respect of contracts entered into at the time the creditor was resident in the IARA country.

These provisions relating to deductions conform closely to the language of article 6A of the Paris reparation agreement,[8] except that the three conditions specified above (a, b, and c) were added to the provision relating to deductions with respect to unsecured legitimate contract claims.

Part VIII provides in general that assets which are under judicial proceedings or are expected to come under judicial proceedings shall be accounted for on the basis of 50 percent of their value until the judicial proceedings are resolved. It did not seem reasonable to require an IARA country to ac-

---

[7] The following illustrates how the deductions with respect to unsecured legitimate contract claims will be applicable: If "A", a national of an IARA country, is owed an unsecured debt by "B", a German in Germany, and the IARA country vests the assets in that country of "B", the IARA country may deduct for the debt claims of "A" which are satisfied out of the assets of "B", even though "A" does not hold a mortgage or lien against these assets of "B". If the IARA country pays the claim of "A", the IARA country would then account to IARA for the value of "B's" assets, less the claim paid to "A". The IARA coun-

urvival of Democracy Dependent on Success of ERP

ADDRESS BY GEORGE C. MARSHALL [1]
Secretary of State

The people in the United States face the greatest ecision in our history. It will have a profound id far-reaching effect on the whole world. Like ll momentous decisions, once made it cannot be ltered. There will be no opportunity for a second uess. The vital decision we are now called upon make with respect to our foreign policy is being ade in the American way. But the danger in his procedure is that we become so preoccupied rith the details that we lose sight of the great ob- ctives of the European Recovery Program.

So much has been said and printed during the ast two months regarding the program that there confusion in the minds of many people about it. uring the hearings before congressional com- iittees, every aspect and detail of the program ave been subjected to analysis. Views not only of he members of the Administration, but also a reat many private individuals from every walk f life—business, agriculture, and labor—have een heard.

It is necessary that Congress should require ustification in complete detail for the amount sked to carry out the program. The discussions ave related to work sheets which are the product f months of study by a highly selected group of eople in and out of government—industrialists, ankers, economists, and businessmen, as well as he Harriman, Krug, and Nourse committees. But he European Recovery Program is far more than mere economic transaction. It represents a tre- nendous effort for constructive leadership. If dopted, it will rank, I think, as one of the great istoric undertakings in the annals of world ivilization.

Therefore, I shall not discuss the details of the nancial, administrative, or economic factors of he program. What I wish to make clear as crystal the great objective of the program and its rela- tionship to the future of the world and this country of ours. Make no mistake, the consequences of its success or failure will determine the survival of the kind of a world in which democracy, individ- ual liberty, economic stability, and peace can be maintained.

The United States and the western democracies have been seeking to bring the postwar crisis to an end as quickly as possible. The Soviet Union and their Communist allies have been seeking to ex- ploit the crisis so as to gain a controlling influence over all of Europe.

As I stated on my return from London, I felt that there must be a decided change in the situa- tion before we would have a basis for a genuine settlement with the Soviet Union. I meant that if a stable and healthy western Europe can be real- ized the Soviet leaders being supreme realists would be much more inclined to reach a settlement on the terms for a peace treaty.

We in this country still have the priceless free- dom of a choice in our foreign relations. We can still decide for ourselves what we should do and not have it decided for us by the march of events or by the dictation of others. But, in my opinion, we are quite literally at the crossroads. The decision we must now make will set the course of history for a long time to come and our own destiny for a distant future.

There are two roads the United States can take at this juncture. We can decide that the difficulties and the risks of this program are too great and therefore to do nothing. We can attempt to meet the situation grudgingly by halfhearted and in- adequate assistance. This in effect would be the equivalent of doing nothing in so far as the result

[1] Delivered by telephone to the National Farm Institute at Des Moines, Iowa, on Feb. 13, 1948, and released to the press on the same date.

is concerned, but at great expense. But even more tragic than the material effect would be the psychological impact of a default in American leadership. If we take such a decision, I think we must expect to see this very vital area of the world—western Europe, its industrial potential, its skills, and its energy—pass under the same control which is now exercised over the satellite nations of eastern Europe. The process would not be the same in each country. It would be faster in some and slower in others, but the pattern and the end result, I believe, would be the same. Under such conditions free institutions would not long survive on the European Continent.

Even if this process halted at the shores of the Atlantic, its impact would be deplorable upon the areas surrounding the European Continent. Geography alone would mean that the Middle East and the entire Mediterranean area would be directly and similarly affected. The position of the British Isles and the whole structure of the British Commonwealth, which has exerted a profound influence on the stability of the world and world trade, would be critically affected. The Continent of Europe with its vast aggregation of resources, manpower, and industrial potential would eventually pass under the control of a system which is plainly antagonistic to our way of government and of life.

After the complete failure of the Moscow conference, and the developments of the succeeding months, I recognized that this Government was faced with but two choices. It could stand aloof, as I have just explained, from the rapidly approaching debacle in western Europe. Or, this Government in its commanding position of acknowledged leadership in the world could take some positive action to save the situation. The negative procedure of the past which had led us into two terrible wars was no longer tolerable.

But it was clearly apparent that our Government would lack an effective basis for its action unless the countries concerned on their own initiative should pledge themselves to a coordinated, outstanding effort to rebuild their economic situation; therefore, my suggestion on June 5 last and the quick response of the 16 European nations which were willing to take the necessary concerted action.

Every nation in Europe was included in the suggestion. I need not go into the reason why a certain group held aloof. But I must emphasize

item are China Aid, Greek-Turkish Military Aid,
Army Request for Japanese-Korean Reconstruction, Inter-American Military Cooperation and
Trieste Aid. Work on the China program has
progressed sufficiently so that I can indicate the
probable amount of the request for this program
at about $570 million though I should like to em-
phasize that this does not represent an official request approved by the President. As to the other
programs mentioned, I cannot yet give you an estimated breakdown but, as indicated, my best present
judgment is that they will total slightly under $500
million. I shall, of course, be glad to furnish more
detailed and definite figures later when I am in a
position to do so.

    I trust this information will be helpful to you.

        Sincerely yours,

                LEWIS W. DOUGLAS

Preparation of Draft Bill on
ERP Legislation

             [Released to the press February 13]

    With respect to the request earlier made to us
in January for estimates of the dates on which
some working draft of the American European
Recovery Program legislation would be ready,
John D. Hickerson, Director, Office of European
Affairs, advised the British and French Ambassadors last Tuesday that the indications were that
the hearings in the Senate Foreign Relations Committee were drawing to a close and that it seemed
appropriate for them to plan on the basis that a
preliminary draft bill, indicating one aspect of
congressional thought, might be ready by the end
of this month.

Supply and Shipping Goal for $522,000,00(

The Department of State announced on February 10 a target supply and shipping prospectus for the $522,000,000 United States foreign aid program to France, Austria, and Italy.[1]

The prospectus, outlining a commodity and dollar breakdown of total projected procurement and costs for each country, allots $284,000,000 to France, $57,000,000 to Austria, and $181,000,000 to Italy.

Some adjustments may have to be made within the over-all target amounts as the program progresses.

French Program

The French target program, including partial programs previously approved in amount of $119,-819,000 under dates December 23, January 9, and January 29, is shown in table I.

TABLE I.

Product	Quantity (long tons)	Estimated freight at ship side cost ($000)	Estimated shipping cost ($000)	Estimated freight at ship-side and shipping cost ($000)
Food				
Cereals	775, 673	$93, 792	$7, 782	$101, 574
Fats and oils	[1] 63, 636	20, 000	(²)	20, 000
Dairy products	6, 013	3, 500	(²)	3, 500
Potatoes	35, 000	450	525	975
Dried fruit (prunes)	5, 000	785	150	935
Dried eggs	200	179	8	187
Coal				
U.S.	3, 800, 000	40, 280	38, 000	78, 280
Ruhr	1, 000, 000	. . . . .	. . . . .	16, 000
Fertilizers				
U.S.	37, 000	2, 200	820	3, 020
Canada	28, 900	1, 800	638	2, 438
Chile	62, 065	. . . . .	. . . . .	2, 729
Petroleum products				
U.S.	³ 140, 500	5, 400	1, 705	7, 105
Offshore	812, 000	15, 050	7, 770	⁴ 24, 895
Miscellaneous				
Pesticides (sulphur)	17, 000	340	160	. . . . .
Cotton and other fibers	28, 000	19, 500	500	20, 000
Medical supplies	. . . . .	. . . . .	. . . . .	1, 000
Reserve	. . . . .	. . . . .	. . . . .	862
TOTAL	. . . . .	. . . . .	. . . . .	$284, 000

[1] Final detailed composition of fats and oils program not yet determined, but will not exceed $20,000,000 in total.
[2] Freight will be paid by the French Government on a nonreimbursable basis.
[3] Subject to adjustment downward after determination of final quantities to come from U.S. sources.
[4] Includes reserve of $2,075,000 for petroleum products not yet specified.

234

TABLE IV.

Item	Estimated freight at shipside and shipping cost ($000)	Percent of total
Food	$38,418	67.40
Fuel (coal only).	10,290	18.05
Seed	3,901	6.86
Fertilizer	2,000	3.50
Medical supplies	1,271	2.23
Pesticides.	483	.85
Incentive goods.	100	.26
Reserve.	537	.85
TOTAL	$57,000	100.00

The Austrian program in general covers the same shipment period as the French program, from December 17, 1947, through March 1948, except for the cereals allocation for April, which will be shipped in April 1948.

Other comments on the Austrian program are as follows:

Sugar. The Austrian Government has agreed to accept and process raw sugar in Austria. This action permits supply of an additional amount of sugar, stated by the Austrian Government and the Commanding General, U.S. Forces in Austria, as urgently needed, without increasing the amount of funds required.

Fuel. No coal is being supplied from the United States as Austrian coal requirements can be met from European sources at a lower unit cost. The proposed program covers Ruhr, Saar, and Czechoslovakian coal for January, February, and March, and Polish coal for February, March, and April. April Polish coal must be paid for on or before March 20, 1948.

Petroleum and petroleum products. No petroleum and petroleum products are included in the program. Such products as are required are being purchased by the Austrian Government.

Pesticides. As a result of having secured British agreement to supply the major portion of the required pesticides, anticipated expenditures for these items have been materially reduced.

Incentive goods. The Austrian Government is most desirous of receiving certain agricultural machinery spare parts as "incentive goods". These parts can be secured from bizonal Germany prior to March 31, 1948.

Reserve. This reserve is set up to cover a possible increase in commodity and shipping costs and certain anticipated administrative charges which might be presented by the Department of the Army and for other contingencies.

A cable from the Commanding General, U.S. Forces in Austria, states that 199 billion calories of import food is required for each 28-day ration period to support an 1,800-caloric ration in Austria. As an indication of its importance to Austria, the proposed food program will provide 772 billion calories or approximately the total import food required for four ration periods.

Italian Program

The target program for Italy, including partial programs previously approved for Italy totaling $93,403,000 under dates of December 23, 1947, January 9, 1948, and January 29, 1948, is shown in table V.

TABLE V.

Product	Estimated quantity (long tons)	Estimated freight at ship-side cost ($000)	Estimated shipping cost ($000)	Estimated freight at ship-side and shipping cost ($000)
Food				
Cereals	641,000	$76,393	$10,749	$87,142
Soya flour	12,000	2,213	252	2,465
Pulses (beans).	17,500	4,329	671	5,000
Dairy products	6,000	1,900	200	2,100
Dried eggs.	1,500	1,344	60	1,404
Rolled oats	6,000	1,035	165	1,200
Macaroni	10,000	2,432	568	3,000
Sugar, raw (Cuba).	28,000	2,661	539	3,200
Potatoes.	28,000	364	840	1,204
Coal				
U.S..	1,800,000	18,900	17,100	36,000
Ruhr	500,000	. . . .	. . . .	8,000
Petroleum				
Petroleum products, U.S.	23,102	1,850	471	2,321
Offshore.	473,683	8,038	4,641	12,679
Fertilizer				
U.S. phosphate rocks	70,000	. . . .	. . . .	1,000
Medical supplies.	. . . .	. . . .	. . . .	1,800
Pesticides	. . . .	. . . .	. . . .	200
Reserve.	. . . .	. . . .	. . . .	12,285
TOTAL	. . . .	. . . .	. . . .	181,000

Table VI is a summary of the Italian program recommended in table V, using the commodity categories specified in Public Law 389. The summary includes estimated cost of commodity and of shipping.

to be carried out in Austria, France, and Italy as authorized under the interim-aid legislation. Because of the reduction of $75,000,000 made by Congress in the administration's request for $597,000,-000 for interim aid, most of the $522,000,000 finally appropriated must be used for essential fuel and food items to these three countries, and only a small amount can be made available to carry out incentive-goods programs. Plans for small incentive-goods programs in these three countries under the interim-aid legislation should be completed within the next two weeks.

ing Target

wheat represents the February and March allocations to China.

The approximately 48,000 long tons of rice from the United States covers about 84 percent of the allocation of 57,085 long tons of United States rice to China for the first six months of 1948.

Hybrid seed corn was requested by the aid mission in China because of its usefulness in certain famine and flooded areas in producing heavy yields of corn to be used as food. It was stated that 2,000 tons of hybrid seed could be distributed to farmers for growing 500,000 acres of corn.

The requirements for pesticides as originally submitted by our mission were considered excessive in view of the distribution problem involved and were reduced by about two thirds.

The $1,000,000 for medical supplies will in considerable part be used to supplement the $4,000,000 already programmed for this purpose under Public Law 84. The $4,000,000 is not sufficient to complete procurement of the China medical program as submitted without some additional funds. Any unexpended balance will be used either for the purchase of medical supplies in addition to those already programmed or for the purchase of more rice.

The $1,000,000 balance is being held in reserve pending final decision as to amounts of petroleum and Diesel oil needed for use in transporting relief supplies.

Status of German Reparation and Dismantling Program

LETTER FROM THE SECRETARY OF STATE TO THE CHAIRMAN OF THE SENATE FOREIGN RELATIONS COMMITTEE

Text of a letter to Senator Arthur H. Vandenberg from Secretary George C. Marshall regarding the German reparation program, and the Department's memorandum on the subject

February 4, 1948

DEAR SENATOR VANDENBERG:

You will recall that during December you indicated the intention of going fully into the German reparation and dismantling program in connection with the consideration of the European Recovery Program by the Senate Foreign Relations Committee. Since that time, the Departments of State and of the Army have submitted to the Congress and to your Committee a considerable amount of information on this subject. During the course of my testimony before your Committee on January 8, I made a number of statements in which I pointed out certain of the reasons in favor of continuing the dismantling program, and indicated that further information and data would be furnished in the near future. Various Army witnesses, including Secretary Royall and Under Secretary Draper, have testified at length before your Committee in support of the dismantling and reparation program, and especially with reference to the more technical aspects of the program, including its effects upon the German economy.

On January 24 Mr. Lovett forwarded to you a copy of the memorandum prepared by the Departments of State and of the Army in reply to the questions contained in House Resolution 365.[2] This resolution called for answers to eleven questions concerning the dismantling program, and the replies (together with the six attachments) went into considerable detail. I understand that the Speaker of the House of Representatives read Mr. Lovett's covering letter of January 24 before the House. It was pointed out in this letter that through both diplomatic channels and through the Office of Military Government (US), the British and French Governments have been asked to supply detailed information with regard to the status of the dismantling program in their respective areas of occupation. Although representatives of these governments have given us assurances that they will make every effort to furnish the requested information, we are still awaiting receipt of detailed replies.

I believe that there are certain very compelling reasons in favor of the reparation program which may not be fully understood by the Congress notwithstanding the quite extensive information which has been made available to the Congress through your Committee and otherwise. For this reason I am submitting to you herewith a further memorandum in which an effort is made to summarize the principal points which are involved. I believe that the information and arguments contained in this memorandum will be of use to your Committee, and it occurs to me that you and other members of the Senate may deem it appropriate to employ this material in any further discussions of the program which may take place. With this thought in mind I am forwarding to you under separate cover additional copies of the memorandum.

I should also like to bring to your attention the fact that the British and French Governments are understood to be opposed to modification of the present dismantling program. We know that they feel themselves justly entitled to and are most anxious to receive delivery of their share of the plants which have been selected for dismantling and of the reciprocal deliveries of commodities which the Soviets are obligated to make to the West. If all dismantling should be halted in our zone, this would be interpreted as the abandonment of the reparation program as far as the United States is concerned. The probable result of such action would be that the United States would find itself in sole opposition to the demands of the other 17 members of the I.A.R.A. group of nations, and would probably be faced with renewed demands for extensive reparation out of current production. The principles for which we have contended so vigorously would thus be placed in jeopardy. Instead of being able to dispose of the reparations problem in short time and at rela-

[1] Released to the press Feb. 9, 1948.
[2] BULLETIN of Feb. 8, 1948, p. 185.

of the Potsdam Agreement we are seeking adequate arrangements with the British regarding further reparation deliveries to the East. These discussions are continuing, and in the meanwhile all deliveries from the US Zone to the USSR (and Poland) have been stopped except for the remnants of three plants which were largely dismantled and delivered before the last meeting of the Council of Foreign Ministers.

After consulting your office, I am taking the liberty of furnishing copies of this letter and memorandum to the Chairmen of the Appropriations Committee of the Senate and the Foreign Affairs and Appropriations Committees of the House of Representatives in view of the interest which these Committees have taken in the reparation and dismantling program.

Faithfully yours,

RMAN REPARATION PROGRAM

In response to these criticisms a fundamental reexamination of all the considerations involved, both economic and political, has been undertaken by the Department of State. The conclusion has been reached that the German reparation program should be continued in its present form, and that such continuance will aid, not hamper, the economic recovery of Europe. Such continuance will, furthermore, leave to the German people adequate resources to enable them to develop a decent standard of life and to contribute through industrial exports to European recovery. The major considerations which led the Department to adopt this conclusion are summarized in the following paragraphs. The question of whether certain of the plants on the dismantling list would be better able to contribute to the world supply of critically short items if retained in Germany is now being investigated.

Political Considerations

The Need for a Final Settlement of the German Reparation Question

The obligation of the aggressor to pay the maximum reparation compatible with economic and political realities is incontestable. The failure after the first World War to arrive at a realistic solution of this problem cost American taxpayers and private investors hundreds of millions of dollars, seriously disrupted European and world trade throughout the interwar period, and gave rise to constant frictions in international political relations.

From this unhappy experience it could be concluded that any reparation settlement, to be satisfactory, should be realistically based on capacity to pay, should be carried to final completion within a relatively short period, and yet should be accepted as equitable by all concerned. It was such a settlement that the United States Government consistently sought from the time when planning for the post-surrender treatment of Germany was begun. Without such a settlement, it was certain that the time when Germany could enter into normal economic and political relations with the rest of the European community would be seriously delayed, and it was probable that American taxpayers and investors would once again find that they had paid the German reparation bill.

The Character of Existing Reparation Agreements

The Potsdam agreement embodies the basic features of a reparation settlement satisfactory to the United States. It very specifically lays down the principle that the German reparation bill must be kept within the bounds of Germany's capacity to pay, and recognizes the necessity for a definitive settlement to be carried through within a few years. It takes into account the fears of European countries of a resurgence of German aggression and yet lays the ground for the establishment of a unified, peaceful, and economically viable Germany capable of self-support.

Providing all parties hereto undertook its implementation in a sincere spirit of cooperation, the Potsdam agreement provided the basis for a definitive settlement of the reparation shares of the Soviet Union and Poland on the one hand, and of all other countries entitled to reparation from Germany on the other. The Paris agreement on reparation, which was negotiated in Paris during the last two months of 1945, represented the practical acceptance by these other countries of the Potsdam reparation settlement. These 18 countries in effect accepted the principle of Germany's capacity to pay and agreed among themselves as to their relative shares in a total volume of German reparation assets which at that time was unknown. Such a reparation settlement is unprecedented in history; and in view of the greatly reduced volume of capital equipment being made available under the revised levels of industry, its continued acceptance is even more remarkable.

The Degree to Which the U.S. Government Is Committed Under Present Reparation Agreements

There can be no doubt that the signatories of the Paris reparation agreement regard the United

its full intensity, although serious difficulties had already appeared. In working on the revised level of industry the American and British authorities in Germany had fully in mind the necessity of providing the basis for a German economy with the resources and flexibility essential not only for its own recovery, but also for the fullest contribution within its power to general European recovery.

Negotiations proceeded over several months, and it was not until August 29, 1947, that the revised level of industry was finally announced. The general effect of the revised level of industry is to permit the retention in the bizonal area of sufficient industrial capacity to produce approximately the same volume of output as was produced in 1936.

1936 was a year of considerable prosperity in Germany and one in which the German standard of living was one of the highest in the world. Not only was the standard of living high in that year, but in addition the Nazi Government found it possible to devote large resources to the construction of the Autobahns, of massive public buildings, and Nazi Brown Houses, and to armaments production.

In 1936 the bizonal area exported, in terms of current prices, roughly $1.75 billions worth of industrial products. The revised level of industry provides the basis for a volume of exports some 15 percent larger than this.

It should be emphasized, in addition, that the revised level in no way constitutes a permanent straitjacket on the German economy. Within the resources left to them, the Germans are free to develop their economy and standard of living to the fullest extent made possible by their enterprise and hard work. Such permanent restriction as may be necessary for reasons of security will be contained in the final peace arrangements. In the meantime, the occupation of Germany will continue.

It is well to recall that, on the basis of the resources available to them in 1936, the Germans established a formidable war machine. Had these resources been devoted to peaceful purposes, the German standard of living could have been greatly raised above its already high level.

It is, of course, true that the population in the bizonal area will be considerably higher than in 1936 and that the volume of industrial output per capita will therefore be lower. Taking into account, however, the fact that resources will no longer be devoted to war purposes, it is considered that full opportunity remains for the development of a decent standard of life.

The level of industry presently contemplated in the French zone is believed to be rather lower, on a relative basis, than that for the bizonal area. Industrial capacity in that area is, however, a relatively small fraction of the total in the three western zones. Even if present French plans are carried out in their entirety, therefore, it is not believed that they will materially reduce the capacity of western Germany as a whole.

The Selection of Individual Plants for Removal

The selection of individual plants for removal was carried out with a view to retaining in Germany the most economically located plants and those best able to contribute to the export program, while at the same time minimizing the local and temporary effects of dismantling. The concentration of production in the plants remaining is expected to improve efficiency in management and in the use of labor, fuel, and raw materials. It should be noted that these lists were drawn up during the period between the end of August 1947 and the middle of October and that the general character of European and world needs, and especially of the needs for specific critical commodities, was well known at this time.

At the time of publication of the list of plants to be dismantled, on October 16, the responsible German authorities were invited to submit suggested amendments. No amendments were submitted in the case of the American list. Some 30 or 40 amendments were suggested for the list of plants in the British zone. Many of these amendments were accepted, and others are still under consideration.

The Relation of German Production to the European Recovery Program

The present level of industrial production in the bizonal area is roughly one third of the capacity scheduled for retention under the revised level of industry. Even this level has been achieved only after more than two years of grinding effort to break the complex log-jam of shortages which is blocking German production—food, coal, raw materials, housing, manpower, transport, etc. In no single branch of industry does production now equal or even approach retained capacity. In no branch of industry will the removal of capacity now scheduled for dismantling materially affect the output of that industry over the next four or five years.

In the light of the above facts it is clear that the real problem of bringing about German recovery, and therefore of enabling Germany to contribute to European recovery, is to increase German production. Even were present German production doubled, it would still be one third lower than is technically possible on the basis of the revised level of industry.

Many suggestions have been put forward in the press and in pamphlets as to possible means of increasing German industrial output to the point where all existing capacity, including that scheduled for dismantling, could be fully utilized. It

western zones of Germany, i.e., in return for 15 of the 25 percent of total removals from the western zones to which they were entitled. Such reciprocal deliveries were to be spread over a period of five years, whereas the capital removal program was to be completed within two years.

Under present plans total capital removals from the western zones would probably amount in 1938 values to approximately 1 billion Reichsmarks, of which the Soviet share would be RM 250 million. In return from this removed plant RM 150 million worth of reciprocal deliveries would be required from the U.S.S.R. Since roughly RM 100 million worth of capital equipment has already been delivered to the Soviet Union, while reciprocal deliveries are only now about to begin, the theoretical debts on both sides are now roughly equal.

In other words, the U.S.S.R. owes to the western powers RM 150 million worth of coal, food, and other commodities, and an equivalent value in deliveries of capital equipment is theoretically owed to the Soviet Union. The extremely urgent demands for commodities in western Europe and the disproportionately great increase in world prices of commodities over capital equipment since 1938, tend to make this possible exchange advantageous to the member nations of the Inter-Allied Reparation Agency.

Conclusions

Analysis of Germany's economic situation shows beyond question that the revised level of industry, and the dismantling program based on it, have no present effect on Germany's ability to produce and to export; nor has the revised level been found an obstacle to planning the maximum feasible contribution by Germany to the general European Recovery Program. It provides for the retention in the bizonal area of sufficient industrial capacity to provide the basis for development of a reasonable standard of living and of a volume of industrial exports greater than prevailed in 1936.

The dismantling and removal of German plants, therefore, represents a transfer of capacity which would otherwise remain idle in Germany to countries which, because of more adequate supplies of manpower, housing, transport, and other scarce factors of production, and because they enjoy more stable monetary and administrative organizations, can make good use of them. Transferred German plants are already contributing to the economic recovery of other European countries and may be expected to reduce the cost of the American contribution to European aid. To a considerable extent recipient nations have no other available source of supply for meeting their requirement for much-needed industrial expansion.

The reparation settlement embodied in the Potsdam and Paris reparation agreements, of which the dismantling program represents the concrete implementation, is one which accords with the best interests both of the United States and, recognizing its obligations, of Germany. It is a settlement to which genuinely friendly European countries, including both Great Britain and France, regard the United States as being fully committed, and one which represents to them the symbol of an attitude towards Germany's past actions and towards their own future, the abandonment of which would cause them the greatest concern.

Arrest of American Officers in Hungary [1]

TEXT OF AMERICAN AND HUNGARIAN NOTES

On instructions of this Government, the American Embassy in Moscow has addressed to the Soviet Foreign Office, under date of February 7, a note ((2) below) protesting the recent arrest in Hungary by Soviet troops of Lt. Cols. Bernard Thielen and Peter J. Kopcsak, Attaché and Assistant Military Attaché, respectively, of the American Legation in Budapest. The American Legation in Budapest has concurrently delivered notes to the Soviet Legation in Budapest ((3) below) and to the Hungarian Foreign Office ((4) below) concerning the matter.

On January 14, Colonels Thielen and Kopcsak were arrested by Soviet troops in Hungary and abducted across the Hungarian frontier to Vienna where intervention by United States authorities effected their release. Following informal representations by the American Minister in Budapest, Selden Chapin, to the Hungarian Foreign Minister on January 16, the Hungarian Foreign Office, in a note dated January 17, stated the Soviet Legation in Budapest would furnish the Foreign Minister, within two or three days, information in regard to the case, which would be forwarded to the American Legation as soon as it was received. The American Legation acknowledged this communication from the Foreign Office in a note of January 19 ((1) below). On January 21, the American Legation received a note from the Soviet Minister in Budapest, who charged, with reference to the case, that Colonels Thielen and Kopcsak had refused to submit proper identification papers and had violated generally known rules in entering a Soviet military area without previous permission from the commander of the Soviet units there. The Soviet Minister added his "hope" that the American Minister would "take the necessary steps that the offenders be punished, lest such incidents should occur in the future."

(1) Text of note of January 19, 1948, from the American Legation, Budapest, to the Hungarian Foreign Office

The Legation of the United States of America presents its compliments to the Ministry for Foreign Affairs and with reference to the Ministry's Note No. 167/pol.–1948, dated January 17, 1948,

has the honor to enclose the gist of the sworn statements of the two officers involved, as to events connected with their recent arrest and abduction across the Hungarian-Austrian border by Soviet military authorities.

The Legation will be happy to receive and will read with keen interest, such documents as may be presented to the Foreign Ministry by the Legation of the Union of Soviet Socialist Republics in Budapest, and which may be forwarded by the former to this Legation, bearing on this case. It is presumably entirely within the competence of the Hungarian Government to decide whether or not Hungary's sovereignty has been violated, and what action if any is necessary as a result; nevertheless the Legation of the United States of America can in advance conceive of no adequate excuse for the exercise of police powers on Hungarian territory by "line of communication" troops of a third power; the arrest of the diplomatic representatives of a foreign government duly accredited to Hungary; refusal by the military authorities of said third power to recognize or to honor the diplomatic identification cards issued by the Hungarian Ministry for Foreign Affairs; refusal by force of arms to permit such diplomatic officers to communicate with their own Legation; and their abduction out of Hungary, to which they are accredited, under armed guard and in such a way as to prevent adequate examination by the Hungarian border guards, the officers being without passports or visas authorizing their departure from Hungary.

The Legation of the United States of America avails itself [etc.]

(Enclosure: Gist of Sworn Statements)

I, Bernard Thielen, Lt. Colonel, United States Army, Attache of the Legation of the United States of America in Budapest and I, Peter J. Kopcsak, Lt. Colonel, United States Army, Assistant Military Attache of the Legation of the United States of America in Budapest make the following joint statements concerning our recent arrest in Hungary and abduction across the Hungarian-Austrian border by Soviet military authorities:

Lt. Colonels Kopcsak and Thielen had departed from Budapest at 8:00 a.m. January 13, 1948, on

---

[1] Released to the press Feb. 11, 1948.

The following day, January 14, 1948, en route to Budapest, at about 11:00 a.m. as they were entering the main square of Papa on the public highway, they stopped to inquire of a Hungarian policeman as to the best route to Zirc. The policeman gave them the information requested and they started to proceed on their journey when after going about one hundred yards they were stopped by a Russian officer and an armed Russian sentry and told that they had to present their documents at the Soviet Kommandatura. The American officers protested that they were merely passing through Papa and offered their documents for the Soviet officer's inspection. The documents were verified as to their authenticity by the Hugarian policeman from whom the officers had previously requested directions, but the Soviet officer refused to discuss the matter and insisted that the American officers accompany him to the Kommandatura. Anticipating only a brief delay, the American officers drove to the Kommandatura. Lt. Col. Kopcsak took his and Lt. Col. Thielen's documents into the Kommandatura office while Lt. Col. Thielen remained in the car which was parked at the Kommandatura entrance and under surveillance of armed Russian sentries. Lt. Col. Thielen was requested several times to drive the car into the Kommandatura courtyard, but each time he refused to do so.

Meanwhile, Lt. Col. Kopcsak had shown his and Lt. Col. Thielen's documents to a Hungarian-speaking Soviet soldier. The latter stated that the Russians understood the status of the two American officers, but that as a matter of routine it would be necessary for the Officer of the Day to telephone the Soviet Town Commandant. After some time, during which no apparent progress had been made, Lt. Col. Kopcsak insisted that he and Lt. Col. Thielen be permitted to continue their journey. A Soviet captain then informed him that he must drive his car into the Kommandatura enclosure, giving as a reason the fact that a large crowd of Hungarians was collecting around the vehicle and the entrance to the Kommandatura. Lt. Col. Kopcsak refused, however.

The Russian captain then requested that the American officer (Lt. Col. Thielen) who was still outside in the car, come into the Kommandatura. After locking the car, Lt. Col. Thielen complied with this request. Upon entering the Kommandatura he pointed out to the senior Russian officer present that he and Lt. Col. Kopcsak had no intention of stopping in Papa. The Soviet officer stated that he was fully aware of that and that it was merely a question of verifying the documents of the American officers. In this connection, he stated that the documents were written in Hungarian. Lt. Colonels Thielen and Kopcsak immediately pointed out that a Hungarian policeman had accompanied them to the Kommandatura and that he could translate the documents or that Lt. Col. Kopcsak could give a literal translation if such were desired and that, furthermore, one of the Russian soldiers obviously spoke fluent Hungarian.

About 2:30 p.m., Lt. Colonels Thielen and Kopcsak informed the officer in charge of the Kommandatura that they were going out to eat lunch. The Soviet officer refused to grant permission for this at first, but after some delay he made a telephone call and then stated that the two American officers might go out for this purpose. The two American officers were accompanied to a nearby restaurant under armed guard of three Russian soilders with submachine guns and one Russian officer.

Upon arrival at the restaurant, the Soviet soldiers forcibly dispersed a crowd which had gathered and kept the curtains drawn during the time when Lt. Colonels Thielen and Kopcsak were having their lunch. The American officers, however, could not help noticing upon leaving the restaurant that this crowd of Hungarian civilians which had again gathered outside, was displaying considerable resentment at the detention of the Americans by the Soviet military.

After lunch the two American officers were escorted, still under armed guard, back to the Kommandatura. There the two officers demanded permission to telephone to the American Legation in Budapest, but were refused, despite continued insistence on this right. It was at this point that the Soviet officials stated that the two American officers were soon to be taken to Budapest. This statement was utilized by the Soviets as an excuse for their repeated refusals to permit any telephone call to be made to the American Legation in Budapest. Lt. Col. Kopcsak continued to insist on his right to telephone and finally said that he would go outside and use another telephone, but when he attempted to leave the office of the Kommandatura, the Russian sentry, upon an order from one of the officials pushed a gun against Kopcsak's chest and told him to sit down.

At this point the Russian captain reentered the room and said that soon the two American officers would be taken to some other place. Lt. Col. Kopcsak immediately asked him where they were to be taken and the captain replied that they would find out later.

About 4:00 p.m. the American officers were told that arrangements had been completed to take them to Budapest and that they would be accompanied by the Town Commandant of Papa, a lieutenant colonel in the Russian Army. The Russian captain then said that while he recognized that it was customary for military officers to carry sidearms, the Commandant had said that he would not accompany them unless they agreed to surrender their weapons. Both Lt. Col. Thielen and Lt. Col. Kopcsak declined to do so unless they were given full assurances as to where they were

of American diplomatic personnel constitutes an arbitrary and unjustified exercise of police power in Hungary by Soviet "line of communication" troops and unwarranted interference with diplomatic officials duly accredited to the Hungarian Government, in derogation of Hungarian sovereignty.

The United States Government protests this unwarranted and unjustified action on the part of the Soviet military authorities and requests that appropriate orders be issued to Soviet troops to ensure that Hungarian sovereignty be respected and that such incidents do not occur in the future.

(3) Text of note of February 7, 1948, from the American Minister in Budapest to the Soviet Minister in Budapest

I have the honor to acknowledge the receipt of Your Excellency's note No. 44 dated January 21, 1948 with regard to the recent arrest by Soviet troops, in the main square of Papa, of Lieutenant Colonels Thielen and Kopcsak of this Legation. I regret to inform Your Excellency that the statements contained in the foregoing communication do not correspond to the facts in the case as set forth in sworn evidence which was previously submitted to the Hungarian Government on January 19, 1948, a copy of which is attached for Your Excellency's information. I should appreciate it if Your Excellency would forward this document to the Soviet Foreign Office in Moscow.

Your Excellency's attention is invited to the significant facts that (1) the Soviet military authorities who arrested the American officers and abducted them from Hungary not only made no effort—despite the latter's possession of valid diplomatic identification—to confirm the identity of the officers by communication with the Hungarian Foreign Office or this Legation but they also refused to permit the officers themselves to telephone this Legation; and (2) this conduct constitutes the arbitrary exercise of police power by Soviet "line of communication" troops and an unwarranted interference with duly accredited diplomatic officials in derogation of Hungarian sovereignty.

In the circumstances, I obviously must reject the contentions in this matter contained in Your Excellency's note under reference, together with the request contained therein that the American officers be punished.

I am informed by my Government that it is lodging a protest through the American Embassy in Moscow with the Soviet Foreign Office regarding this incident; and I am instructed to add that any further correspondence on this matter in so far as relations between the United States of America and the USSR are concerned will be conducted through the American Embassy in Moscow.

Accept [etc.]

(4) Text of Note of February 7, 1948, from the American Legation, Budapest, to the Hungarian Foreign Office

The Legation of the United States of America presents its compliments to the Hungarian Minister for Foreign Affairs and has the honor to refer to a conversation between the Foreign Minister and Minister Chapin on January 16, 1948 with regard to the arrest by Russian troops, in the main square of Papa, of two United States Army officers attached to this Legation, their detention incommunicado for 11 hours and their abduction across the Hungarian-Austrian border to Vienna, involving several flagrant violations of Hungarian sovereignty; as well as to the Ministry's *note verbale* No. 167/POL 1948 of January 17, 1948, stating that the Soviet Legation in Budapest had declared that the incident by no means affected the sovereignty of Hungary, as was to be proven by information and documents which were to be furnished to the Minister in two or three days and which the latter would take pleasure in forwarding to the American Legation. The receipt of this note was acknowledged by this Legation on January 19, 1948.

Italy Notified of Prewar Treaties To Keep

[Released to the press February 11]

The Department of State announced on February 11 that on February 6, 1948, the Italian Government was given official notification, in accordance with the terms of the treaty of peace with Italy signed at Paris, February 10, 1947, regarding the prewar bilateral treaties and other international agreements with Italy which the United States Government desired to keep in force or revive.

Text of note from the American Ambassador at Rome to the Italian Minister for Foreign Affairs giving such notification

I have the honor to refer to the Treaty of Peace with Italy signed at Paris February 10, 1947, which came into force, in accordance with the provisions of article 90 thereof, on September 15, 1947 upon the deposit of instruments of ratification by the Union of Soviet Socialist Republics, the United Kingdom of Great Britain and Northern Ireland, the United States of America, and France. Article 44 of the Treaty of Peace reads as follows:

"1. Each Allied or Associated Power will notify Italy, within a period of six months from the coming into force of the present Treaty, which of its prewar bilateral treaties with Italy it desires

(nciliation

3. Treaty for the advancement of peace. Signed at Washington May 5, 1914. Ratified by the United States March 17, 1915. Ratified by Italy November 29, 1914. Ratifications exchanged at Washington March 19, 1915. Effective March 19, 1915. (Article II was abrogated and replaced by article I of the treaty of September 23, 1931.) [Treaty Series 615; 39 Stat. 1618.]

4. Treaty modifying the terms of article II of the treaty to advance the cause of general peace of May 5, 1914. Signed at Washington September 23, 1931. Ratified by the United States June 25, 1932. Ratified by Italy February 2, 1932. Ratifications exchanged at Rome July 30, 1932. Effective July 30, 1932. [Treaties Series 848; 47 Stat. 2072.]

Consuls

5. Consular convention. Signed at Washington May 8, 1878. Ratified by the United States June 4, 1878. Ratified by Italy July 9, 1878. Ratifications exchanged at Washington September 18, 1878. Effective September 18, 1878. (Article XI, which was annulled by the Convention of February 24, 1881, and article XIII, which was abrogated under Act of Congress approved March 4, 1915, are not to be considered as revived by this notification.) [Treaty Series 178; 20 Stat. 725.]

Debt-Funding

6. Debt-funding agreement. Signed at Washington November 14, 1925. Effective as of June 15, 1925. [Combined Annual Reports of the World War Foreign Debt Commission (1927) p. 222.]

7. Agreement modifying the debt-funding agreement of November 14, 1925 (moratorium). Signed at Washington June 3, 1932. Effective as of July 1, 1931. [Published by the Treasury Department, 1932.]

Extradition

8. Extradition convention. Signed at Washington March 23, 1868. Ratified by the United States June 22, 1868. Ratified by Italy July 19, 1868. Ratifications exchanged September 17, 1868. Effective September 17, 1868. [Treaty Series 174; 15 Stat. 629.]

9. Additional article to extradition convention of 1868. Signed at Washington January 21, 1869. Ratifications exchanged at Washington May 7, 1869. Effective May 7, 1869. [Treaty Series 176 (printed with 174); 16 Stat. 17.]

10. Supplementary convention to extradition convention of 1868. Signed at Washington June 11, 1884. Ratified by the United States April 10, 1885. Ratified by Italy August 8, 1884. Ratifications exchanged at Washington April 24, 1885. Effective April 24, 1885. [Treaty Series 181 (printed with 174); 24 Stat. 1001.]

Narcotic Drugs

11. Arrangement for the direct exchange of certain information regarding the traffic in narcotic drugs. Effected by exchange of notes signed at Rome January 5, and April 27, 1928. Effective April 27, 1928. [Treaty Information Bulletin No. 5 (July 1929) 2nd supp.]

Navigation

12. Agreement relating to the reciprocal recognition of certificates of inspection of vessels assigned to the transportation of passengers. Effected by exchange of notes signed at Washington June 1, August 5, and August 17, 1931. Effective August 15, 1931. [Executive Agreement Series 23; 47 Stat. 2665.]

Passport Visa Fees

13. Agreement relating to the waiver of passport visa fees for nonimmigrants. Effected by exchange of notes

signed at Rome February 11, 21 and 26, 1929. [Not printed.]

Postal

14. Convention relating to exchange of money orders. Signed at Washington March 31, 1877 and at Florence April 20, 1877. Effective July 2, 1877 [20 Stat. 683.]

15. Additional convention to the convention relating to exchange of money orders signed at Washington March 31, 1877 and at Florence April 20, 1877. Signed at Washington August 24, 1880 and at Rome August 9, 1880. Ratified by the United States August 25, 1880. [21 Stat. 788.]

16. Parcel Post Convention. Signed at Washington October 11, 1929. Ratified by the United States October 18, 1929. [Post Office Department print; 46 Stat. 2397.]

Taxation

17. Arrangement for relief from double income tax on shipping profits. Effected by exchange of notes signed at Washington March 10 and May 5, 1926. Effective from January 1, 1921. [Executive Agreement Series 10; 47 Stat. 2599.]

Trade-Marks

18. Declaration for the reciprocal protection of marks of manufacture and trade. Signed at Washington June 1, 1882. Effective June 1, 1882. [Treaty Series 180; 23 Stat. 726.]

This notification will be deemed to be effective on the date of the present note.

It is understood, of course, that either of the two Governments may propose revisions in any of the treaties or other agreements mentioned in the above list.

Further, it shall be understood that any of the provisions in the treaties and other agreements listed in this notification which may be found in particular circumstances to be not in conformity with the Treaty of Peace shall be considered to have been deleted so far as the application of the Treaty of Peace is involved but shall be regarded as being in full force and effect with respect to matters not covered by the latter treaty.

The reciprocal copyright arrangement between the United States and Italy effected pursuant to the exchange of notes signed at Washington October 28, 1892, and the exchanges of notes signed at Washington September 2, 1914, February 12, March 4, and March 11, 1915 will be the subject of a separate communication.

The agreement for the protection of trademarks in Morocco, effected by exchange of notes signed at Tangier June 13, July 29, and December 19, 1903 and March 12, 1904 will also be the subject of a separate communication.

In compliance with paragraph 2 of article 44 of the Treaty of Peace, quoted above, the United States Government will register with the Secretariat of the United Nations the treaties and other agreements which are by this notification kept in force or revived.

Italy Grants Land for American Military

EXCHANGE OF NOTES BETWEEN

[Released to the press February 12]

The Italian Embassy presents its compliments to the Department of State and has the honor to bring to the Department's attention a new provision adopted by the Italian Government with regard to American war cemeteries.

As known to the Department of State, article 3 of the agreement reached through an exchange of notes in September 1946 at Rome, between the Italian Ministry of Foreign Affairs and the United States Embassy, provides that "if in the future the Government of the United States wishes to establish permanent cemeteries or erect memorials in Italy, the Italian Government will exercise its power of Eminent Domain to acquire title to such sites and grant to the United States the right of use therein in perpetuity upon payment by the United States of cost compensation therefor."

Upon instructions received, the Italian Embassy has the honor to inform the Department of State that the Italian Government, wishing to give a token of friendship to the Government and people of the United States, has now decided to grant the American Government the free use of the sites selected for the establishment of war cemeteries.

It would have been the sincere desire of the Italian Government to proceed to a veritable donation of the land involved, but it was not possible to reach such a solution because not consented by existing regulations. On the other hand the advantages that the American Government will draw from such a free cession will be practically the same as those deriving from a donation, since the free use is granted for as long as the selected sites will be destined to military cemeteries.

In the light of the foregoing the Italian Government has the honor to request the American Government to consider the first paragraph of article 3 of the aforesaid agreement modified as follows: "The Italian Government grants gratuitously to the American Government the right of use of the sites selected for permanent American military cemeteries in Italy, to last as long as the American authorities will use such sites as war cemeteries."

WASHINGTON, D.C.,
December 18, 1947.

January 21, 1948.

EXCELLENCY:

I have the honor to acknowledge the receipt of your note no. 11332 of December 18, 1947 stating

Trade and Financial Discussions With Sweden Held [1]

SUMMARY OF DEVELOPMENTS

The Department of State announced on February 11 that at the request of the Government of Sweden, in accordance with paragraph 8 of the understanding with regard to Swedish-American trade reached between the United States and Sweden on June 24, 1947,[2] discussions between representatives of the two Governments have recently been held concerning the financial and trade position of Sweden.

A serious trade and balance-of-payments problem now faces Sweden partly as a result of developments in the exchange position of other countries with which Sweden has important trading relationships and due partly to the operation of temporary regulations imposed to facilitate the transition to the more stringent import controls permitted by the provisions of the June 1947 understanding. In particular, a more serious drain on Sweden's gold and dollar holdings has developed than was anticipated during the conversations between the two Governments at the time this understanding was reached. In the course of the recent discussions the situation facing Sweden was carefully examined and all possible solutions were explored. It was pointed out that Sweden has been and is taking steps to bring its dollar payments and receipts into equilibrium, except for a carry-over of import commitments covered by import licenses issued in 1947 and a seasonal deficit anticipated in the first quarter of 1948.

In order to make it possible for the Swedish Government to take requisite measures to meet its balance-of-payments difficulties and because the quantitative commitments with respect to imports into Sweden from the United States, contained in paragraph 5(c) of the June 1947 understanding between the two Governments, have, in general, been fulfilled, the United States Government has agreed not to invoke the provisions of paragraph 5(c) during the remaining period covered by the understanding, which ends June 30, 1948. During this period, Sweden's import programming will be based on the essentiality of imports, with the exception of cases involving undue hardship for American exporters, which are subject to specific provisions set forth in an exchange of memoranda which is appended to this release. With respect to the period following June 30, 1948, the two Governments have agreed to undertake negotiations with a view to the temporary relaxation of the requirements of articles II and VII of the trade agreement of 1935 along the lines of the balance-of-payments provisions of the general agreement on tariffs and trade concluded at Geneva, Switzerland, on October 30, 1947, between the United States and 22 other signatories. Both Governments consider these provisions appropriate under the circumstances. These provisions would permit countries facing certain balance-of-payment difficulties to program imports on an essentiality basis.

The Government of the United States has also recognized the necessity for Sweden to defer payments to the extent necessary to prevent Sweden's gold and dollar holdings from falling below a minimum working balance.

Under the present circumstances and in view also of the above arrangements, a Government-to-Government credit was agreed not to be appropriate. The Swedish Government, therefore, has not applied for such a credit.

The understanding arrived at between the two Governments has been embodied in an exchange of memoranda and letters, the texts of which follow.

CORRESPONDENCE RELATING TO TRADE AND FINANCIAL DISCUSSIONS WITH SWEDEN

Memorandum from the U.S. to Sweden [3]

The Government of the United States of America wishes to refer to discussions which have recently been held between its representatives and those of the Government of Sweden concerning the problems faced by the Government of Sweden as the result of its serious loss of gold and dollar exchange. These discussions have resulted in a mutual understanding between the two Governments as follows:

1. After a careful examination of the facts relating to the payments position of Sweden it is recognized that a temporary suspension of the commitments undertaken by the Government of Sweden in paragraph 4 of its *aide-memoire* dated June 24, 1947 is necessary to permit the Government of Sweden to meet its present payments difficulties. The principles governing the temporary suspension of paragraph 4 of the cited

---

[1] Released to the press Feb. 11, 1948.
[2] BULLETIN of July 6, 1947, p. 42.
[3] A corresponding memorandum was transmitted from the Government of Sweden to the Government of the United States.

aide-memoire are set forth in a letter dated February 11, 1948 from Mr. Aminoff, Swedish Chargé d'Affaires, to Mr. Thorp, Assistant Secretary of State for Economic Affairs.

2. The Government of the United States recognizes that the commitments undertaken by the Government of Sweden in paragraph 5(c) of its *aide-memoire* dated June 24, 1947 with respect to quotas applicable to the importation of commodities listed in Schedule I of the Commercial Agreement between the two Governments signed May 25, 1935, have, in general, been fulfilled, total imports being in excess of the total of the amounts stipulated. In view of this development, caused substantially by the operation of the transitional rules applied by the Government of Sweden, and because of the serious and unanticipated deficit incurred by Sweden in its balance of payments which has resulted in serious loss of gold and convertible foreign exchange, the Government of the United States agrees not to invoke, for the six months period ending June 30, 1948, the provisions of paragraph 5(c) of the Swedish *aide-memoire* dated June 24, 1947, with respect to the application of Swedish import controls to the importation of items listed in Schedule I of the Commercial Agreement of 1935.

3. In applying quantitative restrictions necessary to safeguard its external financial and balance of payments position to all imports from the United States, including those listed in Schedule I, the Government of Sweden will issue licenses to cover hardship cases in connection with contracts (previously based on valid import licenses, wherever necessary, or assurances thereof) involving goods which have been, or are, in the process of being specifically made or prepared for use in Sweden. Favorable consideration will also be given to cases involving goods for which, in connection with contracts, specific preparations have been made for shipment to Sweden.

4. Because of the large deficit in the Swedish balance of payments with the hard currency areas of the world, it is recognized that the Government of Sweden is faced with the necessity of taking measures to correct its present imbalance of trade, and to conserve its foreign exchange.

5. It is, therefore, understood between the Governments of Sweden and the United States that the balance of payments problems of Sweden are similar to those of other countries which gave rise to the provisions of the General Agreement on Tariffs and Trade, concluded at Geneva, Switzerland, on October 30, 1947 by the United States and twenty-two other signatories and that, therefore, the two Governments agree to undertake negotiations with a view to the temporary relaxation of the requirements of Articles II and VII of the Commercial Agreement of 1935, to become effective July 1, 1948 along the lines of the balance of payments provisions of the General Agreement on

Recovery of American Property Confiscated During Japanese Occupation of China

[Released to the press January 26]

The American Embassy at Nanking has reported that the Chinese Government has extended to June 30, 1948, the time limit for presentation of evidence by American nationals who claim ownership of, or interests in, property which the Chinese Government took over from the Japanese as enemy and puppet property. With respect to property in areas of China not yet recovered by the Chinese Government, documentary evidence of American interests is to be submitted within six months from the date of the recovery of the area. In view of this additional information the Department repeats with appropriate modifications statements which appeared in its announcement of November 14, 1947, on this subject.[1]

Applications for the return of American-owned property which was located in China at the time of the Japanese occupation and which was seized by the Japanese and subsequently found in China should be submitted to the local branch of the Alien Property Liquidation Office of the Central Trust of China within whose jurisdiction such property is located. Branch offices are located in Shanghai, Tsingtao, Tientsin, Hankow, and Canton. Applications from American nationals in the United States should be sent to the American Consulate General in the appropriate one of those cities for forwarding to the branch office of the Central Trust in that city. No application form is prescribed. It is for these applications that the time limit has been extended from December 31, 1947 to June 30, 1948.

Applications for the return of American-owned property located in China at the time of the Japanese occupation and removed to Japan by the Japanese should be submitted to the American Embassy at Nanking for forwarding to the Reparations Commission of the Executive Yuan. No final date for submission of applications for the return of looted property has been established, but prompt submission is strongly recommended. The Far Eastern Commission in a policy decision of July 18, 1946, specified four categories of goods which, if found in Japan and identified as having been removed from an Allied country fraudulently or under duress by the Japanese or their agents, are to be delivered to the Government of the Allied country. The four categories are: industrial and transportation machinery and equipment; gold, other precious metals, precious gems, foreign securities, foreign currencies, and other foreign-exchange assets; cultural objects; agricultural products and industrial raw materials. The specification of the four categories does not exclude the

[1] BULLETIN of Nov. 23, 1947, p. 1000.

possibility that other types of looted property found in Japan may be restored, upon proper identification, to the governments of the countries from which the property was taken.

American owners of property seized by the Japanese, the present location of which is not

Regulations Released Regarding Trade W

[Released to the press February 3]

American businessmen are now to be permitted to enter Japan and remain there for extended periods, the Departments of State and Commerce announced on February 3. The announcement supplements a release of February 3 on the same subject by the Supreme Commander for the Allied Powers (SCAP) in Tokyo.

Since August 15, 1947, American businessmen have been admitted to Japan for trade purposes. During this period original entry permits have been valid for visits of not more than 21 days, although those who have gone to Japan under these conditions have usually been able to secure SCAP permission to remain longer if necessary to conclude particular transactions. It is believed that many American businessmen have postponed travel to Japan until they could secure original entry permits valid for considerably longer periods of stay in that country. Under the new regulations American businessmen approved by the Department of Commerce and by SCAP will obtain entry permits valid initially for visits of 60 days; and in addition they will be permitted after arrival in Japan to apply for permission to remain on indefinitely, to secure entry permits for members of their families, and to establish more or less permanent residences in Japan.

The new regulations now established will permit a certain number of American and other Allied nationals who owned property in Japan prior to the war to go to Japan or send representatives there to act on their behalf in connection with all matters pertaining to their property rights and interests in Japan. Additional information outlining procedures to be followed by persons seeking return of their properties will be furnished later.

The new regulations have eliminated the country quotas which in the past have limited the number of entrants into Japan. Entry permits properly supported by sponsoring governments will now be considered and acted upon in the order of their receipt by SCAP.

Foreign businessmen who go to Japan will find conditions substantially different from those which prevailed in the prewar period, the Departments of State and Commerce caution. Trade continues to be closely controlled by the occupation authori-

PUBLICATIONS

Department of State

For sale by the Superintendent of Documents, Government Printing Office, Washington 25, D.C. Address requests direct to the Superintendent of Documents, except in the case of free publications, which may be obtained from the Department of State.

Eighth Pan American Child Congress, Washington, D.C., May 2–9, 1942. Conference Series 100. Pub. 2847. 647 pp. Limited distribution.

A discussion of the organization, final act, and sessions of the Eighth Pan American Child Congress, held beginning May 29, 1942, in Washington.

Recent Publications of the Department of State, January 1948. 4 pp. Free.

Significant publications released by the Department of State during the past three months.

Food Production: Cooperative Program in Peru. Treaties and Other International Acts Series 1647. Pub. 2956. 9 pp. 5¢.

Agreement Between the United States of America and Peru, Further Extending and Modifying Agreement of May 19 and 20, 1943—Effected by exchange of notes signed at Lima June 11, 1945, and November 22, 1946; entered into force November 22, 1946, effective August 31, 1945.

United States Armed Forces in Guatemala. Treaties and Other International Acts Series 1663. Pub. 2987. 4 pp. 5¢.

Agreement Between the United States of America and Guatemala—Effected by exchange of notes signed at Guatemala August 29, 1947; entered into force August 29, 1947.

Trusteeship for Former Japanese Mandated Islands: Agreement approved by the Security Council of the United Nations April 2, 1947. Treaties and Other International Acts Series 1665. Pub. 2992. 5 pp. 5¢.

Agreement approved by the President of the United States of America July 18, 1947, pursuant to authority granted by joint resolution of the Congress of the United States of America July 18, 1947; entered into force July 18, 1947.

Exchange of Official Publications. Treaties and Other International Acts Series 1668. Pub. 2999. 5 pp. 5¢.

Agreement Between the United States of America and Ecuador—Effected by Exchange of Notes Signed at Quito October 21 and 29, 1947; entered into force October 29, 1947.

---

[1] Supplementing excerpts from *The President's Budget Message for 1949 and Selected Budget Statements,* which were printed in the BULLETIN of Jan. 25, 1948, p. 126.

James Simsarian, author of the article on German assets, is American member of the Committee of Experts on Enemy Property Custodianship of the Inter-Allied Reparation Agency and Special Assistant to the U.S. Delegate to the Inter-Allied Reparation Agency.

The Department of State

For sale by the Superintendent of Documents
U.S. Government Printing Office
Washington 25, D.C.

SUBSCRIPTION:
52 issues, $5; single copy, 15 cents

Published with the approval of the
Director of the Bureau of the Budget

IPACT OF THE UNITED NATIONS UPON DOMESTIC JURISDICTION

By *Ernest A. Gross*

Legal Adviser

With Biblical completeness, article 2 of the arter of the United Nations sets forth "seven" nciples, which the organization and its mem- s, in pursuit of the lofty purposes set forth article 1, accept. The seventh and last of these ds:

'Nothing contained in the present Charter shall thorize the United Nations to intervene in mat- s which are essentially within the domestic isdiction of any state or shall require the Mem- s to submit such matters to settlement under present Charter; but this principle shall not ejudice the application of enforcement measures der Chapter VII."

The framers of the Charter recognized that in carrying out of the terms of the Charter— rthy as the purposes are—there were points which the organization should not impinge on domestic jurisdiction of any state.
The origin of the provisions of article 2 (7) of Charter, for the most part, is found in chapter II (A), paragraph 7, of the Dumbarton Oaks oposals, which reads:

"The provisions of paragraph 1 to 6 of Section (dealing with the 'Pacific Settlement of Dis- tes') should not apply to situations or disputes ising out of matters which by international law e solely within the domestic jurisdiction of the te concerned."

Apart from the difference in wording between is provision and that which later found its y into the Charter, the scope of the provision s greatly broadened by placing it in article 2 of Charter instead of in the chapter dealing with "Pacific Settlement of Disputes", as was done

at Dumbarton Oaks. The setting of the article makes it applicable to the entire Charter, except as to "the application of enforcement measures under Chapter VII".

Dumbarton Oaks Proposals

Numerous amendments of the Dumbarton Oaks Proposals were proposed at San Francisco. A subcommittee of jurists of the sponsoring powers evolved a text on the subject which, with one exception based on a subsequent Australian amendment, forms the text of article 2 (7) as it now stands. That text was introduced by the sponsoring powers as a joint amendment.

The first effect of the paragraph as incorporated in the Charter is that the United Nations cannot "intervene" in certain situations. Messrs. Goodrich and Hambro point out in *Charter of the United Nations, Commentary and Documents* that—

". . . What the provision means is that the Organization shall not exercise any authority, not even make recommendations of any kind, with respect to any matter 'essentially within the domestic jurisdiction' of a state. Nor shall it attempt to promote the solution of any conflict when it is found that the matter falls within the domestic jurisdiction of one of the parties to the dispute."

Limits of the Exception

The only exception contained in the sponsoring powers' joint proposal and in article 2 (7) of the Charter relates to the action which the Security Council may take under chapter VII of the Charter. This exception is not great. Chapter

VII has to do with "Action With Respect to
Threats to the Peace, Breaches of the Peace, and
Acts of Aggression". A situation cannot be imagined which could be said to constitute a threat
to the peace, a breach of the peace, or an act of
aggression, and nevertheless be "essentially within
the domestic jurisdiction" of any state. The concepts are clearly mutually exclusive.

But the exception is even narrower than appears. It was pointed out at San Francisco that
two different types of action are contemplated by
chapter VII of the Charter: (1) "recommendations" and (2) "enforcement" action.

Should measures of enforcement be necessary,
the Security Council should not, it was urged, be
deterred by the contention that a domestic matter
was involved. So far as recommendations by
the Security Council were concerned, it was urged,
there should be no inference that the Security
Council might make recommendations to states
with respect to the settlement of domestic matters.
After considerable debate, this view prevailed
and article 2 (7) was limited to an exception with
respect to "the application of enforcement measures under Chapter VII."

But it should be pointed out that Herbert Vere
Evatt explained, on behalf of the Australian
Delegation, that "To take enforcement action for
restraint of aggression is not intervening in any
way at all in a matter of domestic jurisdiction."[1]
The same view was taken by the Foreign Relations Committee of the Senate of the United
States, which commented in its report on the
Charter that "If the Security Council, acting
under Chapter VII, decided upon enforcement
action, it would be deciding that the matter
threatened international peace and security and,
therefore, had already gone beyond the limits of
domestic jurisdiction."[2]

It is therefore clear that the intention in limiting the exception to article 2 (7) to "the application of enforcement measures under Chapter VII,"
was that other measures contemplated under chapter VII were not to be such as to constitute intervention in matters which are essentially within the
domestic jurisdiction of any state.

---

[1] UNCIO doc. 969. I/1/39, June 14, 1945.
[2] S. Exec. Rept. 8, 79th Cong., 1st sess., pp. 10–11. (Charter of the United Nations.)

was that they were those "in which, by definition, international law permits each state entire liberty of action".

Finally, there was added at San Francisco the provision in article 2 (7) that nothing contained in the Charter "shall require the Members to submit such matters (domestic matters) to settlement under the present Charter". The third of the principles enumerated in article 2 of the Charter reads: "All Members shall settle their international disputes by peaceful means in such a manner that international peace and security, and justice, are not endangered." As explained by Secretary of State Stettinius:

" . . . It is quite conceivable that there might be an international dispute with reference to such matters as tariff, immigration, or the like, but where such a dispute relates to matters which are essentially domestic in character, settlement through international processes should not be required. It would of course remain true that . . . neither party to the dispute would be justified in resorting to force." [5]

Economic and Social Council

But in addition to the drafting of article 2 (7) of the Charter, the San Francisco conference was also faced with the impact of the United Nations upon domestic jurisdiction in other respects.

By article 55 of the Charter, in chapter IX, dealing with "International Economic and Social Cooperation", it was provided that "the United Nations shall promote:

"a. higher standards of living, full employment, and conditions of economic and social progress and development;

"b. solutions of international economic, social, health, and related problems; and international cultural and educational cooperation; and

"c. universal respect for, and observance of, human rights and fundamental freedoms for all without distinction as to race, sex, language, or religion."

Chapter IX (A) of the Dumbarton Oaks Pro-

---

[3] *Report to the President on the Results of the San Francisco Conference,* June 26, 1945, p. 44 (Department of State publication 2349).

[4] *Ibid.,* p. 45.

[5] *Ibid.*

posals had broadly suggested that provision be made in the Charter that "the Organization should facilitate solutions of international economic, social and other humanitarian problems and promote respect for human rights and fundamental freedoms."

The Dumbarton Oaks Proposals, however, contained no provision such as that contained in article 56 of the Charter that the members agree "to take joint and separate action in cooperation with the Organization for the achievement of the purposes set forth in Article 55."

When it came to drafting the Charter, Australia proposed that all members should pledge "to take action both national and international for the purpose of securing for all peoples, including their own, improved labor standards, economic advancement, social security and employment for all who seek it" and to report annually upon steps taken.

Secretary of State Stettinius declared that "the United States Delegation deemed it perfectly appropriate for the member states to pledge themselves to cooperate with the organization for the achievement of these purposes." [6] But he pointed out that the view was advanced "that the further element in the Australian proposal calling for national action separate from the international organization went beyond the proper scope of the Charter of an international organization and possibly even infringed on the domestic jurisdiction of member states in committing them to a particular philosophy of the relationship between the government and the individual." [7] Secretary of State Stettinius concluded in his report to the President:

"The pledge as finally adopted was worded to eliminate such possible interpretation. It pledges the various countries to cooperate with the organization by joint and separate action in the achievement of the economic and social objectives of the organization without infringing upon their right

[6] *Ibid.*, p. 115.
[7] *Ibid.*
[8] *Ibid.*
[9] Report of the Rapporteur of Commission II/3 to Commission II, UNCIO doc. 861, II/3/55 (1), June 8, 1945.
[10] S. Exec. Rept. 8, 79th Cong., 1st sess. (Charter of the United Nations.)
[11] *Report to the President on the Results of the San Francisco Conference*, June 26, 1945, p. 111 (Department of State publication 2349).

first session of the General Assembly. On October 24, 1946, during the meetings of the General Committee, the representative of South Africa requested that the item be removed from the agenda for the reason that the question concerned not Indian nationals, but Indians, nationals of South Africa, and was one essentially within the domestic jurisdiction of South Africa under article 2 (7). The item was retained on the agenda and referred by the General Assembly to the First and Sixth Committees jointly.

The representative of India submitted that the Union of South Africa's discriminatory treatment of Indians on the grounds of race constituted a denial of human rights and fundamental freedoms contrary to the Charter; and that the Union's policy in general and the enactment of the Asiatic Land Tenure and Indian Representation Act of 1946, in particular, impaired friendly relations between the two member states. The Capetown agreement of 1927 and a joint communiqué of 1932 were particularly relied upon by the Representative of India.

The Government of the Union of South Africa admitted that certain restrictive measures had been enacted by the South African Government following World War I. But it stated that the Capetown agreement of 1927 was an attempt to obviate restrictive measures, and that in that agreement India formally recognized the right of South Africa "to use all just and legitimate means for the maintenance of Western standards of life"; that by it, India also pledged herself to cooperate in a scheme of assisted immigration of Indians from South Africa to India, and that South Africa was to assimilate the remaining Indians as far as practicable to western standards of life. India, South Africa asserted, had failed to cooperate in the program of immigration of Indians to India, and though the situation of the Indians was greatly improved, the number of Indians increased rather than decreased. By the Asiatic Land Tenure and Indian Representation Act of 1946, he explained, the situation of Indians was improved by formal recognition, given for the first time to the South African Indian popu-

[12] *Journal of the Security Council*, no. 2, Jan. 24, 1946, p. 15.

[13] *Ibid.*, no. 11, Feb. 15, 1946, pp. 197, 198.

[14] *Ibid.*, pp. 207-208.

[15] *Ibid.*, p. 208.

lation, as members of the South African community. They were given two seats in the Provincial Council of Natal. While the act prevented Indians from acquiring land in certain areas reserved for white occupation, and vice versa, there was no discrimination, South Africa urged, as the law applied equally to Europeans and Indians.

The South African representative maintained that the Capetown agreement of 1927 and the joint communiqué of 1932 were not instruments giving rise to treaty obligations.

The Representative of South Africa strenuously urged that the problems fell within the domestic domain of the state and that its action could not be called into question by other states. He proposed that the General Assembly request an advisory opinion from the International Court of Justice on the question whether the matter was, under article 2 (7) of the Charter, essentially within the domestic jurisdiction of the Union of South Africa.

The matter was the subject of numerous proposals and of prolonged discussion in the Joint Committee. Finally, on December 7, 1946, the Assembly, by resolution, took note of the Indian application regarding the treatment of Indians in the Union of South Africa. It stated that, because of that treatment, friendly relations between the two states had been impaired and that unless a satisfactory settlement were reached, these relations were likely to be further impaired. It expressed the opinion that "the treatment of Indians in the Union should be in conformity with the international obligations under the agreements concluded between the two Governments, and the relevant provisions of the Charter". The two Governments were requested to report at the next session of the General Assembly the measures adopted to this effect.

The issue would have been clarified had an opinion of the International Court been obtained. South Africa proposed this procedure. Many representatives, however, opposed the suggestion on the ground that the political aspects of the question far outweighed its legal aspects.

Human Rights

The preamble to the Charter of the United Nations states that the peoples of the United Nations are determined "to reaffirm faith in fundamental human rights".

tional Clause, the Government of the United States stated that "The declaration does not apply to . . . (b) disputes with regard to matters which are essentially within the domestic jurisdiction of the United States of America as determined by the United States of America."

Nor was such a qualification upon acceptance of the Optional Clause entirely new. For example, the declaration of France accepting compulsory jurisdiction—a declaration filed under the Statute of the Permanent Court of International Justice but which remains still in effect by virtue of article 36 (5) of the Statute of the new Court—excepts therefrom "disputes relating to matters which are essentially within the national jurisdiction as understood by the Government of the French Republic."

The declaration filed on behalf of the United Kingdom (also originally filed under the old Statute), to cite another example, excepts from its scope "disputes with regard to questions which by international law fall exclusively within the jurisdiction of the United Kingdom". Other states, including the Union of South Africa, Australia, Canada, India, Iran, and New Zealand, have a similar exception in their declarations.

Under the old Court, eight other states—Yugoslavia, Albania, Rumania, Poland, Argentina, Brazil, Iraq, and Egypt—also included such an exception in their declarations accepting the compulsory jurisdiction of the Court.

The recent declaration filed by Mexico specified that it shall "not apply to disputes arising from matters that, in the opinion of the Mexican Government, are within the domestic jurisdiction of the United States of Mexico".

Because of the reciprocal character of these declarations, any country which has filed a declaration accepting the compulsory jurisdiction of the Court, may, in any dispute with a country that has filed such a declaration, including a condition of reciprocity, take advantage of such provision and except from the Court's jurisdiction any case which *it* considers within its domestic jurisdiction. Hence, the effects of filing such declarations containing an exception with respect to "domestic" matters, are not limited to the states filing the declaration containing the exception.

A reference may be made here to the celebrated decision of the Permanent Court in the case of the Tunis-Morocco nationality decrees.

By article 13 of the Covenant of the League of Nations, the members of the League agreed to submit disputes, which could not be satisfactorily settled by diplomacy, to arbitration or judicial settlement. Under the provisions of article 15 (1), it was further provided that should "any dispute likely to lead to a rupture . . . (be) not submitted to arbitration or judicial settlement in accordance with article 13," the members agreed that they would submit the matter to the Council of the League.

Article 15, paragraph 8, however, provided:

"If the dispute between the parties is claimed by one of them, and is found by the Council, to arise out of a matter which by international law is solely within the domestic jurisdiction of that party, the Council shall so report, and shall make no recommendation as to its settlement."

On October 4, 1922, the Council of the League adopted a resolution, at the instance of the British Government, concerning a dispute which had arisen between France and Great Britain as to nationality decrees issued in Tunis and Morocco (French Zone) on November 8, 1921, and their application to British subjects, the French Government having refused to submit the matter to arbitration. The Council decided by the resolution to refer to the Permanent Court of International Justice a request for its opinion whether the dispute "is or is not by international law solely a matter of domestic jurisdiction" within the meaning of article 15 (8) of the Covenant.

On February 7, 1923, the Permanent Court of International Justice gave a unanimous opinion that the dispute was, by international law, "not solely within the domestic jurisdiction of France".[16]

At the outset the Court stated that the words "solely within the domestic jurisdiction" contemplated matters which "though they may very closely concern the interests of more than one State, are not, in principle, regulated by interna-

---

[16] Permanent Court of International Justice, series B, no. 4, pp. 7, 32.

[17] *Ibid.*, pp. 23–24.

agreement deals directly with various problems of jurisdiction at the site of the United Nations, and the convention on privileges and immunities deals particularly with problems of immunity from the local jurisdiction of the organization, its officers, of representatives to the organization, and its specialized agencies.

Article 2 (7)—its meaning and significance—comprises, therefore, an exceedingly difficult aspect of the Charter. Its meaning will doubtless be clarified and developed as it is tested in new situations. It is, of course, an utterly hopeless task to endeavor to state what is an "essentially domestic matter" at any given time, or to lay down any slide-rule test for determining what is or is not an "essentially domestic matter". It varies with the particular facts at hand; it varies with the time, with the advance that is made in the area which comes to be recognized by states as proper for international concern and control. It is, in truth, a relative concept dependent upon the development of international relations.

Selected Bibliography [20]

——Fifth Session, Supplement No. 2. Report of the Fiscal Commission (E/440, May 29, 1947, and E/440/Add. 1, July 16, 1947). 9 pp. printed. [10¢.]

Security Council

Letter From the Representative of Yugoslavia Addressed to the President of the Security Council Dated 5 November 1947, and Enclosed Copy of the Note Presented to the Governments of the United Kingdom and the United States of America. (Questions regarding Trieste.) S/598, November 7, 1947. 7 pp. mimeo.

Letter From the Representative of the United Kingdom Addressed to the Secretary-General, Dated 17 November 1947. (Proclamation regarding Trieste.) S/605, November 18, 1947. 2 pp. mimeo.

(*Continued on page 280*)

---

[18] *Ibid.*, p. 26.
[19] *Ibid*, p. 26.
[20] Printed materials may be secured in the United States from the International Documents Service, Columbia University Press, 2960 Broadway, New York City. Other materials (mimeographed or processed documents) may be consulted at certain designated libraries in the United States

FOREIGN AID AND RECONSTRUCTIC

[Released to the press by the White House February 18]

To the Congress of the United States:

On several occasions I have stated that a primary objective of the United States is to bring about, throughout the world, the conditions of a just and lasting peace. This is a cause to which the American people are deeply devoted.

Since V–J Day we have expended great effort and large sums of money on the relief and rehabilitation of war-torn countries to aid in restoring workable economic systems which are essential to the maintenance of peace. A principle which has guided our efforts to assist these war-torn countries has been that of helping their peoples to help themselves. The Congress is now giving careful consideration to a most vital and far-reaching proposal to further this purpose—the program for aid to European recovery.

I now request the Congress to consider the type of further assistance which this country should provide to China.[1]

A genuine friendship has existed between the American people and the people of China over many years. This friendship has been accompanied by a long record of commercial and cultural association and close cooperation between our two countries. Americans have developed a deep respect for the Chinese people and sympathy for the many trials and difficulties which they have endured.

The United States has long recognized the im-

---

[1] Secretary Marshall transmitted on Feb. 18, 1948, to Senator Vandenberg, President pro tempore of the Senate, and to Speaker Martin of the House of Representatives, a copy of the proposed China aid bill.

the Congress authorize a program for aid to China in the amount of 570 million dollars to provide assistance until June 30, 1949.

The program should make provision for the financing, through loans or grants, of essential imports into China in the amount of 510 million dollars. This estimate is based upon prices as of January 1, 1948, since it is impossible at present to predict what effect current price changes may have on the program. Revised dollar estimates can be presented in connection with the request for appropriations if necessary. The essential imports include cereals, cotton, petroleum, fertilizer, tobacco, pharmaceuticals, coal and repair parts for existing capital equipment. The quantities provided for under this program are within the limits of available supplies. The financing of these essential commodity imports by the United States would permit the Chinese Government to devote its limited dollar resources to the most urgent of its other needs.

The program should also provide 60 million dollars for a few selected reconstruction projects to be initiated prior to June 30, 1949. There is an urgent need for the restoration of essential transportation facilities, fuel and power operations, and export industries. This work could be undertaken in areas sheltered from military operations and could help in improving the supply and distribution of essential commodities.

As in the case of aid to European recovery, the conduct of this program of aid should be made subject to an agreement between China and the United States setting forth the conditions and procedures for administering the aid. The agreement should include assurances that the Chinese Government will take such economic, financial, and other measures as are practicable, looking toward the ultimate goal of economic stability and recovery. The United States would, of course, reserve the right to terminate aid if it is determined that the assistance provided is not being handled in accordance with the agreement or that the policies of the Chinese Government are inconsistent with the objective of using the aid to help achieve a self-supporting economy.

Pending establishment of the agency which is to be set up for the administration of the European Recovery Program, the assistance to China should be carried forward under the existing machinery now administering the foreign relief programs. Legislation authorizing the Chinese program should make possible transfer of the administration of the Chinese program to the agency administering our aid to European recovery. The need for authority in the administering agency to make adjustments in the program from time to time will be as great here as in the European Recovery Program.

The proposed program of aid to China represents what I believe to be the best course this Government can follow in the light of all the circumstances. Nothing which this country provides by way of assistance can, even in a small measure, be a substitute for the necessary action that can be taken only by the Chinese Government. Yet this program can accomplish the important purpose of giving the Chinese Government a respite

STATEMENT BY SECR

In consideration of a program of assistance to China, it should be recognized that for the main part the solution of China's problems is largely one for the Chinese themselves. The great difficulty in determining a basis and procedure to justify a program of assistance lies in the conditions which exist in China, military as well as economic.

Thus far, the principal deterrent to the solution of Chinese economic problems is the civil war, which has drained the Chinese Government's internal and foreign-exchange resources, continued the destruction of property and the constant disruption of economic life, and has prevented recovery. The Communist forces have brought about the terrible destruction to wreck the economy of China. This is their announced purpose—to force an economic collapse.

The Chinese Government is in dire need of assistance in its present serious economic difficulties. However, the political, economic, and financial conditions in China are so unstable and so uncertain that it is impossible to develop a prac-

---

[1] Made before the House Committee on Foreign Affairs on Feb. 20, 1948, and released to the press on the same date.

tion, China has certain international financial obligations.

To meet these additional needs for foreign exchange, China will have available certain financial resources of her own. These include proceeds from exports; miscellaneous receipts from such sources as overseas remittances; the sale of surplus property; foreign government and philanthropic expenditures in China; and finally, to be called upon if necessary, China's reserves of gold and foreign exchange which were estimated as totaling the equivalent of 274 million dollars as of January 1, 1948. This amount would be increased to the extent the Chinese are able to bring about an improvement in their net foreign-exchange receipts. On the other hand, the amount will be reduced to the extent that reserves must be used, for lack of other available funds, to make necessary payments after January 1, 1948.

It is proposed, in the program submitted, that it would be administered by the agency or establishment of the Government created by law for the purpose of administering programs of assistance to foreign countries or, pending the establishment of such agency, temporarily by the Department of State in cooperation with the other agencies of the Government directly concerned. The conditions under which assistance is to be extended should be spelled out in an agreement with the Chinese Government, which would be based on the same considerations underlying the conditions for assistance to European countries but of necessity adjusted to the different conditions in China.

Statement by Secretary Marshall Praising Work of AMAG

[Released to the press February 16]

The President's Second Quarterly Report on Assistance to Greece and Turkey was submitted to the Congress today.

It is appropriate at this time to refer to the work of the American Mission for Aid to Greece. In the face of many difficulties, Governor Griswold and his staff are doing an outstanding job in carrying out their mission in accordance with the policies of this Government. I think the members of the Mission have a right to be proud of the work they are doing in this service to Greece and to the United States.

The Greek Situation

ADDRESS BY LOY

Director, Office of Near Ea

. . . .

We must bear in mind general developments in Europe in order to understand American policies in Greece and the character of the difficulties which confront us in that country.

The recent publication of diplomatic documents relating to Soviet–German relations during the years 1939–1941 has helped to refresh our memory of the pact between the Soviet Union and Nazi Germany, which foreshadowed the partition of eastern Europe, the destruction of millions of innocent persons in that area, and the forceful deprivation of a number of eastern European countries of their independence. Unfortunately even after the collapse of the Axis, various peoples of eastern and southeastern Europe continued to be shorn of their liberties. The procedures by which these areas were taken over are also undoubtedly well known to you: use or threat of use of overwhelming armed forces, employment of police-state terror, shamelessly rigged elections, staged mass demonstrations, bluster and machinations by secret agents and terrorists disguised as diplomats or high military or civilian officials of Communist-controlled countries, and treacherous activities of Moscow-trained agents posing as local patriots.

The consequence of such Machiavellian oozing, trickling, and filtering is that the control of international Communism in eastern Europe now extends over a solid belt from the Arctic to the Adriatic and well into the heart of Germany. But it has not yet effectively penetrated to the Mediterranean. In their southward march, the international Communists have encountered some "firm obstacles" which, for the time being, have slowed up their progress. One of these is Turkey. Another is Greece, that sun-blanched pile of rocks which two thousand years ago gave birth to our civilization and which today is struggling for the maintenance of its own independence, is defending its offspring against another of those waves of barbarism which so many times during the centuries have threatened to inundate all of Europe.

The will of the Greeks to retain their freedom was not instilled into them by the United States,

---

[1] Delivered before the Kentucky Women's Action Committee Forum at Louisville, Ky., on Feb. 18, 1948, and released to the press on the same date.

Greeks, an impoverished people ravaged by war, cannot hold the line without aid from abroad, nor should they be expected to do so. For the battle of Greece now being waged is only one sector of the battle for the security of the democratic world. It is more than the struggle of a brave people for their national survival and is by no means merely an international competition over a strategic outpost. It is a battle for decency against darkness, a battle for human freedom and progress against primitive forces of terror and oppression.

The conspiracy against Greece is only a part of a wider plan formulated many years ago. It will be recalled that long before the outbreak of World War II, Communist doctrine stated:

"It is the essential task of the victorious revolution in one country to develop and support the revolution in others. So the revolution in a victorious country ought not to consider itself as a self-contained unit, but as an auxiliary and a means of hastening the victory of the proletariat in other countries.

"Lenin has tersely expressed this thought by saying that the task of the victorious revolution is to do the 'utmost possible in one country for the development, support and stirring up of the revolution in all countries' ".

The groundwork for the "development, support and stirring up of the revolution" in Greece, according to the pattern of the leaders of international Communism, was carefully laid during the war years by the insinuation of Communists into the Greek Government-in-exile and by the creation of EAM, a supposedly nonpartisan Greek resistance group, and ELAS, its associated guerrilla force. It has become only too clear that EAM was in fact a Communist-front organization. Unfortunately, for some time many loyal Greeks as well as friends of Greece abroad were duped as to the real character of the EAM control.

With the liberation of Greece by the British in late 1944, the conspiracy began rapidly to mature. Instead of disbanding when it had no further pretext for existence, ELAS, which turned out to be nothing more than a Communist-controlled army, launched a well-prepared attack on Athens. A brief but appallingly bloody civil war ensued. Defeated in this civil war with the aid of British arms, several thousand members of ELAS, instead of joining other Greeks in the tasks of reconstruction, withdrew individually or in small groups across the northern border of Greece to await and prepare for still another Communist bid for power. This withdrawal was carried on under Communist instructions and with the connivance of the governments of Greece's northern neighbors. Meanwhile, within Greece itself, the Communist Party and its front organization, EAM, were allowed to resume their legal existence and were thus in a position to slander as reactionary

273

and oppressive the very Government which permitted them freedom of speech and press. This campaign of slander was accompanied by attacks on the western Allies and unrestrained praise for the governments of countries already under Communist control.

The conspiracy entered a new phase in 1946—after the Greek people had freely expressed their will and rejected Communism in an internationally observed plebiscite and elections—with the launching of the present guerrilla movement from the training camps of Yugoslavia, Albania, and Bulgaria.

The suggestion is frequently made that the United States should set up in Greece the precise kind of government which the American people would like, headed by leaders of American choosing. The United States is not in the business of making or breaking Greek governments, nor could we go into this business without justifying the charges of intervention and imperialism now so falsely leveled against us by Soviet propaganda or without weakening the confidence of the Greeks in themselves. The present Greek Government is a coalition enjoying the support of the overwhelming majority of the Greek Parliament. That Parliament, in turn, was chosen in elections in March 1946, which were certified by 1,155 foreign observers, including 692 Americans, as representing "a true and valid verdict of the Greek people." There may have been a swing in Greek public opinion one way or the other since 1946. It is difficult without new elections accurately to gage the state of current public opinion, and it would be physically impossible to hold new elections before order is restored without arbitrarily disenfranchising a great many voters. Meanwhile, little purpose is served by petty criticism which magnifies into a major scandal every human failing and every error of judgment of the statesmen freely chosen by the Greek people as their leaders. It seems wise to us to try to cooperate with these leaders. We would be equally disposed to cooperate with any other leaders who might enter the Government regardless of whether they might be of the Right, the Center, or the Socialist Left, provided we are satisfied that they enjoy the support of the democratic Greek people and that they are not the dupes, the fellow travelers, or the accomplices of totalitarian Fascism or Communism.

One of the essential characteristics of a democratic state is a free trade-union movement. Concerted efforts are being made to strengthen such a movement in Greece. These efforts meet certain obstacles, since trade-unionism in Greece has traditionally been weak and in the past has tended to be of political character. Trade-unions were in fact abolished altogether by the prewar Metaxas regime. Since last July, however, elections by secret ballot have been held under the scrutiny

increased approximately 93 percent in the same period. In January 1946 the exchange rate of the drachma was officially pegged at 5 thousand to the dollar. By the end of January 1947, the open-market rate was around 8 thousand, and it stands in the neighborhood of 13 thousand today. From the beginning of 1946 up to the middle of 1947, when the American Mission began its operations in Greece, the open-market rate of the gold sovereign in Athens fluctuated between 130 and 140 thousand drachmas. Today it is fluctuating around 220 thousand drachmas and has been as high as 236 thousand drachmas.

It is clear from these figures that, while runaway inflation has been averted, confidence in the drachma has not been restored. The Greek economic pump has been kept in creaking motion by patchwork repairs and by vigorous priming, but it is not yet operating smoothly and automatically.

What are the reasons for this? Why has more substantial progress not been made?

In the first place, there have been a number of negative factors of an administrative or economic nature which could not be determined in advance and could not therefore be given consideration when the size and scope of the aid-to-Greece program was first presented to Congress.

Among these factors might be mentioned delays in getting the aid project under way. The funds requested by President Truman on March 12 were not actually authorized by Congress until May 22, and the appropriation act itself was not passed until July 30. It was thus August before our operations really began in Greece and necessarily several months later before work projects on a substantial scale could be started. The Greek budget for the period April 1947 through June 1948 was not submitted to the American Mission until September 1947 and was not approved in final form until November. Further time was required to work out and impose the new tax measures.

Among the economic difficulties we might note that the Greek wheat crop for the year 1947–48 was, as a result of the drought, one third less than that of the year 1946–47. The unanticipated wheat deficit thus necessitated heavier imports than had been estimated. The situation was further complicated by a substantial rise in the world price of wheat and other necessary imports during the same period. Furthermore, the yield of foreign exchange from the sale of Greek exports abroad was disappointing. It had been estimated that these exports would yield about 120 million dollars. It now appears that the actual figure will not exceed 70 million dollars. There are several explanations for this: Greece's principal export commodities—tobacco, dried fruits, olive oil—are luxury products which are among the first to be barred by importing nations struggling to curtail imports. Moreover, as a result of the artificial high valuation of the drachma, the export costs of some exportable commodities were higher than world prices. Then we must not forget that Greece's normal foreign markets, Germany and central Europe, which took over 50 percent of her exports before the war, are not now in a position to import what Greece has to export. Serious as they are, the administrative and economic problems are overshadowed by the main difficulty which besets Greece today, the lack of security in the country. The lack of confidence in the drachma and the continued stagnation of Greek capital and enterprise stem in large part from feelings of uncertainty with regard to the future of Greece itself.

In the military field, as in that of economics, the Greeks, with our help, have barely managed to "hold the fort". The situation is still fluid, however, as it was in the middle of 1947. Despite all the fanfare associated with the announcement of the establishment of the Markos junta on Christmas Eve, the guerrillas exercise control over no fixed territory and have not been successful in holding on to any town of significance. There is as yet no "front" in Greece in a military sense. The Greek Army is able physically to go to any point in Greece despite guerrilla opposition. It has not been able, however, to maintain law and order simultaneously in the whole of Greece.

This fluid military situation can best be understood after an examination of a relief map of Greece. The guerrillas exercise predominant influence in most of the mountainous areas, particularly along the northern frontier. They are accustomed to descend in the night from the mountains to raid lowland towns and villages. Usually these settlements are not more than three hours' walking distance from their mountain lairs. Conversely, the Government forces exercise paramount influence in the plains and valleys. They try to protect the towns, villages, and lines of communications. They periodically conduct offensive sweeps and lesser operations against the guerrillas in the mountains.

However, in respect of the numbers, organization, and armament, the guerrillas appear to have gained in strength during the last year. By means of forced recruiting their numbers have been increased from an estimated 10,000 in March 1947 to well over 20,000 at present in spite of the fact that the Government forces have been able to inflict severe losses on them. From isolated bands roaming the hills with an odd assortment of rifles, the guerrillas are developing into a fairly efficient military force, well armed with, and trained in the use of, automatic weapons and artillery. Last December they were able to organize an expedition of over 3,000 men against the town of Konitsa on the Albanian border. The United Nations commission now in Greece, incidentally, has re-

of towns and villages so that the Army could be released for aggressive action against the guerrillas. These measures have required the diversion of 23 million dollars from the contemplated reconstruction program, thereby reducing the amount originally budgeted for reconstruction by about one half. It is unfortunate that in this—the third year after the defeat of the Axis powers—it should still be necessary in a country which, like Greece, suffered so deeply during the war to divert funds, supplies, and energies from the peaceful pursuit of rehabilitation and reconstruction to military purposes. It does not seem necessary to stress here who is responsible for this sad state of affairs.

Do not, however, obtain the impression that the situation in Greece is hopeless. In the economic field some of the factors which have operated against the struggle to preserve a free and independent Greece may disappear. The present Greek crop outlook, for instance, is good. Furthermore, there is a possibility that during the coming year there will not be appreciable rises in the world prices of wheat, foodstuffs, and other supplies needed in Greece. In the near future it should also be possible for Greek economy to begin to feel the beneficial effects of some of the reconstruction projects and financial and administrative reforms which the Greek Government with our aid has carried out during the last year. Improvements may also be expected in the military situation. It is hoped that, when additional military equipment provided for in our program reaches Greece and has been placed in the hands of the Greek Army and National Guard, when the new recruits in the Army and the National Guard have had the requisite training, and when the American military staff officers so recently dispatched to give advice to the Greek Army have reached the field, the Greek Army and National Guard with the enthusiastic backing of all loyal Greeks will set about to liquidate the guerrillas and to free Greece from the paralysis of Communist guerrilla terror.

In case international Communism should find that its advance guard in Greece is in danger, it may decide further to increase its support to the guerrillas. There are, however, definite limits beyond which international Communism and its puppets may hesitate to go in this respect. Even the international Communists must realize the immediate dangers to world peace which might be involved if they resort to more overt forms of aggression, such as the dispatch from the puppet states of heavy reinforcements for the guerrillas in Greece or of heavy shipments of arms. International Communism in its desire to obtain control over Greece may, however, venture so far as to create a situation with which the armed forces of Greece alone could not be expected to cope.

277

The development of such a situation would of course require a reexamination of the whole Greek problem.

It seems likely that the forces of international Communism would pause before launching a policy of overt aggression against Greece if they could only understand that the determination of the United States and other democratic countries to prevent Greece from falling a victim to foreign aggression can be just as firm as that of the aggressor to deprive Greece of her independence and integrity. Nothing is more likely to encourage the weary and disheartened Greek people and to cause the forces of international Communism to reconsider their course of action with regard to Greece than the certainty that, so long as the Greek people desire their freedom and express this desire by cooperating with one another in resisting with all their energy the enemies of their freedom, the United States will not stand idly by while foreign aggressors deprive Greece of its territorial integrity and political independence.

Congress is now giving its consideration to the European Recovery Program, with which the Greek Government has pledged its cooperation and in anticipation of which it has drawn up an ambitious program of self-help through the exploitation of Greece's own resources and through close economic collaboration with the other 15 participating European countries. This program will not be workable in Greece unless the security of Greece can be assured and internal order restored. In fact, unless these conditions are met, the European Recovery Program as a whole will be seriously threatened. For what confidence could other European nations feel in their own security if Greece were allowed to fall victim to aggression? And how can economic reconstruction be envisaged except in an atmosphere of reasonable confidence and security? It is likely, in view of the exigencies of the situation in Greece, that among the various proposals which will be submitted to the Congress in the near future will be one providing for the granting of additional financial aid to Greece for military purposes to supplement the funds destined exclusively for the economic rehabilitation of Greece under the European Recovery Program.

From time to time statements are to be heard to the effect that the Greek problem is incapable of solution, that efforts on the part of the United Nations to prevent Greece from falling victim to aggression will for an indefinite period be offset by increased aid on the part of international Communism and its satellites to the Greek guerrillas, and that so long as we adhere to our present policies with regard to Greece the American taxpayer will, among his other burdens, be compelled to expend large sums in Greece.

tions

that of avoiding "decisions and recommendations on the larger issues" and engaging in "quiet work on the lesser controversial matters", and that of boldly taking hold of "the troubles pouring in upon it" and making "realistic decisions and recommendations". The report shows why that choice arose and, furthermore, gives the framework of events in the world that posed that choice. The United Nations, by taking the bolder course, went into the mainstream of international relations, which is a source of realistic strength for it.

The report, which is a revealing account of history in the making, surveys the difficulties that the principal organs of the United Nations faced. In this connection, it takes account in a forthright manner of the serious problem posed by nonparticipation on the part of certain members in the recommendations approved. In the work of the General Assembly, both Greece and Palestine are treated at length and a fairly full story is given of other important selected matters such as Korea, the Interim Committee, propaganda, and voting in the Security Council. Aside from its consideration of ten political and security problems before the Assembly, the report covers also developments concerning economic and social matters, non-self-governing-territory and legal problems, and various organizational questions, particularly that of the headquarters of the United Nations.

The report succinctly describes the work of the Security Council, covering its powers, responsibilities, and development to 1948. The Indonesian question is given some prominence and the Corfu Channel case is discussed. Also included are the United Kingdom–Egyptian dispute and responsibilities concerning Trieste.

The topic covered most extensively in the report dealing with the Security Council is the international control of atomic energy. Here the extent of agreement and the basic issues in disagreement in the views of the United States and most other members on one hand, and the U.S.S.R. on the other, are defined and brought plainly to light.

An analytical consideration of agreement and disagreement also marks the sections of the report treating the provision of armed forces to be put at the disposal of the Security Council and the problems of the regulation of conventional armaments.

The development of regional economic commissions by the Economic and Social Council during 1947 is highlighted. Discussed are the Economic Commission for Europe and the Economic Commission for Asia and the Far East and the study of further regional commissions for the Near and Middle East and Latin America. The work toward establishing an International Trade Organization is also given considerable attention. The social work of the Economic and Social Council is given due stress, with particular emphasis placed on the preparation of a bill of human rights and the preparations for the forthcoming Conference on Freedom of Information in Geneva beginning March 23.

In considering the work of the Trusteeship Council, the report clearly describes 1947 developments affecting dependent areas, such as colonies and other non-self-governing territories, and the developments affecting the trusteeship system. The trust Territory of the Pacific Islands, administered by the United States, receives special attention, and the work of the Trusteeship Council, now moving into its full scope of functions, is clarified at some length.

The role of the International Court is the subject of a short chapter. A picture of the work of the Secretariat is given, and an up-to-date statement is made on its organization and the problems it confronts. The nature of United States interest toward the Secretariat is also discussed.

The appendix constituting more than half of the report includes 35 of the most important resolutions of the General Assembly and several resolutions of the Security Council, each introduced with a brief statement in nontechnical language. The vote by which a resolution was adopted and in several instances the status of action taken subsequent to the resolution are indicated. Also included are principal papers in connection with the international control of atomic energy, containing certain important statements presenting the American policy during 1947. The plan of work followed in the meetings being held on prob-

OF STATE TO JACOB K. JAVITS

British treaty shipments has interfered with the carrying out of the recommendation of the General Assembly on Palestine embodied in its resolution of November 29, 1947.

(2) "Do the activities of the Arab nations with respect to support of the Arab Higher Committee for Palestine, and the Arab League, or otherwise in their announced violent resistance to the U.N. decision on Palestine, endanger the maintenance of international peace and security in the terms of the U.N. charter?"

While it is true that various Arab Governments and organizations have announced their determined opposition to the General Assembly's recommendation on Palestine, there have thus far been no overt acts which, in the decision of the Security Council of the United Nations, have been determined to endanger the maintenance of international peace and security in the terms of the United Nations Charter. Meanwhile, the United Kingdom, as the Mandatory Power, is responsible for the preservation of peace and security in Palestine. The United States has consistently proclaimed its determination to see the provisions of the United Nations Charter complied with, and its Representative in the General Assembly, in announcing this Government's policy regarding Palestine on October 11, 1947,[1] said that we assumed there would be Charter observance.

(3) "What will be the instructions of the U.S. to its U.N. delegate on the questions referred by the U.N. Palestine Commission to the Security Council regarding the means for making effective the General Assembly's decision on Palestine?"

The United Nations Palestine Commission has thus far submitted its first interim report to the Security Council but the Council has not yet taken action on the report. On February 10 the Council agreed to await the forthcoming special report of the Palestine Commission on the problems of security and enforcement before giving further consideration to the General Assembly's recommendation on Palestine. This report is due February 15. In absence of knowledge as to the contents of the Palestine Commission's next report it has been impossible to formulate instructions to the United States Representative on the Security Council.

---

[1] BULLETIN of Oct. 19, 1947, p. 761.

(4) "What is the U.S. prepared to do to help in the implementation of the U.N. decision on Palestine?"

I believe that much of this question is implicitly answered in my response to Question 3. Until the Security Council has received and studied the report of the Palestine Commission on security and enforcement and has reached a decision it is not possible for this Government to determine in advance the steps which may be necessary to carry out such a decision. However, the United States has been active as a member of certain other principal organs of the United Nations which are dealing with the Palestine problem to implement the resolution of November 29. The United States Representative on the Trusteeship Council and his Deputy have worked with other Members of the Council in preparing a draft statute for the trusteeship of Jerusalem. The United States as

INTERNATIONAL ORGANIZATIONS A

UNITED STATES DELEGATIONS TO FAO MEETINGS IN PHILIPPINES

The Department of State announced on February 20 that the President has approved the composition of the United States Delegations to two meetings sponsored by the Food and Agriculture Organization (FAO). An FAO Regional Meeting To Consider the Formation of a Regional Council for the Study of the Sea is scheduled to open at Baguio, Republic of the Philippines, on February 23, 1948, and an FAO Rice Meeting is scheduled to convene at Baguio on March 1, 1948.

The purpose of the first meeting is to discuss the establishment, organization, and constitution of a Regional Council for the Study of the Sea for waters of the Southwest Pacific and Indian Oceans.

The rice meeting is expected to concern the problems of international trade in rice and the possible formation of an international rice organization.

The United States Delegation to the Meeting To Consider the Formation of a Regional Council for the Study of the Sea is as follows:

Delegate:

Andrew W. Anderson, Chief, Division of Commercial Fisheries, Fish and Wildlife Service, Department of the Interior

Alternate Delegate:

Charles J. Shohan, International Resources Division, Department of State

Advisers:

Edward W. Allen, Acting Chairman, Pacific Fisheries Conference, Seattle, Washington

Directing Council of the Pan American Sanitary Organization Holds First Meeting

ARTICLE BY JAMES A. DOULL

At the Twelfth Pan American Sanitary Conference held at Caracas, Venezuela, from January 2 to 24, 1947, a reorganization plan was adopted which defined the Pan American Sanitary Organization as consisting of four parts: the Pan American Sanitary Conference, meeting once in four years; the Directing Council, meeting annually; the Executive Committee, meeting every six months; and the Pan American Sanitary Bureau, the permanent body of the Organization with headquarters at Washington.

Representatives of all 21 American republics make up the Directing Council. The Executive Committee elected under the new plan included representatives of Argentina (elected for one year), Brazil (three years), Chile (one year), Costa Rica (three years), Cuba (two years), Mexico (three years), and the United States (two years). This Committee held its first meeting from April 28 to May 3, 1947, at Washington and, having received an invitation from the Government of Argentina, decided that the Committee and the Directing Council should meet at Buenos Aires during the second half of September 1947. Accordingly, the original Executive Committee held four sessions in that city from September 22 to 24, the Directing Council held eleven plenary sessions from September 24 to October 2, and the new Executive Committee held a brief concluding session on October 2.

The Executive Committee received at the meetings the report of the Director of the Bureau and prepared draft rules of procedure and a draft agenda for the Council.

Nineteen of the American republics were represented at the meetings of the Directing Council.[1] The Interim Commission of the World Health Organization and the Rockefeller Foundation were represented by observers. The agenda and rules of procedure recommended by the Executive Committee were adopted without significant change. The chief items on the agenda were (1) increase of the quota from 40 cents to one dollar per 1,000 inhabitants and consideration of voluntary supplementary contributions; (2) approval of the constitution of the Pan American Health Organization; (3) approval of the reorganization plan and budget of the Pan American Sanitary Bureau; (4) revision of the Pan American Sanitary Code; (5) relationship of the Pan American Health Organization to the World Health Organization; and (6) election of two countries to succeed Argentina and Chile on the Executive Committee. The following committees were appointed to study and prepare reports on the agenda items: (1) Finance and Reorganization; (2) Constitution; (3) Relations with the World Health and Other Organizations; and (4) Drafting.

Reports of the Committees

1. *Finance and Reorganization.* The Council accepted the report of this Committee and approved the increase in quota from 40 cents to one dollar per 1,000 population. It was agreed to establish an additional optional quota, the amount of which would be in accordance with the economic capacity of each country, and the Director of the Pan American Sanitary Bureau was authorized to take appropriate steps toward securing these funds.

A budget of $1,300,000 for the first year's operation (effective Jan. 1, 1948) was approved subject to availability of funds. From information re-

---

[1] Ecuador and Nicaragua did not send representatives.

ceived from various representatives, the Committee felt justified in taking into account approval by governments of the quota of one dollar per capita and also probably sufficient additional annual contributions to warrant this budget. The Director of the Bureau was authorized to make necessary changes in the budget, subject to subsequent approval of the Executive Committee at the earliest opportunity.

The annual salaries of the Director, Assistant Director, and Secretary and the Representation Fund of the Bureau were approved as follows: Director, $15,000; Assistant Director, $10,000; Secretary, $9,000; and Representation Fund, $6,000. Authorization was also given for the payment by the Bureau of income taxes on the salaries of the employees.

2. *Constitution.* The Committee accepted in the main the draft constitution prepared by the Executive Committee in April and May 1947, and the Committee's report was accepted by the Council with only minor changes. The following features of the constitution are of special interest:

a. NAME—The Executive Committee had recommended the names "Pan American Health Organization" and "Pan American Health Conference". These were rejected in favor of the older terminology, "Pan American Sanitary Organization" and "Pan American Sanitary Conference".

b. MEMBERSHIP—There was much discussion of this point. The relevant provisions as adopted by the Council are:

Article 2 (A) The Pan American Sanitary Organization is at present composed of the 21 American republics. All self-governing nations of the Western Hemisphere are entitled to membership in the Pan American Sanitary Organization.

(B) Territories or groups of territories within the Western Hemisphere which do not conduct their own international relations shall have the right to be represented and to participate in the Organization. The nature and extent of the rights and obligations of these territories in the Organization shall be determined in each case by the Directing Council after consultation with the government or other authority having responsibility for their international relations.

The Final Report

The principal resolutions of the Council included in the final report relate to (1) placing upon the Pan American Sanitary Bureau the solution of the continental problem of urban yellow fever, based fundamentally on the eradication of *Aedes aegypti*, which transmits it; (2) acceptance of the report of the Committee on Relations and authorization of the Executive Committee to act as negotiator with the negotiating subcommittee of the Interim Commission of the World Health Organization; (3) formal authorization of an increase in the annual quota from 40 cents to one dollar per 1,000 inhabitants, and the establishment of an additional voluntary quota; (4) deferment of discussion of the Pan American Sanitary Code until a future meeting; (5) designation of Mexico City as the seat of the 1948 meeting of the Council; and (6) election of Uruguay and Venezuela to the Executive Committee.

Principal Accomplishments of the Meeting

The most important accomplishments of the meeting were agreement on a new constitution, additional progress toward integration with the World Health Organization, approval of a budget that will permit the Pan American Sanitary Organization to put its reorganization plan and its expanded program into effect, and the recognition of the necessity for a new sanitary code of world-wide application.

IONS ON GERMAN MATTERS

resented and the fact that this will be the first occasion on which interested governments will have an opportunity fully to express and examine their respective views, the conclusions reached may necessarily be of a provisional nature, particularly as the time for the conversations may be limited by the need of Ambassador Douglas' return to Washington early in March. A frank interchange of views over the entire range of subjects is contemplated and an effort will be made to obtain agreement on as many points of principle as possible so that clear-cut decisions can be taken at an early date. After the governments have had an opportunity to consider the results of these preliminary discussions, they will determine the next stage.

[Released to the press February 21]

The Department of State refers to the communication of February 13 of His Excellency the Soviet Ambassador relating to the discussions which the Governments of the United States, the United Kingdom and France propose to hold in London respecting Germany.

These discussions have been arranged for the examination of problems in Germany of mutual interest to the three Governments. There is no provision in the Potsdam or other agreements relating to Germany concluded by the four occupying powers which prevents any of the powers from discussing between themselves questions of common concern.

The United States Government is surprised that the Soviet Government should undertake to remind the other powers of their contractual obligations in Germany. The result evoked by the failure of the Soviet Government to observe the principle of economic unity provided for in Section III B 14 of the Potsdam agreement impels the

U. S. Delegation to Conference on Mar

[Released to the press February 10]

The Department of State announced on February 10 that the President has approved the composition of the United States Delegation to the United Nations Conference To Consider the Establishment of an Intergovernmental Maritime Consultative Organization. This meeting is scheduled to open at Geneva, Switzerland, on February 19, 1948, and is expected to last approximately one month. An invitation to the United States Government to attend the Conference was received from the Secretary-General of the United Nations on April 10, 1947. The United States Delegation is as follows

Chairman
Garrison Norton, Assistant Secretary of State

Vice Chairman
Huntington T. Morse, Special Assistant to the Commission, U.S. Maritime Commission

Chief Technical Adviser
John W. Mann, Shipping Division, Department of State

Cooperation in the Americas: Report of the Interdepartmental Committee on Scientific and Cultural Cooperation, July 1946–June 1947. International Information and Cultural Series 1. Pub. 2971. 146 pp. 40¢.

> A discussion of the cooperative scientific and technical projects, the exchange of persons, and the cultural interchanges between the Americas.

Air Transport Services. Treaties and Other International Acts Series 1659. Pub. 2978. 16 pp. 10¢.

> Interim Agreement Between the United States of America and Austria—Signed at Vienna October 8, 1947; entered into force October 8, 1947.

Military Assistance to the Philippines. Treaties and Other International Acts Series 1662. Pub. 2979. 6 pp. 5¢.

> Agreement Between the United States of America and the Republic of the Philippines—Signed at Manila March 21, 1947; entered into force March 21, 1947, effective from July 4, 1946.

Military Mission to Iran. Treaties and Other International Acts Series 1666. Pub. 2997. 10 pp. 5¢.

> Agreement Between the United States of America and Iran—Signed at Tehran October 6, 1947; entered into force October 6, 1947.

National Commission News, February 1, 1948. Pub. 3019. 10 pp. 10¢ a copy; $1 a year.

> Prepared monthly for the United States National Commission for the United Nations Educational, Scientific and Cultural Organization.

Restitution of Property: Transfer to Italian Government of Gold Captured at Fortezza. Treaties and Other International Acts Series 1658. Pub. 2975. 3 pp. 5¢.

> Protocol Between the United States of America, the United Kingdom of Great Britain and Northern Ireland, and Italy—Signed at London October 10, 1947; entered into force September 15, 1947.

The Foreign Service of the United States: Educational Preparation for Foreign Service Officers and Entrance Examinations. Department and Foreign Service Series 1. Pub. 2991. 81 pp. 25¢.

> A comprehensive discussion of the examinations for the U.S. Foreign Service—the requisite educational preparation, general examination information, and sample written examination questions.

Industrial Property: Restoration of Certain Rights Affected by World War II. Treaties and Other International Acts Series 1667. Pub. 2998. 6 pp. 5¢.

> Agreement Between the United States of America and France—Signed at Washington April 4, 1947; entered into force November 10, 1947.

The Turkish Aid Program. Economic Cooperation Series 1. Pub. 3014. 24 pp. 15¢.

> A background of the recent political and economic situations in Turkey leading to the establishment of, and documents relating to, the aid program.

Contributors

James A. Doull, author of the article on the Pan American Sanitary
Organization, served as alternate United States Representative on the
Directing Council of the Pan American Sanitary Organization. Dr.
Doull is Director of the Office of International Health Relations,
United States Public Health Service.

The Department of State bulletin

Vol. XVIII, No. 453 • Publication 3079

March 7, 1948

The Department of State BULLETIN, a weekly publication compiled and edited in the Division of Publications, Office of Public Affairs, provides the public and interested agencies of the Government with information on developments in the field of foreign relations and on the work of the Department of State and the Foreign Service. The BULLETIN includes press releases on foreign policy issued by the White House and the Department, and statements and addresses made by the President and by the Secretary of State and other officers of the Department, as well as special articles on various phases of international affairs and the functions of the Department. Information is included concerning treaties and international agreements to which the United States is or may become a party and treaties of general international interest.

Publications of the Department, as well as legislative material in the field of international relations, are listed currently.

uperintendent of Documents
Government Printing Office
Washington 25, D.C.

SUBSCRIPTION:
sues, $5; single copy, 15 cents

shed with the approval of the
r of the Bureau of the Budget

s of this publication are not
items contained herein may
itation of the DEPARTMENT
ETIN as the source will be

N. Howard

Committee of the General Assembly of the United
Nations on September 29, 1947, the Deputy
Premier and Minister of Foreign Affairs of Greece,
Constantine Tsaldaris, who noted the guerrilla
attempt to overthrow the constitutional Government of Greece and expressed his gratitude for
Anglo-American assistance, stated that each day's
delay in reaching a solution of the Greek question
aided the neighbors of Greece who were threatening Greek independence and "brought further
death and terror in the Greek countryside from
whose farms 250,000 refugees had already fled to
the cities."[2]

That the problem of the refugees was extremely
serious was recognized in the fall of 1947, although
its basic implications in Greek economic and political life were not fully realized at the time of
the organization of the American Mission for Aid
to Greece. Thus, in the first report on assistance
to Greece, dated September 30, 1947, it was pointed
out that the magnitude of the relief problem in
Greece was evident from the fact that out of a
total population of 7,500,000 people, 1,400,000 were
indigents. The report went on to say:[3]

---

[1] See *The United Nations and the Problem of Greece.*
Department of State publication 2909.

[2] U. N. doc. A/C.1/SR.63, pp. 1–3; *The General Assembly
and the Problem of Greece,* Department of State Bulletin
Supplement, Dec. 7, 1947, p. 1110. See also the statement of Mr. Manuilsky, of the Ukraine, on Oct. 3, 1947, in
which he challenged the Tsaldaris estimate and charged
that some 29,000 refugees had gathered from the southern
Peloponnesus to flee "Rightist" bands near Athens and
Piraeus. A/C.1/SR/65, p. 3. Mr. Manuilsky's figures
came from an EAM memorandum submitted to the
Commission of Investigation Concerning Greek Frontier
Incidents (S/AC.4/56/Annex 8).

[3] *1st Report to Congress on Assistance to Greece and
Turkey for the Period Ended September 30, 1947,* p. 8.
Department of State publication 2957.

"The relief problem has been made more acute by the guerrilla warfare, which has impeded and reduced grain collections and has caused an influx of refugees into urban areas in the north of Greece, thus over-taxing distribution facilities and housing to the detriment of public health. . . ."

In the fall of 1947 the problem had grown much more extensive, for in an effort to prevent forcible recruiting and seizure of food and other supplies by the guerrillas, the Greek National Army was compelled to evacuate entire villages, principally in northern and central Greece. During October 1947 the number of refugees was estimated at 300,000, and it was expected that the figure might reach 500,000 by December 1, 1947. The Greek Government estimated that the cost of caring for the refugees would run to approximately 265,000,-000,000 drachmas during the fiscal year, or about 10 percent of the Greek budget. A request was made for an additional $15,000,000 of United States foreign relief program funds to help meet the problem. Moreover, in view of the feeling that a solution of this increasingly serious problem should be worked out, on November 8 the Deputy Premier ordered the Greek National Army to cease forcible evacuation activities.

The agricultural situation deteriorated further in November 1947, since some 400,000 people, mostly farmers, had now fled from mountain villages or villages on the fringes of the mountains. It was noted that about 25 percent of the cereal crops could not be harvested because of guerrilla activity, while some harvested crops were taken by the guerrillas. Moreover, about 40 percent of the potato crop appeared lost for similar reasons, and a considerable amount of the livestock was also lost.

By the middle of January 1948 the number of refugees had reached the significant figure of about 420,000, of whom some 200,000 were in Macedonia, 53,000 in Thrace, 15,000 in Epirus, 150,000 in central Greece, and about 9,000 in the Peloponnesus and the Greek islands. The second report[4] on assistance to Greece declared:

"The chief success of the guerrilla forces has

[4] *Second Report to Congress on Assistance to Greece and Turkey for the Period Ended December 81, 1947*, p. 5. Department of State publication 3035.
[5] *Ibid.*, p. 14.

though progress has been made, the problem is a large one, and the health situation in northern Greece has deteriorated; overcrowding, lack of sanitary facilities, failure to apply DDT and proper immunization measures, insufficient food and a general breakdown in distribution have produced this situation among the refugees from the guerrillas in this region.

In the end, solution of the refugee problem depends upon attainment of security along the Greek frontiers, liquidation of guerrilla warfare, the economic reconstruction and rehabilitation of Greece in all its aspects, and the development of political stability.

Selected Bibliography [7]

mission for the Middle East. E/671, February 16, 1948. 11 pp. mimeo.

General Assembly

Interim Report of the United Nations Special Committee on the Balkans, Adopted by the Special Committee on 31 December 1947. A/521, January 9, 1948. 176 pp. mimeo.

Second Interim Report of the United Nations Special Committee on the Balkans, Adopted by the Special Committee on 10 January 1948. A/522, January 19, 1948. 10 pp. mimeo.

Check List of Reports to the General Assembly, Second Session, 16 September to 29 November 1947. A/INF/14, January 13, 1948. 35 pp. mimeo.

Disposition of Agenda Items of the Second Session of the General Assembly, 16 September–29 November 1947. A/INF/15, January 20, 1948. 65 pp. mimeo.

List of Resolutions Adopted by the General Assembly, Second Session, 16 September to 29 November 1947. A/INF/16, February 2, 1948. 4 pp. mimeo.

Official Records of the Second Session of the General Assembly. Supplement No. 11. United Nations Special Committee on Palestine. Report to the General Assembly, Volume V, Index to the Report and Annexes. 15 pp. printed (A/364/Add. 4, October 9, 1947). [20¢.]

---

[6] *Ibid.*, p. 33.

[7] Printed materials may be secured in the United States from the International Documents Service. Columbia University Press, 2960 Broadway, New York City. Other materials (mimeographed or processed documents) may be consulted at certain designated libraries in the United States.

THE UNITED NATIONS AND SPECIALIZED AGENCIES

Discussion of the Palestine Problem in the Security Council

STATEMENT BY AMBASSADOR WARREN R. AUSTIN [1]

U.S. Representative in the Security Council

The Security Council is now confronted with the complex problem of Palestine as presented to us in the General Assembly recommendation of November 29, 1947, and the two reports from the Palestine Commission. The Council now has before it a number of important questions concerning Palestine for which it must endeavor to find an answer; the situation does not permit any further delay.

The problem has been before the United Nations as a matter of special concern since April 2, 1947. The United States, as a member of the United Nations, has supported since that date those United Nations procedures which we considered most adapted to obtaining a broad and impartial expression of world opinion on the problem which would result in a just and workable solution commending itself to the mandatory power and to the people of Palestine.[2]

As a result of the recommendations of the General Assembly of November 29, 1947, Palestine is now before several of the principal bodies of the United Nations for various types of action under the Charter. The United States as a member of the United Nations and of those bodies will continue to deal with the question of Palestine as a member of the United Nations in conjunction with other members. United States policy will not be unilateral. It will conform to and be in support of United Nations action on Palestine.

While we are discussing the problem of Palestine it is of first importance to the future of the United Nations that the precedent to be established by the action taken in this case be in full accord with the terms of the Charter under which we operate. The interpretation of the terms of the Charter given in the Palestine issue w seriously affect the future action of the Unit Nations in other cases.

Let us turn now to the first and most importa document before us, namely, the General Assemb resolution of November 29.[3] The recommend tions of the General Assembly have great mo force which applies to all members regardless the views they hold or the votes which they m have cast on any particular recommendatio Similarly, the Security Council, although n bound under the Charter to accept and carry o General Assembly recommendations, is neverth less expected to give great weight to them.

Attempts to frustrate the General Assembly recommendation by the threat or use of force, by incitement to force, on the part of the sta or people outside Palestine are contrary to t Charter. You may recall that when the Rep sentative of the United States expressed the vie of my Government to the General Assembly on t Palestine question on October 11, 1947, he said assumed that there would be Charter observanc The life of this union depends upon obedience the law. If any member should violate its oblig tions to refrain in its international relations fr the threat or use of force, the Security Coun itself must act.

The recommendation of the General Assemb makes three separate requests of the Secur Council. The first—(a)—is that the Coun "take the necessary measures as provided for in t plan for its implementation". To determine w these measures are, it is necessary to turn to t plan itself. It will be seen that these are: (1) give guidance to the Palestine Commission; (to take such action as the Security Council m deem proper with respect to either the Jewish the Arab State if by April 1, 1948, a provisio council of government cannot be selected for t State, or, if selected, cannot carry out its functio (3) to issue such instructions to the Commission the Security Council may consider necessary; (to receive and consider periodic progress repo

[1] Made on Feb. 24, 1948, and released to the press in Washington by the Department of State and in New York by the U.S. Mission to the United Nations on the same date.
[2] See *The United States and the United Nations: Report by the President to the Congress for the Year 1947*, pp. 42–57, 164–187. Department of State publication 3024.
[3] *Ibid.*, p. 164.
[4] BULLETIN of Oct. 19, 1947, p. 761.

the outside or from such internal disorder as would itself constitute a threat to international peace.

If the Council finds that a threat to the peace or breach of the peace exists, the Charter authorizes it to follow various lines of action. It is empowered to make recommendations, or to take "provisional measures" under article 40, or to impose economic and other nonmilitary sanctions under article 41, or to take military measures under article 42. The Council is required to follow one or more of these lines of action. It may pursue these lines of action in any sequence it deems proper.

Although the Security Council is empowered to use, and would normally attempt to use, measures short of armed force to maintain the peace, it is authorized under the Charter to use armed force if it considers other measures inadequate. A finding by the Security Council that a danger to peace exists places all members of the United Nations, regardless of their views, under obligation to assist the Council in maintaining peace. If the Security Council should decide that it is necessary to use armed force to maintain international peace in connection with Palestine, the United States would be ready to consult under the Charter with a view to such action as may be necessary to maintain international peace. Such consultation would be required in view of the fact that agreement has not yet been reached making armed forces available to the Security Council under the terms of article 43 of the Charter.

The Security Council is authorized to take forceful measures with respect to Palestine to remove a threat to international peace. The Charter of the United Nations does not empower the Security Council to enforce a political settlement whether it is pursuant to a recommendation of the General Assembly or of the Council itself.

What this means is this: The Council under the Charter can take action to prevent aggression against Palestine from outside. The Council by these same powers can take action to prevent a threat to international peace and security from inside Palestine. But this action must be directed solely to the maintenance of international peace. The Council's action, in other words, is directed to keeping the peace and not to enforcing partition.

The United States Government believes that the first of the three requests made by the General Assembly to the Security Council under its resolution of November 29, 1947, can properly be complied with by the Council. With respect to the second and third requests of the Assembly's resolution—requests (b) and (c)—the Council must act, if necessary, to preserve international peace and security or to curb and reject aggression as provided for in the Charter.

We come now to the second of the documents before us, namely, the First Monthly Report of the Palestine Commission to the Security Council dated February 2, 1948.[5] It reflects the seriousness and the diligence with which the Commission has addressed itself to its difficult task in the course of its 26 meetings in January. The report contains a useful and practical analysis of the tasks set for the Commission by the General Assembly and lists the significant dates which constitute the framework of implementation. Two elements in the report are deeply disturbing to my Delegation. The first is the refusal of the Arab Higher Committee to designate representatives to consult with the Commission. The other is the continued deterioration of the situation in Palestine. The report shows the need for continued negotiations by the Commission with the Mandatory Power, and with representatives of the Jewish and Arab communities of Palestine, if the Commission is to proceed with its task.

My Delegation believes that, with respect to this first report, the Security Council might wish to inform itself of the situation to determine what guidance or instructions it might usefully give to the Palestine Commission. To that end, we suggest that the Security Council itself consult at once, by means of a committee, with the Palestine Commission, the Mandatory Power, and the representatives of the communities of Palestine.

The third document before us is the First Special Report of the Palestine Commission to the Security Council on the problem of security, dated February 16, 1948.[6] This report contains an appraisal by the Commission of the security situation in Palestine as well as the Commission's estimate on the security situation which it believes can be expected upon the termination of the mandate. This special report on security does not allege that a threat to the peace, breach of the peace, or act of aggression has occurred in Palestine. It reports facts which, if accepted or substantiated by the Security Council, would appear to lead to the conclusion that a threat to international peace is present in that situation. With this special report before it, the Security Council must, in our opinion, look into the matter immediately to determine whether such a danger exists.

The report looks ahead to what it considers will happen in the future and clearly implies that a threat to the peace and a breach of the peace will occur if the Commission continues its effort to carry out the Assembly's resolution. Perhaps the most emphatic illustration is found at page 18, VIII, "Conclusion", subparagraph 5:

"It is the considered view of the Commission that the security forces of the Mandatory Power, which at the present time prevent the situation from deteriorating completely into open warfare

---

[5] U.N. doc. A/AC. 21/7, Jan. 29, 1948.
[6] U.N. doc. A/AC. 21/9, Feb. 16, 1948.

nprising the five permanent members, to look at :e into the question of the possible threats to .ernational peace arising in connection with the lestine situation and to consult with the Pales- e Commission, the Mandatory Power, and rep- entatives of the principal communities of Pales- e concerning the implementation of the neral Assembly recommendation; (c) to call on all governments and peoples, particularly in l around Palestine, to take all possible action

to prevent or reduce the disorders now occurring in Palestine.

There is no reason to believe that the Security Council will find this problem any less difficult than others have found it. But there is also no reason for excessive pessimism merely because the question is complicated and involves violence. The responsibilities of the Security Council in this situation are great. We feel confident that all of the members are ready for the Council to address itself at once to its task.

U.S. DRAFT RESOLUTION ON THE PALESTINE QUESTION [7]

THE SECURITY COUNCIL,

Having received the resolution of the General Assembly of 29 November 1947, on Palestine, and having received from the United Nations Palestine Commission its First Monthly Report, and First Special Report on the Problem of Security in Palestine;

Resolves:

1. To accept, subject to the authority of the Security Council under the Charter, the requests addressed by the General Assembly to it in paragraphs (a), (b) and (c) of the General Assembly resolution of 29 November 1947;

2. To establish a committee of the Security Council comprising the five permanent members of Council whose functions will be:

(a) To inform the Security Council regarding the situation with respect to Palestine and to make recommendations to it regarding the

guidance and instructions which the Council might usefully give to the Palestine Commission;

(b) To consider whether the situation with respect to Palestine constitutes a threat to international peace and security, and to report its conclusions as a matter of urgency to the Council, together with any recommendations for action by the Security Council which it considers appropriate;

(c) To consult with the Palestine Commission, the Mandatory Power, and Representatives of the principal communities of Palestine concerning the implementation of the General Assembly recommendation of 29 November 1947.

Appeals to all Governments and peoples, particularly in and around Palestine, to take all possible action to prevent or reduce such disorders as are now occurring in Palestine.

led for Elections in Korea

RESOLUTION ADOPTED BY THE INTERIM COMMITTEE [8]

WHEREAS the Chairman of the United Nations Temporary Commission on Korea, accompanied by Assistant-Secretary-General, consulted the Interim Committee on the following questions:

1. Is it open to or incumbent upon the Commission, under the terms of the General Assembly resolutions of 14 November 1947,[9] and in the light of developments in the situation with respect to Korea since that date, to implement the programme as outlined in resolution II in that part of Korea which is occupied by the armed forces of the United States of America?

If not,

(a) Should the Commission observe the election of Korean representatives to take part in the consideration of the Korean question, as outlined in resolution I of 14 November 1947, provided that it has determined that elections can be held in a free atmosphere? and

(b) Should the Commission consider such

other measures as may be possible and advisable with a view to the attainment of its objectives?"

The Interim Committee,

Bearing in mind the views expressed by the Chairman of the United Nations Temporary Commission on Korea;

Deeming it necessary that the programme set forth in the General Assembly resolutions of 14 November 1947 be carried out and as a necessary step therein that the United Nations Temporary Commission on Korea proceed with the observance of elections in all Korea, and if that is impossible, in as much of Korea as is accessible to it; and

---

[7] U.N. doc. S/685, Feb. 25, 1948. Submitted by the Representative of the United States at the 255th meeting of the Security Council.

[8] U.N. Doc. A/AC.18/31. U.S. draft resolution, which was adopted on Feb. 26, 1948.

[9] BULLETIN of Nov. 30, 1947, p. 1031.

778644—48——2

Considering it important that the elections be held to choose representatives of the Korean people with whom the United Nations Temporary Commission on Korea may consult regarding the prompt attainment of freedom and independence of the Korean people, which representatives, constituting a National Assembly, may establish a National Government of Korea;

Resolves

That in its view it is incumbent upon the United States Nations Temporary Commission on Korea, under the terms of the General Assembly resolution of 14 November 1947, and in the light of developments in the situation with respect to Korea since that date, to implement the programme as outlined in Resolution II, in such parts of Korea as are accessible to the Commission.

FOREIGN AID AND RECONSTRUCTION

Request for Continuing Aid to Greece and Turkey

LETTER FROM THE SECRETARY OF STATE TO THE PRESIDENT PRO TEMPORE OF THE SENATE [1]

[Released to the press February 26]

February 28, 1948.

When the Nazis were still unconquered and Japanese power in the Pacific had not yet been broken, the cooperation that had been engendered among the peoples of the world by their realization of mutual danger led us to hope that, following the successful termination of hostilities, we could expect a period in which the community of nations would work together with good-will and understanding for the common objective of universal peace. Many of the countries which had undergone the ravages of enemy occupation, or which had made sacrifices for the allied cause according to their capabilities, looked forward to the opportunity of pursuing, in peace, their national rehabilitation and democratic development. Unfortunately, events have not justified these hopes.

Greece and Turkey were among those countries which had hoped to be able to face their problems of postwar readjustment with the assurance that, as long as their policies did not encroach upon the rightful interests of other countries, they would be free and even encouraged to reestablish their national life on a peacetime footing, thereby contributing to the early return of normal international relationships. However, hostilities had barely ceased before a concerted campaign against both Greece and Turkey was inaugurated in neighboring countries. The purpose of this campaign was clearly to undermine the territorial integrity and political independence of Greece and Turkey which would deprive the peoples of these countries of the very liberties which they had struggled so hard during the war years to retain.

Turkey has been under constant pressure to

grant military bases in the Straits to a foreign power and to cede to that same power Turkish territory in the Kars-Ardahan region. The northern neighbors of Greece have furnished moral and material support to the Greek communist guerrillas who are attempting to overthrow the legal Greek Government and establish the dictatorship of a foreign-inspired minority. This support is being continued in the face of a resolution adopted by the General Assembly of the United Nations last October.

In the circumstances it has been necessary for Turkey, in the interest of her national security, to maintain a large military establishment which constitutes a severe drain on her economy but which cannot be further reduced without destroying the confidence of the Turkish people in their ability to resist aggression. The conditions are even more critical in Greece, where, as the result of enemy destruction, no extensive rehabilitation was possible with the meager resources of the shattered Greek economy which the Germans left behind as a heritage when they withdrew.

The Congress is well aware, I am sure, that since the liberation of Greece in 1944, several friendly countries have assisted in efforts to restore Greek economic stability, and that large sums have been expended to this end by the British Government, by UNRRA, and by the United States. These efforts have not been unavailing. Without them, I am convinced, Greece would not today be a sovereign nation. They have not, however, accomplished what might have been hoped, primarily because the hostile forces determined to deprive Greece of her sovereignty have, with foreign assistance, intensified their efforts to spread chaos and disintegration.

The importance of assisting Greece and Turkey to maintain their status as free and sovereign na-

[1] Arthur H. Vandenberg. Identical letter was sent on Feb. 26, 1948, to Joseph W. Martin, Speaker of the House. Attached to the letters was a copy of the draft bill.

the ideals which the American people have so recently fought to preserve.

Faithfully yours,

A BILL

To amend the Act approved May 22, 1947, entitled "An Act to provide for assistance to Greece and Turkey".

Be it enacted by the Senate and House of Representatives of the United States of America in Congress assembled, That paragraph (2) of Section 1 of the Act entitled "An Act to provide assistance to Greece and Turkey," approved May 22, 1947 (61 Stat. 103), be, and the same is hereby amended to read as follows:

"(2) by detailing to the United States Missions to Greece or Turkey under this Act, or to the governments of those countries in implementation of the purposes of this Act, any persons in the employ of the Government of the United States; and while so detailed, any such persons shall be considered, for the purpose of preserving his rights and privileges as such, an officer or employee of the Government of the United States and of the department or agency from which detailed. Traveling expenses of such personnel to and from the place of detail shall be paid by the Government of the United States. Such personnel, and personnel detailed pursuant to paragraph 3 of this section, may receive such station allowances or additional allowances as the President may prescribe; and payments of such allowances heretofore made are hereby validated.

Civilian personnel who are citizens of the United States detailed or appointed pursuant to this Act to perform functions under this Act outside the continental limits of the United States shall be investigated by the Federal Bureau of Investigation, which shall make a report thereof to the detailing or appointing authority as soon as possible: *Provided, however,* That they may assume their posts and perform their functions after preliminary investigation and clearance by the Department of State."

Sec. 2. Paragraph (3) of Section 1 of said Act is hereby amended to read as follows:

"(3) by detailing to the United States Missions to Greece or Turkey under this Act, or to the gov-

(Continued on page 319)

INTERNATIONAL ORGANIZATIONS AND CONFERENCES

Calendar of Meetings [1]

Adjourned During Month of February

Icao (International Civil Aviation Organization): First Session of Statistics Division.	Montreal . . . .
Who (World Health Organization):	
Fifth Session of Interim Commission	Geneva . . . .
Expert Committee on Tuberculosis	Geneva . . . .
Ceec (Committee on European Economic Co-operation): European Manpower Conference.	Rome . . . .
Meeting of Special Committee to Make Recommendations for the Coordination of Safety Activities in Fields of Aviation, Meteorology, Shipping and Telecommunications.	London . . . .
International Wheat Council: Special Session	Washington . . . . . .
Iubs (International Union of Biological Sciences): Executive Committee .	Geneva . . . .
Unesco (United Nations Educational, Scientific and Cultural Organization): Sixth Session of Executive Board.	Paris . . . .
Fao (Food and Agriculture Organization):	
Regional Meeting to Consider Creation of Councils for Study of the Sea .	Baguio, Philippines . . .
Regional Meeting of Technical Nutritionists	Baguio, Philippines . . .

In Session as of February 28, 1948

Far Eastern Commission	Washington . . . . . .
United Nations:	
Security Council	Lake Success . . . . . .
Military Staff Committee	Lake Success . . . . . .
Committee on Atomic Energy	Lake Success . . . . . .
Commission on Conventional Armaments	Lake Success . . . . . .
Trade and Employment Conference	Habana . . . .
General Assembly's Special Balkan Committee	Salonika . . . .
Commission for Palestine	Lake Success . . . . . .
Temporary Commission on Korea	Seoul . . . .
Security Council's Committee of Good Offices on the Indonesian Question.	Lake Success . . . . . .

[1] Prepared in the Division of International Conferences, Department of State.

cosoc (Economic and Social Council): Sixth Session	Lake Success	Feb. 2–
nterim Committee of the General Assembly	Lake Success	Feb. 23–
man External Property Negotiations (Safehaven):		**1946**
With Portugal	Lisbon	Sept. 3–
With Spain	Madrid	Nov. 12–
er-Allied Trade Board for Japan	Washington	Oct. 24–
r (Council of Foreign Ministers):		**1947**
Commission of Investigation to Former Italian Colonies	Former Italian Colonies	Nov. 8–
		1948
Deputies for Italian Colonial Problems	London	Jan. 29–
Deputies for Austria	London	Feb. 20–
(International Labor Organization): Permanent Committee on Migration.	Geneva	Feb. 23–28
(Food and Agriculture Organization): Mission to Siam	Siam	Jan. 3–
visional Frequency Board	Geneva	Jan. 15–
er-governmental Maritime Organization	Geneva	Feb. 19–

eduled for March–May 1948

(Food and Agriculture Organization):		
tice Meeting	Baguio, Philippines	Mar. 1–14
econd Meeting of Council	Washington	Mar. 18–31
(Pan American Union): Governing Board	Washington	Mar. 3
ted Nations:		
cosoc (Economic and Social Council):		
Subcommission on Employment and Economic Stability	Lake Success	Mar. 8–
World Conference on Freedom of Information	Geneva	Mar. 23–
Ece (Economic Commission for Europe): Third Session	Geneva	Mar. 31–
Social Commission: Third Session	Lake Success	Apr. 5–
Transport and Communications Commission: Second Session	Geneva	Apr. 12–
Subcommission on Statistical Sampling: Second Session	Lake Success	Apr. 12–
Economic and Employment Commission: Third Session	Lake Success	Apr. 19–
Statistical Commission: Third Session	Lake Success	Apr. 26–
Commission on Narcotic Drugs: Third Session	Lake Success	May 3–
Population Commission: Third Session	Lake Success	May 10–
Human Rights Commission: Third Session	Lake Success	May 17–
Ecafe (Economic Commission for Asia and the Far East)	India	May
ha International Spring Fair	Praha	Mar. 12–21
(International Labor Organization):		
04th Session of Governing Body	Geneva	Mar. 16–20
ndustrial Committee on Chemicals	Paris	Apr. 6–17
st Meeting of Planning Committee on High Frequency Broadcasting	Geneva	Mar. 22–
o (International Civil Aviation Organization):		
eronautical Maps and Charts Division	Brussels	Mar. 22–
Personnel Licensing Division	Montreal	Mar. 30–
tules of the Air and Air Traffic Control Practices Division	Montreal	Apr. 20–
acilitation Division	Europe	May 17–
egal Committee: Annual Meeting	Geneva	May 29–
econd North Atlantic Regional Air Navigation Meeting	Paris	May
econd European–Mediterranean Regional Air Navigation Meeting	Paris	May

Sixth Pan American Railway Congress	Habana	Mar. 27–
Ninth International Conference of American States	Bogotá	Mar. 30–
Conference to Plan for Establishment of an International Institute of Hylean Amazon.	Tingo María, Peru	Mar. 30–
Inter-American Economic and Social Council	Washington	March
Icac (International Cotton Advisory Committee): Seventh Meeting	Cairo	Apr. 1–
Meeting of Technicians in Connection with Final Protocol of Tonnage Measurement of Ships.	Oslo	Apr. 2–
Fifth International Leprosy Conference	Habana	Apr. 3–11
Lyon International Fair	Lyon	Apr. 3–12
Royal Netherlands Industries Fair	Utrecht	Apr. 6–15
26th Milan Fair	Milan	Apr. 12–27
International Conference on Safety of Life at Sea	London	Apr. 23–
22d International Brussels Fair	Brussels	Apr. 17–28
Third Inter-American Travel Congress	Buenos Aires	Apr. 18–28
Central Rhine Commission	Strasbourg	Apr. 20–
Preparatory Conference for World Aeronautical Radio Conference	Geneva	Apr. 24–May 1
Rubber Study Group: Fifth Session	Washington	Apr. 26–
Meeting of the International Commission for the Sixth Decennial Revision of the Lists of the Causes of Death.	Paris	Apr. 26–30
International Conference of Social Work	Atlantic City	Apr. 17–25
Arts and Handicrafts Exhibition of American Elementary School Children.	Montevideo	April
Fifth Pan American Highway Congress	Lima	April
Fourth Pan American Consultation on Cartography	Buenos Aires	April–May
Pan American Institute of Geography and History: General Assembly	Buenos Aires	April–May
Paris International Fair	Paris	May 1–17
Zagreb International Fair	Zagreb	May 8–18
Fourth International Congresses on Tropical Medicine and Malaria (including exhibits).	Washington	May 10–18
International Telegraph Consultative Committee	Brussels	May 10–24
World Aeronautical Radio Conference	Geneva	May 15–
Health Congress of the Royal Sanitary Institute	Harrogate, England	May 24–28
Canadian International Trade Fair	Toronto	May 31–
Iro (International Refugee Organization): Sixth Part of First Session of Preparatory Commission.	Geneva	May
Pan American Sanitary Organization: Meeting of Executive Committee	Washington	May
Who (World Health Organization): Second Session of Expert Committee on Malaria.	Washington	May
Sixth Meeting of the Caribbean Commission	Undetermined	Latter half May.

meeting convened at Geneva, Switzerland, on February 23, 1948. The Department of State submitted the nominations of the delegate and two advisers in concurrence with the Department of Labor. Louis Levine, Chief, Technical Service Division, United States Employment Service, Department of Labor, and Val R. Lorwin, International Labor Economist, Labor Branch, Division of International Labor, Social, and Health Affairs, Department of State, served as advisers.

This session of the Committee was called: (1) to consider proposals for revision of the migration for employment convention of 1939 and related recommendations; (2) to draft a model migration agreement; (3) to consider technical selection and training of migrants; and (4) to discuss cooperation of the International Labor Organization in measures for the coordination of international responsibilities in the field of migration.

FOURTH INTERNATIONAL CONGRESS ON TROPICAL MEDICINE AND MALARIA

[Released to the press February 26]

Replies to the Department of State's invitation to attend the Fourth International Congresses on Tropical Medicine and Malaria, which will be held in Washington, May 10–18, 1948, have been received from 33 nations thus far. Of these, 25 have indicated their acceptance and will send official delegations. They are: Afghanistan, Australia, Austria, Belgium, Bolivia, Dominican Republic, Ecuador, Egypt, Finland, Haiti, Honduras, India, Iraq, Lebanon, Mexico, Netherlands, New Zealand, Pakistan, Panama, Portugal, Saudi Arabia, Siam, Sweden, South Africa, and Venezuela.

Although no formal invitations have been sent to many of the medical, technical, and scientific institutions, societies, and organizations throughout the world, the Department welcomes all interested professional men and women, including students, to participate actively in the congresses. Attendance will be registered. Those who desire to attend should communicate with the Division of International Conferences, Department of State, as soon as possible so that the most suitable hotel reservations may be made.

Correspondents, science editors, and photographers of newspapers, magazines, and journals who wish accreditation should contact the office of the Special Assistant for Press Relations, Department of State, Washington.

The International Congresses on Tropical Medicine and Malaria are meeting again after an interval of ten years, the last joint meeting having been held in Amsterdam. The Fourth Meeting is sponsored by the Department of State in collaboration with other United States agencies and scientific societies interested in tropical medicine.

THE RECORD OF THE WEEK

United States, France, and United Kingdom Condemn Development in Czechoslovakia

DECLARATION

The Governments of the United States, France and Great Britain have attentively followed the course of the events which have just taken place in Czechoslovakia and which place in jeopardy the very existence of the principles of liberty to which all democratic nations are attached.

They note that by means of a crisis artificially and deliberately instigated the use of certain methods already tested in other places has permitted the suspension of the free exercise of parliamentary institutions and the establishment of a disguised dictatorship of a single party under the cloak of a Government of national union.

They can but condemn a development the consequences of which can only be disastrous for the Czechoslovak people, who had proved once more in the midst of the sufferings of the second World War their attachment to the cause of liberty.

[Editor's Note: The above declaration was issued jointly and simultaneously by the United States, the United Kingdom, and France in their respective capitals on February 26. This joint action of the three powers was taken in condemnation of the Communist seizure of power in Czechoslovakia during a Cabinet crisis from February 17 to 25. The crisis was precipitated on the issue whether the organization of the police was to be subject to majority decision of the Cabinet. At the meeting of the Cabinet on February 17 the Communist Premier Klement Gottwald refused to accept or discuss two previous actions of the Cabinet with reference to the police question, and subsequently the non-Communist ministers were unable to obtain satisfaction in this matter. As a result twelve members of the Cabinet representing the National Socialists, People's Party, and the Slovak Democrats, resigned in protest on February 20. During the ensuing days the Communists intimidated the other parties and took over key positions by armed force, mass demonstrations, action committees, and other typical methods in the Communist arsenal of tactics. On February 25 President Benes accepted the resignation of the twelve non-Communist ministers and approved a new Cabinet proposed by Gottwald. The new Cabinet, announced on the same day, consisted chiefly of Communists with limited representation from the other parties subject to complete Communist domination.]

nited States and United Kingdom Sign Civil Air Agreement

The final agreement on the Heads of Agreement itialed in Bermuda on February 11, 1946, proding for civil use of leased air bases in the Caribian area and Bermuda, was signed in Washington ι February 24, 1948, by Lord Inverchapel for reat Britain and Secretary of State George C. arshall for the United States.[1]

This formal agreement will supersede the inrim arrangement which has governed the civil e of the leased bases in the Caribbean area and ermuda for almost two years. It represents the lmination of a sincere and prolonged effort to rmulate the conditions under which civil aircraft ay use the bases, and the two Governments are ippy to announce that they believe these contions will be satisfactory and advantageous to all ncerned. They wish to emphasize, however, that 'e air carriers of third nations will have to be itient, particularly in respect to Kindley Field Bermuda, until the colonial authorities can rovide the necessary terminal facilities to accomodate them. The United States Air Force auorities at Kindley Field have designated a suitile area for civil operations and are cooperating every way possible to assist the colonial authoriis in establishing temporary terminal facilities itil the Bermudan Government can execute its ans for permanent facilities. It is not anticiited that there need be any delay in initiating ie operations of civil users not requiring allocaons of warehousing and terminal facilities. But itil facilities are available, the Government of ermuda regrets that it is compelled to ask airines of the states authorized to use Kindley Field seek to arrange for their passengers and aircraft be handled by one of the existing agencies in ermuda. The Government of Bermuda will also equire well in advance information regarding hedules in order to prevent congestion. The tuation will be reviewed at the earliest possible oment.

ackground of the Agreement

When the United Kingdom undertook in 1940 lease to the United States certain areas in Newundland, Bermuda, and the Caribbean area for aval and air bases, the subsequent agreement expressly provided that, except in special circumances or by agreement between the Governments ncerned, commercial aircraft should not be llowed to operate from the airfields in the leased reas. It also provided that no commercial activiies should be conducted with the leased areas other ian with the consent of the Governments conerned.

After the lease of these bases, the United States constructed a large airfield at each of them. With the end of the war, there were obvious advantages in opening, for use by civil aircraft, airfields in the leased areas in territories lacking other satisfactory civil airfields. Such opening would contribute both to the development of air transport and to the territories concerned. But where satisfactory airfields already existed there was not the same reason for arranging for commercial aircraft to use the base airfields.

Some discussions on this subject between the Governments of the United States and the United Kingdom took place in the autumn of 1945 and later at the Bermuda conference, where Heads of Agreement relating to the bases in the Caribbean area and Bermuda were initialed *ad referendum* on February 11, 1946. The Heads of Agreement left some remaining difficulties and complicated legal problems, but subsequent negotiations have resolved these issues. The agreement which has just been signed contains many improvements over the Heads of Agreement, both as to substance and form. Like the Heads of Agreement, however, it does not relate to the bases in Newfoundland. Separate negotiations have been conducted by the United States with Newfoundland looking towards a formal agreement on the civil use of the bases there as weather alternates, but such negotiations have not yet been concluded.

Features of the Agreement

1. Kindley Field in Bermuda, Coolidge Field in Antigua, Beane Field in St. Lucia, and Atkinson Field in British Guiana will be open for regular use by civil aircraft to the extent that accommodations are available. They are referred to as the regular bases, as distinguished from Carlson and Waller Fields in Trinidad and Vernam Field in Jamaica, which will be open to civil aircraft as weather alternates only.

2. Civil aircraft of the United Kingdom and the United States will be entitled to use the bases on equally favorable terms. The positions of both the United Kingdom and the United States in regard to the exercise of traffic rights on the bases have been safeguarded, and provision has been made to insure that the United States, which will maintain the airfields for military purposes, shall enjoy "most favored nation" treatment. Thus it is agreed that no other civil air carrier, including

---

[1] For text of agreement see Department of State press release 144, Feb. 24, 1948.

civil air carriers of the United Kingdom, will be granted any greater or different traffic rights at the bases than are granted to United States civil air carriers at such bases, with certain exceptions permitted in the case of United Kingdom traffic between two points under its jurisdiction. It is also agreed that the United Kingdom will not grant to civil air carriers of third air nations traffic rights which exceed corresponding rights which such third countries grant to United States civil air carriers in their territory.

3. Civil aircraft of all countries granting in their own territories "two freedom" privileges to both United States and United Kingdom carriers may use the bases for non-traffic purposes, subject to the terms of the present agreement, and article I of the two freedoms agreement.

4. Private and charter operators will be permitted to use the bases, in accordance with the terms of the present agreement, for traffic and non-traffic purposes.

5. The agreement provides for the limitation or suspension of civil use of the bases by the United States military authorities for military reasons or by the government of the colony concerned for security reasons. The agreement protects the right of the United States military authorities to insure that no steps are taken in connection with the commercial air operations which would prejudice in any way the military use of the bases.

6. The United States military authorities will exercise administrative and operational control of the bases except as otherwise specifically provided

U.S. and Norway Sign Lend-Lease Settle

BACKGROUND STATEMENT BY

Representatives of the United States and Norway signed on February 24, 1948, an agreement for over-all settlement of lend-lease and military relief accounts and other war claims.[1] The agreement was signed in Washington by Secretary of State Marshall on behalf of the United States and Ambassador Morgenstierne on behalf of Norway.

The agreement signed constitutes a final settlement for lend-lease, the United States share of civilian supplies furnished by the Allied armies to Norway as military relief, and claims of each Government against the other which arose out of the war.

Total lend-lease aid to Norway amounted to approximately 47 million dollars, including cash reimbursable lend-lease and ships which have been or are to be returned to the United States.

Following the pattern of most previous settle-

[1] For text of agreement see Department of State press release 143, Feb. 24, 1948.

t of financial obligations of the United States
ied Forces, incurred while in Norwegian ter-
ry, and the United States Armed Forces are
iing over to the Norwegian Government their
wegian currency holding. The Norwegian
ernment has agreed also to assume certain
s of Norwegian nationals against the United
es, such as patent, requisitioning, and mari-
salvage claims, and claims arising out of the
ence of United States troops in Norwegian
itory.
s additional provisions of the settlement the
ted States Government reserves the right to
ipture lend-lease arms held by the Norwegian

forces; lend-lease merchant and naval vessels will
be returned in accordance with United States law;
and the wartime claims of each Government
against the other not already settled or excluded
by the agreement are waived.

The two Governments reaffirm their support of
the principles set forth in article VII of the mutual aid agreement of July 11, 1942, and their desire to eliminate discriminatory treatment in international commerce and to reduce tariffs and other
trade barriers.

The agreement was approved in content by the
Norwegian Storting (parliament) before signature.

REMARKS BY AMBASSADOR MORGENSTIERNE

I am particularly happy to be able to sign this
eement on behalf of my Government. It marks
close of an important period of collaboration
ween the governments and peoples of Norway
l the United States in the common struggle
inst and victory over the world aggressors.

I wish to express Norway's deep appreciation of
decisive contribution made by America through
d-lease. History will look upon lend-lease, I
convinced, as an achievement of far-sighted and
lliant statesmanship. In keeping with the spirit
the lend-lease idea the Norwegian economy has

been freed from any burden of repayment for lend-
lease contributions for war purposes.

"Also in the settlement of Norway's obligations
in connection with the civilian relief goods received
just after liberation, the United States Government has shown great understanding of our position in agreeing to terms which do not obligate us
to provide dollar exchange.

"The cultural and educational program for
which means have been provided through this
settlement will be of great and, I am sure, mutual
benefit, and is certain to strengthen the cultural
ties between our two countries."

STATEMENT BY SECRETARY MARSHALL

[am pleased to sign this agreement on behalf of
' Government with the Government of Norway.
e occasion reminds us of the great contribution
de to victory by Norway, and the invaluable and
irageous service rendered to the Allied cause by
ships and men.

The agreement is particularly gratifying since it
not only settles, in a mutually satisfactory way, the
lend-lease accounts arising out of our close and
successful partnership during the war, but, also,
it is evidence of the cordial attitude with which
our two countries are able to solve mutual problems.

---

in Asked To Clarify Position on hwarzkopf Mission

[Released to the press February 26]

*xt of statement released to the Iranian press
February 25, 1948, by the American Embassy
Tehran*

On February 7, 1948, the American Ambassa-
r, G. V. Allen, in the course of a conversation
th Mr. Hakimi, raised the question of the
hwarzkopf mission to the Iranian gendarmerie.
The United States Ambassador then presented
the Prime Minister a note describing the posi-
n of the United States Government in regard
the mission of General Schwarzkopf and re-

quested the Iranian Government to clarify its
position in regard to this mission. It must be an
Iranian decision as to whether the contract should
be continued as heretofore, renegotiated, or terminated. This was not a note of protest but
merely a request for a clear statement of the
Iranian Government's position in the matter.

In as much as no reply has yet been received
from the Iranian Government, the Embassy is
not able to make further comment.

The Embassy, however, must reiterate that the
United States Government has always regarded
the question of United States military advisers in
Iran as entirely a matter for the Iranians themselves to decide.

Draft Agreement of Inter-American Ec

[Released to the press February 25]

The Department of State made available February 25 the text of a draft basic agreement of inter-American economic cooperation which has been prepared by the Economic and Social Council of the Pan American Union as a working document for the Ninth International Conference of American States. This preliminary document has been transmitted by the Pan American Union to each of the 21 American republics. The Conference will convene at Bogotá, Colombia, on March 30, 1948.

The Department pointed out that this draft agreement does not commit the United States Government, or any other government, in any way with respect to the position its Delegation may take at the Conference. In a number of important respects, in fact, the draft is at variance with the views of this Government, and reservations have been entered by the United States, in the Council, particularly with respect to provisions relating

[Released to the press February 25]

The Governments Represented at the Ninth International Conference of American States, Considering:

That it is their desire to maintain, strengthen and develop in the economic field the special relations that unite them within the framework of the United Nations;

That the economic welfare of each State depends in large measure upon the welfare of the others;

That, in accordance with the Charter of the United Nations, they have undertaken to promote social progress and to raise the standard of living within the broadest concept of liberty, as well as to endeavor to obtain opportunities for permanent employment for everyone;

That they have declared, moreover, on various occasions, that they will direct their economic policy toward the creation of conditions which, by means of an increase in production, in domestic and foreign trade, and in national and international investments, may promote everywhere the attainment of high levels of real income, employment and consumption, free from excessive fluctuations, to the end that their people may be fed, housed and clothed in adequate manner and may enjoy the services necessary for health, education and welfare; that industrialization and general economic development are indispensable for the realization of these objectives; and

That at the Inter-American Conference for the Maintenance of Continental Peace and Security they considered that economic security, indispensable for the progress of all the American peoples will be at all times the best guarantee of their political security and of the success of their joint effort for the maintenance of continental peace;

promoting the adoption of sanitary standards with respect to plant and animal quarantine for the purpose of reaching an international understanding to avoid the application of such measures as an indirect means of imposing barriers to international trade.

Article 10. To carry out the functions ascribed to it in Article 9, the Inter-American Economic and Social Council shall have a special organism, of an executive and permanent character, in which the existing inter-American organisms charged with similar functions can be merged, and utilizing the economic services of the Pan American Union. The Council shall determine whether the studies which are requested of it are within its competence, and it may also indicate when it is more appropriate that applications addressed to it should be directed to other national or international institutions or to private institutions.

Article 11. In the development of its activities, the Council and the special organism shall maintain communication and exchange of information with the entities which are concerned, in each country, with the study of basic economic problems or which act as planning organizations for the national economy, as well as with the universities and other technical and scientific institutions in the various countries.

Article 12. The Council may on its own initiative undertake to carry out the functions indicated in Article 9, if it receives the approval of the government or governments in whose territory the studies or investigations are to be realized; moreover, it may do so upon the request of one or more of such governments.

Article 13. The participating States obligate themselves to contribute, in proportion to their resources, the necessary amounts to cover the greater expenditure needed for the maintenance of the organism mentioned in Article 10, within the budget of the Inter-American Economic and Social Council. In the case of a study which may benefit a single country, the Council shall decide in what proportion that country ought to contribute to defraying the necessary expenses.

Article 14. Nothing in this Chapter shall be interpreted as contrary to other arrangements between the American States for the reciprocal extension of technical cooperation in the economic field.

Chapter III: Financial Cooperation

Article 15. The American States reaffirm the principles set forth in the Agreement on the International Monetary Fund and declare that the attainment of the objectives contained therein would facilitate a high level of commercial interchange between the American States and with the rest of the world, and would thereby promote general economic and social progress through stimulating the local investment of domestic savings and attracting private foreign capital. They consider it desirable, therefore, to take all the domestic measures that may be conducive to the achievement of the above objectives.

Although the International Monetary Fund is the intergovernmental institution which can best serve in normal circumstances to attain these objectives through international financial cooperation, the American States agree to complement in appropriate cases the operations of the Fund by means of non-discriminatory bilateral agreements consistent with the purposes of the Articles of Agreement of that organization.

Article 16. The American States reaffirm the purposes of the International Bank for Reconstruction and Development and agree to concert their efforts to make the Bank an increasingly effective instrument for the realization of those purposes, especially those related to the promotion of their mutual economic development. They further declare that they will continue to extend medium and long-term credits to each other through governmental or intergovernmental institutions for economic development and the promotion of international trade, for the purpose of complementing the flow of private investments. The terms of the credits destined for economic development shall be made of sufficient extent so that the services of the loans will not impose excessive burdens on the enterprises which must pay them. Moreover, the American States agree that with respect to these loans an effort will be made to set up a criterion similar to that provided for in paragraph (c), section 4 of Article IV of the Agreement of the International Bank for Reconstruction and Development.

Article 17. The American States recognize that the insufficiency of domestic savings, or the ineffective use thereof, has forced the majority of the countries of America to resort to inflationary practices which may ultimately endanger the stability of their exchange rates and the orderly development of their economies.

The American States agree, therefore, to stimulate the development of local capital markets to provide, from non-inflationary sources, the domestic funds needed to cover investment expenditures in national currency. The American States agree that in general international financing should not be sought for the purpose of covering expenditures in local currency. However, they recognize that as long as the available domestic savings in the local capital markets are not sufficient, expenditures in local currency can, in justified circumstances, be considered for the financing referred to in Article 16.

Chapter IV: Private Investments

Article 18. The American States declare that the investment of private capital and the introduction of advanced techniques from other countries may constitute an important factor in their general economic development and resulting social progress. They also declare that such capital and techniques should be available on reasonable terms and conditions for the countries which need them and should be utilized for productive purposes suited to such countries, and should contribute especially to increasing their national income and giving an impulse to their economic development.

The American States shall reciprocally grant each other appropriate facilities and incentives for the investment and re-investment of capital, and, under normal conditions, for the transfer of capital and earnings.

Foreign capital shall receive equitable treatment. No discriminations shall be applied except when its investment must be limited or conditioned by fundamental principles of public interest.

Article 19. The American States declare that foreign investments should be made with the objective not only of the legitimate profit of those making the investment but also as a means of collaborating in the sound economic development of the receiving countries and of watching over the welfare of the persons dependent upon the enterprises. In the enterprises established by such investments and in accordance with the laws in force in each country just, equitable and non-discriminatory treatment shall be accorded to all personnel, both national and foreign, with respect to employment and conditions thereof.

Article 20. Foreign capital shall be subject to national laws. The American States reaffirm their right to establish, within an order of equity and of legal and judicial guarantees:

a) measures to prevent foreign investments from being utilized directly or indirectly as an instrument for intervening in national politics or for prejudicing the security or the fundamental interests of the receiving country;

b) standards with respect to the extent and terms in which foreign investment will be permitted, as well as reasonable conditions respecting the propriety of existing and future investments.

Article 21. The American States shall take no discriminatory action against investments by virtue of which

Nothing in this Article shall prevent the American States from entrusting the solution of their disputes to other procedures by virtue of agreements already in existence or which may be concluded in the future.

Chapter X: Coordination with United Nations' Economic Organizations

Article 35. Relations between the Inter-American Economic and Social Council and the specialized economic organizations of the Inter-American System, and the United Nations and its specialized agencies, shall be established in accordance with the provisions of the Organic Pact of the Inter-American System.

Chapter XI: Transitory Provision

Article 36. The Inter-American Economic and Social Council shall prepare, where it may be necessary, the drafts of multilateral conventions to carry out the undertakings set forth in the present Basic Agreement of Economic Cooperation, for consideration at the next Inter-American Economic Conference.

Chapter XII: Ratification and Entry Into Force

Article 37. The present Basic Agreement of Inter-American Economic Cooperation shall remain open to signature by the American States, and shall be ratified in accordance with their respective constitutional procedures. The original instrument, whose texts in Spanish, English, Portuguese, and French are equally authentic, shall be deposited with the Pan American Union, which shall send certified copies to the Governments for purposes of ratification. The instruments of ratification shall be deposited in the Pan American Union, which shall notify the signatory Governments of such deposit. Such notification shall be considered an exchange of ratifications.

Article 38. The present Agreement shall enter into effect as among the ratifying States, when two-thirds of the signatory States have deposited their ratifications. The present Agreement shall enter into effect with respect to the other States in the order in which they deposit their ratifications.

Article 39. The present Agreement shall be registered in the General Secretariat of the United Nations through the Pan American Union, upon the deposit of the ratifications of two-thirds of the signatory States.

Article 40. Amendments to the present Agreement may be adopted only at an International Conference of American States held for such purpose. The Amendments shall enter into force under the same terms and in accordance with the procedure established in Article 37.

F STATE TO THE CHAIRMAN OF THE
CHANT MARINE AND FISHERIES

activities, is in Geneva, Switzerland. Mr. Thorp, the Assistant Secretary for economic affairs who is also interested in the matter, is attending the meeting of the Economic and Social Council of the United Nations in New York today.

Therefore, I have asked Mr. Radius, Director of the Office of Transportation and Communication, to present this letter from me and to answer any immediate questions you might desire to ask him.

I understand that the Merchant Marine and Fisheries Committee of the House of Representatives is considering the advisability of the extension of the Merchant Ship Sales Act of 1946.[1] I would like to present to this Committee the position of the Department of State with respect to the extension of the authority of the United States Maritime Commission to sell, charter and operate Government-owned vessels which were built during the war.

On December 1, 1947, the President recommended to Congress that this authority, which will expire on February 29, be extended until June 30, 1949. On February 5 the Senate passed a joint resolution which would extend the authority of the Maritime Commission, as requested by the President, but with an amendment prohibiting the sale or charter of vessels to non-citizens after March 1 of this year.

I strongly urge that this authority now vested in the Maritime Commission be extended without limiting amendments to June 30, 1949. I firmly believe that this Government should have the authority to dispose of surplus vessels to non-citizens when such disposition would be in the national interest and would not endanger our national security.

Fourteen million deadweight tons of vessels are now idle in our laid-up fleet. This tonnage includes vessels for which there is no demand either for charter or purchase by American operators but which could be advantageously operated by citizens of countries whose economic development and political stability are in our national interest. The sale of such vessels would produce revenue to the United States Government, reduce the cost of foreign assistance programs and aid in attaining the objectives of our national policy. In some instances, the sale of only a few vessels would have advantages to the conduct of foreign policy out of proportion to the small number of vessels involved.

I am fully aware that the sale of vessels to non-citizens is related to national security. I consider the Merchant Marine an important element in national defense. The Department of State is vitally concerned with matters affecting national security. Since the Merchant Ship Sales Act of 1946 already provides for consultation with the Secretary of the Navy with respect to sales to non-citizens, I believe that the national defense aspects of any such sales are adequately safeguarded by the present language of the Act. For your further information regarding the national security aspects of this problem, I am attaching a copy of the letter from the Secretary of Defense to Senator Vandenberg dated February 11, 1948.

[1] For a statement by Secretary Marshall before the House of Representatives Committee on Merchant Marine and Fisheries see BULLETIN of June 22, 1947, p. 1225.

military may make it desirable to dispose of some ships to foreign governments or non-citizens in furtherance of national policy. It is entirely possible that a greater ultimate military advantage might in fact be achieved by such use of some of the reserve tonnage now than would result by holding it idle for possible future use under war emergency conditions."

Obviously, there might be changing circumstances as the European Recovery Program progresses, and it would therefore be my suggestion—in which the Secretary of State concurs—that the Act provide that the Administrator, prior to transfer of title to any vessel, shall consult with the Secretary of Defense with regard to the impact on national security of the proposed transfer.

This whole matter, in my opinion, is closely related to the maintenance, by this country, of a healthy domestic shipbuilding industry. It is decidedly in the interest of national security that we maintain our own shipbuilding capacity—and with that end in view, I suggest that your Committee consider the correlation between the transfer of the relatively slow American ships now in the laid-up fleet and the construction, in this country and for our own use, of faster and more modern vessels—perhaps through transfer to an appropriation available for shipbuilding purposes of proceeds derived from the sales of any vessels disposed of under the European Recovery Program.

Sincerely,

JAMES FORRESTAL

The Honorable
ARTHUR H. VANDENBERG
Chairman, Committee on Foreign Relations
United States Senate
Washington, D.C.

MEMORANDUM

NATIONAL INTEREST PASSENGER TRANSPORT

The Department of State submits the following information on national interest passenger transport.

Repatriation of American Citizens.

The following is a summary of the position with respect to the repatriation program of the Department:

The program is practically ended in the north of Europe, the Near East, the Middle East and in the Orient except for stragglers.

By the end of the fiscal year 1948, the programs for Greece and Austria should be completed and that for Hungary nearly completed. Except for special cases repatriation from Germany should also be completed in the present fiscal year.

In the fiscal year 1949 the repatriation program will be chiefly concerned with Americans who have been unable to leave Eastern European territory and Americans from Italy.

In the fiscal year 1945, 5,121 persons were repatriated; in 1946, 20,841; in 1947, 33,475; and in the first six months of fiscal year 1948, 8,619.

There are approximately 34,500 persons remaining to be repatriated as of January 1, 1948. The recapitulation by areas is as follows:

Mediterránean

(Albania, Cyprus, Greece, Italy
Yugoslavia) 13,363

Central Europe

(Germany) 852

Inner Europe

(Austria, Czechoslovakia, Hungary) 897

Baltic Sea

  (Poland) 17,578

Black Sea

  (Rumania, USSR) 1,563

Far East

  (Japan) 240

Other areas

  (N. Europe, Near East, etc.) 81

       TOTAL 34,574

Estimated total to be repatriated between January 1 and June 30, 1948 . . . 8,000.

The foregoing compares with the Department's estimate given last year during consideration of extension of the Maritime Commission's Authority to operate vessels. At that time the number of persons remaining to be repatriated was estimated as 40,000 and the opinion was expressed that if emergency shipping were available, virtually all could be returned to this country by July 1948.

Last year's estimate, like this year's, is based upon the best information available to the Department. The appearance at European consulates of additional Americans who have not heretofore made known their desire for repatriation, sudden shifts to restrictive policies by governments in respect to issuance of exit permits, severe winter conditions which prevent ships entering certain northern ports, and other unexpected conditions, combine to make it next to impossible to estimate any fixed date at which it can positively be asserted that the repatriation program will be finished. On the assumption that present shipping facilities will continue to be available through June 30, 1949, the Department's plans call for the completion of a major portion of the repatriation program by the end of Fiscal Year 1949.

Categories of national interest travellers for whom space is required on Maritime Commission vessels in areas other than Germany and Poland are:

A. Government officials and their families and other official travellers.

B. Business men traveling in the national interest.

C. Officials and employees of relief organizations traveling in the interest of the resumption of normal conditions in afflicted areas abroad.

D. American citizens whose return to the United States was impeded by scarcity of shipping during the war and after.

E. Service dependents in areas where the War and Navy Departments have developed no program for their transportation; service fiancees and Merchant Marine dependents and fiancees in all areas.

F. Dependent alien relatives of American citizens who are properly documented or whose visa issuance is contingent only upon proof of transportation.

G. Students intending to pursue their studies in the United States.

H. American citizens not classifiable under B and C who left the United States after the termination of hostilities despite warning that return transportation might be difficult to obtain.

After all are accommodated, any additional space may be sold to immigrants not included in the priority system.

Displaced Persons

While repatriates are carried on the vessels serving the port of Bremerhaven, they are used principally in transporting displaced persons coming to this country under the President's Directive of December 22, 1945. "Also, all available shipping will be needed if the Congress adopts legislation now pending before it providing for the en-

In view of the attitude of the leaders of the Greek Government and of the Greek labor movement on this question, I am confident that it will be resolved satisfactorily.

Faithfully yours,

February 2, 1948

DEAR MR. MURRAY:

I have received your letter of January 29, expressing the views of the Congress of Industrial Organizations with regard to the anti-strike, anti-lockout law passed by the Greek Parliament on December 7, 1947.

According to our information this measure was enacted hurriedly at a time when the very security of Greece was in grave danger as a result of Communist-inspired terror and violence, and when members of the Greek Parliament feared that the outbreak of a number of strikes might bring an end to the independence of the country.

The representatives of the United States Government in Athens have on several occasions expressed to leading members of the Greek Government our concern over the extreme provisions of the law.

The leaders of the General Confederation of Labor of Greece have also consulted appropriate Greek Government officials with a view to achieving the repeal of the law. The Greek Government has assured them it will propose repeal to Parliament as soon as the democratically elected National Labor Congress, which will meet in March, has chosen a responsible National Executive for the Greek labor movement.

These assurances, which we understand fully satisfy the leaders of Greek labor, were repeated yesterday, February 1, in an official public statement issued jointly by the Prime Minister and the Minister of Foreign Affairs. They expressed the unanimous view of the Greek Government that, with the democratic election of a trade union executive responsible to its members, the emergency which the law was intended to meet will have ceased to exist.

In view of the attitude of the leaders of the Greek Government and of the Greek labor movement on this question, I am confident that it will be resolved satisfactorily.

Faithfully yours,

Ceylon Attains Dominion Status

On February 3, 1948, President Truman addressed a message to Sir Henry Moore, Governor General of Ceylon, extending good wishes of the United States on the attainment by Ceylon of Dominion status within the British Commonwealth of Nations on February 4, 1948. Henry F. Grady, United States Ambassador to India, was designated to be the President's personal representative to attend the independence ceremonies at Colombo, February 10 to 14, 1948.

War Damage Compensation for American Nationals in Rumania

[Released to the press February 18]

The treaty of peace with Rumania, which came into force on September 15, 1947, provides that legal rights and interests of American nationals in Rumania as they existed on September 1, 1939, are to be restored and the Rumanian Government is required to return all property in Rumania of United Nations nationals as it now exists. Where property has not been returned within six months from the coming into force of the treaty (i.e. within six months from Sept. 15, 1947), application for the return thereof is to be made to the Rumanian authorities on or before September 15, 1948, unless claimants are able to show that applications could not be filed within that period. In cases where property cannot be returned or where, as a result of the war, a United Nations national has suffered a loss by reason of injury or damage to property in Rumania, the Rumanian Government is required to make compensation in local currency to the extent of two-thirds of the sum necessary, at the date of payment, to purchase similar property or to make good the loss suffered. To enable claims to receive consideration under the treaty, claimants must have been nationals of one of the United Nations on September 12, 1944 (the date of the armistice with Rumania), and on September 15, 1947 (the date the treaty came into force), or must establish that under the laws in

available in the United States at prevailing wages, and must obtain a permit from the Immigration and Naturalization Service authorizing the bringing in of a specified number of workers. The transportation of the workers from the place of contracting in Mexico to the place of employment in the United States and return must be covered by the employer.

Workers contracted, under the terms of the agreement, cannot be used to replace domestic workers, nor to depress wage standards or other labor conditions.

The text of the agreement, which was dated February 21, 1948, and of the form of contract which has been approved thereunder, is contained in Department of State press release 152 of February 26, 1948.

George H. Butler Joins Policy Planning Staff

[Released to the press February 10]

George H. Butler is relinquishing his post as Ambassador to the Dominican Republic in order to become a member of the Policy Planning Staff of the Department of State. Mr. Butler was detailed temporarily as a member of the Policy Planning Staff during the latter half of 1947. He brings to the Planning Staff a specialized knowledge of inter-American relations from his long experience in the Foreign Service of the United States.

ites Agreement

THE UNITED STATES AND PANAMA

under the express terms of the 1942 Agreement, to the use of the defense sites until one year "after the date on which the definitive treaty of peace which brings about the end of the present war shall have entered into effect", it has nevertheless taken the necessary measures to withdraw from those few remaining sites which had not already been returned to Panama under the provisions of the Agreement. These measures, taken in conformity with the understanding expressed in Article XIII of the 1942 Agreement, were adopted in deference to Panama following the action of its National Assembly on December 22, 1947.

In as much as the evacuation of the defense sites has now been completed, I have the honor, under instructions from my Government, to inform Your Excellency that the Government of the United States of America now considers the Agreement terminated and no longer in effect.

FRANK T. HINES

---

[1] BULLETIN of Dec. 21, 1947, p. 1219, and Jan. 4, 1948, p. 31.

February 20, 1948.

MR. AMBASSADOR: I have the honor to refer to Your Excellency's note No. 566 of February 16, 1948, by which you have been good enough to communicate to me that the government of the US of America, having evacuated all of the defense sites which had been ceded by reason of the recently terminated international conflagration, considers the agreement of May 18, 1942, terminated and of no future effect.

The expressions contained in Your Excellency's note have pleased my government in the sense that the agreement and its execution, through the wholehearted cooperation of both governments, assured the effective protection of the Panama Canal and had an important part in the victorious termination of hostilities. On that occasion, Panama offered loyally and decisively its full cooperation for the defense of this important key to continental security, and my government reiterates at this time its irrevocable intention to cooperate, with all the means within its reach and within its contractual obligations, in the effective protection of this inter-oceanic route, in order to thus assist in the preservation of the democratic ideals common to us both.

Without referring to the difference of interpretation concerning the termination date of the agreement of May 18, 1942, I wish to inform Your Excellency that my government has taken due note of the statements of the government of the United States with regard to the termination of the above-mentioned agreement.

I take this opportunity [etc.]

MARIO DE DIEGO
Minister for Foreign Affairs

Argentine War Minister To Visit U.S.

[Released to the press February 26]

On behalf of the Department of the Army the Department of State has transmitted an invitation to visit the United States to the Minister of War of Argentina, Major General José Humberto Sosa Molina. The Minister has accepted and it is expected that he will arrive in Washington some time in May.

The invitation is another phase of the Army Department's practice of inviting high-ranking military leaders of the other American republics to visit the United States to inspect military installations and to view United States methods of training, organization, and equipment. In conjunction with General Molina's wishes, the itinerary of military installations he will visit is being drawn up by the Department of the Army.

problems presented in 1919, and economic aid and the restoration of normal trade were solutions suggested.

Copies of *Foreign Relations of the United States*, The Paris Peace Conference, 1919, volume XII (xlv, 881 pp.), may be purchased from the Superintendent of Documents, Government Printing Office, Washington, D.C., for $3 each.

PUBLICATIONS

Department of State

For sale by the Superintendent of Documents, Government Printing Office, Washington 25, D. C. Address requests direct to the Superintendent of Documents, except in the case of free publications, which may be obtained from the Department of State.

United States Armed Forces in Guatemala. Treaties and Other International Acts Series 1663. Pub. 2987. 4 pp. 5¢.

Agreement Between the United States and Guatemala—Effected by exchange of notes signed at Guatemala August 29, 1947; entered into force August 29, 1947.

Liquidation of German Property in Italy. Treaties and Other International Acts Series 1664. Pub. 2989. 11 pp. 5¢.

Memorandum of Understanding Between the United States of America, France, United Kingdom of Great Britain and Northern Ireland, and Italy—Signed at Washington August 14, 1947; entered into force August 14, 1947.

Assistance to European Economic Recovery. Economic Cooperation Series 2. Pub. 3022. 20 pp. 15¢.

Statement by Secretary of State Marshall before the Senate Committee on Foreign Relations in regard to basic questions involved in the European Recovery Program, followed by the President's Message to the Congress of Dec. 19, 1947, on a program for United States aid to European recovery. A list of related publications is included.

The United States and the United Nations: Report by the President to the Congress for the Year 1947. Pub. 3024. xiii, 359 pp. 60¢.

Describes the decisions and recommendations made by the United Nations during the past year and the efforts of the United States to contribute to constructive United Nations achievement. Appendixes include selected resolutions adopted at the Second Regular Session of the General Assembly, selected resolutions considered by the Security Council, papers on atomic energy control, armed forces, and regulation of armaments, addresses by United States Representatives, and lists showing membership of the organs and specialized agencies of the United Nations.

Second Report to Congress on Assistance to Greece and Turkey for the Period Ended December 31, 1947. Pub. 3035. 64 pp. 25¢.

The President's report on the progress of the Greek and Turkish aid programs. Charts and biographic notes on personnel of the Mission are included in the appendixes, as well as exchanges of notes facilitating the carrying out of the program.

Harry N. Howard, author of the article on the refugee problem in
Greece, is Special Assistant in the Division of Greek, Turkish, and
Iranian Affairs, Office of Near Eastern and African Affairs, Depart-
ment of State.

The Department of State bulletin

VOL. XVIII, No. 454 • PUBLICATION 3088

March 14, 1948

The Department of State BULLETIN, a weekly publication compiled and edited in the Division of Publications, Office of Public Affairs, provides the public and interested agencies of the Government with information on developments in the field of foreign relations and on the work of the Department of State and the Foreign Service. The BULLETIN includes press releases on foreign policy issued by the White House and the Department, and statements and addresses made by the President and by the Secretary of State and other officers of the Department, as well as special articles on various phases of international affairs and the functions of the Department. Information is included concerning treaties and international agreements to which the United States is or may become a party and treaties of general international interest.

Publications of the Department, as well as legislative material in the field of international relations, are listed currently.

...intendent of Documents
...ernment Printing Office
Washington 25, D.O.

SUBSCRIPTION:
$5; single copy, 15 cents

...with the approval of the
...he Bureau of the Budget

...this publication are not
...s contained herein may
...on of the DEPARTMENT
...as the source will be

COMMITTEE IN INDONESIA

An Article

Netherlands-Indonesian Union. Although the agreement was finally signed by both governments in March 1947, negotiations aimed at its implementation failed and on July 21, 1947, the Dutch began "police action" that brought under their control economically important areas of Java, Madura, and Sumatra and reduced the Republic to three noncontiguous areas—central Java, westernmost Java, and parts of Sumatra.

The conflict was brought to the attention of the Security Council of the United Nations by Australia and India, and on August 1 the Council called upon both parties to cease hostilities and settle their dispute by arbitration or other peaceful means.[1] In an attempt to assist the parties to come to a peaceful settlement, the United States then tendered its good offices, which were accepted by the Netherlands but in effect refused by the Republic, which insisted upon arbitration. On August 25 the Council resolved to set up a consular commission, composed of the career consuls of Security Council member nations posted in the Netherlands East Indies, to observe the implementation of the cease-fire order. By means of the same resolution, the Council also offered to the disputants its good offices.[2] Both parties accepted, and a Good Offices Committee, made up of representatives of three Council members, was established. Two of the members, Belgium and Australia, were selected by the Netherlands and the Republic of Indonesia respectively, while the third member, the United States, was chosen by Belgium and Australia. In late October the Good Offices Committee began its work in Indonesia. On November 1 the Council passed a resolution[3] that gave the Good Offices Committee the additional duty of assisting the parties to arrive at an agreement to implement the Council's cease-fire order of August 1, which a report of the consular commission had indicated was not being observed.

Conferences between the Good Offices Committee and the parties to the dispute were held aboard

[1] U. N. doc. S/459, Aug. 1, 1947.
[2] U. N. doc. S/525, Aug. 26, 1947.
[3] U. N. doc. S/597, Nov. 3, 1947.

323

the U.S.S. *Renville*, which had been made available for the negotiations by the United States Government on the request of the Committee, after it had become apparent that the parties could agree on no other meeting place. The Good Offices Committee explored the military and political viewpoints of both parties and informally offered a detailed program for a military truce and a set of principles to serve as a basis for a political settlement. This program became the basis for the Renville agreement, which was accepted by both parties on January 17, 1948.

The Renville Agreement

The Renville agreement consists of three parts: a truce plan, 12 principles accepted with the truce and designed to serve as a basis for a final political agreement, and six additional principles proposed by the Committee and formally accepted by the parties at a slightly later date. Under the terms of the truce, the Republic accepts the "Van Mook Line", proclaimed by the Dutch in August, as a temporary line of demarcation between Dutch-held and Republican-held territory and as a basis for the establishment of demilitarized zones. Republican troops on the Dutch side of the demarcation line are to be withdrawn to Republican territory under observation of the Committee's military advisers. The truce specifies, however, that establishment of demilitarized zones in no way prejudices the rights, claims, or positions of the parties under Security Council resolutions of August 1, 25, and 26 and November 1, 1947. The 18 political principles provide for the establishment of a sovereign, domocratic, federal United States of Indonesia, of which the Republic is to be a component part, and for the transfer of Netherlands sovereignty to the U.S.I. at the end of a "stated interval". During the interim, Netherlands sovereignty is to be recognized and all states are to be granted fair representation in a central interim government. Plebiscites are to be held in the various territories of Java, Madura, and Sumatra (under observation of the Good Offices Committee if requested by either party) to determine whether these areas desire to form a part of the Republic or another state within the U.S.I. Following this delineation of states, a constitutional convention based upon proportional representation is to be held to frame the constitution of the U.S.I. Upon formation, the U.S.I. is to be linked in equal partnership with the Kingdom of the Netherlands in a Netherlands-Indonesian Union under the King of the Netherlands.

---

[4] U. N. doc. S/649, Feb. 10, 1948, appendix 8, p. 97 (the 6 principles), appendix 13, p. 111 (the 12 principles), and appendix 11, p. 105 (the truce).
[5] U.N. doc. S/649, Feb. 10, 1948.
[6] U.N. docs. S/P.V., 247, 248, 249, 251, 252, 256, and 259.
[7] U.N. doc. S/678, Feb. 18, 1948.

Dutch, in violation of the Renville principles, were organizing new states in territory taken from the Republic during hostilities without waiting for the plebiscites to be held under the observation of the Good Offices Committee and without the freedoms guaranteed by the Renville agreement. The representative of China thereupon proposed a resolution requesting the Committee of Good Offices to pay particular attention to political developments in western Java and Madura, the areas in question, and to report to the Council on these developments at frequent intervals.[10] This resolution was passed by a vote of 8 to 0, with Argentina, the Ukraine, and the Soviet Union abstaining.

In supporting the Chinese resolution, the United States Representative, Mr. Austin, stated that, in the view of the United States Government, under the Renville agreement "any new states temporarily formed in Java, Sumatra and Madura, must be the result of actual popular movements, and that there must be at all times freedom of assembly, of speech and of the press. Whether the situation at any time in West Java meets or violates these requirements may be a question of fact. It is, of course, clear from the agreement that whatever provisional governments may arise in these areas will be subject to the free expression of popular will, expressed through plebiscites held in accordance with the Renville Agreement. Meanwhile, it would be expedient for the Committee of Good Offices on the spot to send reports to the Security Council, whenever necessary, on whether the requirements of freedom of assembly, of speech and of the press have been and are being met. . . . "[11]

Republic shall co-operate to ensure the early establishment of a sovereign, democratic state on a federal basis, to be known as the United States of Indonesia.

Article 3

The United States of Indonesia shall comprise the entire territory of the Netherlands Indies, it being understood that, in case the population of any territory, after possible consultation with the other territories, should notify by means of a democratic procedure that they are not or not yet willing to join the United States of Indonesia, a special relationship to the States and to the Kingdom of the Netherlands can be established for such a territory.

Article 4

1). The component states of the United States of Indonesia shall be the Republic, Borneo and the Great East, without prejudice to the right of the population of any

---

[8] U.N. doc. S/681, Feb. 21, 1948.
[9] U.N. doc. S/682, Feb. 21, 1948.
[10] U.N. doc. S/689, Mar. 1, 1948.
[11] U.N. doc. S/P.V. 259, p. 51.

territory to decide by a democratic procedure that its position in the United States of Indonesia shall be otherwise defined.

2). Without prejudice to the provisions in article 3 and in the first paragraph of this article, the United States of Indonesia will be entitled to make a special arrangement concerning the territory of their capital.

Article 5

1). The constitution of the United States of Indonesia shall be drawn up and enacted by a Constituent Assembly, composed of democratically nominated representatives of the Republic and of the other future partners of the United States, with due observance of the following paragraph of this article.

2). The parties shall consult each other on the method of participation in this Constituent Assembly by the Republic, by the territories, not under the authority of the Republic, and by those groups of the population not or insufficiently represented in the Assembly, the respective responsibility of the Netherlands Government and of the Government of the Republic being duly observed.

Article 6

1). To promote the joint interests of the Netherlands and Indonesia, the Netherlands Government and the Government of the Republic shall co-operate in establishing a Netherlands Indonesian Union, through which the Kingdom of the Netherlands, comprising the Netherlands, the Netherlands Indies, Surinam and Curaçao, shall be converted into the said Union, consisting on the one hand of the Kingdom of the Netherlands, comprising the Netherlands, Surinam and Curaçao, and on the other hand the United States of Indonesia.

2). The foregoing paragraph does not exclude the possibility of any further arrangement affecting the relations between the Netherlands, Surinam and Curaçao.

Article 7

1). In order to promote the joint interests referred to in the preceding article, the Netherlands Indonesian Union shall have organs of their own.

2). These organs shall be formed by the Governments of the Kingdom of the Netherlands and the United States of Indonesia and, if necessary, by the Parliaments of these countries.

3). As joint interests shall be considered co-operation in the field of foreign relations, defence and, as far as necessary, of finance, as well as in economic and cultural matters.

Article 8

At the head of the Netherlands Indonesian Union shall be the King of the Netherlands. The decrees and resolutions for the promotion of joint interests, shall be issued by the organs of the Union in the name of the King.

Article 9

In order to promote the interests of the United States of Indonesia in the Netherlands, and those of the Kingdom of the Netherlands in Indonesia, High Commissioners shall be appointed by the respective governments.

Article 10

The Statute of the Netherlands Indonesian Union shall furthermore contain provisions with a view to:

a. safeguarding the rights of either party in relation to the other, and guaranteeing the fulfilment of their mutual obligations;

b. reciprocal civic rights to be exercised by Netherlands and Indonesian citizens;

Final Clause

his agreement shall be drawn up in the Netherlands in the Indonesian language. Both texts shall be hentic.

DJAKARTA, *November 15th, 1946.*

his twenty fifth day of March, 1947, this agreement been signed by the Delegations, duly authorized to t effect, on behalf of the Governments of the Kingdom

of the Netherlands and of the Republic of Indonesia with due regard to the letters and notes, lastly dated March 15th and March 24th, 1947, exchanged between the two delegations in relation to this agreement and annexed hereto.

Four copies of this agreement in the Netherlands language and four copies in the Indonesian language have been signed.

[Here follow the signatures.]

›cuments Relating to the Indonesian Situation

INITIAL CORRESPONDENCE

ter From the Permanent Liaison Officer of lla to the President of the Security Council [12]

30 July 1947

ɪʀ: The following communication has been received m the Honorable Member in Charge of the External ɪlrs Department in the Government of India:

"I have the honour on behalf of the Government of ndia to draw the attention of the Security Council nder Article 35 (1) of the United Nations Charter o the situation in Indonesia.

During the last few days Dutch forces have embarked rithout warning on large scale military action against he Indonesian people. These attacks began without varning at a time when a delegation of the Indone-ian Republican Government was actually at Batavia or negotiations with the Dutch authorities on the im-ilementation of Linggadjati Agreement.

In the opinion of the Government of India this situ-ition endangers the maintenance of international peace ind security which is covered by Article 34 of the ːharter. The Government of India therefore requests he Security Council to take the necessary measures ›rovided by the Charter to put an end to the present ːituation.

The Government of India earnestly hope that in view 'f its urgency the Council will consider this matter as ioon as possible.

> Jahawarlal Nehru [13]
> Member for External Affairs
> Government of India"

I am, Sir, Your obedient Servant,
(S. SEN)
rmanent Liaison Officer of the Government of India with the United Nations

·tter From the Acting Representative of Australia ı the Security Council to the Secretary-General [14]

30 July 1947 ·

SIR, I have the honour to advise that I have today dressed the following communication to the President ﹐ the Security Council.

"Under instructions from my Government, I have the honour to bring to the attention of the Security Council the hostilities which are at present in progress in Java and Sumatra between armed forces of the Netherlands and of the Republic of Indonesia, and which have been the subject of communiques by their respective Army commanders during the past ten days.

"The Australian Government considers that these hostilities constitute a breach of the peace under Article

39 and urges that the Council take immediate action to restore International Peace and Security.

"In order to prevent an aggravation of the situation the Australian Government proposes that the Security Council, as a provisional measure, and without preju-dice to the rights, claims, or position of the parties concerned, should call upon the Governments of the Netherlands and of the Republic of Indonesia to cease hostilities forthwith and to commence arbitration in accordance with Article 17 of the Linggadjati Agree-ment between the Netherlands and the Government of the Republic of Indonesia signed at Batavia on 25th March 1947. (See letter from the representative of the Netherlands to the United Nations addressed to the Secretary-General, dated 26 March, 1947, Document S/311).

"In view of the urgent circumstances I am instructed to request you to call immediately a meeting of the Security Council for the consideration of this com-munication and that the Provisional Agenda, including this item, be communicated to the representatives on the Security Council simultaneously with the notice of the meeting."

I would be grateful if you could immediately bring this communication to the attention of all representatives on the Security Council.

I have the honour to be, Sir, Your obedient Servant,
> W. R. HODGSON,
> *Minister*

Telegram to the Secretary-General From the Permanent Representative of the Philippines to the United Nations [15]

NEW YORK, *1 August 1947*

THE SECRETARY-GENERAL:

I have been instructed by my Government to transmit its stand in favor of the intervention of the Security Council to halt the armed conflict between the Nether-lands Government and the Government of the Republic of Indonesia. It is urged therefore that the Security Council take such steps as may be necessary to bring about the immediate cessation of hostilities and, without passing judgment on the responsibility on either party for such hostilities, to prevail upon them to submit the controversy to arbitration as provided in Article Seven-teen of the Cheribon Agreement.

---

[12] U.N. doc. S/447, July 30, 1947.
[13] Jawaharlal Nehru.
[14] U.N. doc. S/449, July 30, 1947.
[15] U.N. doc. S/458, Aug. 1, 1947.

The Philippine Government has been moved to take this step because it is vitally interested in the maintenance of peace in that area and because of its humanitarian desire to prevent further blood-shed. Accordingly my Government wishes to express its desire to participate in the discussion of this matter before the Security Council because it considers itself specially affected by any disturbance of peace in that part of the Pacific.

I wish furthermore to communicate to you the availability of my Government to participate in any action that may lead to the settlement of the dispute by arbitration.

With renewed assurances of my highest esteem and consideration.

CARLOS P. ROMULO
Permanent Representative of the Philippines to the United Nations

Letter to the President of the Security Council From the Permanent Representative of the Netherlands to the United Nations [16]

No. 654   *30 July 1947*

SIR, It has come to my knowledge a few hours ago that the Governments of India and Australia have requested to put the question of Indonesia on the agenda of Security Council and that this matter may be dealt with in its meeting of tomorrow 31st July 1947. It goes without saying that—should the Council decide to grant the requests—the interests of the Netherlands would be specially affected.

In case the Security Council should decide to open a discussion on the substance of this matter, I feel that it is my duty to request that this discussion be not begun until my Government has had an opportunity to appoint a representative to take part therein, if the Security Council, as I anticipate, invites the Netherlands to participate in the discussion.

I may add that I presume that the Acting Secretary-General will inform the Netherlands Government if and when the matter will be taken up by the Council, and that in that case a reasonable period of time will be accorded to my Government to send a representative, whom I feel sure my Government would lose no time in appointing.

I would appreciate it very much if you would be so kind as to communicate the contents of this letter to the Members of the Security Council.

I have the honour to be, Sir, Your obedient Servant,

J. W. M. SNOUCK HURGRONJE

SECURITY COUNCIL RESOLUTION ON THE INDONESIAN QUESTION [17]

The Security Council

NOTING with concern the hostilities in progress between the armed forces of the Netherlands and the Republic of Indonesia,

Calls upon the parties

(a) to cease hostilities forthwith, and
(b) to settle their disputes by arbitration or by other peaceful means and keep the Security Council informed about the progress of the settlement.

REPLIES OF THE NETHERLANDS AND THE REPUBLIC OF INDONESIA TO THE SECURITY COUNCIL RESOLUTION

Letter to the President of the Security Council From the Netherlands Ambassador to the United States [18]

NETHERLANDS EMBASSY
WASHINGTON, D. C.   *August 3, 1947.*

SIR, I have the honour to confirm my telegram to Your Excellency of this day, reading as follows:

In a letter dated August 1, 1947, Your Excellency was so good as to communicate to me the text of the resolution adopted that day by the Security Council in respect of conditions in Java and Sumatra. I lost no time in conveying that text by telegraph to the Netherlands Government.

I have now received instructions to inform Your Excellency as follows:

The Netherlands Government, although persisting its denial of the Council's jurisdiction in this matter, fully understands the Council's desire to see the use of arms come to an end in this as in other cases. Moreover the Netherlands Government welcomes the Council's resolution in this sense that it justifies the hope that, under the pressure of world opinion, the Government of the Republic of Indonesia will now be found disposed to carry out what so far it has failed to do in spite of constant and urgent requests and representations on the part of the Netherlands Government and notwithstanding corresponding friendly advice on the part of other powers.

In taking police action the Netherlands Government had, from the outset, strictly limited objectives in view reference may be made in this connection to the communication made on its behalf to the Secretary-General of the United Nations on July 21 in which the limited nature was pointed out of the action aiming at the cessation of a situation whose continuation could no longer be countenanced in the interest of the people.

Having taken into serious consideration the views which led the Security Council to address an appeal to both parties, the Netherlands Government has instructed the Lieutenant-Governor-General of the Netherlands Indies to enter into contact with the authorities of the Republic in order to arrive at the cessation on both sides of hostile action of any kind.

The Netherlands Government confidently anticipate that the good offices offered by the Government of the United States of America and gladly accepted by the Netherlands Government, will contribute greatly toward attaining the result aimed at in the resolution of the Security Council.

Please accept [etc.]   E. N. VAN KLEFFENS

---

[16] U.N. doc. S/450, July 31, 1947.
[17] U.N. doc. S/459, Aug. 1, 1947.
[18] U.N. doc. S/466, Aug. 4, 1947.

Department of State Bulletin

(1) The Government of the Republic of Indonesia, to meet the decision taken by the Security Council on August 1, 1947, and in their earnest desire to restore peace in Indonesia, has decided to order cessation of hostilities to all Republican armed forces on Monday night 2400 hours Indonesian Standard Time.

(2) The Government of the Republic of Indonesia request the attention of the Security Council that aforementioned decision was handed to Republican Government through the Dutch Government in Djakarta only on August 4, 1947, at 0100 hours Indonesian Standard Time. In view of the earliest possible measures to be taken in order to realise the order of cessation of hostilities effectively, the Government of the Republic of Indonesia painfully regret the transfer of the decision of the Security Council being delayed by the Dutch authorities in Djakarta.

(3) In executing the order of the cessation of hostilities, the Government of the Republic of Indonesia request the fullest consideration of the Security Council for some serious technical difficulties to be overcome such as the shortage of time and heavy damage caused by Dutch acts of aggression to Republican communication lines.

(4) In addition, it should be considered, that unlike the military situation on October 14, 1946, when for the first time a cease-fire order was issued by both sides and witnessed by a third party, at the present moment no definite line of demarcation, clearly separating the Republic from the Dutch forces can be traced. Due to the system of a people's defence being followed by the Republican National Army, the fighting has not been restricted to definite frontlines. On the contrary, in many towns and areas which the Dutch military command claimed to have been occupied Republican forces up till now still have maintained its positions.

(5) The Government of the Republic of Indonesia wish to express their grave concern that, as the experience gained during the past two years have learned, unless the execution of the cessation of hostilities be fully and continuously controlled by a third neutral party, there is no guarantee that a cease-fire order will not be violated by Dutch forces onesidedly. Therefore the Republican Government strongly urge the sending of a Committee consisting of the representatives of several countries and appointed by the Security Council to Indonesia at earliest possible time in order to secure the effective and smooth implementation of cessation of hostilities.

(6) The Government of the Republic of Indonesia wish to emphasise that a Dutch order to cease hostilities should imperatively imply the cessation of all kinds of actions, by Dutch military and civil authorities directed against the Indonesian population.

(7) Finally, the Republican Government are of the opinion that cessation of hostilities should be followed by withdrawal of the Dutch armed forces from Republican territory at least behind the demarkation lines fixed by both sides on October 14, 1946.

DR. A. K. GANI
Vice-Premier Republic of Indonesia

JACARTA, *5th August 1947*

COUNCIL RESOLUTIONS

AND WHEREAS it is desirable that steps should be taken to avoid disputes and friction relating to the observance of the "cease fire" orders, and to create conditions which will facilitate agreement between the parties.

[19] U.N. doc. S/466, Aug. 4, 1947.
[20] U.N. doc. S/465, Aug. 4, 1947.
[21] U.N. doc. S/469, Aug. 6, 1947.
[22] U.N. doc. S/525, Aug. 26, 1947.

The Security Council

1. notes with satisfaction the steps taken by the parties to comply with the resolution of 1 August 1947,

2. notes with satisfaction the statement by the Netherlands Government issued on 11 August, in which it affirms its intention to organize a sovereign, democratic United States of Indonesia in accordance with the purpose of the Linggadjati Agreement,

3. notes that the Netherlands Government intends immediately to request the career consuls stationed in Batavia jointly to report on the present situation in the Republic of Indonesia,

4. notes that the Government of the Republic of Indonesia has requested appointment by the Security Council of a commission of observers,

5. requests the Governments members of the Council who have career consular representatives in Batavia to instruct them to prepare jointly for the information and guidance of the Security Council reports on the situation in the Republic of Indonesia following the Resolution of the Council of 1 August 1947, such reports to cover the observance of the "cease fire" orders and the conditions prevailing in areas under military occupation or from which armed forces now in occupation may be withdrawn by agreement between the parties,

6. requests the Governments of the Netherlands and the Republic of Indonesia to grant to the representatives referred to in paragraph 5, all facilities necessary for the effective fulfilment of their mission,

7. resolves to consider the matter further should the situation require.

II. *The Security Council*

RESOLVES to tender its good offices of the parties in order to assist in the pacific settlement of their dispute in accordance with paragraph (B) of the Resolution of the Council of 1 August 1947. The Council expresses its readiness, if the parties so request, to assist in the settlement through a committee of the Council consisting of three members of the Council, each party selecting one, and the third to be designated by the two so selected.[13]

B. Resolution Adopted at the 195th Meeting Held on 26 August 1947

III. *The Security Council*

TAKING into consideration that military operations are

CHRISTMAS DRAFT MESSAGE ADDRES BY THE COMMITTEE

The four resolutions of the Security Council which directly concern the work of the Committee of Good Offices on the Indonesian Question are those of 1, 25, and 26 August and 1 November 1947.

The Committee of Good Offices started its work with a first unofficial meeting in New York on 8 October. It has been at work in Indonesia since 27 October. Today, 24 December, on the eve of Christmas, the symbol of peace on earth, no concrete solution has been given by the parties either to the overall problems, or to the immediate problems of effecting a cease-fire.

---

[13] Part II of this document was introduced as a U. S. draft resolution and issued as U.N. doc. S/514 of Aug. 22, 1947.

[14] U.N. doc. S/597, Nov. 3, 1947. This resolution was submitted by the United States and amended by the subcommittee appointed by the Security Council at its 217th meeting on Oct. 31, 1947.

[15] U.N. doc. S/649, Feb. 10, 1948, p. 70.

y in arriving at an agreement, the Committee wishes to
ind the parties, in a solemn way, of the paramount
importance for them, for the world, and for the ideals of
United Nations, of a prompt and generous imple-
tation of the resolutions of the Security Council on the
onesian question.

he Committee must in good faith warn the parties that
nger delay, however supported by different or divergent
imentation, would certainly be against the spirit of the
olutions, and in particular of the resolution of 1
ember.

he Committee now invites the parties again to re-
sider, immediately, the whole problem with greater
ism, with reciprocal toleration, and with renewed
hasis on all the human aspects of the dispute.

In this spirit, and in consideration of the information
many statements at its disposal, the Committee is
smitting herewith, as Annex I, supplementary sug-
tions for an immediate truce. It recommends to the
ties that they:

(a) Sign immediately and implement forthwith the
everal measures contained in the documents herewith
transmitted, together with those at present before the
ipecial Committees.

At this point, the Committee reminds the parties of
he text of the third paragraph of the resolution of 1
November, which, after the passage concerning the im-
ilementation of a truce, reads as follows: "and pending
igreement to cease any activities or incitement to activ-
ties which contravene that resolution and to take
ippropriate measures for safeguarding life and prop-
rty".

To this end, the Committee suggests that precise
orders be issued or confirmed by the competent authori-
ies of both parties. It further suggests that all methods for the dissemination of such orders be utilized,
ncluding radio broadcasts.

(b) Immediately following the issuance of the foregoing instructions, conclude a truce agreement which
will implement the following part of the third paragraph of the resolution of 1 November, which "calls
upon the parties concerned forthwith to consult with
each other directly or through the Committee of Good
Offices as to the means to be employed in order to give
effect to the cease-fire resolution." The Committee
suggests that the parties accept, without delay, the proposals previously submitted by the Committee to the
parties, at their request, together with the proposals
transmitted herewith as Annex I. All documents submitted by the parties to the representatives of the Committee of Good Offices with the Special Committees,
either spontaneously or in implementation of the truce
plan, should be considered again, in order firstly, to
take stock of all points on which an agreement has been
obtained or is within reach, and secondly, to limit and
define the points on which a compromise between still
conflicting views should be looked for. As part of this
agreement, both parties should fully inform their soldiers still in the territory actually under the authority
of the other of the practical measures devised to effec-

tuate their transport, with arms and equipment, to the
territory of their own party. They should be instructed to comply immediately. The co-operation of
the Committee's military assistants is hereby offered
to help insure a safe and smooth execution of these
movements.

The Committee believes that both of the foregoing
agreements should be an accomplished fact before the
end of this month and should not wait on the settlement
of the political issues. Yet let the Committee make it
clear that in its opinion the several suggestions made in
all three parts of this statement, including Annexes I
and II, constitute one integrated, balanced whole which
the Committee considers essential to the lasting settlement
of the dispute.

4. The Committee is confident that following the
truce, there will be a marked improvement in the atmosphere in which the substantive discussions are to be held.

Here again, the Committee will call upon the parties,
with renewed confidence, to approach the political negotiations in a spirit of deeper understanding, co-operation,
and realism.

The Committee will suggest that each party state in a
new memorandum, and in the most moderate terms, its
views concerning the practical steps to be taken in the
very near future, to insure a lasting settlement of the
political dispute.

Both parties have repeatedly stated that they still hold
to the principles underlying Linggadjati. According to the
statements and explanations the Committee has received
from both parties, the Committee believes that the principles of this Agreement may be summarized as follows:

(a) Independence of the Indonesian peoples;
(b) Co-operation between the peoples of the Netherlands and Indonesia;
(c) A sovereign State on a federal basis, under a constitution which will be arrived at by democratic processes;
(d) A union between the United States of Indonesia
and other parts of the Kingdom of the Netherlands
under the Crown.

What the Committee thinks desirable is a concrete
elaboration of those principles, conceived and drafted by
each of the parties, with the care and the hope to meet
half-way the known or putative views of the other.

The Committee puts itself once more at the disposal of
the parties in the belief that its intervention can help
bring their points of view closer and more quickly together.
The Committee is transmitting herewith, as Annex II,
supplementary suggestions regarding a programme based
upon principles which it believes essential to the attainment of a just and lasting settlement.

As the Committee has already stated, the time has come
for it to send a report to the Security Council on the
progress of the developments of the Indonesian question.
It fervently hopes that the answer of the parties to this
communication will provide a favourable conclusion for
that report.

STATEMENT TO THE SECURITY COUNCIL BY THE U.S. REPRESENTATIVE
ON THE GOOD OFFICES COMMITTEE ON INDONESIA [26]

We were always aware of the wisdom in the statements
both the former Prime Minister of the Republic and
e Netherlands Ambassador to the United States that
ere would be reciprocal relations between progress in
e effectuation of the truce and progress in the settle-
ent of the political dispute. Accordingly, on Christmas
iy, our Committee unanimously adopted a draft plan—
an informal basis—including truce proposals and
mocratic political principles which were submitted in-

formally to the parties as an integrated and balanced
whole. The Republic, though expressing disappointment
in what it considered a rigid truce plan, with a *status quo*
line which for a time would continue to include behind

[26] Made on Feb. 17, 1948, and released to the press by the
U.S. Mission to the United Nations on the same date. This
is a partial text. The U.S. Representative is Frank P.
Graham.

Dutch lines former Republican areas containing millions of people, accepted the plan as a whole for its political principles of freedom and democracy, independence and union. The Netherlands, holding the Christmas message on its continuing informal basis, as counter proposals, accepted most of the suggestions, rejected parts, and accepted other parts with modifications. The Netherlands then made these proposals formal with indications that if not accepted by the Republic, it would not be bound by the twelve political principles. These twelve principles provided, among other things, for the continuance of the assistance of the Committee of Good Offices in the working out of the settlement of the political dispute in Java, Sumatra and Madura; for civil and political liberties; that there would be no interference with the expression of popular movements, looking toward the formation of states in accordance with the principles of the Linggadjati agreement; that changes in the administration of territory would be made only with the full and free consent of the population of the territory at a time of security and freedom from coercion; that, on the signing of the political agreement, there would be gradual reduction of the armed forces of both parties; that, on the signing of the truce agreement, there would be resumption of trade, transportation and communication through the cooperation of the parties; that there would be a period of not less than six months nor more than one year after the signing of the agreement during which uncoerced and free discussion of vital issues should proceed and that at the end of such period free elections would be held for self-determination by the people of their political relations to the United States of Indonesia; provision for the convening of a Constitutional Convention by democratic procedure; provision for serious consideration by one party of the request of the other party for an agency of the United Nations to observe conditions between the signing of the agreement and the transfer of sovereignty from the Netherlands to the United States of Indonesia; provisions for the independence of the Indonesian people and cooperation between the peoples of the Netherlands and Indonesia; provision for a sovereign nation on a federal basis under a constitution to be arrived at by democratic procedures; and provision for the Union of the United States of Indonesia and the other parts of the Kingdom of the Netherlands under the King of the Netherlands.

While deeply appreciative of the fact that the twelve political principles contained many basic provisions for freedom, democracy, independence and cooperation, the Republic was most deeply concerned that there was no guarantee of international observation between the signing of the agreement and the transfer of sovereignty; that there was no provision for the representation of the Republic in the interim government, and that there was no mention of the Republic by name in any of the twelve principles.

Aware of the limitations inherent in a Committee of Good Offices, and in the desperate circumstances of the probable breakdown of negotiations, the Committee decided to make still another new approach to the parties. The Committee suggested for the informal consideration of the parties six additional political principles in addition to the twelve. Pending consideration of the six principles by both parties, the Republic was pondering the acceptance or rejection of the status quo military line and the democratic political principles in which were missing several guarantees of deep concern to the Republic. It soon appeared that the content of the six additional principles, if accepted by the Netherlands, would be decisive as to acceptance by the Republic of the combined plans as, in effect—though not formally—an integrated and balanced whole.

In the six principles were the three things of deep concern to the Republic; specific references to the Repub-

Two things stand out in the Indonesian situation. First, the truce has been signed for the cessation of hostilities and is being kept with the saving of human lives and property. Second, fundamental principles of freedom, democracy, independence, and cooperation have been agreed upon for the early formation of the independent United States of Indonesia in the Union with the Netherlands, both to be free and equal nations in the United Nations.

The two parties to this truce are pledged to stop the killing and the destruction. This contract must be kept. I wish to join the Committee of Good Offices in their faith that this truce will be kept with good faith and good will by both Governments.

The two parties to the agreement are pledged to fulfill the twelve political principles and the six other principles in addition to or in amplification of the twelve. This contract must be kept. I wish to join the Committee of Good Offices in their faith that these principles will be fulfilled by both Governments with good faith and good will.

These political principles are a part of the great tradition of freedom and democracy. Their meaning is known of men. The guarantees of freedom of assembly, speech and the press are unequivocal. A fair plebiscite means a free ballot on a clear issue by the individual in security from coercion or reprisal. The opportunity for advance discussion of the clear issue should be free, full and open to the parties involved. With such other provisions for safeguarding plebiscites, which experience has established for equal participation of the parties and equal guarantee of their political and civil liberties, there can be free and fair self-determination by the people as to whether the population of the various territories of Java, Madura, and Sumatra wish their territory to form part of the Republic of Indonesia or of another state within the United States of Indonesia. These decisions will be based on free ballots and not the force of arms in accordance with the purposes and principles of the United Nations. On the request of either party, the observation of the plebiscite by the Committee of Good Offices is assured by the Agreement between the parties.

In the organization of the constitutional convention by democratic procedure to draft a constitution for the United States of Indonesia representation of the various states in the convention will be in proportion to their populations.

Other provisions in the Renville agreement provide for the gradual reduction of the armies of both parties; the resumption of trade, transportation and communication through cooperation of the parties; fair representation of the Republic in the interim government; and, upon the request of either party, the continuation of the services of the Good Offices Committee in assisting the continuation of the parties to adjust differences which may arise in the interim period relating to the political agreement. All these provisions constitute the foundation for the freedom, independence, and cooperation of the people of the Netherlands and the people of Indonesia.

In a most difficult situation which has seemed almost impossible of solution for so long, the Committee of Good Offices, instead of bringing to us a continuing dispute on the location of a military demarcation line without any agreement on political principles, has brought us both a truce of peace and an agreement on political principles. Members of the Council have already been deeply impressed by the greatness of these principles which became the basis of the truce and under which the military demarcation lines will disappear and the independent, sovereign and democratic United States of Indonesia will take its free and equal place among the Nations of the world.

These principles illustrate the long run value of the basic and historic truth inherent in the statement of the Queen of the Netherlands quoted by Dr. Van Kleffens at our last meeting. Nations which offer their colonies the opportunity to become free and independent Nations will save them for voluntary cooperation, to the mutual benefit of all, in lifting the levels of production, and standards of living, and their opportunities for influence and service in the world.

The great democratic principles in the agreement are in accord with the Charter and the principles of the United Nations. These principles are the heritage of the free peoples of the earth. Many millions of people have died to win them. Two World Wars were fought to save them. The people of the Netherlands and the people of the Republic of Indonesia, and, I trust, all the people of Indonesia will share them as their common heritage.

The Indonesian nationalist movement of half a century, the aspirations for freedom of seventy million Indonesians, the struggles of the people of the Republic of Indonesia, the noble declarations of the Queen and the wise commitments of the Ministers of the Netherlands, are, we are sure, soon to be fulfilled in the transfer of the historic and acknowledged sovereignty of The Netherlands to a free and independent United States of Indonesia as an equal Nation in the new Union of Nations and as an equal Nation in the United Nations. Those of little faith would deny the good faith of the parties and, therefore, doubt the great fulfillment.

We wish to say for the good name of both parties before the World that it is inconceivable to them, that it is inconceivable to the three Member Nations which make up the Committee of Good Offices, and it is inconceivable to this Security Council of the United Nations that either the Kingdom of the Netherlands or the Republic of Indonesia or any representative of either Government would see directly or indirectly to delay or to wear down by attrition or to renounce on a mere pretext or otherwise undermine either the truce or the great principles of human freedom, national independence and mutual cooperation which are now joined in an historic agreement as the latest chapter in the history of the self determination of peoples.

The cooperation of the people of the Netherlands and the people of Indonesia may signal to peoples everywhere on this troubled earth that mankind is again on the upward climb toward a better day.

[27] Made on Feb. 20, 1948, and released to the press by the U.S. Mission to the United Nations on the same date. This is a partial text. The U.S. Representative is Warren R. Austin.

The Government of the Kingdom of the Netherlands and the Government of the Republic of Indonesia, referred to in this agreement as the parties, hereby agree as follows:

1. That a stand fast and cease fire order be issued separately and simultaneously by both parties immediately upon the signing of this agreement and to be fully effective within forty-eight hours. This order will apply to the troops of both parties along the boundary lines of the areas described in the proclamation of the Netherlands Indies Government on 29 August 1947, which shall be called the *status quo* line, and in the areas specified in the following paragraph.

2. That in the first instance and for the time being, demilitarized zones be established in general conformity with the above-mentioned *status quo* line; these zones as a rule will comprise the territories between this *status quo* line and, on one side, the line of the Netherlands forward positions and, on the other side, the line of the Republican forward positions, the average width of each of the zones being approximately the same.

3. That the establishment of the demilitarized zones in no way prejudices the rights, claims or position of the parties under the resolutions of the Security Council of 1, 25, and 26 August and 1 November 1947.

4. That upon acceptance of the foregoing by both parties, the Committee will place at the disposal of both parties its military assistants who will be instructed to assume, in the first instance, responsibility for determining whether any incident requires enquiry by the higher authorities of either or both parties.

5. That, pending a political settlement, the responsibility for the maintenance of law and order and of security of life and property in the demilitarized zones will remain vested in the civil police forces of the respective parties. (The term civil police does not exclude the temporary use of military personnel in the capacity of civil police, it being understood that the police forces will be under civil control.) The Committee's military assistants will be available to advise the appropriate authorities of the parties and to serve in such other proper capacities as may be requested. Among other, they should;

(a) call upon pools of police officers established by each party in its demilitarized zone to accompany the military assistants in their endeavours and moves throughout that demilitarized zone. Police officers of one party will not move into and throughout the demilitarized zone of the other party unless accompanied by a military assistant of the Committee of Good Offices and a police officer of that other party.

(b) promote co-operation between the two police forces.

6. That trade and intercourse between all areas should be permitted as far as possible; such restrictions as may be necessary will be agreed upon by the parties with the assistance of the Committee and its representatives if required.

7. That this agreement shall include all the following points already agreed to in principle by the parties:

(a) To prohibit sabotage, intimidation and reprisals and other activities of a similar nature against individuals, groups of individuals, and property, including de-

---

[28] U.N. doc. S/649, Feb. 10, 1948. The agreement was signed at the 4th meeting of the Committee of Good Offices with the parties on Jan. 17, 1948.

Annex

Clarification of the Agreement

. As regards paragraph 1 of the foregoing agreement, s understood that the two parties will endeavor to im- ment the various points of the truce agreement without ; delay and with all means at their disposal; it is ally understood that, should one of the parties meet :h special difficulties in carrying out fully within a few ys any obligation imposed upon it by the truce agreement, m notification to the other party the time limit of forty- ht (48) hours provided in the first article of the pro- als will be extended up to a maximum of twelve (12) ;s.

. As regards paragraph 2 of the foregoing agreement, it understood that if, as expected, the truce agreement is increasingly implemented and the general situation con- tinues to develop favourably, the demilitarized zones will, as a matter of course, be further extended. The question of an extension of demilitarized zones will upon the re- quest of either party, be considered forthwith by the Com- mittee's military assistants who, acting within the intent of paragraph 5, will advise the appropriate authorities.

3. As regards paragraph 4 of the foregoing agreement, it is understood that the military assistants of the Com- mittee of Good Offices will have every opportunity in the execution of paragraph 4 of the truce agreement, for de- termining whether any incident requires inquiry by the higher authorities of either or both parties, in which case they will of course at the same time refer the matter to their principal, namely, the Committee of Good Offices, whose services will be available to assist in adjusting dif- ferences between the parties in regard to the truce.

PRINCIPLES FORMING AN AGREED BASIS FOR THE POLITICAL DISCUSSIONS [20]

The Committee of Good Offices has been informed by e delegation of the Kingdom of the Netherlands and the delegation of the Republic of Indonesia that, the ace agreement having been signed, their Governments cept the following principles on which the political scussions will be based:

1. That the assistance of the Committee of Good Offices : continued in the working out and signing of an agree- ent for the settlement of the political dispute in the lands of Java, Sumatra and Madura, based upon the inciples underlying the Linggadjati Agreement.

2. It is understood that neither party has the right to event the free expression of popular movements looking ward political organizations which are in accord with the inciples of the Linggadjati Agreement. It is further aderstood that each party will guarantee the freedom ! assembly, speech and publication at all times provided aat his guarantee is not construed so as to include the ivocacy of violence or reprisals.

3. It is understood that decisions concerning changes administration of territory should be made only with ae full and free consent of the populations of those erritories and at a time when the security and free- om from coercion of such populations will have been asured.

4. That on the signing of the political agreement pro- sion be made for the gradual reduction of the armed orces of both parties.

5. That as soon as practicable after the signing of ae truce agreement, economic activity, trade, transporta- ion and communications be restored through the o-operation of both parties, taking into consideration the aterests of all the constituent parts of Indonesia.

6. That provision be made for a suitable period of not ess than six months nor more than one year after the igning of the agreement, during which time uncoerced nd free discussion and consideration of vital issues will iroceed. At the end of this period, free elections will be ield for self-determination by the people of their political elationship to the United States of Indonesia.

7. That a constitutional convention be chosen according to democratic procedure to draft a constitution for the United States of Indonesia.

8. It is understood that if, after signing the agreement referred to in item 1, either party should ask the United Nations to provide an agency to observe conditions at any time up to the point at which sovereignty is trans- ferred from the Government of the Netherlands to the Government of the United States of Indonesia, the other party will take this request in serious consideration.

The following four principles are taken from the Linggadjati Agreement:

9. Independence for the Indonesian peoples.

10. Co-operation between the peoples of the Netherlands and Indonesia.

11. A sovereign state on a federal basis under a con- stitution which will be arrived at by democratic processes.

12. A union between the United States of Indonesia and other parts of the Kingdom of the Netherlands under the King of the Netherlands.

Confirmed for the Government of the Kingdom of the Netherlands

RADEN ABDULKADIR WIDJOJOATMODJO
Chairman of the delegation

Confirmed for the Government of the Republic of Indo- nesia

DR. AMIR SJARIFUDDIN
Chairman of the delegation

The representatives on the United Nations Security Council Committee of Good Offices on the Indonesian Ques- tion, and the Committee Secretary, whose signatures are hereunto subscribed on this 17th day of January 1948, on board the U.S.S. *Renville*, testify that the above principles are agreed to as a basis for the political discussions.

Chairman:	MR. JUSTICE RICHARD C. KIRBY (Aus- tralia)
Representatives:	MR. PAUL VAN ZEELAND (Belgium)
	DR. FRANK P. GRAHAM (United States)
Secretary:	T. G. NARAYANAN

ADDITIONAL PRINCIPLES FOR THE NEGOTIATIONS TOWARD A POLITICAL SETTLEMENT [30]

The Committee of Good Offices is of the opinion that the ollowing principles, among others, form a basis for the egotiations towards a political settlement:

1. Sovereignty throughout the Netherlands Indies is and hall remain with the Kingdom of the Netherlands until, fter a stated interval, the Kingdom of the Netherlands were accepted at the 4th meeting of the Committee of Good Offices with the parties on Jan. 17, 1948.

[30] U.N. doc. S/649, Feb. 10, 1948. These principles were submitted by the Committee of Good Offices with the parties on Jan. 17, 1948, and accepted at the 5th meeting of the Committee with the parties on Jan. 19, 1948.

[29] U.N. doc. S/649, Feb. 10, 1948, p. 111. These principles

transfers its sovereignty to the United States of Indonesia. Prior to the termination of such stated interval, the Kingdom of the Netherlands may confer appropriate rights, duties and responsibilities on a provisional federal government of the territories of the future United States of Indonesia. The United States of Indonesia, when created, will be a sovereign and independent State in equal partnership with the Kingdom of the Netherlands in a Netherlands-Indonesian Union at the head of which shall be the King of the Netherlands. The status of the Republic of Indonesia will be that of a state within the United States of Indonesia.

2. In any provisional federal government created prior to the ratification of the constitution of the future United States of Indonesia, all states will be offered fair representation.

3. Prior to the dissolution of the Committee of Good Offices, either party may request that the services of the Committee be continued to assist in adjusting differences between the parties which relate to the political agreement and which may arise during the interim period. The other party will interpose no objection to such a request; this request would be brought to the attention of the Security Council of the United Nations by the Government of the Netherlands.

4. Within a period of not less than six months or m[??] than one year from the signing of this agreement, a plebiscite will be held to determine whether the populations[?] the various territories of Java, Madura and Sumatra w[?] their territory to form part of the Republic of Indonesia[?] of another state within the United States of Indone[??], such plebiscite to be conducted under observation by [??] Committee of Good Offices should either party, in acco[??]ance with the procedure set forth in paragraph 3 abo[?] request the services of the Committee in this capaci[?] The parties may agree that another method for ascertaining the will of the populations may be employed in place[?] a plebiscite.

5. Following the delineation of the states in accordan[??] with the procedure set forth in paragraph 4 above, a c[??]stitutional convention will be convened, through dem[?] cratic procedures, to draft a constitution for the Unit[?] States of Indonesia. The representation of the vari[??] states in the convention will be in proportion to th[?] populations.

6. Should any state decide not to ratify the constituti[?] and desire, in accordance with the principles of artic[??] 3 and 4 of the Linggadjati Agreement, to negotiate a spec[?] relationship with the United States of Indonesia and t[?] Kingdom of the Netherlands, neither party will object.[?]

DRAFT RESOLUTION SUBMITTED BY THE REPRESENTATIVE OF CANADA REGARDING THE FIRST INTERIM REPORT OF THE COMMITTEE OF GOOD OFFICES [31]

The Security Council,

HAVING considered the Report of the Committee of Good Offices, informing the Council of the steps taken by the Netherlands Government and the Government of the Republic of Indonesia to comply with the Council's resolution of 1 August 1947;

Notes with satisfaction the signing of the Truce Agreement by both parties and the acceptance by both parties of certain principles as an agreed basis for the conclusion of a political settlement in Indonesia;

Commends the members of the Committee of Good Offices for the assistance they have given the two parties in their endeavours to settle their dispute by peaceful means;

Maintains its offer of good offices contained in the resolution of 25 August 1947, and, to this end,

Requests both parties and the Committee of Good Offices to keep the Council directly informed about the progress of the political settlement in Indonesia.

Australian Amendment [32]

Insert the following paragraph between the third and fourth paragraphs of the Canadian draft resolution (document S/678).

CONSIDERS that it is a matter for the Committee of Good

Offices itself as to whether that Committee in the futu[?] should make and at its discretion publish suggestions [?] the parties to help them in reaching a political settleme[?] without necessarily waiting for the parties to request the[?] to do so.

Colombian Amendment [33]

Insert the following before the last paragraph of t[?] Canadian draft resolution (document S/678):

INVITES THE PARTIES:

(a) To direct their efforts, with the assistance of t[?] Committee of Good Offices, toward the early and f[?] implementation of the bases for a political settleme[?] already agreed upon; and

(b) To avail themselves of the Committee's servic[?] for the solution of any differences that may arise betwe[??] them in respect of the interpretation and application [?] such principles.

REQUESTS THE COMMITTEE OF GOOD OFFICES:

To continue, by the means that they consider appropr[?] ate, to assist the parties in their endeavours to attai[?] the ends set forth above.

TEXT OF THE RESOLUTION SUBMITTED BY CHINA AND ADOPTED AT THE 259th MEETING OF THE SECURITY COUNCIL [34]

The Security Council,

REQUESTS the Committee of Good Offices to pay particular attention to the political developments in Western Java and Madura and to report to the Council thereon at frequent intervals.

[31] U.N. doc. S/678, Feb. 18, 1948.
[32] U.N. doc. S/681, Feb. 21, 1948.
[33] U.N. doc. S/682, Feb. 21, 1948.
[34] U.N. doc. S/689, Mar. 1, 1948.

FREEDOM OF INFORMATION [1]

TICLE

According to the American outlook, members of the public should enjoy the right to receive and read printed materials originating at home or abroad, to listen to domestic or foreign broadcasts, to view films produced domestically or in foreign countries, and to proclaim views orally or in writing on political and other subjects. These freedoms are based on the general premise that the public has a moral right to receive and to disseminate information on all sides of controversial issues.

The freedoms applying especially to journalists include, in the American view, the opportunity (subject to laws and regulations aimed at preserving national security) to enter all countries, to travel within them, to have nondiscriminatory access to sources of information, to gather information, to transmit information by telecommunication and by mail without censorship, and to leave without molestation.

The media of mass communication, including the press, radio, and screen, should have the right to acquire information by sending correspondents and photographers to the sources of domestic and international news; to receive dispatches, scripts, and other informational materials originating at home and abroad; to produce and distribute publications and films (freely at home and without undue restrictions in foreign countries); to exhibit films both domestic and foreign; to stage and exhibit plays; and to produce and broadcast radio programs. These privileges imply a corresponding moral obligation to present news comprehensively and without distortion, in order that the public may be adequately informed.

Although all the cherished rights which have been mentioned are inherent in the concept of freedom of information, they are nevertheless subject to certain limitations. Questions naturally arise as to what limitations are proper. In the traditional as well as current answers to these questions, there is general assent to the proposition that restrictions may be imposed upon freedom of information in the interest of military security, public order, public morals, and prevention of

[1] Prepared in the Division of Historical Policy Research, Department of State.

libel. Wide disagreement exists, however, particularly between countries, regarding specific restrictions within these accepted categories.

Origin and Purpose of the Conference

Of the "four freedoms" enunciated by Franklin D. Roosevelt on January 6, 1941, the first was "freedom of speech and expression—everywhere in the world". This freedom was discussed at the San Francisco conference of 1945 which drew up the Charter of the United Nations. Although the Charter refers in various articles to the promotion of human rights and freedoms, without specific allusion to freedom of information, the Chairman of the United States Delegation, Secretary of State Edward R. Stettinius, Jr., reported his understanding that these references were intended to cover freedom of information.

A conference on the subject was first proposed by the Philippine Delegation to the General Assembly of the United Nations, which presented a draft resolution early in 1946 concerning the calling of an "International Press Conference". The resolution was received too late to be included in the agenda for the first part of the first session of the General Assembly, but on February 9, 1946, the Assembly voted to place the question upon the agenda for the second part of the first session, to be held that fall in New York.

At the autumn meeting the Delegation of the Philippine Republic submitted a new draft resolution authorizing a conference of all members of the United Nations on freedom of information. In discussing this resolution, the Representative of the Philippine Republic in the General Assembly's Third Committee, which had the resolution under consideration, explained that his Delegation had proposed the new resolution because it believed that radio and motion pictures must be considered along with the press in dealing with freedom of information.

The resolution, with a slight change in form but not in substance, was unanimously adopted by the General Assembly at its plenary session of December 14, 1946.[2] It declares that freedom of information "is a fundamental human right and is the touchstone of all the freedoms to which the United Nations is consecrated". Implying "the right to gather, transmit and publish news anywhere and everywhere without fetters", freedom of information—according to the resolution—"is an essential factor in any serious effort to promote the peace and progress of the world". It requires, however, "as a basic discipline the moral obligation to seek the facts without prejudice and to spread knowledge without malicious intent". The resolution further states that "Understanding and

[2] For the text of the resolution, see BULLETIN of Feb. 9, 1947, p. 244 n.

) press.[3] The provisional agenda will become finitive upon adoption by the conference.

As finally adopted, the provisional agenda calls st for a general discussion of the principles of eedom of information and next for consideration four fundamental principles which the press, lio, and films as media of information should gard in performing their basic functions of thering, transmitting, and disseminating news d information without fetters. These are:

1. To tell the truth without prejudice and to read knowledge without malicious intent;
2. To facilitate the solution of the economic, cial and humanitarian problems of the world as whole through the free interchange of informa-)n bearing on such problems;
3. To help promote respect for human rights d fundamental freedoms for all, without dis- iction as to race, sex, language or religion, and combat any ideologies whose nature could en- inger these rights and freedoms;
4. To help maintain international peace and curity through understanding and cooperation tween peoples, and to combat forces which in- te war, by removing bellicose influences from the edia of information.

Among the specific problems on the provisional renda is the topic, "Measures to facilitate the athering of information". This includes facili- iting the entry, residence, movement, and travel f accredited news personnel; protecting them against arbitrary expulsion; permitting the widest ossible access to news sources; and eliminating nreasonable or discriminatory taxes.

The conference will also discuss "Measures to acilitate the international transmission of infor- iation". This topic covers the progressive elimi- ation of peacetime censorship as it affects the iternational transmission of information, as well s recommendations for preferential telecom- iunication and postal treatment for news ma- erials, nondiscriminatory transmission rates and ervices for foreign news agencies, alleviation of conomic or commercial restriction on the im- iortation of news material by all media, and pre- ention of such cartelization of news agencies as nay endanger the freedom of the press.

"Measures concerning the free publication and eception of information" is an additional subject 'or conference discussion. This will entail con- iideration of the restrictions imposed by govern- nents on persons or groups wishing to receive and lisseminate information, ideas, and opinions, and recommendation of means to increase the amount)f domestic and international information avail- ible to all peoples and to improve the quality of nformation in the direction of greater accuracy,)bjectivity, comprehensiveness, and representative :haracter.

A further item on the agenda is "Consideration of the drafting of a charter of rights and obliga- tions of the media of information", including (1) a statement of the rights of these media and the means of safeguarding such rights through inter- national agreements within the framework of the United Nations, and (2) a statement of the obli- gations of the media of information and the measures necessary to insure the fulfilment of these obligations.

The conference is also scheduled to discuss "Con- sideration of possible continuing machinery to promote the free flow of true information". Ac- cording to the agenda, the functions of such ma- chinery might include (1) receiving, considering, and reporting on complaints regarding false news, tendentious or defamatory campaigns, obstruc- tions to the flow of information, and violations of any international conventions in this field; (2) suggesting changes in the provisions of such agree- ments, and publishing other recommendations on the question of freedom of information; (3) con- tinuing study of the current performance of news agencies and other processes of international in- formation; and (4) regulating the issuance of in- ternational professional cards for news personnel.

Finally, the provisional agenda provides for "Consideration of the problems involved in the establishment of governmental and semi-govern- mental information services in order to make in- formation available in countries other than their own" and "Consideration of the possible modes of action by means of which the recommendations of the Conference can best be put into effect, whether by resolutions of the General Assembly, international conventions, bilateral agreements, or by the adoption on the part of the individual states of appropriate laws, or other means".

Organization of the Conference

Taking note of the recommendations of the Sub- Commission on Freedom of Information and of the Press, the Economic and Social Council de- cided on August 14 and 15, 1947, that the confer- ence (1) should be held at Geneva beginning March 23, 1948, and (2) should be guided by cer- tain principles. These principles include the following:[4]

That voting rights at the conference shall be ex- ercised only by members of the United Nations.

That in addition to members of the United Na- tions, the following nonmember states shall be in- vited to participate: Albania, Austria, Bulgaria,

[3] For text of the provisional agenda as adopted by the Ecosoc, see U.N. doc. E/573, Sept. 2, 1947, p. 14.
[4] *Ibid.*, p. 11.

Eire, Finland, Hungary, Italy, Pakistan, Portugal, Rumania, Switzerland, Transjordan, and Yemen.

That certain specialized agencies, intergovernmental organizations, and nongovernmental organizations shall be invited to participate in the preparations for the conference and to attend it. Among these are the International Labor Organization and the United Nations Educational, Scientific and Cultural Organization; the International Postal Union, the International Telecommunication Union, and the International Trade Organization (if brought into existence before the conference); and the American Federation of Labor and the International Organization of Journalists.

That delegations to the conference shall consist of not more than five delegates from each state, not more than five alternates, and advisers as required.

Among the papers which the conference will have before it are (1) a memorandum to be prepared by the Secretary-General of the United Nations on the basis of replies to a questionnaire sent to participating governments regarding freedom of information in their respective countries, and (2) three documents adopted by the Sub-Commission on Freedom of Information and of the Press at its second session, namely, draft articles for inclusion in an International Declaration on Human Rights and an International Covenant on Human Rights (sponsored by the Human Rights Commission) and a tentative statement on the rights, obligations, and practices which should be included in the concept of freedom of information.[5] The Sub-Commission also recommended that the conference be apprised of the findings of UNESCO on the technical information needs of war-devastated areas.

The American Position

The first article in the "Bill of Rights" amendments to the Constitution of the United States provides in sweeping terms that "Congress shall make no law . . . abridging freedom of speech, or of the press." Provisions safeguarding freedom of speech and of the press also appear in the constitutions of all 48 of the States of the Union. These legal guaranties do not, however, apply to seditious utterances, obscene publications, or similar categories of expression which are likely to endanger national security, public order, public morals, or the reputations of individuals.

The question of the extent to which freedom of expression may properly be curbed in the interest

---

[5] See U.N. docs. E/437, p. 31; E/441, June 5, 1947; E/547, Aug. 11, 1947. For text of the proposal for a declaration of human rights, see BULLETIN of Dec. 7, 1947, p. 1076.

violent overthrow of the United States Government applies also to journalists who advocate such violent overthrow, unless they are officials of foreign governments or correspondents accredited to the United Nations.

2. Promoting the entry of periodicals, books, and films into countries where now such entry is hindered by political and economic obstacles, such as acknowledged and unacknowledged censorship, currency restrictions, and quotas.

3. Harmonizing the moral responsibility of the press with genuine freedom of the press. For example, how can the problem of so-called "warmongering" be dealt with in democratic countries without destroying freedom of expression?

At the Geneva conference and at other meetings, broad areas of international agreement will be mapped out and international machinery will be developed to give life and strength to real intellectual freedom.

Selected Bibliography[1]

—— Permanent Headquarters Committee. Summary Record of Meetings, 7 November–13 December 1946. ix, 108 pp. printed. [$1.00.]

—— Supplement No. 3. Preliminary Report of the Temporary Sub-commission on Economic Reconstruction of Devastated Areas (London, 29 July–13 September 1946). (A/147, October 26, 1946.) iv, 221 pp. printed. [$2.00.]

—— Supplement No. 5. Text of Agreements for Trust Territories, as approved by the General Assembly on 13 December 1946. 46 pp. printed. [40¢.]

Rules of Procedure of the General Assembly (A/520, December 12, 1947). vii, 29 pp. printed in French and English. [40¢.]

---

[1] Printed materials may be secured in the United States from the International Documents Service, Columbia University Press, 2960 Broadway, New York City. Other materials (mimeographed, or processed documents) may be consulted at certain designated libraries in the United States.

THE UNITED NATIONS AND SPECIALIZED AGENCIES

Discussion of the Palestine Problem in the Security Council

STATEMENT BY AMBASSADOR WARREN R. AUSTIN [1]

U. S. Representative in the Security Council

MR. PRESIDENT:

The pending business is the Belgian amendment to the draft resolution on the Palestine question submitted by the United States, document S/685. The distinguished Representative of Belgium, in speaking upon his amendment, stated, among other things, the following (and I read now from page 45 of SPV/258):

"I have submitted an amendment to the draft resolution of the delegation of the United States. This amendment tends to eliminate from the proposal any provision which constitutes a position on the substance of this question, i.e., partition. Amended in this way the draft resolution would remain within the limits of the present stage in which we find ourselves, the stage of investigation and elucidation of the possibilities. In this way the committee of five would have the greatest possible freedom. It would, nonetheless, be obliged to take into consideration all the elements of the problem, particularly the existence of a resolution of the General Assembly and a partition plan recommended by the General Assembly."

Again on page 46 occurs the following in his address:

"My amendment has but one objective, and that is that the Security Council might avoid pronouncing itself at the present stage of the discussion of this question while it is still insufficiently informed. This amendment does not in any way prejudge the position which the Security Council will take when the proper time comes. The Security Council will not take a position to pronounce itself properly and usefully as long as the committee has not expressed itself upon the results of its investigation."

And outside the record I have come to the understanding that Belgium is against the United States paragraph 1 for the time being. It is understood to be opposed only because Belgium considers that the moment has not yet come to

take a position on it now that the committee of five has not deposited its reports following its talks with the authorities.

Mr. President, the United States, notwithstanding this position, cannot support the Belgian amendment. The substantive issue is on the adoption or postponement of paragraph 1 of the draft resolution proposed by the United States. I read it here for the record:

Resolves:

"1. To accept, subject to the authority of the Security Council under the Charter, the requests addressed by the General Assembly to it in paragraphs (a), (b) and (c) of the General Assembly Resolution of 29 November 1947."

That is the end of it; paragraph 2 implements paragraph 1. A vote for this paragraph would be a vote for partition as a Palestine solution.

The General Assembly voted for partition as a Palestine solution.

The United States of America voted for that solution, and still supports it.

As we have stated before, the United States supports the General Assembly plan for partition as the framework of implementation by pacific means.

Paragraph 1, under consideration, containing the reservation "subject to the authority of the Security Council under the Charter", expresses a Charter principle implied—and we say it must be implied—in every part of the General Assembly resolution. This paragraph 1 in our draft resolution, therefore, interprets the acceptance of the General Assembly requests in the following manner:

"Requests (a) That the Security Council take the necessary measures, as provided for in the plan for its implementation;"

I intend to take them up a, b, c, *seriatim*, and give our interpretation of the effect of the adoption of paragraph 2.

This is accepted, subject to the limitation that armed force cannot be used for implementation of the plan, because the Charter limits the use

.[1] Made on Mar. 2, 1948, and released to the press by the U.S. Mission to the United Nations on the same date. For statement by Ambassador Austin on Feb. 24, 1948, see BULLETIN of Mar. 7, 1948.

This paragraph 1 in the draft resolution interprets Request (c) of the General Assembly resolution as follows:

Under article 39 the Security Council is under a mandate to determine existence of any threat to the peace, breach of the peace, or act of aggression. It may regard attempts to alter by force the settlement envisaged by this resolution as constituting such threat. The obligation must be carried out by the process of determination—note the language of (c)—and not solely at the request of the General Assembly.

As we have stated before, the Special Report of the Palestine Commission, dated February 16, 1948, "reports facts which, if accepted or substantiated by the Security Council, would appear to lead to the conclusion that a threat to international peace is present in that situation". Acceptance of Request (c) through the adoption of paragraph 1 of the United States draft resolution is an undertaking by the Security Council to look into the matter immediately to determine whether such a threat exists. Our subsequent paragraph 2 provides a way of investigation.

Now note the language of this Request (c).

Request (c) reads:

"Requests that the Security Council determine as a threat to the peace, breach of the peace, or act of aggression, in accordance with Article 39 of the Charter, any attempt to alter by force the settlement envisaged by this Resolution."

You cannot drop a word out of that and have the same meaning.

The language of Request (c) had a current construction by my Government at the time of acceptance of it by my Government in the *Ad Hoc* Committee. It excluded the hypothesis that if an attempt to alter by force, the settlement envisaged by the resolution should occur, the Security Council must determine therefore that it constitutes a threat to the peace. That practical current construction was made in the following language by Ambassador Herschel V. Johnson, who was then acting in the *Ad Hoc* Committee, from which I take the following quotation:

"My Delegation, I must say quite frankly, would not have been able to support the original amendment put up by the Delegation of Denmark. We are prepared, however, to accept this revised version. The revised version does not ask the Security Council to act upon a hypothetical situation, but requests that it act in the event that a situation which constitutes a threat to international peace and security should arise. This, at best, can only be an admonition to the Security Council. The Security Council by its own Constitution has the duty to exercise surveillance over such situations, and to determine when a threat to international peace and security exists."

The reservation "subject to the authority of the Security Council under the Charter", in paragraph 1 of our resolution, rests upon the principle upon which the United States stood, as stated by Ambassador Johnson.

As we see it, interpreted in this manner, the acceptance of Request (c) requires determination of the question of fact of threat to international peace, and if such threat is found, action under chapter VII.

Taken all together, paragraph 1 of the United States resolution means that the Security Council will do everything it can under the Charter to give effect to the recommendation of the General Assembly.

Resolution on the Palestinian Question [1]

The Security Council,

HAVING received the resolution of the General Assembly of 29 November 1947, on Palestine, and

Korean Elections To Be Held on May 9

PROCLAMATION BY LIEUTENAN

United States Com

To the People of Korea:

The General Assembly of the United Nations, having established a United Nations Temporary Commission on Korea, recommend that election be held to choose representatives with whom the commission may consult regarding prompt attainment of the freedom and independence of the Korean people, and which representatives, constituting a National Assembly, may establish a national government of Korea; [2]

And the United Nations Temporary Commission on Korea having consulted the Interim Committee of the United Nations, which expressed the view that it is incumbent upon the United Nations Temporary Commission on Korea to implement the program as outlined in the Resolution of the General Assembly in that part of Korea which is accessible to the commission; and

The United Nations Temporary Commission on Korea having concluded to observe such elec-

---

[1] Adopted by the Security Council at its 263d meeting on Mar. 5, 1948. U.N. doc. S/691, Mar. 5, 1948.
[2] Released in Seoul, Korea, on Mar. 1, 1948. Printed from telegraphic text.
[3] BULLETIN of Dec. 14, 1947, pp. 1154, 1162. For resolution adopted by the Interim Committee on Feb. 26, 1948, see BULLETIN of Mar. 7, 1948, p. 297.

Voting is participation in government of one's country, and it is the civic duty of every adult citizen.

Anyone abstaining from voting forfeits his right to complain of actions or policies of a government resulting from an election in which he did not participate.

In a democracy the majority necessarily must govern through duly elected representatives. That imposes upon the minority a duty to accept the results of a fair election. In a democracy the minority defeated in a fair election has the privilege of seeking to become a majority through subsequent persuasion of the voters to adhere to its principles.

In a democracy heads are counted, not broken. Political issues are settled with freely cast ballots, thus avoiding use of force. That calls for discussion, exchange of views on political platforms and candidates as regards attainments and capacity, but not offensive verbal personal attacks or acts of terrorism. Democracy has been called government by discussion.

Elections in Korea, the conduct of the campaign, and the results therefrom, will attract world-wide attention. The actions of the Korean nation and its people will closely be watched by certain groups that wish to be extremely critical and fault finding. Wholehearted acceptance of democratic principles and responsibilities are part and parcel of the accountability and obligations of members of the family of nations.

I hope to see the election supported and carried out by Koreans in a manner which will be creditable to their nation. No individual, group, or combination of groups, can be permitted to nullify the workings of the democratic processes of election. This is the greatest opportunity of all time for all Koreans to demonstrate that they can completely handle their own affairs in a democratic manner and can conduct fair and free elections under laws developed by Koreans themselves. Korean political leaders and interim government officials and members of the Korean election committees carry great responsibility in development of a free atmosphere for truly democratic elections and in guaranteeing freedom of speech, press, orderly assembly and campaigning by candidates, to the end that representatives chosen in the election will be the actual choice of the people. I sincerely believe that they can and will assume and carry out this responsibility, and I urge all Koreans to work together to this end.

---

[4] Released in Seoul, Korea, on Mar. 4, 1948. Printed from telegraphic text.

FOREIGN AID AND RECONSTRUCTION

Extension of Aid to Greece and Turkey

STATEMENT BY GEORGE C. MARSHALL [1]

Secretary of State

On March 12, 1947, Congress was requested to authorize assistance to Greece and Turkey in the amount of 400 million dollars for the period ending June 30, 1948. The President then stated that such action was made necessary by the gravity of a situation which involved the foreign policy and national security of the United States.

Congress authorized the requested aid by act of May 22, 1947, and appropriated the necessary funds by act of July 30, 1947. There has been presented to the Congress a request for additional military assistance to Greece and Turkey in the amount of 275 million dollars, covering the period through the fiscal year 1949.

In Turkey the supply of equipment destined for the strengthening of the Turkish defense forces is under the general supervision of Ambassador Edwin C. Wilson, who also serves as Chief of the American Mission for Aid to Turkey. In Greece the work of supporting and rehabilitating the Greek economy and of strengthening the Greek armed forces is being carried on by the American Mission for Aid to Greece under the leadership of Dwight P. Griswold.

The program of American aid to Greece has had the important substantial result that Greece continues to exist as a free nation. Economic recovery has been seriously impeded, in spite of American aid, because guerrilla warfare, supported from neighboring countries, has been intensified and continues to disrupt Greek economy.

One hundred seventy-two million dollars, or about 57 percent of the total funds provided for the Greek aid program, is being expended for the strengthening of the Greek armed forces and the creation of local National Guard units to take over from the mobile army the protection of towns, villages, and lines of communications threatened by the guerrilla forces.

When the President addressed Congress on this subject in March 1947, a commission of the Security Council of the United Nations was in the Balkans to investigate alleged border violations along

Greece's northern frontier. The majority report of this committee, submitted on June 27, 1947, concluded that Yugoslavia, Albania, and Bulgaria had supported the guerrilla warfare in Greece. Action on the basis of this report by the Security Council was blocked by a Soviet veto. The matter was accordingly referred, on American initiative, to the General Assembly which, on October 21, 1947, adopted a resolution calling upon Albania, Bulgaria, and Yugoslavia "to do nothing which could furnish aid or assistance" to the guerrillas. It also called upon these powers and Greece "to cooperate in the settlement of their disputes by peaceful means", making certain specific recommendations to this effect. It established a special committee to observe the compliance by the four governments with these recommendations and to be available to assist in their implementation.

The Government of Greece reiterated its willingness to cooperate with the Special Committee. It has in fact done so. On the other hand, the Government of Yugoslavia informed the Secretary-General of the United Nations that it "will not extend any cooperation to the Commission or its observation groups and will not permit their entry into Yugoslav territory". Similar announcements were made by the Governments of Albania and Bulgaria. The Delegates of the Soviet Union and Poland in the General Assembly had already made it clear that their Governments would take no part in the activities of the Special Committee, though membership on the Committee was, and still is, reserved for them.

This attitude on the part of the Union of Soviet Socialist Republics, Poland, Yugoslavia, Bulgaria, and Albania led the Committee in its first interim report to comment on its inability "to report any evidence of bi-lateral compliance with any of the recommendations of the General Assembly". In its second interim report, the Committee called attention to the large-scale guerrilla attack of Christmas Day against the Greek town of Konitsa on the Albanian border and declared, on the basis of the report of its observation group in the region, "that aid in the form of logistic

[1] Made before the House Foreign Affairs Committee on Mar. 3, 1948, and released to the press on the same date.

ipport is being furnished from Albania to guerillas operating on Greek territory".

There was an announcement on December 24,)47, over the Belgrade radio, of the establishent of a Greek junta under the guerrilla leader [arkos. Propaganda against the United States ad in favor of the Greek guerrillas has been arried on by the Government-controlled press ad radio in the Communist-dominated countries f eastern Europe, and, like support extended to ie Greek guerrillas, has been intensified since ie inception of the American aid program.

The President, in transmitting to the Congress ie second report on assistance to Greece and 'urkey, stated: "It is significant that the guerrilla arfare is directed not against the Greek Army at against the people of Greece. The deliberate ad wanton destruction of Greek villages does not sult from military engagements. It is determined and ruthless destruction intended to render eople homeless and drive them from the soil; to arce them into overcrowded urban centers where iey become charges of an already overburdened ate; and to create for them conditions of misery ad hardship in the hope that this will make them isceptible to political agitation". The accuracy f this statement is confirmed by the fact that ver 400,000 of the Greek people have left their omes in the villages of the districts where the aerrillas operate and have sought refuge in the ties of northern Greece. They have fled from ie guerrillas. They have not joined them.

By such means the independence and territorial itegrity of Greece are being threatened and all forts of the Greeks and their friends to promote ie economic rehabilitation of the country are aing systematically undermined. The Greek overnment has been obliged to divert to military arposes and for refugee relief increasing amounts " money and supplies needed for economic rebilitation. The American Aid Mission also has aen obliged to divert some 23 million dollars of e American funds originally intended for economic purposes in order to build up the Greek med forces.

The situation is serious, but it is not without' pe. The Greek Government, in its efforts to eet its many critical problems, has shown a commendable resistance to the pressure to depart from mocratic principles and to apply totalitarian ethods to meet the situation. A coalition government headed by the Chief of the Liberal Party ad supported by a large majority of the freely acted Greek Parliament still is in power. An tensification of the Greek military effort against e guerrillas, with the forces and equipment esently authorized and now proposed and with e help of the American military officers now aching the field, gives promise of greater success. With such success in the elimination of guer-

rilla warfare, the economic part of the American aid program which already has begun to show results will have a greatly increased effectiveness in the strengthening of Greek economy.

Extension of further American military aid to Greece and Turkey which is now before the Congress, as well as early and favorable action on the European Recovery Program, will be of tremendous importance in discouraging more overt aggression against Greece. Conversely, nothing could be more calculated to encourage the enemies of Greece in their designs than a show of weakness or hesitation on the part of the United States.

When request for appropriation for aid to Greece and Turkey was made last year the Department of State expressed the hope that, with funds provided under the initial year's program, recovery in Greece would have progressed to such a point that further financing of Greek rehabilitation could be obtained from the international fiscal institutions. The intensification of guerrilla warfare brought about by increased support by Greece's northern neighbors has unfortunately not only made this impossible but has in fact increased the need for both economic and military assistance to Greece.

As a member of the Paris conference of the Committee of European Economic Co-operation, Greece participated in the development of a program for European recovery which it was calculated would require four years for realization. Funds provided under the ERP will not, of course, be available for military assistance to the Greek armed forces in their fight against the guerrillas. Although there is expectation that the guerrilla menace can be brought under control during the period for which additional military action is now requested, ultimate success in the guerrilla war and termination of military assistance to Greece depends in large part upon the degree to which Greece's northern neighbors give assistance to the guerrillas in their efforts to secure Communist domination of Greece against the wishes of the Greek people.

I call your attention to the following passage from the recent report on Greece of the subcommittee of the House of Representatives Select Committee on Foreign Aid:

"Should the United States now withdraw its support from Greece, which would almost certainly result in the establishment of a Communist government, the Communist parties throughout Europe would undoubtedly utilize the opportunity to point out to those who are now valiantly resisting Communist infiltration in other countries the uncertainty of relying on United States help. The effects of such withdrawal would greatly weaken the determination of the constitutional forces resisting Communism elsewhere".

The continuation of military assistance to Turkey, which has since the war been under such constant foreign pressure that she has had to maintain a large and burdensome military establishment, is equally important. Intensification of Communist pressure against Turkey during the past year, coupled with clear evidence in Greece and Czechoslovakia of Communist intentions against all independent nations who stand in the way of their plans for expansion, have foreclosed the expectation that the military assistance we are furnishing Turkey in this year's aid program will be sufficient. While the proposed program involves no commitment, moral or otherwise, as to continuation of assistance to Turkey beyond the fiscal year 1949, no assurance can be given that additional aid will not be required as long as there

Continuation of Assistance to Free Terri

LETTER FROM THE SECRETARY OF ST
OF THE

[Released to the press March 3]

I enclose herewith for consideration by the Congress draft legislation which would authorize the extension by the United States Government of economic assistance to the Free Territory of Trieste. This legislation is in the form of a bill to amend the Foreign Aid Act of 1947, Public Law 389, 80th Congress. The proposed amendment would make this law applicable to the Free Territory of Trieste or either of its zones, and would extend through June 30, 1949, the period during which aid may be given Trieste. Authorization of further funds is not requested, for funds already authorized under PL 389 but not yet appropriated are adequate to cover the $20,-000,000 program of economic assistance here proposed.

Trieste's status as a Free Territory was agreed upon at the Paris Peace Conference, after the failure of the conferees to reach agreement on its incorporation into either Italy or Yugoslavia. The United States played an important part in determining Trieste's status as a Free Territory, and United States troops, jointly with troops of the United Kingdom, at present occupy the city of Trieste itself and a small part of the adjacent territory. After the Security Council of the United Nations agrees on a Governor for the Free Territory of Trieste, the occupation troops will

---

[1] Arthur H. Vandenberg. An identical letter was also sent on Mar. 3, 1948, to Joseph W. Martin, Speaker of the House. Attached to the letters was a copy of the draft bill.

States. Assistance by this Government has been supplied first under the Army's Plan A program to prevent disease and unrest, and more recently under the United States Foreign Relief Program (Public Law 84). The funds available under the latter program will be exhausted before the end of March 1948. Funds should be appropriated by April 1 to cover certain of Trieste's dollar exchange needs for the second quarter of 1948 and for the whole of fiscal 1949. No provision of funds for aid to Trieste was included in the European Recovery Program, for Trieste is not yet a member of the Committee of European Economic Cooperation, although the European Recovery Program legislation would make it possible for Trieste to be included at some later time.

The proposed program of economic assistance requiring dollar funds totals $20,000,000 for the period April 1, 1948 through June 30, 1949. This program would continue economic assistance for relief purposes, as specified in Public Law 389, but does not make provision for recovery and reconstruction. It is intended to prevent disease and unrest in the zone of Trieste still occupied by US–UK troops, and to prevent the economic situation there from deteriorating further. It continues assistance to the US–UK zone at approximately present levels, but makes no provision for aid to the Yugoslav zone of occupation. Should a Governor be appointed for Trieste and UN funds become available the amount needed for the present program would hereby be reduced.

It is proposed that this program be administered by the State Department until other administrative arrangements are made upon the establishment of an agency to administer the European Recovery Program. Provision is made in Section 14 of PL 389 for the transfer of functions, applicable records, and funds to any organization for general foreign aid which Congress may provide.

Faithfully yours,

A BILL

To amend the Foreign Aid Act of 1947 in order to provide for assistance to the Free Territory of Trieste.

Be it enacted by the Senate and House of Representatives of the United States of America in Congress assembled, That the Foreign Aid Act

March 14, 1948

of 1947 (Public Law 389, 80th Congress) is hereby amended in the following particulars:

(*a*) In section 2 after the comma following the word "France" insert the words "The Free Territory of Trieste or either of its zones (hereinafter referred to as Trieste)".

(*b*) In subsection (b) of section 5 after the date "June 30, 1948" insert the following words "or in the case of Trieste, September 30, 1949".

(*c*) In subsection (d) of section 5 after the date "March 31, 1948" insert the words "or in the case of Trieste, June 30, 1949".

(*d*) In subsection (b) of section 11 before the period at the end of the subsection insert a comma and the words "provided that the provisions of this subsection shall not be applicable in respect of wheat, wheat flour, or cereal grain acquired for Trieste after June 30, 1948".

(*e*) In section 15 before the period at the end of the section, insert a comma and the words "provided that funds may be obligated for the procurement of commodities for Trieste until June 30, 1949".

(*f*) Add a new Section 19 as follows: "Pending the appointment of a Governor for the Free Territory of Trieste, either of the zones of the Territory shall be considered as a country and the respective Allied Military Commands as the governments thereof for the purposes of this act.

Address on European Recovery Program

On March 6, Charles E. Bohlen, Counselor, made an address on European aid before the Herald Tribune Forum in New York City; for the text of this address, see Department of State press release 170 of March 6, 1948.

THE FOREIGN SERVICE

Consular Offices

The American Legation and Consulate at Dublin, Ireland, have been combined, effective February 4, 1948.

The American consular agency at Puerto Cortas, Honduras, was established on February 21, 1948.

The Vice Consulate at Fredericton, New Brunswick, Canada, was closed to the public on January 24, 1948.

The American Consulate General at Changchun, China, was closed on February 3, 1948.

The American Consulate at Bergen, Norway, was opened to the public on February 24, 1948.

Report on United States Foreign Aid Shipments

[Released to the press March 2]

Status report of shipments under the United States foreign aid program and the Greek-Turkish aid program as of February 27, 1948

Under Public Law 84

Country	Program as of 2/27/48 [1]	Procurement initiated	Shipments made
Austria......	$72,786,129	$72,786,129	$69,106,800
Freight.......	12,142,590	12,185,187	11,566,756
Subtotal....	84,928,719	84,971,316	80,673,556
China........	40,853,189	38,600,482	12,721,007
Freight......	4,339,362	4,265,506	1,469,078
Subtotal....	[2]45,192,551	42,865,988	14,190,085
Greece........	33,251,182	33,250,075	31,363,153
Freight.......	4,633,977	4,620,063	4,386,912
Subtotal....	37,885,159	37,870,138	35,750,065
Italy.........	96,630,355	96,630,355	95,582,622
Freight.......	20,677,980	20,583,834	20,558,261
Subtotal....	117,308,335	117,214,189	116,140,883
Trieste........	9,759,328	9,759,330	7,385,232
Freight.......	2,448,452	2,406,481	1,823,261
Subtotal....	12,207,780	12,165,811	9,208,493
All countries...	253,280,183	251,026,371	216,158,814
Freight......	44,242,361	44,061,071	39,804,268
TOTAL C & F cost...	$297,522,544	$295,087,442	$255,963,082

[1] Source: Office of Assistant Secretary of State for economic affairs.
[2] Includes $18,000,000 specifically appropriated for China under Public Law 393 dated Dec. 23, 1947.

Under Public Law 389

Country	Program as of 2/27/48 [1]	Procurement initiated	Shipments made
Austria.......	$52,142,520	$46,077,797	$5,443,2?
Freight.......	4,857,480	4,363,437	803,2?
Subtotal....	57,000,000	50,441,234	6,246,4?
France.......	225,942,000	147,799,248	66,931,1?
Freight......	58,058,000	42,774,153	24,354,4?
Subtotal....	284,000,000	190,573,401	91,285,6?
Italy........	144,494,000	93,472,579	38,178,7?
Freight......	36,506,000	25,719,041	9,642,7?
Subtotal....	181,000,000	119,191,620	47,821,5?
All countries..	422,578,520	287,349,624	110,553,5?
Freight......	99,421,480	72,856,631	34,800,3?
TOTAL C & F cost.....	$522,000,000	$360,206,255	$145,353,6?

[1] Source: Office of Assistant Secretary of State economic affairs.

Under Public Law 78
(GREEK-TURKISH AID PROGRAM)

Country	Procurement initiated	Shipments made
Greece..................	$40,894,946	$17,654,0?
Freight..................	7,043,362	2,911,8?
TOTAL..................	$47,938,308	$20,565,??

THE DEPARTMENT

Transfer of Personnel From UE to A–T

On February 18, 1948, the personnel assigned to the Office of the Under Secretary for economic affairs was transferred to the Office of the Assistant Secretary for economic affairs.

The Assistant Secretary for economic affairs will continue to advise and assist the Secretary in the development and implementation of foreign economic policy with respect to international trade, finance, and economic development and security; and the Assistant Secretary for transportation and communications will continue to advise and assist the Secretary in the development and implementation of foreign economic policy, principally with respect to transport and communications affairs.

Appointment of Officers

Willard L. Thorp, Assistant Secretary for economic affairs, as Coordinator for the European Recovery Program (ERP), effective January 19, 1948.

Paul H. Nitze as Deputy to the Assistant Secretary for the coordination of European recovery matters, and James A. Stillwell as Principal Assistant to Mr. Nitze, effective February 18, 1948.

nsion of Reciprocal Trade Agreements Act[1]

MESSAGE OF THE PRESIDENT TO THE CONGRESS

[Released to the press by the White House March 1]

e Congress of the United States:

ecommend that the Congress extend the Re-
cal Trade Agreements Act in its present form
hree years, until June 12, 1951. This Act
rizes the President, under well-defined pro-
es and limitations, to conclude agreements
other countries for the reciprocal reduction
iffs and other obstacles to international trade.
r fourteen years the Reciprocal Trade Agree-
s Act has been an essential element of United
s foreign policy. It was first enacted in 1934,
as been extended by the Congress four times,
ch occasion after thorough study of its oper-
and results. It is well known to the Ameri-
eople and has drawn their constant and in-
ing support, regardless of party affiliation.

e basic reason for this constant popular sup-
and repeated Congressional approval is that
ct has provided a sound method for increas-
orld trade through progressive lowering of
barriers, to the benefit of living standards
here and abroad.

e importance of the Act is greater today than
s ever been. Together with other nations we
ngaged in a mighty endeavor to build a pros-
s and peaceful world. The financial assist-
we have already contributed, and the further
ve shall give to nations in Europe and else-
e, constitute a tremendous investment toward
l economic recovery. The Reciprocal Trade
ements Act, by stimulating an increasing flow
ade between nations, will contribute strongly
e achievement of this objective. Its extension
ential if we are to complete the work we have
n.

e trade-agreements program contributes not
to the restoration of a prosperous world econ-
; it also contributes directly to the welfare and
erity of the people of the United States. Our
le need to import many commodities from
d; we need equally to export many of our
ucts. Both needs are served by agreements
h reduce or eliminate obstacles to commerce
een the United States and other countries.

ese agreements recognize the fundamental
that trade is a two-way business, and that our
gn commerce depends upon a balanced rela-
hip between imports and exports. Foreign
tries must be able to sell to us if they are to
the dollars to pay for our exports and to re-

pay our loans. Adequate markets for our agricultural and industrial producers depend upon the
lowering of trade barriers by other countries. Imports of goods needed in this country improve the
standard of living of our people as consumers at
the same time that they make possible the maintenance of markets for our people as producers.

Currently, we are exporting far more than we
are importing. But this is a temporary condition
made necessary by considerations of overriding
importance. The trade-agreements program is a
sound method for achieving a more balanced relationship in the future within the broader framework of the expanding world trade so necessary
to economic reconstruction.

In addition, by contributing to the lowering of
trade barriers the United States can support the
expansion of private trading as distinct from government trading. The existence of trade restrictions is too often accompanied by government participation in trading operations—extending even
to trading by government agencies. The preservation of our private enterprise system at home is
closely bound up with the reduction of trade
restrictions and the encouragement of private
international trade.

The Reciprocal Trade Agreements Act is a
proven instrument for achieving these objectives.
Prior to 1945 the United States had concluded
agreements with 29 countries, affecting about one-
half of our foreign commerce. These agreements
helped greatly to reduce trade barriers and to
stimulate the foreign commerce of the United
States and the other countries concerned.

Since 1945 we have continued our efforts to reduce the strains imposed upon the world economy
by narrow concepts of economic nationalism. Last
summer at Geneva the United States and twenty-
two other countries concluded the most important
and comprehensive trade agreement in history.
By this agreement these twenty-three nations
agreed to reduce their tariffs, or to maintain low
tariffs or none at all, on a wide variety of products.
The products affected accounted in 1938 for over
half the world's international trade. In addition,
the Geneva agreement included commitments to
curb the use of other trade restrictions, such as
import quotas and preferential treatment of imports from one country as against those from another.

[1] H. Doc. 551, 2d sess.

This agreement is a landmark in international economic relations. Never before have so many nations combined in such an intensive effort to reduce barriers to trade. While it will be some time before the benefits of the agreement can be fully felt, it is clear that it will make a substantial contribution to the expansion of world trade and to the recovery of the world economy.

We expect that many other countries will wish to join the Geneva Agreement. The continuance of the Reciprocal Trade Agreements Act is necessary to enable the United States to play its part in extending this reduction of trade barriers to these other countries. Furthermore, we shall need the authority of the Act to make appropriate revisions in the Geneva Agreement as they are made necessary by changing world conditions.

The trade-agreements authority will also be needed to enable us, in concert with other nations, to carry out the International Trade Organization charter, now being completed at Havana. The United States has actively sponsored the creation of this Organization to encourage the conduct of trade between nations on fair and liberal principles and to provide a forum where nations can consult on points of economic difference and on cooperative measures to solve common economic problems. The proposed charter, which will be presented to the Congress at a later date, includes as one of its cardinal points the undertaking that all member countries will stand ready to negotiate for the reduction of tariffs and other trade barriers on a reciprocal and mutually advantageous basis. The extension of the Reciprocal Trade Agreements Act will enable us to carry out this undertaking.

For all these reasons I am convinced that we should continue the Reciprocal Trade Agreements Act. The positive benefits to world trade, to United States export industries and agriculture and to our domestic consumers are beyond question. Furthermore, we need have no fear of serious harm to any domestic producer. An expanding foreign trade promotes the most efficient use of our productive resources and contributes to the growing prosperity of the whole Nation.

In addition, the interests of domestic producers are carefully protected in the negotiation of each trade agreement. I assured the Congress, when the Reciprocal Trade Agreements Act was last extended in 1945, that domestic producers would be safeguarded in the process of expanding trade. That commitment has been kept. It will continue to be kept. The practice will be continued of holding extensive public hearings to obtain the view of all interested persons before negotiations are even begun. The practice will be continued whereby each agreement before its conclusion will be carefully studied by the Departments of State, Treasury, Agriculture, Commerce and Labor, the National Military Establishment, and the United

D L. THORP [1]

for Economic Affairs

tarization, denazification, and the elimination of war industries—policy has assumed a more positive and constructive orientation.

The failure of the Council of Foreign Ministers to reach four-power agreement on basic questions with respect to the political and economic treatment has led the United States to seek other and more immediate means of making progress toward its objectives—seeking agreement from as many of the occupying powers as possible. The division into zones creates an artificial and non-economic situation. This condition has been met in part by the economic fusion of the United States and United Kingdom zones to deal with the economic problems of the combined area. At present tripartite conversations are in progress in London to determine the extent to which cooperation can be extended among the three western zones.

As to the first objective, demilitarization and security, great progress has been made toward the achievement of the task. The demobilization of armed forces and quasi-military organizations has been completed in the United States zone. By the end of this year, all military installations will have been destroyed or converted to peacetime uses. War material and equipment has been destroyed or otherwise disposed of. Military training, research activity, and propaganda are banned. The production, importation, and use of designated war materials, including aircraft and equipment, is forbidden. War industries in the primary sense are prohibited, as well as such indirect potential war industries as the production of magnesium, radioactive material, and seagoing ships. In the United States zone, 130 first-priority war plants will have been dismantled by June 30, 1948. Other steps in the economic and political field will also contribute to reducing the military hazard for the future.

American policy cannot be content merely with these immediate steps. It demands adequate safeguards that no future German government will be

---

[1] An address delivered before the Herald Tribune Forum, New York, N. Y., Mar. 6, 1948, and released to the press on the same date.

able to return to paths of aggression. To this end, a 40-year four-power treaty was proposed which would have established a continuing system of inspection to assure no revival of a German military establishment. This proposal was, in effect, rejected by the U.S.S.R. However, in the absence of four-power agreement, the United States is ready to support constructive measures by the western European powers to guard against German military revival.

With regard to the second main objective, that in the economic field, there are two main headings: first, compensation to the Allied and associated powers for the damage done to them by the German war machine; and second, economic recovery.

Here in the United States, it is difficult for us to appreciate fully the point of view of those countries where devastation was tremendous and who ask for reparations from Germany. Obviously, there is no possibility of equivalent compensation. However, countries have been permitted to take over German external assets within their own territories and German shipping has been distributed. The United States has also favored the payment of reparations by the transfer of surplus capital goods from Germany, such transfers to be so limited as to leave Germany able to be self-sustaining and able to contribute her appropriate share to European recovery.

The United States has consistently opposed reparations from current production as either imposing an impossible burden on the German economy or requiring indirect payment of these reparations by the United States by increasing the assistance which it must provide. Because of Soviet failure to accede to the Potsdam principle of the economic unity of Germany, deliveries to the U.S.S.R. from the U.S. zone have been largely suspended since May 1946.

The effect of the reparations program on the operation of the German economy, at least as applied in the western zones of Germany, has been somewhat exaggerated. The program based on the revised bizonal level-of-industry agreement is intended to remove only plants or equipment which are surplus to a peaceful German economy and which will contribute more effectively to European recovery if transferred to the claimant countries. The German economy today is operating far below its capacity, even if the removals had been much greater than these actually scheduled.

But the economic problem of Germany lies much more in the future. Germany is not a going concern. Its present rate of industrial production is less than one half that of the prewar years. Devastation, destruction, deterioration, and disorganization have led to persisting food and coal shortages, transportation bottlenecks, inadequate supplies of consumers' goods and raw materials, inadequate housing, unstable currency, black mar-

basic objectives can best be accomplished if there is no excessive concentration of either economic or political power.

I should not wish even to suggest that any of the objectives, the destruction of militarism, the achievement of economic health, and the firm establishment of democratic political institutions, has been fully accomplished as yet. The difficulties and problems are many. The quadripartite stalemate is a tremendous obstacle.

It is possible to achieve and maintain the negative goal of demilitarization from the outside. The constructive economic and political goals require more than external direction. Neither a healthy economy nor an effective democracy can be achieved by compulsion or legislation, although a contrary regime could possibly be forced upon Germany by organized political penetration and interferences from the outside. Such a course is not the American way. We would prefer to offer Germany the opportunity to develop along constructive lines. We can provide substantial assistance. Nevertheless, the basic fact remains that, in our view, the ultimate responsibility must rest upon the German people themselves. As victors, we prefer to establish certain limits and suggest general patterns.

In the last analysis, it is the German people alone who can make effective our hope that they will rebuild their nation upon the principles expressed in the Charter of the United Nations, recognizing "the equal rights of men and women and of nations large and small". It is the profound hope of the United States that the Germany of the future will be a peace-loving nation, enjoying economic health and democratic political institutions.

Procedure for Filing War Claims in Luxembourg

[Released to the press March 2]

The Department of State has been informed by the American Legation at Luxembourg that American nationals may request the assistance of the Luxembourg Office of Recuperation with a view to recovering property which has been taken or is presumed to have been taken from Luxembourg territory during the war.

The Department has also been informed that, although Luxembourg legislation does not at the present time provide for compensation to nationals of the United States, the Luxembourg authorities will accept for registration war-damage claims of American nationals. These claims should be filed with the Office de l'État des Dommages de Guerre, 27 rue Aldringer, Luxembourg, which office will provide the necessary forms. Residents and nonresidents may file claims using the English, French, or German languages. No time limit has been fixed within which claims must be filed.

The Department has been further informed that all transfers which were based upon confiscation, seizure, forced sale, or any other means have been declared null and void and that claims for the restitution of such property should be filed with the Office des Sequestres, 19 rue Nord, Luxembourg. In the event that office denies the validity of the claim, ordinary legal proceedings may be instituted against the Sequests in the Tribunal d'Arrondissement (District Court) at Luxembourg, with the assistance of member of the Luxembourg bar. The three-year limit within which such claims must be filed will begin to run with the coming into force of the German peace settlement.

Rumania Notified of Prewar Treaties U.S. Will Keep in Force or Revive

TEXT OF NOTE FROM THE AMERICAN MINISTER AT BUCHAREST TO THE RUMANIAN MINISTER FOR FOREIGN AFFAIRS

[Released to the press March 2]

The Department of State announced on March 2 that on February 26, 1948, the Rumanian Government was given official notification in accordance with the terms of the treaty of peace with Rumania signed at Paris February 10, 1947 regarding the prewar bilateral treaties and other international agreements with Rumania which the United States Government desired to keep in force or revive.

February 26, 1948.

I have the honor to refer to the Treaty of Peace with Rumania, signed at Paris February 10, 1947, which came into force, in accordance with the provisions of article 40 thereof, on September 15, 1947 upon the deposit of instruments of ratification by the Union of Soviet Socialist Republics, the United Kingdom of Great Britain and Northern Ireland, and the United States of America. Article 10 of the Treaty of Peace reads as follows:

"1. Each Allied or Associated Power will notify Roumania, within a period of six months from the coming into force of the present Treaty, which of its pre-war bilateral treaties with Roumania it desires to keep in force or revive. Any provisions not in conformity with the present Treaty shall, however, be deleted from the above-mentioned treaties.

"2. All such treaties so notified shall be registered with the Secretariat of the United Nations in accordance with Article 102 of the Charter of the United Nations.

"3. All such treaties not so notified shall be regarded as abrogated."

I have the honor, by direction of the Government of the United States of America and on its behalf, to notify the Rumanian Government, in accordance with the provisions of the Treaty of Peace quoted above, that the Government of the United States of America desires to keep in force or revive the following pre-war bilateral treaties and other international agreements with Rumania:

Arbitration

1. Arbitration treaty. Signed at Washington March 21, 1929. Ratified by the United States June 4, 1929. Ratified by Rumania June 20, 1929. Ratifications changed at Washington July 22, 1929. Effective July 1929. [Treaty Series 794; 46 Stat. 2336.]

Commerce

2. Provisional commercial agreement. Signed at Bucharest August 20, 1930. Effective September 1, 1930. [Executive Agreement Series 8; 47 Stat. 2593.]

Conciliation

3. Conciliation treaty. Signed at Washington March 21, 1929. Ratified by the United States June 4, 1929. Ratified by Rumania June 20, 1929. Ratifications changed at Washington July 22, 1929. Effective July 1929. [Treaty Series 795; 46 Stat. 2339.]

Consuls

4. Consular convention. Signed at Bucharest June and 17, 1881. Ratified by the United States April 6, 18. Ratified by Rumania March 4, 1883. Ratifications changed at Bucharest June 13, 1883. Effective June 1883. (Articles XI and XII, which were abrogated under Act of Congress approved March 4, 1915, are not to be considered as revived by this notification.) [Treaty Series 297; 23 Stat. 711.]

Extradition

5. Extradition treaty. Signed at Bucharest July 1924. Ratified by the United States February 26, 19. Ratified by Rumania February 24, 1925. Ratifications exchanged at Bucharest April 7, 1925. Effective April 1925. [Treaty Series 713; 44 Stat. 2020.]

6. Supplementary extradition treaty. Signed at Bucharest November 10, 1936. Ratified by the United States May 19, 1937. Ratified by Rumania July 7, 1937. Ratifications exchanged at Bucharest July 27, 1937. Effective July 27, 1937. [Treaty Series 916; 50 Stat. 1349.]

In compliance with paragraph 2 of article 10 of the Treaty of Peace, quoted above, the United States Government will register with the Secretariat of the United Nations the treaties and other agreements which are by this notification kept in force or revived.

Time Limit Extended for Filing Claims in Austria

[Released to the press March 5]

The Department of State has been informed that the time limit for filing claims under the first, second, and third restitution laws in Austria is being extended to December 31, 1948. Until this extension, the time limit for such filing under the three restitution laws was set for the end of March 1948. Claimants will now have an additional nine months in which to file their claims.

On April 4, 1947, the Department announced the restitution program which the Austrian Government put into effect. At that time it was stated that claimants should deal directly with the appropriate Austrian authorities. If the claimant is unable to determine with which authorities to file, claims, together with supporting documents in the German language, may be sent to the Austrian Federal Ministry for Safeguarding Property and Economic Planning (Bundesministerium fuer Vermoegenssicherung und Wirtschaftsplanung) in Vienna.

According to recent information from Vienna, the implementation of the restitution program has been progressing in a satisfactory manner. Statistics submitted by the Austrian Government indicate, however, that all claims may not have been presented. The Department urges, therefore, that all persons who have claims falling within the purview of the first, second, and third restitution laws file them before December 31, 1948.

Grants-in-Aid Extended to Three U.S. Professors

Grants-in-aid have been extended by the Department of State to the following: Arthur M. McAnally, librarian of the University of New Mexico, to serve as visiting librarian at the University of San Marcos at Lima, Peru, for a period of seven months; A. C. Howell, professor of English, and James C. Andrews, professor of biological chemistry, both of the University of North Carolina, to teach at the University of San Carlos, Guatemala, for a period of six months; Ralph Hayward Keniston, professor of romance languages and dean of the College of Literature, Science, and the Arts, University of Michigan, to serve as a consultant at the National University, Mexico.

357

Air-Transit Agreement With Portugal Concluded

GENERAL STATEMENT

Another chapter in cooperation between the Portuguese and American Governments was opened in Lisbon on February 2, 1948, with the signing of an agreement on the continuation of facilities for the transit of American military aircraft through Lagens Airfield on Terceira Island in the Azores. Following several months of friendly negotiation between the Portuguese Minister for Foreign Affairs, Dr. José Caeiro da Matta, and Ambassador John C. Wiley, notes were exchanged on that date embodying a new agreement.

This new arrangement takes the place of the agreement of May 30, 1946.[1] That one, in turn, took effect at the expiration of an agreement made during the war for the joint construction and operation of a military airfield on Santa Maria Island in the Azores. The Azores were an important step in the system of communications linking the European theater of war with the United States and the Far East, and the facilities made available there to the American and British Governments were of invaluable assistance in the prosecution of the war. At an impressive ceremony on June 2, 1947, the Santa Maria Airfield was turned back to the full control of the Portuguese Government, and it is now a key point in the network of international civil aviation.

On the occasion of the conclusion of the new agreement of February 2, 1948, letters were also exchanged between the Portuguese Foreign Minister and the American Ambassador, stressing the close ties existing between the two Governments and the desire of both Governments to continue to work in close collaboration in building the peace. The texts of the documents exchanged on February 2 follow.

CORRESPONDENCE RELATING TO AGREEMENT

[Released to the press February 13]
Note from the Portuguese Minister for Foreign Affairs to Ambassador Wiley

February 2, 1948.

MR. AMBASSADOR:

I have the honor to communicate to Your Excellency that the request of the Government of the United States relative to the continuance of transit facilities granted to American aircraft under the agreement of May 30, 1946 has been considered attentively and in the most friendly spirit. The Portuguese Government believes that the following formula will give satisfaction to the interests in question:

I

The Government of Portugal and the Government of the United States:

Considering that the facilities granted for the transit of American aircraft servicing the occupation troops in Germany and Japan terminated on December 2, 1947 under the terms of the agreement of May 30 of the preceding year;

Considering the manifest utility to the Government of the United States, given its international responsibilities with which at the moment it is burdened, in continuing the transit through Lagens of the referred to aircraft;

Having in mind the advantages which the facilities will achieve for the security of Europe and for the reestablishment and consolidation of world peace as well as the indirect value which the same may bring about for the common defense and security;

Examining the execution of the program agreed upon for the carrying out of the May 30 agreement between the Portuguese military authorities and the ATC Command in the Azores;

Agree:

That the Portuguese Government will continue to grant to the Government of the United States transit facilities for American aircraft through Lagens aerodrome in the following terms:

(a) The granting of facilities refers to a period of three years beginning December 2, 1947 tacitly extendable from year to year for two years more, if not denounced by the Portuguese Government with three months' notice. The Government of

---

[1] BULLETIN of June 23, 1946, p. 1082.

e United States may denounce the agreement nd relinquish the facilities at any moment.

(b) There shall not be due for the utilization f the aerodrome and of the various installations e payment of any tax or rental and for the purose of customs and other facilities the special aaracter of the aircraft in transit will be rejected. The Government of the United States ill, however, be responsible for the expenses hich may have to be made for those improvements of the aerodrome which are not necessary or the utilization by the Portuguese services as ell as the replacement if necessary of deteriorated stallations which are destined to the services or ving quarters of its personnel, it being undertood that all constructions shall be immediately onsidered property of the Portuguese Government.

(c) The Government of the United States will ontinue to furnish the necessary facilities for the pprenticeship and training of Portuguese peronnel having in mind the perfect functioning f the services of the air base including those utized by the ATC during the three year period entioned in Paragraph A, as well as the acquision by the Portuguese Government of material eemed indispensable for the services of the base.

(d) The special conditions of a technical nature ecessary for the carrying out of the present greement will be stipulated between the Portuuese military authorities and the ATC Command t Lagens and will be subject to confirmation of e Ministry of War in Lisbon, as well as a peodic revision at the request of either of the pares. It is understood, however:

1. The personnel of American nationality norally in service may not exceed the minimum ached during the last 12 months, except in case f emergency or extraordinary military measures ommunicated as far as possible in advance to the ortuguese Government and there then can be auhorized the entry and utilization of personnel ecessary to the anticipated traffic.

2. Among the material the acquisition of which ill be facilitated, the material needed for the new ontrol tower will be given urgent consideration.

3. There may be authorized the residence in raia da Victoria of persons of the families of e personnel on service and there will be granted a consequence of this authorization the necessary cilities.

(e) The Portuguese Government reserves the ght to grant the Government of Great Britain ansit facilities analogous to those mentioned in us agreement.

In case the Government of the United States ccepts the formula mentioned above, the affirmave reply of Your Excellency will constitute with us the agreement of the two Governments con-

cerning this matter, which will enter into force together with the arrangements contemplated in item (d) above.

CAEIRO DA MATTA

Ambassador Wiley replied to the foregoing note on the same date accepting the formula mentioned therein.

———

Note from the American Ambassador to the Portuguese Foreign Minister

February 2, 1948.

EXCELLENCY:

I have the honor to inform Your Excellency that the Government of the United States of America has long recognized and appreciated the whole-hearted desire of the Government of Portugal to cooperate and participate in the maintenance of international peace and security and the reconstruction of Europe. During the war the Portuguese Government granted the United States Government the use of important facilities on Santa Maria Island in the Azores which constituted an extremely valuable contribution to the war effort of the United Nations. Since the expiration of this wartime agreement, the United States Government has continued to receive the full cooperation of the Portuguese Government in providing for transit facilities at Lagens airfield in the Azores for United States aircraft serving the American forces of occupation in Germany and Japan.

The responsibilities of the United States to the nations of the world for the occupation of the ex-enemy nations still continue. Therefore, acting under instructions, I wish to take this opportunity to express to Your Excellency the warm appreciation of my Government for the enlightened spirit of international cooperation which has motivated the Government of Portugal in concluding with the Government of the United States the new agreement announced today.

The conclusion of this agreement demonstrates once more the increasingly close ties existing between our two governments and peoples. I am confident that, animated by the noble principles which traditionally guide our two nations, we will continue to work in close and friendly collaboration in building the peace.

I avail myself [etc.] JOHN C. WILEY

———

Note received February 7 from the Portuguese Foreign Minister to the American Ambassador

MR. AMBASSADOR:

I have the honor to refer to the note which Your Excellency so kindly delivered to me on the occasion of the conclusion of the agreement which extended for a new period the transit facilities through Lagens granted to American aircraft.

The expressions of friendship addressed to the Portuguese Government are all the more appreciated when it is realized that they are inspired by a perfect understanding of the spirit which predominated in the agreement we have just concluded.

For its part, the Portuguese Government has duly appreciated the efforts and sacrifices which the American Government and people have made and continue to make in the pursuit of European security and reconstruction and for the consolidation of peace; and insofar as the collaboration of Portugal towards the realization of that common aspiration is concerned, my country has always considered, and will continue to consider, that the United States, with its power for order and merited prestige, is in the vanguard of the nations which are endeavoring to secure for mankind a future of dignity, tranquility and well-being.

Standing close in the vast field of world problems, it is with gratification that I express the hope that the United States and Portugal, while progressively cementing a friendship which will be most helpful in the attainment of their respective destinies, will at the same time furnish an unequivocal example of international cooperation based on principles of mutual respect which are so necessary to the objectives of peace.

U.S. Accepts Membership in the Caribbea

[Released to the press March 5]

The President signed on March 5 the joint resolution (H.J. Res. 231) authorizing membership by the United States in the Caribbean Commission and the instrument approving, on behalf of the United States Government, the agreement for the establishment of the Caribbean Commission. Accordingly, the Secretary of State is taking steps to notify the other member governments (France, the Netherlands, and the United Kingdom) of this Government's formal approval of the agreement.

Purpose and Activities

The Caribbean Commission is an advisory body which makes recommendations to the member governments on economic and social matters of common interest to the territories of the Caribbean area, particularly on agriculture, communications, education, fisheries, health, housing, industry, labor, social welfare, and trade. This purpose is in accordance with the declaration regarding non-self-governing territories contained in chapter XI of the Charter of the United Nations.

tories within the Commission's scope is entitled to send two delegates to the Conference and these are designated in accordance with the particular territory's constitutional procedure. The conference held sessions in Barbados in 1944, in St. Thomas in 1946, and the third session is scheduled to be convened in Guadeloupe toward the end of 1948.

The Caribbean Research Council fosters a regional approach to research and advises the Commission on scientific, technological, social, and economic problems. Members of the Council are appointed by the Commission with special regard to their scientific competence.

Relations With Other International Bodies

While the Commission has at present no organic relationship with the United Nations, the agreement provides that the Commission and its auxiliary bodies shall cooperate as fully as possible with the United Nations and with appropriate specialized agencies on matters of mutual concern within the terms of reference of the Commission. Cooperation between the Commission and the United Nations has been established at the secretariat level.

THE DEPARTMENT

Confirmation of George V. Allen

The Senate on February 25, 1948, confirmed the nomination of George V. Allen to be Assistant Secretary of State for public affairs.

PUBLICATIONS

Department of State

For sale by the Superintendent of Documents, Government Printing Office, Washington 25, D.C. Address requests direct to the Superintendent of Documents, except in the case of free publications, which may be obtained from the Department of State.

Second Year of the United Nations: The Role of the United States. International Organization and Conference Series III, 3. Pub. 3072. vi, 10 pp. Free.

> Excerpts from *The United States and the United Nations: Report by the President to the Congress for the year 1947* (Department of State publication 3024).

Sovereignty and Interdependence in the New World: Comments on the Inter-American System. Inter-American Series 35. Pub. 3054. 32 pp. Free.

> An article by William Sanders describing various phases of inter-American cooperation as it has developed during the past 60 years.

An International Bill of Human Rights. International Organization and Conference Series III, 2. Pub. 3055. 30 pp. Free.

> An article by James P. Hendrick giving the background work and plans for further progress in preparing an international bill of rights.

The Department of State

For sale by the Superintendent of Documents
U.S. Government Printing Office
Washington 25, D.C.

SUBSCRIPTION:
52 issues, $5; single copy, 15 cents

Published with the approval of the
Director of the Bureau of the Budget

HE UNITED STATES RECIPROCAL TRADE-AGREEMENTS PROGRAM
ND THE PROPOSED INTERNATIONAL TRADE ORGANIZATION

An Article

ntroduction

The economic foreign policy of the United tates is aimed at expansion of trade between ations on a reciprocal and mutually advantageous asis. It is designed to help: (*a*) increase employment; (*b*) increase the production, exchange, nd use of goods and services; (*c*) raise living tandards in all countries; (*d*) eliminate trade auses of international friction and hostility; and *e*) create economic conditions in the world that ill be conducive to the maintenance of world eace.

As evidence of its belief in the importance of his policy, the United States has taken action in number of important directions. Since 1934 his country has carried on a well-organized pro- ram for reciprocal reduction of tariff and other arriers to our trade with foreign countries by greements with them. This Government is also negotiating numerous treaties of friendship, commerce, and navigation with other countries. The United States has taken a leading part in establishing the Food and Agriculture Organization, he International Monetary Fund, and the International Bank for Reconstruction and Development. To assure the minimum economic and political conditions under which these international organizations can effectively operate and under which our long-range foreign policy can be successfully implemented is the purpose of the Marshall Plan.

Development of the Reciprocal Trade-Agreements Program

Between the two world wars, especially during the depression, practically all governments applied rigid foreign-trade controls. These controls were usually designed to restrict imports into their countries and, at the same time, to force domestic products into foreign markets regardless of supply and demand or the effects on other countries. Some countries took this course because of necessity or fear of another war. Some followed this course through mistaken ideas of nationalistic self-sufficiency and prosperity. A few were deliberately bent on economic and political aggression and domination.

The measures which were employed included exchange restrictions, bilateral and discriminatory trade-balancing agreements, tariff and other trade preferences, excessively high import duties, and export subsidies designed to dump surplus goods abroad. They amounted to an international trade war.

Up to about 1928 the American Government and American investors made extensive foreign loans, some of them unwise. Meanwhile, United States tariff policy (in 1921 and again in 1922 the United States raised its tariffs against imports) was making it practically impossible for many foreign borrowers to repay the loans fully through sales of their goods and services in the United States. In 1930 the United States raised its import duties to record levels, through passage of the Hawley-Smoot Tariff Act of 1930.

As a result of this action and other causes, the annual value of United States foreign trade fell from $9,640,000,000 in 1929 to $2,934,000,000 in 1932—a drop of more than two thirds. Many American export industries were shut down and many American workers joined the bread lines. American crop surpluses broke down the home markets. American producers of automobiles, machinery, petroleum products, pork, wheat, cotton, tobacco, fruit, and many other important products were hard hit by the loss of foreign markets. Unemployed workers and struggling farmers dropped out of the domestic market. The same thing was happening in foreign countries. The world-wide depression was intensified and prolonged by the collapse of international commerce.

Passage of the Trade Agreements Act in 1934

In 1934 Congress passed the Trade Agreements Act—since renewed four times—for the purpose of restoring lost foreign markets for American products.

The act authorizes the President to conclude trade agreements with foreign countries and, in return for reduction of their barriers against American goods, to reduce United States tariffs and other import restrictions on goods from abroad. Since high trade barriers hinder this exchange of goods, it is obvious that other countries can and will buy and pay for more American goods if they can sell more of their own in this country.

The act requires the President to obtain advice and assistance for certain specified government agencies in formulating the agreements. The 1934 act specified the Departments of State, Agriculture, and Commerce, and the Tariff Commission. That act also forbade the reduction of any United States tariff in a trade agreement by more than one half of the rate in effect when the act was passed. The initial term of each agreement is fixed at not more than three years, after which the agreement remains in effect unless either country terminates it on six months' notice.

A very important provision of the act specifies that interested persons or groups shall have full opportunity to present information and views on any agreement before it is concluded. This provision is carried out under Executive orders of the President (see page 5). The duration of the authority given to the President in the 1934 act was limited to three years from June 12, 1934. In 1937 Congress extended this authority for another three-year period; in 1940 for another three years; in 1943 for two years; and in 1945 for three years, or until June 12, 1948.

Renewal and Expansion of the Act in 1945

In extending and amending the act in 1945, Congress enlarged the authority of the President to modify United States tariffs and other important restrictions. Under the amended act he may reduce a tariff rate by not more than one half of the rate in effect on January 1, 1945. Thus an original rate which had been reduced before January 1, 1945, may now be further reduced in a trade agreement by not more than one half of the January 1, 1945, level, but an original rate which had not been reduced before January 1945, may only be reduced by not more than one half of the rate in effect when the act was passed in 1934.

For example:

If the rate in effect in 1934 were	$1.00 per unit
And if the rate was reduced by one half before January 1, 1945, on that date it would be	.50 per unit
It could be reduced, in a future trade agreement, by one half of 50 cents per unit, to	.25 per unit

However:

If the 1934 rate of	1.00 per unit
Had not been reduced at all before January 1, 1945, it would remain, on that date, at	1.00 per unit
And could be reduced, in a future trade agreement, only by one half of $1.00 to . .	.50 per unit

receives written statements on any phase of the trade-agreements program.

The information and views of interested persons received through the Committee for Reciprocity Information are analyzed and studied by the interdepartmental trade-agreements organization along with data developed through official studies before final recommendations are made by the Trade Agreements Committee.

Public Notice, Hearings, and Lists of Possible Concession Products. The Secretary of State is required to give public notice of intention to negotiate a trade agreement not less than 30 days before the agreement is concluded. Actually, much longer notice is given. At the same time that the Secretary of State issues this public notice, the Committee for Reciprocity Information announces the closing date for receiving written statements on the proposed agreement and the date for opening public hearings on it.

Simultaneously, there is published a list of all United States import commodities on which United States tariff concessions will be considered in the negotiations. The fact that a given commodity appears on this list does not necessarily mean that a United States tariff concession on it will be made. Decisions on concessions are reached only after the studies and hearings have been completed, after the President has approved the recommendations, and after negotiation has determined that adequate foreign concessions can be obtained in return.

Provisions of Trade Agreements

"Tariff concessions" in trade agreements may take the form of reductions in import duties, the guaranteeing or "binding" of such duties against increase during the life of the agreement, or the "binding" of a free-list item against imposition of an import duty during the life of the agreement.

In addition to commitments with regard to tariffs on imports or exports, trade agreements contain provisions for reduction or elimination of other forms of import restrictions such as quotas. They likewise provide for reduction or elimination of trade discriminations such as tariff preferences and assurances against imposition of discriminatory taxes or other regulations on imported products.

Each new trade agreement signed by the United States must contain a commitment that, in import matters, each government will treat the goods of the other no less favorably than it treats the goods of any third country. This commitment puts into effect what is called the "most-favored-nation" principle.

In addition, each future agreement must also include a clause providing that the United States shall be free to withdraw or modify a concession made with respect to any particular article to the extent and for such time as may be necessary to protect against any unforeseen situation threatening injury to producing interests which may develop as a result of a concession made by the United States.

Trade agreements also contain other so-called escape clauses or exceptions which permit each contracting country, for reasons of security, protection of health, or other specified purposes, to take measures which might otherwise be in conflict with the letter of the agreement.

Agreements Concluded Up to October 1947

On October 30, 1947, the General Agreement on Tariffs and Trade (see page 13) was signed at Geneva. Up to October 30, 1947, trade agreements had been concluded between the United States and 29 foreign countries. Following is a list of the countries and of the dates of signing and of coming into effect of the agreements:

Country	Signed	Effective
Cuba	Aug. 24, 1934	Sept. 3, 1934
Brazil	Feb. 2, 1935	Jan. 1, 1936
Belgium (and Luxembourg)	Feb. 27, 1935	May 1, 1935
Haiti	Mar. 28, 1935	June 3, 1935
Sweden	May 25, 1935	Aug. 5, 1935
Colombia	Sept. 13, 1935	May 20, 1936
Canada (superseded)	Nov. 15, 1935	Jan. 1, 1936
Honduras	Dec. 18, 1935	Mar. 2, 1936
The Netherlands	Dec. 20, 1935	Feb. 1, 1936
Switzerland	Jan. 9, 1936	Feb. 15, 1936
Nicaragua [1]	Mar. 11, 1936	Oct. 1, 1936
Guatemala	Apr. 24, 1936	June 15, 1936
France	May 6, 1936	June 15, 1936
Finland	May 18, 1936	Nov. 2, 1936
Costa Rica	Nov. 28, 1936	Aug. 2, 1937
El Salvador	Feb. 19, 1937	May 31, 1937
Czechoslovakia [2]	Mar. 7, 1938	Apr. 16, 1938
Ecuador	Aug. 6, 1938	Oct. 23, 1938
United Kingdom	Nov. 17, 1938	Jan. 1, 1939
Canada (second agreement)	Nov. 17, 1938	Jan. 1, 1939
Turkey	Apr. 1, 1939	May 5, 1939
Venezuela	Nov. 6, 1939	Dec. 16, 1939
Cuba (first supplementary agreement)	Dec. 18, 1939	Dec. 23, 1939
Canada (supplementary fox-fur agreement) [3]	Dec. 13, 1940	Dec. 20, 1940
Argentina	Oct. 14, 1941	Nov. 15, 1941
Cuba (second supplementary agreement)	Dec. 23, 1941	Jan. 5, 1942
Peru	May 7, 1942	July 29, 1942
Uruguay	July 21, 1942	Jan. 1, 1943
Mexico	Dec. 23, 1942	Jan. 30, 1943
Iran	Apr. 8, 1943	June 28, 1944
Iceland	Aug. 27, 1943	Nov. 19, 1943
Paraguay	Sept. 12, 1946	Apr. 9, 1947

[1] The duty concessions and certain other provisions of this agreement ceased to be in force as of Mar. 10, 1938.
[2] The operation of this agreement was suspended as of Apr. 22, 1939, and terminated on July 5, 1945.
[3] This replaced a previous supplementary agreement relating to fox furs, signed on Dec. 30, 1939, and was terminated on May 1, 1947.

orted, although domestic production of these goods was low in efficiency and high in cost. Prices also rose in these countries.

World-Wide Trend Toward Trade Restrictions

Under these conditions most nations tended to retain and intensify rigid wartime trade controls and also to resort to discriminatory bilateral deals—some of them on a barter basis. Their governments limited foreign purchases to the goods most urgently needed. Such foreign exchange as they could obtain was strictly controlled and reserved for the purchase of essentials from abroad. Import quotas, import licensing systems, and exchange controls were imposed. War-born "infant industries" established vested interests and demanded protection against imports, regardless of their own less efficient and more costly production.

Dependence of the United States on Foreign Markets

At the same time, the United States industrial and agricultural plant was vastly expanded as a result of the war. Agricultural production in 1946 was almost a third larger than during the 1935–39 period and the Federal Reserve Index for February 1947 showed that the physical volume of manufacturing production, as a whole, is almost double that of the 1935–39 period. In general, moreover, the increase in the production of goods which have been exported in large amounts in the past was relatively much greater—for machinery, ¾ times the 1935–39 period, for transportation equipment, 1⅓, and for rubber products, almost ½. Our expanded agricultural and industrial system is selling much larger amounts abroad than in prewar years. The temporary reductions in exports of a few of these products might reduce some inflationary pressures within the United States, but in the long run, such a course would prove disastrous. Foreign markets, on a sound commercial basis, are of crucial importance to the American economy as a whole. Disappearance of these markets would soon result in a surplus of many products, serious price declines for certain key commodities, and eventual unemployment in some of our most efficient industries.

The Marshall Plan

Present critical circumstances, both economic and political, necessitate large-scale measures of assistance merely to assure the continued existence of our largest customers in Europe as going concerns. The economic dislocations in Europe and throughout the world have proved to be far more severe than was at first realized, and European economic recovery will be a long and difficult problem. The interim-aid bill passed by Congress on December 16, 1947, and the European Recovery Program (Marshall Plan) are primarily concerned with the immediate problem of economic relief and reconstruction over the next four years with the chief emphasis on certain European countries. This assistance toward recovery, important as it is, could be ineffectual unless world trade in the next four years expands to the point where these countries are able to sell their own goods and services abroad in sufficient amounts to pay for the imports they need and desire. Consequently, in American self-interest the long-run trading policies of the United States and the rest of the world must provide the best possible conditions for a revival of international trade. The maze of restrictions, bilateralism, and discriminations must be eliminated so that trade may flow more freely. Unless decisive action is taken now, current restrictive and discriminatory practices could easily develop into a mold too hard to break after the emergency has lessened.

The Long-run Program

The United States has, consequently, been developing a program, concurrently with the European Recovery Program, to implement its long-run policy. This program stems from the reciprocal trade-agreements program but is broader and more comprehensive. Nevertheless, the new program will have the same elements of caution, reciprocal advantage, careful analysis, and assurances of the welfare of the American economy which have characterized the reciprocal trade-agreements program in the past.

The program now under way will consist of concrete steps toward realizing United States ideas of a world-wide system of international commercial relationships which will help to make possible greater production, exchange and use of goods, increased employment, and higher living standards in all countries, as an economic foundation for world peace and security.

United States Proposals for World Trade Expansion

At the same time that the United States was participating in setting up the United Nations structure, our experts were engaged on concrete plans for multilateral expansion of world trade and, after two years of work, published in 1945 our *Proposals for Expansion of World Trade and Employment.*[1]

These *Proposals* suggested the establishment of an International Trade Organization to coordinate and assist the cooperative efforts of member countries to improve their economic positions by facilitating international commerce. They also laid down certain principles which the United States believed should underlie such efforts. These principles related chiefly to relaxation and re-

[1] Department of State publication 2411.

moval of governmentally imposed trade restrictions and discriminations, to curbing trade barriers created by private combines and cartels, to remedying disorder in world markets for certain primary commodities, and to reducing irregularities in employment and production.

Suggested Charter for an International Trade Organization

The United States *Proposals* were published in this country and sent to foreign governments as a basis for discussion. The United Kingdom, France, and other countries declared their agreement with all important points in the *Proposals* and their willingness to support them in international discussions. The *Proposals* were then spelled out and elaborated in the *Suggested Charter for an International Trade Organization of the United Nations*,[2] also prepared by United States Government experts in the form of an international agreement or convention.

Preparatory Committee of United Nations Conference on Trade and Employment

In February 1946, the Economic and Social Council of the United Nations resolved to call the United Nations Conference on Trade and Employment to consider the establishment of such an agency as the United States had suggested. The Council set up a Preparatory Committee composed of 19 nations (Australia, Belgium, Brazil, Canada, Chile, China, Cuba, Czechoslovakia, France, India, Lebanon, Luxembourg, Netherlands, New Zealand, Norway, Union of South Africa, Union of Soviet Socialist Republics [3], United Kingdom, and the United States) to arrange for such a conference, prepare an agenda for it, and draft a charter for the proposed organization to be considered at the international conference.

This Preparatory Committee opened its work at London in October 1946, with both the United States *Proposals* and the United States *Suggested Charter* as basic working documents. A drafting committee of the Preparatory Committee met in New York during January and February of 1947 and made further modifications in the proposed charter. The United States Government held public hearings on the draft charter in seven cities during February and March 1947 and asked for criticisms and suggestions. Most of the points raised at these hearings were incorporated in the final draft completed by the Preparatory Committee at Geneva after continuous meetings commencing in April and terminating at the end of

---

[2] Department of State publication 2598.
[3] Although a member, the Union of Soviet Socialist Republics has not participated in the work of the Preparatory Committee.
[4] The Union of Soviet Socialist Republics did not participate in the tariff and trade negotiations.

ally the agreement in accordance with procedures required by their constitutions or laws. Since a number of countries did not put the agreement into force on January 1, 1948, this Government has exercised its right under the agreement generally to withhold concessions which are of primary interest to those countries which were represented at Geneva until they have put their new tariff schedules into effect.

The agreement will enter definitively into force upon deposit with the Secretary-General of the United Nations of formal acceptances on behalf of countries making up 85 percent of the foreign trade of all negotiating countries. The general agreement is accompanied by supplemental agreements between the United States and Belgium-Luxembourg, Canada, France, the Netherlands, and the United Kingdom suspending the existing trade agreements which the United States has with those countries, and similar provisions were contained in an exclusive supplementary trade agreement between the United States and Cuba.

Relationship of the General Agreement to the International Trade Organization

The General Agreement on Tariffs and Trade is a concrete indication on the part of the major trading nations of the world in advance of the United Nations Conference on Trade and Employment at Habana, that the commitment in the draft charter to negotiate toward the substantial reduction of tariffs and other trade barriers and elimination of preferences can be implemented. It proves the willingness of these important countries to start together on the long road back to economic sanity in international relations. It is significant evidence that the principles of the charter can become not mere words but the guides and signposts toward a more rational world.

Addresses on World Trade and Reciprocal Trade-Agreements Program

On March 15 Assistant Secretary Thorp made an address on world trade and European recovery before the World Trade Conference in Pittsburgh, Pa.; for the text of this address, see Department of State press release 197 of March 15, 1948.

On March 12 C. Tyler Wood, Deputy to the Assistant Secretary for economic affairs, made an address on the International Trade Organization and the reciprocal trade-agreements program before the New Jersey Forum on the United Nations in Newark, N. J.; for the text of this address see Department of State press release 193 of March 12, 1948.

FOREIGN AID AND RECONSTRUCTION

Cool Judgment Urged in Solving World Crisis

BY GEORGE C. MARSHALL [1]

Secretary of State

•

The world is in the midst of a great crisis inflamed by propaganda, misunderstanding, anger, and fear. At no time has it been so important for cool judgment, for an appeal to one's self for a proper sense of justice, for a realization of conditions—material, political, and spiritual—in other parts of the world. Virtually everything we do in connection with our foreign relations is misunderstood by some abroad. Our most generous motives are suspected, our good intentions are condemned, and we on our side are apt to grow passionate or fearful—overzealous in our passions or failing in action because of our fears.

In the midst of this turmoil, complicated by the distractions of an election campaign, it is important to express one's feelings on the situation in moderate terms. We should, I think, calmly and prayerfully appraise the facts, so nearly as we can judge them to be the facts, and then search for a firm conclusion in keeping with our sense of justice.

In the midst of this clamor of propaganda and vigorous and sometimes reckless statements, I personally, in my responsibility as Secretary of State, have tried to keep a level head. And in my approach to the situation, I have tried to understand the point of view of other peoples, other nations, other conditions than those surrounding us here at home.

I think you must realize that it is not possible for us in America to reach a full understanding of the reactions of people who not only suffered terribly and bitterly during the war but are still struggling against grim poverty and cold, uncertainty of the future, and acute dread of tomorrow. We must realize that they look to us either with hope because of our riches and security or with dislike, if not hatred, for the very same reason. In considering the reactions, the situation of these peoples, we should consider, by comparison, our own blessings, our comforts and prosperity, our great liberties and our freedom to say what we please and do pretty much as we please, and our right to worship in whatever manner or faith our conscience dictates. With these great privileges, I suppose we never can be brought to a full realization of the dilemma of the peoples of Europe.

Now with these thoughts in mind, I turn to what we should do affirmatively and immediately. The proposal was made last summer for what is taken form as the European Recovery Program. That proposal had as its basis a desire to help and in no way to hinder, a desire to promote the peace and in no way to threaten war. It was not an easy decision last June to submit a proposal which would involve the American people in large contributions for the next four years. Frankly I anticipated immediate and emphatic expressions of opposition from many in this country. Actually, there was at the time little of public opposition. Instead, there was astonishment at the speed with which the countries of western Europe reacted and the remarkable demonstration of 16 sovereign nations making concessions one to the other among themselves, banding together for the good of all. That had never occurred before in history. It probably would not have occurred last summer except for the tragic dilemma which faced them. And it has led today to a strong and promising effort to form a political association which may be the first step to what has been the dream of many great minds troubled by the dangers of the existing uncoordinated situation.

Since I have been Secretary of State I have received countless messages from people in the United States telling me that they were praying that my efforts would be successful in establishing a firm basis for peace. These messages have been of comfort to me because mine has not been an easy task. So far it has been one of many frustrations.

The appeal to prayer has a powerful influence

[1] An address delivered before the Federal Council of Churches, Washington Cathedral, Washington, D.C., on Mar. 11, 1948, and released to the press on the same date.

American life because we are at heart a deeply religious people, though we do not always admit . I think the church and the school are two institutions in American life which must play a very important part in meeting the world problems. There is, therefore, a heavy responsibility resting on the minister of the church and the teacher of the young. The police-state official dictates to preacher and teacher alike. The truth suppressed. That presents one of our great difficulties in securing a fair judgment of what we are sincerely endeavoring to do for the good of the world at large. Prayer is one of the great means of keeping alive our belief in the ultimate triumph of the Christian principles which underlie our civilization. This faith in our ideals is particularly important when we are forced to be realistic in face of an extremely serious world situation. The influence of the church, of you churchmen, will be a tremendous factor in reaching wise decisions.

Exploratory Discussions on Import Programs Within Scope of ERP

[Released to the press March 12]

A series of informal conversations was started March 12 by the Department of State with representatives of the 16 countries which participated in the Committee of European Economic Co-operation last summer. While, of course, no economic assistance can be extended unless and until the Congress acts on the proposed European Recovery Program and the use of any ERP funds shall have been approved in accordance with the terms of the act, it is considered desirable to enter into preliminary discussions of the present plans and programs of the participating countries so that the administrator of the program will have available the information necessary to act promptly. This is of especial importance in the case of certain countries whose economic position will be precarious in April.

Procurement of supplies under the interim aid program for Austria, France, and Italy will, under present legislation, terminate on March 31, 1948. Even if Congress approves the additional 55 million dollars requested, interim aid funds will be sufficient to cover placement of contracts only during the early part of April. Although these supplies will continue to flow for some weeks after procurement has been concluded, the prompt initiation of procurement action during April under the ERP is necessary if a later gap in shipments is to be avoided.

The current discussions, it is stressed, are merely tentative and exploratory and in no sense are to be construed as involving any commitments on the part of the United States. Their purpose is merely to explore the types of import programs which would be within the purpose and scope of the ERP under the pending Senate bill.

THE UNITED NATIONS AND SPECIALIZED AGENCIES

Korean Elections To Conform to Views of Interim Committee

STATEMENT BY SECRETARY MARSHALL

[Released to the press March 10]

The Interim Committee voted by a majority of 41 to 2, with 11 abstentions, to advise the United Nations Temporary Commission on Korea to observe elections in the areas of Korea accessible to it. Included in the majority vote were the votes of a majority of the countries represented in the Temporary Commission. On March 1, Dr. Y. W. Liu, Chinese member of the Commission and its acting chairman, at a public celebration in Seoul announced that "in conformity with the views expressed by the Interim Committee of the General Assembly in its resolution adopted on 27 February 1948, the United Nations Temporary Commission on Korea will discharge its duties, that is to say, observe elections in such parts of Korea as are accessible to the Commission not later than 10 May 1948 . . ." General Hodge has informed us that after the Commission had arrived at this decision announced by Dr. Liu, he consulted with the Commission, and it was agreed that he would announce the date for holding the elections as May 9, 1948.

INTERNATIONAL ORGANIZATIONS AND CONFERENCES

The Second Inter-American Conference on Social Security

ARTICLE BY WILBUR J. COHEN

Seventeen countries were represented at the Second Inter-American Conference on Social Security which was held at Rio de Janeiro, Brazil, November 10–21, 1947. This was the first meeting of the Conference since it was established in September 1942 to promote cooperation among the social-security institutions of the various countries.[1] The chairman of the United States delegation was Arthur J. Altmeyer, Commissioner for Social Security of the United States and Chairman of the Inter-American Committee on Social Security.[2]

The other countries represented were: Argentina, Bolivia, Brazil, Canada, Chile, Colombia, Cuba, the Dominican Republic, Ecuador, Guatemala, Mexico, Panama, Paraguay, Peru, Uruguay, and Venezuela. Observers from the International Labor Organization, the Pan American Union, the Pan American Sanitary Organization, the International Social Security Association, the Inter-American Statistical Institute, the World Health Organization, and the United Kingdom also attended.

Opening Session

The first plenary session was formally opened by Mr. Altmeyer as Chairman of the Committee on Social Security. In his opening speech Mr. Altmeyer referred to the task before the Inter-American Conference on Social Security and the Inter-American Committee on Social Security as

the development of a cooperative program of action throughout the Americas, which will enlist the cooperation of all inter-American and international institutions concerned.

Agenda of the Conference

The agenda of the Conference consisted of a consideration of four reports: (1) the report of the secretary general; (2) insurance of occupational risks; (3) unemployment insurance; and (4) conclusions of the Joint Meeting of the Medical and Statistical Technical Commissions (January 1947, at Washington, D.C.).

The report of the secretary general included a summary of the work of the secretariat, the financial situation of the organization, a brief review of recent social-security developments in the Americas, a discussion of child nutrition in relation to social security, and a summary of investment of social insurance funds. These topics were discussed by the delegates, and at the same time delegates described new developments and problems in social security in their respective countries.

A summary of the conclusions set forth in the 10 resolutions adopted by the Conference is presented below.

Resolutions Adopted

1. *Social Security and International Collaboration.* This resolution points out the necessity of economic progress to provide for comprehensive social-security services.

2. *Social Security and Social Services.* The Conference expressed the wish that the ninth International Conference of American States, which is scheduled to open at Bogotá, Colombia, on March 30, 1948, devise a plan of action for the encouragement of social services in the Americas.

---

[1] For a summary of the 1942 Conference, see "The First Inter-American Conference on Social Security", *Social Security Bulletin*, October 1942, pp. 4–7. See also "Permanent Committee of the Inter-American Conference on Social Security", *ibid.*, October 1945, pp. 3–4.

[2] The U. S. Delegation, in addition, consisted of: Clara M. Beyer, Department of Labor; Wilbur J. Cohen, Social Security Administration; Edward J. Rowell and Roy Tasco Davis, Jr., American Embassy, Rio de Janeiro.

nology. The Conference requested "the Inter-American Committee on Social Security to study, for inclusion in the agenda of the next Conference, the question of the standardisation of American social security terminology, bringing the various terms used into uniformity and giving the equivalent of each in the four official languages of the Conference."

9. *Coordination of Social Security Services with Public Social Services.* The Conference resolved that consideration be given by a future Conference "to the question of the bases, scope and methods of coordination of social insurance services with Government services pursuing similar objects; and That this question should include a sufficiently comprehensive study of questions connected with the maintenance of medical benefit in cases where that provided by social security institutions to insured persons and their families ceases or is not due."

10. *Principle of Tripartite Representation at the Sessions of the Conference.* The Conference advocated that the tripartite representation system of the International Labor Organization, whereby government, employer, and worker delegates participate, be used in its own sessions as far as possible.

Third Meeting of the Inter-American Committee on Social Security

During the Conference, the third meeting of the Inter-American Committee on Social Security took place. The Committee is generally responsible for handling the business and administrative aspects necessary for effectuating the work of the Conference and of carrying out the work of the organization between conferences.

Among the important actions taken by the Committee were adoption of a budget of $30,000 for 1948; agreement to convene the Medical and Statistical Technical Commissions in 1948; and publication of a new edition of the *Inter-American Handbook of Social Security Institutions.*

The Committee re-elected Mr. Altmeyer as chairman. Antonio Diaz Lombardo, Director General of the Mexican Institute of Social Security, was elected vice chairman.

The Executive Body, which acts for the Committee during intervals between its sessions, was elected by the Committee. The four elected members were: Helvécio Xavier Lopes of Brazil; Nicasio Silverio of Cuba; Edgardo Rebagliati of Peru; and Amadeo Almada of Uruguay. The chairman and vice chairman also were members of the Executive Body. It was agreed to hold the next Conference at Bogotá, Colombia.

---

[2] See "Meeting of the Medical and Statistical Commissions of the Inter-American Committee on Social Security", article by Wilbur J. Cohen, BULLETIN of Feb. 23, 1947, p. 337.

U.S. DELEGATION TO U.N. CONFERENCE ON FREEDOM OF INFORMATION

[Released to the press March 12]

The Department of State announced on March 12 that the President has approved the composition of the United States delegation to the United Nations Conference on Freedom of Information scheduled to be held at Geneva, March 23–April 24, 1948. The United States Delegation is as follows:

Chairman:

William Benton, Member, United States National Commission for the United Nations Educational, Scientific and Cultural Organization (UNESCO)

Delegates:

Sevellon Ledyard Brown, Editor and Publisher, Providence *Journal*

Erwin D. Canham, Editor, *Christian Science Monitor*

Zechariah Chafee, Jr., Professor, Harvard Law School; Member, United Nations Economic and Social Council Subcommission on Freedom of Information and the Press

Harry Martin, President, American Newspaper Guild

John Carter Vincent, United States Minister to Switzerland

Alternate Delegates:

Walter A. Graebner, European Director, Time-Life International

Oveta Culp Hobby, Executive Vice President, Houston *Post;* Executive Director, Radio Station KPRC

Frank McCarthy, Manager, Motion Picture Association of America

Howard K. Smith, Chief European Correspondent, CBS

Legal Consultant:

George Washington, the Assistant Solicitor General of the United States, Department of Justice

Advisers:

Lloyd A. Free, Special Assistant to the Director, Office of Information and Educational Exchange, Department of State

Allan Dawson, Office of American Republic Affairs, Department of State

Donald Dunham, Public Affairs Officer, United States Mission, Bucharest

Dorothy Fosdick, Office of European Affairs, Department of State

David H. Henry, 2d, Second Secretary, American Embassy, Moscow

Joseph M. Jones, Special Assistant to the Director, Office of Public Affairs, Department of State

Walter M. Kotschnig, Chief, Division of International Organization Affairs, Department of State

Hertzel Plaine, Office of the Assistant Solicitor General, Department of Justice

Special Assistant to the Chairman:

John Howe, *Encyclopaedia Britannica*, New York

Press Relations Officer:

Luther J. Reid, Special Assistant to the Assistant Secretary of State for Public Affairs, Department of State

378

Robert N. De Hart, Engineer in Charge of Shortwave
Broadcast, CBS

Charles R. Denny, Vice President and General Counsel,
NBC

George E. Hughes, Vice President and East Coast Representative, Associated Broadcasters, Inc.

James P. Veatch, Manager, Frequency Bureau, RCA Laboratories Division, RCA

U.S. DELEGATION TO SEVENTH MEETING OF INTERNATIONAL COTTON ADVISORY COMMITTEE

The Department of State announced on March
12 the United States Delegation to the seventh
meeting of the International Cotton Advisory
Committee. This meeting, the first meeting of the
Committee to be held outside the United States, is
scheduled to convene at Cairo, Egypt, on April 1,
1948. The Delegation is as follows:

Chairman

Edwin D. White, Assistant to the Secretary of Agriculture,
Department of Agriculture

Advisers

Read Dunn, Director of Foreign Trade, National Cotton
Council of America, Washington, D.C.

Robert Bailey Elwood, Assistant Agricultural Attaché,
American Embassy, Cairo

Arthur W. Palmer, Head, Division of Cotton and Other
Vegetable Fibers, Office of Foreign Agricultural Relations, Department of Agriculture

Clovis D. Walker, Chief, Cotton Branch, Production and
Marketing Administration, Department of Agriculture

Adviser and Secretary

James G. Evans, Chief, Fibers Section, International
Resources Division, Department of State

The tentative agenda for the meeting includes:
(1) a review of the world cotton situation; (2)
statements from the delegations on the situation
and the current problems with respect to cotton in
their countries; (3) a program of work for the
secretariat and financial provision for 1948–49;
(4) reports of the officers of the Committee; and
(5) other subjects.

EIGHTH WORLD'S POULTRY CONGRESS SCHEDULED TO MEET

The eighth World's Poultry Congress is scheduled to be held at Copenhagen, August 20–27,
1948, under the patronage of King Frederik IX
of Denmark. About 35 countries have accepted
the invitation of the Danish Government to participate in the Congress, and 15 countries have announced the formation of national committees.
The United States will send an official delegation,
which will be named at a later date. A national
committee representing all segments of the poultry industry in the United States has been set up
to prepare for United States participation.

THE RECORD OF THE WEEK

Triparti

TEXT OF CO

The informal discussions of German problems which began in London on 23rd February between the representatives of the United States, United Kingdom and France, and as from February 26th with the representatives of the Benelux countries, went into recess today.

At the request of the other delegations, the meetings were held under the chairmanship of the U.K. representative, Sir William Strang. The U.S. and French delegations were led by Mr. Douglas and M. Massigli, the U. S. and French Ambassadors in London. At the first meeting it was agreed to invite the Benelux countries to take part, on an equal footing, in the discussions of all items on the agenda, except those dealing with administrative matters which are the direct responsibility of the occupying powers controlling the three occupied areas. The chief representatives of the Benelux delegation were Jenkheer Michiels van Verduynen, the Netherlands Ambassador, Vicomte Obert de Thiesieus, the Belgian Ambassador, and M. Claessen, the Luxembourg Minister.

Important progress has been made and it has been decided that these discussions will be resumed during April for the purpose of reaching conclusions on the remaining question, so that the delegations may be in a position to submit to their governments, at the end of the next session, their recommendations over the whole field. In the meantime various aspects of certain of these problems will be the subject of more detailed examinations.

The continuous failure of the Council of Foreign Ministers to reach quadripartite agreement has created a situation in Germany which if permitted to continue, would have increasingly unfortunate consequences for western Europe. It was therefore necessary that urgent political and economic problems arising out of this situation in Germany should be solved. The participating powers had in view the necessity of ensuring the economic reconstruction of western Europe in-

[1] Released to the press in London on Mar. 6, 1948, and in Washington on Mar. 8, 1948.

sideration was given of all delegations to the establishment of an international control of the Ruhr on which Germany would be represented. The purpose of this international control would be to ensure that the economic resources of this area should not again be used for the purposes of aggression and that there should be adequate access to the coal, coke and steel of the Ruhr for the benefit of extensive parts of the European community including Germany. Agreed recommendations in this respect will be submitted to the governments concerned on the scope and form of this control.

A constructive discussion among all the delegations took place on the present situation and the possible evolution of the political and economic organization of Germany in the combined U.S./U.K. zone and the French zone. A wide measure of agreement was reached on a number of controversial points. In particular it was agreed that a federal form of government, adequately protecting the rights of the respective states but at the same time providing for adequate control authority, is best adapted for the eventual reestablishment of German unity, at present disrupted. Moreover, in order to facilitate the association of western Germany with the European Recovery Programme the three delegations concerned further agreed that prompt action should be taken to coordinate as far as possible the economic policies of the three zones, in such matters as foreign and inter-zonal trade, customs, and freedom of movement for persons and goods.

slovakia

CRETARY MARSHALL

fall of Czechoslovakia. This alarm ranges all the way from fears that Italy might fall to the Communists and, in the extreme, to talk of war. I wonder if we could have your assessment of the situation so far as you can go."

The Secretary replied as follows:

I think you correctly described the situation in your question—that there are great fears as to the developments. There are also very strong feelings regarding these developments and a considerable passion of view on the part of a great many in this country. The situation is very, very serious. It is regrettable that passions are aroused to the degree which has occurred. It is tragic to have things happen such as just occurred in Czechoslovakia, particularly what has happened to some of the officials, as in the affair today of the death of Jan Masaryk, all of which indicates very plainly what is going on. It is a reign of terror in Czechoslovakia and not an ordinary due process of government by the people.

Hungary and Bulgaria Notified of Prewar Treaties U.S.

Will Keep in Force or Revive

HUNGARY

[Released to the press March 11]

The Department of State announced on March 11 that on March 9, 1948, the Hungarian Government was given official notification, in accordance with the terms of the treaty of peace with Hungary signed at Paris, February 10, 1947, regarding the prewar bilateral treaties and other international agreements with Hungary which the United States Government desires to keep in force or revive.

Text of note from the American Minister at Budapest to the Hungarian Minister for Foreign Affairs giving such notification

I have the honor to refer to the Treaty of Peace with Hungary, signed at Paris February 10, 1947, which came into force, in accordance with the provisions of article 42 thereof, on September 15, 1947 upon the deposit of instruments of ratification by the Union of Soviet Socialist Republics, the United Kingdom of Great Britain and Northern Ireland, and the United States of America. Article 10 of the Treaty of Peace reads as follows:

"1. Each Allied or Associated Power will notify Hungary, within a period of six months from the coming into force of the present Treaty, which of its pre-war bilateral treaties with Hungary it desires to keep in force or revive. Any provisions not in conformity with the present Treaty shall, however, be deleted from the above-mentioned treaties.

"2. All such treaties so notified shall be registered with the Secretariat of the United Nations in accordance with Article 102 of the Charter of the United Nations.

"3. All such treaties not so notified shall be regarded as abrogated."

I have the honor, by direction of the Government of the United States of America and on its behalf, to notify the Hungarian Government, in accordance with the provisions of the Treaty of Peace quoted above, that the Government of the United States of America desires to keep in force or revive the following pre-war bilateral treatie[s] and other international agreements with Hungary[:]

Arbitration

1. Arbitration treaty. Signed at Washington Januar[y] 26, 1929. Ratified by the United States February 2[,] 1929. Ratified by Hungary July 6, 1929. Ratificatio[n] exchanged at Washington July 24, 1929. Effective Jul[y] 24, 1929. [Treaty Series 797; 46 Stat. 2849.]

Commerce

2. Treaty of friendship, commerce and consular right[s] and exchanges of notes. Signed at Washington June 2[4,] 1925. Ratified by the United States June 16, 1926. Rat[i]fied by Hungary April 1, 1926. Ratifications exchanged [at] Budapest September 4, 1926. Effective October 4, 192[6.] [Treaty Series 748; 44 Stat. 2441.]

Conciliation

3. Conciliation treaty. Signed at Washington Januar[y] 26, 1929. Ratified by the United States February 28, 192[9.] Ratified by Hungary July 6, 1929. Ratifications exchange[d] at Washington July 24, 1929. Effective July 24, 192[9.] [Treaty Series 798; 46 Stat. 2353.]

Copyright

4. Copyright convention. Signed at Budapest Januar[y] 30, 1912. Ratified by the United States July 31, 191[2.] Ratified by Hungary August 12, 1912. Ratifications e[x]changed at Washington September 16, 1912. Effectiv[e] October 16, 1912. (Revived May 27, 1922.) [Treaty S[e]ries 571; 37 Stat. 1631.]

Debt-funding

5. Debt-funding agreement. Signed at Washingto[n] April 25, 1924. Effective as of December 15, 1923. [Co[m]bined Annual Reports of World War Foreign Debt Com[m]ission (1927) 132.]

6. Agreement modifying the debt-funding agreement [of] April 25, 1924 (moratorium). Signed at Washington Ma[y] 27, 1932. Effective as of July 1, 1931. [Printed by th[e] Treasury Department 1932.]

Extradition

7. Treaty for the extradition of fugitives from justic[e.] Signed at Washington July 3, 1856. Ratified by the Unit[ed] States December 12, 1856. Ratified by Austria-Hunga[ry] November 16, 1856. Ratifications exchanged Decembe[r] 13, 1856. Effective December 13, 1856. (Revived Ma[y] 27, 1922.) [Treaty Series 9; 11 Stat. 691 and 18 Stat. 26[.]

Passport Visa Fees

8. Reciprocal arrangement for temporary waiver [of] visitors' visa fees. Signed April 6 and 21, 1936. Ter[m] extended to March 31, 1937, by notes exchanged at Bud[a-]

382

This notification will be deemed to be effective on the date of the present note.

It is understood, of course, that either of the two Governments may propose revisions in any of the treaties or other agreements mentioned in the above list.

Further, it shall be understood that any of the provisions in the treaties and other agreements listed in this notification which may be found in particular circumstances to be not in conformity with the Treaty of Peace shall be considered to have been deleted so far as application of the Treaty of Peace is involved but shall be regarded as being in full force and effect with respect to matters not covered by the latter treaty.

In compliance with paragraph 2 of article 10 of the Treaty of Peace, quoted above, the United States Government will register with the Secretariat of the United Nations the treaties and other agreements which are by this notification kept in force or revived.

GARIA

"3. All such treaties not so notified shall be regarded as abrogated."

I have the honor, by direction of the Government of the United States of America and on its behalf, to notify the Bulgarian Government, in accordance with the provisions of the Treaty of Peace quoted above, that the Government of the United States of America desires to keep in force or revive the following pre-war bilateral treaties and other international agreements with Bulgaria:

Arbitration

1. Arbitration treaty. Signed at Washington January 21, 1929. Ratified by the United States February 14, 1929. Ratified by Bulgaria July 2, 1929. Ratifications exchanged at Washington July 22, 1929. Effective July 22, 1929. [Treaty Series 792; 46 Stat. 2332.]

Certificates of Origin

2. Agreement for the waiver of legalization on certificates of origin. Effected by exchange of notes signed at Sofia January 5, 1938. Effective January 5, 1938. [Executive Agreement Series 124; 52 Stat. 1509.]

Commerce

3. Provisional commercial agreement. Effected by exchange of notes signed at Sofia August 18, 1932. Effective August 18, 1932. [Executive Agreement Series 41; 48 Stat. 1753.]

Conciliation

4. Conciliation treaty. Signed at Washington January 21, 1929. Ratified by the United States February 14, 1929. Ratified by Bulgaria July 2, 1929. Ratifications exchanged at Washington July 22, 1929. Effective July 22, 1929. [Treaty Series 793; 46 Stat. 2334.]

Extradition

5. Extradition treaty. Signed at Sofia March 19, 1924. Ratified by the United States May 15, 1924. Ratified by

Bulgaria June 10, 1924. Ratifications exchanged at Sofia June 24, 1924. Effective June 24, 1924. [Treaty Series 687; 43 Stat. 1886.]

6. Supplementary extradition treaty. Signed at Washington June 8, 1934. Ratified by the United States April 10, 1935. Ratified by Bulgaria July 27, 1935. Ratifications exchanged at Sofia August 15, 1935. Effective August 15, 1935. [Treaty Series 894; 49 Stat. 3250.]

Naturalization

7. Naturalization treaty. Signed at Sofia November 23, 1923. Ratified by the United States February 26, 1924. Ratified by Bulgaria March 30, 1924. Ratifications exchanged at Sofia April 5, 1924. Effective April 5, 1924. [Treaty Series 684; 43 Stat. 1759.]

Passport Visa Fees

8. Arrangement for the reduction of passport visa fees for non-immigrants. Effected by exchange of notes signed at Sofia June 19 and 29, 1925. Effective August 1, 1925. [Not printed.]

Postal

9. Parcel post convention. Signed at Sofia August 2, 1922 and at Washington August 26, 1922. Ratified by the United States August 31, 1922. Effective as of November 11, 1919. [Post Office Department print; 42 Stat. 2205.]

10. Convention for the exchange of postal money orders. Signed at Washington April 3, 1922. Effective October 1, 1923. [Not printed.]

11. Protocol to money order convention signed at Washington April 3, 1922. Signed at Washington September 6, 1923. Effective October 1, 1923. [Not printed.]

This notification will be deemed to be effective on the date of the present note.

It is understood, of course, that either of the two Governments may propose revisions in any of the treaties or other agreements mentioned in the above list.

Further, it shall be understood that any of the provisions in the treaties and other agreements listed in this notification which may be found in particular circumstances to be not in conformity with the Treaty of Peace shall be considered to have been deleted so far as application of the Treaty of Peace is involved but shall be regarded as being in full force and effect with respect to matters not covered by the latter treaty.

In compliance with paragraph 2 of article 8 of the Treaty of Peace, quoted above, the United States Government will register with the Secretariat of the United Nations the treaties and other agreements which are by this notification kept in force or revived.

Inclusion of Communists a Matter for Chinese Government To Decide

[Released to the press March 11]

In view of misunderstandings that have arisen concerning the Secretary's statements about China at his March 10 press conference, it is pointed out that the Secretary referred to President Truman's statement of December 15, 1945.[1] That statement

[1] BULLETIN of Dec. 16, 1945, p. 945.
[2] Identic notes were delivered Mar. 4, 1948, to the Ambassadors of Yugoslavia, Czechoslovakia, and Poland.
[3] Not printed.

Proposed Foreign Policy Legislation

LETTER FROM THE COUNSELOR OF THE DEPARTMENT OF STATE TO THE CHAIRMAN OF THE HOUSE FOREIGN AFFAIRS COMMITTEE

[Released to the press March 8]

March 4, 1948.

MY DEAR DR. EATON:

I refer to your letter of February 18, 1948 to the Secretary transmitting a copy of the resolution adopted that day by the Committee on Foreign Affairs.

The Resolution requested that the State Department "furnish the Committee with a statement of all foreign policy legislation needed for this session immediately and the estimated authorizations and appropriations to be requested together with an agenda of any other steps proposed to be taken by the State Department to support the financial aspects of its foreign policy. . . .".

In response to questioning by Committee members during both the open hearing and the executive session on February 20, Secretary Marshall discussed the Department's legislative program, including certain of its financial aspects. There are enclosed in response to the Committee's resolution and in supplement to the Secretary's answers during the hearings:

(1) A statement of all foreign policy legislation needed this session, and

(2) The estimated authorizations and appropriations to be requested this session.

The first enclosure amends in some respects and brings up to date the list of proposed foreign policy legislation which Mr. Lovett sent you on December 1, 1947. The second enclosure is in effect a supplement to the information which Secretary Marshall sent you by letter on February 6, with particular reference to the item therein described as "other foreign aid (including China)".[1] The China Aid request for $570 million has already been submitted as has the Greek-Turkish Aid amendment, requesting authorization for additional appropriations in the amount of $275 million. The item in enclosure II on Economic Development of Latin America was not mentioned in the Secretary's letter of February 6 because decisions were not sufficiently definite at that time to warrant its inclusion.

As you know, instability in world conditions is such that it would be impossible to give your Committee positive assurance that no additional foreign policy legislation will be requested during this session. In the estimate of the Department, however, the enclosures list all foreign policy legislation which the Department now foresees as likely to be requested during this session of the Congress, except for several treaties which will be submitted to the Senate and for several relatively unimportant and non-controversial items which may be submitted this session for action but upon which final decisions have not been reached.

In response to that portion of the resolution which requested "an agenda of any other steps proposed to be taken by the State Department to support the financial aspects of its foreign policy", the Department has no further comments to offer than those which the Secretary submitted during the hearings on February 20.

Sincerely yours,

For the Secretary of State:
CHARLES E. BOHLEN
Counselor

February 27, 1948

I. Statement in Response to Request of House Committee on Foreign Affairs for a "Statement of all Foreign Policy Legislation Needed this Session"

For convenience and clarity the following list is divided into three parts.

Part I includes, in a suggested order or priority, all Department sponsored legislation now before the House Committee on Foreign Affairs upon which there has not been final action by either House and legislation which has not yet been submitted to the Congress by the Executive and which, as in the case of the renewal of the Reciprocal Trade Agreements Act, may be referred to Committees other than the Foreign Affairs Committee.

Part II lists, without reference to any suggested order of priority, foreign policy legislation upon which the Senate has completed action but which awaits House action or the convening of a conference.

Part III lists foreign policy legislation which the Department is sponsoring by itself, or jointly with other Departments, but which has been referred to Committees other than the Committee on Foreign Affairs.

---

[1] BULLETIN of Feb. 22, 1948, p. 233.

I. *Foreign Policy Legislation Submitted by the Department of State Upon Which Final Action has not Been Taken by Either House (in suggested order of priority)*

1. The European Recovery Program.
2. Amendments to Greek-Turkish Aid Legislation (PL 75).
3. China Aid Program.
4. Trieste Legislation.
5. Renewal of Reciprocal Trade Agreements Act (not yet submitted to the Congress).
6. The Inter-American Military Cooperation Act (H.R. 3836, reported out by House Foreign Affairs Committee but not yet acted upon).
7. Munitions Control Act (submitted on April 15, 1947 and referred to House Foreign Affairs Committee, H. Doc. 195).
8. Organic Legislation for Government of Trust Territories of the Pacific Islands (not yet submitted to the Congress).
9. Authorization for loan of $65 million to finance construction of the United Nations Headquarters (not yet submitted to the Congress).
10. Amendment of the United Nations Participation Act (PL 264, 79th Congress). To authorize the appointment of an additional representative to the United Nations and for other purposes. (Not yet submitted to the Congress).
11. Authorization for Extension of Aid to Destitute Americans Abroad. (Submitted to the Congress on July 14, 1947 and referred to House Committee on Foreign Affairs.)
12. Authorization for the State Department to perform certain consular type functions for German nationals in the United States. (H.R. 4330 favorably reported upon by House Foreign Affairs Committee on July 23, H. Report 1045).
13. Authorization to Participate in the Pan American Railway Congress (S.J. Res. 177. Not introduced in House. Railway Congress is scheduled to meet in late March and legislation should, if possible, be enacted before then.)
14. Procedural Amendments to Charter of Institute of Inter-American Affairs (PL 369), amendments introduced by Mr. Jonkman on January 26, 1948.
15. Authorization for detail of United States personnel to International Organizations (submitted by letter dated January 19, 1948 and referred to House Foreign Affairs Committee).
16. Authorization for Basic Authority for Assistant Secretaries of State Positions in Department of State.

II. *Foreign Policy Legislation Upon Which Senate Action Has Been Completed and Which is Now Pending Before the House Committee on Foreign Affairs or Awaiting Action by the House of Representatives*

1. World Health Organization (H.J. Res. 161, passed by Senate as S.J. Res. 98, July 7, 1947).

4. *Loan for United Nations Headquarters Construction.*

An agreement between the United States and the United Nations is expected to be signed in the near future, setting forth the terms of a proposed United States interest-free loan of $65 million for the construction of United Nations headquarters. After the agreement is signed, the President is expected to transmit the agreement to the Congress for approval and request the necessary authorizing legislation and appropriation. The loan is to be repaid over a period of 30 years.

5. *Inter-American Military Cooperation.*

Final figures are not yet available on the amount that will be needed to implement this legislation which is now pending before the House of Representatives.

SAGE OF TRANSMITTAL

Seventy-ninth Congress, as required by that law.

HARRY S. TRUMAN.

THE WHITE HOUSE, *March 8, 1948.*

Enclosure: Report from the Secretary of State concerning Public Law 584.

OF THE DEPARTMENT OF STATE

tions under paragraph 32 (b) (2) of the act during the period January 1 through December 31, 1947.

Introduction

The Department of State has proceeded, during the calendar year 1947, with the preparation and negotiation of the executive agreements which, pursuant to the terms of the act, underlie the educational exchange programs in the participating countries. This broad program of long-range educational exchanges, setting a new precedent in international intercourse, has called for meticulous attention to many details of cultural, financial, political, and economic relations. The agreements concluded during this year were under active negotiation with the countries concerned for over 6 months. Now that a pattern has been established, however, negotiations may be expected to move more rapidly and the first few months of 1948 should see many more programs under way.

The reception accorded the proposals of the United States for the establishment of the educational exchange program by the governments of the various foreign countries and the popular interest in the program demonstrated at home and abroad give every promise of fulfillment to the objectives of the Congress in providing, through this program, improved understanding between the peoples of the world.

China

The executive agreement required by the act was signed in Nanking at 4:30 p.m. November 10, 1947, Nanking time.[2] The signatories were the Honorable J. Leighton Stuart, American Ambassador to China, on behalf of the Government of the United States of America, and His Excellency, the Minister of Foreign Affairs, Dr. Wang Shih-chieh, on behalf of the Government of the Republic of China. The complete text of the agreement follows as annex A.

The agreement provides for the establishment of the United States Educational Foundation in China as an organization created and established to facilitate the administration in China of the program of educational exchanges authorized by the act. The management and direction of the affairs of the Foundation are vested in a Board of Directors and the following members have been appointed by Ambassador Stuart:

The Honorable J. Leighton Stuart, American Ambassador to China, Chairman;
Dr. Robert Briggs Watson, acting regional director for the Far East of the Rockefeller Foundation;
George H. Green, Jr., submanager, Shanghai branch of the National City Bank of New York;
John F. Melby, second secretary of the American Embassy, Nanking;
George L. Harris, cultural relations attaché to the American Embassy, Nanking.

The agreement provides that the Chinese Government shall appoint not more than five advisers to the Board. Four such appointments have been made as follows:

Dr. Hu Shih, president of Peita, Peiping, Chairman;
Dr. Sah Pen-Tung, secretary general of Academia Sinica;
Dr. Wui Yi-Fang, president, Ginling Women's College;
Dr. Han Lien-Ching, chief, Department of Cultural Relations, Ministry of Education.

While the agreement provides that the Government of the Republic of China should deposit with the Treasurer of the United States an amount of Chinese national currency equivalent to $250,000 (United States currency) within 30 days of the signing of the agreement, Embassy, Nanking, was authorized to accept an initial deposit of Chinese national currency equivalent to only $5,000 to cover immediate administrative expenses, the balance payable on demand of the United States Gov-

[2] BULLETIN of Nov. 23, 1947, p. 1005.
[3] BULLETIN of Jan. 4, 1948, p. 27.

THE FOREIGN SERVICE

Board of Examiners for Foreign Service To Hold Examination

The Department of State announced on March 4 that the Board of Examiners for the Foreign Service had determined to hold on September 27–30, 1948, a written examination for appointment as Foreign Service officer.

The examination will be held at American diplomatic posts and consulates and at the following 18 Civil Service examination centers: Atlanta, Boston, Chicago, Cincinnati, Dallas, Denver, Honolulu, Los Angeles, New Orleans, New York, Philadelphia, St. Louis, St. Paul, San Francisco, San Juan, Seattle, Washington, D.C., and Winston-Salem. Application blanks may be obtained from the Board of Examiners for the Foreign Service, Department of State, Washington 25, D.C. All applications must be received by the Board of Examiners on or before July 1, 1948. Applicants must be at least 21 and under 31 years of age as of July 1, 1948, and must have been citizens of the United States for at least 10 years before July 1, 1948. If married, they must be married to American citizens.

Regional Consular Conference To Be Held

[Released to the press March 4]

The Office of the Foreign Service announced on March 4 that a regional consular conference will be held at the American Embassy in Mexico City, April 5–9, at which diplomatic and consular officers from 20 posts in Mexico will discuss plans to improve American Foreign Service operations in that country.

The sessions will be addressed by prominent Foreign Service officers and by Departmental officials whose duties in Washington keep them in constant communication with American representatives in Mexico. Speakers will stress the importance of keeping the Foreign Service in constant alinement with changing demands and performance criteria so that the Service will always be responsive to the needs of American business, agriculture, labor, and industry.

Other matters to be considered include border and visa problems, administrative procedures, and ways to effect a better coordination of the activities of the officers stationed in the Capital and the field.

A similar conference was held last fall in Ottawa for Foreign Service personnel in Canada. Plans are under way to arrange consular sessions later in the year in South Africa.

---

[1] BULLETIN of July 27, 1947, p. 198.
[2] Included in the report are Annex A, text of the agreement with China, for which see BULLETIN of Nov. 23, 1947, p. 1005, and also TIAS 1687, and Annex B, text of the agreement with Burma, for which see TIAS 1685.

Lincoln MacVeagh Appointed Ambassador to Portugal

The White House announced on March 5 the appointment of Lincoln MacVeagh, former Ambassador to Greece, as Ambassador to Portugal, replacing John C. Wiley, who has been named Ambassador to Iran. Mr. MacVeagh's successor at Athens has not yet been selected.

THE DEPARTMENT

Loyalty of State Department Employees

Statement by Secretary Marshall

[Released to the press March 10]

Charges have been made regarding the loyalty of State Department employees. I am aware of the importance of insuring the loyalty of personnel serving the Department. Our special authority to terminate employment obviously places a heavy responsibility on us to see that the personnel is dependable and that we act with fairness and decency.

The Department's policy gives the benefit of doubt to the Government when questions of employees' loyalty arise. But the doubt must be based on reliable evidence. We must careful avoid action based on spiteful, unsupported, or i responsible allegations.

I have confidence in the loyalty of the personnel I regret the undermining of the confidence of th people in the Department, especially at this cri cal juncture.

U.S. Professor and Chilean Physician Extended Grants-in-Aid

A grant-in-aid has been extended by the D partment of State to the following: Santiago F esco MacClure of Santiago, Chile, to enable hi to spend a year as research consultant at the Was ington University, St. Louis, Missouri; Philip Thayer of Washington, D.C., for a two weel visit to Habana, Cuba, to confer with officials the University of Habana and others regarding international faculty exchange program in t field of law.

Transfer of Nondemilitarized Combat Matériel

[Released to the press Mar]

The following is a list of authorizations and transfers of surplus nondemilitarized and demilitariz combat matériel effected by the Department of State in its capacity as foreign-surplus and lend-lea disposal agent, during the months of February, May, July, October, November, and December 19 and not previously reported to the Munitions Division:

Country	Description of matériel	Procurement cost	Sales price	Date transf
				1947
Argentina...	One J 2F-5 aircraft (Navy utility amphibian biplane)...	$10,000.00	$3,500.00	Feb.
Brazil....	Miscellaneous cartridges and metallic belt links....	271,906.81	27,180.79	Dec.
	8,020 100-lb. practice bombs and charges........	26,867.00	2,686.70	Dec.
Canada....	21 light tanks, M5A1, and 100 assembly stabilizers with fin, for use with practice rifle grenade M11.	568,224.00	17,454.00	Dec.
China	50 LST'S or landing ships, tank (demilitarized). (Partial sale of landing craft located at Subic Bay, Republic of the Philippines).	80,890,000.00	1,400,000.00	Octo
Cuba.....	Miscellaneous cartridges, shells, shell fins, percussion primers, canisters, shot, grenades, signals.	345,430.63	30,695.45	Dec.
	6 tank engines, 36 bundles of track assemblies, and miscellaneous spare parts for light tanks. M3A1.	99,422.60	4,971.13	Dec.
Ecuador ...	Miscellaneous shells, shot, cartridges, and canisters...	49,085.53	2,451.41	Dec.
	Miscellaneous cartridges, clips, shells, grenades, and rockets.	151,732.27	12,847.23	Dec.
El Salvador..	3 tank engines, 18 bundles of shoe-track assemblies and miscellaneous spare parts for light tanks, M3A1.	49,711.31	2,485.57	Dec.
France	15 P-51 aircraft and spare parts for one year's maintenance.	787,335.00	157,467.00	Nov.
Netherlands..	2 B-17, 3 P-47 and 3 P-51 aircraft, (demilitarized, nonflyable, for ground instruction only, in educational institutions).	877,158.00	1,300.00	July
Uruguay ...	Miscellaneous cartridges, metallic belt links, practice bombs, and charges.	22,513.31	2,254.53	Nov.
Venezuela ..	Miscellaneous cartridges, metallic belt links, practice bombs, charges, bombs, fuzes, assembly fins, and aiming wire assemblies.	70,264.93	7,029.21	Dec.

Quito January 22, 1945; entered into force January 22, 1945.

Mobile Radio Transmitting Stations. Treaties and Other International Acts Series 1670. Pub. 3005. 3 pp. 5¢.

Interim Arrangement Between the United States of America and Canada—Effected by exchange of notes signed at Washington June 25 and August 20, 1947; entered into force August 20, 1947.

Diplomatic List, February 1948. Pub. 3048. 186 pp. 20¢ a copy; $2 a year.

Monthly list of foreign diplomatic representatives in Washington with their addresses.

National Commission News, March 1, 1948. Pub. 3053. 10 pp. 10¢ a copy; $1 a year.

Prepared monthly for the United States National Commission for the United Nations Educational, Scientific and Cultural Organization.

Selected Bibliography [1]

British–United States Zone of the Free Territory of Trieste. S/679, Feb. 18, 1948. iv, 46 pp. mimeo.
Official Records
——First Year: First Series. Supplement No. 1, 83 pp. printed. [75¢.]
——Second Year. No. 54, 151st meeting, 3 July 1947. 13 pp. printed. [10¢.]
——Second Year. No. 55, 152nd and 153rd meetings, 8 July 1947. 40 pp. printed. [40¢.]
Letter from the Chairman of the United Nations Palestine Commission to the President of the Security Council [Transmitting the first special report to the Security Council, The Problem of Security in Palestine]. S/676, Feb. 16, 1948. 19 pp. mimeo.
Official Records:
——First Year, Second Series, Supplement No. 12A. 20 pp. printed. [35¢.]
——Second Year. No. 40, 134th meeting, May 16, 1947. 22 pp. printed. [20¢.]
——No. 41, 135th meeting, May 20, 1947. 23 pp. printed. [40¢.]
——No. 42, 136th and 137th meetings, May 22, 1947. 60 pp. printed. [60¢.]
——No. 43, 138th meeting, June 4, 1947. 16 pp. printed. [15¢.]
——No. 48, 143d and 144th meetings, June 20, 1947. 22 pp. printed. [20¢.]
——No. 49, 145th meeting, June 24, 1947. 27 pp. printed. [20¢.]
——No. 50, 146th meeting, June 25, 1947. 21 pp. printed. [20¢.]
——No. 51, 147th and 148th meetings, June 27, 1947. 42 pp. printed. [40¢.]

[1] Printed materials may be secured in the United States from the International Documents Service, Columbia University Press, 2960 Broadway, New York City. Other materials (mimeographed or processed documents) may be consulted at certain designated libraries in the United States.

Wilbur J. Cohen, author of the article on the second Inter-American
Conference on Social Security, is Assistant Director, Bureau of
Research and Statistics, Social Security Administration.

The Department of State bulletin

VOL. XVIII, No. 456 • PUBLICATION 3103

March 28, 1948

·intendent of Documents
·ernment Printing Office
Washington 25, D.C.

SUBSCRIPTION:
, $5; single copy, 15 cents

with the approval of the
he Bureau of the Budget

this publication are not
s contained herein may
on of the DEPARTMENT
as the source will be

*The Department of State BULLETIN,
a weekly publication compiled and
edited in the Division of Publications,
Office of Public Affairs, provides the
public and interested agencies of
the Government with information on
developments in the field of foreign
relations and on the work of the Department of State and the Foreign
Service. The BULLETIN includes
press releases on foreign policy issued
by the White House and the Department, and statements and addresses
made by the President and by the
Secretary of State and other officers
of the Department, as well as special
articles on various phases of international affairs and the functions of
the Department. Information is included concerning treaties and international agreements to which the
United States is or may become a
party and treaties of general international interest.*

*Publications of the Department, as
well as legislative material in the field
of international relations, are listed
currently.*

L WHEAT AGREEMENT

d G. Cale

Wheat Council indicated, a number of other questions on which full agreement was not reached in the.London conference. In its final meeting, that Conference entrusted to the International Wheat Council the task of bringing the negotiations to a successful conclusion. Membership in the Council had been increased to 13 prior to the London conference, the following countries having accepted an invitation of membership issued by the Council in March 1946: Belgium, Brazil, China, Denmark, France, India, Italy, and the Netherlands. The Union of Soviet Socialist Republics and Yugoslavia, which were also issued invitations at the same time, did not become members.

In entrusting the task of negotiating the agreement to the Wheat Council, the London conference recommended that invitations to membership in the Council be extended to all countries that were represented at the Conference. Between the time of the London conference and the meeting of the Special Session of the Wheat Council in which the wheat-agreement negotiations were completed, 15 additional countries became members of the Council, namely: Austria, Colombia, Czechoslovakia, the Dominican Republic, Egypt, Greece, Ireland, Lebanon, Mexico, New Zealand, Norway, Peru, Poland, Portugal, and Uruguay, thus bringing membership in the Council to 28.

The. first important step taken by the Council pursuant to the request of the London conference occurred at the Council's meeting on December 8, 1947, when a Special Session was agreed upon for January 28 for the purpose of negotiating and signing an international wheat agreement. It also established a Special Committee (consisting of the representatives of Australia, Brazil, Canada, France, India, the Netherlands, the United Kingdom, and the United States), instructing it to do any preparatory work which would expedite the proceedings of the Special Session. This Committee met on December 9 and 29, 1947, and on January 5 and 6, 1948, and prepared a report to the International Wheat Council stating what it considered to be the substantive issues facing the Special Session, namely: the questions of

---

[1] For a discussion of this Conference and a brief summary of the negotiations leading up to it see BULLETIN of June 1, 1947, p. 1053.

duration of the agreement, the maximum and minimum prices for which it should provide, the equation of guaranteed import and export quantities, and the inclusion in the agreement of provisions giving the Council added responsibility and authority to deal with emergency needs for wheat that might arise. It was necessary to devise a way of bringing the guaranteed import and export quantities provided for in the agreement into equality, since importing countries had indicated in London a desire to purchase substantially larger quantities of wheat than exporting countries were in a position to commit themselves to supply.

In its December 8, 1947, meeting, the Council agreed to invite to its Special Session all countries which had been invited by the United Kingdom Government to attend the Wheat Conference in London in March and April 1947, namely, all countries which were members either of the United Nations or of the Food and Agriculture Organization. Each of the 28 countries which were members of the Wheat Council were represented by delegations at the Special Session. In addition, 13 other countries accepted the Council's invitation and were represented by delegates or observers. These were Afghanistan, Cuba, Ecuador, Finland, Guatemala, Iran, Liberia, Pakistan, Philippines, Sweden, Switzerland, Union of South Africa, and Venezuela. The Special Session was therefore attended by representatives from 41 countries, and by observers from United Nations, Food and Agriculture Organization, International Bank for Reconstruction and Development, and the International Monetary Fund.

A number of governments sent specially instructed representatives to the Special Session. The United Kingdom, for example, sent Sir Herbert Broadley and John Wall of the British Ministry of Food from London. Other governments were represented by their regular delegations to the International Wheat Council who were, of course, under special instructions regarding the subject matter before the Special Session. The United States was represented at the Special Session by its regular delegation to the International Wheat Council. This is composed of N. E. Dodd, Under Secretary of Agriculture; Leroy K. Smith, Director, Grain Branch, Department of Agriculture; L. A. Wheeler, until March 1, 1948, Director, Office of Foreign Agricultural Relations, Department of Agriculture, and since then a member of the United States Foreign Service; and Edward G. Cale, Associate Chief, International Resources Division, Department of State.

Mr. Wheeler, who is Chairman of the Council, presided at all meetings of the Special Session. The Secretary of the Council, Andrew Cairns, served as Secretary of the Special Session.

Since the major issues to be faced at the Special Session were already well understood, the organi-

vernments regarding the outstanding unsettled ues at the time. The recess was agreed upon by e Special Session in the hope that the negotia-ns could be completed within a short time after e Session reconvened.

All meetings of the Special Session except the al meeting on March 6 were in executive session. rrangements were made, however, for the Chair-an and the Secretary of the Special Session to eet with representatives of the press from time to ne and to issue releases in order that the press d the public might be kept advised of the prog-ss of the negotiations. At the final session on arch 6, which was open to the public, copies of e agreement that had been negotiated and of a lease describing its principal features were stributed to the press.

The agreement consists of a preamble and 22 ticles. The preamble indicates that the coun-ies signing the agreement have done so "recog-zing that there is now, a serious shortage of heat, and that later there may be a serious sur-us; believing that the high prices resulting from e present shortage and the low prices which uld result from a future surplus are harmful to eir interests, whether they are producers or con-mers of wheat; and concluding therefore that eir interests, and the general interest of all coun-ies in economic expansion, require that they ould cooperate to bring order into the interna-nal wheat market". The agreement's objec-ves, as stated in article I, "are to assure supplies wheat to importing countries and to assure mar-ts to exporting countries at equitable and stable ices".

The essence of the agreement is contained in ticles II through VI. Article II, dealing with ghts and obligations of importing and export-g countries, contains two annexes. Annex I ves in metric tons and in bushels the "guaranteed rchases" of each of the signatory importing untries. Annex II gives the "guaranteed sales" each of the exporting countries.

Article III provides for the supplying to the uncil by the contracting governments of the in-rmation regarding sales for export, and export, d purchases for import, and import, of wheat hich is necessary for the record keeping by the uncil that will be required in the administration the agreement.

Article IV deals with the enforcement of rights. provides that any importing country which at y time finds difficulty in making its guaranteed rchases at the maximum price may, through the uncil, call upon the exporting countries to sup-y wheat up to the amount which the exporting untries have guaranteed to supply the importing untry in question and that any exporting coun-y which at any time finds difficulty in making its aranteed sales at the minimum price may,

through the Council, call upon the importing countries to purchase wheat up to the amount which the importing countries have guaranteed to purchase from the exporting country in question. The exporting countries may be called upon by the importing countries to deliver wheat only at the maximum price. The importing countries may be called upon by the exporting countries to purchase wheat only at the minimum price. Transactions in wheat over and above the guaran-teed quantities are not subject to the terms of the agreement.

Article V deals with the adjustment of obliga-tions. It provides that any contracting govern-ment which fears that it may be prevented by circumstances, such as a short crop in the case of an exporting country or such as the necessity to safeguard its balance of payments or monetary reserves in the case of an importing country, from carrying out its obligations and responsibilities under the agreement shall report the matter to the Council. It also provides that the Council, if it finds that the country's representations are well-founded, shall seek to bring about an adjustment in obligations through the voluntary assumption of those obligations by other contracting countries. It provides further that in the event it is not possible to adjust the obligations on a voluntary basis the Council shall reduce the quantities in the appropriate annex to article II, on a propor-tional basis, in order to bring the total quantities in the annexes into equality with each other.

Article VI deals with prices. This article, as was the case in London, raised the most difficult problems that had to be considered. As finally negotiated, the article provides for a uniform maximum price of $2.00 per bushel and for a minimum price of $1.50 in the first year, $1.40 in the second year, $1.30 in the third year, $1.20 in the fourth year, and $1.10 in the fifth year. These prices are for no. 1 Manitoba Northern wheat in store Fort William/Port Arthur, expressed in terms of Canadian currency per bushel at the parity for the Canadian dollar determined for the purposes of the International Monetary Fund as of February 1, 1948. Under this definition one dollar Canadian currency is equal to one dollar United States currency. Under the definition of "wheat" used in the agreement, wheat includes flour in terms of wheat equivalent in every case where the term occurs, except in this article and in article IX dealing with stocks which are to be held by exporting and importing countries.

No provision was incorporated in the agreement specifically for the purpose of moderating fluc-tuations within the limits set by the basic maxi-mum and minimum prices, although a provision which was contained in the London draft agree-ment was included, under which the Council may, by a two-thirds majority of the votes held by the exporting and importing countries voting separately, determine the minimum and maximum prices for the third, fourth, and fifth years of the agreement, provided that the minimum price so determined is not lower than the basic minimum price and the maximum price so determined is not higher than the basic maximum price referred to earlier (i.e., the minimum may not be lower than $1.50 in the first year, $1.40 in the second year, et cetera, and the maximum may not be higher in any year than $2.00).

With one exception, voting under the agreement is on a weighted basis with the weight of the vote being determined by the quantity of wheat which a country is committed to buy or sell and with 50 percent of the total vote being exercised by exporting countries and 50 percent by importing countries. The exception relates to voting on the seat of the Council under paragraph 10 of article XI in which case each delegate has one vote.

From the foregoing discussion it is evident that of the problems mentioned in its report to the Council by the Council's Special Committee, the question of duration was settled on the basis of five years, that the price range question was settled on the basis of a uniform ceiling of $2.00 and a floor beginning at $1.50 and dropping by 10-cent stages to $1.10 in the fifth year, and that no provision for narrowing price fluctuations within these limits was made which can take effect without a two-thirds majority vote of exporters and importers, voting separately. Since Canada and the United States each hold more than one third of the exporter vote and since the United Kingdom holds more than one third of the importer vote, it is apparent that no change in the maximum and minimum prices can be made without the concurrence of each of these countries.

The problem of equating the guaranteed export and import quantities, as indicated earlier, arose from the fact that the importing countries which had expressed a desire to participate in the agreement wished to commit themselves to purchase larger quantities of wheat under the agreement than the exporting countries were in a position to agree to supply. Some of the countries desiring to purchase additional quantities were prepared to commit themselves to do so for each of the five years of the agreement. Others needed substantially larger quantities of wheat in the earlier years than in the later years, since they expected their domestic production, which in many instances had been reduced by the war, to increase materially during the life of the agreement. In equating the guaranteed export and import quantities, the relationship of those quantities to the allocations of the importing countries that have been recommended by the International Emergency Food Committee of the Council of the Food and Agriculture Organization and the allocations it is likely

that are members of the agreement as to the level
of supplies in relation to need. During meetings
of the Special Session the United States Delegation pointed out that so long as the cereals shortage continues it anticipates that the needs of the
occupied areas will be screened by IEFC in the same
way as in the past. Should the United States ever
find it necessary to invoke the above-mentioned
provision, under these conditions, it would hope
to be able to come to the Council with a figure as to
the requirements of the occupied areas that had
been unanimously agreed to by the members of
IEFC. Membership in IEFC and the Wheat Council
are virtually the same, but it is the responsibility
of IEFC, rather than the Wheat Council, to recommend the international distribution of wheat on
the basis of relative need.

The responsibility of IEFC in this connection
was recognized by the Special Session in the unanimous adoption of the following resolution which
also met the second and third problems mentioned
above:

"The Special Session of the International Wheat
Council, held in Washington January–March
1948, recognizes that the International Emergency
Food Committee of the FAO Council is the appropriate body to recommend the international distribution of wheat and other grains used for human consumption during the continuation of the
present severe food emergency, and that international trade in wheat and other grains during this
emergency should be in accordance with that Committee's recommendations, provided that the recommended distribution of wheat to no country is
less than its guaranteed purchases under the International Wheat Agreement after adjustments,
if any, effected in accordance with the provisions
of Article V of that Agreement."

Since certain of the importing countries feared
that this resolution might be taken by IEFC to imply that the countries' total requirements for wheat
were covered by their guaranteed purchases under
the agreement, the Special Session also unanimously adopted the following resolution:

"The Special Session of the International Wheat
Council, held in Washington January–March
1948, hereby instructs its Secretary to inform the
International Emergency Food Committee of the
FAO Council that as the figures in Annex I to Article II of the International Wheat Agreement,
signed in Washington in March–April 1948, do
not represent the total requirements of the signatory countries they should not be regarded as a
measure of these countries' needs."

The fourth problem was met by the addition of
a new paragraph (paragraph 6) to article V on
"Adjustment of Obligations". This paragraph
states that:

"If, in order to meet a critical need which has arisen or threatens to arise, a contracting Government should appeal to the Council for assistance in obtaining supplies of wheat in addition to its guaranteed quantity, the Council may, by two-thirds of the votes held by the Governments of importing countries and by two-thirds of the votes held by the Governments of exporting countries, reduce the guaranteed import quantities of the other contracting importing countries for the current crop-year, on a *pro rata* basis, by an amount sufficient to provide the quantity of wheat which the Council determines to be necessary to relieve the emergency created by the critical need, provided that the Council agrees that such emergency cannot be met in any other manner."

In view of the fact that the agreement is, in effect, a multilateral bulk-purchase contract, the initial signatories will be limited to those countries which have indicated an intention to participate in it by signifying the quantity of wheat which they are willing to guarantee to sell or purchase pursuant to its provisions. There are 36 such countries, 3 exporting countries and 33 importing countries. These include all of the countries attending the conference with five exceptions, namely: Argentina, Finland, Iran, Pakistan, and Uruguay. Of these, two, Argentina and Uruguay, are members of the present Wheat Council. At the Special Session the Argentine Representative indicated, as he had in London, that his Government was not prepared to accept the provisions in the agreement under which a maximum price would have been established for wheat exported from Argentina.

Uruguay is in a position of having to import wheat in some years and to export wheat in others. During the Special Session a provision was added to the London draft of the agreement (paragraph 2 of article XI) under which a country that is in this position may become a nonvoting member of the Council provided it agrees to supply the Council with the statistical information regarding its transactions in wheat which is required of other participating countries and that it agrees to pay the membership fee determined by the Council. Such a nonvoting member need not sign the agreement but may become a nonvoting member by indicating to the Council its willingness to meet the conditions stated immediately above. Any such country or any other country may become a voting member of the Council by accession in accordance with the provisions of article XXI. This article states that subject to unanimity, any government may accede to the agreement under such condi-

⁵ By Mar. 25 seven additional countries had signed: Australia, bringing exports covered by countries which had signed to 100 percent, and Belgium, Cuba, New Zealand, Norway, Republic of the Philippines, and Switzerland, bringing imports covered to more than 70 percent.

International Wheat Council, which is established by article XI, shall be convened in July 1948 Washington by the Government of the United tes of America. At this meeting any government which has formally accepted the agreement which is of the opinion that the guaranteed rchases or guaranteed sales of the countries ose governments have formally accepted it are ifficient to insure its successful operation may ct its withdrawal by notification to the Government of the United States. In the event of failure accept by a government or by governments ose guaranteed purchases or sales are, in the nion of the governments which have ratified, of sufficient importance to prevent the effective eration of the agreement, the Council would be uired to make adjustments in the guaranteed antity or quantities in the appropriate annex article II.

The Council in its final meeting of the Special ssion recognized that a considerable amount of rk would have to be done between the close the Session and the first meeting of the new teat Council in July 1948. It therefore apinted a Preparatory Committee to make recomndations for the consideration of the new Council, including recommendations on rules of prolure, the records to be kept in accordance with provisions of article III, the budget for the p year 1948–49, the work of the new Council's retariat, and any other draft plans which, in opinion of the Preparatory Committee, would ist the new Council to make at its July meeting

the arrangements necessary to commence the operation of the agreement on August 1, 1948. Sir Herbert Broadley of the United Kingdom Delegation was appointed chairman of the Committee which includes representatives of the following countries in addition to the United Kingdom: Australia, Brazil, Canada, Egypt, France, India, Benelux, and the United States. The Council provided further that the Preparatory Committee should hold at least three formal meetings, the first and second in London in April and May, respectively, and the third in Washington early in June 1948.

This agreement is the result of an attempt on the part of the participating countries to find a multilateral solution to serious problems in respect of wheat which either exist at present or are expected to arise in the near future. The multilateral approach to such problems is envisioned in the chapter on intergovernmental commodity agreements of the charter for an International Trade Organization which was sponsored by the United States Government and which during the negotiations at the Habana Conference proved acceptable to all the governments that indicated their intention of participating in the organization. From this viewpoint the agreement assumes added importance since it is the first agreement negotiated in the light of the principles regarding commodity agreements that are contained in the Iro charter, and since it will therefore, in a sense, be a test case as to whether the multilateral approach envisioned is capable of being applied in the case of a specific commodity.

atements, Addresses, and Broadcasts of the Week

e President	Toward securing the peace and preventing war. Printed in this issue.	Address before the Congress on Mar. 17.
e President	On foreign and domestic policies. Not printed. Released to the press by the White House on Mar. 17.	Address made before the Society of the Friendly Sons of St. Patrick in New York City on Mar. 17.
retary Marshall	World-wide struggle between freedom and tyranny. Printed in this issue.	Address made in Berkeley on Mar. 19.
retary Marshall	On the present world situation. Not printed. Text issued as press release 221 of Mar. 20.	Address made in Los Angeles on Mar 20.
retary Marshall	Relation of military strength to diplomatic action. Printed in this issue.	Statement before the Armed Services Committee of the Senate on Mar. 17.
sistant Secretary Norman Arnour	On questions to be considered at the forthcoming International Conference of American States. Not printed. Text issued as press release 224 of Mar. 20.	Broadcast over the NBC network on Mar. 20.
ilip C. Jessup	On problem of voting in the Security Council. Printed in this issue.	Statement made in the Interim Committee on Mar. 15.
nthrop G. Brown, Acting Director, Office of International Trade Policy	U.S. foreign economic policy. Not printed. Text printed as Department of State publication 3097.	Address made before the Texas Cotton Association in Corpus Christi on Mar. 19.

781476—48——2

THE UNITED NATIONS AND SPECIAL

STATEMENT BY AMBASSA

U.S. Representative in

The resolution adopted by the Security Council on 5 March 1948 requested the permanent members of the Security Council "to consult and to inform the Security Council regarding the situation with respect to Palestine . . ."

A brief report on the above part of the resolution was made this morning. With respect to that report, I wish to comment upon paragraph 4, which reads:

"The Palestine Commission, the mandatory power, the Jewish Agency and the Arab Higher Committee have indicated that the partition plan cannot be implemented by peaceful means under present conditions."

The representative of the Jewish Agency, Dr. Silver, apparently had no complaint with respect to paragraph 4 provided the emphasis was in the right place. He laid the emphasis on the last words, "under present conditions". So do we.

Paragraph 5 of the report given this morning reads:

"The mandatory power has confirmed that a considerable number of incursions of illegal arms and armed elements into Palestine have occurred by land and sea."

For the information of the Security Council, I shall read the testimony obtained from the mandatory power on this point. The members have before them a document submitted by the Secretary-General. The portion which I shall read is found on the ninth page of the document. The questions referred to were addressed to the mandatory power.

"QUESTION 1: Have any incursions by armed elements from outside Palestine occurred in addition to those already reported to the Palestine Commission by the mandatory power?"

The members will note that the incursions referred to are in addition to those already reported. The following is the answer given to question 1.

"ANSWER 1: The following information is now available in addition to that already supplied:

"(a) On or about 24 February, between 500 and

---

¹ Made in the Security Council on Mar. 19, 1948 (U.N. doc. S/P. V. 271, Mar. 19, 1948).

Commission was "No." It observed, in this connection, that the Jews of Palestine generally accepted the plan, that the Arabs of Palestine generally opposed the plan; and that the mandatory power had declined to take any action which might be interpreted as involving implementation of the plan.

The Palestine Commission has repeated its view that it could not discharge its responsibilities on the termination of the mandate without the assistance of an adequate non-Palestinian armed force for the preservation of law and order. The Palestine Commission does not consider it possible to implement the plan by peaceful means either as a whole or in substantial part so long as the existing vigorous Arab resistance to partition exists.

The Palestine Commission considered itself unable, within the terms of the Resolution of the General Assembly, to consider whether any modification of the recommended plan might offer a basis for agreement among the people of Palestine.

With regard to the establishment of the provisional council or councils of government in the proposed Jewish and Arab States by 1 April 1948, the Palestine Commission has concluded: (a) that the attitude of the Arab Higher Committee and Arab resistance in Palestine preclude any possibility of selecting a provisional council of government for the proposed Arab State by 1 April, (b) that while the Palestine Commission can take and has in fact taken some preliminary steps toward the selection of the provisional council for the Jewish State, the provisional council will not be able to carry out its functions, in the sense of the plan, prior to the termination of the mandate, (c) the position of the mandatory power precludes any possibility of fulfilling by 1 April the provisions of the plan as regards either the Arab or the Jewish provisional council of government.

With regard to the City of Jerusalem, the Palestine Commission's view is that the administration of the City of Jerusalem by the United Nations is possible if the plan of partition with economic union is generally accepted by the Arab and Jewish communities of Palestine and peacefully implemented.

The permanent members of the Security Council held two discussions with the representative of the mandatory power last week. One of these was devoted to security problems, and the other to the implementation of the partition plan.

From the information supplied by the mandatory government, it appeared that several thousand Arabs have entered Palestine in bands of varying size, and have infiltrated the Palestinian population. The identification of these Arabs has not been firmly established, but it appears to be common knowledge in Palestine that they include nationals of most of the neighbouring Arab States and that they have entered from Lebanon, Syria, Transjordan, and Egypt. The United Kingdom reports that these bands are irregular formations and are not organized units of any national armed force.

The representative of the mandatory power was asked whether his Government considers that there is a threat of force against Palestine which now constitutes a threat to international peace, and also whether the existing situation in Palestine is a situation which constitutes a threat to the peace. He replied that his Government would furnish all the facts available but that the question of what constitutes a threat to the peace is for the Security Council to decide.

In response to questions concerning implementation of the General Assembly recommendation, the mandatory power stated that it has "accepted" the Plan of Partition with economic union recommended by the General Assembly, but that it cannot participate in its implementation. While it wished to avoid any action which might be considered as obstructive, it could not itself be instrumental in putting into effect a plan which is not accepted by both the Arabs and the Jews of Palestine.

The representative of the mandatory power informed the permanent members that his Government considered that it would be very difficult to carry out the Plan without the backing of force; that even if the Jewish militia were sufficiently armed to ensure the organization and protection of the Jewish State, such action would not be the equivalent of a settlement; that the United Kingdom did not believe that there were any modifications in detail which would make the Plan acceptable both to the Jews and Arabs of Palestine; and that no change in the timetable of British withdrawal from Palestine is contemplated by the United Kingdom. The representative of the United Kingdom further stated that his Government had no suggestions to make with regard to means by which the Jews and Arabs of Palestine might be brought together although successful efforts in this direction would be welcomed.

Representatives of the mandatory Government further indicated that there would be a very substantial deficit in the Palestinian budget following British withdrawal and that, while the Palestinian Government has been financially self-sufficient, the cost of maintaining British forces in Palestine is considerably larger than the total Palestinian budget of $96,000,000 annually.

Representatives of the Jewish Agency stated that the Jews of Palestine accept the partition Plan. The Agency claimed that the Plan represents, however, an irreducible minimum for the Jews of Palestine since it already involves a great reduction in what they consider their rightful claims. Also that, although there is no perfect or easy solution, the present Plan is the only practical solution reached after many other plans had failed

". . . whatever procedure the United Nations may decide to adopt with a view to assuming responsibility for the Government of Palestine on 15 May . . ."

He concluded with the statement:

"Finally, I must repeat that the United Kingdom must not enter into any new or extended commitment in regard to Palestine. Our contribution has already been made over the years and the date of termination of responsibility is irrevocably fixed."[1]

The status of Palestine will be equivocal because the United Kingdom seeks to give up the mandate. Article 5 of the mandate in respect of Palestine provides:

"The mandatory shall be responsible for seeing that no Palestine territory shall be ceded or leased to, or in any way placed under the control of, the government of any foreign power."

In the premises there is the urgent need for early clarification of the United Nations responsibility toward Palestine. The General Assembly and the Security Council have broad responsibilities and fidelity to the principles of justice and the aims of the Charter to assist in bringing about a pacific settlement of situations and disputes placed before them. The Security Council has specific obligations and powers where it finds a threat to the peace, breach of the peace, or act of aggression. I have already dealt, in my statements to the Security Council on 24 February and again on 2 March, with these responsibilities.

The assumption of administrative or governmental responsibility by the United Nations is another matter. If the United Nations is to act as a government, a large administrative task is involved. The Organization itself becomes directly responsible for all phases of the life of the people over whom such powers are exercised. It is a formidable responsibility, and a heavy financial commitment is incurred by all fifty-seven members of the Organization.

The United Nations does not automatically fall heir to the responsibilities either of the League of Nations or of the mandatory power in respect of the Palestine mandate. The record seems to us entirely clear that the United Nations did not take over the League of Nations mandate system.

The League of Nations Assembly on 18 April 1946, at its final session, passed a resolution which included the following two paragraphs:

"THE ASSEMBLY . . .

"3. RECOGNIZES THAT, on the termination of the League's existence, its functions with respect to the mandated territories will come to an end, but notes that Chapters XI, XII, and XIII of

[1] U.N. doc. S/P. V. 260, pp. 49-50.

the Charter of the United Nations embody principles corresponding to those declared in Article 22 of the Covenant of the League;

"4. TAKES NOTE of the expressed intentions of the Members of the League now administering territories under mandate to continue to administer them for the well-being and development of the peoples concerned in accordance with the obligations contained in the respective mandates,"— note these words—"until other arrangements have been agreed upon between the United Nations and the respective mandatory powers."

At the First Part of the First Session of the United Nations General Assembly, on 12 February 1946, the General Assembly passed a resolution regarding the transfer of certain functions, activities, and assets of the League of Nations to the United Nations. No transfer of functions concerning mandates was mentioned. The resolution included the statement that:

"The General Assembly will itself examine, or will submit to the appropriate organ of the United Nations, any request from the parties that the United Nations should assume the exercise of functions or powers entrusted to the League of Nations by treaties, international conventions, agreements, and other instruments having a political character."

Provision was made in the United Nations Charter for the voluntary placing of mandates under a trusteeship system by means of trusteeship agreements between the General Assembly or the Security Council and the states directly concerned, including the mandatory power. By such an agreement, the United Nations itself, under article 81 of the Charter, could become the administering authority for a trust territory. But no such proposal has been made by the mandatory power with respect to Palestine, and no action has been taken by the United Nations itself which would have that result.

A unilateral decision by the United Kingdom to terminate the Palestine mandate cannot automatically commit the United Nations to responsibility for governing that country. We think it clear that the United Nations does not succeed to administrative responsibility for Palestine merely because the latter is a mandate. Signing the Charter did not commit the signatories to a contingent liability for mandates, to become operative by the decisions of mandatory powers to abandon their mandates. On the facts reported by the permanent members, Palestine is a land falling under chapter XI of the United Nations Charter, a non-self-governing territory.

Does the General Assembly recommendation of 29 November 1947 constitute an acceptance by the United Nations of governmental responsibility for Palestine? Let us examine the facts.

On 2 April 1947, the United Kingdom directed

the Jews and Arabs of Palestine, who must live together, further opportunity to reach an agreement regarding the future government of that country. Such a United Nations trusteeship would, of course, be without prejudice to the character of the eventual political settlement, which we hope can be achieved without long delay. In our opinion, the Security Council should recommend the establishment of such a trusteeship to the General Assembly and to the mandatory power. This would require an immediate special session of the General Assembly, which the Security Council might call under the terms of the Charter. Pending the meeting of the special session of the General Assembly, we believe that the Security Council should instruct the Palestine Commission to suspend its efforts to implement the proposed partition plan.

I shall now read three propositions which are being submitted by the United States. I am not making any representation for any other one of the permanent members. The United States propositions are contained in a paper entitled "Additional Conclusions and Recommendations Concerning Palestine", which has been circulated to the members. It reads as follows:

"1. The plan proposed by the General Assembly is an integral plan which cannot succeed unless each of its parts can be carried out. There seems to be general agreement that the plan cannot now be implemented by peaceful means.

"2. We believe that further steps must be taken immediately not only to maintain the peace but also to afford a further opportunity to reach an agreement between the interested parties regarding the future government of Palestine. To this end we believe that a temporary trusteeship for Palestine should be established under the Trusteeship Council of the United Nations. Such a United Nations trusteeship would be without prejudice to the rights, claims or position of the parties concerned or to the character of the eventual political settlement, which we hope can be achieved without long delay. In our opinion, the Security Council should recommend the establishment of such a trusteeship to the General Assembly and to the mandatory power. This would require an immediate special session of the General Assembly, which the Security Council should request the Secretary-General to convoke under article 20 of the Charter.

"3. Pending the meeting of the proposed special session of the General Assembly, we believe that the Security Council should instruct the Palestine Commission to suspend its efforts to implement the proposed partition plan."

Draft resolutions which would give effect to the above suggestions will be circulated shortly for the consideration of the Security Council.

The position of the United States on Palestine was stated by Ambassador Austin in the Security Council on Friday.

The course of action with respect to the Palestine question which was proposed on March 19 by Ambassador Austin appeared to me, after the most careful consideration, to be the wisest course to follow. I recommended it to the President, and he approved my recommendation.

The primary and overriding consideration in that situation is the need to maintain the peace and to prevent chaos and wide-spread disorder upon the termination of the mandate on May 15, 1948. We believe that the United Nations should do everything it can to bring the fighting to an end and save the lives of the men, women, and children which would be lost in the bitter fighting which could otherwise be expected to follow the withdrawal of British troops.

The grave international situation which the President described in his message to the Congress on March 17 further emphasizes the compelling importance of preventing the outbreak of open warfare in Palestine. The interest of the United States in a peaceful settlement in Palestine arises not only out of deep humanitarian considerations but also out of vital elements of our national security.

The United States supported the partition plan for Palestine in the General Assembly last autumn.

Since that time we have explored every possibility of a peaceful implementation of that recommendation. We sought to have the Security Council accept the plan as a basis for its own action in the matter. This it refused to do on March 5, 1948. We then sought to find through consultations among the five principal powers some basis of agreement on which the partition plan might go forward by peaceful means. These consultations were unsuccessful in developing any measure

Current United Nations Documents: A

Trusteeship Council

Second Session. Draft Statute for the City of Jerusalem. T/118, Jan. 26, 1948. 29 pp. mimeo.

³ Made at a press conference in Los Angeles, Calif., on Mar. 20, 1948, and released to the press on the same date.

⁴ Printed materials may be secured in the United States from the International Documents Service, Columbia University Press, 2960 Broadway, New York City. Other materials (mimeographed, or processed documents) may be consulted at certain designated libraries in the United States.

Regarding Czechoslovakia

PRESENTATIVE OF CHILE [1]

In the opinion of the Permanent Representative of Czechoslovakia, these facts involve a violation of the Treaty of Friendship and Mutual Assistance of 12 December 1943, constitute an obvious threat to world peace and security and a flagrant violation of Article 2, paragraph 4, of the San Francisco Charter. The Security Council should therefore investigate them, in accordance with Article 34 of the Charter.

My Government has been informed that you have refused the request of the Permanent Representative of Czechoslovakia, because you consider it as coming from a non-governmental organization and not, therefore, as a communication from a Member State.

Without wishing to give an opinion on the propriety of the step you have taken with regard to the Czechoslovak Representative's request, and without implying that I accept his status as a private individual and not the legitimate representative of his Government, as you have suggested, I have the honour on behalf of Chile, which I represent before the United Nations, on personal and direct instructions from the President of the Republic, to request you to refer the question raised by the Permanent Representative of Czechoslovakia in the above-mentioned letter, to the

sentatives of the Government of the Union of Soviet Socialist Republics who came to Praha for that purpose, led by V. A. Zorin, Deputy Minister of Foreign Affairs.

"The political independence of Czechoslovakia, a member of the United Nations, has thus been violated by threat of use of force of another member of the United Nations, the Union of Soviet Socialist Republics, in direct infringement of Paragraph 4, Article 2 of the Charter.

"As representative of the Sovereign state of Czechoslovakia, I bring this situation, referred to in Article 34 of the Charter, to the attention of Security Council, asking its investigation, as one that is suppressing freedom and independence of Czechoslovakia, and which is likely to endanger the maintenance of international peace and security.

"It is very clear that the *coup* by the Communist minority by force was effectuated successfully only because of official participation of representatives of the Union of Soviet Socialist Republics and because of the threat of the use of military force of the Union of Soviet Socialist Republics in readiness on the north-west boundaries of Czechoslovakia. Official and military representatives of the Union of Soviet Socialist Republics participated in closed and public meetings of the Communist party and stayed long enough to see organized terror take hold of the free democratic Czechoslovakia people. Pictures taken in the streets of Prague, published in the world press, show

Security Council, for the purposes set forth in that letter.

In making this request, I am using the right conferred by Article 35, paragraph 1, of the Charter on all Members of the United Nations.

The Chilean Government considers that the responsible and authoritative accusation of the Permanent Delegate of Czechoslovakia is of such a serious nature that a mere reason of formality, such as the alleged lack of status of Mr. Papanek, cannot be allowed to prevent the institution whose specific task is to safeguard world peace and security, from making the necessary investigations to prove the truth of this accusation. If the events mentioned in Mr. Papanek's denunciation prove to be true—and everything seems to indicate that they are—it would mean that the world is again facing an exact repetition of the actions and methods which were employed by Nazi Germany in the years preceding the last World War, and were its immediate cause. It would therefore

---

the officers of the Soviet Union with armed police, clad in new Czechoslovak uniforms, participating in the meetings and demonstrations.

"Since the *Coup* of the Communist minority, the President of the Republic has not been permitted to make any public appearance, or public utterance, has been allowed to receive no visitors, except Vabrian Zorin, the Deputy Foreign Minister of the Soviet Socialist Republics whom he refused to receive, and is not a free agent, while the Communist usurpers spread terror and break every law which establishes and protects the freedom of men and democratically established institutions, even while they say they are carrying out the will of the people.

"The Constitution of Czechoslovakia, adopted in 1920, states that the people are the sole source of state power and provides for general secret elections through which the people express their will. Masses of people driven by terror and the threat of the loss of their jobs into public squares of Czechoslovak cities and towns to demonstrate or to strike, cannot be considered as expressing the will of the people. Yet, claiming that such demonstrations with the participation of official and military representatives of the Union of Soviet Socialist Republics express the will of the people, a minority party usurped the power of the government of Czechoslovakia and is imposing its rule upon all the people without regard for the Constitution or the law.

"The President is prevented from executing his constitutional powers. Political parties have been forced to change their leaders. Many regularly elected members of Parliament have not only been removed from Office, but deprived of their Parliamentary immunity. Many have been brutally beaten and jailed. University professors, judges, high officials in all governmental departments who refuse to bow to the communist dictatorship have been dismissed or demoted. Students who refuse to pledge loyalty to the new "order" are expelled from the universities. The rights and privileges of citizens guaranteed by the Constitutions are being flagrantly violated. The Official lists of names of individuals faithful to the democratic principles who have been arrested without legal grounds are increasing daily. Personal liberty is restricted. Many dismissed intellectuals are forced to manual labour. The right of private ownership of property is violated. To travel or emigrate is prohibited except for the chosen few. The inviolability of the home no longer exists. The freedom of the press has been

an solidarity, Chile cannot remain indifferent ›re the events described by the representative of choslovakia. No country which is a Member he United Nations, however small or however ote from the theatre of events in question, can de the responsibilities of solidarity deriving m the Charter and from the conviction that ther world war would be a catastrophe whose sequences no part of the world could escape. taking the present attitude, my Government eves that it is making the only possible contri- ion, within its limited means and the present umstances, to the common task of preventing disaster. It believes also that it is thereby illing its duty, as a signatory to the San Fran- o Charter, of ensuring that the Organization ms its status as a decisive instrument for the ntenance of world peace. It is not difficult to ›cast that failure by the United Nations to rvene in the situation before us would result in of its prestige and a consequent reduction of future effectiveness. The Chilean Govern- t's attitude, therefore, is motivated by its ›tion to the United Nations' cause and its ere respect for democracy and human dignity. ut there is another moral reason which leads Government to sponsor the Czechoslovak dele- e's request that his country's case should be estigated and considered. In October last ile was obliged to sever diplomatic relations h the Union of Soviet Socialist Republics and th Yugoslavia, because those countries were erfering in her internal affairs (trying to dis- ›t and hamper production of the basic raw terials such as copper and nitrates, which Chile ›orts to friendly countries) through the illegal 'olutionary action of a national group working their interest. The objects of this action, which ncide completely with those of her intervention Czechoslovakia, demonstrate the extent and ture of the Union of Soviet Socialist Republics' ıns and prove that neither geographical situa- n nor greater or lesser degrees of strength or e, or a country's love of peace, or indifference it, are factors which can have any influence in ıbling a country to avoid becoming involved in onflict such as a great power like the Union of viet Socialist Republics might undertake. ıus the Chilean Government on that occasion ıst reluctantly felt obliged to extend its sever-

ance of relations to the Czechoslovak Government. It did so because it had proof that agents of that Government were taking part alongside those of the other countries mentioned, in truly aggressive activities, by paralyzing the economic life of Chile, as I have stated. The Chilean Government under- stood that this was happening without the knowl- edge of President Benes and Mr. Masaryk, his Minister for Foreign Affairs, whose democratic and pacifist opinions have always been beyond doubt, and that it was merely the international manifestation of action being taken inside the country by elements which, shielded by the demo- cratic National Coalition Government, were pre- paring the *coup* of 22 February. However, we were obliged to break off our traditional friendly relations with Czechoslovakia, in defence of our elementary duty to defend the country against the intervention of foreign powers desirous of dis- turbing production and overthrowing the demo- cratic constitutional regime which Chile has en- joyed since achieving her independence.

Now that events have proved the rightness of the Chilean point of view and justified the true reasons which led my Government to take such steps, we wish to render homage to the noble Czech people—for whom we feel a deep admira- tion and respect—by supporting in our capacity as a Member of the United Nations, the just de- mands made in their name by their Permanent Representative to the United Nations.

In view of the foregoing considerations, I re- peat to you, in the name of my Government, our request that the case be brought before the Secu- rity Council, in order that, in accordance with Article 34 of the United Nations Charter, it may investigate the events reported by the Permanent Representative of Czechoslovakia, Mr. Jan Papanek, which constitute a threat to interna- tional peace and security.

I also request you to communicate to the Secu- rity Council, our petition that, in conformity with Article 31 of the Charter, my country be invited to participate in the discussion of this matter, when it is brought before the Security Council.

I have the honour to be [etc.]

HERNAN SANTA CRUZ
Ambassador, Permanent Representative of Chile to the United Nations.

STATEMENT BY AMBASSADOR WARREN R. AUSTIN [1]
U.S. Representative in the Security Council

A decision on the question now pending is not lecision on the substance, and it will not con- ‌tute a judgment upon the merits. But when the ›stion is raised, as it is here, as to whether an m should be placed on the agenda for discussion not, there must be a consideration of the char- ‌er of the question in order to learn whether the

competence of the Security Council reaches the item.

[1] Made in the Security Council on Mar. 17, 1948, and re- leased to the press by the U.S. Mission to the United Na- tions on the same date. At the time of going to press only an unofficial transcript of remarks was available. For text of remarks see U.N. doc. S/P. V. 268, Mar. 17, 1948.

Now, here we have charges made in a formal complaint which are grave and which involve two members of the United Nations, and now we have countercharges. Briefly, the item involves this issue: On its face the Chilean complaint, by reference to Mr. Papanek's communication, alleges that the political independence of Czechoslovakia, a Member of the United Nations, has been violated by threat of the use of force by another Member of the United Nations, namely, the Soviet Union. It further refers to the statement in that communication that the Czechoslovakian *coup* was effectuated successfully only because of official participation of representatives of the Soviet Union and threat of the use of military forces of the Soviet Union in readiness on the northwestern boundaries of Czechoslovakia. The Chilean complaint requests investigation of these allegations.

If these allegations are true, the matter would clearly not be essentially within the jurisdiction of Czechoslovakia because it would be a situation resulting from illegal action by one Member against another. Secondly, the Security Council, in order to be able to determine whether the case comes within the meaning of article 2, subparagraph 7, must consider the Chilean complaint, and, of course, it cannot consider the Chilean complaint if it is not put on the agenda.

But, since we opened our hearing on the question of adding this item to the agenda, the remarks made by the distinguished representative of the Soviet Union constitute a countercharge. M. Papanek, who has represented a distinguished Member of the United Nations, is charged here as being a "traitor". This matter is also rendered very much more important by the opprobrious attack upon Chile. The suggestion that Chile is not acting upon her own initiative as a distinguished Member of the United Nations, but is a "puppet" commanded by "external circles" who work through their "lackeys", is a charge which renders this item much more important than it was solely upon the complaint made by Chile.

But there are other allegations in the statement by the representative of the Soviet Union that reflect upon the press of the United States of America—"venal and calumnious American newspapers"; another charge of "yellow" newspaper. I could not follow this fast enough to get the exact language, but you recall "yellow press of America", and the charge of "warmongering" against people in the United States of America, including very highly placed persons.

Now, I ask the Security Council if it can evade or avoid the responsibility that is placed upon it to give these charges a hearing—all of them. For this reason the United States will vote to place this item on the agenda.

Discussion in the Interim Committee on the Problem of Voting in the Security Council [1]

U. S. PROPOSALS [1]

I. Study of Categories of Security Council Decisions

A. The Interim Committee should study the categories of decisions which the Security Council is required to make in carrying out the functions entrusted to it under the Charter and the Statute of the International Court of Justice, and should report to the General Assembly those categories of decisions which in its judgment, in order to ensure the effective exercise by the Security Council of its responsibilities under the Charter, should be made by an affirmative vote of seven members of the Security Council, whether or not such categories are regarded as procedural or non-procedural. (A provisional proposed list of such categories is attached.)

B. The Interim Committee should recommend to the General Assembly:

"3. Report, with its conclusions, to the third session the General Assembly, the report to be transmitted the Secretary-General not later than 15 July 1948, and by the Secretary-General to the Member States and the General Assembly."

On Jan. 9, 1948, the Interim Committee, by resolution asked that proposals on the problem of voting in the Security Council be transmitted to the Secretary-General on or before Mar. 15, 1948.

[1] U.N. doc. A/AC.18/41, Mar. 10, 1948. By a resolution adopted on Nov. 21, 1947, the General Assembly requested its Interim Committee to—
"1. Consider the problem of voting in the Security Council, taking into account all proposals which have been or may be submitted by Members of the United Nations to the second session of the General Assembly or to the Interim Committee;
"2. Consult with any committee which the Security Council may designate to cooperate with the Interim Committee in the study of the problem;

412

11. Decisions concerning the time and place of its regular and periodic meetings pursuant to Article 28 (2) and Article 28 (3).

12. Establishment of subsidiary organs pursuant to Article 29.

13. The election of a President pursuant to Article 30.

14. Adoption of Rules of Procedure pursuant to Article 30.

15. Decisions to permit the participation of Members of the United Nations in the discussion of any question where the Council considers that the interests of the Member are specially affected pursuant to Article 31.

16. Decisions to invite a Member State which is not a Member of the Security Council, or a State not a Member of the United Nations which is a party to a dispute under consideration by the Council, to participate without vote in the discussion relating to the dispute pursuant to Article 32.

17. Decisions with respect to conditions for the participation of a State which is not a Member of the United Nations in the Security Council discussions in accordance with Article 32.

18. Decisions to consider and discuss a matter brought to the attention of the Council.

19. Decisions to call upon the parties to a dispute to settle their dispute by peaceful means of their own choice pursuant to Article 33 (2).

20. Decisions to investigate a dispute or a situation which might lead to international friction or give rise to a dispute, pursuant to Article 34.

21. Decisions to recommend appropriate procedures or methods of adjustment of a dispute or situation endangering the maintenance of international peace and security, pursuant to Article 36 (1).

22. Decisions of the Security Council pursuant to Article 36 (3) to recommend to the parties to a legal dispute that the dispute should be referred by the parties to the International Court of Justice in accordance with provisions of the Statute of the Court.

23. Decisions to make recommendations at the request of all parties to a dispute with a view to its pacific settlement, pursuant to Article 38.

24. Decisions to request assistance from the Economic and Social Council pursuant to Article 65.

25. Reference of a legal question to the International Court of Justice for an advisory opinion pursuant to Article 96 (1).

26. Decision to convoke a conference to review the Charter prior to the Tenth Annual Session of the General Assembly pursuant to Article 109 (1).

27. Decision to convoke a conference to review the Charter subsequent to the Tenth Annual Session of the General Assembly pursuant to Article 109 (3).

[2] 28. Election of judges of the International Court of Justice pursuant to Article 4 (1), Article 10 (1) of the Statute of the Court. (Article 10 (2) of the Statute).

29. Decisions of the Security Council determining the conditions under which a State which is a party to the present Statute of the International Court of Justice, but which is not a Member of the United Nations, may participate in electing

STATEMENT BY P

U.S. Deputy Representative

The Interim Committee is considering the veto at the request of the General Assembly contained in its resolution of November 21, 1947, which "requests the Interim Committee of the General Assembly . . . to consider the problem of voting in the Security Council, taking into account all proposals which have been or may be submitted by Members of the United Nations to the second session of the General Assembly or to the Interim Committee."

The Interim Committee in order to give effect to the request of the General Assembly, on January 9, 1948, adopted a resolution which requested the Members of the United Nations who desire to submit proposals on the problem of voting in the Security Council to transmit them to the Secretary-General on or before March 15, 1948, and further requested the Chairman to bring up the problem before the Interim Committee not later than March 15, 1948.

The General Assembly resolution contemplated three phases of action on this problem: action by this Committee, continued action by the Security Council and conferences between our Committee and a committee of the Security Council.

In addition the General Assembly resolution requested consultations among the Permanent Members "in order to secure agreement among them on measures to ensure the prompt and effective exercise by the Security Council of its functions."   .

It would seem appropriate at this time to indicate the progress which has been made since January 9 in the direction of giving effect to the General Assembly program.

In the first place a number of proposals are now before the Interim Committee. We believe that these proposals furnish an excellent starting point for the studies of this Committee.

As to the second phase of action contemplated in the General Assembly resolution, Committee 1 of

---

[2] These decisions are made by 'an absolute majority of votes in the General Assembly and in the Security Council".

[3] Made on Mar. 15, 1948, before the Interim Committee and released to the press by the U.S. Mission to the U.N. on the same date.

cedure to matters essential to the maintenance of international peace and security. The Charter requires unanimity of the major powers only in substantive decisions by the Security Council. There is no requirement for unanimity in the Assembly, in the Economic and Social Council and in the Trusteeship Council. . . .

"This does not mean that unanimity or the closest possible approximation to it is not to be desired and striven for in all these organs. It means only that it was not deemed essential to apply the principle to the voting procedures.

"Those organs and agencies do not have the power to enforce the law. That power rests with the Security Council and that is the reason why the Members of the United Nations applied the principle of unanimity to the voting procedures of the Security Council and not to the voting procedures in any of the other institutions of the United Nations.

"The large nations that are Permanent Members of the Council possess the power to keep peace in the world—to enforce observance of the law. The Charter does not give them that power. It recognizes that power and places obligations upon these nations to use that power in accordance with the law."

The United States continues to adhere to the viewpoint which Ambassador Austin expressed so forcefully more than two years ago. The proposals of the United States suggest 31 separate items which come up in a study of the veto. The proposals of China, the United Kingdom, and New Zealand contain other suggestions, and additional ones may be raised in the course of our discussion. I agree that the study of those items will necessarily be a technical study. The problem is a technical one. There is no simple formula which can be applied as a "cure-all" and which will automatically result in the liberalization of the voting procedure and immediate improvement in the effectiveness of the Security Council. The United States feels that progress can best be achieved in the General Assembly through careful study. To quote Mr. Dulles concerning the nature of the study: "It is not a study which is designed to produce any predetermined result or to produce any specific diminution of the veto power, but it is a study of the problem to the end that the General Assembly next year will be able to approach this problem with more light and less heat than was the case at the last General Assembly. We felt that a good deal of violence and antagonism which marked the discussions in the General Assemblies both in 1946 and 1947 was largely due to the fact that the problem had not been adequately studied and its difficulties adequately perceived."

To come to the specific United States proposals

which are now before this Committee, the United States first suggests that the Interim Committee should study the categories of decisions which the Security Council is required to make in carrying out the functions entrusted to it under the Charter and the Statute of the International Court of Justice and should report to the General Assembly those categories of decisions which in its judgment, in order to insure the effective exercise by the Security Council of its responsibilities under the Charter, should be made by an affirmative vote of seven members of the Security Council.

It is apparent from the resolution of November 21 that in giving the Interim Committee this task the General Assembly was exercising its power to make recommendations "relating to the powers and functions of any organs of the United Nations" (article 10 of the Charter). It therefore seemed most appropriate to us that the study in the Interim Committee should deal primarily with the functioning of the Security Council and that the Interim Committee conclusions and the General Assembly recommendations should be directed to the desired result; namely, to the liberalization of voting procedures in connection with those decisions of the Security Council where such liberalization is most likely in fact to result in the improved operation of the Council.

The United States proposal goes on to recommend that the General Assembly accept the conclusions which the Interim Committee may reach on this subject and "that the General Assembly as a first step recommend to the Permanent Members of the Security Council that they mutually agree that such voting procedures be followed and that steps be taken to make their agreement effective." We recognize that after the General Assembly has made recommendations for liberalization of the voting procedures, the task of accomplishing such liberalization may be a difficult one. The most effective way of securing improvement in the operations of the Security Council would be through agreement of the permanent members. Mr. Dulles stated this to the First Committee of the General Assembly and Ambassador Austin repeated the statement before this Committee on January 9. "We realize that without such agreement, it will be difficult to accomplish great practical results. Charter amendment requires the approval of all five. It may perhaps prove possible to get agreement on certain Charter amendments and certainly there is an important area in which existing procedures could be liberalized without alteration of Article 27."

We believe that the permanent members will all give great weight to whatever recommendations may be made by the General Assembly on this subject and we are therefore proposing that the General Assembly recommend to the permanent members that they mutually agree to follow the voting

ability of such consultations. The General Assembly resolution of December 13, 1946 "requests the Permanent Members in consultation with one another, to insure that the use of the special voting privilege does not impede the Security Council in reaching decisions promptly." The General Assembly resolution of November 21, 1947 requests consultations among the permanent members on the problem of voting. The United States proposal goes somewhat further than either of the previous General Assembly resolutions but goes no further than the statements of the permanent members themselves. All of the permanent members have stated in the General Assembly that such consultations are desirable. We believe that the second part of our proposal complements the first part and that its adoption will assist the Security Council in effectively performing its functions.

In conclusion, we sincerely hope that the studies in this Committee will result in a fuller understanding of this extremely difficult and technical subject, and that as a result of this study, this Committee will reach enlightened and constructive conclusions that have the support of the overwhelming force of world opinion. If those conclusions are converted into realities through their adoption in practice, the United Nations will be a more effective instrument for the accomplishment of its great purposes.

U.S. Delegation to Ninth International Conference of American States

[Released to the press by the White House March 19]

The President on March 19 named the following as members of the United States Delegation to the Ninth International Conference of American States, to be held at Bogotá, Colombia, beginning March 30, 1948:

Chairman:

George C. Marshall, Secretary of State

Delegates:

Willard L. Beaulac, Ambassador to Colombia
John W. Snyder, Secretary of the Treasury
W. Averell Harriman, Secretary of Commerce
Norman Armour, Assistant Secretary of State for political affairs, Department of State
Ernest A. Gross, Legal Adviser, Department of State
William D. Pawley, Ambassador to Brazil
Walter J. Donnelly, Ambassador to Venezuela
William McC. Martin, Jr., Chairman, Board of Directors Export-Import Bank of Washington
Paul C. Daniels, Director, Office of American Republic Affairs, Department of State

The Delegation will be accompanied by a group of advisers and a technical and administrative staff.

THE RECORD OF THE WEEK

Toward Securing the Peace and Preventing War

ADDRESS BY THE PRESIDENT TO THE CONGRESS[1]

March 17, 1948

MR. PRESIDENT, MR. SPEAKER, MEMBERS OF THE CONGRESS:

I am here today to report to you on the critical nature of the situation in Europe, and to recommend action for your consideration.

Rapid changes are taking place in Europe which affect our foreign policy and our national security. There is an increasing threat to nations which are striving to maintain a form of government which grants freedom to its citizens. The United States is deeply concerned with the survival of freedom in those nations. It is of vital importance that we act now, in order to preserve the conditions under which we can achieve lasting peace based on freedom and justice.

The achievement of such a peace has been the great goal of this nation.

Almost three years have elapsed since the end of the greatest of all wars, but peace and stability have not returned to the world. We were well aware that the end of the fighting would not automatically settle the problems arising out of the war. The establishment of peace after the fighting is over has always been a difficult task. And even if all the Allies of World War II were united in their desire to establish a just and honorable peace, there would still be great difficulties in the way of achieving that goal.

But the situation in the world today is not primarily the result of the natural difficulties which follow a great war. It is chiefly due to the fact that one nation has not only refused to cooperate in the establishment of a just and honorable peace, but—even worse—has actively sought to prevent it.

The Congress is familiar with the course of events.

You know of the sincere and patient attempts of the democratic nations to find a secure basis for peace through negotiation and agreement. Conference after conference has been held in different parts of the world. We have tried to settle the questions arising out of the war on a basis which would permit the establishment of a just peace. You know the obstacles we have encountered. But the record stands as a monument to the good faith and integrity of the democratic nations of the world. The agreements we did obtain, imperfect though they were, could have furnished the basis for a just peace—if they had been kept.

But they were not kept.

They have been persistently ignored and violated by one nation.

The Congress is also familiar with the developments concerning the United Nations. Most of the countries of the world have joined together in the United Nations in an attempt to build a world order based on law and not on force. Most of the members support the United Nations earnestly and honestly, and seek to make it stronger and more effective.

One nation, however, has persistently obstructed the work of the United Nations by constant abuse

---

Statement by Ambassador Warren R. Austin

The President's declaration of the acts necessary to support the purposes and principles of the United Nations Charter has my full support. I am more persuaded than ever that we need universal military training as a permanent policy and I believe that right now we need the reenactment of selective service. The European Recovery Program has had my hearty endorsement from the beginning.

I think the President was moderate in his statements on the critical situation now confronting the people of the world. The issues that have confronted the United Nations from the outset have been difficult in themselves; but they have become increasingly serious in their reflection of the division between the Soviet Union and the rest of the United Nations.

The position of the United States in its discharge of its inescapable responsibilities and as a force for the solution of the problems before us by agreement, will be improved if our military posture is strengthened. The President's emphasis on the United Nations demonstrates that everything he said is aimed toward the pacific solution of our problems.

---

[1] This address was also printed as Department of State publication 3102, General Foreign Policy Series 2.

a movement toward common self-protection in the face of the growing menace to their freedom.

At the very moment I am addressing you, five nations of the European community, in Brussels, are signing a 50-year agreement for economic cooperation and common defense against aggression.

This action has great significance, for this agreement was not imposed by the decree of a more powerful neighbor. It was the free choice of independent governments representing the will of their people, and acting within the terms of the Charter of the United Nations.

Its significance goes far beyond the actual terms of the agreement itself. It is a notable step in the direction of unity in Europe for the protection and preservation of its civilization. This development deserves our full support. I am confident that the United States will, by appropriate means, extend to the free nations the support which the situation requires. I am sure that the determination of the free countries of Europe to protect themselves will be matched by an equal determination on our part to help them to do so.

The recent developments in Europe present this nation with fundamental issues of vital importance.

I believe that we have reached a point at which the position of the United States should be made unmistakably clear.

The principles and purposes expressed in the Charter of the United Nations continue to represent our hope for the eventual establishment of the rule of law in international affairs. The Charter constitutes the basic expression of the code of international ethics to which this country is dedicated. We cannot, however, close our eyes to the harsh fact that through obstruction and even defiance on the part of one nation, this great dream has not yet become a full reality.

It is necessary, therefore, that we take additional measures to supplement the work of the United Nations and to support its aims. There are times in world history when it is far wiser to act than to hesitate. There is some risk involved in action—there always is. But there is far more risk in failure to act.

For if we act wisely now, we shall strengthen the powerful forces for freedom, justice, and peace which are represented by the United Nations and the free nations of the world.

I regard it as my duty, therefore, to recommend to the Congress those measures which, in my judgment, are best calculated to give support to the free and democratic nations of Europe and to improve the solid foundation of our own national strength.

First, I recommend that the Congress speedily complete its action on the European Recovery Program. That program is the foundation of our policy of assistance to the free nations of Europe.

Prompt passage of that program is the most telling contribution we can now make toward peace.

The decisive action which the Senate has taken without regard to partisan political considerations is a striking example of the effective working of democracy.

Time is now of critical importance. I am encouraged by the information which has come to me concerning the plans for expeditious action by the House of Representatives. I hope that no single day will be needlessly lost.

Second, I recommend prompt enactment of universal training legislation.

Until the free nations of Europe have regained their strength, and so long as Communism threatens the very existence of democracy, the United States must remain strong enough to support those countries of Europe which are threatened with Communist control and police-state rule.

I believe that we have learned the importance of maintaining military strength as a means of preventing war. We have found that a sound military system is necessary in time of peace if we are to remain at peace. Aggressors in the past, relying on our apparent lack of military force, have unwisely precipitated war. Although they have been led to destruction by their misconception of our strength, we have paid a terrible price for our unpreparedness.

Universal training is the only feasible means by which the civilian components of our armed forces can be built up to the strength required if we are to be prepared for emergencies. Our ability to mobilize large numbers of trained men in time of emergency could forestall future conflict and, together with other measures of national policy, could restore stability to the world.

The adoption of universal training by the United States at this time would be unmistakable evidence to all the world of our determination to back the will to peace with the strength for peace. I am convinced that the decision of the American people, expressed through the Congress, to adopt universal training would be of first importance in giving courage to every free government in the world.

Third, I recommend the temporary reenactment of selective-service legislation in order to maintain our armed forces at their authorized strength.

Our armed forces lack the necessary men to maintain their authorized strength. They have been unable to maintain their authorized strength through voluntary enlistments, even though such strength has been reduced to the very minimum necessary to meet our obligations abroad and is far below the minimum which should always be available in the continental United States.

We cannot meet our international responsibilities unless we maintain our armed forces. It is of vital importance, for example, that we keep our

Relation of Military Strength to Diplomatic Action

BY GEORGE C. MARSHALL [1]

Secretary of State

MR. CHAIRMAN: You gentlemen have asked me to give my views on the need of our country taking at this time further measures to assure the national security. Any such measures must obviously relate to the foreign policy of the United States. In the world in which we live our national security can no longer be effectively weighed and dealt with in terms of the Western Hemisphere alone.

The President has spoken to the Congress this morning in joint session. You have before you the text of his address. It is not necessary for me to repeat what he said.

I wish to express in person to you my own concern over the accelerated trend in Europe. In the short years since the end of hostilities this trend has grown from a trickle into a torrent. One by one, the Balkan States, except Greece, lost all semblance of national independence. Then two friendly nations—first Hungary and last week Czechoslovakia—have been forced into complete submission to the Communist control.

Within one month the people of Italy, whose Government we had a large part in reconstituting, will hold a national election. The outcome of that election has an importance far beyond local Italian affairs. It will decide not only whether Italy will continue with its restoration into a true democracy. It will foretell whether the disintegrating trend to which I have referred may reach the shores of the Atlantic.

It is said that history never repeats itself. Yet as these free people one by one are subjugated to police-state control even the blind may see in that subjugation of liberty a deadly parallel.

The Government of the United States has undertaken steps to meet this disintegrating trend in the heart of Europe. The comprehensive proposal in this regard is the Recovery Program legislation now under active consideration in the House. This program, I believe, is a fundamental requirement for the strengthening of the western nations of Europe.

But this economic program in the existing situation is not a complete answer. It is said that one cannot buy peace and prosperity with dollars. The accelerating march of events in European areas has now made it clear that reliance for the future safety of those areas cannot be placed alone on the slow processes of reconstruction financed with our help. There is something more for the United States to do. We must show, conclusively, by decisive legislative action, to all the nations of the world that the United States intends to be strong and to hold that strength ready to keep the European world both at peace and free.

Diplomatic action, without the backing of military strength, in the present world can lead only to appeasement. The President today indicated that we have made every effort of negotiation, and of organization in the United Nations, to find a way to understandings and agreement. I said in my final report as Chief of Staff in 1945, "War is not the choice of those who wish passionately for peace; it is the choice of those who are willing to resort to violence for political advantage".

I regard the present military policy of this Government as one based largely on meeting the problems of attrition, with the contrasting necessity for larger and larger appropriations to give us security.

Perhaps my meaning could be made clearer by a comparison of the German procedure under Hitler with that proposed under a policy of universal military training. The Nazis devoted all the resources of Germany in preparation for war on a given date, September 1, 1939. The purpose and procedure under universal military training is exactly the opposite. We would be striving to avoid such dates. We want peace; we want to avoid war. Therefore, among other things, we want a system which will be bearable financially, which will not bankrupt the country, a system which, adjusted to world conditions, can be continued at a minimum of cost and personal contribution, a system in accordance with our traditions and strong desires.

I see no possible way financially to maintain a reasonable military posture except on the foundation of universal military training. The consideration of this subject has been confused by discussions of amounts, requirements, administration, and various conflicting beliefs. The clear-cut issue is whether or not this country will stand before the world for at least the next five or ten years in a position appropriate to its leadership in furthering the perpetuation of free governments and avoiding their transition into police states. We desire a state of affairs which would make repetitions of the fate of Hungary and Czechoslovakia, the intimidation of Finland, the

---

[1] Made before the Armed Services Committee of the Senate on Mar. 17, 1948, and released to the press on the same date.

subversive operations in Italy and France, and the cold-blooded efforts to destroy the Greek Government unlikely, because they would definitely be fraught with real danger to those who would attempt such action.

Many of the measures complementary to universal military training would be strengthened and facilitated by the latter. The maintenance of the Army, the Navy, and the Air Force at suitable strength on a volunteer basis would be made easier, I am sure. But what is much more important, the National Guard would be greatly strengthened and made a vital citizen force immediately available in an emergency, which it cannot be under existing conditions. The quality of the R.O.T.C. would be much improved, the training put on a higher level, and the time for such training materially shortened. Finally, universal military training would bring to millions of American families a sense of individual and collective responsibility of the duty to help assure security and peace for ourselves and for the world. There is evidence that the majority of American men and women are ready to follow courageous leadership toward that end.

Due to the rapid dwindling in the strength of our armed forces, the temporary application of selective service is also necessary. A reconsideration of our air program is necessary, but first of all I am convinced that the decision of the American people to adopt the democratic procedure of universal training would strengthen every free government. The combination of two things, the enactment of the European Recovery Program on the one hand and a decision by the American people that clearly indicates that they are determined their course, is necessary now, I think, to the maintenance of peace in the world.

Referring to a discussion of universal military training in my final report as Chief of Staff, September 1945, I closed with these words: "I can fortify ourselves against disaster, I am convinced, by the measures I have here outlined. In these protections we can face the future with reasonable hope for the best and with quiet assurance that even though the worst may come, we are prepared for it."

World-Wide Struggle Between Freedom and Tyranny

BY GEORGE C. MARSHALL [1]
Secretary of State

I am honored by the invitation of the University of California to participate in this Charter Day celebration. I am particularly glad to be present because, except for hurried military inspections of a few hours' duration during the war or brief stopovers en route to and from the Far East, I had no opportunity to accept any of the numerous hospitable invitations I have received from California. My first contact with the University was to assist the then Dean Barrows in the instruction of a few of your R.O.T.C. students on a week-end camping trip. That, I think, was in 1916. During the holiday period of that year I was asked to speak at the first convention of the personnel of the Forestry Department on the west coast which was held in one of your lecture rooms. Those represent my previous contacts with the University.

For a number of years I have been deeply interested in educational procedures. You may not have realized it, but effective and expeditious instructional procedure has been a very important requirement imposed by our military policy—a policy which has always involved the hasty development of military forces after the arrival of the emergency. Your tremendous plant, instructional procedure, and large student body are of great interest to me, particularly during these days when so many former service men are students in the colleges and universities. In that connection, I must be frank to admit that I once felt the Government would receive only a small return for its financial outlay in guaranteeing to our veterans their present educational opportunities. I have been proved completely wrong in my anticipation, for I am told, wherever I go in the educational world, that the veterans have not only done extraordinarily well, but that they have set a high standard for the universities and future students to maintain. At Amherst last June I addressed graduating class of which 80 percent were veterans, and the experience there led me to speculate regarding the future effect on this country of a citizenship dominated by men and women who have seen much of the world, not hurriedly, but intimately for years at a time and have had their own characters tested by the hardships and dangers to which they were exposed. This broad experience, followed later by a college or university education at a mature age, will be productive of a new brand of citizen whose wisdom and foresight may avoid the dangers of our past mistakes.

Everyone's thoughts turn today to the situation abroad—Europe, the Middle East, and the Far

[1] An address delivered at the University of California at Berkeley, Calif., on Mar. 19, 1948, and released to the press on the same date.

of freedom and justice we have always upheld by every means available.

I would make the same comment regarding the general world situation but in this case applying it more to the problem of just where and how we should exert our influence. Unfortunately, critical situations are not confined to Europe. They exist in the Middle East, in Indonesia, in China—and we cannot ignore Latin America, or our direct responsibilities in Japan and Korea. Therefore, very important decisions must be made by our Government as to exactly what we should do to meet these various crises. Our means are not unlimited—we must not spend our efforts unwisely.

As a matter of fact, I find the present situation disturbingly similar to that with which I labored as Chief of Staff. I watched the Nazi Government take control of one country after another until finally Poland was invaded in a direct military operation. For several years I had to withstand heavy pressures from various theaters of operation in the world for assistance—support in the form of matériel—without regard to our then extremely limited resources available in the United States. Later, after our entry into the war, these pressures greatly increased in the demand for support to an extent which if met would have rendered us ineffective, I think, on almost every field of action. This situation continued up to the time of our landings in Normandy and even after the liberation of France still continued regarding our forces in Italy and in the western Pacific.

I find myself in virtually the same position today as I was during those war years, and the decisions are just as difficult and equally important. Rich and powerful as we are, we cannot afford to disperse our efforts to a degree which would render all ineffective. Every region has its claims and its proponents, and it is therefore necessary to decide on a general strategy to be employed, having in mind the entire world situation.

One factor I especially wish to make clear today is the importance of timely action on our part in the face of the dictatorial procedure with which we are confronted in Europe. Take, for example, the Recovery Program. It has not been a question of a small group of men deciding what was the best thing to do and then immediately giving directions for carrying out that decision. On the contrary, the initial suggestion which resulted in this program was made June 5, 1947. Sixteen nations responded immediately and early in September submitted a statement of their agreements and their proposals. At the same time three highly representative committees of distinguished citizens in this country studied the various aspects of the matter and made their reports in September and early October. Finally, the matter was carried to the Congress which had been convened in a special session last fall. There have been committee hearings; there have been the recommendations and proposals of a Congressional group who-studied matters abroad last summer. There has just been completed the debate on this subject in the Senate, followed by a highly favorable vote. The House Committee makes its report this week, I think. The debate and vote in the House are soon to follow. Yet the original suggestion was made almost a year ago.

All of this procedure is as we would have it. It is but an expression of a democracy of free men carefully considering and debating what had best be done. In one sense it represents much of what we fought for during the last war. But our problem is how, with the rapid march of events in Europe, to meet the situation. Earlier in this talk I used the expression "initial advantage". What I meant to imply was that the initial advantage is almost always on the side of the dictators, as it was overwhelmingly in the last war. In the long run, I am sure, the democracies will invariably win out. But the trouble is that the lapse of time may result in such a serious loss of position and strength that the task of the democracies may involve a long, hard struggle to recover the ground thus lost.

A special effort is now being made to carry through the European Recovery Program promptly to final approval. This program, as you know, is based on economic factors. I agree that the economic reinforcement of the free nations will not alone guarantee their safety under existing conditions. But it should so strengthen them that they will have a far better chance of defending themselves and their governments against transition into police states dominated by the central committee of the Communist Party in Europe. My concern is to see us reach a prompt decision in regard to this program and not delay action while discussing new conceptions or proposals regarding related matters.

In connection with the electoral campaign now in progress in Italy, the leaders of the Communist Party have given their interpretation to the policy of the United States in connection with the outcome of these elections. They publicly asserted that if their party, the Communist Party, is victorious at the polls American assistance to Italy will continue without change.

I have only this comment to make regarding that interpretation of the policy of the United States:

The European Recovery Program has been created on the basis of the voluntary association of 16 nations who came together of their own free will and drew up a program of mutual self-help for their economic recovery. There has been no compulsion or pressure of any sort in regard to

prompt enactment and immediate application of the European Recovery Program. This is fundamental to all our future decisions in dealing with a situation as grave as any that has ever confronted this Nation. The President has presented to the Congress the further measures which should be taken.

rritory of Trieste to Italy

TS OF THE U.S., U.K., AND FRANCE

nitely compromise the possibility of applying the statute.

In these circumstances the three Governments have concluded that the present settlement cannot guarantee the preservation of the basic rights and interests of the people of the Free Territory.

The Governments of the United States, the United Kingdom, and France have therefore decided to recommend the return of the Free Territory of Trieste to Italian sovereignty as the best solution to meet the democratic aspirations of the people and make possible the reestablishment of peace and stability in the area.

In as much as the Security Council has assumed the responsibility for the independence and territorial integrity of the Free Territory of Trieste, the Governments of the United States, the United Kingdom, and France will submit to the Security Council for approval the arrangements to be jointly agreed upon.

Intentions of Czechoslovakia To Sign ITO Agreement Studied

[Released to the press March 20]

The Government of Czechoslovakia has informed this Government that on March 20, 1948, it intends to sign the protocol of provisional application of the general agreement on tariffs and trade and to put the agreement provisionally into effect on April 20, 1948. The general agreement is a comprehensive trade agreement among 23 nations, the negotiations concerning which were completed October 30, 1947, at a meeting in Geneva, Switzerland.

The United States Government is examining the implications and obligations of the agreement in the light of the recent developments in Czechoslovakia.

Petroleum is in short supply in the United States as in many other countries throughout the world. As a result, repeated urgent requests are being received from foreign countries for United States Government assistance in obtaining the petroleum supplies necessary to meet their essential requirements.

The Oil-Industry Committee in the United States, appointed by a Senate committee, under the chairmanship of Senator Tobey, to study the petroleum situation in the United States, has recently reported that for the period of December 1947 through March 1948 in the New England and Middle Atlantic States there will be a 15 percent shortage of gas and distillate fuel oil and that for the entire area east of the Rockies the shortage will be 10 percent. It is anticipated that the shortage in gasoline and other products in season will be approximately the same order of magnitude and that there may not be a general improvement for some time. The Committee recommended that every effort be made to conserve fuel, that petroleum products be used only for essential purposes, and that wherever conversion from oil to coal is practicable, the change should be made. The Committee asked all consumers to cooperate in economizing in the utilization of petroleum products.

Since shortly before the war world-wide petroleum requirements have grown at a more rapid rate than at any other time in the history of the industry. World-wide consumption was approximately 5,000,000 barrels a day in 1938, is approximately 8,500,000 barrels a day today, and the requirements estimated in the Krug Committee Report for 1951 will be 10,000,000 barrels a day. World consumption grew to 5,000,000 barrels a day in about eighty years; it is expected to double in the succeeding twelve or thirteen years. The industry believes that this 10,000,000 barrel-a-day rate will be reached before 1951, probably in 1950.

The supply of petroleum products is limited by the availability of crude oil and the capacity of the world's transportation and refining facilities. Although there may be a small amount of available crude-oil productive capacity in the Middle East, it is not available because of lack of transportation and refineries. On a world-wide basis the facilities for the production and distribution

---

[1] Memorandum submitted by the United States Representative to the Inter-American Economic and Social Council of the PAU on Mar. 8, 1948, and released to the press on Mar. 19.

The Department of State on June 9, 1947, received a letter from the Governor of Oklahoma stating that a joint resolution ratifying the proposed amendment had failed to pass.

THE FOREIGN SERVICE

Consular Offices

The American Consulate General at Bratislava, Czechoslovakia, was opened to the public on March 1, 1948.

PUBLICATIONS

Department of State

For sale by the Superintendent of Documents, Government Printing Office, Washington 25, D.C. Address requests direct to the Superintendent of Documents, except in the case of free publications, which may be obtained from the Department of State.

Austria: Zones of Occupation and the Administration of the City of Vienna. Treaties and Other International Acts Series 1600. Pub. 2861. 9 pp., 2 maps. 35¢.

> Agreement Between the United States of America and Other Governments—Signed at London July 9, 1945; entered into force July 24, 1945.

United States Educational Foundation in Burma. Treaties and Other International Acts Series 1685. Pub. 3051. 7 pp. 5¢.

> Agreement Between the United States of America and Burma—Signed at Rangoon December 22, 1947; entered into force December 22, 1947.

Twenty-fifth Report to Congress on Lend-Lease Operations: Lend-Lease Fiscal Operations, March 11, 1941 through June 30, 1947. Pub. 3064. 77 pp.

Diplomatic List, March 1948. Pub. 3086. 189 pp. 20¢.

> Monthly list of foreign diplomatic representatives in Washington, with their addresses.

American Trade Policy. Commercial Policy Series 110. Pub. 3091. 13 pp.

> An article by Woodbury Willoughby describing the background of present U.S. policy for the elimination of trade discriminations and reduction of trade barriers, and the charter for an International Trade Organization which came out of the Habana trade and employment conference.

United States Foreign Economic Policy. General Foreign Policy Series 1. Pub. 3097. 11 pp. Free.

> Address by Winthrop G. Brown discussing our stake in the European Recovery Program, the International Trade Organization, and the trade agreements program.

Toward Securing the Peace and Preventing War: Address by the President to the Congress of the United States, March 17, 1948. General Foreign Policy Series 2. Pub. 3102. 5 pp. Free.

> The President's report on the critical international situation, requesting prompt passage of the European Recovery Program and universal military training and temporary revival of selective service.

Contributors

Edward G. Cale, author of the article on the international wheat agreement, is Associate Chief of the International Resources Division, Office of International Trade Policy, Department of State. Mr. Cale is a member of the United States Delegation to the international Wheat Council.

The Department of State bulletin

VOL. XVIII, No. 457 • PUBLICATION 3110

April 4, 1948

For sale by the Superintendent of Documents
U.S. Government Printing Office
Washington 25, D.C.

SUBSCRIPTION:
52 issues, $5; single copy, 15 cents

Published with the approval of the
Director of the Bureau of the Budget

The Department of State BULLETIN, a weekly publication compiled and edited in the Division of Publications, Office of Public Affairs, provides the public and interested agencies of the Government with information on developments in the field of foreign relations and on the work of the Department of State and the Foreign Service. The BULLETIN includes press releases on foreign policy issued by the White House and the Department, and statements and addresses made by the President and by the Secretary of State and other officers of the Department, as well as special articles on various phases of international affairs and the functions of the Department. Information is included concerning treaties and international agreements to which the United States is or may become a party and treaties of general international interest.

Publications of the Department, as well as legislative material in the field of international relations, are listed currently.

'ORLD HEALTH ORGANIZATION—PROGRESS AND PLANS

By H. van Zile Hyde, M.D.

Alternate U. S. Representative, Interim Commission

The first World Health Assembly, which is heduled to meet in Geneva on June 24, 1948, will ark the beginning of full-scale Wнo activity and e termination of the interim phase of the devel-ment of the international health agency planned the International Health Conference in New ork during the summer of 1946. The completion planning for the Assembly by the Fifth Session the Interim Commission, which met in Geneva nuary 22–February 7, 1948, provides an appro-iate point for reviewing the work and accom-ishments of the Commission and for previewing e potentialities and work of the Wнo itself.

The gap between the International Health Con-rence and the World Health Assembly has been rolonged well beyond the most pessimistic predic-ons. At the time of the Assembly the Interim ommission will have been in existence two years. .t the Conference in New York, plenipotentiaries 62 governments, representing essentially the tal population of the world, signed on July 22, 46, the constitution of the Wнo in an atmosphere enthusiasm and confidence. It was anticipated at confirmation of these signatories would be pidly forthcoming. China and the United ngdom had signed without reservation. Then ings slowed down. Nineteen months after the gning, when only 20 [1] of the required 26 members the United Nations had deposited instruments acceptance, the Interim Commission set the ne date for the Assembly in trust that the re-ired number of deposits would be rapidly rthcoming.

This decision was taken when neither the United ates, the Union of Soviet Socialist Republics, nor ance, all active members of the Interim Com-ission, had deposited their instruments of ac-ptance. It was taken in the belief that further olongation of the interim phase would be dam-ing to international cooperation in health. The ates serving on the Interim Commission have come acutely sensitive to the fact that they, as small group, have been directing international alth activities on behalf of all signatories to

the constitution over a long period, even though some of them have not accepted the constitution and others who are not members of the Commission have done so long since. It is to be hoped that the action taken in calling the Assembly will serve as a stimulant to this important movement.

Assuming that 26 members of the United Na-tions deposit instruments of acceptance of the constitution before June 24 (which must be the case if the Assembly is to meet) there will be at least 34 members of the Wнo at that time, since 8 non-members [2] of the United Nations have al-ready deposited their instruments of acceptance.

The Interim Phase

The International Health Conference recognized that there would be an interval between its con-clusion and the first meeting of the World Health Assembly. In order to provide for this interval, it established, through an arrangement signed by 61 governments, an Interim Commission composed of representatives of 18 members [3] of the United Nations. The arrangements laid down the re-sponsibilities of the Commission. Chief among these were the development of proposals for the program and budget for the first year of the Wнo; the provisional agenda of the first World Health Assembly, with necessary documents and recommendations relating thereto; studies in re-

---

[1] China, the United Kingdom, Canada, Iran, New Zea-land, Syria, Liberia, Ethiopia, the Netherlands, Saudi Arabia, the Union of South Africa, Haiti, Norway, Sweden, Iraq, Siam, Yugoslavia, India, Turkey, and Egypt. Aus-tralia, Czechoslovakia, Greece, and the Union of Soviet Socialist Republics have since deposited their instruments of acceptance, making a present total of 24 members of the United Nations who have become members of the Wнo.

[2] Switzerland, Transjordan, Italy, Albania, Austria, Fin-land, Ireland, and Portugal.

[3] Australia, Brazil, Canada, China, Egypt, France, India, Liberia, Mexico, the Netherlands, Norway, Peru, the Ukrainian Soviet Socialist Republic, the United Kingdom, the United States of America, the Union of Soviet Socialist Republics, Venezuela, and Yugoslavia.

gard to headquarters and regional organization; and the relationship of the WHO to the United Nations and to other specialized agencies as well as to nongovernmental organizations interested in fields related to health. The arrangement also provided that the Interim Commission should take the steps necessary to effect the transfer to it, and later to the WHO, of the functions and duties of the League of Nations Health Organization and the International Office of Public Health of Paris.

The Commission has met at quarterly intervals to carry on this work. At its first session, which was held in New York immediately following the International Health Conference, Dr. Brock Chisholm of Canada was elected Executive Secretary. Under his direction, a staff has been developed and offices established in New York, Geneva, and Singapore. At its fifth session, held in Geneva, the Commission concluded its major work. In the near future its recommendations regarding the agenda of the World Health Assembly and the program and relationships of the World Health Organization will be transmitted to signatories of the WHO constitution and to the Interim Commission. A final session of the Commission will be held on June 18, 1948, just prior to the World Health Assembly, to review and approve a narrative report to the World Health Assembly and such other supplemental reports and recommendations as may be required by circumstances.

Despite the frequency of meetings and the travel involved, the sessions of the Interim Commission have been attended by never less than 14 of its 18 members, showing continued active interest in international health on the part of the member governments.

The United Nations has made funds available for the work of the Commission, authorizing loans amounting to $3,000,000 for the two-year life of the Commission. Present estimates indicate that the Commission will draw approximately $2,700,000 against this authorization. In addition, by agreement with UNRRA, $3,000,000 has been transferred to the Interim Commission from that agency for the continuation of certain health functions in UNRRA-receiving countries.

The work of the Commission has fallen under three quite distinct headings, namely:

(1) Planning for the WHO;
(2) Consolidation and continuation of the work of pre-existing international health agencies;
(3) Continuation of certain health functions of UNRRA by arrangement with UNRRA.

Planning for the WHO

The major task of the Interim Commission has been to lay the groundwork for the WHO. This planning is certain to shape the course of the WHO for many years to come. Although the

a truly world problem toward the solution of which the WHO can make a major contribution by the rapid extension and application of existing technical knowledge.

Tuberculosis

Tuberculosis is, of course, one of the great enemies of mankind. During the war, deaths from this disease increased almost everywhere as a result of crowding, malnutrition, and the intimate association of open cases of the disease with the general population due to the breakdown of control measures. Indeed, during 1944 and 1945, the death rates in Europe reached most alarming heights, in many places doubling the prewar rate. Since that time there has been a deceptive reduction in current tuberculosis death rates, due to the fact that many of those persons who would normally have survived to swell the present death rate died earlier than would have been their expected lot. The rate of infection, however, remains high, as revealed by mass X-ray and tuberculin surveys, threatening a progressive increase in death rates during ensuing years. Important steps can be taken to ward off this increase and reduce, progressively, the rate of infection. Long-established methods of control, which have proved highly effective where they have been well developed, require extension and strengthening. The essence of these control measures is the finding and isolation of contagious cases.

There is, however, a relatively new tool, which only of late has won wide acceptance. The Scandinavian and other countries including France, Canada, and the United States, have produced convincing evidence of the effectiveness, in the control of tuberculosis, of the use of a vaccine known as BCG (Bacillus Calmette-Guérin) which was developed in France almost three decades ago. It remains now to determine the exact place of BCG, in relation to other control measures, in the over-all control of tuberculosis. It is quite fully agreed however that BCG has a vital role to play in the international control of tuberculosis. It is the tool that offers hope of immediate benefit, while the world attempts to build the economic foundations which are essential to the control of tuberculosis by older, more orthodox control measures. These latter measures depend upon a sound economic structure which makes available to all proper food, clothing, housing, medical care, and hospitalization. Internationally, the final conquest of tuberculosis is in the hands of the United Nations itself and those of its specialized agencies concerned with world economic health. Tuberculosis is a disease that can be suppressed by a planned attack. The low death rate of 32 per 100,000 in Denmark, as contrasted with rates of 200 to 400 per 100,000 in several other areas of Europe, is a direct result of such attack.

The Interim Commission has recognized that the WHO can contribute significantly toward its control through the extension of professional knowledge by fellowships, demonstrations, and expert advice to governments, through the extension of public knowledge concerning the disease and its method of spread, by the promotion of the eradication of tuberculosis in cattle, and particularly, now, by the extension of the use of BCG vaccine.

The Commission has not felt it prudent to wait for the WHO in order to extend the use of BCG vaccine in areas in which tuberculosis is epidemic. It is therefore sending teams to India, at the request of that Government, to demonstrate the technique of vaccination in the hope of extending its use there on a wide basis. At the same time it is providing to the International Children's Emergency Fund a panel of experts to advise the Fund on the technical aspects of a program upon which the Fund is embarking to vaccinate an estimated 15 million children in Europe. The Commission has, as well, accepted the responsibility for conducting studies to determine the effect on tuberculosis rates of this vast vaccination program.

Venereal Disease

As is usual during and following war, there has been a tremendous upsurge of venereal disease over wide areas. The movement of masses of peoples, troops, and displaced civilians, the shattered economy of nations and degradation of morals which are inherent in warfare form the basis of this increase. Concurrently, in countries not directly affected by war, the incidence of venereal disease is exceedingly high as a concomitant of social backwardness. There are, for instance, extensive areas in Africa in which over 75 percent of the population is infected with syphilis. By way of contrast, certain countries, with high social and health standards, had reduced venereal disease prior to the war to a problem of minor significance. This was the case, particularly, in the Scandinavian countries, but even those countries reported a six to tenfold increase in the incidence of syphilis during the war. Venereal disease, particularly syphilis, is a serious economic burden upon the generation which tolerates it and places upon the successor generation a heavy burden of congenitally infected dependents.

Even while the war-caused increase in venereal disease was occurring, a momentous event took place in the discovery of the effectiveness of penicillin in the treatment of both syphilis and gonorrhea. At last, a quick-acting, highly effective curative agent had been found and was in production on a large scale. It is important that this new agent be used to its full effectiveness, as rapidly as possible, in the treatment and control of venereal

by the World Health Assembly after decisions have been taken as to the date of termination of the Interim Commission, the site of the headquarters of the WHO, and the level of activity during the first full year. This period, of perhaps four months, will constitute a transitional period from the interim to the full initial level of WHO activities, and its financing will require supplementation of the approved 1948 Interim Commission budget. It is hoped that this transitional budget may include provisions for repayment of indebtedness to the United Nations and for the establishment of a working capital fund so that the WHO may begin its first full year on a sound financial base.

The budget proposed for 1949 totals $6,473,991. The Interim Commission is presenting it as a working document for the World Health Assembly rather than as a definitive budget. It is intended to present the Commission's views as to the requirements for carrying out effective initial programs in the various fields in which the Commission feels the WHO should take action during its first year or must take action to meet its statutory or inherited obligations. It is being presented in a form which lends itself readily to modification in emphasis on specific programs and in organizational structure. It can be reduced or expanded, in whole or in part, and refined to meet the wishes of the Health Assembly. In this way it can serve as a guide to the World Health Assembly, with no attempt being made by the smaller interim group to force an organizational pattern upon the larger group.

Headquarters

The arrangement establishing the Interim Commission charged it with making studies in regard to site of headquarters. The Commission has circularized governments to determine their interest in the matter and to elicit any offers of land or

---

[4] The League of Nations Health Organization ceased to exist with the dissolution of the parent body. The United Nations assumed responsibility for certain of its activities. This responsibility was transferred to the Interim Commission of the World Health Organization in the fall of 1946.

A protocol, signed on the same day as the constitution of the World Health Organization, provides for the ultimate dissolution of the International Office of Public Health and the transfer of its assets, duties, and functions to the World Health Organization. By agreement between the Interim Commission and the Permanent Committee of the Office, the Commission is now carrying on the duties assigned to the Office by international conventions. The Office was established by the Rome agreement of 1907, which can be terminated only by the consent of all 45 states which are parties. By becoming a party to the protocol the states have agreed to the termination of the agreement of 1907. They have further agreed that if all the parties to the agreement of 1907 have not agreed to its termination by Nov. 15, 1949, they will then denounce the agreement of 1906. Such denunciation will take effect on Nov. 15, 1950.

facilities that might be forthcoming. It has been indicated that France and Switzerland and perhaps other governments will lay before the World Health Assembly specific offers of land and buildings. In addition, the plan for the United Nations building in New York includes facilities for such specialized agencies as may settle there.

The studies made by the Interim Commission on this matter are not complete or definitive. A special committee composed of the Representatives of India, Egypt, France, Mexico, and Norway was appointed to study this matter and has presented a report calling attention to factors which should be taken into account in arriving at a decision in regard to the site of the headquarters, such as proximity to other related agencies; availability of adequate space, communications, transport, and other facilities; economic and social stability; cultural and scientific environment, et cetera. The report of the Committee, however, does not include a careful evaluation of these factors, but rather leaves the impression that despite such real considerations, the final choice will rest on other less tangible factors. The leading contenders at the present time would appear to be Geneva, London, New York, and Paris.

The position held consistently by the United States Representative, since the preparatory meeting in early 1946, is that the dominant consideration should be the scientific quality of the environment. It is felt that the WHO will attract a staff of high scientific attainment more readily if located in a place at which its staff can maintain close daily contact with outstanding specialists in the various fields of its interest. Isolation from such an environment could well lead to stagnation. Brussels, Copenhagen, London, New York, and Paris, among places that have been considered, would appear to excel as scientific centers.

Regional Arrangements

The arrangement establishing the Interim Commission instructed it to make studies in regard to regionalization of the WHO. Except for negotiations with the Pan American Sanitary Organization [5] leading toward integration of that organization as the regional organ in the Western Hemisphere, as provided in the constitution of the WHO, little has been done in this field. Replies to an inquiry on the subject have been tabulated and will be presented to the WHO. These include detailed suggestions as to regional structure from the Governments of France, India, the Union of South Africa, and the United Kingdom. Outside of the Western Hemisphere, no general pattern has emerged, with the exception of the Pan Arab

---

[5] Pan American Sanitary Organization consists of the Pan American Sanitary Bureau and the Pan American Sanitary Conference and its directing council.

436

greatly increased force behind internationalism, particularly the broader thinking of Americans and American agencies, there is a new drive within these organizations, giving promise of their increasing initiative and effectiveness. The Interim Commission has recognized that the WHO would do well to support this development.

The Commission itself has not entered into formal relationship with voluntary organizations, but has developed close working relationships with the International Union Against Tuberculosis, the International Union Against Venereal Disease, the International Congresses on Tropical Medicine and Malaria, the International Congress on Mental Health, the International Congress on Microbiology, and others. As an example of the value of such relationship, one can cite the establishment by the Commission of a world influenza center in London for the world-wide study, through regional and national laboratories, of the viruses causing influenza in local outbreaks. This program is a direct result of consultation with the International Congress on Microbiology and is considered by exports the world over as of the highest importance.

The Commission is recommending to the World Health Assembly a mechanism whereby international voluntary agencies in the health field may, after establishment of their truly representative international character, become related to the WHO and have the privilege of consultative status. It can be hoped that liaison will be established with the more important organizations on a permanent basis and that some of these organizations will establish their headquarters in close association with that of the WHO, so that all major resources for the attack upon world health problems will be closely coordinated and mutually supporting. Meanwhile, as pointed out above, the Interim Commission, jointly with UNESCO, is establishing as a first step a central bureau to assist the voluntary technical organizations in developing and coordinating international congresses in their technical fields.

Absorption of Pre-existing Health Agencies

Certain rather extensive routine operating functions of the Interim Commission have been derived directly from the health organizations of the League of Nations and the International Office of Public Health in Paris, both of which have been or are being absorbed by the Interim Commission on behalf of the WHO. These functions have the solidity of international acceptance over a period of years. They perhaps lack the glamour of novelty but constitute a firm base for the new organization. These functions include the following:

The routine exchange of information between

nations on the occurrence of pestilential disease, such as cholera, plague, smallpox, and typhus;

The administration of the international sanitary conventions;

The delineation of yellow-fever zones and approval of yellow-fever vaccines;

The revision of international sanitary convention procedures;

The development and maintenance of international standard preparations;

The preparation of monographs on drugs in the development of an international pharmacopoeia;

The analysis and presentation of statistical material regarding the occurrence of infectious diseases; and

The publication of bulletins, journals, fasciculi, and international lists covering scientific, legal, and statistical matters important to international control of disease and improvement of health.

International Epidemic Control

The most extensive operation of the Interim Commission in this field is the conduct of the international exchange of epidemiological information with regard to the pestilential diseases. A world center is maintained in Geneva into which flows constantly all information concerning the occurrence of these diseases. The information is sent to Geneva directly by many countries and from others, indirectly, through the Pan American Sanitary Bureau, the Alexandria (Egypt) Epidemiological Bureau, and the Singapore Station of the WHO. The information received is transmitted throughout the world in a weekly epidemiology and vital-statistics report and, more rapidly, to the affected countries through telegram and radio. The Singapore Station maintains regular broadcasts in which it keeps shipping constantly informed of health conditions in the many ports of the Far East.

This service is of vital importance in maintaining the free movement of sea and air traffic without undue risk of transmission of disease. The epidemiological service proved its value most recently in connection with the cholera epidemic in Egypt when it kept the world continuously and reliably informed of the course of the epidemic. It was able at the same time to counter rumors that were serving as a serious impediment to maritime and air traffic.

The experience of the Egyptian cholera epidemic has indicated the need for improvement in the service as taken over from the League of Nations and has led to a decision to use telegraphic and radio means of distributing information more freely during emergencies. Further, as part of its responsibility for the administration of international sanitary conventions, the Interim Commission has instituted an investigation of the excessive quarantine restrictions imposed by nu-

strike hard at all the urgent problems in the countries in which it was operating. The WHO will have a much larger field in which to operate, all countries being potentially its beneficiary. At the same time, its financial resources will be more restricted. It will therefore be necessary for the WHO to focus its attention upon a limited number of general health problems, giving assistance on a wide geographical basis in regard to these specific problems. As progress is made in the solution of these, emphasis can be shifted to other problems of general importance.

In view of the importance of the field-services program as a basis for future WHO work, it would be well to look briefly at some of the Interim Commission activities in certain of the receiving countries.

The Interim Commission maintains missions, varying in size from 1 to over 30 experts, in Austria, Greece, China, Ethiopia, Poland, Hungary, and Italy. The composition and functions of these missions vary in accordance with the need of each recipient country.

In Greece, the mission has been largely concerned with providing technical advice to the Government in the control of malaria and tuberculosis. This has included the close supervision of widespread use of DDT both by airplane spraying in marsh areas and hand spraying of houses in communities throughout the malarious areas of the country.

In Ethiopia, the mission has been conducting courses for sanitary inspectors and hospital dressers in an attempt to provide foci for the spread of elementary concepts of sanitation and nursing care.

In China, where the largest mission of experts is maintained, the Commission is training both the faculties and students of the schools of medicine, nursing, and public health. It also provides to the Government technical advice concerning the control of cholera, plague, kala azar, tuberculosis, and malaria, as well as advice and assistance aimed at the improvement of port sanitation and quarantine.

In Italy, a small mission is maintained, at the request of that Government, to assist and advise in the wise use of local funds that were accumulated from the internal sale of UNRRA-supplied goods. This mission is working with the Italian Government and the Rockefeller Foundation in an effort to eradicate malaria-carrying mosquitoes on the Island of Sardinia and in other malarious areas of Italy.

In Austria, Hungary, and Poland the missions consist of a single medical officer, serving in a liaison capacity. These officers assist in selecting and making arrangements for professional personnel granted fellowships by the WHO Interim Commission for foreign study. They also assist in arranging for visits of specialists and lecturers and in providing current medical literature, periodicals, and teaching apparatus made available by the Commission. These officers also give technical advice and assistance on the many problems faced by the health authorities of these countries.

Assistance to Yugoslavia and Finland has been limited to the award of fellowships, and in the Ukraine to the supply of current medical literature.

This brief review indicates the diversity of the activities of the Interim Commission under its field-service program.

Fellowship Program

The aim of the fellowship program has been to foster the spread of medical knowledge to the widest possible extent and particularly to aid in rehabilitating public health and medical education in the countries to which it has been possible to extend aid. Essentially, one third of the field-services funds has been allocated for this program. The WHO Interim Commission staff experts have assisted governments in the selection of fellowship candidates and in arranging study schedules for them. Although the universities and medical schools in nearly all countries receiving fellows are overcrowded, they, as well as hospitals, laboratories, and governmental health administrations, have cooperated consistently in providing training.

The majority of fellows are experienced specialists engaged in teaching at universities or hospitals; their fields of study include practically all the specialized medical techniques. The awards to this group provide for three to six months of study and observation, often at a number of different institutions. A second group is composed of specialists in the technical and administrative public-health services; most of these fellows are on leave from responsible posts in the health administrations of their own countries. Their studies, covering periods of three to six months, include advanced work in universities and observation in public-health agencies and field projects. A limited number of fellowships for a full year of study are awarded to young men and women who are preparing for careers in various branches of public health and nursing. In view of the necessary emphasis placed on the rehabilitation of medical schools during this period of the program, a large number of fellowships have been in basic medical sciences and clinical fields. There have been 175 fellowships awarded in Europe.[*]

[*] Fellowships have been distributed in the following fields: public-health administration, 28; cancer, 12; venereal disease, 7; tuberculosis, 6; child health, 12; clinical specialties, 56; mental health, 11; basic medical sciences, 35; public-health nursing, 2; dentistry, 3; and legal medicine, 3.

Fellows have been placed largely in the United States, Canada, England, and Switzerland.

Medical Literature

Assistance in the selection and procurement of medical books and periodicals has been given to eight of the eleven countries which have requested such aid. Members of the WHO Interim Commission staff have taken part in this highly specialized task, which is essential to the restoration of medical education in countries cut off from scientific developments during the war.

The World Health Assembly

As the meeting of the World Health Assembly approaches, one can look back upon the development and international acceptance of a broad WHO constitution, followed by a long interim period during which useful work has been done and valuable experience gained.

The World Health Assembly will have before it recommendations based upon this experience. These recommendations are being submitted to the World Health Assembly by the Interim Commission in the anticipation of lively and fruitful discussions, not as a finished product for rubber stamping by the Assembly. It will be necessary for the Assembly to give careful and detailed study to all elements of the proposed program in order to mature the recommendations and fit them into a sound budget structure, scaled to fit the available funds. The program adopted by the Assembly will cast the die, shaping the WHO for many years to come. Other matters, in addition to the general program which will be before the Assembly requiring exploration, and in most cases decision, are the pattern of relationships between the WHO and other organizations; the regional pattern of the WHO, with particular reference to the integration of the Pan American Sanitary Organization as a regional organization of the WHO; the location of WHO headquarters; and the selection of a Director General.

The World Health Assembly will be composed of the health leaders of the countries constituting the organization. The International Health Conference in New York, which was climaxed by the signing of three important international instruments, and the successful course of the Interim Commission since that time have confirmed the historical fact that, in the field of health, nations can meet together in a spirit of friendship and understanding and arrive at firm decisions which are carried through to an effective conclusion for the betterment of mankind. The first World Health Assembly can be expected to be another example of this historical fact. It will be the first in a series of annual World Health Assemblies, which can be an important focus of the world's hope of peace and life.

ompletion of ITO Charter Hailed as Hope for Troubled World

STATEMENT BY THE DEPARTMENT OF STATE

[Released to the press March 25]

The Department of State announces the signg of the final act of the United Nations Confer ce on Trade and Employment at Habana, mark g the completion of a charter for an Interna nal Trade Organization. The representatives about 60 nations participated in the preparation the final draft of the charter.

The charter is a momentous achievement and one om which the whole world will benefit. It is the oduct of more than two years of constant and nscientious labor by experts and representatives the many nations who worked long and weary urs to reach agreement on a code of international onomic activity which would be acceptable to l. First, the United States issued in December 45 its *Proposals for the Expansion of World rade and Employment* [1] which suggested the for ation of an International Trade Organization. his was expanded by the United States into a *uggested Charter* in September 1946.[2] The fol wing month a Preparatory Committee of 18 na ons established by the United Nations modified is draft at London; in February 1947 further anges were made at a meeting at Lake Success; d in August 1947 a fourth draft was drawn up at eneva. Finally, at Habana from November 21, 47, to March 24, 1948, the present charter was epared. Through this series of conferences the oposed charter received the fullest possible con deration and the utmost care in its formulation. The charter will now be submitted to the various untries for acceptance according to the consti tional procedures established by each country. the United States it will be submitted to the ongress for approval.

The completion of the charter is a clear and un istakable demonstration of the ability of a major rt of the world to work together for the common od. It goes far beyond study and recommenda on. It contains numerous and detailed commit ents which are mutually beneficial to the mem rs. It is broader in scope and greater in detail an most, if not all, previous agreements between tions on economic relations.

Many of the changes and modifications made in bsequent drafts of the charter were suggested

by interested groups in this country. The charter includes provisions recommended by the Finance Committee of the United States Senate, by busi ness, labor, farm, and other organizations. As a result the charter is a live and meaningful docu ment concerned with practical rules for encourag ing the flow of international trade.

The main objective of the charter is the raising of living standards throughout the world. It pro poses to do this by promoting the expansion of international trade on a basis of multilateralism and general nondiscrimination, by fostering the growth of production and employment, and by encouraging the economic development of back ward areas. Its substantive chapters set forth a series of international commitments with respect to national policies regarding tariffs, customs ad ministration, hidden restrictions on trade, import and export quotas, exchange controls, preferences and other forms of discrimination, state trading, subsidies, restrictive business practices in inter national trade, intergovernmental commodity agreements, the international aspects of domestic employment policies, economic development, and international investments. Other chapters outline the structure, functions, and procedures of the International Trade Organization.

The chapter on employment and economic ac tivity emphasizes the fact that employment, pro duction, and demand for goods and services are not only of domestic concern but are necessary for the well-being of all countries. Members agree to take action designed to achieve and maintain full and productive employment through measures appropriate to their political, economic, and social institutions.

The chapter dealing with economic develop ment and reconstruction was, as it had been in the previous conferences on the charter, one of the most hotly debated sections at the Habana con ference. Under the provisions of this chapter, members agree to cooperate with other countries through the medium of international agencies for the purpose of promoting general economic devel opment as well as the reconstruction of those coun tries whose economies have been devastated by the

[1] Department of State publication 2411.
[2] Department of State publication 2598.

war. The chapter specifies the principles which shall apply to the promotion of economic development and reconstruction and the treatment of international investment. It indicates the conditions and specifies the procedures under which particular measures, otherwise inconsistent with the commercial-policy provisions of the charter and with trade agreements made pursuant thereto, may be used to promote economic development and reconstruction. Similarly, the chapter delineates the particular conditions and procedures under which preferential agreements for economic development and reconstruction may be employed.

Almost a third of the charter is devoted to provisions on commercial policy. Under the provisions of the chapter dealing with this subject, members agree to extend to each other general most-favored-nation treatment and to undertake negotiations directed toward the reduction of tariffs and the elimination of preferences on a reciprocal and mutually advantageous basis. In general, the charter also prohibits the imposition of discriminatory internal taxes and regulations on foreign products. In view of the peculiar features of moving pictures as a commodity in international trade, special provisions were included to deal with cinematographic films.

Since quantitative restrictions on imports and exports can have an even more limiting effect than tariffs, taxes, or other similar charges, it was agreed that basically such quantitative restrictions would not be allowed. It was recognized, however, that under certain conditions and with regard to certain commodities it might be advisable to allow exceptions. The permitted exceptions are carefully enumerated and circumscribed, with safeguards to prevent their possible abuse. These exceptions include the use of import quotas on agricultural and fisheries products if they are necessary in connection with governmental programs restricting domestic marketing or production. Import quotas are also permitted for the purpose of safeguarding a member's balance of payments.

Safeguards are also included to insure that the interests of other members are not unreasonably prejudiced by the indiscriminate use of subsidies. A modification of considerable interest to the United States was made in the provisions dealing with export subsidies. Such subsidies may now be used without the prior approval of the organization, as had been previously required under the Geneva draft over the objection of the United States. They, however, must not be employed by a member to acquire more than its equitable share of world trade in the particular commodity.

Since state trading has become of growing importance in recent years, the charter has included a section dealing with this aspect of commerce. This section provides that countries carrying on trade through state enterprises should conduct

he general principles which are to govern inter-governmental commodity agreements, the circumstances under which they are to be used, and the procedures for developing and administering them. These provisions seek to safeguard the interests both of producer and consumer countries and to afford an effective solution to the particular commodity problem involved.

The remaining articles of the charter deal with the structure and functions of the International Trade Organization, procedures for the settlement of differences, and a number of general matters, including relations with nonmembers, general exceptions for national security reasons, methods of amending the charter, procedure for withdrawal of a member from the Organization and for termination of the charter, and requirements to be met for entry of the charter into force. The principal organs of the Organization will consist of a Conference, an Executive Board, and a Secretariat, including a Director-General and his staff. Differences may be settled by consultation or arbitration between the members, or by reference to the Executive Board or Conference, or to the International

Court of Justice under certain circumstances. The charter prohibits a member from entering into a preferential arrangement with a nonmember which prevents the latter from according to other members any benefit of such an arrangement. In general, members are prohibited from according to nonmembers treatment which, being more favorable than that accorded to other members, would injure the economic interests of the latter. Members are free under the charter to discriminate against nonmembers if they so wish.

The charter is to enter into force when a majority of the countries which signed the final act of the Habana conference have approved the document. However, if a majority fail to approve at the end of one year after the signature of the final act, then the charter may come into force whenever 20 countries approve the charter. If the charter has failed to come into force by September 30, 1949, those countries which have approved the charter may consult among themselves as to whether and on what terms to bring the charter into force.

STATEMENT BY THE PRESIDENT

[Released to the press by the White House March 24]

I am deeply gratified that representatives of more than 50 nations are signing today in Habana the charter for the International Trade Organization. This charter will now be sent to the government of each nation for ratification.

The charter for the International Trade Organization is a code of fair dealing in international trade. Member nations agree to work out mutually beneficial employment policies and ways of promoting economic development. The charter provides for limitations upon cartels and defines the proper scope of intergovernmental commodity agreements. It establishes standards for the conduct of international trade. The charter thus deals comprehensively with economic problems which heretofore have been dealt with piecemeal, if at all, in international agreements.

The charter has immediate significance to the

efforts of the nations now working to repair the devastation and dislocation caused by World War II. Acceptance of the charter, in the spirit in which it has been framed, will stimulate the expansion of international trade upon which world prosperity depends. By supporting the growth of a prosperous international trade, this code of fair dealing will contribute greatly to our efforts for a just and lasting peace.

The development of this charter is an example of the finest type of international cooperation. The action in Habana today marks the conclusion of one of the most difficult and important tasks ever undertaken at international conferences.

This achievement demonstrates that many countries can work together through the United Nations to reach sound agreement on complex international issues.

STATEMENT BY GEORGE C. MARSHALL
Secretary of State

[Released to the press March 25]

It is gratifying that the United Nations Conference on Trade and Employment has succeeded in producing a charter for an International Trade Organization.

Completion of the charter follows two years and more of intensive effort, including four meetings held under the auspices of the United Nations, to formulate a generally acceptable code of fair prac-

tice in matters affecting international commerce. Representatives of more than fifty nations have now produced a document which, when approved by the governments concerned, will bring into being an organization dedicated to these purposes.

In the development of the charter, widely divergent interests and points of view had to be reconciled. The present economic difficulties and special situations of many of the countries represented at

Habana added to the difficulty of this task. The fact that agreement was finally made possible in these circumstances demonstrates that the most difficult common problems are susceptible of cooperative solution where there exists a common determination to succeed.

The course and outcome of the Habana conference also demonstrate the great immediate importance attached to both the ends and the means set forth in detail in the charter. Participating governments sent some of their leading men to the meetings and were intensely concerned, to the end of the negotiations, with the exact final terms of agreement. Chaotic economic conditions at present brought home the vital need for a statement of long-range objectives and for agreement upon the fair trade policies to be used in seeking these objectives. The charter for the Ito is an answer to both needs.

The charter represents agreement on basic economic policies never before treated in a single general international agreement. It recognizes the degree to which national action over a wide area

STATEMENT BY WI

Chairman, U.

This is a day for history. There have been other conferences on international economic affairs. But none of them has undertaken a task so difficult as the one that is completed here today. None of them has come to an agreement concerning so many vital economic interests of so many states. None of them has produced a document so comprehensive as the Habana charter for world trade. Few, if any of them, have attained so notable a measure of success.

This is a momentous day for the United Nations. It marks the culmination of an enterprise that had its beginnings in the declarations of policy that were made in the Atlantic Charter in 1941 and in article VII of the mutual aid agreements in 1942. It marks the completion of three years of careful planning and almost two years of continuous negotiations. It marks the embodiment in a charter, produced by more than 50 nations, of the principles contained in the *Proposals* that were published by the United States in 1945.[2] It marks the

---

[1] Made on Mar. 23, 1948, at final plenary session of U.N. Conference on Trade and Employment and released to the press on the same date.

[2] *Proposals for Expansion of World Trade and Employment* (Department of State publication 2411).

international trade, was old-fashioned and impractical. The disorganization caused by the war was too great. The problems of reconstruction were too pressing. Nations were too much preoccupied with immediate difficulties. They would not look to the future. The future, in any case, was too uncertain. It could not be done.

It has been done!

The charter is now ready for submission to the legislatures of the participating nations for approval.

This conference has afforded the world an impressive demonstration of the ability of nations to work out a comprehensive agreement on matters of vital importance under conditions of great difficulty. Interests have differed at Habana, but efforts to understand, to explain, and to agree have never failed. We have all gained in knowledge and understanding. We have achieved, through these years of working together, a voluntary agreement for our mutual benefit. In this achievement, a troubled world may well take hope.

DOR WARREN R. AUSTIN [1]

Seat of the United Nations

higher standards of living. The Iᴛᴏ influence on the flow of international trade can be expected to aid also in achieving international monetary stability. In short, commercial frictions are diminished, and energies can increasingly be devoted to peaceful pursuits.

Hand in hand with the Iᴛᴏ goes the reciprocal trade-agreements program, now up for renewal in Congress. The Iᴛᴏ charter pledges member states to negotiate for the reduction of tariffs and the elimination of trade preferences in much the same way that the United States, almost alone, has pursued reductions over the last 14 years. Consequently, the Reciprocal Trade Agreements Act is the essential vehicle for carrying out Iᴛᴏ objectives and achieving our own aims under the Iᴛᴏ charter.

Moreover, extension of the act by Congress would be evidence of the good will of the United States toward world trade expansion. It would offer to the trade of other countries the prospect of entering the American market, but only in return for concessions providing wider markets for American goods. It would stimulate the expansion of commerce, increase production, and stabilize employment.

---

[1] Made on Mar. 24, 1948, and released to the press by the U.S. Mission to the U.N. on the same date.

U.S. Position in the United Nations Regarding Chilean Complaint

STATEMENT BY AMBASSADOR WARREN R. AUSTIN [1]
U.S. Representative in the Security Council

MR. PRESIDENT: My speech will not be long. The Council has before it charges against the Soviet Union and against the present rulers of Czechoslovakia. In the main, they allege interference by the Soviet Union in various ways in the affairs of Czechoslovakia, including the threat of force and the support which the Soviet Union has rendered to the Communist minority in its disruption of the Government of Czechoslovakia.

My Government views these charges with concern. It feels that the Security Council has an obligation to consider these charges with care. The Council has heard the Representative of Chile and Dr. Papanek. Many points have been made on which we should have clarification. We have yet to hear anything which amounts to an answer to any of the charges. The Ukraine's Representative yesterday did not answer. The distinguished Representative of the Soviet Union today has not answered. The Ukrainian Representative devoted all of his discourse to an attempt to draw a red herring across the whole situation by making a mass of unsubstantiated and fanciful allegations about the conduct of others, some of which were directed toward my Government. This could not help to determine the question now before the Security Council. Today the distinguished Representative of the Soviet Union interprets the conduct of the United States as crude interference in the internal affairs of other countries and other states, as blackmail and bribery; even charges of incitement to treason against Czechoslovakia by the United States.

Well now, Mr. President, if that were so—if it were correct—if we, the United States, were willing to recognize a semblance of truth in these charges, I affirm that it could not convince the unfortunate and unhappy people of Czechoslovakia that the charges against the rulers of the Soviet Union are spurious. The poor people of Czechoslovakia are redeemed from bondage by being told that other peoples have suffered from indirect aggression. However, such fantastic stories about the United States have been told throughout my attendance upon the General Assemblies and Security Council meetings of the United Nations. And it has always been obvious to all the world why such statements were made and that they are propaganda of the arbitrary rulers of the Russian people. They have not changed any since the first time they were uttered. They are just the same as ever and they are not worthy of a detailed answer.

The main point that interests us as a responsible body of this great international institution is to apply the test to such conduct that it deserves and ask the question: wherein do you find any answer whatever to the charges that are revealed here, that the Soviet Union has reduced the good people of Czechoslovakia to slavery; that their great system of democracy has been turned topsy-turvy; and that their economic structure has been so corrupted already that freedom of acquiring and holding property is now destroyed?

Probably the Representative of the Ukraine has not been in so favorable a position as the doormen and the cowboys of the United States of America. I am certain that the distinguished Representative of Russia does not have the opportunity that the very well-informed taxi driver in the city of Washington or in the city of New York has to have knowledge about the external affairs of the United States. But his comment, which was intended to be witty, operates as a great compliment to the democratic system of the United States, in which taxi drivers and doormen and cowboys can know and have something to say about the external affairs of their beloved country.

Now, there is one witness—that is, he might be a witness—of the actual facts in Czechoslovakia. He represents the present rulers of the inhabitants of Czechoslovakia, and I do not see him sitting here at this "horseshoe".

I assume the Czechoslovakian Representative will say that we are dealing with a domestic matter, but how does he explain the coincidence of the arrival in Prague of Deputy Soviet Foreign Minister Zorin immediately preceding the crisis? Members of the Council will realize that it was not in character for a Deputy Foreign Minister of the Soviet Union to travel to other countries on business such as distribution of wheat. On the contrary, it is customary for representatives of such

[1] Made before the Security Council on Mar. 23, 1948, and released to the press by the U.S. Mission to the United Nations on the same date.

the Minister of Trade made that statement on behalf of the present rulers of Czechoslovakia. If so, to what aid from the Soviet Union was the Minister referring? It might also enlighten the Council to be informed as to the reasons for withdrawing the original press statement.

We have a series of charges relating to the claim that the Communist minority has by a *coup d'état* taken control of the machinery of the state. On the other hand, we have the contrary claim that all that has happened has been in accordance with the will of the Czechoslovakian people and is therefore an internal matter with which we cannot deal.

In this connection, the Representative of the new Czechoslovakian Government released a statement to the press yesterday giving the position of his Government with regard to the issues before the Security Council. This statement raised certain additional questions to which the Council would, I imagine, be glad to have the answers. The allegation was made that the developments which took place in Czechoslovakia in February resulted from the *deviation of certain political parties* from the ideas for which the best Czechoslovakian patriots fought during the terrible years of German occupation and from the abandonment of the principles on which the Czechoslovakians based the building of their liberated country. Is it the position of the new Czechoslovakian Government that the Communist Party alone of all the political parties which made up the National Front before February is true to the ideals of democracy and freedom which had been the mainstay of the Czechoslovak people for hundreds of years? If this is the case it might be interesting to hear the Czechoslovakian Government's explanation of the necessity for the sudden change from the policy of traditional Czechoslovakian democracy to the policy of a police state.

The allegation was also made to the press that the Czechoslovakian crisis was settled according to constitutional principles and parliamentary practice. Is it consistent with the Constitution of Czechoslovakia for the present rulers to deprive regularly elected members of Parliament of their parliamentary immunity and to remove them from office, or to dismiss judges and other high officials of the Government who disagree with them?

We would be glad to have information concerning the charges which have been made before us. Do the inhabitants of Czechoslovakia welcome the domination of Russian-trained officials? Is every influential citizen of Czechoslovakia regarded as a traitor or as "a person who betrayed his country", solely because he deviates from the ideas of the present officials ruling the inhabitants?

It is charged that President Benes has been prevented from speaking to the people of Czechoslovakia and that three separate speeches prepared by him were censored by the present rulers of the people. It would be useful to know whether this statement is accurate and, if so, the reasons for the decision of the Government to refuse the President facilities for making these speeches publicly. If these allegations are not true, it would be helpful if some explanation could be given to the Security Council as to why the President has not made a statement to his people at this time of crisis.

Czechoslovakia was a nation which understood democracy and a country in which democratic principles and procedures prevailed. If, as the Czechoslovakian Representative has asserted to the press, the recent developments were spontaneous internal developments, how can he reconcile that assertion with actions which were taken by the Communist minority, such as breaking up meetings of other established parties, the arrest of opposition political leaders, the expulsion from universities of well-known professors, the imposition of a complete censorship on the press and radio of the country? Why have editors of leading Czechoslovakian papers disappeared; why have leaders in all walks of Czechoslovakian life fled; why have a number of Czechoslovakian diplomatic representatives abroad resigned; why did the Foreign Minister of Czechoslovakia commit suicide; and, I repeat, why has the President of Czechoslovakia remained silent?

Too much has happened which is not in character with the Czechoslovakian people and Czechoslovakian tradition. Too much has happened which bears a striking similarity to what happened in other countries for the Security Council to be satisfied with perfunctory or categorical denials or with further red herrings. The Council deserves and should receive from the Czechoslovakian Representative the fullest explanation with respect to the points which I have raised. We should also hear what the Representative of the Soviet Union has to say as to these points.

The Security Council should realize that grave charges have been made, charges to which it cannot close its eyes. The Security Council should, therefore, consider these charges in all of their aspects. All sides of the case should be heard.

No member should draw conclusions prematurely or lightly. Certainly my Government does not intend to do so. The Council should realize, furthermore, that if these charges should be established they would constitute a case of indirect aggression. The United Nations would then be called upon to develop effective collective measures designed for the preservation of the territorial integrity and political independence of states, however small.

Whether the charges are traversed or admitted, my Government's position is to support continued consideration by the Security Council aimed at saving other peoples from indirect aggression.

ndar of Meetings [1]

ssion as of April 4, 1948		
		1946
astern Commission	Washington	Feb. 26–
i Nations:		
urity Council	Lake Success	Mar. 25–
itary Staff Committee	Lake Success	Mar. 25–
mic Energy Commission	Lake Success	June 14–
		1947
nmission on Conventional Armaments	Lake Success	Mar. 24–
urity Council's Committee of Good Offices on the Indonesian Question.	Lake Success	Oct. 20–
ieral Assembly Special Committee on the Greek Question	Salonika	Nov. 21–
		1948
nmission for Palestine	Lake Success	Jan. 9–
aporary Commission on Korea	Seoul	Jan. 12–
erim Committee of the General Assembly	Lake Success	Feb. 23–
isoc (Economic and Social Council):		
ubcommission on Employment and Economic Stability	Lake Success	Mar. 22–
Vorld Conference on Freedom of Information	Geneva	Mar. 23–
Council of Foreign Ministers):		**1947**
nmission of Investigation to Former Italian Colonies	Former Italian Colonies . . .	Nov. 8–
		1948
juties for Italian Colonial Problems	London	Jan. 29–
juties for Austria	London	Feb. 20–
Food and Agriculture Organization): Mission to Siam	Siam	Jan. 3–
sional Frequency Board	Geneva	Jan. 15–
Meeting of Planning Committee on High Frequency Broadcasting .	Geneva	Mar. 22–
Pan American Railway Congress	Habana	Mar. 27–
International Conference of American States	Bogotá	Mar. 30–
(International Civil Aviation Organization): Personnel Licensing Division.	Montreal	Mar. 30–
(International Cotton Advisory Committee): Seventh Meeting . .	Cairo	Apr. 1–
ng of Technicians in Connection With Final Protocol of Tonnage Measurement of Ships.	Oslo	Apr. 2–
International Leprosy Congress	Habana	Apr. 3–11
International Fair	Lyon	Apr. 3–12

Prepared in the Division of International Conferences, Department of State.

vities and Developments»

UTY CHAIRMAN OF POLICY GROUP ON OTÁ CONFERENCE DESIGNATED

iul C. Daniels, Director for American Re-
ic Affairs, has been designated Deputy Chair-
of the Policy Group on the Bogotá confer-
, effective March 5, 1948.

U.S. OBSERVERS TO SIXTH PAN AMERICAN RAILWAY CONGRESS

The Secretary of State has announced the composition of the United States observer group to the
Sixth Pan American Railway Congress scheduled
to convene at Habana, March 27, 1948. United
States representation will consist of William T.
Faricy, president, Association of American Railroads; Julian Duncan, Bureau of Statistics, Interstate Commerce Commission; and Seymour T. R.
Abt, Transport and Communications Branch, Office of International Trade, Department of Commerce.

U.S. DELEGATION TO FIRST SESSION OF CHEMICAL INDUSTRIES COMMITTEE

[Released to the press March 26]

The Department of State has announced the composition of the United States Delegation to the First Session of the Chemical Industries Committee as recommended to the Secretary of State by the Secretary of Labor. This meeting which was called by the International Labor Office is scheduled to convene at Paris on April 6 and is expected to last 10 days. The Delegation is tripartite, composed of representatives of the Government, employers, and workers of the United States, as follows:

GOVERNMENT DELEGATES

Arthur J. White, Wage and Hour and Public Contracts Division, Department of Labor
Thomas W. Delahanty, Associate Chief, Chemical and Health Products Branch, Office of International Trade, Department of Commerce

Advisers

W. Duane Evans, Chief, Productivity and Technical Developments Division, Bureau of Labor Statistics, Department of Labor
Richard Eldridge, Labor Attaché, American Embassy, Paris

EMPLOYERS' DELEGATES

E. W. Dwyer, Head, Industrial Relations Section, Monsanto Chemical Company, St. Louis, Mo.
Howard R. Huston, Assistant to the President, American Cyanamid Company, New York City

WORKERS' DELEGATES

John J. Mates, International Board Member, United Mine Workers of America, Washington, D.C.
H. A. Bradley, President, International Chemical Workers Union, Akron, Ohio

The meeting has been called to consider the problems of the chemical industries in the light of recent events and changes and of conditions of labor and the organization of industrial relations in those industries.

U.S. DELEGATION TO FIFTH INTERNATIONAL LEPROSY CONGRESS

[Released to the press March 25]

The Department of State has announced the following United States Delegation to the Fifth International Leprosy Congress which is scheduled to be held at Habana, April 3–11, 1948:

Chairman

Perry Burgess, President, American Leprosy Foundation, New York City

Delegates

Frederick A. Johansen, Medical Director, U.S. Public Health Service; Director, U.S. Marine Hospital, Carville, La.; Member, Advisory Medical Board, American Leprosy Foundation
Eugene R. Kellersberger, General Secretary, American Mission to Lepers, Inc., New York City

STATEMENT BY THE PRESIDENT [1]

It is vital that the American people have a clear derstanding of the position of the United States the United Nations regarding Palestine.

This country vigorously supported the plan for rtition with economic union recommended by the nited Nations Special Committee on Palestine d by the General Assembly. We have explored ery possibility consistent with the basic princi-es of the Charter for giving effect to that solu-n. Unfortunately, it has become clear that e partition plan cannot be carried out at this ne by peaceful means. We could not undertake impose this solution on the people of Palestine the use of American troops, both on Charter ounds and as a matter of national policy.

The United Kingdom has announced its firm tention to abandon its mandate in Palestine on ay 15. Unless emergency action is taken, there ll be no public authority in Palestine on that te capable of preserving law and order. Vio-ce and bloodshed will descend upon the Holy nd. Large-scale fighting among the people of at country will be the inevitable result. Such hting would infect the entire Middle East and uld lead to consequences of the gravest sort in-lving the peace of this Nation and of the world. These dangers are imminent. Responsible gov-nments in the United Nations cannot face this ospect without acting promptly to prevent it. e United States has proposed to the Security uncil a temporary United Nations trusteeship

for Palestine to provide a government to keep the peace. Such trusteeship was proposed only after we had exhausted every effort to find a way to carry out partition by peaceful means. Trustee-ship is not proposed as a substitute for the parti-tion plan but as an effort to fill the vacuum soon to be created by the termination of the mandate on May 15. The trusteeship does not prejudice the character of the final political settlement. It would establish the conditions of order which are essential to a peaceful solution.

If we are to avert tragedy in Palestine, an im-mediate truce must be reached between the Arabs and Jews of that country. I am instructing Am-bassador Austin to urge upon the Security Council in the strongest terms that representatives of the Arabs and Jews be called at once to the council table to arrange such a truce.

The United States is prepared to lend every appropriate assistance to the United Nations in preventing bloodshed and in reaching a peaceful settlement. If the United Nations agrees to a temporary trusteeship, we must take our share of the necessary responsibility. Our regard for the United Nations, for the peace of the world, and for our own self-interest does not permit us to do less.

With such a truce and such a trusteeship, a peaceful settlement is yet possible; without them, open warfare is just over the horizon. American policy in this emergency period is based squarely upon the recognition of this inescapable fact.

eport on Fifth Meeting of Preparatory Commission for IRO

ARTICLE BY GEORGE L. WARREN

The Preparatory Commission for the Interna-nal Refugee Organization (PCIRO) met for the th time at Geneva on January 20, 1948.[2] The rpose of the meeting was to consider the status adherences to the IRO constitution, to adopt dgets for the current and ensuing fiscal years, d to take action indicated by consideration of e report of the Executive Secretary. The Com-ission had assumed operating responsibilities on half of IRO on July 1, 1947, for the care, repatria-n, and resettlement of displaced persons.

Status of the International Refugee Organization

The French and Belgian Delegates advised the Commission that their Governments had com-pleted the required legislative actions and would soon deposit certificates of ratification to the IRO constitution with the Secretary-General of the United Nations. It was noted that the deposit of ratifications by France and Belgium would bring

[1] Released to the press by the White House on Mar. 25.
[2] For the report of the 4th meeting of the Preparatory Commission for IRO, see BULLETIN of Sept. 28, 1947, p. 638.

the number of adherences to IRO to 13 and that the adherence of two additional governments would be required to bring the IRO into being. The total percentage of governments' contributions, including those of France and Belgium, would be 75.24 percent. The Brazilian Delegate announced the intention of his Government to introduce appropriate legislation in the Congress immediately upon the signing of an interim working agreement with the Commission. The hope was expressed that Brazil might complete its adherence by March 31, 1948.

Budget Discussions

Budgets authorizing expenditures of $119,000,-000 in the current fiscal year and of $155,000,000 for the fiscal year 1948–49 were approved by the Preparatory Commission. Together the two budgets provide funds for the resettlement of 679,000 displaced persons and the repatriation of 179,000. The budget for the current fiscal year is $3,443,000 higher than that approved at the October meeting of the Preparatory Commission. This was made possible by an increase in anticipated revenue, by receipt of $1,500,000 from the assets of UNRRA, and anticipated reimbursements from the Australian Government of $580,760 for the transportation of displaced persons to Australia and the return of prisoners of war to Europe in PCIRO ships.

A comparison of the budgets for the fiscal years 1947–48 and 1948–49 reveals the extent to which PCIRO hopes to increase the rate of resettlement of refugees. The budget for the current fiscal year devotes 12 percent to resettlement costs as compared with 36 percent in the budget for 1948–49. Increased resettlement will result in a decrease in care and maintenance costs from 68 percent of the current year's budget to 48 percent of the 1948–49 expenditures.

Resettlement Overseas

The discussion on the budgets developed the information that PCIRO has seven ships in operation in moving displaced persons overseas for resettlement in Australia, Brazil, Canada, and Venezuela. Four of these are chartered from the U. S. Army. Displaced persons numbering 17,300 have already been recruited by immigration selection missions or are in possession of immigration visas and are awaiting transportation from Austria, Germany, and Italy. It was estimated that four extra ships would be required to move these persons immediately.

Cut-off Date

In the discussion of the budget for 1948–49 the United Kingdom Delegate took the initiative in proposing a cut-off date before which a refugee must have left his country of origin or former habitual residence in order to qualify for IRO assistance. This proposal was advanced for the purpose

ly Accepts Proposal of U.S., U.K., and France To Place
⋅e Territory of Trieste Under Italian Sovereignty [1]

MEMORANDUM OF DEPARTMENT OF STATE OF MARCH 20, 1948

he Government of the United States desires
ɔropose to the Government of Italy that it
ɜe to the early consideration, jointly with the
ʹernments of the United Kingdom, France and
Union of Soviet Socialist Republics of the
otiation of a Protocol to the Treaty of Peace
ɩ Italy to provide for the return of the Free
ritory of Trieste to Italian sovereignty.
ɩ will be recalled that the Government of the
ted States has consistently maintained that
entire area of the Free Territory is ethnically
historically Italian territory and that this
ʹernment agreed to its separation from Italy
ɣ on the condition that it should be truly inde-
dent and that the human rights of the people
ʹully protected and guaranteed against all pos-
lity of suppression or infringement. This con-
on is now apparently impossible of achieve-
ɩt and therefore this Government has concluded
ɩ the rights and interests of the overwhelmingly
ian population of the area can be assured
ɣ through the return of the Free Territory to
ɩan sovereignty.
ʹhe Government of the United States has de-
ɩd upon this proposal in view of the proven
ʹorkability of the provisions of the Treaty of
ɩe with Italy establishing the Free Territory.
s the considered opinion of this Government
ɩ certain elements of the population have suc-
ɩed in establishing conditions which make in-
rative the guarantees of true independence for
Territory and the protection of the basic rights
the people as envisaged in the Permanent
tute of the Free Territory. The successful es-
ɩshment of a Free Territory was recognized
ɩ the first as being entirely dependent upon the
est cooperation and good will of all concerned.
ɰever, from the first hours of the history of
area as a Free Territory it became all too

apparent that certain elements were intent upon
preventing the establishing of a truly independent
Free Territory of Trieste. Subsequent events have
further proven that the most fundamental human
rights have been denied and a totalitarian system
has been established in the Zone of the Territory
placed under the temporary administrative responsibility of the Commander of the Yugoslav
forces in the Free Territory of Trieste. These developments have convinced the Government of the
United States that the settlement envisaged in the
Treaty of Peace with Italy cannot successfully
guarantee freedom for the people of the area or
true independence for the Free Territory of
Trieste.

The Government of the United States, after
consultation with the Governments of the United
Kingdom and France, has therefore decided to
recommend the return of the Free Territory of
Trieste to Italian sovereignty as the best solution
to meet the democratic aspirations of the people
and make possible the reestablishment of peace
and stability in the area. It is hoped that the
Government of Italy will concur in this view and
agree to the immediate negotiation of a protocol
to the Treaty of Peace with Italy to effect this
solution of the problem.

It is proposed that such protocol as may be
agreed to by the Powers concerned would, prior to
coming into force, be submitted to the Security
Council for its approval in view of the special
responsibilities assumed by the Council in connection with the Free Territory of Trieste.

A similar communication is being addressed to
the Government of the Union of Soviet Socialist
Republics.

[1] Released to the press Mar. 23. For recommendations
of the three Governments, see BULLETIN of Mar. 28, 1948,
p. 425.

March 22, 1948

MR. SECRETARY OF STATE,

With reference to the memorandum delivered by the Department of State on the 20th instant concerning the proposal of the Government of the United States to consider, together with the Governments of the United Kingdom, France and the Soviet Union, the negotiation of a protocol to the Treaty of Peace with Italy providing for the return of the Free Territory of Trieste to Italian sovereignty, I have the honor, on instructions from my Government, to communicate to you the following:

1. The Italian Government learned with very keen and legitimate satisfaction that the Governments of the United States, the United Kingdom and France had reached the conclusion that the reestablishment of a free order and respect for the democratic aspirations of the great majority of the population of the Free Territory of Trieste can only be guaranteed by the return of the Territory to Italian sovereignty.

2. The Italian Government is prepared to participate to that end together with the Governments of the United States, the United Kingdom, France and the Soviet Union through the drawing up of protocol which will be submitted to the Security Council for approval.

3. The Italian Government speaks for the entire Italian people and the people of the Free Territory in expressing their rejoicing. It realizes fully the importance and significance of the proposal jointly put forward by the Governments of the United States, the United Kingdom and France. This proposal not only constitutes the recognition of a fundamental principle of international justice, but, when realized, can likewise constitute a guaranty of peace and of that sincere collaboration which Italy desires with the neighboring Yugoslav people.

Please accept [etc.]

ALBERTO TARCHIANI
Ambassador of Italy

Transfer of Passenger and Cargo Vessels to Italy

STATEMENT BY THE PRESIDENT

[Released to the press by the White House March 16]

Fourteen of the ships transferred to Italy today are Italian vessels seized by the United States during the war. The other 15 are the equivalent tonnage of Italian ships which were seized by the United States and lost during the conflict or reduced to such a condition that they could not be returned.

The Italian vessels seized by the United States during the early years of the war played an important part in the victory against dictatorship to which the Italian people contributed so much after

their own liberation from Fascism. They are now turned now to rejoin the Italian Merchant Marine and work again for the rebuilding of peace and the restoration of a prosperous Italy.

In making this transfer, I am happy to express again the feeling of friendship and admiration for the American people for the Italian people, who, in these brief years since the war ended in Europe, have made such courageous strides forward in the democratic faith and repeatedly shown the world that, supported with courage and wisdom, the faith cannot and will not falter or fail.

EXECUTIVE ORDER 9935

[Released to the press by the White House March 16]

By virtue of the authority vested in me by the Constitution and laws of the United States, including the Trading With the Enemy Act of October 6, 1917 (40 Stat. 411), as amended, and the act of August 5, 1947, Public Law 370, 80th

Congress, 1st Session, it is hereby ordered as follows:

1. The Attorney General and the United States Maritime Commission are authorized and directed to transfer to the Government of Italy all right, title, interest, and possession of the United States, the Attorney General, or the Maritime Commission in the following vessels, which were under Italian registry and flag on September 1, 1939

---

[1] 13 *Federal Register* 1395.

(f) Delivery of the *Hermitage* (ex. *Conte Biancamano*) and *Monticello* (ex. *Conte Grande*) pursuant to this order shall be without prejudice to any rights of the Government of the United States, under existing agency agreements with the Government of Italy, with respect to (1) accounting for revenues of such vessels accruing prior to the date of delivery of such vessels pursuant to this order, and (2) the operation of the S.S. *Saturnia* and S.S. *Vulcania*, or either, in accordance with existing agreements between the United States and Italy.

4. The Liberty ships to be transferred to the Government of Italy shall be selected by the United States Maritime Commission, in consultation with the Government of Italy, such vessels to be operated by Italy for commercial use. Provision shall be made that such Liberty ships are to be operated under the Italian flag and shall not be sold to any person or corporation not a national of Italy, without the consent of the Government of the United States.

5. The Attorney General and the United States Maritime Commission shall act in consultation with the Secretary of State in carrying out the terms of this Executive order with all possible promptness in a manner which will effectuate the foreign policy of the United States to assist friendly and democratic European nations to rebuild their economies without delay.

THE WHITE HOUSE,
March 16, 1948.

Additional Treaties With Italy U.S. Will Keep in Force or Revive

[Released to the press March 16]

Text of a note from Ambassador Dunn delivered on March 12, 1948, to the Italian Foreign Office by the American Embassy at Rome

I have the honor to refer to my note of February 6, 1948 giving official notification, in accordance with Article 44 of the Treaty of Peace with Italy dated at Paris February 10, 1947, regarding the pre-war bilateral treaties and other international agreements with Italy which the United States desires to keep in force or revive.[3] It was stated

---

[2] The names of the Liberty ships transferred are as follows: Fort Wedderburne, Fort Gasperau, Fort Charnisay, Fort Hudson's Hope, Fort Maurepas, Fort Fork, Fort MacMurray, Fort Simpson, Fort Kootenay, Fort La Traite, Fort Walsh, Fort Rae, Fort Frederick, Fort Gibraltar, and Fort Acton.

[3] BULLETIN of Feb. 22, 1948, p. 248.

in that notification that the reciprocal copyright arrangement between the United States and Italy and the agreement for the protection of trademarks in Morocco would be the subject of a separate communication.

I have the honor to inform you now that the Government of the United States of America wishes to include the reciprocal copyright arrangement between the United States and Italy effected pursuant to the exchange of notes signed at Washington October 28, 1892, and the exchanges of notes signed at Washington September 2, 1914, February 12, March 4, and March 11, 1915, among the pre-war bilateral treaties and other international agreements with Italy which the United States desires to keep in force or revive. Accordingly, it is understood that the aforementioned arrangement will continue in force and that the Government of each country will extend to the nationals of the other country treatment as favorable with respect to copyrights as was contemplated at the time the arrangement was entered into by the two countries.

The Government of the United States of America also desires to continue in force or revive the agreement for the protection of trademarks in Morocco, effected by exchange of notes signed at Tangier June 13, July 29, and December 19, 1903 and March 12, 1904.

Reiteration of Four Power Responsibilities in the ACC

Statement by Secretary Marshall

[Released to the press March 25]

The Representatives of this Government have tried diligently and patiently for nearly three years and are still trying to make the Allied Control Council an effective organization for the administration of Germany as an economic and political unit. Their efforts have to a large extent been frustrated by the tactics of the Soviet Representatives on the Council. The Acc in Berlin as well as the joint occupation of the city are established by governmental agreement. Any further attempt to disrupt the functioning of the Allied Control Authority, as initially suggested by the conduct of the Soviet Representative on March 20, could only be construed as reflecting an intention, which the United States does not share, to renounce efforts to obtain Four Power agreement on policies for Germany and would be regarded as unilateral action aimed against the unification of Germany. In accordance with the international agreement binding on all four control powers, the United States intends to continue to fulfill its responsibilities as a member of the Control Council and as a joint occupant of the city of Berlin.

[Released to the press March 26]

XCELLENCY : I have the honor to acknowledge receipt of your note, No. 50, of March 6, 1948, erning the discussions which the Governments he United States, the United Kingdom and nce held in London respecting Germany.

ι its note of March 6, the Soviet Government rated the views expressed in the Soviet Emy's communication of February 13, 1948, to the t that the London discussions were in contraion to the Potsdam Agreement and to the eement on Control Machinery for Germany. ts memorandum of February 21, 1948, the Dement of State pointed out that these talks were nged for a discussion of problems in Germany ιutual interest to the three governments, and there is no provision in the Potsdam Agreet, or other agreements relating to Germany ιluded by the four occupying powers, which ents any of the powers from discussing ben themselves questions of common concern.

he United States Government notes that the iet Government continues to fail to recognize the three powers have been obliged to consult ng themselves at this time as a result of the illingness of the Soviet Government to implet the principles of economic unity as well as r principles of the Potsdam Agreement. The iet Government claims that the other occupying ers have undertaken a series of unilateral acs, contrary to the four-power agreement with ect to Germany.

he Soviet Government cites, as the first expresof such policy, the agreement between Great ain and the United States with respect to the omic fusion of their respective zones of occuon in Germany. The note of the Soviet Govnent states : "It is well known that the question reating a unified Anglo-American Zone was even submitted for the consideration of the trol Council". This statement does not corred to the facts. At the meeting of the Allied trol Council in Berlin on July 20, 1946, General Varney made the following statement on behalf is Government :

The United States Government is of the view no zone in Germany is self-sustaining. The tment of two or more zones as an economic unit ld improve conditions in the zones concerned. Therefore, the United States Government has ιorized its representative on the Allied Control

Council to join with the representatives of any other occupying power or powers in measures for the treatment of our respective zones as an economic unit, pending quadripartite agreement which would permit the application of the Potsdam decision to treat all of Germany as an economic unit so as to attain a balanced economy throughout Germany.

"While the United States would prefer quadripartite agreement to implement the Potsdam decision for the establishment of central German administrative agencies for Germany as a whole, its representative is prepared to cooperate with the representatives of any or all of the other occupying powers in Germany in establishing administrative arrangements to secure economic unity.

.   .   .   .   .

"The United States does not intend by its present proposal to divide Germany but rather to expedite its treatment as an economic unit.

"Any arrangements which representatives of the United States may make with the representatives of any other occupying power will be open on equal terms to the representatives of all other occupying powers at any time they are prepared to participate.

"The United States Government proposes this arrangement because of its belief that Germany can no longer be administered in four air-tight compartments without free economic interchange unless economic paralysis is to result. The United States Government is unwilling to permit creeping economic paralysis to grow if it is possible to attain economic unity between its zone and any other zone in Germany as a prelude to economic unity for all Germany."

According to the official minutes of the Allied Control Council (CONL/M(46)19), the meeting agreed in view of the unpreparedness of the other delegations to defer consideration of the United States proposal. At the next meeting on July 30, 1946, according to the official minutes (CONL/M (46)20), the Control Council considered the United States Government's proposal. At this meeting Marshal Douglas announced that after full consideration the British Government had authorized him to accept, in principle, General McNarney's offer. Comments on the United States proposal were made by the Soviet representative at this meeting and by the French representative at subsequent meetings.

It should be recalled that the same offer of the United States Government to join its zone economically with that of any other occupying power had previously been made before the Council of Foreign Ministers by the Secretary of State, Mr. Byrnes, on July 11, 1946, at Paris, and was subsequently reiterated by him in an address at Stuttgart on September 6, 1946. The responsibility for rejection of this offer and for failure to include its zone in this economic arrangement lies upon the Soviet Union itself.

The threat to the authority of the Allied Control Council does not arise from the actions of the United States, but rather from the consistent pursuit by the Soviet Government in the eastern zone of Germany of a systematic unilateral policy of its own. The Soviet Government has failed to observe the principle of economic unity provided for in Section III, B, 14, of the Potsdam Agreement. It has likewise failed to insure, as provided in Section III, B, 15 (c), of the same agreement, "the equitable distribution of essential commodities between the several zones so as to produce a balanced economy throughout Germany and reduce the need for imports". It has carried out reparation removals of industrial capital equipment from the eastern zone without regard to agreed limitations on such removals and without consideration of the legitimate peace-time requirements of the German economy. It has also continuously taken reparation in the form of resources and current production, contrary to the understanding at Potsdam. The Soviet Government under the guise of reparation has taken into its possession in gigantic trusts (the so-called Soviet A. G's) major industrial establishments in the eastern zone accounting for 25 to 30 per cent of the total remaining industrial productive capacity.

The Soviet Government has furthermore carried out in its zone a unilateral policy with respect to political activity. The Potsdam Agreement envisaged that local self-government would be re-established throughout Germany on democratic principles; that all political parties with rights of assembly and of public discussion should be allowed and encouraged; and that representative and elective principles should be introduced in the various levels of government. In actual practice, however, the Socialist Party was suppressed by the imposed amalgamation with the Communist Party into the Socialist Unity Party, which has become the new bulwark for a totalitarian regime in eastern Germany, while the other authorized political parties have been subjected to pressure, discrimination and intimidation, and have not been enabled to function freely. Basic human rights are being denied the population, while concentration camps are being used anew for individuals unwilling to accept this new totalitarianism. It is the unilateral policy of the Soviet Union which

Department of State

For sale by the Superintendent of Documents, Government Printing Office, Washington 25, D.C. Address requests direct to the Superintendent of Documents, except in the case of free publications, which may be obtained from the Department of State.

American Mexican Claims Commission: Report to the Secretary of State, under the act of Congress set up December 18, 1942. Arbitration Series 9. Pub. 2859. iii, 676 pp. $1.50.

> Relevant documents with decisions of the Commission showing reasons for the allowance or disallowance of the claims.

Liquidation of German Property in Sweden. Treaties and Other International Acts Series 1657. Pub. 2970. iii, 52 pp. 15¢.

> Accord Between the United States of America, France, the United Kingdom, and Sweden—Signed at Washington July 18, 1946; entered into force March 28, 1947.

Food Production: Cooperative Program in Peru. Treaties and Other International Acts Series 1669. Pub. 3000. 23 pp. 10¢.

> Agreement Between the United States of America and Peru Further Extending and Modifying Agreement of May 19 and 20, 1943—Signed at Lima December 4, 1946, and January 29, 1947; entered into force January 29, 1947, effective January 1, 1947.

American Dead in World War II. Treaties and Other International Acts Series 1672. Pub. 3007. 10 pp. 5¢.

> Agreement Between the United States of America and Belgium—Signed at Brussels June 6 and July 23, 1947; entered into force July 23, 1947.

United States Educational Foundation in China. Treaties and Other International Acts Series 1687. Pub. 3050. iii, 25 pp. 10¢.

> Agreement Between the United States of America and China—Signed at Nanking November 10, 1947; entered into force November 10, 1947.

Digest of UNESCO Program for 1948. International Organization and Conference Series IV, United Nations Educational, Scientific and Cultural Organization 2. Pub. 3081. 9 pp. 5¢.

> A six-point program for promoting peace and security by marshaling the cultural and educational resources of the world.

UNESCO and the National Commission: Basic Documents. International Organization and Conference Series IV, United Nations Educational, Scientific and Cultural Organization 3. Pub. 3082. 17 pp. 10¢.

> Constitution of UNESCO, act providing U.S. membership, and list of officers and members of the U.S. National Commission for UNESCO.

National Commission News, April 1, 1948. Pub. 3090. 10 pp. 10¢ a copy; $1 a year; foreign subscription $1.35 a year.

> Prepared monthly for the United States National Commission for the United Nations Educational, Scientific and Cultural Organization.

The Department of State

For sale by the Superintendent of Documents
U.S GoVernment Printing Office
Washington 25, D.C.

SUBSCRIPTION:
52 issues, $5; single copy, 15 cents

Published with the approval of the
Director of the Bureau of the Budget

Article

convention for air navigation drawn up in Habana in 1928; but the permanent American aeronautical commission was never formally constituted.

Cognizant that a postwar international organization was needed that not only would set up air-navigation standards and practices for the whole world, but would deal with the economic problems of international air transport, the United States took the lead by calling an international conference on civil aviation. On November 1, 1944, representatives of 54 nations met at Chicago.[4]

The International Civil Aviation Conference lasted until December 7, 1944. The final act of the Conference, signed by the representatives of all participating governments, contained the texts of the following instruments: interim agreement on international civil aviation; convention on international civil aviation; international air-services transit agreement; and international air-transport agreement; as well as 12 technical annexes.

Each of the four instruments was opened for signature on December 7, 1944. The first two instruments not only set forth general principles for international air navigation but also provided respectively for a provisional and a permanent international aviation organization. The international air-services transit agreement, incorporating the "two freedoms" of the air—the right

---

[1] As of Feb. 17, 1948.

[2] During the period June 6, 945, to Apr. 4, 947, the Organization was called PICAO (Provisional International Civil Aviation Organization).

[3] Relating to the regulation of air navigation.

[4] The only major nonenemy or nonenemy-occupied states which did not participate were Argentina, which was not invited, and the U.S.S.R., which did not attend. Argentina in June 1946 adhered to the interim agreement, the convention, and the transit agreement, but the U.S.S.R. has taken no action in this direction.

to fly over sovereign territory and the right to land for noncommercial purposes—and the international air-transport agreements incorporating the "five freedoms," including commercial air rights, were only the beginning of an attempt to handle the economic problems of international air transport through reciprocal granting of privileges on a multilateral basis. The technical annexes were only a start in the direction of international standardization of air-navigation procedures. It would be the work of the new international aviation body to develop and revise the work of the Chicago conference.

By June 6, 1945, the interim agreement had been accepted by the number of states (26) required to bring it into force, and the Provisional International Civil Aviation Organization was accordingly established. On August 15, 1946, the first meeting of PICAO was held at Montreal, Canada.

Structure of the Organization

The structure of the provisional Organization—an annual Assembly of all member states, a Council of 21 member states elected by the Assembly, and an international Secretariat—has been preserved in the permanent Organization, which came into existence on April 4, 1947, 30 days after the twenty-sixth instrument of ratification of the Chicago convention had been deposited with the United States Government.[5] The Assembly,[6] which elects its own officers and determines its own rules of procedure, has the function of taking appropriate action upon the reports of the Council and handling all other matters referred to it by the Council or not specifically assigned to the Council. The Council, or executive body, complies with the directives of the Assembly, maintains liaison with member states and with other international bodies, and is generally responsible for carrying out the work of the Organization. In session about eight months of the year, the Council is assisted by subsidiary working groups such as the Air Navigation and Air Transport

[5] The United States is the depositary government for the instruments of ratification of or adherence to the interim agreement and to the convention on international civil aviation.

[6] First Interim Assembly held in Montreal, Canada, May 21–June 8, 1946; First Assembly of ICAO held in Montreal, Canada, May 6–27, 1947; Second Assembly of ICAO scheduled to be held in Geneva, Switzerland, in June 1948.

the various regions, and develop special regional operating "procedures."[7]

One of the most interesting developments which had its beginning at a regional meeting is the North Atlantic Ocean weather ship station program. In the spring of 1946, the North Atlantic Route Service Conference recommended to the Interim Council the establishment of 13 ocean weather ship stations. The stations not only would provide essential weather data to permit safe and economical operation of the heavily troubled North Atlantic routes, but also would provide electronic air-navigation aids and would serve in emergencies as search and rescue units.

Following approval of the program by the Council, the Interim Assembly of PICAO in May 1946 decided that the ocean weather stations could not be financed from the PICAO general fund. Instead, the Assembly resolved that the program should be carried out by contributions "in kind or in cash" from interested states. At the London Conference on North Atlantic Ocean Weather Stations, held under the auspices of PICAO in September 1946, an international agreement was reached whereby the 13 weather stations were to be established and maintained by eight different states, with PICAO assuming responsibility for coordination of the program.[8]

The Organization's authority for carrying out the ocean weather ship station program and other "joint-support" projects is contained in chapter XV of the Chicago convention, which places on the Council the responsibility for consulting with

---

[7] To date, the following regional air-navigation meetings have been held: North Atlantic Route Service Conference in Dublin, from Mar. 4–27, 1946; European-Mediterranean Route Service Conference in Paris, from Apr. 24–May 15, 1946; Caribbean Regional Air Navigation Meeting in Washington, from Aug. 26–Sept. 13, 1946; Middle East Regional Air Navigation Meeting in Cairo, from Oct. 1–18, 1946; South Pacific Regional Air Navigation Meeting in Melbourne, from Feb. 4–22, 1947; South American Regional Air Navigation Meeting in Lima, from June 17–July 7, 1947; and South Atlantic Regional Air Navigation Meeting in Rio de Janeiro, from July 15–31, 1947.

[8] The London agreement has not yet been fully implemented. As of Feb. 17, 1948, only seven ocean weather stations were in operation: two maintained by the United States, two by the United Kingdom, one by France, one by Belgium and the Netherlands jointly, and one maintained part time by Canada.

a member state which, in its opinion, fails to provide adequate air-navigation facilities for international carriers. The Council is also to consult with other states affected by the lack of proper air-navigation facilities—airports, radio, and meteorological services, etc.—and make recommendations for improvements. If the member state is willing to remedy the situation but unable to bear the cost of the new facilities, the Council may agree to provide all or a portion of the funds. The Organization may finance "joint support" projects to a limited extent by drawing on its general fund, but for the most part will make special assessments, as in the case of the ocean weather ship stations, against the various member states in proportion to their use of the air-navigation facilities in question.

The "joint support" program of ICAO promises to be one of the most valuable contributions of the Organization to international civil aviation. In addition to the North Atlantic Ocean weather ship stations, the Organization is at the present time sponsoring the joint operation of the loran station at Vik, Iceland. Member states furnishing financial and technical assistance for operation of the station are Canada, France, Iceland, the Netherlands, the United States, and the United Kingdom, whose flag lines use this air-navigation facility when flying across the Atlantic.

Work in the Economic Field

The Chicago Aviation Conference, in drawing up two separate agreements—the international air-services transit agreement and the international air-transport agreement—for signature and acceptance by states members of the Organization, anticipated the difficulties inherent in postwar attempts to solve the problem of international exchange of aviation privileges on a multilateral basis. Thirty-six states accepted the transit agreement, incorporating the "two freedoms", but only 17 states accepted the transport agreement,

---

[9] The United States, Nicaragua, the Dominican Republic, and China, which accepted the air-transport agreement, subsequently withdrew from the agreement.

[10] The FAL Division's terms of reference also include matters pertaining to financial and monetary regulations, taxes, police and immigration requirements, military restrictions, and regulations imposed by national and international aeronautical authorities.

Air Transport Committee through the Council to the next Assembly of all member states, which is scheduled to be held in Geneva in June 1948.

Work in the Legal Field

With the creation of a permanent Legal Committee by the First Assembly of ICAO in May 1947, the Organization took over the work of unifying and codifying private international air law, which formerly had been handled by the Comité International Technique d'Experts Juridiques Aériens (CITEJA).[11] At its first meeting held in Brussels, in September 1947, the Legal Committee reached agreement on a draft convention on international recognition of rights in aircraft, which would facilitate the financing of aircraft engaged in international civil aviation. The draft convention will be presented to the 1948 ICAO Assembly for approval by both member and nonmember states. In addition to handling private air-law matters, the Legal Committee is charged with advising the Organization on public air law, e. g., in connection with the sovereignty of a state over the air space above its territory and the elimination of discriminatory national regulations.

The convention on international civil aviation defines the aims and objectives of ICAO as follows:

"to develop the principles and techniques of international air navigation and to foster the planning and development of international air transport so as to:

"(a) Insure the safe and orderly growth of international civil aviation throughout the world;

"(b) Encourage the arts of aircraft design and operation for peaceful purposes;

"(c) Encourage the development of airways, airports, and air navigation facilities for international civil aviation;

"(d) Meet the needs of the peoples of the world for safe, regular, efficient and economical air transport;

"(e) Prevent economic waste caused by unreasonable competition;

"(f) Insure that the right of contracting States

(Continued on page 491)

---

[11] Established at Paris on May 7, 1926, and dissolved following its sixteenth and final session, held in Montreal (May 10–22, 1947), concurrently with the First Assembly of ICAO.

FOREIGN AID AND RECONSTRUCTION

Foreign Assistance Act of 1948 [indep?]

STATEMENT BY THE PRESIDENT

[Released to the press by the White House April 3]

Few Presidents have had the opportunity to sign legislation of such importance as the Foreign Assistance Act of 1948.

The signing of this act is a momentous occasion in the world's quest for enduring peace.

I commend the Congress of the United States for the cooperation it has evidenced in the prompt passage of this measure.

Its passage is a striking manifestation of the fact that a bipartisan foreign policy can lead to effective action. It is even more striking in its proof that swift and vigorous action for peace is not incompatible with the full operation of our democratic process of discussion and debate. Those who are skeptical of the effectiveness of a democratic system should ponder the lesson of the enactment of this measure.

Our program of foreign aid is perhaps the greatest venture in constructive statesmanship that any nation has undertaken. It is an outstanding example of cooperative endeavor for the common good.

The Foreign Assistance Act is the best answer that this country can make in reply to the vicious and distorted misrepresentations of our efforts for peace which have been spread abroad by those who do not wish our efforts to succeed. This measure is America's answer to the challenge facing the free world today.

It is a measure for reconstruction, stability, and peace. Its purpose is to assist in the preservation of conditions under which free institutions can survive in the world. I believe that the determination of the American people to work for conditions of enduring peace throughout the world, demonstrated by this act, will encourage free men and women everywhere and will give renewed hope to all mankind that there will one day be peace on earth, good will among men.

Statement by George C. Marshall

[Released to the press by the White House April 3]

The decision of the United States Government as confirmed by the Foreign Assistance Act of 1948 is, I think, an historic step in the foreign policy of this country.

The leaders in the Congress and the membership generally have faced a great crisis with courage and wisdom and with legislative skill, richly deserving of the approval and the determined support of the people.

Program for Development of Sicily and Southern Italy

STATEMENT BY ROBERT A. LOVETT
Acting Secretary of State

[Released to the press April 1]

Representatives of the Committee for Economic and Social Development of Italy, composed of prominent American citizens of Italian origin, called on the Acting Secretary of State on April 1 to inform him of their program for assisting in the development of Sicily and southern Italy. During the course of the conversations Mr. Lovett made the following remarks

I am happy to receive the Committee for Eco-
nomic and Social Development of Italy, and to hear of your program to contribute to the welfare of the people of Sicily and southern Italy.

The Government and people of the United States have already done much to help the Italians help themselves back to economic recovery and the restoration of a truly democratic way of life. The efforts and the progress which the Italian nation have already made in this direction have inspired the admiration of the world.

(*Continued on following page*)

---

¹ Public Law 472 (80th Cong., 2d sess.).

NINTH INTERNATIONAL CONFERENCE OF AMERICAN STATES

terdependence of the Americas

ADDRESS BY GEORGE C. MARSHALL [1]

Chairman, U.S. Delegation

t is a genuine pleasure for me to meet again h the distinguished delegates of the American ublics, and especially so under the hospitable pices of the Republic of Colombia. I wish to ress through His Excellency Doctor (Laure-) Gómez, Foreign Minister of Colombia, our tinguished presiding officer, the very sincere ap-ciation we feel for the Government of Colombia our host, our respectful admiration for His cellency President Ospina Pérez, and our strong ling of friendship and regard for the people of lombia.

t is my privilege and duty to convey to the con-ence warm greetings from President Truman h his earnest wish that our efforts here will be cessful in behalf of all the peoples of the ericas.

en years have passed since the Eighth Inter-tional Conference of American States was held Lima. The momentous events of that period layed this Ninth Conference but did not halt ogress in inter-American cooperation.

The emergency meetings of the Foreign Min-ers, which enabled us to coordinate our wartime orts, were followed by the all-important confer-ce at Mexico City in 1945 which resulted in the t of Chapultepec, and the Conference on the aintenance of Continental Peace and Security so ccessfully concluded last August at Rio de Ja-iro with the treaty of reciprocal assistance.

We are here to consolidate and to carry forward e decisions of these previous conferences. We ve to consider a lengthy agenda to give effect to e provisions of the ninth resolution of the Mex-

ico City conference, pertaining to the reorganiza-tion, consolidation, and strengthening of the inter-American system. This is no small undertaking, for what we do in this respect will have an im-portant bearing on the future of all our joint un-dertakings. The proposed organic pact will be the very heart of our hemispheric organization.

Cooperation among our countries has been greatly broadened and intensified during recent years. We need for this cooperation an organiza-tional structure which will on the one hand be adequate to the increased responsibilities placed upon it, and on the other hand, efficiently adminis-tered so that duplication of effort may be avoided. The inter-American conferences and meetings of Foreign Ministers are the instruments through which the inter-American system formulates policy and reaches decisions on questions of major importance. The drafters of the organic pact have wisely concluded that to insure that these policies and decisions are effectively carried out, the Pan American Union, as the central permanent agency of the inter-American system, must be given a greater responsibility and commensurate staff. Under the direction of the inter-American confer-ences and meetings of Foreign Ministers the Pan American Union should play an increasingly sig-nificant role in the effective functioning of the inter-American system.

I am sure we all are agreed that the development

[1] Made before the second plenary session in Bogotá, Co-lombia, on Apr. 1, 1948, and released to the press on the same date. The Secretary of State is serving as Chairman of the U.S. Delegation to the Conference.

(Continued from preceding page)

But a further effort is required before we can y the task is done. That effort is the European ecovery Program, which has just been approved y the Senate and House of Representatives. Its rimary purpose is to make possible the economic covery of the peoples of Europe by providing merican aid to reinforce their self-help and co-peration so that they can live together in peace d security. Certain basic plans for economic habilitation drawn up by the Italian Govern-

ment itself form part of the European Recovery Program for Italy. These plans include the re-habilitation of southern Italy and Sicily—land reclamation, the building of roads and electric power lines, the modernization of agriculture, and the establishment of local industries.

I should like to say again that I am happy to hear of your plans to support and assist the Italian people in this great project, and I am sure you can make a most valuable contribution towards the aim for which we are all working.

of the inter-American system is within the concept of the United Nations and contributes to the attainment of its objectives.

The urgent need of effective methods of economic cooperation presents us with problems that call for the utmost good will and understanding in order to accommodate complex interests.

Agreement on a convention setting forth the procedures for the pacific settlement of disputes is one of the necessary aims of this conference. By this means we will establish a broad juridical basis for the peaceful adjudication of any differences that may arise among the American states. At the same time we will set an example to a distracted world in the maintenance of peace among neighbor states under an accepted system of law that assures justice and equity to all nations, large and small.

Significant questions related to social progress and the rights of the individual man are to receive full consideration in the deliberations of the conference. These are matters in which all our peoples are deeply concerned. They rightfully expect us to take positive action for their protection and welfare. That, in reality, is the purpose of our endeavors.

The overwhelming desire of the people of the world is for peace and security, freedom to speak their thoughts, freedom to earn a decent living in their own way. It is the earnest, the very genuine desire of the people of my country to continue to assist, so far as they are able to do so, the other people of the world to attain these objectives.

We have encountered, as you are aware, the determined and open opposition of one group of states. If the genuine cooperation of the Soviet Union could be secured, world recovery and peace would be assured. Until such cooperation is secured, we must proceed with our own efforts.

My Government has assumed heavy responsibilities in this undertaking, but we cannot do the job alone. We need the understanding and the cooperation of other nations whose objectives are the same as ours.

We must face reality. Allow me to talk to you frankly regarding the tremendous problems the United States is facing. After four years of supreme effort and a million casualties, we had looked forward to a state of tranquillity which would permit us to reorganize our economy, having made vast expenditures in natural resources and money. Instead my people find themselves today faced with the urgent necessity of meeting staggering and inescapable responsibilities—humanitarian, political, financial, and military—all over the world, in western Europe, in Germany and Austria, in Greece and Turkey, in the Middle East, in China, Japan, and Korea. Meeting these unprecedented responsibilities has demanded tremendous drafts on our resources and imposed burdensome

ient of national economies. The charter pointed ie way toward realization of this aim through the ncouragement of private enterprise and the fair :eatment of foreign capital.

Our specific task here is to find workable iethods by which our principles may be effectively pplied in practical affairs. In a few moments I iall discuss the proposals of the United States)elegation for achieving this objective. But first wish to draw attention to the general back-round from which they proceed. I do so because believe that the experience of my country in its :onomic development offers some useful prece-ents.

One of the principal needs of the United States fter it achieved independence was private capital)r development of its resources and for western xpansion. From overseas, and this is the point wish to emphasize, at first cautiously and often ith misunderstanding on both sides, the venture ipital of Europe was invested in the new United tates of America.

The great benefits accruing to the people of the inited States from its material development were :tributable in an important degree to this assist-nce received from abroad which together with ie economic and political freedom of action en-bled our people to capitalize rapidly upon the reat natural resources of the country, and thus evelop the production which has enabled us to ear today the heaviest responsibilities ever placed pon a single nation.

By 1900 the people of the United States them-lves were becoming large investors in enterprises)road. But internal development continued un-oated. Despite the transformation from debtor) creditor nation and the accumulation of capital)r foreign investments of its own, the United tates continues to welcome money and technical ssistance from other countries.

The point I wish to make is that even after the nited States had achieved economic maturity and ad become a major source of venture capital)reign investors continued to participate in the idustrial and commercial growth of the nation ithout discrimination.

This policy has enabled the United States to rosper. The large-scale exchange of capital,)ods, and services; the system of free enterprise; ie confidence of other people in our future and ie protection afforded foreign investments; the)ntributions made by skilled, energetic immi-rants—all these helped immeasurably in making ir nation not only productive and vigorous, but ee. I repeat, this policy has enabled the United tates to prosper, and I wish here to stress that has enabled the United States to do a great deal)r other countries, including the protection of ieir freedoms along with our own.

May I at this time invite your attention to a

fact of particular significance related to the broad benefits to which I have just referred? That is, the fact that these benefits have been transferred into human values through the elevation of the real wages of labor to a point higher than has been achieved under any other system of enterprise in the history of mankind. These benefits auto-matically transfer themselves into the cultural and physical advancement of all of the people.

The United States is qualified, I submit, by its own historical experience to respond understand-ingly to the purpose of other American republics to improve their economic status. We understand the wish to achieve balanced economies through the development of industries, mechanization of agriculture, and modernization of transportation.

My Government is prepared to increase the scale of assistance it has been giving to the economic development of the American republics. But it is beyond the capacity of the United States Govern-ment itself to finance more than a small portion of the vast development needed. The capital re-quired through the years must come from private sources, both domestic and foreign.

As the experience of the United States has shown, progress can be achieved best through in-dividual effort and the use of private resources. Encouragement should therefore be given to the increase of investment capital from internal as well as external sources. It is obvious that foreign capital will naturally gravitate most readily to countries where it is accorded fair and equitable treatment.

For its part, the United States fully supports the promotion of economic development in the American republics. We advocate the prompt preparation of sound development programs, which will set specific and realistic goals to be accomplished in the next few years.

The United States supports the International Bank for Reconstruction and Development as an important source of long-term capital for develop-ing the economies of the American republics. My Government confidently expects the role of this in-stitution to be one of increasing usefulness.

The President of the United States is submitting to Congress a request for an increase in the lending authority of the Export-Import Bank which will be available for sound projects. These Govern-ment funds will be in addition to the private fi-nancing which will be needed for a much greater number of development projects.

The United States has studied the proposals regarding the taxation of foreign investments, with a view to avoiding double taxation and to encouraging the flow of private capital into other countries desiring it. I am glad to report that the President has under consideration measures to liberalize taxes on capital invested in foreign countries. These measures are designed to encourage not only initial investment but also the retention and reinvestment abroad of earnings derived from such capital. These measures also would liberalize the tax treatment of United States citizens residing abroad, and should therefore encourage technical experts to accept employment in other countries.

My Government attaches special importance to efforts to improve health, sanitation, education, and agricultural and industrial processes throughout the Hemisphere. We look forward to an expansion of the cooperative efforts of the American republics in these fields. We are surveying the availability of technical experts who may collaborate in the progress and development of the American republics, as recently authorized by the Congress on a more flexible basis.

The economic advancement and security of the Hemisphere are supremely important to all countries, large and small, and to every citizen of our countries. Through joint endeavor, with each country accepting its share of responsibility and seeking faithfully to carry out its obligations, I am confident that the American republics will consistently move forward and attain the objectives which we all so earnestly desire.

Before concluding I wish to call attention to the close relationship between the solemn pacts we are here to conclude at Bogotá and the treaty of reciprocal assistance signed at Rio de Janeiro last September. Together, these pacts, when ratified, will form a harmonious whole guaranteeing the social, cultural, and economic progress of the Americas and at the same time the preservation of their independence, security, and sovereignty. I am informed that ten countries have already ratified the treaty of reciprocal assistance and that several other nations plan to take positive action along this line. It is to be hoped that during our labors here we may receive the gratifying word that the required number of ratifications have been deposited to enable the treaty to enter into effect. Such action is particularly important in the present world situation. We need the other vital measures we are to consider here as indispensable contributions to the welfare of the Americas. The peoples for whom we speak are impatient to launch this promising cooperative endeavor, for they see in it their greatest hope for achieving a better life for themselves, their children, and their children's children. They look to this conference to set in motion the concerted effort that will make their constant dream of peace and plenty a living, satisfying reality. We must not fail them.

[*Following the conclusion of his formal address to the conference, Secretary Marshall spoke extemporaneously substantially as follows*]

As has been the case with my predecessors here, it has been necessary for me to speak formally

Alternate Delegates

John C. Dreier, Chief, Division of Special Inter-American Affairs, Department of State

M. B. Ridgway, Lt. Gen., U.S.A., Department of the Army

William Sanders, Associate Chief, Division of International Organization Affairs, Department of State

Leroy D. Stinebower, Deputy U.S. Representative on the Economic and Social Council of the United Nations

Jack B. Tate, Deputy Legal Adviser, Department of State

Advisers

Thomas C. Blaisdell, Jr., Director, Office of International Trade, Department of Commerce

Henry Chalmers, Commercial Policy Adviser, Office of International Trade, Department of Commerce

John S. deBeers, International Finance Division, Department of the Treasury

John J. Haggerty, Office of Foreign Agricultural Relations, Department of Agriculture

John Halderman, Assistant Chief, Division of International Organization Affairs, Department of State

Osborne B. Hardison, Rear Admiral, U.S.N., Department of the Navy

Hubert Harmon, Lt. Gen., U.S.A.F., Department of the Air Force

Edward Hidalgo, National Security Resources Board

Edward A. Jamison, Division of Special Inter-American Affairs, Department of State

Muna Lee, Division of American Republics, Office of Information and Educational Exchange, Department of State

Cecil B. Lyon, Special Assistant to Assistant Secretary for political affairs, Department of State

Kenneth Meiklejohn, Assistant Solicitor, Department of Labor

Otis E. Mulliken, Division of International Organization Affairs, Department of State

Oscar M. Powell, Regional Director for the West Coast, Social Security Administration, Federal Security Agency

Sherman S. Sheppard, Chief, International Activities Branch, Bureau of the Budget, Executive Office of the President

H. Gerald Smith, Special Assistant to the Assistant Secretary for economic affairs, Department of State

Joseph H. Taggart, Economic Adviser to Chairman, Munitions Board, The National Military Establishment

Lloyd Tibbott, Assistant to the Chief, Division of Regulations, Maritime Commission

Marjorie M. Whiteman, Office of Assistant Legal Adviser for International Organization Affairs, Department of State

Simon N. Wilson, Division of Special Inter-American Affairs, Department of State

Special Assistant to the Chairman

Marshall S. Carter, Special Assistant to the Secretary of State

Special Assistant for Press Relations

Michael J. McDermott, Special Assistant for Press Relations, Department of State

Secretary General

Clarke L. Willard, Associate Chief, Division of International Conferences, Department of State

Special Assistant to the Secretary General

Frances E. Pringle, Division of International Conferences, Department of State

Technical Secretary

Ward P. Allen, Division of International Organization Affairs, Department of State

(*Continued on next page*)

(Continued from preceding page)

Assistant Technical Secretaries

Donald M. Dozer, Acting Chief, Division of Research for Latin America, Department of State
Laura Iredale, Division of International Organization Affairs, Department of State
John L. Kuhn, Executive Secretariat, Department of State

Documents Assistant

Margaret L. Moore, Division of Special Inter-American Affairs, Department of State

Archivist

Patricia Ann Foster, Division of Central American and Panama Affairs, Department of State

Administrative Secretary

Orion J. Libert, Division of International Conferences, Department of State

Assistant Administrative Secretary

Anthony A. Covins, Division of Foreign Service Administration, Department of State

Administrative Assistant

Ann Jablonski, Division of Finance, Department of State

Secretaries of Delegation

Howard E. Chaille, Division of Communications, Department of State
Joseph W. Musick, Office of Controls, Department of State
R. Richard Rubottom, Jr., Second Secretary of Embassy, Bogotá

INTERNATIONAL ORGANIZATIONS AND CONFERENCES

INTERNATIONAL WHEAT AGREEMENT SIGNED

[Released to the press April 2]

The international wheat agreement, which was open for signature in Washington from March 6 until April 1, has been signed on behalf of all the importing and exporting countries listed in annexes I and II to article 2 of the agreement.[1]

The 36 signatory countries are Afghanistan, Australia, Austria, Belgium, Brazil, Canada, China, Colombia, Cuba, Czechoslovakia, Denmark, Dominican Republic, Ecuador, Egypt, the French Union and Saar, Greece, Guatemala, India, Ireland, Italy, Lebanon, Liberia, Mexico, Netherlands, New Zealand, Norway, Peru, Republic of the Philippines, Poland, Portugal, Sweden, Switzerland, Union of South Africa, United Kingdom of Great Britain and Northern Ireland, United States of America, and Venezuela.

The agreement is subject to formal acceptance by the signatory governments.

The objectives of the agreement, as provided in article 1, are to assure supplies of wheat to importing countries and to assure markets to exporting countries at equitable and stable prices.

INVITATIONS TO ATTEND THE INTERNATIONAL AIR EXPOSITION EXTENDED

At the request of William O'Dwyer, Mayor of the City of New York, the Department of State has transmitted on behalf of the City of New York, to all foreign governments having diplomatic missions at Washington, invitations to send representatives to attend the International Air Exposition on Mayor's Day, August 7, 1948. The representatives of the foreign governments will be the official guests of the City of New York on Mayor's Day. Although this event is not sponsored by the United States Government, the Department of State is transmitting the invitations of the Mayor of the City of New York in consideration of the general interest in the Golden Anniversary Air Exposition.

U.S. TO ACT AS HOST TO FIFTH MEETING OF RUBBER STUDY GROUP

[Released to the press March 29]

The Department of State has announced that the United States Government will act as host to the fifth meeting of the Rubber Study Group which will convene at Washington April 26-May 1, 1948, to review the world rubber situation. Invitations have been issued to the following countries whose Governments are members of the Group: Australia, Belgium, Canada, Ceylon, Czechoslovakia, Denmark, France, Hungary, Italy, Liberia, the Netherlands, and the United Kingdom. The United Nations, the Food and Agriculture Organization of the United Nations, and the Pan American Union have been invited to send observers.

The Rubber Study Group was organized in 1944 by the Governments of the Netherlands, the United Kingdom, and the United States. France has participated in all but the first meeting. At its fourth meeting at Paris in July 1947, the Rubber Study Group established a Management Committee which meets periodically at London. A permanent secretariat was set up at London by the Management Committee in 1947 to provide the Study Group with a full information service covering both the statistical situation and the general economic position as it relates to rubber

[1] For comments on the wheat agreement, see BULLETIN of Mar. 28, 1948, p. 395.

For the convenience of those in attendance and to conserve time, the meeting halls will be provided with a simultaneous interpretation system so that speeches and papers will be heard in any one of the three official languages, English, French, and Spanish. Up to four scientific meetings will be held at one time. The subjects to be considered at the congresses cover a wide range. Consideration will be given to human diseases which debilitate and kill as well as interfere with production and trade. The problems of nutrition of man in the tropics together with the maladies of domestic animals will be discussed. Emphasis will be placed on the most effective uses of the insecticides which have given a new power over disease-spreading insects, as well as on the drugs which have recently been synthesized. To cover so wide a field the scientific program has been organized in 12 sections. There will be about 180 papers in all presented by outstanding scientists from 37 countries. Daily programs of technical motion pictures have been scheduled.

Highlights of the working program will be two special evening sessions, the first of which will commemorate the demonstration by Walter Reed of the mosquito transmission of yellow fever. The second will commemorate the fiftieth anniversary of the discovery by Ronald Ross of the method of malaria transmission. Tours will be made to the National Institute of Health, the Naval Medical Research Institute, and the Army Medical Department Research and Graduate School. There will be a whole day of demonstrations at the Agricultural Research Center at Beltsville, Maryland, including the spraying of insecticides from the air.

Entertainment for the delegates and members, in addition to private dinners and social functions, will include an official reception at the Pan American Union; a social gathering at the Shoreham Hotel; a garden party at Dumbarton Oaks; a trip by boat to Mount Vernon; and an official dinner at the Mayflower Hotel. The wives of members and delegates will be feted officially at a White House tea by Mrs. Truman and at a special luncheon at the Army-Navy Country Club in Arlington.

Physicians, doctors of veterinary medicine, sanitary engineers, nurses, bacteriologists, parasitologists, entomologists, chemists, and other professional persons should find much of value in the program and also in the association with other scientists in the same fields from other lands. Any reputable professional person with qualifications and interest in any phase of tropical medicine will be eligible to become a member of the congresses. Anyone desiring further information should write to the Executive Secretary, Fourth International Congresses on Tropical Medicine and Malaria, Department of State, Washington 25, D.C.

THE RECORD OF THE WEEK

Progress of Human Liberty in Democratic Form

BY GEORGE V. ALLEN [1]

Assistant Secretary for Public Affairs

*　　*　　*　　*　　*

Having taken my oath of office only yesterday, this is my first public address in my new capacity, which carries the somewhat vague title—Assistant Secretary for Public Affairs. One might logically conclude that since diplomacy and the conduct of foreign affairs are traditionally secret operations, there would be little for a State Department official to do in the field of public affairs. The Department has often been accused of dissimulating rather then disseminating the truth. The creation of an Assistant Secretaryship for Public Affairs was decided upon, I believe, in an effort to bring about the widest possible dissemination of the truth.

Serious efforts have been made and are being made to change the traditional attitude toward diplomacy. This can be accomplished best by a change in the traditional conduct of diplomacy. The Department of State has a responsibility not only to keep the public informed in foreign affairs but to seek public support and assistance in the formulation of foreign policy.

In my capacity as public-affairs officer, I shall make every effort to deal as openly with the public as is humanly possible. I do not promise that there shall be no longer any secrets. Public officials, when first taking office, are under the temptation to make pleasing promises of the determination to "let the public in on what is going on". If they make such promises, however, they may discover later that the promises are impossible of fulfilment. There is point to the complaint of some commentators that our national interests have at times suffered from too much publicity during negotiations.

Although I am unable to give you assurances of a wide-open policy in the public-affairs section of the State Department, I do want to say this with the utmost genuineness. My job is with the public, and I shall at all times be your advocate. I hope you will be mine. I hope we can work together as a team, all seeking to achieve the same end.

One is often asked, "What is the end we seek to achieve in our foreign policy?" A more frequent question is, "Do we have a foreign policy?" Moreover, there is considerable confusion regarding what foreign policy is anyway—ours or any other nation's. Can it be defined so the ordinary man can understand it, or must one search through volumes of learned studies to begin to comprehend the subject?

I shall be bold enough today to try to answer, simply as I can, my own personal understanding not only of what foreign policy is in general but also what the major policy is which we Americans are seeking to achieve today.

Let us consider briefly what foreign policy is. I believe the broad answer to this is fairly easy. The foreign policy of any nation or government consists of the aims which that nation seeks to achieve *outside* its own borders. The contrast is with domestic policy, which is the goal or goals which a government seeks to attain within its frontiers.

The foreign policy of a country may include aims which remain constant over a long period of time, such as, for example, Russia's effort to gain control of the Dardanelles during more than four centuries. On the other hand, a policy may be entirely discarded. At one time, for example, Americans clamored loudly for "54′40″ or fight" in a dispute with Canada over the northwest frontier. This aim has long since been forgotten.

State Department officials have been asked to define American foreign policy ever since Thomas Jefferson organized the Department in 1789. Moreover, I have no doubt that British, French, and all other foreign-office officials in democratic countries have often been asked a similar question by their own citizens. It would not generally occur that a Soviet citizen would ask his foreign office the question, "What is Soviet foreign policy?" To do so might imply either that there were some doubts in the citizen's mind on the subject or that he was critical.

Fortunately, the question can be freely asked in America. I hope this will always be true. To answer the question has sometimes been difficult, but I believe the answer is easier today perhaps than it has been at any time in our history.

During the early days of our Republic, our f...

[1] Address made before the Overseas Press Club in Washington, D.C., on Apr. 1, 1948, and released to the press on the same date.

ȝn policy was concerned primarily with staying
ȝt of European quarrels—the no-entangling-alli-
ȝce policy. Later we were concerned, outside our
ȝrders, with the question of extending those very
ȝrders to the Pacific Ocean. Since the turn of the
ȝntury we have been increasingly concerned with
ȝproving our relations in this Hemisphere, cul-
ȝinating some years ago in the keystone of óur
ȝlicy in this field, the policy of the good neighbor.
Today, it seems to me clear that the chief aim
ȝhich the United States seeks to achieve abroad is
ȝe triumph, on the broadest possible scale, of the
ȝinciples of democracy. Practically everything
ȝe do, in big and little matters, is directed toward
ȝat goal. We seek to support in every way we
ȝn the democratic way of life, the dignity of the
ȝman individual, freedom of religion, and free-
ȝm of thought and expression.

Additional elements in our foreign policy, co-
ȝdinated with this chief aim, include strongest
ȝpport for the United Nations and an effort to
ȝake it a more effective instrument. We seek to
ȝphold the principles of the Atlantic Charter,
ȝcluding notably freedom from fear. We strive
ȝ free the world from the fear of aggression. We
ȝek the triumph of justice, of decency, and stabil-
ȝy in international relations.

I should point out that our foreign policy, like
ȝat of every other nation, is a national one. Our
ȝovernment, in the final analysis, must seek to
ȝhieve goals which will have the best results for
ȝr own nation. We seek the preservation of de-
ȝocracy in the world essentially in order to assure
ȝs preservation in our own country. Happily, our
ȝational aims coincide with the interests of free
ȝen everywhere.

One may well ask, "Is there anything new in our
ȝoreign policy today? We Americans have al-
ȝ'ays believed in democracy and fought for it.
ȝ'hy do you suddenly put it at the head of the list,
ȝominating all else in our foreign policy at the
ȝresent time?"

The answer, I believe, lies in the fact that democ-
ȝacy has only recently been brought under serious
ȝhreat. From the beginning of our Republic until
ȝecent times, democracy has been on the increase in
ȝhe world. Human liberty and freedom of thought
ȝade steady progress during the nineteenth cen-
ȝury. We Americans came to regard its triumph
ȝs rapidly being achieved and to believe there was
ȝot much we need to do about it except stand by
ȝnd wish it godspeed.

But with the 1917 revolution in Russia a new
ȝoncept came into prominence—the concept of the
ȝule of a great nation through an ideological dic-
ȝatorship conceived in bloodshed and maintained
ȝy the chains of mental slavery. For a number of
ȝears this dictatorship was too busy with its in-
ȝernal affairs to cause much concern to the out-
ȝide world. Our foreign policy was affected, cer-

tainly, but the existence of an anti-democratic
regime in Russia was not at first a major concern
to us.

Then came the rise of a similar regime in Germany, different in certain acts and concepts but
entirely similar in its totalitarianism and its ruthless destruction of any opportunity for the people
to make their voices heard. The German brand
of totalitarianism was more immediately dangerous. Its aggressive actions galvanized our people
into the realization, for the first time, that democracy as a principle of government could be lost.
We began to realize that Sinclair Lewis was not
living in a dream world when he preached, "It
can happen here."

Today the vast majority of American people are
thoroughly aroused to the fact that our democratic
way of life is under most serious attack, and some
even fear that democracy is losing the battle.

If you grant that the preservation of democracy
is the chief aim of our foreign policy, the next
question is, "What are we doing about it? How
do we implement this policy?" I would like to
emphasize that there is an important distinction
between foreign policy and its implementation,
although the difference is not generally or sufficiently appreciated.

In my own view, the single most important
implement we are using at the moment, in our
effort to achieve the preservation of democracy, is
to assist in the economic recovery of the democratic world.

Perhaps I should explain why I do not list economic recovery itself as a major goal of our
foreign policy. Why should ERP, for example,
be called merely an instrument of foreign policy?
Certainly, the relief of misery and want, the attainment of food and clothing and the material
things of life, are good ends in themselves. But
only materialists would list those ends as final
goals. There is a better and higher goal, toward
which economic recovery is merely a way station.
The political and spiritual freedom of the human
soul and the human personality is the ultimate
goal we must keep constantly in our minds.

Economic recovery is merely one of the many
implements of our foreign policy. We are doing
and attempting many other things at the same
time—but all are directed toward the same overwhelmingly important task of the democratic
world today.

In the field of public affairs, you and I are concerned with information and education as instruments in achieving our foreign-policy objectives.
The astonishingly widespread misrepresentation
and misunderstanding of our motives make it
imperative that American policy be better understood, not only behind the Iron Curtain and
elsewhere abroad but even in our own country.
After two years abroad, I am shocked to return

THE RECORD OF THE WEEK

and find the extent to which Mr. Henry Wallace, to take an outstanding example, goes about parroting the misrepresentation of our foreign-policy aims. Very many of the things he says are the same sort of villification of our motives I have listened to over the Moscow radio during the past two years in Iran.

I shall, in conclusion, undertake to consider whether there is a reasonable likelihood that the democratic way of life will suffer extinction, whether it will hold its own in a stalemate with totalitarianism, or whether it will triumph.

There are people devoted to human liberty on both sides of the Iron Curtain, just as there are on both sides people who are willing to sell their liberties for the false promise of a worker's paradise under Communism. If two things are accomplished, it is my personal conviction that democracy will prevail. In the first place, economic development throughout the democratic world must be achieved, to give the masses of the people, the industrial workers and the farmers, a high stand-

Reduction of Trade Barriers—Rhetoric

BY WINTHR

Acting Deputy Director, Offi

Ten days ago at Havana, the representatives of 54 nations, meeting under the auspices of the United Nations, reached agreement on a charter for an International Trade Organization, to be submitted to their governments for acceptance. This charter is a broad code of international economic conduct. It is the culmination of over two years of international effort, and at the final session of the conference William L. Clayton, head of the United States Delegation, had this to say:

"There have been other conferences on international economic affairs. But none of them has undertaken a task so difficult as the one that is completed here today. None of them has come to an agr ement concerning so many vital economic interests of so many states. None of them has produced a document so comprehensive as the Havana charter for world trade. Few, if any, of them have attained so notable a measure of success."

Five months ago, at Geneva, the representatives of 23 nations, also meeting under the auspices of the United Nations, reached agreement on a general agreement on tariffs and trade, containing rules for the conduct of many aspects of their trade with each other and providing for the tariff treatment of products accounting for over half the

[1] Address made before the World Trade Conference of the Cleveland World Trade Association on Apr. 2, 1948, and released to the press on the same date.

nations. We have seen the results of trade discriminations during the years between two world wars—nations playing off trade with one country against that with another in a global game of political chess. Almost inevitably trade discriminations develop political aspects, and the competitive clashes which in private enterprise are merely stimulating become national issues and involve national pride when they occur in government-to-government dealings.

Fourth, the belief that progressive trade policies must be supported by consistent policies for stabilization in the field of certain primary commodities. Prolonged and drastic fluctuations in world markets for these commodities can create widespread hardship and unemployment and thus undermine the very foundations of a cooperative world economy. Machinery and rules should be provided for reaching intergovernmental agreements to govern temporarily the production and marketing of such commodities when they are in burdensome world surplus.

Fifth, the belief that though nations may choose to use different systems of trading, it is possible for them to work in harmony. Therefore, an effort should be made to find rules which, for example, will govern the operation of state trading enterprises in international trade so as to place those countries using such a system as nearly as possible on the same basis as those relying on private enterprise.

Sixth, the belief that it is essential to develop the resources of underdeveloped areas and to make the fullest use of the resources of all areas. Increased production and increased consumption lead the way hand in hand to increased prosperity, and one's most highly developed neighbors turn out to be one's best markets.

Seventh, the belief that the availability of machinery for easy international consultation, the obligation to consult, and agreement in advance on the rules of the game are the surest guaranties against economic warfare.

And so, under this *Charter*, nations which join the Ito would agree:

1. To take measures designed to maintain productive employment and buying power within their own borders as a means to stimulating trade, avoiding measures which would create difficulties for the economies of others.

2. To encourage private and public international investment and to recognize the need for economic advancement of less well-developed areas.

3. To negotiate for mutual reduction of trade barriers.

4. To eliminate discrimination in international

---

² Department of State publication 2598.

trade, except in exceptional and clearly defined circumstances.

5. To lower the "invisible tariff" of customs administration.

6. To conduct international trade between private and public enterprises according to principles of nondiscrimination and fair dealing.

7. To curb and regulate international monopolies and cartels.

8. To accept a code of principles to govern the formation and operation of intergovernmental commodity agreements, which should be fair to producer and consumer alike and give producers and consumers an equal voice in their negotiation and operation.

9. To consult with other members about contemplated action which might affect them adversely.

The same basic beliefs also underlie the general agreement on tariffs and trade, which, you will recall, is the second document which I mentioned at the beginning of this talk. When the United States put forward to the world its proposals for rules to govern international trade and for an International Trade Organization, it had available also a mechanism for more concrete action—the mechanism of the Trade Agreements Act. Accordingly, as I said, it invited a considerable number of other nations to negotiate with it and with each other for the reduction of tariffs. As a result 23 countries, representing over three quarters of the world's international trade, met at Geneva, and after seven months of negotiation, reached agreement on the text of an agreement which specifies the tariff treatment of products which account for over half of the world's trade. Imports of these products by the Geneva countries prewar amounted to over ten billions of dollars, of which United States imports were about a billion and three quarters.

The tariff concessions granted were of three kinds: reductions in rates of duty; binding of existing rates against increases; and binding of duty-free status. The United States obtained reductions in duty from other countries on products of principal interest to us accounting in 1939 for about 500 million dollars of imports. We granted reduction in duty on imports into the United States accounting in 1939 for about 500 million dollars. We bound the existing tariff rates on about 150 million dollars of imports and bound the duty-free status of about a billion one hundred million dollars of imports. We obtained corresponding concessions for our exports of approximately the same magnitude.

The general agreement also contains provisions designed to prevent the participants from canceling out tariff concessions by imposing discriminatory and restrictive measures such as import quotas, exchange controls and manipulations,

flict. And this, throughout the entire range of trade relationships, is what the signatories of the charter agree to do. Each will surrender some part of its freedom to take action that might prove harmful to others; and thus each will gain the assurance that others will not take action harmful to it."

The general agreement on tariffs and trade also contains exceptions to its general provisions which I mentioned earlier. These exceptions are, of course, made to allow for the present extreme shortages abroad in production and foreign exchange. But these exceptions, like those in the charter, are closely defined, their use limited, and the conditions under which they must be abandoned are clearly set forth.

It would be less than honest of me to say that our foreign sales of exportable products will increase immediately because of these tariff concessions from other countries. They will not. In the long run, United States commercial exports cannot increase until the rest of the world is better able to pay for them. Profitable trade must be reciprocal and there is very little real reciprocity when our exports of goods and services are exceeding our imports by 11 billion dollars a year, as they did in 1947.

But tariff concessions in a wide area of world trade—such as were achieved at Geneva and are looked forward to under the ITO—will inevitably facilitate, liberalize, and encourage world trade. People work and produce when they see a chance to exchange their products for things which they want and cannot produce for themselves. That is human nature. As world production and trade conditions begin to return to normal, as exceptions cease to be operative, as United States producers again face competition in foreign markets, the tariff concessions embodied in the general agreement will give easier access to those markets for the goods which United States agriculture and industry must sell abroad in order to maintain the level of economic activity in this country. Even while shortages of dollars exist, the concessions will help to expand trade between so-called "soft currency" countries, and the general provisions will limit the use of controls to the cases where they are really needed.

The general agreement was negotiated by the United States under the authority of the Trade Agreements Act, which expires on June 12. The President has asked the Congress to renew this tried and tested instrument of our foreign economic policy, already four times renewed, for a further period of three years. Why?

There were only 23 countries at Geneva. It is important to bring many other countries into the general agreement. To do so they must negotiate reductions in their tariffs with the Geneva countries. The President needs the trade-agreements authority to participate in these negotiations.

. If he does not have effective authority to negotiate because of failure to renew the act, we will simply have to say to countries wishing to come into the agreement that it is uncertain whether we can give effect to the results of any negotiation. Since the trade of most countries with the United States is highly significant to them, they will hesitate to come in on this basis. We will be keeping friendly countries out of this cooperative economic effort.

In the European Recovery Program we will be embarking on a tremendous effort to help western Europe get back on its feet. The program recognizes the elementary fact that one of the prerequisites to their staying on their feet is to reduce the barriers to their trade between each other and between themselves and the rest of the world. They should get into a position to earn their own way by selling their goods. The reduction of their tariffs on each other's goods and the extension of tariff reductions in their trade with the rest of the world is one good way of enabling them to pay their own way. We should not, just as we embark on the European Recovery Program, give up our ability to participate with these countries in working out arrangements by which they can more completely pay their own way.

The Trade Agreements Act is a symbol to the rest of the world of the United States willingness to participate in international economic cooperation. Its first enactment, 14 years ago, marked the reversal of the policy of economic isolationism which we pursued after World War I. Any action which could be interpreted as a repudiation by the United States of the trade-agreements policy

Restitution of Looted Property in Japan

UNITED STATE

The United States interim directive, dispatched by the Joint Chiefs of Staff to the Supreme Commander for the Allied Powers on 17 March 1948, follows

1. The instructions here below are additions to and do not derogate from the full force and effect of FEC–011/12.

2. The SCAP should accord the same treatment to all property found in Japan, and identified as having been located in an Allied country either at or during the time of occupation, and which was removed therefrom by fraud or duress by the Japanese or their agents, as that which he accords to objects in the four categories listed in para. 1 of FEC–011/12 (JCS Directive # 57) identified as

5. The Supreme Commander for the Allied Powers shall create an agency comprising one representative from each of the restitution and reparations teams in Japan of the eleven member countries of the Far Eastern Commission, who desire to participate, to advise on restitution matters. In addition, the Supreme Commander or his deputy should act as the non-voting chairman of the agency. It may meet at the call of the Supreme Commander or at the request of any member. The Supreme Commander should notify the United States Government of the views of the agency when his views conflict with those of the majority of the member countries.

6. In cases of doubt as to the adequacy of the evidence of ownership submitted to support a claim for an object known to have been looted, the Supreme Commander shall inform the other members of the advisory agency of the existence of the claim. The advisory agency, after examining the evidence, shall give its advice to the Supreme Commander as to whether the claim should be approved or the provisions of paragraph 4 above applied.

7. No claims for the restitution of looted property should be lodged with SCAP after eight months from the issuance of this directive to SCAP; provided that after such terminal date, claims may, with the concurrence of SCAP, be lodged for property known to have been looted but not previously identified.

MENTS OF STATE AND COMMERCE

would permit them to remain in Japan longer, must not only demonstrate that their continued presence will contribute to the objectives of the occupation but must also provide their own support outside the facilities of the Japanese Government-operated hotels.

Individual applications must be sponsored by the applicant's own government and forwarded through established diplomatic channels. United States property owners or their representatives desiring to take advantage of the arrangements outlined herein, should make application to the Office of International Trade, U. S. Department of Commerce, through its field offices. Applications will be considered by the Supreme Commander in priority of their receipt, and entry permits will be valid during a period of 60 days, assigned by the General Headquarters in Japan. Passport applications should be filed with the clerk of Federal or State courts or with the passport agents located in Washington, San Francisco, and

New York. Transportation will be obtained by the entrants via established transportation facilities.

Procedures governing the restitution of properties to American and other United Nations owners are chiefly the following. After his arrival in Japan the U.S. owner, or his duly authorized agent, will make application to the Supreme Commander through the U. S. Reparations and Restitution Mission in Tokyo for the return of his property. Attention is drawn to Department of State press release no. 532, June 27, 1947, which described the instructions under which powers of attorney may be drawn by American property owners outside of Japan. Regardless of whether the property was sold or liquidated by the Japanese Government during the war, owners are entitled to return of their property. However, in such cases, the owner must agree, as a condition of the return of his property, to refund to the Japanese Government the amount of money received as payment or that was deposited in a blocked account in the owner's name at the time of sale or liquidation. Repayment of such amounts, however, will only be due after the settlement of any claims for loss or damage that the owner may make against the Japanese Government. If the property has been leased to a third party by the Japanese custodian or administrator, the owner will have the opportunity of terminating the lease and obtaining vacant possession. If, however, the property has been requisitioned by the occupation forces for their use, vacant possession will not be obtained by the owner until the property is released by the occupation forces.

In accepting the return of the property, the owner will not be required to renounce any claim he may have against the Japanese Government or its nationals for damages to the property. Since the procedures for adjudicating or settling claims against the Japanese Government or its nationals have not yet been determined, it is not possible to state the extent or nature of compensation which may be provided in respect to claims for loss or damage suffered before return of the property nor when such claims will be acted upon. A owner who is unable or unwilling to assume control of his property at the present time will not b compelled to accept its return, nor will any right he may have be prejudiced by his not resumin control at present. Until the property is returne to the owner, the Japanese Government has so responsibility for its preservation and protectio under the direction of the Supreme Commande but after its return its future maintenance and an rehabilitation costs are the responsibility of th owner.

At present SCAP regulations do not perm postwar commercial entrants to engage in busines and investment activities in Japan except as spe cially authorized. Business entrants are now pei mitted to engage in international trade throug Boeki Cho (Japanese Board of Trade), and SCA licenses have been issued to banking, shipping, an insurance companies to service foreign trad Resident Allied and neutral nationals who hav been in Japan continuously since September 1945, are permitted to engage in business activ ities on the same basis as Japanese nationals an it is contemplated that commercial entrants whos activities will contribute to the economic rehabil tation of Japan will be accorded the same pri ileges.

No procedure has yet been established whereb foreign exchange can be converted to yen excep at the military exchange rate of 50–1 and all in port-export of raw materials and other commod ities must be through Boeki Cho and subject t SCAP approval and validation. In addition, the present time there is no provision for conver sion of Japanese yen into foreign currencies.

Commercial entrants wishing to investigate ir vestment possibilities must realize there is a crit ical shortage of materials, services, and facilitie which may handicap their operations, and permis sion to do business in Japan, if granted, will i no way constitute special grounds for such mate rials, facilities, or services.

STATEMENT BY GEORGE C. MARSHALL

Secretary of State

[Released to the press March 25]

The terms of reference of the Far Eastern Commission provide that the United States may issue interim directives to SCAP pending action by the Far Eastern Commission whenever urgent matters arise which are not covered by policies already formulated by the Commission. In this case there was agreement among the countries on a portion of the policy of restitution and, since the restitution program is considered urgent b many of the countries which suffered at the hand of the Japanese, the United States felt it necessar to provide SCAP with policy guidance. The direc tive issued by the United States covers only thos aspects of the restitution program on which ther are no differences. The unagreed aspects of th restitution policy are still under discussion in th FEC.

possible during the war. The agreement of April 4, 1947, was entered into in accordance with the provisions of Public Law 690, 79th Congress, approved August 8, 1946. Since the signature of that agreement the Congress of the United States enacted legislation (Public Law 220, 80th Congress, approved July 23, 1947) permitting extension of periods during which the above-mentioned benefits might be obtained. The supplementary agreement is designed to extend periods specified in the earlier agreement to the later dates permitted by act of Congress.

Procedure for Filing Claims With Hungary

[Released to the press March 18]

The treaty of peace with Hungary which came into force on September 15, 1947, provides that legal rights and interests of American nationals in Hungary as they existed on September 1, 1939, are to be restored, and the Hungarian Government is required to return all property in Hungary of United Nations nationals as it now exists. Where property has not been returned within six months from the coming into force of the treaty (i. e., within six months from September 15, 1947), application for the return thereof is to be made to the Hungarian authorities on or before September 15, 1948, unless claimants are able to show that applications could not be filed within that period. In cases where property cannot be returned or where, as a result of the war, a United Nations national has suffered a loss by reason of injury or damage to property in Hungary, the Hungarian Government is required to make compensation in local currency to the extent of two thirds of the sum necessary, at the date of payment, to purchase similar property or to make good the loss suffered. To enable claims to receive consideration under the treaty, claimants must have been nationals of one of the United Nations on January 20, 1945 (the date of the armistice with Hungary), and on September 15, 1947 (the date the treaty came into force), or must establish that under the laws in force in Hungary during the war they were treated as enemies. Claimants must also be nationals of this Government at the time of the filing of their claims.

The Department of State has recently been advised of the requirements of the Hungarian Government in connection with the preparation of claims and will communicate directly in the near future with all claimants of whom the Department has a record, advising them of such requirements.

[1] Not printed.
[2] BULLETIN of Nov. 9, 1947, p. 912.
[3] BULLETIN of Apr. 20, 1947, p. 725.

American nationals, including individuals, corporations, and associations, resident outside Hungary, who desire to file claims under the treaty, should, upon being advised of the requirements in that connection, prepare and submit their claims to the Office of the Legal Adviser, Department of State, Washington, D.C., at the earliest practicable date. Claimants residing in Hungary should, upon receipt of instructions as to the method of preparing claims, prepare and file their claims with the American Legation in Budapest.

Claimants who desire to file claims of the character indicated but who have not previously communicated with the Department of State regarding that subject, should do so at once.

The Department of State and the American Legation in Budapest will endeavor to render claimants such assistance as is practicable in connection with the preparation of their claims and in the transmittal thereof to the Hungarian Government. Full responsibility for the actual preparation of claims, however, and for the submission of the necessary documentary evidence to establish their validity rests with the claimants and their attorneys.

When information regarding the procedure for preparing and filing claims under the treaty of peace with Italy becomes available, a similar announcement will be made. Announcements have already been made with respect to claims under the Bulgarian and Rumanian treaties.[1]

Income Tax Convention With New Zealand Signed

[Released to the press March 16]

A convention between the United States and New Zealand for the avoidance of double taxation and the prevention of fiscal evasion with respect to taxes on income was signed at Washington on March 16, 1948, by George C. Marshall, Secretary of State, and Walter Nash, P.C., Minister of Finance and Minister of Customs for New Zealand.

The provisions of the convention are similar in general to those contained in conventions now in force between the United States and Canada, France, Sweden, and the United Kingdom.

The convention provides that it shall be ratified, and that, upon the exchange of instruments of ratification, it shall become effective, as to United States tax, for the taxable years beginning on or after January 1 in the calendar year in which the exchange occurs, and, as to New Zealand tax, for the year of assessment beginning on April 1 next following the calendar year in which the exchange occurs.

[1] BULLETIN of Mar. 14, 1948, p. 356.

Fulbright Act

Grants for Burma
[Released to the press March 31]

The Board of Foreign Scholarships and the Department of State announce a limited number of grants available for visiting professors and research scholars under the first-year Fulbright program approved for Burma. The grants will be awarded under the provisions of Public Law 584, 79th Congress (the Fulbright act). All grants will be paid in Burmese currency and may include salary, maintenance, and travel. Partial grants may be made in Burmese currency to supplement any financial assistance the candidate is receiving from his institution in this country or from other sources.

Eight grants will be awarded United States professors to teach at institutions of higher learning in Burma, in the following fields:

University of Rangoon:
  industrial chemistry
  hydroelectric engineering
  fresh-water biology
  economics
State Training College for Teachers, Rangoon:
  educational research
  educational psychology
  abnormal psychology
  physical education

Five grants will be awarded to citizens of the United States for post-doctoral research in connection with institutions of higher learning in Burma.

Application blanks and additional information concerning these awards will be available from the Committee on International Exchange of Persons, Conference Board of Associated Research Councils, 2101 Constitution Ave., Washington 25, D.C.

Student Ships Assigned
[Released to the press March 30]

The Department of State announced on March 30 that the *Marine Tiger* and the *Marine Jumper* have been assigned by the United States Maritime Commission at the request of the Department and numerous private organizations, to transport American and foreign students, teachers, and other academic personnel between the United States and Europe during the summer of 1948. Each vessel will make four special transatlantic round trips between June and September, calling on all sailings at British and French ports and on two sailings at Olso.

Each of these former troop transports has room for 600 passengers. The number of staterooms is limited, the majority of the accommodations being in dormitories and large compartments. Rates will vary from $140 to $200 one way, depending upon the class of accommodation and port of destination.

The Netherlands Government, through its Office for Foreign Student Relations, is also operating student ships, the *Kota-Inten* and the *Tabinta*, which will make one voyage each from Quebec to Rotterdam on June 18 and July 1, respectively. Each of these vessels has a capacity of 750. Early in September the *Volendam*, with a capacity of 1,500, will sail from Rotterdam for New York to provide return transportation for the students traveling to Europe on the two smaller ships. The cost of round-trip passage will be $280.

The Institute of International Education, 2 West Forty-fifth Street, New York 19, N. Y., will administer the entire student-ship program. Requests for information, schedules, and application for passage on both the Dutch and the American vessels should be addressed to the Institute. American diplomatic missions in Europe will assist foreign students and teachers who wish to arrange passage for the United States on the ships.

The American Friends Service Committee of Philadelphia will conduct a shipboard orientation program for passengers on the *Marine Jumper* and the *Marine Tiger*. This committee enjoyed conspicuous success in carrying out this kind of program on the ships last summer. There will be a similar program on the Dutch vessels, with the cooperation of the Friends.

The determination of priorities to be assigned applicants will be the responsibility of an executive committee composed of representatives of a number of the organizations sponsoring travel to Europe this summer. All organizations and individuals applying for passage on the student ships will be required to demonstrate that their purpose is formal study, attendance at conferences, or participation in cultural or reconstruction projects.

Statement by Assistant Secretary Allen

The action of the Maritime Commission in assigning two vessels for facilitation of educational travel between the United States and Europe next summer is very gratifying to the Department. By enabling several thousands of young Americans to visit Europe for a summer's study, this project will make a definite contribution toward the furthering of good will and amity among the free peoples of the world. I regard the assignment of these ships for such a purpose as an outstanding example of the way in which Government is able to supplement and encourage the initiative of private organizations in carrying on educational exchange with other nations.

ng and that all other necessary funds are
d from other sources.

nts to American scholars for research and
:ional projects in the Philippines will act as
ulus to cultural rehabilitation, it is believed,
ition to giving Filipino scholars the benefit
ctical training with American specialists.

ss on Freedom of Information

March 25 William Benton, Chairman of the
Delegation to the Conference on Freedom of
ation at Geneva, made an address at the
g plenary session on freedom of information
le press. For the text of this address, see
tment of State press release 231 of March
48.

an Lawyer Visits U.S.

Moises Poblete-Troncoso, professor of labor
tion and director of the Institute of Social

and Economic Sciences, University of Chile, arrived in Washington March 16, accompanied by
his wife, for a four months' visit under the travel-
grant program of the Department of State. Dr.
Poblete-Troncoso's visit is being made at the request of the Library of Congress for the purpose
of serving as consultant in social legislation.

John N. Andrews Appointed to Board of Foreign Scholarships

The Department of State announced on April 2
that the President has appointed Col. John N.
Andrews to the Board of Foreign Scholarships
under the Fulbright act. Colonel Andrews, the
personal representative of the Administrator of
Veterans Affairs since 1946, will fill the unexpired
term of Gen. Omar N. Bradley who represented
veterans on the Board until his appointment as
Chief of Staff.

THE DEPARTMENT

al for Restoration of Funds for Efficient Conduct of Foreign Relations

STATEMENT BY GEORGE C. MARSHALL [1]
Secretary of State

ro months ago, I appeared before the House
'opriations Subcommittee to present the 1949
et request of the Department of State. It was
l at that time that the budgetary estimates
e Department did not include requests for
i which could be eliminated without actually
iring the conduct of foreign relations. There
een no reason to change that view.
orld conditions with which the Department
ncerned have in recent weeks deteriorated,
r than improved, as is well known to you.
there are the still unresolved problems of
iany, Japan, and Korea. And the United
ons demands increasing attention and support
problems multiply.
is against this background that I ask you to
der the appropriations which are being reed today.
r most important request at this time is for
estoration of $4,050,000 for the Department
ce. A reduction of this extent requires the
arge of 780 employees before June 30—one

out of every six members of the staff—the discharge
of even a larger number if the action is delayed
beyond that date.
This cut, I think, would impair major activities
and cripple supporting activities. The year 1949,
undoubtedly to be a critical one in world affairs,
would find us definitely weakened because of budget
limitations.
During the past 14 months, the size of the Department staff, including the information program, has been reduced by more than 1,300 employees. In the course of this 20-percent reduction, many of the duplications arising from the
sudden absorption by the Department of five war
agencies have been eliminated, and the organizational structure has been steadily improved.
We cannot eliminate those administrative and
policy activities which function to support the
work and the staff of the Foreign Service abroad.

[1] Made before the Senate Appropriations Subcommittee
on Mar. 23, 1948, and released to the press on the same
date.

Nor can we curtail our public-service activities—the issuance of passports and visas and the protection of American interests in foreign countries. Our United Nations Delegation and our delegations to other international organizations are to be maintained. The negotiation of technical agreements with other governments must continue. Curtailment of our economic-planning activities will mean a substantial decrease in the effectiveness of the Department at a time when economic matters are fundamental considerations in foreign policy. In the same manner, our planning and policy-making activities must be based on continuing intelligence activities.

Viewed organizationally, the picture is exactly the same.

The geographic offices, organized on a country basis, employ only 300 persons. These country desks are already taxed beyond their capacity, and reductions would be impossible.

The economic offices of the Department are engaged in work related to the European Recovery Program and the proposed China relief program. They are promoting a revival of world trade and furthering the establishment of a permanent International Trade Organization. They are engaged in many other activities related to postwar economic problems and the task of reconstructing a stable world economy.

Reduction of the United Nations Affairs staff is impossible without jeopardizing our interests in the United Nations and the specialized agencies.

The work of the intelligence offices increases in importance as direct sources of information are closed to us in eastern Europe.

The administrative offices of the Department are hardpressed to provide essential services to the public, the Department, the Foreign Service, and other agencies of the Government which participate in international relations. Sharply reduced in the last several years and hardest hit by last year's reduction-in-force program, these offices cannot absorb further cuts without drastic reductions in the services which they must render.

Second in importance only to the Department Service is a request for the restoration of the $2,672,615 which has been cut from the estimates for the Foreign Service.

Such a reduction will require the discharge of about 500 employees of the Foreign Service. Most of the reduction would be applied to consular clerks and staffs engaged in observing and reporting political and economic developments around the world. The ability of the Foreign Service to meet its basic responsibilities would be impaired.

The legislative framework for the reorganization and improvement of the Foreign Service is contained in the Foreign Service Act of 1946. The Department has been working on plans for the implementation of this act for over a year.

U.S. and Afghanistan To Raise Legations to Embassy Status

[Released to the press March 18]

The Governments of the United States and Afghanistan have agreed to raise their respective Legations to Embassy status, effective upon a date to be mutually determined. Diplomatic relations between the two countries were established on May 4, 1935, when the first American Minister presented his credentials to the King of Afghanistan. The first Afghan Minister to the United States was received by the President on June 4, 1943.

In the early years of United States–Afghanistan relations, the American Minister to Iran, resident at Tehran, was concurrently accredited to Afghanistan. On June 6, 1942, an American Legation was opened in Kabul. The present step reflects the continued growth of close and cordial relations between the two countries.

Corrections

In the BULLETIN of March 14, 1948, page 360, first column, first line of the article on the Caribbean Commission, *read* "signed on March 4" *instead of* "signed on March 5" the joint resolution (H. J. Res. 231) authorizing membership by the United States in the Caribbean Commission and the instrument approving the agreement for the establishment of the Caribbean Commission.

In the BULLETIN of April 4, 1948, page 453, second column, the next to the last paragraph should read as follows:

"It is proposed that such arrangement as may be agreed to by the Powers concerned should be submitted to the Security Council for its approval in view of the special responsibilities assumed by the Council in connection with the Free Territory of Trieste."

—Continued from page 467

are fully respected and that every contracting State has a fair opportunity to operate international airlines;

"(*g*) Avoid discrimination between contracting States;

"(*h*) Promote safety of flight in international air navigation;

"(*i*) Promote generally the development of all aspects of international civil aeronautics."

The groundwork for achieving the aims and objectives of the Organization has been carefully laid. By supporting Icao's work, the United States and other nations of the world will derive the maximum benefit from the continued development of international civil aviation.

The Department of State

For sale by the Superintendent of Documents
U.S. Government Printing Office
Washington 25, D.C.

SUBSCRIPTION:
52 issues, $5; single copy, 15 cents

Published with the approval of the
Director of the Bureau of the Budget

JNITED NATIONS MARITIME CONFERENCE

by John Martin Cates, Jr.

The United Nations Maritime Conference met n Geneva, February 19 to March 6, 1948, at the nvitation of the United Nations Economic and iocial Council. In a little over two weeks it had oncluded a convention establishing the Intergovrnmental Maritime Consultative Organization o be known as IMCO, had adopted a draft agreenent of relationship with the United Nations, nd had established a Preparatory Committee to erve as an interim body for preparation for the irst Assembly.[1] The major share of the credit or this accomplishment is due to the president f the Conference, Dr. J. J. Oyevaar of the Netherands, who, with firmness and tact, kept the Conerence at its task until the job was accomplished. The establishment of IMCO upon the ratification f the convention by 21 states will complete the rganization of those specialized agencies believed y the United Nations to be necessary to deal with echnical and economic problems existing or exected to arise in the fields of transport and comnunication.

The delegates to the Conference benefited greatly rom the experience of several Allied wartime hipping agencies and two successive postwar oranizations, the United Maritime Consultative Council (UMCC) and the Provisional Maritime Consultative Council (PMCC).[2] The UMCC, at a onference in Washington in October 1946, had repared the so-called "Washington Draft", a proosed convention which, with the express approval f the Economic and Social Council, served as he basic working document for the Maritime Conference.

The representatives of the 32 Governments and observers[3] who convened in Geneva approached he problems before the Conference with unusual lirectness. By the end of the first full day's sesion the Conference had brought to light the three asic questions before it:

(1) Should a separate maritime organization e established, or should a commission of the Jnited Nations deal with maritime problems as hey arise?

(2) Should the scope of the organization be imited to a narrower scope than the Washington Draft to include only technical matters, or should he scope be broadened beyond that of the Washngton Draft to include matters of private shipping economics?

(3) How should a balance be obtained in the Council between the ship-providing nations and the ship-using nations?

The United States position on the general problem of whether there should be a separate maritime organization was set forth by Garrison Norton, Assistant Secretary of State and chairman of the United States Delegation,[4] in the opening session of the Conference as follows:

The United States favored the creation of an intergovernmental maritime organization in order that there might be a shipping organization to participate on an equal basis with aviation, telecommunication, and meteorological organizations in the coordination of such matters as safety of life at sea; to supply continuity of effort necessary for effective intergovernmental cooperation in shipping in place of the present practice of sporadic diplomatic conferences; to establish the principle that certain shipping problems should, as a general rule, be handled through normal commercial processes without unnecessary governmental interference; to facilitate the handling of shipping problems by governmental and industry personnel experienced in shipping matters; to contribute to world peace by the establishment of a forum where differences of opinion on shipping questions could be discussed and resolved by persons familiar with the problems. The United States position was that an organization established on the basis of the Washington Draft would achieve these ends.

[1] The convention and the final act are contained in U.N. docs. E/Conf. 4/61 and E/Conf. 4/62 of Mar. 6, 1948. See pp. 499 ff.

[2] BULLETIN of Jan. 25, 1948, p. 99, and Feb. 1, 1948, p. 131.

[3] The Governments represented by Delegations were Argentina, Australia, Belgium, Brazil, Canada, Chile, China, Colombia, Czechoslovakia, Denmark, Dominican Republic, Egypt, Finland, France, Greece, India, Ireland, Italy, Lebanon, Netherlands, New Zealand, Norway, Pakistan, Panama, Peru, Poland, Portugal, Sweden, Switzerland, Turkey, United Kingdom, United States of America. Governments represented by observers: Cuba, Ecuador, Iran, Union of South Africa. In addition the following organizations were represented by observers: International Civil Aviation Organization, International Labor Office, International Meteorological Organization, International Telecommunication Union, World Health Organization, International Chamber of Commerce, International Cooperative Alliance, International Law Association, International Transport Workers Federation.

[4] For membership on the U. S. Delegation, see BULLETIN of Feb. 29, 1948, p. 286.

After several days of general discussion by the full Conference, a working group, which came to be known as the Main Working Party, was set up under the chairmanship of the president of the Conference, consisting of representatives of the following countries: Argentina, Australia, Belgium, Brazil, China, France, India, Ireland, Norway, Poland, United Kingdom, and United States. This group, after meeting for several days in closed sessions and then alternately with the full Conference, was able to develop the majority of the proposals which became the basis of the final convention.

The first major issue as to whether shipping problems should be handled by an independent maritime organization or by a commission of the United Nations was raised by Australia and New Zealand, which opposed the establishment of a separate maritime organization, preferring that, in the interests of coordination and economy, maritime problems be dealt with by commissions of the United Nations. Australia and New Zealand were alone in their support of this proposal, and the Conference, although not actually voting upon this matter until almost its final session, proceeded in its discussions on the assumption that there should be a separate organization. One of the most effective arguments against placing shipping matters under a commission of the United Nations was made by Sir Ramaswami Mudaliar, the Representative of India and a former chairman of the United Nations Economic and Social Council, who stated that in the light of his experience he did not believe United Nations commissions were so organized as to be able to carry out the functions proposed for the Maritime Organization. Further, he believed the International Trade Organization (Ito) would be too burdened by other matters to take up the special problems arising in the shipping industry.

The second major issue was raised by the Scandinavian countries and Finland by the proposal that Imco be established as a technical organization only, and that matters of discrimination and unfair restrictive practices, that is, commercial practices, be left to the United Nations or to the proposed Ito.

This proposal, which would have meant an organization of narrower scope than that proposed in the Washington Draft, which had been agreed to by the Scandinavians at the Washington Umcc conference in 1947, launched a long and thorough debate on the advisability of defining the terms "discrimination" and "unfair" or "restrictive" practices; the proposed scope of the International Trade Organization; ship-operating subsidies; bilateral agreements to divide tonnage; the definition of "technical matters"; shipping conferences; the need to guard against the new organization's being so constituted as to prevent

elected with regard to the desirability of adequate geographical representation. The Argentine proposal, as finally adopted in article 17 of the convention, provided that six members should represent governments "with the largest interest in providing international shipping services"; six should represent "other nations with the largest interest in international seaborne trade"; and of the four remaining, two should represent governments "having a substantial interest in providing international shipping services", and two should represent governments "having a substantial interest in international seaborne trade".

It was apparent that until some agreement was reached as to which nations would be represented on the Council, the Conference would make little progress on this important article. Accordingly, a working group in an all-night session developed a list of 12 countries to make up groups (a) and (b) under article 17 as well as a procedure for the selection of the Council as subsequently provided in article 18 of the convention.

The six nations chosen as having the largest interest in providing international shipping services were determined by the Working Party to be Greece, Netherlands, Norway, Sweden, United Kingdom, and United States; and the six Governments with the largest interest in international seaborne trade were Argentina, Australia, Belgium, Canada, France, and India.

The motivating purpose behind this distribution of Council seats was to maintain a balance between ship-providing nations and ship-using nations. The next step was to work out procedures for choosing such nations. Having no definite formula before it, the Working Party chose the original 12 on the basis of tonnage figures and the expert knowledge of the various delegates present. In order that this balance might be maintained in the future, the Working Party further proposed that the Council itself should determine, for purposes of membership on the Council, those governments with the largest interest in providing international shipping services, those having a substantial interest in providing such services, and those having the largest interest in international seaborne trade. The Assembly then would elect two nations from among those nominated by the Council as having "a substantial interest in providing" shipping services and two nations to represent those "having a substantial interest in international seaborne trade".

When these proposals were placed before the Conference, discussion was directed toward the necessity for geographic distribution, alleged undemocratic processes followed in choosing the Council, and what was referred to as the "veto power" of the Council. It was evident, however, that regardless of selection procedures, not all nations represented at the Conference would be able to obtain seats on the Council. Recognition of this fact was made by the Delegate of Brazil who, in one of the most effective speeches of the Conference, pointed out the fact of the limited number of seats on the Council and the fact that Brazil itself was not included among the first 12 nations selected, but expressed the willingness of Brazil to cooperate in this attempt to reach a compromise, with the hope that Brazil's importance to world trade might be recognized when the four remaining members of the Council were chosen. This conciliatory proposal by the Representative of Brazil had much the same effect as the earlier move by the United States Delegate in accepting a compromise proposal on the functions of the Organization.

Acceptance of the final language on the Council was aided also by the realization of the majority of delegates that the interests of the older shipowning nations, the "common carriers", deserved the amount of protection afforded by the election procedures and by the referral procedure (referred to in debate as the "veto power" of the Council) provided in article 16 (h), at least during the formative years of the Organization. The final vote on the adoption of articles 17 and 18 was 21 in favor and 4 opposed.

Failure to include Panama among the 12 original members of the Council and as a member of the Main Working Party was cited by the Delegate of Panama as evidence that the Conference was systematically overlooking the interests of Panama and as the reason for Panama's formal withdrawal from the Conference.

Following agreement on this third major issue, the Conference was divided for discussion and drafting purposes into three additional working parties, Maritime Safety, Legal Questions, and Relationship With the United Nations. These groups, together with the Main Working Party and a subsequently appointed drafting committee, worked out the language as finally adopted for the balance of the convention.

So far as the final language differs from the Washington Draft, the following points deserve notice:

The membership provision (part III) was amended to provide that those states not members of the United Nations, but which were invited to the Conference, might become original members of the Organization. Provision was also made for nonvoting associate members.

The Maritime Safety Committee (part VII) was given enlarged functions and its own secretary. The chief change in the functions of the Maritime Safety Committee was that it should "provide machinery for performing any duties assigned to it by the Convention, or by the Assembly, or any duty within the scope of this Article which may be assigned to it by any other intergovernmental instrument". This language was in-

Italy, Lebanon, Netherlands, Poland, Portugal, Switzerland, Turkey, United Kingdom, and United States.

Following the termination of the Conference, the Preparatory Committee held a special meeting at which it was decided that a representative of Canada should serve as chairman; that the first regular meeting of the committee would be held at Lake Success in October 1948; that all interim secretariat functions should be performed on behalf of the Preparatory Committee by the Secretariat of the United Nations.

The success of the Conference clearly demonstrates the achievements in international cooperation possible under a specialized agency when the delegates are familiar with technical matters under discussion, as well as with the related political problems, and are sincerely devoted to the cause of international cooperation. Prior to the convening of the Conference, doubts were voiced as to whether a maritime organization could be established, so divergent were certain national views. However, during the Conference there was apparent not only a sincere desire to reach an agreement on an Intergovernmental Maritime Consultative Organization but also a willingness to work out compromises recognizing opposing points of view in order to make an agreement possible. The success of the Maritime Conference in concluding, in less than two and one-half weeks, a workable agreement in such a controversial field, evidences the atmosphere of conciliation and cooperation which pervaded the Conference as well as the determination of the delegates to reach agreement.

The Imco convention provides an organization representing shipping interests which can act with the other international organizations in the transport and communications field to effect the coordination necessary in matters of safety procedures at and over the sea, and the planning necessary to work out the effective integration of transport systems throughout the world.

Consultative Organization[6]

tices relating to technical matters of all kinds affecting shipping engaged in international trade, and to encourage the general adoption of the highest practicable standards in matters concerning maritime safety and efficiency of navigation;

(b) to encourage the removal of discriminatory action and unnecessary restrictions by Governments affecting shipping engaged in international trade so as to promote the availability of shipping services to the commerce of the world without discrimination; assistance and encour-

---

Italy, Netherlands, Poland, Portugal, Switzerland, Turkey, United Kingdom, and United States. Against: China. Abstentions: Denmark, Egypt, Lebanon, Norway, New Zealand, Pakistan, and Sweden. Absences: Czechoslovakia, Panama, and Peru.

[6] U.N. doc. E/Conf. 4/61 of Mar. 6, 1948.

agement given by a Government for the development of its national shipping and for purposes of security does not in itself constitute discrimination, provided that such assistance and encouragement is not based on measures designed to restrict the freedom of shipping of all flags to take part in international trade;

(c) to provide for the consideration by the Organization of matters concerning unfair restrictive practices by shipping concerns in accordance with Part II;

(d) to provide for the consideration by the Organization of any matters concerning shipping that may be referred to it by any organ or Specialized Agency of the United Nations;

(e) to provide for the exchange of information among Governments on matters under consideration by the Organization.

PART II

Functions

Article 2

The functions of the Organization shall be consultative and advisory.

Article 3

In order to achieve the purposes set out in Part I, the functions of the Organization shall be:—

(a) subject to the provisions of Article 4, to consider and make recommendations upon matters arising under Article 1 (a), (b) and (c) that may be remitted to it by Members, by any organ or Specialized Agency of the United Nations or by any other intergovernmental organization or upon matters referred to it under Article 1(d);

(b) to provide for the drafting of conventions, agreements, or other suitable instruments, and to recommend these to Governments and to intergovernmental organizations, and to convene such conferences as may be necessary;

(c) to provide machinery for consultation among Members and the exchange of information among Governments.

Article 4

In those matters which appear to the Organization capable of settlement through the normal processes of international shipping business the Organization shall so recommend. When, in the opinion of the Organization, any matter concerning unfair restrictive practices by shipping concerns is incapable of settlement through the normal processes of international shipping business, or has in fact so proved, and provided it shall first have been the subject of direct negotiations between the Members concerned, the Organization shall, at the request of one of those Members, consider the matter.

PART III

Membership

Article 5

Membership in the Organization shall be open to all States, subject to the provisions of Part III.

Article 6

Members of the United Nations may become Members of the Organization by becoming parties to the Convention in accordance with the provisions of Article 57.

Article 7

States not Members of the United Nations which have been invited to send representatives to the United Nations Maritime Conference convened in Geneva on the

Article 19

Members represented on the Council in accordance with Article 17 shall hold office until the end of the next regular session of the Assembly. Members shall be eligible for re-election.

Article 20

(*a*) The Council shall elect its Chairman and adopt its own rules of procedure except as otherwise provided in the Convention.

(*b*) Twelve members of the Council shall constitute a quorum.

(*c*) The Council shall meet upon one month's notice as often as may be necessary for the efficient discharge of its duties upon the summons of its Chairman or upon request by not less than four of its members. It shall meet at such places as may be convenient.

Article 21

The Council shall invite any Member to participate, without vote, in its deliberations on any matter of particular concern to that Member.

Article 22

(*a*) The Council shall receive the recommendations and reports of the Maritime Safety Committee and shall transmit them to the Assembly and, when the Assembly is not in session, to the Members for information, together with the comments and recommendations of the Council.

(*b*) Matters within the scope of Article 29 shall be considered by the Council only after obtaining the views of the Maritime Safety Committee thereon.

Article 23

The Council, with the approval of the Assembly, shall appoint the Secretary-General. The Council shall also make provision for the appointment of such other personnel as may be necessary, and determine the terms and conditions of service of the Secretary-General and other personnel, which terms and conditions shall conform as far as possible with those of the United Nations and its Specialized Agencies.

Article 24

The Council shall make a report to the Assembly at each regular session on the work of the Organization since the previous regular session of the Assembly.

Article 25

The Council shall submit to the Assembly the budget estimates and the financial statements of the Organization, together with its comments and recommendations.

Article 26

The Council may enter into agreements or arrangements covering the relationship of the Organization with other organizations, as provided for in Part XII. Such agreements or arrangements shall be subject to approval by the Assembly.

Article 27

Between sessions of the Assembly, the Council shall perform all the functions of the Organization, except the function of making recommendations under Article 16 (i).

PART VII

Maritime Safety Committee

Article 28

(*a*) The Maritime Safety Committee shall consist of fourteen Members elected by the Assembly from the

Members, governments of those nations having an important interest in maritime safety, of which not less than eight shall be the largest ship-owning nations, and the remainder shall be elected so as to ensure adequate representation of Members, governments of other nations with an important interest in maritime safety, such as nations interested in the supply of large numbers of crews or in the carriage of large numbers of berthed and unberthed passengers, and of major geographical areas.

(b) Members shall be elected for a term of four years and shall be eligible for re-election.

Article 29

.(a) The Maritime Safety Committee shall have the duty of considering any matter within the scope of the Organization and concerned with aids to navigation, construction and equipment of vessels, manning from a safety standpoint, rules for the prevention of collisions, handling of dangerous cargoes, maritime safety procedures and requirements, hydrographic information, log-books and navigational records, marine casualty investigation, salvage and rescue, and any other matters directly affecting maritime safety.

(b) The Maritime Safety Committee shall provide machinery for performing any duties assigned to it by the Convention, or by the Assembly, or any duties within the scope of this Article which may be assigned to it by any other intergovernmental instrument.

(c) Having regard to the provisions of Part XII, the Maritime Safety Committee shall have the duty of maintaining such close relationship with other intergovernmental bodies concerned with transport and communications as may further the object of the Organization in promoting maritime safety and facilitate the co-ordination of activities in the fields of shipping, aviation, telecommunications and meteorology with respect to safety and rescue.

Article 30

The Maritime Safety Committee, through the Council, shall:

(a) submit to the Assembly at its regular sessions proposals made by Members for safety regulations or for amendments to existing safety regulations, together with its comments or recommendations thereon;

(b) report to the Assembly on the work of the Maritime Safety Committee since the previous regular session of the Assembly.

Article 31

The Maritime Safety Committee shall meet once a year and at other times upon request of any five of its members. It shall elect its officers once a year and shall adopt its own rules of procedure. A majority of its members shall constitute a quorum.

Article 32

The Maritime Safety Committee shall invite any Member to participate, without vote, in its deliberations on any matter of particular concern to that Member.

PART VIII

The Secretariat

Article 33

The Secretariat shall comprise the Secretary-General, a Secretary of the Maritime Safety Committee and such staff as the Organization may require. The Secretary-General shall be the chief administrative officer of the

governmental, such functions, resources and obligations within the scope of the Organization as may be transferred to the Organization by international agreements or by mutually acceptable arrangements entered into between competent authorities of the respective organizations. Similarly, the Organization may take over any administrative functions which are within its scope and which have been entrusted to a government under the terms of any international instrument.

PART XIII
Legal Capacity, Privileges and Immunities
Article 50

The legal capacity, privileges and immunities to be accorded to, or in connection with, the Organization, shall be derived from and governed by the General Convention on the Privileges and Immunities of the Specialized Agencies approved by the General Assembly of the United Nations on the 21st November, 1947, subject to such modifications as may be set forth in the final (or revised) text of the Annex approved by the Organization in accordance with Sections 36 and 38 of the said General Convention.

Article 51

Pending its accession to the said General Convention in respect of the Organization, each Member undertakes to apply the provisions of Appendix II to the present Convention.

PART XIV
Amendments
Article 52

Texts of proposed amendments to the Convention shall be communicated by the Secretary-General to Members at least six months in advance of their consideration by the Assembly. Amendments shall be adopted by a two-thirds majority vote of the Assembly, including the concurring votes of a majority of the Members represented on the Council. Twelve months after its acceptance by two-thirds of the Members of the Organization, other than Associate Members, each amendment shall come into force for all Members except those which, before it comes into force, make a declaration that they do not accept the amendment. The Assembly may by a two-thirds majority vote determine at the time of its adoption that an amendment is of such a nature that any Member which has made such a declaration and which does not accept the amendment within a period of twelve months after the amendment comes into force shall, upon the expiration of this period, cease to be a party to the Convention.

Article 53

Any amendment adopted under Article 52 shall be deposited with the Secretary-General of the United Nations, who will immediately forward a copy of the amendment to all Members.

Article 54

A declaration or acceptance under Article 52 shall be made by the communication of an instrument to the Secretary-General for deposit with the Secretary-General of the United Nations. The Secretary-General will notify Members of the receipt of any such instrument and of the date when the amendment enters into force.

PART XV
Interpretation
Article 55

Any question or dispute concerning the interpretation or application of the Convention shall be referred for set-

503

tlement to the Assembly, or shall be settled in such other manner as the parties to the dispute agree. Nothing in this Article shall preclude the Council or the Maritime Safety Committee from settling any such question or dispute that may arise during the exercise of their functions.

Article 56

Any legal question which cannot be settled as provided in Article 55 shall be referred by the Organization to the International Court of Justice for an advisory opinion in accordance with Article 96 of the Charter of the United Nations.

PART XVI

Miscellaneous Provisions

Article 57. Signature and Acceptance

Subject to the provisions of Part III the present Convention shall remain open for signature or acceptance and States may become parties to the Convention by:

(a) Signature without reservation as to acceptance;
(b) Signature subject to acceptance followed by acceptance; or
(c) Acceptance.

Acceptance shall be effected by the deposit of an instrument with the Secretary-General of the United Nations.

Article 58. Territories

(a) Members may make a declaration at any time that their participation in the Convention includes all or a group or a single one of the territories for whose international relations they are responsible.
(b) The Convention does not apply to territories for whose international relations Members are responsible unless a declaration to that effect has been made on their behalf under the provisions of paragraph (a) of this Article.
(c) A declaration made under paragraph (a) of this Article shall be communicated to the Secretary-General of the United Nations and a copy of it will be forwarded by him to all States invited to the United Nations Maritime Conference and to such other States as may have become Members.
(d) In cases where under a trusteeship agreement the United Nations is the administering authority, the United Nations may accept the Convention on behalf of one, several, or all of the trust territories in accordance with the procedure set forth in Article 57.

Article 59. Withdrawal

(a) Any Member may withdraw from the Organization by written notification given to the Secretary-General of the United Nations, who will immediately inform the other Members and the Secretary-General of the Organization of such notification. Notification of withdrawal may be given at any time after the expiration of twelve months from the date on which the Convention has come into force. The withdrawal shall take effect upon the expiration of twelve months from the date on which such written notification is received by the Secretary-General of the United Nations.
(b) The application of the Convention to a territory or group of territories under Article 58 may at any time be terminated by written notification given to the Secretary-General of the United Nations by the Member responsible for its international relations or, in the case of a trust territory of which the United Nations is the administering authority, by the United Nations. The Secretary-General of the United Nations will immediately inform all Members and the Secretary-General of the

(b) Representatives of Members including alternates and advisers, and officials and employees of the Organization shall similarly enjoy such privileges and immunities as are necessary for the independent exercise of their functions in connection with the Organization.

Section 3. In applying the provisions of Sections 1 and 2 of this Appendix, the Members shall take into account as far as possible the standard clauses of the General Convention on the Privileges and Immunities of the Specialized Agencies.

Maritime Conference [7]

In carrying out the functions of this section due consideration shall be given to the deliberations and decisions of the United Nations Maritime Conference.

3. The first meeting of the Preparatory Committee shall be held in Geneva immediately after the conclusion of this Conference.

4. The Preparatory Committee shall elect a Chairman and adopt its own Rules of Procedure.

5. The expenses of the Preparatory Committee other than those of the Members of the Committee shall be met from funds which Governments may advance to the Committee or from funds which may be loaned by the United Nations. The Preparatory Committee shall explore the feasibility of obtaining a loan from United Nations and, if mutually acceptable, may enter into a loan agreement. The obligation under any such loan would be considered by the Governments represented at the Conference as a first claim for repayment by the Intergovernmental Maritime Consultative Organization within the first two years of its existence. In the event of advances of funds to the Preparatory Committee from Governments, such advances may be set off against the contributions of the Governments concerned to the Organization.

6. The Preparatory Committee may enter into agreement with the Secretary-General of the United Nations concerning the possible provision of personnel and other secretarial services under mutually satisfactory arrangements.

7. The Preparatory Committee shall cease to exist upon resolution of the First Session of the Assembly of the Intergovernmental Maritime Consultative Organization.

ANNEX B
United Nations Maritime Conference

A DRAFT RESOLUTION ON THE SAFETY OF LIFE AT SEA CONFERENCE

WHEREAS The United Nations Maritime Conference has approved a convention for the establishment of an Intergovernmental Maritime Consultative Organization whose scope includes matters relating to maritime safety, and

WHEREAS The conference for the purpose of revising the Convention on Safety of Life at Sea of 1929, will be held in London in April 1948, and

WHEREAS The matters to be considered by the Safety of Life at Sea Conference fall within the field of responsibilities covered by the International Maritime Consultative Organization Convention,

The United Nations Maritime Conference

Recommends That the Safety of Life at Sea Conference examine the convention on the Intergovernmental Maritime Consultative Organization with a view to drafting provisions in its final acts which will take into account the duties and functions relating to maritime safety which have been accorded to the Intergovernmental Maritime Consultative Organization.

(Continued on page 523)

FIRST MEETING OF THE LEGAL COM
CIVIL AVIATION ORGANIZATION

by G. Nathan

No better place could have been found for the first meeting of the Legal Committee of the International Civil Aviation Organization than the city of Brussels in early September. This ancient city, combining as it does the charm of the old world with the modern approach of the new, lent just the right atmosphere for substantial accomplishment. Every representative of the 29 countries taking part in the September meeting will long remember with warmth the kindness and attention which were shown the delegates by our Belgian hosts.

Although this was the first meeting of the Icao Legal Committee, an organization had existed for many years known as the Citeja [1] which had been charged with the development of private international air law, a function now assumed by the Legal Committee. Perhaps the most famous achievement of the Citeja is the convention, signed at Warsaw in 1929, dealing with the limitation of liability of international air carriers to passengers and shippers.

The Citeja, however, was not part of, nor directly connected with, any international technical aviation organization, and after the Chicago conference of 1944 it was felt by many member states that this organizational separation of the Citeja from Icao was not conducive to the most rapid attainment of practical results. It was, therefore, the desire of the various states comprising Icao to bring into that organization the Citeja work, with the intention of combining the benefits which the Citeja meetings had offered with the broader program of the Legal Committee of Icao, which will deal with public as well as private international air law problems. This merger was accomplished in effect by the adoption of a resolution by the First Assembly of Icao in May 1947 creating the new Legal Committee and the allied resolution of dissolution adopted by the Citeja.

Prior to the assembly resolution there had been much discussion in United States Government

---

[1] Comité Internationale Technique d'Experts Juridiques Aériens, or International Technical Committee of Aerial Legal Experts.

settled the relationship of the Legal Committee to the Council and other agencies of the Organization but they did enumerate the objectives of the committee and the manner in which draft conventions should be processed.[2]

It has been necessary to go into a considerable amount of background detail in order to present the picture of the organizational problems which confronted the Legal Committee at its first meeting. Although the question of the relationship of the Legal Committee to the Council and the Organization was directly raised only once,[3] the members of the Legal Committee were fully aware of the problem. While the rules of procedure, as drawn up by the Legal Committee, do not completely solve the problem in theory, it is believed they represent an eminently fair and workable compromise solution.

Generally, the rules do not depart markedly from the usual organizational rules for any working group. The membership of the Committee is comprised of individuals rather than member states, as is the case with the Air Transport and Air Navigation Committees, and each such individual must be a legal expert designated by his government. Each government may designate as many such experts as it chooses. On the other hand, no individual can represent more than one contracting state. Although the membership is composed of individuals, the voting is by countries, each country having one vote.

national organizations as may be determined by the Council;

"2. That any such draft convention shall either (a) be placed upon the agenda of the first annual meeting of the Assembly of the Organization convened after the expiration of a period of not less than four months following the transmission of the draft convention as provided in paragraph 1, or (b), in special circumstances, be submitted to an extraordinary meeting of the Assembly or a conference of Contracting States convened for that purpose by the Organization;

"3. That in matters relating to international air law Non-contracting States and international organizations shall be invited to participate in meetings of the Assembly or any conference to the greatest extent consistent with the general policy of the Organization;

"4. That, if agreement is reached, the Assembly or conference shall approve the draft and thereafter the Convention shall be open for signature and ratification or adherence by Contracting States and for adherence by such other States as may be determined by the Assembly or conference;

"5. That, in the meetings of the Legal Committee at which a draft convention is considered and approved, Non-contracting States and international organizations, as may be determined by the Council, shall have the right to participate (without the right to vote) to the full extent provided in the Rules of Procedure of the Legal Committee."

[3] The United States Delegation announced that the United States Government would seek to have the question of the relationship of the Legal Committee to the Council and the Organization placed on the agenda of the Second Assembly.

Provision is made for observers to take part in the deliberations of the committee, but without the right to vote and with a rather unique provision relating to presentation of motions, resolutions, and amendments. Observers will have such rights if their motion, resolution, or amendment is seconded by two members of different contracting states.

The officers of the committee are to be a chairman and one or two vice chairmen, each of whom is to be elected at the annual session of the committee. No such officer can be elected to hold the same position for two consecutive terms, although a former vice chairman may be elected chairman and *vice versa*. Since the committee relies entirely upon the secretariat of the Organization for its secretarial help and the management of its meetings, it is provided that the members of the secretariat of the Organization, who have been designated for that purpose by the Secretary General of the Organization, shall constitute the secretariat of the committee and of its subcommittees.

The question of the time at which the annual meeting is to be held by the committee gave rise to considerable discussion. It was apparent to the conferees at Brussels that an annual meeting held at the same time and place as the annual Assembly of the Organization would be subject to some disadvantages. In the first place, for many committee members there would be the necessity for participating in the more general work of the Organization rather than in the specialized work of the committee. This would mean that committee projects would not advance so rapidly in a meeting held in conjunction with the Assembly as in one which was entirely separate.

Secondly, there was the undesirable feature of nonconformity with the other committees of ICAO, which are not in session during an Assembly. Despite these disadvantages there appeared to be more to be gained from the point of view of committee organization and functioning, by holding the annual meeting in conjunction with the Assembly than there was to be lost. It was considered that the annual Assembly offered the best opportunity for obtaining representation by the greatest number of states. Moreover, by commencing its sessions three or four days earlier than the Assembly sessions and possibly continuing them after the Assembly ended, some committee work could be accomplished.

Most of the representatives to the Legal Committee would be serving as representatives for their respective countries on either the Legal Commission of the Assembly or on some other commission of the Assembly. However, there might be times during Assembly sessions when the work of the commission would not be so severe as to prevent the Legal Committee from meeting.

As a result of these considerations, it was decided to hold the formal annual meeting of the

appropriate procedure for dealing with the subject at hand, taking into account as far as is practicable any time limits which may be recommended by the Assembly or the Council of the Organization.

Another indication of the subordination of the committee to the desires of the Council is the provision contained in article XIV relating to the handling of special requests under paragraph II(b) of the committee constitution. These special requests, if referred to the committee while it is in session, must be handled at that time. Special requests made while the committee is not in session must be referred by the chairman to any existing subcommittee dealing with the general subject matter or, if no such subcommittee is in existence, then to a special committee named in accordance with article VIII for report to the next session of the committee.

There is one respect, however, in which the Legal Committee did not subordinate itself in its rules to the Council. That relates to the question of special advice requested by the Assembly. Here the rules provide that the opinion or document requested by the Assembly shall be transmitted directly to that body rather than through the Council. However, as a means of keeping the Council informed and of permitting the Council to make recommendations for possible changes in the documents submitted by the Legal Committee, provision has been made for the transmission to the Council of a copy of such document at the same time it is transmitted to the Assembly.

As a tribute to the working methods of the CITEJA, the rules of procedure provide, in addition to subcommittees, for the appointment of "rapporteurs" when necessary and desirable.

The foregoing comments indicate generally the outline of the rules of procedure adopted by the Legal Committee at Brussels.[4] Although they go a long way toward placing the committee at the disposition of the Council, it is apparent from the rules that a certain amount of independence has been provided for. To the extent that compromise between two incompatible positions is possible in respect to the working of the Legal Committee these rules represent such a compromise. It is believed that this is a workable solution and will foster the development of conventions on private international air law better than either the plan of complete independence followed by CITEJA on the one hand or the establishment of a full-time committee of the Council on the other.

Earlier in this article mention was made of the outstanding accomplishment of the Legal Committee in the preparation of a draft convention on the international recognition of rights in aircraft. This subject had been under consideration by the CITEJA since 1931. The question with which the draft deals is perhaps one of the most highly technical and involved that has been studied by an international air law committee to date, but the very reasons which make the subject so complex are the ones which make such a convention necessary. At the present time the law on conflicts of law of the various countries relating to the recognition of a status in an aircraft of foreign registry is highly divergent. Some countries recognize that a security interest validly created under the law of the state of registry of the aircraft and constituting a lien or charge on the aircraft is a valid charge. Other countries do not recognize that any such status can be created in aircraft, due to the fact that they are considered "movables". Security interests in movables generally are considered contrary to the public policy of many countries following the Roman law. Between these two points of view there are possibilities of many variations, with the result that international financing of aircraft has been rendered difficult and uncertain.

Since the Chicago Aviation Conference was held in 1944, the United States Government has been one of the leaders in the attempt to reconcile the differences and conflicting points of view of the various states and to come to an agreement on a workable convention. It was believed that the advantages which would accrue to American aviation interests through such a convention would be twofold: (1) it would permit United States airlines operating internationally to obtain credit and financing for the purchase of new equipment; and (2) it would facilitate the financing by foreign operators of American equipment by opening the way for them to obtain credits from private sources.

However, the convention in order to be workable would have to provide a reasonable measure of security for those who advance the necessary capital. Without such reasonable security, it is probable that sufficient money to finance fleets of aircraft would be difficult to obtain. A convention which did not recognize this problem and meet it realistically would be of little practical value.

Basically it appeared that a convention must provide for six principal measures of protection for secured interests in aircraft. In the first place, no liens of any substantial amount should be permitted to be placed ahead of the secured lender's claim after his claim has been duly recorded. This means in effect that all hidden privileges should be reduced to an absolute minimum and that contracting countries must agree not to place other claims such as tax claims ahead of the secured interest on foreign aircraft.

The second requisite for a valid convention relates to what is known as "fleet-mortgage doctrine". That doctrine provides in brief for the

[4] The rules of procedure as adopted at Brussels may be found in appendix "A" (ICAO doc. 4607-LC/43) to the report of the Legal Committee to the Second Assembly of the International Civil Aviation Organization (ICAO doc. 4629-LC/65).

joint liability of each aircraft in the fleet for the entire loan made to the operating airline. Each aircraft of the fleet being financed therefore constitutes security for the entire amount of the loan rather than merely for the proportionate part of the debt attributable to it. A rough analogy from everyday business life is the joint liability of co-signers of a note. Each co-signer is liable for the face amount of the note, although obviously the lender cannot collect from all co-signers together more than the amount due. The same is true of the fleet mortgage. Each individual airplane is answerable for the total amount of the loan on the entire fleet to the extent of the unpaid balance.

The importance of the fleet-mortgage principle to the financing of international airlines cannot be overemphasized. Conservative financial interests are extremely reluctant to lend large sums of money secured by individual aircraft because of the operational hazards and the obsolescence factors involved in aircraft generally and because of the limited market for single luxury-type transport airplanes. If a fleet of aircraft is made security for the loan, however, the lender will be in a better position to be paid in full. In case of insolvency or bankruptcy of the airline, the aircraft may be disposed of either singly or as a fleet, whichever will bring the most money. If one of the aircraft is lost at sea or in foreign territory, the remaining planes will still constitute security for the loan. These factors tend to overcome the obsolescence disadvantages, and consequently, under the fleet-mortgage doctrine, bankers have been willing to lend up to 80 percent of the purchase price on fleets, whereas the amounts they have been willing to lend on individual aircraft have been considerably less.

Since most airlines do not have the ready cash available to pay for more than 20 percent of the original cost of a fleet of aircraft at the time of acquisition, the importance of this doctrine becomes apparent. In many cases its recognition would mean the difference between obtaining a fleet of aircraft or doing without.

A third desirable feature of any international convention dealing with rights in aircraft is the elimination of what the French term *la purge*. This doctrine, in brief, is that upon the judicial sale of an aircraft, the purchaser at the sale will receive an unencumbered title, despite the fact that the sale may have been made at the behest of a junior lienor or even a general creditor. The purchaser would not be required to assume prior secured interests or to take the aircraft subject to such liens, and the prior security holder would have to look to the proceeds of the sale for repayment.

Ordinarily under the "purge" doctrine, if the chattel is encumbered by a lien prior to that of the attaching creditor, the holder of the prior lien will be paid in full before the attaching creditor

favor. Concepts which are familiar to American lawyers and bankers were completely unfamiliar to foreign lawyers who appear to have an aversion to the detailed corporate indentures so common in American financing.

The principal objection which was voiced by the lawyers of other nations was to the fleet-mortgage principle. This objection appeared to stem from a fear that persons residing in their countries and injured by a foreign airplane would have no recourse against the assets of the airline concerned if recognition were given to the prior liens of secured creditors. Since under the fleet-mortgage principle each aircraft is burdened with an encumbrance many times the value of the aircraft, the effect is to separate the risk of the operation from the capital which gives it birth. For this reason, the delegate of Norway at the meeting of the First Assembly of ICAO in May of 1947 strongly objected to the recognition of the fleet-mortgage principle beyond 80 percent of an amount proportionate to the total amount loaned as the weight of the aircraft bears to the total weight of the fleet. By this "apportionment", provision would be made for the involuntary creditors at home. Obviously, the apportionment doctrine eliminated much of the value of the fleet mortgage as a security device.

The foreign lawyers also objected to the recognition of a variety of types of security devices, many of which were completely unknown to them. These, of course, included the equipment trust, the conditional sale, and the hire-purchase agreement. Such devices in many countries, even though they may be known, are not enforced because they are deemed to be contrary to the general public policy of the country. Even mortgages, which appear to be more generously treated than other financing methods in this respect, are not recognized in many countries abroad.

In regard to spare parts, there had been almost unanimous objection to the doctrine that such parts should receive protection different from that afforded other chattels by the domestic law of the territory where they were kept. This position stems from the traditional view that chattels maintained in the territory of a country are subject to the protection of the laws of that country and consequently should be governed entirely by those laws. Many foreign countries do not recognize mortgages or other liens on movable chattels located on their soil.

Prior to the Brussels meeting of the Legal Committee of ICAO, the tremendous gulf which lay between the point of view of many foreign lawyers and that of the United States was evident to all parties. Deep differences of national approach had to be resolved, old prejudices forgotten, and new methods devised which would bring about substantial compromise and achievement. It is obvious that some compromises would have to be made in the United States position. The fears voiced by foreign representatives had their root in national commercial customs of far longer standing than ours, and even if that had not been so, it would hardly be possible to have lasting agreement on matters which had been so highly controversial if the viewpoint of one country were the sole one represented. Consequently, in the draft convention proposed by the Brussels meeting of the Legal Committee there are many compromises and no small number of legal novelties.

The large majority of the Legal Committee was finally won over to the recognition of all types of security devices when these were presented in a form which separated them into their various vital constituent parts. Thus when the proposal was made that each contracting state undertake to recognize (1) rights of property in aircraft, (2) rights to acquire aircraft by purchase coupled with possession of the aircraft, (3) rights to the possession of aircraft under leases of six months or more, and (4) mortgages, hypothecs, and similar rights, the committee members perceived what was involved more clearly than they would have been able to do if the rights had been presented to them under the familiar names of conditional sale, equipment trust, hire-purchase agreement, and chattel mortgage. Since it is believed that these four categories of rights represent the constituent parts of every recognized security interest now known, the United States position would appear to be fully covered by the terms of article I.

The draft convention is also substantially satisfactory in the treatment accorded the fleet mortgage. As has been stated before, the basic objection to the fleet-mortgage doctrine on the part of other countries was the fact that under that doctrine the commercial risks of the enterprise are separated completely from the capital which sets it in motion. The effect of this separation may be to cause injustice to those involuntary creditors who had in no way intended to deal with the airline. For the main part they will be victims of aircraft accidents or accidents involving surface vehicles operated by the airline concerned. Unless they have a right of recourse against the property of the airline or some equivalent thereof in their country, it is very probable that they will not be able adequately to protect their interests. The American Delegation recognized the fairness of this point of view, and consequently no pains were spared to obtain a satisfactory compromise.

With respect to contract or other voluntary creditors, the position appeared entirely different. Here the creditor has ample opportunity to judge the credit position of the airline prior to entering into negotiations and it was felt that this was a matter where in all justice the creditor should assume the risk.

What is believed to be an eminently fair compromise was finally worked out. No limitation

and pay a price equal to the total outstanding debt. Since that amount in most cases will be many times the value of the aircraft attached, it is obvious that few such sales will take place. While it is true that in the case of mortgages or other liens on single aircraft, the security holder is in a more disadvantageous position than he would be under the doctrine urged by the American Delegation, nevertheless, it is believed that the result will be substantially adequate.

The subject of recognition of security rights in spare parts located in foreign countries also called for a substantial compromise. The position taken by the American Delegation was that spare parts should be treated in the same manner as aircraft, so far as the recognition and protection of security interests are concerned. It was argued that there was no greater reason for affording a contract creditor recourse against spare parts than against the aircraft, and that the spare parts themselves would rarely if ever cause damage to a foreign claimant. No occasion could therefore arise where the public interest required such parts to be made available for attachment by local creditors.

This argument, however, was not completely convincing to the other delegations. It was pointed out that there are various types of claims which, although contractual in nature, are traditionally granted liens by operation of law, as for example, the claim of a landlord for arrears in rent. Employees are usually accorded prior liens against the goods of their employer. Such employees in the large majority of cases would be natives of the country where the parts are located. Moreover, it is also possible that the spare parts themselves might cause damage.

As a result, a compromise solution was finally reached applying the apportionment doctrine to spare parts. The machinery whereby this is set up is contained in article VIII of the proposed draft. It provides that the minimum bid for which the spare parts may be sold shall be two thirds of the value of the parts, as determined by experts appointed by the authority responsible for the sale. Upon their sale, the court (or other authority responsible for the sale) may refuse to recognize the claim of the secured creditor in an amount in excess of two thirds of the proceeds. As a consequence, the maximum security which a lender can count on as to spare parts located in a foreign jurisdiction would be two thirds of the current value of the parts.

The draft convention is believed satisfactory with respect to the ease with which valid liens can be created. Recording in countries foreign to the registry of the aircraft is not necessary. In the case of spare parts a sign must be posted on the premises setting forth the fact that the spare parts are subject to a secured interest, the name and address of the holder of such interest, and the record where such interest is recorded. This obligation, however, should not prove to be an onerous burden. Further recording is not required by the convention for the replacement of stocks of spare parts and this may be accomplished without diminishing the security of the lender in the stockpile.

In another connection the convention would appear to be entirely satisfactory to the American position. Preferred claims as set forth in article III have been limited to compensation due for salvage of the aircraft and extraordinary expenses indispensable for preservation of the aircraft. It was the consensus of the committee that these expenses would never exceed relatively minor sums.

In the treatment of priority claims a rather novel approach was included at the request of the United Kingdom Delegation. These claims were made subject to recording as ordinary secured claims upon the expiration of their priority at the end of three months. In this way the holder of a preferred claim may record his claim and enjoy the benefits of a secured creditor from the date of recordation. Of course, this would not mean that a claim so recorded would be prior to other secured claims previously recorded, but it would outrank all mortgages and other liens which were recorded subsequently.

By article III, paragraph 7, the contracting states are enjoined from admitting or recognizing any right other than the priority rights set forth in article III which would displace recorded secured rights. In this connection it should be noted that the paragraph containing this prohibition was originally placed in article IV. During the last day of the Conference, this paragraph was moved up into article III as paragraph 7 in order to avoid a cross reference between article IV and article III. The effect of this removal is greater than at first meets the eye, for under the terms of article IX the provisions of article III must be applied by contracting states to all aircraft, including domestic aircraft operating on home soil.

The result of article III (7), read in conjunction with article IX, is that a contracting state is prohibited from placing tax liens and other charges ahead of recorded mortgages, even though the aircraft stays at home and the secured creditor is a national and resident of such contracting state. There is nothing to indicate in the Conference proceeding that this result was intended, and it will be a simple matter to correct. It will be necessary to correct it, however, since it is understood that the constitutions of a number of countries prohibit the enactment of any law which deprives the state of its right to place tax liens ahead of all other charges with respect to domestic chattels.

(Continued on page 523)

THE UNITED NATIONS AND SPECIALIZED AGENCIES

Request for a Special Session of the General Assembly on Palestine

STATEMENT BY AMBASSADOR WARREN R. AUSTIN [1]
U.S. Representative in the Security Council

The time appears suitable to offer to the Security Council resolutions to carry out part II of the paper representing the views of four of the permanent members (S/P.V.270, 19 March 1948, page 7), as follows:[2]

As a result of the consultations of the permanent members regarding the situation with respect to Palestine, they find and report that a continuation of the infiltration into Palestine, by land and by sea, of groups and persons with the purpose of taking part in violence would aggravate still further the situation, and recommend

"(a) that the Security Council should make it clear to the parties and governments concerned that the Security Council is determined not to permit the existence of a threat to international peace in Palestine, and

"(b) that the Security Council should take further action by all means available to it to bring about the immediate cessation of violence and the restoration of peace and order in Palestine."

The statement made by the President of the United States on March 25 indicates the urgent necessity of exerting every effort in the Security Council to arrange a truce between the Jews and Arabs of Palestine.

Such a truce should be based on two fundamental considerations:

First, it is absolutely essential that violence and bloodshed in Palestine cease. This is demanded by humanitarian considerations. We must pre-

vent anarchy. It is required to keep international peace. Cessation of hostilities is imperative.

Second, both the Jews and Arabs of Palestine must be prepared to accept truce arrangement which would not prejudice the claims of either group. The truce should include suspension of political as well as military activity.

My Government considers it essential that representatives of the Jewish Agency and of the Arab Higher Committee be called upon to state their views on the necessary arrangements for a truce. Such representatives should, of course, be fully authorized to enter into definitive truce arrangements with the Council.

To provide for the immediate cessation of hostilities and the basis for a truce, Mr. President, I have submitted for the consideration of the Council the following resolution.[4]

The Security Council,

In the exercise of its primary responsibility for the maintenance of international peace and security,

Notes the increasing violence and disorder in Palestine and believes that it is of the utmost urgency that an immediate truce be effected in Palestine;

Calls upon the Jewish Agency for Palestine and the Arab Higher Committee to make representatives available to the Security Council for the purpose of arranging a truce between the Arab and Jewish communities of Palestine, and emphasizes the heavy responsibility which would fall upon any party failing to observe such a truce,

Calls upon Arab and Jewish armed groups in Palestine to cease acts of violence immediately.

It is the view of my Government that the immediate cessation of hostilities and the establishment of a truce in Palestine are the most urgent objectives. We believe that the Council should also proceed as promptly as possible to the consideration of the additional conclusions and recommendations concerning Palestine. I alluded to these in my statement to the Council at its 271st meeting on Friday, March 19.

[1] U.N. doc. A/530, Apr. 7, 1948. Note by the Secretary-General, acting under provisions of rules 7 and 9 of the rules of procedure of the General Assembly, has, by telegram dated Apr. 1, 1948, summoned the second special session of the Assembly to meet at Flushing Meadows, N.Y., on Apr. 16, 1948. Provisional agenda for the second special session of the General Assembly is contained in U.N. doc. A/531, Apr. 7, 1948.

[2] Made on Mar. 30, 1948, in the Security Council and released to the press by the U.S. Mission to the United Nations on the same date.

[3] U.N. doc. S/714, Apr. 7, 1948.

[4] U.N. doc. S/704 of Mar. 30, 1948. Adopted unanimously by the Security Council at its 277th meeting on Apr. 1, 1948.

to consider further the question of the future government of Palestine.

It will be noted that this resolution does not mention trusteeship. The United States adheres to the view I stated in the Security Council on March 19, and which was reaffirmed by the Secretary of State on March 20 and again by the President of the United States on March 25, that a temporary trusteeship should be established to maintain the peace. This trusteeship would be without prejudice to the character of the final political settlement in Palestine. We believe that a trusteeship is essential to establish order, without which a peaceful solution of this problem cannot be found or put into effect.

The exigencies of the time limits confronting the Security Council require prompt decision and issue of the call for a Special Session. This should not be delayed by debate over details of the temporary trusteeship. The United States is ready to offer and consider with other members of the Security Council proposals regarding such details while the necessary notice period is running.

DOR WARREN R. AUSTIN [6]

In the Security Council

urgency that an immediate truce be effected in Palestine;

"*Calls upon* the Jewish Agency for Palestine and the Arab Higher Committee to make representatives available to the Security Council for the purpose of arranging a truce"—not for the purpose apparently indicated in the speeches which have been made here today, but—

"a truce between the Arab and Jewish communities of Palestine; and emphasizes the heavy responsibility which would fall upon any party failing to observe such a truce;

"*Calls upon* Arab and Jewish armed groups in Palestine to cease acts of violence immediately."

This calls for a standstill; this calls for a cessation of hostilities; this calls for the stopping of the slaughter, the civil disobedience, the destruction of property, and the anarchy which exists in a territory that is under a mandate. Just remember that this is not a free territory. It does not belong to anybody. If you search out the title to it, I think you will find that it has a legal position as a result of the war.

---

[5] U.N. doc. S/705 of Mar. 30, 1948.
[6] Made on Mar. 30, 1948, in the Security Council and released to the press by the U.S. Mission to the United Nations on the same date.

This is a mandatory property under a mandatory administrator. Events are occurring there which are a shame to humanity, and it is up to the Security Council, of all organizations in the world, to put a stop to them.

This resolution, if passed, would impose an obligation under the Charter upon every member of the United Nations to carry out the decision made in this resolution. Our position would be somewhat different after the adoption of a resolution like this from what it is under a recommendation made by the General Assembly.

There is no mystery about the word *truce*. It requires two things above all others: one is the cessation of hostilities and the other is the cessation of provocation. And it is that part of the duty of the Security Council that is indicated in the third paragraph of the resolution, which reads as follows:

"*Calls upon* the Jewish Agency for Palestine and the Arab Higher Committee to make representatives available to the Security Council for the purpose of arranging a truce between the Arab and Jewish communities of Palestine . . ."

No such effective change in the military aspect of this matter could be had without arranging the terms of the truce, that is, reaching an agreement between the parties which are now violating the peace. Now this standstill idea is not new. It was recognized when the United Nations Charter was made, and it was recognized largely at the instigation of those who represented the Jews in Palestine. Article 80 which deals with a trusteeship or a mandatory, is contained in chapter XII, international trusteeship system. It reads as follows:

"1. Except as may be agreed upon in individual trusteeship agreements, made under articles 77, 79 and 81, placing each territory under the trusteeship system, and until such agreements have been concluded"—that is for how long: until such agreements have been concluded—

"nothing in this Chapter shall be construed in or of itself to alter in any manner the rights whatsoever of any states or any peoples or the terms of existing international instruments to which Members of the United Nations may respectively be parties."

I understand that this article was suggested at San Francisco by the Zionists in order to assure continued recognition of their national home in Palestine. But the text equally protects the rights of Arabs to maintain the continuity of the unity of Palestine in their civil and religious rights in the territory protected by the mandate.

Discussion in the Security Council of the Czechoslovak Question

STATEMENT BY AMBASSADOR WARREN R. AUSTIN [1]

U.S. Representative in the Security Council

At an earlier meeting on this matter I raised the question with reference to the participation of the representative of the new Czechoslovak regime in this proceeding.

It has been a consistent practice which is firmly rooted in the Charter, for a state nonmember of the Security Council against whom charges were made or whose interests appear to be specially affected in a matter before the Council, to petition for permission to take part in the proceedings. Such request has invariably been granted. It is quite obvious that the current proceeding is of grave concern for the Czechoslovak Government. It was for that reason that I suggested informally the invitation of the Czechoslovak Representative to the Council table. However, thus far his Representative has not found it advisable to request, in accordance with the established procedure, permission to participate. On the contrary, I am told that in a statement to the press he indicated that his Government did not wish to participate in the proceedings because the proceedings related to matters essentially within the domestic jurisdiction of Czechoslovakia.

Now, members of the Council will recall that it has been alleged that a police regime has been established in Czechoslovakia with foreign assistance. The complaint was validly placed on the Council agenda by a vote of a large majority of Council members. One of the aims of the Council proceedings is to establish whether or not the matter before the Council is essentially within the domestic jurisdiction of Czechoslovakia as is alleged by the Czechoslovak Representative in statements made outside of the Council.

We can not help but wonder what causes the new Czechoslovak Government to be so reluctant about requesting an opportunity to be heard by this Council. Can it be that the Czechoslovak Government is afraid of participating in an open debate? Is it apprehensive that its case will not stand up before world opinion following open and free debate in this Council? This strange reluctance stands in stark contrast to the active participation in the past of the old democratic Czechoslovak Government in international conferences. In the League, the Czechoslovak Government spoke with authority based on its democratic institutions at home and on its adherence to justice in its foreign policies. Members of the Council will also recall the contribution which the Czechoslovak Delegation under the leadership of the late

Jan Masaryk made at the San Francisco conference. In summary, I can only say that the reluctance of the present Czechoslovak regime to request a hearing certainly has not instilled in my delegation a feeling that this regime has a strong case to present.

I feel that the Council, in view of the seriousness of the charges which have been made before it, should proceed in the most impartial manner. I think the Council should go on record as inviting the Representative of this new Czechoslovak regime to appear before us in order that he may state his Government's side of the case and in order that he may be available to answer questions which we may wish to put before him. For my part, I have a number of questions which I desire to direct to him. In an earlier statement during this case, I gave the Council an indication of the nature of some of these questions which I would like to ask. I am therefore presenting a resolution on this point to the Council reading as follows: [2]

The Government of Czechoslovakia is invited to participate without vote in the discussion of the Czechoslovak question now under consideration by the Security Council, and the Secretary-General is instructed to notify the Czechoslovak Representative to the United Nations accordingly.

THE FOREIGN SERVICE

Consular Offices

The American Consulate at Port Limón, Costa Rica, was officially closed on March 31, 1948.

The American Consulate at Cebu, Republic of the Philippines, was opened to the public on April 5, 1948.

The American Consulate at Palermo, Italy, has been raised to the rank of Consulate General, effective April 8, 1948.

Confirmations

On April 7, 1948, the Senate confirmed the following nominations: Lincoln MacVeagh to be Ambassador Extraordinary and Plenipotentiary to Portugal and Felix Cole to be Ambassador Extraordinary and Plenipotentiary to Ceylon.

[1] Made on Apr. 6, 1948, in the Security Council and released to the press by the U.S. Mission to the United Nations on the same date.
[2] Adopted by the Security Council at its 278th meeting on Apr. 6, 1948. U.N. doc. S/711, Apr. 6, 1948.

Freedom of Information Throughout World Insures Peace

ADDRESS BY WILLIAM BENTON [1]

Chairman, U.S. Delegation to the Freedom of Information Conference

Our conference at Geneva, as was to be expected, is sharply divided. The Soviet Union, with the small states which echo its views, daily proclaims that the state, the Communist dictatorship, is the source of all good, the purveyor of all freedom—by decree. On the other side are ranged the representatives of those countries whose people yet dare freely to express their opinions and to call themselves rational, self-governing men. These hold that freedom of information means primarily freedom from the state, or from any monopoly whatever, public or private.

The free are thus face to face with those whose ideology drives them toward the destruction of freedom. This is the stark reality. It is more clearly illuminated with each passing day at the Geneva conference.

There are nevertheless ludicrous as well as grave aspects to this cleavage. To hide the most complete censorship and thought dictation known to history, the Soviet propagandists have erected elaborate Potemkin villages of freedom along the route of international scrutiny. They have built gilded facades labeled "freedom from exploitation by monopoly capitalism". They have created monumental stage sets labeled "true freedom of expression".

I find it not at all ludicrous that around the clock and in several dozen languages Soviet propagandists appropriate, degrade, and bastardize the words which are the hard-earned and world-accepted currency of free men. Liberty, equality, fraternity, independence, justice, freedom, democracy. For these, brave men have died at the hands of tyrants for thousands of years.

Now the U. S. S. R. insists with a thousand amplified voices that repression is freedom, and that true freedom elsewhere in the world is slavery; they insist that the police state is democracy, and that democracy in other countries is dictatorship by monopoly capitalists. They assert that aggression is peace and liberation, and that true liberation is aggression; that complete state control of man's thought and expression is freedom of expression; and that true freedom of expression among free men is dictatorship.

The age-old trick of the propagandists, from the day of the Sophists to the day of Dr. Goebbels,

has been to confuse and confound the listener b[y] labeling black as white and white as black. I[ts] latest manifestation is this official attempt to d[e] preciate the word currency of free men, to dri[ve] the sound currency of clear meanings from th[e] market place of ideas.

Thus it became apparent from the earliest da[y] of the conference that the Soviet Union is [in] Geneva primarily to create propaganda that, the[y] hope, will further undermine freedom of expre[s] sion in the world.

Day after day, in each of the committees of th[e] conference, the delegates have been obliged to liste[n] to harangues upon the evils of the American pres[s] the British press, and others throughout the worl[d] We have had thrown back at us admissions of gui[lt] of all of the defects in the operation of a free pre[ss] that have been unearthed by our own schola[rs] our own statesmen, and our own press itself in [its] effort to remedy them.

We readily admit the imperfections of our ow[n] free press. We seek always to correct them, a[nd] it is a continuous job. Nevertheless, it becom[es] boring to have these defects brought up, time aft[er] time, as reasons for abolishing freedom of expre[s] sion. We refuse to burn down the palaces of fre[e] dom merely in order to smoke out the rats. Hect[or] McNeil, Chief of the British Delegation, aft[er] sitting through endless hours of attacks of th[at] kind, during the course of an impressive addre[ss] turned to the Soviet Representative and remarke[d] "If I wanted I could in this speech have point[ed] to the inconsistencies, the variations, the treache[r] ous, and the unjustifiable changes in the views a[nd] the news given publication by the authoritari[an] presses of Soviet Russia and of eastern Europe. I have not attacked it, it is not because I la[ck] ammunition."

Similarly, the United States Delegation does n[ot] lack ammunition for attack of that kind. W[e] could provide chapter and verse on how the Sovi[et] press and radio, domestically within the Sovi[et] Union and internationally through its world-wi[de] broadcasting and its controlled publications, s[e] lects, distorts, and perverts the news, especia[lly] news about the non-Communist world. With r[e] spect to the United States, all Soviet organs ha[ve] for many months, day in and day out, hammer[ed] out variations on a series of simple themes: T[he] United States is imperialistic and militaristic; t[he] United States is undemocratic and reactionar[y;]

[1] Delivered before the Anglo-American Press Club in Paris, France, on Apr. 7, 1948, and released to the press on the same date.

United States is culturally backward; the United States is on the verge of a catastrophic depression from which it is trying to extricate itself by imperialistic adventures.

If the United States refuses loans and favors to other nations, it is portrayed as rich and selfish. If it makes loans or grants favors, it is seeking to enslave foreign peoples. If it takes a firm position on any issue, it is militaristic and imperialistic. If it yields, this is evidence of the inner decay of capitalism.

I have a file of Tass Agency reports of the Geneva conference. If an American or British or French news agency here were to be guilty of such shockingly one-sided, malicious reporting, the enraged readers would put it out of business. But not Tass. The Tass News Agency is the official disburser of the Soviet Government.

There are two reasons why we have not used our ammunition about this deliberate incitement to hatred. One reason is that we are not at Geneva to make propaganda. We are there to do all that we can to reduce barriers to the flow of information among men and nations. The second reason is that nations which believe in freedom of information tend to lack skill in propaganda, except as efforts to spread the truth over a period of years is the best propaganda. We are deeply wedded to fact and fair argument. Our social, political, and moral patterns would not permit us to use the Soviet type of propaganda. We make a mistake when we try it.

But in spite of the diversionary propaganda attacks that have impeded the work of the conference, real progress has been made. Issues and the meaning of words have been clarified; we know now more precisely what it may be possible to accomplish.

In my opening speech at the conference I expressed doubt that unanimous agreement would be possible. I indicated that in some areas it was not desirable even to seek unanimous agreement.

These doubts are now shared, I believe, by the great majority of the delegates at the conference. Impassable unbridgeable crevasses divide free peoples from states who claim to be the people who have been more fully exposed. As the chairman of one of the delegations at Geneva remarked to me, if free nations reach any agreement with the Soviet bloc on any resolution or convention on freedom of information, it will be because the U.S.S.R. and ourselves do not share a common understanding of the words used.

What we can achieve in Geneva, as I now see it, is general agreement—agreement by countries not hostile to freedom—on an international convention guaranteeing greater access to news, greater freedom in its transmission from country to country and freedom within states to receive news. Several countries—Great Britain, France, and others—as well as the United States—have pro-

posed conventions aimed at these objectives. We of the United States are pressing hard for this goal, and I am hopeful that one or more conventions will be adopted that will be strong and meaningful.

The second thing we hope to achieve at the conference is general agreement upon sending the conference's recommendations and agreements not only to the Economic and Social Council but directly to governments, and immediately to appeal to them and to private groups for implementation and at once.

A final major objective of the American Delegation at the conference is to secure agreement upon the establishment of continuing machinery in the United Nations that will keep world attention focused on the vital subject of freedom of expression within and among nations.

The continuing machinery we envisage would extend the life of the U.N. Subcommission on Freedom of Information and direct it to study and report on barriers to the free flow of information, the extent to which freedom of information is actually accorded to the peoples of the world, the adequacy of the news available to them.

These are our hopes and expectations in terms of specific objectives. Looking back upon the last two weeks in Geneva, however, it seems to me that never have the official representatives of nations in conference assembled probed so deeply into the ultimate causes of war. This may surprise you.

But consider that freedom of expression is the father and protector of all other freedoms enjoyed by a free society of happy men.

Consider that freedom of expression is the basis of democratic self-government wherever in the world men have attained it.

Consider that in the Soviet Union and its satellite states ruling groups hold freedom of expression to be more dangerous than cancer or atomic power.

Consider that the extinction of freedom of expression wherever in the world it exists is avowedly and observedly a primary aim of Soviet policy.

Consider finally that the United Nations, instinctively seeking to rout out the causes of war, has called together representatives of the people of the world in a conference at Geneva to discuss ways and means of promoting a free flow of information.

Consider these things, gentlemen, and perhaps you will agree that in our conference at Geneva we are hacking away at the taproot of war.

There was a time, perhaps, when love of glory, or prospect of gain, or ideological fanaticism caused powerful rulers to embark upon wars of aggression. But not today, when the front lines are the city boulevards, and no prospect of gain could possibly be imagined, even by a fanatic, to offset the colossal cost of modern war. Fear—stark, elemental fear—is today the chief threat to peace.

Today we must concede that fear is rampant and it is not inappropriate to ask why this is so. We are only three years removed from the most devastating war in history. The enemies of the victorious Allies are crushed. No people in the world have the desire to fight again. And yet, fear has seized the world.

Fear on the part of whom?

Fear on the part of what?

Fear is by its nature infectious and self-compounding. The Soviet Union and its satellites profess to be fearful of the West. The western powers doubt and fear the intentions of the Soviets. No nation escapes this universal infection. Actions based on fear set off a cycle of greater fears and ever more antagonistic actions.

And what is the source and the focus of this world-wide infection? I say without hesitation that its greatest single continuing source is the policy of the Soviet Union toward freedom of information. I do not say that the only thing the world has to fear is fear itself, because I will not presume to analyze the motives of the Soviet Government or of any other government. I will not presume to analyze the mixture of ideological evangelism, or of lust for power; or of the desire for national security, or of so-called historic national aspirations.

But I will presume to say flatly that, had it not been the policy of the Soviet Government to deny the Russian people the right to express themselves and to communicate freely with other peoples, and to deny the right of other peoples to communicate with them, the world would not now find itself in the grip of such an acute fear psychosis.

At the war's end, no foreign danger to the U.S.S.R. even remotely appeared on the horizon. The American, British, French, Chinese, and other Allied peoples, grateful to the Russian people for their tremendous effort in helping to defeat the common enemy, had poured out their treasure, their confidence, and their admiration to their ally. Yet the Soviet Government would not permit contact between their people and those in other countries who enjoy freedom. The Russian people have not been permitted to learn for themselves the nature and intentions of other peoples, or the achievements and ways of life of other peoples. Higher went the barriers insulating Soviet citizens from contact with the outside. Turned on was the campaign of hatred against foreign countries. Set into motion was a foreign policy of expansionism that has resulted in the seizure and control of neighboring states which might serve as buffers against free peoples. Revived was the old Comintern in new dress to press revolution and Communist control in all parts of the world, to preach everywhere that repression is freedom and that

ions of Interzonal Boundaries of the Free Territory of Trieste

'EXT OF NOTE FROM THE UNITED STATES TO THE YUGOSLAV FOREIGN OFFICE [1]

April 6, 1948

Embassy of the U.S.A. presents its com-
s to the Minister of Foreign Affairs of the
ed People's Republic of Yugoslavia and
nstructions of the Secretary of State of
ted States has the honor urgently to bring
[inister's attention a series of incidents con-
z flagrant violations of the interzonal
ies of the Free Territory of Trieste on the
the Yugoslav occupational forces.
[arch 29 at 12:15 o'clock the personnel of
tish observation post situated approxi-
3,000 yards southeast of Basovizza and 300
nside the British-U.S. zone of the Free
ry of Trieste were fired upon from the zone
l by Yugoslav forces. Two members of
;oslav Military Government police (*Difesa*
i) were seen to fire a number of rifle shots
t the above-mentioned post.
however, was not the first instance in which
s of the Yugoslav occupation forces and of
goslav Military Government police have
. members of the Anglo-American zone of
e Territory of Trieste. On December 12,
ugoslav troops opened fire in this same area

shooting over the heads of the Venezia Giulia police who were stationed in the British-U.S. zone.
Again, on March 22, 1948, two members of the
Venezia Giulia police force who were patroling
the railway line which runs from St. Antonio to
the border of the two zones were fired upon by
members of the Yugoslav forces, and one of them
was wounded.

The Government of the United States most
firmly protests against this series of violations of
the interzonal boundaries of the Free Territory
of Trieste by Yugoslav occupation forces and
against these provocative acts toward personnel
of the British-American zone in the performance
of their duty. The Government of the United
States trusts and expects that the Yugoslav Government will promptly issue the necessary instructions to its responsible representative to the end
that there will be no repetitions of such incidents
which seriously endanger the lives of members of
the British-U.S. forces and the Venezia Giulia
police in the discharge of their responsibilities in
the area of the Free Territory of Trieste under
British-American administration.

The Embassy avails itself [etc.]

'roposes Discussion of Protocol for Return of Free Territory of Trieste

NOTE FROM THE ACTING SECRETARY OF STATE TO THE ITALIAN AMBASSADOR [2]

April 9, 1948.

Acting Secretary of State presents his com-
s to His Excellency the Italian Ambassa-
l has the honor to acknowledge the receipt
Excellency's note of March 22, 1948, re-
; the proposal of the Governments of
the United Kingdom and the United
for the return of the Free Territory of
to Italian sovereignty.

e no reply has yet been received from the
ment of the Union of Soviet Socialist Re-
it is the view of the United States Govern-
at, should the Soviet Government agree to
posal, a preliminary meeting of the repre-
es of the powers principally, concerned

might be convened in Paris early in May to negotiate a draft of the necessary protocol to the Treaty
of Peace with Italy. The United States Government feels that in the interest of terminating the
present unsettled situation in the Free Territory
of Trieste and restoring peace and stability in the
area, early action by the interested powers is required. The Government of the United States
would be glad to have the views of the Italian
Government regarding this suggested precedure.

---

[1] Delivered on Apr. 6, 1948, and released to the press on
Apr. 7.
[2] Delivered on Apr. 9, 1948, and released to the press on
the same date.

April 9, 1948.

The Acting Secretary of State presents his compliments to His Excellency the Ambassador of the Union of Soviet Socialist Republics and has the honor to refer to the United States Government's communication of March 20, 1948, in which it was proposed that the Soviet Government agree to early consideration, jointly with the Governments of the United Kingdom, France and Italy, of the negotiation of a protocol to the Treaty of Peace with Italy to provide for the return of the Free Territory of Trieste to Italian sovereignty. As His Excellency is aware, similar communications were addressed by the Governments of France and the United Kingdom to the Government of the Union of Soviet Socialist Republics, and by the Governments of France, the United

International Joint Commission Meets To Discuss

[Released to the press April 8]

At its regular meeting in Washington on April 7, the International Joint Commission (on boundary waters, United States and Canada) appointed the Engineering Boards which will conduct investigations under the two references which the Governments of Canada and of the United States made to the International Joint Commission on January 12, 1948.[4] These studies will concern numerous streams in the vicinity of the international boundary from the Continental Divide on the west to and including the basin of the Red River of the North on the east.

Later that same day the Engineering Boards, all members of which were in Washington, held an organizational meeting and established operating procedures and outlined steps to make the necessary investigations and reports to the Commission.

Since the matters referred by the two Governments to the International Joint Commission fall in two separate areas, two Boards with identical membership were established, one to be known as the International Waterton-Belly Rivers Engineering Board and the other as the International Souris-Red Rivers Engineering Board.

The initial steps in each of the two references will be to investigate and report upon the water requirements arising out of the existing dams and other works or projects located in the waters which

---

[3] Delivered on Apr. 9, 1948, and released to the press on the same date.
[4] BULLETIN of Feb. 1, 1948, p. 151.

WHEREAS A special Preparatory Committee of Experts, representing intergovernmental organizations in the fields of aviation, meteorology, shipping and telecommunications, has recently met in London to consider principles for the co-ordination of activities in those four fields,

WHEREAS The report of the Preparatory Committee (circulated to the Conference as Document E/CONF. 4/8) will be considered at the forthcoming conference to revise the Convention for the Safety of Life at Sea, to be held in London in April 1948.

Resolves That this Conference direct its President to inform the Conference on Safety of Life at Sea that the Conclusions contained in paragraph 21 of the Report of the Preparatory Committee of Experts were taken into consideration by this Conference when drafting Part VII of the Intergovernmental Maritime Consultative Organization Convention which establishes the Maritime Safety Committee.

[Here follows Annex D: Draft Agreement on Relationship Between the United Nations and the Intergovernmental Maritime Consultative Organization.]

PUBLICATIONS

Soviet Supply Protocols Made Public

[Released to the press April 9]

The Department of State released to the public on April 9 the texts of four protocols which formed the basis of United States, British, and Canadian material assistance to the Union of Soviet Socialist Republics during the war against the Axis. The document, Department of State publication 2759, European Series 22, entitled *Soviet Supply Protocols*, may be obtained in pamphlet form from the Superintendent of Documents, United States Government Printing Office, Washington 25, D.C., at 35 cents a copy.

The *Soviet Supply Protocols*, while indicating the quantities of supplies which the United States committed itself to provide, does not indicate the extent to which materials were actually delivered to the Soviet Union. United States offerings were reduced under the terms of the protocols by Soviet selections to accord with available shipping. Additional requests of the Soviet Government for urgently needed items were met wherever possible by additions to protocol schedules or by substitution for scheduled items. Shipping failures and resultant production curtailment and, in the third and fourth protocols, shipments in excess of protocol commitments, were factors which caused variance with original protocol plans. Information covering the supplies actually delivered to the Soviet Union during the war period may be found in the *Twenty-First Report to Congress on Lend-Lease Operations* and other publications of the United States Government.

---

[5] The full text of the draft convention as approved by the Legal Committee at Brussels on Sept. 25, 1947, may be found in Appendix "C" (ICAO doc. 4627–LC/63) to the report of the Legal Committee to the Second Assembly of the International Civil Aviation Organization (ICAO doc. 4629–LC/65).

DOCUMENTS AND STATE PAPERS: A New Monthly Periodical

The first issue of *Documents and State Papers*, a new official monthly periodical of the Department of State, was released on April 16. It contains a specially prepared policy paper surveying Allied policy in the Japanese reeducation program, the basic directive to SOAP for the occupation of Japan, and a translation of the Constitution of the Italian Republic.

The need for a periodical to provide an additional source for documentary data has long been recognized. Rapidly changing developments in international affairs have made it necessary to document this Government's position more fully and adequately.

The weekly DEPARTMENT OF STATE BULLETIN will continue to carry current official announcements, articles, and statements on principal international developments. *Documents and State Papers* will include documentary reports and texts, specially prepared policy papers, texts of treaties and international agreements, basic background studies, and selected official documents and statements. Such subjects as United States occupation policies, participation in the United Nations, international conferences, foreign economic policies, and treaty developments, as well as general aspects of foreign policy, will be treated.

Under the direction of E. Wilder Spaulding, Chief of the Division of Publications, Office of Public Affairs, Angelo.Eagon will be Editor of *Documents and State Papers* and will continue as Editor of the DEPARTMENT OF STATE BULLETIN.

Documents and State Papers may be obtained from the Superintendent of Documents, U.S. Government Printing Office, Washington 25, D.C. (Subscription $3.00 a year; single copy 30¢.) ·

Contributors

G. Nathan Calkins, Jr., author of the article on the Legal Committee on ICAO, is Chief of the International and Rules Division, Civil Aeronautics Board. Mr. Calkins served as Chairman of the U.S. Delegation to the meeting in Brussels.

John M. Cates, Jr., author of the article on the United Nations Maritime Conference, is an officer in the Division of International Organization Affairs, Office of United Nations Affairs, Department of State. Mr. Cates is a member of the U.S. Delegation to that conference.

The Department of State

For sale by the Superintendent of Documents
U.S. Government Printing Office
Washington 25, D.C.

SUBSCRIPTION:
52 issues, $5; single copy, 15 cents

Published with the approval of the
Director of the Bureau of the Budget

GNIFICANCE OF TEXTILES IN THE JAPANESE ECONOMY

by *Stanley Nehmer and Marguerite C. Crimmins*

To achieve the objective of creating a perma-
ntly peaceful, democratic state in Japan, it is
cessary to establish in that country a self-sup-
rting economy. Japan must import many raw
iterials and at least one fifth of her food to
rvive; and in order to pay for those imports,
e must redevelop her international trade. The
ost important industries to rehabilitate in Japan,
th an objective of enabling the Japanese to be
lf-supporting, are the textile industries. This
ticle is designed to point up the significance of
e textile industries in the domestic economy and
the foreign trade of Japan.

PREWAR SIGNIFICANCE OF JAPAN'S
TEXTILE INDUSTRIES

ntribution to Production and Employment

During the prewar period, the textile industries
ere among the more important segments of the
ipanese economy. In 1928, textiles accounted
ir 40 percent of the total value of Japan's fac-
ry production and absorbed 52 percent of all
idustrial labor. This high proportion of value
f production and employment was not main-
ined, however, over the next decade. Changes
i the character of the Japanese economy, which
ivolved the rapid expansion of the war-support-
ig metal, machinery, and chemicals industries,
ere responsible for the decline in the relative im-
ortance of the textile industries although they
ill ranked among Japan's major industries. By
)36, textiles accounted for 29 percent of the total
ilue of factory production and about 38 percent
f total industrial employment.

Measured by both of the above criteria, in 1928
ie cotton and silk industries were the largest and
iost active ones, while wool ranked third and
iyon had not yet been developed significantly.
y 1936 such changes as the decline in the price of
lk and the further development of cotton, wool,
id rayon caused a shift in the relative importance
f the various textiles. Chart 1 summarizes the
intribution of each of the textile industries in
)28 and 1936.

pril 25, 1948

Contribution to Trade

Important as the textile industries were to the
internal economy of Japan, they had equal or
greater significance in Japan's foreign trade. In
1930 the value of exports of all textile raw materials and products amounted to 501 million dollars, or 55 percent of the value of Japan's total
exports. In the same year the cost of imports of
textile raw materials and products totaled 271 million dollars, or 27 percent of the cost of Japan's
total imports. By 1936 the textile industry contributed somewhat less to Japan's total foreign
trade; textile exports accounted for 485 million
dollars, or 48 percent of Japan's total exports, and
textile imports of 349 million dollars represented
33 percent of total imports.

Each of the branches of the textile industry differed with respect to its net contribution to
Japan's foreign exchange. Silk, a native product
of Japan, required no imported raw materials in
its manufacture. The entire value of exported
silk, therefore, was an addition to Japan's foreign
exchange. Cotton, wool, and rayon textiles, on the
other hand, required heavy raw-material imports

Chart 1

COMPARATIVE POSITION
OF JAPAN'S TEXTILE INDUSTRIES, 1928-36

Value of Textile Production

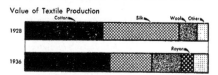

Textile Employment

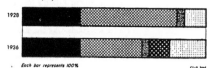

Each bar represents 100%

CI-G 3665

since no cotton or wool was grown in Japan and because sufficient good-quality rayon pulp was not available. Since the cost of raw cotton and wool absorbed a large percentage of the value of the finished product, cotton and wool textile exports were not such good sources of foreign exchange as were silk exports. In fact, in the period 1928–36 the value of identifiable cotton and wool exports did not cover the cost of raw cotton and wool imports. The reason for this "deficit", of course, was that Japanese domestic consumption of cotton and wool absorbed a large proportion of these two imports. With restricted domestic consumption, however, both of these branches of the textile industry could yield a net addition to the foreign-exchange account. In the case of imported pulp for rayon, its cost does not absorb such a large proportion of the value of the finished product as do raw cotton and wool, and since the value added by manufacture in the rayon industry is relatively large, the rayon industry can pay its own way more easily than either the cotton or wool industries and can probably make a net contribution to Japan's foreign-exchange position.

Raw Silk Trade. Japan's silk industry encountered serious difficulties during the 1930's. Exports of raw silk fluctuated between 470,000 bales in 1930 and 553,000 bales in 1935, and then declined to 386,000 bales in 1939. The price of raw silk dropped from $5.07 a pound in 1928 to a low of $1.30 in 1934 and then rose gradually to a peak of $2.79 in 1940. Some of the factors responsible for the falling value of Japan's raw-silk exports were Japan's devaluation of the yen, which appears to have had no prolonged effect on increasing silk exports; a declining market after 1935 in the United States, which had absorbed an average of 95 percent of Japan's raw-silk exports in 1928-32, because of growing competition from rayon; and the world-wide depression, which affected the foregoing factors and generally unstabilized the world silk market. Consequently, the contribution which raw silk made to Japan's foreign exchange dropped severely during this period. In 1928 exports of raw and waste silk totaled 350 million dollars, but by 1936 this figure had fallen to 142 million dollars. Even so, in the latter year raw-silk exports still played a major role in Japan's foreign trade, contributing 11 percent of the value of all exports.

Cotton Trade. Of Japan's cotton textiles, cotton piece goods was the most outstanding item in Japan's export trade. In 1928 exports of cotton piece goods totaled 189 million dollars and in 1936 amounted to 151 million dollars. These same exports contributed 17 percent of the value of total

[1] U.S. Tariff Commission, *Japan's Competitive Position in International Trade*, May 1935, part II, pp. 52–68.
[2] Quoted in International Labour Office, *The World Textile Industry*, 1937, vol. I, p. 181; from Manchester Chamber of Commerce, *Monthly Record*, no. 9, Sept. 30, 1936, p. 369.

modity Credit Corporation (Ccc), and the Department of State, as a concurring agency, entered into an agreement under which about 900,-000 bales of raw cotton, held by Ccc, was sent to Japan during the ensuing year and a half for manufacture. At least 60 percent of the finished yarn and piece goods was to be sold by the Uscc and the proceeds applied to the cost of the raw cotton. Under the agreement the balance of the textiles could be used for domestic consumption, but the need to maximize foreign-exchange receipts to pay for food and other essential imports resulted in the decision that a smaller quantity would be retained than allowed in the contract. Under an extension of this agreement executed in July 1947 an additional 350,000 bales of raw cotton and spinnable cotton waste was supplied Japan from the United States.

In addition, Scap-negotiated agreements with India and Egypt have provided for Japanese imports of 170,000 bales of Indian cotton and 5,000 bales of Egyptian cotton. From July 1946, when raw-cotton imports were first reflected in increased cotton-yarn production, through September 1947, Japan produced 330,500,000 pounds of cotton yarn, part of which was woven by the latter date into 705,800,000 square yards of cloth.[4]

With the encouragement of the United States Government and Scap, the Japanese Government and the textile industries formulated plans for the rehabilitation of the industries. On December 30, 1946, Scap granted the cotton-spinning industry permission to borrow 600 million yen for rehabilitation purposes.[5] On February 7, 1947, Scap authorized the rebuilding of the cotton-textile industry to the level of four million spindles;[6] and on April 4, 1947, Scap authorized the rebuilding of rayon capacity to a level of 150,000 metric tons annually.[7]

Scap encouraged raw-silk production in the belief that large quantities could be sold, especially to the United States, although in smaller quantities than in the prewar period. During 1946 and 1947, however, it became clear that competition from synthetic fibers and high prices for raw silk had reduced the raw-silk market even more than had been anticipated, although it appeared that the market for Japanese-produced silk fabric had perhaps been underestimated. In July 1947, Scap authorized the release of 10,000 bales of raw silk a month to Japanese weavers for manufacture into silk fabric for export.

[3] *The Textile Mission to Japan*, Report to the War Department and to the Department of State, January–March 1946 (Department of State publication 2619).
[4] Scap report to Chief of Staff, U.S. Army, Washington; radio no. Z28684, Nov. 13, 1947.
[5] Scapin 1427 (Memorandum for the Japanese Government).
[6] Scapin 1512.
[7] Scapin 1600.

Chart 2

INDEXES OF JAPANESE TEXTILE PRODUCTION

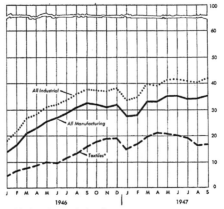

*Includes only raw silk, cotton, wool and spun silk
yarn; and cotton, wool, and rayon woven goods.

In August 1947 SCAP released a program for the rehabilitation of the woolen industry. This program envisaged the rebuilding of the industry's capacity to a level of 733,000 worsted spindles and 815 woolen cards and the consumption of.665,000 bales of wool annually.[8]

FEC Policies

Certain policy decisions by the Far Eastern Commission have created a framework within which the textile industry must function. One such decision, issued January 23, 1947, determined "that the peaceful needs of the Japanese people should be defined as being substantially the standard of living prevailing in Japan during the period of 1930–34". Although this policy does not fix a specific maximum level for any particular industry, with reference to the textile industry this policy might be taken to mean that domestic consumption of textiles in peacetime Japan should average not more than about 8.7 pounds per capita, the average 1930–34 consumption. However, this level is far above present levels and is unattainable at the present time owing to the low level of textile production and the need to maximize exports.

Another FEC policy decision, issued February 27, 1947,[9] established the policy on grounds of the

[8] SCAP, *A Program for the Japanese Woolen Industry,* Aug. 25, 1947.
[9] BULLETIN of Mar. 30, 1947, p. 574. See also a correction in BULLETIN of May 25, 1947, p. 1041.
[10] SCAP, *Japanese Economic Statistics,* Bulletin No. 13, September 1947, pp. 7–9.

The major reasons for low textile production lie
ot so much in the slow rehabilitation of produc-
ve capacity as in the means for putting present
pacity into operation. In each of the textile in-
ustries more machinery is in operable condition
an is actually in operation. Shortages of raw
aterials, labor, and fuel have presented the most
rious problems in the effort to increase textile
roduction. Trade and credit difficulties have
sulted in such an inadequate and uneven flow of
w cotton, wool, and rayon pulp that production
hedules have been disrupted. Many textile
orkers who moved to rural areas as a result of
rban bombings during the war have been reluc-
nt to leave those areas, where food is compara-
vely ample, to work in industrial communities
here there are serious food shortages. Power
gs, which become particularly serious during the
y season (one fourth of the year), have forced
rtain textile mills to close down one or more days
week. Aggravating these operational difficul-
es, the general problem of inflation and uncer-
inties concerning financial issues have militated
ainst investment and thus against increased
roduction in the textile industry.

xtiles in Japan's Postwar Trade

Although the textile industries have not rees-
blished their prewar position relative to the
her industries in Japan since the surrender, a
ajor portion of Japanese foreign trade has been
xtiles. In 1946, one third of the value of Japan's
ports consisted of textile raw materials, almost
l of which was raw cotton. Textiles, mostly raw
lk, represented over two thirds of Japan's total
ports. It should be noted, however, that almost
l of the raw silk exported in 1946 was on con-
gnment to the Usco and more than two thirds of
is silk remained unsold at the end of 1946.
It was not before 1947 that the raw cotton im-
orted in 1946 was available for export, and trade
atistics for the first eight months of 1947 are
mewhat more realistic as a pattern of Japanese
ostwar trade. Textile raw-material imports dur-
g this period amounted to 31 million dollars,
most all of which was spent for raw cotton, or
pproximately 9 percent of total imports.[11] Tex-
le exports, on the other hand, accounted for 94
illion dollars, or 77 percent, of total exports;[12]
f total textile exports, cotton yarn and piece
ods contributed 74 million dollars, or 79 per-
nt; raw silk and silk piece goods, 11 million dol-
rs, or 12 percent; rayon yarn and piece goods and
ool yarn and piece goods, approximately 3 mil-
on dollars apiece, or 3 percent each. It is ap-
arent from these figures that silk exports suffered
great decline between 1946 and 1947 and that
tton exports had become much more significant.
silk-fabric exports expand in the future, as
ems very likely, this relation between silk and
tton exports—the major textile-export items in

Japan's prewar trade—may be less far apart in
the future.

Until August 15, 1947, trade with Japan was
conducted almost entirely on a government-to-
government basis.. The Japanese Government
Board of Trade, *Boeki Cho*, was the nominal principal on the Japanese side of all export and all
import transactions. In practically every such
transaction the buyer from or seller to Japan was
a foreign government or government corporation
(the U. S. Commercial Company in the case of
exports to the United States) or private firms
specifically designated by their governments to
carry on trade with Japan. Private businessmen were invited to Japan for the first time under
the occupation in the summer of 1947 with August 15 as the opening date. Beginning September 1, *Boeki Cho* was authorized to enter into sales
contracts with private foreign traders in Japan
for the export of practically all types of Japanese
goods currently being produced for export, with
the exceptions of cotton textiles, raw silk, and the
1947 tea crop. With reference to cotton textiles,
the U. S. Commercial Company's sales policy was
to sell only to governments in order to keep sales
on a large-scale basis, to keep selling expenses
low, and to avoid the problem of discriminating
among competing private firms in foreign countries. Raw silk was not at first offered to private
buyers because the Usco had given certain price
guaranties to the silk trade in the United States,
and price and sales policies to be followed by
Boeki Cho had to be carefully coordinated with
those of Usco. When this coordination was accomplished, raw silk was added to the list of commodities which could be purchased by private foreign traders in Japan.

Restrictions on the entry of businessmen into
Japan were relaxed in February 1948 so as to
provide for longer stays in Japan and for semipermanent residence.[13] It is hoped that these
changes in SCAP regulations will increase substantially the number of foreign traders in Japan
and lead directly to an expanded volume of
foreign trade. It is assumed, for example, that
many American and foreign firms specializing in
the textile trade will consider establishing offices
or agencies in Japan through which they can
arrange to secure Japanese textiles to fill the needs
of their customers. Eventually Japanese nationals will be permitted to travel abroad for commercial purposes and the marketing of textiles
will undoubtedly be a fruitful commercial activity
for such travelers. In the meantime, however, it

[11] SCAP, Economic and Scientific Section, *Report on
Japanese Trade for the Far Eastern Commission*, Dec. 5,
1947.
[12] It is reported that for all of 1947, textiles represented
56 percent of Japan's exports.
[13] BULLETIN of Feb. 22, 1948, p. 254.

will be necessary for foreign textile merchants to market Japanese production.

A change in trade procedure occurred at the end of 1947 when the USCC terminated its Japanese program. Its responsibility for the sale of raw silk, silk piece goods, cotton yarn, and cotton piece goods in the United States was transferred to a newly established "SCAP Foreign Trade New York Office" under the supervision of a SCAP representative who also acts as an agent of *Boeki Cho*. This office will be maintained only until private trade channels have been opened up sufficiently to assure a maximizing of Japanese export proceeds without such an agency. The office is empowered to negotiate contracts with American dealers for Japanese commodities, in addition to the ones mentioned above, although American dealers and foreign traders will be able to buy goods in Japan on the same terms and at the same prices as those quoted by the New York office. The office also maintains a showroom, makes Japanese trade information available to the United States market, and supplies United States market information to SCAP and *Boeki Cho*.

THE FUTURE UNDER THE OCCUPATION: PROBLEMS AND PROSPECTS

The significance of textiles in the Japanese economy makes the rehabilitation of Japan's textile industries essential to a self-supporting economy, and consequently, to the successful achievement of the aims of the occupation and a minimization of the costs to the United States and its Allies of supporting Japan. The rehabilitation of the Japanese textile industries is dependent partly upon the solution or amelioration of Japan's domestic economic problems, partly upon United States and Allied policies, and partly upon the world conditions of supply and demand for textile raw materials and finished products. The extent to which these industries are rehabilitated will be a factor in determining the post-occupation status of the Japanese economy and the contribution which Japan can make to the rehabilitation of the world economy.

Japan's internal economic problems, such as the availability of trained labor and of fuel and power for textile mills, are affected by occupation policy even though it is not within the purview of the Allied occupation to engage in the operations of Japanese industry. For example, the availability of labor can be correlated with the availability of food in urban areas; the adequacy of food, in turn, is determined partly by the amount of United States outlays, partly by the volume of Japanese exports to pay for food imports, and partly by world food supplies.

As long as the occupation continues and the Japanese are not permitted to participate freely in world trade, Allied policies will affect the procurement of textile raw materials and the mar-

[he Japanese woolen industry has both a raw-terial and a market problem. The industry is most wholly dependent upon imported wools ich before the war came chiefly from Australia. small quantity of Australian wool was shipped ring the latter part of 1947 on a virtual cash lar basis. At the beginning of 1948 the Aus-lian Government announced that Australia uld exchange raw wool for Japanese textiles 1 other products, in amounts depending upon volume of Japanese goods which Australia is e to use. No details as to quantities of ma-ials concerned have at present been announced. [apan's major wool-textile markets before the r were China, Manchuria, Korea, and other Far stern countries. As long as present political l economic conditions in the Far East continue, pan will have to look elsewhere for its wool tile export markets. It would appear that both v material and market problems will limit the ent of rehabilitation of the Japanese wool lustry.

yon

[he Japanese rayon industry could probably l its products without much difficulty in world rkets today because of the current rayon short-age. In order for Japan to manufacture rayon of suitable quality for export, however, rayon pulp must be imported since most domestic rayon pulp is of inferior quality. A world shortage of rayon pulp as well as credit difficulties have prevented significant rayon-pulp purchases. Internally, Japanese producers have faced the problem of securing coal for rayon production, a serious obstacle because of the coal shortage. A larger quantity of coal is required to produce a given quantity of rayon textiles than is required to pro-duce a comparable quantity of cotton, wool, or silk textiles. As long as Japan suffers from an acute shortage of coal, it may be uneconomical to divert to the rayon industry coal which otherwise could be used by other branches of the textile industry (e.g., cotton) in production for export. In addi-tion, certain essential chemicals—caustic soda and sulphuric acid—are produced in Japan only from imported raw materials and coal, and hence are also in short supply. Thus, the rehabilitation of the rayon industry will be determined by the avail-ability of rayon pulp, coal, and chemicals.

It may take from five to ten years to solve the problems which are facing Japan's textile in-dustries today. The significance of these indus-tries to the Japanese economy and to United States and Allied policies make these problems of concern to us.

THE CONGRESS

)evelopment and Control of Atomic Energy. S. Rept. , 80th Cong., 2d sess., pursuant to Public Law 585, 79th g. 9 pp.

he United States Information Service in Europe. Re-t of the Committee on Foreign Relations, pursuant to Res. 161, a resolution authorizing the Committee on 'eign Relations to make an investigation of the effects ertain State Department activities. S. Rept. 855, 80th g., 2d sess. vii, 23 pp.

[ational Aviation Policy. Report of the Congres-al Aviation Policy Board, Congress of the United tes, pursuant to Public Law 287, 80th Cong., an act provide for the establishment of a temporary congres-al aviation policy board. S. Rept. 949, 80th Cong., sess. vi, 57 pp.

mending section 13 of the Surplus Property Act of 4, as amended, to provide for the disposition of surplus l property to states, political subdivisions, and munici-ities for use as public parks, recreational areas, and oric monument sites. S. Rept. 970, 80th Cong., 2d sess. p.

rganization of Federal Executive Departments and ncies. S. Rept. 983, 80th Cong., 2d sess. 3 pp.

rotocol Extending the International Coffee Agreement: sage from the President of the United States trans-ting the protocol for the extension for one year from ober 1, 1947, subject to certain conditions, of the er-American Coffee Agreement signed in Washington November 28, 1940. The protocol was signed September November 1, 1947. S. Doc. Executive A, 80th Cong., sess. 6 pp. [Department of State, pp. 2–3.]

onsular Convention with Costa Rica. Message from President of the United States, transmitting the con-ar convention between the United States of America and the Republic of Costa Rica, signed at San José on January 12, 1948. S. Doc. Executive D, 80th Cong., 2d sess. 14 pp. [Department of State, 2–3.]

Aid to Greece and Turkey. Report of the Committee on Foreign Relations on S. 2358. A bill to amend the act approved May 22, 1947, entitled "An act to provide for assistance to Greece and Turkey". S. Rept. 1017, 80th Cong., 2d sess. iii, 38 pp. [Department of State, 2–3, 17–38.]

Aid to China. Amended report of the Committee on Foreign Relations on S. 2393. A bill to promote the gen-eral welfare, national interest, and foreign policy of the United States by providing aid to China. S. Rept. 1026, 80th Cong., 2d sess. iii, 20 pp.

Investigation of the Shortage of Petroleum, Petroleum Products, and Natural Gas. S. Rept. 1048, 80th Cong., 2d sess., to accompany S. Res. 210. 2 pp.

First Report of the Joint Committee on Atomic Energy to the Congress of the United States. H. Rept. 1289, 80th Cong., 2d sess. 9 pp.

Transportation as it Affects the European Recovery Program. Preliminary Report Seventeen of the House Select Committee on Foreign Aid, pursuant to H. Res. 296, a resolution creating a special committee on foreign aid. H. Rept. 1504, 80th Cong., 2d sess. ii, 61 pp.

Report on Greece. Preliminar Report Twelve, Subcom-mittee on Italy, Greece, and Trieste, of the House Select Committee on Foreign Aid, pursuant to H. Res. 296, a resolution creating a special committee on foreign aid. H. Rept. 1505, 80th Cong., 2d sess. ii, 12 pp.

Report on Germany. Preliminary Report Thirteen, Recommendations by Subcommittee on Germany, of the House Select Committee on Foreign Aid, pursuant to H. Res. 296, a resolution creating a special committee on foreign aid. H. Rept. 1500, 80th Cong., 2d sess. ii, 6 pp.

SECOND SESSION OF THE ADMINIST INTERNATIONAL TELECOMMUNICAT

By Helen

The Administrative Council of the International Telecommunication Union held its second session at Geneva, from January 20 to February 11, 1948. The Administrative Council, which was set up by the International Telecommunication Conference at Atlantic City in the autumn of 1947, constituted one of the outstanding innovations in the reorganization of the Union. Its particular purpose was to assure the continuity of the authority of the Union in the interval between plenipotentiary conferences, as well as to assure the coordination of the activities of the other permanent organs of the Union and of the Union with other international organizations such as the United Nations and the International Civil Aviation Organization (ICAO). The Telecommunication Conference elected the following 18 countries as members of the Council: Argentina, Brazil, Canada, China, Colombia, Egypt, France, Italy, Lebanon, Pakistan, Poland, Portugal, Switzerland, Turkey, the Union of Soviet Socialist Republics, the United Kingdom, the United States, and Yugoslavia.

---

[1] The Council, at its first day's meeting, was presented with a difficult problem. The Soviet Administration, three days before the convening of the Council, sent a telegram to the Secretary General of the Union advising that its Representative was ill and would be unable to attend. The Soviet Administration requested that the Council session be deferred until March 1. Considering this problem as the first item on its agenda, the Council reached the conclusion that the meeting should not be postponed. It based its decision on the fact that by the time the Soviet Administration had notified the Secretary General most of the representatives had either arrived at Geneva or were en route thereto. Since many had come long distances, it was felt that the expenditure of funds was too great to allow a postponement. In addition, it was maintained that the members of the Council are countries and not individuals and that a second representative should be designated in the event that the first one is unable to attend.

No provision had been made in the convention for the appointment of an acting chairman, and the second problem confronting the Council was one of interpretation of the new convention. The Council finally elected by unanimous vote the United States Representative, Mr. de Wolf, as acting chairman. It included a provision in the rules of procedure that in the future, should a similar situation arise, the four vice chairmen would choose an acting chairman by agreement or by lot.

534

of the United Nations and to discuss it informally with the Director of the Transport and Communications Division of the United Nations Secretariat.

The Council also considered the question of ITU representation at international conferences (other than ITU conferences) in which the Union is interested. There was some thought that the Union could be represented by one of the officials of the General Secretariat or by a member of the Administrative Council. After discussion it was finally agreed that no one person could make decisions for the Union at such meetings but that it was desirable to have the Union represented by the Secretary General or a person designated by him who would supply information concerning the Union but who would go no further.

The Council approved the calling of the International Administrative Aeronautical Radio Conference at Geneva on May 15, 1948.[2] In accordance with the decision of the Council, a telegram was sent to the signatories of the Atlantic City convention, requesting their approval of the calling of this Conference. The approval of a majority, as required before the Conference could be convened, was attained. It was decided that a preparatory group of experts would proceed to Geneva three weeks before the Conference convenes to prepare its agenda.

The Council also approved the calling of the Administrative Telephone and Telegraph Conference at Paris on May 1, 1949, by the French Government. In addition it approved a recommendation by the Provisional Frequency Board (PFB) of the Union for the convening of certain regional conferences to implement the decisions of the Atlantic City Radio Conference.

Various political questions arose and were forwarded to the Council while it was in session. The first was a request for an expression of opinion from the preparatory committee of experts of eight countries at Brussels preparing for the European Broadcasting Conference at Copenhagen. The Soviet Delegation to the Committee of Eight had requested a provision in the rules of procedure requiring unanimity in all decisions reached. The Council advised the Committee of Eight that, while the latter was free to adopt its own rules of procedure, the Council looked with disfavor on the adoption of a rule contrary to the long-established custom and spirit of the ITU.

The second resulted in the approval by the Council of the participation of the International Broadcasting Organization (OIR) in the forthcoming International Radio Consultative Committee (CCIR) Conference at Stockholm.

The third was the report of the chairman of the Provisional Frequency Board (PFB), which outlined the progress of the Board up to date and included a statement on the divergence of views between the Soviet Delegation and the United

(Continued on page 555)

U.S. Regards Information to Security Council on Political Developmen₁ in Czechoslovakia Necessa₁

STATEMENT BY AMBASSADOR WARREN R. AUSTIN [1]

U.S. Representative in the Security Council

The Security Council has been considering the serious charges made before it both against the Soviet Union and the present Czechoslovak Government with respect to the recent events that have taken place in Czechoslovakia.

It is charged that the Government of the Czechoslovak Republic, legally constituted by the parliamentary election of May 1946, has been undermined by a Communist minority which was encouraged and given promise of help by the representatives of the U.S.S.R.

It is said that the Communist coup was successful only because of the violence of a Soviet-supported Communist minority; because of the participation of Soviet representatives; and the threat of military force of the Soviet Union in readiness near the boundaries of Czechoslovakia. Soviet officials and military representatives are alleged to have taken part in meetings and demonstrations in Prague during the crisis. It was further alleged that Soviet officers participated in the arrest of non-Communist political leaders; that Soviet agents worked in the Ministry of Interior which controls the police and the security troops; and that Soviet agents were also among the armed militia in the streets of Prague.

Allegations were made in support of the charge that Czechoslovakia was subject to indirect aggression and political infiltration which led to the subversion of the parliamentary regime and to the establishment of a terroristic police rule under the present regime.

It is further charged that the political independence of Czechoslovakia, a member of the United Nations, has been violated by threat of use of force on the part of another member of the United Nations, the U.S.S.R., in violation of paragraph 4 of article 2 of the Charter, and that as a result a situation exists which is likely to endanger the maintenance of international peace and security.

It has been argued that these charges cannot be considered by the Security Council because of the provision contained in article 2 (7) of the Charter providing that the United Nations cannot intervene in matters which are essentially within the domestic jurisdiction of a state. However, the charges are based on the allegation of an illegal

intervention of one state in the internal affairs ₀ another state leading to the impairment of ₃ political independence. Moreover, the restorati₀ and maintenance of democratic institutions ʼ₁ liberated Europe, including Czechoslovakia, w₁ made the subject of an international agreeme₂ concluded at Yalta by Marshal Stalin, Pri₁ Minister Churchill, and President Roosevelt ₁ February 1945. Consequently, if the charges a₁ true, article 2(7) could clearly not be a bar ₀ Security Council jurisdiction over the Czech-slovak question. The taking of evidence is t₁ way to settle whether the charges are a preme₀ tated quota of slander, as charged by the Sovi₁ Union.

In the charges before us we are not faced wi₁ an account of armed forces moving across t₀ frontier from one state to another in pursuance ₀ an aggressive purpose. In such case of a "use ₀ force" the problem of evidence for all practic₁ purposes would not arise. However, the charg₁ before us are that a "threat of force" was use₁ The Security Council must determine wheth₁ "threat of force" was used or some other form ₀ pressure or illegal interference was applied. A₁ the facts in this case are not readily apparent, b₀ the seriousness of the charges is such that the S₁ curity Council is bound to make every effort ₁ "get at the facts".

The Chilean Government, which brought t₀ Czechoslovak question before the Security Council₁ cil originally, requested the Security Council ₀ conduct an investigation. A proposal has now be₁ submitted by the Chilean Government for the cr₁ ation of a subcommittee to hear witnesses and r₁ port to the Security Council on the nature of the testimony. We believe that this might be a co₁ venient method for the Security Council to unde₁ stand the Czechoslovak situation. I assert th₁ the United States is behind this proposition if ₁ is made by a member of the Council.

What were the events that led up to the death ₀ the Foreign Minister of that country and to t₁ numerous resignations of Czechoslovak dipl₁ matic representatives in the United States, Ca₁ ada, Netherlands, Norway, France, and elsewher₁ Is the death of Masaryk propaganda poison? A₁ these resignations deceit circulated abroad? Wh₁ is there present along the Czechoslovak fronti₁ an unusually heavy frontier guard and what ₀ the significance of the flight from that country ₀

---

[1] Made in the Security Council on Apr. 12, 1948, and released to the press by the U.S. Mission to the United Nations on the same date.

umerous refugees and particularly political fig-
res whose reputation and integrity were not
rown into question prior to the rise of the new
gime?

Certain facts on the developments in Czecho-
ovakia itself are a matter of common knowledge.
hey have not been reviewed in detail here, how-
er, and they should be. They constitute the
amework of internal developments against
hich the charges of external interference must
considered.

The Czechoslovak Government crisis was pre-
pitated by the unwillingness of Premier Gott-
ald and the Communist ministers to respect two
ajority decisions of the Cabinet with reference
the administration of the police power under
e Communist Ministry of Interior. The latter
as making arbitrary appointments of police of-
ials in a process of extending Communist con-
ol. The 12 non-Communist ministers resigned in
otest as an appropriate parliamentary response
a refusal of a Cabinet minority to abide by the
ish of the Cabinet majority. The Communists
ized upon this as an occasion for breaking the
position, discrediting its leaders, and taking
er full control of the Government. How was it
ssible that this minority party could successfully
erthrow the elected Government of Czechoslo-
kia and establish in effect a police regime?

At the time of the crisis the Communist Party
as already in control of the security police, the
ate broadcasting apparatus, and had also secured
portant influence in the armed forces. This
ntrol arose as a result of a series of circumances, beginning with the signing of a friend-
ip treaty between Czechoslovakia and the
S.S.R. on December 12, 1943. This was an ex-
ession of a desire on the part of the Czecho-
ovak Government to maintain close relations
th the Soviet Union in the genuine belief that
echoslovakia, when liberated from German oc-
pation, would be able to continue its democratic
vernment and institutions without intervention
m her powerful neighbor. This treaty, in fact,
luded a clause stipulating nonintervention by
her of the parties in the other's domestic affairs.
is perhaps significant to note that this treaty
as one of a series of treaties signed between the
S.S.R., Bulgaria, Hungary, Rumania, and Po-
d, all of which contained this guaranty. Now
sk you, are these allegations based on newspaper
orts, or are they based on solemn conventions?
the same time, the Czechoslovak leaders de-
red their willingness to include representatives
the Communist Party in a new Cabinet, al-
ugh it had never before participated in any
echoslovak Government. They showed more
n good will to cooperate with the Soviet Union
d with the Communists. In the negotiations
t took place in 1945 in Moscow among Czecho-
vak leaders with regard to the formation of a

new Cabinet, the Communists managed to secure
the key posts of Interior, Information, Agriculture, and Education. In addition, the Communists
had a stronghold in the Ministry of Foreign Affairs through the Undersecretary of State and in
the Ministry of National Defense, which was
headed by General Ludvig Svoboda, a professional
soldier who had led the first Czechoslovak brigade
in the U.S.S.R. and whose pro-Soviet sentiments
are well known. These key positions as a rule, according to the Czechoslovak parliamentary practice, went to the party that received the strongest
support in the elections. We can only speculate on
what basis the Communists obtained them during
the Moscow discussion.

Control of key posts in the Government placed
the Communists during the period immediately
after Czechoslovak liberation in a dominant position entirely out of proportion to their popular
support. Through the Ministry of Interior they
controlled the police, which they soon reorganized
into the National Security Corps based on the
Soviet model. The Ministry of Information gave
them control over the use of mass media of communication for propaganda purposes, and the
Ministry of Agriculture placed them in a position
to compel allegiance from agricultural workers
and small peasants.

Moreover, it will be recalled that at the time
of the liberation from the German occupation four
fifths of the country was occupied by Soviet troops
and remained so occupied for eight subsequent
months.

Despite these advantages enjoyed by the Communist Party, 62 percent of the vote in the first
postwar election went to the non-Communist
parties. Nevertheless, in subsequent developments the Communists ignored the fact that they
were a minority and attempted to discredit and
undermine non-Communist parties such as the
Slovak Democrats and the National Socialists.

The Communists had given sufficient evidence
before the recent seizure of power that they could
not and would not tolerate any political opposition, which they identified as treason to the state.
This was brought out at the time of the coup by
immediate formation of action committees, the
sudden appearance of a well-disciplined and fully
armed factory militia in Prague, and the swift and
ruthless purge of the non-Communist leaders.
These steps reveal a high degree of preparation,
a high degree of organization, for seizure of power.
It is a pattern designed to usurp control of a state.
We should ascertain to what extent outside assistance contributed to this thorough preparation.
It shows how impossible it is for those who believe in government through democratic processes
and parliamentary methods to cooperate in good
faith with the Communists. At the time of the
coup the tension in Czechoslovakia was height-
ened by reports of Soviet intervention and of the

ril 25, 1948

presence of a large number of Soviet agents in the country. It was at this time that Soviet Deputy Foreign Minister Zorin arrived in Prague. Shortly thereafter during the crisis there appeared on the streets of Prague special heavily armed police shock regiments. These regiments under the command of the Communist Minister of Interior were called out to patrol the streets and to search the headquarters of opposition parties. Great numbers of armed factory militia also appeared in Prague, marching in military formation, wearing red arm bands, and carrying the Soviet flag.

All the indications of the birth of a police state were evident: complete seizure of control over broadcasting facilities, elimination of non-Communist newspaper editors, suppression of a number of non-Communist periodicals, and the imposition of complete censorship. Since the *Putsch* no true opposition publications exist in Czechoslovakia. Virtually all journalists hitherto critical of the Communists have been purged. A large number of journalists have been expelled from the association of Czech journalists, among them Lev Sychrava, Delegate to the United Nations Commission on Freedom of Information and winner of a 1947 prize as the best Czech journalist.

All non-Communist parties were purged and a number of non-Communist functionaries were arrested.

"Action committees" were formed and given full administrative control over the duly constituted organs of the Republic. There was no existing basis in Czechoslovak law for any such act.

Yet according to reports available here very little overt opposition to the Communist coup was apparent. How are we to understand that the majority of the Czechoslovak people, known for their traditional adherence to democratic majority rule, acquiesced to the Communist minority? Could it be that the coup occurred because over the shoulder of the minority glared the face of a foreign power? Is it not significant that the minority was led by individuals indoctrinated by a foreign power who had been in close association with its authorities?

There are men of universally respected reputations who have for years been a part of Czechoslovak political life and who have now found it necessary for a second time in ten years to flee their homeland. They were present during the crisis and can perhaps shed some light on the question of how it was that totalitarian police-state methods were substituted for traditional Czech democratic procedure without any significant overt expression of protest on the part of the Czechoslovakian people.

As has been pointed out in the Security Council discussions, the Czechoslovak story assumes added significance when compared with developments that have taken place throughout eastern and cen-

ever that it is important for the Security Council to get to the bottom of this situation.

We have also now been told that there are groups of men outside of Czechoslovakia who were leaders in the political life of this country prior to the coup. The Representative of Chile has made a suggestion for the creation by the Council of a subcommittee to hear the stories of these leaders who were in Czechoslovakia when the coup occurred and presumably should have firsthand knowledge of the events at that time and those which led up to the coup. My Government feels the Council would not be discharging fully its obligations if it did not hear these people. It feels that the creation of a sub-group to receive such testimony and to obtain other available information and to report back to the full Council on it is a convenient and feasible procedure.

We feel the subcommittee should consist of representatives of five states of the Council. In our view the terms of reference should be very simple. The subcommittee should be authorized to hear the testimony of these Czech political leaders and to report on this testimony to the Security Council.

My Government feels that it is essential that such information be obtained in order that the Council will be better able to decide what further steps should be taken on this matter. I should add that we would not consider the activity of such a sub-group to be in any way an investigation. The proposal before us has the full support of my Government.

---

[2] BULLETIN of Apr. 18, 1948, p. 517.

[3] A letter dated Apr. 8, 1948, to the Secretary-General from Dr. Vladimir Houdek, Representative of Czechoslovakia to the U.N. (see U.N. doc. S/718 of Apr. 10, 1948), follows:

SIR: Referring to your letter dated April 6, 1948 and upon instructions from my Government, I have the honour to bring the following to your attention:

The discussion of internal matters before the Security Council is in contradiction to the provisions of the Charter. Such matters are exclusively within the domestic jurisdiction of any state. The Czechoslovak Government therefore rejects with indignation the unfounded complaint which has been put before the Security Council.

Czechoslovakia has been and will remain a peace-loving state and wishes to maintain friendly relations with peace-loving nations on the basis of mutual respect in accordance with the purposes and principles of the United Nations. The discussion on the changes in the composition of the Czechoslovak Government based on slanderous allegations has confirmed our conviction that it is only a pretext to stir up the hostile campaign against the Soviet Union and other states of Eastern Europe with which Czechoslovakia has strong bonds of friendship. Such action is in flagrant contradiction to one of the fundamental tasks of the United Nations which is to promote friendly relations between nations in order to strengthen international peace and security.

Since the discussion of internal matters of Czechoslovakia in the Security Council is contrary to the basic principles of the Charter, inspired by the aim of protecting the sovereignty and independence of states, the Czechoslovak Government does not find it possible to take in any way part in such discussion.

U.S. Observers Invited to World Health

TEXT OF LETTER FROM THE EXECUTIVE
OF "WHO" TO THE U.S. REPRE

8 April 1948

Sir, Article 80 of the Constitution of the World
Health Organization stipulates that that Act shall
enter into force immediately 26 Member States
of the United Nations have become parties to it.
This number has, at the present date, been
exceeded.

By Article 2 of the Arrangement establishing
the Interim Commission of the World Health Organization, the Commission is required to convoke
the first session of the World Health Assembly as
soon as practicable and not later than six months
after the date on which the Constitution of the
Organization comes into force.

During its fifth session the Interim Commission,
in view of the imminent entry into force of the
Constitution fixed 24 June 1948 as the opening
date for the first session of the World Health
Assembly, and decided that it should be held in
Geneva.

Accordingly, letters of convocation have now
been sent to the Governments of the member States
of the Organization, i.e., those which, in accordance with Article 79 of the Constitution have
either signed that Act without reservation, or ratified their signatures and deposited the instruments
of ratification with the Secretary-General of the
United Nations.

1. As the Government of your country has not
yet accomplished the formalities required for
membership by the above-mentioned article, it
cannot at present be convoked under that provision. But, in view of the desirability of its presence at the Assembly, I have pleasure in inviting
you to be good enough to appoint one or more
observers to follow, in that capacity, the work
of the session. I should be very grateful if you
would furnish me as soon as possible with the
names of the observers appointed.

May I remind you that the rôle of observer does
not carry the right of taking part in the discussions or the voting. Furthermore, no provision has been made for reimbursement or
expenses to this category.

2. However, it goes without saying that if your
Government, as is greatly to be desired, should
ratify and deposit the instrument of ratification
before 24 June, it would be admitted to participation in the work of the Assembly in the capacity

rth American Broadcasting Engineers' Meeting

ARTICLE BY DONALD R. MACQUIVEY

\t the First North American Broadcasting En-
eers' Conference at Habana, Cuba, in 1937 [1]
) problems, suppression of interference and
)vision of adequate service, were the pri-
ry concern of those who negotiated the first
rth American regional broadcasting agreement
ARBA). Radio waves, of course, recognize no
:ional boundaries. It is therefore absolutely es-
tial, if the best use of the radio spectrum is to
realized, to agree internationally concerning the
iditions under which these waves shall be trans-
tted.

The NARBA is an affirmation of international co-
eration and an example of an international
reement that is really effective. Although prob-
us have arisen under the NARBA, there is no doubt
it the agreement works, and it works to the
itual benefit of all countries concerned. An ad-
ntage to one country in one particular instance
compensated by an advantage to another in an-
ier instance. The sum of all advantages ex-
)ds by far the disadvantages experienced, as the
jective is not to take from one and give to an-
ier but rather to determine how each can ob-
.n the greatest service while interfering as little
possible with service in other countries.

Those in the United States Government con-
rned with the operation of the NARBA have
iny rather definite views on how it could be
proved, as do similarly placed persons in other
)rth American countries. Some of those views
ire first expressed at the Second North Ameri-
n Regional Broadcasting Conference held at
ashington, D.C., in February 1946 to consider
iat should be done because of the impending
piration of the 1937 treaty. Persons attending
at conference found that they had neither the
ne nor the necessary data to rewrite the treaty
mpletely, and so they agreed to extend the old
:aty by means of what is called the "interim
reement", *modus vivendi*. [2]

The interim agreement incorporated some of the
sired modifications, but of principal interest here
the provision that the governments concerned
)uld circulate their more complete proposals and
at a group of radio engineers would meet at Ha-
.na on November 1, 1947. Eight United States
)vernment representatives and 10 industry ad-
sers attended under the chairmanship of George
. Sterling of the Federal Communications Commission, the Meeting of Technicians on the North
American Regional Broadcasting Agreement.
Technical aspects of the proposals from the various countries were discussed and a number of
agreements reached.

Unfortunately many of the international interference and service-expansion problems are not
purely matters of finding the best technical engineering solution. After all, radio broadcasting is
a means to an end, not the end in itself. If, for
example, each among a number of political parties,
as in Cuba, wants to sponsor its own station, the
problem of finding radio-spectrum space is much
more acute than would be the case if there were
fewer stations, each prepared to serve all.

Another question with mixed policy and engineering aspects is the question of use of clear
channels—those spots in the broadcast frequency
band assigned almost exclusively to each of a few
high-power stations. Many considerations not
strictly of an engineering character must be taken
into account in determining how best to provide
broadcasting service to persons in sparsely populated areas. From a purely engineering standpoint, without much consideration being given to
the economics of the problem, it would be possible
to render such service either by means of a few
clear-channel stations or by means of a larger
number of stations on the same frequency, each
serving its own smaller region. An essentially
nonengineering question related to this problem is
whether or not clear-channel stations should be
located in or near large cities and carry programs
and advertising of purely local interest. There
are many details of these clear-channel problems
and the complexity and need to hear all controversial views have been two of the principal
reasons why the Federal Communications Commission has conducted extensive hearings on the
subject. A decision in the matter is essential before any substantial amount of preparation for
the next North American regional broadcasting
conference can be completed. Until this and related decisions are reached, it will be impossible
to determine the potential interference to or from
foreign stations on the same or adjacent channels
to stations in this service.

---

[1] Treaty Series 962.
[2] Treaties and Other International Acts Series 1533.

Suffice it to say that these matters could not be discussed at Habana without prejudice to future Federal Communications Commission decisions. The delegation was limited not only to discussion of the technical aspects of the proposals presented but also, within that limitation, it could discuss only those technical questions which had little or no bearing on the major questions yet to be decided at home. This situation resulted in much discussion and delay because the Mexican Delegation was authorized to discuss much broader policy matters than were the delegates from any other nations represented.

In spite of these difficulties, however, the meeting proved valuable to all who attended. Certain technical definitions were clarified so that, when the terms are referred to in the future, all parties concerned will know exactly what is involved. Agreement on definitions is more important than may appear on the surface. For example, a provision in the agreement on the measures to be taken to suppress interference from spurious radiations would be relatively ineffective if one nation considered such radiations to be only undesirable harmonics of the desired signal while another nation considered them to be only parasitic emissions not related to the desired signal in any particular way. It costs money to suppress either type. Such expenditures bring in no revenue to the station making them. Unless they are made, however, service from other stations will be degraded, if not completely destroyed. It is necessary that all agree, therefore, on the conditions under which action will be taken.

The most important benefit from the meeting at Habana was the mutual exchange of views concerning the requirements of each nation. The Mexican Delegation discussed a proposal of that country that the broadcast band be reallocated so that stations providing local service would be assigned frequencies at the high-frequency end of the band, regional stations would be assigned adjacent but lower frequencies, and clear-channel stations would be assigned frequencies at the low end of the band. From the single standpoint of effectiveness of propagation of radio waves for the purposes indicated, the proposal might well have been considered had its merits been known some two decades ago. To adopt such a plan now, however, would cost the United States broadcasting industry literally millions of dollars as hundreds of stations would have to be shifted in frequency and, as a result, almost entirely rebuilt.

The size of many of the components used in a broadcast transmitting system depends upon the frequency at which they operate. New antennas would have to be designed and constructed, transmitters rebuilt, and power would have to be increased in hundreds of installations in order to maintain consistent coverage. Worst of all would be the necessity of reworking completely the scores

An informal discussion was held concerning the applicability of frequency-modulation broadcasting to the solution of some of the broadcasting problems in the North American region, particularly those in the lower latitudes and densely populated areas. Although this discussion was not a part of the discussions concerning the North American regional broadcasting agreement and although the question of whether or not any provisions relating to frequency modulation should be included in that agreement is still unsettled, it was decided to exchange information on trials of frequency-modulation broadcasting and monitoring results obtained. There was considerable agreement that the noise-suppression characteristics and the propagation limitation to be expected from frequency-modulation broadcasting would help materially to provide high-quality broadcasting service to the nations located in areas of high-noise level and with relatively large population centers.

Because the meeting was a technical conference and dealt, in general, with quantities quite susceptible to measurement, there was somewhat less room for disagreement than would be the case at a nontechnical conference. Many of the engineers were acquainted with each other from previous meetings. All in all, both the United States broadcasting-industry representatives who assisted the Government Delegation immeasurably and those responsible Government officials who made up the Delegation considered the meeting highly valuable and essential as a preparation for the forthcoming conference for the purpose of rewriting the NARBA.

U.S. DELEGATION TO INTERNATIONAL AERONAUTICAL RADIO CONFERENCE

[Released to the press April 14]

The Acting Secretary of State approved on April 12 the composition of the United States Delegation to the Preparatory Conference for the International Administrative Aeronautical Radio Conference which is scheduled to be held at Geneva, April 24–May 15, 1948. The United States Delegation is as follows:

Chairman

Arthur L. Lebel, Assistant Chief, Telecommunications Division, Department of State

Vice Chairman

Edwin L. White, Chief, Aviation Division, Federal Communications Commission

Advisers

James D. Flashman, Lieutenant Colonel, Department of the Air Force

Edmund V. Shores, Chief, Mobile Aeronautics Communications Center, Civil Aeronautics Administration, Department of Commerce

---

[1] Executive Agreement Series 196.

The Preparatory Conference will (1) prepare a draft agenda for the International Administrative Aeronautical Radio Conference which is scheduled to open at Geneva on May 15, 1948, immediately following the Preparatory Conference; (2) consider technical principles on which a frequency-assignment plan is to be based; (3) prepare the framework for such a plan; and (4) arrange for the compilation of world frequency requirements for aeronautical mobile services. It is expected that Argentina, Australia, Belgium, Canada, China, France, the Union of Soviet Socialist Republics, the United Kingdom, and the United States will be represented at this meeting.

The International Administrative Aeronautical Radio Conference, suggested by the Belgian Delegation at the Atlantic City telecommunication conferences, has been called by the Administrative Council of the International Telecommunication Union. This meeting will develop a world-wide plan for specific assignment of the individual frequencies included in the bands allocated to the aeronautical mobile services at Atlantic City.

U.S. DELEGATION TO INTERNATIONAL CONFERENCE ON SAFETY OF LIFE AT SEA

[Released to the press April 12]

The Department of State announces that the President has designated Admiral Joseph F. Farley, Commandant of the U. S. Coast Guard, to serve as Chairman of the United States Delegation to the International Conference on Safety of Life at Sea which is scheduled to convene at London, April 23, 1948. Jesse E. Saugstad, Chief, Shipping Division, Department of State, has been designated Vice Chairman. Other members of the United States Delegation are:

Advisers

David Arnott, American Bureau of Shipping, New York City
James L. Bates, Chief, Technical Bureau, Maritime Commission
Martin D. Berg, Lt. Comdr., U. S. Coast Guard
Charles L. Brand, Rear Admiral, Assistant Chief, Bureau of Ships, Department of the Navy
David P. Brown, American Bureau of Shipping, New York City
Raymond F. Farwell, Capt., U.S.N.R., U. S. Coast Guard
Arthur R. Gatewood, Shipbuilders Council of America, New York City
Robert O. Glover, Rear Admiral, Hydrographer of the Navy, Department of the Navy
Hoyt S. Haddock, Executive Secretary, Cio Maritime Committee, Washington
Norman R. Hagen, U. S. Weather Bureau, American Embassy, London
Henry T. Jewell, Captain, Chief, Merchant Vessel Personnel Division, Office of Merchant Marine Safety, U. S. Coast Guard
William N. Krebs, Assistant Chief Engineer, Federal Communications Commission
J. Lewis Luckenbach, President, American Bureau of Shipping, New York City
John W. Mann, Shipping Division, Department of State

at approximately 10-year intervals. The 1929 conference decided that a useful purpose would be
served if classification were made the subject of
a definite convention between governments. A
protocol was annexed to the report of the 1929
conference, and the agreement relating to statistics of causes of death was signed on July 19, 1934.

The delegates to the Meeting of the International Commission for the Fifth Decennial Revision of the International Nomenclature of Diseases met at Paris in October 1938 and adopted
resolutions requesting the Government of the
United States to form a subcommittee to study
the problem of obtaining international consistency
in the methods of selecting the primary causes of
death. In accordance with these resolutions an
American subcommittee, appointed by the Secretary of State, prepared a draft report which was
adopted with few changes by an Expert Committee of the Interim Commission of the World
Health Organization. With other documents, this
amended text will serve as the basis for the work
of the forthcoming Conference.

PROGRAM OF FOURTH INTERNATIONAL CONGRESSES ON TROPICAL MEDICINE AND MALARIA

The Department of State released on April 17
the program of the Fourth International Congresses on Tropical Medicine and Malaria, which
will be held in Washington May 10–18.[1] The
meetings are being sponsored by the United States
Government and scientific societies to encourage
and facilitate the pooling of useful knowledge for
the prevention and treatment of tropical diseases.

Organization of the Congresses is headed by
Dr. Leonard A. Scheele, Surgeon General of the
United States Public Health Service, who is act-
ing as chairman. Vice chairmen are Dr. George
K. Strode, Director of the International Health
Division of the Rockefeller Foundation, and
Clarke L. Willard, Associate Chief, Division of
International Conferences, Department of State.
Dr. Rolla E. Dyer, Director of the National In-
stitute of Health, is program director. The enter-
tainment committee and the exhibits committee
are being handled respectively by Dr. Fred L.
Soper, Director of the Pan American Sanitary
Bureau, and Dr. E. M. Gunn, United States Army
Institute of Pathology. Dr. Wilbur A. Sawyer,
former Director of the International Health Division of the Rockefeller Foundation and Director
of Health for Unrra, is acting for the Department
of State in preparing and directing the program.

---

[1] Bulletin of Apr. 11, 1948, p. 475.

THE RECORD OF THE WEEK

Pan American Day,

BY GEORGE

Assistant Secretaı

Because they are very much in all our minds, I must refer at the outset to the tragic events that have momentarily interrupted the deliberations of the Bogotá conference in the last few days. I shall not undertake to comment extensively on these events. However, there are two things that I must say to you, knowing that they express the sentiments of the American people and of all of you here tonight. The first is that we sympathize from the bottom of our hearts with the people of Colombia in their hour of sudden tragedy and are confident that nothing can prevent Colombia from continuing its forward march as one of the most progressive and respected of the American republics. The other is that only persons who have momentarily lost their perspective will allow themselves to believe that the occurrences in Bogotá can represent any kind of setback to pan-Americanism or in any way alter its progress. The Ninth International Conference of American States will, like its predecessors over more than half a century, serve to knit still more closely the sturdy fabric of inter-American relations.

Pan American Day, which has dawned for us here a few hours ahead of the calendar, is an occasion on which we celebrate friendship among nations—not friendship as an ideal only, but friendship as an accomplished fact among 21 sovereign states. That friendship is epitomized in this gathering. It is epitomized in the person of my good friend at this table, the Ambassador of Honduras, who, in the course of many years as the well-beloved representative of his country in Washington, has become a personal symbol of the friendliness and good will that animates the relations of the good-neighbor republics. The friendship among our countries is, in fact, reflected in the personal respect and liking that we all feel for the distinguished representatives from our neighbor countries who have foregathered with us this evening.

The answer to any question that might be raised as to whether we, in this country, appreciate the blessing of our inter-American friendship is sug-

---

[1] Address made at a Pan American dinner tendered by the citizens of Washington, D.C., on Apr. 13, 1948; released to the press on the same date.

tend that the good-neighbor policy is no more. The contrast between the range of our cooperation today and the extent of our cooperation ten years ago, when the good-neighbor policy was growing up, sufficiently refutes that silly pretense.

Another substantial refutation is provided by the common preoccupation of the Bogotá conferees today—and the conference is *not* over—with the strengthening of an inter-American system that has been steadily growing in strength for the past 15 years. The process of building our good-neighbor system continues year by year. It is a stronger, more closely knit system today than it was at the end of the war in 1945. It will, I am confident, be still stronger when the present conference in Bogotá concludes its interrupted deliberations.

The one concept I should like to stress above all others tonight is that cooperation among the American republics is founded, and must always be founded, on the concept of mutuality. All of the republics must help each other and must learn from each other. The United States can make and is making a positive contribution to the economic and social development of the republics to the south through means which have already been discussed—through lending the technical knowledge of our public-health officials, agricultural experts, and scientists to other American republics which feel that we can be of help and which ask us for them.

But this is not all. We are receiving and must continue to receive in return the great social and cultural contributions which other of our sister republics have to offer the United States. Effective cooperation represents the will to give and to receive by all parties.

I attended an impressive reception given by Mrs. Truman a few days ago to the foreign students in and around Washington. The number of students and government trainees from other American republics in this one city was a wonderful revelation to me. And I may add that the charm and good looks of the young ladies in the group lent an added pleasure to the occasion.

I asked each of them to whom I talked about their work—what they were studying, and where, and how. All the while the thought kept recurring to my mind that they were contributing, perhaps unwittingly but very positively, to the cultural progress of the United States. While they were obtaining their education here, we were gaining from them. Their cultural backgrounds and points of view are enriching our own. The literature, the art, and the music of the other American republics are becoming ever better known in the United States through the cooperative exchange that characterizes our relations with them. Our own culture is being substantially strengthened by their constructive influence and their contributions. We are anxious to benefit as much as we can from the long and distinguished cultural heritage of our sister republics.

I sometimes think that the great Pan American Highway, which we hope will some day add so much to the communications network that ties us together, might very appropriately be called "the two-way passage highway".

To one who, like myself, has for some years past been preoccupied with international relations in other parts of this turbulent globe, it is impossible not to view the relations that have developed and are continuing to develop in this Hemisphere with a sense of vast encouragement and gratification. We Amercan republics have

our differences, but we manage to settle tho: differences peacefully and amicably. Our frien ship grows stronger in the process of their settl ment. Now, when we talk about peace on ear we don't mean an earth on which there are r differences of opinion. We mean, simply, an ear on which differences of opinion are settled l peaceful means. In that light, the long-ter achievement of the American republics is ou standing in history and in the context of prese relations among nations generally. It is a achievement that, without due complacency, v can celebrate this evening with very good co sciences indeed.

Export-Import Bank To Finance Economic Development in Other American Republics

MESSAGE OF THE PRESIDENT TO THE CONGRESS

To the Congress of the United States:

In recent months the United States has been considering a number of measures to further the achievement of the primary objective of our foreign policy—the establishment throughout the world of the conditions of a just and lasting peace.

One of the essential requirements for the attainment of that objective is continuing cooperation among the American republics and collaboration in the development of their resources and industries.

Genuine friendship has long existed between the people of the United States and our neighbors to the south. This friendship has been marked by cultural and economic association and close cooperation. The people of the United States have strongly supported the policy of the Good Neighbor and have a special regard for the peoples of the countries to the south of us.

The United States has long recognized the importance of economic and political stability in the Western Hemisphere. Such stability rests substantially upon the continuation of a satisfactory rate of economic progress. In this respect, we must fairly recognize that the economies of the other American republics are relatively undeveloped. In these countries, natural resources are abundant, but the expansion of production has been restricted due to the lack of capital and of modern production methods. Production can be increased only by means of a considerable volume of capital investment in transportation and power facilities, processing plants and other installations.

To some extent the need for capital in these countries is met by domestic savings, but such savings in general are insufficient to secure the necessary equipment and technical skills. Substantial and continued progress in the development of the re-

sources and industries of the other American r publics therefore requires foreign financing. T United States, by reason of its close relations wi these countries and its strong economic positio is the principal source to which the other Americ republics look for equipment, materials, and tec nology as well as for their financing.

I recommend, therefore, that the Congress i crease the lending authority of the Export-Impo Bank by 500 million dollars. The proposed i crease in the lending authority of the Bank wou not involve any change in the statutory requir ments under which the Bank has been operating.

This increased lending authority would place tl Bank in a position to assist in meeting essenti: requirements for the financing of economic d velopment in the other American republics. would permit the Bank to make loans for wel planned development projects which are econom cally justified and to cooperate most effectivel with private funds.

Such an increase would not, of course, be a sul stitute for necessary action that the other Amer can republics can and should take to attract priva investment capital and to mobilize fully their ow investment resources.

The proposed increase represents, I believe, a important step which this Government should tak to assist the economic development of the countrie to the south of us.

It is of great importance to the United State as a member of the American community, tha there be continued expansion of production, ir creasing trade activity, and rising standards c living in the other American republics. It is i our mutual interest to help develop in the countrie to the south those essential materials which ar becoming less abundant in the United States, a

ll as others regularly imported from distant
rions.
Above all, it is in our mutual interest to assist
: American republics to continue their economic
ogress, which can contribute so much to the
operative strength of the independent American
oublics.
I request the Congress, therefore, to give favor-
le consideration to the proposed increase in the
iding authority of the Export-Import Bank.

HARRY S. TRUMAN

THE WHITE HOUSE,
April 8, 1948.

Commitment for Reconstruction in Colombia Approved

The Board of Directors of the Export-Import
Bank of Washington announced on April 15 the
approval, at a special meeting, of a commitment of
10 million dollars to the Republic of Colombia to
assist that Government in financing the acquisition
of United States supplies, materials, and equipment
needed for the speedy reconstruction of properties
destroyed or damaged in the recent disturbances in
Colombia. Details as to requirements and arrangements will be worked out on a mutual basis.

S.S.R. Rejects Procedure for Drafting of Protocol to Italian Treaty

MEMORANDUM FROM THE U.S.S.R.

79   [Translation]

With reference to the memorandum of the De-
rtment of State of March 20 and in reply to the
te of the Department of State of April 9 the
viet Embassy has the honor to communicate the
llowing.

In connection with the urgency of the question
ntioned in the note of April 9 the Embassy
ems it necessary to point out that in the memo-
ndum of the Department of State of March 20,
which reference is made in said note, no indica-
n is contained of the urgency of this question.
Simultaneously, the Soviet Government draws
e attention of the Department of State to the
ct that the treaty of peace with Italy, as with
ner states that participated in the war, was pre-

pared by the Council of Foreign Ministers and examined in detail at the Paris Conference, with the
participation of 21 states, which subsequently
signed and ratified it, and that it entered into force
only several months ago.

Hence it stands to reason that the proposal to
decide the question of the revision of the treaty of
peace with Italy in respect to one or another of its
parts by means of correspondence or the organization of private conferences is considered unacceptable by the Soviet Government as violating the
elementary principles of democracy.

EMBASSY OF THE UNION OF
SOVIET SOCIALIST REPUBLICS
Washington, April 13, 1948

U.S. REPLY TO THE U.S.S.R.

[Released to the press April 15]

The Acting Secretary of State presents his
npliments to His Excellency the Ambassador of
: Union of Soviet Socialist Republics and has
: honor to refer to the Soviet Embassy's memo-
ndum No. 79 of April 13, 1948, concerning the
urn of the Free Territory of Trieste to Italian
ereignty.

While regretting that the Soviet Government
s not found it possible to act favorably in this
tter, the Government of the United States is at
oss to understand why the procedure suggested
' the negotiation of a draft protocol to the Ital-
Treaty is considered unacceptable. It was the
ention of the Government of the United States
t the preliminary meeting of the powers prin-
ally concerned to negotiate a draft protocol
ould be followed by consultation with all other
erested governments. In the view of the Gov-

ernment of the United States the suggested preliminary meeting is in fact the first step of the procedure followed in the drafting of the Treaty of
Peace with Italy. As pointed out in the Soviet
Embassy's memorandum the Treaty of Peace was
prepared by the Council of Foreign Ministers and
subsequently submitted for the consideration of the
twenty-one states at the Paris Conference.

Should the Soviet Government find it possible
to agree in principle to the return of the Free Territory of Trieste to Italian sovereignty the Government of the United States will be glad to consider any suggestions which the Soviet Government may have regarding the procedure for the
drafting of the necessary protocol to the Italian
Treaty.

DEPARTMENT OF STATE,
Washington, April 16, 1948.

Treaty of Friendship, Commerce, and Nar
Transmitted to the Senate

[Released to the press April 14]

The President on April 14 transmitted to the
Senate, for the purpose of obtaining that body's
consent to ratification, the treaty of friendship,
commerce, and navigation between the United
States and Italy, signed at Rome February 2, 1948.
The President recommended early Senate action
on the treaty, as follows:

To the Senate of the United States:

With a view to receiving the advice and consent of the Senate to ratification, I transmit herewith a treaty of friendship, commerce and navigation between the United States of America and
the Italian Republic, together with a protocol and
an additional protocol relating thereto, signed at
Rome on February 2, 1948.

The enclosed treaty, together with the two related protocols, was negotiated on a basis of com-

SUMMARY OF

[Released to the press April 14]

The new treaty is designed to provide an effective
legal framework for economic intercourse between
the United States and Italy, such a framework
having been lacking since December 1937 when a
former commercial treaty, concluded in 1871, was
terminated by mutual consent. It is regarded by
the Department of State as a significant step in
strengthening the cordial relations between the
United States and Italy. It is the first instrument
of the type that has been signed by Italy since the
war.

The present treaty is similar to treaties now in
force between the United States and a number of
countries. In agreeing to it, Italy accepts the liberal principles of business and commercial intercourse which the United States is seeking to advance through the proposed charter for an International Trade Organization, as well as through
the conclusion with other countries of bilateral
treaties of friendship, commerce, and navigation
embodying like principles. It is believed that the
present instrument creates a framework within
which business, trade, and cultural relations may,
through liberal principles, develop effectively and
to the mutual advantage of the two countries.

---

[1] Not here printed.

shipped to Italy for preparation and transship-
ment. It was never intended that this material
would remain in Italy, and in shipping it there
in the first place it was hoped to give employment
to Italian facilities and workers. No Italian scrap
is being shipped to the United States.

The United States recognizes the urgent need of
the Italians for scrap and the fact that the output
of steel in Italy as well as production in the metal-
fabricating industries are to a considerable extent
dependent on adequate supplies of scrap for Italian steel furnaces. In recognition of this situation,
some 80,000 tons of captured German ammunition and American ammunition are being made
available to Italy from the United States zone of
Germany for use as scrap. In addition, about 80,-
000 tons of ship scrap has recently been made available to Italy by the United States Maritime
Commission.

An additional important source of scrap metal
has been made available to Italy by the United
States through this Government's renunciation of
its allocation of excess Italian Naval vessels. This
action by the United States has contributed to the
Italian economy more than 40,000 tons of unusually valuable scrap material at no cost whatsoever
to the Italian Government.

American Scientists To Survey
Southern Italy and Sicily

The United States Government has sent two
prominent officials of the Departments of Agriculture and the Interior on a survey trip to southern
Italy and Sicily on the invitation of the Italian
Government.[1]

Dr. Max A. McCall, Assistant Chief of the
Bureau of Plant Industry, Soils, and Agricultural
Engineering of the Department of Agriculture,
and Mr. George E. Tomlinson, Assistant Director
of Project Planning of the Bureau of Reclamation, Department of the Interior, arrived in Rome
April 13 for the purpose of conducting jointly with
Italian scientists in the same fields an inquiry into
possibilities of developing industry and expanding agricultural production in southern Italy
through hydroelectric, irrigation, and land-recla-
mation projects.

After preliminary discussions in Rome on the
13th, the American experts together with their
Italian colleagues proceeded to Naples to meet with
technicians of south Italy and inspect projects in
the vicinity of Naples. After a brief return to
Rome, the group will make a detailed tour of
Sicily and southern Italy. The inquiries being
made by Dr. McCall and Mr. Tomlinson and the
Italian officials are preliminary to later detailed

[1] BULLETIN of Apr. 11, 1948, p. 468.

consideration of specific projects by a larger group of professional scientists.

The need for projects of the type under study in southern Italy has long been recognized. Ever since the end of Fascism, the Italian Government has felt the increasing urgency of coping with the problems presented by this area. It has therefore requested help from the United States in alleviating the situation along lines which have been developed to the immense benefit of farmers in similar areas in this country.

Coal Exports to Italy To Aid Gas-Producing Industry

[Released to the press April 14]

The Italian Purchasing Mission in Washington has been authorized to proceed immediately with purchase of emergency supplies of United States coal vitally needed for the Italian gas-producing industry.

Even though full-scale production of coal has not yet been resumed in this country, this action was taken because the Italian Government has informed the United States Government that the gas-producing industry of Italy is faced by a reduction in operation unless additional coal supplies are obtained.

The coal will be licensed for export by the Department of Commerce under the "hardship" provision of the recent order suspending bituminous-coal export licenses as a result of the coal-production stoppage.

Chilean Technologist Awarded Grant-in-Aid

Francisco Mardones Otaiza, of Santiago, Chile, director of the National Institute of Technological Research and Standards, arrived in Washington April 8 for a six weeks' visit as the recipient of a grant-in-aid from the Department of State under the program administered by the Division of International Exchange of Persons for the interchange of specialists and professors with the other American republics. The purpose of his visit, which is being planned in cooperation with the Bureau of Standards of the Department of Commerce, is to familiarize himself with the organization and the functions of the Bureau of Standards. On his return to Chile he expects to organize an Office of Weights and Measures. On his present visit Mr. Mardones hopes to awaken interest in this country in the creation of an Inter-American Committee of Standards. There is already in existence, as an organ of the United Nations, an International Standard Organization (Iso), but as yet the only countries of the Western Hemisphere to join it are the United States, Brazil, Chile, and Canada.

work. Both schools accept graduates of primary schools located throughout the Shan and Kachin States. A knowledge of the Burmese language will not be required.

Application blanks are available at the Division of International Educational Relations, United States Office of Education, Federal Security Agency, Washington 25, D.C. The deadline for the receipt of applications is May 15, 1948.

ement With Mexico

(*b*) A change, in November 1947, to the ad valorem equivalent of the duty in 1942 or higher, of the rates of duty on some 5000 items *not* in the trade agreement.

5. In December 1947 it became evident that Mexico would raise the duty on items in the trade agreement. At this point the United States

(*a*) Could have announced its intention of denouncing the agreement in the event of such action by Mexico or

(*b*) Could have sought a solution to the problem through negotiation and agreement.

6. Denunciation of the agreement

(*a*) Would have resulted in a major, and it is believed, unnecessary breach in United States economic relations with Mexico.

(*b*) Would have lost for the United States the opportunity to influence the amount by which Mexico would increase rates and to obtain compensation for such increases by further bargaining.

7. Therefore, after full consideration by the interdepartmental trade-agreements organization of all phases of the problem, and with over-all United States–Mexico relations in mind, the United States agreed to provisional increases in duties on trade-agreement items to levels equivalent, on an ad valorem basis, to those provided in the trade agreement when it first came into effect. In return Mexico agreed to negotiations intended to restore the balance in the agreement through revision of the new Mexican rates on items not now in the agreement.

8. If a satisfactory adjustment of Mexican tariff rates should prove impossible to negotiate, the United States is not precluded from seeking agreement on the basis of withdrawing concessions previously made by this country to Mexico or from terminating the agreement in accordance with its provisions.

---

[1] BULLETIN of Jan. 11, 1948, p. 59, and Feb. 15, 1948, p. 212.

Second Report to Congress on U.S. Foreign Relief Program

President Truman transmitted to the Congress on April 13 the second report on the United States Foreign Relief Program, which was authorized by joint resolution of the 80th Congress, Public Law 84, to provide assistance to the people of countries devastated by war.[1] The countries which have received relief under the program are Austria, Greece, Italy, the Free Territory of Trieste, and China. Foods of various kinds, principally cereals, and seeds, fertilizer, fuel, and medical supplies have been shipped under the relief program. Foods represent about 95 percent of the total cost.

Of the $350,000,000 appropriated for this purpose, the Congress stipulated, among other things, that up to $40,000,000 was to be set aside as a contribution to the International Children's Emergency Fund and $5,000,000 to cover the ocean transportation of supplies provided by private American relief agencies. On December 31, 1947, the amount reserved for supplies to the countries

receiving relief was $285,900,000. The value of shipments made totaled $229,520,292 which included the ocean freight.

Shipments of supplies in the three months from October 1 through December 31, 1947, totaled 3,736,813 long tons, compared to the 1,006,401 long tons shipped in the previous period.

The report notes the acknowledgement of recipient countries for the part United States relief supplies have played in their economy. This acknowledgement has been marked by religious blessing ceremonies on the arrival of the first vessels in a dozen Greek ports, by ceremonies greeting the 200th vessel bearing relief to Italy, by the attendant newspaper and radio publicity, by colored posters prominently displayed in retail stores and elsewhere, identifying the United States relief supplies, or emphasizing the proportion of the United States contribution toward the food ratio, or stating that the local proceeds from the sale of United States commodities remain in the country to be used for relief projects.

[1] This report was released by the Department of State on Apr. 13 as publication 3101.

Transfer of Nondemilitarized Combat Matériel

[Released to the press April 13]

The following is a list of sales of surplus non-demilitarized and demilitarized combat matériel effected by the Department of State in its capacity as foreign surplus and lend-lease disposal agent during the months of July and October 1947 and January and February 1948, and not previously reported to the Munitions Division:

Country	Description	Procurement cost	Sales price	Date of transfer
				1948
Chile.	Miscellaneous cartridges, metallic belt links, 100-lb. practice bombs, and spotting assembly charges.	$115, 576. 87	$11, 561. 74	Jan. 20
				1947
China	One LCI (demilitarized) to T. Y. Fong, Asia Development Corporation, Shanghai, China.	373, 400. 00	6, 500. 00	October
				1948
Cuba.	Miscellaneous cartridges, metallic belt links, bombs, fuzes, assembly fins, spotting assembly charges, and arming wire assemblies.	62, 074. 60	6, 210. 84	Feb. 6
	Eight machine gun mounts	1, 124. 00	124. 00	Feb. 6
Peru	Miscellaneous spare parts for combat matériel	2, 899. 79	347. 91	Feb. 25
				1947
Singapore. . .	Seven LST's (demilitarized) to Tung Hwa Trading Co., Ltd., Singapore.	11, 324, 600. 00	122, 000. 00	1 on July 2 6 on Oct. 7
				1948
Venezuela. . .	Nine tank engines, 54 bundles of track assemblies, miscellaneous spare parts for tank, light, M3A3.	166, 096. 89	8, 304. 84	Jan. 6
	Miscellaneous cartridges, shells, percussion primers, shell fins, canisters, shot, projectiles, charges, and signals.	251, 937. 73	18, 351. 18	Feb. 19

PUBLICATIONS

Department of State

For sale by the Superintendent of Documents, Government Printing Office, Washington 25, D.C. Address requests direct to the Superintendent of Documents, except in the case of free publications, which may be obtained from the Department of State.

UNESCO and You. International Organization and Conference Series IV. Pub. 2904. (Reprint.) vi, 41 pp. 15¢.

> Questions and answers on the How, What, and Why of UNESCO—together with a six-point program for individual action.

Information for Bearers of Passports. January 1, 1948. Passport Series 7. Pub. 3012. iv, 65 pp. Free.

> Information of interest to American citizens, dealing with loss of nationality and with their status in certain countries with which the United States has or has not concluded treaties of naturalization.

Passport and Visa Information for Clerks of Courts Who Take Passport Applications, 1948. Passport Series 8. Pub. 3029. 17 pp. Free.

> Replaces edition of 1947.

Publications of the Department of State, January 1, 1948. Pub. 3030. 56 pp. Free.

> A semi-annual list cumulative from October 1, 1929.

Postal Union of the Americas and Spain. Treaties and Other International Acts Series 1680. Pub. 3043. 51 pp. 15¢.

> Convention, and Final Protocol and Regulations of Execution of the Convention, Between the United States and Other Governments—Signed at Rio de Janeiro September 25, 1946; entered into force January 1, 1947.

Second Report to Congress on the United States Foreign Relief Program, for the quarter ended December 31, 1947. Economic Cooperation Series 5. Pub. 3101. v, 62 pp. 25¢.

> Report to the Congress on the U.S. Foreign Relief Program, under Public Law 84, approved May 31, 1947, which authorized an appropriation for relief assistance to the people of countries devastated by war.

Work of the United Nations Good Offices Committee in Indonesia. International Organization and Conference Series III, 4. Pub. 3108. 14 pp. Free.

> An article and documents relating to the Indonesian situation.

The United States Reciprocal Trade-Agreements Program and the Proposed Trade Organization. Commercial Policy Series 112. Pub. 3112. 7 pp. 10¢.

Havana Charter for an International Trade Organization and Final Act and Related Documents, March 24, 1948. Commercial Policy Series 113. Pub. 3117. viii, 77 pp. 25¢.

> Final text of the charter to be submitted to the governments represented at the Havana conference for their acceptance.

Contributors

The article on the significance of textiles in the Japanese economy is by *Stanley Nehmer*, research analyst in the Division of Research for Far East, Office of Intelligence Research, Department of State, and by *Marguerite C. Crimmins*, who was formerly a research analyst in that office.

Helen G. Kelly, author of the article on the second session of the Administrative Council of the International Telecommunication Union, is an officer in the Telecommunications Division, Department of State. Miss Kelly served as adviser to the United States Delegation to the second session of the Administrative Council.

Donald R. MacQuivey, author of the article on the North American Broadcasting Engineers' Meeting, served as vice chairman of the U.S. Delegation to the conference. Mr. MacQuivey is an officer of the Telecommunications Division, Office of Transport and Communications, Department of State.

U. S. GOVERNMENT PRINTING OFFICE: 1948

The Department of State

For sale by the Superintendent of Documents
U.S. Government Printing Office
Washington 25, D.C.

SUBSCRIPTION:
52 issues, $5; single copy, 15 cents

Published with the approval of the
Director of the Bureau of the Budget

In many respects they are not only an indication of present problems but also a preview of the constitutional debates which may be expected in the period of federal reconstruction, which, one hopes, lies ahead.

The occupation forces which took over the U. S. zone in May 1945 were confronted with political and administrative chaos as the result of the collapse of the whole Nazi system. Democracy, as a political theory, as a personal philosophy, and as a system of governmental organization, had almost disappeared under the force of National Socialist theory and practice. Basic laws, administrative personnel, and daily operations alike had been thoroughly nazified.

Government and party had become so completely enmeshed and comingled that action which was immediately undertaken to destroy the Nazi Party inevitably paralyzed many essential public services. The German people as a whole had neither the energy nor the tools with which to create and support a democratic government. The occupation forces had to start rebuilding from the ground up.

In the months which have elapsed since the conclusion of hostilities, the U. S. Military Government endeavored to assist the Germans in their efforts to revive the will to democracy and to assist that will to express itself in practical political, economic, and social forms. Vital to this broader effort was the specific program for creating democratic political processes and institutions.

Basic also was the necessity of appointing public officials on all levels of government who, as trustees for the German people, would begin the long process of reestablishing popular government. These officials had to carry the dual responsibilities of preparing for a more stable period of democratic controls and exercising the interim functions of government.

The first step in the reestablishment of democracy was the reorganization of local and state units of government. At the outset it was necessary that German officials of all levels should work under the detailed direction and control of Military Government officers, but a degree of independence and responsibility was rapidly developed, first in local and then in state governments. At the suggestion of Military Government, the three

EDITOR'S NOTE: This article on the German constitutions is reprinted from the *Information Bulletin*, magazine of U.S. Military Government in Germany, issue of Mar. 9, 1948, p. 3.

states prepared municipal government codes which were reviewed, revised, and approved by Military Government in November 1945.

Codes for county government were approved in February 1946. Thus the necessary legal foundations were laid at municipal and county levels. The next step was the introduction of popularly elected local representative bodies. In September 1945 a schedule of elections was prepared under which municipal councils were elected in January 1946; councils in the rural counties in April 1946; and in the larger cities in May 1946.

It still remained ·to frame the structure for democratic state governments, each with an elected legislature, a responsible executive, and an independent judiciary. The aim was to clothe the state governments with authority and to charge them with responsibility to the greatest extent commensurate with the continued military occupation of Germany and the attainment of occupation objectives, bearing·in mind that no central German government existed to exercise those powers which must be centrally vested.

In February 1946 the three ministers-president were authorized to appoint preparatory constitutional commissions. These commissions reviewed constitutional problems and prepared draft constitutions for consideration by state constitutional assemblies. The delegates to these assemblies were elected by popular vote on June 30, 1946, and began their work in the following month.

The constitutions of the states in the U. S. zone are German in origin, spirit, and preparation. They spring from no Military Government dictate but from the needs and minds of the German people. Military Government insisted that the reestablishment of democracy cannot spring from a dictated constitution, that to enlist the wholehearted support of the German people, the constitutions must represent their will and not that of the occupation forces.

The specific process of constitution-making was guided by Military Government only through a general statement of basic principles of democratic organization which is contained in the September 30, 1946, directive, entitled "Relationships Between Military and Civil Government (U. S. Zone) Subsequent to Adoption of Land Constitutions". The statement of democratic principles was specifically interpreted and applied to certain provisions of the constitutions.

The constitutional conventions which were elected in June varied materially in party composition. The Hesse convention consisted of 90 members made up of 43 Social Democrats, 34 Christian Democrats, 7 Communists, and 6 Liberal Democrats. In Württemberg-Baden the 100 members included 41 Christian Democrats, 32 Social Democrats, 17 Democratic People's Party representatives, and 10 Communists.

Baden clearly provide for the parliamentary form of government; the Bavarian constitution is somewhat ambiguous on this point and reflects convention sentiment favoring a more independent type of executive. An independent judiciary is established with a power of judicial veto which German court have usually lacked in the past, namely, to declare laws passed by the legislature unconstitutional.

Each constitution contains a long bill of rights—rights that are guaranteed to individuals or to groups, rights that are of a political, social, and economic character. In part, these rights are the traditional rights of the individual as formulated in the English revolution of the seventeenth century and the American and French revolutions of the eighteenth century; in part, they are the newer social and economic rights so much stressed in twentieth-century thought. Through the ordinary courts and through the administrative courts, these rights will be protected against legislative and administrative violation.

At the same time the constitutions recognize that no rights are absolute and that, particularly in times of emergency, restrictions are necessary.

Among the more controversial questions dealt with by the constitutions are relationships of the states to the future German government and to interim authorities, such as the Council of States (*Länderrat*) and the bizonal economic agencies; the socialization of industry; land reform; and problems of church and state with respect to such matters as state subsidies to churches, church taxes, and church control of public education.

Viewed as a whole, the constitutions represent notable attempts by the Germans themselves to rebuild democratic constitutionalism. The legislatures elected under the constitutions convened in December 1946, and each chose a minister-president and cabinet. Thus, at the beginning of 1947, 20 months after the cessation of hostilities, municipal, county, and state governments in the U. S. zone were all operating under democratically adopted constitutions and with popularly elected representative bodies.

In the Soviet zone, the Soviet Military Administration was obliged to begin managing essential civil services through their military commanders on all levels of government, utilizing such Germans as were available and trustworthy. Cooperation came most readily from former members of the German Communist Party and from Germans specially trained for administrative tasks and in communist ideology in Russia.

States and provinces were immediately organized on the basis of existing traditional units. However, certain territorial adjustments were made in the interests of administrative efficiency and convenience. Pomerania, west of the Oder–Neisse line, was attached to Land Mecklenburg.

The small section of Lower Silesia which re-mained within the present boundaries of Ger-many was incorporated into the Land Saxony.

Brandenburg was reestablished as a political unit, minus those parts which are now under Polish administration. The former independent Land Anhalt was joined to the Prussian province of Saxony, and Thuringia was extended by the in-clusion of a small amount of former Prussian territory. Enclaves existing in the zone were eliminated. After quadripartite agreement on the dissolution of the State of Prussia, the former Prussian provinces received state status. There are now five states in the Soviet Zone: Branden-burg, Saxony-Anhalt, Saxony, Thuringia, and Mecklenburg.

Municipal and city councils were elected in Sep-tember 1946, and county councils and state as-semblies, legislatures, or parliaments, in October of the same year. These legislatures drafted state constitutions which, after review by the Soviet Military Administration, were promulgated be-tween December 1946 and the end of February 1947.

The constitutions of the Soviet Zone states are almost identical in their provisions and occasion-ally identical in phraseology as a result of the dominant position of the Soviet-sponsored So-cialist Unity Party.

The legislative power is vested in a unicameral legislature elected by universal suffrage and secret ballot, according to the principles of proportional representation. The legislature exercises legisla-tive authority and control over the administration and the judiciary of the state. In certain specified cases provision is made for popular referenda.

The executive power is exercised by a minister-president who is chosen by and responsible to the legislature. The cabinet is composed of ministers who are nominated by the minister-president and confirmed by the legislature and are individually responsible for their activities and must resign if the confidence of the legislature is withdrawn.

A judiciary is established consisting of profes-sional and lay judges nominated by democratic parties and organizations and elected by the rep-resentative bodies. While they are subject only to law, they are not permitted to question the con-stitutionality of properly enacted laws. When the question of the constitutionality of a law arises, de-cision is rendered by a special committee consist-ing partly of the legislative executives, partly of members of the high state courts and the univer-sity law faculties.

The communities and counties are recognized as self-supporting corporations. However, they execute those governmental functions that may be assigned to them by the legislature or the state government. Local governments and popularly elected officials are fully responsible to their as-semblies and can be removed by them.

lature. The ministers are responsible to the minister-president on matters of over-all policy and to the legislature on matters falling within their functional fields.

A constitutional court is established to review legislation and pass upon its constitutionality. All three constitutions take special pains to guard church interest. Religious instruction is to be imparted in all schools and to be supervised by the churches. Permissive clauses for the socialization of basic industries are included in all the constitutions. Adequate compensation is required in all cases. Property rights, especially land and real-estate rights, are safeguarded.

All constitutions give the minister-president power in cases of emergency to suspend for brief periods certain of the basic rights granted to the citizens. In all such cases the legislature must immediately be informed of this action. Denazification laws are specifically exempted from the constitutional provisions of the bill of rights.

On June 9, 1947, the French High Command in Germany issued Ordinance No. 95, a document comparable to the September 30 directive of the American Military Government. This ordinance makes the constitutions subject to Control Council and French High Command orders. Furthermore, certain spheres of activity pertaining to reparations, movements of population, dismantling, and occupational requirements are removed from the competence of the German authorities.

Proposals pertaining to decartelization, denazification, and democratization must be communicated to the French High Command before being introduced in the legislature. The state budget must make provisions for occupation costs. All laws must receive French Military Government approval before promulgation.

Although the French zone constitutions give the impression that the state governments are independently functioning entities, they are actually supervised by French Military Government to an extent even greater than that which would be suggested by a reading of Ordinance No. 95.

In addition to the specific subjects reserved to French Military Government by this order, there are also "legislative powers in the field of economics for which coordination between the states is required." On the strength of this latter provision the states have been forbidden to legislate on any branches within the fields of economics, food and agriculture, or transport.

While laws outside the prohibited and restricted categories may be introduced in a legislature without prior Military Government review, the Germans have been "advised" to submit them for prior review so that, for all practical purposes, there is advance clearance of everything the legislature does, in addition to a review, before promulgation, of legislation already enacted.

FOREIGN AID AND RECONSTRUCTION

International Law and the European Recovery Progra

BY ERNEST A. GROSS [1]
Legal Adviser

Mr. Justice Holmes said that a page of history is worth a volume of logic. I propose to outline some of the facts of history which have necessitated the formulation of the European Recovery Program and to indicate its relation to certain other aspects of American foreign economic policy. I hope thus to put the Economic Cooperation Act of 1948 in perspective so that we who are concerned with the dynamics of international law may see the problem whole, rather than as a fragment.

The report of the Senate Committee on Foreign Relations enumerates some of the reasons why Europe is in need: "Economic nationalism, political tensions and uncertainty, war devastation, the prolonged interruption of international trade, the loss of foreign income and dollar funds, internal financial disequilibrium, shortage of supplies from southeast Asia, the wartime movement of peoples to certain areas of western Europe, and a 10-percent increase of population have all contributed to economic break-down in Europe. Germany, a focal point in the European economy, is paralyzed. Inflation is rampant. Subversive elements are hampering recovery and engineering social chaos."

This summary is of particular interest because it starts with "economic nationalism" and ends with a reference to subversive elements "engineering social chaos". Neither of these is, of course, unique to the postwar history of Europe and, as has been recently pointed out, the European revolutions of just a century ago posed the still unsolved problems of nationalism and Marxian socialism. It remained for the supreme demagogy of Hitler to select a name for his party which suggested a twin solution; and it remained for the National Socialist Party to prepare the fields in which subversion thrives.

Economic conditions at the end of World War II resulted in the decision of most nations—the United States being a notable exception—to retain, if not to intensify, rigid trade controls and

to resort to discriminatory bilateral deals. Eac country desperately conserved its small and pr cious stock of foreign exchange by limiting forei purchases to goods and services most urgent needed, while at the same time attempting to p suade other countries, most of whom were in like situation, to accept those nonessentials whi had to be exported in order to provide necessa foreign exchange. Under such pressures a syste of ever-increasing discriminations and restrictio on foreign trade tended to arise; and restrictic ism and protection, once sampled, are stro drugs, the habit of which is not easy to bre At the time when increased international tra was an obvious necessity, restrictionism, bilater ism, and special dealism threatened effectively strangle such trade.

Against this background, the Secretary of Stat on June 5, 1947, in his now famous Harva speech, announced that the United States Gover ment would make efforts to "help start the Eur pean world on its way to recovery", if the cou tries of Europe would agree on the requiremen and upon the part they themselves would take " give proper effect to whatever action might undertaken by this Government". Shortly aft Secretary Marshall's statement, the Foreign Mi isters of the United Kingdom and France invit the Foreign Minister of the U.S.S.R. to meet wi them to consider whether a joint program for t economic recovery of Europe might be devise The U.S.S.R. refused to cooperate on the grou that such a program "would lead to interferen in the internal affairs of European countries She also refused to permit Poland and Czech slovakia to subject themselves to such interferen

In July 1947 the United Kingdom and Fran invited all European countries, other than Spai to attend a conference to formulate such a pr gram. The 14 nations which accepted this inv tation, together with its initiators, formed a Cor mittee of European Economic Co-operation, th members of which have now formed by treaty European economic organization which will be long-range and vital importance. The Comm tee of European Economic Co-operation issued

[1] Address made before the American Society of International Law in Washington on Apr. 23, 1948, and released to the press on the same date.

internal law of nations, so this change in international relations—this weaving together of economies—will affect international law. It is our task to see that international law is a ready tool, not for change for the sake of change, but for the real interests of nations and peoples.

To carry out our task we must see whether such programs for economic cooperation as ERP have already modified—or indeed violated—what are established principles of international law. One question which leaps to mind is, of course, whether the effort toward economic cooperation conflicts with the concept of territorial sovereignty—a charge which might be lightly dismissed did it not indicate misconception or mischief.

It is a charge which must be appraised in the context in which it is most frequently made, and which was keynoted by the declaration adopted at the first meeting of the Cominform: "The Truman-Marshall plan is only a constituent part, the European subsection, of a general plan for the policy of global expansion pursued by the United States in all parts of the World".

The hollowness of the charge is most apparent when viewed against the dogma of the Chief of the Soviet State, announced more than 15 years before the so-called "Truman-Marshall Plan", that the premises of the proletarian revolution must start "from the point of view of the state of world economy, inasmuch as the individual countries and individual national economies are no longer independent economic units . . . and inasmuch as the old 'civilizing' capitalism has grown into imperialism and imperialism is a world system of financial bondage . . . (Stalin, *Foundations of Leninism*, 1932).

There is, indeed, in the two programs of economic cooperation I am discussing, no conflict with established concepts of sovereignty. The charter of the International Trade Organization will come into effect, when it does, by the ratification of the states making up the Organization—a ratification which will in itself be a re-affirmation of the rights of sovereignty. So also the charter of the European cooperation organization is to be ratified by the members, and the provision of assistance to the members will be made possible by agreements to be negotiated between the United States and the other cooperating states.

The Senate Foreign Relations Committee report reveals the legislative consideration of this subject:

"In stressing the importance of these obligations (i.e., those embodied in the multilateral undertakings), the Committee was sensitive to the fact that the countries of western Europe are highly developed sovereign nations and would be properly resentful of any interference from the outside in their internal affairs. There can be no possible criticism on this score inasmuch as the undertakings were voluntarily assumed by the Committee of European Economic Co-operation countries upon their own initiative and in no sense represent an attempt on the part of the United States to impose restrictions on the sovereign rights of the participating countries."

It is appropriate to recall the remarkable treatise of Fedor Martens, who served 40 years in the Russian Foreign Office and who, long before his death in 1909, had earned the sobriquet of "the Chief Justice of Christendom" for his work as an arbitrator. In 1883 he wrote: "Looking to their own progress and that of their citizens, states must enter into relations among themselves, seek in other countries the resources which they may lack and in return offer their assistance to other peoples for the attainment of legitimate purposes. In fulfilling their essential duties they depend upon one another. The degree of their mutual dependence is in proportion to the degree of their civilization and education". This is not far from the language of article 1 of the charter of the ITO nor from the language of section 102(a), title I of the Economic Cooperation Act of 1948. The latter states:

"Recognizing the intimate economic and other relations between the United States and the nations of Europe, and recognizing that disruption following in the wake of war is not contained by national frontiers, the Congress finds that the existing situation in Europe endangers the establishment of a lasting peace, the general welfare and national interest of the United States, and the attainment of the objectives of the United Nations."

In fulfillment of this policy, the Act goes on to offer to the cooperating nations that very assistance of which Martens spoke.

Still less substantial is the question whether the economic policies of the United States, as exemplified in these two programs, are in conflict with the Charter of the United Nations. The preparation of the charter of the International Trade Organization was in fact sponsored by the Economic and Social Council of the United Nations. The European Recovery Program accords with the procedures and the objectives of the Charter of the United Nations and explicitly contemplates coordination with the specialized agencies of the United Nations. The Committee of European Economic Co-operation was careful to point out in its general report that, wherever suitable international machinery exists, it is the desire of the participating countries that their collective tasks be undertaken within the framework of the United Nations.

But although existing institutions and established concepts have been respected, it remains true that fundamental changes in economic relations among nations may well develop new inter-

ing countries will agree with us to cooperate with each other in reducing barriers to trade among themselves and other countries. Further, each participating country must take measures to locate and identify and put into appropriate use the assets and earnings therefrom belonging to its citizens where such assets are located within the United States, its territories, or possessions. This provision, which the legislative history makes clear does not require forced liquidation of the assets, is based on the concept that idle, hoarded, or unproductive assets should be put to use. The concept is not a new one; wartime decrees of, for example, the United Kingdom and the Royal Netherlands Government-in-exile, were directed at placing into use the assets in this country belonging to their citizens. In this instance, however, the requirement that the participating countries put these assets to use in furtherance of the recovery program stems from our legislation. The problem for the lawyer, recognizing the need for and the justice of such action, is to assure accomplishment of the objective in a manner that does not prejudice the legitimate stability of private international investment in its important role in the modern international economy.

The bilateral agreements are also to provide that the participating countries will agree to negotiate suitable protection for the right of access for any United States citizen to the sources of materials, required by the United States as a result of the deficiencies or potential deficiencies in its own resources, on terms of treatment equivalent to those afforded the nationals of the participating countries.

The participating country is also to agree to submit for decision of the International Court of Justice, or any arbitral tribunal mutually agreed upon, any case espoused by this Government involving compensation for a national of the United States for governmental measures affecting his property rights. It can be expected that difficult problems will arise in connection with decisions which must be made by this Government as to which cases it will espouse under this provision and the extent to which we will require of citizens a demonstration that the local remedies are inadequate.

An over-all problem with respect both to the multilateral agreements among the participating countries and the bilateral agreements with the United States will be the applicability of article 36 of the Statute of the International Court of Justice, which provides that the states parties to the Statute may declare that they recognize "as compulsory *ipso facto* and without special agreement in relation to any other state accepting the same obligation, the jurisdiction of the Court in all legal disputes concerning: (a) the interpreta-

(*Continued on page 585*)

THE UNITED NATIONS AND SPECIAL[

STATEMENT BY AMBASSAD

U.S. Representative at the S

Since the United States introduced the resolution in the Security Council which led to the calling of this Special Session of the General Assembly, we believe it appropriate for us to outline at this early stage of our proceedings the nature of the problem which now confronts us.   In essence, it is the establishment of peace in Palestine and the creation of conditions for a constructive political settlement.

The Palestine question first came before the United Nations at a Special Session of the General Assembly which convened in New York on April 28, 1947, in response to a request made by the United Kingdom on April 2, 1947.   In that Special Session the United States supported the idea that a Special Committee, made up of neutral and disinterested members, should review the situation in Palestine and report to the regular session of the General Assembly which was to meet in September of last year.   We supported such a Committee because we were aware that earlier efforts to find a solution for Palestine had been unavailing and because we were anxious to see the question dealt with by the United Nations on its merits, free from special interests and other factors which did not bear directly upon Palestine itself.

While the United Nations Special Committee on Palestine was at work, from May 26, 1947, until the submission of its report to the General Assembly on September 3, 1947, the United States Government scrupulously refrained from statements of policy or from acts which might in any way prejudice the work of that Committee.   We were eager for it to have every possible opportunity to make an impartial study of the question and to recommend what seemed to it to be a fair solution.

Inherent in our attitude was a desire to give very great weight to the work of such a Committee.

---

[1] Made on Apr. 20, 1948, to the Political and Security Committee (First Committee) at the Second Special Session of the General Assembly ; released to the press by the U.S. Mission to the United Nations on the same date. Mr. Austin is Chairman of the U.S. Delegation to the Special Session.

favor, none against. The paragraph was rejected.

Amendments to the remainder of our resolution were proposed. We accepted most of these suggestions in the hope that the consultation among the five permanent members called for in the resolution would facilitate agreement on a course of action and promote peaceful implementation of the Assembly resolution. The resolution was then adopted by a vote of 8 to 0 with Argentina, Syria, and the United Kingdom abstaining.[3]

During a period of intensive consultation—many meetings being held—among the permanent members, the mandatory power, the Palestine Commission, and the representatives of the Jews and Arabs of Palestine, the following finding was reported to the Security Council (I refer to S/PV 270, page 7, no. 4) : "The Palestine Commission, the mandatory power, the Jewish Agency and the Arab Higher Committee have indicated that the partition plan cannot be implemented by peaceful means under present conditions".

By the middle of March we recognized that time was fast running out.[4] The only certainty was that grave disorders were occurring daily in Palestine and that even greater bloodshed could be expected after May 15th. That prospect presented a hard choice to the United States as a member of the United Nations. We could take an inactive position and let the situation move on to inevitable chaos. The alternative was to suggest some emergency action to preserve the peace, running the risk of the misunderstanding which would accompany any such effort on our part. My Government considered that the only decent course lay in an effort to save lives, and we found that our colleagues in the Security Council were ready to move in the same direction.

Truce Efforts

The United States, therefore, along with other members of the Security Council, turned to an attempt to effect a truce in order to bring to an end the serious fighting now occurring daily in Palestine and to forestall even greater bloodshed after May 15th.[5]

The report of the United Nations Palestine Commission directed to this Special Session states that "Arab elements, both inside and outside of Palestine, have exerted organized, intensive effort toward defeating the purposes of the resolution of the General Assembly. To this end, threats, acts of violence, and infiltration of organized, armed, uniformed Arab bands into the Palestinian terri-

---

[3] BULLETIN of Mar. 7, 1948, p. 297.

[3] *Ibid.*, Mar. 14, 1948, p. 344.

[4] *Ibid.*, Mar. 28, 1948, p. 402. See also *ibid.*, Apr. 4, 1948, p. 451.

Ibid., Apr. 18, 1948, p. 514.

tory have been employed". Our own information confirms this part of the Palestine report. The primary reason why the General Assembly's resolution of November 29th could not be carried out by peaceful means was Arab resistance. Some of this resistance, arising from outside Palestine, is in clear violation of the Charter of the United Nations and must be halted.

The Jewish Agency for Palestine has demonstrated that it is prepared to accept the resolution of the General Assembly of last November 29, despite the fact that this resolution did not represent the full measure of their claims. We must recall, however, that elements in the Jewish Community have resorted to wide-spread terrorism and wilful murder since November 29, 1947. Such activities have shocked the entire world, have served to inflame still further the Palestine question, and have made is more difficult for the United Nations to find a peaceful solution to the Palestine problem.

Responsibility of Palestinians

It seems to us clear that the primary responsibility for reaching a peaceful settlement of this problem rests upon the people of Palestine. Instead of serious and responsible efforts to resolve their differences, we see bitter retaliatory fighting and an apparent determination to seek a solution by force of arms rather than by force of reason, adjustment, and persuasion. We do not believe that the peoples of Palestine are entitled to appear before the United Nations to assert demands which must be accepted by the other party and the world community as the only alternative to war.

Meanwhile, the United Kingdom has steadfastly held to May 15 as the terminal point of the mandate and to August 1 as the final departure date of the remaining British forces.

Faced with these British deadlines and mounting conflict in Palestine, the Security Council in the early hours of last Saturday morning acted to establish a truce. This action of the Council needs and deserves the full support of all the members of the United Nations.

Cooperation Essential for Truce

Further action on the truce by the Security Council may be required. It may be necessary to establish in Palestine a truce commission of the Council and to make available to the commission a limited number of police to assist in supervising the truce and to reinforce the local police in controlling irresponsible elements. At the heart of the matter is the need for those who control the Arab and Jewish populations of Palestine to cooperate to the fullest in the enforcement of the truce called for by the Security Council.

---

* Not printed here.

therefore, that the First Committee will ask the Fourth Committee to undertake this task immediately.

Trusteeship a Standstill—Not a Solution

We do not suggest a temporary trusteeship as a substitute for the plan of partition with economic union or for any other solution of the Palestine problem which may be agreed upon by the Jews and Arabs of that country. We consider it an emergency measure to insure public order and the maintenance of public services. The truce and trusteeship together envisage a military and political standstill to save human life and to make possible further negotiations on a final political settlement. As we see it, the truce and trusteeship would be entirely without prejudice to the rights, claims, or position of the parties or to the character of the eventual political settlement.

Economic Development of Palestine

It is not enough to provide only for law and order in Palestine. If the United Nations accepts temporary responsibility for the Government of Palestine, everything possible should be done to promote the economic recovery and development of the country for the mutual benefit of all of its inhabitants. The record shows that the peoples of Palestine can and will work together for their mutual welfare if given a reasonable chance to do so. All over Palestine Jews and Arabs have collaborated on such fundamental problems as irrigation and water supply, transportation, and sanitation. It should be an important function of a temporary government to promote such collaboration. If we really want to reduce and prevent violence, we will take measures to substitute tools for weapons. That will be much less costly and much more successful than attempting solely to maintain police authority. It will also reduce the emphasis on political bitterness.

We are dealing with people who, like people everywhere, are interested in the common things of life—the education of their children, the improved cultivation of their land, more and better food, more power for their industries, greater opportunities for themselves and their children in jobs and business and farming. Peace is not an ominous quiet but a substitution of the tractor for the tank.

Role of United Nations Agencies

Here, the many resources of the United Nations might be mobilized. The United Nations is not concerned solely with the solution of conflict and with the maintenance of peace. The Organization and its members are obligated by the Charter to promote international economic and social cooperation. We believe that when the fighting stops, a real opportunity will open up for joint action by Jews and Arabs, assisted by the United ·

571

Nations, its specialized agencies, and the proposed Economic Commission for the Middle East, to develop the economic potentialities of Palestine. Attention might be given to plans for harnessing the River Jordan, for draining the swamplands near its source, and for reclaiming new areas of arid land in order that they might bloom once again as in Biblical times. Attention could be given to other proposals, such as the one for digging a canal to allow the water of the Mediterranean to flow into the Dead Sea depression, thereby affording people electric power, not only for Palestine but for surrounding countries.

Practical projects for the development of hydroelectric power might be unfolded in such a way as to warrant the financial assistance of the International Bank for Reconstruction and Development. The Food and Agriculture Organization might assist in the fruitful utilization of reclaimed areas. The World Health Organization might be asked to assist in combating the danger of malaria around the headwaters of the Jordan. The International Labor Organization might contribute to the improvement of working and living conditions. In the fields of education and culture and of scientific experimentation, the temporary government of Palestine might enlist the advice and assistance of the United Nations Educational, Scientific and Cultural Organization.

A peaceful Palestine should also attract private investments which would contribute, in many ways, to its economic development.

People who now disagree concerning the form of government which should ultimately be established for Palestine have in common a devotion to that land and a desire for its development. On projects such as those which I have mentioned, they could collaborate for the promotion of the common weal.

Basic United Nations Purposes

From the beginning our purposes as members of the United Nations have been to prevent a situation likely to endanger peace in Palestine and in the world and positively to facilitate a peaceful settlement with self-government and a chance for orderly social and economic development.

RESOLUTION CONCERNING DRAFT STAT

WHEREAS, the General Assembly by its Resolution of 29 November 1947, requested the Trusteeship Council to elaborate and approve a detailed Statute for the City of Jerusalem within five months of the date of passage, i.e., by 29 April 1948; and

The Trusteeship Council,

Taking note of the resolutions adopted by the Security Council concerning the future govern-

---

[1] U.N. doc. US/T/15. Adopted by the Trusteeship Council on Apr. 21, 1948.

The Little Assembly of the United Nations

BY PHILIP C. JESSUP [1]

Deputy U.S. Representative on the Interim Committee of the United Nations

This first national conference of the regional officers of the International Relations Clubs is a significant event. I have followed for a good many years the work of the International Relations Clubs with a great deal of interest and admiration for the results of your work. The establishment and operation of these clubs constitute one of the substantial contributions of the Carnegie Endowment toward the attainment of international peace. I hope this is merely the first of a series of similar national conferences. You regional officers of International Relations Clubs are in key positions. Your own opinions are important, and you have an opportunity to exercise an influence on the thinking of an important section of American opinion.

In giving you tonight a thumb-nail sketch of the work of the Little Assembly of the United Nations, I should warn you that I approach the subject from an optimistic point of view. One of the most subtle definitions of the difference between the optimist and the pessimist is the one which says that the optimist is a person who *thinks* this is the best of all possible worlds while the pessimist is one who *knows* that it is. The pessimist sees no hope for improvement. The basic reason for optimism in considering the United Nations is the fact that there is ample opportunity for development and change. We are witnessing rather rapid developments and rather notable changes. The organization is still in its infancy, and one cannot expect that the developments and changes will constantly be revolutionary. A pessimistic outlook in regard to the United Nations comes from a concentration on the headlines in which you find stress on the crises and the difficulties.

The optimistic outlook comes from a detailed examination of the facts and from putting those facts in their proper perspective. A good example of what I have in mind is afforded by the dispute between Albania and Great Britain regarding the damage to British warships in the Corfu Channel. That event in 1946 and the British charge that Albania was responsible for the damage made the headlines. Public attention was still concentrated on the case during the rather violent debates in the Security Council. The Russian defense of the Albanian position against the British contentions seemed to illustrate once again the so-called split between the "East and West". As soon as the case neared peaceful settlement when the Security Council decided to recommend to the parties that they refer the legal questions involved to the International Court of Justice, the case began to drop out of the news. When on March 25 of this year, the Court handed down its decision, it received only minor coverage on inside pages of the papers. People's attention was not drawn to the fact that the United Nations Court in its first decision had rendered a unanimous opinion concurred in by all 15 of the regular judges, with no split between the "East and West". There was very little in any of the news coverage of the trial to reveal the atmosphere of complete courtesy and good will which characterized all of the proceedings.

Membership

The seriousness of the international situation is apparent, and I have no desire to minimize it. Its essential nature has been made clear in recent addresses and statements by the President and by the Secretary of State. The address by the President to the Congress on March 17 contained far-reaching recommendations concerning the steps necessary to enable the United States to make the peace secure and to prevent war. It is not my purpose tonight to discuss the recommendations regarding the military measures which the President has recommended. I do wish to remind you that he placed equal emphasis on our support of the United Nations. He repeated the point which had previously been stressed on behalf of the Administration that "the door has never been closed, nor will it ever be closed to the Soviet Union or any other nation which will genuinely cooperate in preserving the peace." However, the refusal of the Soviet Union to cooperate at any stage cannot and does not deter the other Members of the United Nations from pressing forward with the development and use of that organization. Fifty-one members of the United Nations are continuing their cooperation in the Little Assembly. The Soviet Union and the five other states which follow the Soviet lead are entitled to seats in the Little Assembly and may occupy them whenever they wish to join in this particular process of international cooperation. They could have taken their places this week, and they can take them next week.

[1] Address made before the First National Conference of the Regional Officers of International Relations Clubs of the Carnegie Endowment for International Peace, St. Louis, Mo., on Apr. 10, 1948 and released to the press by the U.S. Mission to the U.N. on the same date.

The 51 states which are participating in the work of the Little Assembly are doing so in a spirit of broad accommodation and mutual confidence. The six other members would be free to participate in that same spirit or even to participate in angry and vituperative opposition. They are free to choose their own method. At present they choose the method of non-cooperation.

It cannot be denied that their absence from the Little Assembly makes the process of discussion and negotiation and study easier than it would be if they were present. It must also be recognized that their absence may make some of the results of the Little Assembly's work less conclusive than they would be if all 57 members participated. However, I repeat, the absence of the six does not prevent progress; progress is being made.

Origin and Functions

Before discussing what the Little Assembly is doing and what it hopes to accomplish, I should like to go back briefly to the creation of this new subsidiary organ of the General Assembly. I should like to point out why it exists and just what its function is.

The Little Assembly, or as it is officially called, "the Interim Committee of the General Assembly", was sponsored by the United States in the General Assembly last fall. It was not, however, a sudden invention of the United States. It was not the product of any immediate crisis in Soviet-American relations. The general notion of creating some General Assembly machinery which would be able to operate between sessions had been under discussion for some time. The Netherlands Delegation had raised it at an earlier session of the General Assembly. Various nongovernmental organizations in the United States had been studying the problem and had worked out certain proposals. Various individuals had been giving the matter their consideration. The Department of State was in touch with these various currents of thought and was able to utilize them.

During the spring and summer of 1947, it began to be apparent that if the United Nations was to succeed in reducing the atmosphere of tension which was becoming increasingly evident throughout the world, it would be necessary for the General Assembly, as the great forum of world opinion, to take up seriously the role assigned to it under the Charter in the political and security field. It was realized that the move to develop the General Assembly's role might momentarily heighten the impression of basic political disagreement, but in balance it was believed that the results would counteract these impressions and make general cooperation more possible in the future. It might be said that the treatment was analogous to that in which the patient's temperature is temporarily increased with the expectation that a cure

ian member of the Commission refused to take his seat, and the Soviet military authorities refused even to receive a letter from the Commission. As Mr. Gromyko informed the Secretary-General of the United Nations, the Soviet Union took a "negative attitude" toward the Korean Commission and its work. Faced with these developments, the Commission decided to exercise the privilege which the General Assembly had conferred upon it of consulting with the Interim Committee. The chairman of the Commission and its secretary flew back to Lake Success and laid the problem before us. The matter was discussed very fully, very frankly, and without acrimony. The Interim Committee was not given the authority to issue instructions to the Korean Commission, and it did not attempt to do so. It did as a result of its discussions conclude the consultation by expressing its view to the Korean Commission that it was incumbent upon it to proceed to observe elections in as much of Korea as is accessible to it. The southern zone, which is under American occupation and where full cooperation is afforded, contains two thirds of the population. It was hoped that the Soviet Union would change its attitude and cooperate with the United Nations by permitting the Korean people to take part in free elections in the northern zone as well. So far, that cooperation has not been given. I shall not attempt to discuss all the angles of the Korean situation, which is still a difficult one, but I may say that from the point of view of the history of the Little Assembly, the consultation with the Korean Commission seems to have been useful and to have demonstrated the value of this subsidiary organ in matters of this kind. If the Little Assembly had not been in existence, it is quite possible that a Special Session of the General Assembly would have had to be called to deal with the problem. The Little Assembly affords a more convenient and far less expensive instrumentality for general discussions on such a matter, even though the Little Assembly does not have the power to make recommendations to anyone except its parent body.

Veto Question

The other question which was specifically referred by the General Assembly to the Interim Committee was the question of the veto. It is not necessary to remind you of the nature of this problem. When the Little Assembly began its sessions in January, there was a definite feeling of disappointment on the part of some delegations when the United States suggested that proposals on the veto problem should be submitted to the Interim Committee on or about March 15. Some had evidently hoped that the United States would come forward at once with a fully worked out program which would serve as a basis of the Interim Committee's work. The United States, however, has always had the view in regard to the Interim Committee that one of its chief values would lie in its nature as a study group. The United States has consistently avoided anything which might suggest an attempt to regiment the discussion in that body. When matters are brought before the Security Council or before the General Assembly, the proposing states are apt to take definite positions and to feel that their prestige is involved in sustaining those positions and in securing for them general approval. The Interim Committee is especially useful in affording an opportunity to states to advance tentative suggestions, for the purpose of free discussions. This is particularly true in regard to the veto. That subject has in the past elicited strong statements illustrating various points of view, most of them uncomplimentary to the right of veto. Some of them have pointed out that the trouble has not been with the right of veto as such but with the abuse of that right. The subject had never been fully explored in a dispassionate and thorough way in an international gathering since the Charter was adopted at San Francisco. Actually, the Interim Committee is now engaged in that kind of study. Currently, a working group of a subcommittee of the Little Assembly composed of the representatives of 10 states is studying one by one a list of 98 possible decisions which the Security Council might make in applying the Charter or the Statute of the International Court of Justice. Of those 98 possible decisions, the working group has already reached agreement that 36 of them are procedural in nature. In regard to some six others, it has already been agreed that whether procedural or not, it would be desirable that they should be decided by vote of any seven members of the Security Council, that is, that the veto should not apply. This approach is in line with the proposal submitted by the United States to the Interim Committee on March 10. In that proposal, we suggested 31 categories of Security Council decisions, all of which the United States feels should be made by a vote of any seven members of the Security Council in order to insure the effective exercise by the Security Council of its responsibilities under the Charter. The United States list included some questions which are clearly procedural and some in regard to which there is a good deal of controversy. The first item on the United States list is that having to do with the admission of states to membership in the United Nations. As you know, the veto has so far been exercised by the Soviet Union on 10 occasions to prevent the approval of applications for membership. The working group of the Interim Committee has agreed that it would be desirable to have these questions decided by the vote of any seven members of the Security Council. The United States proposals also suggest that the

principles of cooperation in the maintenance of international peace and security.

One should not expect that the Little Assembly will now provide the final answers. If one looks back over the history of the League of Nations one will find that there was a continuing series of studies ranging from 1920 up through the early 1930's, all designed to elaborate the means of pacific settlement of disputes. Those efforts resulted in the drafting of a number of important and valuable documents, such as the General Act of Geneva of 1928. This League of Nations experience is being restudied and re-evaluated. So is the comparable experience in the Inter-American system which is now being re-examined at the Bogotá conference. The Little Assembly can only break ground for a continuation of studies which ought to go on over a great many years. Some people seem to think that it is futile to start studies of this kind now in the midst of a period of political tension. The same objection was raised to the first steps taken in regard to the progressive development and codification of international law. The answer to these objections is that when one deals with long-range problems of this character, it is never too soon to begin. Moreover, the very fact that states are embarking on work involving a concentration on peace may make a contribution to the relief of the tension which superficially seems to make the work itself inappropriate.

Future Status

The General Assembly also asked the Interim Committee to study itself. It asked it to report to the session which meets in September on the advisability of establishing a permanent committee of the General Assembly to perform such duties as those now entrusted to the Interim Committee. The Interim Committee, was, of course, established on an experimental basis, and it goes out of existence when the General Assembly meets in the fall. The Little Assembly has appointed another subcommittee which is studying the implications of this problem. Various suggestions have been made concerning additional powers which might be given to the Interim Committee if it is continued beyond this year, for example, the suggestion made by the Belgian Delegation that the Interim Committee, if continued, should be given the power to request advisory opinions from the International Court of Justice. It is too soon to give a final answer to the question whether the experience of the Interim Committee justifies its continuance.

I have already suggested that the Korean consultation and the work on the veto and the study of political cooperation indicate the value of a body of this kind. There has not yet been an opportunity to determine how useful it can be in smoothing the path for the General Assembly and reducing the burden of its work. If the Little Assembly lives up to expectations in that respect as well, it is not unreasonable to suppose that the General Assembly will want to continue it at least on an experimental basis for another year.

Accomplishments

The Little Assembly has not been a spectacular body. Because the Korean question involves the relations between the United States and the Soviet Union, the consultation with the Korean Commission attracted some attention, but in general its work has received only brief notice in the press. This is not surprising, and it is not to be deplored. On the other hand, it is not to be taken as an index of the value of the work. The studies of the veto problem may prove to be of considerable political and constitutional significance in the history of the United Nations. At any time, some state may bring up before the Interim Committee for study some new suggestion, perhaps one designed to promote cooperation in the maintenance of international peace and security by some other method. Whether spectacular or not, the work which is being done is a current indication of the vitality and utility of the United Nations.

There is a danger that in attempting to explain the operations of a body which is not widely known, one will give the impression of exaggerating its importance. Compared, for instance, to the problems currently being handled in the Security Council, the work of the Little Assembly may be said to be of relatively minor significance, but the kind of long-range study which is being made and the precedent for continued cooperative study which is being set, may quite possibly have an effect long after the specific political issues before the Security Council at any one time have been settled and have passed from the arena of political conflict.

If it should unhappily prove to be the case that the Security Council should continue to meet with serious difficulty in discharging its primary responsibilities in the field of international peace and security, it is hard to escape the conclusion that the emphasis on the potential role of the General Assembly in this field will increase. It must not be forgotten that the General Assembly represents the entire membership of the United Nations and so does the Little Assembly. The history of the League of Nations indicates a natural trend toward the democratization of any international organization of this character through the development of the functions of those organs on which the membership is most broadly represented. If the General Assembly continued to meet only once a year, the difficulty in the way of its dealing with current political issues would be apparent. If it decides to keep in existence, between its sessions, some body which represents it and on which all

INTERNATIONAL ORGANIZATIONS AND CONFERENCES

endar of Meetings[1]

iession as of May 1, 1948		**1946**
Eastern Commission	Washington	Feb. 26–
ed Nations:		
curity Council	Lake Success	Mar. 25–
ilitary Staff Committee	Lake Success	Mar. 25–
tomic Energy Commission	Lake Success	June 14–
		1947
mmission on Conventional Armaments	Lake Success	Mar. 24–
curity Council's Committee of Good Offices on the Indonesian Question.	Lake Success	Oct. 20–
eneral Assembly Special Committee on the Greek Question	Salonika	Nov. 21–
		1948
mmission for Palestine	Lake Success	Jan. 9–
mporary Commission on Korea	Seoul	Jan. 12–
terim Committee of the General Assembly	Lake Success	Feb. 23–
eneral Assembly: Second Special Session on Palestine	Flushing Meadows	Apr. 16–
osoc (Economic and Social Council):		
Transport and Communications Commission: Third Session	Geneva	Apr. 12–
Economic and Employment Commission: Third Session	Geneva	Apr. 19–
Statistical Commission: Third Session	Lake Success	Apr. 26–May 7
Ece (Economic Commission for Europe): Third Session	Geneva	Apr. 26–
(Council of Foreign Ministers):		**1947**
mmission of Investigation to Former Italian Colonies	Former Italian Colonies	Nov. 8–
		1948
puties for Austria	London	Feb. 20–
sional Frequency Board	Geneva	Jan. 15–
Meeting of Planning Committee on High Frequency Broadcasting	Geneva	Mar. 22–
(International Civil Aviation Organization): Rules of the Air and Air Traffic Control Practices Division.	Montreal	Apr. 20–
rnational Conference on Safety of Life at Sea	London	Apr. 23–
rnational Administrative Aeronautical Radio Conference: Preparatory Committee.	Geneva	Apr. 24–
erence To Plan for Establishment of an International Institute for Hylean Amazon.	Iquitos, Peru	Apr. 30–
duled for May 1948		
(Council of Foreign Ministers): Deputies for Italian Colonial Problems.	London	May 1[2]–
ed Nations:		
osoc (Economic and Social Council):		
Commission on Narcotic Drugs: Third Session	Lake Success	May 3–
Population Commission: Third Session	Lake Success	May 10–
Human Rights Commission: Third Session	Lake Success	May 20–
E (Economic Commission for Europe):		
Committee on Electric Power	Geneva	May 10–
Panel on Housing	Geneva	May 13–
Committee on Coal	Geneva	May 25–
sco (United Nations Educational, Scientific and Cultural Organization):		
ternational Teachers Organization	Paris	May 3–4
mmittee of Experts for the Study of a Plan for Translations of Great Books.	Paris	May 10–14
eeting of Experts on Art and General Education	Paris	May 11–15

[1] Prepared in the Division of International Conferences, Department of State.
[2] Tentative.

Activities and Developments »

U.S. DELEGATION TO IRO PREPARATORY MEETING

[Released to the press April 19]

The Department of State announced on April 19 the composition of the United States Delegation to the Sixth Part of the First Session of the Preparatory Commission for the International Refugee Organization (IRO) which is scheduled to be held at Geneva, May 4–14, 1948. The United States Delegation is as follows:

Chairman

George L. Warren, Adviser on Refugees and Displaced Persons, Department of State; U.S. Representative on the Preparatory Commission for the IRO

Adviser

John D. Tomlinson, Assistant Chief, Division of International Organization Affairs, Department of State

Administrative Assistant

Helen Norman, U.S. Delegation, International Telecommunication Union High Frequency Board, Geneva

The meeting will consider, among other things, the status of adherences to the IRO constitution, the operating reports of the Executive Secretary, and appropriate action in the determination of policies as indicated in these reports.

The Preparatory Commission for the IRO was established in order to insure the continuity of service to displaced persons after July 1, 1947 when UNRRA and the Intergovernmental Committee on Refugees went out of existence, and to take the necessary measures to bring the permanent organization into operation as soon as possible.

The IRO will come into existence when 15 states whose contributions amount to 75 percent of the operational budget have signed the constitution. The United States, in addition to signing the constitution, is a signatory to the agreements establishing the Preparatory Commission and *ipso facto*, a member of the Preparatory Commission.

The Fifth Part of the First Session of the Preparatory Commission for the IRO was held at Geneva, January 20–31, 1948.

U.S. DELEGATION TO ICAO MEETINGS

[Released to the press April 22]

The Acting Secretary of State announced on April 22 the composition of the United States Delegation to the second European-Mediterranean Regional Air Navigation Meeting and to the Second North Atlantic Regional Air Navigation Meeting, both of which have been called by the International Civil Aviation Organization (ICAO). These regional meetings are scheduled to convene

ations, air-traffic control, communications, search and rescue, meteorology, aerodromes and ground aids, and manuals. Subsequently, several committee meetings were held to define further and to clarify air-traffic control and operations problems, and a regional office was established at Paris.

It is expected that delegations from approximately 25 countries will attend the European-Mediterranean Regional Meeting and that delegations from 18 countries will attend the North Atlantic Regional Meeting.

U.S. PARTICIPATION IN WHO ASSEMBLY PENDING

[Released to the press April 24]

Acting Secretary of State Robert A. Lovett on April 24 informed Dr. Brock Chisholm, the Executive Secretary of the Interim Commission of the World Health Organization, that this Government would, for the time being, refrain from naming observers to the World Health Assembly scheduled to meet in Geneva, on June 24, 1948, since legislation providing for United States membership in the World Health Organization is pending before the Congress.[1]

Mr. Lovett expressed his hope that it might be possible for the United States to participate fully in the World Health Assembly as a member of the World Health Organization.

The text of Mr. Lovett's letter is as follows:

April 24, 1948

SIR: I acknowledge receipt of your letter of April 7, 1948, transmitted to me by the United States Representative, inviting the United States to send one or more Observers to the World Health Assembly, which will be convened in Geneva, Switzerland, on June 24, 1948. I also note that you invite the United States to send a Delegation to the World Health Assembly in the event this Government becomes a Member of the World Health Organization prior to June 24, 1948.

Legislation providing for United States membership in the World Health Organization is still pending before the Congress. In view of my continued hope that the United States will become a Member of this organization in sufficient time to participate fully in the World Health Assembly, I refrain from naming Observers at the present time. However, in due course, you will be notified of the names of such Observers or Delegates as the United States may find it possible to send to the Assembly.

Very truly yours,

ROBERT A. LOVETT
Acting Secretary of State
of the United States of America

---

[1] BULLETIN of Apr. 25, 1948, p. 540.

THE RECORD OF THE WEEK

Fift

MR. PRESIDENT, MR. SPEAKER, MEMBERS OF THE CONGRESS, DISTINGUISHED GUESTS:

It is eminently fitting that we should assemble here today to pay solemn tribute to the heroic champions of human freedom who brought about the liberation of Cuba. The commemoration of half a century of Cuban independence recalls the valor of the Cuban patriots and American soldiers and sailors who gave liberally of their strength and their blood that Cuba might be free. From that chapter in man's age-old struggle for freedom, we can draw inspiration for the hard tasks that confront us in our own time.

The struggle for Cuban independence, like every other effort of its kind, was fraught with hardship and disappointment. But the unconquerable determination of the Cuban people to win freedom overcame all obstacles. From the first, the fight for liberation by Cuban patriots evoked the sympathy of the people of the United States. Those in quest of independence have always had the support of the people of this Nation.

Americans watched with admiration the beginning of the final struggle for independence led by José Martí and his valiant compatriots, Gómez, Maceo, and García. Our people made increasingly plain their desire to assist the Cuban patriots. The sinking of the United States battleship *Maine* in Havana harbor on February 15, 1898, crystallized the growing sentiment in this country for joining forces with the Cuban people in their fight for self-government.

The Congress passed a joint resolution expressing in clear terms the conviction of the men and women of the United States that the people of the Island of Cuba should be free and independent. It also expressed our determination that once the Cuban people were liberated, they, and they alone, should govern the Island of Cuba. It is the passage of this joint resolution, 50 years ago today, which we are commemorating in this ceremony.

This joint resolution, the foundation upon which our relations with the Cuban Republic are based, brought the military and naval forces of the

---

[1] Delivered on Apr. 19, 1948, before a joint session of the Congress in observance of the Cuban anniversary, and released to the press by the White House on the same date.

the mettle of men and their institutions of government. Our own moment of history also calls for calmness, for courage, for strength, and above all for the steadfast resolution that, come what may, we shall stand for the right.

We honor today the memory of a noble few among the countless heroes who have fought to advance the cause of human freedom through the ages.

Let us avail ourselves of this occasion to refresh our faith in freedom and to rededicate this Nation and ourselves to the principles of liberty, justice, and peace.

STATEMENT BY SECRETARY MARSHALL[2]

On the occasion of the fiftieth anniversary of the independence of Cuba and concurrently with the meetings of the Ninth Conference of American States the United States joins with the other free and independent nations of the earth in an expression of fraternity and friendship addressed to the Cuban nation. The Congress of the United States is meeting today in joint session in honor of the occasion and we here in Bogotá join with our Congress and the people of my country in extending warm felicitations to a sister republic.

for Return of Trieste

N ITALY AND THE UNITED STATES

Text of the Italian Ambassador's letter to the President

March 20, 1948

MY DEAR MR. PRESIDENT:

Allow me to convey to you the feelings of the deepest gratitude of the Italian Government and the Italian people for the momentous decision taken by this Country in view of the return of the Free Territory of Trieste to its Motherland.

I am sure that this just and generous decision will be received with the greatest exultation, not only by the entire Italian nation, but also by the inhabitants of the Free Territory of Trieste who have never abandoned their hopes of being restored to their country and will be welcomed in Italy as a further proof of the fraternal friendship of the United States towards her.

I take the liberty of adding to these feelings of my fellow-citizens my own personal sentiments of the profoundest appreciation and gratitude.

Accept [etc.]   TARCHIANI
Italian Ambassador

American War Claims in Italy[1]

session t
Economi

Departs
tl Hous
tig Ell
ding t
t on t
of Aus
Economi
to note f

t: On t
tecnic Co
t has dire
tient an
ts, on be
tud Aust
toralled
te notice
t: Progre
tig to re
tpatificat
tinment t
tote.
Accept

PAYMENT OF $5,000,000 BY ITALY

The Italian Ambassador, on behalf of the Government of Italy, on April 23 presented to the Department of State a check in the amount of $5,000,000 in fulfilment of the obligation assumed by Italy pursuant to article 2 of the memorandum of understanding between the Government of the United States and the Government of Italy regarding Italian assets in the United States and certain claims of United States nationals against Italy, signed at Washington on August 14, 1947. The check was accepted for the Secretary of State by Willard Thorp, Assistant Secretary of State for economic affairs. Mr. Thorp headed the American delegation during the negotiations with the Italian financial and economic delegation to the United States which resulted in the conclusion two memoranda of understanding and supplementary notes concerning various financial and economic questions relating to the treaty of peace with Italy. This payment by Italy is to be utilized in such manner as the Government of the United States may decide to be appropriate, in application to the claims of United States nationals arising out of the war and not otherwise provided for.

The Italian Ambassador made the following statement on this occasion:

EXCHANGE OF REMARKS BETWEEN AMBASSADOR TARCHIANI AND ASSISTANT SECRETARY THORP

"I am particularly gratified that I should be entrusted with the task of handing over this check representing the lump sum with which certain claims of American citizens arising out of the war and not otherwise provided for will be satisfied. In spite of her foreign-exchange situation, Italy desires to show once more that she intends strictly to abide by her international obligations and that she desires to settle as promptly as possible all outstanding problems between our two countries."

Mr. Thorp replied as follows:

"I am happy to receive, on behalf of the United States Government, this further evidence of the Italian Government's desire to discharge its international obligations. This action by your government, taken despite Italy's difficult foreign exchange situation, clearly emphasizes Italy's desire to settle as promptly as possible the various problems of mutual concern to our two countries which remain outstanding from the war period

national
tun—Cont
d a treat
t(f) the
ted, wil
tal oblig
tparation
tal oblig
t: United
tipating
taternatio
tal States
tor comm
tipating
ture, and
tution of
tof any q
tise.
tare sugg
tational
t: Intern
tropean
taration:
the econo
tre huma
talism, a
ton of it
this task
tuire v
tnuire y
taining
t, 1948

PROCEDURE FOR FILING CLAIMS

Under provisions contained in the peace treaty with Italy which came into force on September 15, 1947, American nationals are entitled to have returned to them property in that country which was sequestrated or placed under control of authorities of the Italian Government during the war. The treaty provides that where such property has not already been returned application for its return must be filed before September 15, 1948, except in cases where the claimant is able to show that an application could not be filed before that date.

Such applications should be prepared in the form of an affidavit in duplicate stating the name and address of the claimant, the date, place, and circumstances under which he acquired American citizenship, a description of the property to be returned, its location, and, if known, the date and place possession or control thereof was taken by the Italian authorities. If the claimant was not the owner of the property at the time it was taken, the date and manner of the claimant's acquisition of ownership thereof should be stated.

Applications are to be made to the *Ufficio Beni Alleati e Nemici*, Rome, Italy. However, to assist American nationals desiring to obtain the return of their properties, the American Embassy in Rome will transmit such applications to the proper Italian authorities.

Claimants will be notified by the Italian Government of the time and place of the return of their property and should make arrangements for receipt either personally or through a designated representative.

The filing of applications for the return of property is not to be confused with the filing of claims for loss or damage to property sustained by American nationals in Italy during the war. Instructions with respect to the latter will be furnished claimants by the Department of State and by the American Embassy in Rome as soon as possible.

[1] Released to the press Apr. 23.

Proposed Legislation on Gift of Statue From Uruguay

[Released to the press April 23]

The Department of State on April 23 transmitted to the presiding officers of Congress proposed legislation to authorize the acceptance and erection of a statue of Gen. José Gervasio Artigas, offered to the Government of the United States as a gift from the Government of Uruguay. The text of the letter to Senator Vandenberg follows:[1]

MY DEAR SENATOR VANDENBERG: I enclose for your consideration a draft of proposed legislation entitled "A bill to provide for the acceptance on behalf of the United States of a statue of General José Gervasio Artigas, and for other purposes".[2]

This legislation is necessary in order to authorize the acceptance and erection in Washington, D.C., of a statue of General Artigas offered to the Government of the United States as a gift from the Government of Uruguay; and to authorize the appropriation of funds for the cost of erection, construction of a pedestal, landscaping the adjacent area, and necessary plans and specifications.

An officer of the Uruguayan Army, Egardo Ubaldo Genta, is the proponent of the idea of donating a bronze statue of the Uruguayan national hero, General Artigas, to the United States in keeping with a plan to exchange bronze statues of heroes among the American republics. Such exchanges have been consummated by Uruguay with at least six other American republics. The donation of the Artigas bronze dates back to December, 1940 when the Uruguayan Chamber of Deputies authorized an appropriation for the casting of the statue of Artigas to be donated to the City of Washington, D.C. A part of the total cost of the statue was contributed by the school children of Montevideo. Because of the war and the limitations on shipping facilities, arrangements were delayed until April, 1947 when the statue was shipped to the United States. The Department received a communication from the Uruguayan Embassy officially offering the statue to the United States as a gift from the Government of Uruguay.

The Department is of the opinion that the acceptance of the gift of a statue of General Artigas would serve to strengthen the friendly relations now existing between the Governments of Uruguay and the United States and to further the concept of hemispheric solidarity for which we strive.

The Department further believes that the Government of the United States should consider re-

---

[1] The same letter was sent to Speaker Martin.
[2] Not printed.

turning this expression of friendship and esteem by the donation of a statue of our national hero, General George Washington, to the Government of Uruguay for erection in the City of Montevideo. Information is now being developed that may be required in support of legislation to authorize a casting of a reciprocal statue of George Washington to be donated to the Government of Uruguay, and it is contemplated that such legislation will be proposed at a later date. ·

I hope that the Congress will find it possible t act upon this draft legislation this session.

A similar communication is being sent to th Speaker of the House.[3] .

The Department has been informed by th Bureau of the Budget that there is no objectio to the submission of this proposal to the Congres

Sincerely yours,

For the Acting Secretary of State:

CHARLES E. BOHLEN
Counselor

Procedure for Handling International Fisheries Problems

EXCHANGE OF LETTERS BETWEEN THE DEPARTMENT OF STATE AND THE DEPARTMENT OF THE INTERIOR

[Released to the press April 12]

April 5, 1948

MY DEAR MR. SECRETARY:

Following your conversation of several weeks ago with Secretary Marshall on the means for improving the handling of international fisheries and wildlife matters, there were several discussions between officials of our two Departments and an agreement was reached which, I believe, will accomplish this objective. This letter confirms the agreement.

It is my understanding that in the field of international fisheries and wildlife relations the Department of the Interior will keep the State Department advised at all times on the need for international action; will prepare on its own initiative or at the request of the State Department studies and reports on the foreign and domestic scientific and technological aspects and on the domestic economic, industrial and sports aspects of the problems; will recommend action which may be taken by the Department of State; and will advise the Department of State during international negotiations.

Since the Fish and Wildlife Service is staffed with specialists to obtain and analyze promptly and effectively information similar to that needed by the Department of State, it is agreed that there will be a substantial increase in emphasis by the Service upon keeping the Department of State informed on the need for international action and on investigating and reporting to the Department in preparation for negotiations or other international action. The effective performance of these functions by the Service will relieve the Department of such work of this character as it is presently performing. It is agreed that the Service should expand its consultation with American interests on international fisheries and wildlife matters and

its activity in making recommendations on actio which the Department may take on such problem

The Department of State will shortly reorgani the fisheries work of the Department. In this co nection, the Department anticipates confining i activities to the formulation and determination general policy on the conduct of internation fisheries and wildlife relations and expects to loo to other agencies for advice and guidance on oth phases of the problem. It will be necessary, course, for the Department to continue its prepar tion of the background work on pertinent dipl matic history and international law.

Representatives of the two Departments will, understand, meet immediately to develop plans f regularly constituted groups of industry and sta government representatives to advise the two D partments on international fisheries and wildli matters. Although the establishment of suc groups will not preclude the present practice consulting on particular problems with grou having a knowledge of and interest in such speci problems, the general groups will provide couns which our Departments would find difficulty obtaining by other means and which will aid of two Departments in the promotion of the gener welfare in this field.

It is recognized that there exists an excelle spirit of cooperation between the Fish and Wil life Service and the Department and that there a high degree of flexibility in meeting the vari problems of common concern. It is understo that this agreement is not intended in any degr to formalize the relations now existing betwe the two organizations or to formalize the mann of handling any particular problem. Thus, whi it is anticipated that the Department will, occasion requires, participate in planning studi and investigations which may be needed for inte national action and will consult, from time to tim directly with State officials, industry and spor representatives, and other interested and inform

PUBLICATIONS

Department of State

For sale by the Superintendent of Documents, Government Printing Office, Washington 25, D.C. Address requests direct to the Superintendent of Documents, except in the case of free publications, which may be obtained from the Department of State.

Parcel Post Service Within the Postal Union of the Americas and Spain. Treaties and Other International Acts Series 1681. Pub. 3044. 19 pp. 10¢.

Agreement, and Final Protocol, Between the United States and Other Governments—Signed at Rio de Janeiro September 25, 1946; entered into force January 1, 1947.

General Agreement on Tariffs and Trade. Vol. I. Commercial Policy Series 111. Pub. 3107. 82 pp. 25¢.

Final Act adopted at the conclusion of the Second Session of the Preparatory Committee of the United Nations Conference on Trade and Employment with the general clauses of the General Agreement on Tariffs and Trade and Protocol of Provisional Application of the Agreement.

Diplomatic List, April 1948. Pub. 3118. 189 pp. 20¢ a copy; $2.00 a year.

Monthly list of foreign diplomatic representatives in Washington, with their addresses.

Reciprocal Trade. Treaties and Other International Acts Series 1702. Pub. 3033. 5 pp. 5¢.

Agreement and Accompanying Letters Between the United States of America and Canada; rendering inoperative the agreement of November 17, 1938, and supplementing the general agreement on tariffs and trade of October 30, 1947—signed at Geneva October 30, 1947; entered into force October 30, 1947, effective January 1, 1948.

Restitution of Monetary Gold. Treaties and Other International Acts Series 1683. Pub. 3046. 5 pp. 5¢.

Protocol Between the United States of America, the United Kingdom of Great Britain and Northern Ireland, and France and Austria—signed at London November 4, 1947; entered into force November 4, 1947.

Fur Seals. Treaties and Other International Acts Series 1686. Pub. 3057. 2 pp. 5¢.

Agreement Between the United States of America and Canada; amending the provisional agreement of December 8 and 19, 1942—effected by exchange of notes signed at Washington December 26, 1947; entered into force December 26, 1947.

Exchange of Official Publications. Treaties and Other International Acts Series 1688. Pub. 3058. 3 pp. 5¢.

Agreement Between the United States of America and Sweden—effected by exchange of notes signed at Stockholm December 16, 1947; entered into force December 16, 1947.

Correction

In the BULLETIN of April 11, 1948, page 476, the footnote in the lefthand column should state that the address by Mr. Allen was made before the Overseas Press Club in New York rather than in Washington.

The Department of State bulletin

Vol. XVIII, No. 462 • Publication 3140

May 9, 1948

The Department of State BULLETIN,
a weekly publication compiled and
edited in the Division of Publications,
Office of Public Affairs, provides the
public and interested agencies of
the Government with information on
developments in the field of foreign
relations and on the work of the Department of State and the Foreign
Service. The BULLETIN includes
press releases on foreign policy issued
by the White House and the Department, and statements and addresses
made by the President and by the
Secretary of State and other officers
of the Department, as well as special
articles on various phases of international affairs and the functions of
the Department. Information is included concerning treaties and international agreements to which the
United States is or may become a
party and treaties of general international interest.

Publications of the Department, as
well as legislative material in the field
of international relations, are listed
currently.

uperintendent of Documents
. GoVernment Printing Office
Washington 25 ,D.C.

SUBSCRIPTION:
sues, $5; single copy, 15 cents

shed with the approval of the
: of the Bureau of the Budget

s of this publication are not
items contained herein may
Itation of the DEPARTMENT
ETIN as the source will be

rusalem

PHILIP C. JESSUP [1]

Resolution on Protection of Jerusalem*

The General Assembly,
Considering that the maintenance of order and security in Jerusalem is an urgent question which concerns the United Nations as a whole,
Resolves to ask the Trusteeship Council to study, with the Mandatory Power and the interested parties, suitable measures for the protection of the City and its inhabitants, and to submit within the shortest possible time proposals to the General Assembly to that effect.

---

* U.N. doc. A/543, Apr. 26, 1948; adopted by the General Assembly at its 132d Plenary Session on Apr. 26, 1948.

Greek Orthodox Church. These leaders, declaring themselves as representatives of "Religion, not of politics or of Government Policies," united in asking the leaders of Arabs and Jews "to establish a 'truce of God' which means a holy area of peace and freedom from violence in the City of Jerusalem . . . .".

The United States is not primarily concerned with the procedure by which we move on to deal with this question of Jerusalem but we believe we should act expeditiously. We welcome the amendment introduced by the Representative of

---

[1] Made in Committee 1 (Political and Security) of the Second Special Session of the General Assembly on Apr. 26, 1948, and released to the press by the U.S. Mission to the United Nations on the same date. Mr. Jessup is a member of the U.S. Delegation to the Special Session.

[2] France: Draft Resolution (U.N. doc. A/C.1/280, Apr. 22, 1948).
The First Committee
Considering that the maintenance of order and security in Jerusalem is an urgent question which concerns the United Nations as a whole,
Recommends the General Assembly,
to ask the Trusteeship Council to study and, in consultation with the Mandatory Power and the interested parties, take suitable measures for the protection of the City and its inhabitants.

Sweden to the original French proposal (document A/C.1/281)[3] because we hope that it will eliminate any controversy concerning procedure and enable work to begin at once upon the practical details of the plan.

As the Delegation of the United States declared in the debate on Friday, we hope that the proposal of France as amended by the Representative of Sweden, will be promptly approved, that we shall then return to the general debate, and that upon the conclusion of the general debate the committee will then proceed to deal specifically with the United States suggestion for dealing with Palestine as a whole.

Questions Involved in Concept of Trusteeship for Palestine

STATEMENT BY PHILIP C. JESSUP [4]

Since our first meeting a week ago the Committee has been discussing the question of the future government of Palestine as referred to it by the General Assembly. Many delegations have expressed their views on the plan of partition with economic union and others have spoken on a military and political truce and a temporary trusteeship for Palestine.

Meanwhile, the Mandatory for Palestine has reiterated its position that it will relinquish the Mandate on May 15th. The question now in everyone's mind is what governmental authority will succeed the Mandatory authority when the Mandate is relinquished. The plan of partition with economic union recommended by the General Assembly last November is not materializing in the form in which it was recommended. Both of the principal communities of Palestine have announced their intention of establishing states in that country upon the termination of the Mandate, unless irreconcilable conditions are met. Despite the action of the Security Council calling for an immediate cessation of hostilities, each day that passes reveals new acts of violence and threats of violence on an unprecedented scale. Since our paper was prepared, the Security Council has established a Truce Commission and this Committee has just requested the Trusteeship Council to make

a special study of measures to protect Jerusalem. These developments must, of course, be taken into account. In our opinion they could be helpful integrated in any temporary trusteeship administration. So the question still stands, What will the form and nature of the governmental authority in Palestine three weeks from today?

In the working paper circulated a week ago it was suggested that the Committee should consider the possibility of a United Nations trusteeship for Palestine on a temporary basis and with the United Nations itself as the administering authority. The views expressed thus far in the general debate indicate a general desire on the part of most members of the Committee to continue with substantive discussion of the trusteeship idea. We accordingly welcome such a discussion at this time before the Committee takes action on the United States draft resolution in document A/C.1/278.

I think it may be helpful to the Committee if I were to indicate what seem to us the principal questions involved in the concept of trusteeship for Palestine. Other questions may occur to other members of the committee.

At the outset may I recall that the suggestion of temporary trusteeship is a part of what Ambassador Austin called "a military and political standstill to save human life and to make possible further negotiations on a final political settlement". This idea of a standstill is reflected in the preamble to the draft agreement contained in the working paper. There it is stated that the General Assembly, in approving terms of trusteeship for Palestine, would be acting—and I quote the language of the preamble—"without prejudice to the rights, claims, or position of the parties concerned or to the character of the eventual political settlement." This general principle should be kept in mind in the Committee's consideration of specific parts of the question before us.

Every delegation in the Committee is interested in the arrangements suggested for securing a trusteeship. According to the working paper, the organization and direction of the police force

[3] Sweden: Amendment to Draft Resolution of France (U.N. doc. A/C.1/281, Apr. 23, 1948). The Swedish amendment called for deletion of words in brackets and addition of italicized words.

The First Committee
Considering that the maintenance of order and security in Jerusalem is an urgent question which concerns the United Nations as a whole,
Recommends the General Assembly,
To ask the Trusteeship Council to study [and, in consultation] with the Mandatory Power and the interested parties [take] suitable measures for the protection of the City and its inhabitants, and to submit within the shortest possible time proposals to the General Assembly to that effect.

[4] Made in Committee 1 (Political and Security) of the Second Special Session of the General Assembly on Apr. 27, 1948, and released to the press by the U.S. Mission to the United Nations on the same date. Mr. Jessup is a member of the U.S. Delegation to the Special Session.

of Palestine "in which there shall be no limitation on the sale, purchase, lease or use of land on grounds of race, nationality, community or creed". Are the principles in this statement of land policy just and equitable? The same article provided that the criteria upon which the land system shall be based shall be recommended to the governor-general by a commission of impartial experts neither Arab nor Jew. Does this provision of the draft agreement recommend itself?

It is important to consider the means of facilitating the economic and social development of Palestine. The United Nations Economic and Social Council, the specialized agencies related to it, and the Proposed Economic Commission for the Middle East, could be useful in this regard. In this connection the article of the draft trusteeship agreement dealing with external affairs should be considered. By article 35, the conduct of external affairs would be placed in the hands of the governor-general. This article also deals with the adherence by Palestine to international conventions and recommendations drawn up by the United Nations or by the specialized agencies referred to by article 57 of the Charter. The role of the Trusteeship Council in adhering to such conventions and recommendations is covered by the same article.

Are the provisions of article 35 appropriate for obtaining the maximum use of these United Nations agencies in developing the human and material resources of Palestine for the benefit of its inhabitants and of the world?

In considering these and other features of a temporary trusteeship for Palestine it will be helpful, I feel, to bear constantly in mind the primary responsibility of Jews and Arabs. In his address last Monday, the Representative of the United States said "that the primary responsibility for reaching a peaceful settlement of this problem rests upon the people of Palestine . . . We do not believe that the peoples of Palestine are entitled to appear before the United Nations to assert demands which must be accepted by the other party and the world community as the only alternative to war."

In a political sense, it is axiomatic that government cannot be established nor maintained without the cooperation of the governed. In saying this, the United States Delegation merely wishes to apply this general truth to the specific situation in Palestine. If a temporary trusteeship for Palestine is established the United States would anticipate the fullest possible measure of participation by Jews *and* Arabs in positions of the highest responsibility and trust within the central administration. The success or failure of a temporary trusteeship, or of any other form of government for Palestine, will turn upon the degree of cooperation existing among the various elements of the population.

Security Council Resolution on Establisl Commission for Palestine [1]

Referring to its resolution of 17 April 1948 calling upon all parties concerned to comply with specific terms for a truce in Palestine,

The Security Council

Establishes a Truce Commission for Palestine composed of representatives of those members of the Security Council which have career consular Officers in Jerusalem, noting, however, that the representative of Syria has indicated that his Government is not prepared to serve on the Commission. The function of the Commission shall be to assist the Security Council in supervising the implementation by the parties of the resolution of the Security Council of 17 April 1948;

United States Delegation to Second Spec

Representatives

Warren R. Austin, U.S. Representative at the Seat of the United Nations and Representative in the Security Council, Ambassador

Francis B. Sayre, U.S. Representative in the Trusteeship Council, Ambassador

Philip C. Jessup, Deputy Representative on the Interim Committee of the General Assembly

Alternate Representatives

Dean Rusk, Director, Office of United Nations Affairs, Department of State

John C. Ross, Deputy to the Representative at the Seat of the United Nations

Advisers

Frank P. Corrigan, Adviser on Latin American Affairs, U.S. Mission to the United Nations

Donald C. Blaisdell, Special Assistant to the Director, Office of United Nations Affairs, Department of State

William I. Cargo, Division of Dependent Area Affairs, Department of State

Benjamin Gerig, Deputy Representative in the Trusteeship Council; Chief, Division of Dependent Area Affairs, Department of State

Raymond A. Hare, Foreign Service officer; Chief, Division of South Asian Affairs, Department of State

John E. Horner, Office of European Affairs, Department of State

Gordon Knox, Adviser on Security Council and General Affairs, U.S. Mission to the United Nations

Samuel K. C. Kopper, Special Assistant to the Director,

[1] U.N. doc. S/727, Apr. 23, 1948. This Resolution was submitted by the U.S. Delegation and was adopted by the Security Council at its 287th meeting on Apr. 23, 1948. See also BULLETIN of Apr. 18, 1948, p. 515.

RINE F. LENROOT

the opening and closing sessions, were held. The commission's reports and the report of the resolutions committee, after approval in the plenary sessions, were incorporated in the final act, which was signed at the closing session. A copy of the final act was to be deposited with the Pan American Union and with the American International Institute for the Protection of Childhood and is to be published by the latter organization.

Each country invited to participate in the Congress had been advised by the Venezuelan Organizing Committee that it would be responsible for preparing a paper on one of the official topics in one of the four sections. To Argentina, for example, had been assigned the topic of organization and financing of maternal and child-health services; to Brazil and Bolivia, prevention of tuberculosis in childhood; to a group of Central American countries, symptoms of deficiency disease; all to be studied and discussed in *section I*. To the United States had been assigned the organization of social services for mothers and children; to Chile and Peru, the child under social security; to Uruguay, the care of the dependent child; to Venezuela, the children's code—all included in *section II*. Cuba, Ecuador, Colombia, Mexico, Costa Rica, and Panama shared responsibility for the five topics on the agenda of the section on education. All countries had the privilege of preparing "co-relatos" or joint reports on the major topics, and many of these joint reports were important documents which contributed greatly to the discussions.

Commission I reported on three recommendations. The first, dealing with organization and financing of maternal and child-health services, recognized the need for extension of such services in all American countries and recommended that these services be integrated with local public-health services; that sanitary units, health centers, or rural health stations be set up; that agencies which include health services in their programs (mental hygiene, dental health, nurseries, kindergartens, et cetera) work in close relationship and as a part of the maternal and child-health service; that the work of the generalized public-health nurse be recognized as the best for study and solution of matters affecting the health of mothers and children; that activity in the maternal and child-health field be adapted to available technical and economic resources, preference being given to

595

fundamental work in the field of child care; that maternal and child-health services be financed through participation of federal, state, and local and private contributions, in accordance with the characteristics of each country but with technical direction, centralized under a single command; and that services for care of sick children be closely related to the maternal and child-health service, preferably integrated with the local public-health service.

The second resolution, dealing with deficiency diseases, recommended greater protection of family life through extension of social insurance and family subsidies; creation of nutrition institutes for the study of food values and popular education; mass feeding; training of personnel for nutrition work; measures for increasing food production, reducing the cost of living, avoiding speculation and hoarding, adulteration of food products, and excessive advertising of dietary and food products. The resolution specifically recommended that the topic of child nutrition and diseases due to malnutrition be put on the program of the next Congress.

The third resolution of the Commission dealt with tuberculosis. It urged early discovery and isolation of cases; adoption of a resolution of the Twelfth Pan American Sanitary Conference concerning systematic and periodical mass examination by the Abreu method; intensification of preventive measures, including the raising of living standards, and B.C.G. vaccination in addition to, but not as a substitute for, recognized preventive measures; international cooperation of bacteriologists, physicians, and statisticians with a view to achieving greater uniformity in procedures for reporting, applying, and evaluating results of B.C.G. vaccination; and greater attention to control of bovine tuberculosis than is now given in some American countries.

Because of the great interest in the major topic assigned to the Venezuelan Delegation, namely, the children's code, the Technical Commission on Social Welfare and Legislation divided into two subcommissions, one to deal with this topic and the other with those pertaining to care of dependent children, organization of social services, and the child under social security. As revised by the Technical Commission and approved by the Congress, the code contains 20 separate headings and a brief preamble referring to the desirability of codifying laws relating to the protection of minors and recommending this proposed code to the American countries, subject to adaptation to the constitutional requirement and social and cultural conditions of each country. The full text of the code was included in the final act.

The eight-point recommendation submitted by the United States Delegation as part of its paper

A Costa Rican resolution urged the Institute to consider the problem of children who cross national frontiers, on their own initiative or at the instigation of others for reasons contrary to their interests.

The Institute was applauded for the cooperation it had given during the past year in connection with the organization of seminars on social work at Medellín, Colombia, and Montevideo, Uruguay, under the auspices of the United Nations. It was praised for the progress it had made in carrying out resolutions of the Eighth Pan American Child Congress dealing with inter-American cooperation and was directed to consult with the Pan American Union and with inter-American agencies operating in related fields as to the best way of carrying out resolutions and recommendations of the Ninth International Conference of American States relative to inter-American cooperation in matters pertaining to health, education, social services, and social insurance as they affect children. Recognizing the importance of the problem of nutrition and the efforts which international organizations are making to deal with it, both through the United Nations and various inter-American agencies, the Institute was asked to study ways in which the experience of the International Children's Emergency Fund of the United Nations, the Food and Agriculture Organization of the United Nations, and the Pan American Sanitary Bureau can serve to promote efforts to raise the level of child nutrition in the American countries. As for the resolution recommending support of the International Children's Emergency Fund, the Institute was entrusted with the responsibility of sending copies of the resolution to the Fund, to the United Nations, to the Pan American Union, to the American Governments, and to the agencies and press of the Continent.

All of these resolutions of an inter-American and international character, including the declaration of Caracas on child health, were reported to the Congress by Commission IV on Inter-American Cooperation. Others included in this group were a resolution recommending that the Ninth International Conference of American States, at its meeting at Bogatá, recognize the need of giving special attention to the protection of children and youth and the importance of inter-American cooperation in solving problems related to the health, welfare, and education of children and the training of personnel for work in these fields. This resolution also recommended that all American countries adhere to and support the work of the American International Institute for the Protection of Childhood.

In view of the fact that more adequate statistics will be needed to enable the American countries and agencies to carry out many of the resolutions of the Congress, a special resolution recommended that the agencies in each country responsible for taking the 1950 census arrange to obtain statistical data which will contribute to a knowledge of the real situation of the child in America. A copy of this resolution was to be sent to the American Statistical Institute for submission to the organizing committee for the 1950 census of the Americas which is scheduled to meet later in the year.

APPOINTMENT OF U.S. COMMISSIONERS ON THE SOUTH PACIFIC COMMISSION

The Secretary of State announced on April 28 that the President has appointed the United States Commissioners and Alternate Commissioners on the South Pacific Commission. The following persons have been appointed:

Senior Commissioner: Felix Keesing, professor of anthropology at Stanford University and an outstanding authority on the South Pacific
Commissioner: Milton Shalleck, lawyer of New York, with a distinguished record in law and government
Alternate Commissioner: Karl C. Leebrick, vice president of the University of Hawaii and an expert on Pacific affairs
Alternate Commissioner (for the first Commission meeting): Orsen N. Nielsen, American Consul General at Sydney, Australia, and U.S. Representative in the Interim Organization of the South Pacific Commission

The purpose of the South Pacific Commission is to facilitate international cooperation in promoting the social and economic advancement of the dependent peoples of the South Pacific. The Commission, while not an organic part of the United Nations, is expected to develop close relations with the United Nations and its specialized agencies. The South Pacific Commission, like the Caribbean Commission (established in 1942 as the Anglo-American Caribbean Commission), is a pioneer venture in regional cooperation among governments responsible for the administration of dependent areas.

The Governments which will participate in the work of the mission are those of Australia, France, the Netherlands, New Zealand, the United Kingdom, and the United States. By action of the President on January 28, 1948, the agreement establishing the South Pacific Commission was accepted on behalf of the United States Government.[1]

The Commission, assisted by a Research Council and periodical conferences of representatives of the local inhabitants, has a great opportunity to render an important service both to the member governments and to the people in the region.

---

[1] BULLETIN of Feb. 15, 1948, p. 214.
[2] For article on the Institute, see BULLETIN of Nov. 9, 1947, p. 891.

Morgan Heiskell, European Representative, Paris

MACKAY RADIO AND TELEGRAPH COMPANY

Leroy F. Spangenberg, Vice President, New York, N. Y.

RCA COMMUNICATIONS, INC.

Glen McDaniels, Vice President and General Attorney, New York, N. Y.

John H. Muller, Assistant to Executive Vice President, New York, N. Y.

WESTERN UNION TELEGRAPH COMPANY

K. Bruce Mitchell, Director, International Communications, New York, N. Y.

Marion M. Newcomer, Manager, Western Union Telegraph Company in Germany, Frankfurt

The Sixth Meeting of the Committee has been called jointly by the International Telecommunication Union and the Government of Belgium to study technical questions relating to telegraphy and to formulate recommendations for the solution of these problems.

Invitations to attend the forthcoming meeting have been sent to member governments of the International Telecommunication Union and to private companies and international organizations interested in the subject matter.

U.S. DELEGATION TO INTERNATIONAL TIN STUDY GROUP

[Released to the press April 16]

The United States acted as host to the Second Meeting of the International Tin Study Group, which convened April 19–23, 1948, in Washington. The address of welcome was delivered by Willard L. Thorp, Assistant Secretary of State.

The Tin Study Group is composed of 14 members which have primary interest in the production or consumption of tin. The Group maintains a permanent secretariat with headquarters at The Hague.

The United States Delegation is headed by Donald D. Kennedy, Chief, Division of International Resources, Department of State, assisted by the following:

Advisers

George Jewett, Associate Director, Office of Metals Reserve, Reconstruction Finance Corporation

Erwin Vogelsang, Chief, Tin and Antimony Section, Metals Division, Department of Commerce

Carl N. Gibboney, International Commodity Arrangements Adviser, Department of Commerce

Charles Merrill, Chief, Metal Economics Branch, Bureau of Mines, Department of the Interior

Fred Bartlett, U.S. Embassy, London

Carl Ilgenfritz, Vice President, United States Steel Corporation

Secretary

Virginia D. Karchere, Division of International Resources, Department of State

THE RECORD OF THE WEEK

Treaty of Economic, Social and Cultural Collaboration and Collective Self-Defence

BETWEEN GREAT BRITAIN AND NORTHERN IRELAND, BELGIUM, FRANCE, LUXEMBOURG, AND THE NETHERLANDS

Brussels, 17th March, 1948

His Royal Highness the Prince Regent of Belgium, the President of the French Republic, President of the French Union, Her Royal Highness the Grand Duchess of Luxembourg, Her Majesty the Queen of the Netherlands and His Majesty The King of Great Britain, Ireland and the British Dominions beyond the Seas,

Resolved

To reaffirm their faith in fundamental human rights, in the dignity and worth of the human person and in the other ideals proclaimed in the Charter of the United Nations;

To fortify and preserve the principles of democracy, personal freedom and political liberty, the constitutional traditions and the rule of law, which are their common heritage;

To strengthen, with these aims in view, the economic, social and cultural ties by which they are already united;

To co-operate loyally and to co-ordinate their efforts to create in Western Europe a firm basis for European economic recovery;

To afford assistance to each other, in accordance with the Charter of the United Nations, in maintaining international peace and security and in resisting any policy of aggression;

To take such steps as may be held to be necessary in the event of a renewal by Germany of a policy of aggression;

To associate progressively in the pursuance of these aims other States inspired by the same ideals and animated by the like determination;

Desiring for these purposes to conclude a treaty for collaboration in economic, social and cultural matters and for collective self-defence;

Have appointed as their Plenipotentiaries:

His Royal Highness the Prince Regent of Belgium
    His Excellency Mr. Paul-Henri Spaak, Prime Minister, Minister of Foreign Affairs, and

---

¹ Great Britain. Cmd. 7367. Miscellaneous No. 2 (1948).

His Excellency Mr. Gaston Eyskens, Minister of Finance,

The President of the French Republic, President of the French Union
    His Excellency Mr. Georges Bidault, Minister of Foreign Affairs, and
    His Excellency Mr. Jean de Hauteclocque Ambassador Extraordinary and Plenipotentiary of the French Republic in Brussels,

Her Royal Highness the Grand Duchess of Luxembourg
    His Excellency Mr. Joseph Bech, Minister of Foreign Affairs, and
    His Excellency Mr. Robert Als, Envoy Extraordinary and Minister Plenipotentiary of Luxembourg in Brussels,

Her Majesty the Queen of the Netherlands
    His Excellency Baron C. G. W. H. van Boetzelaer van Oosterhout, Minister of Foreign Affairs, and
    His Excellency Baron Binnert Philip van Harinxma thoe Slooten, Ambassador Extraordinary and Plenipotentiary of the Netherlands in Brussels,

His Majesty the King of Great Britain, Ireland and the British Dominions beyond the Seas for the United Kingdom of Great Britain and Northern Ireland
    The Right Honourable Ernest Bevin, Member of Parliament, Principal Secretary of State for Foreign Affairs, and
    His Excellency Sir George William Rendel K.C.M.G., Ambassador Extraordinary and Plenipotentiary of His Britannic Majesty in Brussels,

who, having exhibited their full powers found in good and due form, have agreed as follows:

ARTICLE I

Convinced of the close community of their interests and of the necessity of uniting in order to

affecting in any way the authority and responsibility of the Security Council under the Charter to take at any time such action as it deems necessary in order to maintain or restore international peace and security.

ARTICLE VI

The High Contracting Parties declare, each so far as he is concerned, that none of the international engagements now in force between him and any other of the High Contracting Parties or any third State is in conflict with the provisions of the present Treaty.

None of the High Contracting Parties will conclude any alliance or participate in any coalition directed against any other of the High Contracting Parties.

ARTICLE VII

For the purpose of consulting together on all the questions dealt with in the present Treaty, the High Contracting Parties will create a Consultative Council, which shall be so organized as to be able to exercise its functions continuously. The Council shall meet at such times as it shall deem fit.

At the request of any of the High Contracting Parties, the Council shall be immediately convened in order to permit the High Contracting Parties to consult with regard to any situation which may constitute a threat to peace, in whatever area this threat should arise; with regard to the attitude to be adopted and the steps to be taken in case of a renewal by Germany of an aggressive policy; or with regard to any situation constituting a danger to economic stability.

ARTICLE VIII

In pursuance of their determination to settle disputes only by peaceful means, the High Contracting Parties will apply to disputes between themselves the following provisions:

The High Contracting Parties will, while the present Treaty remains in force, settle all disputes falling within the scope of Article 36, paragraph 2, of the Statute of the International Court of Justice by referring them to the Court, subject only, in the case of each of them, to any reservation already made by that Party when accepting this clause for compulsory jurisdiction to the extent that that Party may maintain the reservation.

In addition, the High Contracting Parties will submit to conciliation all disputes outside the scope of Article 36, paragraph 2, of the Statute of the International Court of Justice.

In the case of a mixed dispute involving both questions for which conciliation is appropriate and other questions for which judicial settlement is appropriate, any Party to the dispute shall have the right to insist that the judicial settlement of the legal questions shall precede conciliation.

The preceding provisions of this Article in no way affect the application of relevant provisions or agreements prescribing some other method of pacific settlement.

ARTICLE IX

The High Contracting Parties may, by agreement, invite any other State to accede to the present Treaty on conditions to be agreed between them and the State so invited.

Any State so invited may become a Party to the Treaty by depositing an instrument of accession with the Belgian Government.

The Belgian Government will inform each of the High Contracting Parties of the deposit of each instrument of accession.

ARTICLE X

The present Treaty shall be ratified and the instruments of ratification shall be deposited as soon as possible with the Belgian Government.

It shall enter into force on the date of the deposit of the last instrument of ratification and shall thereafter remain in force for fifty years.

After the expiry of the period of fifty years, each of the High Contracting Parties shall have the right to cease to be a party thereto provided that he shall have previously given one year's notice of denunciation to the Belgian Government.

The Belgian Government shall inform the Governments of the other High Contracting

COMMUNIQUÉ ON FIRST MEETING OF THE

The French Foreign Office published the following communiqué on the meeting of signatories to the Brussels treaty

April 18, 1948

The five Foreign Ministers of the signatory powers of the treaty of Brussels meeting Paris April 17, 1948 in consultative council according to Article 7 agreed on the following provisions to insure application of accord of March 17:

1. The permanent consultative council is composed of the five Ministers of Foreign Affairs. The council will meet in each of the capitals of the signatory states in turn each time that such a meeting appears necessary and at least once every three months.

2. The permanent organ of the council will be constituted by diplomatic representatives in London of Belgium, France, Luxembourg, Netherlands and designated representative of the British Government. It will be assisted by a secretariat. It will meet at least once a month.

' Printed from telegraphic text.

nearly 35 percent and in imports, about 11 percent. For most other countries, the figures are in reverse order of magnitude. Thus, in very brief summary, is pictured the world disequilibrium of today.

Never have our own exports and imports been so seriously out of balance. Never before have American products been needed so badly, yet never has the means with which to purchase them been so inadequate. Largely through the medium of the extension of grants, credits, and the liquidation of foreign gold reserves and dollar assets, American goods have moved in this great quantity but the present pattern, necessary as it is for immediate economic progress, cannot be long maintained. To be sure, the gap between commodity exports and imports is never identical with the financial elements in the balance of payments. However, in the long run, the invisible items cannot possibly begin to meet an unbalanced situation such as the present. In fact, our position as a creditor nation, a state which is steadily becoming greater as we extend more and more credit and as foreign assets in the United States are liquidated, points increasingly to the necessity of bringing commodity exports and imports more nearly into line. Our American foreign policy must be based on these fundamental economic facts.

The European Recovery Program has been discussed largely in terms of the extent to which exports to western Europe from the Western Hemisphere are necessary for the economic operation and recovery of these war-devastated areas. However, the fundamental economic objective of the European Recovery Program is the reestablishment of the ability of European countries to support themselves without outside assistance. The fact is that Europe, and particularly western Europe, is a workshop and must import materials and export finished goods in order to live. The report of the Committee on European Economic Co-operation recorded last summer the intention of the member countries to increase their exports to the United States in the course of the next four years from an estimated 848 million dollars in 1948–49 to 1,484 million dollars in 1951–52. Greater increases were planned for other areas of the world so as to reestablish the prewar pattern which made it possible for Europe to live. The

[1] Address made before the National Council of American Importers in New York City on Apr. 22, 1948, and released to the press on the same date.

estimates for European exports to the United
States which have been presented to the appropriations committees by the Executive branch of the
Government are somewhat higher, namely 1,587
million dollars for 1948–49 (measured at July 1,
1947, prices). The comparable figure for 1947
was 1,279 million dollars and the target for
1951–52, a most uncertain estimate of course, is
2,759 million dollars. These new figures are on a
different basis from the CEEC estimates, since they
include western Germany as well as substantial
quantities of raw materials such as rubber and tin
from colonies and dependencies of the 16 countries.

European exports to the United States are of
particular importance at the moment because payments are made in dollars, which may be used anywhere in the world as needed. Europe used to
export more substantially to other parts of the
world, which in turn frequently earned their capacity to pay Europe in dollars by exporting to the
United States in greater volume than they imported from us. Europe also had a substantial
invisible income from these other sources. However, the non-European countries which used to
transfer dollars to Europe in such quantities are
now also in trouble with respect to trade with the
United States, i.e., they also have import surpluses,
and are unable to do an adequate job of financing
even their own dollar needs. Hence, they are reluctant to pay Europe in dollars or other convertible currency. The salvation of European countries in terms of self-support cannot immediately
be achieved by means of exports to non-European
areas outside the United States. However, one of
the more hopeful aspects of the situation is the
expectation that the deficit between the European
countries and countries outside the Western Hemisphere will change to a surplus after about two
years, and the triangular process of balancing payments can be gradually resumed.

It therefore becomes clear that importing by the
United States of increased quantities of goods
from Europe is one step which can assist the
Europeans in achieving their recovery objectives.
It is equally clear that American imports from
other parts of the world which trade with Europe
are of similar consequence in terms of European
recovery. In a general economic sense, as we increase our imports from any part of the world,
we make it more possible for other countries to
recover their equilibrium and to make further
progress.

This is the determinant of our immediate and
short-run foreign economic policy. Our imbalance of trade is so great that we must finance
the deficit, not to keep ourselves going, but to enable other countries to obtain absolute necessities
for their consumers and their recovery. Our objective should be not to get accustomed to this
sort of arrangement ourselves, nor allow our
friends abroad to get accustomed to it. It is

as possible. High tariffs are inconsistent with our position as a creditor nation. We have made significant progress along this line since the enactment of the reciprocal trade agreements act in 1934. The most recent major step in this direction was, of course, the signature of the general agreement on tariffs and trade at Geneva in 1947, with the consequent duty reductions which were put into effect on January 1 of this year. The charter recently initialed in Geneva provides the long-run program for permitting the expansion of trade by the reduction of trade barriers.

But all these conditions of which I have been speaking are not enough to meet the problem. Goods do not move of their own accord. The American importer is the hero in the piece. Traditionally, our major efforts in foreign trade have been oriented in the direction of our exports, and too little attention has been directed toward increasing our purchases from other countries. The well-known American skill in salesmanship must be brought into play to show the American people the desirability of acquiring goods from abroad. Many products of European countries are highly desirable for consumers in the United States. There is great importance in the possibilities of increased imports of raw materials and industrial goods from European countries and their dependencies. The future health of our foreign trade, as well as our ability to benefit from our creditor position, depends primarily upon our imports and our importers.

It is true that foreign goods in various lines compete with our own products, but our system is one which has always believed that competition is the life of trade, and it is clear that if we do not buy other people's exports, they will not be able to buy ours. The European Recovery Program has been called a calculated risk, and the United States has accepted this risk as a major feature of foreign policy. To the extent that we buy goods produced by other countries in increasing quantities, so that we enable other countries to gain in their ability to support themselves, we reduce the element of risk in our foreign economic operations. Nor is it enough to call it a reduction of risk. It is also the path to the expansion of trade with the concurrent promise of rising standards of living both at home and abroad.

Address on Reciprocal Trade Agreements

On April 16 Winthrop G. Brown, Acting Director, Office of International Trade Policy, Department of State, made an address on reciprocal trade agreements and their effects on imports before the Import Session of the Third Mississippi Valley World Trade Conference in New Orleans; for the text of this address, see Department of State press release 293 of April 16, 1948.

International Wheat Agreement Transmitted to the Senate

MESSAGE OF THE PRESIDENT TO THE SENATE

To the Senate of the United States:

With a view to receiving the advice and consent of the Senate to ratification, I transmit herewith, in certified form, the International Wheat Agreement,[1] in the English and French languages, which was open for signature in Washington from March 6, 1948 until April 1, 1948 and was signed, during that period, by representatives of this Government and the governments of 35 other countries.

The purpose of the Agreement, described in greater detail in the enclosed report of the Secretary of State and letter from the Acting Secretary of Agriculture, is to provide supplies of wheat to importing countries and to assure markets to exporting countries at equitable and stable price.

In view of the fact that the Agreement requires formal acceptance by the signatory governments by July 1, 1948, I urge that the Senate give the Agreement the earliest possible consideration.

HARRY S. TRUMAN

THE WHITE HOUSE,
April 30, 1948.

(Enclosures: (1) Report by the Secretary of State; Letter from the Acting Secretary of Agriculture.)

REPORT OF THE SECRETARY OF STATE

April 29, 1948

THE PRESIDENT:

The undersigned, the Secretary of State, has the honor to lay before the President, with a view to its transmission to the Senate to receive the advice and consent of that body to ratification, if his judgment approve thereof, a certified copy of the International Wheat Agreement which was open for signature in Washington from March 6, 1948 until April 1, 1948 and was signed, during that period, by representatives of the Government of the United States of America and representatives of the Governments of 35 other countries.

The Agreement is the result of approximately fifteen years of negotiation in an effort to conclude an agreement providing a framework within which there might be stabilized the greatest possible portion of the international wheat trade. Negotiations reached a successful conclusion at the Special Session of the International Wheat Council held in Washington from January 28, 1948 until March 6, 1948.

The objectives of the Agreement, as set forth in Article I thereof, are "to assure supplies of wheat to importing countries and to assure markets to exporting countries at equitable and stable prices." In general the Agreement is in the nature of a multilateral contract requiring member exporting countries to supply designated quantities of wheat to member importing countries, when requested to do so by those importing countries, at the maxi-

mum prices established in the Agreement and, conversely, requiring member importing countries to purchase designated quantities of wheat from member exporting countries, when requested to do so by those exporting countries, at the minimum prices established in the Agreement. The market which the Agreement assures to United States producers of wheat should eliminate to a great extent the serious disadvantages to those producers which are the result of bilateral contracts between other exporting countries and certain of the importing countries signatory to the Agreement. The number and coverage of such bilateral contracts, moreover, undoubtedly would have been increased if the Agreement had not been negotiated.

It is believed that in addition to assuring markets, at guaranteed prices, to exporting countries for a substantial portion of the exportable wheat production of those countries, thus encouraging the maintenance of production during the current cereals shortage, the Agreement will have the effect, by assuring importing countries of designated quantities of wheat at specified prices, of encouraging those countries whose cost of wheat production is relatively high to meet a larger part of their requirements with imported wheat and, accordingly, to plan their agricultural production with a view to increased diversification of crops and employment of land resources to greater advantage.

The Agreement, in accordance with the provisions of Article XXII thereof, is to remain in force for a five-year period. Provision is made in

[1] See *Documents and State Papers*, May 1948, pp. 102–111.

Department of State Bulletin

in effect during the next wheat-marketing year, to provide, in Article XX, that instruments of acceptance of the Agreement be deposited no later than July 1, 1948 by all Governments except those of importing countries which are prevented by a recess of their respective legislatures from accepting the Agreement by that date. In order to bring the Agreement into force on the part of the United States it is necessary, therefore, that the United States instrument of acceptance be deposited by July 1, 1948. Accordingly it is recommended that the Senate be requested to give consideration to the Agreement at the earliest opportunity.

Respectfully submitted,

G. C. MARSHALL

HEAT AGREEMENT

provides for the reporting to the Council by a country which fears that it may be prevented by circumstances from fulfilling its obligations under the Agreement; for a finding by the Council as to whether that country's representations in this connection are well-founded; and, if so, for an adjustment in the obligations in question, through the voluntary assumption of those obligations by other contracting countries, if this is possible, and, if it is not, through a reduction by the Council, on a pro rata basis, of the quantities in the appropriate annex to Article II.

Article VI establishes the following minimum and maximum prices for the duration of the Agreement for no. 1 Manitoba Northern wheat in store at Fort William or Port Arthur:

	Minimum	Maximum
1948/49	$1.50	$2.00
1949/50	1.40	2.00
1950/51	1.30	2.00
1951/52	1.20	2.00
1952/53	1.10	2.00

The Article provides further that during the last three years of the five-year period during which the Agreement is to remain in force the price range may be narrowed, within the minimum and maximum limits, by the Council by a two-thirds majority of the votes held by the exporting and importing countries voting separately.

There are established in Article VI formulas for determining the price equivalents for no. 1 Manitoba Northern wheat in store in Vancouver, f. a. q. wheat f. o. b. Australia, no. 1 Hard Winter wheat f. o. b. Gulf/Atlantic ports of the United States, and no. 1 Soft White/no. 1 Hard Winter wheat f. o. b. Pacific ports of the United States. Article VI provides also that the Executive Committee, in consultation with the Standing Technical Advisory Committee on Price Equivalents, established by Article XV, may determine the price equivalents for other descriptions of wheat.

Article VII authorizes the Council, upon request by a member country, to use its good offices in facilitating transactions in wheat in amounts in addition to those provided for elsewhere in the Agreement.

Article VIII authorizes any exporting country to export wheat at special prices for use in nutritional programs that are approved by the Food and Agriculture Organization, provided the wheat is exported under conditions that are approved by the Council, it being understood that the Council will not give its approval unless it is satisfied that the full commercial demand of the importing countries will be met throughout the period in question at not more than the minimum price.

Article IX provides that the minimum stockholdings of the exporting countries shall be as follows, subject to the proviso that stocks may be permitted to fall below these figures if the Council decides that this is necessary in order to provide the quantity of wheat needed to meet either the domestic requirements of the exporting countries or the import requirements of the importing countries:

Australia . . . 25 millions of bushels (excluding farm
     stocks).
Canada . . . 70 millions of bushels (excluding farm
     stocks).
United States . 170 millions of bushels (including farm
     stocks).

This Article further places an obligation upon exporting and importing countries to operate price-stabilization reserves up to 10 percent of their guaranteed export and import quantities, respectively.

Article X sets forth the areas to which the Agreement applies with respect to each contracting country.

Article XI establishes an International Wheat Council, provides that each contracting government shall be a member thereof, and makes provision for such administrative matters as frequency of meetings, election of officers, and rules of procedure.

Article XII provides for the distribution among importing and exporting countries of votes in the Council on the basis of the quantities of wheat which those countries have guaranteed to purchase or sell under the Agreement.

Article XIII requires the Council to perform the duties assigned to it under the Agreement and confers on the Council such powers in addition to those expressly conferred upon it as may be necessary to achieve its effective operation and to realize its objectives. Article XIII provides also for the settlement by the Council of any dispute arising out of the interpretation of the Agreement or regarding an alleged breach of its provisions.

effective upon its acceptance by importing countries which hold a simple majority of the votes of the importing countries (including the Government of the United Kingdom) and by acceptance by the Governments of Australia, Canada, and the United States; that any government not accepting the amendment may withdraw from the Agreement at the end of the current crop year; and that any contracting government which considers its national security endangered by the outbreak of hostilities may withdraw from the Agreement upon the expiry of 30 days' written notice to the Council.

SECRETARY OF AGRICULTURE
TARY OF STATE

tices, have also helped our wheat growers to reach this goal of organized and realistic abundance. But the problem posed by the production level achieved in this effort involves ways and means of gaining our further objective of *sustained* abundance. ·.

The problem is particularly significant in the large specialized areas of the Pacific Northwest and the Great Plains. In these areas, crop shifts are limited and full employment of agricultural resources involves production of considerable quantities of wheat in excess of normal domestic needs. Measured in terms of acreage, the United States has at present several million acres producing wheat for export or for non-food uses other than feed and seed. The impact of this acreage holds in large measure the key to the well-being of American agriculture. Markets which the proposed Agreement helps to assure, however, would absorb this excess and would minimize the need for considering costly restrictions on the production of wheat in the United States for several years to come.

Our stake in the world wheat market is important. The average annual value of United States exports of wheat and flour during the past 25 years exceeds 200 million dollars or nearly 14 percent of the total value of exports of agricultural products during that period. We all remember the effects of economic developments in many of our formerly important foreign markets for wheat during the decade of the thirties. It was during this period that a natural tendency towards self-sufficiency developed in many of the principal importing countries of Europe by increasing domestic production of bread grains. This development was accompanied, in turn, by increasing trade barriers and restrictions that resulted in

(Continued on page 611)

General Agreement on Tariffs and Trade

The President issued on April 22 a proclamation putting into effect as of April 21, 1948, the provisions of the general agreement on tariffs and trade with respect to Czechoslovakia.[1] The proclamation implements an obligation entered into by this Government last October 30 when the general agreement was concluded at Geneva with 22 other countries.

The attitude of the Government of the United States towards the events of last February in Czechoslovakia was publicly indicated in the joint statement of February 26, 1948, by the Secretary of State of this Government and by the Foreign Ministers of the Governments of the United Kingdom and France. It has not changed. These events, however, do not directly affect the legal status of the reciprocal obligations under the general agreement.

The President's action followed receipt of a communication from the Secretary-General of the United Nations informing this Government that the Government of Czechoslovakia had signed the protocol of provisional application of the general agreement and had thereby obligated itself to put the general agreement into effect. Since Czechoslovakia has now placed the general agreement in effect with respect to the United States and the other contracting parties, this country as well as the other contracting parties are obligated to apply the agreement to Czechoslovakia.

It is part of a world-wide program, sponsored by the United Nations and actively participated in by the United States, designed to reduce trade barriers and to restore international trade to an orderly and stable basis. It is the most comprehensive agreement with respect to tariffs and other trade barriers ever negotiated.

Czechoslovakia is the tenth of the Geneva countries to give effect to this agreement. The other countries which have done so, in addition to the United States, are the United Kingdom, France, Belgium, the Netherlands, Luxembourg, Canada, Australia, and Cuba. The remainder of the 23 participants in the negotiations have until June 30, 1948, to put the agreement provisionally into effect. The obligations assumed by Czechoslovakia under this agreement and those assumed by other countries to Czechoslovakia are integral parts of the agreement.

Under the general agreement, Czechoslovakia grants concessions on products of interest to the

---

[1] *13 Fed. Reg.* 2211.

Income Tax Convention With the Netherlands Signed

[Released to the press April 29]

A convention between the United States and the Netherlands for the avoidance of double taxation and the prevention of fiscal evasion with respect to taxes on income and certain other taxes was signed at Washington on April 29, 1948, by Secretary Marshall and E. N. van Kleffens, Netherlands Ambassador in Washington.

Statement by Secretary Marshall

[Released to the press April 29]

Mr. Ambassador, the signing of this treaty represents the culmination of a long period of negotiations.

Double taxation upon the same income is a major obstacle to international trade. When this treaty enters into force, that obstacle will be eliminated to a very large extent as between our two countries. The nationals and corporations of both countries will benefit.

It has been a pleasure for me to join with you in signing the treaty.

The provisions of the convention are similar in general to those contained in conventions now in force between the United States and the United Kingdom, Canada, France, and Sweden.

The convention provides that it shall be ratified and that it shall become effective on January 1 of the year last preceding the year in which the instruments of ratification are exchanged.

Mexican Housing Authority Visits U.S.

Adolfo Zamora, Managing Director of the Banco de Fomento de la Habitación, S.A., of Mexico, D.F., arrived in Washington April 10 for a series of conferences with the officials of the Housing and Home Finance Agency. Mr. Zamora is visiting this country as the recipient of a grant-in-aid from the Department of State under the program administered by the Division of International Exchange of Persons for the interchange of specialists and professors with the other American republics. His visit is being planned in cooperation with the Housing and Home Finance Agency. After two weeks in Washington he expects to spend some time in New York studying further the housing program as it is administered in the United States. He is particularly interested in the problems of finance, administration, and organization of the program.

Status of Civil Aviation Documents as of April 1, 1948

DATES OF SIGNATURES

Country	Final Act	Interim Agreement	Convention	Transit Agreement (Two Freedoms)	Transport Agreement (Five Freedoms)
Afghanistan	[1]S	S	S	S	S
Australia	S	S	S	7/4/45	
Belgium	S	4/9/45	4/9/45	4/9/45	
Bolivia	S	S	S	S	S
Brazil	S	5/29/45	5/29/45		
Canada	S	S	S	2/10/45	
Chile	S	S	S	S	
China	S	S	S		S
Colombia	S	5/24/45	10/31/47		
Costa Rica	S	3/10/45	3/10/45	3/10/45	3/10/4
Cuba	S	4/20/45	4/20/45	4/20/45	4/20/4
Czechoslovakia	S	4/18/45	4/18/45	4/18/45	
Dominican Republic	S	S	S	S	S
Ecuador	S	S	S	S	S
Egypt	S	S	S	S	
El Salvador	S	5/9/45	5/9/45	5/9/45	5/9/4
Ethiopia	S	3/22/45	2/10/47	3/22/45	3/22/4
France	S	S	S	S	
Greece	S	S	S	S	
Guatemala	S	1/30/45	1/30/45	1/30/45	1/30/4
Haiti	S	S	S	S	S
Honduras	S	S	S	S	S
Iceland	S	S	S	4/4/45	4/4/4
India	S	S	S	S	
Iran	S	S	S	S	8/13/4
Iraq	S	S	S	S	
Ireland	S	S	S		
Lebanon	S	S	S	S	²S
Liberia	S	S	S	S	S
Luxembourg	S	7/9/45	7/9/45	7/9/45	
Mexico	S	S	S	S	S
Netherlands	S	S	S	S	³S
New Zealand	S	S	S	S	
Nicaragua	S	S	S	S	S
Norway	S	1/30/45	1/30/45	1/30/45	
Panama	S	5/14/45			
Paraguay	S	7/27/45	7/27/45	7/27/45	7/27/4
Peru	S	S	S	S	S
Philippines	S	S	S	S	
Poland	S	S	S	S	
Portugal	S	S	S		
Spain	S	S	S	S	
Sweden	S	S	S	S	S
Switzerland	S	S	7/6/45	7/6/45	
Syria	S	S	7/6/45	⁴7/6/4	
Turkey	S	S	S	S	⁵S
Union of South Africa	S	6/4/45	6/4/45	6/4/45	

Country	Final Act	Interim Agreement	Convention	Transit Agreement (Two Freedoms)	Transport Agreement (Five Freedoms)
d Kingdom	S	S	S	⁶ S	
d States	S	S	S	S	S
ıay	S	S	S	S	S
ːuela	S	⁷ S	. . . . .	⁷ S	⁷ S
¡lavia	S	. . . . .	. . . .	. . . .	. . . .
h Minister	S	S	S	S	S
Minister	S	S	S	S	S

ɛservation accompanying signature of the *United lom:* "I declare that, failing later notification of ion, my signature to this Agreement does not cover ɔundland". (Reservation withdrawn by United lom Feb. 7, 1945.)
ɛservation accompanying signature of *Venezuela:*

"La Delegación de Venezuela firma *ad referendum* y deja constancia de que la aprobación de este documento por su Gobierno está sujeta a las disposiciones constitucionales de los Estados Unidos de Venezuela." (Interim, transit, and transport agreements accepted by Venezuela Mar. 28, 1946.)

SUBSEQUENT ACTION TAKEN

Country	Interim Agreement (Date of Acceptance)	Convention ¹ (Date of Deposit of Ratification or Adherence)	Transit Agreement (Date of Receipt of Note of Acceptance)	Transport Agreement (Date of Receipt of Note of Acceptance)
anistan	5/16/45	4/ 4/47	5/17/45	² 5/17/45
ıtina	6/ 4/46	ᴬ 6/ 4/46	6/ 4/46	
·alia	5/19/45	3/ 1/47	8/28/45	
um	4/17/45	5/ 5/47	7/19/45	
ia	5/17/46	4/ 4/47	4/ 4/47	4/ 4/47
ıl	5/29/45	7/ 8/46	. . . .	
ːda	12/30/44	2/13/46	2/10/45	
	6/ 4/45	3/11/47	. . . .	
a	6/ 6/45	2/20/46	. . . .	³ 6/ 6/45
nbia	6/ 6/45	10/31/47	. . . .	
ı Rica				
	6/20/47	. . . . .	6/20/47	
hoslovakia	4/18/45	⁴ 3/ 1/47	4/18/45	
nark	11/13/45	2/28/47	. . . .	
inican Republic	1/25/46	1/25/46	. . . .	⁵ 1/25/46
ɖor				
ɔt	4/26/45	3/13/47	3/13/47	
ɪlvador	5/31/45	6/11/47	6/ 1/45	6/ 1/45
ɔpia	3/22/45	3/ 1/47	3/22/45	3/22/45
ce	6/ 5/45	3/25/47	. . . .	
ce	9/21/45	3/13/47	9/21/45	⁶ 2/28/46

ʰhe convention entered into force Apr. 4, 1947.
ndicates adherence.
.fghanistan denounced the International Air Trans-Agreement Mar. 18, 1948; effective Mar. 18, 1949.
ɪeservation accompanying acceptance of *China:* "The ɔtances are given with the understanding that the isions of Article IV Section 3 of the International ʈransport Agreement shall become operative in so far ɪe Government of China is concerned at such time as ɔonvention on International Civil Aviation . . . shall ıtified by the Government of China." (Chinese instru-t of ratification of the Convention on International ˡ Aviation deposited Feb. 20, 1946. China denounced International Air Transport Agreement Dec. 11, 1946; ːtive Dec. 11, 1947.)
ʰhe Ambassador of *Czechoslovakia* made the following ɛment in the note transmitting the Czechoslovak in-ment of ratification: "The Czechoslovak Ambassador

wishes to bring to the attention of His Excellency that the Convention on International Civil Aviation was ratified by the President of the Czechoslovak Republic on the assumption that the International Civil Aviation Organization will carry out fully the resolution passed by the United Nations Organization on December 12, 1946 concerning the exclusion of the Franco Spain from coopera-tion with the United Nations".
⁵ The *Dominican Republic* denounced the International Air Transport Agreement Oct. 14, 1946; effective Oct. 14, 1947.
⁶ Reservation accompanying acceptance of *Greece:* "In accepting this Agreement [transport] in accordance with Article VIII, paragraph two thereof, I am directed to make a reservation with respect to the rights and obligations contained in Article I, Section 1, paragraph (5) of the Agreement, which, under Article IV, Section 1, Greece does not wish, for the time being to grant or receive."

Country	Interim Agreement (Date of Acceptance)	Convention[1] (Date of Deposit of Ratification or Adherence)	Transit Agreement (Date of Receipt of Note of Acceptance)	Transport Agreement (Date of Receipt of Note of Acceptance)
Guatemala	4/28/47	4/28/47	4/28/47	
Haiti	6/ 2/45	3/25/48		
Honduras	11/13/45		11/13/45	11/13/5
Iceland	6/ 4/45	3/21/47	3/21/47	
India	[7]5/ 1/45	3/ 1/47	[7]5/ 2/45	
Iran	12/30/46			
Iraq	6/ 4/45	6/ 2/47	6/15/45	
Ireland	4/27/45	10/31/46		
Italy		[8]10/31/47		
Lebanon	6/ 4/45			
Liberia	3/17/45	2/11/47	3/19/45	3/19/5
Luxembourg	7/ 9/45			
Mexico	5/22/45	6/25/46	6/25/46	
Netherlands	1/11/45	3/26/47	1/12/45	[9]1/12/5
New Zealand	[10]4/18/45	3/ 7/47	[10]4/19/45	
Nicaragua	12/28/45	12/28/45	12/28/45	[11]12/28/5
Norway	1/30/45	5/ 5/47	1/30/45	
Pakistan		[A]11/ 6/47	[12]8/15/47	
Panama				
Paraguay	7/27/45	1/21/46	7/27/45	7/27/5
Peru	5/ 4/45	4/ 8/46		
Philippines	3/22/46	3/ 1/47	[13]3/22/46	
Poland	4/ 6/45	4/ 6/45	4/ 6/45	
Portugal	5/29/45	2/27/47		
Siam	3/ 6/47	4/ 4/47	3/ 6/47	3/ 6/7
Spain	7/30/45	3/ 5/47	7/30/45	
Sweden	7/ 9/45	11/ 7/46	11/19/45	11/19/5
Switzerland	7/ 6/45	[14]2/ 6/47	7/ 6/45	
Syria	7/ 6/45			
Transjordan	3/18/47	[A]3/18/47	3/18/47	
Turkey	6/ 6/45	12/20/45	6/ 6/45	[15]6/ 6/5
Union of South Africa	11/30/45	3/ 1/47	11/30/45	
United Kingdom	[16]5/31/45	3/ 1/47	[16]5/31/45	
United States	2/ 8/45	8/ 9/46	2/ 8/45	[17]2/ 8/5
Uruguay				
Venezuela	3/28/45	[A]4/ 1/47	3/28/46	3/28/6
Yugoslavia				

A indicates adherence.

[7] Reservation accompanying acceptance of *India:* "In signifying their acceptance of these agreements [interim and transit], the Government of India . . . do not regard Denmark or Thailand as being parties thereto . . . ". (Reservation respecting Denmark on interim agreement withdrawn by India July 18, 1946. Reservation respecting Siam on transit agreement withdrawn by India June 6, 1947.)

[8] The participation of *Italy* effected in accordance with the provisions of Article 93 of the convention and resolution of May 16, 1947, by Assembly of ICAO. Effective Nov. 30, 1947.

[9] Reservation accompanying acceptance of the *Netherlands:* " . . . the signatures . . . affixed to the . . . International Air Transport Agreement (with reservation set forth in Article IV Section 1) constitute an acceptance . . . by the Netherlands Government and an obligation binding upon it." (Reservation relinquished by the Netherlands Sept. 21, 1945.)

[10] Reservation accompanying acceptance of *New Zealand:* " . . . the New Zealand Government does not regard Denmark or Thailand as being parties to the Agreements mentioned [interim and transit] . . . ". (Reservation respecting Denmark on interim agreement withdrawn by New Zealand Apr. 29, 1946.)

[11] *Nicaragua* denounced the International Air Transport Agreement Oct. 7, 1946; effective Oct. 7, 1947.

[12] The Ambassador of *Pakistan* informed the Secretary of State by note no. F 96/48/1 of March 24, 1948 " . . . that by virtue of the provisions in Clause 4 of the Schedule of the Indian Independence (International Arrangemen) Order, 1947, the International Air Services Transit Agreement signed by United India continues to be binding after the partition on the Dominion of Pakistan." The acceptance by India on May 2, 1945, of the transit agreement applied also to the territory, then a part of India, which later, on Aug. 15, 1947, became Pakistan.

[13] Reservation accompanying acceptance of the *Philippines:* "The above acceptance is based on the understanding . . . that the provisions of Article II, Section 2 of the International Air Services Transit Agreement shall become operative as to the Commonwealth of the Philippines at such time as the Convention on International Civil Aviation shall be ratified in accordance with the Constitution and laws of the Philippines." (Philippine instrument of ratification of the Convention on International Civil Aviation deposited Mar. 1, 1947.)

[14] The Minister of *Switzerland* made the following statement in the note transmitting the Swiss instrument of ratification: "My government has instructed me to notify you that the authorities in Switzerland have agreed

(Continued on next page)

eorganization of the Public Affairs Area

(a) The Department announced on April 22 the
)llowing organization changes in the area under
ıe jurisdiction of the Assistant Secretary—Pub-
c Affairs, effective as of April 22, 1948:

(1) The Office of Information and Educational
xchange (OIE) is abolished.

(2) The Office of International Information,
ıe Office of Educational Exchange, and an
xecutive Staff are established.

(3) The organization units and special assist-
ıts previously reporting to the Assistant Secre-
ıry—Public Affairs or the Office of Information
ıd Educational Exchange will be under the fol-
)wing jurisdiction:

Office of International Information: Program
oordinator (now acting as Chief of Staff for the
ınternational Policy Programming Staff (IPPS);
pecial Assistant for Freedom of Information;
pecial Assistant for Interdepartmental Informa-
on Coordination; Special Assistant for Interde-
artmental information Planning; Special As-
stant for Utilization of Private Information
Iedia; Division of International Broadcasting;
)ivision of International Motion Pictures; Divi-
on of International Press and Publications.

Office of Educational Exchange: Secretariat of
ıe Interdepartmental Committee on Scientific
ınd Cultural Cooperation; Division of Libraries
ınd Institutes; Division of Exchange of Persons
including the Special Assistant for the Fulbright
rogram).

Executive Staff: Area Divisions (RPD); all
)ecial assistants and staff of the immediate office
f the Assistant Secretary—Public Affairs except
ıs noted below.

(4) No change will be made in the organization
of the Office of Public Affairs (PA) and the
UNESCO Relations Staff.

(b) The following Officers are hereby designated to assume responsibility in the key positions
listed below in an acting capacity, other existing
appointments remaining unchanged until further
notice:

(1) Director, Office of International Information (OII)—William T. Stone; Executive Officer—Parker May.

(2) Director, Office of Educational Exchange
(OEX)—Kenneth Holland; Executive Officer—
(to be announced later; pending such announcement, all OEX Executive Officer functions will be
carried out by the OII Executive Officer).

(3) Director, Executive Staff—Leland Barrows.

Assistant Secretary—Public Affairs

(a) *Purpose.* To advise and assist the Secretary in the development and implementation of
United States foreign policy with respect to programs for international information and educational exchange and to domestic programs designed to inform the American public concerning
foreign relations.

(b) *Major functions.* The Assistant Secretary,
in coordinating and supervising the activities of
the offices under his supervision, performs the following functions:

(1) Plans and develops the information and
educational exchange policies of the Department.

(2) Directs the relations of the Department of

(Continued from preceding page)

ıith the authorities in the Principality of Liechtenstein
ıat this Convention will be applicable to the territory of
ıe Principality as well as to that of the Swiss Con-
ıderation, as long as the Treaty of March 29, 1923 inte-
rating the whole territory of Liechtenstein with the
ıwiss customs territory will remain in force."
ıⁱ Reservation accompanying acceptance of *Turkey:*
ı . . . the reservation made by the Turkish Delegation
ın the fifth freedom of the air contained in the Inter-
ıtional Air Transport Agreement is explained in the
)llowing article of the law by which the aforementioned
ıstruments have been ratified: 'The Turkish Government,
ıhen concluding bilateral agreements, shall have the
ıuthority to accept and apply for temporary periods the
rovision regarding the fifth freedom of the air contained
ı the International Air Transport Agreement.' "
ıˢ Reservation accompanying acceptance of the *United
:ingdom:* "In signifying their acceptance of the said

Agreement [interim and transit], the Government
of the United Kingdom . . . neither regard the Governments of Denmark and Siam as being parties
thereto . . .". (Reservation respecting Denmark on
interim agreement withdrawn by United Kingdom Mar.
30, 1946.)
ıⁱ Reservation accompanying acceptance of the *United
States:* "These acceptances by the Government of
the United States of America are given with the
understanding that the provisions of Article II, Section 2,
of the International Air Services Transit Agreement and
the provisions of Article IV, Section 3, of the International
Air Transport Agreement shall become operative as to
the United States of America at such time as the Convention on International Civil Aviation . . . shall be ratified by the United States of America". (The United States
of America denounced the International Air Transport
Agreement July 25, 1946; effective July 25, 1947. United
States instrument of ratification of the Convention on
International Civil Aviation deposited Aug. 9, 1946.)

State with other Federal agencies on all matters of international information and educational exchange policies.

(3) Stimulates and facilitates the activities of public and private information and educational exchange agencies in the foreign field and services domestic private and public agencies as they deal with foreign relations.

(4) Insures that the programs and policies recommended by the United States Advisory Commissions on Information and Educational Exchange are considered in the development and execution of the international information and educational exchange program; insures that the Secretary of State's responsibilities are discharged with respect to the National Commission for UNESCO, the Board of Foreign Scholarships, and other advisory boards and commissions.

(c) *Organization.* The Assistant Secretary, assisted by a deputy, directs the work of the UNESCO Relations Staff, the Office of Public Affairs, the Office of International Information, the Office of Educational Exchange, and an Executive Staff.

(1) The Deputy Assistant Secretary is authorized to take all necessary action relating to international programs for information and educational exchange and to domestic programs designed to inform the American people concerning foreign relations.

(a) Such delegation of authority does not extend to any duties or functions which, under existing law, can only be exercised by the Secretary of State or by an Assistant Secretary of State in his behalf. In the absence of the Assistant Secretary—Public Affairs, such duties are performed by the Assistant Secretary—Political Affairs, or, in his absence, the Assistant Secretary—Economic Affairs.

(b) Such delegation of authority is exercised under the general direction and control of the Assistant Secretary—Public Affairs, or during his absence, the Secretary of State.

(c) Such delegation of authority does not affect any delegation of authority to any subordinate officials below the rank of Assistant Secretary of State.

(d) *Relationships with other agencies.* The Assistant Secretary serves as—

(1) Chairman of the Interdepartmental Committee on Scientific and Cultural Cooperation.

(2) A member of the Board of Directors of the Institute of Inter-American Affairs.

Office of International Information

(a) *Purpose.* To support United States foreign policy by giving foreign peoples a true pic-

agement units of the Department, to insure that over-all management policies and methods of the Department are applied in the Offices under the Assistant Secretary's jurisdiction.

(b) *Major functions.*

(1) Prescribes and insures the effective execution of a system of field and departmental reporting and a system of program evaluation; maintains Congressional liaison, under the auspices of the Office of the Counselor, and prepares any necessary reports for the Secretary, the Congress, and the general public.

(2) Prescribes and insures the application of a system of administrative reports for the Offices under the jurisdiction of the Assistant Secretary; maintains liaison, on behalf of the Assistant Secretary and the Deputy, with the Office of Foreign Service and the several offices of the Assistant Secretary—Administration; directs the internal administration and procedures of the immediate Office of the Assistant Secretary and Deputy Assistant Secretary—Public Affairs; coordinates and reviews for the Assistant Secretary the preparation of the annual budgets for the Offices under the jurisdiction of the Assistant Secretary.

(3) Maintains liaison with the geographic offices of the Department and provides regional guidance to the Office of International Information and the Office of Educational Exchange; in collaboration with the appropriate administrative divisions of the Department, and with the concurrence of the two previously named offices, has responsibility for, (a) initiating and processing requests concerning foreign service personnel actions and administrative services for the program overseas, (b) preparation of the budget for foreign activities.

(c) *Organization.* The Director of the Executive Staff is responsible to the Assistant Secretary and the Deputy Assistant Secretary—Public Affairs. The Director's Staff includes officers responsible for activities in the following fields: Reports and Evaluation; Administrative Coordination and Liaison; Regional Program Guidance.

Edward W. Beattie, Jr., Will Head News Operations of International Broadcasting Division

George V. Allen, Assistant Secretary of State for Public Affairs, announced on April 29 the appointment of Edward W. Beattie, Jr., as head of the news operations of the State Department's International Broadcasting Division.

Mr. Beattie, a veteran of 15 years of service with the United Press, will assume his new duties immediately with headquarters in New York City (224 West 57th Street). He will direct all news operations for the broadcasts of the Voice of the United States of America.

John H. Hilldring Appointed as Special Assistant for Palestine Affairs

[Released to the press April 28]

John H. Hilldring, former Assistant Secretary of State for occupied areas, on April 28 accepted appointment as Special Assistant to the Secretary of State for Palestine Affairs.

General Hilldring served as Assistant Secretary of State for occupied areas from April 17, 1946, until his resignation on August 31, 1947. He was appointed an adviser to the United States Delegation to the Second Session of the General Assembly of the United Nations on September 10, 1947, and four days later was appointed an alternate representative on the Delegation, in which capacity he was a principal spokesman for this Government on matters pertaining to the Palestine question. His services terminated on December 2, 1947.

THE FOREIGN SERVICE

Teaching of Arabic in Foreign Service Institute

[Released to the press May 1]

The Foreign Service Institute, which for the past year has gone all out to provide overseas personnel with instruction in some three dozen languages so as to make them more useful in representing American political and economic interest abroad, has launched a course in a real "toughie"—Arabic.

Five officers of the Foreign Service, selected from among those desiring to specialize in Near Eastern affairs, are working eight hours a day with native speakers of Arabic, seeking to imitate and master the un-English sounds which some day they will use in communicating with the peoples of Syria, Lebanon, Iraq, Saudi Arabia, Egypt, and other Arabic-speaking areas. In the course, which will last six months, the officers concentrate on the spoken language, with the objective of speaking Arabic as the Arab speaks it. By September it is expected that they will be well along in conversational Arabic, and they should be able to carry on talks in the language and make sense of what they hear in the streets of Damascus, Jidda, Baghdad, or Cairo.

In this new course, the textbook is tossed out the window. Dr. Charles Ferguson, 26-year-old Philadelphian who supervises the instruction, is applying the new techniques and insights developed by modern linguistic science and uses his own scientific transcriptions. His students won't see an alphabet until the course is three fourths completed. Nor will there be much in the way of writing, since his theory is that "language is the

Department of State

For sale by the Superintendent of Documents, Government Printing Office, Washington 25, D.C. Address requests direct to the Superintendent of Documents, except in the case of free publications, which may be obtained from the Department of State.

Health and Sanitation: Cooperative Program in Venezuela. Treaties and Other International Acts Series 1661. Pub. 2988. 13 pp. 5¢.

> Agreement Between the United States of America and Venezuela Extending Agreement of February 18, 1943, as amended, until June 30, 1948—Effected by Exchange of Notes Signed at Caracas June 30, 1947; entered into force June 30, 1947, effective January 1, 1947.

Settlement of Certain War Accounts and Claims. Treaties and Other International Acts Series 1675. Pub. 3027. 5 pp. 5¢.

> Agreement and Accompanying Notes Between the United States of America and Czechoslovakia—Signed at Praha July 25, 1947; entered into force July 25, 1947.

Headquarters of the United Nations. Treaties and Other International Acts Series 1677. Pub. 3038. 5 pp. 5¢.

> Interim Agreement Between the United States of America and the United Nations—Signed at Lake Success, New York, December 18, 1947; entered into force December 18, 1947.

Exchange of Money Orders. Treaties and Other International Acts Series 1682. Pub. 3045. iii, 35 pp. 15¢.

> Agreement, and Final Protocol, Between the United States of America and Other Governments—Signed at Rio de Janeiro September 25, 1946; Ratified and Approved by the Postmaster General of the United States of America February 20, 1947; Approved by the President of the United States of America February 27, 1947; entered into force January 1, 1947.

National Commission News, May 1, 1948. Pub. 3120. 10 pp., 10¢ a copy; $1 a year; foreign subscription $1.35 a year.

> Prepared monthly for the United States National Commission for the United Nations Educational, Scientific and Cultural Organization.

World Health Organization—Progress and Plans. International Organization and Conference Series IV, World Health Organization 1. Pub. 3126. 23 pp. 15¢.

> A study of the World Health Organization, at the time of its becoming a specialized agency of the United Nations; an article on its progress and future plans, its constitution; an intergovernmental arrangement on the establishment of an interim commission; and a selected bibliography.

Address by the Secretary of State Before the Second Plenary Session of the Ninth International Conference of American States, Bogotá, Colombia, April 1, 1948. International Organization and Conference Series II, American Republics 2. Pub. 3139. 14 pp. Free.

Contributors

Katharine F. Lenroot, author of the article on the Ninth Pan American Child Congress, is Chief of the Children's Bureau, Social Security Administration, Federal Security Agency. Miss Lenroot served as Chairman of the United States Delegation to the Congress.

The Department of State bullet

VOL. XVIII, No. 463 • PUBLICA

May 16, 1948

The Department of State BU
a weekly publication comp
edited in the Division of Pub
Office of Public Affairs, pro
public and interested age
the Government with infor
developments in the field o
relations and on the work o
partment of State and the
Service. The BULLETIN
press releases on foreign poli
by the White House and the
ment, and statements and
made by the President an
Secretary of State and othe
of the Department, as well
articles on various phases
national affairs and the fun
the Department. Informati
cluded concerning treaties
ternational agreements to u
United States is or may b
party and treaties of gener
national interest.

Publications of the Depart
well as legislative material in
of international relations, a
currently.

Superintendent of Documents
. Government Printing Office
Washington 25, D.C.

SUBSCRIPTION:
ssues, $5; single copy, 15 cents

shed with the approval of the
r of the Bureau of the Budget

s of this publication are not
items contained herein may
itation of the DEPARTMENT
ETIN as the source will be

RGE C. MARSHALL [1]

of State

ment of the United Nations machinery would not in itself solve the problem. Since the most important of the peace settlements have not been agreed upon, the United Nations has been compelled to carry on its activities under world conditions far different from those contemplated by the Charter.

It was obvious to the framers of the Charter of the United Nations that an effective organization to preserve the peace must include every major power. The San Francisco conference created an organization, the purposes and principles of which corresponded with the objectives of the United States foreign policy. The organization as developed at San Francisco received the overwhelming endorsement of the American people and had the virtually unanimous approval of the United States Senate.

This organization was designed to consolidate and strengthen over a long period of time the foundations of peace through common action in solving political, economic, social, cultural, and health problems. Machinery was established for the settlement of international disputes by peaceful means so that the advice and assistance of all members, and the mobilization of world public opinion, might be brought to bear in the pacific settlement of disputes. It was found possible to go considerably farther than the League of Nations in the establishment of enforcement machinery, but at the San Francisco conference none of the major powers was prepared to grant to this organization the right of enforcement against a major power.

When universal agreement to the Charter was achieved, the strength of the major powers in relation to one another was such that no one of them could safely break the peace if the others stood united in defense of the Charter. Under existing

---

[1] Made before the House Foreign Affairs Committee on May 5, 1948, and released to the press on the same date.

world circumstances the maintenance of a comparable power relationship is fundamental to world security.

The aspirations of the people of the world as set forth in the Charter of the United Nations have been shaken by developments since the summer of 1945. It gradually became apparent that the postwar conditions anticipated at San Francisco were not being realized. The failure of concerted action by the major Allies rendered it necessary for the United States Government to attempt to create the desired postwar conditions in cooperation with other states willing to do so.

It became progressively clearer that serious misconceptions prevailed in the minds of the leaders of the Soviet Union concerning western civilization and the possibilities for developing stabilized working relations between the Soviet Union and the other members of the community of nations. It is a misconception to suppose that domination of the world by a single system is inevitable. It is a misconception to suppose that differing systems cannot live side by side in peace under the basic rules of international conduct prescribed by the Charter of the United Nations. These rules are obligatory upon all members.

A fundamental task of the United Nations and of our foreign policy is to dispel the misconceptions of the Soviet leaders and to bring about a more realistic view of what is possible and what is impossible in the relationship between the Soviet Union and the world at large. In this way there can be restored to international society the equilibrium necessary to permit the United Nations to function as contemplated at San Francisco.

Our realization of the need for this equilibrium has led to action along several lines, all designed to create conditions favorable to the working of the United Nations. The first necessary step was to insure the freedom and independence of the members. The ability of democratic peoples to preserve their independence in the face of totalitarian threats depends upon their determination to do so. That determination in turn depends upon the development of a healthy economic and political life and a genuine sense of security.

Therefore, the United States Government is responding to requests to provide economic assistance to various countries in Europe and elsewhere. The United States is cooperating with 16 European countries in a recovery program providing for self-help and mutual aid.

The United States Government is now considering the steps necessary to bring the national military establishment to the minimum level necessary to restore the balance of power relationships required for international security.

The United States is acutely aware that the return of a sense of security to the free nations of the world is essential for the promotion of con-

task of recovery. What is needed for the achievement of a world order based on law and dedicated to peace and progress is a widespread improvement in the material and social well-being of the peoples of the world. The responsibility for such improvement will always rest primarily upon the peoples and governments themselves. In this field the United Nations, however, can play an increasingly active role.

The factor of military strength is of immediate and major importance in the present world situation, but is not the element which will be paramount in the long run. The emphasis often placed solely on the military aspects of world affairs does a disservice to the cause of peace. The more that present differences are talked about and treated exclusively as a military problem, the more they tend to become so.

The problems today presented to those who desire peace are not questions of structure. Nor are they problems solvable merely by new forms of organization. They require performance of obligations already undertaken, fidelity to pledges already given. Basic human frailties cannot be overcome by Charter provisions alone, for they exist in the behavior of men and governments.

The suggestion that a revised United Nations, or some form of world government, should be achieved, if necessary, without those nations which would be unwilling to join, deserves special attention. Such a procedure would probably destroy the present United Nations organization. The result would be a dispersal of the community of nations, followed by the formation of rival military alliances and isolated groups of states. This result would weaken us and expose us to even greater dangers from those who seek domination of other states.

It is not changes in the *form* of international intercourse which we now require. It is to changes of *substance* that we must look for an improvement of the world situation. And it is to those changes of substance that our policy has been directed. When the substance of the world situation improves, the United Nations will be able to function with full effectiveness. Meanwhile we will continue our efforts in cooperation with other governments to improve the working of the United Nations under the Charter.

The United Nations was created after years of study and after many months of difficult negotiations. It now has 58 members. It is the symbol of the aspirations of mankind. Its success is the hope of mankind. All new efforts to attain order and organization in the affairs of men require time to grow roots in the loyalties of men. The history of our own people testifies to this necessity. Let us not in our impatience and our fears sacrifice the hard-won gains that we now possess in the United Nations organization.

I am deeply moved by the desire to strengthen the United Nations that is demonstrated by the Congress in calling these hearings. Earnest and continuing support of the United Nations is clearly needed in a world which has suffered two devastating wars in 25 years, which faces the danger (which is filled with fear) of a third, and in which over half the people are both hungry and illiterate.

Building peace and security in such a world is a tremendous job. Fortunately, the work of securing agreement among sovereign nations on the plan for an international organization to maintain peace was begun while a majority of them were united in fighting a common enemy.

Structure of the United Nations

The men who wrote the Charter at Dumbarton Oaks and San Francisco realized that an international organization formed to preserve the peace must include every major power in its membership, with no exceptions. That was true in 1945; it is true today. To attain that goal, each member had to pay a price. Each had to yield on some of its own desires as to the shape of the Organization and to accommodate itself to the wishes of others.

The Charter which resulted clearly defined the effort which would be required if the peoples of the world were to find the peace, the freedom, and the decent living which they earnestly sought.

The first task was the removal of the causes of war.

The Charter was framed to combine the efforts of the members of the United Nations in creating the conditions of peace through joint action.

The second task was to substitute for war pacific settlement of disputes.

The third task was to insure collective security by peace forces voluntarily agreed upon by members.

Assuming that the numerous and varied efforts of the Congress, of state legislatures, of towns and cities, as well as of important civic organizations, recognize the need for the United Nations and are intended to strengthen it—then there must be a reconciliation among them and with the members of the United Nations which is based on reality. It goes without saying that such a reconciliation cannot occur if the purpose is something else. If the purpose should be to discredit the United Nations as impotent or to dissolve it in order to try erecting a new organization with its rubble, there cannot be reconciliation.

---

[*] Made before the House Foreign Affairs Committee on May 5, 1948, and released to the press on the same date.

forward toward all reasonable measures for strengthening the capacity of the United Nations to perform its second task.

Chapter VI, "Pacific Settlement of Disputes," is by far the most important part of the Charter. Experience in the United Nations with disputes, "the continuance of which is likely to endanger the maintenance of international peace and security", leads to the judgment that we should stay within chapter VI just as long as it is humanly possible to do so.

The frailty in the Security Council to which I wish to point is one of procedure. We have encountered a misuse of the veto. It is in chapter VI, where we seek to substitute for war the great principle of agreement, that the misuse of the veto has caused skepticism, criticism, and search for improvement. Right here it is necessary to reconcile with the facts the efforts at strengthening the United Nations.

The Soviet Union has exercised the veto 23 times—eleven times on membership applications, nine times on issues of pacific settlement, and three times on the Balkan issue.

It is not true that the United Nations has failed because of this veto. On the contrary, it has succeeded in spite of the veto, as I will demonstrate. However, it is true that the United Nations could expedite its service and accomplish more effective solutions of disputes and situations if the veto privilege were not permitted to interfere with pacific settlement of disputes.

I wish to persuade you, from the facts. Your earnest work toward strengthening the United Nations is encouraging because of the influence which your views may have upon the adoption of improved practices and procedures within the Charter. When it becomes feasible to amend the Charter in respect of chapter VI, as well as in respect of admission of new members, the strong position you will have taken in criticism of this frailty should prove to be of great assistance to the members of the United Nations. That time has not arrived, as I will point out.

Now, first let me show what has actually happened in the use of the United Nations to substitute pacific solutions for war.

1. The Security Council succeeded in inducing the Soviet Union to withdraw its troops from the territory of Iran.

2. The withdrawal of British and French troops from Syria and Lebanon was a result of a Security Council expression of strong views.

3. The Security Council has helped to protect the political independence and territorial integrity of Greece, even though the Soviet Union three times vetoed efforts to deal with the situation. Twice the vetoes overcame a majority of nine, which supported resolutions finding that assistance to and support of guerrillas on the northern bor-

ders of Greece constituted a threat to the peace within the meaning of chapter VII of the Charter. The third veto was on a resolution requesting the General Assembly to make recommendations in the Greek case. The veto failed in its purpose; it did not bar all United Nations service for peace. The Security Council merely divested itself of the subject, and the General Assembly, five weeks later, passed a resolution calling upon Albania, Bulgaria, and Yugoslavia to do nothing which could furnish assistance to the guerrillas.

The General Assembly also established the Balkan Commission with headquarters at Salonika to observe the compliance with the recommendations and to assist in implementing them. These recommendations outlined specific methods for settlement of their disputes by peaceful means. This Balkan Commission is now at work on the ground. The tremendous moral effect of surveillance by all of the rest of the world is now being witnessed.

The United Nations certainly has upset the timetable of the aggression of Communism in Greece. The United Nations is helping Greece in her struggle for freedom. The United States in cooperation with the United Nations has helped Greece to preserve her independence.

4. Indonesia was another situation, the continuance of which might have led to a threat to international security and peace. War had already begun between the Dutch and Indonesians, but the Security Council was able to obtain a truce. Moreover, a Good Offices Committee was set up, which helped to determine lines of demarcation between the forces and to obtain agreement on 18 principles to guide the setting up of the United States of Indonesia. Progress is now being made on the basis of those principles. This was an achievement which involved the peace and security of a population equal to half of that of the United States. In addition, one of the great consequences of the pacific settlement of this dispute is to give strength to the movement away from the old colonial system toward self-government and independence. This movement is of critical importance to a vast area both in Asia and Africa. We find it involved indirectly in the next item—India-Pakistan.

5. India and Pakistan brought their dispute over Kashmir to the Security Council with representations that, if the conditions continued, war of communal intensity might break out all over the subcontinent. Four hundred million inhabitants of the newly established free dominions of India and Pakistan were on the verge of war. If the United Nations had not been available to them, the conditions, now bad enough, would certainly have been much worse by this time.

Their case was kept within chapter VI. Prolonged, difficult negotiations were tried without agreement between the parties; whereupon the Security Council adopted recommendations for a

Council consideration of the coup in Czechoslovakia is a good example. This entire proceeding has been conducted in the face of Soviet veto threats. But their threats cannot halt the Council's examination of evidence. If and when the veto occurs, the evidence will become part of the record.

Changes Are Needed

Notwithstanding t h e s e accomplishments, changes are needed. There are ways of working for them within the Charter.

Vigorous efforts are under way now to improve the machinery of the United Nations for the pacific settlement of disputes.

The United States was largely responsible for the establishment of the Interim Committee of the General Assembly. This Little Assembly, as it is generally known, is now studying a number of proposals aimed toward strengthening the machinery for the pacific settlement of disputes. Moreover, it is working on a series of suggestions to restrict the application of the veto and liberalize the voting procedures of the Security Council. The results of this work will be taken up at the next regular session of the General Assembly in September.

I believe that this distinguished Committee has a copy of a provisional list of Security Council decisions which the United States proposes should be made by an affirmative vote of seven members whether or not such decisions are regarded as procedural or non-procedural. Your views touching this effort could stimulate it. They would strengthen us in our efforts to obtain what is really needed : agreement among the permanent members that such voting procedures could be followed and the establishment of these voting procedures by rules.

This approach has a chance of success, it is realistic, and it recognizes the one essential in building a genuine system of collective security—Big Power unity.

No abandonment of universality should be tolerated. There is no real security without universality. We must not tear down this powerful buttress of the world organization. Instead; the structure should be braced on the inside.

East and West Relations the Core

The core of the world-security problems is the relationship between the East and the West. Since the end of the war, the rift between these two powerful groups has gradually widened. No matter what the machinery, no matter how stringent the Charter limitations, the operators of the machinery would still be the member states. If these states will observe the obligations contained in the present Charter and cooperate within the present framework of the Organization, its gravest problems will be solved.

Creation of additional machinery would not affect the basic political situation with which we are confronted. What is necessary is a fundamental adjustment between East and West. This will have to be undertaken at the suitable time.

The fact that in the short span of its existence, the United Nations has not been able to solve this basic problem has profoundly affected the thinking of many members of Congress and of some of our most forward-looking civic leaders and organizations. But I have yet to find a single radical revision of the United Nations Charter which could, as a practical matter, be adopted at this time by any appreciable number of states and which, if adopted, would solve that crucial problem which is at the basis of present world insecurity. The most likely result of revision, under the present circumstances, would be the destruction of the United Nations.

U.N.—The Bridge Between East and West

The end of the United Nations would lead to the complete destruction of the political, economic, social, and technical activities of the United Nations. The present effectiveness of these activities stems to a great degree from the fact that all major powers and an overwhelming majority of other states take part in the organization. Once this relative universality of membership is destroyed, such collaboration as now exists would cease, and a complete break between the East and the West would occur. The only possible bridge between the East and West would collapse; and yet, the problem of bridging the gap between the East and West is precisely the crucial problem of our time.

The U.S. and the U.N.

Meanwhile, the United Nations affords us an equal opportunity to mobilize world opinion and action against activities which threaten peace and security. It provides an unsurpassed forum for explaining our policies to other states and peoples and for mobilizing their support. It serves as an instrument of negotiation with other powers. It permits the United States to act in concert with other powers in carrying out enterprises which this country could not or would not undertake unilaterally. It is the outstanding instrumentality for solving economic and social problems, safeguarding human rights and fundamental freedom, and improving the welfare of all the peoples. It is and should continue to be the cornerstone of our foreign policy.

Since the desire of the overwhelming majority of the American people is the strengthening of the United Nations, what, then, is the best course to pursue?

Nations is ready to begin construction. The "world capital" foreseen by Congress in 1945 can at last become a permanent physical reality.

No Political Strings to Hospitality

Through all this period, the United States has scrupulously refrained from attaching political conditions to its hospitality. We did not ask that the United Nations should take this or that course, or develop in a particular direction, or amend its Charter, or revise its organizational structure, before it could establish its headquarters in this country. We invited the United Nations to these shores in the full knowledge of its possible limitations. We had signed and ratified the Charter. We did not "buy a pig in a poke". (See the 723 pages of hearings before the Committee on Foreign Relations, U.S. Senate, 79th Congress, 1st session.)

Now, however, the loan is associated with the Ferguson–Judd resolution. The implication is that until certain actions such as the calling of a special session of the General Assembly to debate a particular problem, or until the United Nations is reorganized so as to perform more effectively certain of its political functions, the loan may be retarded.

If the Congress should now take the view that we should not proceed with the loan agreement or begin construction of the headquarters until these things were done, a heavy blow would be struck both at the organization and at the sincerity and prestige of the United States. It would be unfortunate if other members of the United Nations should feel that we were attempting to use our financial resources in this case to achieve a political end. It would be equally unfortunate if they were to feel that we had so little faith in the United Nations that we were unwilling to make this demonstration of our support.

Provisions of the Loan

It is proposed that we lend the organization a sum not to exceed 65 million dollars. This will be repaid from the ordinary budget of the United Nations, to which we now contribute 39.89 percent of the total. What we would actually be advancing beyond our own proportionate share of the cost, therefore, is the balance over 60 percent of the principal of the loan. We would also, of course, in effect be making a gift to the United Nations of some 60 percent of the interest which might have been earned had the money been invested in some other enterprise.

It will be clear to the Congress, I am certain, that there is no feasible alternative to financing the construction of the headquarters by a loan.

Ordinarily it would have been desirable to raise the necessary funds through immediate cash contributions by all member states. But at this particular juncture, when so many are struggling to recover from the devastation of war and when all must contend with a critical shortage of dollar exchange abroad, dollar payments on the scale required would have imposed a very heavy burden on many states. Some would certainly have felt that, since the money was to be spent in this country, the United States might reasonably have been expected to make a higher proportionate contribution toward the cost of the buildings than it makes to the ordinary budget of the United Nations.

In my opinion, such an arrangement would have been most unfortunate. We have directed our efforts in the United Nations toward a reduction in our general budget quota. Our offer of an interest-free loan forestalled any suggestion that we should pay a disproportionate share of the construction costs.

Other Alternatives Surveyed

A number of possibilities for financing were explored before the United States consented to enter into the loan agreement. Arrangements for private financing would have been far from satisfactory. Under the most favorable terms, a large part of the total cost would still have had to be contributed in cash. The interest rate quoted was high. It would have been necessary to mortgage the buildings as security—a step which would have involved serious legal problems and which would have required legislative action by State and possibly Federal authorities. The plans themselves would have had to be reviewed with the lenders to assure the convertibility of the headquarters to other uses in the theoretical event of foreclosure. Finally, there is a strong psychological objection to placing the United Nations under obligation to private financial interests.

Other methods of financing were also canvassed without encouraging results. It was discovered that under its charter the International Bank for Reconstruction and Development could make loans only to member nations, or to business enterprises with a guaranty from the government concerned. Similarly, neither the Reconstruction Finance Corporation nor the Export-Import Bank appeared to have the statutory authority to make such a loan without specific congressional authorization.

These were the circumstances in which the United States Government entered the picture. A thorough study of the problem by experts in the Department of State and the Treasury resulted in the preparation of the plan suggested by the President to the United Nations.

Reasons for Interest-Free Feature

The interest-free feature of the proposed loan may be regarded as an offset to the financial advantages gained by the United States because the headquarters is located here. Quite apart from

MATTERS OF WHICH THE SECURITY COUNCIL IS SEIZED AND THE STAGE REACHED IN THEIR CONSIDERATION

A. Pursuant to Rule 11 of the Provisional Rules Procedure of the Security Council, I submit e following summary statement of matters of iich the Security Council is seized and of the ige reached in their consideration on 24 April 48. [For omitted materials, see U.N. doc. .728 or consult the semiannual BULLETIN lexes.]

The Iranian Question

.   .   .   .   .

Special Agreements under Article 43 and the Organization of the Armed forces made available to the Security Council

.   .   .   .   .

Rules of Procedure of the Security Council

.   .   .   .   .

By letter dated 5 September 1947 (document 540/Corr.1) the representative of the United ngdom suggested several additional rules of ocedure concerning meetings of the Security uncil. This letter has not yet been considered the Council.

Statute and Rules of Procedure of the Military Staff Committee

.   .   .   .   .

The General Regulation and Reduction of Armaments and Information on Armed Forces of the United Nations

.   .   .   .   .

Appointment of a Governor of the Free Territory of Trieste

By letter dated 13 June 1947, the representative the United Kingdom requested that an early te be fixed for the discussion by the Security uncil of the question of the appointment of a vernor of the Free Territory of Trieste. The estion was placed on the agenda at the 143rd eting of the Security Council, and discussed in vate at the 144th and 155th meetings on 20 June l7 and 10 July 1947. The Council set up a sub-nmittee composed of the representatives of

Australia, Colombia and Poland to collect additional information about the candidate.

At its 203rd meeting held in private on 24 September 1947, the Council examined the report of its sub-committee and also examined a new candidate proposed by the representative of China. The Council decided to ask the permanent members to hold an informal consultation.

The Council took up this matter again at its 223rd meeting held in private on 18 December and decided in pursuance of Article 11 (paragraph 1) of the Permanent Statute for the Free Territory of Trieste to request the Governments of Italy and Yugoslavia to consult with each other in an effort to reach agreement on a candidate and to report on their progress to the Council not later than 5 January 1948.

At its two hundred and thirty-third meeting held in private, the Council discussed the replies from the Governments of Italy and Yugoslavia to the Security Council's request of 19 December. The representative of the Union of Soviet Socialist Republics suggested that the members of the Council should express their opinion regarding the new candidates mentioned in the above replies. Some permanent members of the Council, however, declared that they were not yet in a position to discuss those candidates. The Council decided to ask the permanent members to have a further consideration on the matter next week and also decided to have another meeting of the Council on this question as soon as possible.

At its two hundred and sixty-fifth meeting held in private, the Security Council agreed, after some discussion, to postpone further consideration of this question until such time as it was requested by any Member of the Council.

7. *The Egyptian Question*

.   .   .   .   .

The Council further considered the question at its 201st meeting on 10 September 1947. A draft resolution submitted by the representative of China (document S/547) and amendments thereto submitted by the representative of Australia (document S/549) failed to receive a majority of votes

---

[1] U.N. doc. S/728, Apr. 27, 1948.

and were not adopted. The President then stated that the Egyptian question would remain on the agenda and that the Council would continue its consideration of the question at the request of any member of the Council or of either of the two parties concerned.

8. *The Indonesian Question*

.   .   .   .   .

At the 181st meeting the representative of Australia introduced a draft resolution (document S/488) and amendments to this resolution were submitted by the representative of Poland (document S/488/Add.1) and China (document S/488/Add.2) at the 185th and 187th meetings. At the 192nd meeting the representatives of Australia and China introduced a joint draft resolution (document S/513) and the representative of Australia introduced a new separate draft resolution (document S/512. The representative of the United States also submitted a draft resolution (document S/514). At the 193rd meeting the representative of Belgium introduced a draft resolution (document S/517).

At the 195th meeting the draft resolutions were put to a vote. An amendment submitted by the representative of the Union of Soviet Socialist Republics to the joint Australian-Chinese resolution (S/513), providing for the establishment of a Commission of the Security Council to supervise the "cease fire" order received seven votes in favour, two against (Belgium and France) with two abstentions (China and the United Kingdom) and was not adopted since one of the permanent members voted against it. The joint Australian-Chinese resolution was then adopted by seven votes in favour with four abstentions (Colombia, Poland, United Kingdom and the Union of Soviet Socialist Republics).

The Polish amendment (S/488/Add.1) to the original Australian draft resolution was re-submitted as an amendment to the second Australian resolution (S/512). The Polish amendment received three votes in favour, four against (Belgium, France, United Kingdom and the United States) with four abstentions (Australia, Brazil, China and Colombia), and was not adopted. The Australian resolution received three votes in favour (Australia, Colombia and Syria), none against with eight absentions, and was not adopted.

The United States draft resolution (S/514) received eight votes in favour, none against with three abstentions (Poland, Syria and the Union of Soviet Socialist Republics) and was adopted.

The Belgian draft resolution (S/517) received four votes in favour, (Belgium, France, United Kingdom and the United States) one against (Poland) with six abstentions and was not adopted.

ote and were not adopted as they did not obtain he necessary affirmative votes.

The representative of Australia then submitted n amendment to the United States revised draft esolution (document S/593).

A Sub-Committee consisting of the representatives of Australia, Belgium, China and the United States was created with the task of trying to nerge the revised United States draft resolution nd the various amendments thereto into one text. A proposal by the representative of the United Kingdom to use both the revised United States raft resolution (document S/588) and the Polish esolution (document S/589) as a basis was rejected by the Council.

The above-mentioned Sub-Committee met on 1 November and submitted a combined draft resolution to the Security Council (document S/594). The combined draft resolution was considered by he Security Council at its 218th and 219th meetngs on 1 November 1947.

The representative of the United States, in support of the draft resolution submitted by the Sub-Committee, withdrew his own revised draft resolution. He further stated that he was authorized y the representatives of Australia, Belgium and China to announce that they, for the same reason, lso withdrew their amendments to the United States revised draft resolution.

An amendment introduced by the representative f Colombia (document S/595) to the draft resolution submitted by the Sub-Committee was not arried.

The revised United States draft resolution as submitted by the Sub-Committee (document /594) was put to a vote and adopted.

The Polish draft resolution (document S/587) as then put to a vote and rejected as it did not btain the required number of affirmative votes.

At its 222nd meeting on 9 December 1947, the Council took note of a report from the Committee f Good Offices regarding the place for holding neetings with the two parties concerned (document S/611).

At its 224th meeting, held on 19 December 1947, ne Security Council agreed that the Committee f Good Offices should continue with its present omposition after 31 December 1947.

At the same meeting of the Council the President nformed that the Committee of Good Offices was reparing an interim report to the Security Council on the progress of its work and that it hoped o cable the report on or about 22 December 1947.

At its 225th meeting on 30 December 1947, the ecurity Council took note of a cablegram from ne Chairman of the Committee of Good Offices ating that the Committee was now preparing a nore comprehensive report than originally anticpated, and that the report would be forwarded pon its early completion.

At its 229th meeting of the Security Council on 17 January, the President read a cablegram from the Chairman of the Committee of Good Offices (document S/650) stating that delegations of the Republic of Indonesia and the Netherlands would sign a truce agreement on 17 January 1948 on board the USS "Renville" and that immediately thereupon, both parties would sign an agreement on twelve political principles which were to form the agreed basis for discussions concerning the settlement of the dispute.

The first interim report of the Security Council's Committee of Good Offices on the Indonesian Question (documents S/649 and S/649/Corr.1) was considered by the Security Council at its 247th, 248th, 249th, 251st, 252nd, 256th and 259th meetings with representatives of Australia, India, Netherlands, the Philippines, the Republic of Indonesia and the Committee of Good Offices participating without a vote. A draft resolution regarding the interim report was introduced by the representative of Canada (document S/678) and amendments thereto were submitted by the representatives of Australia (document S/681) and of Colombia (document S/682).

The representative of China introduced a new draft resolution (document S/689) which was adopted at the two hundred and fifty-ninth meeting with eight votes in favour, none against and three abstentions (Agentina, Ukrainian Soviet Socialist Republic and the Union of Soviet Socialist Republics). The Colombian amendments (document S/682) to the Canadian draft resolution (document S/678) were then put to a vote paragraph by paragraph but did not obtain the required number of affirmative votes. The Canadian draft resolution (document S/678) was adopted with seven votes in favour, none against, and four abstentions (Colombia, Syria, Ukrainian Soviet Socialist Republic and the Union of Soviet Socialist Republics).

9. *Voting Procedure in the Security Council*

At the 197th meeting on 27 August, the Council discussed the resolution adopted by the General Assembly at its sixty-first plenary meeting, held on 13 December 1946, concerning voting procedure in the Security Council (document S/237). It was decided to refer the resolution to the Committee of Experts with instructions to consider the matter and to make recommendations as to action the Council might take to comply with the recommendations.

By letter dated 2 December 1947, (document S/620), addressed to the President of the Security Council, the Secretary-General drew the attention to the resolution concerning the Voting Procedure in the Security Council adopted by the General Assembly on 21 November 1947.

The Security Council considered this communication at its 224th meeting on 19 December 1947.

The President of the Council confirmed the receipt of the above-mentioned letter.

10. *Procedure in Application of Articles 87 and 88 of the Charter With Regard to the Pacific Islands under Strategic Trusteeship of the United States of America*

By letter dated 7 November 1947 addressed to the President of the Security Council, the Secretary-General drew attention to certain questions in connection with the procedure to follow in application of Articles 87 and 88 of the Charter in relation to the Pacific Islands under strategic trusteeship of the United States of America (document S/599).

The Security Council, at its 220th meeting on 15 November discussed the above-mentioned letter and decided to refer all questions arising from that letter to the Committee of Experts for study and report.

By letter dated 2 December 1947 (document S/613) addressed to the President of the Security Council the representative of the United States informed the Security Council that Eniwetok Atoll, part of the Pacific Islands under strategic trusteeship by the United States had been closed for security reasons in order that the United States Government might conduct experiments relating to nuclear fission there.

The Security Council at its two hundred and twenty-second meeting on 9 December 1947 took note of the above-mentioned communication and unanimously decided to defer further consideration of the matter until the report from the Committee of Experts now examining the functions of the Security Council in relation to strategic areas had been received.

By letter dated 12 December 1947 (document S/621) the Chairman of the Committee of Experts announced that due to unexpected complications the Committee of Experts had not been able to report to the Council within the time specified, and that it would do so at the earliest possible moment.

The Security Council considered this letter at its 224th meeting on 19 December 1947. A resolution submitted by the representative of Poland (document S/625) giving further instructions to the Committee of Experts and setting new time limits was ruled out of order by the President of the Council. The ruling was challenged, but confirmed by a vote with nine affirmative votes. The representative of Poland reserved his right to reintroduce his draft resolution under a separate agenda item later.

The President stated that the Council took note of the above-mentioned letter.

11. *Applications for Membership*

At its 118th plenary meeting held on 17 November 1947, the General Assembly adopted resolutions requesting the Security Council to recon-

sixty-third meetings continued consideration of the First Monthly Progress Report to the Security Council of the United Nations Palestine Commission (document S/663) and the First Special Report to the Security Council on the Problem of Security in Palestine submitted by the United Nations Palestine Commission (document S/676).

At the two-hundred and sixty-second meeting, the President requested that the representatives of the United States and the Union of Soviet Socialist Republics consult together in an effort to formulate a mutually acceptable version of the United States draft resolution (document S/685). At the two-hundred and sixty-third meeting the representatives of the United States and the Union of Soviet Socialist Republics reported on the results of their consultation and the representative of the United States amended his draft resolution accordingly. The representative of Belgium announced that he accepted certain of the changes made in the United States amended resolution and wanted them to be incorporated in the Belgian amendment (document S/688). Thereupon, the Belgian amendment as revised was put to a vote paragraph by paragraph, but failed to obtain the required number of affirmative votes and consequently was not carried. The amended resolution of the United States was also voted upon paragraph by paragraph. The preamble, the first part of paragraph 2 and the final paragraph were adopted. The accepted paragraphs of the amended United States Resolution were then put to the vote as a whole and adopted by eight affirmative votes, none against and three abstentions (Argentina, Syria and the United Kingdom. For the text of the resolution as finally adopted see document S/691).

At its two hundred and sixty-seventh meeting, the Security Council heard statements by the representatives of Lebanon and Syria. At the two hundred and seventieth meeting, Members of the Council who had participated in the consultations of the permanent members reported to the Council on the results of their discussion. At the two hundred and seventy-first meeting, the representative of the United States outlined the contents of a proposed resolution which would be submitted at a later date.

Discussion was continued at the two hundred and seventy-fourth, two hundred and seventy-fifth and two hundred and seventy-seventh meetings. At the two hundred and seventy-seventh meeting the draft resolution (document S/704) introduced by the representative of the United States as amended by the representative of the Ukrainian Soviet Socialist Republic, calling for a truce in Palestine was adopted unanimously. The draft resolution (document S/705) also introduced by the representative of the United States, requesting the Secretary-General to convene a special session of the General Assembly regarding Palestine, was adopted by nine votes in favour with two abstentions (Ukrainian Soviet Socialist Republic and the Union of Soviet Socialist Republics). The Secretary-General announced that the special session of the General Assembly called for by the terms of the United States resolution (S/705) would be convoked on 16 April 1948.

Discussion was continued at the 282nd and 283rd meetings. The representative of Colombia introduced a draft resolution containing the terms of a truce in Palestine. The resolution as amended (document S/723) was adopted by a vote of nine in favour, none against, and two abstentions (Ukrainian Soviet Socialist Republic and the Union of Soviet Socialist Republics).

A the 287th meeting, the representative of the United States introduced a draft resolution calling for the establishment of a Truce Commission to supervise the implementation of the resolution adopted by the Council on 17 April (document S/723). The resolution (document S/727) was adopted by a vote of eight in favour, none against and three abstentions (Colombia, Ukrainian Soviet Republic and the Union of Soviet Socialist Republics).

13. *The India-Pakistan Question*

By letter dated 1 January 1948 (document S/628), the representative of India, under Article 35 of the Charter, drew the attention of the Council to the present situation in Jammu and Kashmir and requested the Security Council to ask the Government of Pakistan:

1. to prevent Pakistan Government personnel, military and civil, from participating or assisting in the invasion of the Jammu and Kashmir State:

2. to call upon other Pakistan nationals to desist from taking any part in the fighting in the Jammu and Kashmir State:

3. to deny to the invaders:

(*a*) access to and use of its territory for operations against Kashmir,

(*b*) military and other supplies,

(*c*) all other kinds of aid that might tend to prolong the present struggle.

The Security Council admitted this question to its agenda at its 226th meeting on 6 January. Representatives of the Governments of India and Pakistan were, in pursuance of Article 31 of the Charter, invited to participate in the discussion without a vote.

At the request of the representative of Pakistan, the Council postponed further consideration of the question until a meeting to be held not later than 15 January 1948.

In a letter addressed to the Secretary-General (document S/646) the Minister of Foreign Affairs of Pakistan answered to the application to the

The question was further considered at the 36th, 237th, 238th, 239th, 240th, 241st and 242nd meetings and the President reported on his continuing conversations with the parties. At the 37th meeting the representative of Belgium introduced two draft resolutions (documents S/661 and S/662). At the 239th meeting, the representative of India introduced two proposals.

Further consideration of the question was postponed until 10 February 1948, the conversations between the President and the two parties to be continued in the meantime.

Discussion continued at the two hundred and forty-third, two hundred and forty-fourth, two hundred and forty-fifth and two hundred and forty-sixth meetings. At the two hundred and forty-sixth meeting, the Council, concurred with request of the representative of India to postpone indefinitely the consideration of the situation in Jammu and Kashmir (document S/628) in order to give the representative of India an opportunity to return to India for consultation with his Government. The representative of India was urged to be at the disposal of the Council for continuation of the consideration of this question at as early date as possible, and the Council reserved its right to take up the Jammu and Kashmir question again at its discretion before the return of the Indian representative. Consideration of aspects of the India-Pakistan question other than those relating to the situation in Jammu and Kashmir would be resumed on Wednesday, 18 February 1948.

At its 250th and 257th meetings the Security Council considered aspects of the India-Pakistan question other than those relating to the situation in Jammu and Kashmir.

Discussion was continued at the 264th, 265th and 269th meetings. The representative of China introduced a draft resolution (document S/699) which resulted from his consultations with the delegations of India and Pakistan. At the 284th, 285th and 286th meetings, the Council considered a revised draft resolution submitted jointly by the representatives of Belgium, Canada, China, Colombia, the United Kingdom and the United States of America, (document S/726) outlining the terms of a general settlement of the dispute. At the 286th meeting, this resolution was voted on paragraph by paragraph, and adopted. At the 287th meeting the nomination of Belgium and Colombia, to the Commission provided for in the terms of the resolution (document S/726) was approved by a vote of seven in favour, none against and four abstentions (Belgium, Colombia, Ukrainian Soviet Socialist Republic and the Union of Soviet Socialist Republics). It was agreed that the President of the Security Council should continue to meet with both parties in an effort to find a solution to the question of Junagadh.

14. The Czechoslovakian Situation

By letter dated 12 March 1948 (document S/694) the permanent representative of Chile to the United Nations requested that, in accordance with Article 34 of the Charter, the Security Council, "investigate the events reported by the permanent representative of Czechoslovakia, Dr. Jan Papanek, which constitute a threat to international peace and security". At the two hundred and sixty-eighth meeting this item was admitted to the Agenda and the representative of Chile invited to participate in the discussion in accordance with Article 31 of the Charter. The representative of Chile requested that, in accordance with Rule 39 of the Provisional Rules of Procedure, the Security Council should invite Dr. Jan Papanek to supply it with information.

At the two hundred and seventy-second meeting, on the request of the representative of Argentina, and in accordance with Rule 38 of the Provisional Rules of Procedure, the proposal of the representative of Chile to invite Dr. Jan Papanek to supply the Security Council with information, in accordance with Rule 39 of the Provisional Rules of Procedure, was adopted by a vote of nine to two.

Discussion was continued at the 273rd, 276th and 278th meetings. The resolution (document S/711) introduced by the representative of the United States, inviting the Government of Czechoslovakia to participate in the discussion of the Czechoslovakian question, was adopted by nine votes to none with two abstentions (the Ukrainian Soviet Socialist Republic and the Union of the Soviet Socialist Republics). In response to this invitation the Government of Czechoslovakia stated that it did not find it possible to take part in the discussion (document S/718).

At the 281st meeting, the representative of Chile submitted a draft resolution proposing that a sub-committee of the Council be appointed to hear statements and testimony relative to this question, and to submit a report thereon to the Security Council as soon as possible.

Current U.N. Documents: A Selected Bibliography[1]

International Children's Emergency Fund. Programme Committee. Report of the Sub-Committee on Medical Projects. E/ICEF/43, Feb. 18, 1948. 56 pp. mimeo.
—— Executive Board. Report of the Executive Director to the Nineteenth Meeting of the Executive Board, 9 March 1948. E/ICEF/46, Feb. 27, 1948. 15 pp. mimeo.

[1] Printed materials may be secured in the United States from the International Documents Service, Columbia University Press, 2960 Broadway, New York City. Other materials (mimeographed or processed documents) may be consulted at certain designated libraries in the United States.

FOREIGN AID AND RECONSTRUCTION

Economic Cooperation Act of 1948

STATEMENT BY THE DEPARTMENT OF STATE AND THE
ECONOMIC COOPERATION ADMINISTRATION

The Department of State and the Economic Cooperation Administration released on May 8 copies of the exchanges of notes between the United States and 11 member nations of the Organization for European Economic Co-operation.[1]

The purpose of the notes is to record certain assurances which the Economic Cooperation Act specifies are to be received from the participating countries before the Administrator can proceed with a full assistance program with respect to them. According to subsection 115(c), each country is expected to signify its adherence to the purposes of the Act and its intention to conclude an agreement with the United States. Each note contains statements to this effect, and further states that the country in question is carrying out the provisions of subsection 115(b) which are applicable to it and is also engaged in continuous efforts to bring about a joint recovery program. In addition, those countries which will probably receive some assistance in the form of grants agree to make deposits in their own currency commensurate with the dollar amount of assistance furnished as a grant. These deposits are to be available for certain United States expenses abroad and for other purposes agreed to by the two countries.

EXCHANGES OF NOTES BETWEEN THE U.S. AND ELEVEN MEMBER NATIONS OF THE
ORGANIZATION FOR EUROPEAN ECONOMIC CO-OPERATION [2]

The Acting Secretary of State to the Netherlands Ambassador

EXCELLENCY: I have the honor to inform you that the Economic Cooperation Act of 1948 (Title I of the Foreign Assistance Act of 1948) became law on April 3, 1948.

You will note the general requirement of the Act

that, before assistance may be provided by the United States to a country of Europe which participates in a joint recovery program based on self-help and mutual cooperation, an agreement must have been concluded between that country and the United States as described in subsection 115(b) of the Act. However, before such an agreement is concluded and until July 3, 1948, the Government of the United States proposes, under the terms of subsection 115(c), to arrange for the performance with respect to your country, of those functions authorized by the Act which may be determined to be essential in furtherance of its purposes. This action by the Government of the United States is contingent upon the requirements of subsection 115(c) of the Act being fulfilled.

Accordingly, I should appreciate your notifying me whether your Government adheres to the purposes and policies in furtherance of which the Act authorizes assistance to be provided, and is engaged in continuous efforts to accomplish a joint recovery program through multilateral undertakings and the establishment of a continuing or-

[1] Released to the press by the Department of State and the Economic Cooperation Administration on May 8.
[2] While all the notes are similar, there are certain slight differences. For this reason copies of the notes which do differ are included in this release. On the list of countries which have exchanged notes with the United States are: Austria, Denmark, France, Iceland, Ireland, Italy, Luxembourg, the Netherlands, Norway, Sweden, and the United Kingdom. Notes have not been exchanged as of this date with Greece, Portugal, Switzerland, and Turkey, nor with the western zones of Germany.

Copies of the notes exchanged are with (1) the Netherlands (exchanges with Denmark, Luxembourg, and Norway are in the same form); (2) Ireland (these are in the same form as those with Iceland and Sweden); (3) Italy (which are in the same form as those with France); (4) the United Kingdom; and (5) Austria.

The Netherlands Ambassador to the Acting Secretary of State

NETHERLANDS EMBASSY
Washington 9, D.C.
April 20, 1948

SIR: I have received your note of April 20th, concerning the Economic Cooperation Act of 1948.

My Government has authorized me to inform you of its adherence to the purposes and policies of the Economic Cooperation Act of 1948, which are stated in the whole of subsection 102(b) and in subsection 102(a), respectively, and in furtherance of which the Act authorizes assistance to be provided to my country.

My Government has taken careful note of the provisions of subsection 115(b) of the Economic Cooperation Act of 1948 and intends to conclude an agreement with your Government pursuant to that section. It is understood that your Government would be required by the Act to terminate assistance if at any time it should find that my Government was not complying with such provisions of subsection 115(b) of the Act as your Government considered applicable. My Government is complying with and, for so long as assistance may be made available to it under the Act pursuant to your letter, is prepared to comply with all the applicable provisions of subsection 115(b) of the Act and is also engaged in continuous efforts to accomplish a joint recovery program through multilateral undertakings and the establishment of a continuing organization for this purpose.

Pending the determination of the terms of the future agreement between our two Governments under subsection 115(b) of the Act, my Government agrees to make deposits, in guilders, upon notification by your Government, in amounts commensurate with the dollar amount of assistance furnished hereunder which is designated by your Government as a grant. These deposits will be available for the administrative expenses incurred by your Government in my country under the Economic Cooperation Act of 1948, and will be held or used for such other purposes as may be agreed to between our two Governments. It is understood that the provisions of the future agreement between our two Governments concerning any deposits to be made pursuant to paragraph (6) of subsection 115(b) will apply with respect to all of such assistance for my Government which is determined to have been made by grant during the period covered by your letter.

In the event that your Government should decide to offer some part of the assistance to be furnished to my Government pursuant to your letter as a loan, or on other terms of payment, it is understood that the terms of payment will be determined in accordance with the Act.

I am authorized to state that my Government

understands that the proposals contained in your letter do not constitute an obligation on the part of your Government to make assistance available to my country.

Accept [etc.]   E. N. VAN KLEFFENS

The Undersecretary of State to the Irish Minister

April 28, 1948

SIR: I have the honor to refer to the Economic Cooperation Act of 1948, which became law on April 3, 1948.

I should like to call your attention to the general provisions of section 115 of the Act regarding the conclusion of an agreement between each of the participating countries and the United States.

In accordance with your Government's stated desire to cooperate with the United States and with the other participating countries in accomplishing the objectives of a joint recovery program, I should appreciate being notified that your Government adheres to the purposes and policies which the Act as a whole is designed to carry out. The purposes of the Act are stated in the whole of subsection 102(b), and the policies referred to in subsection 102(b) are those designated as such in subsection 102(a). I should also like to know whether your Government intends to conclude an agreement with the United States in accordance with section 115 of the Act, and whether your Government is now acting consistently with the applicable provisions of subsection 115(b), and intends to continue acting consistently with these provisions. Among them is one regarding continuous efforts of the participating countries to accomplish a joint recovery program through multilateral undertakings and the establishment of a continuing organization for this purpose.

I hope that in the near future representatives of our two countries may begin negotiations for an early conclusion of the agreement contemplated in the Act.

Accept [etc.]

For the Secretary of State:
ROBERT A. LOVETT

The Irish Minister to the Secretary of State

IRISH LEGATION
Washington, D. C.
April 28, 1948

SIR: I have the honour to acknowledge the receipt of your note of this date, concerning the Economic Cooperation Act of 1948 which became law on April 3, 1948.

As you know, my Government desires to cooperate with the United States, and with the other

hole of subsection 102(b) and the policies re-
erred to in subsection 102(b) are those designated
s such in subsection 102(a).

Since subsection 115(c) of the Act predicates
he furnishing of assistance upon continuous com-
liance with such provisions of subsection 115(b)
s my Government may consider applicable, I
hould appreciate your advising me whether your
Government is already taking the national meas-
ires necessary to carry out the applicable provi-
ions of subsection 115(b) and will continue to take
uch measures as long as assistance is made avail-
ble to it pursuant to this note.

During the period covered by this note, assist-
nce may be furnished to your Government under
he Act on terms of payment or by grant. It is
ontemplated that, during the period covered by
his note, such assistance will be furnished to your
Government for the most part by grant. I suggest that pending the determination of the terms
f the future agreement between our two Govern-
nents under subsection 115(b) of the Act, deposits
n the currency of your country in respect of any
ıssistance furnished hereunder which is designated
y my Government as a grant be made in accord-
ınce with the agreement between our two Govern-
nents concluded in Rome on January 3, 1948, and
relating to economic aid. I further suggest that
:hese deposits may be used for administrative expenses of the Government of the United States in
:he currency of your country, incident to my Gov-
ırnment's operations within your country under
:he Economic Cooperation Act of 1948 and for such
other purposes as may be agreed upon by our two
Governments. The provisions of the future agreement between our two Governments concerning
any deposits to be made pursuant to paragraph (6)
of subsection 115(b) will apply with respect to all
of such assistance for your Government which
is determined to have been made by grant during
the period covered by this note.

It is anticipated that my Government may offer
some part of the assistance to be furnished pursuant to this note as a loan, or on other terms of
payment, and in that event the terms of payment
will be determined in accordance with the Act.

The Act authorizes my Government to appoint
a special mission for economic cooperation to your
country. I trust that you will extend the same
degree of cooperation to this mission that you have
extended to the representatives of my Government
concerned with the operations under the aforementioned agreement concluded between our two Governments on January 3, 1948.

I am sure your Government understands that
the proposals set forth in this note cannot be
viewed as constituting an obligation on the part of
my Government to make assistance available to
your country.

Accept [etc.] ROBERT A. LOVETT

The Italian Ambassador to the Acting Secretary of State

ITALIAN EMBASSY
Washington, D. C.
April 21, 1948

EXCELLENCY: I have received your note of April
21st, 1948 concerning the Economic Cooperation
Act which became law on April 3rd, 1948.

My Government has authorized me to inform
you of its adherence to the purposes and policies
of the Economic Cooperation Act of 1948, which
are stated in the whole of subsection 102(b) and
in subsection 102(a), respectively, and in furtherance of which the Act authorizes assistance to be
provided to my country.

My Government has taken careful note of the
provisions of subsection 115(b) of the Economic
Cooperation Act of 1948 and intends to conclude
an agreement with the Government of the United
States of America, pursuant to that section.

Since subsection 115(c) of the Act predicates the
furnishing of assistance upon continuous compliance with such provisions of subsection 115(b),
as the Government of the United States of America may consider applicable, I wish to inform you
that the Italian Government is already taking the
national measures necessary to carry out the
applicable provisions of subsection 115(b) and
will continue to take such measures as long as
assistance is made available to it pursuant to this
note.

My Government is engaged in continuous efforts
to accomplish a joint recovery program and to that
end has signed on April 16, 1948 an agreement related to economic European cooperation which
contains multilateral undertakings and provides
for a permanent organization of the participating
Governments.

My Government understands that, during the
period covered by your note, assistance may be furnished to it for the most part by grant. Pending
the determination of terms of the future agreement
between our two Governments, under section
115(b) of the Act, deposits in the currency of my
country in respect of any assistance which is designated by your Government as a grant will be made
in accordance with the bilateral agreement between
our two Governments signed in Rome on January
3rd, 1948 related to economic aid. These deposits
may be used for administrative expenses of your
Government in the currency of my country, incident to your Government's operations within my
country under the Economic Cooperation Act of
1948 and for such other purposes as may be agreed
to by our Governments. It is understood that the
provisions of the future agreement between our
two Governments, concerning any deposits to be

made pursuant to paragraph (6) of subsection 115(b), will apply with respect to all of such assistance for my Government which is determined to have been made by grant during the period covered by your note.

In the event that your Government should decide to offer some part of the assistance to be furnished to my Government pursuant to your note as a loan, or on other terms of payments, it is understood that the terms of payment will be determined in accordance with the Act.

My Government notes with satisfaction that your Government will appoint a special mission for economic cooperation to my country. My Government will extend the same degree of cooperation to this mission that it has extended to the representatives of your Government concerned with the operations under the bilateral agreement signed in Rome between our two Governments on January 3rd, 1948, relating to economic aid.

I am authorized to state that my Government understands that the proposals contained in your note do not constitute an obligation on the part of your Government to make assistance available to my country.

I wish to express [etc.]

ALBERTO TARCHIANI
Ambassador of Italy

The Undersecretary of State to the British Ambassador

April 30, 1948

EXCELLENCY: I have the honor to refer to the Economic Cooperation Act of 1948 (Title I of the Foreign Assistance Act of 1948) which became law on April 3, 1948.

You will note the general requirement of the Act that, before assistance may be provided by the United States to a country of Europe which participates in a joint recovery program based on self-help and mutual cooperation, an agreement must have been concluded between that country and the United States as described in subsection 115(b) of the Act. However, before such an agreement is concluded and until July 3, 1948, the Government of the United States proposes, under the terms of subsection 115(c), to arrange for the performance, with respect to the United Kingdom, of those functions authorized by the Act which may be determined to be essential in furtherance of its purposes. This action by the Government of the United States is contingent upon the requirements of subsection 115(c) of the Act being fulfilled.

Accordingly, I should appreciate your notifying me whether the British Government adheres to the purposes and policies in furtherance of which the Act authorized assistance to be provided, and is engaged in continuous efforts to accomplish a

The British Ambassador to the Secretary of State

BRITISH EMBASSY
Washington, D. C.
30th April, 1948

SIR, I have the honour to acknowledge the receipt of your note of today's date regarding the passage into law of the Economic Cooperation Act of 1948.

2. I am directed by His Majesty's Principal Secretary of State for Foreign Affairs to inform you that His Majesty's Government in the United Kingdom have taken note of the provisions of the Act and of the various points made in your note under reply. I am authorized to declare on behalf of His Majesty's Government in the United Kingdom that they adhere to the purposes and policies of the Economic Cooperation Act of 1948, which are stated in the whole of sub-section 102(b) and in sub-section 102(a) respectively, and in furtherance of which the Act authorizes assistance to be provided to the United Kingdom. His Majesty's Government also intend to conclude an agreement with the United States Government pursuant to sub-section 115(b) of the Act.

3. Since sub-section 115(c) of the Act predicates the furnishing of assistance upon continuous compliance with such provisions of sub-section 115(b) as the United States Government may consider applicable, His Majesty's Government wish me to inform you that they are already taking the national measures necessary to carry out the applicable provisions of sub-section 115(b) of the Act, and will continue to do so as long as assistance is made available to them in accordance with your note.

4. His Majesty's Government are making continuous efforts to bring about, together with the other participating governments, a joint programme of European recovery, and to that end His Majesty's Principal Secretary of State for Foreign Affairs signed on April 16th the Convention for European Economic Cooperation, which contains multilateral undertakings and establishes a continuing organization of the participating governments.

5. His Majesty's Government have noted the contents of paragraphs 5 and 6 of your note and agree to make deposits in pounds sterling, upon notification by the United States Government, in amounts commensurate with the dollar amount of assistance furnished under the terms of your note and designated by the United States Government as a grant. These deposits will be available for the administrative expenses incurred by the United States Government in the United Kingdom under the Economic Cooperation Act of 1948, and will be held or used for such other purposes as may be agreed to between the two Governments.

It is understood that the provisions of the future agreement between His Majesty's Government and the Government of the United States concerning any deposits to be made pursuant to paragraph 6 of sub-section 115(b) will apply with respect to all assistance for His Majesty's Government which is determined to have been made by grant during the period covered by your note.

6. Finally, I am directed to state that His Majesty's Government understand that the proposals set out in your note do not constitute an obligation on the part of the United States Government to make assistance available to the United Kingdom.

I have the honour [etc.] INVERCHAPEL

**The Acting Secretary of State
to the Austrian Minister**

April 15, 1948

SIR: I have the honor to inform you that the Economic Cooperation Act of 1948 (Title I of the Foreign Assistance Act of 1948) became law on April 3, 1948.

You will note the general requirement of the Act that, before assistance may be provided by the United States to a country of Europe which participates in a joint recovery program based on self-help and mutual cooperation, an agreement must have been concluded between that country and the United States as described in subsection 115(b) of the Act. However, before such an agreement is concluded and until July 3, 1948, the Government of the United States proposes, under the terms of subsection 115(c), to arrange for the performance, with respect to your country, of those functions authorized by the Act which may be determined to be essential in furtherance of its purposes. This action by the Government of the United States is contingent upon the requirements of subsection 115(c) of the Act being fulfilled.

Accordingly, I should appreciate your notifying me whether your Government adheres to the purposes and policies in furtherance of which the Act authorizes assistance to be provided, and is engaged in continuous efforts to accomplish a joint recovery program through multilateral undertakings and the establishment of a continuing organization for this purpose, and also whether your Government intends to conclude an agreement with the United States in accordance with subsection 115(b). The purposes of the Act are stated in the whole of subsection 102(b) and the policies referred to in subsection 102(b) are those designated as such in subsection 102(a).

My Government would be required by the Act to terminate assistance authorized by subsection 115(c) to your country if at any time it should find that your Government was not complying with such provisions of subsection 115(b) of the

Act as my Government might consider applicable. I should appreciate being notified whether your Government is complying with and, for so long as assistance may be made available to it under the Act pursuant to this note, is prepared to comply with the applicable provisions of subsection 115(b).

It is contemplated that, during the period covered by this note, such assistance will be furnished to your Government by grant. I suggest that pending the determination of the terms of the future agreement between our two Governments under subsection 115(b) of the Act, deposits in the currency of your country in respect of any assistance furnished hereunder which is designated by my Government as a grant to be made in accordance with the agreement between our two Governments under the Foreign Aid Act of 1947. I further suggest that these deposits may be used for administrative expenses of the Government of the United States in the currency of your country, incident to my Government's operations within your country under the Economic Cooperation Act of 1948 and for such other purposes as may be agreed upon by our two governments. The provisions of the future agreement between our two Governments concerning any deposits to be made pursuant to paragraph (6) of subsection 115(b) will apply with respect to all of such assistance for your Government which is determined to have been made by grant during the period covered by this note.

I trust that your Government will concur in these arrangements.

The Act authorizes my Government to appoint a special mission for economic cooperation to your country. I trust that you will extend the same degree of cooperation to this mission that you have extended to the representatives of my Government concerned with the operations under the agreement concluded between our two Governments pursuant to the Foreign Aid Act of 1947.

I am sure your Government understands that the proposals set forth in this note cannot be viewed as constituting an obligation on the part of my Government to make assistance available to your country.

Accept [etc.]   ROBERT A. LOVETT
Acting Secretary of State

The Austrian Minister to the Acting Secretary of State

April 15, 1948

SIR: I have received your letter concerning the Economic Cooperation Act of 1948.

My Government has authorized me to inform you of its adherence to the purposes and policies of the Economic Cooperation Act of 1948, which are stated in the whole of subsection 102(b) and in

terms of the future agreement between our two Governments under Section 405 of the Act, deposits in the currency of your country in respect of any assistance furnished hereunder which is designated by my Government as a grant be made in accordance with the agreement between our two Governments dated October 27, 1947. I further suggest that these deposits may be used for administrative expenses of the Government of the United States in the currency of your country, incident to my Government's operations within your country under the China Aid Act of 1948, and for such other purposes as may be agreed upon by our two Governments. The provisions of the future agreement between our two Governments concerning any deposits in Chinese currency to be made will apply with respect to all of such assistance for your Government which is determined to have been made by grant during the period covered by this letter.

I trust that your Government will concur in the understandings expressed above.

The Act authorizes my Government to appoint a special mission for economic cooperation to your country. I should appreciate receiving the assurances of your Government that the fullest cooperation will be extended to the representatives of my Government concerned with operations in implementation of the Act.

I am sure your Government understands that the proposals set forth in this letter cannot be viewed as constituting an obligation on the part of my Government to make assistance available to your country.

Accept [etc.]

GEORGE C. MARSHALL

The text of Ambassador Koo's note:

April 30, 1948

SIR:

I have the honor to acknowledge the receipt of your note of April 30, 1948, in which you are good enough to inform me that in view of the China Aid Act of 1948 (Title IV of the Foreign Assistance Act of 1948) which became law on April 3, 1948, the Government of the United States, pending the conclusion of an agreement between China and the United States under Section 405 of the Act and until July 3, 1948, proposes to arrange for the performance of those functions authorized by the Act which may be determined to be essential in furtherance of those purposes of the Act which apply to the funds authorized under Section 404(*a*) thereof, and that this action of the Government of the United States is contingent upon certain requirements, as therein set forth, being fulfilled.

In reply my Government has authorized me to inform you of its adherence to the purposes and policies set forth in Section 402 of the China Aid Act of 1948 in furtherance of which the Act authorizes assistance to be provided to China. My Government has also authorized me to inform you of its intention to conclude an agreement with the United States in accordance with Section 405 of the Act.

Pending the conclusion of such an agreement, it is understood by my Government that the extension, pursuant to your note, of aid to China hereunder as authorized by Section 404(*a*) of the Act will be provisionally governed by the Agreement between our two Governments dated October 27, 1947, subject to such modifications, particularly with respect to the types of assistance and the terms and methods of procurement and distribution, as may hereafter be agreed to by our two Governments, having regard to the different character of the assistance under said Act from the relief aid extended under the Agreement of October 27, 1947, and subject, as preliminary arrangements, to the understandings set forth below.

During the period covered by your note, it is anticipated that assistance other than that relating to the reconstruction projects will be furnished to my Government under the Act with funds authorized under Section 404(*a*) thereof by grant. Terms of payment, if any, for recon-

First Report to Congress on the U.S. For

[Released to the press May 5]

The first report on the United States Foreign Aid Program under Public Law 389, transmitted by the President to the Congress on May 5, 1948, covers the period immediately before and during the brief period from the approval of the Foreign Aid Act on December 17, 1947, through December 31, 1947.

The report describes the administrative steps taken by the Department of State and by its overseas missions; the findings of the Cabinet Committee on World Food Programs; the negotiation of agreements with Austria, France, and Italy; the development of initial supply programs, procurement policies, and procedures for reimbursing the foreign governments for purchases made by them under the supply programs; and the establishment of local currency funds.

In his letter of transmittal to the Congress, President Truman noted:

ments signatories of the International Telecommunication Convention of Atlantic City, 1947.

The purpose of the Aeronautical Radio Conference is to develop a world-wide plan of specific assignment of the individual frequencies included in the bands allocated to the Aeronautical Mobile Service at Atlantic City.

A Preparatory Committee, on which the United States is represented, has been meeting at Geneva since April 24 to prepare the agenda for the Aeronautical Radio Conference and to consider the technical principles on which the frequency plan is to be based.

U.S. DELEGATION TO SIXTH CONGRESS OF INTERNATIONAL COLLEGE OF SURGEONS

[Released to the press May 6]

The Department of State announced on May 6 the composition of the United States Delegation to the Sixth International Congress of the International College of Surgeons scheduled to be held at Rome, May 18–23, 1948. The United States Delegation is as follows:

Chairman

Albert A. Berg, M.D., Director of Surgery, Beth Moses Hospital, Brooklyn

Delegates

O. Anderson Engh, M.D., Chief Orthopedic Consultant to U. S. Public Health Service Dispensary, Washington

James H. Forsee, Colonel (M.C.), U.S.A., Chief of the Surgical Service, Fitzsimmons General Hospital, Denver

Custis Lee Hall, M.D., Consultant in Orthopedic Surgery, U.S. Veterans Hospital, Washington

Robert F. Schultz, Commander (M.C.), U.S.N., Officer in Charge, Audio-Visual Training Section, Professional Division, Bureau of Medicine and Surgery, Department of the Navy

Max Thorek, M.D., Professor of Surgery, Cook County Graduate School of Medicine, Chicago

The program of the Congress will consist mainly of the presentation of reports and films covering scientific subjects in the various surgical fields and the visiting of hospitals, clinics, museums, and medical libraries.

The International College of Surgeons was established in 1935 for the purpose of fostering the international advancement of surgery. To carry out its aim, the organization has promoted within various countries the formation of boards in surgical specialties. The American Chapter of the College has approximately 2,500 members. The fifth Congress was held at Lima, Peru, in 1946.

Fifth Meeting of the Rubber Study Gro

The Fifth Meeting of the Rubber Study Group, held in Washington under the chairmanship of Donald D. Kennedy, Chief, Division of International Resources, Department of State, ended on April 29, 1948.

The principal objects of the meeting were:

1. To examine the statistical position regarding production, consumption, and stocks of rubber throughout the world;

2. To review the world rubber situation in the light of the changes in that position since the Fourth Study Group Meeting, held at Paris in July 1947;

3. To consider measures designed to expand world consumption.

1. The Group examined the statistical position and made estimates for natural-rubber production and the total consumption of natural and synthetic rubber during the year 1948 and provisionally for 1949. During 1948 it was estimated that world production of natural rubber would be in the neighborhood of 1,390,000 tons while total consumption of natural and synthetic rubber might be in the region of 1,745,000 tons, of which about 1,310,000 tons would be natural rubber. In regard to 1949 it was estimated that natural-rubber production would be of the order of 1,550,000 tons, while total consumption of natural and synthetic might again be 1,745,000 tons.

Tables giving the estimates made by the Group are attached. The Group felt the need for projecting its estimates beyond the current year but the figures for 1949 should be treated with the greatest caution.

2. There was an exchange of views on the subject of the price of natural rubber. The discussion covered the field of commodity agreements, government control of the sale and purchase of natural rubber, and special arrangements for the purchase of natural rubber by governments from governments for stock-piling at fixed prices.

The Group reached the conclusion that the time had not arrived for any consideration or examination of a commodity agreement.

3. The Group continued its policy of examining all means for encouraging the expansion of the world consumption of rubber.

It considers that every effort consistent with national-security requirements should be made to insure that exchange and trading in rubber should be freed.

It again expressed the hope that maximum assistance would be given to the countries desiring to make an extensive use of rubber but which, on account of the war, cannot afford to pay in foreign currencies for the rubber imports they require.

RGE C. MARSHALL [1]
of State

selves and between themselves and other nations. This is a wise provision because the recovery of Europe depends upon a great increase in the production of goods, and markets for these goods wait upon a lowering of barriers to the exchange of such goods.

The ERP was a vital step; but only a first step. We must now follow through with measures to make ourselves and the other free nations stronger. We must work closer together in commerce. No economic bond is closer than the friendly ties of mutually satisfactory trade. No force is more decisive than the introduction or maintenance of unnecessary barriers to such trade.

So the first fundamental reason for my conviction that renewal of the Trade Agreements Act is particularly important at this time is because that act is a well-tried, useful, and effective instrument by which we can further develop economic ties with other nations which believe as we do and want the kind of world that we want.

There is another reason for this conviction. We in the United States, perhaps more than in any other part of the world, believe in private enterprise. We are convinced that trade within our country and between our country and other nations can best be so conducted. And we further believe in equality of opportunity. As stated in the Atlantic Charter, every country should have equal access to the trade and raw materials of the world. There are, we must admit, some exceptions to this principle; we do not always follow it ourselves. But we sincerely believe it to be an objective which we should seek to achieve. I was referring to Cuba and the Philippines.

Since World War II economic conditions in most of the rest of the world have been chaotic in the extreme. Shortages have been the rule for most countries since the war as they were during the war. And during the war techniques for the control and direction of trade by governments have been brought to a high degree of perfection. Principally because of shortages of goods the international trade of a large part of the world has since the war been governed by bilateral agreements between governments. Imports and exports have been directed and controlled by governments as to

[1] Made before the Subcommittee on Tariffs and Reciprocal Trade of the House Ways and Means Committee on May 6.

source, destination, and quantity. In such a world the private trader is at a serious disadvantage, and in the long run would be forced out of business. Moreover, international trade cannot be controlled and directed by government in isolation from domestic trade. If international trade is to be controlled by government, the tentacles of such control must inevitably reach down into the operation of domestic trade. We do not want this to happen to the trade of the United States, either domestic or foreign.

And so the other great task confronting us in the economic field today is to build the kind of international trading conditions in which private trade can survive and grow. It is to this end that the United States has taken the lead since World War II in securing international agreement as to the rules which should govern international trade and the reduction of the barriers imposed by governments against that trade. It is for that reason that we have sought and obtained agreement that equality of opportunity rather than discrimination should be the rule, that quotas would not be used for protective purposes, and that tariffs would be maintained at moderate levels. If the international trade of the world cannot be

General Agreement on Tariffs and Trade

The President issued on May 4 a proclamation putting into effect, with respect to China, as of May 22, 1948, the provisions of the general agreement on tariffs and trade.[1] The agreement was entered into last October 30 at Geneva with 22 other countries. The President's action followed receipt of information that the Government of China had signed the protocol of provisional application of the general agreement on April 21, 1948; pursuant to provision of the protocol, China will give effect to the agreement on the expiration of 30 days from date of signature.

China is the eleventh of the Geneva countries and the first country in the Far East to give effect to this agreement. The other countries which have done so, in addition to the United States, are the United Kingdom, France, Belgium, the Netherlands, Luxembourg, Canada, Australia, Cuba, and Czechoslovakia.

Under the general agreement, China grants concessions on products of interest to the United States representing approximately 52 million dollars in terms of 1939 trade. Existing import duties were reduced on such products as office machines, light trucks and chassis, canned milk, lubricating oil and grease, and tires and tubes; on an extensive list of other items, on which existing duties are

---

[1] Proclamation 2769 (13 *Fed. Reg.* 467).

possessions of Germans not resident in Spain to whom the previous blocking law of May 1945 continues to apply.

Agreement has been reached concerning identifiable looted gold acquired by the Spanish Government from Germany. The Spanish Government has stated that although it was not aware of the looted origin either at the time of acquisition or subsequently, it will make immediate restitution of all looted gold now identified as being in the possession of the Spanish Government and of any additional such gold found and claimed prior to April 30, 1949. As a result of this agreement, the international movement of gold held by the Spanish Government is now free from the restrictions of the Gold Declaration of February 22, 1944.

Signing of Income Tax Convention With Denmark

[Released to the press May 6]

A convention between the United States and Denmark for the avoidance of double taxation and the prevention of fiscal evasion with respect to taxes on income was signed at Washington on May 6, 1948, by George C. Marshall, Secretary of State, and Henrik de Kauffmann, Danish Ambassador in Washington.

The provisions of the convention are similar in general to those contained in income-tax conventions now in force between the United States and the United Kingdom, Canada, France, and Sweden.

The convention provides that upon the exchange of instruments of ratification it shall be effective (*a*) in the case of United States tax, for the taxable years beginning on or after January 1 of the year in which the exchange takes place, and (*b*) in the case of Danish tax, for the taxable years beginning on or after April 1 of the year in which the exchange takes place.

Statement by Secretary Marshall

[Released to the press May 6]

Mr. Ambassador, in signing this treaty we have completed a long period of negotiations between our two countries for a treaty to eliminate double taxation upon income.

We believe that the system of exemptions and credits provided by this treaty—mutually beneficial to the citizens and enterprises of both countries—will go far to overcome, in the field of income taxation, one of the major obstacles to international trade and business.

It has been a pleasure for me to join with you in signing the treaty.

Educational Exchange Program Under Fulbright Act

AGREEMENT WITH GREECE SIGNED

[Released to the press May 3]

The Government of the United States and the Government of Greece signed in Athens on April 23 an agreement putting into operation the program of international educational exchanges authorized by the Fulbright act (Public Law 584, 79th Congress). This was the fourth agreement signed by the United States Government under the Fulbright act, the previous agreements having been signed with the Governments of China, Burma, and the Philippine Republic.[1]

The agreement with the Greek Government establishes the United States Educational Foundation in Greece to administer certain funds resulting from the sale of surplus property to that country. The present agreement provides for an annual program of from $100,000 to $400,000 in Greek currency for certain educational purposes. These purposes include the financing of "studies, research, instruction, and other educational activities of or for citizens of the United States of America in schools and institutions of higher learning located in Greece, or of the citizens of Greece in United States schools and institutions of higher learning located outside the continental United States . . . including payment for transportation, tuition, maintenance and other expenses incident to scholastic activities; or furnishing transportation for citizens of Greece who desire to attend United States schools and institutions of higher learning in the continental United States . . .

whose attendance will not deprive citizens of the United States of America of an opportunity to attend such schools and institutions."

The Foundation in Greece will have a seven-man board of directors consisting of the principal officer in charge of the United States Diplomatic Mission in Greece as honorary chairman; the chief public-affairs officer of the United States Embassy in Greece, or such other Embassy officer as designated by the Chief of Mission, as chairman; two other members of the Embassy staff; two citizens of the United States of America resident in Greece, and two nationals of Greece, one of whom shall be prominent in the field of education.

Information about specific opportunities for American citizens to pursue studies, teach, or do research in Greece will be made public in the near future. Further inquiries about these opportunities and requests for application forms should be addressed to the following three agencies: Institute of International Education, 2 West 45th Street, New York 19, N.Y. (for graduate study); United States Office of Education, Washington 5, D.C. (for teaching in national elementary and secondary schools); and the Conference Board of Associated Research Councils, 2101 Constitution Avenue, NW., Washington 25, D.C. (for teaching at the college level, for post-doctoral research, and for teaching in American elementary and secondary schools in Greece).

GRANTS FOR CHINA UNDER FULBRIGHT ACT

The Department of State and the Board of Foreign Scholarships announce opportunities for grants to six American librarians to staff three library institutes to be established in cooperation with the American Library Association under the Fulbright program in China.

The institutes will be located at National Peiping University, Peiping; National College of Social Education, Soochow; and Lingnan University, Canton.

The staff of each of the institutes will consist of a senior librarian in charge and an assistant librarian. Applicants will be selected on the basis of successful experience in the field of library work and will serve for one year. A knowledge of the Chinese language is not required. Veterans will be given preference provided that their qualifications are approximately equal to those of other

candidates. Grants are payable in Chinese currency and will include salary and living allowance.

The United States Educational Foundation in China will have general supervision over the institutes. It is planned that each of the sponsoring universities will appoint an advisory committee of Chinese librarians to assist in arranging the programs and may assign Chinese librarians to assist in the work of the institutes.

The institutes will serve as a medium for the exchange of information between scholars, administrators, and librarians of China and those of the United States, especially in regard to the philosophy of librarianship and the functioning of libraries. The librarians selected will also give instruction in the technical processes of librarianship, especially in regard to selection and cataloging of western books, and will have an opportunity to visit regional libraries to observe and advise.

[1] BULLETIN of Apr. 11, p. 487.

Addresses on European Recovery Program

On April 19, George C. McGhee, Special Assistant to the Under Secretary and Coordinator for Aid to Greece and Turkey, made an address on aid to Greece before the East Texas Chamber of Commerce annual meeting held at Temple, Texas; for the text of this address, see Department of State press release 305 of April 19, 1948.

On April 26, Assistant Secretary Thorp made an address on the European Recovery Program before the American Supply and Machinery Manufacturers' Association, Inc., at Atlantic City, New Jersey; for the text of this address, see Department of State press release 321 of April 26, 1948.

PUBLICATIONS

Department of State

For sale by the Superintendent of Documents, Government Printing Office, Washington 25, D.C. Address requests direct to the Superintendent of Documents, except in the case of free publications, which may be obtained from the Department of State.

Narcotic Drugs. Treaties and Other International Acts Series 1671. Pub. 3006. iii, 60 pp. 20¢.

> Protocol, with Annex, Between the United States and Other Governments; amending the agreements, conventions, and protocols of January 23, 1912, February 11, 1925, February 19, 1925, July 13, 1931, November 27, 1931, and June 26, 1936; ratified by the President July 15, 1947—protocol entered into force with respect to the United States August 12, 1947.

Health and Sanitation Cooperative Program in Peru. Treaties and Other International Acts Series 1673. Pub. 3017. 15 pp. 10¢.

> Agreement Between the United States and Peru; extending the agreement of May 11, 1942, as amended, until June 30, 1948—effected by exchange of notes signed at Lima June 18 and 25, 1947; entered into force June 25, 1947, effective July 1, 1947.

Relief Assistance. Treaties and Other International Acts Series 1674. Pub. 3026. iii, 43 pp. 15¢.

> Agreement and Exchange of Notes Between the United States and China—signed at Nanking October 27, 1947; entered into force October 27, 1947.

Foreign Service List, January 1, 1948. Pub. 3076. iv, 201 pp. 50¢. Subscription price $1.00 a year; $1.25 foreign.

> A quarterly list of officers in the American Foreign Service, their classification, assignments, etc.; also description of consular districts and tariff of Foreign Service fees.

First Report to Congress on the United States Foreign Aid Program. Economic Cooperation Series 6. Pub. 3119. iv, 32 pp. 15¢.

> For period ended December 31, 1947; contains statements on the basis for interim aid and on the administration and operation of the program; also includes the pertinent legal documents.

The Department of State bulletin

Vol. XVIII, No. 464 • Publication 3151

May 23, 1948

The Department of State BULLETIN, a weekly publication compiled and edited in the Division of Publications, Office of Public Affairs, provides the public and interested agencies of the Government with information on developments in the field of foreign relations and on the work of the Department of State and the Foreign Service. The BULLETIN includes press releases on foreign policy issued by the White House and the Department, and statements and addresses made by the President and by the Secretary of State and other officers of the Department, as well as special articles on various phases of international affairs and the functions of the Department. Information is included concerning treaties and international agreements to which the United States is or may become a party and treaties of general international interest.

Publications of the Department, as well as legislative material in the field of international relations, are listed currently.

For sale by the Superintendent of Documents
U.S. Government Printing Office
Washington 25, D.C.

SUBSCRIPTION:
52 issues, $5; single copy, 15 cents

Published with the approval of the Director of the Bureau of the Budget

SIGNIFICANCE OF THE INSTITUTE OF INTER-AMERICAN AFFAIRS IN THE CONDUCT OF U.S. FOREIGN POLICY

By Louis J. Halle, Jr.

I

Among the paradoxical but logical developments of our times is the growth of international cooperation that has accompanied the spread of international chaos over the past several generations. More countries cooperate with one another than in the past; moreover the fields of activity in which they now cooperate officially include, besides the traditional fields of politics and commerce, almost all the larger aspects of cultural, social, and economic affairs.

In the more secure and orderly circumstances of the last century, our Government did not feel it need be actively concerned if, say, the inhabitants of some land thousands of miles away were chronically hungry or handicapped by illiteracy. The dangers, advantages, and responsibilities of "one world" had not clearly emerged in the unfolding of history. Although our people may often responded generously to dramatic appeals from famine-stricken countries, distant lands were far more distant than today, and we did not conceive that we had official responsibility where we lacked jurisdiction.

With the necessity of adjusting ourselves to spreading disorder in a shrinking world, we have now come to identify the welfare of our own people—spiritual, cultural, economic, or political—with the welfare of peoples everywhere. The thinking of other nations has followed a similar course, so that this development is one which we share with all the other nations that represent our common civilization. If there is a difference, it is simply that our stake and our responsibility are greater by virtue of our resources and our position.

Within the Western Hemisphere we must take realistic account of the fact that any aggression from outside, political as well as military, though it occurred 5,000 miles away, would be directed at the United States as the ultimate target. The im-

mediate action would be merely an attempt to establish or extend what was, with respect to us, a beachhead. The point of view of any other country in the Hemisphere, if realistic, must likewise be that any weakness of the United States that invites aggression, political or military, also exposes the other country to aggression, whether as a preliminary target, an incidental target, or the target of a mopping-up operation. No country in the Hemisphere is likely to preserve its independence if the independence of the United States is lost; and the independence of the United States would certainly be jeopardized if any other American nation were subjugated by an overseas power. In a world where aggression is more than an academic possibility, active cooperation would be imposed on the nations of the Hemisphere by self-interest, if by nothing else, as a vital necessity. All the American nations have, in fact, agreed on the need for cooperation and are cooperating on a broad and well-established basis. Canada, while not a member of the Organization of American States, is certainly to be included among the cooperating good neighbors in the Hemisphere.

In this situation, the American republics are continuing and developing long-range cooperation on a broad front to strengthen their own social systems so that those systems may stand firm against the threat of political aggression taking the form of chaos fomented from abroad. They have recognized that the maintenance of freedom depends on the maintenance of the basic conditions that enable men to be free. Hungry peoples will not cherish their freedom because they cannot enjoy it. Peoples that are ridden by disease lack the strength to defend their freedom. Uneducated peoples do not know how to exercise freedom. Hunger, disease, and ignorance are the principal allies of totalitarianism in the modern world. They are the only popular allies it has. They give it what political strength it commands. Taking this kind of cause-and-effect into account, the American republics are agreed on the long-term strategy of cooperatively dealing with the threat of totalitarianism by eliminating the allies on which it depends. The proceedings of Inter-American conferences may be cited for repeated expressions of their determination to work together for the reduction of ignorance, poverty, and disease.

II

The broadening range of intergovernmental cooperation in recent times has been accompanied by necessary innovations in the machinery of government. The basic machinery developed for the purpose has been that of international organization.[1] The cooperating nations being many and having common interests, it is natural that the machinery should be multilateral and based on common participation. Such organizations as the Food and Agriculture Organization of the United Nations (FAO), the United Nations Educational, Scientific and Cultural Organization (UNESCO), and the Inter-American Institute of Agricultural Sciences are, however, in their infancy. Their resources are still inadequate to the total needs of their members. The Pan American Sanitary Organization, although much older, faces much the same dilemma. Under the circumstances, the active participation of the United States in these organizations has not obviated the necessity of developing, within its own Government, machinery for effective bilateral cooperation with other governments in these diverse fields. Through this machinery, cooperative activities are carried on that could not be carried on at all if it did not exist.

The two main agencies that have been developed within this Government for the purpose are the Interdepartmental Committee on Scientific and Cultural Cooperation and the Institute of Inter-American Affairs. The history, the methods, and the substantial accomplishments of the former have already been reported in the BULLETIN.[2] The latter is the subject of this report, as it will be of three others to follow. The three to follow will set forth what, specifically, is being accomplished through the Institute in the fields of agriculture, public health, and education. This first one is concerned with the purpose already suggested and the means.

---

[1] For a discussion on the development of the Inter-American System see *Sovereignty and Interdependence in the New World* (Department of State publication 3054).

[2] Reprinted from the BULLETIN as *The Program of the Interdepartmental Committee on Scientific and Cultural Cooperation* (Department of State publication 2994) and also *Cooperation in the Americas* (Department of State publication 2971).

offices in the ministry building you will not find that it presents a fundamentally different appearance from any other division of the ministry or of our own Government departments in Washington.

The financial arrangements are no less intimate. The project contributions of each government go into a joint bank account in which it is impossible to distinguish the pesos of the one from the dollars of the other.

The arrangement just described is typical and is tending to become standard, but in each country there are variations, greater or lesser, adapted to local circumstances and the character or origin of particular programs. It is an arrangement that has now been adopted by our Government, in its essentials, for carrying on the present programs of assistance in Greece and Turkey.

At this point it is well to say what, in fact, these programs are. In governmental parlance, we often use the terms "program" and "project" interchangeably. With respect to the activities of the Institute, "projects" are the parts into which a "program" may be analyzed. A program is, in itself, a long-range developmental enterprise, covering a large geographical area and, to the extent possible, projected forward in its planning over a period of years. A typical agricultural program, for example, is designed permanently to improve the productivity of the agriculture of a country as a whole by introducing and establishing new devices and new methods. This may mean the importation of improved varieties of seed and cattle; it may mean the establishment of machinery pools for making agricultural machinery available to farmers on a rental basis where and when they need it; it may mean the introduction of pasteurization and bottling in the processing of milk; it may mean varied extension work over a wide area; it may mean improving the design of fishing craft; and it will probably mean most of these things together with many others not listed here. All the programs involve, moreover, the training of technicians, either locally or in the United States, with a view to establishing a national supply of technical experts sufficient for the national needs. These technicians are trained specifically to take part in the programs and carry them on. In a similar manner, the public health and sanitation and the educational programs are designed to establish permanent high standards, organization, and facilities.

Further reports in the BULLETIN will describe actual programs in the three fields of operation. It therefore suffices to add here that all these programs are more than long-range in conception; they are intended to be permanent. This is not to say that anybody has a notion of making United States participation in any of them permanent. On the contrary, the policy of this Government is to withdraw from these programs as soon as they have become sufficiently developed and established so that what has been begun may be effectively continued with the resources available to the local government. To that end, the contribution of the United States, normally, is reduced from year to year while the contribution of the local government increases. The burden is shifted gradually. Although the United States makes the preponderant contribution initially to all these programs, some of the programs have developed to such an extent that the local government is now contributing funds at the rate of eight or ten or even twelve times our contribution.

To give these matters their due proportion, it is necessary to note that these programs are primarily programs of technical assistance and only incidentally of financial assistance by the United States. Far more important than the relatively small amounts of money we supply are the know-how, experience, and training embodied in our technical experts or taking the form of the technical training that we give to nationals of the countries in which the programs operate.

A final word on operating policy. This Government does and must scrupulously refrain from urging its cooperative assistance on any country, since its participation in these essentially domestic programs would be improper if it were not in response to the invitation and full welcome of the local governments. One does not help one's neighbor put up his barn unless he indicates that he needs help and requests it. The Institute is merely the device by means of which our Government is able to meet, when it appears to be in the common interest, the desires and the specific requests of other American republics.

V

The programs in which this Government participates through its Institute of Inter-American Affairs represent, simply, one important aspect of the aggressive action without which the paper resolutions in which the American republics have expressed their determination to cooperate for the economic and social welfare of their peoples would be meaningless. What they are accomplishing in this respect will be set forth in the reports that follow this. Their purpose, however, is also "to strengthen friendship and understanding among the peoples of the American republics". Our diplomatic missions, the representatives of cooperating governments, and qualified observers generally agree that the programs are, in fact, accomplishing this purpose. They are accomplishing it, not merely by the benefits they confer by their contributions to the general welfare, but also by processes that are no less important if less tangible.

I revert to the intimate nature of the cooperation that is provided by the *servicio* and similar administrative devices. In them you have what is in

America's Responsibility in World Trade

By Norman Burns

When the Secretary of State recommended to Congress on May 6 that the Reciprocal Trade Agreements Act be renewed for another three years, he observed that the United States, through force of circumstance, had become the rallying point for the free peoples of the earth. Our leadership in world affairs, he stated, depended, in considerable measure, upon the continuity and consistency of our policy in the international economic field. He concluded that "No economic bond is closer than the friendly ties of mutually satisfactory trade."[1]

United States Needs To Export

The United States has a vital economic stake in world trade because we are now the world's principal foreign trading country. United States exports are larger than those of any other country. United States imports are second only to those of the United Kingdom.

Approximately 10 percent of our total agricultural and industrial production is sold abroad. Some people may think that an average export of only 10 percent of total production is not important, but businessmen know that a change of 1 percent in a company's sales may make the difference between black and red ink. Moreover, the 10-percent average obscures the fact that for many products exports take a fifth to a half of their total production.

In the industrial field we have about one half of the world's productive capacity and we need foreign markets if we are to keep that productive capacity at work. We need to export to prosper, and so do other nations. Exports furnished a market for 14 percent of our total production of automobiles, 26 percent of aircraft, 22 percent of office appliances, 18 percent of printing machinery, 5 percent of industrial machinery, 12 percent of radios, 17 percent of agricultural machinery, 15 percent of drugs, 38 percent of rosin, 52 percent of phosphate rock, and 36 percent of our output of borax, etc. (1938 basis). Since the production of many of these products is concentrated in particular localities a loss of exports would have particularly sharp repercussions on such areas.

In the agricultural sphere there is the need of foreign markets to absorb our potential agricultural surpluses. United States agricultural production in 1947 was 35 percent above the prewar volume. In the crop year 1946–47, we exported over one third of our production of wheat, rice, and dried milk, between 10 and 25 percent of our production of dried beans and peas, condensed and evaporated milk and cheese, from 5 to 10 percent of our edible fats and oils, eggs, and fruit; we normally export one third or more of our cotton, tobacco, and dried fruits.

From the point of view of labor, it is estimated that 2.5 million nonfarm workers are directly or indirectly dependent for their jobs upon exports. This constitutes 5½ percent of our total nonagricultural employment. In iron and steel, electrical machinery, motor vehicles, nonferrous metals, coal, chemicals, and rubber from 11 to 18.5 percent of the workers are directly or indirectly dependent upon exports for their jobs.

Obviously, in an integrated economy such as ours, city and farm are highly dependent upon each other and both have a major stake in exports. A substantial shrinkage in our export trade in any single important product would affect adversely that product and would reverberate throughout our whole economy.

United States Needs To Import

Many people favor large exports but are highly dubious about the benefits of imports. They want to export much and import little.

The unavoidable fact is that we cannot export unless we import, except by continuing foreign loans indefinitely without repayment. The corner grocery store cannot sell unless it buys.

The real question is not whether we want to import but whether we want to import and export—that is, whether we want a large foreign trade which means large exports and large imports; or a small foreign trade with small exports and small imports; or no foreign trade. However we may feel on this question, it is hardly an accident that the prosperous countries of the world are those that have a large foreign trade. The poor countries are those that have a small per capita foreign trade.

Imports are beneficial, not only because they help to sustain exports, but also because of their direct usefulness in domestic production and consumption. Over one half of our total imports consists of crude and semi-crude materials used by domestic manufacturers as raw materials in their further fabrication of finished goods. Many of these are primary materials either not produced at all in this country or not produced in sufficient volume to fill our needs at a reasonable price. For example, the Bureau of Mines reported to Con-

[1] BULLETIN of May 16, 1948, p. 651.

gress in May 1947 that our known commercial reserves of 24 major minerals were less than sufficient to supply 35 years of domestic requirements at current rates of consumption. Among these are copper, lead, zinc, manganese, chrome, tungsten, mica, tin, bauxite, cadmium, vanadium, tantalum, asbestos, graphite, nickel, industrial diamonds, and petroleum—all vital materials in an industrial economy. Imports of such materials are necessary (a) to conserve dwindling domestic reserves in the event of an emergency and (b) to supply our manufacturers with raw materials at costs that will permit them to compete against foreign manufacturers of fabricated goods.

A second large category of imports consists of such products as coffee, tea, cocoa, bananas, and spices, which are not produced at all in the United States. These are essential to maintain our standard of living.

A third, and smaller class, consists of imports which compete directly or indirectly with more or less similar domestic products. Such imports are frequently of a different grade, quality, and price range than the domestic product. Among such imports are high-priced British woolens, French lace (of finer count than domestic lace), Wedgewood chinaware from the United Kingdom, and specialty French and Italian cheese and wine. Lower tariffs on such imports would benefit consumers. On the other hand, drastic reduction of tariff rates might disrupt the domestic producers. In practice, the United States has followed a policy of selective tariff reductions on such products with due regard to competitive and other factors.

The elimination of foreign competition through the device of high tariffs runs counter to American ideas of increasing efficiency through the force of free competition. In the long run, highly protected industries, when not stimulated by free competition, lag in technological developments. Protection frequently spells stagnation. The American economy owes its vigor and driving force to competition.

American industrial and agricultural efficiency is so great that even before the war our exports exceeded our imports. Hourly labor rates were lower abroad than in this country but the efficiency of our management, labor, and machinery was so great that the labor cost per unit of product, for practically all mass-production goods, was actually lower here than abroad.

Because of America's high industrial efficiency and productivity American labor can compete to advantage with free labor anywhere in the world. Otherwise we could not sell in world markets.

Crucial Problem in Our Foreign Trade

The crucial fact, today, is that our exports have increased far more than imports since the war. Before the war, exports slightly exceeded imports.

regard for the effect on other countries, who often felt impelled to retaliate. Such practices in the 1920's and 1930's tended to "dry up" international trade.

International Trade Organization

The United States participated with 52 other countries in the formulation of a Charter for an International Trade Organization at Habana (November 21–March 24) for a set of rules that countries would follow in their conduct of trade with each other. In international trade, as in private business, countries need to follow certain rules so that trade can expand in an orderly fashion. In the past, different countries followed many trade practices. The result, some said, resembled a playing field where, at the same time, the English were playing rugby, the French tennis, the Cubans pelota, and the Americans baseball.

The new rules cover such matters as trade barriers, nondiscrimination and equal trade treatment, import quotas, export subsidies, customs formalities, cartel regulations, international commodity agreements, and the protection of foreign investments.

The charter for an International Trade Organization will be submitted to Congress, possibly within the next year, to decide whether the United States shall become a member.

Renewal of the Reciprocal Trade Agreements Act

The Trade Agreements Act, first passed in 1934, has been renewed four times since then. It expires June 12, 1948. The Act permits the President to enter into trade agreements with other countries whereby the United States tariffs may be reduced (by not more than 50 percent below the rate of January 1, 1945—after public hearing) in return for equivalent concessions from the other country.

The Geneva Trade Agreement, and other trade agreements concluded since 1934, were negotiated under this Act. If the Act is not renewed, the old agreements continue in force, unless terminated by the President, but no new agreements can be made.

The President recommended to Congress on March 1, 1948, that the Act be renewed without change for another three years. He stated that renewal was necessary: (1) to enable the United States to negotiate tariff agreements with other countries that might want to join the Geneva Agreement, (2) to enable the United States to negotiate revisions in the Geneva Agreement when changing world conditions necessitated revision, and (3) to permit continued leadership of the United States in its program of expanding international trade in a "mighty endeavor to build a prosperous and peaceful world".[2]

---

[2] BULLETIN of Mar. 14, 1948, p. 351.

NINTH INTERNATIONAL CONFERENCE OF AMERICAN STATES

International Organization of American Stat[es]

TEXT OF CHARTER

IN THE NAME OF THEIR PEOPLES,
THE STATES
REPRESENTED AT THE NINTH INTERNATIONAL
CONFERENCE OF AMERICAN STATES,

CONVINCED that the historic mission of America is to
offer to man a land of liberty, and a favorable environment
for the development of his personality and the realization
of his just aspirations;

CONSCIOUS that that mission has already inspired numerous agreements, whose essential value lies in the desire of
the American peoples to live together in peace, and, through
their mutual understanding and respect for the sovereignty
of each one, to provide for the betterment of all, in independence, in equality and under law;

CONFIDENT that the true significance of American solidarity and good neighborliness can only mean the consolidation on this Continent, within the framework of democratic institutions, of a system of individual liberty and
social justice based on respect for the essential rights of
man;

PERSUADED that their welfare, and their contribution to
the progress and the civilization of the world, will increasingly require intensive continental cooperation;

RESOLVED to persevere in the noble undertaking that
humanity has conferred upon the United Nations, whose
principles and purposes they solemnly reaffirm;

CONVINCED that juridical organization is a necessary
condition for a security and peace founded on moral order
and on justice; and

In accordance with Resolution IX of the Inter-American
Conference on Problems of War and Peace, held at Mexico
City,

HAVE AGREED upon the following

Charter of the Organization of American States

PART ONE

Chapter I: Nature and Purposes

Article 1

The American States establish by this Charter the
international organization that they have developed to
achieve an order of peace and justice, to promote their
solidarity, to strengthen their collaboration, and to defend
their sovereignty, their territorial integrity and their
independence. Within the United Nations, the Organization of American States is a regional agency.

Article 2

All American States that ratify the present Charter
are Members of the Organization.

Article 3

Any new political entity that arises from the union
several Member States and that, as such, ratifies the pr[es]ent Charter, shall become a Member of the Organizati[on].
The entry of the new political entity into the Organizat[ion]
shall result in the loss of membership of each one of t[he]
States which constitute it.

Article 4

The Organization of American States, in order to [put]
into practice the principles on which it is founded a[nd]
to fulfill its regional obligations under the Charter of [the]
United Nations, proclaims the following essential p[ur]poses:

a) To strengthen the peace and security of the contine[nt];
b) To prevent possible causes of difficulties and to ens[ure]
   the pacific settlement of disputes that may arise am[ong]
   the Member States;
c) To provide for common action on the part of th[ose]
   States in the event of aggression;
d) To seek the solution of political, juridical and e[co]nomic problems that may arise among them; and
e) To promote by cooperative action their economic, soc[ial]
   and cultural development.

Chapter II: Principles

Article 5

The American States reaffirm the following principl[es]:

a) International law is the standard of conduct of sta[tes]
   in their reciprocal relations.
b) International order consists essentially of respect [for]
   the personality, sovereignty and independence [of]
   states, and the faithful fulfillment of obligations [de]rived from treaties and other sources of internation[al]
   law.
c) Good faith shall govern the relations between stat[es].
d) The solidarity of the American States and the hi[gh]
   aims which are sought through it require the politi[cal]
   organization of those states on the basis of the effect[ive]
   exercise of representative democracy.
e) The American States condemn war of aggression: [vic]tory does not give rights.
f) An act of aggression against one American State is [an]
   act of aggression against all the other American Stat[es].
g) Controversies of an international character arisi[ng]
   between two or more American States shall be sett[led]
   by peaceful procedures.
h) Social justice and social security are bases of last[ing]
   peace.
i) Economic cooperation is essential to the comm[on]
   welfare and prosperity of the peoples of the contine[nt].
j) The American States proclaim the fundamental rig[hts]
   of the individual without distinction as to ra[ce],
   nationality, creed or sex.

internal or external affairs of any other state. The foregoing principle prohibits not only armed force but also any other form of interference or attempted threat against the personality of the state or against its political, economic and cultural elements.

Article 16

No state may use or encourage the use of coercive measures of an economic or political character in order to force the sovereign will of another state and obtain from it advantages of any kind.

Article 17

The territory of a state is inviolable; it may not be the object, even temporarily, of military occupation or of other measures of force taken by another state, directly or indirectly, on any grounds whatever. No territorial acquisitions or special advantages obtained either by force or by other means of coercion shall be recognized.

Article 18

The American States bind themselves in their international relations not to have recourse to the use of force, except in the case of self-defense in accordance with existing treaties or in fulfillment thereof.

Article 19

Measures adopted for the maintenance of peace and security in accordance with existing treaties do not constitute a violation of the principles set forth in articles 15 and 17.

Chapter IV: Pacific Settlement of Disputes

Article 20

All international disputes that may arise between American States shall be submitted to the peaceful procedures set forth in this Charter, before being referred to the Security Council of the United Nations.

Article 21

The following are peaceful procedures: direct negotiation, good offices, mediation, investigation and conciliation, judicial settlement, arbitration, and those which the parties to the dispute may especially agree upon at any time.

Article 22

In the event that a dispute arises between two or more American States which, in the opinion of one of them, cannot be settled through the usual diplomatic channels, the Parties shall agree on some other peaceful procedure that will enable them to reach a solution.

Article 23

A special treaty will establish adequate procedures for the pacific settlement of disputes and will determine the appropriate means for their application, so that no dispute between American States shall fail of definitive settlement within a reasonable period.

Chapter V: Collective Security

Article 24

Every act of aggression by a state against the integrity or inviolability of the territory or against the sovereignty or political independence of an American State shall be considered an act of aggression against the other American States.

667

Article 25

If the inviolability or the integrity of the territory or the sovereignty or political independence of any American State should be affected by an armed attack or by an act of aggression that is not an armed attack, or by an extra-continental conflict, or by a conflict between two or more American States, or by any other fact or situation that might endanger the peace of America, the American States, in furtherance of the principles of continental solidarity or collective self-defense, shall apply the measures and procedures established in the special treaties on the subject.

Chapter VI: Economic Standards

Article 26

The Member States agree to cooperate with one another, as far as their resources may permit and their laws may provide, in the broadest spirit of good neighborliness, in order to strengthen their economic structure, develop their agriculture and mining, promote their industry and increase their trade.

Article 27

If the economy of an American State is affected by serious conditions that cannot be satisfactorily remedied by its own unaided efforts, such State may place its economic problems before the Inter-American Economic and Social Council to seek through consultation, the most appropriate solution for such problems.

Chapter VII: Social Standards

Article 28

The Member States agree to cooperate with one another to achieve just and decent living conditions for their entire populations.

Article 29

The Member States agree upon the desirability of developing their social legislation on the following bases:

a) All human beings, without distinction as to race, nationality, sex, creed or social condition, have the right to attain material well-being and spiritual growth under circumstances of liberty, dignity, equality of opportunity and economic security;

b) Work is a right and a social duty; it shall not be considered as an article of commerce; it demands respect for freedom of association and for the dignity of the worker; and it is to be performed under conditions that ensure life, health and a decent standard of living, both during the working years and during old age, or when any circumstance deprives the individual of the possibility of working.

Chapter VIII: Cultural Standards

Article 30

The Member States agree to promote, in accordance with their constitutional provisions and their material resources, the exercise of the right to education, on the following bases:

a) Elementary education shall be compulsory and, when provided by the state, shall be without cost;

b) Higher education shall be available to all, without distinction as to race, nationality, sex, language, creed or social condition.

Article 31

With due consideration for the national character of each State, the Member States undertake to facilitate free cultural interchange by every medium of expression.

ments, of any matter referred to it by the Inter-American Conference or the Meeting of Consultation of Ministers of Foreign Affairs.

Article 51

The Council shall be responsible for the proper discharge by the Pan American Union of the duties assigned to it.

Article 52

The Council shall serve provisionally as the Organ of Consultation when the circumstances contemplated in Article 43 of this Charter arise.

Article 53

It is also the duty of the Council:

a) To draft and submit to the Governments and to the Inter-American Conference proposals for the creation of new Specialized Organizations or for the combination, adaptation or elimination of existing ones, including matters relating to the financing and support thereof;

b) To draft recommendations to the Governments, the Inter-American Conference, the Specialized Conferences or the Specialized Organizations, for the coordination of the activities and programs of such organizations, after consultation with them;

c) To conclude agreements with the Inter-American Specialized Organizations to determine the relations that shall exist between the respective agency and the Organization;

d) To conclude agreements or special arrangements for cooperation with other American organizations of recognized international standing;

e) To promote and facilitate collaboration between the Organization of American States and the United Nations, as well as between Inter-American Specialized Organizations and similar international agencies;

f) To adopt resolutions that will enable the Secretary General to perform the duties envisaged in Article 84.

g) To perform the other duties assigned to it by the present Charter.

Article 54

The Council shall establish the bases for fixing the quota that each Government is to contribute to the maintenance of the Pan American Union, taking into account the ability to pay of the respective countries and their determination to contribute in an equitable manner. The budget, after approval by the Council, shall be transmitted to the Governments at least six months before the first day of the fiscal year, with a statement of the annual quota of each country. Decisions on budgetary matters require the approval of two-thirds of the members of the Council.

Article 55

The Council shall formulate its own regulations.

Article 56

The Council shall function at the seat of the Pan American Union.

Article 57

The following are organs of the Council of the Organization of American States:

a) The Inter-American Economic and Social Council;
b) The Inter-American Council of Jurists; and
c) The Inter-American Cultural Council.

Article 58

The organs referred to in the preceding article shall have technical autonomy within the limits of this Charter; but their decisions shall not encroach upon the sphere of action of the Council of the Organization.

Article 59

The organs of the Council of the Organization are composed of representatives of all the Member States of the Organization.

Article 60

The organs of the Council of the Organization shall, as far as possible, render to the Governments such technical services as the latter may request; and they shall advise the Council of the Organization in matters within their jurisdiction.

Article 61

The organs of the Council of the Organization shall, in agreement with the Council, establish cooperative relations with the corresponding organs of the United Nations and with the national or international agencies that function within their respective spheres of action.

Article 62

The Council of the Organization, with the advice of the appropriate bodies and after consultation with the Governments, shall formulate the statutes of its organs in accordance with and in execution of the provisions of this Charter. These organs shall formulate their own regulations.

A) THE INTER-AMERICAN ECONOMIC AND SOCIAL COUNCIL.

Article 63

The Inter-American Economic and Social Council has for its principal purpose the promotion of the economic and social welfare of the American nations through effective cooperation for the better utilization of their natural resources, the development of their agriculture and industry and the raising of the standards of living of their peoples.

Article 64

To accomplish this purpose the Council shall:

a) Propose the means by which the American nations may give each other technical assistance in making studies and formulating and executing plans in order to carry out the purposes referred to in Article 26 and to develop and improve their social services;
b) Act as coordinating agency for all official inter-American activities of an economic and social nature;
c) Undertake studies on its own initiative or at the request of any Member State;
d) Assemble and prepare reports on economic and social matters for the use of the Member States;
e) Suggest to the Council of the Organization the advisability of holding Specialized Conferences on economic and social matters;
f) Carry on such other activities as may be assigned to it by the Inter-American Conference, the Meeting of Consultation of Ministers of Foreign Affairs or the Council of the Organization.

Article 65

The Inter-American Economic and Social Council, composed of technical delegates appointed by each Member State, shall meet on its own initiative or on that of the Council of the Organization.

Article 66

The Inter-American Economic and Social Council shall function at the seat of the Pan American Union, but it may hold meetings in any American city by a majority decision of the Member States.

Foreign Affairs, the Specialized Conferences, and the Council and its organs.

Article 82

The Pan American Union, through its technical and information offices, shall, under the direction of the Council, promote economic, social, juridical and cultural relations among all the Member States of the Organization.

Article 83

The Pan American Union shall also perform the following functions:

a) Transmit *ex officio* to Member States the convocation to the Inter-American Conference, the Meeting of Consultation of Ministers of Foreign Affairs, and the Specialized Conferences;

b) Advise the Council and its organs in the preparation of programs and regulations of the Inter-American Conference, the Meeting of Consultation of Ministers of Foreign Affairs, and the Specialized Conferences;

c) Place, to the extent of its ability, at the disposal of the Government of the Country where a conference is to be held the technical aid and personnel which such government may request;

d) Serve as custodian of the documents and archives of the Inter-American Conferences, of the Meetings of Consultation of Ministers of Foreign Affairs and, insofar as possible, of the Specialized Conferences;

e) Serve as depository of the instruments of ratification of Inter-American agreements;

f) Perform the functions entrusted to it by the Inter-American Conference, and the Meeting of Consultation of Ministers of Foreign Affairs;

g) Submit to the Council an annual report on the activities of the Organization;

h) Submit to the Inter-American Conference, a report on the work accomplished by the organs of the Organization since the previous Conference.

Article 84

It is the duty of the Secretary General:

a) To establish, with the approval of the Council, such technical and administrative offices of the Pan American Union as are necessary to accomplish its purposes.

b) To determine the number of department heads, officers and employees of the Pan American Union; to appoint them, regulate their powers and duties, and fix their compensation, in accordance with general standards established by the Council.

Article 85

There shall be an Assistant Secretary General, elected by the Council for a term of ten years and eligible for reelection. In the event of a vacancy in the office of Assistant Secretary General, the Council shall, within the next ninety days, elect a successor to fill such office for the remainder of the term.

Article 86

The Assistant Secretary General shall be the Secretary of the Council. He shall perform the duties of the Secretary General during the temporary absence or disability of the latter, or during the ninety-day vacancy referred to in Article 79. He shall also serve as advisory officer to the Secretary General, with the power to act as his delegate in all matters that the Secretary General may entrust to him.

Article 87

The Council, by a two-thirds vote of its members, may remove the Secretary General or the Assistant Secretary

General, whenever the proper functioning of the Organization so demands.

Article 88

The heads of the respective departments of the Pan American Union, appointed by the Secretary General, shall be the Executive Secretaries of the Inter-American Economic and Social Council, the Council of Jurists and the Cultural Council.

Article 89

In the performance of their duties the personnel shall not seek or receive instructions from any government or from any other authority outside the Pan American Union. They shall refrain from any action that might reflect upon their position as international officials responsible only to the Union.

Article 90

Every Member of the Organization of American States pledges itself to respect the exclusively international character of the responsibilities of the Secretary General and the personnel and not to seek to influence them in the discharge of their duties.

Article 91

In selecting its personnel the Pan American Union shall give first consideration to efficiency, competence and integrity; but at the same time importance shall be given to the necessity of recruiting personnel on as broad a geographical basis as possible.

Article 92

The seat of the Pan American Union is the City of Washington.

Chapter XIV: The Specialized Conferences

Article 93

The Specialized Conferences shall meet to deal with special technical matters or to develop specific aspects of inter-American cooperation, when it is so decided by the Inter American Conference or the Meeting of Consultation of Ministers of Foreign Affairs; when inter-American agreements so provide; or when the Council of the Organization considers it necessary, either on its own initiative or at the request of one of its organs or of one of the Specialized Organizations.

Article 94

The program and regulations of the Specialized Conferences shall be prepared by the organs of the Council of the Organization or by the Specialized Organizations concerned; they shall be submitted to the Member Governments for consideration and transmitted to the Council for its information.

Chapter XV: The Specialized Organizations

Article 95

For the purposes of the present Charter, the Inter-American Specialized Organizations are the inter-governmental organizations established by multilateral agreements and having specific functions with respect to technical matters of common interest to the American States.

Article 96

The Council shall, for the purposes stated in Article 53, maintain a register of the Organizations that fulfill the conditions set forth in the foregoing article.

Article 97

The Specialized Organizations shall enjoy the fullest technical autonomy and shall take into account the recom-

Organization of American States does not recognize restriction on the eligibility of men and women to participate in the activities of the various Organs and to hold ~ons therein.

ter XVIII: Ratification and Entry Into Force

Article 108

present Charter shall remain open for signature by American States and shall be ratified in accordance :heir respective constitutional procedures. The origi nstrument, the Spanish, English, Portuguese, and h texts of which are equally authentic, shall be de 'd with the Pan American Union, which shall transmit ied copies thereof to the Governments for purposes of :ation. The instruments of ratification shall be de 'd with the Pan American Union, which shall notify .gnatory States of such deposit.

Article 109

~ present Charter shall enter into force among the 'ing States when two-thirds of the signatory States deposited their ratifications. It shall enter into force respect to the remaining States in the order in which ieposit their ratifications.

Article 110

The present Charter shall be registered with the Secretariat of the United Nations through the Pan American Union.

Article 111

Amendments to the present Charter may be adopted only at an Inter-American Conference convened for that purpose. Amendments shall enter into force in accordance with the terms and the procedure set forth in Article 109.

Article 112

The present Charter shall remain in force indefinitely, but may be denounced by any Member State upon written notification to the Pan American Union, which shall communicate to all the others each notice of denunciation received. After two years from the date on which the Pan American Union receives a notice of denunciation, the present Charter shall cease to be in force with respect to the denouncing State, which shall cease to belong to the Organization after it has fulfilled the obligations arising from the present Charter.

In Witness Whereof the undersigned Plenipotentiaries, whose full powers have been presented and found to be in good and due form, sign the present Charter at the City of Bogotá, Colombia, on the dates that appear opposite their respective signatures.

THE UNITED NATIONS AND SPECIALIZED AGENCIES

el Proclaimed as an Independent Republic

TEXT OF LETTER FROM THE AGENT OF THE PROVISIONAL GOVERNMENT OF ISRAEL TO THE PRESIDENT OF THE U.S.

[Released to the press by the White House on May 15]

Y DEAR MR. PRESIDENT: I have the honor to fy you that the state of Israel has been pro ned as an independent republic within fron : approved by the General Assembly of the :ed Nations in its Resolution of November 29, , and that a provisional government has been ged to assume the rights and duties of govern t for preserving law and order within the idaries of Israel, for defending the state nst external aggression, and for discharging >bligations of Israel to the other nations of the ld in accordance with international law. The of Independence will become effective at one ute after six o'clock on the evening of 14 May l, Washington time.

'ith full knowledge of the deep bond of sym iy which has existed and has been strengthened ' the past thirty years between the Government he United States and the Jewish people of ~stine, I have been authorized by the provi

sional government of the new state to tender this message and to express the hope that your government will recognize and will welcome Israel into the community of nations.

Very respectfully yours,

ELIAHU EPSTEIN
Agent, Provisional Government of Israel

Statement by President Truman

[Released to the press by the White House May 14]

This Government has been informed that a Jewish state has been proclaimed in Palestine, and recognition has been requested by the provisional government thereof.

The United States recognizes the provisional government as the *de facto* authority of the new State of Israel.

The Rome Manpow

BY VAL R

The importance of manpower problems in the European Recovery Program was recognized by the Committee of European Economic Co-operation (CEEC) conference at Paris in 1947. That Conference's Manpower Committee called for more effective transfers of workers from countries of manpower surplus to countries with manpower shortages, and indicated some of the types of measures to be taken for more effective utilization of labor within each country. It asked also that the Italian Government call a conference of the "interested governments" at Rome early in 1948, to review the progress made in recruiting foreign workers and to "plan and coordinate any further measures which may be necessary".

Participation

Late in November 1947 the Italian Government sent invitations to all the CEEC countries for such a conference, to open on January 26. All the CEEC countries with the exception of Iceland accepted the invitation to the Conference, as did the occupying authorities of the three western zones of Germany.

The specialized agencies with an interest in the problem—the International Labor Organization, Economic Commission for Europe, Food and Agriculture Organization, International Bank, and International Refugee Organization—were represented by observers. The International Trade Organization, in view of its preliminary state of organization, chose not to send an observer.

The Italian Government asked the United States to send observers to the Conference. The United States observers were: Val R. Lorwin of the Division of International Labor, Social, and Health Affairs, Department of State, Senior Observer; Lt. Col. Thomas A. Lane, then Chief Labor Officer, Allied Military Government, British–United States Zone, Free Territory of Trieste, and now labor attaché at Rome; and William Shaughnessy, then of the United States Employment Service, Department of Labor, now with the International Refugee Organization.

Since it was the first international conference in Italy since the end of the Fascist regime, its arrangements were of particular interest. These arrangements can certainly be regarded as having come off successfully. The hospitality of the

Conference Work

The Rome conference elected as president
Giuseppe Saragat, vice-president of the Italian
Council of Ministers and president of the Inter-
ministerial Committee for Social and Welfare
Questions. As rapporteur general it named M.
Bousquet, head of the French Delegation, and
director general for administrative affairs at the
Quai d'Orsay. As vice-presidents it chose A. F.
Rouse, head of the United Kingdom Delegation
and head of the Foreign Labor Branch of the
Ministry of Labor; and Jean Cuvelier, of the
Ministry of Foreign Affairs, head of the Belgian
Delegation. Of its two major working committees,
Committee I was concerned with domestic labor-
utilization measures, and Committee II with inter-
national manpower movements. Chairman of
Committee I was Mr. Rouse, with M. Delperée of
the Belgian Ministry of Labor as rapporteur.
Committee II chose a chairman from the Portu-
guese Delegation, Alexandre Ribeiro da Cunha,
associate director general of the National Insti-
tute of Labor and Social Insurance, with Albert
Tobin, of the Federal Office of Industry, Arts,
Crafts and Labor of Switzerland, as rapporteur.
A statistical committee was also set up, with M.
Duon, of the French National Institute of Statis-
tics, as chairman.

The conclusions took the form of recommendations to the governments represented, or to "interested governments" among those represented.[1]
The Conference's immediate and most tangible
results were in the field of international migration.
There was serious consideration of many domestic
manpower issues. But the preoccupation with
international issues was inevitable, first, because the Conference was meeting in Rome, under
the shadow of the present Italian unemployment
problem; and, second, because by the nature of
things, the Conference could propose forms of immediate action on emigration and immigration,
whereas internal manpower problems require
action, which is often quite gradual, within each
country.

Rome Committee

The major development of the Conference was
its recommendation to the governments represented for the setting up at Rome of a Committee
for the Coordination of European Manpower
Movements. In contrast to its rather formidable
title, the Committee is to work on the practical
day-to-day operational questions involved in the
implementation of bilateral emigration agreements, as a sort of "trouble shooter", or "progress
chaser" as the English would call it. It is to suggest practical ways and means of facilitating manpower movements under the bilateral accords. It
is to concern itself, at least for the time being,
largely with Italian manpower movements to
other European countries.

The emphasis is on the practical as distinct from
long-range studies, and on the day-to-day type
of operational problem, as distinct from policy-
setting or the promotion of emigration. Problems on which the Committee would work may
include:

(a) Accelerating, simplifying, and reducing
the costs of travel documents;
(b) Language and vocational "pre-training"
for emigration;
(c) Simplification of medical controls;
(d) Simplified occupational classification, for
immediate bilateral use in recruitment of workers;
(e) Travel and reception arrangements;
(f) Housing;
(g) Transfer of emigrant savings and family
allowances;
(h) Maintenance of social-security rights of
temporary emigrants.
(i) Current exchange of information on labor
requirements and availabilities.

These are not spectacular tasks; they are modest
but practical and specific.

The Conference recognized the long-established
jurisdiction and competence of the ILO in its field,
and the special concern of the Preparatory Commission of IRO, as well as the general work of the
ECE. Where the ILO had work under consideration or in preparation, it was clearly noted. Thus
the recommendation on occupational classification
begins by requesting the ILO to establish as rapidly
as possible "standards accepted internationally
for the occupational classification of workers".
Only then does the recommendation go on to
charge the Rome Committee with establishing
"without delay", "as a provisional measure", a simplified classification which will facilitate recruiting, "for use in bilateral relations".

The ILO, specifically, and "any other institutions
concerned with migration problems" are invited
to take part in the work of the Committee.

The organization of the Committee is to be
simply a council, with one representative from
each member state, set up and instructed to draw
up its own rules of procedure. Chairmanship is
to rotate among the members.

The Committee will have headquarters in Rome.
Expenses, it was declared, would be very small,

[1] The findings and recommendations of the Conference
were issued in mid-April (Committee of European Economic Co-operation, *Manpower Conference, Rome, January–February 1948: Reports*, English edition published by
H.M. Stationery Office, London, 1948). These reports combine the general report of the Conference and the reports
of its three working committees, as approved by the delegates of all the countries participating in the Conference
and the observers of the International Labor Organization,
the Economic Commission for Europe, and the Preparatory Commission for the International Refugee Organization.

since the Italian Government would furnish the premises and as much clerical staff as was wanted. It was understood that the professional staff would be small. In addition to Italy, several of the other interested countries indicated they might be willing to send second technicians to help staff the Committee. It was recognized that the fate of the project would depend to a considerable extent on the competence of its staff.

Membership was open originally to all CEEC countries and to other "European or non-European" states. The Committee was to come into being as soon as three Governments had agreed to join it.

The likely future organization of the CEEC countries was much in the minds of delegates to the Conference, and they realized that they were broaching some of the general problems of European cooperative organization and of relation to existing international organizations. As the first committee of the CEEO to meet since the 1947 meetings in Paris, they were, as a United Kingdom Delegate said, "the victims of their own initiative". The resolution recommending the creation of the Rome Committee therefore stated that it was being proposed pending the decisions to be taken with regard to the final structure of the body or the bodies to be established for the continued application of European reconstruction programs.

Displaced Persons

The Conference gave recognition to the "task at once humanitarian and of vital importance for European reconstruction" of the PCIRO in the "resettlement of displaced persons in productive work." It recommended the creation by the PCIRO of a Committee, similar in function to the Rome Committee, to aid in solving the practical problems of displaced-person recruitment.

With regard to displaced persons in Italy, it was generally agreed, although not specified, that the Rome Committee should be competent, with IRO participation, to assist in any way it could along the lines of its general terms of reference.

European Manpower Balance Sheet

The Conference gave the CEEC countries a chance to bring up to date the picture of needs and availabilities of emigrant workers. It was fairly generally understood that the figures offered at the CEEC sessions in Paris in August 1947, particularly on the requirements side, were far from firm. Of course such figures of requirements for foreign workers are in all cases dependent, not only on economic conditions, but also upon various political considerations. The figures produced at the Rome conference, therefore, even in their indications of totals—not to mention the breakdowns by skilled and unskilled workers—can be only tentative approximations.

this manpower" recommended, among other things, that:

1. Countries with labor shortages give priority to essential industries, improving living and working conditions, developing training programs, and—where Governments intervene directly in wage policy—offering wage advantages to workers in key industries.

2. Countries with labor shortages "study—in collaboration with unions and employer organizations—any measures of control conducive to the increase or recruitment of manpower in key industries, while safeguarding the legitimate rights of the workers in question". It was recognized that some countries, notably the United Kingdom, had successfully introduced (or since the war, reintroduced) the direction of labor. But several countries which had suffered German occupation insisted that, as the report states, "general coercive methods of controlling manpower come up against the spontaneous opposition of workers and trade union organizations, in whose memory the effects of similar measures imposed during the war are still fresh. For this reason, in countries which were occupied by Germany, measures to control manpower are necessarily mainly indirect."

All delegations agreed on the necessity of improving national employment services.

3. New classes of workers—women, older workers, disabled—be drawn into the labor market in countries of labor shortage, and that hours of work might be increased.

4. Vocational training and apprenticeship programs be further developed, with the aid of the Ilo.

5. Action be taken on housing programs.

Further exchanges of ideas and experience on problems of domestic manpower policy should and will undoubtedly take place among the technicians of the various countries. The English, notably, offered to exchange visits with technicians of other countries.

Rome Committee Begins Work

The Council of the Rome Committee held its first meeting between April 6 and April 12, with delegates present from Belgium, France, Greece, Italy, the Netherlands, Portugal, and the United Kingdom. Luxembourg, although not represented, had also notified the Italian Government of its adherence. Present as observers were representatives of Ireland, Norway, and Switzerland. The Council adopted its statutes, prepared a provisional budget for submission to the member states, and proposed a formula for the sharing of expenses. It named Mario Tomasini, director general of emigration in the Italian Foreign Office, as secretary general of the Committee. It decided to "approach the Organization for European Economic Co-operation (Oeec) for recogni-

tion as one of the subsidiary organizations envisaged in the draft agreement of the Oeec (articles 8, 15c and 19) and in paragraph 3 of the draft resolution on the tasks of the Oeec" and remarked that "recognition would imply monetary aid from Oeec sources."

The Council proposed to hold its next meeting in Paris, in view of the importance of the question of relations with Oeec. But the nature of that relationship remains to be defined.

U.S. OBSERVERS TO CONFERENCE ON REVISION OF INTERNATIONAL CONVENTION FOR PROTECTION OF LITERARY AND ARTISTIC WORKS

[Released to the press May 11]

The Department of State has announced the United States Observer Delegation to the Diplomatic Conference for the Revision of the International Convention for the Protection of Literary and Artistic Works, scheduled to convene at Brussels, June 5, 1948. The United States Observer Delegation is as follows:

Chairman

Thomas E. Bracken, Assistant Legal Adviser, Department of State

Observers

Arthur Fisher, Associate Register of Copyrights, Library of Congress

John Schulman, Hays, St. John, Abramson, and Schulman, 120 Broadway, New York City

The International Union for the Protection of Literary and Artistic Works was given its charter by the Bern convention of September 9, 1886, effective December 5, 1887. This convention was amended and completed at Paris on May 4, 1896, by a supplementary act and an interpretative declaration which went into effect on December 9, 1897.

A complete revision was made at Berlin on November 13, 1908. The act of Berlin, known as the revised convention of Bern for the protection of literary and artistic works, went into force on September 9, 1910.

A supplementary protocol was agreed upon at Bern in 1914. The last revision before World War II was made at Rome in 1928. At that conference the Belgian Government was designated as the member state to call the next conference at Brussels.

Although the United States is not a member of the International Union for the Protection of Literary and Artistic Works, never having adhered to the Bern-Berlin-Rome convention, particular importance is attached to the conference at Brussels, since proposed changes in the international copyright convention may affect the interests of United States authors and producers.

U.S. DELEGATION TO SECOND SESSION OF FACILITATION DIVISION OF ICAO

[Released to the press May 13]

The Department of State has announced the composition of the United States Delegation to the Second Session of the Facilitation Division of the International Civil Aviation Organization (ICAO), which is scheduled to convene at Geneva on May 17, 1948. The United States Delegation is as follows:

Chairman

John R. Alison, Assistant Secretary of Commerce

Advisers

H. Alberta Colclaser, Divisional Assistant, Aviation Division, Department of State

Horace S. Dean, Assistant Division Leader, Division of Foreign Plant Quarantines, Bureau of Entomology and Plant Quarantine, Department of Agriculture

Gilbert Lee Dunnahoo, Chief, Foreign Quarantine Division, United States Public Health Service, Federal Security Agency

Burke H. Flinn, Customs Air Coordinator, Bureau of Customs, Department of the Treasury

Josh Lee, Member, Civil Aeronautics Board, Department of Commerce

Albert E. Reitzel, Assistant General Counsel, United States Immigration and Naturalization Service, Department of Justice

Harry G. Tarrington, Chief International Services Officer, Staff Programs Office, Civil Aeronautics Administration, Department of Commerce

John R. Young, Jr., Director of International Affairs, Air Transport Association, Washington, D.C.

The Facilitation Division of ICAO is one of the groups established in accordance with the convention on international civil aviation which was adopted by the Chicago Civil Aviation Conference in 1944 and which became effective April 4, 1947. The purpose of the Facilitation Division is to study the problems involved in and to prepare recommendations which would facilitate and expedite navigation by aircraft between territories of contracting states and prevent unnecessary delays to aircraft, crews, passengers, and cargo, especially in the administration of laws relating to immigration, public health, agricultural quarantine, and customs. Member states of ICAO are entitled to participate in the Division's meetings.

The agenda for the forthcoming meeting includes: (1) review of progress made by the member states in the field of facilitation of international air transport; (2) consideration of a draft set of international standards and recommended practices on facilitation of international air transport prepared by the ICAO Secretariat; (3) preparation of international standards and recommended practices on facilitation of international air transport in such final form as can be acted

upon by the ICAO Council pursuant to articles [54, and 90 of the convention on international ci aviation; (4) consideration of means other th standards and recommended practices where effect can be given to the measures necessary f the facilitation of international air transport; a (5) consideration of measures which would he the implementation of the facilitation progra

U.S. DELEGATION TO HEALTH CONGRESS OF ROYAL SANITARY INSTITUTE

[Released to the press May

The Department of State announced on May the composition of the United States Delegati to the Health Congress of the Royal Sanita; Institute which is scheduled to be held at Harr gate, England, May 24–28, 1948. The invitati to attend the Congress was transmitted by t United Kingdom on behalf of the Royal Sanita Institute. The United States Delegation is follows:

Chairman

Capt. John M. Bachulus (M.C.), U.S. Navy, Staff Medi Officer to the Commander-in-Chief, U.S. Naval Forc Eastern Atlantic and Mediterranean

Delegates

Burnet M. Davis, M.D., Surgeon, U.S. Public Health Se ice, Federal Security Agency; Liaison Officer, Britl Ministry of Health

Barton P. Jenks, U.S. Delegation, Economic Commissi for Europe

Lt. Col. John W. Regan (M.C.), U.S. Army, Chief, E vironmental Sanitation Branch, Office of the Surge General, Department of the Army

The Health Congress will be divided into se tions where papers will be presented and discu sions held on subjects relating to public healt and sanitation. There will be a section of trop cal hygiene, in which a discussion is planned c "yellow fever and its transmission". Anothe section will deal with sanitation conditions at ai ports all over the world, especially health-contr measures and the present and future uses of ne insecticides.

The Royal Sanitary Institute is the leadin public-health society of the British Commor wealth and could be considered as the Britis counterpart of the American Public Health Ass ciation. The Institute brings together at its ar nual health congresses representatives of gover ments, municipalities, and health instituti̇or from all parts of the world, thereby affordin opportunity for public-health workers to discus subjects of common interest. The last Healt Congress of the Royal Sanitary Institute was he at Torquay, England, June 2–6, 1947.

U.S. Policies and Purposes Regarding the Soviet Union

STATEMENTS OF AMBASSADOR SMITH AND FOREIGN MINISTER MOLOTOV [1]

[Released to the press May 11]

On May 4 Ambassador Walter Bedell Smith called on V. M. Molotov, Soviet Minister for Foreign Affairs, and made to him, on behalf of the United States Government, the following oral statement

Two years ago during my initial conversation with Generalissimo Stalin and yourself, I stated as clearly as possible my estimate of the inevitable reaction of the American people to the continuance of a policy by the Soviet Government which would appear to have as its purpose the progressive expansion of the area of Soviet power. At that time I pointed out that it would be a grave misinterpretation of the fundamentally pacific character of the American people to believe that they would not react strongly and vigorously to the progressive domination by one country of its neighbors and the clear threat to the world community which such actions would imply.

I emphasized at that time that the United States had no desire whatever to see the world divided into two major groupings, nor to divert a large part of its income to the maintenance of a military establishment which such a world situation would necessitate in elementary self-defense. It seemed apparent then that such a line of policy as that described would lead inevitably to a crystallization of the non-Soviet areas of the world, whose people would quite understandably feel themselves progressively threatened by such developments. It seemed also inevitable in such a case that the United States, as the strongest nation in this community, would be forced to take a leading part in this movement and to divert a large portion of its energy, which by preference our people would prefer to utilize for assistance in the reconstruction of the ravages of the war, to the maintenance of a military establishment adequate to meet the developing world situation.

Unhappily the apprehensions I felt at that time have been realized.

Since that date, Soviet policies in eastern Europe have produced the reaction which was predicted. The situation which has resulted is obviously one of great seriousness.

The European community and the United States have become alarmed at the implications of Soviet policy, and are drawing closer together in mutual self-protection, but only in self-protection.

It is for this reason that my Government desires me to outline to you with complete clarity and frankness the position of the United States Government.

There should be no mistake about the determination of the United States to play its part in these cooperative movements for recovery and self-defense. The concern and the determination of the people of the United States have been intensified by the inexplicable hostility of the Soviet Government to the European Recovery Program—a measure which in its inception and subsequent development is so obviously only a measure of American assistance for reconstruction on a cooperative basis without menace or threat to anyone.

The situation which has been produced by the actions of the Soviet Government or by political groups obviously under its control, and the natural and inevitable reaction on the part of other countries, including the United States, to these actions is obviously one of great seriousness.

My Government has no idea what conclusions the Soviet Government has reached concerning the present attitude of the United States. It has noted that the picture of this attitude given by the Soviet press is dangerously distorted and erroneous. Whether, or in what degree, the members of the Soviet Government themselves believe this distorted version my Government has no means of estimating. For this reason I wish to make plain certain points on which my Government considers it extremely important that there be no misunderstanding at this time.

1. The policies of the United States Government in international questions have been made amply clear in recent months and weeks. They have the support of the overwhelming majority of the American people. They will continue to be vigorously and firmly prosecuted.

It would be a grave error if others were to assume that domestic considerations, such as the forthcoming elections, would in any way weaken the determination of the United States to support

---

[1] Printed from telegraphic text.

what it believes to be right. The American people have always known how to separate domestic and foreign policy at the proper moment.

Similarly, my Government is aware that Communist organizations here and there have been disseminating propaganda to the effect that a forthcoming economic crisis in the United States will soon produce a radical change in American policies. It is hoped that no one will be so foolish as to forfeit the chances of progress toward world stability for the sake of an economic prognostication which has been proven wrong time and time again. Even those who persist in believing such a prognostication must, at the very least, realize that an economic crisis would not affect in any way our basic productive capacity nor our concept of the basic factors underlying our foreign policy.

It must be emphasized that the present state of world affairs involves issues which the people of the United States consider to be vital to United States national security and to world peace. No one should deceive himself as to the seriousness of United States policy with respect to these issues.

2. On the other hand, my Government wishes to make it unmistakably clear that the United States has no hostile or aggressive designs whatever with respect to the Soviet Union. Assertions to the contrary are falsehoods which can result only from complete misunderstanding or malicious motives. United States policies have been so devised that they cannot possibly affect adversely the interests of a Soviet Union which seeks to live at peace with its neighbors and to refrain from attempts to exercise undue influence, directly or indirectly, in their affairs.

In fact, many of the elements of United States foreign policy to which the Soviet press takes such strong exception today would never have come into existence if it had not been necessary for the United States to aid other countries to defend their own political integrity from attempts, on the part of Communist minorities, to seize power and to establish regimes subservient to foreign interests. Should these attempts cease, the necessity for some of the manifestations of United States foreign policy, which are apparently unwelcome in Moscow, would cease with them.

The present state of United States–Soviet relations is a source of grievous disappointment to the American people and to the United States Government. As far as we are concerned, it represents a painful and undesired alternative toward which we have been driven, step by step, by the pressure of Soviet and world Communist policy. We still do not despair by any means of a turn of events which will permit us to find the road to a decent and reasonable relationship between our two countries, with a fundamental relaxation of those

It is common knowledge that the United States
f America also is carrying out the policy of
rengthening its relations with bordering coun-
ies, for example, with Canada, Mexico, and also
ith other countries of America, and this is fully
nderstandable. It is likewise understandable that
1e Soviet Union also is conducting a policy of
rengthening its relations with bordering and
:her countries of Europe. The Union of Soviet
ocialist Republics will pursue in the future as
ell its policy of strengthening friendly relation-
iips with these countries of Europe.

In the declaration of the Government of the
nited States of America it is stated that certain
f the external political measures of the United
tates of America in other countries, which have
:oked the dissatisfaction of the Union of Soviet
ocialist Republics, are explained by the excessive
ifluence of the Union of Soviet Socialist Repub-
cs in the internal affairs of these countries. The
oviet Government is unable to agree with this
ind of explanation.

In the countries of eastern Europe which are
nder consideration, following the war, as is well
nown, there took place serious democratic re-
orms which are a means of defense against the
ireat of a new war and which created favorable
nditions for the growth of friendly relations
:tween these countries and the Union of Soviet
ocialist Republics. It would be absolutely in-
orrect to attribute the democratic reforms which
ive taken place here to interference of the Soviet
nion in the internal affairs of these countries.
his would mean ignoring the indubitable fact
iat the above-mentioned reforms are a natural
jsult of the victory of democratic forces over
[azism and Fascism and are regarded by the peo-
les of eastern Europe as guaranties against the
ireat of a new war. In this connection, the
nergence of Communists in positions of leader-
iip is completely understandable, since the people
f these lands consider Communists the most ef-
:ctive fighters against a new war.

No one has the right to dispute the fact that the
urrying through of democratic reforms is an in-
:rnal affair of each state. However, from the
jove-mentioned communication of the Govern-
ent of the United States it is clear that it holds
1other viewpoint and tolerates on its own part
iterference in the internal affairs of other states
hich cannot but call forth serious objections on
ie part of the Soviet Government. Events in
,reece are not the only example of such inter-
:rence in the internal affairs of other states.

The Government of the United States of
merica explains the present unsatisfactory state
: Soviet-American relations also by the position
f the Soviet Government on the question of the
>-called European Recovery Program.

At the same time it is absolutely clear that if
ie question of the economic recovery of the

European countries had been set up, not as has
been done in the indicated program, but on the
basis of normal conditions of international economic cooperation within the framework of the
United Nations organization and with the
necessary regard of the national rights and
sovereignty of states, there would be no reason
for the Union of Soviet Socialist Republics' negative attitude toward the ERP, all the more since
the Union of Soviet Socialist Republics, as one
of the states which suffered most, economically, in
the war, is fully interested in the development of
postwar international economic cooperation.

At the same time the Soviet Government thinks
it necessary to state that the present unsatisfactory
condition of Soviet-American relations and the
tense state of the international situation are the
result of the recent policy of the Government of
the United States of America.

The creation of such a tense situation has been
fostered in the first place by such steps of the
Government of the United States of America as
the increasing development of a network of naval
and air bases in all parts of the world, including
territories adjacent to the Union of Soviet Socialist Republics, about which the press and a series
of official representatives of the United States of
America frankly declare that the establishment of
these bases has the aim of the encirclement of the
Union of Soviet Socialist Republics. Such
measures cannot be explained by the interests of
self-defense. It is likewise impossible to overlook
the fact that the present atmosphere of international relations is poisoned by warlike threats
of all kinds directed against the Union of Soviet
Socialist Republics, issuing from certain circles
closely connected with the Government of the
United States of America. In contrast to this,
the Soviet Government is conducting a consistently
peaceful policy with respect to the United States of
America and other states, is not establishing military bases in other countries and is not emitting
any kind of threat toward anyone at all. .

Further, there was recently formed a military
union of western countries, including England,
France, Belgium, Holland, and Luxembourg. At
a time when all the treaties of mutual assistance
concluded by the Soviet Union with the eastern
countries, as well as with England and France,
have as their aim the prevention of a new aggression on the part of Germany and are not directed
against any allied state, the newly founded military alliance of the five western states, as is clear
from the treaty, has in view not only Germany
but may equally be directed against those states
which were allies in the second world war. In
all the English, French, and American press it is
openly said that this union is directed against the
Union of Soviet Socialist Republics. Furthermore, it cannot be overlooked that the formation

of the stated military union was possible only thanks to the patronage of the Government of the United States of America. It is clear that the military treaty of the five western states can in no way be regarded as a treaty of self-defense.

The unfriendly character of the policy of the Government of the United States of America with regard to the Union of Soviet Socialist Republics has its effect also in the realm of Soviet-American commerce. In accordance with the commercial agreement concluded between our two states, the Government of the United States of America is obliged not to apply in regard to the export of goods from the United States of America to the Union of Soviet Socialist Republics any more burdensome regulations or formalities than are applied in regard to any third country. However, the policy now conducted by the Government of the United States of America ignores this obligation and is in complete contradiction to the Soviet-American commercial agreement, setting up discrimination in regard to the Union of Soviet Socialist Republics, regardless of the fact that the Union of Soviet Socialist Republics is fulfilling in good faith its obligations under the aforementioned agreement. As a result thereof, the export into the Union of Soviet Socialist Republics of American goods is disrupted, goods on which the Union of Soviet Socialist Republics has paid deposits or even the full cost, a fact which injures the American firms concerned as well. The intolerability of such a situation is completely evident.

At the present time the Government of the United States of America declares that the United States has no hostile or aggressive intentions with regard to the Union of Soviet Socialist Republics, and expresses the hope of the possibility of finding a way to the establishment of good and reasonable relations between our two countries, together with a fundamental relaxation of the tension in international relations, and expresses its readiness to cooperate in such a stabilization of world conditions as would correspond as well to the interests of the security of the Soviet people.

The Soviet Government can only welcome this declaration of the Government of the United States of America, for, as is known, it has always carried on a peace-loving policy and one of collaboration with regard to the United States of America which has always met with unanimous approval and support on the part of the peoples of the Union of Soviet Socialist Republics. The Government of the Union of Soviet Socialist Republics declares that in the future as well it intends to carry out this policy with complete consistency.

The Soviet Government also expresses the hope for the possibility of finding the means to eliminate present disagreements and to establish between our countries good relations which would correspond to the interests of our peoples, as well as to the consolidation of universal peace.

what I am sure he already knows, i.e., that the only provision of this agreement which had not been violated by the Union of Soviet Socialist Republics was that permitting the presence of an American clergyman in Moscow.

However, these were matters which it would be profitless for us to pursue to the exclusion of the major issues. I had, I believed, made completely clear the policies of the United States and the reasons which prompted the adoption of these policies. I appreciated Mr. Molotov's statement of the policies of his Government, which I would communicate at once to Washington.

THE PRESIDENT

The statement made by Ambassador Smith represented no new departure in American policy. It was a reiteration of the American position as it has been repeatedly expressed both publicly and privately.

The two salient points of the statement made by Ambassador Smith were these:

"The policies of the United States Government in international questions have been made amply clear in recent months and weeks. They have the support of the overwhelming majority of the American people. They will continue to be vigorously and firmly prosecuted."

.   "   .   .   .

"On the other hand my Government wishes to make it unmistakably clear that the United States has no hostile or aggressive designs whatsoever with respect to the Soviet Union."

RETARY MARSHALL

tinguish it from the mass of unofficial statements, our responsibility was to make clear the position of the United States Government, and of the United States alone.

General Smith did not ask for any general discussion or negotiation. We have had a long and bitter experience with such efforts. This Government had no intention of entering into bilateral negotiations with the Soviet Government on matters relating to the interests of other governments. The discussion of any proposals in regard to outstanding issues which the Soviet Government may have in mind must, as a matter of course, be conducted in the body charged with responsibility for these questions. What we want is action in the fields where action is possible and urgently necessary at the present time. I refer to the matters before the Security Council and other United Nations bodies, such as the situation in

Korea, questions before the Allied Control Council in Berlin and the Austrian treaty negotiations, where the utmost of difficulties have arisen and stalemates generally resulted. It would be very unfortunate if an attempt were made to sit down at a table and enter into general discussions and have the discussions result in failure to reach agreements, or result in disputes over the obligations which might be undertaken in such agreements. That would do the world great harm. We cannot afford a continuation of such failures. What we must have is successful action where such action is now sorely needed.

The following is a summary of Secretary Marshall's press and radio news conference on May 12

When asked if he planned to send any further information, note, or statement to Mr. Molotov on this subject, Mr. Marshall replied that he had nothing in mind at the present time.

Asked if the Russians proved willing to enter into negotiations in a spirit of compromise and harmonization, the United States would in consultation with the other great powers be willing to do this, the Secretary replied in the affirmative. He explained that we would do so if specific proposals, not general discussions, were involved. The Secretary pointed out that this merely affirmed what the President had already said and what had been our policy throughout as to continuing negotiations. He said that the negotiations must have a practical possibility of getting us somewhere.

When asked if this were what was meant by the statement that the door is always wide open, Mr. Marshall replied in the affirmative, explaining that our statement was a reaffirmation of what the President had said.

A correspondent asked if there were any thought being given by this Government concerning a two-power negotiation with the Russians on international problems other than the ones that directly affected the two countries. Mr. Marshall replied that no thought whatever was being given to such negotiations.

When asked to amplify his remark that the confusion of statements would increase as our political campaign became more intense, Mr. Marshall commented that his audience would probably know more about that subject than he would.

The Secretary was then asked if he thought that it was now up to the Soviet Union to take the initiative for discussions. Mr. Marshall said that it went much further than that. He said that Mr. Molotov had said:

"The Soviet Government can only welcome this declaration of the Government of the United

agreement. He felt that the United States ust guard with great care the integrity of these tions in such matters but that there was a special zard as to what might happen. He said it had ppened in this particular case. When asked if ere were any way in which this could be prented, the Secretary shrugged his shoulders.

Mr. Marshall, when asked if this had been an change of notes or just an exchange of verbal ews, replied that it had been done orally but with irm preliminary understanding of what was to be id. Asked if it had been a note or an *aide-mém-re*, the Secretary replied that he was not enough a diplomat to answer such a technical question.

When asked if Ambassador Smith left a piece paper with Mr. Molotov for the one he had sent, Mr. Marshall replied that he thought that it d been sent afterwards. Asked if the paper had en marked "confidential", Mr. Marshall replied at he had not seen it. He remarked that Mr. olotov had sent Ambassador Smith a copy of the bstance of his remarks after the interview was er.

The Secretary, when asked if we would still be terested in carrying on the confidential discusns through diplomatic channels since a settlent has not been reached in other councils, replied at we would always be endeavoring to do this henever there was an opportunity to get a benecial result.

When asked if the State Department seemed to gard the disclosure as somewhat unfortunate, t not to the point of regarding it as unfortunate, e Secretary said he had tried to point out that is was the only field for such diplomatic interanges where we could proceed without having a neral public response at a moment which would obably disturb the process of views or any possility of agreement. When a correspondent said did not see how this disclosure had hurt the use of peace in any way, Mr. Marshall replied at it might not have hurt it, and it might have lped it. He said he was not disputing that part it. But, he pointed out, in the conversations tween an Ambassador and a Foreign Minister, e understanding had been that there was no disosure unless the other party was first notified that ch a disclosure would be made. Mr. Marshall id that we were not quibbling over this and would oceed with the tenor of our ways along the lines had in the past.

A correspondent asked why, since the United ates communication of May 4 did not involve y invitation to voice a reply directly, Ambassa-r Smith had not made this clear when he replied Mr. Molotov's acceptance on May 9. Mr. Marall replied that he had not talked to Ambassador nith. He said he knew exactly what the Ambassador said, pointing out that General Smith d had no indication that there was going to be

a release or that only a portion of his statement would be released while all of Mr. Molotov's statement would be released.

The Secretary was asked what the insuperable objection to inviting Mr. Stalin in person to Washington would be if the Soviet Government would submit a concrete proposal for discussions. He declined to discuss this question, saying that it was a matter for the President to comment on.

A correspondent asked what was left to do in order to maintain our relations with Russia if the field of verbal exchange of views was the only field left and was no longer safe. Mr. Marshall said that we were going ahead. He explained that we had not broken off any negotiations and had asserted and reasserted the desire to continue with them. He stated that we would go ahead with the negotiations and accept the hazards.

When the Secretary was asked if there were not a long list of pending Soviet-American issues on which Ambassador Smith had been trying to get discussion and whether this list would be an appropriate subject for diplomatic negotiations, he replied that the list had been a continuing subject for diplomatic negotiations.

Secretary Marshall, when asked if he felt that the Russian reply indicated any change in attitude on the part of the Russian Government, replied that in the statement of the fundamentals it revealed no change of view. He went on to say that he had read one portion which he thought had a particular significance for the future and he felt that the Soviet reply and the release indicated the willingness of the Soviet Government to proceed with negotiations. Asked if he were encouraged by this, the Secretary declined to comment.

When asked if Ambassador Smith's original statement had been predicated on the assumption that the Soviet Government might become either confused or would misinterpret some statements in our political campaign, Mr. Marshall said that probably the primary purpose was to make unmistakably clear to the Soviet Government the terms of the American foreign policy and its intentions and views with regard to the Soviet Government because there had been so much said in the various debates and speeches, and in the papers that we thought it necessary to avoid any possibility of misunderstanding which might lead to tragic consequences. He said we wished to make the policy of the United States Government entirely clear, no matter what might be said here or there. The Secretary mentioned Soviet propaganda, pointing out that sometimes there was a tendency to believe your own propaganda if you heard it often enough. He said the Soviet propaganda was going full force so that there was a general confusion of statements which might result in a very unfortunate reaction. It was to guard against this, he said, that we undertook to make as clear as possible the position of the United States Government as to its policy, its attitude toward the Soviet Union, its firm purpose and its willingness in relation to its efforts to reach an accord.

When asked if he had a practical hope that the Soviet Government would take the actions, or some of the actions, which he had said were necessary to proceed with negotiations, Mr. Marshall replied that he had hope that we would see evidence in these various fields of more of a spirit of reaching an accord.

. Mr. Marshall, when asked if there had been any other overtures, however informal, on the part of the Soviet Government in the last few months looking toward a United States–Soviet conference, said he did not recall any overtures at any time for a United States–Soviet conference that would be on a purely bilateral basis. He remarked here that he had just read a teletype from Paris saying that General Smith had left Paris on a fishing trip in the Normandy area. He said that the General had pointed out that he was going with personal friends and not officials in order to squelch rumors that his trip was taken in order to talk with high officials concerning Soviet-American relations.

A correspondent remarked that the Secretary's statement said that we would want to have some assurances before entering into negotiations with Russia if there were to be an agreement reached. Mr. Marshall replied that he had not said this. He explained that he had said that we wanted assurances that we would have to get practical results. Mr. Marshall pointed out that there was a vast difference between general negotiations and ones specifically for a particular purpose.

Henry F. Grady Presents Credentials to King of Nepal

Henry F. Grady, American Ambassador to India, presented on May 3 to His Majesty King Tribhubana his credentials as Envoy Extraordinary and Minister Plenipotentiary of the United States to the Kingdom of Nepal. Accompanied by other American Foreign Service personnel of the Embassy at New Delhi and the Consulate General at Calcutta, Dr. Grady traveled to Katmandu, Nepal's capital, where he was received by the King and by the Maharajah Mohan Shum Shere Jung Bahadur Rana, who recently succeeded to the prime ministership.

Dr. Grady will represent the United States concurrently in New Delhi as Ambassador and in Katmandu as Minister, with his residence in the former capital.

THE FOREIGN SERVICE

ınge of Ambassadors Between ınd Ceylon

[Released to the press April 26]

ı Government of the United States and the ʹnment of Ceylon have agreed to initiate diplic representation by the exchange of amlors.

ʹlon achieved fully responsible status within ritish Commonwealth of Nations on Febru-, 1948. The President of the United States , Personal Representative with the rank of ıl Ambassador to Colombo, Ceylon, to attend ecial ceremonies by which the people of Ceyelebrated the establishment of their new ıhood on that day.

ı United States first opened a Consulate at ıbo, Ceylon, in 1850. In August 1947 the ılate was raised to a Consulate General. Cole has been appointed the first United ı Ambassador to Ceylon. He has been in the ʹn Service for many years, having just served nister to Ethiopia. It is expected that Mr. ʹvill arrive in Ceylon and present his letters ıdence to Sir Henry Moore, the Governorʹal of Ceylon, and formally establish the d States Embassy sometime in June this ʹ The Government of Ceylon expects to ʹe early action to establish its Embassy in ıngton.

s exchange of ambassadors between the d States and Ceylon reflects the continued ı of close and cordial relations between the ıuntries.

PUBLICATIONS

Department of State

For sale by the Superintendent of Documents, Government Printing Office, Washington 25, D.C. Address requests direct to the Superintendent of Documents, except in the case of free publications, which may be obtained from the Department of State.

Inter-American Conference for the Maintenance of Continental Peace and Security. International Organization and Conference Series II, American Republics 1. Pub. 3016. iv, 225 pp. 40¢.

Report of the American Delegation, together with text of treaty of reciprocal assistance, signed at Rio de Janeiro September 2, 1947, and a small map of the region defined by article 4 of the treaty.

European Recovery Program: Commodity Reports Including Manpower. Economic Cooperation Series 4. Pub. 3093. xii, 448 pp. Free.

Commodity reports on food and agriculture, fertilizer, agricultural machinery, coal, coal mining machinery, electric power, petroleum, iron and steel including steel making equipment, inland transport, maritime transport, timber, and manpower.

Convention for European Economic Co-operation With Related Documents. Economic Cooperation Series 7. Pub. 3145. i, 52 pp. Free.

Text of the convention and pertinent protocols and resolutions preceded by text of the final act of the Second Session of the Committee of European Economic Co-operation.

Confirmation

On April 14, the Senate confirmed the nomination of Herschel V. Johnson to be American Ambassador Extraordinary and Plenipotentiary to Brazil.

ıments and Addresses of the Week

ınt Secretary Allen	Continuing Partnership in Educational Exchange. Not printed. Text issued as press release 353 of May 10.	Address made before the Conference on International Student Exchange at the University of Michigan, Ann Arbor, Michigan, on May 10.
	On the subject of UNESCO. Not printed. Text issued as press release 370 of May 13.	Address made before the Pacific Regional Conference of UNESCO in San Francisco on May 13.
ınt Secretary Thorp	On the International Wheat Agreement. Not printed. Text issued as press release 374 of May 14.	Statement made before a subcommittee of the Senate Foreign Relations Committee on May 14.
ıry Marshall	On the Fourth International Congresses on Tropical Medicine and Malaria. Not printed. Text issued as press release 358 of May 10, 1948.	Statement made at opening ceremonies of the Fourth International Congresses on Tropical Medicine and Malaria on May 10.
ıry Marshall	On observance of World Trade Week. Not printed. Text issued as press release 381 of May 15.	Statement made on May 15.

Louis J. Halle, Jr., author of the article on the Institute of Inter-
American Affairs, is Special Assistant to the Director of the Office of
American Republic Affairs, Department of State, and is also a member
of the Board of Directors of the Institute.

Norman Burns, author of the article on America's responsibility in
world trade, is an adviser in the Division of Commercial Policy, Office
of International Trade Policy, Department of State.

Val R. Lorwin, author of the article on the Rome Manpower Confer-
ence, is an officer in the Division of International Labor, Social and
Health Affairs. ' He served as senior United States observer at the
Manpower Conference held at Rome January 26–February 9, 1948, on
the invitation of the Italian Government, under the auspices of the
Committee of European Economic Co-operation.

The Department of State bulletin

Vol. XVIII, No. 465 • Publication 3160

May 30, 1948

For sale by the Superintendent of Documents
U.S. Government Printing Office
Washington 25, D.C.

Subscription:
52 Issues, $5; single copy, 15 cents

Published with the approval of the
Director of the Bureau of the Budget

*The Department of State BULLETIN,
a weekly publication compiled and
edited in the Division of Publications,
Office of Public Affairs, provides the
public and interested agencies of
the Government with information on
developments in the field of foreign
relations and on the work of the Department of State and the Foreign
Service. The BULLETIN includes
press releases on foreign policy issued
by the White House and the Department, and statements and addresses
made by the President and by the
Secretary of State and other officers
of the Department, as well as special
articles on various phases of international affairs and the functions of
the Department. Information is included concerning treaties and international agreements to which the
United States is or may become a
party and treaties of general international interest.*

*Publications of the Department, as
well as legislative material in the field
of international relations, are listed
currently.*

: Six Years of Progress [1]

Article

ernments to encourage and strengthen cooperation among themselves and their territories in the
Caribbean area with a view to improving the economic and social well-being of the peoples of these
territories. The political aspects of the problems
of non-self-governing territories do not come
within the terms of reference of the Caribbean
Commission. The member governments have
agreed to promote scientific, technological, and
economic development in the Caribbean area and
to facilitate the use of resources and the treatment
of mutual problems, especially in the field of
research.

The member governments have further agreed
that the objectives of the Caribbean Commission
are in accord with the principles of the Charter of
the United Nations. It will be recalled that article
73 of that Charter recognizes the principle that the
interests of the inhabitants of non-self-governing
territories are paramount and accepts as a sacred
trust the obligation to insure their political, economic, social, and educational advancement, the
development of self-government, and the furtherance of international peace and security.

Commissioners and the West Indian Conferences

Both by custom and by specific provision of the
agreement, the Commission must draw heavily
and importantly on the wishes, the needs, and the
advice of the people of the Caribbean area. To
insure that recommendations from the people in
social and economic matters are brought to the
attention of both the local and metropolitan governments, two organizational devices are used.
One is the appointment of West Indians and those
closely identified with the interests of the people
of the West Indies to the Commission, and the
other is the convening under the auspices of the
Commission of the biennial West Indian Conference. This conference consists of two representatives of each territory who discuss the social and
economic problems of the region and make spe-

---

[1] This article has been condensed from draft of a speech
unrevised by the late Charles W. Taussig, Chairman of
the United States Section of the Caribbean Commission.
It had been written for delivery at the Sixth Meeting of
the Commission, May 24–29, 1948, at San Juan, Puerto
Rico.

cific recommendations to the local governments
and the metropolitan governments through the
Commission.

The independence of their activities as commissioners and their relationship to their metropolitan governments is also to a large degree dependent on the customs and the constitutional
procedures of their respective home governments.

All of the United States Commissioners are appointed by the President of the United States.
Three out of four of the United States Commissioners are from Puerto Rico and the Virgin
Islands of the United States. Puerto Rico has
two distinguished representatives on the Commission, Governor Piñero and Dr. Rafael Picó,
Chairman of the Planning, Urbanizing, and Zon-
ing Board. The third commissioner from the area
is Governor William H. Hastie of the Virgin
Islands of the United States, who has been closely
associated with the Caribbean for many years.

It is the policy of the United States Section to
depend largely on the advice of the three commissioners resident in this region. It is somewhat
handicapped by geographical distance, but visits
of the Puerto Rican and Virgin Islands Commissioners to Washington and telephone consultations
which frequently occur between the Co-chairman
in Washington and the West Indian Commissioners enable them to work closely together. The
policy of the United States Section is to assign
to the West Indian Commissioners a maximum of
responsibility.

At the last meeting of the Caribbean Commission at Trinidad in December 1947, Governor
Hastie acted as Co-chairman for the United
States and Chairman of that meeting. Rafael
Picó is the United States Representative on the
Panel of Experts which is now engaged in making
an important industrial survey of the Caribbean
area for the Commission. Governor Piñero has
only recently been appointed to the Commission
by President Truman, but because of the Governor's interest in Commission activities when he was
Resident Commissioner for Puerto Rico in Washington, it is certain that he will assume all the
responsibilities and activities in the Commission
that are consistent with his arduous duties as
Governor of Puerto Rico.

To increase further the influence and activity
of the West Indian Commissioners, it is the intention of the United States Section to convene
periodically the four United States Commissioners
so that the four commissioners can act as nearly
as possible as a unit in forwarding the interests
of the region. The first of these periodic meetings of the United States Commissioners will take
place immediately following the present series of
meetings.

The Caribbean Commission may recommend on
its own initiative specific measures to improve the
social and economic conditions of the Caribbean

by representatives from Jamaica, Trinidad, British Guiana, the Leeward Islands, the Windward Islands, Puerto Rico, the Virgin Islands of the United States, Surinam, and from the United States, the United Kingdom, and the Netherlands. In addition, guest representatives from Cuba, Haiti, and the Dominican Republic were present. The subject of land reforms of the area was discussed in considerable detail. Among the various systems reviewed and publicized at this Conference was the imaginative and comprehensive land-reform program of Puerto Rico.

International Cooperation

The Caribbean Commission is making every effort to avoid duplication of activities with other international organizations. Although the Commission has at present no organic relationship with the United Nations, it has issued a directive to its Secretary General to maintain the closest contact with the United Nations at the secretariat level. This arrangement, now functioning, is of benefit to both organizations.

At a result of the pioneering work of the Caribbean Commission, a South Pacific Commission has been created to carry on similar work with the non-self-governing territories in that area. That Commission consists of the four governments participating in the work of the Caribbean Commission and in addition Australia and New Zealand. It is holding its first meeting this month in Sydney, Australia.

None know better than the commissioners themselves of the shortcomings of the Caribbean Commission and how difficult it is for it to reach quickly many of its goals. The role that has been assigned to it in the field it covers is among the most difficult in international organization. At the sixth meeting, the Commission will discuss among other matters the ways and means of improving its organization, of speeding up its work, of becoming more vital to the people of the Caribbean.

The members of the Commission, both present and past, representing France, the Netherlands, the United Kingdom, and the United States, have labored hard and have acted in genuine international and interterritorial friendship to help make the lives of the people of the Caribbean happier and more fruitful.

Furth

A

Resolution Adopted on the Report of the First Committee

The General Assembly,

TAKING ACCOUNT of the present situation in regard to Palestine,

I

Strongly affirms its support of the efforts of the Security Council to secure a truce in Palestine and calls upon all Governments, organizations and persons to co-operate in making effective such a truce.

II

1. *Empowers* a United Nations Mediator in Palestine, to be chosen by a committee of the General Assembly composed of representatives of China, France, the Union of Soviet Socialist Republics, the United Kingdom and the United States of America, to exercise the following functions:

(*a*) To use his good offices with the local and community authorities in Palestine to:

(*i*) Arrange for the operation of common services necessary to the safety and well-being of the population of Palestine;

(*ii*) Assure the protection of the Holy Places, religious buildings and sites in Palestine;

(*iii*) Promote a peaceful adjustment of the future situation of Palestine.

(*b*) To co-operate with the Truce Commission for Palestine appointed by the Security Council in its resolution of 23 April 1948.[2]

(*c*) To invite, as seems to him advisable, with a view to the promotion of the welfare of the inhabitants of Palestine, the assistance and co-

---

[1] U.N. doc. A/554, May 17, 1948. Adopted at the 135th plenary meeting of the General Assembly on May 14, 1948.
[2] BULLETIN of May 9, 1948, p. 594.

Further Discussion in the Security Council of the Palestine Situation

STATEMENTS BY AMBASSADOR WARREN R. AUSTIN [1]

U.S. Representative at the Seat of the United Nations

Mr. President, the Security Council has now dequate information to demonstrate that its arlier efforts to bring an end to the fighting in 'alestine have been unsuccessful. Actual fighting ow in progress in Palestine, together with state- 1ents being made by all parties directly involved, learly indicates to the United States Government 1at there is a threat to the peace and breach of the eace within the meaning of article 39 of the 'harter.

We believe, therefore, that the Security Council 1ould find that the situation with respect to Pal- 1tine constitutes a threat to the peace and breach f the peace under article 39.

We believe that the Security Council should sue an order as a provisional measure under rticle 40, calling upon all authorities who are 1 control of armed elements now operating in any art of Palestine to bring about an immediate andstill in all military operations.

I will read at this point a draft resolution on 1e Palestine question submitted by the Repre- 1ntative of the United States at the 293d meeting f the Security Council, 17 May, 1948, which is 1cument S/749:

"The Security Council

"TAKING INTO CONSIDERATION that previous res- 1utions of the Security Council in respect to Pal- 1tine have not been complied with and that mili- 1ry operations are taking place in Palestine;

"*Determines* that the situation in Palestine con- 1itutes a threat to the peace and a breach of the 1ace within the meaning of Article 39 of the 1arter;

"*Orders* all Governments and authorities to 1ase and desist from any hostile military action 1d to that end issue a cease-fire and stand-fast 1der to their military and para-military forces 1 become effective within 36 hours after the adop- 1n of this resolution;

"*Directs* the Truce Commission established by 1e Security Council by its resolution of 23 April, 48 to report to the Security Council on the com- 1iance with these orders."

Mr. President, in the meantime, in order to per- 1t the Security Council Truce Commission to 1oceed with maximum speed, the Security Coun- 1 should ascertain which Arab authorities are responsible for Arab aspects of the situation in Palestine and insure that such Arab authorities have designated representatives to deal with the Security Council Truce Commission. The United States considers additional information on Palestine to be desirable. The Council may wish to put to the principal parties a number of questions. Some of these questions will be familiar to you, but it seems necessary to bring together in compact form all of the relative facts that can be obtained for the further information of the Security Council and to obtain these facts before a decision is made. I am submitting the type of questions that we think should be propounded to all of the parties interested in the following substance, namely:

1. To: Egypt, Saudi Arabia, Transjordan, Iraq, Yemen, Syria, and Lebanon:

(*a*) Are elements of your armed forces or irregular forces sponsored by your government now operating in Palestine?

(*b*) If so, where are such forces now located, under what command are they now operating, and what are their military objectives?

(*c*) On what basis is it claimed that such forces are entitled to enter Palestine and conduct operations there?

(*d*) Who is now responsible for the exercise of political functions in the Arab areas of Palestine?

(*e*) Is such authority now negotiating with Jewish authorities on a political settlement in Palestine?

(*f*) Have the Arab governments entered into any agreements among themselves with respect to Palestine?

(*g*) If so, what are the terms of the agreements?

2. Questions to the Arab Higher Committee:

(*a*) Is the Arab Higher Committee exercising political authority in Arab sections of Palestine?

(*b*) What governmental arrangements have been made to maintain public order and to carry on public services in Arab sections of Palestine?

---

[1] Made before the Security Council on May 17, 1948, and released to the press by the U. S. Mission to the United Nations on the same date.

(c) Have the Arabs of Palestine requested assistance from governments outside of Palestine?

(d) If so, what governments and for what purpose?

(e) Have you named representatives to deal with the Security Council Truce Commission for the purpose of effecting the truce called for by the Security Council?

3. *Questions to the Provisional Government of Israel:*

(a) Over which areas of Palestine do you actually exercise control at the present time?

(b) Do you have armed forces operating outside areas claimed by your Jewish State?

(c) If so, on what basis do you attempt to justify such operations?

(d) Are you negotiating with Arab authorities regarding either a truce or a political settlement in Palestine?

(e) Have you named representatives to deal with the Security Council Truce Commission for the purpose of effecting the truce called for by the Security Council?

(f) Will you agree to an immediate and unconditional truce for the City of Jerusalem and the Holy Places?

_____

[The following extemporaneous remarks were made by Ambassador Austin before the Security Council on May 22, 1948, and released to the press by the U.S. Mission to the U.N. on the same date.]

Mr. President, the paragraph before us reads:

"Determines that the situation in Palestine constitutes a threat to the peace and a breach of the peace" within the meaning of article 39 of the Charter.

During the brief time in which we have been considering this resolution, events have been reported to us by our Truce Commission and by others, and statements have been made here by the member states and by others, including a message from King Abdullah, and information has reached us in other ways emphasizing a fact which should have been obvious to us all the time: that the situation in Palestine is not merely a threat to the peace; it is a breach of the peace of a very serious nature.

Never before have I argued the phase of the matter which involves the consequences of that, that is to say, its reaching out into international life. But the time has come when we are about to vote on this matter, when I think we cannot ignore the international character of this breach of the peace. Probably the most important evidence and the best evidence we have on that subject is the admissions of the countries whose five

untry, which has had no government according his claim.

Thereby he admitted the international character whatever act this is. He walked right into the harter of the United Nations, which is an international charter, and saw fit to call to our attention articles 51 and 52 of the Charter as a justification for this invasion. He omitted, probably by inadvertence, to refer to that article which ows that this act of regional organization in alestine is contrary to the Charter and in violation of it and is strictly an illegal act.

He omitted to refer to article 53, which provides, nong other things, "but no enforcement action all be taken under regional arrangements or by gional agencies without the authorization of the curity Council, with the exception of measures ainst an enemy state, as defined in paragraph of this Article, provided for pursuant to Article 7 or in regional arrangements directed against newal of aggressive policy on the part of any ch state, until such time as the Organization ay, on the request of the Governments concerned, charged with the responsibility for preventing rther aggression by such a state."

Those states defined in paragraph 2 were the emy states of World War II. Of course, that not the position here. Therefore, we have evince of the highest type of the international violation of the law here—an admission by those who mmit the violation.

Now, it is not necessary to pass upon the jurid al status of Palestine in order to have a cease- e resolution adopted here. Therefore, we do t push any claim about any juridical status here, t it is perfectly obvious to all of us that that rt of Palestine which is under the de facto vernment of the Provisional Government of rael is not a part of the regional organization which he refers, and therefore, this is not that operative effort that he would have us believe is. This is hostility by a group, a coalition, a gion—call it a regional organization—against organized community that least claims before that it is a state. We do not have to pass upon e question of whether it is or not. All we have consider is the fact of what is going on there. But here is something of considerable signifi nce, it seems to us. We are informed that the vernment of Syria in agreement with the Arab ague states has proclaimed a blockade of the gional waters of Palestine and has issued warn gs to foreign shipping. It is elementary that a oclamation of a blockade constitutes a claim of lligerent rights. The exercise of belligerent ghts depends upon the existence of war, whether be international war or civil war. The claim to ercise belligerent rights must rest upon a recog tion of the belligerency of the opposing party.

I do not intend now to discuss the grave questions involved in this claim, nor do I intend to dis- cuss here and now the validity of the blockade which has been proclaimed. I refer to the proc- lamation of the blockade alleged to be applicable to foreign shipping off the coast of Palestine merely for the purpose of adding another bit of evidence to establish the fact that there is a threat to the peace and a breach of the peace in Palestine.

It is impossible to maintain that foreign ship- ping off the coast of Palestine is subject to the exercise of belligerent rights and at the same time to assert that there is no threat to the peace or breach of the peace within the meaning of article 39 of the Charter. This is equivalent in its ab- surdity to alleging that these five armies are there to maintain peace and at the same time are con- ducting bloody war.

If this is a genuine position, Mr. President— that their purpose is to maintain peace—would it hurt them to adopt this resolution? No! They could perform their obligations if that is their true position. Everyone knows that this resolution adopted here by the Security Council would have a binding effect.

This would be a finding, a decision by the Se- curity Council, and every member of the United Nations would be bound by it and bound to help keep King Abdullah where he belongs. We find in article 2, paragraph 5: "All Members shall give the United Nations every assistance in any action it takes in accordance with the present Charter, and shall refrain from giving assistance to any state against which the United Nations is taking preventive"—that is what this is—"or enforce- ment action," and, 6: "The Organization shall en- sure that states which are not Members of the United Nations act in accordance with these prin- ciples so far as may be necessary for the mainte- nance of international peace and security."

Now again turn to article 48. This would apply to every member of the United Nations if we adopt it in this resolution proposed by the United States. This would be a decision and article 48 provides: "The action required to carry out the decisions of the Security Council for the maintenance of in- ternational peace and security shall be taken by all the Members of the United Nations or by some of them, as the Security Council may determine. Such decisions shall be carried out by the Members of the United Nations directly and through their action in the appropriate international agencies of which they are members." And this resolution points directly at certain members of the United Nations and calls upon them to cease fire. But article 25—what does article 25 do to members of the United Nations? Let us read it:

"The Members of the United Nations agree to accept and carry out the decisions of the Security

Council in accordance with the present Charter."

Now, Mr. President, there are certain consequences that follow disobedience of the decisions of the Security Council. It is not necessary to step right off immediately into action under articles 41 or 42. There are other sanctions against disobedience of the decisions. Therefore, since there is no reasonable ground for difference about the existence of a threat to the peace, about the existence of disturbance of the peace, about the character—the international character—of it, the Security Council should take care of the situation under its obligations found in article 1. I had better read it. It is unsafe for me to try to quote. I found that out before.

"The Purposes of the United Nations are:

"1· To maintain international peace and se-

Resolution on the India-Pakistan Questio

The Security Council,

Having considered the complaint of the Government of India concerning the dispute over the State of Jammu and Kashmir, having heard the representative of India in support of that complaint and the reply and counter complaints of the representative of Pakistan,

Being strongly of opinion that the early restoration of peace and order in Jammu and Kashmir is essential and that India and Pakistan should do their utmost to bring about a cessation of all fighting,

Noting with satisfaction that both India and Pakistan desire that the question of the accession of Jammu and Kashmir to India or Pakistan should be decided through the democratic method of a free and impartial plebiscite,

Considering that the continuation of the dispute is likely to endanger international peace and security;

Reaffirms the Council's Resolution of January 17th,

Resolves that the membership of the Commission established by the Resolution of the Council of January 20th, 1948, shall be increased to five and shall include in addition to the membership mentioned in that Resolution, representative of —— and —— and that if the membership of the Commission has not been completed within ten days from the date of the adoption of this Resolution the President of the Council may designate

[1] U.N. doc. S/726, Apr. 22, 1948. Submitted jointly by the Representatives of Belgium, Canada, China, Colombia, the United Kingdom, and the United States. Adopted at the 286th meeting of the Security Council on Apr. 21, 1948.

:aphs provide full freedom to all subjects of the tate, regardless of creed, caste, or party, to express their views and to vote on the question of the :cession of the State, and that therefore they ιould co-operate in the maintenance of peace and ·der.

2. The Government of India should:

(a) When it is established to the satisfaction : the Commission set up in accordance with the ouncil's Resolution of 20 January that the tribesen are withdrawing and that arrangements for ιe cessation of the fighting have become effective, it into operation in consultation with the Comission a plan for withdrawing their own forces ·om Jammu and Kashmir and reducing them cogressively to the minimum strength required)r the support of the civil power in the mainteιnce of law and order,

(b) Make known that the withdrawal is taking lace in stages and announce the completion of ιch stage;

(c) When the Indian forces shall have been reuced to the minimum strength mentioned in (a))ove, arrange in consultation with the Commison for the stationing of the remaining forces to ϱ carried out in accordance with the following rinciples:

(i) That the presence of troops should not afford any intimidation or appearance of intimidation to the inhabitants of the State,
(ii) That as small a number as possible should be retained in forward areas,
(iii) That any reserve of troops which may be included in the total strength should be located within their present Base area.

3. The Government of India should agree that ntil such time as the plebiscite administration reιrred to below finds it necessary to exercise the)wers of direction and supervision over the State)rces and police provided for in Paragraph 8 they ill be held in areas to be agreed upon with the lebiscite Administrator.

4. After the plan referred to in paragraph 2(a))ove has been put into operation, personnel reuited locally in each district should so far as ossible be utilized for the reestablishment and ιaintenance of law and order with due regard to rotection of minorities, subject to such additional ϛquirements as may be specified by the Plebiscite dministration referred to in paragraph 7.

5. If these local forces should be found to be indequate, the Commission, subject to the agreeιent of both the Government of India and the overnment of Pakistan, should arrange for the ϱe of such forces of either Dominion as it deems fective for the purpose of pacification.

B. PLEBISCITE

6. The Government of India should undertake to ensure that the Government of the State invite the major political groups to designate responsible representatives to share equitably and fully in the conduct of the administration at the Ministerial level, while the plebiscite is being prepared and carried out.

7. The Government of India should undertake that there will be established in Jammu and Kashmir a Plebiscite Administration to hold a Plebiscite as soon as possible on the question of the accession of the State to India or Pakistan.

8. The Government of India should undertake that there will be delegated by the State to the Plebiscite Administration such powers as the latter considers necessary for holding a fair and impartial plebiscite including, for that purpose only, the direction and supervision of the State forces and police.

9. The Government of India should at the request of the Plebiscite Administration make available from the Indian forces such assistance as the Plebiscite Administration may require for the performance of its functions.

10. (a) The Government of India should agree that a nominee of the Secretary-General of the United Nations will be appointed to be the Plebiscite Administrator.

(b) The Plebiscite Administrator, acting as an officer of the State of Jammu and Kashmir, should have authority to nominate his Assistants and other subordinates and to draft regulations governing the Plebiscite. Such nominees should be formally appointed and such draft regulations should be formally promulgated by the State of Jammu and Kashmir.

(c) The Government of India should undertake that the Government of Jammu and Kashmir will appoint fully qualified persons nominated by the Plebiscite Administrator to act as special magistrates within the State judicial system to hear cases which in the opinion of the Plebiscite Administrator have a serious bearing on the preparation for and the conduct of a free and impartial plebiscite.

(d) The terms of service of the Administrator should form the subject of a separate negotiation between the Secretary-General of the United Nations and the Government of India. The Administrator should fix the terms of service for his Assistants and subordinates.

(e) The Administrator should have the right to communicate direct with the Government of the State and with the Commission of the Security Council and, through the Commission with the Security Council, with the Governments of India and Pakistan and with their Representatives with the Commission. It would be his duty to bring to the notice of any or all of the foregoing (as he in his discretion may decide) any circumstances arising which may tend, in his opinion, to interfere with the freedom of the Plebiscite.

11. The Government of India should undertake to prevent and to give full support to the Administrator and his staff in preventing any threat, coercion or intimidation, bribery or other undue influence on the voters in the plebiscite, and the Government of India should publicly announce and should cause the Government of the State to announce this undertaking as an international obligation binding on all public authorities and officials in Jammu and Kashmir.

12. The Government of India should themselves and through the Government of the State declare and make known that all subjects of the State of Jammu and Kashmir, regardless of creed, caste or party, will be safe and free in expressing their views and in voting on the question of the accession of the State and that there will be freedom of the Press, speech and assembly and freedom of travel in the State, including freedom of lawful entry and exit.

13. The Government of India should use and should ensure that the Government of the State also use their best endeavours to effect the withdrawal from the State of all Indian nationals other than those who are normally resident therein

U.N. Temporary Commission To Observe

At its 33d meeting, the United Nations Temporary Commission on Korea today (April 28) adopted the following resolution:

"In order to comply with the provisions of the resolution passed at its 22nd meeting, on 12 March,

"Having satisfied itself as a result of its extensive field observations in various key districts of south Korea that there exists in south Korea in a reasonable degree a free atmosphere wherein the democratic rights of freedom of speech, press and assembly are recognized and respected,

"The United Nations Temporary Commission on Korea *resolves:*

"To confirm that it will observe the elections announced by the commanding General of the United States Forces in Korea to be held on 10 May 1948."

In its resolution of March 12, 1948, the Temporary Commission decided "to observe elections

[1] Released to the press by the U.N. Department of Public Information on Apr. 28, 1948.
[2] BULLETIN of Mar. 14, 1948, p. 344.

Thirty-first Session of the International Labor Conference [1]

The Thirty-first Session of the International Labor Conference is scheduled to convene at San Francisco on June 17, 1948, and is expected to continue at least three weeks. The Thirtieth Session was held at Geneva in June and July 1947. The forthcoming session will be the fifth to be held in the United States, others having met at Washington in 1919, New York in 1941, Philadelphia in 1944, and Seattle in 1946.

It is expected that the Conference will be attended by delegations from most, if not all, of the 55 member countries of the International Labor Organization (ILO). The delegations will be "tripartite", that is, composed of two members representing the Government, one representing management, and one representing labor. Countries which are members of the United Nations but not members of the ILO have been invited to be represented by observers at the Conference.

The ILO is an intergovernmental agency, financed by contributions from its member governments, whose purpose is to further social justice and thus provide the basis for universal and lasting peace. The Organization provides machinery for concerted international action to improve working conditions, raise standards of living, and promote social and economic stability. Established in 1919, it is now a specialized agency of the United Nations.

The principal function of the International Labor Conference is the formulation of international minimum standards governing workers and living conditions. These standards are embodied in multilateral treaties, called international labor conventions, and in formal recommendations. The member countries are obligated to consider conventions for possible ratification. If a country ratifies a convention, it is under obligation to apply its provisions and to submit annual reports to the International Labor Office on the manner in which it is doing so. Recommendations are not required to be considered for possible ratification, but countries are obligated to consider them "with a view to effect being given to them by national legislation or otherwise". Eighty-six conventions and 82 recommendations have been adopted by the 30 sessions of the Conference to date. Fifty-three of the conventions are currently in force. A total of 972 national ratifications of the conventions has been registered.

The agenda of the forthcoming session will comprise the following items: (1) the Director-General's report on the work of the Organization during the year and on social and economic trends throughout the world; (2) financial and budgetary questions, including the approval of the budget for the 1949 operations of the Organization; (3) examination of reports supplied by the member governments on the way in which they are implementing the conventions they have ratified; (4) consideration of the adoption of one international labor convention and one recommendation providing for national employment services and consideration of the adoption of a convention revising the convention on fee-charging employment agencies adopted by the Conference in 1933; (5) preliminary considerations of the question of vocational guidance with a view to framing international standards at the 1949 session; (6) wages, including the questions of wage policy, fair-wage clauses in public contracts, and the protection of wages; (7) consideration of a convention to safeguard freedom of association of workers and employers and to protect their right to organize; (8) the question of industrial relations, including the application of the principles of the right to organize and bargain collectively, collective agreements, conciliation and arbitration, and cooperation between the public authorities and employers' and workers' organizations; (9) consideration of adoption of a convention revising the conventions regulating the employment of women on night work; (10) consideration of a convention partially to revise the convention regulating the night work of young persons; (11) substitution for the provisions of the night-work (women) convention (revised), 1934, and of the night-work of young persons (industry) convention, 1919, contained in the schedule to the labor-standards (nonmetropolitan territories) convention, 1947, of the corresponding provisions of the revising conventions proposed under items 9 and 10 above; and (12) approval of an annex, relating to the ILO, to the convention on the privileges and immunities of the U.N. specialized agencies.

The Conference will be preceded on June 12 and 14 by the 105th session of the Governing Body.

[1] Prepared by the Division of International Conferences, Department of State.

Seventh Meeting of the International Cotton Advisory Committee

By James

The Seventh Plenary Meeting of the International Cotton Advisory Committee was held at Cairo and Alexandria, Egypt, April 1–8, 1948. Nineteen member governments and the Food and Agriculture Organization of the United Nations were represented. His Excellency Mahmoud Fahmy Nokrashy Pasha, Prime Minister of Egypt and Minister of Finance, addressed the meeting at the opening session. His Excellency Osman Abaza Bey, Under Secretary of State, Ministry of Finance, and head of the delegation of the host country, served as chairman of the meeting.

The International Cotton Advisory Committee was organized in 1939 " (*a*) to observe and keep in touch with developments in the world cotton situation and (*b*) to suggest as and when advisable to governments represented on it any measure suitable and practicable for the achievement of ultimate international cooperation." In order to achieve the effectiveness of its work, the Advisory Committee at its fifth meeting (Washington, May 7–14, 1946) recommended to the member governments the establishment of an Executive Committee which would cooperate with international organizations concerned with the world cotton situation, thereby providing for the exchange of views in regard to current developments. The Committee also recommended that a secretariat be organized at Washington which would assemble and make available to member governments information on world cotton production, trade, consumption, stocks, and prices.[1]

Following the pattern of previous plenary meetings the agenda for the seventh meeting as recommended by the Executive Committee provided for: (1) consideration of proposals relating to organizational changes and the expenditure of funds; (2) consideration of the work program for the following year; (3) consideration of recommendations to member governments looking toward further international cooperation; and (4) a review of the cotton situation in each of the member countries and in the world as a whole. Final action of the seventh meeting consisted of 14 reso-

[1] The sixth meeting of the Advisory Committee (Washington, June 9–11, 1947) approved minor organizational changes within the established structure.

tanding and cooperation . . . ". Accordingly the Secretariat was instructed to compile and publish, with respect to the world cotton situation, monthly commentaries, quarterly and annual statements, and a quarterly statistical bulletin for cotton and competing fibers. The Secretariat was also instructed to initiate studies of national statistical procedures relating to cotton (Resolution III).

Recommendations to Member Governments

It was also recognized by the Advisory Committee that the statistical and other data essential to full knowledge of the world cotton situation must be made available to the Secretariat as a basis for the work program. The Advisory Committee therefore resolved to recommend to member governments that they make every effort to provide the Secretariat with specific data, including information concerning stocks; ginnings; imports; consumption; losses by destruction; exports; reexports; prices; indication of area to be planted; forecasts and estimates of areas planted, areas harvested, yields, and production; rayon fiber and yarn production, imports, exports, and prices; elucidating comment on the information furnished; and semi-annual statements on economic developments affecting the supply and distribution of cotton. The Secretariat was authorized to take steps to secure similar information for countries whose governments are not members of the Advisory Committee. It was suggested that the Standing Committee consider the advisability of assembling statistical data on the output of textile machinery (Resolution III).

Cotton Situation

Each delegation presented a statement of the cotton situation in the country it represented. The Secretariat presented a review of the current world cotton situation, a summary of which follows:

"The world cotton situation for the 1947–48 season is characterized by:

1) Production of cotton below the prewar level and considerably less than indicated consumption.

2) A general level of world mill activity below prewar and mill output of cotton textiles much less than world needs.

3) Stocks of cotton apparently ample to meet mill requirements for the current season but decreasing at a rapid rate as a result of the continuing excess of cotton consumption over production since the end of the war.

4) International trade in cotton hampered by financial difficulties but with prospects that total trade for the current season may be sufficient for the maintenance of mill activity during the latter part of the season.

(5) Prices for cotton high enough to suggest increasing substitutions of synthetic fibers for cotton but too low, in relation to returns from the production of foodstuffs and other competing enterprises to stimulate the rapid expansion of cotton cultivation in countries where governmental production control measures are not in effect.

(6) A continuation of the upward trend in synthetic fiber production with prospects for an accelerated increase in the rate of production and substitutions for cotton as war-damaged rayon plants are repaired and new plants constructed."

U.S. DELEGATION TO SECOND ANNUAL ASSEMBLY OF ICAO

[Released to the press May 21]

The Department of State announced on May 21 that the President has approved the composition of the United States Delegation to the Second Annual Assembly of the International Civil Aviation Organization (ICAO), scheduled to convene at Geneva June 1, 1948.

The United States Delegation will be headed by Russell B. Adams, Board Member, Civil Aeronautics Board. J. Paul Barringer, Deputy Director, Office of Transport and Communications, Department of State, will serve as vice chairman.

Invitations have been extended to both Houses of Congress to send congressional advisers as part of the Delegation.

Designated as consultants to the Delegation are: John R. Alison, Assistant Secretary of Commerce for Aeronautics, and Paul Aiken, Second Assistant Postmaster General.

The following have been named as Government advisers: John M. Cates, Jr., Division of International Organization Affairs, Department of State; Leo G. Cyr, Assistant Chief, Aviation Division, Department of State; Paul T. David, U.S. Representative on the Air Transport Committee of ICAO; Charles F. Dycer, Director, Aircraft and Components Service, Civil Aeronautics Administration, Department of Commerce; Glen A. Gilbert, Chief of Technical Mission, Civil Aeronautics Administration, Department of Commerce; Alfred Hand, Director, Staff Programs Office, Office of the Administrator, Civil Aeronautics Administration, Department of Commerce; Robert D. Hoyt, Chief, International Standards Division, Civil Aeronautics Board; Robert J. G. McClurkin, Assistant Director, Economic Bureau, Civil Aeronautics Board; Emory T. Nunneley, Jr., General Counsel, Civil Aeronautics Board; H. Walker Percy, Acting U.S. Representative on the Air Navigation Committee of ICAO; Edward S. Prentice, Assistant Chief, Aviation Division, Department of State; Carl H. Schwartz, Assistant Chief, Estimates Division, Bureau of the Budget; Brackley Shaw, General Counsel, Department of the Air Force; Paul A. Smith, Rear Admiral, U.S. Coast and Geodetic Survey, representing the United States on the Council of ICAO; and Theodore C. Uebel, liaison officer, Staff Program Offices, International Services, Civil Aeronautics Administration, Department of Commerce.

Included in the Delegation as industry advisers are Hall L. Hibbard, Vice President and Chief Engineer, Lockheed Aircraft Corporation, and Stuart G. Tipton, General Counsel, Air Transport Association of America.

Lyle L. Schmitter, Division of International Conferences, Department of State, will serve as executive secretary; and Norman P. Seagrave, Air Coordinating Committee, will serve as technical secretary to the Delegation.

United States positions on the specific agenda items to be discussed and acted upon at the Second Assembly of Icao have been prepared within the framework of the Air Coordinating Committee, where opportunity was provided for full and complete industry participation in United States positions.

The Second Annual Assembly of Icao will not only review and approve actions taken by the Council of Icao during the past year but will also discuss matters of policy and operation during the forthcoming year. Icao now has a membership of 48 nations, most of which are expected to send representatives to the Assembly. Among the more important matters to come before the Assembly is the expected signing of an international convention concerning the protection of the rights of mortgage holders of aircraft engaged in international air commerce.

The Second Assembly is the first full meeting of the Organization since it began operations one year ago in accordance with the Chicago convention on international civil aviation. The Assembly represents a significant step in international cooperation by an important specialized agency of the United Nations.

AEC TO SUSPEND ACTIVITIES

On May 17, the Atomic Energy Commission, at its 16th meeting since it began its work on June 14, 1946, decided to suspend its activities.

The vote on the draft report of the Commission to the Security Council presented on May 7 by François de Rose of France on behalf of the Delegations of France, the United Kingdom, and the United States, was 9 to 2. The two negative votes were cast by the U.S.S.R. and the Ukrainian S.S.R.

The Report of the Atomic Energy Commission to the Security Council, the third report to be submitted by the Commission, recommends in view of the failure to achieve agreement on the international control of atomic energy "at the Commission level", that the "negotiations in the Atomic Energy Commission be suspended" until the General Assembly finds that this situation no longer exists or until such time as the permanent members of the Atomic Energy Commission (Canada, China, France, U.S.S.R., U.K., U.S.) find "through prior consultation, that there exists a basis for agreement".

The Commission further recommends that the three reports be transmitted to the next regular session of the General Assembly, convening in Paris on September 21, "as a matter of special concern".

THE RECORD OF THE WEEK

Major Problems Existing Between U.S. and U.S.S.R. Are Not Bilateral Issues

[Released to the press May 18]

The Department of State has seen the press reports of a statement by Premier Stalin in response to an "open letter" from Henry Wallace. Premier Stalin's opinion that a peaceful settlement of outstanding problems is possible and necessary in the interests of a general peace is encouraging, but the specific issues listed in Premier Stalin's statement are not bilateral issues between this country and the Soviet Union. They are of intimate and compelling interest to many countries and have been under negotiation for the past two years or more in bodies where other countries are represented, such as the United Nations and the Council of Foreign Ministers. For example, the United Nations Atomic Energy Commission and its subcommittees have held over 200 meetings and the Commission on May 17 reported its inability to reach an agreement because of the adamant opposition of two of its members—the Soviet Union and the Ukraine—to proposals which were acceptable to the other nine nations represented on the Commission. A similar situation exists with regard to other issues mentioned in Premier Stalin's statement.

The Department of State on May 19 made the following information available to the press in connection with the Stalin statement:

1. Reduction of Armaments

The problem of the regulation of conventional armaments was discussed in the 1946 General Assembly of the United Nations, and has since been under consideration in the Commission for Conventional Armaments of the Security Council.

2. Atomic Energy

In the field of atomic energy, agreement on an effective plan for international control has so far been blocked by the Soviet Union.

The presentation of the Third Report of the Commission marks the recognition of an impasse which has existed practically since the negotia-

tions began almost two years and 220 meetings ago. Fourteen out of 17 of the nations which are now or have been represented on the Commission are agreed on the basic and indispensable requirements of an international control plan; the Soviet Union, Poland, and the Ukraine have been the only members of the Commission to disagree.

Despite its unceasing efforts, the Commission has now been forced to declare that: "It has been unable to secure the agreement of the Soviet Union to even those elements of effective control considered essential from the technical point of view, let alone their acceptance of the nature and extent of participation in the world community required of all nations in this field by the First and Second Reports of the Atomic Energy Commission." In this situation, the Commission has concluded that for the present no useful purpose could be served by carrying on negotiations at the Commission level and has referred the whole problem to the Security Council with a recommendation that it be forwarded to the General Assembly.

The conclusion that further work at the Commission level would be futile does not mean that the efforts to achieve international control of atomic energy are to be terminated, but it does mean that the Commission has recognized that factors necessary to bring about agreement on an effective system for the international control of atomic energy are outside the competence of the Commission. The United Nations is still confronted with the problem of international control of atomic energy and the United States Government is still ready to participate in genuinely effective control.

3. German Peace Settlement

By common agreement the question of a German peace settlement is one for the Council of Foreign Ministers. The Council has held two long meetings devoted to this subject. Soviet opposition to virtually every proposition put forward by the United States, Great Britain, and France has thus far blocked all progress on this question.

4. *Japanese Peace Settlement*

In July 1947 the United States proposed to the ten other members of the Far Eastern Commission that a preliminary conference be held to discuss a peace treaty for Japan, the voting procedure of such a conference to be by two-thirds majority. Eight states indicated general agreement with this proposal. The Soviet Union held that the peace-treaty problems should be considered by the Council of Foreign Ministers, composed in this instance of the United Kingdom, China, the U.S.S.R., and the United States. China proposed that the peace treaty be considered by a conference of the eleven Far Eastern Commission countries and that decisions be taken by a majority which must include the four powers named above. It has so far been impossible to resolve the conflict between these widely different concepts as to the basis on which the Japanese peace-treaty conference should be convened.

5. *Evacuation of Troops From China*

As of March 31, 1948, there were stationed in China, of the armed forces of the United States, 1,496 Army personnel and 4,125 Navy and Marine personnel. These forces remain in China at the request of the National Government.

6. *Evacuation of Troops From Korea*

With respect to the suggestion that United States and Soviet occupation forces be withdrawn from Korea, the United Nations General Assembly, by resolution of November 14, 1947, recommended a plan for the early achievement of Korean independence, to be followed promptly by the withdrawal of all foreign armed forces.

The General Assembly constituted a United Nations commission to assist in this program. The Ukraine was elected to membership on the commission but refused to serve. The U.S.S.R. denied the United Nations commission entry into the northern zone of Korea. It has not only refused to collaborate in any way in the implementation of the United Nations plan but has attempted to proceed unilaterally with a plan of its own which threatens to lead to civil war among the Koreans themselves.

7. *Respect for National Sovereignty and Noninterference in Domestic Affairs*

The facts bearing on this subject are too voluminous for recapitulation here. The actions and policies of the two Governments in this respect are a matter of public record, and speak for themselves.

8. *Military Bases*

The policy of the United States in this respect

False Accusations by Yugoslav Press Against American Officials Protested

TEXT OF U.S. NOTE TO YUGOSLAV FOREIGN OFFICE [1]

[Released to the press May 19]

Text of a note dated May 18 delivered to the Yugoslav Foreign Office by the American Embassy at Belgrade on that date

The Embassy of the United States presents its compliments to the Yugoslav Minister of Foreign Affairs and has the honor to bring to the Minister's attention various false accusations reported by the Yugoslav press as having been made against American officials in the course of the trial of one Ilija Mangovic before the Circuit Court at Cacak. It is not the purpose of the Embassy to raise any question as to the conduct of this trial. As a matter of record, however, the Embassy feels that it must make mention of the allegations put forth, which were to the effect that Lieutenant Colonel Stratton and W. O. La Plante had employed the accused, knowing him to be a criminal, and that Lieutenant Colonel Stratton had concealed him from the Yugoslav authorities and had assisted him to escape.

On the first point it is noted from the Yugoslav press that prosecution admitted that the accused, prior to his employment by Americans, had been granted amnesty by the Yugoslav Government for his past actions. The Minister will doubtless agree that American Embassy personnel cannot be approached for employing amnestied persons.

On the second point, the Embassy is in a position formally to declare that it is completely untrue that Colonel Stratton concealed the accused from the Yugoslav authorities. Incontestable proof of this fact will be found in the Embassy's *note verbale* No. 720 of August 5, 1947, in which the Embassy furnished to the Minister the names of all domestic servants employed by Embassy personnel. The name of the accused was duly listed therein.

It surely would not be seriously maintained that Colonel Stratton attempted to assist the accused in avoiding arrest. On one occasion an unidentified person did in fact intercept Colonel Stratton at his gate with what Colonel Stratton understood to be an inquiry about servants. Quite properly this stranger was invited to call at the Embassy where an interpreter would be available for any appropriate inquiries. The person in question did not then or at any other time appear at the Embassy.

In view of the publicity given to the defamatory imputations against two officers of this Embassy, the Embassy feels certain that the Minister will wish publicly to correct the false statements made about these officers.

The Embassy avails itself [etc.]

Procedure for Filing Ownership Declaration in Yugoslavia

[Released to the press May 19]

The American Embassy at Belgrade has been informed by the Yugoslav Ministry of Foreign Affairs that foreign owners of Yugoslav Government prewar internal debt claims and securities must submit a declaration of ownership relative to their holdings by May 31, 1948, or forfeit them to the state.

The Ministry explained that some owners declared their titles before June 30, 1947, as prescribed by law, and later transmitted their securities for conversion prior to December 31, 1947, but did not submit a declaration of ownership. In order to permit claimants to file this declaration of ownership, the Yugoslav authorities have extended the period for filing to May 31, 1948. This extended period applies also to claimants who did not declare and deposit their claims and securities within the prescribed period. Claimants who have already submitted a declaration of ownership need not do so again, however.

The foregoing applies to Yugoslav internal-debt obligations payable in dinars and originating prior to April 18, 1941, and to nonfunded claims of all kinds against the Yugoslav Government.[2] The Yugoslav Ministry of Finance at Belgrade was to receive the declarations relative to the Government securities, while those pertaining to nonfunded claims were to be sent to the agencies where such claims originated.

[1] Printed from telegraphic text.
[2] BULLETIN of June 22, 1947, p. 1219.

Greece and Bipartite Board for U.S.–U.K. Zones of Germany Adhere to Economic Cooperation Act

[Released to the press by the Department of State and the ECA May 18]

The Department of State and the Economic Cooperation Administration on May 18 released copies of the exchange of notes between the United States and Greece signifying Greek adherence to the purposes of the Economic Cooperation Act. Also released on May 18 were copies of the corresponding exchange of letters between the United States and the American and British Military Governors in Germany, who constitute together the Bipartite Board for the United States and United Kingdom zones of occupation of Germany. The publication of these texts follows the release on May 8 of exchanges between the United States and 11 participating European countries, namely: Austria, Denmark, France, Iceland, Ireland, Italy, Luxembourg, the Netherlands, Nor-

way, Sweden, and the United Kingdom.[1] Sin that time the Belgian Government authorized t publication of the text of its exchange of not with the United States, which is similar to th between the United States and the Netherland Notes have not been exchanged as of this date wi Portugal, Switzerland, Turkey, and the Fren zone of occupied Germany.

The primary difference between the Greek l ter and those signed by other countries is that provides that assistance rendered to Greece duri the period covered by the letter will be extend through the American Mission for Aid to Gree in substantially the same manner as for the e nomic assistance being provided under the prese Greek Aid Program and pursuant to the existi aid agreement of June 20, 1947.

EXCHANGE OF NOTES BETWEEN THE UNITED STATES AND GREECE

The American Chargé d'Affaires at Athens to the Greek Foreign Minister

April 15, 1948

EXCELLENCY: I have the honor to inform you that the Economic Cooperation Act of 1948 (Title I of the Foreign Assistance Act of 1948) became law on April 3, 1948.

You will note the general requirement of the Act that, before assistance may be provided by the United States to a country of Europe which participates in a joint recovery program based on self-help and mutual cooperation, an agreement must have been concluded between that country and the United States as described in subsection 115(b) of the Act. However, before such an agreement is concluded and until July 3, 1948 the Government of the United States proposes, under the terms of subsection 115 (c) to arrange for the performance, with respect to your country, of those functions authorized by the Act which may be determined to be essential in furtherance of its purposes. This action by the Government of the United States is contingent upon the requirements of subsection 115(c) of the Act being fulfilled.

Accordingly, I should appreciate your notifying me whether your Government adheres to the purposes and policies in furtherance of which the Act authorized assistance to be provided, and is engaged in continuous efforts to accomplish a joint recovery program through multilateral undertak-

ings and the establishment of a continuing orga ization for this purpose, and also whether yo Government intends to conclude an agreeme with the United States in accordance with su section 115(b). The purposes of the Act a stated in the whole of subsection 102(b) and t policies referred to in subsection 102(b) are tho designated as such in subsection 102(a).

My Government would be required by the A to terminate assistance authorized by subsecti 115(c) to your country if at any time it shou find that your Government was not complyir with such provisions of subsection 115(b) of t Act as my Government might consider applicabl I should appreciate being notified whether yo Government is complying with and, for so lor as assistance may be made available to it und the Act pursuant to this letter, is prepared to cor ply with the applicable provisions of subsectic 115(b).

It is contemplated that, during the period co ered by this letter, such assistance under the A as may be furnished to your Government wi be by grant and will be extended through tl American Mission for Aid to Greece in substa tially the same manner as for economic assistan being provided under the present Greek aid pr gram, including the provisions for deposits Greek currency against imports at the full lande cost including the foreign exchange certifica charge. The existing agreement of June 20, 19 between our Governments shall continue to r main in force. The economic assistance to be fu

[1] BULLETIN of May 16, 1948, p. 640.

nished to your Government during the period covered by this letter will be under the terms of that agreement as they apply to economic matters, and pursuant also to other relevant undertakings of your Government within the framework of that agreement. The provisions of the future agreement between our two Governments concerning any deposits to be made pursuant to paragraph (six) of subsection 115(b) of the Economic Cooperation Act will apply with respect to all assistance for your Government which is determined to have been made by grant during the period covered by this letter. I trust that your Government will concur in these arrangements.

I am sure your Government understands that the proposals set forth in this letter cannot be viewed as constituting an obligation on the part of my Government to make assistance available to your country.

Please accept [etc.]   K. L. RANKIN

The Greek Foreign Minister to the American Chargé d'Affaires at Athens

May 12, 1948

DEAR MR. RANKIN: Referring to your letter sub. No. 346 of April 15, 1948 I have the honor to advise that the Greek Government has authorized me to inform you of its adherence to the purposes and policies of the Economic Cooperation Act of 1948, which are stated in the whole of subsection 102 (b) and in subsection 102 (a), respectively, and in furtherance of which the Act authorizes assistance to be provided to my country.

The Greek Government has taken careful note of the provisions of subsection 115 (b) of the Economic Cooperation Act of 1948 and intends to conclude an agreement with your Government pursuant to that section. It is understood that your Government would be required by the Act to terminate assistance if at any time it should find that the Government of Greece was not complying with such provisions of subsection 115 (b) of the Act as your Government considers applicable.

The Greek Government is complying with and for so long as assistance may be available to it under the Act pursuant to your letter, is prepared to comply with all the applicable provisions of subsection 115 (b) of the Act, and is also engaged in continuous efforts to accomplish a joint recovery program through multilateral undertakings and the establishment of a continuing organization for this purpose.

The Greek Government understands that, during the period covered by your letter, it is contemplated by your Government that such assistance under the Act as may be furnished hereunder will be by grant and that such assistance will be extended through the American Mission for Aid to Greece in substantially the same manner as the economic assistance being provided under the present Greek aid program, including the provisions for deposits of Greek currency against imports at the full landed cost including the foreign exchange certificate charge. It is understood that the existing agreement of June 20, 1947, between our Governments shall continue to remain in force, and the economic assistance to be furnished to the Greek Government during the period covered by your letter will be under the terms of that agreement as they apply to economic matters and pursuant also to other relevant undertakings of the Greek Government within the framework of that agreement. It is understood that the provisions of the future agreement between our Governments concerning any deposits to be made pursuant to paragraph (6) of subsection 115 (b) of the Economic Cooperation Act will apply with respect to all assistance for the Greek Government which is determined by your Government to have been made by grant during the period covered by your letter.

I am authorized to state that the Government of Greece understands that the proposals contained in your letter do not constitute an obligation on the part of your Government to make assistance available to my country.

Please accept [etc.]   C. S. TSALDARIS

EXCHANGE OF LETTERS BETWEEN THE UNITED STATES AND THE BIPARTITE BOARD FOR U.S.–U.K. ZONES OF OCCUPATION OF GERMANY

The U.S. Political Adviser on German Affairs at Berlin to the Bipartite Board

May 1, 1948

SIRS: 1. The Economic Cooperation Act of 1948 (title one of the Foreign Assistance Act of 1948) became law on 3 April 1948.

2. You will note the general requirement that, before assistance may be provided by the United States to a participating country as defined in subsection 103(A) of the act, an agreement must

have been concluded between that country and the United States as described in subsection 115(B) of the act. However, before such an agreement is concluded and until 3 July 1948, the Government of the United States proposes, under the terms of subsection 115(C) to arrange for the performance, with respect to the United States and United Kingdom Zones of Occupation of Germany, of those functions authorized by the act which may be determined to be essential in furtherance of its purposes. This action by the Government of the United States is contingent upon the requirements of subsection 115(C) of the act being fulfilled.

3. Accordingly, I should appreciate your notifying me whether the Bipartite Board, on behalf of the United States and United Kingdom Zones of Occupation of Germany, adheres to the purposes and policies in furtherance of which the act authorizes assistance to be provided, and is engaged in continuous efforts to accomplish a joint recovery program through multilateral undertakings and the establishment of a continuing organization for the purpose, and also whether the Bipartite Board, on behalf of the United States and United Kingdom Zones of Occupation of Germany, intends to conclude an agreement with the United States in accordance with subsection 115(B). The purposes of the act are stated in the whole of subsection 102(B) and the policies referred to in subsection 102(B) are those designated as such in subsection 102(A).

4. The Government of the United States would be required by the act to terminate assistance authorized by subsection 115(C) to the United States and United Kingdom Zones of Occupation of Germany if at any time it should find that such zones were not complying with such provisions of subsection 115(B) of the act as the Government of the United States might consider applicable. I should appreciate being notified whether the United States and United Kingdom Zones of Occupation of Germany are complying with and, for so long as assistance may be made available to them under the act pursuant to this letter, are prepared to comply with the applicable provisions of subsection 115(B).

5. It is contemplated that all assistance to the United States and United Kingdom Zones of Occupation of Germany hereunder will be made available upon terms of payment. The proceeds of exports from all future production and stocks of the United States and United Kingdom Zones of Occupation of Germany will be available for payment for such assistance at the earliest practicable time consistent with the rebuilding of the German economy on healthy, non-aggressive lines. Such proceeds shall be applied for such payment on a basis at least as favorable to the United States as that agreed upon respecting payment for imports under the memorandum of agreement between the United States and the United Kingdom dated 2 December 1946, as amended, relating to the economic integration of the United States and the United Kingdom Zones of Occupation of Germany. Detailed terms of payment will be determined in accordance with the act at a later time.

6. I should also like to have the agreement of the Bipartite Board, on behalf of the United States and United Kingdom Zones of Occupation of Germany, that deposits in German marks in

hat the proceeds of exports from all future pro-
luction and stocks of US/UK zones of occupation
)f Germany will be available for payment for
such assistance at the earliest practicable time
:onsistent with the rebuilding of the German
:conomy on healthy, non-aggressive lines. It fur-
her understands that such proceeds shall be ap-
)lied for such payment on a basis at least as
:avorable to the United States as that agreed upon
·especting payment for imports under the memo-
·andum of agreement between the United States
and the United Kingdom dated 2 December 1946,
as amended, relating to the economic integration
)f the United States and United Kingdom zones
)f occupation of Germany. It is further under-
:tood that detailed terms of payment will be de-
ermined in accordance with the act at a later time.
5. The Bipartite Board, on behalf of the United
States and United Kingdom zones of occupation
)f Germany, agree that deposits in German marks,
n respect of assistance furnished pursuant to your
etter, will be made pursuant to procedures as
nay be required by the administrator in accordance with the provision of the act, and will be held
)r used for such purposes as may be agreed between the administrator of the Economic Coopera-
ion Administration and the Bipartite Board.
6. The Bipartite Board, on behalf of the United
States and United Kingdom zones of occupation
)f Germany, understands that the proposals con-

tained in your letter do not constitute an obligation on the part of the Government of the United
States to make assistance available to such zones.

GENERAL LUCIUS B. CLAY,
United States Military Governor

GENERAL BRIAN ROBERTSON,
United Kingdom Military Governor

Registration of Property Claims in Bulgaria

[Released to the press May 14]

The Department of State announced on May 14
that a recent Bulgarian law for the nationalization
of urban real property requires that foreigners
owning such property should register, by June 15,
1948, their ownership with the Municipal People's
Council of the municipality in which the property
is located.

The Bulgarian law defines urban real property
subject to nationalization as property situated
within the limits of urbanization plans and owned
by private persons and corporations for the receipt of income from invested capital. Such
property in villages is apparently exempt from
the terms of the law.

The Department of State is requesting an extension of the dead line for registering the above-
mentioned statements of ownership but is unable
to state whether favorable action will be taken on
the request.

Signing of Protocol With France Modifying Double Taxation Convention

Summary of Provisions

[Released to the press May 17]

A protocol between the United States and France
for the purpose of modifying in certain respects
the convention of October 18, 1946, between the
two countries relating to double taxation was
signed at Washington on May 17, 1948, by George
C. Marshall, Secretary of State, and Henri Bonnet, French Ambassador in Washington.

The object of the protocol is to effect certain
modifications in the provisions of the convention,
signed at Paris October 18, 1946, for the avoidance
of double taxation and the prevention of evasion
n the case of taxes on estates and inheritances and
for the purpose of modifying and supplementing
certain provisions of the convention of July 25,
.939, between the two countries relating to income
axation.

The convention of October 18, 1946, is under consideration in the Senate Committee on Foreign
Relations and has been the subject of hearings
before a subcommittee of that Committee. The
protocol has been negotiated with France as a

result of proposals made in the course of those
hearings.

The protocol provides that it shall be ratified
and that it shall become effective and continue
effective as though it were an integral part of the
convention of October 18, 1946.

**Remarks of Secretary Marshall and
Ambassador Bonnet**

[Released to the press May 17]

Mr. Ambassador, the signing of this protocol
will, we hope, hasten the coming into force of the
double-taxation convention concluded by the
United States and France in 1946.

Upon the entry into force of that convention,
together with this protocol, the taxpayers—both
citizens and enterprises—of the two countries will
benefit by the elimination, for the most part, of
double taxation affecting the settlement of estates, and also by increased advantages under the
income-tax convention of 1939, now in force.

In this way the two Governments have shown

their mutual desire to relieve still further the burdens which arise from double taxation.

———

Mr. Secretary, I am glad that the signing of this protocol will make possible the prompt ratification both of the convention signed in 1946 and of this protocol which is an integral part of it.

I believe that the coming into force of that Co vention will not only permit to rectify unfair i dividual situations resulting from double taxatio but will also tend to facilitate harmonious cor mercial relations between our two countries, keeping with the principles upon which they a in full agreement.

American Citizens Removed From Vessel by Lebanese Authorities at Beirut

[Released to the press May 21]

The Department of State has been informed by the American Minister to Lebanon, Lowell C. Pinkerton, that 40 American citizens, together with 29 persons of other nationalities, were removed by Lebanese authorities May 19 at Beirut from the American S.S. *Marine Carp.* All were men between 19 and 55 years of age. The Legation was informed that all of these persons were being interned in the former French barracks at Beka, Lebanon.

The Legation made representations to the Lebanese authorities against the removal of these American passengers. A short time earlier the American Minister had intervened with the Lebanese Foreign Office on behalf of the Americans when it appeared possible that search of these passengers and baggage aboard the vessel might lead to their removal from the vessel. The American Minister, upon learning of the search action, had sent aboard an officer of the Legation who remained during the incident.

At the time of the American intervention the Lebanese authorities stated that passengers it chose to remove from the vessel would be removed by force if necessary. The Legation thereupon advised American citizens aboard the vessel that physical resistance might lead to bloodshed. The result was that the removal of selected passengers was accomplished without use of force and without violence. Some pistols, ammunition, and certain electrical equipment were seized. The ship then sailed for Haifa.

In addition to the 40 American citizens removed, the Lebanese authorities also removed 24 Palestinians, three Canadians, one Pole, and one Mexican.

The American citizens removed were:

George Alper	Leon Goldstein
David Beinin	Bernard Goobich
Oded Bouria	Bernard Greene
Meyer Braiterman	Martin Gross
George Brodsky	Nadar Halevi
David Crohn	Victor Hoffer
Benjamin de Roy, Jr.	Nahmin Horwitz
Steven Esrater	Robert S. Jacobs
Samuel Frazin	Ahud Kadish
Harlow Geberer	Murray Kadlsh

Eli Kalamanowitz	Abraham Rosenthal
Raymond Kaplin	Max H. Rosenweig
Bernard Kasan	Abraham H. Sharaby
Robert Keller	Herman Sklar
Nathan Kramer	Ernest Sokal
Nathan J. Krothinger	Theodore Steinberg
Leonard Loeb	Michael Stomachin
Irwin Maurer	David Taub
Jeash Nagdimon	Gilbert Ziff
Lee Dov Rappoport	K. Jakie Zucker

Sweden and Luxembourg File Letters of Intent Under Foreign Assistance Act

[Released to the press by ECA May

Two additional European countries—Swede and Luxembourg—have filed letters of intent an have qualified for assistance under the Foreig Assistance Act, Paul G. Hoffman, Administrato for Economic Cooperation, announced on May

This brings the total of countries which have qualified to 13, including France, Italy, Austri the Netherlands, Denmark, Norway, the Unite Kingdom, Iceland, Belgium, Ireland, and Chin Countries still to file such letters are Greece, Portu gal, Switzerland, Turkey, and western German

At the same time, Mr. Hoffman announced add tional authorizations for shipment of commoditi to four European countries as follows:

Country	Commodity	Quantity	Authorization
Austria	Wheat	18,000 long tons .	$1,976,0
Denmark	{Crude soya-bean oil . . .	536 long tons . .	328,0
	{Protein feed (peanut meal).	2,000 long tons .	200,0
Greece	Fertilizer	2,250 short tons .	214,9
The, Netherlands	Linseed oil	4,400,000 lbs . .	1,291,0

After allowances for adjustments and revisior in previously announced authorizations, this a(tion brings the total authorizations to $110,629,33 This is exclusive of ocean transportation, amoun ing to $5,851,000.

CBS Correspondent Slain in Greece

[Released to the press May 19]

The body of George Polk, Columbia Broadcasting System correspondent in Greece, with arms and legs trussed, was washed ashore in Salonika Bay on the morning of May 16. A preliminary autopsy indicated that he had been shot through the back of the head and that his body had been in the water for some days. Personal effects were still on the body.

The American Consul General at Salonika had reported on May 12 that Polk had been reported missing following his departure from his hotel on Sunday morning, May 9. He had taken no baggage or personal effects with him and left no word of his plans or destination. Polk had made a dinner engagement for the following night and had requested his wife to proceed from Athens to Salonika on May 12 in order to accompany him on a trip to Kavalla.

Although a copy of a letter found in Polk's room indicated that he had visited Salonika for the purpose of contacting Markos, it is not known whether his death was connected with such a trip. He had made no request for the permit required to visit a military zone, although he was familiar with the regulations in this respect.

American Consul General Gibson at Salonika has reported that the local Salonika police, with the aid of British Police Mission officials, have been carrying on an intensive investigation in an endeavor to locate the perpetrators of this crime. Moreover, Prime Minister Sophoulis has announced that he has given instructions to alert the entire police force of the country to assist in this case. Minister of Public Order Constantine Rendis and his Director General are now in Salonika and have offered a reward of 25 million drachmas (approximately $2,500) to anyone furnishing information.

On May 17, Greek Prime Minister Sophoulis addressed the following letter to American Chargé l'Affaires Rankin at Athens

I wish to express to you the deep regret of the Government for the terrible and shocking murder of Mr. Polk, the American correspondent, which has aroused indignation and horror and has deeply moved the Greek people. The Government considers it a matter of honor to spare no effort toward arresting the assassin, clearing up this matter, and turning over the criminal immediately into the hands of justice, in order that the sense of hospitality of the Greek people which has been deeply hurt may be fully satisfied. The Greek people will not tolerate such crimes which may indeed soil and humiliate our ancient civilization, a civilization which the sound thinking Greek people are determined to uphold intact and which they consider as the most honorable continuation of their history.

Assassination of Greek Minister of Justice

[Released to the press May 4]

Secretary of State Marshall has sent the following message to Constantine Tsaldaris, Deputy Prime Minister and Minister for Foreign Affairs of Greece

I have been deeply shocked by the brutal assassination of the Greek Minister of Justice, Christos Ladas. Please convey my most sincere sympathy and that of the United States Government to the Greek Government and to the families of Christos Ladas and the other victims of this cowardly and criminal attack.

Discussions on Gold Transferred by Germany to Bank for International Settlements

[Released to the press May 14]

Representatives of the Governments of the United States, the United Kingdom, and France, on the one hand, and of the Bank for International Settlements on the other, have met in Washington to discuss the subject of gold transferred by Germany to the Bank for International Settlements. During these discussions it was found that the Bank had inadvertently acquired gold which had been looted by Germany. By an exchange of letters dated May 13, 1948, the Bank for International Settlements agreed to deliver to the three Governments, on demand, 3,740 kilograms of fine gold, valued at about $4,200,000, in full settlement of all looted gold acquired by it from Germany.

Upon receipt, the gold will be distributed by the Tripartite Commission for the Restitution of Monetary Gold at Brussels pursuant to the Paris Reparation Agreement.

Generalissimo Chiang Kai-shek Inaugurated as President of Chinese Republic

[Released to the press May 20]

The United States Government notes with pleasure the occasion of the inauguration of Generalissimo Chiang Kai-shek as the first President of the Republic of China and Marshal Li Tsung-jen as the first Vice President of the Republic of China under the new constitution. The election of these outstanding leaders of China by secret ballot in the National Assembly was an auspicious beginning for constitutional government in China. The United States Government looks forward to the success of their joint efforts directed toward promoting economic recovery and stability in China and thus alleviating the hardships which the Chinese people are suffering. It is hoped that the China Aid Program will assist them in their efforts to this end.

Achievements of the Bogotá Conference

BY NORMAN ARMOUR [1]

Assistant Secretary for Political Affairs

Charter for the Organization of American States

The first task of the Bogotá conference was to draft a charter for the Organization of American States. This job was completed in a form that was highly satisfactory to all delegations including our own. The new charter sets forth the basic principles that guide the American nations in their mutual relations. Those principles clearly affirm the sovereign equality of all nations, their determination to settle all their disputes by peaceful means, and the consideration that an attack against one of them is an attack against all. The charter, and the Organization which gives it form, is founded upon the highest principles of law and justice, under which nations of varying size and power agree to live together in mutual respect and cooperation.

The principal features of the organization for which the charter provides are likewise of a thoroughly democratic character. Every five years—and in special circumstances at other times—the Inter-American Conference will meet. This Conference is the top representative body of the Organization, empowered to deal with any matter relating to the friendly relations among American states. For emergency purposes, there is a meeting of consultation of Ministers of Foreign Affairs of the 21 republics. This body is called together when needed, for example, in the event that the peace and security of the Americas is threatened by a fact or situation requiring important decisions as to joint defensive measures to be taken. Finally, there is the Council of the Organization sitting in permanent session in Washington. An outgrowth of what was formerly the Governing Board of the Pan American Union, the Council is assisted in its work by three subordinate bodies: the Economic and Social Council, the Cultural Council, and the Council of Jurists. In all these representative bodies each state has one vote, and none of them has a veto.

The permanent Organization of American States and the secretariat of the entire Organization, retain the familiar name of the Pan American Union. There are, in addition, a number of specialized conferences and organizations which deal with technical matters of common interest such as public health, agricultural sciences, child welfare, the status of women, and others. All these conferences and agencies together comprise the Organization of American States.

For the first time, the new charter of the Or-

ganization brings together the principles a basic organizational structure through which t 21 republics will continue their cooperative r lations. The charter, signed in Bogotá by all republics, will be transmitted by the Departme of State to the President with a view to his seekir the advice and consent of the Senate to its rat fication at the appropriate time.

Economic Agreement

Another basic field of endeavor at Bogotá w that of economic cooperation. Last summer tl conference of Rio de Janeiro called upon tł Bogotá conference to formulate a basic agreemer for economic cooperation. This task was lik wise satisfactorily executed at Bogotá.

In the economic agreement, which will also l submitted to the Congress for approval, the Amer can republics set forth certain basic ideas ar plans which are considered essential to their eco nomic development.

It is recognized that technical cooperation is c great importance to the improved use of the nat ural resources of the Americas. To this end ir creased facilities, in the form of a trained tech nical staff, will be made available to the Inter American Economic and Social Council, and th various governments agree to intensify their pres ent efforts to extend technical advice and hel to each other.

Financial cooperation forms another major par of the economic agreement signed at Bogotá Recognizing the responsibility of every countr to take steps within its own borders to improv its financial position, the agreement nevertheles points to the desirability of continuing mediun and long-term loans from one government tc another to supplement the role of private invest ment in the over-all development of economic re sources. Such government-to-government financ ing must, it is agreed, be restricted to economically sound projects which do not require excessive pro tection or subsidies.

Private investment is recognized as playing a major role in the expected economic development of the American republics, and the economic agreement of Bogotá points to the importance of creating satisfactory opportunity and security for

[1] Excerpts from remarks delivered over the national net work of the Columbia Broadcasting System at Washing ton, D.C., on May 12, and released to the press on the same date.

the foreign as well as domestic investor. The agreement declares that just as foreign investors must respect the laws of the country in which they engage in business and must accept a responsibility for contributing to the economic and social improvement of its people, so must the governments accord fair and equitable treatment to foreign capital as well as to domestic. The American governments, in the Bogotá agreement, undertake not to take discriminatory action against foreign investments. They specifically agree that any expropriation shall be accompanied by the payment of a just price in a prompt, adequate, and effective manner.

It is generally believed that these and other provisions of the basic economic agreement of Bogotá will go far toward meeting the fundamental needs of the other American republics for capital and technical skills with which to develop their rich and varied resources. Government loans in appropriate amounts and for appropriate purposes will continue to play their part in this process. But of greater importance are the provisions of the agreement which are directed toward the attraction of private capital in the building up of the other American republics. Effective application of the guaranties offered to foreign investors in the Bogotá agreement should make it possible for increasing amounts of United States capital to be invested in Latin America for productive and mutually advantageous purposes. This process and its ensuing raising of purchasing power and living standards will, of course, be of benefit to United States industry and commerce as well as to that of other countries of the Hemisphere.

Peaceful Settlement and Rights of Women

The United States Delegation signed two other treaties at Bogotá. One of these was a treaty which brings together the various procedures for the peaceful settlement of international disputes among the American states. The other was a convention agreeing to grant to women the right to vote and hold national office—an important step forward in the process of enabling the women of all the Americas to achieve the broader rights to which they are entitled. For constitutional reasons the Delegation of the United States was not able to sign a similar convention according women equal civil rights, since in our country the major responsibility for such matters rests with our States rather than with the Federal Government.

Resolutions

The United States also abstained from approving a resolution adopted by the Conference with respect to the termination of colonies and other territories of European states in the Americas.

Among the various resolutions approved by the Conference, the one relating to the continuity of diplomatic relations among the American republics is of particular significance in our inter-American relations. This resolution establishes the principle that continuity of diplomatic relations among the American republics is desirable as a contribution to their increasing solidarity and cooperation. At the same time, it is provided that the establishment or maintenance of diplomatic relations with a given government does not imply any judgment in regard to the internal policies of that government; nor can the establishment or severance of diplomatic relations with another government be used as a means for obtaining unjustified advantages of any character. The policy embodied in this resolution is entirely consistent with the policy of nonintervention adopted at Montevideo in 1933 and embodied in the new charter of the Organization of American States.

A number of other important resolutions and declarations were adopted at Bogotá. Several of these had to do with the broad field of social welfare and human rights. In fact, it should be noted that all through the discussions at Bogotá, including the debates on economic affairs, there was a constant emphasis placed upon the ultimate goal of inter-American cooperation—the raising of living standards of all the people and an increased respect for the dignity of the human individual in all classes of society.

I should like to mention the declaration in which the American republics unanimously condemned the aims and methods of international Communism and other forms of totalitarianism as hostile to the political principles and the ideas of economic and social justice which the American republics have long upheld. In this resolution the American republics took notice of a world situation far beyond the bounds of their own Continent. The reality of international Communism's opposition to all that the American states stand for was thrust forcibly upon the consciousness of the delegates at Bogotá by the obvious efforts of Communist adherents to sabotage the Conference. It is comforting to know of the united stand which the Americas took at Bogotá in opposition to new forms of totalitarianism and in stronger determination to achieve the ideals of political and economic democracy that are set forth in all their constitutions.

The United States and its sister republics of Latin America may well be proud of the record of achievement of the conference at Bogotá. In the face of great difficulties it succeeded in establishing new and firmer foundations for the cooperative relations of the Americas. Its work will have lasting and material benefits for the future peace, security, and economic and cultural advancement of the peoples of all our 21 American nations.

Colombia Expresses Gratitude for American Red Cross Aid During Bogotá Demonstrations

Exchange of Messages

[Released to the press May 13]

May 2, 1948.

I convey to Your Excellency·my most sincere and cordial salutations and express to you the thanks of the Government and people of Colombia for the most helpful and effective collaboration and assistance rendered by the American Red Cross on the occasion of the distressing events of recent days which placed the stability of our democratic institutions in grave jeopardy. The invaluable and opportune demonstration of solidarity of the great nation and Government of which Your Excellency is President is a proof of the bonds of sincere and loyal friendship which unite our two peoples and Governments and which have been strengthened on this occasion. I renew to Your Excellency the assurances of my highest consideration and of my deep and undying gratitude.

MARIANO OSPINA PEREZ
President of the Republic of Colombia

————

May 12, 1948

I thank you sincerely for your courteous telegram of May 2, the contents of which have been communicated to the American Red Cross. I speak for myself and for the American people in saying that we have esteemed it a privilege to be able to furnish neighborly assistance to the Colombian people.

HARRY S. TRUMAN

U.S. Prepared To Resume Diplomatic Relations With Nicaragua

[Released to the press May 6]

In view of the resolution of the Ninth International Conference of American States at Bogotá concerning the desirability of continuity of diplomatic relations among the American republics, the United States Government has informed the Government of Nicaragua that it is prepared to appoint a new Ambassador to Nicaragua and has requested the *agrément* of the Nicaraguan Government for a candidate for nomination to this position.

Prior to this action, the Governments of the other American republics were informed that the United States Government contemplated appointing an Ambassador to Nicaragua.

Letters of Credence
Paraguay

The newly appointed Ambassador of Paraguay, Señor Dr. Don Juan Felix Morales, presented his credentials to the President on April 23. For the text of the Ambassador's remarks and for the President's reply, see Department of State press release 318 of April 23, 1948.

Tourist Travel to Philippines

[Released to the press April 12]

The Department of State announces that the Philippine Government welcomes tourist travel and that the food supply, taxis, and other facilities are now adequate for a normal flow of visitors. The Department will issue passports to tourists upon assurance that they have adequate maintenance while in the Philippines.

Philippine Republic Extended Time for Renewing Trade-Mark Registration

The extension until June 30, 1948, of time for renewing trade-mark registrations with respect to the Philippines was granted by the President in Proclamation 2786 (13 *Federal Register* 2565) on May 11, 1948.

or Sanitary

CANADA AND THE UNITED STATES

If such an agreement is acceptable to the United States Government, it is the proposal of the Canadian Government that this Note and its Annex together with a reply agreeing thereto, constitute an agreement between the two Governments effective from the date of the reply from the United States authorities.

Canadian Embassy,
WASHINGTON, D.C.
4th March 1948.

ANNEX

MEMORANDUM OF AGREEMENT

4th March 1948

In order to improve the sanitary practices prevailing in the shellfish industries of Canada and the United States, it is agreed as follows:

1. Whatever manual of recommended practice for sanitary control of the shellfish industry is approved by both the United States Public Health Service and the Canadian Department of National Health and Welfare, will be regarded as setting

717

forth the sanitary principles that will govern the certification of shellfish shippers.

2. The degree of compliance with those principles obtained by the State authorities of the United States will be reported to the Canadian Department of National Health and Welfare by the United States Public Health Service, and the degree of compliance obtained by the Provincial and other competent authorities in Canada will be reported by the Canadian Department of National Health and Welfare to the United States Public Health Service.

3. Whenever inspections of shellfish handling facilities or of shellfish growing areas are desired by either party to this Agreement, the other party will endeavour to facilitate such inspections.

4. This Agreement may be terminated by either party giving thirty days' notice.

The Secretary of State presents his compliments to His Excellency the Ambassador of Canada and has the honor to refer to his note No. 106 of March 4, 1948 proposing that an agreement be entered into between the Governments of the United States of America and Canada in the following terms:

[The above memorandum of agreement is here repeated.]

The Memorandum of Agreement as set forth above is acceptable to the Government of the United States of America. As proposed in His Excellency's note, therefore, that note and the present reply are regarded as constituting an agreement between the two Governments, effective on the date of the present note.

DEPARTMENT OF STATE,
Washington, April 30, 1948.

Field Investigation of Dredging Operations in Niagara River

[Released to the press May 14]

On February 13, 1948, the International Joint Commission, United States and Canada, was requested by Canada and the United States to conduct an investigation into certain dredging operations that were conducted on Strawberry Island in the Niagara River with a view to ascertaining whether these operations might lead to removal of obstructions that would result in pollution of waters of the Niagara River. On April 2, 1948, the reference was amended to include all questions relating to the pollution of the Niagara River.

The Commissioners have arranged for a field investigation of conditions existing in the Niagara River with respect to these matters, beginning at

Secretary on activities and progress under the Act;

9 Perform such other tasks relating to the Department's participation in foreign aid and assistance programs as may be assigned by the Secretary or Under Secretary.

C Organization. The Coordinator, as a staff aid to the Under Secretary, will be provided with the necessary assistants to carry out the responsibilities of his post.

D Relationships within the Department. The Coordinator will:

1 Serve as the normal channel for the formal interchange of information between the Department and ECA as required by the Act;

2 Facilitate and expedite the development of uniform Departmental policies on foreign aid and assistance matters.

E Relationships with other agencies. The Coordinator will have continuing relationships with:

1 The ECA, as the principal liaison officer of the Department;

2 Committees of Congress and inter-agency committees through or in concert with appropriate officers of the Department.

Appointment of Officers

The State Department announced on May 6 the appointment of Frederick C. Oechsner as Special Assistant to the Director of the Office of International Information.

Resignation of Clair Wilcox

The Department of State announced on April 30 the resignation of Clair Wilcox as Director of the Office of International Trade Policy.

THE FOREIGN SERVICE

Confirmations

On May 21, 1948, the Senate confirmed the following nominations:

Robert Butler to be American Ambassador Extraordinary and Plenipotentiary to Cuba;

Ralph H. Ackerman to be American Ambassador Extraordinary and Plenipotentiary to the Dominican Republic;

George P. Shaw to be American Ambassador Extraordinary and Plenipotentiary to Nicaragua.

On May 5, 1948, the Senate confirmed the nomination of Ely E. Palmer to be Ambassador Extraordinary and Plenipotentiary to Afghanistan.

Contributors

James G. Evans, author of the article on the seventh plenary meeting of the International Cotton Advisory Committee, is an officer in the International Resources Division, Department of State. Mr. Evans served as an adviser and secretary of the U.S. Delegation to the meeting.

The Department of State bulletin

VOL. XVIII, No. 466 • PUBLICATION 3168

June 6, 1948

The Department of State BULLETIN,
a weekly publication compiled and
edited in the Division of Publications,
Office of Public Affairs, provides the
public and interested agencies of
the Government with information on
developments in the field of foreign
relations and on the work of the Department of State and the Foreign
Service. The BULLETIN includes
press releases on foreign policy issued
by the White House and the Department, and statements and addresses
made by the President and by the
Secretary of State and other officers
of the Department, as well as special
articles on various phases of international affairs and the functions of
the Department. Information is included concerning treaties and international agreements to which the
United States is or may become a
party and treaties of general international interest.

Publications of the Department, as
well as legislative material in the field
of international relations, are listed
currently.

For sale by the Superintendent of Documents
U.S. Government Printing Office
Washington 25, D.C.

SUBSCRIPTION:
52 issues, $5; single copy, 15 cents

Published with the approval of the
Director of the Bureau of the Budget

Preceding Resolutions of the General Assembly

On December 11, 1946, the General Assembly unanimously adopted a resolution to the following effect:

"Genocide is a denial of the right of existence of entire human groups, as homicide is the denial of the right to live of individual human beings; such denial of the right of existence shocks the conscience of mankind, results in great losses to humanity in the form of cultural and other contributions represented by these human groups, and is contrary to moral law and to the spirit and aims . of the United Nations.

Many instances of such crimes of genocide have occurred when racial, religious, political and other groups have been destroyed, entirely or in part.

The punishment of the crime of genocide is a matter of international concern.

The General Assembly therefore,

Affirms that genocide is a crime under international law which the civilized world condemns, . and for the commission of which principals and accomplices—whether private individuals, public officials or statesmen, and whether the crime is committed on religious, racial, political or any other grounds—are punishable;

Invites the Member States to enact the necessary legislation for the prevention and punishment of this crime;

Recommends that international co-operation be organized between States with a view to facilitating the speedy prevention and punishment of the crime of genocide, and, to this end,

Requests the Economic and Social Council to undertake the necessary studies, with a view to drawing up a draft convention on the crime of genocide to be submitted to the next regular session of the General Assembly."

A further resolution was adopted by the General Assembly on November 23, 1947, stating:

"The General Assembly,

REALIZING the importance of the problem of combating the international crime of genocide;

REAFFIRMING its resolution 96(I) of 11 December 1946 on the crime of genocide;

DECLARING that genocide is an international crime entailing national and international responsibility on the part of individuals and States;

---

[1] U.N. doc. E/794, May 24, 1948.

NOTING that a large majority of the Governments of Members of the United Nations have not yet submitted their observations on the draft Convention on the crime of genocide prepared by the Secretariat and circulated to those Governments by the Secretary-General on 7 July 1947;

CONSIDERING that the Economic and Social Council has stated in its resolution of 6 August 1947 that it proposes to proceed as rapidly as possible with the consideration of the question of genocide, subject to any further instructions which it may receive from the General Assembly,

Requests the Economic and Social Council to continue the work it has begun concerning the suppression of the crime of genocide, including the study of the draft Convention prepared by the Secretariat, and to proceed with the completion of a convention, taking into account that the International Law Commission, which will be set up in due course in accordance with General Assembly resolution 174(II) of 21 November 1947, has been charged with the formulation of the principles recognized in the Charter of the Nurnberg Tribunal, as well as the preparation of a draft code of offences against peace and security;

Informs the Economic and Social Council that it need not await the receipt of the observations of all Members before commencing its work; and

Requests the Economic and Social Council to submit a report and the Convention on this question to the third regular session of the General Assembly."

History of the Committee's Work

The first meeting of the Committee was held on April 5, 1948, at Lake Success. The Committee continued to sit through May 10, 1948.

The United States Representative was elected chairman of the Committee, the Soviet Representative, vice-chairman, and the Lebanese Representative, rapporteur.

The Committee, upon the motion of the Soviet Representative, voted that before proceeding to the actual drafting of a convention on genocide, it would discuss and make preliminary decisions on ten basic principles outlined in a paper presented by the Soviet Representative. (U.N. doc. E/AC.25/7.) After a discussion of the principles, the Committee proceeded to the actual work of drafting.

A special subcommittee was elected by the Committee to draft the formal articles of the treaty (articles 11 through 19). The subcommittee consisted of the Representatives of the United States, as chairman, Poland, and the Union of Soviet Socialist Republics. The articles prepared by the subcommittee were adopted by the Committee substantially as drafted.

To aid it in its work, the Committee had before it a draft convention on genocide prepared by the

Secretariat of the United Nations (U.N. doc E/447), a draft convention submitted by the French Government (U.N. doc. E/623/Add.1) a draft convention circulated informally by the Soviet Representative, and a draft convention submitted by the United States on September 30 1947 (U.N. doc. E/623, pp. 35–40). It was pointed out by the United States Representative that it had been specifically stated in the United States Mission's press release no. 376 of February 10, 1948, that this draft did "not represent the final position of the United States Government".

The Committee at first decided to give priority to no one text, but later decided to use as a basis of discussion a draft text submitted by the Chinese Representative. (U.N. doc. E/AC.25/9.)

The draft convention finally agreed upon is attached as annex A. The text of the convention as a whole was adopted by a vote of 5 to 1 (the U.S.S.R. dissenting), with 1 abstention (Poland)

Summary of the Draft Convention

Briefly stated, the draft convention declares genocide to be a crime under international law (article 1), and defines it in terms of "deliberate acts committed with the intent to destroy a national, racial, religious or political group, or grounds of the national or racial origin, religious belief, or political opinion of its members (article 2). In other words, to fall within the category of genocide, an act must have the above specified intent and motive. The "deliberate acts' are listed as:

"(1) killing members of the group;

"(2) impairing the physical integrity of members of the group;

"(3) inflicting on members of the group measures or conditions of life aimed at causing their deaths;

"(4) imposing measures intended to prevent births within the group."

Article 3 defines so-called "cultural genocide" as any deliberate act committed with the intent to destroy the language, religion, or culture of a national, racial, or religious group on grounds of the national or racial or religious belief of its members, such as:

"(1) prohibiting the use of the language of the group in daily intercourse or in schools, or the printing and circulation of publications in the language of the group;

"(2) destroying or preventing the use of libraries, museums, schools, historical monuments, places of worship or other cultural institutions and objects of the group."

In article 4, not only genocide, but also conspiracy, attempt, and direct public or private incitement to commit genocide and complicity in any of these acts are declared punishable.

Article 5 states that heads of state, public officials, or private individuals shall be punished.

The parties to the convention undertake in article 6 to enact the necessary legislation in accordance with their constitutional procedures to give effect to the provisions of the convention.

Article 7 recognizes the jurisdiction of "a competent international tribunal" as well as the jurisdiction of the tribunals of the country where the offense is committed.

Under article 8, the parties to the convention may call upon any competent organ of the United Nations to take appropriate action under the Charter for the prevention and suppression of genocide, and may bring to the attention of any such organ any cases of violation of the convention.

Article 9 provides for extradition for genocide and other acts enumerated in article 4.

Article 10 refers disputes as to the interpretation or application of the convention to the International Court of Justice.

The remaining articles 11–19 contain the formal provisions (language, etc.).

Comments on the Draft Convention

The United States Representative opposed the inclusion of so-called "cultural genocide" in the convention (article 3), feeling that the subject should more properly be taken up in connection with the protection of minorities. He stated that the act of creating the new crime of genocide was one of extreme gravity, and the United States felt that the convention should be confined to those barbarous acts directed against individuals which form the basic concept of public opinion on this subject. The French Representative, not being satisfied with the formula worked out in article 3, also opposed its inclusion.

The United States Representative was also opposed to the inclusion of "direct incitement" as a punishable act under article 4. He stated that incitement to commit genocide should be punishable only so far as it constituted "attempt" or "conspiracy" (which are made punishable under the same article), but that incitement to commit genocide should not be separately listed as a punishable offence.

ANNEX A: DRAFT CONVENTION ON GENOCIDE

As adopted by the Ad Hoc Committee on Genocide [1]

PREAMBLE

The High Contracting Parties,

DECLARING that genocide is a grave crime against mankind which is contrary to the spirit and aim of the United Nations and which the civilized world condemns;

HAVING BEEN PROFOUNDLY SHOCKED by many recent instances of genocide;

HAVING TAKEN NOTE of the fact that the International Military Tribunal at Nurnberg in its judgment of September 30th–October 1st 1946 has punished under a different legal description certain persons who have committed acts similar to those which the present Convention aims at punishing, and

BEING CONVINCED that the prevention and punishment of genocide requires international cooperation,

Hereby agree to prevent and punish the crime as hereinafter provided:

Article I

(Genocide: a crime under international law)

Genocide is a crime under international law whether committed in time of peace or in time of war.

Article II

("Physical" and "biological" genocide)

In this Convention genocide means any of the following deliberate acts committed with the intent to destroy a national, racial, religious or political group, on grounds of the national or racial origin, religious belief, or political opinion of its members:

(1) killing members of the group;

(2) impairing the physical integrity of members of the group;

(3) inflicting on members of the group measures or conditions of life aimed at causing their deaths;

(4) imposing measures intended to prevent births within the group.

Article III

("Cultural" genocide)

In this Convention genocide also means any deliberate act committed with the intent to destroy the language, religion, or culture of a national, racial or religious group on grounds of the national or racial origin or religious belief of its members such as:

(1) prohibiting the use of the language of the group in daily intercourse or in schools, or the printing and circulation of publications in the language of the group;

(2) destroying or preventing the use of libraries, museums, schools, historical monuments, places of worship or other cultural institutions and objects of the group.

Article IV

(Punishable acts)

The following acts shall be punishable:

(a) genocide as defined in Articles II and III;

(b) conspiracy to commit genocide;

(c) direct incitement in public or in private to commit genocide whether such incitement be successful or not;

[1] The notes in parentheses placed before the articles which indicate the subject dealt with therein are not intended to be part of the convention.

(d) attempt to commit genocide;
(e) complicity in any of the acts enumerated in this article.

Article V
(Persons liable)

Those committing genocide or any of the other acts enumerated in Article IV shall be punished whether they are Heads of State, public officials or private individuals.

Article VI
(Domestic legislation)

The High Contracting Parties undertake to enact the necessary legislation in accordance with their constitutional procedures to give effect to the provisions of this Convention.

Article VII
(Jurisdiction)

Persons charged with genocide or any of the other acts enumerated in Article IV shall be tried by a competent tribunal of the State in the territory of which the act was committed or by a competent international tribunal.

Article VIII
(Action of the United Nations)

1. A party to this Convention may call upon any competent organ of the United Nations to take such action as may be appropriate under the Charter for the prevention and suppression of genocide.
2. A party to this Convention may bring to the attention of any competent organ of the United Nations any case of violation of this Convention.

Article IX
(Extradition)

1. Genocide and the other acts enumerated in Article IV shall not be considered as political crimes and therefore shall be grounds for extradition.
2. Each party to this Convention pledges itself to grant extradition in such cases in accordance with its laws and treaties in force.

Article X
(Settlement of disputes by the International Court of Justice)

Disputes between the High Contracting Parties relating to the interpretation or application of this Convention shall be submitted to the International Court of Justice provided that no dispute shall be submitted to the International Court of Justice involving an issue which has been referred to and is pending before or has been passed upon by a competent international criminal tribunal.

FINAL CLAUSES

Article XI
(Languages, date of the Convention)

The present Convention of which the Chinese, English, French, Russian and Spanish texts are equally authentic shall bear the date of . . .

---

¹ The dates for the time limits will have to be filled in according to the date of the adoption of the Convention by the General Assembly.

2. A certified copy thereof shall be transmitted to all Members of the United Nations and to the non-member States referred to under Article XII.

Article XIX

(Registration of the Convention)

The present Convention shall be registered by the Secre-tary-General of the United Nations on the date of its com-ing into force.

E V. ALLEN

State for Public Affairs

strong roots in the minds of men. UNESCO's job is to enrich the soil and help strengthen the roots. Like good gardeners, we must go on with that spade work, without looking for miracles of rapid fruition, and undeterred by fears of drouth or blight.

UNESCO is a small organization with a large job. If you could see UNESCO in action it would look something like this. In an old hotel in Paris, about 400 people are at work. While they are engaged in a tremendous enterprise, they are spending only about seven million dollars a year. In one room a former school superintendent from Poland is gathering information about the de-struction of schools and laboratories and libraries in the war-devastated countries. A Frenchman in another office is studying the needs in those same countries for radio sets and film projectors and newsprint.

Reports are coming to them from field staffs in Europe and China, Burma, the Philippines, and other countries ravaged by war.

In another office at UNESCO House, Professor James Quillen, of Stanford, is preparing sugges-tions which will come back to educators in this country and in all the member states on ways in which textbooks and teaching materials can be improved so as to contribute to international understanding.

At the same time UNESCO will be promoting the publication of books which explain national tradi-tions and viewpoints of its member states to one another.

In another corner of UNESCO House you would see three or four men busily drawing up sugges-tions for radio scripts and for educational films which will be submitted to producers in each coun-try. These programs and films emphasize themes of human cooperation, and the common heritage of the arts and sciences of mankind.

---

[1] Excerpts from an address made before the Pacific Regional Conference on UNESCO at San Francisco on May 13, 1948, and released to the press on the same date.

These are but a few illustrations of Unesco at work.

Unesco's work originates in Unesco House, but in its accomplishment it draws upon the educational and intellectual resources of all its member nations. Unesco House is a physical center of international cooperation. It provides what has never existed before—a continuing home for international conferences of educators and scientists and scholars. It provides such humdrum, but indispensable, services as conference rooms, secretarial staff, and interpreters. It is a meeting point and a growing point for the international mind.

One of Unesco's activities is international communication. This embraces the international use of radio and films and press; the free flow of ideas across national boundaries; the interchange of books; and the development of public libraries. We seek to destroy any barriers to the freest flow of information and thought between nations. We seek, moreover, to prevent the great instruments of mass communications from being manipulated in order to warp the minds of men.

An incident which occurred in Poland recently illustrates the unfortunate barriers to the free interchange of information which exist. In our Embassy in Warsaw, we have an information office where Polish citizens may obtain information about the United States—texts of speeches made in the United States and of editorials published in the American press. A few days ago, the Polish Government promptly began to detain for questioning any Poles who visited our information office. A high Polish official declared that the American Embassy in Warsaw was placing Polish citizens in jeopardy by making information available to them!

I am glad to point out that copies of *Izvestia* and *Pravda* are sold alongside the *Wall Street Journal* on the newsstands of New York. Volumes by Karl Marx and Adolf Hitler are found alongside the works of Voltaire and Rousseau on library shelves throughout this country.

The Unesco effort to increase communication among nations embraces not only the interchange of ideas but also of persons. Unesco seeks the widest flow of students, scholars, and cultural leaders among the nations of the world, in all directions.

There are now approximately 20,000 foreign students in the United States and about half as many Americans abroad. It is my view that the United States, in keeping with the principles of Unesco, should always ask to keep open the door for the widest interchange of visits between Americans and the people of every other country. I would not be warranted in leading you to expect that the interchange of persons with eastern Europe is likely to increase in the near future, either under Unesco or any other program. The Ameri-

Urges all Governments and authorities concerned to take every possible precaution for the protection of the holy places and of the City of Jerusalem, including access to all shrines and sanctuaries for the purpose of worship by those who have an established right to visit and worship at t lem,

Instructs the United Nations Mediator for Palestine, in concert with the Truce Commission, to supervise the observance of the above provisions, and *decides* that they shall be provided with a sufficient number of military observers.

Instructs the United Nations Mediator to make contact with all parties as soon as the cease fire is enforced with a view to carrying out his functions as determined by the General Assembly.

Calls upon all concerned to give the greatest possible assistance to the United Nations Mediator,

Instructs the United Nations Mediator to make a weekly report to the Security Council during the cease fire,

Invites the states members of the Arab League and the Jewish and Arab authorities in Palestine to communicate their acceptance of this resolution to the Security Council not later than 6.00 p.m., New York Standard Time, on 1 June 1948,

Decides that if the present resolution is rejected by either party or by both, or if, having been accepted, it is subsequently repudiated or violated, the situation in Palestine will be reconsidered with a view to action under Chapter VII of the Charter.

Calls upon all Governments to take all possible steps to assist in the implementation of this resolution.

U.S. Asks Jewish and Arab States To Cooperate In Cease-Fire Order

[Released to the press May 24]

The Department on May 24 telegraphed the chiefs of the American Missions in Egypt, Iraq, Syria, Lebanon, Saudi Arabia, and the Yemen directing them to approach either the Chief of State or the Foreign Minister in the country to which each is accredited to say that the United States Government is gravely disturbed at the present course of developments in Palestine and that the United States Government hopes that the

---

[1] U.N. doc. S/773, May 22, 1948. Resolution adopted at the 302d meeting of the Security Council on May 22.

[2] BULLETIN of May 9, 1948, p. 594.

[3] U.N. doc. S/801, May 29, 1948. Resolution adopted by the Security Council on May 29, 1948.

government to which he is accredited will, as a fellow member of the United Nations, give full cooperation in respect to the cease-fire resolution adopted May 22 by the Security Council.

The Department followed this action by telegraphing similar instructions to the American Vice Consul in charge of the Consulate General in Jerusalem, William C. Burdett, to approach the Government of Transjordan.

The appeal of the United States Government was taken unilaterally and follows numerous representations made on the question of Palestine to both the Arab states and Jewish leaders.

Current United Nations Documents: A Selected Bibliography [1]

Official Records. First Year, Second Session. Special Supplement No. 2. Summary Records of the Meetings of the Committee of the Whole on Refugees and Displaced Persons. 64 pp. printed. [70¢.]

—— Second Year, Fifth Session. Supplement No. 4. Report of the Second Session of the Economic and Employment Commission. [E/445 and E/445/Add. 1] 21 pp. printed. [20¢.]

—— Supplement No. 5. Commission on Human Rights. Report of the Sub-Commission on Freedom of Information and of the Press. [E/441 and E/441/Add. 1] 16 pp. printed. [20¢.]

—— Supplement No. 6. Report of the Economic Commission for Asia and the Far East and Report of the Committee of the Whole. [E/452 and E/491] 27 pp. printed. [30¢.]

—— Supplement No. 1. Report of the Commission on Human Rights. [E/600] 59 pp. printed. [60¢.]

Index to the Resolutions of the Economic and Social Council. First to Fifth Sessions Inclusive, 1946–1947. E/INF/20, Feb. 18, 1948. 53 pp. mimeo.

Composition of the Economic and Social Council and Subsidiary Organs. E/INF/21, Feb. 4, 1948. 18 pp. mimeo.

THE CONGRESS

Fascism in Action: A Documented Study and Analysis of Fascism in Europe. H. Doc. 401, 80th Cong., 1st sess. ii, 206 pp.

The Strategy and Tactics of World Communism: Supplement I, One Hundred Years of Communism, 1848–1948; Supplement II, Official Protests of the United States Government Against Communist Policies or Actions, and Related Correspondence. H. Doc. 619, 80th Cong., 2d sess. iv, 129 pp.

Loan to the United Nations to Finance Construction of Permanent Headquarters in the United States: Message from the President of the United States, transmitting an agreement between the United States and the United Nations concerning a loan of $65,000,000, without interest, to be made by the United States to the United Nations to finance the construction of the permanent headquarters of the United Nations in the United States. H. Doc. 595, 80th Cong., 2d sess. 4 pp.

[1] Printed materials may be secured in the United States from the International Documents Service, Columbia University Press, 2960 Broadway, New York City. Other materials (mimeographed or processed documents) may be consulted at certain designated libraries in the United States.

Israel, received June 1, based its acceptance of the cease-fire on five "assumptions". The Arab League reply, transmitted June 2, accepted in the light of certain "explanations". In both cases the qualifications were chiefly concerned with interpretation of the resolution's provisions governing importation of arms and fighting personnel during the cease-fire period.

Atomic Energy

On June 2 the Security Council received the Third Report of the Atomic Energy Commission. Adopted on May 17 by a 9-2 vote (U.S.S.R., Ukraine), the report says that the Commission has "reached an impasse" because the Soviet Union will not "agree to even those elements of effective control considered essential from the technical point of view, let alone their acceptance of the nature and extent of participation in the world community required of all nations in this field by the first and second reports of the Atomic Energy Commission."

The Third Report is submitted to the Security Council for consideration and transmittal, together with the two previous reports to the General Assembly as "a matter of special concern".

The report states that "this situation" is beyond the competence of the Commission and recommends that negotiations at the Commission level be suspended until the General Assembly finds "that this situation no longer exists" or until the Commission's six permanent members (Canada, China, France, U.S.S.R., U.K., U.S.) "find that there exists a basis for agreement on the international control of atomic energy."

The Soviet Union flatly rejects the majority plan on the ground that it constitutes an unwarranted infringement of international sovereignty.

The Commission's majority "is fully aware of the impact of its plan on traditional prerogatives of national sovereignty," the report adds, "but in the face of the realities of the problem it sees no alternative to the voluntary sharing by nations of their sovereignty in this field".

The report notes that the majority plan is a "substantial achievement" in that it will serve as the basis of any further discussion of this subject". The majority plan calls for an international agency, established by treaty, which would control in some degree all phases of atomic-energy activities and have broad powers of inspection to prevent clandestine activities. The plan specifies in great detail the powers and functions of the control agency.

Referring to the insistence of the Soviet Union that a convention outlawing atomic weapons and providing for destruction of existing weapons must precede any control agreement, the report asserts that the Commission's majority "considered that such a convention, without safeguards, would offer no protection against non-compliance."

Annexes to the Third Report (U.N. doc. AEC/31) include a summary of the majority plan, the U.S.S.R. proposals, the analysis and rejection of the U.S.S.R. proposals which the Commission's Working Group adopted on April 5, 1948, and two speeches by Andrei Gromyko in rebuttal.

Kashmir

The Security Council's Commission on Kashmir, at an informal meeting May 28, decided to hold its first formal meeting in Geneva on June 15 and then to proceed to the Indian subcontinent. Charles P. Noyes, adviser to Ambassador Austin on Security Council and general affairs, represented the U.S. at the meeting.

The Commission's roster was completed June 2 by appointment of J. Klahr Huddle as U.S. Representative. Mr. Huddle, a veteran Foreign Service officer, is the first U.S. Ambassador to the Union of Burma.

On June 3 the Security Council voted to instruct the Commission not only to give priority to the India-Pakistan dispute over the affiliation of Kashmir and Jammu but also to investigate three other issues which are troubling the two countries' relations.

U.S. Representation

The Senate confirmed on June 1 the President's appointment of Philip C. Jessup to be Deputy U.S. Representative in the Security Council. He succeeds Herschel V. Johnson, who has been named Ambassador to Brazil. Dr. Jessup is on leave from Columbia University, where he has the Hamilton Fish chair of international law and diplomacy. Since January 1948, he has represented the U.S. in the Interim Committee of the General Assembly, a post he will continue to hold.

The President on May 28 named Joseph E. Johnson to be an additional Deputy Representative of the U.S. in the Interim Committee. Dr. Johnson, now professor of history at Williams College, was associated with the Department of State from 1942 to 1947, participating in activities which led to the organization and early operation of the United Nations.

ıdar of Meetings [1]

rned During May		1948
. Nations:		
nic Energy Commission	Lake Success	June 14, 1946– May 17, 1948
ımission for Palestine	Lake Success	Jan. 9–May 17
soc (Economic and Social Council):		
ːonomic and Employment Commission: Third Session	Lake Success	Apr. 19–May 6
atistical Commission: Third Session	Lake Success	Apr. 26–May 7
ɔmmission on Narcotic Drugs: Third Session	Lake Success	May 3–20
ɔpulation Commission: Third Session	Lake Success	May 10–
ːE (Economic Commission for Europe):		
Third Session	Geneva	Apr. 26–May 7
Committee on Electric Power	Geneva	May 10–
Panel on Housing	Geneva	May 13–15
Committee on Coal	Geneva	May 25–
ıl of Foreign Ministers: Deputies for Austria	London	Feb. 20–May 24
Meeting of Planning Committee on High Frequency Broadcasting	Geneva	Mar. 22–May 22
International Civil Aviation Organization):		
ɪs of the Air and Air Traffic Control Practices Division	Montreal	Apr. 20–May 12
nd North Atlantic Regional Air Navigation Meeting	Paris	May 19–
ational Administrative Aeronautical Radio Conference: Prepara- ry Conference.	Geneva	Apr. 24–May 15
·ence To Plan for Establishment of an International Institute of ylean Amazon.	Iquitos, Peru	Apr. 30–May 10
merican Sanitary Organization: Meeting of Executive Committee	Washington	May 3–
ɔ (United Nations Educational, Scientific and Cultural Organiza- ɔn):		
·rnational Teachers Organization	Paris	May 3–4
ımittee of Experts for the Study of a Plan for Translations of Great Books.	Paris	May 10–14
ting of Experts on Art and General Education	Geneva	May 11–15
nternational Refugee Organization): Sixth Part of First Session of :eparatory Commission.	Geneva	May 4–
‚World Health Organization):		
·ert Committee for the Preparation of the Sixth Decennial Revision of the International Lists of Diseases and Causes of Death.	Geneva	May 4–11
·ert Committee on Malaria: Second Session	Washington	May 19–25
Meeting of South Pacific Commission	Sydney	May 10–
ı International Congresses on Tropical Medicine and Malaria	Washington	May 10–18
ational Telegraph Consultative Committee	Brussels	May 10–29
ational Administrative Aeronautical Radio Conference	Geneva	May 15–
ı Congress of the Royal Sanitary Institute	Harrogate, England	May 24–28
Meeting of the Caribbean Commission	San Juan, PR	May 24–29
ısion as of May 1, 1948		1946
‘astern Commission	Washington	Feb. 26–
ı Nations:		
ırity Council	Lake Success	Mar. 25–
·tary Staff Committee	Lake Success	Mar. 25–

Prepared in the Division of International Conferences, Department of State.

Calendar of Meetings—Continued

United Nations—Continued

		1947
Commission on Conventional Armaments	Lake Success	Mar. 24–
Security Council's Committee of Good Offices on the Indonesian Question.	Lake Success	Oct. 20–
General Assembly Special Committee on the Greek Question	Salonika	Nov. 21–
		1948
Temporary Commission on Korea	Seoul	Jan. 12–
Interim Committee of the General Assembly	Lake Success	Feb. 23–
General Assembly: Second Special Session on Palestine	Flushing Meadows . . .	Apr. 16–
Ecosoc (Economic and Social Council): Human Rights Commission: Third Session.	Lake Success	May 20–
German External Property Negotiations (Safehaven):		**1946**
With Portugal	Lisbon	Sept. 3–
With Spain	Madrid	Nov. 12–
		1947
Council of Foreign Ministers: Commission of Investigation to Former Italian Colonies.	Former Italian Colonies .	Nov. 8–
		1948
Provisional Frequency Board	Geneva	Jan. 15–
International Conference on Safety of Life at Sea	London	Apr. 23–
Icao (International Civil Aviation Organization):		
Second European-Mediterranean Regional Air Navigation Meeting . .	Paris	May 4–
Legal Committee: Annual Meeting	Geneva	May 28–

Scheduled for June 1-30, 1948

Icao (International Civil Aviation Organization):		
Second Session of General Assembly	Geneva	June 1–
Conference of North Atlantic States Concerned in Joint Support of Iceland Air Navigation Services.	Geneva	June 21–
United Nations:		
Ecosoc (Economic and Social Council):		
Economic Commission for Asia and the Far East: Third Session . .	Ootacamund, India . . .	June 1–
Economic Commission for Latin America	Santiago	June 7–
Subcommission on Economic Development	Lake Success	June 14–
Permanent Central Opium Board: 50th Session	Geneva	June 14–
Trusteeship Council: Third Session	Lake Success	June 16–
Diplomatic Conference on Revision of Convention for Protection of Literary and Artistic Works.	Brussels	June 5–19
Meeting of International Association for Hydraulic Structures Research . .	Stockholm	June 6–
International Conference on Textiles	Buxton, England	June 7–12
International Telephone Consultative Committee: Rates and Traffic and Technical Meetings.	Stockholm	June 7–22
Ilo (International Labor Organization):		
105th and 106th Sessions of Governing Body	San Francisco	June 9–
31st General Session of Conference	San Francisco	June 17–
Third International Conference on Large Dams	Stockholm	June 10–
Specialist Conference on Tropical and Sub-tropical Soils	Hertfordshire, England .	June 14–28
WHO (World Health Organization):		
Sixth Session of Interim Commission	Geneva	June 18–
First General Assembly	Geneva	June 24–
Second International Soil Mechanics and Foundation Engineering Conference.	Rotterdam	June 21–30
Eleventh International Conference on Public Education	Geneva	June 24–

Regarding Danube River [1]

, FRENCH, AND SOVIET GOVERNMENTS

part in the conference after the question of a treaty with Austria has been settled".

In notes to the three European powers, the United States, on February 27, 1948, initiated discussions to obtain agreement among the Four Powers regarding a time for calling the conference. The notes expressed United States concern for a meeting at the "earliest practicable time."

The United States has urged full participation for Austria. This position has been based on the importance of Austrian interests as a major riparian nation and the part Austria can play in development of more abundant commerce beneficial to all Danubian interests. The United States also had in mind its frequently stated position that Austria should enjoy the status of a liberated nation. On these considerations, and because treaty discussions then getting under way in London might settle the treaty question without much delay, the United States in its initial note of February 27 suggested that the time for issuing a conference call be extended beyond March 15 to some time later in 1948.

The United Kingdom and France agreed; the Union of Soviet Socialist Republics recognized the "grave importance" of settlement of questions about Danube navigation but rejected Austria's unresolved status as a factor in determining a time for the conference. Thus, there was agreement with the United States desire for a meeting at the earliest practicable time, but there were differences of opinion as to what that time would be.

The United States responded April 12, again urging the importance of Austrian participation, reiterating its desire for an early conference, and suggesting that work of the conference could be facilitated and speeded if the Four Powers would exchange views in Washington beforehand.

The Soviet Government replied on May 8, terming the idea of preliminary discussions in Washington unacceptable, again rejecting Austrian participation, stating its understanding that Yugoslavia would "make it possible for a Danube conference to be held in the city of Belgrade", and suggesting May 30 as a date.

The United States notes of May 25 point out that arrangements could not possibly be concluded for

---

[1] Released to the press May 26, 1948.
[2] Not printed.

May 30, propose the practicable date of July 30, and again urge Austrian participation—in at least a consultative capacity, as it now participates in deliberations of other international bodies, such as the Economic Commission for Europe.

Without seeking any special rights, commercial or other, for itself, the United States has evidenced active interest in the freedom of Danube navigation ever since the end of the recent war in pursuance of its permanent interest in opening the way to fuller international trade and facilitating commerce. It has consistently pursued the inter-

DECISIONS AT THE COUNCIL OF
IN DECEM

1. Danube provisions in the Balkan peace treaties (identical articles 34 in the Bulgarian, 38 in the Hungarian and 36 in the Rumanian treaty, signed February 10, 1947) :

"Navigation on the Danube shall be free and open for the nationals, vessels of commerce, and goods of all States, on a footing of equality in regard to port and navigation charges and conditions for merchant shipping. The foregoing shall not apply to traffic between ports of the same State."

2. Four Power Declaration, adopted December 6, 1946, regarding the calling of a Danube conference:

"1. The Governments of the United States, the United Kingdom, the U.S.S.R., and France agree

STATEMENT BY SEC

Following a preliminary exchange of views initiated by this Government, the United States yesterday proposed to the British, French, and Soviet Governments that a conference be called for July 30 on certain questions regarding the Danube River.

This vital European waterway normally affords the nations of eastern and western Europe their principal means of carrying on commerce. Its free

Gail A. Hathaway, Special Assistant to Chief of Engineers, Corps of Engineers, Department of the Army

B. F. Jakobsen, Chief, Plans and Specifications Section, South Pacific Division, Corps of Engineers, Department of the Army

Charles J. Merdinger, Lt. Comdr., Civil Engineer Corps, United States Navy, Oxford, England

Clarence Rawhouser, Engineer, Dams Division, Bureau of Reclamation, Department of the Interior

James B. Thompson, Assistant to Head of Soil Mechanics and Paving Section, Bureau of Yards and Docks, Department of the Navy

Carl P. Vetter, Chief, Office of River Control of the Colorado River, Bureau of Reclamation, Department of the Interior

Walker R. Young, Chief Engineer, Bureau of Reclamation, Department of the Interior

The Conference will discuss the utilization of soil as a building material in dams and other structures and compare findings of experiments and exchange information on experiences in soil mechanics since the First Conference, which was held at Harvard University, Cambridge, June 22–27, 1936.

The agenda of the meeting includes the following topics: (1) theories, hypotheses, and considerations of common nature; (2) tests in the laboratory; (3) investigations in the field; (4) stability and deformation of artificial fills; (5) slides in natural ground; (6) earth pressure on artificial supports; (7) settlement of buildings on footings and mats; (8) pile foundations; (9) problems in road and railway construction; (10) improvement of the mechanical properties of the soil; (11) ground-water observations and drainage; (12) survey of the work of laboratories and individuals in the field of soil mechanics; and (13) suggestions for exchange of information.

To stimulate interest in and to encourage the preparation of papers for the Second International Conference, national committees were organized in a number of countries. The United States National Committee on Soil Mechanics was created in February 1947. Philip C. Rutledge of Northwestern University is the chairman of the Committee.

U.S. DELEGATION TO THIRD INTERNATIONAL CONGRESS ON LARGE DAMS

[Released to the press May 26]

The Department of State announced on May 26 the composition of the United States Delegation to the Third International Congress on Large Dams, scheduled to be held at Stockholm, June 10–17, 1948. The United States Delegation is as follows:

Chairman

Gail A. Hathaway, Special Assistant to Chief of Engineers, Corps of Engineers, Department of the Army

Vice Chairmen

Joel D. Justin, Consulting Engineer, Cornell University

(*Continued on page 751*)

THE RECORD OF THE WEEK

Soviet Violations of Treaty Obligations:

Department of State to the Senate C

I. GERMANY

Agreements

1. The final delimitation of German-Polish frontier should await the peace settlement (Potsdam protocol, VIII, B).

2. Payment of reparations to leave enough resources to enable German people to subsist without external assistance. Reparation claims of U.S.S.R. to be met by removals of capital goods and appropriation of external assets. Economic controls in Germany to be limited to those essential to curb German war potential and insure equitable distribution of essential goods among zones (Potsdam protocol, II, B, 15, 19; III, 1).

3. Economic Directorate of ACA agreed, May 24, 1946, that each member would submit report on reparations removals from its zone.

4. Germany to be treated as a single economic unit (Potsdam protocol, II, B, 14).

5. All democratic political parties to be allowed and encouraged throughout Germany (Potsdam protocol, II, A, 9).

6. Control Council agreed to prevent German political leaders or press from making statements criticizing allied decisions or aimed at disrupting allied unity or creating hostile German attitude toward any of occupying powers (Control Council Directive No. 40).

7. The Allied Control Authority has authorized the free exchange of printed matter and films in the different zones and Berlin (Control Council Directive No. 55).

8. Freedom of speech and press are guaranteed (Potsdam protocol, II, A, 10). Germany is to be prepared for eventual reconstruction of political li: e on democratic basis (Potsdam protocol, II, A§ 3).

9. German external assets in Finland, eastern Austria, Hungary, Bulgaria, and Rumania, to be vested in the German External Property Commission (Control Council Law No. 5).

10. Quadripartite legislation has been enacted to provide for tax uniformity and stabilization of wages in all zones (Control Council Laws Nos. 12 and 61; Control Council Directive No. 14).

Violations

1. U.S.S.R. has repeatedly maintained that the Oder-Neisse line constitutes the definitive German-

[1] Reproduced from the Senate Foreign Relations Committee print of the report on S. Res. 213.

Commission as required by Control Council Law No. 5.

10. Soviet authorities have permitted the land governments of Brandenburg and Saxony-Anhalt to grant partial tax exemptions to large groups of wage and salary earners in violation of this legislation. This move is intended to stop the exodus of skilled workers to the western zones, encourage qualified workers to take jobs in Soviet-owned factories, and make propaganda for the improving living standards of Soviet-zone workers.

II. AUSTRIA

Agreements

1. The Allied Council would insure the removal of all restrictions on movement within Austria of persons, goods, or other traffic; economic unity to be promoted (new control agreement of June 28, 1946, art. 4,*a*).

2. Obligation to open the way for the Austrian people to find economic security (Moscow declaration). Obligation of Allied Council (i.e. occupying powers) to assist Austrian Government to recreate a sound national life based on stable economic and financial conditions (new control agreement, art. 3,*c*).

3. Obligation to assist Austrian Government to recreate a sound national life based on stable economic and financial conditions; to assist Austrian Government to assume full control of affairs of state in Austria; to facilitate full exercise of Austrian Government's authority equally in all zones; to promote the economic unity of Austria (new control agreement, arts. 3,*c*; 3,*d*; and 4,*a*).

4. Obligations with respect to stable economic and financial conditions, free movement within Austria as a whole, and economic unity (new control agreement, arts. 3,*c*; 4,*a*).

5. Obligation to assist Austrian Government to recreate a sound and democratic national life based on respect for law and order (new control agreement, art. 3,*c*).

6. Obligations with respect to law and order, assumption by Austrian Government of full control of affairs of state, full exercise of Austrian Government's authority equally in all zones (new control agreement, arts. 3,*c*; 3,*d*; and 4,*a*).

7. Obligation with respect to full exercise of Austrian Government's authority equally in all zones (new control agreement, art. 4,*a*).

Violations

1. Soviet-instituted system of licensing specified categories of goods for shipment from eastern to other zones (December 1947) impedes free movement of goods and traffic throughout Austria as a whole.

2. Properties seized by Soviets as oil in 1945,

land in February 1946, industrial plants in April 1946, and later exceed what might reasonably be construed as legitimate German assets under the Potsdam protocol. Removals of equipment and materials under guise of "German assets" and "war booty".

3. Withholding of certain food and industrial production from Austrian economy and from application of Austrian law.

4. Soviets designate certain railroad cars as "war booty", prohibit their movement from Soviet to other zones, and propose Austrians "repurchase" these cars (April 1948).

5. Soviet interference with Austrian efforts to maintain law and order through arbitrary arrest or abduction of Austrians (i.e., abduction of transport official from a train in December 1947).

6. Confiscation in eastern zone and Soviet sector of Vienna of certain issues of the United States-sponsored *Wiener Kurier* and other publications; threats to distributors of such publications.

7. Local Soviet military authorities insist that 17 nonelected Communist mayors remain in office in Soviet zone against authority of provincial and national governments.

III. EASTERN AND SOUTHEASTERN EUROPE

Poland

Agreements

"This Polish Provisional Government of National Unity shall be pledged to the holding of free and unfettered elections as soon as possible on the basis of universal suffrage and secret ballot. In these elections all democratic and anti-Nazi parties shall have the right to take part and to put forward candidates" (Crimean Conference, February 12, 1945).

"The three powers note that the Polish Provisional Government in accordance with the decisions of the Crimea Conference has agreed to the holding of free and unfettered elections as soon as possible on the basis of universal suffrage and secret ballot in which all democratic and anti-Nazi parties shall have the right to take part and to put forward candidates . . ." (Potsdam agreement, August 2, 1945)

Violation

On several occasions prior to the elections and following persistent reports of reprehensible methods employed by the Government against the democratic opposition, this Government reminded the Polish Provisional Government of its obligations under the Yalta and Potsdam agreements and was joined on these occasions by the British Government. On January 5, 1947, the British and Soviet Governments were asked to associate themselves with this Government in approaching the Poles on this subject, and the British Government made

similar representations to the Soviet Government
reiterating the request that the Soviet Government
support the British and American Governments in
calling for a strict fulfillment of Poland's obligations. The Soviet Government refused to participate in the proposed approach to the Polish Government. The British and American representations were summarily rejected by the Polish Government as "undue interference" in the internal
affairs of Poland.

Of the 444 deputies elected to the parliament in
the elections of January 19, 1947, the Polish Peasant Party (reliably reported to represent a large
majority of the population) obtained only 28
places, thus demonstrating the efficiency with
which the government had prepared the ground.
On January 28, the Department of State issued a
release to the press stating that reports received
from our Embassy in Poland immediately prior to
and subsequent to the elections, based upon the
observations of American officials, confirmed the
fears which this Government had expressed that
the election would not be free.

Hungary

Agreement

1. Under the armistice agreement an Allied Control Commission was established under the chairmanship of the U.S.S.R. and with participation
of the United States and United Kingdom (armistice agreement, January 1945, art. 18 and annex F).

2. The three heads of the Governments of the
Union of Soviet Socialist Republics, the United
States, and United Kingdom declared their mutual
agreement to concert during the temporary period
of instability in liberated Europe the policies of
their three Governments in assisting the peoples
liberated from the domination of Nazi Germany
and the peoples of the former Axis satellite states
of Europe to solve by democratic means their
pressing political and economic problems (Yalta
agreement, February 1945).

3. Upon the cessation of hostilities, it was agreed
at Potsdam that the United States, United Kingdom and Union of Soviet Socialist Republics
would consult with a view to revising the procedures of the Allied Control Commissions for Rumania, Bulgaria, and Hungary to provide for
effective participation by the United States and
United Kingdom in the work of those bodies
(Potsdam protocol XI, August 1945).

Violation

1. The U.S.S.R. representative on the Acc for
Hungary consistently acted unilaterally in the
name of the Acc without consultation with or
notice to his United States and United Kingdom
colleagues, thus denying them any semblance of
effective participation in the work of the Acc.

effective three-power participation in the commissions (Potsdam protocol XI, August 1945).

6. The U.S.S.R. undertook to give friendly advice to the Bulgarian Government regarding the desirability of the inclusion in the government of two representatives of democratic groups, "who (a) are truly representative of the groups of the parties which are not participating in the Government, and (b) are really suitable and will work loyally with the Government" (Moscow Conference, December 1945).

Violation

1. The Soviet chairman of the Acc repeatedly took unilateral action in the name of the Acc and without consultation with his United States or United Kingdom colleagues, thus effectively negating the United States and United Kingdom participation in that body.

2. The U.S.S.R. has aided and abetted the Bulgarian Government in failing to fulfill these provisions of the armistice to varying degrees. The Soviets have refused to consider with the United States and United Kingdom Bulgaria's obligation to restore and restitute United Nations property and interests and, while deliveries of foodstuffs were made to the Yugoslavs unilaterally, the U.S.S.R. has blocked three-power consideration of amounts to be shipped to Greece. None has been shipped to that country.

3. The Soviet Government has consistently refused to concert policies with the United States and United Kingdom to assist the people of Bulgaria to solve their political and economic problems democratically. On the contrary the Soviet Government, through the local Communist Party, has unilaterally subverted representative democratic processes in Bulgaria and assisted in denying the Bulgarian people the exercise of fundamental freedoms. For example, in 1945 the Soviets unilaterally interfered in the internal affairs of Bulgaria's largest political party by demanding and obtaining the replacement of Dr. G. M. Dimitrov as Secretary General of the Agrarian Union.

4. The Soviet Chairman of the Acc consistently thwarted American press coverage of Bulgarian developments by negative or extremely dilatory action on United States Government requests for entry permits for reputable American correspondents. Conversely, representatives of the *Daily Worker* and other left-wing periodicals were permitted to enter Bulgaria without difficulties.

5. The Union of Soviet Socialist Republics refused repeated United States and United Kingdom requests to consult as agreed, and continued to operate the Acc's unilaterally without effective participation of or even, on occasion, knowledge

of the United States and United Kingdom members.

6. The Soviet authorities, despite the Moscow agreement, aided and abetted a minority Bulgarian Communist regime in thwarting the implementation of that agreement and prevented the broadening of the Bulgarian Government envisaged therein.

Rumania

Agreement

1. The three heads of the Governments of the Union of Soviet Socialist Republics, the United States, and United Kingdom declared their mutual agreement to concert during the temporary period of instability in liberated Europe the policies of their three Governments in assisting the peoples liberated from the domination of Nazi Germany and the peoples of the former Axis satellite states of Europe to solve by democratic means their pressing political and economic problems (Yalta agreement on liberated Europe, February 1945).

2. Upon the cessation of hostilities, it was agreed at Potsdam that the allied control Commission procedure should be revised to provide for effective United States and United Kingdom participation in the work of those bodies (Potsdam protocol XI, revised Allied Control Commission procedure in Rumania, Bulgaria, and Hungary).

3. The three Governments stated that they had no doubt that, in view of the changed conditions resulting from the termination of the war in Europe, representatives of the allied press would enjoy full freedom to report to the world upon developments in Rumania.

Violation

1. Contrary to its agreement at Yalta, the U.S.S.R., acting through the Rumanian Communist Party and its own agencies and armed forces in Rumania, systematically and unilaterally subverted the democratic will of the Rumanian people to totalitarianism in negation of their fundamental freedoms. Major examples of such U.S.S.R. actions may be cited as follows:

(1) Unilateral intervention by Soviet occupation authorities and by Vishinsky (February–March 1945) in effecting the overthrow of Premier Radescu's interim representative government and the installation of a Communist-controlled regime. Refusal in this connection to concert either with the United States representatives in Rumania or on a governmental level.

(2) Unilateral support of Premier Groza's retention of office in defiance of the King's demand for his resignation and the United States request for tripartite consultation in response to the King's appeal (August 1945).

4. The U.S.S.R. delegation refused to adhere to the agreement when an attempt was made to schedule the party consultations. The U.S.S.R. delegation unilaterally asserted that, despite the signature of communiqué No. 5, and despite assurances of cooperation with the Commission, and a pledge to refrain from fomenting or instigating active opposition, the members of a so-called antitrusteeship committee could not be consulted by the Joint Commission.

V. MANCHURIA

Agreements

1. "The high contracting parties agree to render each other every possible economic assistance in the postwar period with a view to facilitating and accelerating reconstruction in both countries and to contributing to the cause of world prosperity" (Sino-Soviet treaty and agreements of August 14, 1945, art. VI).

2. ". . . In accordance with the spirit of the aforementioned treaty, and in order to put into effect its aims and purposes, the Government of the U.S.S.R. agrees to render to China moral support and aid in military supplies and other material resources, such support and aid to be entirely given to the National Government as the central government of China.

"2· In the course of conversations . . . the Government of the U.S.S.R. regarded the three eastern provinces (i.e. Manchuria) as part of China" (note of V. M. Molotov, August 14, 1945, relating to the treaty of friendship and alliance).

3. "The administration of Dairen shall belong to China" (agreement concerning Dairen of August 14, 1945).

Violations

1. "Industry . . . (in the three eastern provinces, also known as Manchuria) . . . was directly damaged to the extent of $858,000,000 during Soviet occupancy . . . the greatest part of the damage to the Manchurian industrial complex . . . was primarily due to Soviet removals of equipment" (Department of State press release No. 907 of December 13, 1947, citing Pauley report).

2. The Chinese Government has failed to receive from the U.S.S.R. since August 14, 1945, the promised military supplies and other material resources. But when Russian troops withdrew from Manchuria. "Chinese Communists in that area appeared with Japanese arms in very substantial quantities . . . the natural assumption is that they were taken with the acquiescence, at least, of the Russians." (Quotation is from testimony of W. W. Butterworth at hearing before the Committee on Appropriations, United States Senate, December 17, 1947.)

3. Chinese Government troops attempting to en-

render were denied the right to land at Dairen by the Soviet authorities there and were forced to utilize less advantageous landing points.

China has up to the present time been unable to tablish a Chinese Government administration Dairen.

Firm and Determined Course for the Democracies

BY GEORGE C. MARSHALL [1]

Secretary of State

It is unnecessary I think for me to re-outline what has taken place recently between the United States and the Soviet Union in particular and the western European countries and the Soviet and satellite countries in general. However, there are certain aspects of the situation which it might be profitable to discuss. For example, in our intense desire for peace, in our longing for some firm basis of accord between or among the principal nations of the world, we are apt to be confused as to the actual facts and conditions involved in achieving our desires. The method of modern totalitarian propaganda is to twist, pervert, and confuse and to create an impression which may not in any way represent the true situation or the possibilities for successful action. As I have explained in public statements we have reached a virtual stalemate in a number of courts of action. The Conference of Foreign Ministers has struggled unsuccessfully for months and days on end to find a basis of agreement for a settlement regarding Austria. We have had similar experiences with relation to a peace settlement for Germany, making virtually no progress whatever. As a matter of fact, in London last December it required 10 days to reach agreement merely on the agenda for the meeting, and the meeting itself was seized upon largely by the Soviet authorities as an opportunity for propaganda statements for wide distribution, particularly in Germany and the satellite states. You are probably more familiar with the efforts of the Security Council of the United Nations with regard to the problem of atomic energy and a number of other matters pertaining to the regulation of the peace of the world. The Assembly of the United Nations, not afflicted by the veto power, has been able to dispatch groups of its members to observe conditions in Greece and Korea, but these groups have been seriously limited or handicapped by the refusal of the Soviet Union and other governments of eastern Europe to participate, or even to permit the free movement and action of these representatives of the United Nations Assembly on territories under their control. Endless discussions or negotiations have failed to secure the coop-

eration which is imperative to the stabilization the world situation and the development of a sou basis for continuing peace.

There is an overwhelming demand for so agreement to wipe out fear of war and to br about a return to normal conditions, and theref strong resentment of any statement or lack of tion that appears contrary to the fulfilment that desire. These great desires are impelled deep emotions but those emotions must not le us into ill-advised and trustful actions which h ard the future of this country. I am sure that one's desire is greater than mine to find a basis peaceful security and a return of general prosp ity to the world. But it is my official duty to that this country is not misled by its emotions ir commitments or actions which would threaten future.

As a matter of fact, I think excellent progr has been made since the first of the year. It I been history-making and will later on be so rec nized. I feel certain that the continuation of t firm course we have been following will lead to t solution of the worst of our difficulties and w eventually clear the way to a sound basis for pea I am absolutely certain that only such a firm a determined course can save the situation for t democracies.

In this connection, it is of the utmost importan that all Americans realize the significance of o position in the world today. Our leadership is recognized the world over, but the obligations such leadership are not completely recognized I us Americans ourselves. We are generous, som times to a fault, but it is just as important that be understanding. By this I mean that we mt try our best to realize the situation of other peopl and their point of view and their inevitable rea tions to many things that are publicly proclaim in this country. We often defeat our own gene osity or aims by ignoring the sensitivity of peop their national pride, and the utterly different su roundings in which they live compared to ours he in America. This applies not only to the natio of western Europe; it applies also to those behir the Iron Curtain. There, however, the people a fed on the diet of a controlled press and an asto ishing propaganda, astonishing because of its utt

[1] Excerpts from an address made before the General Federation of Women's Clubs in Portland, Oreg. on May 28, 1948, and released to the press on the same date.

certain tactical vulnerability arising from the complete freedom of expression and the generosity of debate within their countries, in contrast to the procedure on the other side of the fence where a carefully agreed upon line of action is set in motion, with no possibility of criticism because a strong hand compels complete support. Such a method enjoys great advantages for the moment. In the end, I think it will defeat itself, if history is a true indication of probabilities. But in the short-term issues, like those of the present period, it does present great difficulties for us.

For example, we have today a heated public discussion as to what is the proper procedure for this Government in its relations with the Soviet Union, a discussion which largely ignores the fact that we are faced with a deliberate, a cynical propaganda campaign to offset a sincere effort on our part to establish a basis for profitable negotiations and agreements leading to a stabilization of the world situation.

Now that is a very general statement. I will particularize. A diplomatic interchange took place as you all know between our Ambassador in Moscow and the Soviet Foreign Minister.[2] Contrary to diplomatic precedent, the one Government chose to release without notice to the other a portion of the discussion. All of its own statements were released to the press but only a portion of the statements of our Ambassador. However, the procedure went much further than that. In the last and the most important paragraph—one of only four sentences, two of the sentences were omitted, completely distorting the meaning so as to form the basis for the Soviet propaganda purpose.

In Ambassador Smith's statement, the closing paragraph contained the following sentences:

"My Government earnestly hopes that the members of the Soviet Government will not take lightly the position of the United States Government, as here expressed. They have it in their power to alleviate many of the situations which today weigh so heavily on all international life. It is our earnest hope that they will take advantage of these possibilities. If they do, they will not find us lacking in readiness and eagerness to make our own contribution to a stabilization of world conditions entirely compatible with the security of the Soviet peoples."

This statement clearly meant that if the Soviet Government would abandon certain courses of conduct and action which have kept the world in a state of uneasiness and confusion since the close of hostilities, they would thereby produce an entirely new international atmosphere—and that if they did, then they would not find any lack of response from this Government.

[2] BULLETIN of May 23, 1948, p. 679.

In the version published by the Soviet Government, the second and third sentences I have just read above were omitted, and in the radio broadcast from Moscow the first three words of the last sentence were also omitted.

By this means it was possible momentarily to create the impression that the United States had proposed direct or unilateral negotiation, when the full text was not susceptible of any such interpretation.

What does that mean to you? It meant to me that the officials of the Soviet Government knew we would recognize that the purpose of their release was to gain a propaganda advantage in order

U.S. Answers Soviet Protest Regarding American Aircraft Near Japan

[Released to the press May 27]

On May 25 the American Embassy in Moscow replied to various Soviet notes of protest [1] concerning the activities of American aircraft over waters adjoining Japan.

The Embassy's note informed the Soviet Government that a thorough investigation had been conducted of the instances cited in the Soviet notes and that careful study had been given to the allegations of the Soviet Government that the activities of United States aircraft in these waters violated the freedom of commercial navigation. In no single one of the more than 50 cases to which objection had been made by the Soviet Government, however, was there evidence, either in the Soviet notes or from the investigation undertaken by the United States authorities, that the aircraft in question were in such an attitude or position, regardless of their altitude, that they constituted any interference with commercial navigation. The note continued that the Government of the United States desired to point out that under the Moscow Agreement the Supreme Commander for the Allied Powers issues all orders for the occu-

Suspension of Austrian Treaty Negotiat

GENERAL

[Released to the press May 26]

The meetings of the Foreign Ministers' Deputies for Austria in London have been temporarily suspended while it is ascertained whether there exists a justifiable basis for continued negotiations. In view of the progress which had been made in the Austrian treaty negotiations and of the ever-narrowing area of disagreement still remaining, the Department of State hoped that the

---

[1] Not here printed.

Yugoslavia was fixed by plebiscite in accordance with the Treaty of St. Germain and sanctioned by international recognition since 1920. The revision of this frontier would be an unwarranted imposition on a small liberated country, inconsistent with the spirit of the Moscow Declaration, and prejudicial to the stability of this area and Austria's hope of becoming a self-supporting nation. It had always been assumed by the United States Government, and has been repeatedly so stated, that the restoration of Austria as a state liberated from German domination in accordance with international commitment involved the restoration of the whole state and not merely a part thereof.

The United States, likewise, has never concealed, nor deviated from, its intention to uphold the principle of no reparations from Austria. The Governments of the United States, U.S.S.R. and United Kingdom agreed at the Potsdam Conference "that reparations should not be exacted from Austria". The United States by many forms of material assistance has been faithful to its pledge under the Moscow Declaration to assist Austria to obtain economic security. It could not now be party to an agreement which would place Austria in economic servitude to Yugoslavia for an indefinite period.

The problem of concluding an Austrian treaty should have permitted a swift and easy solution.

Since the first meeting of the Council of Foreign Ministers, the United States Government has endeavored to obtain consideration of this problem. Its repeated attempts to bring about a speedy solution were consistently frustrated by the delaying tactics of the Soviet Union. When the machinery was finally established in January of 1947 to negotiate the treaty, it was believed that a fair and just solution would be achieved. Now, after almost a year and a half of continuous negotiations, and more than 325 meetings of the representatives of the Four Powers, we again find the solution deferred.

The conclusion of an acceptable Austrian treaty permitting a reestablished Austrian state to develop freely on a sound basis is regarded as essential to the peace and security of Europe. The future course of the treaty negotiations offers a test of the desire for the development of international cooperation. The machinery has been established and continues available; the issues are clear and simple; the tasks of occupation have been fulfilled; the Austrian nation three years after liberation deserves the right to manage its own affairs freely; the necessity for final settlement of the Austrian problem is long over-due. The United States Government stands ready to resume discussions whenever there is hope that the basic issues of the Austrian treaty can be resolved.

LETTER FROM THE U.S. DEPUTY ON THE AUSTRIAN TREATY NEGOTIATIONS TO THE SECRETARY GENERAL OF THE COUNCIL OF FOREIGN MINISTERS[1]

[Released to the press May 24]

May 24, 1948

As chairman of the next meeting of the Council of Foreign Ministers, deputies for Austria, I am informed that the delegations are unable to remain indefinitely in London. In these circumstances, it is difficult for me to set a date for the resumption of the Austrian treaty negotiations, but I am prepared at any time to call the next meeting of the deputies as soon as possible upon receiving information that there exists a justifiable basis for continued negotiation, particularly with respect to assurances concerning the maintenance of Austria's 1937 frontiers and the principle of no reparations.

In order to ensure continuity and to facilitate communications with a view of avoiding delay in convocation of the next meeting, I am authorized to inform you that Mr. Gerald Keith, Counselor of the United States Embassy, London, has been designated to act as liaison for exchange of information with the secretariat or with the representatives of other governments. He will act in

this capacity upon my departure. I shall be grateful if you would be kind enough to inform the other deputies of this communication.

SAMUEL REBER

_____

Letters of Credence

Costa Rica

The newly appointed Ambassador of Costa Rica, Señor Don Mario A. Esquivel, presented his credentials to the President on May 26. For texts of the Ambassador's remarks and the President's reply, see Department of State press release 422 of May 26, 1948.

Correction

In the BULLETIN of April 25, 1948, page 541, footnote 2 should read "Treaties and Other International Acts Series 1553" instead of "1533".

_____

[1] Printed from telegraphic text.

Greek Investigation Into Death of CBS

STATEMENT BY SE

[Released to the press May 26]

The American Chargé d'Affaires at Athens, Mr. Karl L. Rankin, has reported that the Greek investigation into the tragic death of George Polk,[1] whose body was found in Salonika Bay on May 16, is being efficiently handled by the Greek police and national security agency. The two Columbia Broadcasting System representatives who are conducting an independent investigation in Salonika, Messrs. Winston Burdett and John Secondari, have also reported that they are getting the fullest cooperation of the Greek police.

The American Chargé is in constant touch with the Greek Ministers of Justice and Public Order and describes the investigation being carried out under their supervision as "vigorous and thorough". At Athens, First Secretary George Edman and Third Secretary Oliver M. Marcy have been specially designated to follow this investiga-

TEXT OF NOTE FROM AMBASSADOR

[Released to the press May 29]

May 28, 1948

The Ambassador of Greece presents his compliments to His Excellency the Secretary of State and has the honor to inform him that the Greek Government has instructed him to report on the Polk case as follows:

The investigation of the horrible murder of George Polk continues to be vigorously prosecuted by all appropriate agencies of the Greek State. A summary of the activities to date follows:

(1) On the day of the discovery of the body at Salonika, the Prime Minister, Mr. Sophoulis, and the Minister of Press and Information, Mr. Alianos, issued statements condemning the crime and promising a full and exhaustive enquiry.

(2) On the day following the discovery of the body the Minister of Public Order, Mr. Rentis, himself proceeded to Salonika to supervise the investigation. On the same day, Mr. Rentis, in the name of the Greek State, offered a reward of 25 million drachmae for information leading to

---

[1] BULLETIN of May 30, 1948, p. 713.
[2] Printed from telegraphic text.

STATEMENT BY THE GREEK UNDER SECRETARY FOR PRESS AND INFORMATION

[Released to the press May 26]

ı view of the great interest of the American ːnalistic world in the case of the murder of rge Polk, the Greek Government would wele and facilitate any correspondent or comːee of correspondents from America to asceron the spot the urgent steps taken by the ɛk Government in carrying out a thorough investigation, in every direction, with a view to discovering those guilty and punishing them most severely.

Such correspondents or a committee of correspondents will at the same time have the opportunity of ascertaining, while in Greece, that there exists a regime of absolute freedom of press for every journalist.

ɪanon Rejects U.S. Demand for Release of American Citizens

ɒTE FROM THE LEBANESE FOREIGN OFFICE TO THE AMERICAN MINISTER TO LEBANON [1]

[Released to the press May 23]

May 22, 1948

eferring to your letter No. 151 of May 20, 1948, tive to the landing and internment, effected ɾ 19, of a certain number of Jewish immigrants eling on board the S. S. *Marine Carp,* I have honor to inform you that this measure has ι taken by the military authorities in view of safety of the Lebanese Army of Occupation alestine and for order and security in Palestine ɪtory occupied.

he said passengers were traveling to Haifa, not ɾided with regular immigration permits, and time when this post, reserved for operations nbarkation of British forces, has been declared ne forbidden to all landing of passengers.

was manifest that the able-bodied men among e illegal immigrants were going, as some ιsands of others who have preceded them, to elements of trouble and anarchy in Palestine to attack the Lebanese forces which have interːd with other Arab forces to reestablish order put an end to the violence and acts of terrorism mitted by the Zionists.

ou know, in effect, Mr. Minister, that the ɑnese Army and the other Arab armies have rvened in Palestine, with the consent and at request of the large majority of its inhabitants, ɾotect those inhabitants against the crimes of ɪonist minority constituted into terrorist orizations—Haganah, Irgun or Stern—reined by a continuous illegal immigration which been admitted by the Minister of Immigration he so-called state of Israel.

hese organizations whose origin dates back ɪ beyond the UNO recommendation for parɪn were created under the mandate outside the and have been responsible for the most atrocious crimes perpetrated in Palestine, Egypt, Italy, the Orient, Britain, and which the Jewish Agency itself had discredited before the so-called Jewish state had assembled these organizations and had incorporated them in its armed forces.

Their ill deeds which have gone beyond national limits and have affected the most sacred rights of humanity—such as at Deir, Yassin, Haifa or Tiberias—have justified intervention of the Arab Governments. The latter have moreover been injured in their essential right: violation of frontiers before all intervention; attack upon Arab consular representations at Jerusalem of which the Secretary of the Lebanese Consulate was a victim and especially the will for expansion into aggressive Zionism expressed by the words of the Ben Gurion or of one Shertok before they were chief of government of [and] Minister of Foreign Affairs of the pretended state of Israel.

It is in fact to fulfil the mission arising from the. intervention in Palestine which has been forced upon the Lebanese Army and to secure its own security and that of Arab armies that it has had to take the measure in question.

I should, moreover, point out that certain of the illegal Jewish immigrants debarked and bearers of American passports far from claiming American citizenship and protection, and gloried in obedience to the state of Israel.

The able-bodied men of every nationality so debarked and detained, numbering 69, follow the list of names attached.[2] They have been directed to the detention camp of Baalbek where they are lodged and fed in care of Lebanese authorities and can be visited at any time by the representatives of the American Legation.

[1] Printed from telegraphic text.
[2] BULLETIN of May 30, 1948, p. 712.

ɪ ·6, .1948

Extension of the Trade Agreements Act

EXCHANGE OF CORRESPONDENCE BETWEEN REPRESENTATIVE DOUGHTON
AND SECRETARY MARSHALL

[Released to the press May 24]

The Secretary of State released on May 24 the exchange of correspondence with Representative Doughton, ranking minority member of the Committee on Ways and Means of the House of Representatives. Representative Doughton wrote to the Secretary of State requesting an expression of views regarding H.R. 6556, a bill to extend the Trade Agreements Act.

May 21, 1948

MY DEAR MR. SECRETARY:

As you know, H.R. 6556, which provides for an extension of the Trade Agreements Act for one year, makes drastic changes in the procedure for negotiation of reciprocal trade agreements.

In your opinion, in view of the scope of the proposed changes, would the best interests of the Nation be better served if the Reciprocal Trade Agreements Act were permitted to expire than for H.R. 6556 to be enacted in its present form?

Your expeditious reply to this inquiry will be of great value to, and much appreciated by, the Minority Members in their consideration of the bill in the House of Representatives. It is now contemplated that the bill will be debated in the House on Wednesday, May 26, 1948.

With expressions of high esteem, I am

Sincerely yours,

R. L. DOUGHTON

May 24, 1948

DEAR MR. DOUGHTON:

I have your letter of May 21 asking my opinion whether our national interests would be better served by permitting the expiration of the Trade Agreements Act than by the passage of HR-6556 with its drastic changes in procedure.

The Trade Agreements Program has been a cornerstone of our foreign economic policy for fourteen years. Through it we have exercised a significant part of our leadership in world economic affairs.

The principle of the Trade Agreements Program is incorporated in the European Cooperation Act of 1948. The present Congress so provided because it recognized that European recovery waits upon a great expansion in European production for which there must be markets and that

markets in turn wait upon a lowering of barrier to trade among the European countries and be tween such countries and other nations.

Although HR-6556 extends the Trade Agreements Act for one year, it does so with such crip pling amendments that only a shadow of th original Act is preserved while its substance is destroyed.

HR-6556 provides for a cumbersome procedur which would involve interminable delays and ser ous questions of responsibility.

It substitutes a single Agency (Tariff Commi sion) for the present Trade Agreements Con mittee composed of representatives of seve government agencies all directly interested in th tariff, as the body responsible for investigation an recommendation to the President.

Most serious of all it, in effect, makes pure pr tection the sole criterion for tariff action and fo bids the Tariff Commission from participating i deliberations of the Trade Agreements Committee in which, under the present system, other impo tant aspects of the national interest are also take into account.

In my judgment enactment of HR-6556 woul make the Reciprocal Trade Agreements Progra unworkable.

Under the circumstances I think our nation interests would be better served to permit tl Trade Agreements Act to expire than for HR-65! to be enacted. But it is my earnest hope that th Congress will extend the Reciprocal Trade Agre ments Act for three years without the propose crippling amendments.

Faithfully yours,

[signature]

THE CONGRESS

Conventions and Recommendations Formulated at t Twenty-Ninth Session of the International Labor Conf ence: Message from the President of the United Stat transmitting authentic texts of three conventions and t recommendations formulated at the twenty-ninth sess of the International Labor Conference, held at Montre from September 19 to October 9, 1946. H. Doc. 603, 80 Cong., 2d sess. 29 pp.

Large Dams—*Continued from page 737*

Walker R. Young, Chief Engineer, Bureau of Reclamation, Department of the Interior

Members of the Delegation

E. Robert de Luccia, Chief, Bureau of Power, Federal Power Commission

B. F. Jakobsen, Chief, Plans and Specifications Section, South Pacific Division, Corps of Engineers, Department of the Army

T. A. Middlebrooks, Chief, Soils Branch, Office of Chief of Engineers, Corps of Engineers, Department of the Army

Clarence Rawhouser, Engineer, Dams Division, Bureau of Reclamation, Department of the Interior

Dr. Karl Terzaghi, Consulting Engineer, Graduate School, Harvard University

Carl P. Vetter, Chief, Office of River Control of the Colorado River, Bureau of Reclamation, Department of the Interior

The purpose of the Congress is to discuss and demonstrate recent developments in the building of large dams. Invitations have been issued to the 20 governments which are members of the International Commission on Large Dams. Dams higher than the Hoover (Boulder) Dam, the highest in the world, are now being planned in both Europe and India. The Congress will review the subject and attempt to draw some conclusions as to the practicability of dams of this size. The Congress will also discuss experiences arising from the testing and the actual use of special cements for large dams. Other topics to be considered are a critical exposition of the measurement of uplift pressures and stresses arising therefrom, research methods and instruments for the measure of stresses and deformation in earth and concrete dams, and the most recent precautions to avoid the formation of pipings.

The first two days of the Congress will be devoted to the presentation of reports and to discussions, while the following five days will be spent on a study tour of a number of dams and hydroelectric power plants and of one of Sweden's large industries.

The First Congress was held at Stockholm in 1933, simultaneously with the sectional meeting of the World Power Conference. The Second Congress was held at Washington, in 1936, simultaneously with the plenary meeting of the World Power Conference.

The International Commission on Large Dams, which arranges for the congresses, was constituted in 1928 for the purpose of promoting research in matters connected with large dams and of collecting experiences in regard to their design, construction, maintenance, and operation. The member nations of the Commission function through national committees. The United States Committee on Large Dams is headed by Michael W. Straus, Commissioner, Bureau of Reclamation, Department of the Interior.

Contents of *Documents and State Papers* for
June 1948

★ The Interim Committee or "The Little Assembly"

★ Arms for the United Nations

★ Compulsory Jurisdiction of the Court

★ Third Anniversary of the U.N. Charter

★ U.N. Conference on Fredom of Information

U. S. GOVERNMENT PRINTING OFFICE: 1948

The Department of State bulletin

VOL. XVIII, No. 467 • PUBLICATION 3172

June 13, 1948

The Department of State BULLETIN, a weekly publication compiled and edited in the Division of Publications, Office of Public Affairs, provides the public and interested agencies of the Government with information on developments in the field of foreign relations and on the work of the Department of State and the Foreign Service. The BULLETIN includes press releases on foreign policy issued by the White House and the Department, and statements and addresses made by the President and by the Secretary of State and other officers of the Department, as well as special articles on various phases of international affairs and the functions of the Department. Information is included concerning treaties and international agreements to which the United States is or may become a party and treaties of general international interest.

Publications of the Department, as well as legislative material in the field of international relations, are listed currently.

For sale by the Superintendent of Documents
U.S. Government Printing Office
Washington 25, D.O.

SUBSCRIPTION:
52 issues, $5; single copy, 15 cents

Published with the approval of the
Director of the Bureau of the Budget

"AID FROM AMERICA": Foreign Relief Operations in Italy

by Durand Smith

What happens to foreign-aid funds after they have been appropriated by the Congress? Few taxpayers know, except in a vague and general way, how that portion of their tax dollars is spent. This article tells something of what has been done and is being done with the money allocated to Italy under the post-UNRRA relief program [1] and the interim-aid program. [2]

Italy received $121,000,000 in relief assistance under the first program, now virtually completed; the second program, which is also nearing completion, is providing Italy with approximately $182,000,000 in aid.

To keep its people from going hungry and to keep its economy running Italy must import wheat and coal. The bulk of the American funds therefore has been used to purchase these two basic commodities. In addition, fats, pulses, petroleum products, blister copper, sugar, medical supplies, dairy products, pesticides, fish, and canned meat have been procured. All the wheat (including flour) has been bought in the United States and almost all the coal. Offshore purchases have consisted of coal from the Ruhr, wet salt fish from Iceland, raw sugar from Cuba, canned meat from Mexico, and blister copper from Chile.

Lack of dollars and other foreign exchange made it impossible for Italy to purchase these vitally important supplies; they were given to the Italian Government by the American Government.

In July 1947 the U.S. Relief Mission to Italy [3] was organized. It consisted of nine Americans: the relief adviser, two assistant advisers, four field observers, and two secretaries, all of whom were appointed to the Foreign Service Reserve or Staff. The seven men were given diplomatic status as attachés of the American Embassy in Rome. Office space was provided by the Italian Government in a building on the well-known Via Veneto a few steps from the Embassy. Italian personnel eventually numbering about 40 were employed there for clerical and administrative duties.

An agreement between the two Governments concerning the rendering of assistance was signed on July 4 in Rome. The Ambassador, James Clement Dunn, signed for the American Government; Alcide de Gasperi, President of the Council of Ministers, and Carlo Sforza, Minister for Foreign Affairs, signed for the Italian Government. [4]

From mid-July through August negotiations were carried on between the Mission and the Italian Government regarding the implementation of the agreement. Many discussions took place about the reception, allocation, distribution and sale of supplies, about pricing and local currency proceeds, about publicity and labeling. A milestone was reached on August 27 when the first shipload of relief supplies, 9,620 tons of coal, arrived in Genoa. Another milestone was passed during the first week of September when the field observers left Rome to make a preliminary survey of their areas and to establish regional offices. One field observer made his headquarters in Milan, another in Venice, a third in Naples; the fourth operated out of Mission headquarters in Rome.

It was a constant problem to make clear to the Italian people how "Aid From America" actually was a gift; Italians still had to pay normal prices

---

[1] The United States foreign-relief program was authorized by Public Law 84, 80th Cong., 1st sess., approved May 31, 1947 (61 Stat. 125).

[2] The United States foreign-aid program was authorized by Public Law 389, 80th Cong., 1st sess., approved Dec. 17, 1947 (61 Stat. 934).

[3] The name was changed to U.S. Foreign Aid Mission to Italy when the second program came into being.

[4] Another agreement, under the foreign-aid program, was signed on Jan. 3, 1948, by the same three representatives.

for their bread and their household gas, although American flour was used in baking more than half of their bread and American coal produced their gas.

The programed supplies—approved by the Department of State and the Italian Technical Delegation in Washington after they had received comments and recommendations from the Mission and Italian Government officials in Rome—were upon arrival in Italy distributed in great part through commercial channels. They were sold for lire at agreed-upon prices which were calculated not to disturb the economy of the country. The proceeds derived from the sale of the commodities were placed in a special account which came to be known as the lire fund. Under the post-UNRRA relief program it amounted to approximately 41 billion lire. Relief and work-relief projects approved by the Mission were then financed by this fund, which also paid the local administrative expenses of the Mission.

Certain products were, however, not sold. Soap was turned over to hospitals and sanitoria; streptomycin for the treatment of specific types of tuberculosis was given to low-income patients in institutions; evaporated milk was donated to institutions serving luncheons to poor children; 20 percent of the penicillin was distributed free of charge.

The job of the field observers was a varied and comprehensive one: to check on the distribution and utilization of supplies, to advise and report on the expenditures from the lire fund, to observe and report on economic conditions, and to publicize to the greatest extent possible the purpose, source, character, amounts, and progress of the programs.

The Italian Government provided each field observer as well as the adviser and assistant advisers with an automobile. Each field observer engaged locally an assistant, who acted as interpreter, a secretary, and a driver. The field observer in Naples was responsible for south Italy and Sicily, a territory which embraces five regions (Campania, Lucania, Puglia, Calabria, and Sicily) consisting of 24 provinces. During the eight months the Naples office was maintained, he visited every province. Two of the more remote Sicilian provinces were visited once, the others from two to six times.

inadequate equipment; windows lacked glass; children sometimes had to eat their lunches standing because there were no benches.

Signs giving credit to "Aiuti dell' America" were distributed to these institutions to be prominently displayed. It was with considerable satisfaction that these signs were observed in kindergartens in Taranto and Siracusa run by the Unione Donne Italiane (Union of Italian Women), a Communist organization. In Marsala the Communist mayor and the field observer together visited the principal institution where the child-feeding program was operating and were tumultuously received. The mayor later insisted on being host to the field observer and his assistant for the traditional cup of coffee. His cordiality and appreciation for American aid were genuine if paradoxical.

The lire fund was likewise used to help a number of "Boys' Towns" or "Children's Villages". One was the Villaggio Norma de Martino, beautifully and healthfully situated on the bay five miles south of Salerno. Private gifts permitted the reconstruction and renovation of about 100 units of Quonset and Nissen huts to make them serviceable as school rooms, dormitories, refectories, kitchens, and so on, for housing, feeding, and teaching 500 abandoned, orphaned, or poor children. The lire fund paid the operating expenses for the first six months. The village was dedicated and opened on April 15, three days before the elections, with appropriate ceremonies in which Ambassador Dunn participated.

A malaria-control compaign, an anticholera campaign, the building of a penicillin plant, highway and bridge reconstruction, land reclamation, irrigation, labor on state railroads, food parcels for the unemployed—in all the lire fund made possible or contributed to approximately one hundred projects.

Every feasible method to achieve publicity was used. Weekly bulletins issued by the Mission kept newspapers, periodicals, officials, and others informed of the progress of the programs. The field observers called on journalists and secured local coverage of their visits. The Italian radio was likewise helpful with announcements and interviews; upon the arrival of each hundredth ship it broadcast the ceremonies: the three hundredth in late January in Bari, the four hundredth in early March in Reggio Calabria, the five hundredth

on April 2 in Taranto, the six hundredth on April 15 in Naples. Ambassador Dunn's participation and speeches always gave great prominence to the occasions.

Newsreels and documentary films publicized "Aid from America" throughout Italy. During the election campaign window displays in 10 cities told the story. An ideal spot was found in Naples; the display there consisted of an effective photomontage of unloading operations, using genuine samples of American wheat, flour, coal, penicillin, streptomycin, and DDT.

More than a dozen posters, a common and accepted medium in Italy, plastered building walls in the cities as well as the villages. They were designed to attract attention to the amount of aid and also to explain graphically the use of the lire fund.

Suitable labels and markings on commodities were used where practicable. Bills for household gas bore a rubber-stamped notice that the gas was produced by free American coal. When an Italian employee of the Mission in Naples received her gas bill the day before the elections she noticed that someone had almost entirely obliterated the familiar notice. The Communist newspaper of Naples, La Voce, had attacked the Italian Government months before for its "servility" to American capitalists in requiring the gas companies to give credit on their bills.

Leftist newspaper propaganda proved quite helpful. At first it minimized the extent of American aid, then it admitted the size of the programs but denied that supplies were entirely free, and finally it changed to charges of misuse of the lire fund.

The Italian people, especially in the south, were cheerful, hospitable, and grateful for the help America was giving them. In Sicily the courtesy and hospitality shown the field observer on many occasions were all but overwhelming; the subsequent publicity value was considerable. In spite of the most vigorous efforts he was forced, in order to avoid offending Sicilians, whose hospitality is legendary, to accept during one trip three bottles of various liqueurs, a box of typical Sicilian sweets, a leather album, innumerable bouquets of flowers (not boutonnieres but armfuls), and countless meals and drinks. In Ragusa, accompanied by the prefect and the mayor, wherever

(Continued on page 777)

THE INSTITUTE OF INTER-AMERICA
AGRICULTURAL PROGRAMS

by Louis J.

I

The picture of the tropics that most of us once entertained is of distant Edens in which nature is so bountiful that men need only gather the fruits that fall from overhead. Writers of popular romance have perpetuated this picture, which doubtless harks back to the days when thinly populated tropical wildernesses provided rich cargoes for the densely populated centers of power to the north. The north looked toward the undeveloped equatorial regions for wealth. One clue to the course of empire in modern times may be found in the extent to which this situation has been reversed over large areas, so that pópulations in the tropics now look to the north for means to achieve a reasonably safe and comfortable living.

The tropics, by and large, are not rich in the most fundamental form of wealth, good agricultural soil. Slopes that support luxuriant rainforest will not support corn for more than a few seasons, as tropical farmers often learn to their sorrow. Sparseness of population, in relation to the agricultural soil available, has largely accounted for the fact that tropical peoples in times past have been able to feed themselves adequately. Quantity of agricultural land, which allows the farmer to move on as the soil becomes exhausted, is a satisfactory substitute for quality as long as it lasts. With the doubling of populations in 25 to 50 years and the progressive disappearance of frontiers, however, the problem has acquired its practical aspects.

The great majority of the other American republics lie within the tropics, and all of them are primarily agricultural. Nevertheless, most of them must supplement the production of their own farms by imports from abroad, and many of their people know what it is to be hungry. Those who work the land may be less articulate on this point than those concentrated in the centers of population, who get their food from public markets and complain of high costs when what they actually have to complain of may be low agricultural pro-

emergency. As it passed, however, it became increasingly practicable to survey what had been accomplished in the long-range development of agricultural processes, to envisage the permanent benefits toward which the programs were making their way, and to plan accordingly. Our general policy of cooperation had, from the beginning, been viewed as a vital permanent aspect of the good-neighbor policy, even if the initial direction taken by these cooperative programs had been largely determined by the immediate needs of a Hemisphere at war. It represented a historical development rather than a temporary expedient.

III

While the Institute formerly participated in ten agricultural programs, its participation is now limited to four—in Costa Rica, Haiti, Paraguay, and Peru. The Paraguayan program will serve as an illustration of the magnitude and character of these programs. A report of the Food Production Division sums up the original problem of Paraguay in the following concise terms:

"December 31, 1947 marks the completion of five years of experience for STICA (Servicio Técnico Interamericano de Cooperación Agrícola), the *servicio* which was created in 1942 by the Paraguayan and U.S. Governments to study, propose and attempt to carry out solutions for Paraguay's agricultural problems. When U.S. technicians, who were sent by the Food Supply Division to join Paraguayan personnel in this task, first arrived they discovered that Paraguay possesses tremendous agricultural resources which more than compensate for absence of a seaport: a tropical climate suitable for production of most temperate and tropical zone crops, wide expanses of fertile soil awaiting development, abundant virgin forests, and one of the greatest concentrations in the world of undeveloped hydroelectric energy. Yet, despite these natural advantages, agricultural production there was insufficient to satisfy domestic demands, much less to provide a surplus for foreign markets and build up dollar supplies. Its subsistence-type economy, based on farming, cattle-raising and timber exploitation, supports a population of over one million, more than two-thirds of whom live within a hundred miles of Asunción, the capital city, yet almost all of whom know little of modern agricultural techniques. STICA's task

759

then was to build a program, based on these conditions, which would serve as a beginning for an integrated agricultural economy."

It is to be noted that the balance between population and practicably arable land is more favorable in Paraguay than in most other American republics. Approaching the capital, Asunción, from the south, you fly over vast areas of fertile grasslands that are all but unpopulated. Paraguayans, in conversation with you, express their concern at the lack of an adequate population to exploit the possibilities of the land—a complaint that has a certain music for those who have confronted the more common and more direful problem of inadequate land. This land is ready to produce in abundance, awaiting simply the application of proper tools and techniques. The average Paraguayan farmer lives well enough, by the standards he knows, but he could live a great deal better. The Paraguayan Government is seriously concerned with dealing with this situation, and looks to our country for the experience and technical "know-how" that can provide the remedy.

Here is what Paraguay and the United States have done so far to meet this situation, through the cooperative *servicio* known as STICA.

A 500-acre farm has been established 30 miles from Asunción, called the National Institute of Agronomy. It is one of several foundation-stones of the joint agricultural program. On it, the seeds of new crops and of improved varieties are produced, tested, and labeled for distribution, while experimentation in agricultural methods is conducted to determine those best adapted to the needs of the country and the means of the farmer. The experimentation also serves to demonstrate such principles as contour-plowing, crop-rotation, and the use of green fertilizers.

Another foundation-stone is a model dairy farm established by STICA on the outskirts of Asunción. It demonstrates proper methods of pasturage and experiments with new varieties of pasture grass. It demonstrates pasteurization and the sanitary handling of milk, including bottling. It demonstrates the improvement of dairy stock. And, finally, it markets excellent milk of its own production in Asunción.

The third foundation-stone is a 27,000-acre ranch owned by the Paraguayan Government and supporting 6,000 head of beef cattle, which in turn support it. Here STICA demonstrates the improve-

inaugurated the cooperative agricultural program in Haiti in 1944, it had to deal with what was already an emergency. Trees that held the soil on mountain slopes had been destroyed, the topsoil had washed away, and what was left in large part was desert marked by gulleys. The familiar alternation of drought and flood had ensued. Irrigation works constructed in colonial times had fallen into disrepair and once fertile valleys had been ruined by salt. The problem was not simply one of improving agricultural methods with a view to eventually increasing the wealth and welfare of the country. It was one of getting food for hungry mouths.

The average Haitian farmer could not have been expected to understand the relatively abstruse principle of land use and soil conservation. His methods were primitive and ingrained in his thinking by generations of tradition. Hunger had not increased any disposition he might have had to take the long view rather than preoccupy himself exclusively with the immediate problem of getting something to eat for his increasing family. During 1944 and 1945 the Institute's agricultural mission was also preoccupied with this immediate problem. Emergency-aid organizations were set up; seeds and the cuttings from fruit trees and vegetables were distributed; information on planting, cultivation, and insect control was given out; emergency irrigation and drainage projects were undertaken.

It was not until 1946 that it became possible to think in terms of plans for the longer future. The decision then taken was to concentrate on projects of education and demonstration, since it was necessary to improve the pattern of Haitian agriculture as it existed, initially, in the mind of the Haitian farmer. Rather than a few large demonstration areas having been established, many small demonstration plots were developed in various parts of the country to illustrate soil-conservation practices, crop development, irrigation, and the use of machinery. Assistance was given in re-establishing a 1,200-acre farm for livestock demonstration work and as a training center for students of animal husbandry. Emergency rehabilitation was undertaken on La Gonave Island, a formerly rich agricultural region, once serving as one of the chief suppliers of corn and millet to the mainland, now reduced to dire poverty by soil exhaustion, drought, and pests. At the same time, the work of training

Haitian agriculturists in Haiti and Puerto Rico was expanded.

The most ambitious project of rehabilitation that the Haitian Government has under way, with the cooperation of the Institute, is in the 150,000-acre Artibonite Valley, potentially the richest agricultural area in the country but already half ruined for agriculture by salting and in danger of being wholly ruined. A Haitian Government commission is now making plans for over-all development of the Valley's resources, including projects for irrigation, drainage, flood-control, and hydroelectric power. Meanwhile, certain pilot-projects being carried out under the agricultural program involve drainage and diversion of flood waters to bring about the deposit of silt on land made useless by salting. Already wasteland has been successfully reclaimed for agriculture by these projects.

As is the case with most other Central American countries, the chief threat to Costa Rica's future is the rapid erosion of her mountain slopes as a result of deforestation, with the ensuing complex of desert, drought, flood, hunger, economic deterioration, and political instability. The general progress of soil-exhaustion is less advanced here than in Haiti, but its pace is alarming. The problem is to stop it in time. Consequently, the agricultural program in Costa Rica has put its chief emphasis on conservation through contour-plowing, bench-terracing, use of manures, crop-rotation, and similar devices. It has established an extension service which is gradually expanding throughout the country, and in the course of time the farmers have been coming in increasing numbers to seek advice and assistance from the extension agents and to buy agricultural tools provided at cost. This has been so effective that airplane travelers have noted the transformation taking place in Costa Rica as the landscape is increasingly featured by slopes plowed on the contour, by curving hillside ditches, and by terraces.

By far the largest agricultural program in which the Institute participates is one that has assumed the proportions of a great national development in Peru, that of the SCIPA (Servicio Cooperativo Inter-Americano de Producción de Alimentos). The Peruvian Government, for one thing, is able to pay by far the major share of the costs, while the economic circumstances in Peru are such that important aspects of the program there are self-sustaining. Its foundation is an extension service

THE UNITED NATIONS AND SPECIALIZED AGENCIES

Acceptance of Four-Week Truce Resolution by Jewish and Arab Leaders

STATEMENT BY AMBASSADOR WARREN R. AUSTIN [1]

U.S. Representative at the Seat of the United Nations

Mr. President: My government feels encouraged by the unconditional acceptance of the terms of this resolution of May 29.[2] We recognize that the present situation involves the obligations, whatever they are, that arise out of the resolution of the General Assembly of May 17 (document A/554), plus the resolution of the Security Council of May 29 represented by document S/801. We realize that nothing we can say in our speeches can change in any manner the obligations contained in those resolutions.

The spirit of the resolutions, however, is exceedingly important, and, as I have said on several occasions, I am very anxious to take the pressure off the political question somewhat if it can be done. If our mediator and our Truce Commission can lay some stress upon that part of the resolution of the General Assembly which empowers the United Nations mediator in Palestine to invite as seems to him advisable, with the view to the promotion of the welfare of the inhabitants of Palestine, the assistance and cooperation of appropriate specialized agencies of the United Nations, such as the World Health Organization and the International Red Cross and other governmental and nongovernmental organizations of a humanitarian and nonpolitical character, to start in motion the resources which the United Nations can deliver to the people of the Middle East, something will arise out of it, I am sure, that will aid further to bring together all people who reside in the Middle East, because they have a common interest. Many times the relationship of Jews and Arabs to each other on a racial basis has been referred to here and the need they have for each other to collaborate and to live together in peace has been emphasized on both sides. I expect that perhaps this movement cannot be inaugurated in four weeks, but it certainly can be envisaged—it can be contemplated in the negotiations which are about to take place.

I would like to have the mediator feel that the Security Council is greatly interested in this element. Of course the parties know that. They have sat right here with us at this table, and they know of our interest. Also, being in the United States they know of the activity in the United States as a member nation to promote these activities of the United Nations through its various specialized agencies.

Now, as to the proposal of our distinguished President with respect to the communication S/814 from the mediator, I accept the ruling and, of course, will back it so far as it is necessary, and I want to say in passing that my Government is ready to do everything that it can under the two resolutions that command the situation; to do its full share in the effort of maintaining the cease-fire effectually and at finding an ultimate solution for the problem by pacific means. But, as to this communication, may I suggest that without in any way disturbing the ruling of the President of the Security Council, which is in full accord with the request of the mediator. There are two points which I do not think will do harm to bring out in connection with the mediator's request. He speaks of controls here and of setting a date. He says:

"For practical reasons hope Security Council, in event acceptance by both parties, would not set effective date so early that the controls would not be operative, thus inducing immediate charges of violation both sides."

Now, Mr. President, we think that that should be interpreted liberally and reasonably so that it will not become an impractical construction of the situation. If he has to wait before his deadline until after controls covering all aspects of these two resolutions are set up and in operation, it will be a long time probably. Under the General Assembly resolution he has to arrange the operation of common services necessary to the well-being of the population of Palestine; secondly, assure the protection of the Holy Places, buildings, and sites in Palestine. Those two affairs, if he regards them as in the meaning of controls, might take all of the time that is involved in these four weeks. And we cannot have the fighting going on. It seems to me reasonable to suggest as a limit three days as enough in which to determine the exact time of the hour and minute for the cessation of hostilities.

[1] Made before the Security Council on June 2, 1948, and released to the press by the U.S. Mission to the United Nations on the same date.
[2] S/801, May 29, 1948 (BULLETIN of June 6, 1948, p. 729).

Now, I am not offering this as a modification of the ruling. I merely suggest it as a point of view which might be communicated to him from the President of the Security Council. Certainly, if no one objects to it, it would be suitable to convey that idea to him that it will expedite the cease-fire and get that into effect right away, for I think all parties now are well satisfied that there is nothing to be gained in continuing the hostilities. Whatever temporary advances might be made would not mean anything. After lives have been lost nothing would be gained on the ultimate question of the solution of the problem of Palestine. In fact, a little something would have been lost instead because there would have generated bitterness which always interferes with a negotiation such as we have before us.

I conclude, Mr. President, by saying I wish to encourage the mediator and the Truce Commission and the parties concerned that the United Nations will continue to help all it can toward a solution that will be just and will be acceptable.

CABLEGRAM FROM THE UNITED NATIONS' MEDIATOR IN PALESTINE TO THE SECRETARY-GENERAL [1]

June 2, 1948

In event Security Council resolution 29 May be accepted by both parties, assumption is that a date would have to be set for truce coming into effect. I talked to Tel Aviv and Amman and my preliminary study problem of controls convinced me that a limited time must be allowed between the date acceptance of resolution and date its application. From standpoint application of controls this might be some days.

For practical reasons hope Security Council, in event acceptance by both parties, would not set effective date so early that the controls would not be operative, thus inducing immediate charges of violation both sides. My suggestion for procedure is that the mediator be authorized fix effective date in consultation with two parties and Truce Commission. I assume the four week period computed from this effective date.

[COUNT FOLKE BERNADOTTE]

JEWISH AND ARAB STATES REPLY TO ORDER FOR A FOUR-WEEK TRUCE

Text of letter from the Representative of the Jewish Agency for Palestine, addressed to the Secretary-General, transmitting a telegram from the Foreign Minister of the Provisional Government of Israel [4]

June 1, 1948

SIR: On Saturday, May 29, I transmitted to the Provisional Government of Israel the text of the resolution adopted by the Security Council with reference to a cease-fire in Palestine for a period of four weeks.[5] I now have the honor to convey the following reply from Mr. M. Shertok, Foreign Minister in the Provisional Government of Israel:

"The Provisional Government of Israel has given full consideration to the resolution of the Security Council adopted on May 29, 1948 calling upon all governments and authorities to order the cessation of all acts of armed force for a period of four weeks.

"The Provisional Government of Israel has decided to respond to this call and to instruct the High Command of the Defense Army of Israel to issue a cease-fire order to Israeli forces on all fronts

to be observed as from Wednesday, June 2, 3:00 AM Israeli time (corresponding to 7:00 PM New York Daylight time) if the other side acts likewise. The Provisional Government of Israel will also comply with all the injunctions and obligations imposed by the resolution, provided that a similar undertaking is entered into by the other governments and authorities concerned.

"The readiness of the Provisional Government of Israel to cooperate in the execution of the cease-fire as laid down in the Security Council's resolution is based on the following assumptions which, in the opinion of the Provisional Government, are clearly implied in the terms of the resolution:

"1. That the ban on the import of arms into the territory of the Arab states enumerated in the resolution should apply also to the deliveries of arms from stocks owned or controlled by foreign powers within those territories.

"2. That during the cease-fire, the armed forces of neither side will seek to advance beyond the areas controlled by them at the announcement of the cease-fire and that each side will be entitled to maintain the positions in its military occupation at that time.

"3. That freedom of access to Jerusalem will be

[1] U.N. doc. S/814, June 2, 1948.
[4] U.N. doc. S/804, June 1, 1948.
[5] BULLETIN of June 6, 1948, p. 729.

ensured for the supply of food and other essentials, as well as for normal civilian entry and exit.

"4. That any attempt by the parties concerned to stop or impede the normal transport of goods assigned to Israel and other states concerned will be regarded as an act of armed force.

"5. That while the Provisional Government of Israel is ready to comply with the injunction that persons of military age admitted during the cease-fire period should not be mobilized or submitted to military training, its freedom to admit immigrants, regardless of age, will not be impaired."

Although all these consequences seem to flow naturally from the text and spirit of the cease-fire resolution which the Provisional Government of Israel accepts without reservation, it seems important for the avoidance of misunderstanding that they should be placed on the record at this stage.

In addition to this letter, I have been instructed to seek an early occasion, at the discretion of the Security Council, for explaining the views of the Provisional Government of Israel in an oral submission. May I request that the contents of this letter be made available to members of the Security Council.

I have the honor [etc.]

AUBREY S. EBAN
Acting Representative
Provisional Government of Israel

Text of telegram to the Secretary-General from the Minister for Foreign Affairs of Egypt dated June 1, 1948[6]

June 1, 1948

I have the honour to acknowledge receipt of Your Excellency's telegram of 29 May 1948 in which you kindly give me the text of the resolution adopted on that day by the Security Council with a view to ceasing hostilities in Palestine for a period of four weeks. The Governments of the states members of the Arab League, to which you communicated the said resolution, have considered it and have taken the following decision which they have instructed me to transmit to you. I hereby transmit the following communication to you from the Arab League:[7]

The governments of the Arab states stated in their replies to the first invitation to the same effect that the Security Council addressed to them on 22 May last that they greatly wished peace to be re-established in Palestine and both the Arab and Jewish people of that country to live side by side in perfect harmony and mutual understanding. The Arab states also gave the reasons why they would not accept that invitation and drew attention to the guarantees without which the suspension of the hostilities taking place in Palestine

would only constitute a temporary respite giving rise to disorder on a greater scale and more serious acts of terrorism. It is pleasant to note that the Security Council has taken these considerations into account. The suspension of hostilities is merely a means of finding the just solution of the Palestine problem which would be so welcome. The Arab states also note with satisfaction that the Security Council's resolution instructs the United Nations mediator to make contact with all parties, as soon as the cease-fire is in force, with a view to carrying out his functions as determined by the General Assembly in its resolution of 14 May last. One of the most important of these functions is that of reaching a peaceful and just solution of the problem.

The governments of the Arab states are confident that the United Nations mediator and the members of the Truce Commission appointed by the Security Council on 23 April 1948 will realise that any solution which does not ensure political unity for Palestine nor respect the will of the majority of the population of that country will not have the least chance of success. There is not the least doubt that it will have exactly the opposite effect from that for which the suspension of hostilities was resolved: it will open the gates of Palestine, at the present time controlled by the Zionists, to receive hordes of Jewish immigrants of military age who are waiting at the ports of Europe and America for the first chance to go to Palestine in large numbers. Most of these immigrants have received a thorough combatant training, and their entry into Palestine will have the effect of reinforcing the bands of Zionist terrorists, which constitute a serious threat to the Arabs of Palestine and to the security of the middle eastern Arab countries. It is inconceivable that the Security Council could have intended to place the Zionists in a position to profit by the period of cessation of hostilities in order to receive a reinforcement of men who, although they come to Palestine as immigrants, are in reality nothing but trained fighters and thus come within the definition in the second paragraph of the Security Council resolution prohibiting the introduction of combatant personnel into Palestine during the period of the armistice.

Finally, the governments of the Arab states consider it necessary that a body should be set up under all the necessary safeguards, charged with the most careful supervision of the provisions and conditions of the Security Council resolution on the cessation of hostilities and capable of performing this delicate function. The governments of

---

[6] U.N. doc. S/810, June 1, 1948.
[7] For communications to the Secretary-General from the Governments of Syria, Saudi Arabia, Iraq, and Lebanon, see, respectively, the following U.N. docs.: S/815, June 2, 1948, S/811, S/807, and S/805, June 1, 1948.

the Arab states consider that in this regard the Security Council resolution does not give them full assurance that the other party will respect the provisions and conditions of the armistice. Therefore, as members of a regional organisation responsible for maintaining security in their zone, they are bound to collaborate whole-heartedly with the United Nations mediator and the members of the Truce Commission for Palestine in order to supervise the carrying out of the aforesaid provisions and conditions.

In the light of the above explanations the Arab states which are anxious to see peace re-established in Palestine and the way prepared for a just and fair solution of the Palestine problem, accept the

Security Council's invitation to cease fire for a period of four weeks from the date to be determined for this purpose. In accepting this invitation, in spite of the obstacles with which all the attempts hitherto made to solve the Palestine problem justly and fairly have been confronted owing to the systematically obstructive attitude taken up by the Zionists, the Arab states are proving their sincere wish to collaborate with the United Nations in achieving such a solution at a moment when their armies which have entered Palestine have the situation in hand.

I have the honour [etc.]

AHMED MOHAMMED KHASHABA Pasha,
Minister for Foreign Affairs of Egypt

Current United Nations Documents: A Selected Bibliography [1]

Security Council

Official Records:
Second Year:
—— No. 68, 172d and 173d Meeting, August 1, 1947. 62 pp. printed. 60¢.
Third Year:
—— No. 56, 281st Meeting, April 12, 1948, 34 pp. printed. 35¢.
—— No. 60, 285th Meeting, April 19, 1948. 52 pp. printed. 50¢.
Committee of Good Offices on the Indonesian Question :
Report to the Security Council on Political Developments in Madura. S/786. May 26, 1948. 20 pp. mimeo.
Second Interim Report of the Committee to the Security Council. S/787. May 26, 1948. 37 pp. mimeo.
Report of the Administration of the British/United States Zone of the Free Territory of Trieste for the First Quarter of 1948 (letter of transmittal included). S/781. May 25, 1948. 48 pp. mimeo.

Economic and Social Council

Official Records, Second Year:
Supplement No. 7. Second report on post-UNRRA activities. 74 pp. printed. 75¢.
Supplement No. 8. Report of the Transport and Communications Commission. 68 pp. printed. 70¢.
Official Records, Third Year: Supplement No. 2. Report of the Commission on narcotic drugs. 88 pp. printed. 90¢.
Resolutions Adopted by the Economic and Social Council during its sixth session from February 2 to March 11, 1948. 48 pp. printed. 50¢.
Report of the Interim Commission of the World Health Organization. E/786. Apr. 28, 1948. 19 pp. mimeo.
Commission on Narcotic Drugs: Report to the Economic and Social Council on the Draft Protocol To Bring Under Control Certain Drugs Not Covered by the 1931 Convention. E/798. May 26, 1948. 24 pp. mimeo.

Report on the Activities of the United Nations Educational, Scientific and Cultural Organization. E/804. May 25, 1948. 13 pp. mimeo.
Report of the Population Commission. E/805. May 26, 1948. 30 pp. mimeo.
Disposition of Agenda Items at the Sixth Session. E/INF/22. 74 pp. Also E/INF/22/Add. 1. May 10, 1948. (Index) 49 pp. mimeo.
Arrangements of the Economic and Social Council of the United Nations for Consultation with Non-Governmental Organizations: Guide for Consultants. E/INF/23. Apr. 30, 1948. 46 pp. mimeo.
Commission on Human Rights: Third Session International Law Association. E/CN4/89. May 12, 1948. 63 pp. mimeo.

Sales Prices for U.N. Documents

The following sales prices were approved on April 22, 1948, for mimeographed United Nations documents which are to be sold to institutions, libraries, and the public by the U.N. Department of Public Information. The sales will replace the system of free distribution to depository libraries except so far as such libraries have reciprocal arrangements with the United Nations for exchange of publications.

The prices are as follows. All figures are for documents in one language:

A Documents	$30.00
A Committee Documents	65.00
Both A Documents and A Committee Documents	75.00
E Documents	30.00
E Committee Documents	90.00
Both E Documents and E Committee Documents	100.00
S Documents	100.00
AEC Documents	20.00
TC Documents	30.00

Yearly subscription price for all documents. $225.00

[1] Printed materials may be secured in the United States from the International Documents Service, Columbia University Press, 2960 Broadway, New York City. Other materials (mimeographed or processed documents) may be consulted at certain designated libraries in the United States.

of course change the wording of the resolution if it chose to do so, and the United States would naturally be bound by any such change. But the arrangement already established, Mr. Jessup said, seems to the United States to be "a simple and practical one which the Council has already authorized."

Mr. Gromyko replied that Mr. Jessup's statement showed that the United States had a "negative attitude" toward the participation of Soviet Union observers. He reserved the right to submit a formal resolution on observer arrangements at the Council's next meeting on Palestine.

Techniques of Pacific Settlement

The Interim Committee of the General Assembly is making "substantial progress" in developing general principles of international cooperation and improved methods for pacific settlement of disputes, Philip C. Jessup, Deputy U.S. Representative, said in a press statement released June 7.[2]

This aspect of the work assigned to the Interim Committee by the General Assembly's resolution of November 13, 1947, is in the hands of a 15-nation subcommittee, which plans to complete its work in July. The United States is a member.

The subcommittee is studying pacific settlement procedures, which are mentioned in article 33 of the Charter as including negotiation, enquiry, mediation, conciliation, arbitration, and judicial settlement, in the light of existing treaties and of League of Nations and inter-American experience. Mr. Jessup noted that the subcommittee is emphasizing the obligation of U.N. members to try settling their disputes by these methods before bringing them to the Security Council or the General Assembly.

The subcommittee also has under consideration proposals for improving the machinery of international conciliation. "For example," Mr. Jessup said, "China and the U.S. have suggested the creation of a panel . . . of competent persons who might be selected by states or by U.N. organs for service on commissions of enquiry and conciliation. . . . There have been several instances in which competent personnel has been urgently needed for N.U. commissions, as in the cases of Indonesia, Kashmir and the Balkans."

India-Pakistan Disputes

The Security Council met June 8 to discuss a letter from Prime Minister Nehru of India which protested the Council's June 3 decision to enlarge the scope of its Kashmir Commission.

---

[2] U.S. Mission to U.N. press release 469.

Mr. Nehru's letter also reaffirmed India's objections to the plan approved by the Council on April 21 for a plebiscite in Kashmir and Jammu and said there "can be no question of the Commission proceeding to implement the resolution on Kashmir until objections by the Government of India have been met."

The Indian contention is that Pakistan's charges of Indian aggression against the state of Junagadh, genocide, and violation of certain inter-dominion agreements do not constitute threats to peace and are outside the Security Council's jurisdiction.

The Council informally agreed that its President, Mr. El Khouri of Syria, should reply to Mr. Nehru that, first, the Council had come to no conclusion about the three Pakistan complaints but had merely asked its Commission for information on them, and, secondly, the Commission itself would discuss with Indian and Pakistan authorities, upon its arrival, the question of implementing the Kashmir plan.

Mr. El Khouri said he would draft such a letter and submit it to a later meeting of the Council, but Philip C. Jessup of the United States said he was sure the Council would prefer to have the letter sent off promptly without review.

Human Rights

The Human Rights Commission will find it necessary to revise its timetable for the preparation of a "Bill of Human Rights" in the light of experience gained at its current session, the U.S. Delegation believes.

When the Commission convened its third session on May 24, it was hoped that by June 18 it could complete the drafts of a Declaration of Human Rights, a Covenant of Human Rights, and suggestions for implementation of the Covenant.

The Commission has found that the drafting of the declaration alone is a bigger job than was anticipated. It is likely that only the declaration will be completed at this session.

Subsequent procedure had not been determined as of June 10. The declaration alone could be sent to the Economic and Social Council for review at its Geneva session, opening July 19, or the Com-

Production of Rice

B. Ellis

monies Joaquin M. Elizalde, Philippine Ambassador to the United States and chairman of the Philippine Delegation, was unanimously elected chairman of the Meeting.

Rules of procedure and an agenda were adopted. The following four committees were established to consider principal items of business listed in the agenda: I—Expansion of Rice Production; II—Rice Marketing and Distribution; III—International Organization; and IV—Three-Year Rice Program. The working committees and their subcommittees met daily until they had completed reports on the subjects assigned to them.

Decisions and Recommendations of the Meeting

In view of the existing world shortage of rice and the belief that shortages will continue for several years because of the war devastation of extensive producing areas and the rapid increase in population in the major rice-consuming areas, the Meeting concentrated its attention on measures to conserve supplies and increase production in the immediate future. While many of the measures recommended were of long-term duration, it was believed they would be of great assistance also in meeting the immediate problem.

A brief summary of some of the more important actions of the Meeting follows:

1. One of the principal limiting factors in achieving increased production is the extreme shortage of workstock in Asia, and since rinderpest infestation is a serious obstacle to the rehabilitation of herds, the Meeting recommended that prompt action be taken by the Fao, in consultation with the International Office of Epizootics, to form a Far East Veterinary Committee to eradicate rinderpest in Southeast Asia through a coordinated program.

2. In order to speed up the rehabilitation of abandoned rice lands, the Meeting recommended that the producing countries "conduct investigations to ascertain the practical usefulness" of mechanized equipment and that the Council of Fao endeavor to obtain such equipment for countries where its use would be practical.

3. The Meeting further recommended that countries submit data to the Council of Fao on their production requisites and requested that the Council consider the establishment of advisory services to aid governments in obtaining their production requirements.

4. In order to provide necessary irrigation for bringing additional lands into production, the

Meeting recommended that the Fao "do its utmost to help governments secure the financial assistance, machinery and equipment" needed for the construction of irrigation and drainage works where detailed projects could be demonstrated to be economically sound.

5. It was the opinion of the Meeting that substantial losses occur at all stages from production through final consumption and that much could be done to alleviate the existing shortage by reducing such losses. The Meeting recommended that "all rice producing countries undertake during 1948 a vigorous campaign to conserve rice supplies" and that every country establish "a National Rice Conservation Committee to serve as a planning body" for carrying out such a campaign. It was also recommended that the Fao serve as a coordinating body to assist individual governments in setting up and carrying out the conservation campaign.

6. One of the principal proposals made by the Rice Study Group concerned the establishment of an international organization to deal with rice. This proposal was of major interest to the delegations attending the Meeting, particularly those delegations from Southeast Asia. Accordingly, the Meeting agreed unanimously to recommend to the Council of Fao that an International Rice Council be established. In general, the proposed International Rice Council would seek to facilitate cooperative action in matters relating to the production, conservation, distribution, and consumption of rice but would not deal with matters relating to international trade. Under the proposed constitution, membership in the Rice Council would be open to all Fao member governments and the Council would be organized upon approval by the Council of Fao and after acceptance of at least ten countries representing in the aggregate not less than half of the world production of rice in the crop year 1947–48. The seat of the Council would be at the site of the Southeast Asia regional office and would work in close cooperation with the regional office, making annual reports on its activities to the Council of Fao.

7. The Meeting was of the unanimous opinion "that the solution of the pressing production problems requires the mobilization and full utilization of the scientifically trained personnel and research facilities of the rice producing countries" and therefore recommended that Fao sponsor a Far East Rice Investigation Committee with subcommittees on "(a) utilization and control of water, (b) machinery and equipment, and (c) soil, agronomy and plant improvement". It was also urged that these recommendations be considered by the proposed International Rice Council when established.

8. The Meeting recognized the importance of international price agreements but agreed that a considerable amount of preliminary investigation

the ILO [1]

ence. In pursuance of the Conference's resolutions, the Governing Body decided to call a Technical Conference on the Organization of Labor Inspection, and an agenda for this meeting was approved. In response to an invitation from the Government of Ceylon, it was decided that the Conference should meet in that country, if possible before the end of the current year.

Report on the Regional Meeting for the Near and Middle East

The Director General reported that, in accordance with the authorization given to him by the Governing Body at its previous session, he had communicated to governments the resolutions adopted at the Regional Meeting for the Near and Middle East, held at Istanbul in the autumn of 1947. He stated that he had taken the action called for by the resolutions to the extent to which he could do so without prejudicing any decisions which the Governing Body might take later.

Joint Maritime Commission's Report

The Governing Body considered the report of the Joint Maritime Commission which had met at Geneva, December 2-5, 1947. After presentation of the report, the Governing Body authorized the Director General of the ILO to convene a tripartite subcommittee in the autumn of 1948. This subcommittee will examine the information supplied by governments concerning the reasons which have prevented them from ratifying the conventions approved at the Seattle Maritime Conference in June 1946 and concerning the extent to which some of the provisions of the conventions have been applied in their respective countries. The Governing Body also authorized the ILO to continue the study of certain aspects of seamen's welfare.

Amendments to the Constitution of the ILO

A document was submitted by the Director General concerning ratification of the amendments to the constitution of the ILO adopted by the Twenty-ninth Session of the International Labor

---

[1] Prepared by the Division of International Conferences, Department of State.
[2] The 94th Session of the Governing Body of the ILO (January 1945) established seven major industrial committees: Inland Transport; Coal Mining; Petroleum Production and Refining; Metal Trades; Iron and Steel Production; Building, Civil Engineering and Public Works; and Textiles. The Industrial Committee on Chemicals was set up at the 101st Session of the Governing Body, May 1947.

Conference at Montreal in 1946. These amendments must be ratified by two thirds of the states members of the organization, including five of the eight states of chief industrial importance, before they can come into force. As the number of members at present is 55, the required two-thirds majority is 37. At the time of the Governing Body's session, ratifications from 34 countries, including seven members of chief industrial importance, had been formally communicated to the ILO. Furthermore, ratifications had been authorized by the competent national authority in five other countries.[3]

ILO Budget for 1949

The Finance Committee presented budget estimates for 1949 amounting to a total of $5,109,270. This budget was adopted unanimously. According to the established procedure, the 1949 budget as approved by the Governing Body must be laid before the coming session of the International Labor Conference for final adoption. This Conference is scheduled to open at San Francisco on June 17, 1948.

Problem of Manpower .

Another problem to be discussed was one which is now receiving attention in a number of countries, namely, the best means of using available manpower to enhance economic development and increase production. The Governing Body examined the tasks which the Manpower Subcommittee of the Economic Commission for Europe had asked the ILO to undertake. Meeting after the International Manpower Conference at Rome, January 26–February 9, 1948, the Manpower Subcommittee recommended that the ILO: (1) establish an international service for exchange of information and experience regarding vocational guidance and training; (2) collect and disseminate data on manpower available and required, making every effort to render interchangeable the occupational nomenclatures of the different countries and to improve methods of compiling manpower statistics; (3) draft minimum standards for migration in Europe; and (4) take all other necessary action to accelerate manpower movements between European countries.

The Director General of the ILO pointed out that the proposed work is in fact within the normal sphere of activity of the ILO. He stressed its immediate and urgent character and expressed the view that the organization should not be too formalistic about it. The Governing Body unanimously decided to accede to the requests made by the Manpower Subcommittee of the Economic

---

[3] The official deposit of the thirty-seventh ratification occurred on Apr. 20, 1948. The constitution of the International Labor Organization instrument of amendment, 1946, is, therefore, now in effect.

II. *Representing the Employers of the United States*

DELEGATE

J. David Zellerbach, President, Crown Zellerbach Corporation, San Francisco

III. *Representing the Workers of the United States*

DELEGATE

Frank P. Fenton, International Representative, AF of L, Washington

The delegation also will include a staff comprising the following:

Advisers

G. Russell Bauer, Field Representative, Wage and Hour and Public Contracts Divisions, Department of Labor, Chicago

Clara M. Beyer, Associate Director, Bureau of Labor Standards, Department of Labor

Anna F. Blackburn, Principal Attorney, Office of the Solicitor, Department of Labor

Millard Cass, Special Assistant to the Under Secretary of Labor, Department of Labor

L. Wendell Hayes, Specialist in International Organization Affairs, Office of United Nations Affairs, Department of State

Harry A. Jager, Chief, Occupational Information and Guidance Service, Office of Education, Federal Security Agency

Rachel F. Nyswander, Labor Economist, Women's Bureau, Department of Labor

Charles Sattler, Commissioner, West Virginia State Department of Labor, Charleston, W. Va.

Collis Stocking, Assistant Director for Program Policy, U.S. Employment Service, Department of Labor

Oscar Weigert, Chief of Section, Foreign Labor Conditions Staff, Bureau of Labor Statistics, Department of Labor

Aryness Joy Wickens, Assistant Commissioner for Program Operations, Bureau of Labor Statistics, Department of Labor

Bernard Wiesman, Division of International Labor, Social and Health Affairs, Department of State

Special Assistant to Head of Delegation

Edith G. Boyer, Administrative Assistant to the Under Secretary of Labor, Department of Labor

Representing the Employers of the United States

ADVISERS:

William B. Barton, in charge of Labor Relations, U.S. Chamber of Commerce, Washington

Miss L. E. Ebeling, Director of Personnel, Sherwin Williams Paint Company, Cleveland

Carroll French, Director of Research, Department of Industrial Relations, National Association of Manufacturers, New York City

M. M. Olander, Director of Industrial Relations, Owens-Illinois Glass Company, Toledo

Maitland S. Pennington, Office of the Vice President, Pacific Transport Lines, Inc., San Francisco

H. M. Ramel, Vice President, Ramsey Corporation, St. Louis

Thomas R. Reid, Vice President, Human Relations, McCormick and Company, Inc., Baltimore

Charles E. Shaw, Manager, Industrial Relations, Standard Oil Company of New Jersey, New York City

James Tanham, Vice President, The Texas Company, New York City

Representing the Workers of the United States

ADVISERS:

Dave Beck, Representative, International Brotherhood

773

of Teamsters, Chauffeurs, Warehousemen, and
Helpers, Seattle
Nelson Cruikshank, Director of Social Security Activi-
ties, American Federation of Labor, Washington
C. W. Doyle, Secretary, Seattle Central Labor Union,
Seattle
H. W. Fraser, President, Order of Railway Conductors
of America, Cedar Rapids, Iowa
C. J. Haggerty, Secretary, California State Federation of
Labor, San Francisco
Bert M. Jewell, Representative, Railway Labor Execu-
tives Association, Washington
George Meany, Secretary-Treasurer, American Federa-
tion of Labor, Washington
Rose Schneiderman, President, Women's Trade Union
League, New York City
Serafino Romualdi, Secretary, International Relations,
Inter-American Confederation of Workers, Wash-
ington
John F. Shelley, President, San Francisco Central Labor
Council, San Francisco
E. M. Weston, President, Washington State Federation
of Labor, Seattle

Secretary of the United States Delegation

Millard L. Kenestrick, Division of International Conferences, Department of State

The agenda for the Thirty-first Session includes
the following items: (1) the Director General's
report; (2) financial and budgetary questions; (3)
reports on the application of conventions; (4) consideration of the adoption of one convention and
one recommendation providing for national employment services and consideration of the adoption of a convention revising the convention on fee-
charging employment agencies adopted by the
Conference in 1933; (5) preliminary consideration
of the question of vocational guidance with a view
to framing international standards at the 1949
session; (6) wages, including questions of wage
policy, fair-wage clauses in public contracts, and
the protection of wages; (7) consideration of a
convention to safeguard freedom of association
of workers and employers and to protect their
right to organize; (8) the question of industrial
relations, including the application of the principles of the right to organize and bargain collectively, collective agreements, conciliation and
arbitration, and cooperation between the public
authorities and employers' and workers' organizations; (9) consideration of a convention partially
revising the night-work (women) convention,
1919, and the night-work (women) convention (revised), 1934; (10) consideration of a convention
partially revising the night work of young persons
(industry) convention, 1919; (11) substitution of
the provisions of the night-work (women) convention (revised), 1934, and of the night work of
young persons (industry) convention, 1919, contained in the schedule to the labor-standards (nonmetropolitan territories) convention, 1947, for the
corresponding provisions of the conventions proposed under items (9) and (10) above; and (12)
approval of an annex to the convention on the
privileges and immunities of the specialized agen-

ting of the Second Assembly of ICAO

STATEMENT BY THE CHAIRMAN OF THE U.S. DELEGATION [1]

[Released to the press June 2]

, President: The United States of America it least four main opportunities for this sec- ssembly to promote the sound growth of inter- nal civil aviation.

rst, there is the opportunity which exists for evelopment of wider and deeper mutual un- andings and friendships. The International Aviation Organization now has a member- of 48 contracting states. This assembly, fore, constitutes a large gathering—a large n—of the nations of the world.

the work of the assembly, my Government s that each delegation present will contribute lly to the discussion and solution of the prob- presented. Only by such widespread and)cratic participation can we come to appre- each other's individual problems. And only ich appreciation—and by a tempering where- possible of the firmness of our respective posi- —can we define sound common objectives and lately reach agreements which all of us can ort with conviction and enthusiasm.

cond, the assembly provides the opportunity he full membership of ICAO to review and to nent constructively on the work of the Council,)mmittees, and the secretariat over the past . This is especially important to non-Council ber states. Benefit to all member states is the :tive of the organization as reflected in the isions of the convention. And at this meet- ill member states have not only the oppor- y but the obligation to comment upon all the : of ICAO in its first year of operation.

the opinion of the United States, much of the rtant work of the organization has progressed what slowly through the Council over the year. For example, it must be a source of it to all of us that today, despite the excellent : done by the technical divisions, and despite irgent recommendation of the first assembly,)ne ICAO standard or recommended practice yet in force under article 90 of the convention. 7 Government believes that the assembly ld place increasing emphasis upon the effi- y and effectiveness of the existing organiza- and its present activities. Expansion by the ably and the Council either of the organiza-)r the scope of its activities at this time would se us to the serious risk of simply broadening rea of possible inefficiency and ineffectiveness. does not mean that we must shun new prob- of importance. It means simply that a

happy balance must be struck between the urgency of undertaking new projects and the necessity of pressing forward vigorously with those of greater or equal importance upon which we have already embarked. In striking this balance, we must re- member that there is no virtue in providing a program of ideal scope without reasonable assur- ance of positive accomplishment.

Third, the United States delegation believes that in its deliberations, the assembly should be keenly conscious of the fact that its function is one of policy-making. Its opportunity to make policy will be gravely impaired if it allows itself to be distracted by details of administration. Techno- logical and economic developments will continue to change the detailed pattern of the international civil aviation picture. We would be ill-advised here to attempt to formulate minute and inflexible instructions to the Council on all the phases of ICAO's work in the year ahead. The assembly should establish sound and broad policies. The Council, in its executive actions, should implement those policies in detail for the benefit of all mem- ber states.

Fourth, it is the important privilege of this sec- ond assembly to arrive at final agreement on a con- vention on international recognition of rights in aircraft. The United States believes that the adoption and ratification by member states of this convention is urgently required to serve the pub- lic interest by providing means whereby operators of aircraft can obtain equipment so essential to a full realization of the potentialities of interna- tional air commerce. The need for such a treaty has long been pressing. Surely the many years of study by CITEJA plus the thorough review and redrafting performed by the ICAO Legal Committee at its Brussels meeting last October should insure that the legal commission will report for adoption a workable and mutually satisfactory document which can be approved in Geneva by all states represented.

The President of the United States of America has provided me with full powers to act for him in signing such a convention. We earnestly hope that this convention can be completed at this as- sembly and submitted for ratification.

These four main lines of action which I have dis- cussed provide us with opportunities for real achievement at this assembly. If we seek other

---

[1] Russell B. Adams. Made at the opening meeting at Geneva on June 1, 1948.

opportunities, we should remember that nations sometimes display wisdom not only in what they do but also in what they refrain from doing. We shall make a wise decision if we do not undertake now a revision of the organization's basic charter. That should wait at least until 1950. Not the trappings of form and procedure but good faith and intelligence, applied in a spirit of cooperation, constitute the ingredients of all achievement. Several years of operating experience are required to provide us with the wisdom for taking the important step of revision of the fundamentals of our mutual undertakings in the convention.

One last word. As we put aside from day to day the work of the assembly, I hope that we may all become better known to each other. Let us not spend all our energy at the formal conference table. Our delegation hopes to have the time to form personal friendships as well as official acquaintanceships. Thus all of us can acquire friendly understandings of differing viewpoints which will redound to the mutual advantage of all countries and of the organization throughout the year ahead. More than that, and however unconsciously, we shall be building a better world, knitted closer together by the bonds of personal friendship and understanding.

U.S. DELEGATE TO PROTECTION OF CHILDHOOD MEETING

[Released to the press June 3]

The Department of State announced on June 3 the designation of Elizabeth Munro Clarke, Child Welfare Consultant, Children's Bureau, Social Security Administration, Federal Security Agency, as United States Alternate Technical Delegate to the regular annual meeting of the Council of the American International Institute for the Protection of Childhood. The meeting is scheduled to convene on June 5, 1948, at Montevideo, Uruguay.

The agenda for this meeting of the Council includes: (1) consideration of the annual report of the Director of the Institute; (2) review of the resolutions and recommendations of the Ninth Pan American Child Congress, held at Caracas, Venezuela, January 1948; (3) consideration of the future development of the Institute in the light of the resolutions of the Ninth International Conference of American States, held at Bogotá, Colombia, March-April 1948; and (4) consultation concerning article 9 of the statutes of the Institute, which deals with representation of member states.

The Council, composed of representatives of the 19 member states (Haiti and Nicaragua are not members of the Council), directs the activities of the American International Institute for the Protection of Childhood. The Institute was established with headquarters at Montevideo in accord-

Carl Z. Berry, Lt. Col., M.C., U.S.A., Assistant Military Attaché for Medicine, American Embassy, London
John W. Regan, Lt. Col., M.C., U.S.A., Chief, Environmental Sanitation Branch, Office of the Surgeon General, Department of the Army

The Congress is being organized by the Institut Pasteur under the patronage of the President of the Republic of France and members of the French Government. Its purpose is to commemorate the application of B.C.G. vaccine to mankind and to estimate the scope of its use in different countries. The meeting will also celebrate the fiftieth anniversary of the establishment of the Institut Pasteur at Lille, France. The Institut was founded by Dr. Albert Calmette and is the scene of his main research in cooperation with Dr. Camille Guérin on B.C.G. vaccine.

'Aid From America"—*Continued from page 757*

he went he encountered bows, salutes, hand-clapping, or cheers; photographers walked backward snapping shutters as he approached; no one was permitted to precede him into a building or room. The hotels of Ragusa were not suitable, he was told, to shelter him, and he was therefore lodged, wined, and dined by the prefect in a modern and magnificient governor's palace whose ballroom walls were inscribed with quotations from Mussolini's speeches and decorated with a 30-foot portrait of Il Duce and another of the late King, both covered with paper.

The weeks before the national elections on April 18 and 19 were marked by economic paralysis, tenseness, some violence, and fear for the future. But when the voting took place, throughout the peninsula and the islands an unexpected calm prevailed. Naples was if anything quieter than on a normal Sunday; the atmosphere was somewhat festive and casually cheerful. There was much less evidence of police and *carabinieri* activities than during the previous 10 days. Balloon sellers did their usual business; fishermen peacefully mended their nets; sleeping figures topped the sea wall; sailboats and racing shells dotted the bay; the crowds turned out for their regular Sunday-evening *corso;* and the restaurants served nothing stronger than mineral water.

Immediately after the elections a great feeling of relief and much greater confidence in the future were evident. One of the great issues of the campaign had been settled: "Aid From America" was necessary, it was understood and appreciated, and it was welcome.

THE RECORD OF THE WEEK

Agreement of London Conference on German

Statement by the Department of State

[Released to the press June 2]

The Department of State is gratified that agreement has been reached on all points of substance at the London conference on Germany. In addition to his many other tasks, Ambassador Douglas represented the United States as chief delegate during the long and arduous sessions which lasted almost six weeks, and he did a masterful job in contributing to the successful conclusion reached. The conference results will be submitted as agreed recommendations to the respective governments for their approval. The delegations are putting the finishing touches to their report to their governments, and it is understood that a more complete announcement will be made shortly. Until this information is officially available, the Department is unable to add anything further to the brief communiqué issued at London except to express the hope that the governments themselves will be able to agree at an early date to the program drawn up at London, which seems to offer the prospect

of constructive achievement in solving the problems facing us in Germany.

Communiqué Issued by U.S., U.K., France Belgium, Netherlands, Luxembourg

[Released to the press June 2]

June 2, 1948

The informal discussions on Germany between Representatives of the United States, United Kingdom, France and the three Benelux countries, which began in London on February 23 and which, after a recess beginning on March 6, were resumed on the 20th of April, have resulted in agreements on the items discussed. Agreed recommendations over the whole field are being submitted for approval to the Governments concerned, as envisaged in the communiqué issued on March 6. A report of these recommendations will shortly be made public.

U.S.S.R. Urged To Give Views on Return of Free Territory of Trieste to Italy

Note From Secretary Marshall to the Soviet Ambassador [1]

[Released to the press June 1]

June 1, 1948

The Secretary of State presents his compliments to His Excellency the Ambassador of the Union of Soviet Socialist Republics and has the honor to refer to his note of April 16, 1948 regarding the proposal that the Free Territory of Trieste be returned to Italian sovereignty.[2] In that note the Soviet Government was informed that the Government of the United States would welcome any suggestions which the Soviet Government might desire to propose concerning the procedure for

drafting the necessary protocol to the Treaty of Peace with Italy to effect the return of the Free Territory to Italian sovereignty.

As the Government of the United States is convinced that the protection of the rights and interests of the people of the Free Territory require the very early resolution of the problem, it is hoped that the Soviet Government will communicate its views at an early date concerning the procedure to be followed for the joint consideration of the matter by the powers concerned.

[1] Alexander S. Panyushkin is the Soviet Ambassador the United States.

[2] BULLETIN of Apr. 25, 1948, p. 549. See also BULLETIN of Apr. 4, 1948, p. 453, and Apr. 18, 1948, p. 522.

THE UNITED STATES AND TURKEY

As you know, my Government desires to co-operate with the United States, and with the other countries participating in a joint recovery program to effectuate the purposes of this program. I am, accordingly, authorized to inform you that my Government adheres to the purposes and policies of the Economic Cooperation Act of 1948, which are stated in the whole of subsection 102(b) and in subsection 102(a) respectively, and which the Act as a whole is designed to carry out.

My Government has taken careful note of the provisions of subsection 115(b) of the Act, and intends to conclude an agreement with your Government pursuant to that subsection. It is my Government's understanding that the details of the applicability to Turkey of paragraphs (1) through (10) of subsection 115(b) will be covered in the discussions of the terms of this agreement. My country is already acting consistently with the provisions of subsection 115(b) that are applicable to it, and is engaged in continuous efforts to accomplish a joint recovery program through multilateral undertakings and the establishment of a continuing organization for this purpose. I join in the hope that negotiations for the conclusion of the agreement between our two countries may be started soon.

Please accept [etc.] HUSEYIN RAGIP BAYDUR

Transportation Survey To Be Conducted in Greece

[Released to the press June 5]

A comprehensive transportation survey is scheduled to start in Greece the middle of June. The survey is designed to determine the need and priority for rehabilitation and development of the Greek rail and highway systems, coastal shipping, and civil aviation. The survey, which was requested by the Greek Government, will be carried out jointly by the American Mission for Aid to Greece and the Economic Cooperation Administration. American and Greek transport experts will conduct the survey.

Results of the survey are expected to provide a guide to determining the best types of transport to assure efficient distribution of commodities and at the same time provide a transport system which the Greeks will be able to support and maintain. Emphasis will be placed on the cost of transportation, particularly as its development and rehabilitation are related to contributions from United States aid sources. Consideration will also be given rail and highway transport necessary to enable Greece to maintain international connections with other European countries. Agricultural areas still undeveloped or now served by inadequate transportation will be studied with a

U.S. Views Lebanese Detention of Ameri of Principles of International Law

[Released to the press May 30]

Upon instruction of the Department of State, the United States Minister to Lebanon, Lowell C. Pinkerton, on May 29, delivered a formal note of protest to the Lebanese Foreign Office.[1] The note informed the Lebanese Government that this Government considers the grounds for the detention of the Americans taken from the SS *Marine Carp* unsatisfactory. The note stated that so far as the United States Government has been advised, Lebanese authorities do not purport to have acted under the authority of any law or legal process of Lebanon; the Lebanese Government has made

Supplemental Appropriation for Surp for Extending Credit to Iran

[Released to the press May 28]

A subcommittee of the Senate Appropriations Committee, under the chairmanship of Senator Styles Bridges, on May 28 opened hearings on a request by the President, on the recommendation of the Secretary of State, for a supplemental appropriation for the care, handling, and disposal of surplus property abroad. The requested appropriation was for $19,155,000, of which $15,675,000 is designed to cover the cost of repairing, packaging, and shipping surplus military equipment to be sold to Iran.

As stated by representatives of the Department of State and the Department of the Army before the Senate Subcommittee on May 28, the appropriation is requested in order to enable the Foreign Liquidation Commissioner to extend credit to the Iranian Government up to the amount specified for expenses which would be incurred in connection with the sale to Iran of certain items of surplus military equipment needed by the Iranian Army and *gendarmerie* to maintain internal secu-

---

[1] Not printed.

to Iran does not differ in any way from numerous other sales of surplus material to other countries, except that in this particular case the Iranian Government finds itself unable to pay in cash dollars the costs involved in delivery of the equipment in question. The negotiations have been carried out in routine fashion, and each important step has been made public both in the United States and Iran. In this connection, reference is made to the Department's press releases 304 of April 10, 1947, and 509 of June 20, 1947.[1] The objective of the Iranian Government in seeking these supplies, as announced in those press releases, has been to re-equip the Iranian Army and *gendarmerie* in order to maintain internal security in Iran. The equipment of both forces is at present below standard because they have been unable to obtain adequate replacements since the outbreak of World War II. In the light of the declaration of Tehran of December 1, 1943, in which the United States, Great Britain, and the Soviet Union declared their desire for the maintenance of the sovereignty, independence, and territorial integrity of Iran, and in view of the interest of the United States in the maintenance of security in the Middle East, the Department of State considers it in the interest of the United States as well as of Iran to meet the request of the Iranian Government.

Mixed Nationality Commission in Poland

American citizenship who had been arrested by Polish authorities.

The United States Government regrets that none of these objectives has been accomplished. No citizenship cases have been determined and American consular representatives have not been allowed to visit persons under arrest who claim United States citizenship. The already difficult work of the Commission was further complicated when the Polish Foreign Office on April 12 notified the American Embassy of a recently evolved official interpretation of the Polish nationality law wherein the Polish Government takes the position that all persons born abroad of Polish parents are Polish citizens exclusively, regardless of date of birth. Previously the Polish Government had held that only those children born abroad of Polish parents subsequent to the promulgation of the Polish nationality law of January 31, 1920, would be considered to possess Polish citizenship exclusively.

The United States reserves the exclusive right to determine the validity of claims of any persons to United States citizenship and does not admit the right of any other government to decide this question. It will therefore continue to press vig-

---

[1] BULLETIN of July 6, 1948, p. 47.

orously through diplomatic channels for its rights in this regard as well as for the right to interview and protect the interests of claimants to American citizenship who are under arrest in Poland.

American citizens of Polish parentage who are contemplating trips to Poland are advised to consider carefully the new Polish interpretation of Polish nationality law and the possible difficulties which might be encountered in returning to the United States.

U.S. Ships To Proceed to Weather Stations in Canadian Arctic Waters

[Released to the press June 4]

Three United States ships—a Navy icebreaker, a Coast Guard icebreaker, and a Navy cargo ship—will proceed to Canadian Arctic waters this summer to resupply the existing weather stations which, as previously announced,[1] have been jointly established there by the Canadian and United States Governments, and to reconnoiter sites for further weather stations to be jointly installed next year. Canadian representatives will participate in the expedition.

The ships will be commanded by Capt. George J. Dufek, United States Navy, embarked in the U.S.S. *Edisto*, icebreaker. Other vessels participating in the cruise will be the U.S.C.G. *Eastwind*, icebreaker, and the U.S.S. *Wyandot*, cargo vessel.

The primary purpose of the expedition is the resupply of the four weather stations that have been established at Slidre Fjord, Eureka Sound; Resolute Bay, Cornwallis Island; southeastern Prince Patrick Island; and the Isachsen Peninsula, Ellef Ringnes Island. Its secondary purpose is such icebreaker reconnaissance as is practicable in nearby areas in which the Canadian and United States authorities plan to establish two further weather stations in 1949.

Helicopters carried aboard the vessels will make short-range flights to assist in navigation through the ice pack.

The *Edisto* will be commanded by Commander E. C. Folger, United States Navy; the *Wyandot* by Capt. J. D. Dickey, United States Navy; and the *Eastwind* by Capt. J. A. Flynn, U.S. Coast Guard.

Fulbright Grant Awarded Yale Professor

The Department of State announced on June 3 that Dr. John Langdon Brooks, instructor in zoology, Osborne Zoological Laboratory, Yale University, has been selected by the Board of Foreign Scholarships for an award under the Fulbright act to serve as a visiting professor of fresh-water biology at the University of Rangoon in Burma.

---

[1] BULLETIN of July 13, 1947, p. 82.

of October 30, 1947—Signed at Geneva October 30, 1947; entered into force October 30, 1947, effective January 1, 1948.

12th Report to Congress on Operations of UNRRA; Under the Act of March 28, 1944, as of June 30, 1947. Pub. 3111. iii, 56 pp. 20¢.

The President's report, including the supply program, health and welfare services, displaced-persons operation, administration, amount of U.S. contribution, and over-all operation of program.

Selected Publications and Materials Relating to American Foreign Policy, April 1948. Pub. 3130. iv, 23 pp. Free.

Lists Department publications on the Department and the Foreign Service, U.S. foreign policy as a whole, United Nations, peace, economic reconstruction, reciprocal trade, U.S. policy in occupied areas, refugees and displaced persons, Europe, Near and Far East, and American republics.

United Nations Conference on Freedom of Information, Geneva, Switzerland; March 23–April 21, 1948. International Organization and Conference Series III, 5. Pub. 3150. 45 pp. 15¢.

Report of U.S. Delegates, with related documents, including final act, General Assembly resolutions on measures to be taken against propaganda and the inciters of a new war, and list of U.S. Delegates.

Strengthening the United Nations. International Organization and Conference Series III, 6. Pub. 3159. 10 pp. 10¢.

Reprinted from BULLETIN of May 16, 1948. Statement made by Secretary Marshall before the House Foreign Affairs Committee on May 5, 1948, outlining the views of the State Department on the structure of the United Nations and the relationship of the Government to the United Nations.

Durand Smith, author of the article on foreign-relief operations in Italy, is a Foreign Service Staff officer and was an attaché of the American Embassy in Rome from July 22, 1947, to May 7, 1948, serving as a field observer of the United States Foreign Aid Mission to Italy.

Louis J. Halle, Jr., author of the article on cooperative agricultural programs of the Institute of Inter-American Affairs, is Special Assistant to the Director of the Office of American Republic Affairs, Department of State, and is also a member of the Board of Directors of the Institute.

Leonard B. Ellis, author of the article on the international rice meeting, is Rice Commodity Specialist, Production and Marketing Administration, Department of Agriculture. Mr. Ellis was head of the U.S. Delegation to the international rice meeting.

The Department of State bulletin

Vol. XVIII, No. 468 • Publication 3187

June 20, 1948

The Department of State BULLETIN, a weekly publication compiled and edited in the Division of Publications, Office of Public Affairs, provides the public and interested agencies of the Government with information on developments in the field of foreign relations and on the work of the Department of State and the Foreign Service. The BULLETIN includes press releases on foreign policy issued by the White House and the Department, and statements and addresses made by the President and by the Secretary of State and other officers of the Department, as well as special articles on various phases of international affairs and the functions of the Department. Information is included concerning treaties and international agreements to which the United States is or may become a party and treaties of general international interest.

Publications of the Department, as well as legislative material in the field of international relations, are listed currently.

For sale by the Superintendent of Documents
U.S. Government Printing Office
Washington 25, D.C.

SUBSCRIPTION:
52 issues, $5; single copy, 15 cents

Published with the approval of the Director of the Bureau of the Budget

DANUBE

L. Hadsel

the lower part of the river. At the same time, Austria and Great Britain became more and more concerned with navigation conditions on the Danube, since their commercial interests in the Balkans were expanding. The Austrian Government had given a monopoly of traffic within its domain to a semiofficial navigation company and by diplomatic efforts sought to obtain navigation rights for this firm both on the upper Danube and at the mouth of the river. The British trade to the Black Sea ports of the Danube increased approximately sixfold during the years between the treaty of Adrianople and the Crimean War. Both Great Britain and Austria were therefore concerned when Russia, on the one hand, imposed quarantine measures and tolls which helped Russian trade from the competing Black Sea port of Odessa and, on the other hand, neglected the channel of the Danube so that sand bars and other obstacles made navigation extremely hazardous. On the eve of the Crimean War the European nations were thus faced with the fact that although Russia did not deny legal right of entry, the Government in St. Petersburg made shipping difficult on the Danube.[4]

The treaty of Paris at the end of the Crimean War made provision both to remove the physical obstacles to traffic on the Danube and to eliminate discrimination in favor of the ships of any one nation. Article XVII provided for the establishment of a commission of riparian states, composed of Austria, Bavaria, Turkey, Württemberg, and the Danubian principalities to regulate traffic and

---

[1] Edward Hertslet, *Map of Europe by Treaty* (London, 1875–1891), vol. I, p. 270.
[2] Arts. XV to XIX of the treaty of Paris, Mar. 30, 1856, *ibid.*, vol. II, p. 1257.
[3] *Documents and State Papers*, July 1948.
[4] Joseph P. Chamberlain, *The Danube* (Department of State House Inquiry Handbooks, 1918, no. 5), pp. 17–24.

remove obstacles to commerce throughout the course of the river. Austria, however, sought to use this commission as an instrument for establishing its ascendancy on the Danube and as a means for nullifying the provision for freedom of navigation for all countries. The other parties to the treaty of Paris, particularly Great Britain, protested this policy, and the proposed commission never came into existence.[5]

The treaty of Paris also provided for the creation of a second commission, in which Great Britain, Austria, France, Prussia, Russia, Sardinia, and Turkey would participate, for the purpose of clearing the mouth of the Danube of sand bars and other impediments to navigation. In contrast to the riparian commission, this body, which became known as the European Commission, began functioning immediately and with a large measure of success. By 1861, for example, it had cleared and improved the mouth of the middle channel of the Danubian delta, the Sulina arm. It found, however, that navigation was also impeded by the lack of police and port administration. As a result, the European Commission assumed, with the approval of the member governments, police and regulatory powers. These powers were confirmed by the Public Act of 1865.

The European Commission continued as a temporary body until the treaty of London in 1883, at which time its life was extended for 21 years, with provision for further extension unless one of the contracting parties should object. In the meantime, the powers of the Commission were strengthened by the treaty of Berlin in 1878 and the Public Act of 1881. The Commission was given greater regulatory powers and a flag of its own, and its jurisdiction was extended upstream to the city of Galati. The principle was generally recognized, moreover, that fiscal charges should not exceed a reasonable contribution to the maintenance and improvement of the river.

The London treaty of 1883, in addition to giving the European Commission a semipermanent status, also further defined its powers. The northern branch of the Danubian delta, the Chilia arm, was taken from under the Commission's direct jurisdiction, and Russia and Rumania were authorized to exercise control over that part of the

---

[5] *Ibid.*, pp. 33–34.
[6] Art. 24. For text see Georges Kaeckenbeeck, *International Rivers* (London, 1920), pp. 63–64.

dom, Greece, Italy, Rumania, Yugoslavia, Czechoslovakia, Germany, Austria, Bulgaria, and Hungary, became the basis of the international regulation of the Danube during the interwar years.[8] The statute reaffirmed the principle of freedom of navigation on the Danube and defined the river system to be under international authority.[9] The statute also stated that the European Commission, composed provisionally of France, Great Britain, Italy, and Rumania, should retain the powers it possessed before the war. The authority of the European Commission should extend over the maritime Danube, and its powers could be terminated only by an international agreement concluded by all of the states represented on the Commission.

The statute of 1921 created a new regime for the fluvial Danube, the International Commission, thus bringing to fruition a development of over 75 years in the direction of regulating Danubian commerce for the benefit of all nations. The International Commission, composed, in accordance with the peace treaties, of two German representatives, one representative of each of the other riparian states, and the members of the European Commission, was entrusted with supervision of the Danube from Ulm to Braila. It was responsible for seeing (1) that no obstacles were interposed to unrestricted navigation on the river, (2) that navigation dues were levied in a nondiscriminatory fashion and only for the improvement of commerce, and (3) that tolls and taxes of riparian states were levied without distinction of flag and in such a manner as to cause no hindrance to navigation. The International Commission was also charged with drawing up a program of works to be carried out in the interests of navigability of the river system. This program, executed and paid for by the riparian states, would be super-

---

[7] Treaty of Versailles, June 28, 1919, arts. 327, 331–353; treaty of Saint-Germain, Sept. 10, 1919, arts. 290–308; treaty of Neuilly-sur-Seine, Nov. 27, 1919, arts. 218–235; and treaty of Trianon, June 4, 1920, arts. 274–291.
[8] Great Britain, Foreign Office, Treaty Series, 1922, no. 16.
[9] The system was defined as including the Danube from Ulm to the Black Sea; the Morava and Thaya where they formed the frontier between Austria and Czechoslovakia; the Drave from Barcs; the Tisza from the mouth of the Szamos; the Maros from Arad; and all lateral canals or waterways which might be constructed.

vised by the International Commission. Cabotage, the transport of goods and passengers between two or more ports in the same state, was unrestricted.

The International Commission was authorized to establish such administrative, technical, sanitary, and financial services as it considered necessary. Its headquarters for the first five years at least was to be located at Bratislava. The Commission was also empowered to establish in conjunction with Rumania and Yugoslavia a special administration for the Iron Gates and cataracts on the Danube between Turnu-Severin and Moldova.[10]

For the first time a system of international administration participated in by both riparian and nonriparian states was in effect on the entire navigable course of the Danube. The results of this broad participation were apparent during the interwar years, when the efforts of the two Commissions comprising this system to maintain freedom of navigation met with a large measure of success. Along the upper course, blasting and dredging operations deepened and straightened the channel to accommodate large vessels. In the middle Danube, canals shortened the river where it meanders across the plainland of northern Yugoslavia. At the Iron Gates, blasting and construction projects facilitated traffic. In the delta, the Sulina arm was further dredged, additional breakwaters built, and other aids to navigation constructed. In the peak year of 1936 over ten million tons were reported to have been moved upon the river by the Danube fleets, and on the eve of

[10] This special administration was set up in 1932, by an agreement relating to the setting up of special services at the Iron Gates, with annexes and full protocol signed at Semmering June 28, 1932. See League of Nations Treaty Series, vol. 140, pp. 191–227.

[11] Permanent Court of International Justice. Series B. Advisory Opinion No. 14. *Jurisdiction of the European Commission of the Danube between Galatz and Braila* (Leyden, 1927), pp. 68–71.

[12] Great Britain, Foreign Office, Treaty Series, 1939, no. 38.

[13] *Ibid.*, no. 37.

[14] Provisional arrangement regarding the Danube regime between Germany, Bulgaria, Hungary, Italy, Rumania, Slovakia, and Yugoslavia, signed at Vienna, Sept. 12, 1940. This agreement also provided for a special committee composed of Germany, Rumania, and Yugoslavia to take over the administration of the Iron Gates established by the agreement at Semmering of June 28, 1932.

As World War II drew to a close, the Soviet Union assumed a dominant role in Danubian affairs. Not only did Soviet troops occupy the area from the Black Sea to the Soviet zone of Austria, but the armistice agreements signed with Rumania, Bulgaria, and Hungary gave the Soviet High Command control of shipping facilities on large sections of the river.[18] Soviet control of the bulk of the Danubian fleets and port facilities was perpetuated through the formation of joint shipping companies with Rumania in July 1945, Hungary in March 1946, and Yugoslavia in March 1947. These companies, in which the Soviet Union obtained a decisive voice, were granted special privileges, such as freedom from taxes and preferential treatment in obtaining foreign exchange, and were also potentially empowered to monopolize loading, repair, and fuel facilities on the river. At the end of the war the Soviet Union also organized a special company within its zone of Austria, which though primarily military was also engaged in commercial shipping on the Danube.

During 1945–46 the United States made several attempts to open up navigation on at least part of the Danube. One of the first efforts was a proposal submitted to the Berlin (Potsdam) conference of July–August 1945, in which the Danube, as well as other waterways of Europe, would be opened in order to hasten European recovery. This proposal was not accepted at this conference nor at the first session of the Council of Foreign Ministers from September 11 to October 2, 1945. The United States next sought action by the Allied Control Council for Austria and pressed in January 1946 for open navigation on the Danube throughout Austria. The question was again raised in May and in August, but the Soviet Union refused to permit navigation be-

---

[15] Moscow *News*, Sept. 19, 1940.

[16] U.S.S.R. communiqué of Oct. 26, 1940.

[17] Moscow *News*, Nov. 4, 1940, p. 24.

[18] Armistice with Rumania, Sept. 12, 1944, in Bulletin of Sept. 17, 1944, pp. 289–292; Armistice with Bulgaria, Oct. 28, 1944, *ibid.*, Oct. 29, 1944, pp. 492–494; and Armistice with Hungary, Jan. 20, 1945, *ibid.*, Jan. 21, 1945, pp. 83–86. For problems of postwar shipping, see also Doris S. Whitnack and David Handler, "Danubian Transportation Problems in Relation to Development of the Basin", *ibid.*, June 30, 1946, pp. 1108–1110.

tween its zone and the rest of Austria.[19] The United States also sought to obtain freedom of navigation of the Danube by action through the United Nations, and on October 3, 1946, the Economic and Social Council passed a resolution introduced by the United States in favor of convening a conference in Vienna to consider ways of opening navigation on the Danube. When, however, the Secretary-General of the United Nations ascertained that many of the nations concerned with the Danube, including the Soviet Union, would refuse to attend, the conference was not held.[20]

In the meantime, the United States had made a sustained effort throughout 1946 to obtain recognition of freedom of navigation on the Danube in the treaties of peace with the former Axis satellites, Bulgaria, Rumania, and Hungary. The United States Delegation went to the Paris session of the Council of Foreign Ministers, which opened April 25, 1946, with the hope of inserting provisions in the satellite treaties insuring (1) freedom of commerce, (2) reasonable sanitation and police regulations, (3) removal of obstacles in the main channel of the river, (4) nondiscriminatory tolls, and (5) equal status for the ex-enemy countries in any temporary or permanent regime. The Soviet Union, however, opposed any mention of freedom of navigation in the treaties with Bulgaria, Hungary, and Rumania on the grounds that it would impair the sovereignty of these countries and that Yugoslavia and Czechoslovakia should be consulted. The head of the American Delegation, Secretary of State Byrnes, countered with a compromise proposal: that only a declaration of freedom of navigation should be inserted in the treaties. The United Kingdom, while supporting the position of the United States, declared that it also favored convocation of a conference to regulate commerce on the Danube. The United Kingdom, having a direct commercial interest in Danubian shipping and having been a member

---

[19] Allied Council, Minutes, 14th Meeting, Jan. 22, 1946, and Allied Commission for Austria, Executive Committee, Minutes of the 52d Meeting, Aug. 16, 1946.

[20] U.N. doc. E/254, Jan. 28, 1947.

[21] BULLETIN of Oct. 13, 1946, p. 656.

[22] Paris Peace Conference, 1946: Selected Documents (Department of State publication 2868), p. 818.

states: the Soviet Union, the Ukrainian S.S.R., Bulgaria, Rumania, Yugoslavia, Hungary, and Czechoslovakia. Any changes in the resulting convention should take place at a conference composed of these nations. Austria should take part in the above-mentioned conference after the question of the treaty with Austria had been settled.[24]

V. Background of the Conference on the Danube

Prior to the expiration of the six-month period after the Balkan peace treaties came into force, the United States, in a note of February 27, 1948, to the Soviet Union, the United Kingdom, and France, reaffirmed its desire for a conference but suggested the time for calling the conference be extended until the end of 1948 in order to allow the Austrian Government to participate on a basis of equality. This was on the assumption that representatives of the Four Powers, whose talks were just getting under way at that time in London, would make genuine progress towards settling the Austrian treaty. France and the United Kingdom, in notes respectively of March 12 and 13, stated their approval of the American suggestion. The Soviet Union, however, rejected, in its reply of March 15 the suggestion that the time for calling the conference be extended and proposed that the conference be convened in Belgrade not later than April or May.

The United States agreed on April 12 to the holding of the conference at Belgrade as soon as practicable. The United States also stated that in view of the general desire to begin discussions on the Danube, it assumed that the Soviet Union was prepared to discuss practical arrangements to give effect to freedom of navigation on the Danube in the Soviet zone of occupation or where the river was used as a Soviet line of communication. In the same reply, the United States restated its view that "because of Austria's recognized position as an important riparian," the Austrian Government should participate in the conference. The message also referred to the principle of freedom of navigation incorporated in the treaties of peace with Bulgaria, Rumania, and Hungary, and suggested an exchange of views among the Four Powers concerning preliminary arrangements for the conference. In its reply of May 8, the Soviet Union, however, rejected the proposal for an informal exchange of views, remained adamant on exclud-

(*Continued on page 797*)

Cease-Fire and Truce Proposals Submitted to Jewish and Arab States

NOTE FROM U.N. MEDIATOR IN PALESTINE TO THE ARAB STATES AND THE PROVISIONAL GOVERNMENT OF ISRAEL [1]

June 7, 1948

1. I have the honour to inform you that, in pursuance of the action of the Security Council at its 311th meeting, 2 June, authorizing the Mediator to fix the effective date for the truce in Palestine, and following extensive consultations on this matter with representatives of the two parties, and with the support of the Truce Commission, I herewith give formal notice of the effective date and hour for the commencement of the cease-fire and truce in Palestine as envisaged in the resolution of the Security Council of 29 May.

2. The effective date and hour of the cease-fire and truce, including the application of supervision envisaged in the resolution of 29 May, shall be Friday, 11 June 1948, at six o'clock in the a. m. GMT. As of this date and hour, there is to be cessation of all acts of armed force in Palestine for a period of four weeks and all commanders in the field should be notified accordingly.

3. In view of the urgency of the time factor and the necessity of giving final confirmation of this decision in ample time to each party concerned, I must ask that notification to me of your acceptance or rejection of this date and hour shall be in my hands not later than Wednesday noon GMT, 9 June. If this decision is accepted by all parties, final confirmation will be dispatched to you by me not later than 6 p. m. GMT, Wednesday, 9 June, in order to reach you on the same day. Should the decision be rejected, or accepted only conditionally, by any of the parties, no further consultations on the matter will be undertaken by me, but I will promptly report the circumstances fully to the Security Council for such action as that body may deem appropriate. It is, of course, my earnest hope that the decision will be accepted unconditionally.

4. In the event of acceptance of this decision, the date and hour for public announcement of the beginning of this truce will be communicated to you in my message of final confirmation 9 June, in order that publication shall be made simultaneously by all concerned.

5. This decision has been taken in the light of the following considerations:

(1) The clear intent of the truce as envisaged in the Security Council resolution of 29 May is to bring about the cessation of hostilities without prejudice to the rights, claims and position of either Jews or Arabs, and to ensure that no military advantage shall accrue to either side as a result of the application of the truce;

(2) The President of the Security Council has informed me that all parties concerned have accepted the resolution of 29 May unconditionally and that the Mediator should fix the date for the cease-fire in consultation with the two parties and the Truce Commission in as short a period as possible;

(3) I am aware, of course, that each side, in accepting the resolution, notified the Security Council of certain "assumptions and explanations" in connection with some of the provisions of the resolution, and that as a result, there were conflicting views of the intent of particular clauses, especially those relating to "fighting personnel and men of military age";

(4) In the course of the amicable consultations with representatives of the parties concerned on 3, 4, 5 and 6 June, I exerted every effort to reconcile these divergent interpretations and as a result of these consultations and explanations and interpretations made to me by each party, I am firmly convinced that any remaining differences are altogether insufficient to warrant any further delay in the beginning of the truce.

6. As I have carefully explained to each side, it is my earnest intention to apply the truce and controls required in such a manner as to ensure that no military advantage will accrue to either side during the period of the truce or as a result of its application. To this end, I have made certain interpretations of the resolution and certain decisions as to its application which have been thoroughly explained to representatives of both sides and which in summary follow:

(1) No fighting personnel, which shall include persons identified as belonging to organized military units as well as all persons bearing arms, shall be introduced into any of the Arab States or into any part of Palestine.

[1] Cablegram of June 7, 1948, U.N. doc. S/829, June 8, 1948. Count Folke Bernadotte is U.N. mediator in Palestine.

shall be no increase in the fighting strength deployed along the fronts and lines, nor in the war materials on hand. Routine replacement of personnel may be undertaken.

(7) War materials shall not be imported into the country or territory of any interested party.

(8) Relief to populations of both sides in municipal areas which have suffered severely from the conflict, as in Jerusalem and Jaffa, shall be administered by an International Red Cross Committee in such a manner as to ensure that reserves of stocks of essential supplies shall not be substantially greater or less at the end of the truce than they were at its beginning.

(9) All warlike acts, whether on land, sea or air, shall be prohibited during the truce.

7. I recognize fully that both the effectiveness of the truce and its fairness depend in large measure on the manner in which it is supervised and applied. A detailed plan for its application is in preparation and will be put into operation when the truce begins. No doubt numerous questions will arise in connection with the details of supervising the truce. Consultations on such matters of detail may be undertaken when the truce is in effect.

8. I am deeply appreciative of the spirit of cooperation manifested by both sides in the difficult negotiations over the truce. I trust that this same spirit will continue in order that the truce may be achieved and the larger work of mediation may proceed constructively in an atmosphere of peace in Palestine.

BERNADOTTE

UCE BY ARAB STATES [3]

shall begin as from Friday 11 June 1948 at 6:00 o'clock in the morning, GMT.

I would like to point out that the Arab States have complete confidence in your determination to effect a just application of the Security Council resolution.

I avail myself of this opportunity to renew to you, Monsieur le Comte, the assurance of my very high consideration.

The President of the Council of Ministers.

[Egyptian Prime Minister]

M. F. NOKRASHY

---

[3] Message to U.N. mediator. U.N. doc. S/833, June 10, 1948. Similar replies were received from the Governments of Iraq, Transjordan, and Yemen.

1. The Provisional Government of Israel has given careful consideration to the communication addressed by you to the undersigned on June 8, 1948, indicating the date and hour on which the proposed cease-fire and truce arrangement is to come into effect, and setting out interpretations of the resolution and decisions as to its application adopted by you.

2. The Provisional Government of Israel desires to inform you that it has decided to accept the cease-fire and truce proposal and is prepared, if the other side accepts likewise, to issue an order for a cease-fire and the cessation of acts of armed force for the period of four weeks commencing on Friday, June 11, 1948, at six o'clock in the morning, G.M.T., corresponding to ten o'clock in the morning Israeli time.

3. While the Provisional Government of Israel attaches no conditions to this decision, it finds it necessary to make certain observations which are set forth in the following paragraphs. In this connection we beg to point out that forty-eight hours elapsed between your last meeting with the undersigned in Haifa and the receipt of your communication under reply here. We cannot but assume that during this time the representatives of the Arab League, or of the governments composing it, had opportunities for further consultation with you by direct contact and by oral elucidation of various points at issue, opportunities denied us by the fact that you were in Cairo.

4. The Provisional Government of Israel maintains the position set forth in my message to you of June 7 as regards restrictions you intend to impose on the entry into Israel of Jewish immigrants of military age during the truce period. It regrets its inability to agree that the policy you propose to adopt in this regard accords with the resolution of the Security Council of May 29, inasmuch as that Resolution embodies no other limitation on the immigration of men of military age than that they should not be mobilized or trained for military service during the truce, which limitation the Provisional Government of Israel had accepted from the outset.

As a result of the interview between the undersigned and yourself at Haifa on June 3, and your oral message transmitted through Mr. Reedman on June 4,[4] the Provisional Government of Israel

---

[3] Transmitted by Acting Representative of the Provisional Government of Israel, Aubrey S. Eban, in letter to Secretary-General dated June 10, 1948. U.N. doc. S/834, June 10, 1948.

[4] John Reedman is a member of the U.N. Secretariat and has been acting as liaison officer in Tel Aviv.

nent of Israel welcomes your assurance that will adjust your policy accordingly.

If the truce is rejected by the other party the whole matter is referred back to the ırity Council, the Provisional Government of ‚el reserves the right to revert to its original tion regarding interpretation of the provi- s of the Resolution of May 29, without it being

committed to any concessions implied in the pres- ent acceptance of the cease-fire and truce proposal.

10. The Provisional Government of Israel con- fidently hopes that if the cease-fire and truce ma- terializes, you may find it possible to make such arrangements as will ensure complete equality of contact with you and access to you for both par- ties concerned.

MESSAGE FROM U.N. MEDIATOR ANNOUNCING ACCEPTANCE OF TRUCE[1]

have the honour to transmit the following sage from the United Nations mediator to the rested governments concerning the acceptance he truce:

I. I have the honor to inform you that in re- ıse to my note of June 7 setting forth my pro- ıls as United Nations Mediator for truce in ıstine, I have today, 9 June, received uncon- onal acceptance of my proposals from all in- sted parties. The cease-fire and truce, efore, will be effective Friday, 11 June 1948, :00 o'clock in the morning, GMT.

2. Public announcement of the acceptance of truce by the parties concerned will be made ne in Cairo tonight, 9 June, at 8:00 o'clock, T. Simultaneous announcement may be made your Government at the corresponding hour, in any case should not be made before 8:00 ɔck (GMT).

"3. I take this opportunity to express to your Government my deepest gratitude for the splendid co-operation which has been given to me in this difficult task and my warm appreciation of the high motives which have led your Government to accept the proposals for the truce.

"I am, of course, highly gratified that my efforts toward the truce have now borne fruit. I will do my utmost to supervise the terms of the truce fairly and efficiently and will immediately turn my attention to the broader aspects of my task as mediator, namely the promotion of a peaceful ad- justment of the future situation of Palestine.

Count BERNADOTTE"

TRYGVE LIE
Secretary-General.

ıdom of Navigation on the Danube—*Continued from page 793*

Austria from the conference, and pressed for vocation of the conference by the end of that ıth.

he United States, in turn, pointed out in a note Iay 25, 1948, that convocation of a conference he end of the month was clearly impracticable, , in order to give adequate time for the partici- ng nation to prepare for the discussions, pro- ed July 30 as the convening date. The United :es asked the Soviet Union to reconsider its tion on the participation of Austria. The ted States also requested that Yugoslavia, as : nation, be asked to grant conference facilities lar to those which this country would accord if meetings were held in the United States, that freedom of communication, including air- ʻier service and freedom from censorship on ference reporting for press and radio repre- atives of the participating nations. The So- Union, in a note of June 12, accepted the date ɔosed by the United States and agreed to the ʻicipation of Austria on a consultative basis.

Final arrangements for the conference are there- fore in the process of being completed.

The attitude of the United States toward the proposed conference on the Danube is indicated by the statement of Secretary Marshall on May 26, 1948:

"This vital European waterway normally affords the nations of eastern and western Europe their principal means of carrying on commerce. Its free and open navigation, with the resultant bene- fits of more abundant trade, is of very real urgency to the peoples of all Europe in their daily lives. It is our conviction that a beneficial new conven- tion for the regime of navigation on the Danube should be worked out as soon as possible. Until we reach agreement on a new convention, this im- portant sphere remains an unsettled area in inter- national relations. It should be, instead, an area of constructive cooperation."[2]

---

[1] U.N. doc. S/830, June 9, 1948, as corrected.
[2] BULLETIN of June 6, 1948, p. 736.

U.S. Position and Views on Atomic Energy

STATEMENT BY PHILIP C. JESSUP [1]

Deputy U.S. Representative In the Security Council

The position and views of the United States on the international control of atomic energy have been clearly stated on many occasions and are well known to the Security Council.

Atomic weapons were first developed during the war against the Axis powers. How terrible would have been the consequences had this weapon been developed in Germany and used against our great Allies in the war. Fortunately it was developed in the United States, with the participation of the United Kingdom and Canada and the collaboration of scientists from many nations.

Immediately after the use of this weapon, the United States proposed international control in order to ensure that this new discovery might be used for peaceful purposes only, for the welfare of all nations, instead of as an instrument of destruction. Toward this end the United States has made and will continue to make every possible effort. Subject to the putting into effect of a system of control, the necessary basis of which has been set forth in the first and second reports of the Atomic Energy Commission, the United States is proposing to dispose of its atomic bombs, to give up all its activities in the production of dangerous quantities of atomic materials, and to turn over its knowledge of these processes to an International Agency.

Two and one half years ago the General Assembly by unanimous vote created the Atomic Energy Commission of the United Nations and laid down its terms of reference. At the first meeting of the Commission the United States made certain proposals for the control of atomic energy for peaceful purposes only and the elimination of atomic weapons from national armaments. As the negotiations progressed, other delegations made important contributions, so that shortly the search for effective control became a truly cooperative effort on the part of 14 of the 17 nations who are or have been members of the Atomic Energy Commission.

During a period of two years and in over 200 meetings, this cooperative effort has resulted in the preparation of a plan which would meet the terms of reference laid down by the General Assembly by controlling atomic energy to the extent necessary to ensure its use for peaceful purposes only, by eliminating atomic weapons from national armaments, and by providing safeguards necessary to the security of all nations. This plan provides for an international control agency which would own all source material and nuclear fuel, own, operate, and manage all dangerous facilities, license all non-dangerous activities in this field, and conduct inspections to prevent diversions of material or clandestine operations.

Further, the plan of the majority provides that a system of quotas, assigning to each signatory state its specific proportion of atomic fuels and power plants, should be written into the treaty itself so that the international agency would have no arbitrary powers in this respect, but would simply carry out the provisions of the treaty. Furthermore, in the interests of security, it is agreed that production of nuclear fuel be kept to the minimum required for actual beneficial purposes.

The Commission has examined other solutions and rejected them because in the opinion of the Commission they did not meet the known facts of the problem created by the discovery of atomic energy and thus failed to provide the safeguards required by the terms of reference set out by the General Assembly. Over a period of two years the Commission has found no alternative to the plan now proposed by the majority.

Specifically the Commission examined the Soviet Union amendments to the first report during the spring of 1947. Thereafter the Soviet proposals of June 11, 1947, were considered in numerous meetings in the summer of 1947. Finally, three months during the winter of 1948 were devoted to a further intensive study of all Soviet proposals in the light of questions asked by the Delegate of the United Kingdom and by delegates of other nations and the replies of the Soviet Delegate. As a result of these exhaustive discussions, the majority of the Commission was forced to recognize the inadequacy of the Soviet proposals and rejected them in the following terms:

". . . the Soviet Union proposals ignore the ex-

---

[1] Made before the Security Council on June 11, 1948, and released to the press by the U.S. Mission to the United Nations on the same date.

the First and Second Reports of the Atomic Energy Commission."

In view of the nature of the impasse in the Atomic Energy Commission, it is now proposed to transfer these negotiations to a higher level. It is the hope of my Government that the debate in the Security Council and in the General Assembly will enable the nations of the world to assess this situation in the light of the experience of the Atomic Energy Commission, the findings it has made, the lessons it has drawn from the difficulties it has met, and the conclusions it has reached.

All governments are faced with one or the other of two alternatives: either a continuation of the race in atomic armaments, or agreement on a system of international control in which all nations would have confidence because they believed it to be effective. There is no middle ground between these two alternatives.

No government can fail to recognize the nature and extent of the sacrifice which would be required of them by the acceptance of an effective system of control of atomic energy to ensure the prohibition of atomic weapons. Such a sacrifice seems at the moment very large. But in the longer view it weighs little against the advantages of security and the benefits which will accrue to all nations by the pooling of knowledge in this field, and its cooperative development for the common well-being.

My Delegation is of the opinion that the Security Council, in keeping with its responsibility, should state clearly its position. My Delegation hopes that in the consideration of these matters in the Security Council and in the General Assembly the Soviet Union, together with all other nations, may come to recognize the soundness of the plans . so painstakingly developed by the Atomic Energy Commission.

In this hope the Delegation of the United States presents the following resolution:

OLUTION[1]

Approves the "Report and Recommendations of the Atomic Energy Commission" (Part I) of the Third Report of the United Nations Atomic Energy Commission, and

Directs the Secretary-General to transmit to the General Assembly and to the member nations of the United Nations, the First, Second, and Third Reports of the United Nations Atomic Energy Commission, together with the record of the Security Council's approval thereof.

---

[1] U.N. doc. S/836, June 11, 1948.

Suggestions to Korean Assembly on Form

LETTER FROM GENERAL HODGE

$$\left(May\ 27,\ 1948 \right)$$

I congratulate you upon your election as representative of the Korean people to participate in
forming a government and in uniting the Korean
nation. You carry great responsibilities of which
I am sure you are well aware and which I am confident you will handle with great honor to yourself
and the fine people you represent.

The most important feature of the election is
that it puts the fate and future of Korea into
Korean hands. The manner and method in which
the elected representatives in South Korea make
their approach to handling the affairs of their nation will have tremendous and lasting effect on the
future of the Korean people.

The policy of the United States has always been
that Korea shall be a united, independent nation
under democratic government free of foreign
domination. That same policy is reflected internationally in the forty-three to nothing vote of the
United Nations General Assembly when it voted
to observe elections in Korea as a step toward
establishing a Korean national government and to
advise Korean elected representatives in the
formation of that government. This policy also
reflects the wishes of the thirty million Korean
people, and we all regret exceedingly that the free
election could not be held in Korea north of the
thirty-eight degree parallel at the same time as in
South Korea. The United States and United
Nations hope that this can be done and that representatives from North Korea can join those of
South Korea·in the establishment of a truly national Korean Government, joining North and
South Korea together in one nation.

It is my hope, the hope of the United States
Government, and the hope of the members of the
United Nations Temporary Commission on Korea
as expressed to me on numerous occasions, that the
newly elected representatives will do everything
in their power to form a truly democratic government and to unite Korea.

I am sure that members of the Assembly, both as
individuals and as members of party groups, have
ideas as to how these objectives can be accomplished. In that connection, I have three suggestions for your possible early consideration when
you meet to begin your deliberations toward the
formation of a government. They are as follows:

---

[1] Printed from telegraphic text. Lt. Gen. John R. Hodge
is Commanding General, U.S. Forces in South Korea.

United States in the United Nations

Trusteeship

Ambassador Francis B. Sayre, U.S. Representative in the Trusteeship Council, retired from the Council's presidency when it convened at Lake Success June 16 for its third session. To succeed him the Council elected Liu Chieh of China. Sir Alan Burns of the United Kingdom was chosen Vice President.

Among agenda items for the session is review of annual reports by France, Belgium, the United Kingdom and Australia regarding their administration of various trust territories in Africa and the southwestern Pacific.

An item of direct concern to the United States is discussion of the relations of the Trusteeship Council and the Security Council with respect to trusteeships for strategic areas. The only strategic trusteeship now in force is that of the United States over the Pacific islands formerly mandated to Japan. Article 83 of the U.N. Charter provides that all U.N. functions relating to strategic-area trusteeships shall be exercised by the Security Council, which "shall . . . avail itself of the assistance of the Trusteeship Council" to perform U.N. functions related to welfare of the trust territory's inhabitants.

Human Rights

The Human Rights Commission on June 17 was putting the finishing touches on its draft of an International Declaration of Human Rights. The third session of the Commission was scheduled to end on June 18.

Drafting the Declaration proved to be a much bigger job than was anticipated when the Commission convened at Lake Success on May 24. As a result, the projected Covenant on Human Rights did not come up for discussion, and the question of implementation of rights stated in the Covenant was touched upon only briefly.

As the session neared its close, the Commission had not decided whether to submit the Declaration to the Economic and Social Council and thence to the General Assembly for approval. Some delegates favored delay until agreement was reached on the Covenant and the implementation provisions. The U.S. Representative, Mrs. Franklin D. Roosevelt, was prepared to propose that the Declaration be transmitted to Ecosoc and the General Assembly, leaving to the Assembly the final decision as to whether approval should await completion of the Covenant.

The Declaration draft appeared to have won unexpectedly wide support within the 18-nation Commission. It is a "tighter" document—shorter, simpler, and easier to understand—than any earlier draft. It consists of a preamble and some 30 articles.

Beginning in article 1 with the declaration that "all human beings are born free and equal in dignity and rights," it proceeds with several articles generally resembling the guaranties contained in the U.S. Constitution. Among them are the right to life and liberty, freedom from arbitrary arrest and involuntary servitude, the right to own property, and freedom of thought, conscience, and religion.

The Commission adopted without change the draft article on freedom of speech and of the press prepared by its subcommission in that field and subsequently approved by the U.N. Conference on Freedom of Information at Geneva.

Other articles deal with economic, social, and cultural rights. They include the right to work and to protection from unemployment; the right to an "adequate" standard of living, including food, clothing, housing, medical care, and provision against sickness, disability, and old age; the right to an education, to rest and leisure; and the right to participate in the cultural life of the community.

Future of the "Little Assembly"

United States support for continuance in some form of the Interim Committee of the General Assembly was announced by Joseph E. Johnson, Deputy U.S. Representative, at a Lake Success meeting on June 17.

The General Assembly resolution of November 13, 1947, which established the Interim Committee (popularly known as the "Little Assembly"), limited its life to the period between the close of the 1947 Assembly and the opening of the 1948 Assembly but asked the Committee to report back on the advisability of establishing a permanent interim organ. Subcommittee 4, to which Mr. Johnson's statement [1] was made, is drafting recommendations on this point.

After reviewing the accomplishments of the Interim Committee since it began functioning in January 1948, Mr. Johnson said the United States favored its continuance for at least another year. "My Government feels", he said, "that the experience of this Committee demonstrates that its continuance will strengthen the United Nations and will contribute to its sound and orderly development."

Mr. Johnson said the boycott of the Interim Committee by the Soviet Union and "the five other states which follow its lead" had been a handicap but had not prevented progress. "I leave it to the members of the Interim Committee," he added, "whether the record does not show that Mr. Vyshinsky has been proven mistaken in his estimate that the Interim Committee would be but a crude

---

[1] U.S. Mission to the United Nations, press release 476.

device to bypass the Security Council and would, as a principal organ, usurp its functions. Indeed, I suggest that an examination of the record of the Interim Committee may well convince the Soviet Union that it will wish to participate in its work if the General Assembly decides to continue it."

Atomic Energy

On June 11 and June 16 the Security Council debated the Atomic Energy Commission's Third Report. Philip C. Jessup, U.S. Deputy Representative, opened the debate with a review of the Commission's work, of the majority plan for control, and of the inadequacy of the Soviet Union's position.[2] He introduced a draft resolution under which the Security Council would approve the majority plan of control as "the necessary basis for establishing an effective system of international control of atomic energy" and would refer to the General Assembly the situation resulting from the impasse in the Commission.

At the June 11 session the Representatives of Canada and the United Kingdom joined the United States in arguing for suspension of the Commission's work pending negotiations at a "higher level" to break the impasse in the Commission. On June 16, Belgium, China, and France also endorsed the Commission's findings.

In an hour-long speech on June 16, Andrei Gromyko restated the U.S.S.R.'s opposition to the majority plan and said that the draft resolution for Security Council approval of the Commission's reports "must be rejected".

Palestine

A bid by the Soviet Union for representation on the corps of military observers assigned to the U.N. mediator in Palestine failed to win Security Council approval at a June 15 meeting. The Ukraine voted with the U.S.S.R., but the other nine members abstained.

The Soviet Union's draft resolution would have had the Security Council itself decide to provide military observers for the mediator, the observers to be appointed by Council members "wishing to participate in the designation of such observers, excluding Syria".

On June 10 the Council's majority had agreed that Count Bernadotte should make the arrange-

---

[2] For text of Mr. Jessup's statement, see p. 798.

of the World's Poultry Science Association, organized in 1912 and composed of leaders of the world's poultry industry. The First Congress was held in the Netherlands in 1921. The last Congress, the Seventh, held at Cleveland in July 1939 was one of the world's largest agricultural gatherings. A national committee, headed by Mr. Termohlen, has been preparing for United States participation in the Congress. It is expected that approximately 35 countries will participate in this meeting.

U.S. DELEGATION TO EIGHTH INTERNATIONAL CONGRESS OF ENTOMOLOGY

[Released to the press June 7]

The Department of State announced on June 7 the United States Delegation to the Eighth International Congress of Entomology, scheduled to be held at Stockholm, August 8–14, 1948. The Delegation is as follows:

Chairman

Dr. Percy N. Annand, Chief, Bureau of Entomology and Plant Quarantine, Department of Agriculture

Delegates

Dr. George H. Bradley, Chief of the Entomology Division, Communicable Disease Center, U. S. Public Health Service, Atlanta, Ga.
Dr. J. Chester Bradley, Professor of Entomology, Cornell University, Ithaca, N. Y.
Dr. Ernest N. Cory, State Entomologist of Maryland, University of Maryland, College Park, Md.
Dr. Herbert L. Haller, Assistant to the Chief, Bureau of Entomology and Plant Quarantine, Department of Agriculture
Dr. William P. Hayes, Professor of Entomology, University of Illinois, Urbana, Ill.
William H. W. Komp, Sanitary Engineer Director, Division of Tropical Diseases, National Institute of Health, U. S. Public Health Service, Federal Security Agency
Dr. Zeno P. Metcalf, Professor of Zoology and Entomology, North Carolina State College, Raleigh, N. C.
Col. Charles H. Morehouse, M.C., U.S.A., Chief, Department of Preventive Medicine, School of Aviation Medicine, Randolph Field, Tex.

The Congress, one in a triennial series which held its last meeting at Berlin in 1938, has as its main purpose the study and investigation of methods for preventing the spread of noxious insects. This meeting is of significance in view of the importance of insect control in the international food situation and because it will offer an opportunity to appraise recent extensive developments in the field of insect control both here and abroad.

THE RECORD OF THE WEEK

President Sproul, distinguished guests, ladies and gentlemen:

I deeply appreciate the privilege you have given me of taking part in these exercises at this great university.

I regret that I could not arrange my schedule to permit me to be here next week at the time for which you first invited me. Under these circumstances, I am pleased that an adjustment could be made on the part of the university so as to make it possible for me to be here today.

Three years ago this month, across the bay in San Francisco, I witnessed the signing of the Charter of the United Nations. That Charter represents man's hope for a world order based on law and for lasting peace based on justice.

Today, I have come back to the shores of San Francisco Bay to discuss with you recent world events and, in particular, to appraise the progress we are making toward world peace.

Many students here today and in colleges across the country are veterans. They fought for peace, peace with freedom and justice. They, above all, have reason to expect a plain statement of the progress we are making in that direction.

The American people know from experience that our daily lives are affected not only by what happens in this country but also by events abroad. Most American families bear the scars and memories of a war which began thousands of miles from this Nation. Every American wants to be sure that this country is doing everything in its power to build a lasting peace and a just peace. We believe that such a peace can be achieved by the nations of the world.

Anyone can talk of peace. But only the work that is done for peace really counts.

I propose to describe the specific steps the United States has taken to obtain peace in the world. I propose, also, to discuss what further measures we must take, and what measures others must take, if our hopes for peace are to be fulfilled.

I submit to you that the United States has consistently done its part in meeting the requirements for a peaceful world.

---

[1] Delivered at the commencement exercises at the University of California, Berkeley, on June 12, 1948, and released to the press by the White House on the same date.

only the United States and the Soviet Union; they affect all nations.

Whether it be control of atomic energy, aggression against small nations, the German or the Austrian peace settlements, or any of the other questions, the majority of nations concerned have found a common basis for action. But in every case the majority agreement has been rejected, denounced, and openly attacked by the Soviet Union and her satellites whose policies it controls.

Let me repeat: The division has not been between the United States and the Soviet Union but between the Soviet Union and the free nations of the world.

The United States is strongly devoted to the principle of discussion and negotiation in settling international differences. We do not believe in settling international differences by force. There are certain types of disputes in international affairs which can and must be settled by negotiation and agreement.

But there are others which are not susceptible to negotiation.

There is nothing to negotiate when one nation disregards the principles of international conduct to which all members of the United Nations subscribed. There is nothing to negotiate when one nation habitually uses coercion and open aggression in international affairs.

What the world needs in order to regain a sense of security is an end to Soviet obstruction and aggression. I will give you two clear illustrations of what I have in mind.

The situation in Greece has caused great uneasiness throughout the world. It has been the subject of a series of investigations on the part of commissions of the United Nations. The facts have been established over and over again by these investigations. They are clear beyond dispute. Some 20,-000 Greek guerrillas have been able to keep Greece in a state of unrest and to disrupt Greek recovery, primarily because of the aid and comfort they have been receiving from the neighboring countries of Bulgaria, Yugoslavia, and Albania.

Last October the United Nations General Assembly adopted a resolution calling upon Bulgaria, Yugoslavia, and Albania to stop their illegal aid and comfort to the Greek rebels. This resolution was agreed to by more than two thirds of the membership of the United Nations. But it has been boycotted by Russia.

The situation in Greece requires no special negotiation, or discussion, or conference.

On its own initiative the Soviet Government can cease its boycott of the United Nations recommendation. It can join with other nations in stopping illegal foreign support of the Greek guerrillas so that Greece may have an opportunity for peaceful reconstruction.

If the Soviet Union genuinely desires to make a contribution to peace and recovery in the world it can prove it in Greece.

The situation in Korea is also disturbing. There the Soviet Government has defied the clearly expressed will of an overwhelming majority of the United Nations by boycotting the United Nations Temporary Commission on Korea. This commission was created last fall by the General Assembly to help set up a Korean national government based on free and democratic elections.

The Soviet boycott has prevented the residents of the northern zone of Korea from electing representatives to establish a unified national government for Korea.

The situation in Korea requires no special negotiation, or discussion, or conference.

On its own initiative the Soviet Government can abandon its boycott of the United Nations Commission. It can permit the people of North Korea to work with their compatriots in the south in creating an independent and democratic nation.

If the Soviet Union genuinely desires to make a contribution to peace and recovery in the world, it can prove it in Korea.

In these questions, as in all others, there are practical ways for the Soviet Union to show its good faith by proper action.

The United States will always respond to an honest move by any nation to further the principles and purposes of the Charter of the United Nations.

But no nation has the right to exact a price for good behavior.

What is needed is a will for peace. What is needed is the abandonment of the absurd idea that the capitalistic nations will collapse and that instability in international affairs will hasten their collapse, leaving the world free for communism.

It is possible for different economic systems to live side by side and in peace, one with the other, provided one of these systems is not determined to destroy the other by force.

I have said before and I repeat now: The door is always open for honest negotiations looking toward genuine settlements.

The door is not open, however, for deals between great powers to the detriment of other nations or at the expense of principle. We refuse to play fast and loose with man's hope for peace. That hope for peace is too sacred to be trifled with for propaganda purposes, or selfish advantage, by an individual or nation. We are interested in peace—not in propaganda.

We shall judge the policy of every nation by whether it advances or obstructs world progress toward peace, and we wish our own policy to be judged by the same standard.

I stated our American policy for peace at the end of the war. It has been restated many times, but I shall repeat essential elements of our policy again so that there can be no misunderstanding anywhere by anyone.

TEXT OF COMMUNIQUÉ

[Released to the press June 7]

[n accordance with an announcement issued on ne 2 at the conclusion of informal discussions Germany between representatives of United ates, United Kingdom, France and three Bene- ɩ countries [Belgium, Netherlands, Luxem- urg] a report containing agreed recommenda- ns on all items discussed was submitted to their ipective governments. These recommendations ve been submitted as a whole since their main ovisions are mutually dependent and form an livisible program. Principal features of this ɔort are the following:

ASSOCIATION OF BENELUX COUNTRIES IN POLICY ¡GARDING GERMANY

The recommendations include specific provisions ɩ a close association between military govern- ɩnts and Benelux representatives in Germany matters affecting Benelux interests. Moreover ll opportunities will be given the Benelux rep- ¡entatives to be kept informed of developments the western zones.

, ROLE OF THE GERMAN ECONOMY IN THE EURO- AN ECONOMY AND CONTROL OF THE RUHR

(A) As stated in the communiqué of March 6 had been agreed that for the political and eco- mic well-being of the.countries of western Eu- pe and of a democratic Germany, there must be close association of their economic life. This ɔse association, which will enable Germany to ntribute to and participate in European recov- y, has been ensured by the inclusion on April 16 the combined zone and French zone in the or- nization for European economic cooperation as ll members.
(B) It was agreed to recommend the establish- ɩnt of an international authority for the control the Ruhr in which United States, United ingdom, France, Benelux countries and Ger- any would participate, and which does not volve the political separation of the Ruhr area om Germany. It does, however, contemplate ntrol of distribution of coal, coke and steel of uhr in order that on the one hand industrial ɩncentration in that area shall not become ɩ instrument of aggression, and on the other ll be able to make its contribution to all countries

participating in a European cooperative economic program, including, of course, Germany itself. A draft agreement containing the provisions for its establishment is attached as annex I. This agree- ment is to be concluded by the United States, United ·Kingdom and France as occupying pow- ers. Moreover the Benelux countries are to be fully associated with the preparation of the more detailed agreement provided for in article 12, and are to be consulted as to the time when the author- ity begins to exercise its functions.
(C) Arising out of the discussions on the Ruhr it has been recommended that the principle of non- discrimination against foreign interests in Ger- many be reaffirmed, and that each government should promptly study the problem of safeguard- ing foreign interests in order that there may be subsequently established as soon as possible an intergovernmental ·group to review the question and make recommendations to their governments.

III. EVOLUTION OF POLITICAL AND ECONOMIC ORGANIZATION OF GERMANY

(A) Further consideration has been given by all delegates to the problem of the evolution of the political and economic organization of Ger- many. They recognize, taking into account the present situation, that it is necessary to give the German people the opportunity to achieve on the basis of a free and democratic form of government the eventual re-establishment of German unity at present disrupted. In these circumstances they have reached the conclusion that it would be de- sirable that the German people in the different states should now be free to establish for them- selves the political organization and institutions which will enable them to assume those govern- mental responsibilities which are compatible with the minimum requirements of occupation and con- trol and which ultimately will enable them to as- sume full governmental responsibility. The dele- gates consider that the people in the states will wish to establish a constitution with provisions which will allow all the German states to subscribe as soon as circumstances permit.
Therefore the delegates have agreed to recom- mend to their governments that the military gov- ernors should hold a joint meeting with the Minis- ters-President of the western zone in Germany.

At that meeting the Ministers-President will be authorized to convene a Constituent Assembly in order to prepare a constitution for the approval of the participating states.

Delegates to this Constituent Assembly will be chosen in each of the states in accordance with procedure and regulations to be determined by the legislative bodies of the individual states.

The constitution should be such as to enable the Germans to play their part in bringing to an end the present division of Germany not by the reconstitution of a centralized Reich but by means of a federal form of government which adequately protects the rights of the respective states, and which at the same time provides for adequate central authority and which guarantees the rights and freedoms of the individual.

If the constitution as prepared by the Constituent Assembly does not conflict with these general principles the military governors will authorize its submission for ratification by the people in the respective states.

At the meeting with the military governors the Ministers-President will also be authorized to examine the boundaries of the several states in order to determine what modifications might be proposed to the military governors for the purpose of creating a definitive system which is satisfactory to the peoples concerned.

(B) Further discussions have taken place between the United States, United Kingdom and French delegations on measures for coordinating economic policies and practices in the combined zone and the French zone. Agreed recommendations have been reached on the joint conduct and control of the external trade of the whole area. It has been recognized that a complete economic merger of the two areas cannot effectively take place until further progress has been made in establishing the necessary German institutions common to the entire area.

IV. PROVISIONAL TERRITORIAL ARRANGEMENTS

The delegations have agreed to submit for the consideration of their governments proposals for dealing with certain minor provisional territorial adjustments in connection with the western frontiers of Germany.

V. SECURITY

This problem was considered in three aspects: (A) General Provisions. (B) Measures during the period in which the occupying powers retain supreme authority in Germany. (C) Measures after the period in which the occupying powers retain supreme authority in Germany.

General Provisions

The United States, United Kingdom and

RECOMMENDATION BY THE LONDON CONFERENCE OF REPRESENTATIVES OF THE UNITED STATES, UNITED KINGDOM, FRANCE AND BELGIUM, NETHERLANDS AND LUXEMBOURG ON INTERNATIONAL CONTROL OF THE RUHR

Whereas international security and general economic recovery require:

that the resources of the Ruhr shall not in the future be used for the purpose of aggression but shall be used in the interests of peace;

that access to the coal, coke and steel of the Ruhr, which was previously subject to the exclusive control of Germany, be in the future guaranteed without discrimination to the countries of Europe cooperating in the common economic good;

Whereas it is desirable for the political and economic well-being of these countries and a democratic Germany that there be close association of their economic life;

Whereas it is important that trade between the countries mentioned in the preceding paragraph should be facilitated by lowering trade barriers and by any other means,

The Governments of the United States, United Kingdom and France, after consultation with the Governments of the Netherlands, Belgium and Luxembourg, have agreed as follows:

1. An international control shall be set up in the Ruhr and exercised by an International Authority for the Ruhr (hereinafter called the International Authority); the International Authority shall be organised forthwith and shall begin to exercise its functions at a time to be determined by the contracting Governments, and in any case before the establishment of a provisional German government.

2. The International Authority shall be composed of representatives of the United States, United Kingdom, France, Netherlands, Belgium, Luxembourg and Germany.

3. The International Authority shall take its decisions by majority vote. The United States, United Kingdom, France and Germany shall have three votes each, and the Netherlands, Belgium and Luxembourg one vote each.

4. Until the contracting Governments decide otherwise, the representative of Germany shall be designated and the vote for Germany exercised by those Powers which share the responsibility for the economic administration of that part of Germany which includes the Ruhr (hereinafter called "the Occupying Powers concerned").

5. The functions of the International Authority shall, subject to existing or future international agreements among the contracting governments concerning the allocation of coal, coke and steel, be as follows:

(a) subject to the provisions of Article 6 below,

to make the division of coal, coke and steel from the Ruhr as between German consumption and export, in order to ensure adequate access to supplies of these products, taking into account the essential needs of Germany

(b) to ensure that the German authorities do not institute, carry out or permit artificial measures or discriminatory practices which would distort the movement of Ruhr coal, coke and steel in international trade, except for measures of protection approved by the International Authority

(c) to exercise, in the circumstances envisaged in Article 10(b) below, the powers described in Article 9(b) below.

(d) During the period in which the Occupying Powers concerned exercise supreme authority (which period is hereinafter called "The Control Period") to bring to the attention of the occupation authorities concerned measures which would ensure, and thereafter itself to ensure, safeguard and protection for coal, coke and steel enterprises in the Ruhr involving foreign interests, within the framework of existing or future agreements between the Allied Governments represented on the Authority.

6. (a) The findings of the International Authority under the provisions of Article 5(a) shall be consistent with the programmes of the C.E.E.C. for the recovery of the participating countries.

(b) During the Control Period, or until such earlier time as may be agreed upon by the contracting Governments, the findings of the International Authority under the provisions of Article 5(a) will be transmitted to the Military Governors for implementation. The Military Governors will proceed with the implementation of these findings (1) to the extent consistent with any agreements relative to the provision of financial assistance to Germany which are now or may come in effect between any two or more of the contracting Governments; and (2) in accordance with the terms of any existing international agreement among the contracting Governments, or extension thereof, with respect to the allocation of coal and coke.

7. The International Authority shall have the right:

(a) to receive regular reports on production, distribution and consumption of Ruhr coal, coke and steel;

(b) to demand additional reports on these subjects whenever necessary;

(c) to verify the information at its disposal by enquiries on the spot and by subpoena and examination of witnesses;

(d) to call for information about supplies of coal, coke and steel from sources other than the Ruhr.

8. During the Control Period the occupation authorities concerned will maintain adequate control over the management in the Ruhr coal and coke industry.

9. During the Control Period, or until such earlier time as may be agreed upon by the contracting Governments, the occupation authorities concerned will maintain

(a) such powers in respect of the coal, coke and steel industries of the Ruhr as will enable the International Authority to perform the functions and exercise the rights assigned to it in Articles 5 and 7 above, and as may be necessary to ensure that the decisions with respect to the export of these products from Germany are carried out;

(b) such further powers as may be necessary to enforce the disarmament of Germany, including power to control the supply of Ruhr coal, coke and steel to any industries which may be prohibited or limited in the interests of security by agreement among the contracting Governments or under the terms of any international agreement to which they shall become party.

10. (a) When the occupation authorities concerned relinquish the powers referred to in Article 9(a) the German authorities shall be responsible to the International Authority for enabling it to perform the functions and exercise the rights assigned to it in Articles 5 and 7 above and shall take such measures as may be necessary to ensure that the decisions of the International Authority are carried out.

(b) When the occupation authorities concerned relinquish the further powers referred to in Article 9(b) these powers shall be transferred to such international body as may be designated for these purposes by the Peace Settlement or by any international Agreement to which the Allied Governments represented on the Authority are parties, and the Authority shall cooperate with that international body in such ways as shall be prescribed by the Peace Settlement or by such international agreement. If no such international body is set up, these powers shall be transferred to the Authority but shall be exercised only by the Allied representatives on the Authority.

11. Should the German Government not carry out the decisions of the International Authority, the latter may, by a majority vote of the Allied representatives, find that the German Government is in default on its obligations and recommend, to the occupation authorities during the Control Period, and thereafter to the Allied Governments represented on the Authority, the application of the necessary enforcement measures, provided however that before such enforcement measures are applied the German Government shall be given a reasonable opportunity for a hearing. At the expiry of the Control Period, these enforcement measures shall be applied in accordance with the relevant provisions of the Peace Settlement or any international agreement to which the Allied Governments represented on the Authority are parties.

12. This Agreement constitutes a statement of principles which shall form the basis for a more detailed agreement setting up the International Authority.

STATEMENT BY SECRETARY MARSHALL

[Released to the press June 9]

I wish to announce that the U.S. Government approves and accepts the recommendations of the London conference of the western powers respecting Germany.

The U.S. Government believes that the London recommendations, which at the outset will apply to the larger part of Germany, represent a major step toward a comprehensive solution of German problems. The recommendations are the product of intensive study and prolonged negotiation in the course of which mutually beneficial agreements were reached. These agreements, including that relating to the Ruhr, constitute a program which, while continuing adequate security safeguards and reenforcing controls over demilitarization, offers the Germans the opportunity of peaceful reconstruction and self-government in keeping with the principles of the Potsdam agreement.

The U.S. favors a united Germany but has consistently stressed that political unity must proceed from economic unity and that both must be based on a recognition of individual liberties. Economic unity embraces the free movement of persons throughout all of Germany, the free movement of trade, a common export-import program, and the cessation by the Soviets of reparation removals from current production. The three western powers tried without success to obtain Soviet acceptance of these principles, which are fair and just and offer the only means for the establishment of German unity.

The governments represented at London consider that to the greatest extent possible Germany should be united economically and be permitted to contribute to, and share in, the welfare of those countries of Europe which are cooperating in the common economic good. It was likewise agreed that the Germans in the western area should now be free to proceed with the assumption of govern-

the ultimate adherence of all the German states as soon as circumstances permit.

The United States believes that the London program will stand the test of experience and that if conditions can be developed for its application to Germany as a whole it would resolve the issues which have thus far divided Germany under the occupation powers and would thereby remove the principal obstacle to the development of a peaceful Europe.

F THE CONFERENCE

The most important agreements relate to the role of the German economy in European recovery, allocation of Ruhr products, constitutional government, territorial questions, and security.

1. Germany and European Recovery

It has lately become apparent, even to those most fearful of the consequences of German economic revival, that German reconstruction is essential to the well-being of Europe. Not only would a chronically depressed Germany be unable to contribute sorely needed goods and materials to the participating countries of the ERP, but it would constitute a positive menace to the prosperity and security of these countries. It has now been fully agreed that the bizonal area, including the critical Ruhr industrial complex, and the French zone should participate in the recovery program and should be enabled to make a major contribution to its success. In these plans there is no intent that German recovery shall have priority over the needs of other participating countries but only the intent that Germany shall share in the common effort and the common welfare.

2. International Authority for the Allocation of Principal Ruhr Products

For years there has been controversy, often embittered, concerning the position of the vital industrial area of the Ruhr in the new Europe. It has come to be generally admitted that there can be neither (*a*) liquidation of the Ruhr industrial potential nor (*b*) restoration of Ruhr industries to exclusive German control. Two major objectives must be assured; first, that Ruhr resources may never be used for warlike purposes and second, that their exploitation must serve the general European welfare, not Germany exclusively, yet not excluding Germany.

To this end an agreement was reached whereby an International Authority should determine the allocation of the most vital Ruhr industrial resources as between domestic consumption and export. Germany is to be represented on the Authority, and the partnership of the countries immediately concerned should result in a closer association of their economic life. The Ruhr is to remain German, and hence this solution should not give rise to dangerous irredentist sentiments. The Authority will have ample competence to insure that the Ruhr is not converted into a military arsenal. Allocation of needed materials will be on a fair and nondiscriminatory basis. Moreover on the basis of existing and possible future agreements regarding financial responsibility in Germany, the interests of the United States will be protected during such time as it may make the major financial contribution.

3. German Government

The three western powers have been for some time deeply concerned that there is no political organization in Germany capable of regulating economic matters and serving as a focus for the revival of democratic political life. It is moreover clear that the European Recovery Program for western Germany can only be administered successfully by a competent German government.

The western powers have continuously endeavored to obtain quadripartite agreement to setting up a German government which would avoid dangerous over-centralization, yet which would insure democratic rights and practices and would be empowered to participate in a program for German and European economic recovery. The Union of Soviet Socialist Republics has persistently obstructed such agreement by holding to terms inconsistent with these objectives. The western powers have now agreed to a series of procedures leading to the creation by the Germans of a democratic government on a federal basis and resting on the foundation of a popular constitution. This government is to be provisional in character but will represent the first major step since the war toward the realization of German unity. It will adequately protect the rights of the participating states and the freedoms of the individual while insuring adequate central authority to deal with the urgent problems of western Germany as a whole. In this process the Germans will have an opportunity to manifest their wish for self-government, and the constitution essentially will be one of German devising and acceptance.

The vital prerogatives of the occupying powers will be safeguarded by an occupation statute which will delimit the powers reserved to the occupation authorities while granting broad executive, legislative, and judicial powers to the German government. Such a statute, to be drafted by the military governors in consultation with German representatives, will clarify the legal basis for actions either by the occupation authorities or the German federal and state governments. The grant of broad powers and responsibility to the Germans should give a greater reality to German political

among the western nations in the evolution of a policy which it can be hoped will lead to a peaceful and fruitful association of Germany with western Europe. At the same time it does not exclude the participation of the rest of Germany whenever the people of that area are free to join. At this critical stage, only constructive measures, not procrastination, can offer hope of an eventual German settlement and the consolidation of the peace of Europe on the basis of economic stability and political freedom.

American Policy in Japan

BASSADOR STUART [1]

Powers who destroyed Japanese power, proceeded to disband the Japanese Army, Navy, Air Force, and General Staff. I defy anyone to produce a single shred of evidence that any part of Japanese military power is being restored or that there is any intention on the part of the United States other than to assure that it will never rise again. The basis of Japanese aggression was its overseas empire. It has now lost that empire and cannot regain it without military power. You may rest assured the American people and government will make sure it does not do so.

As for Japanese economic and industrial power, the United States again on behalf of the Allied Powers, proceeded to destroy or dismantle all Japanese war industries. We are now faced with a situation where we must restore enough of Japanese economic life to enable the Japanese people to become self-supporting. No one can expect the American taxpayer to continue indefinitely paying the Japanese bills. Japan must be allowed a chance for self-support or it will be a continuing liability not only to the United States but also to China. An indigent country can never become a peace-loving and democratically-minded people. If it be argued that industry can be converted to war-time purposes, I admit the truth of the allegation. In modern warfare, any production is susceptible of war uses. Food is a war product. Textiles are a war product. Any of the articles of consumption are necessary in modern warfare. It will be our responsibility to insure that these products are used for peaceful purposes. This task will be made immeasurably easier if we cooperate thereon. It will be immeasurably more difficult if we squabble among ourselves.

If it be charged that the revival of Japanese economy will be a threat to Chinese economy, then I deny it. Certainly the demands of the peoples

---

[1] Made by J. Leighton Stuart, American Ambassador to China, on June 4, 1948, and released to the press by the American Embassy at Nanking on the same date. Printed from telegraphic text.

of the world for goods and services are far greater than anything all the countries in the world in the predictable future can hope to satisfy. On the contrary, the indefinite continuation of an indigent Japan will continue to lower the standards of living of the world. The world will be deprived of what Japan can produce. It will continue to be a drain on our already depleted resources. As a hungry and restless people, it will continue to be a threat to peace. Such a situation is made to order for Communism. If we are sincere in our profession that Communism, in the general interest, must be stopped, then we must remove the causes which encourage Communism.

If those of you who agitate or who participate in the agitation against the United States on the question of Japan disagree with what I have said, then you must be prepared to face the consequences of your actions. If in your hearts you know that I am right and still continue your agitation for other and secret purposes, then I say to you that it is time you examined your consciences. If by dishonest means you are attempting to accomplish some clandestine purpose, you are not only damaging the United States, you are also damaging your own country. You are also damaging your own standing and reputation as students and intellectuals of China whose best and most honest efforts are so desperately needed today by your country. You are the ones who are in the best position in China to know the truth. If you betray it you also betray yourselves. If you are not true to yourselves then most assuredly you cannot be true to any one or any thing else.

I hardly need protest my affection for Chinese student groups. If my life has not proven that, then it has been a total failure. I trust then that you will take the harsh words I have felt compelled to speak in the spirit in which they are intended. My greatest wish is the peace and welfare of all peoples of the world. Unless China and the United States can approach each other with mutual trust and confidence, that peace and welfare are endangered. I have confidence that the students of China will not knowingly lend themselves to evil purposes or betray the trust which has been placed in them by their country.

At the same time I want to assure you that I am fully aware of how much the Chinese people suffered at the hands of the Japanese and how heroically China resisted aggression. I was a prisoner of the Japanese myself and I know what it meant. I also know that the American people are aware of the tremendous Chinese sacrifices and are deeply grateful for that selfless contribution to the defeat of our common enemy. But I would also say that despite the understandable bitterness of China to-

the importance of the census, are cooperating to make it a success. Special interest is felt in the agricultural census, which is the first ever to be made in El Salvador.

Proclamation of the 1947 Sugar Protocol

[Released to the press June 8]

The President on June 1, 1948, proclaimed the protocol dated at London, August 29, 1947, prolonging for one year after August 31, 1947, the international agreement regarding the regulation of production and marketing of sugar signed at London May 6, 1937.

The protocol was signed on behalf of the Governments of the United States of America (with a reservation "subject to ratification"), the Union of South Africa, the Commonwealth of Australia, Belgium, Brazil, Cuba, Czechoslovakia, the Dominican Republic, the French Republic, the United Kingdom of Great Britain and Northern Ireland, Haiti, the Netherlands, Peru, the Republic of the Philippines, Poland, Portugal, and the Federal People's Republic of Yugoslavia.

The Senate gave its advice and consent to ratification of the protocol on April 28, 1948, and on May 14, 1948, the protocol was ratified by the President. The instrument of ratification by the United States was deposited in the archives of the British Government on May 25, 1948.

THE FOREIGN SERVICE

Regional Conference To Be Held in Bangkok

[Released to the press June 7]

A regional conference will be held in Bangkok from June 21 to June 26 under the chairmanship of Edwin F. Stanton, U.S. Ambassador to Siam. Attending will be officers assigned to the U.S. diplomatic and consular posts in southeast Asia as well as to missions in countries adjacent thereto. Three State Department officers will be present. This conference is similar to those held previously in other parts of the world, where problems common to a specific area are discussed by officers in the field who would not otherwise be able to meet and exchange views.

THE DEPARTMENT

Wilbert Chapman Appointed Special Assistant to the Under Secretary

The Department of State announced on June 8 the appointment of Dr. Wilbert M. Chapman as Special Assistant to the Under Secretary. Dr. Chapman will handle coordination of international fisheries matters for the Department.

 *Contributors*

Fred L. Hadsel, author of the article on freedom of navigation on the Danube, is an historian in the Division of Historical Policy Research, Office of Public Affairs, Department of State.

U. S. GOVERNMENT PRINTING OFFICE: 1948

The Department of State bulletin

VOL. XVIII, No. 469 • PUBLICATION 3201

June 27, 1948

The Department of State BULLETIN,
a weekly publication compiled and
edited in the Division of Publications,
Office of Public Affairs, provides the
public and interested agencies of
the Government with information on
developments in the field of foreign
relations and on the work of the Department of State and the Foreign
Service. The BULLETIN includes
press releases on foreign policy issued
by the White House and the Department, and statements and addresses
made by the President and by the
Secretary of State and other officers
of the Department, as well as special
articles on various phases of international affairs and the functions of
the Department. Information is included concerning treaties and international agreements to which the
United States is or may become a
party and treaties of general international interest.

Publications of the Department, as
well as legislative material in the field
of international relations, are listed
currently.

uperintendent of Documents
Government Printing Office
Washington 25, D.C.

SUBSCRIPTION:
sues, $5; single copy. 15 cents
hed with the approval of the
of the Bureau of the Budget

s of this publication are not
items contained herein may
itation of the DEPARTMENT
ETIN as the source will be

HE INSTITUTE OF INTER-AMERICAN AFFAIRS

Cooperative Programs in Health and Sanitation

by Louis J. Halle, Jr.

I

Some students of human ecology, going back Malthus, have maintained that diseases perform vital function in keeping populations down to e "carrying capacity" of the land on which they re. Malaria, according to this grim view, may some places be an alternative to starvation. nprovement in peoples' health, however, may so contribute to an increase in the "carrying pacity" of the land by making it possible for em to work the land more effectively. I recall eing a settlement of bush huts on the Mexican-uatemalan boundary where malaria had reduced e population to below the "carrying capacity" the land—to zero, in fact. The empty huts were lling into ruin. While this is an extreme case, in remote region beyond the frontiers of civiliza-)n, most of us who have traveled extensively in)pical America have seen rural populations so bilitated by disease that their ability to work e land was impaired. Disease is an appreciable ctor in the low agricultural productivity of iny regions in the American tropics. It also iltifies progress in the other branches of human complishment.

The achievement of public health throughout e Hemisphere is more a matter of providing latively simple means than of applying abstruse ills to complex and varied situations. Tablets at are sold in drugstores would have saved the :tlement that was exterminated by malaria, if ey had been at hand. Hookworm is easily pre-nted and easily cured, but only where the means e available. Chlorine can make a water supply fe, but you have to have the chlorine. You also ve to have men and women who know how to ply the remedies. The United States is more rtunate than most American republics in the mber of physicians, nurses, sanitary engineers, d other public-health experts available to look

after its population. The shortage of such trained persons is acute throughout most of Latin Amer-ica, especially outside the great centers of popu-lation.

The essential simplicity of the problem accounts for the fact that the cooperation of this Govern-ment with other American governments, through the Institute of Inter-American Affairs, yields more immediate benefits in the field of public health than in other fields. When the Peruvian and United States Governments, through the *servicio* administering the health and sanitation program in Peru, attacked the problem of malaria in the coastal town of Chimbote, the incidence of malaria there was 25 percent. Four years later it was 2 percent. Chimbote has the finest harbor on the Peruvian coast, with coal mines and iron ore not far away. The economic possibilities in-herent in this situation were not realized before 1943 because the conditions of health were such as to weaken the native population and deter im-migration. From 1942 to 1947, however, the population of Chimbote rose from 5,000 to 10,000, and it now has what appears to be an expanding future. This illustrates the kind of effectiveness that can be achieved by cooperation in health and sanitation.

Effectiveness in time, however, in the achieve-ment of improvements that are permanent and pro-gressive, depends upon a substantial increase in the locally available supply of trained professionals. Consequently, the Health and Sanitation Division of the Institute has given special emphasis to training in the fields of preventive medicine, sani-tary engineering, nursing, and medical education. The need of this training is suggested by statistics showing that, even today and in a progressive country, a population of 47 million people will have a total of 800 nurses to look after it—that is, one nurse for every 58,750 persons. By the end of 1947, some form of training in nursing or midwifery had been given, under the cooperative programs, to over 4,000 women from 14 of the other American republics, training that ranged from that of nurse aides to that of graduate nurses in public health. Over 1,100 persons, including nurses, had received grants for study in the United States, and the great majority of these have now returned to their countries to assume positions of responsibility in public health and to work with United States technicians in carrying on the health programs. At the same time, over 5,000 persons have had local training courses, and assistance has been given in the development of nursing schools in 13 countries. Activities in health education, originally organized by the cooperative health *servicios* and now operated by national departments of health, are being taken over and expanded by the local nationals who have been trained in the United States.

The Institute has, since 1942, cooperated in health programs in 18 of the other American republics. It operates, today, in 14 of these 18. In each country, the objectives are the control of major diseases and the alleviation of conditions that bring about low levels of health. The program in Brazil may be taken as an example of how these programs operate and what they accomplish.

II

The Amazon valley, transported to the United States, would reach about two thirds of the distance from our eastern seaboard to the Pacific coast. It represents the kind of hot, humid tropics in which organisms that compete with man or are hostile to him have an advantage. Weeds require no cultivation and parasites all but take possession of the human population. The attainment of a satisfactory life, by civilized standards, is a challenge to science. The possibilities for economic development in the valley, however, have strongly attracted those who think in ample terms. The Brazilian Government has been considering a plan to increase the valley's economic value and is, in fact, appropriating funds for a large program of development. The foundation of such a program must necessarily effect the creation of conditions that insure a minimum standard of public health. Men cannot engage in pioneer exploitation, even today, by remote control alone.

When, in 1942, the Governments of Brazil and of the United States undertook to cooperate in a program of public health and created the Serviço Especial de Saude Publica (SESP) for the purpose, immediate as well as long-range considerations dictated the Amazon valley as the first scene of operations. World War II was in its most desperate phase and raw materials obtainable in the valley were needed in the common struggle of the United Nations. The men who went in to get those raw materials had to be protected against disease.

A logical first step in the program would have been to establish a health center in each municipal seat, but the funds were insufficient. The more important towns were selected and 30 health centers established with a physician in charge of each. These centers were staffed by visiting nurse aides, laboratory technicians, sanitary inspectors, and administrative personnel. Not enough public-health nurses were available to have one for each, but a few were found and assigned to key posts. The main work of these centers has been control of communicable diseases, maternal and infant care, health education for the public, health examinations, public-health nursing, sanitation, sanitary inspection, vital statistics, and some medical care. Each center has a laboratory and a small pharmacy for the preparation of drugs and other necessities. No charge is made for services rendered.

In order to extend the area of their influence, these 30 centers are supplemented by 34 secondary health posts, manned by sanitary inspectors under the constant supervision of the doctors at the main posts. Some of the centers have launches for itinerant service.

SESP constructed hospitals in Belém, Breves, Fortaleza, Manáus, and Santarém and is responsible for their operation. As the scope of the health work increased, laboratories were established in Belém and Manáus to augment the clinical research work of the hospitals and health centers. Here the SESP technicians of both nationalities have been studying means for the control of malaria, yaws, filariasis, intestinal parasites, brucellosis, Chagas's disease, and trichinosis.

From the beginning, the program on the Amazon has been characterized by important projects for the reduction of malaria. At Belém, a large dike

water-supply or sewerage systems had been undertaken in nine towns.

Extensive laboratory work is carried on at various localities in the valley of the Rio Doce and in a railroad car that facilitates studies and surveys throughout the area. The treatment, prophylaxis, and general control of malaria are also pursued actively. Wherever DDT has been used, a marked reduction in the number of persons coming to malaria-control posts for treatment has ensued.

These activities, specifically located in the Amazon and Rio Doce valleys, are supplemented by country-wide activities that include leprosy control, nursing, the training of professional and technical personnel, and general health education. A nursing school has been built in São Paulo. Nurses from Brazil and the United States are working in this and other schools for the improvement and extension of hospitals and public-health nursing services. One objective is to have four or five nursing schools so well developed that they constitute a permanent reservoir for the supply of nurses who can develop other schools and nursing services generally. Women selected for outstanding qualities of leadership are sent to the United States for thorough training. In courses of training conducted in Brazil and averaging six months, 102 visiting nurse aides and 83 hospital aides have been trained.

Up to the end of 1947, SESP had graduated 23 doctors in public health from its own staff and granted four fellowships to other doctors. Fellowships had been granted to 117 doctors in the United States, and 36 fellowships had been granted to engineers. Twenty-two women had been sent to take the basic three-year course of nursing in the United States; 14 to take one-year postgraduate courses in the United States; and 42 had been granted fellowships for the three-year course at nursing schools in Brazil.

As this training goes forward, a campaign is being conducted to teach the public the need for competent nursing and the benefits that can result. This is being done by the establishment of libraries, health clubs, and boards of health; by instruction for school teachers; by distribution of pamphlets, posters, and movies; and by radio broadcasts.

There are indications that public opinion in Brazil is responding favorably to the work of the health program. In Aimores, a town of 5,000, from 20 to 30 cases of typhoid fever occurred every year, many resulting in death. In 1943 Sesp started work on a water-supply system that was completed in 1946. Not a single case of typhoid fever occurred in 1947, to the amazement of the people, who now speak with pride of the wonderful effects produced by their drinking water. Recently a letter was written to the mayor of a town asking if he had money available for spraying the houses of the town with DDT. He replied that there were no funds for this purpose. A few days later, Sesp received an urgent telegram stating that the funds had been secured. What had happened was that the people of the town had learned of the mayor's reply, a meeting of the town council had been held, and the mayor had been persuaded to change his mind.

It appears safe to say that the cooperative health program in Brazil, in addition to improving conditions of health over a large part of the country, has contributed to laying a foundation for further and permanent improvements.

III

The features of the Brazilian health program that I have cited above are, for the most part, features of the other health programs as well. The purpose of describing the one program in some detail was thereby to describe all programs in rough outline. No two are quite the same, of course, since the particular problems and the range of problems they have to solve are often peculiar to each country. The importance of mining in Bolivia, for example, has led to special emphasis on industrial hygiene and safety in the cooperative health program there. The extent of tuberculosis in Chile prompted the construction under the Chilean program of a large tuberculosis hospital near Santiago. Specialized nutrition projects were developed to deal with the prevalence of goiter in Colombia. The acute need of hospitals in Ecuador led to the construction or remodeling of 25 hospitals. In Haiti, the program has worked particularly on the control of yaws and malaria. The program in Mexico has been characterized, in part, by cooperation with

THE UNITED NATIONS AND SPECIALIZED AGENCIES

uture of the Interim Committee

STATEMENT BY JOSEPH E. JOHNSON [1]

Deputy U.S. Representative in the Interim Commission

This Subcommittee is meeting today, after some ree months, to consider the reports of its two rking groups, and to address itself to the ultiate question which is now before it. To use the nguage of the Philippine resolution which eated this Subcommittee, it must "make a recomndation on the advisability of establishing a rmanent committee of the General Assembly . . ." (/AC.18/10). You, Mr. Chairman, suggested your plan for these working groups that implicit this question is the possibility of recommendg the continuance of such a committee on a rther temporary basis.

When Secretary Marshall, on September 17, 47, introduced the proposal for a standing comttee of the General Assembly, he said in the urse of the general debate:

"In our opinion every member of the United tions should be seated on this body. The crean of the Interim Committee will make the facilis of the General Assembly continually available ring the next year to all its members. It will engthen the machinery for peaceful settlement d place the responsibility for such settlement oadly upon all the members of the United Nans. Without infringing on the jurisdiction of e Security Council, it will provide an unsurssed opportunity for continuing study, after the journment of this Assembly, of the problems th which the United Nations must contend if it to succeed."

The Interim Committee was established and it at work. As the Bolivian Representative obrved at an early meeting of this Subcommittee, has permitted "calm and serene consideration" questions and has enabled all nations repreted to express opinions on a wide horizon. This, my opinion, has been a good thing. Recently a

member of the press commented to me that there are not many headlines in the Interim Committee's work. That too is a good thing. Headlines are apt to reflect conflict, and one of our chief purposes is to minimize conflict.

Let me refer briefly to three areas in which the Interim Committee has been working.

1. Implementation

In this field the Interim Committee has already made a signal contribution. Its existence made one special session of the General Assembly unnecessary. I refer, of course, to the Korean consultation. Through this consultation the Committee provided most effective assistance and support to the Korean Commission in carrying through a difficult task. The Commission in this manner obtained the advice of the membership of the United Nations in a convenient, effective, and inexpensive manner.

Also in the field of implementation is the Interim Committee's study of voting procedures in the Security Council. The Committee has been the forum in which members of the United Nations have for the first time since San Francisco had an opportunity for a full exchange of views on voting procedures. It is already apparent that the report of the Interim Committee will be a valuable document on which further important decisions can be based. This subject is one to which the United States attaches great importance.

These two matters have demonstrated the value of a subsidiary organ in carrying out *ad hoc* tasks for the General Assembly between its sessions.

---

[1] Made in Subcommittee 4 on June 17, 1948, and released to the press by the U.S. Mission to the United Nations on the same date.

It is reasonable to suppose that in the future the General Assembly will find it useful to deal with other important matters in like fashion. A practice of this kind is most likely to develop out of experience. Our experience to date would justify further reliance on a body such as this.

2. Pacific Settlement Studies

Subcommittee 2 has begun work which the United States and, if I am not mistaken, many other members, hope will continue for a period of years, and which will probably involve a continuing process of reexamination. Its discussions have gone forward in an atmosphere removed from the tension of immediate political issues. These studies relate to chapter VI of the Charter, which Ambassador Austin has recently characterized as the most important part of that document. They also relate to the General Assembly's responsibilities under articles 11(1) and 13(1, a). We have been impressed with the insight characterizing the discussions in that Subcommittee.

3. Preparatory Work

The Interim Committee has not yet undertaken any preparatory work for the next regular session of the General Assembly, and there is the possibility that it may not do so in the weeks to come. But it has a potentiality in that field. The representatives who have sat through the sessions of these subcommittees and the Interim Committee, and have had an opportunity to compare them with the hectic meetings of the First Committee, cannot but be impressed with that potentiality.

In summary, my Government feels that these have been important, useful, and productive months for the Interim Committee in spite of the fact that the calling of the Second Special Session of the General Assembly forced it substantially to cease its operations for a considerable time.

The Soviet Union and the five other states which follow its lead have not occupied the seats to which they are entitled. Their absence has made some of the results of the Interim Committee's work less conclusive than they might otherwise have been. However, the absence of these six members has not prevented progress. I leave it to the members of the Interim Committee, Mr. Chairman, whether the record does not show that Mr. Vyshinsky has been proven mistaken in his estimate that the Interim Committee would be but a crude device to by-pass the Security Council and would, as a principal organ, usurp its functions (A/P. V. 84, page 97). Indeed, I suggest that an examination of the record of the Interim Committee may well convince the Soviet Union that it will wish to participate in its work if the General Assembly decides to continue it.

The Future

Let me now turn to the future and relate these experiences to it. With such a promising beginning, it seems to my Government that the conclusion must follow that the Interim Committee should be continued. The important thing is its continuance. The term for which it is continued is relatively unimportant; perhaps this should be another experimental year, as a minimum. But the view of the United States, I venture to think, is well known to the other representatives. Speaking last month before the House of Representatives Committee on Foreign Affairs, Secretary Marshall considered how the existing machinery of the United Nations could be strengthened and in this connection he recalled that "by means of this [Interim] Committee the far-reaching influence of the General Assembly is being brought more effectively to bear in fulfilling the purposes and principles of the Charter."

We feel that a firm foundation has been laid. The United States is earnestly concerned with strengthening the United Nations. It recognizes the part that a continuing committee of the General Assembly has played and can play.

At this stage of the discussion I do not propose, Mr. Chairman, to comment upon the various tentative conclusions contained in the reports of the working groups or to anticipate the discussion of the Subcommittee upon them. That I would reserve for later. But one observation is appropriate. My Government feels that the sound development of a committee of the General Assembly functioning between sessions will evolve from the confident belief by the members that it will not encroach upon the functions of the principal organs or other agencies of the United Nations. One of the outstanding facts about the Interim Committee thus far is that it has not so encroached. I suggest that such confidence will continue to evolve from use of the Committee along the lines already developed rather than from substantial alteration of its terms of reference. It is because of this conviction that the United States has not itself, in the working group in which it has participated, suggested any considerable changes in the terms of reference of a future committee. We feel that its orderly development will result from continuing substantially those powers which it now has; and from actual use of these powers including the development of its potentiality for both preparatory work and implementation.

The United States urges the continuance of a committee of the General Assembly in the nature of the present Interim Committee, at least for another year. My Government feels that the experience of this Committee demonstrates that its continuance will strengthen the United Nations and will contribute to its sound and orderly development.

Why and How We Came To Find Ourselves at the Havana Conference

BY WILLIAM L. CLAYTON[1]

Adviser to the Secretary of State

"Why and How We Came To Find Ourselves [a]t the Havana Conference" is a good story, but [,] will take us over a long and difficult road.

The story needs to be told because it will help [)] a better understanding of the Havana charter.

No doubt the inspiration for that great enter[r]ise lay in the general realization that the na[t]ons of the world made a tragic mess of their [i]nternational economic relationships following the [fi]rst world war and in a determination that this [t]ime road should not be traveled again.

It is only necessary to mention such matters as [r]eparations, the handling of the war debts, [r]ising to fantastic heights of tariffs and other [t]rade barriers, the practice of bilateral and barter [t]rading, and the bitter retaliations and discrimi[n]ations which flowed from these actions.

The first significant declaration of a determina[t]ion to prevent a recurrence of these tragic mis[t]akes was contained in the Atlantic Charter in [A]ugust 1941. The victorious German Army was [t]hen far inside Russia, having long since swept [w]estern Europe. There were no illusions in the [U]nited States regarding the peril with which we [w]ould be faced if Germany should win the war.

Under these dramatic circumstances President [R]oosevelt and Prime Minister Churchill met upon [t]he Atlantic and signed a pledge which became [k]nown as the Atlantic Charter. The Atlantic [C]harter announced, among other things, that the [t]wo Governments: ". . . will endeavor, with [d]ue respect for their existing obligations, to [f]urther the enjoyment by all States, great or small, [v]ictor or vanquished, of access, on equal terms, [t]o the trade and to the raw materials of the [w]orld . . ."

By 1943 thirty-four other nations had subscribed [t]o the principles of the Atlantic Charter.

Four months after the publication of the At[l]antic Charter the Japanese attack on Pearl Harbor [b]rought the United States into the war.

Within a short time thereafter we concluded [t]he first of a series of master lend-lease agreements [w]ith our European Allies.

Article VII of this agreement committed the [s]ignatory Governments to the principle of "the expansion, by appropriate international [a]nd domestic measures, of production, employ[m]ent, and the exchange and consumption of goods, [w]hich are the material foundations of the liberty [a]nd welfare of all peoples; . . . the elimina[ti]on of all forms of discriminatory treatment in [i]nternational commerce; and . . . the reduc[ti]on of tariffs and other trade barriers."

The United States Government lost no time,

even in the agonizing years of the war, in taking energetic action to mobilize the thinking in other governments and to prepare measures to carry out these declarations.

In November 1943, a distinguished British delegation led by Lord Keynes came to Washington by invitation to discuss with us the shaping of a world economic program. A broad range of economic subjects including trade and finance were discussed at that time. Similar discussions were held in January 1944 with the Canadian Government. Following these talks, we began work in Washington to shape up a program of action. For this purpose, an interdepartmental committee was formed, headed originally by Mr. Myron Taylor and later by Mr. Dean Acheson as Chairman of the Executive Committee on Economic Foreign Policy, established by the President. As Assistant Secretary of Commerce, I took part in the deliberations of this Committee and later, as Assistant Secretary of State for Economic Affairs, succeeded Mr. Acheson as Chairman of the Committee.

The international trade policies formulated by this group were presented in a document called *Proposals for the Expansion of World Trade and Employment*. Before publication in December 1945, these proposals were discussed with the British Government and were mutually agreed to. Subsequently, in the early months of 1946, other governments expressed their approval of the principles contained in the U.S. proposals.

Having achieved a wide measure of agreement on basic economic principles, the United States then drafted a charter to give effect to these principles. This document was known as *Suggested Charter for an International Trade Organization*. It was circulated to all United Nations governments for their consideration.

Meanwhile, the United Nations had been organized and in February 1946, the Economic and Social Council called a preliminary meeting of 18 countries to prepare for a conference on trade and employment. This meeting was held in London from October 15 to November 30, 1946. The draft charter suggested by the United States was used as the basis of discussion.

The text of the draft resulting from the London meeting was put into better shape by a drafting committee convened at Lake Success in January and February 1947. This became known as the "New York draft" and served as the basis for the Second Preparatory Conference convened in

---

[1] Delivered at the Economic Institute of the Chamber of Commerce of the U.S. at Washington, D.C., on June 15, 1948, and released to the press on the same date.

Geneva in April 1947. Prior thereto, however, this Government diligently endeavored to acquaint the American public and the Congress with the project in hand. Conferences were held with numerous business groups including the United States Chamber of Commerce. A representative group selected from departments of the Government held informal public hearings in seven major cities of the United States to receive "grass roots" opinions about the proposed Ito. The Senate Committee on Finance conducted a detailed inquiry, the record of which covers several thick volumes.

This "referendum" of public and congressional opinion was extremely valuable. Over 100 specific suggestions were received for revising or extending the charter. The entire record was carefully studied to pick out every meritorious suggestion for use in the Geneva negotiations. Both the Geneva draft and the present Havana Charter bear the imprint of these suggestions.

As you probably know, there were 19 countries represented at Geneva, and negotiations there lasted some five months. They were complicated and prolonged by the fact that these same countries were also negotiating a General Agreement on Tariffs and Trade which required bargaining on thousands of specific items. In addition, agreement on general undertakings had to be reached to give value to the tariff reductions on these items. This enormous and very difficult task was successfully concluded and now stands as a landmark in international trade relations.

The charter negotiations at Geneva were concluded late in August 1947. On November 21, 1947, the World Conference on Trade and Employment convened at Havana to perfect the final draft of the charter. Representatives of 56 countries attended the Conference. This meant that two thirds of the countries at Havana had not participated in the preliminary conferences at London and Geneva. The charter was finally initialed by representatives of 54 countries.

.   .   .   .

In retrospect it seems almost inconceivable that representatives of 54 nations, great and small, developed and undeveloped, with divergent interests, and speaking many different languages, could agree on a constitution of principles to govern their international economic relationships.

The drafters of the American Constitution didn't have an easy time reaching agreement on that document, but just suppose they had neglected to forbid the States of this Union to erect tariff barriers. In that case, today, 160 years later, we would certainly have a flourishing crop of protectionist measures dividing the United States into 48 economic principalities.

For example, I am quite sure that my State of Texas would have prohibitive tariffs, among other

than that; it would be regarded as a repudiation of much that has been accomplished under that leadership.

If we deliberately vacate our rightful place in this field, does anyone believe that there is another nation in the world today prepared to step into our shoes?

What, then, would the consequence of such action be?

It is certain that every country in the world would feel that it was again on its own, that it was compelled to rely on unilateral action, in short that it had no other recourse except to return to the practices of the international economic jungle—everyone for himself and the devil catch the hindmost.

Bilateralism, import quotas, export quotas, exchange controls, cartels, subsidies, discriminations, retaliations—all the devices known to man for limiting the international exchange of goods and services—would again become standard procedure throughout the world.

Do we want to see a return to that kind of world? Is that in our interest? We must realize that the United States could not long remain an island of free enterprise in a sea of state-controlled international trade. The United States would be forced into the international trading practices of the rest of the world.

But that is not all.

We would find it extremely difficult to carry on international trade in isolation from domestic trade.

There are two roads we can take here.

One road leads in the direction of free enterprise and the preservation of democratic principles.

The other road leads in the direction of Socialism and state trading.

We must soon choose which road we will take.

The Twentieth Century Fund recently issued a report recommending strongly a broad anti-cartel policy by the United States and declaring that support by the United States of the International Trade Organization is essential to such a policy.

The report further states that if the United States refuses the Ito charter, the result will be not a better agreement but a looser one or perhaps no agreement at all.

There are only two questions we have to ask ourselves in trying to decide what we will do about the Ito charter; and those two questions are:

1. Would the United States and the world be better off if there were no Ito, leaving each country to act on its own as heretofore?

2. If the present charter is rejected, would we be able later on to obtain agreement on a better charter?

In my opinion the answer to both questions is NO.

Termination of International Institute

The Permanent Committee:
Meeting in accordance with the Statutes of the IIA;
noting the formal statement made by the FAO in a circular letter dated February 2, 1948 that the Protocol of Dissolution of the International Institute of Agriculture became effective on January 28, 1948;
and
desiring to carry out the provisions of the Protocol in accordance with its provisions and as instructed by the XVIth General Assembly of the IIA;
adopts on this day, the 27th day of February 1948 the following Final Act:

In conformity with Art. VI, item I of the Protocol of Dissolution of the International Institute of Agriculture (including the International Forestry Centre), the said Protocol was not subject to ratification unless a special reservation to that effect was made at the time of signing.

The following countries, 30 in number, signed unreservedly: Australia, Belgium, Bulgaria, Canada, China, Cuba, Denmark, El Salvador, Finland, France, Greece, Hungary, India, Iran, Ireland, Luxembourg, Netherlands, Norway, Paraguay, Poland, Portugal, Rumania, San Marino, Siam, Spain, Sweden, Switzerland, Union of South Africa, United Kingdom, Uruguay.

In conformity with item 2 of Art. VI, the Protocol "will come into effect when accepted by at least thirty-five Government Members, of the Institute".

The following countries, six in number, have filed with FAO the instrument of ratification (chronological order):

United States, February 10, 1947.
Egypt, October 13, 1947.
Turkey, October 25, 1947.
Nicaragua, November 15, 1947.
Czechoslovakia, January 28, 1948.
Italy, January 29, 1948.

The Protocol, by the terms of Art. VI, therefore became operative at the time of the thirty-fifth ratification, namely on January 28, 1948, when

A Selected Bibliography[1]

Economic and Social Council

Official Records, Third Year, Seventh Session:

Supplement No. 1. Report of the Economic and Employment Commission. [E/790, May 10, 1948.] 21 pp. Printed. 25¢.

Supplement No. 8. Report of the Social Commission. [E/779, May 6, 1948.] 58 pp. Printed. 60¢.

Economic Commission for Europe. Annual Report. E/791, May 18, 1948. 58 pp. mimeo.

Report of the Committee and Draft Convention Drawn up by the Committee. (Ad Hoc Committee on Genocide). E/794, May 24, 1948. 59 pp. mimeo.

United Nations International Children's Emergency Fund. Financial Report and Statements . . . and the Report of the Board of Auditors. E/796, May 26, 1948. 10 pp. mimeo.

Supplementary Report of the Food and Agriculture Organization . . . E/797, May 24, 1948. 57 pp. mimeo.

Commission on Narcotic Drugs. Report to the Economic and Social Council on the Third Session of the Commission. E/799, May 28, 1948. 44 pp. mimeo.

Report of the Secretary-General on the Allocation of Functions Among the Various Organs Concerned in the Field of Migration. E/806, May 28, 1948. 111 pp. mimeo.

Transfer to the United Nations of the Functions Exercised by the French Government . . . for the Suppression of the White Slave Traffic, and . . . the Suppression of Obscene Publications. E/809, June 4, 1948. 7 pp. mimeo.

THE FOREIGN SERVICE

Consular Offices

A consular agency was established at Curitibá, Brazil, on May 24, 1948.

Confirmations

On June 17, 1948, the Senate confirmed the nomination of Harold H. Tittmann, Jr., to be Ambassador Extraordinary and Plenipotentiary to Peru.

---

[1] Printed materials may be secured in the United States from the International Documents Service, Columbia University Press, 2960 Broadway, New York City. Other materials (mimeographed or processed documents) may be consulted at certain designated libraries in the United States.

The United States in the United Nations

Palestine

Steps taken by the United States in accordance with the Security Council's Palestine truce resolution of May 29 and in support of the U.N. mediator's truce proposals were listed in a letter sent to Trygve Lie, Secretary-General of the United Nations, on June 22 by Philip C. Jessup, Acting U.S. Representative to the United Nations in the absence of Ambassador Warren R. Austin. The Security Council had decided on June 15 at the request of Count Bernadotte, U.N. mediator for Palestine, to ask all U.N. members for such reports.

Mr. Jessup's letter [1] stated that (1) appropriate authorities of the U.S. Government have been instructed to prevent departure from the United States for Palestine or Arab League countries, during the truce period, of "fighting personnel", as specified in the May 29 resolution; (2) attention of the authorities concerned, including the Chairman of the U.S. Maritime Commission, has been called to the stipulations in the mediator's June 7 truce proposals regarding immigration of "men of military age"; (3) the U.S. embargo on arms shipments to the Near East, instituted November 17, 1947, meets the resolution's injunction on this point; (4) as a member of the Security Council's Truce Commission in Palestine, the U.S. Government has supplied the mediator, at his request, with military observers, transport aircraft, communications facilities, and three naval patrol vessels.

Atomic Energy

On June 22 the Security Council concluded a series of three meetings devoted to the reports of the Atomic Energy Commission. It decided by a vote of 9–0 (U.S.S.R. and Ukraine abstaining) that the Commission's three reports and the record of the Council's debates on them should be transmitted to the General Assembly "as a matter of special concern".

Agreement on simple referral to the General Assembly followed the defeat, by a Soviet Union veto, of a draft resolution which Philip C. Jessup, U.S. Deputy Representative, had tabled on June 11. The U.S. proposal was that the Council should refer the Commission's reports to the General Assembly along with its express endorsement of the majority plan of atomic control outlined in the general findings and recommendations of the First Report and the specific proposals of the Second Report, as well as of the Third Report's

[1] Printed in this issue.

on June 26. On June 23, the Commission approved resolutions calling for a general economic survey of Latin America and defining the working relations between Ecla and the Inter-American Economic and Social Council.

U.S. Representation

On June 24 the President appointed W. Averell Harriman, U.S. Special Representative in Europe of the Economic Cooperation Administration to serve as U.S. Representative on the U.N. Economic Commission for Europe, a regional economic organ of the U.N. Economic and Social Council. On that date the President also appointed John J. Macdonald as U.S. Representative on the Security Council Truce Commission for Palestine and as U.S. Consul General in Jerusalem to succeed Thomas C. Wasson, who was killed by a sniper's bullet while serving in that capacity. Mr. Macdonald has been a Foreign Service officer since 1930, serving most recently as Consul General in Bombay. Both appointments are recess appointments, pending Senate confirmation.

Aviation Conference

The International Civil Aviation Organization concluded its second assembly on June 22 after a three-week session in Geneva. Russell B. Adams, chief of the U.S. Delegation, called particularly important Conference approval of a proposed international legal convention on recognition of rights in aircraft. The United States is one of the 14 states out of a total of 49 Icao members who have signed the convention, which recognizes in all contracting states the rights in aircraft granted by any one of them and which is designed to afford the international airline operators with the largest possible measure of assistance in arranging and financing aircraft purchases. Other accomplishments of the conference were recommendations to simplify aviation border crossings, approval of the right of punishment of airmen who infringe local air regulations, establishment of an Air Navigation Commission, and recommendations for the development of international standards and recommended practices.

Correction

It was erroneously stated in "The United States and the United Nations" in the BULLETIN of June 13, 1948, p. 768, that the U.N. Special Commission on the Balkans had moved its headquarters from Geneva to Salonika. The Commission is currently writing its report in Geneva, having moved there from Salonika.

---

[1] U.S. Mission to the United Nations press release 479.

INTERNATIONAL ORGANIZATIONS AND CONFERENCES

Veterinary Science

[Released to the press June 14]

The Department of State announced on June 14 that Dr. Banner B. Morgan, associate professor of veterinary science, University of Wisconsin, Madison, Wis., and Dr. Harry Ellis Kingman, Wyoming Hereford Ranch, Cheyenne, Wyo., have been designated as members of the United States Delegation to the First International Congress on the Physiopathology of Animal Reproduction and Artificial Insemination. The Congress, sponsored by the Italian Government, is scheduled to be held at Milan from June 23 to 30, 1948.

The purpose of the meeting is to examine the problem of animal reproduction, both from the scientific side and from the standpoint of its technical and economic aspects. Special attention will be given to methods of artificial insemination. Among the other topics to be discussed are: (1) biological problems of animal reproduction; (2) livestock reproduction; (3) pathological problems of animal reproduction; and (4) legislative problems concerning artificial insemination and animal reproduction.

The Congress will be divided into sections for discussions and there will be special exhibitions of scientific and educational material.

World Health

[Released to the press June 19]

The Department of State has announced that the President has given approval to the United States Delegation to the First Session of the World Health Assembly, which is scheduled to convene at Geneva on June 24, 1948. The United States Delegation is as follows:

Delegates

Thomas Parran, M.D., Medical Director, U.S. Public Health Service, Federal Security Agency (Chairman of the Delegation)

Martha M. Eliot, M.D., Associate Chief, Children's Bureau, Federal Security Agency

James R. Miller, M.D., Trustee, American Medical Association

Alternates

Frank P. Corrigan, M.D., Political Adviser on Latin America, U.S. Mission to the United Nations, Lake Success, N.Y.

James A. Doull, M.D., Medical Director, U.S. Public Health Service, Chief, Office of International Health Relations, Federal Security Agency

Wilton Halverson, M.D., Director, Public Health, State of California, San Francisco, Calif.

H. Van Zile Hyde, M.D., Alternate U.S. Representative, Interim Commission of the World Health Organization; Division of International Labor, Social and Health Affairs, Department of State

Durward V. Sandifer, Deputy Director, Office of United Nations Affairs, Department of State

Advisers

Howard B. Calderwood, Division of United Nations Economic and Social Affairs, Department of State

Nelson H. Cruikshank, Director, Social Insurance Activities, American Federation of Labor, Washington, D.C.

Albert W. Dent, M.D., President, Dillard University, New Orleans, La.

Morton Kramer, Ph.D., Chief, Research and Information, Office of International Health Relations, U.S. Public Health Service, Federal Security Agency

Mrs. David M. Levy, President, Citizens Committee on Children of New York City

James E. Perkins, M.D., Managing Director, National Tuberculosis Association, New York City

Miss Lucile Petry, Director, Division of Nursing, U.S. Public Health Service, Federal Security Agency

Alvin Roseman, Deputy Director, International Activities Branch, Bureau of the Budget

Paul F. Russell, M.D., Malariologist, Rockefeller Foundation, The Rockefeller Institute, New York City

James S. Simmons, Brigadier General, M.C., U.S. Army, (Retired), Dean, School of Public Health, Harvard University, Cambridge, Mass.

John Tomlinson, Assistant Chief, Division of United Nations Economic and Social Affairs, Department of State

Tom Whayne, Colonel (M.C.), U.S. Army, Chief, Preventive Medicine Division, Office of the Surgeon General, Department of the Army

Abel Wolman, Professor, Sanitary Engineering, Johns Hopkins School of Public Health and Hygiene, Johns Hopkins University, Baltimore, Md.

Executive Secretary

William H. Dodderidge, Division of International Conferences, Department of State

The convening of the World Health Assembly marks the beginning of full-scale activity of the World Health Organization (WHO) and the termination of the interim phase of the development of the international health agency planned by plenipotentiaries of 62 governments at the International Health Conference at New York City during the summer of 1946.

The Constitution of the WHO provides that each member nation be represented at the Assembly by three delegates having only one vote. It also provides that the Assembly will be the governing body of the WHO and that it will, among other things, determine policies, name member nations entitled to designate persons to serve on the Executive Board of the WHO, appoint the Director General, review reports of the WHO Interim Commission,

Howard L. Melvin, chief consulting engineer, Ebasco Services, Inc., New York, N.Y.
Wendall A. Morgan, head, Power System Technical Group, Bureau of Reclamation
Philip Sporn, president, American Gas and Electric Services Corporation, New York, N. Y.

The objects of the Conference are to study and discuss developments and progress in the construction, operation, and maintenance of large high-tension electric systems by bringing together every two years eminent specialists from many countries. The Conference will study the most recent advances in: (1) the manufacture of machinery for generation, transformation, and circuit breaking of electric currents; (2) the construction, insulation, and maintenance of overhead lines and underground cables; and (3) the operation, protection, and interconnection of networks.

Founded in March 1921, under the aegis of the International Electrotechnical Commission, the International Conference on Electric Systems operates with the support and assistance of all the large international electrotechnical organizations. It is not only one of the oldest of all international electrotechnical organizations, but it is also the largest, having more than 1,000 permanent members. Its biennial sessions have become the periodic meeting place of electrical engineers from all over the world.

The forthcoming meeting is of particular interest at the present time because of its bearing on the increased power production for Europe contemplated under the European Recovery Program.

Public Education

[Released to the press June 14]

The Department of State announced on June 14 the appointment of the United States Delegation to the Eleventh International Conference on Public Education to be held at Geneva from June 28 to July 3, 1948. The Delegation is as follows: Galen Jones, Director of Secondary Education, U.S. Office of Education, Chairman, and Ruth Emily McMurry, UNESCO Relations Staff, Department of State.

The Conference is jointly sponsored by the United Nations Educational, Scientific and Cultural Organization (UNESCO) and the International Bureau of Education. Progress reports on the development of educational standards and facilities in each country will be submitted by the delegations. In addition, the Conference will study three main questions: (1) the role of school psychologists; (2) the teaching of writing; (3) the teaching about the U.N. and its specialized agencies. The Conference will offer opportunities for an exchange of information on the present features of educational movements in the various countries. It will also afford an opportunity for studying, on an international plane, educational problems of present interest which have formed the subject of inquiries or study on the part of the United Nations Educational, Scientific and Cultural Organization and the International Bureau of Education.

The Tenth International Conference held last year under the sponsorship of IBE and UNESCO was attended by delegates from more than 40 countries. Seventy-one nations have been invited to participate in the Conference this year.

The materials submitted and the text of the discussions at the forthcoming Conference will be published jointly by UNESCO and IBE in French and English editions.

Genetics

[Released to the press June 17]

The Department of State announced on June 17 the United States Delegation to the Eighth International Congress of Genetics scheduled to convene at Stockholm on July 7, 1948. The United States Delegation is as follows:

Chairman

Dr. Forrest V. Owen, senior geneticist, Division of Sugar Plant Investigations, Bureau of Plant Industry, Soils and Agricultural Engineering, Department of Agriculture

Delegates

Dr. Milislav Demerec, Carnegie Institution, Cold Spring Harbor, Long Island, N.Y.

Dr. Walter E. Heston, principal geneticist, National Cancer Institute, Bethesda, Md.

Dr. Hermann J. Muller, president of the International Congress of Genetics, professor of zoology, Indiana University, Bloomington, Ind.

The seventh and last International Congress of Genetics was held at Edinburgh from August 23 to 29, 1939. The forthcoming congress will bring together leading scientists for the presentation of papers and discussions on human genetics as well as experiments on plant and animal breeding.

Recent advances in the field of genetics will prove of great interest both to the scientific world and to the layman by their practical application to plant and animal breeding.

Radiocommunications

[Released to the press June 17]

The Department of State announced on June 17 the United States Delegation to the Fifth Meeting of the International Radio Consultative Committee of the CCIR (Comité Consultatif International des Radiocommunications) of the International Telecommunication Union, scheduled to be held at Stockholm July 12–31, 1948. The United States Delegation is as follows:

Chairman

Harvey B. Otterman, Associate Chief, Telecommunications Division, Department of State

GOVERNMENT IN FRANKFURT

possible at any time to establish economic unity on the basis of free movement of goods and persons, joint export-import controls and the cessation of Soviet reparations from current production, it should not be difficult to arrange for a common currency for Germany as a whole.

The currency to be used was printed in the United States in 1947 and 1948. The decision on printing at that time contemplated use of currency either on a quadripartite or western basis, depending on whether quadripartite agreement was reached. If it had been reached, the currency already printed in the United States would have been available for its immediate implementation, and it was hoped that several months' delay between the agreement and actual implementation would thus be avoided. If, on the other hand, quadripartite agreement were not reached, as has been the case, the currency would be available for use in the western zones.

OF CURRENCY REFORM

a family of four, 240 marks of old money can be paid in, for which the family receives immediately 160 deutsche marks and an additional 80 marks one month later.

Other money held by the German public, as well as savings accounts in banks, savings banks, and postal-savings institutions will be converted into deutsche marks at a later date. The conversion rate, which will drastically reduce the total amount of money in circulation, as well as other details concerning the exchange of these amounts of money, will be published shortly in further laws. During this later conversion operation, the per capita quota already received will be deducted from the deutsche mark funds then converted or credited to the individual. Thus, if a person has an account with a bank which, through this later conversion, is reduced to 200 deutsche marks, he will still have deducted from this the sixty marks which he already received as his per capita quota in the new currency.

The per capita quota will be paid this coming Sunday by the same offices issuing food rationing stamps. In order to receive the new money, all persons must observe the following instructions:

Individuals must show their food ration and

identity cards and hand in 60 marks in old money. As far as families are concerned, the per capita quota for the whole family will be delivered to the head of the family after he has produced the food ration and identity cards for each family member and has handed in 60 marks for each person. Persons who are physically incapable of appearing themselves may send a representative who, however, must be authorized by a letter stating the reason for nonappearance of the person concerned. If the head of a family is incapacitated, by sickness or otherwise, from appearing, another member of the family can pick up the per capita quota, again submitting an authorization. Special regulations will apply to travelers; they will find them at the nearest food-ration office.

Wages and salaries must be paid in the new currency as of Sunday. Wage and salary recipients who are paid on a bi-monthly or monthly basis in advance will get a reimbursement of 70 percent, in new money, for the days between the tenth day after currency reform and their next pay day (for which they were paid in advance in old currency).

There will be a moratorium of one week for all money obligations in reichsmarks. That is to say, during this week (ending June 26) no debts should be paid.

Prices will not be affected by the currency reform. In all laws, administrative regulations, contracts, etc., the new currency will simply replace the old.

Business enterprises will, upon application, receive advances to tide them over. This aid in new deutsche mark will depend on the number of employees and the size of their holdings in old money. In principle, they will receive 80 marks per employee, the total aid not to exceed their holding in old currency.

In preparation for the exchange of old money in circulation and bank accounts, the old money now in the western zones must be turned in or registered by June 26. All money not turned in or registered by that date will become worthless.

In order to guarantee a full utilization of all property, the German legislative authorities will be charged with working out a law for the equalization of financial burdens within six months

STATEMENT BY THE UNITED STATES, T

By virtue of the attempt by the Soviet military administration to usurp for itself the authority to dominate the economic affairs of Berlin and issue its own currency for the quadripartite city, the western powers find it necessary to introduce the deutsche mark in the three western sectors of Berlin.

At the time of the monetary reform in the three

---

[1] Released in Berlin on June 23, 1948. Printed from telegraphic text.

The three western occupying powers specifically
vited the Soviet military administration to dis-
ss on a quadripartite basis the most feasible
ethod of protecting the economy of the people
Berlin.   At the meeting on Tuesday 22 June on
e finance and economic experts from the four
cupying powers of Germany, the western zone
presentatives offered to consider and work out
th the Soviet authorities a reasonable and satis-
ctory method for the handling of the currency
d monetary reform measures for Berlin as a
tole.   It was and still is the desire of the three
estern powers to have a uniform currency for the
tole of Berlin.

The western proposals were refused by the
iviet military authorities.   Instead, the Soviet
ilitary authorities insisted that it alone would
ite the currency law for the city of Berlin.
irthermore, the Soviet administration refused
recognize the prerogatives of the Kommanda-
ra as the supreme law making body of Berlin.
stead the SMA announced this morning laws
nich would presumably be applicable to greater
erlin—the same laws the SMA has promulgated
r the Soviet zone.

The western powers cannot submit to such arbi-
iry action which is in violation and total

disregard of the actual quadripartite status of
Berlin and which disregards and violates all
agreements respecting the managements of money
and banking affairs of the city.   The three western occupying powers in Berlin found it necessary,
therefore, to issue orders that laws promulgated
by the Soviet military administration will not
apply to the three western sectors of Berlin.   The
three western powers, therefore, find themselves
forced to introduce into the three western sectors
of Berlin the deutsche mark which is now legal
tender in the three western zones.

Details of the manner and time of the conversion
of existing money and bank account holdings of the
population of the U.S., U.K., and French sectors
of Berlin will be announced shortly.   Meantime,
an order calling for the immediate closing of all
banks in the three western sectors and declaring a
moratorium on all financial obligations pending
the announcement of details of the monetary conversion operation, has been published.

In order to minimize undue hardships among
the civilian population of the three western sectors
of Berlin, the occupying powers have decreed that
food and chemists shops will remain open during
the period of conversion.

---

ie IIAA—Continued from page 822

nperature and heavy rainfall are ideal for the
ltivation of manioca, cocoa, tea, rice, yucca,
paya, pineapple, and citrus fruits, and of rubber,
ichona, and barbasco.   The community grew
om 668 in 1940 to 5,000 in 1942 and in that year
e total health facilities and services consisted
a small out-patient clinic with one physician,
rking part time only.   In 1943, a Cooperative
ialth Service survey of all school children
owed that 99 percent were infected, 67 percent
th hookworm and 67 percent with parasites
ier than hookworm.   The Cooperative Health
rvice conducted a campaign for the construction
privies and the building of safe walls, for an
preciation of the need for shoes, clean drinking
ter, and wholesome foods, and for the examina-
n and treatment of children.   A 40-bed hospital
s built and operated.   Visiting and hospital
rse aides were trained and child-health confer-
ces held.   A mobile dispensary servicing work-
n on the Tingo María - Pucalpa highway at-
ded 11,692 patients during the 18 months it was

in operation.   Recent examinations made by the
Cooperative Health Service show that the percentage of school children infected with intestinal
parasites has declined from 99 percent in 1943 to
58 percent in 1947; infections with ascaris and
trichocephalus have dropped from 67 to 5 percent.
The incidence of malaria has dropped from 17
percent in 1945 to less than 1 percent in 1947.

These cases do not, of course, represent the ultimate achievement of the health programs that our
neighbors have undertaken with our cooperation.
The ultimate achievement must be the substantial
permanent improvement of physical health in the
Hemisphere, with all that means for the progress
of men in the accomplishments of civilization.
The way to this goal is long, but there is reason
to believe that the good-neighbor policy, expressed
in this kind of cooperation, is making progress
along this road.[1]

[1] For articles by Mr. Halle on the significance of the
IIAA in the conduct of U.S. foreign policy and on the
cooperative agricultural programs of the IIAA, see BULLE-
TIN of May 23, 1948, p. 659, and June 13, 1948, p. 758.

French Zone of Germany Adheres to Ec

[Released to the press jointly with the ECA June 4]

Ambassador Caffery to General Guillaume [1]

June 3, 1948

SIR: The Economic Cooperation Act of 1948 (title I of the Foreign Assistance Act of 1948) became law on 3 April 1948.

You will note the general requirement that, before assistance may be provided by the United States to a participating country as defined in subsection 103 (*a*) of the Act, an agreement must have been concluded between that country and the United States as described in subsection 115 (*b*) of the Act. However, before such an agreement is concluded and until 3 July 1948, the Government of the United States proposes under the terms of subsection 115 (*c*) to arrange for the performance, with respect to the French Zone of Occupation of Germany, of these functions authorized by the Act which may be determined to be essential in furtherance of its purposes. This action by the Government of the United States is contingent upon the requirements of subsection 115 (*c*) of the Act being fulfilled.

Accordingly, I should appreciate your notifying me whether the French Military Government, on behalf of the French Zone of Occupation of Germany, adheres to the purposes and policies in furtherance of which the Act authorizes assistance to be provided, and is engaged in continuous efforts to accomplish a joint recovery program through multilateral undertakings and the establishment of a continuing organization for this purpose, and also whether the French Military Government, on behalf of the French Zone of Occupation of Germany, intends to conclude an agreement with the United States in accordance with subsection 115 (*b*). The purposes of the Act are stated in the whole of subsection 102 (*b*) and the policies referred to in subsection 102 (*b*) are those designated as such in subsection 102 (*a*).

Since subsection 115 (*c*) of the Act predicates the furnishing of assistance upon continuous compliance with such provisions of subsection 115 (*b*) as my Government may consider applicable, I should appreciate your advising me whether the French Zone of Occupation of Germany is already taking the measures necessary to carry out the applicable provisions of subsection 115 (*b*) and will continue to take such measures as long as assistance is made available to it pursuant to this note.

It is contemplated that all assistance under the

---

[1] Ambassador Caffery representing the U.S. Government and General Guillaume the French Military Government.

such assistance at the earliest practicable time consistent with the rebuilding of the German economy on healthy non-aggressive 'lines. Detailed terms of payment will be determined by joint agreement in accordance with the Act at a later time.

The French Military Government, on behalf of the French Zone of Occupation of Germany, agrees that deposits in German marks in respect of assistance furnished pursuant to your letter will be made in accordance with procedures to be determined by the Government of the United States of America and the French Military Government and that such deposits will be held or used for such purposes as may be agreed to between the Government of the United States of America and the French Military Government.

The French Military Government, on behalf of the French Zone of Occupation of Germany, understands that the proposals contained in your letter do not constitute an obligation on the part of the Government of the United States to make assistance available to such Zone.

. Military Services

ATIONS WITH PORTUGAL

sion of a new agreement. The new agreement was finally signed on February 2, 1948.[2]

The transit facilities which United States military aircraft have enjoyed at Lagens Airfield since May 30, 1946, have been extended by this new agreement for three years. Thereafter the agreement may be extended for two years more, making the agreement valid, in effect, for five years. The negotiations were carried out by the Portuguese Government in an atmosphere of complete cooperation and good will and their assistance has permitted the United States to maintain lines of communication with its forces abroad which are of the utmost value at this time. These same conditions exist between the Portuguese military authorities and United States military technicians responsible for servicing American military aircraft which pass through the Lagens Airfield. Consequently, the most satisfactory operating conditions exist at the field.

The facilities which the United States has enjoyed in the Azores since 1944 have been provided by the Portuguese Government without the requirement of any *quid pro quo*. During the war, the extension of military air-base facilities in the Azores was not without its problems to Portuguese neutrality. Since the war, the Portuguese Government has continued to permit the United States to use these facilities in its usual spirit of international cooperation.

---

[1] BULLETIN of June 23, 1946, p. 1080.
[2] BULLETIN of Mar. 14, 1948, p. 358.

[Released to the press June 17]

The following communication from Secretary of Defense James V. Forrestal to Dr. Antonio de Oliveira Salazar, Prime Minister of Portugal, was delivered June 15 by the new Ambassador to Portugal, Lincoln MacVeagh, when he presented his credentials

June 15, 1948

EXCELLENCY: I would like to take the occasion of Ambassador MacVeagh's first call on you to send by his hand this expression of my appreciation for the generous assistance and cooperation which we have received from the Government of Portugal in the agreement concluded on February 2, 1948. Ambassador Wiley expressed the gratitude of the Government of the United States at the time the agreement was signed. I would now like to add my own thanks on behalf of the military services of the United States.

The important military facilities on Santa Maria Island in the Azores which your Government permitted us to use during the recent war proved to be an invaluable asset in the final victory of the United Nations. Since the war, our military aircraft have been permitted by your Government to use transit facilities at Lagens Field in the Azores. These facilities have been of great value to us in maintaining safe and efficient lines of communication with the American forces of occupation in Germany and Japan. In the agreement of February 2, 1948 your Government has very generously made it possible for us to continue to maintain these lines of communication through the Azores in the most satisfactory manner.

The responsibilities of the United States Government as one of the occupying powers still continue and we appreciate with deep gratitude the goodwill and spirit of international cooperation which the Government of Portugal has displayed in its willingness to assist us and to participate in the maintenance of international peace and security and the reconstruction of Europe.

Accept [etc.]   JAMES FORRESTAL
                             Secretary of Defense

Proclamations Issued on General Agreement on Tariffs and Trade With Union of South Africa and Cuba

Union of South Africa

The President on June 12, 1948, issued a proclamation [1] putting into effect, as of June 14, 1948, the concessions in the General Agreement on Tariffs and Trade initially negotiated with the Union of South Africa, which had not yet been made effective. The agreement was entered into last October 30 at Geneva, with 22 other countries. The President's action followed receipt of information that the Government of the Union of South Africa had signed the Protocol of Provisional Application of the General Agreement on May 14, 1948; pursuant to the agreement and the protocol, the Union of South Africa will be a contracting party to the agreement on the expiration of 30 days from the date of signature.

The Union of South Africa is the twelfth of the Geneva countries to give effect to this agreement. The other countries which have done so, in addition to the United States, are the United Kingdom, France, Belgium, the Netherlands, Luxembourg, Canada, Australia, Cuba, Czechoslovakia, and China.

Under the General Agreement the Union of South Africa grants concessions on products of interest to the United States representing approximately $32.5 million in terms of 1939 trade. Existing import duties were reduced on such products as tractors, certain industrial machinery, typewriters, air compressors, lumber, barbed wire, sprayers, sprinklers, sporting goods, and lard on an extensive list of other items, on which existing duties are recognized for the most part to be generally low, duties are bound. These include such items of interest to the United States as certain industrial and mining machinery, lubricating oil, bottles, calculating machines, cash registers, clocks, watches, and radios. The duties on passenger automobiles and on truck chassis were bound at various rates ranging from 3 percent on truck chassis to 20 percent and 30 percent on passenger automobiles. The Union of South Africa is one of the largest foreign markets for American automobiles.

The Union of South Africa and the other contracting parties to the agreement are committed to certain undertakings with respect to the application of quotas, import restrictions, valuation for

[1] Proclamation 2791 (13 *Fed. Reg.* 3272).

oil, crude talc, ostrich feathers, wattle extract, wool finer than 44's and mohair. Continued duty-free entry is assured on such items as diamonds, Persian lamb and caracul, sheep and lamb skins, spiny lobsters, asbestos, wattle bark, chrome ore, and corundum ore.

Cuba

On June 11, 1948, the President issued a proclamation [2] putting into effect a few additional rectifications of schedule XX of the General Agreement on Tariffs and Trade with Cuba and of prior proclamations relating to this agreement, and announcing that the special protocol modifying article XIV of this agreement, concluded at Habana on March 24, 1948, entered into force on April 19, 1948 (for text of special protocol, see Department's press release 261, March 31, 1948).

ns

them more responsive to scientific developments and technical improvements in the field.

Upon entry into force the convention, with final protocol, and the Radio Regulations annexed thereto will abrogate and replace, in relations between the contracting governments, the international telecommunication convention signed at Madrid on December 9, 1932, and the Cairo revision of the General Radio Regulations signed on April 8, 1938.

Under article 49 of the Atlantic City convention, it will enter into force on January 1, 1949, between those countries, territories, or groups of territories in respect of which instruments of ratification or accession have been deposited by that date.

Double Taxation With France

[Released to the press June 19]

The President has signed the ratification, dated June 18, by the United States of America of (1) the convention between the United States and France, signed at Paris on October 18, 1946, for the avoidance of double taxation and the prevention of evasion in the case of taxes on estates and inheritances, and for the purpose of modifying and supplementing certain provisions of the convention between the two Governments relating to income taxation signed at Paris on July 25, 1939; and (2) the protocol between the United States and France, signed at Washington on May 17, 1948, for the purpose of modifying in certain respects the convention of October 18, 1946.

The convention was submitted by the President to the Senate on January 10, 1947, with a view to

---

[2] Proclamation 2790 (13 *Fed. Reg.* 3269).

obtaining advice and consent to ratification (S. Exec. Doc. A, 80th Cong., 1st sess.). As a result of hearings before a subcommittee of the Senate Committee on Foreign Relations, the supplementary protocol was negotiated and concluded with France and was submitted by the President to the Senate on May 19, 1948 (S. Exec. Doc. G, 80th Cong., 2d sess.).

On June 2, 1948, the Senate approved a resolution advising and consenting to the ratification of the convention and protocol. Upon the exchange of instruments of ratification by the two Governments, the convention and protocol will enter into force (1) in respect of the provisions relating to taxes on estates and inheritances, on the day of that exchange, and (2) in respect of the provisions relating to taxes on income, on January 1 following that exchange.

Role of the Library in the Overseas Information Program

BY HOWLAND H. SARGEANT [1]

Deputy Assistant Secretary for Public Affairs

Too often we Americans take library service, like freedom, for granted. We come to expect certain services of the trained librarian, who performs them with grace and courtesy.

It is precisely because we take these matters—and so many others—for granted that we frequently lose sight of the fact that they are simply manifestations, temporary manifestations to be sure, of a system of government which has been created and strengthened in war no less than in peace. In other lands not so fortunate as our own, people are trying to take heart from our triumphs and learn from our experience, brief as it has been as a nation, how to better their own lives.

Because American ideas, American techniques, and American progress have become of paramount concern to millions of people around the globe, the United States Government—in close cooperation with private agencies—has established an information and education program to present what we in the State Department like to call "a full and fair picture" of the United States of America.

In presenting this picture to the world, we employ the media of press, radio, and motion pictures; we are getting into full swing on an exchange-of-persons program which we hope will result in an increasing two-way flow of deserving students, professors, and technicians. And, last but certainly not least, we maintain 50 United States Information Libraries abroad to bring the assistance of American experience to people in other nations who are working on problems which have been studied in this country.

In a word, these libraries are designed to make available to the general public, educators, government officials, and professional people in other nations current materials of both general and specialized interest which present, once again, a full and fair picture of the United States of America. When we say full and fair picture, we must be careful lest we be suspected of bending over backwards to depict the United States under soft lights. That would be propaganda, a word as difficult to define as it is to understand. When a former colleague of mine in the State Department was asked once to define propaganda, he said: "I cannot define propaganda any more than a cat can define a rat. But a cat knows a rat when he smells one."

Recently a young man in French Indochina told our librarian there he was finally convinced we were not propagandists. Why? he was asked. Because, he said, he had recently discovered a criticism of the Truman administration in a copy of *Time* magazine on our shelves.

The original suspicion of the young man in Indochina is illustrative of an attitude our librarians encounter in many parts of the world. The overseas edition of *Life* carries the same news reports and editorial comment as the American edition but omits all advertisements. This lack of complete identity with the publication read in the United States causes criticism. Library visitors complain that the material is edited and slanted for their benefit. Peoples have been subjected to propaganda from so many sources for so many years that even this small variation arouses suspicion. Our United States Information Libraries make available factual reports, varying opinions on problems of concern to the American people, and experienced American librarians present and assist in the evaluation of sources. In

---

[1] Excerpts from an address made before the Special Libraries Association Meeting at Washington, D. C., on June 10, 1948, and released to the press on the same date.

other words, these libraries give good reference service to the serious inquiries, and this in itself is considered a phenomenon. It is a manifestation of the democratic attitude from which some have become separated and of which they are deeply appreciative.

From your own experience, you know how much more stimulating is the task of the librarian when the resources of the library are in demand. That is one of the experiences which nearly all of our overseas librarians have in common. For in almost every nation of the world today there is an insatiable thirst for knowledge about the Western Hemisphere. The people of those nations have formed the habit of going directly to the United States Information Library for knowledge about this country. They have developed a high degree of confidence in our libraries and in our librarians, especially in nations where our libraries represent their only contact with the United States.

This has frequently proved somewhat aggravating to officials of countries behind the Iron Curtain. These officials are fully aware of the dangers in popular contact with democracy and in several countries are exerting every effort to discourage the use of those libraries. In this connection, you may be interested to learn what happened to our library in Czechoslovakia when the Communists took over. Here is an extract from the monthly report of our librarian in Prague:

"During March 10,632 people visited the library. This number shows that intimidation has had but a temporary effect on regular users of the library. There are some days when the reading rooms are crowded beyond capacity and people won't leave even after closing time is announced. Despite the changed political situation, people continue to be interested in the United States, and in some cases more so than ever."

I might add as a footnote that during the rioting in Prague four Czech policemen marched in front of the library to protect the Americans from some of the more irresponsible elements in the city. During a lull one of the policemen dropped into the library to borrow a copy of the *Reader's Digest*. That, I believe, illustrates rather forcefully that the desire for knowledge comes to the fore even amid revolutions.

Far too often we tend to think of libraries as mere collections of books. This, as you well know, is a grave mistake. Libraries are people. For want of a trained librarian, the value of much information has been lost. During the war a great deal of intelligence work was found to be nothing more than the efficient use of authoritative information already available but in need of collection, evaluation, and proper channeling to meet specific problems.

That is where the trained librarian comes in. For only a trained librarian, knowing both the

subjects under his jurisdiction and the people with whom he deals, is in a position to evaluate to the best possible advantage the knowledge at his disposal. As Herbert Spencer once said, "When a man's knowledge is not in order, the more of it he has the greater will be his confusion". To arrest this confusion, the librarian must bring into play the best features of a courteous host and a dependable source of information.

This is doubly true in the case of a librarian assigned to duty abroad in the Government service. There he must take on the added role of an *ex officio* ambassador from the United States. The American librarian assigned to overseas duty must be a good administrator who is able to organize and maintain excellent library service with limited professional assistance and a limited collection. He must also have that intangible quality that is a talent for establishing pleasant relations with individuals and organizations. This is important, for failure to promote friendly relations would be, in effect, a failure of our mission to further mutual understanding among peoples through our information and education program.

He must also have a sense of selecting those people in the foreign community who are active and are anxious to make practical use of the information and knowledge contained in the library collection. In many remote areas of the world access to American books is not easy, and the librarian who goes abroad must be prepared to supplement the library's collection through local contacts with individuals and organizations in the community possessing American publications.

The librarian must also have a broad knowledge of the problems and duties of other American officials in the community so he may keep them informed of any new published developments in their field which will make their work more effective. Close liaison must be maintained in cities and small communities abroad where Americans are few in number. Contact with developments back home is not easy, and any new publications, especially if they are of general interest, are likely to be objects of intense interest.

The basic foundation of any collection in an overseas library is a group of reference books which make it possible to answer inquiries concerning the United States and the American people. No matter how well a librarian thinks he knows our country, he will find that there is much he neglected to learn. Of course, the value of an individual collection will depend upon the interests and needs of the community in which the library is located. The people in some areas of the world are especially interested in American industrial and engineering developments; other areas are particularly interested in American agriculture. Material on American history—and especially constitutional development—is important and adaptable nearly everywhere. So are community-wide problems, such as child welfare, public health, and sanitation.

The librarian abroad will come into contact with all types of people with all types of inquiries. They are certain they can find the answer to nearly any question about America from the United States librarian, and we try not to let them down. For example, a public-health commissioner in one community was interested in obtaining information on American techniques for the control of tuberculosis, how the disease was treated in community hospitals, and the means by which American communities obtained public support for such programs. Engineers frequently ask for scientific reports on road construction and the building of dams. A manufacturer recently asked the librarian for information on how air conditioning affects . efficiency of the workers in textile manufacturing.

I pointed out earlier that many of these questions are elementary to Americans who deal with them daily. But to a resident of another country out of touch with American developments, they seem quite extraordinary. When the librarian answers a question to the satisfaction of a visitor, he is doing more than supplying necessary information. He is telling the story of America. He is spreading good will. He is promoting peace.

Frequently we hear criticism of the passive role of libraries in a world struggling for peace. Is the criticism justified? Here is what a Hungarian writes from Budapest: "The Library and the reading room maintained by the American legation in Budapest is the greatest benefit imaginable for us

Grants-in-Aid Awarded to Cultural Lead

Dominican Republic

The Reverend Oscar Robles Toledano, vice rector of the University of Santo Domingo, Dominican Republic, is spending two weeks in Washington as a part of a three months' visit to the United States for the purpose of observing the methods of university administration and academic organization in this country. His visit has been arranged under the travel-grant program of the Department of State.

United States

Dr. H. Claude Horack, dean of the Law School of Duke University, Durham, North Carolina, has been awarded a grant by the Department of State in cooperation with the Inter-American Bar Association to enable him to make a survey of law schools in the other American republics.

The project, under auspices of the Inter-Ameri-

Presentation of Student-Exchange Record

A pictorial record of last year's student-exchange project was presented to Secretary Marshall on June 15 by representatives of the Institute of International Education and the American Friends' Service Committee on behalf of the 35 organizations which sponsored the program.

The presentation was made to the Secretary in appreciation of the State Department's aid in carrying out the project last summer which took some 3,000 American students to Europe for study and brought a number of foreign students to the United States.

The album presented to the Secretary contains photographs of all phases of the project taken in Europe and aboard the *Marine Tiger* and the *Marine Jumper*, the two ships made available for the project by the Maritime Commission.

THE DEPARTMENT

Henry Labouisse Named Foreign Aid Coordinator

[Released to the press June 16]

The Department of State announced on June 16 the appointment of Henry R. Labouisse, Jr., as Coordinator for Foreign Aid and Assistance in the Office of the Under Secretary.

The post of Coordinator was created to facilitate the discharge of the Department's responsibilities under the Foreign Assistance Act of 1948 and to insure that the Department's foreign-aid policy formulation and execution is adequately related to programs administered by the Economic Cooperation Administration.

Mr. Labouisse will advise and assist the Secretary and Under Secretary in coordinating Departmental planning and operations on foreign aid and assistance programs administered by the Eca; and will serve as the Department's principal liaison officer with Eca.

Appointment of Officers

William T. Stone as Special Assistant to the Assistant Secretary for public affairs, effective June 18, 1948.

Lloyd A. Dehrbas as Director of the Office of International Information, effective June 21, 1948.

Paul H. Nitze as Deputy to the Assistant Secretary for economic affairs, effective June 17, 1948.

William D. Wright as Special Assistant to the Director General of the Foreign Service, effective June 15, 1948.

Thomas Fitch as Special Adviser to the Director of the Office of Controls, effective June 15, 1948.

Sales and Transfers of Nondemilitarized Combat Matériel

[Released to the press June 8]

The following is a list of authorizations and transfers of surplus combat matériel effected by the Department of State in its capacity as foreign surplus disposal agent during the months of Ap and December, 1947, and January, March, a April, 1948, and not previously reported to t Munitions Division of the Department:

Country	Description of matériel	Procurement cost	Sales price	Date of transfe
				1948
ARGENTINA . .	Miscellaneous shells, directors, machine guns, gun mounts, height finders, aiming circles.	$4, 413, 946. 40	$248, 604. 20	Mar. 19
BELGIUM . . .	One 500-ton netlayer (ex-German vessel), demilitarized, to Ets. Van Heyghen of Ghent, Belgium.	(Captured enemy equipment)	8, 000. 00	Feb. 16
CANADA	Miscellaneous radar and radio equipment	2, 594. 85	391. 40	Apr. 6
CHINA	Miscellaneous cartridges, charges, shells, grenades .	842. 727. 50	81, 247. 34	Apr. 29
ECUADOR . . .	Miscellaneous cartridges, metallic belt links, bombs, charges, assembly fins, fuzes, arming wire assemblies.	49, 294. 33	4, 931. 00	Apr. 2
	Miscellaneous cartridges and shells	16, 164. 61	1, 618. 70	Apr. 20
	21 tank engines, 126 bundles of track assemblies, and spare parts for tank, light, M3A3.	409, 193. 73	20, 459. 68	Apr. 20
				1947
GREECE . . .	6 LCI's, demilitarized	2, 240, 000. 00	240, 000. 00	April
				1948
	11 minesweepers, nondemilitarized	12, 809, 500. 00	1, 320, 000. 00	January
GUATEMALA . .	Miscellaneous cartridges, metallic belt links, shells, shot, and shell fins.	224, 506. 10	14, 948. 47	Mar. 25
	3 tank engines, 18 bundles of shoe track assemblies, and miscellaneous spare parts for tank, light, M3A1.	49, 711. 31	2, 485, 57	Mar. 25
HAITI	Miscellaneous cartridges, shells, grenades, rockets .	91, 469. 21	7, 035. 82	Mar. 5
	One AT-11 aircraft	83, 401. 00	20, 000. 00	Apr. 16 -
PHILIPPINES . .	847 automatic pistols, cal. .45; 662 carbines, cal. .30, M-1; 15 Thompson submachine guns, cal. .45, M-1; 2 Garand rifles, cal. .30, M-1, and related parts and accessories to the Manila Police Department, Philippine Government.	57, 501. 01	53, 904. 70	Feb. 24
	One patrol craft and 3 submarine chasers to T. Y. Egan (demilitarized, poor condition, for salvage).	2, 450, 000. 00	8, 198. 07 (approx.)	March–Apr
	One LCI to E. S. Yeaton (demilitarized, poor to fair condition).	373, 400. 00	5, 500. 00	Dec. 17, 19 Mar. 11, 1
	One LCI to T. Y. Egan (demilitarized, poor to fair condition).	373, 400. 00	2, 500. 00	Dec. 17, 19 Mar. 1, 1
	10 LCT's to Compania Maritima (demilitarized, seriously damaged).	1, 393, 000. 00	2, 500. 00	Dec. 17, 19 Mar. 1, 1
	One patrol craft to T. Y. Egan, and one submarine chaser (demilitarized, poor condition, for salvage).	1, 250, 000. 00	1, 250. 00	Dec. 17, 19 Mar. 1, 1
URUGUAY . . .	One submarine chaser (demilitarized), one aircraft rescue boat, one motor launch, and one picket boat (fair condition).	1, 323, 883. 00	35, 361. 00	Mar. 30
	Miscellaneous cartridges, canisters, sheels, shot, smoke grenades, signals, and rockets.	578, 569. 66	47, 010. 23	Mar. 9

A report to the Secretary of State on the Second Session of the UNESCO General Conference, including the program, budget, the administration and external relations of UNESCO, the personnel involved, and selected documents.

Third Report to Congress on Assistance to Greece and Turkey For the Period Ended March 31, 1948. Economic Cooperation Series 9. Pub. 3149. v, 63 pp. 20¢.

The President's quarterly report on the financial, military, economic, public-welfare, and agricultural aspects of assistance to Greece and Turkey (with detailed tables and map).

Problems of American Foreign Relations. General Foreign Policy Series. Pub. 3169. 16 pp. Free.

Address by Charles E. Bohlen, Counselor in the Department of State, before the graduating class of the University of Arizona, Tucson, on May 26, 1948.

American Peace Policy: Address by the President June 12, 1948. General Foreign Policy Series 5. Pub. 3195. 12 pp. Free.

Delivered at the commencement exercises of the University of California, Berkeley.

Contributors

Louis J. Halle, Jr., author of the article on cooperative programs in health and sanitation of the Institute of Inter-American Affairs, is Special Assistant to the Director of the Office of American Republic Affairs, Department of State, and is also a member of the Board of Directors of the Institute.

Publication 3344

INDEX 𝒹𝒾𝓈𝓉𝑜𝓇𝓎

Volume XVIII: Numbers 444-469, January 4-June 27, 1948

Atomic Energy Commission—Continued
  Reports to UN—Continued
    Transmittal of 1st, 2d, and 3d reports to General
      Assembly, 830.
    UN resolution accepting 1st, 2d, and 3d reports, 799.
  Suspension of negotiations, recommendation in 3d re-
    port to Security Council, 704.
Austin, Warren R.:
  Address on tensions in UN, 14.
  Appointment to Interim Committee of UN General As-
    sembly, 47.
  Note to Secretary-General of UN regarding accreditation
    of UN correspondents, 48.
  Statements:
    Czechoslovak situation, 411, 446, 517, 536.
    Indonesian situation, 333.
    ITO charter, completion of, 445.
    Military training, universal, 418.
    Palestine situation, 294, 342, 402, 514, 515, 568, 695, 763.
    UN, strengthening of, 626.
Australia, treaties:
  General agreement on tariffs and trade:
    Signature of protocol of provisional application, 120,
      373, 652.
    Tariff concessions, U.S. proclamation, 120, 373, 652.
  Wheat agreement, signature, 474.
Austria:
  Aid from U.S.:
    Allocation under interim-aid program, 138.
    Expression of gratitude for, 82.
    Note to U.S. on passage of act, 585.
    Streptomycin, shipment from U.S. under interim-aid
      program, 611.
    Supply and shipping goal for foreign-aid program,
      234.
    Tabular report, 350.
  Treaties, agreements, etc.:
    Aid agreement, interim, with U.S., remarks by U.S.
      High Commissioner (Keyes) on signature, 52.
    Economic Cooperation Act of 1948, adherence to
      purposes of, exchange of notes with U.S., 645,
      686, 712.
    Peace treaty with Allies, negotiations in Council of
      Foreign Ministers:
      Resumption, 213.
      Suspension, 746.
    Wheat agreement, signature, 474.
  Treaty obligations, Soviet violation, 739.
  U.S. property in, extension of time for filing claims, 357.
Aviation (see also International Civil Aviation Organiza-
    tion; Treaties):
  Aeronautical radio conference, administrative and
    preparatory conference, U.S. delegations, 543, 649.
  Air Policy Commission, President's, report of, discussed
    in statement by Mr. Kuter, 116.
  Cooperation in, necessity for, statement by Mr. Kuter,
    116.
  International Air Exposition, invitations to, 474.
  U.S. aircraft, activities over waters adjoining Japan,
    U.S. reply to Soviet protests, 746.
  U.S. military aircraft, transit through airfield in Azores,
    agreement between U.S. and Portugal (1946), ex-
    tension, 221, 358, 839.
Azores. See Aviation.

Balkans, UN Special Committee on:
  Action in UN, 768, 831.
  Dates of meetings, 25, 144, 300.
Bangkok, Siam, regional Foreign Service conference to be
  held in, 815.
Bank for International Settlements, relinquishment of
  monetary gold looted by Germany, agreement with
  U.S., U.K., and France, 713.
Barrows, Leland, designation in State Department, 63,
  615.
B.C.G. vaccine, 1st international congress, U.S. delegation,
  777.
Beattie, Edward W., Jr., designation in State Department,
  617.

Caribbean Commission:
Organization and function, article by Mr. Taussig, 691.
Relation to UN, 693.
U.S. acceptance of membership, 360, 491.
Carnegie Endowment for International Peace, regional conference, St. Louis, Mo., address by Mr. Jessup, 573.
Cates, John M., articles:
Conference of directors of International Meteorological Organization, 43.
UN maritime conference, 495.
Cebu, Republic of the Philippines, opening of U.S. Consulate, 517.
CEEC. See European Economic Co-operation, Committee of.
Census of Americas, 1950, consultation by El Salvador with Census Bureau on, 815.
Centennial celebration of State of Wisconsin, Madison, Wisc., address by Mr. Bohlen, 78.
Central America. See American republics and the individual countries.
Ceylon:
Dominion status achieved, U.S. attitude, 316.
Exchange of Ambassadors with U.S., 687.
U.S. Ambassador (Cole), appointment, 517.
CFM. See Foreign Ministers, Council of.
Chamber of Commerce, Pittsburgh, Pa., address by Secretary Marshall, 108.
Changchun, China, closing of U.S. Consulate General, 349.
Chapman, Wilbert M., designation as Special Assistant to Under Secretary of State, 815.
Charts analyzing Inter-American System, 164, 166, 180.
Chemical Industries Committee, U.S. delegation, 450.
Chiang Kai-shek, Generalissimo, inauguration as President of Chinese Republic, 713.
Chicago Council of Foreign Relations, address by Mr. Austin, 14.
Child congress, 9th Pan American, 62, 595.
Children's Emergency Fund, International, Executive Board, 25.
Chile (see also American republics):
Bond service, new, plans for, 486.
Combat matériel, transfer by U.S. to, table, 122, 554.
Cultural leader, visit to U.S., 390, 489, 552, 751.
Czechoslovak situation, request for investigation by Security Council:
Letter from Chilean representative to UN Secretary-General, 409.
Statement by U.S. representative (Austin), 446.
Interference by U.S.S.R. in internal affairs charged by representative to UN, 411.
China:
Aid from U.S.:
China Aid Act of 1948, proposals regarding, exchange of notes between Secretary Marshall and Ambassador Koo, 647.
Foreign Assistance Act of 1948, qualification for aid under, 686.
Proposed extension of aid, message of President Truman to Congress and statement by Secretary Marshall, 268.
Supply and shipping target, 237.
Tabular report, 350.
Technical mission, Chinese, to U.S., 115.
Chiang Kai-shek, Generalissimo, inauguration as President of Chinese Republic, 713.
Combat matériel, transfer by U.S. to, and retransfer to U.S., table, 123, 390, 554, 846.
Communists in Government of, U.S. position, 384.
Educational-exchange program, with U.S., under Fulbright act:
Grants under, 487, 654.
Signing of agreement establishing, 388.
Property of U.S. citizens confiscated during Japanese occupation of, procedure for filing claims, 253.
Surplus-property contract for, statement by Secretary Marshall, 384.

China—Continued
Treaties, agreements, etc.:
General agreement on tariffs and trade:
Signature of protocol of provisional application, 652.
Tariff concessions, U.S. proclamation, 652.
U.S. Educational Foundation in China, agreement establishing (1947), signature, 388.
Wheat agreement, signature, 474.
U.S. Consulate General at Changchun, closing, 349.
U.S. policy in Japan, statement by U.S. Ambassador (Stuart) on attitude of Chinese students toward, 813.
Chisholm, Dr. Brock, correspondence with U.S. regarding attendance at World Health Assembly, 540.
Citizens, U.S. See Protection of U.S. nationals.
Civil aviation. See Aviation; ICAO; Treaties.
Civil Aviation Organization, International. See International.
Claims. See Property; Protection of U.S. nationals and property.
Clayton, William L.:
Address on United Nations conference on trade and employment, 825.
Statement on completion of ITO charter, 444.
Coal exports to Italy, aid for gas-producing industry, 552.
Coffee Board, Inter-American, 26.
Cohen, Wilbur J., article on 2d inter-American conference on social security, 376.
Cole, Felix, appointment as U.S. Ambassador to Ceylon, 517, 687.
Colombia (see also American republics) :
American Red Cross, aid during Bogotá demonstrations, correspondence between President of Colombia (Ospina Perez) and President Truman, 716.
Cultural leader, visit to U.S., 815.
Reconstruction in, commitment for, by Export-Import Bank, 549.
Wheat agreement, signature, 474.
Columbia Broadcasting System correspondent (Polk), Greek investigation of murder, 713, 748.
Combat matériel, nondemilitarized, transfer of :
Iran, supplemental appropriation for, proposed, 780.
Tables showing, 122, 390, 554, 846.
Commerce. See Trade.
Commerce, Department of, joint announcement on restitution of looted property in Japan, 483.
Commissions, committees, etc., international (see also name of commission; Conferences; United Nations) :
Allied Control Council for Germany, 456.
American States, Organization of, 666.
Bar Association, Inter-American, 844.
Bipartite Board for U.S.–U.K. Zones in Germany, 708.
Cancer Research Commission, International, 148.
Caribbean Commission, 360, 491, 691.
European Economic Co-operation, Committee of, 138, 375, 674.
European Economic Co-operation, Organization for, 640.
European Manpower Movements, Committee for Coordination of, 675.
Far Eastern Commission, 92, 93, 213, 482, 530.
Fisheries Commission, International Pacific Salmon, 95.
Food and Agriculture Organization, 26, 145, 282, 300, 301, 449, 769.
Inter-Allied Reparation Agency, 227, 240.
Inter-Allied Trade Board for Japan, 25, 144, 301.
Inter-American Affairs, Institute of, 659, 758, 819.
Inter-American Economic and Social Council of Pan American Union, 426.
International Civil Aviation Organization, 116, 463, 704, 776.
International Joint Commission, U.S.-Canada, 150, 522, 718.
Literary and Artistic Works, International Union for Protection of, 677.
Maritime Consultative Organization, Intergovernmental, 286, 495.

Conferences, congresses, etc., international—Continued
History, Commission on, of Pan American Institute of
Geography and History, 1st consultation, 87.
Hydraulic structures research, International Associa-
tion of, meeting, 734.
International Civil Aviation Organization, meetings, 25,
145, 301, 449, 506, 580, 678, 703, 733, 775, 776, 831.
International Joint Commission, U.S.-Canada, meeting,
522.
International labor conference, 31st session, 701, 773.
International Labor Organization, meetings, 25, 139,
301, 303, 378, 450, 771.
Journées Médicales de Bruxelles, 22d session, 777.
Leprosy congress, 5th international, 450.
Literary and artistic works, international convention
for protection of, diplomatic conference for revision,
677.
Lyon international fair, 145, 302, 449.
Malaria and tropical medicine, 4th international con-
gresses, 303, 475, 545.
Manpower conference, 138, 674.
Maritime Consultative Organization, Intergovern-
mental, conference to consider establishment, 286,
495.
Meteorological Organization, International, conference
of directors, 43.
Milan fair (26th), 146, 302.
Ministers of Foreign Affairs, Permanent Consultative
Council, meeting, 602.
North American regional broadcasting agreement, meet-
ing of technicians, 25, 541, 747.
Ophthalmology, 3d Pan American congress, 26, 144.
Pan American child congress (9th), 62.
Pan American Institute of Geography and History, Com-
mission on History, 1st consultation, 87.
Pan American Sanitary Organization, 1st meeting of
directing council, 283.
Paris international fair, 302.
Physiopathology of animal reproduction and artificial
insemination, 1st international congress, 832.
Poultry congress, 8th world, 379, 803.
Praha international spring fair, 26, 145, 301.
Protection of Childhood, American International Insti-
tute for, Council of, annual meeting, 776.
Public education, 11th international conference, 833.
Radio conference, aeronautical, 543.
Radio Consultative Committee of CCIR, 5th meeting,
834.
Railway congress, 6th Pan American, 449.
Refugee Organization, International, meetings of Pre-
paratory Commission, 21, 49, 451, 580.
Resources, renewable natural, 1st inter-American con-
ference on conservation, 146.
Rhine Commission, Central, meeting, 302.
Rice meeting, international, 282, 769.
Royal Netherlands industries fair, 146, 302.
Royal Sanitary Institute, health congress, 678.
Rubber Study Group, 5th meeting, 474, 650.
Safety activities in fields of aviation, meteorology,
shipping, and telecommunications, meeting of com-
mittee to make recommendations on, 26, 145, 300.
Safety of life at sea, international conference on, 544.
Ships, tonnage measurement of, meeting of technicians,
302, 449.
Social security, inter-American committee on, 3d meet-
ing, 377.
Social security, 2d inter-American conference on, 376.
Social work, international conference on, 146, 302.
Soil mechanics and foundation engineering, 2d inter-
national conference on, 734, 737.
Soils, tropical and subtropical, specialist conference,
734.
Sugar Council, international, meeting, 580.
Surgeons, International College of, 6th congress, 649.
Telecommunication Union, International, meetings spon-
sored by, 22, 122, 379, 534, 543, 599, 649, 834.
Telegraph and consultative committee, 6th plenary meet-
ing, 302, 580, 599, 733.

Conferences, congresses, etc., international—Continued
Telephone consultative committee, rates, traffic, and
technical meetings, 146, 734.
Textiles conference, 734.
Tin Study Group, 2d meeting, 475, 599.
Trade-marks rights, German, preliminary discussions on
treatment of, 25.
Travel congress, 3d inter-American, 146, 302.
Tropical medicine and malaria, 4th international con-
gresses, 303, 475, 545.
UNESCO, meetings sponsored by, 25, 145, 300, 302, 579,
598, 733.
Wheat Council, International, special session, 215, 300,
395.
World health assembly, 440, 540, 581, 734, 832.
World Health Organization, Interim Commission, meet-
ings, 23, 144, 300, 734, 774.
World Health Organization, meetings sponsored by, 26,
144, 300, 580, 733.
Zagreb international fair, 302.
Conferences, congresses, etc., national:
Pacific regional conference on UNESCO, 727.
Regional consular conferences:
Bangkok, 815.
Capetown, 450.
Mexico City, 389, 450.
Congress, U.S.:
Aid, proposed, to—
China, 268.
Greece and Turkey, 298, 346.
Trieste, 348.
Economic Cooperation Act. See Economic Cooperation
Act.
Educational-exchange programs, report on operations
of State Department, transmittal to Congress, with
text of report, 387.
Foreign-aid program, transmittal of 1st report, 648.
Foreign Assistance Act. See Foreign Assistance Act.
House Committee on Foreign Affairs:
China, aid to, statement by Secretary Marshall, 270.
ERP, relation to foreign policy, statement by Secre-
tary Marshall, 112.
Foreign-policy legislation, proposed, letter from Coun-
selor of State Department (Bohlen), 385.
Greece and Turkey, extension of aid to, statement by
Secretary Marshall, 346.
Palestine situation, UN solution of, letter from Secre-
tary Marshall, 281.
UN, strengthening of, statements by Secretary Mar-
shall and Ambassador Austin, 623.
House Committee on Merchant Marine and Fisheries,
letter and enclosures from Secretary Marshall re-
garding extension of Ship Sales Act of 1946, 311.
House Committee on Ways and Means, statement and
correspondence by Secretary Marshall on renewal
of Trade Agreements Act, 651, 750.
Legislation, listed, 123, 230, 533, 619, 730, 750, 782.
Messages from President Truman:
Annual message, 90.
China, proposed aid to, 268.
Cuban anniversary (50th), joint session on, 582.
Export-Import Bank financing of economic develop-
ment in American republics, 548.
Friendship, commerce, and navigation, treaty with
Italy, transmittal to Senate, 550.
Peace, means of securing, 418.
Trade Agreements Act, Reciprocal, extension of, 351.
Wheat agreement, international, transmittal to Sen-
ate, 606.
Presidential term, Constitutional amendment, status of
ratifications, 427.
Publications. See Legislation supra.
Senate Committee on Armed Services, address by Secre-
tary Marshall concerning relation of military
strength to diplomatic action, 421.
Senate Committee on Foreign Relations:
ERP legislation, preparation of draft bill, 233.

Congress, U. S.—Continued
Senate Committee on Foreign Relations—Continued
European economic recovery, statement by Secretary
Marshall, 71.
Foreign financial aid (1948–49), estimates, 233.
U.S. participation in UN, 1947, résumé of report, 279.
Uruguayan gift, legislation proposed on acceptance of,
letter from Counselor of State Department (Bohlen)
to President pro tempore of Senate (Vandenberg),
585.
Congress of Industrial Organizations (CIO), protests to
Department of State concerning Greek anti-strike,
anti-lockout law, letter from Secretary Marshall,
315.
Constitution of U.S., status of ratifications of proposed
amendment regarding term of office of the President,
427.
Constitutions of German states, article discussing, 559.
Consular convention, U.S. with—
Costa Rica, signature, 314.
U.K., negotiations, 191.
Consultative Council, Permanent, of Ministers of Foreign
Affairs of U.K., Belgium, France, Luxembourg, and
Netherlands, communiqué on first meeting, 602.
Conventions. *See* Conferences; Treaties.
Copyright protection, convention on (1886), as revised,
U. S. observer delegation to conference for revision of,
677.
Correspondents. *See* Information.
Costa Rica:
Agricultural program, cooperative, with Institute of
Inter-American Affairs, 762.
Ambassador to U.S. (Esquivel), credentials, 747.
Consular convention, with U.S., signature, 314.
U.S. Consulate at Port Limón, closing, 517.
Cotton, trade of, in Japan, discussed in article by Mr.
Nehmer and Miss Crimmins, 528.
Cotton Advisory Committee, International, 7th meeting:
Agenda and U.S. delegation, 379.
Article by Mr. Evans, 702.
Council of Foreign Ministers. *See* Foreign Ministers.
Credentials. *See* Diplomatic representatives in U.S.
Crimmins, Marguerite C., article on significance of textiles
in Japanese economy, 527.
Cuba (*see also* American republics):
Combat matériel, transfer by U.S. to, table, 122, 390, 554.
Cultural leader, visit to U.S., 845.
Independence, 50th anniversary, address by President
Truman and statement by Secretary Marshall, 582.
Treaties, agreements, etc.:
General agreement on tariffs and trade:
Exclusive supplementary agreement with U.S., text,
signature, and proclamation, 28, 29, 60, 841.
Signature of protocol of provisional application,
120, 373, 652.
Tariff concessions, U.S. proclamation, 120, 373, 652.
Trade agreement, with U.S. (1934, 1939, 1941), procla-
mation rendering inoperative, 29.
Wheat agreement, signature, 474.
U.S. Ambassador (Butler), appointment, 719.
U.S. educator, visit to Habana, 390.
Cultural cooperation (*see also* Educational exchange pro-
gram):
Law schools in other American republics, survey, 844.
Student exchange, pictorial record, 845.
Visitors from U.S. to: Cuba, 390; Guatemala, 357; Mexi-
co, 357; other American republics, 716; Peru, 357.
Visitors to U.S. from: Argentina, 751; Bolivia, 716;
Brazil, 716, 751, 845; Chile, 390, 489, 552, 751; Colom-
bia, 815; Cuba, 845; Dominican Republic, 814, 844;
El Salvador, 844; Guatemala, 31; Mexico, 611; Peru,
716; Uruguay, 814, 845.
Cyprus, opening of U.S. Consulate at Nicosia, 619.
Czechoslovakia (*see also* Europe):
Combat matériel, retransfer to U.S., table, 123.
Communist seizure of power:
Joint U.S., French, and U.K. declaration, 304.
Statement by Secretary Marshall, 381.

Documents and State Papers, State Department publication, announcement on initiation of, 524.
Dodd, Norris E. (Acting Secretary of Agriculture), letter to Secretary Marshall recommending Senate approval of international wheat agreement, 609.
Domestic jurisdiction, impact of UN upon, article by Mr. Gross, 259.
Dominican Republic (*see also* American republics) :
Cultural leaders, visit to U.S., 814, 844.
U.S. Ambassador (Ackerman), appointment, 719.
Wheat agreement, signature, 474.
Donnelly, Walter J. (American Ambassador to Venezuela), attendance at inauguration of Venezuelan President-elect, 222.
Double-taxation conventions, U.S. and—
Denmark, signature and statement by Secretary Marshall, 653.
France, modification of, signature, remarks, and ratification, 711, 841.
Netherlands, signature and statement by Secretary Marshall, 611.
New Zealand, signature, 486.
Douglas, Lewis W. (Ambassador to Great Britain), letter to Senator Vandenberg regarding estimate for foreign financial aid for 1948–49 : 233.
Doull, James A., article on 1st meeting of directing council of the Pan American Sanitary Organization, 283.
Dublin, Ireland, conversion of U.S. Legation and Consulate to combined office, 349.
Dunn, James C. (U.S. Ambassador to Italy), remarks regarding interim-aid agreement with Italy, 51.

ECA. *See* Economic Cooperation Administration.
ECE. *See* Economic Commission for Europe.
Economic, social and cultural collaboration and collective self-defence, treaty between U.K., Belgium, France, Luxembourg, and Netherlands, text, 600.
Economic agreement, inter-American, text of draft, 308.
Economic and Social Council, Inter-American, 184, 426.
Economic and Social Council of UN (ECOSOC) :
Commissions, committees, etc. :
Dates of meetings, 25, 26, 144, 145, 301, 449, 579, 733, 734.
Economic Commission for Asia and Far East, 768.
Economic Commission for Europe, 27, 737, 831.
Economic Commission for Latin America, 828, 831.
Economic Commission for Mid-East, proposed, 732.
Genocide, *ad hoc* Committee on, 723.
Human Rights Commission, 195, 264, 732, 768, 801, 831.
Transport and Communications Commission, 131.
Freedom of information, conference on, 337, 378, 518.
Resolution on Yugoslav gold reserves in U.S., 209, 448.
Sixth session, statement by U.S. representative (Thorp) and agenda, 209.
Economic Commission for Asia and the Far East, discussion in UN, 768.
Economic Commission for Europe (ECE) :
Appointment of Mr. Harriman as U.S. representative, 831.
Coal, Committee on, 579, 733.
Electric Power, Committee on, 579, 733.
Housing, Panel on, 579, 733.
Inland Transport Committee :
Designation of highways for truck transport, 737.
Discussed by Acting Secretary Lovett, 27.
Economic Commission for Latin America :
First session, 831.
U.S. representative, appointment, 828.
Economic Commission for Mid-East, proposed by UN, 732.
Economic Cooperation Act of 1948 (*see also* Foreign Assistance Act) :
Adherence to purposes of, by : Austria, 645, 686 ; Belgium, 686 ; Denmark, 640 n., 686 ; France, 640 n., 686 ; French zone of Germany, 838 ; Greece, 708 ; Iceland, 640 n., 686 ; Ireland, 642, 686 ; Italy, 642, 686 ; Luxembourg, 640 n., 712 ; Netherlands, 640, 686 ; Norway, 640 n., 686 ; Sweden, 640 n., 712 ; Turkey, 779 ; U.K., 644, 686 ; U.S.–U.K. zones of Germany, 708.

Economic Cooperation Act of 1948—Continued
Passage of, note of thanks to U.S. from Austria, 585.
Statement by Department of State and Economic Cooperation Administration, 640.
Economic Cooperation Administration (ECA) :
Appointment of Mr. Hoffman as Administrator, 516.
Cooperation with State Department, 718.
Economic Cooperation Act of 1948, joint statement with State Department, 640.
Transportation in Greece, joint survey with AMAG, 779.
ECOSOC. *See* Economic and Social Council.
Ecuador (*see also* American republics) :
Ambassador to U.S. (Dillón), credentials, 62.
Combat matériel, transfer by U.S. to, table, 122, 846.
Wheat agreement, signature, 474.
Educational-exchange program, under Fulbright act :
Agreements with : Burma, 27, 388 ; China, 388 ; Greece, 654 ; Philippine Republic, 488.
Educational Exchange, Office of, establishment, 615.
Foreign Scholarships, Board of, membership, 389, 489.
Grants for : Burma, 487, 552, 782 ; China, 487, 654.
Operations of State Department, report by Secretary Marshall, 387.
Educational-exchange program with other American republics. *See* Visitors *under* Cultural cooperation.
Egypt :
Combat matériel, transfer by U.S. to, table, 122.
Palestine situation. *See* Palestine.
Question in Security Council, summary statement by Secretary-General (Lie), 633.
Steamship service to U.S., inauguration, 486.
Wheat agreement, signature, 474.
Elections in Korea :
Date proclaimed by U.S. commander in Korea (Hodge), 344.
Need for, resolution by Interim Committee of UN, 297.
Views of Interim Committee of UN, conformity with, statement by Secretary Marshall, 375.
Electric systems, large, 12th biennial session of international conference, U.S. delegation, 833.
Elisabethville, Belgian Congo, opening of U.S. Consulate, 619, 751.
Ellis, Leonard B., article on international rice meeting of FAO, 769.
El Salvador (*see also* American republics) :
Census, 1950, consultation with U.S. Census Bureau on, 815.
Combat matériel, transfer by U.S. to, table, 123, 390.
Cultural leader, visit to U.S., 844.
Embargo on exportation of arms and scrap iron, 318.
Embassies, U.S. *See* Foreign Service.
Employment and trade, UN conference on. *See* Trade and employment.
Enemy assets, German. *See* Germany.
Entomology, 8th international congress, U.S. delegation, 803.
ERP. *See* European Recovery Program.
Esquivel, Mario A., credentials as Costa Rican Ambassador to U.S., 747.
Europe. *See* Aid to foreign countries ; Displaced persons ; European Recovery Program.
Europe, Economic Commission for, 26, 27, 145, 301, 579, 733, 737, 831.
European Economic Co-operation, Committee of (CEEC) :
Exploratory discussions with U.S. on import program under ERP, 375.
Manpower conference (Rome) :
Article by Mr. Lorwin, 674.
Observers from U.S., 138.
European Economic Co-operation, Organization for, 138, 640.
European Manpower Movements, Committee for Coordination of, establishment, article by Mr. Lorwin, 675.
European-Mediterranean regional air-navigation meeting of ICAO, 2d, U.S. delegation, 580.

Foreign Service, U.S.:
Ambassadors, appointment:
Afghanistan (Palmer), 719; Brazil (Johnson), 687; Ceylon (Cole), 517, 687; Cuba (Butler), 719; Dominican Republic (Ackerman), 719; European countries (Harriman), 619; Greece (Grady), 782; Iran (Wiley), 390; Nicaragua (Shaw), 719; Peru (Tittmann), 829; Portugal (MacVeagh), 390, 517.
Arabic, teaching of, in Foreign Service Institute, 618.
Consular conferences, regional:
Bangkok, 815.
Capetown, 450.
Mexico City, 389, 450.
Consular convention, with—
Costa Rica, signature, 314.
U.K., negotiations, 191.
Consular offices: Aruba, West Indies, elevation to rank of Consulate, 124; Bergen, Norway, opening, 349; Bratislava, Czechoslovakia, opening, 427; Cebu, Republic of the Philippines, opening, 517; Changchun, China, closing, 349; Curitiba, Brazil, opening, 829; Dublin, Ireland, conversion of Legation and Consulate to combined office, 349; Elisabethville, Belgian Congo, opening, 619, 751; Fredericton, New Brunswick, Canada, closing, 349; Haifa, Palestine, opening, 619; Kabul, Afghanistan, elevation to rank of Embassy, 491, 782; Nicosia, Cyprus, opening, 619; Palermo, Italy, elevation to rank of Consulate General, 517, 619; Port Limón, Costa Rica, closing, 517; Port-of-Spain, Trinidad, British West Indies, elevation to rank of Consulate General, 124; Puerto Cortes, Honduras, opening, 349; St. Stephen, New Brunswick, Canada, closing, 63.
Ministers, appointment: Nepal (Grady), 686; Union of South Africa (Winship), 491.
Written examinations for, 389.
France:
Aid from U.S.:
Economic Cooperation Act of 1948, adherence to purposes of, 640 n., 686.
Foreign-aid program, supply and shipping goal, 234.
Foreign-aid shipments from U.S., tabular report, 350.
Interim-aid agreement, with U.S., 50.
Interim-aid allocation, 138.
Combat matériel, transfer by U.S. to, and retransfer to U.S., table, 123, 390.
Communist seizure of power in Czechoslovakia, joint declaration with U.S. and U.K., 304.
Customs union, with Italy, U.S. attitude, 253.
Danube, conference to consider free navigation of, exchange of views with U.S., U.K., and Soviet Governments, 735.
Expropriation of German assets in Spain, 653.
Foreign Minister, meeting with U.S. and U.K. Foreign Ministers, discussed, 456.
Prisoners of war, status of release of, 221.
Treaties, agreements, etc.:
Double taxation (1946), protocol modifying:
Ratification, 841.
Signature and remarks, 711.
Economic, social and cultural collaboration and collective self-defence, with U.K., Belgium, Luxembourg, and Netherlands, text, and communiqué of meeting of Permanent Consultative Council, 600, 602.
Economic Cooperation Act of 1948, adherence to purposes of, 640 n., 686.
General agreement on tariffs and trade:
Signature of protocol of provisional application, 120, 373, 652.
Tariff concessions, U.S. proclamation, 120, 373, 652.
Industrial-property agreement, supplementary, with U.S. (1947), entry into force, 485.
Interim-aid agreement, with U.S., signature and remarks, 50.
Trade agreement (1936), proclamation rendering inoperative, 30.
Wheat agreement, signature, 474.

France—Continued
Trieste, Free Territory of, return to Italy proposed, joint statement with U.S. and U.K., 425.
Tripartite conversations with U.S. and U.K. on German economic unity. See Tripartite.
Franks, Oliver Shewell, appointment as British Ambassador to U.S., 782.
Fredericton, New Brunswick, Canada, closing of U.S. Vice Consulate, 349.
Free Territory of Trieste. See Trieste.
Freedom and tyranny, world-wide struggle between, address by Secretary Marshall, 422.
Freedom of information. See Information.
Freezing of assets in U.S., Yugoslav complaint and U.S. attitude, 117.
Friendship, commerce, and navigation, treaty with Italy:
Signature, 219.
Summary of provisions and transmittal to Senate, 550.
Fulbright act. See Educational-exchange program.
Fund, International Children's Emergency, 25.
Fur seals, protection of, provisional agreement, U.S. and Canada (1942), extension (1947), 94.

Gallegos, Rómulo (President-elect of Venezuela), U.S. diplomatic representation at inauguration of, 222.
General Assembly and the Problem of Greece, BULLETIN supplement, 49.
General Assembly of UN:
Balkans, Special Committee on, 25, 144, 300, 768, 831.
Economic accomplishments of, address by Mr. Thorp, 83.
Greek question, special committee on, 449, 579, 734.
Indians in South Africa, discussion, 263.
Interim Committee. See Interim Committee.
International Law Commission, action regarding, 732.
Korea, Temporary Commission on, 297, 344, 375, 575, 700, 768, 800.
Palestine situation. See Palestine.
Statements by U.S. representative (Austin), 514, 568.
Genetics, 8th international congress of, U.S. delegation, 834.
Geneva agreement. See Tariffs and trade, general agreement on.
Genocide, report of U.S. representative on ECOSOC committee and text of draft convention, 723.
Geography and History, Pan American Institute of, Commission on History, article by Mr. Whitaker, 87.
Germany:
Allied Control Council, statement by Secretary Marshall on Four Power responsibilities, 456.
Assets, external:
Agreement relating to resolution of conflicting claims to, 3, 93.
Rules for accounting for, in countries members of Inter-Allied Reparation Agency, 227.
Soviet proposals on, 191.
Spain, expropriation of, 653.
Currency reform, statements regarding, and summary, 835.
Declaration on problems in, by Yugoslavia, Czechoslovakia, and Poland, U.S. position, 384.
Documents on Soviet-German relations, release of, by State Department, 150.
Future of, address by Mr. Thorp, 353.
Gold, monetary, looted by, agreement between Bank for International Settlements and U.S., U.K., and France, 713.
Level-of-industry plan in bizonal area, 188, 241.
"People's Congress", U.S. and U.K. position, statement by Secretary Marshall, 456.
Reparation program:
Memorandum of State Department, with letter from Secretary Marshall to Senator Vandenberg, 288.
Removal of industrial plants, letter from Under Secretary Lovett to House Speaker Martin, with data requested, 185.
State constitutions, article from Information Bulletin of U.S. Military Government in Germany, 559.

Germany—Continued
  Treaty obligations, Soviet violation, 738.
  Tripartite conversations on economic unity in (U.S., U.K., and France with Benelux representation), 285, 380, 457, 778, 807.
  Zone of occupation, French, adherence to purposes of Economic Cooperation Act, 838.
  Zone of occupation, Soviet, lack of information regarding, discussed in letter by Under Secretary Lovett, 185.
  Zone of occupation, U.S.:
    Civil administration:
      Study by State Department survey group proposed, 352.
      To remain under Department of the Army, 456.
    Military tribunals, appointments to, 316.
  Zones of occupation, U.S. and U.K.:
    Bipartite Board for U.S.–U.K. Zones, adherence to purposes of Economic Cooperation Act, 708.
    Level-of-industry plan, revised, discussed in questions and answers on removal of industrial plants from Germany, 188.
    Plants, industrial, removal by reparation, correspondence and questions and answers concerning, 185.
Gitchev, Dimiter, indictment of, in Bulgaria, statement by Department of State, 219.
Gold:
  Looted by Germany, restitution:
    Agreement between Bank for International Settlements and U.S., U.K., and France, 713.
    Spain, expropriation in, 653.
    Tripartite Commission for, share allowed to Italy, 551.
  Yugoslav, reserves in U.S., ECOSOC resolution, 448.
Gonzalez-Arevalo, Ismael, credentials as Guatemalan Ambassador to U.S., 486.
Good Offices Committee of the Security Council, negotiations for settlement of Netherlands-Indonesia dispute, 143, 323, 634, 802.
Grady, Henry F.:
  Appointment as U.S. Ambassador to Greece, 782.
  Credentials as U.S. Minister to Nepal, 686.
Graham, Frank P., statement to Security Council on Good Offices Committee on Indonesia, 331.
Great Britain. *See* United Kingdom.
Greece:
  Address by Mr. Henderson, 272.
  Aid from U.S.:
    Addresses by Mr. McGhee and Mr. Henderson, cited, 491, 655.
    American Mission for Aid to Greece (AMAG), 115, 271, 272, 291, 779.
    Request for continuation of, 298, 346.
    Tabular report, 350.
  Anti-strike, anti-lockout law, U.S. attitude, 315.
  Assassination of Minister of Justice (Ladas), message from Secretary Marshall to Greek officials, 713.
  Combat matériel, transfer by U.S. to, and retransfer to U.S., table, 123, 846.
  Communists in, attempt to overthrow recognized Government, U.S. position, 59.
  Economic situation, relation to AMAG, address by Mr. Henderson, 275.
  General Assembly and the Problem of Greece. BULLETIN supplement, 49.
  General Assembly special committee on Greek question, 449, 579, 734.
  Murder of CBS correspondent (Polk):
    Announcement, 713.
    Investigation, 748.
  Refugee problem, article by Mr. Howard, 291.
  Transportation in, joint survey by ECA and AMAG, 779.
  Treaties, agreements, etc.:
    Economic Cooperation Act of 1948, adherence to purposes of, exchange of notes with U.S., 708.

Kashmir Commission of Security Council of UN:
Appointment of Mr. Huddle as U.S. Representative, 732, 828.
Security Council resolutions, 143, 698.
Summary statement by Secretary-General (Lie) at Security Council, 638.
UN action, 732, 767.
Keith, Gerald, designation as liaison officer to act between meetings of Deputies for Austria of Council of Foreign Ministers, 747.
Kelly, Helen G.:
Appointment to ITU Administrative Council, 122.
Article on International Telecommunication Union, 534.
Kentucky Women's Action Committee Forum, Louisville, address by Mr. Henderson, 272.
Keyes, Gen. Geoffrey, remarks regarding interim-aid agreement with Austria, 52.
Knapp, J. Burke, designation in State Department, 751.
Kopcsak, Lt. Col. Peter J., arrest of, in Hungary, texts of U.S.-Hungarian notes, 244.
Korea:
Elections, observance of:
Interim Committee of UN, resolutions and relation to UN Temporary Commission on Korea, 297, 375, 575.
Lieutenant General Hodge, proclamation and statement, 344, 345.
Statements by Secretary Marshall, 375, 700.
UN Temporary Commission on Korea, activities in observance of elections, 375, 700, 768, 800.
U.S. draft resolution, 297 n.
Government, new, formation of, letter from Lieutenant General Hodge to Assemblymen, 800.
Treaty obligations, Soviet violation, 742.
Kuter, Laurence S., statement on necessity for international cooperation in aviation matters, 116.
Kyriazides, Nicolas (alien correspondent at UN), case of, statement by Acting Secretary Lovett, 20, 48.

Labor Organization, International. *See* International.
Labouisse, Henry, designation in State Department, 845.
Lagens Airfield in Azores, agreement between U.S. and Portugal, 358, 839.
Landon, Herman R., appointment as U.S. delegate to 2d session of Permanent Migration Committee of ILO, 303.
Latin America, Economic Commission for, 828, 831.
Latin American countries. *See* American republics.
Lebanon:
Detention of U.S. nationals removed from S.S. *Marine Carp*, exchange of notes with U.S., 749, 780.
Removal of U.S. nationals from S.S. *Marine Carp*, 712.
Truce with provisional government of State of Israel, acceptance, 795.
Wheat agreement, signature, 474.
Legal Committee of ICAO, 1st meeting, 506.
Legations, U.S. *See* Foreign Service.
Legislation. *See* Congress, U.S.
Lehrbas, Lloyd A., designation in State Department, 845.
Lend-lease (*see also* Surplus war property), settlement agreements, U.S. and—
Brazil, 552.
Norway, 306.
Lenroot, Katharine F., article on 9th Pan American child congress, 595.
Leprosy, 5th international congress, U. S. delegation, 450.
Level-of-industry plan in bizonal area of Germany:
Discussed in questions and answers on removal of industrial plants from Germany, 188.
State Department memorandum, 241.
Liberia, wheat agreement, signature, 474.
Libraries, in overseas information program, 842.
Lie, Trygve (Secretary-General of UN), summary of matters under consideration by Security Council, 633.
Linggadjati agreement between the Netherlands and Indonesia, text, 325.

Literary and artistic works, diplomatic conference for revision of international convention for protection of, U.S. observer delegation, 677.
Little Assembly of UN. *See* Interim Committee.
London conference on economic unity of Germany. *See* Germany; Tripartite conversations.
Lorwin, Val R., article on Rome manpower conference, 674.
Lovett, Robert A.:
Addresses, statements, etc.:
Alien correspondents at the UN, 20.
Inland transport, international, facilitation of, in Europe, 27.
Sicily and southern Italy, development, 468.
Trade agreement with Mexico, Schedule I, negotiations for revision of, 59.
Correspondence:
Ambassadors of Yugoslavia, Czechoslovakia, and Poland, regarding declaration on German problems, 384.
Burmese President (Sao Shwe Thaike), on establishment of Union of Burma, 61.
European Economic Co-operation, Organization for, members of, on Economic Cooperation Act of 1948: 640.
Gurney, Senator, on disposition of captured Hungarian horses, 221.
Secretary of Interior (Krug), on procedure for handling international fisheries and wildlife problems, 586.
Soviet Ambassador (Panyushkin), memorandum regarding tripartite conversations (U.S., U.K., and France) on German economic unity, 286.
Soviet Ambassador (Panyushkin), on use of Mellaha airfield by U.S. Air Force, 220.
Soviet Ambassador (Panyushkin), on visit of U.S. vessels to Italian ports, 219.
Speaker of the House of Representatives (Martin), on removal of industrial plants from Germany as reparation, 185.
Turkish Ambassador (Baydur), regarding adherence of Turkey to Economic Cooperation Act, 779.
World health assembly, U.S. representation, 581.
Loyalty of State Department employees, statement by Secretary Marshall, 390.
Luxembourg:
Trade-mark registrations, extension of time for renewal of, 222.
Treaties, agreements, etc.:
Economic, social and cultural collaboration and collective self-defence, with U.K., Belgium, France, and Netherlands, text and communiqué of meeting of Permanent Consultative Council, 600, 602.
Economic Cooperation Act of 1948, adherence to purposes of, 640 n., 712.
General agreement on tariffs and trade:
Signature of protocol of provisional application, 120, 373, 652.
U. S. proclamation, 120.
Tripartite conversations on German economic unity, U.S., U.K., and France (representation at), 285, 380, 457, 778, 807.
U.S. property in, filing claims for, 355.

MacQuivey, Donald R., article on North American broadcasting-engineers' meeting, 541, 747.
MacVeagh, Lincoln, appointment as U.S. Ambassador to Portugal, 390, 517.
Malaria and tropical medicine, 4th international congresses, 303, 475, 545.
Manchuria, treaty obligations, Soviet violation, 743.
Mandated islands, Japanese. *See* Pacific Islands, Territory of.
Manpower conference (Rome):
Article by Mr. Lorwin, 674.
U.S. observer to, 138.
Marine Carp, removal of U.S. nationals by Lebanese authorities at Beirut, 712, 749, 780.

Military government in Germany, statement by Secretary Marshall on Four Power responsibility in Allied Control Council, 456.
Military Staff Committee of UN, dates of meetings, 25, 144, 300, 449, 579, 733.
Military strength, relation to diplomatic action, statement before Senate Armed Services Committee by Secretary Marshall, 421.
Military training, universal. See Universal military training.
Military tribunals for Germany, appointments to, 316.
Mission, American, for Aid to Greece (AMAG), 115, 271, 272, 291, 779.
Mission, to U.S. from China, aid, 115.
Mississippi Valley world trade conference (3d), New Orleans, La., address by Mr. Brown, cited, 605.
Molotov, Vyacheslav M. (Soviet Foreign Minister), statement on Soviet-American relations, 680.
Monetary gold. See Gold.
Moore, Charles E., appointment to AMAG, 115.
Morales, Juan Felix, appointment as Paraguayan Ambassador to U.S., 717.
Morgenstierne. See Munthe de Morgenstierne.
Morse, David A., appointment as Director General of ILO, 802.
Munthe de Morgenstierne, Wilhelm (Norwegian Ambassador), remarks on signing of lend-lease settlement agreement between U.S. and Norway, 307.

Nabuco, Mauricio, appointment as Brazilian Ambassador to U.S., 782.
Nationality Commission, Mixed, in Poland, request for termination by U.S., 781.
Navigation, free, on the Danube, conference to consider, 793.
Nazi-Soviet Relations, 1939–1941, 150.
Near East, regional meeting of ILO for, article by Mr. Tobin, 139.
Nehmer, Stanley, article on significance of textiles in Japanese economy, 527.
Nepal:
Minister to U.S. (Kaiser), credentials, 215, 318.
U.S. Minister (Grady), credentials, 686.
Netherlands:
Combat matériel, transfer by U.S. to, table, 390.
Indonesian dispute with Netherlands. See Indonesian situation.
Treaties, agreements, etc.:
Double taxation, convention with U.S., signature and statement by Secretary Marshall, 611.
Economic, social and cultural collaboration and collective self-defence, with U.K., Belgium, France, and Luxembourg, text, and communiqué of meeting of Permanent Consultative Council, 600, 602.
Economic Cooperation Act of 1948, adherence to purposes of, exchange of notes with U.S., 641, 686, 712.
German enemy assets, resolution of conflicting claims to, with U.S. and Canada (1947), signature, 3.
General agreement on tariffs and trade:
Signature of protocol of provisional application, 120, 373, 652.
Tariff concessions, U.S. consultation, 120.
Trade agreement (1935), proclamation rendering inoperative, 30.
Wheat agreement, signature, 474.
Tripartite conversations on German economic unity, U.S., U.K., France (representation at), 285, 380, 457, 778, 807.
Wheat from U.S., message to U.S. on receipt of, 611.
New Brunswick, U.S. Vice Consulate at Fredericton, closing, 349.
Newspapermen. See Information.
New Zealand:
Combat matériel, retransfer to U.S., table, 123.
Treaties, agreements, etc.:
Double taxation, with U.S., signature, 486.
Wheat agreement, signature, 474.

Niagara River, investigation of dredging operations, 718.
Nicaragua (see also American republics):
U. S. Ambassador (Shaw), appointment, 719.
U.S. diplomatic relations with, resumption of, proposal, 716.
Nicosia, Cyprus, opening of U.S. Consulate, 619.
Nitze, Paul H., designation in State Department, 350, 845.
Nonintervention of UN in domestic jurisdictions, article by Mr. Gross, 259.
Non-self-governing territories. See Trusteeship.
North Atlantic regional air-navigation meeting of ICAO, 2d, U. S. delegation, 580.
North Atlantic States concerned in joint support of Iceland air-navigation services, ICAO conference of, U.S. delegation, 776.
Norway:
Combat matériel, transfer by U.S. to, table, 123.
Treaties, agreements, etc.:
Economic Cooperation Act of 1948, adherence to purposes of, 640 n., 686.
Lend-lease settlement agreement, with U.S. (1942):
Signature and statements by Secretary Marshall and Ambassador Morgenstierne, 306, 307.
Wheat agreement, signature, 474.
Trade-mark registrations, renewal of, by, 93.
U.S. Consulate at Bergen, opening, 349.

Occupied areas (see also Austria; Germany; Japan; Korea), administration of Germany by State Department, plans for, 352, 456.
Oechsner, Frederick C., designation in State Department, 719.
OIE. See Information and Educational Exchange.
Oil, world supply, memorandum by U.S. representative to Inter-American Economic and Social Council of Pan American Union, 426.
Opium Board, UN, Permanent Central, 145, 734.
Organization for European Economic Co-operation (OEEC), 138, 640.
Organization of American States, charter, 666.
Overseas Press Club, Washington, D.C., address by Mr. Allen, 476, 587.

Pacific Islands, Territory of, trusteeship, summary statement by Secretary-General (Lie) at Security Council, 636.
Pacific settlement of disputes, action in Interim Committee of General Assembly, 576, 767.
Pakistan:
Dispute with India on Kashmir:
Proceedings of Security Council, 732, 767.
Resolutions of Security Council, 143, 698.
Summary statement by Secretary-General (Lie) at Security Council, 638.
Palermo, Italy, elevation of U.S. Consulate to rank of Consulate General, 517, 619.
Palestine, U.S. Consulate at Haifa, opening, 619.
Palestine situation:
Addresses, statements, etc.:
Mr. Austin, 294, 342, 402, 514, 515, 568, 695, 763.
Secretary-General (Lie), 636.
Secretary Marshall, 281, 408.
President Truman, 451.
Arab Higher Committee, attitude, 402, 514, 569, 695.
Arab States, countries of, 795.
Cease-fire order of May 22 and U.S. support, 695, 729.
Congress, House Committee of Foreign Affairs, letter from Secretary Marshall to member of, 281.
General Assembly, 2d Special Session:
Appointment of United Nations Mediator, resolution, 694.
Statement by Mr. Austin requesting special session and presenting in Security Council a draft resolution, 514, 515.
Trusteeship for Palestine, statement by Mr. Jessup, 592.
U.S. attitude reviewed by Mr. Austin, 568.

Palestine situation—Continued
Jerusalem, protection of:
  Cease-fire order of Security Council (May 22), resolution, 729.
  French resolution and Swedish amendment in General Assembly, 591 n., 592 n.
  Trusteeship Council resolution, 572.
  U.S. position on French resolution, statement by Mr. Jessup, 591.
Jewish attitude, 402, 569, 695.
Lebanon:
  Removal of U.S. citizens from S. S. *Marine Carp*, 712.
  U.S. and Lebanon, exchange of notes, 749, 780.
Security Council:
  Proceedings in, 731, 767, 802, 830.
  Resolutions: creating committee (Feb. 25), 297; calling on permanent members for recommendations (Mar. 5), 344; establishing Truce Commission (Apr. 23), 594; cease-fire order (May 22), 729; four-week truce (May 29), 729.
  Summary of, statement by Mr. Austin, 568.
Truce beginning June 11:
  Acceptance by Arab States, text, 795.
  Acceptance by provisional government of State of Israel, text, 796.
  Cease-fire and truce proposals submitted to Arab States and Israel, note from UN mediator (Bernadotte), presenting, 794.
  Message to interested governments from UN mediator (Bernadotte), announcing acceptance of truce, 797.
Truce Commission, Security Council resolution on establishment, 594.
Truce resolution of May 29:
  Acceptance of Security Council resolution by Jewish and Arab leaders, 764, 765.
  Cablegram from UN mediator (Bernadotte) to Secretary-General Lie, 764.
  U.S. support, 763, 830.
Trusteeship for, U.S. proposal, statements by Mr. Austin and Mr. Jessup, 570, 592.
UN mediator in Palestine, creation of position by General Assembly (*see also* Bernadotte, Count), 694.
UN Palestine Commission:
  Reports of, discussed, 281, 296.
  Liquidation, 694.
U.S. support of efforts to solve, 568, 729, 830.
Palmer, Ely E., appointment as U.S. Ambassador to Afghanistan, 719.
Pan American child congress (9th), 62, 595.
Pan American Day, Washington, D. C., address by Mr. Allen, 546.
Pan American Institute of Geography and History, Commission on History, article by Mr. Whitaker, 87.
Pan American organizations, chart showing, 164.
Pan American Sanitary Organization, 1st meeting of directing council of, article by Mr. Doull, 283.
Pan American Union (*see also* American States, Ninth International Conference):
  History and functions, article by Mr. Sanders, 159.
  Inter-American Economic and Social Council, 184, 426.
Panama (*see also* American republics):
  Ambassador to U.S. (Jaén Guardia), credentials, 486.
  Defense sites, withdrawal of U.S. armed forces, 31.
  Treaties, agreements, etc.:
    Defense sites in, use of, with U.S. (1942), exchange of notes and termination, 317.
    Defense sites in, use of, with U.S. (1947), rejection of ratification by Panama, 31.
Panyushkin, Alexander Semenovich, credentials as Soviet Ambassador to U.S., 62.
Papanek, Jan, letter concerning Czechoslovak coup, 409 n.
Papers Relating to Foreign Relations of the United States: 1932, vol. II, released, 459; *The Paris Peace Conference*, 1919, vol. XII, published, 319.

Paraguay (*see also* American republics):
  Agricultural program, cooperative, with Institute of Inter-American Affairs, 759.
  Ambassador to U.S. (Morales), credentials, 717.
Paris Peace Conference 1946: Selected Documents, 125.
Passports, tourist, for Philippines, 717.
Pawley, William D., assistance of, in preparatory work for inter-American conference at Bogotá, 149.
Peace treaties. *See* Austria, Italy, Rumania.
Peru (*see also* American republics):
  Agricultural program, cooperative, with Institute of Inter-American Affairs, 762.
  Ambassador to U.S. (Ferreyros Ayulo), credentials, 318.
  Combat matériel, transfer by U.S. to, table, 554.
  Cultural leaders, visit to U.S., 357, 716.
  U.S. Ambassador, appointment, 829.
  Wheat agreement, signature, 474.
Petroleum, world supply, 426.
Philippines, Republic of the:
  Combat matériel, transfer by U.S. to, table, 846.
  Opening of U.S. Consulate at Cebu, 517.
  Property, transfer to (Ex. Or. 9921), 124.
  Tourist passports, 717.
  Trade-mark registrations, extension of time for renewal, 717.
  Treaties, agreements, etc.:
    Educational-exchange program, with U.S. (1947), signature, 488.
    Wheat agreement, signature, 474.
Physiopathology of animal reproduction and artificial insemination, first international congress, U.S. delegation, 832.
Poland:
  Declaration on German problems, U.S. position, 384.
  Nationality Commission, Mixed, request by U.S. for termination, 781.
  Treaty obligations, Soviet violation, 739.
  Wheat agreement, signature, 474.
Policy Planning Staff, appointment of Mr. Butler as member of, 317.
Polk, George, murder of, in Greece:
  Correspondence and statements concerning, 713.
  Greek investigation, 748.
Port Limón, Costa Rica, closing of U.S. Consulate, 517.
Port-of-Spain, Trinidad, British West Indies, elevation of U.S. Consulate to rank of Consulate General, 124.
Portugal:
  Treaties, agreements, etc.:
    Transit of U.S. military planes through airfield in Azores, with U.S. (1946), extension of, signature and exchange of notes, 221, 358, 839, 840.
    Wheat agreement, signature, 474.
  U.S. Ambassador (MacVeagh), appointment, 390, 517.
Poultry congress, world, 8th:
  Plans, 379.
  U.S. delegation, 803.
Preparatory Commission for IRO. *See* Refugee Organization, International.
President, U.S. *See* Truman, Harry S.
Presidential term, constitutional amendment, status of ratifications, 427.
Press. *See* Information.
Prisoners of war, release, status of, from French, British, and Soviet Governments, 221.
Proclamations:
  Sugar protocol (1947), 815.
  Tariffs and trade, general agreement on (1947):
    China, 652.
    Cuba, 60, 841.
    Czechoslovakia, 610.
    Supplementary proclamations, 250, 841.
    Union of South Africa, 840.
  Trade agreements, termination, 30.
  Trade-mark registrations, extension of time for renewal of:
    Luxembourg and Denmark, 222.
    Norway, 93.
    Philippine Republic, 717.

Publications—Continued
  Lists—Continued
    State Department, 35, 63, 124, 151, 255, 287, 319, 361, 391, 427, 459, 555, 587, 619, 655, 687, 783, 847.
    United Nations, 208, 267, 293, 341, 391, 408, 448, 639, 730, 766, 829.
  Nazi-Soviet Relations, 1939–1941 : 150.
  Paris Peace Conference 1946 : Selected Documents, 125.
  Soviet Supply Protocols, 523.
  United States and the United Nations: Report by the President to the Congress for the Year 1947 : 279.
Puerto Cortes, Honduras, opening of U.S. consular agency, 849.

Radio (*see also* Telecommunication) : Broadcasting-engineers' meeting, North American, article by Mr. MacQuivey, 541, 747.
Railway congress, 6th Pan American, U.S. observers, 449.
Railway-transport equipment, German, questions and answers concerning, 189.
Ramsey, Fred W., designation in State Department, 520.
Rayon, in Japan, discussed in article on textiles in Japanese economy, 533.
Reber, Samuel :
  Designation as U.S. Deputy for Austrian treaty at proposed meeting of Deputies of Council of Foreign Ministers, 213.
  Letter to Secretary General of CFM on suspension of meetings of Council's Deputies for Austria, 747.
Reciprocal assistance, inter-American treaty of (1947), U.S. ratification, 60.
Reciprocity Information, Committee for, public notice of, regarding revision of Schedule I of trade agreement with Mexico, 60.
Recognition of new governments. *See* Diplomatic relations.
Recovery Program, European. *See* European Recovery Program.
Red Cross, American, aid to Colombia during Bogotá demonstrations, exchange of messages, 716.
Refugee Organization, International (IRO), Preparatory Commission :
  Agenda, 63.
  Fourth and fifth meetings, articles by Mr. Warren, 21, 451.
  U.S. delegations, 49, 580.
Refugees and displaced persons. *See* Displaced persons.
Reparation :
  Germany :
    Letter from Secretary Marshall to Senator Vandenberg, 238.
    Memorandum of Department of State, 239.
    Removal of industrial plants from, letter from Under Secretary Lovett to Speaker Martin, with data requested, 185.
  Inter-Allied Reparation Agency, 227, 240.
  Japan, Far Eastern Commission, policy decision, 92.
Repatriation, State Department memorandum regarding, 313.
Republic of the Philippines. *See* Philippines.
Resources, renewable natural, conservation of, 1st inter-American conference on, agenda, 146.
Restitution of Monetary Gold, Tripartite Commission for (*see also* Gold), 551.
Revival of prewar bilateral treaties. *See under* Treaties, prewar.
Rhine Commission, Central, 302.
Rice meeting of FAO, 282, 769.
Royal Sanitary Institute, health congress, U.S. delegation, 678.
Rubber Study Group, International, 5th meeting, 474, 650.
Rumania :
  Nonenemy status of, statement by Secretary of the Treasury, 121.
  Property of UN nationals in, procedure for filing claims, 316.

Rumania—Continued
Treaties, agreements, etc.:
Peace treaty, with Allies, violations of, U.S. letter to Rumanian Government, 216.
Revival of prewar, by U.S., text of U.S. note, 356.
Soviet violation, 742.

Saar, French Union and, signatory to wheat agreement, 474.
Safety of life at sea, conference on, U.S. delegation, 544.
St. Stephen, N.B., Canada, closing of U.S. Consulate, 63.
Salmon Fisheries Commission, International Pacific, 95.
Sanders, William, article on the Inter-American System, 155.
Sandifer, Durward V., designation in Department of State, 215.
Sanitary Organization, Pan American, 283.
Santa Cruz, Hernan, letter concerning Czechoslovak coup, 409.
Sargeant, Howland H., article on role of libraries in the overseas information program, 842.
Saudi Arabia, truce with provisional government of State of Israel, acceptance, 795.
SCAP. See Supreme Commander for Allied Powers.
Scheele, Leonard A., article on 4th international cancer research congress, 147.
Schwarzkopf mission, in Iran, clarification requested by U.S., 307.
Science, survey, U.S., of southern Italy and Sicily, 551.
Scrap metal:
Embargo on export, 318.
For Italian shipments, sources, 551.
Sea, regional meeting to consider formation of a regional council for study of, 282.
Secretary of State. See Marshall, George C.
Securities. See Property.
Security Council of UN:
Appointment of Mr. Jessup as deputy U.S. representative, 732.
Atomic energy. See Atomic energy; Atomic Energy Commission.
Austin, Warren R. (U.S. representative). See Austin.
Czechoslovak question. See Czechoslovakia.
Date of meeting, 25, 144, 300, 449, 579, 733.
Egyptian question, summary statement by Secretary-General Lie, 633.
Good Offices Committee of. See Indonesian situation.
Greek question. See Greece.
India-Pakistan dispute. See Kashmir.
Indonesian-Netherlands dispute. See Indonesian situation.
Iranian question, summary statement by Secretary-General Lie, 633.
Jammu and Kashmir. See Kashmir.
Kashmir situation. See Kashmir.
Membership in UN, application for, summary statement by Secretary-General Lie, 636.
Pacific Islands, Territory of, summary statement by Secretary-General Lie, 636.
Palestine situation. See Palestine.
Resolutions:
Atomic Energy Commission, 799.
India-Pakistan, 143, 698.
Indonesian situation, 328, 329, 336.
Kashmir, 143, 698.
Palestine situation, 297, 344, 729.
Status of matters under consideration, summary statement by Secretary-General Lie, 633.
Trieste. See Trieste, Free Territory of.
Trusteeship Council, 572, 734, 801, 830.
Voting problem, U.S. draft resolution and proposals in Interim Committee of General Assembly, 86, 412.
Voting procedure, summary statement by Secretary-General Lie, 635.
Security program, State Department, loyalty of employees, statement by Secretary Marshall, 390.

Treaties, agreements, etc.—Continued
  Prewar treaties, revival by U.S., text of U.S. note to—
    Bulgaria, 383.
    Hungary, 382.
    Italy, 248, 455.
    Rumania, 356.
  Shellfish industry, sanitary control of, with Canada, text and correspondence, 717.
  Sugar, international agreement regarding production and marketing (1937), protocol prolonging (1947), proclamation, 815.
  Tariffs and trade, general agreement on (1947):
    Addresses, statements, etc.:
      Mr. Brown, 478.
      Mr. Wilcox, 39, 125.
      Mr. Willoughby, 67.
    Article XIV, protocol modifying, 841.
    Cuba, exclusive supplementary agreement, 28, 29 (text), 60, 841.
    Czechoslovakia, attitude, 425, 610.
    Proclamations putting into effect for—
      China, 652.
      Cuba, 60, 841.
      Czechoslovakia, 610.
      Union of South Africa, 840.
    Relationship to ITO, discussed, 373.
    Signature of protocol of provisional application by—
      China, 652.
      Czechoslovakia, 610.
      Original signatories, 120, 373, 652.
      Union of South Africa, 840.
    Supplementary proclamations, 250, 841.
    Trade agreements rendered inoperative upon proclamation, 30, 60.
  Telecommunication convention, international, final protocol and Radio Regulations, ratification, 841.
  Trade, with Mexico (1942), revision of Schedule I, 59, 212, 553.
  Trade agreements, proclamation rendering certain inoperative for contracting parties to general agreement on tariffs and trade, 30, 60.
  Treaty Committee, establishment, 491.
  Whaling, international agreement (1937), protocol amending (1946), proclamation, 318.
  Wheat agreement, international:
    Article by Mr. Cale, 395.
    Letter from Acting Secretary of Agriculture to Secretary of State recommending Senate approval, 609.
    Principal provisions, summary, 607.
    Signature, 474.
    Transmittal to Senate, 606.
Treaty obligations, Soviet violations, State Department report to Senate Committee on Foreign Relations, 738.
Trieste, Free Territory of:
  Aid from U.S.:
    Draft bill for continuation of aid (to amend Public Law 389), 349.
    Letter from Secretary Marshall to Senator Vandenberg enclosing draft bill, 348.
    Tabular report, 350.
  Boundary, violations, U.S. note to Yugoslavia, 521.
  Return to Italy, proposed:
    Italian Ambassador (Tarchiani), note to Secretary of State accepting proposal, 454.
    Joint proposal by U.S., U.K., and France, 425.
    Memoranda of Department of State to Italy and U.S.S.R. submitting proposal, 453, 491, 521, 522.
    President Truman and Italian Ambassador (Tarchiani), exchange of notes, 583.
    Secretary Marshall to Soviet Ambassador, note requesting Soviet views on, 778.
    Soviet attitude, exchange of memoranda, 549.
  Summary statement by Secretary-General (Lie) to Security Council, 633.

Tripartite conversations (U.S., U.K., and France), on German economic unity:
  Announcement, 285.
  Benelux countries, entry of, 380.
  Communiqué, joint, by U.S., U.K., France, Belgium, Netherlands, and Luxembourg on agreement at London conference, 380, 778.
  Purpose, 811.
  Report of agreed recommendations, 807.
  Statement released to press by Department of State, 778.
  U.S. attitude:
    Secretary Marshall, notes to Soviet Ambassador, 286, 457.
    Secretary Marshall, statements, 380, 810.
Truce. See Palestine.
Truman, Harry S.:
  Addresses, statements, etc.:
    Foreign Assistance Act of 1948, 468.
    Israel, recognition by U.S. of provisional government, 673.
    Italy, transfer of vessels to, 454.
    ITO charter, completion of, 443.
    Palestine, U.S. position in UN regarding, 451.
    Peace policy, U.S., 47, 418, 804.
    United Nations, as means of world peace, 47.
    U. S.-Soviet relations, 683.
  Budget on international affairs and finance, 126, 255.
  Correspondence:
    Burmese President (Sao Shwe Thaike), on establishment of Union of Burma, 61.
    Colombian President (Ospina Perez), on American Red Cross aid to Colombia during Bogotá demonstrations, 716.
    Italian Ambassador (Tarchiani), on proposed return of Trieste to Italy, 583.
  Executive orders. See Executive orders.
  Messages to Congress:
    Annual message, 90.
    China, proposed aid to, 268.
    Cuban independence, 50th anniversary, joint session on, 582.
    Economic development in other American republics, financing by Export-Import Bank, 548.
    Peace, means of securing, 418.
    Reciprocal Trade Agreements Act, extension of, 351.
    Congress, transmitting—
      Report of UN activities and U.S. participation, 279.
      Educational-exchange programs, operations of State Department, with report by Secretary Marshall, 387.
      Foreign-aid program, 1st report, 648.
    Senate, transmitting—
      Friendship, commerce, and navigation treaty, with Italy, 550.
      Wheat agreement, international, with report by Secretary Marshall and letter from Acting Secretary of Agriculture, 606.
  Proclamations. See Proclamations.
Trusteeship:
  Pacific Islands, Territory of, summary statement by Secretary-General (Lie) at Security Council, 636.
  Palestine, question of, statement by Mr. Jessup, 592.
  Security Council discussion, 830.
Trusteeship Council of UN:
  Jerusalem, City of, resolution concerning draft statute for, 572.
  Strategic trusteeships, action in UN, 801, 830.
  Third session, 734.
Turkey:
  Aid from U. S.:
    Address by Mr. McGhee, cited, 491.
    Draft bill (to amend Public Law 75), 299.
    Extension of, statement by Secretary Marshall, 346.
    Secretary Marshall, letter to Senator Vandenberg, requesting continuation, 298.

Turkey—Continued
Combat matériel, transfer by U.S. to, and retransfer, table, 123.
Economic Cooperation Act of 1948, exchange of notes with U.S. regarding adherence to purposes of, 779.

UNESCO (United Nations Educational, Scientific and Cultural Organization):
Accomplishments, address by Mr. Allen, 727.
Appointment of Mr. Holland as U.S. counselor, in Paris, 212.
Art and general education, meeting of experts on, 579, 733.
General Conference, 2d session in Mexico, 25.
Executive Board, 6th session, 145, 300.
Hylean Amazon, International Institute of, calling of conference for establishment of, 598.
Pacific regional conference, address by Mr. Allen, 727.
Teachers organization, international, 579, 733.
Theatre Institute, International, conference on, 580.
Translation of great books, experts for study of plan for, committee of, 579, 733.

Union of South Africa:
General agreement on tariffs and trade (1947):
Signature of protocol of provisional application, 840.
Tariff concessions, U.S. proclamation, 840.
Treatment of Indians in, discussion in General Assembly, 263.
U.S. Minister (Winship), appointment, 491.
Wheat agreement, signature, 474.

Union of Soviet Socialist Republics:
Ambassador to U.S. (Panyushkin), credentials, 62.
Arrest of American officers in Hungary by Soviet troops, texts of notes regarding, 244.
Czechoslovak independence. See Czechoslovakia.
Danube, conference to consider free navigation of, exchange of views with U.S., U.K. and French Governments, 735.
Germany, tripartite discussions on, U.S. reply to Soviet objections regarding, 457.
Interference in Chilean internal affairs, accusation, 411.
Italy, peace treaty, rejection of drafting procedure, exchange of memoranda with U.S., 549.
Mellaha airfield, use of, by U.S. Air Force, U.S.–U.S.S.R. notes concerning, 220.
Prisoners of war, status of release of, 221.
Propaganda methods, discussion by Secretary Marshall, 744.
Protests regarding activities of U.S. aircraft over waters adjoining Japan, U.S. reply to, 746.
Relations with Germany, documents bearing on, release by State Department, 150.
Marshal Stalin, statement responding to open letter from Mr. Wallace, U.S. attitude, 705.
Supply protocols, with U.S., U.K., and Canada, publication of, by U.S., 523.
Treaty obligations, violations, State Department report to U.S. Senate Committee on Foreign Relations, 738.
Trieste, notes from U.S. regarding return to Italy, 522, 778.
Trieste, return to Italy, attitude, 549.
U.S. relations with:
Statements by President Truman and Secretary Marshall, 683.
Statements by Ambassador Smith and Foreign Minister Molotov, 679, 682.
U.S. vessels, visits to Italian ports, correspondence with U.S. concerning, 218.
Zone of occupation in Germany, position on information regarding, 185.

United Kingdom:
Ambassador to U.S. (Franks), credentials, 782.
Bipartite Board for U.S.-U.K. Zones in Germany, 708.
Communist seizure of power in Czechoslovakia, joint declaration with U.S. and France, 304.

United Kingdom—Continued
Danube, conference to consider free navigation of, exchange of views with U.S., French, and Soviet Governments, 735.
Dominion status for Ceylon, 316.
Expropriation of German assets in Spain, 653.
Foreign Minister, meeting with U.S. and French Foreign Ministers, discussed, 456.
German "People's Congress", U.S. and U.K. position, statement by Secretary Marshall, 456.
Prisoners of war, status of release of, 221.
Treaties, agreements, etc.:
Air bases in Caribbean area and in Bermuda, civil use of, with U.S., expansion of 1941 agreement, signature, 305.
Consular treaty, with U.S., negotiations, 191.
Economic, social and cultural collaboration and collective self-defence, with Belgium, France, Luxembourg, and Netherlands, text, and communiqué of meeting of Permanent Consultative Council, 600, 602.
Economic Cooperation Act of 1948, adherence to purposes of, exchange of notes with U.S., 645, 686.
General agreement on tariffs and trade:
Signature of protocol of provisional application, 121.
Tariff concessions, U.S. proclamation, 120.
Trade agreement (1938), proclamation rendering inoperative, 30.
Wheat agreement, signature, 474.
Trieste, Free Territory of. See Trieste.
Tripartite conversations with U.S. and France on German economic unity. See Tripartite.
Union of Western Europe, proposal by Mr. Bevin for, statement by Department of State, 138.

United Nations:
Addresses and statements:
Mr. Austin, 14, 446, 626.
Secretary Marshall, 623.
President Truman, 47.
Atomic energy, action on, 731, 802, 830.
Atomic Energy Commission. See Atomic Energy Commission.
Charter, invocation of, in Palestine situation, Security Council resolution, 695.
Children's Emergency Fund, International, 25.
Correspondents:
Review of accrediting of, note from U.S. Mission to Secretary-General Lie, 48.
Statement by Acting Secretary Lovett, 20.
Documents, listed, 208, 267, 293, 341, 391, 408, 448, 639, 730, 766, 829.
Economic and Social Council. See Economic and Social Council.
General Assembly. See General Assembly.
Human Rights, Commission on. See Human Rights.
Inter-American regional system, coordination with:
Chart showing, 180.
Discussed by Mr. Sanders, 177.
Interim Committee. See Interim Committee.
Korea, Temporary Commission on. See Korea.
Little Assembly. See Interim Committee.
Maritime conference, international:
Annexes of final act, text, 505.
Article by Mr. Cates, 495.
Mediator in Palestine. See Bernadotte, Count.
Membership in, summary statement by Secretary-General (Lie) at Security Council, 636.
Nonintervention in domestic jurisdictions, article by Mr. Gross, 259.
Palestine situation. See Palestine.
Property in Rumania belonging to nationals of, procedure for filing claims, 316.
Publications. See Documents supra.
Security Council. See Security Council.
Specialized agencies. See name of agency.

United Nations—Continued
Trade and employment conference at Habana. *See* Trade and employment, United Nations conference on.
United Nations Newsletter, 655.
United States and the United Nations: Report by the President to the Congress for the Year 1947, 279.
United States in, special reports, 731, 767, 801, 830.
United States citizens. *See* Protection of U.S. nationals.
Universal military training, addresses, statements, etc.:
Mr. Austin, 418.
Secretary Marshall, 421.
President Truman, 420.
University of California, Berkeley:
Address by Secretary Marshall, 422.
Address by President Truman, 804.
Uruguay (*see also* American republics):
Combat matériel, transfer by U.S. to, table, 123, 390, 846.
Cultural leaders, visit to U.S., 814, 845.
Gift to U.S., proposed legislation for acceptance, 585.

Venezuela (*see also* American republics):
Combat matériel, transfer by U.S. to, table, 390, 554.
Inauguration of President (Gallegos), attendance of American Ambassador (Donnelly), 222.
Treaties, agreements, etc.:
Air-transport agreement with United States, signature, 716.
Wheat agreement, signature, 474.
Vessels (*see also* Maritime):
Egypt–U.S. steamship service, inauguration, 486.
Finnish, requisitioned during war, compensation for, 63.
Italian, return to Italy by U.S., statement by President Truman and Executive order, 454.
Marine Carp, removal of U.S. nationals from, by Lebanese authorities at Beirut, 712, 780.
Merchant Ship Sales Act of 1946, extension of, letter from Secretary Marshall to House Committee on Merchant Marine and Fisheries, 311.
Student ships:
Assignment of, for educational-exchange program, 487.
Statement by Mr. Allen, 488.
U.S., to resupply Canadian Arctic weather stations, 782.
U.S., visit to Italian ports, U.S.–U.S.S.R. correspondence concerning, 218.
Veto question in Interim Committee of UN, discussion, 575.
Voting in the Security Council, 635.

Wallace, Henry, statements of Department of State on Marshal Stalin's response to letter of, 705.
War-damage claims. *See* Protection of U.S. nationals.
Warren, George L., articles on IRO, 21, 451.
Weather stations in Canadian Arctic, resupply program by U.S. and Canada, 782.
West Indies, elevation of U.S. Vice Consulate at Aruba to rank of Consulate, 124.
Western European Powers, treaty of economic, social and cultural collaboration and collective self-defence, and communiqué on 1st meeting of Permanent Consultative Council, texts, 600, 602.
Western Union. *See* European Union.
Whaling, international agreement (1937), proclamation of protocol (1946) concerning, 318.
Wheat, U.S., shipment to Netherlands, message of thanks from Queen, 611.

Wheat agreement, international:
Acting Secretary of Agriculture, letter to Secretary of State recommending Senate approval, 609.
Article by Mr. Cale, 395.
Signature, summary, and transmittal to Senate, 474, 606, 607.
Wheat Council, International:
Article by Mr. Cale, 395.
Special session, at Washington, 215.
Whitaker, Arthur P., article on first consultation of Commission on History, 87.
Wilcox, Clair:
Resignation as director of Office of International Trade Policy, 719.
Statement at UN conference on trade and employment, 39, 125.
Wiley, John C., appointment as U.S. Ambassador to Iran, 390.
Willoughby, Woodbury, article on postwar commercial policy of U.S., 67.
Winship, North, appointment as U.S. Minister to Union of South Africa, 491.
Wood, C. Tyler, address on ITO and reciprocal trade-agreements program, cited, 373.
Wool, in Japan, discussed in article on textiles in Japanese economy, 533.
World conference on trade and employment. *See* Trade and employment, UN conference on.
World health assembly. *See* World Health Organization.
World Health Organization (WHO):
Administration and Finance Committee, meetings, 26, 144.
Diseases, international lists of, and causes of death, expert committee on, meetings, 580, 733.
Interim Commission, 5th session, agenda and U.S. delegation, 23.
Interim Commission, 6th session, work of and U.S. delegation, 734, 774, 833.
Malaria, expert committee on, meetings, 302, 580, 733.
Membership, listed, 431 n., 802.
Progress and plans, article by Dr. Hyde, 431.
Tuberculosis, expert committee on, meetings, 26, 145, 300.
U.S. membership, 802.
World health assembly, 1st session, and U.S. representation, 540, 581, 734, 832.
World health assembly, discussed, 440.
World Trade Conference of Cleveland World Trade Association, address by Mr. Brown, 478.
Wright, William D., designation in State Department, 845.

Yemen, truce with provisional government of State of Israel, acceptance, 795 n.
Yugoslavia:
Accusations against U.S. officials by press of, U.S. position, 707.
Assets frozen in U.S., demand for release, U.S. position, 117.
Comments on personal American activities, U.S. position, text of note from Secretary Marshall, 485.
Declaration on German problems, U.S. position, 384.
Gold reserves in U.S., ECOSOC resolution, 448.
Property of U.S. nationals:
Procedure for filing claims, 707.
U.S. position, 117.
Trieste, zonal boundary, note from U.S, 521.

Zones of occupation. *See* Germany.

U. S. GOVERNMENT PRINTING OFFICE: 1948

Lightning Source UK Ltd.
Milton Keynes UK
UKHW012016220219
337761UK00009B/338/P